C000026414

1 MONTH OF
FREE
READING

at

www.ForgottenBooks.com

By purchasing this book you are
eligible for one month membership to
ForgottenBooks.com, giving you
unlimited access to our entire
collection of over 1,000,000 titles via
our web site and mobile apps.

To claim your free month visit:

www.forgottenbooks.com/free919788

* Offer is valid for 45 days from date of purchase. Terms and conditions apply.

ISBN 978-0-265-98918-0
PIBN 10919788

This book is a reproduction of an important historical work. Forgotten Books uses
state-of-the-art technology to digitally reconstruct the work, preserving the original format
whilst repairing imperfections present in the aged copy. In rare cases, an imperfection in
the original, such as a blemish or missing page, may be replicated in our edition. We do,
however, repair the vast majority of imperfections successfully; any imperfections that
remain are intentionally left to preserve the state of such historical works.

Forgotten Books is a registered trademark of FB &c Ltd.
Copyright © 2018 FB &c Ltd.
FB &c Ltd, Dalton House, 60 Windsor Avenue, London, SW19 2RR.
Company number 08720141. Registered in England and Wales.

For support please visit www.forgottenbooks.com

JOURNAL

OF THE

ROYAL

STATISTICAL SOCIETY.

(𝔉oundeð 1834.)

INCORPORATED BY ROYAL CHARTER 1887.

VOL. LXX.—YEAR **1907**.

LONDON:

THE ROYAL STATISTICAL SOCIETY,
9 ADELPHI TERRACE, STRAND, W.C.

1907.

v.70

NOTICE.

The Council of the Royal Statistical Society wish it to be understood that the Society is not responsible for the statements or opinions expressed in the Papers read before the Society or inserted in its *Journal*.

ROYAL STATISTICAL SOCIETY.

Patron.

HIS MOST GRACIOUS MAJESTY THE KING.

Honorary President.

H.R.H. THE PRINCE OF WALES, K.G.

COUNCIL AND OFFICERS.—1907-8.

Honorary Vice-Presidents
(having filled the Office of President).

RT. HON. LORD EVERSLEY.	RT. HON. SIR H.H. FOWLER, G.C.S.I., M.P.
RT. HON. LORD BRASSEY, G C.B.	RT. HON. LORD AVEBURY, F.R.S.
SIR ROBERT GIFFEN, K.C.B., LL.D, F.R.S.	MAJOR P. G. CRAIGIE, C.B.
RT. HON. CHARLES BOOTH, D.Sc., F.R.S.	SIR FRANCIS SHARP POWELL, BART., M.P.
SIR ALFRED E. BATEMAN, K.C.M.G.	RT. HON. THE EARL OF ONSLOW, G.C.M.G.
RT. HON. LORD COURTNEY.	SIR RICHARD BIDDULPH MARTIN, BART.

President.

THE RIGHT HON. SIR CHARLES WENTWORTH DILKE, BART, M.P.

Vice-Presidents.

ARTHUR L. BOWLEY, M.A.	TIMOTHY A. COGHLAN, I.S.O.
SIR E. W. BRABROOK, C.B., V.-P.S.A.	BERNARD MALLET.

Treasurer.

SIR RICHARD BIDDULPH MARTIN, BART.

Honorary Secretaries.

R. H. REW.   A. WILSON FOX, C.B.   G. UDNY YULE.

Honorary Foreign Secretary.

SIR J. ATHELSTANE BAINES, C.S.I.

Other Members of Council.

WILLIAM M. ACWORTH, M.A.	FREDERICK HENDRIKS, F.I.A.
EDWARD BOND.	NOEL A. HUMPHREYS, I.S.O.
G. G. CHISHOLM, M.A., B.Sc., F.R.G.S.	A. W. WATERLOW KING, J.P.
SIR ERNEST CLARKE, M.A., E.L S., F.S.A.	PROF. C. S. LOCH, D.C.L.
NATHANIEL L. COHEN.	THEODORE MORISON, M.A.
RICHARD F. CRAWFORD.	SIR SHIRLEY F. MURPHY, M.R C.S.
REGINALD DUDFIELD, M.A., M.B.	FRANCIS G. P. NEISON, F.I.A.
SIR WILLIAM C. DUNBAR, BART., C.B.	GEORGE PAISH.
PROF. F. Y. EDGEWORTH, M.A., D C L.	L. L. PRICE, M.A.
SIR JOHN GLOVER, J.P.	SIR LESLEY PROBYN, K.C.V.O.
EDGAR J. HARPER.	DAVID A. THOMAS, M.A., M.P.

Assistant Secretary.

J. H. MAGEE, B.A.

Chief Clerk and Librarian.

JOHN A. P. MACKENZIE.

Bankers.—MESSRS. DRUMMOND, CHARING CROSS, S.W., LONDON.

Offices.—9, ADELPHI TERRACE, STRAND, W.C., LONDON.

CONTENTS.

Vol. LXX.—Year 1907

March, 1907.

	PAGE
Correlation of the Weather and Crops. By R. H. HOOKER, F.R.Met.S.	1— 42
Discussion on Mr. R. H. Hooker's Paper	42— 51
Statistics of Production and the Census of Production Act (1906). By G. UDNY YULE	52— 87
Discussion on Mr. G. Udny Yule's Paper	87— 99

MISCELLANEA :—

I.—The late Viscount Goschen (President, 1886-88)	100—102
II.—On the Representation of Statistical Frequency by a Series. By Professor F. Y. EDGEWORTH, D.C.L.	102—106
III.—Prices of Commodities in 1906. By A. SAUERBECK	107—121
IV.—Roumania's Forty Years of Progress, 1866-1907. By LEON GASTER	122—129
V.— Correspondence	129—131

Book Reviews	132—155
Statistical and Economic Articles in Recent Periodicals	156—164
Quarterly List of Additions to the Library	165—183
Periodical Returns	184—202

June, 1907.

PAGE

The Alleged Increase of Insanity. By NOEL A. HUMPHREYS, I.S.O. .... 203—233

Discussion on Mr. Noel A. Humphreys' Paper .... 233—241

The Herring Fishery. By ALBERT E. LARK, F.C.A. .... 242—259

Discussion on Mr. A. E. Lark's Paper .... 259—266

The Decline in Number of Agricultural Labourers in Great Britain. By LORD EVERSLEY .... 267—306

Discussion on Lord Eversley's Paper .... 307—319

Annual Report, Accounts, &c. .... 320—329

Proceedings of the Seventy-third Annual General Meeting... 330, 331

MISCELLANEA :—

Dr. Joseph Körösy—M. G. Olanesco 332, 333

Book Reviews .... 334—376

Statistical and Economic Articles in Recent Periodicals .... 377—386

Quarterly List of Additions to the Library .... 387—406

September, 1907.

Some Considerations relating to the Position of the Small Holding in the United Kingdom. By W. G. S. ADAMS, M.A. .... 411—437

Discussion on Mr. W. G. S. Adams's Paper........................ 438—448

MISCELLANEA :—

I.—Congress of the International Statistical Institute...... 449—454

II.—Note on the Mortality from Tuberculosis, 1851-1905. By R. DUDFIELD, M.A., M.B................................ 454—470

III.—Meeting of the British Association. Discussion on Modern Methods of treating Observations .... 471—476

IV.—Agricultural Returns of Great Britain 477, 478

PAGE

Book Reviews .... 479—520

Statistical and Economic Articles in Recent Periodicals .... 521—529

Quarterly List of Additions to the Library .... 530—551

December, 1907.

The Presidential Address of THE RIGHT HON. SIR CHARLES
    W. DILKE, BART., M.P., for the Session 1907-08. Delivered
    to the Royal Statistical Society, 19th November, 1907 ...... 553—582

    Proceedings on the 19th November, 1907 .... 583—586

✓ An Inquiry into the Rent of Agricultural Land in England
    and Wales during the Nineteenth Century. By ROBERT
    J. THOMPSON .... 587—616

    Discussion on Mr. R. J. Thompson's Paper .... 617—624

MISCELLANEA :—

    I.—Memorandum as to Birth-Rates and Marriage-Rates
        in England and Wales. By THOMAS A. WELTON,
        F.C.A. .... 625—629

    II.—The Assize of Bread at Oxford, 1794-1820. By
        ADOLPHUS BALLARD, B.A., LL.B. (Lond.). Hon.
        M.A. (Oxon.) .... 629—637

    III.—The Differential Law of Wages. By HENRY L. MOORE,
        Columbia University, New York .... 638—651

    IV.—Agricultural Returns of Great Britain, 1907 .... 651—653

    V.—The International Congress on Tuberculosis, Washing-
        ton, 1908...................................... 654

Book Reviews .... 655—695

Statistical and Economic Articles in Recent Periodicals .... 696—705

Quarterly List of Additions to the Library .... 706—727

INDEX to vol. lxx (1907) .... 729—743

APPENDIX.   List of Fellows, Bye-Laws, Rules, &c. .... 1—71

Vol. LXX.]   [Part I.

JOURNAL

OF THE ROYAL STATISTICAL SOCIETY.

MARCH, 1907.

Correlation *of the* Weather *and* Crops.

By R. H. Hooker, F.R.Met.S.

[Read before the Royal Statistical Society, 15th January, 1907.
Sir Richard B. Martin, Bart., President, in the Chair.]

In his paper upon "Seasons in the British Isles from 1878,"[*] read in 1905 before this Society, Dr. W. N. Shaw drew attention to the great importance of the rainfall during autumn to the yield of wheat in the following summer. In the subsequent discussion upon this paper, Mr. D. A. Thomas[†] thought that the relation was not so close as Dr. Shaw seemed to think, and questioned whether the autumn rainfall were the dominant factor: to me, however, it appeared that Dr. Shaw had shown it to be of more importance than had hitherto been supposed. It occurred to me that the method of correlation might quite possibly enable us to determine whether the meteorological conditions during autumn were or were not the predominant factor in our wheat supply.

The method, although somewhat laborious, is in theory exceedingly simple and obvious. The correlation coefficients between the yield of wheat and the rainfall of various periods are calculated in the usual way, and it is then assumed that the maximum coefficient indicates the period of greatest influence. The primary problem suggested by the discussion on Dr. Shaw's paper is, therefore, to ascertain whether the correlation coefficient between the wheat yield and rainfall is higher during autumn than at any other period of the year.

It occurred to me also that it was worth while extending the scope of this inquiry to include other crops, and, in addition, to

[*] *Journal of the Royal Statistical Society*, vol. lxviii, part ii, p. 285. See also " Proc. Roy. Soc.,' 1905, p. 552, and 1906, A, p. 70 ; and " Report of the " Meteorological Committee, 1905-06," p. 20-22.

[†] *Journal*, 1905, p. 315.

ascertain similarly the effect of variations in temperature.   The tables at the end of this paper therefore comprise the correlation coefficients for successive periods of the year between (*a*) rainfall, (*b*) temperature, and the following ten crops :—wheat, barley, oats, beans, peas, potatoes, turnips and swedes, mangolds, hay from clover and rotation grasses, and hay from permanent grass.*

It will be observed that the treatment of such a subject pre-supposes a knowledge of the conditions of plant growth, practical agriculture, and of statistics, far beyond what I possess, more particularly in the case of the two former; and my grateful thanks are accordingly due to Sir William Thiselton-Dyer, F.R.S., Dr. W. Somerville, and Mr. G. U. Yule, for much information on fundamental elementary points in connection with these subjects. I hope it will be recognised that I have done my best to supplement my ignorance, by securing the help of the best authorities in their respective branches of science.

The first consideration is the selection of a suitable tract of country.   Climatic conditions differ so materially in England and Scotland, and even in different parts of England, that it is necessary to select an area sufficiently small to ensure reasonable uniformity of climate over the whole of it.   That is to say, that, if one portion is experiencing heavy rain, we want to be pretty certain that the remainder is also receiving an excess of precipitation.   On the other hand, the area must not be too small, since it is necessary, in order to attribute any results to the weather, to be fairly safe in assuming that other possible factors more or less balance each other. It is quite conceivable, for instance, that a given rainfall may have a different effect upon a crop grown on a limestone soil to what it has upon one grown on alluvium or granite ; hence the area should, if possible, be of sufficient size to comprise various geological formations, &c.   It should, moreover, include a considerable amount of each of the crops under investigation.   The area must therefore be somewhat of the nature of a compromise, and should be as large as is compatible with reasonable uniformity of climatic conditions.

These desiderata seem to me best secured in the district known in our Agricultural Returns as " Division I : England, east and " north-east."   From this I have, however, omitted the East Riding of York (as being rather too far north), Middlesex and London ; and the selected area thus consists of the counties of Lincoln, Huntingdon, Cambridge, Norfolk, Suffolk, Essex, Bedford, and Hertford.   I shall call this area Eastern England.   The average area under each of these crops in the last two decades is shown in

---

* For brevity, I shall describe these two classes of hay as "seeds' hay" and " meadow hay," respectively.

Table II. It may be pointed out, as evidence of the importance of this district in this connection, that it includes the county with the largest acreage under each of the ten crops named, except only permanent grass: it may therefore not inaptly be described as comprising the centre of production of each crop.* The yield per acre of each crop (see Tables II and III) is of course calculated from the figures of area and production given for each county in the Annual Agricultural Returns during the twenty-one years 1885-1905 (1886-1905 only in the case of the two classes of hay).

The district is also very uniform as regards climate. My data are taken from the weekly returns of the Meteorological Office, and represent the average rainfall, accumulated temperature above 42°, and accumulated temperature below 42°, in each of the periods under consideration, of the following eight stations: Hillington, Yarmouth, Geldeston, Cambridge, Felixstowe, Clacton-on-Sea, Rothamsted, Shoeburyness.† These are the stations comprised in the Meteorological District known as " England East," and are all within the agricultural area specified above, which latter, however, includes Lincolnshire. This county is so important from an agricultural point of view, that I could not omit it; there are situated within it two meteorological stations, but the data for them do not materially affect the averages I have taken.

As regards the periods of the year selected, Dr. Shaw took the usual quarters. It seemed conceivable, however, that the critical period for a crop might be a shorter time than three months: comparison with autumn rainfall indicated that conditions at the time of sowing wheat are of importance, possibly therefore a single month might prove the dominant period. On the other hand, farming operations, and the period of growth of a plant, may be delayed (for a limited length of time, doubtless varying with the crop); and consequently on an average of many years the limits of the dominant period may be more extended and ill-defined. For instance, among the problems to which an answer might be expected from this inquiry is: Is the weather at time of sowing important for turnips ? If it is, then June will be important in an

---

* Potatoes may possibly be regarded as an exception. Lincoln has, on the average, the greatest area, but owing to the higher yield per acre, Lancaster frequently surpasses it in total production.

† These averages are calculated from the data published in the " Weekly " Weather Report," but I have been saved the considerable trouble of actually working them out, as the Meteorological Office have allowed me to copy the weekly averages for the district from their books. It should be mentioned that the 53rd week, when it occurs, has been ignored: I satisfied myself that in no case was the weather in this week abnormal, and that the general average was representative of it.

early year, and possibly July in a late year; hence we must choose a period sufficiently long to cover all reasonable delays. Eight weeks seem sufficient for this in the majority of cases. The periods tested are therefore successive (and overlapping) periods of eight weeks.

I anticipated that the 33rd—40th weeks (approximately second half of August to first week in October) would be the earliest period to affect the earliest sown crop (wheat). When these calculations were practically completed, however, I found that the autumn seemed to have an important influence upon certain crops that were not sown until after the succeeding winter. I suppose a practical agriculturist might have anticipated this. I accordingly carried the calculations back for a further six months. I end with the 37th—44th weeks of the harvest year itself (approximately mid-September to early November) as being probably the last to affect the latest harvested crops (roots). I have thus examined the effect, upon each crop, of the weather during a period extending over twenty months, viz., from the 9th week (beginning of March) until the 44th week (beginning of November) of the following year. I have also taken the seasons (autumn,* winter, spring and summer), and the approximate cereal year (36th week to 35th week of the following year) as a whole, with a view to seeing whether the average of the whole year, or a three-monthly period, were more important than any particular eight weeks.

As regards the meteorological statistics, the actual rainfall figures were naturally taken. But as regards temperature, it seemed to me that the variations in the number of degrees Fahrenheit between one year and another were hardly sufficiently large to bring out the differences with sufficient clearness. I have therefore utilised the accumulated temperatures above $42°$ F.; that is to say the total number of day-degrees† above $42°$ in each period. The selection of $42°$ as a base temperature below which it is assumed that plants make (practically) no growth is, I believe, due to A. de Candolle, but I do not know how far it is supposed to apply to all plants alike. In any case, it forms the accepted base-line, and is quite convenient for the present purpose. I have also correlated the crops with the accumulated temperatures below $42°$; but these rarely appear to yield any significant information (beyond what

* These terms will throughout be used to denote approximately the three calendar months, viz., autumn = September, October, November, &c. Strictly speaking, they are periods of thirteen weeks: autumn is taken as including the 36th–48th weeks, &c.

† See, *e.g.*, Dr. Shaw's paper (*Journal*, 1905, p. 265) for an explanation of accumulated temperatures, also regarding the base temperature of $42°$ F.

may be learnt from the accumulated temperatures above 42°, with which they are of course closely correlated), and I have not as a rule discussed them.

Some explanation is perhaps desirable concerning the correlation coefficients. I have in the first place formed the ordinary coefficient[*] $r = \dfrac{\Sigma\,(xy)}{\sqrt{n}\,\sigma_1\sigma_2}$, between the crop and (a) rainfall, (b) accumulated temperature above 42°. But rainfall and temperature are themselves correlated; hence an apparent influence of, say, rainfall upon a crop may really be due to the rainfall conditions being dependent upon temperature, or *vice versâ*. Hence it seemed desirable to calculate the *partial* or *net* correlation coefficients, *i.e.* (following the notation given in Mr. Yule's paper of 1897).[†]

$$\rho_{12} = \frac{r_{12} - r_{13}\,r_{23}}{\sqrt{(1 - r_{13}{}^2)\,(1 - r_{23}{}^2)}}, \quad \rho_{13} = \frac{r_{13} - r_{12}\,r_{23}}{\sqrt{(1 - r_{12}{}^2)\,(1 - r_{23}{}^2)}}.$$

This partial coefficient (ρ) may be regarded as a truer indication of the connection between the crop and each factor alone, inasmuch as, speaking approximately, we may say that the effect of the other factor is eliminated. It may be observed, moreover, that the relative influence of rainfall and temperature upon the crop is given by $\dfrac{\rho_{12}}{\rho_{13}}$; or, more accurately, this fraction measures the relative effect of changes equal in amount to their respective standard deviations in the rainfall and temperature.[‡] In discussing the figures in the tables I shall accordingly utilise the partial correlation coefficients rather than the others. Finally, I have worked out what Mr. Yule calls the coefficient of double correlation[§] between the crop and rainfall and accumulated temperature above 42°, $R = \sqrt{\dfrac{r_{12}{}^2 + r_{13}{}^2 - 2r_{12}\,r_{23}\,r_{13}}{1 - r_{23}{}^2}}$, or as it may also be written, $R = \sqrt{1 - (1 - r_{12}{}^2)(1 - \rho_{13}{}^2)}$, a form which is quicker to calculate. This may be regarded as a measure of the joint influence of the rainfall and temperature upon the crop. For the sake of brevity, I shall speak of R as measuring the effect of the

---

[*] See, *e.g.*, Yule "On the Theory of Correlation" (*Journal*, vol. lxi. 1897, p. 812, *et seq.*, or Bowley, "Elements of Statistics."

[†] *Journal*, 1897, p. 833.

[‡] *Cf.* Hooker and Yule, "Note on Estimating the Relative Influence of Two "Variables upon a Third" (*Journal*, 1906, p. 197). In that paper we gave a method of estimating the relative influence of equal *percentage* changes in two factors, the fraction there given being equivalent to $\dfrac{\rho_{12}}{\rho_{13}} \cdot \dfrac{\sigma_2}{\sigma_3}$.

[§] *Journal*, 1906, p. 199; also 1897, p. 833.

" weather," using this term in the strictly limited sense of consisting only of these two factors.

Before discussing the actual results of the calculations, several cautions are necessary. In the first place, what value of the correlation coefficient may we safely regard as significant of a causal connection between the crops and rainfall or temperature? Clearly, with the very small number of observations at our command, a very small coefficient can no more be regarded as absolute evidence of such than, say, 3 successive throws of sixes with a die can be taken as proof positive that the die is loaded. In this case, we have records of the yield of crops for only 21 years, *i.e.*, we have but 21 observations. Mr. Bowley suggests[*] that when the correlation coefficient (r) is greater than six times its probable error we may be practically certain that two phenomena are not independent of each other. Now the probable error of the correlation coefficient $= 0\cdot67 \dfrac{1 - r^2}{\sqrt{n}}$; on this assumption, then, the correlation coefficient may be regarded as satisfactory evidence of causal connection when $r = 6 \times 0\cdot67 \dfrac{1 - r^2}{\sqrt{n}}$ or more, *i.e.*, when $r = 0\cdot58$. With a large number of observations, such a coefficient would be a very high one; but in the present instance we must ignore many values that would generally be regarded as significant. The chance that there is no real connection when the coefficient is as high as six times its probable error is, I believe, something like one in 15,000, and I think we shall be fairly safe in assuming a real connection whenever the coefficient is over 0·5. It must be observed, however, that with lower coefficients the probability of there being interdependence is still very great; we should for instance only be wrong once in about seven times by assuming connection when the correlation coefficient is 0·3 (probable error = 0·135). I propose accordingly to regard a coefficient between 0·3 and 0·5 as *suggestive* of dependence. Values below 0·3 I shall, as a rule, ignore, in the absence of any corroborative evidence. Perhaps I may remark that I believe that some statisticians would consider themselves justified in drawing deductions from lower coefficients than those I have adopted as my limits.

The probable error of ρ, Mr. Yule informs me, is similar to that of r, viz., $0\cdot67 \dfrac{1 - \rho^2}{\sqrt{n}}$. I, therefore, take the same limits as above indicated, namely, 0·5 and 0·3 as satisfactory evidence, and as suggestive, of causal connection respectively.

---

[*] " Elements of Statistics " (1st edition), p. 320.

The double correlation coefficient (R) is not so simple. This value can of course never fall below 0, and the square root of the mean square of all accidental values should theoretically (Mr. Yule estimates) be 0·31 in the present instance, corresponding to a somewhat lower arithmetic mean value of about 0·25, if the variables were really independent. The probable error would seem to be less, rather than greater, than the value of

$$0·67\frac{1 - R^2}{\sqrt{n}}.$$

I may perhaps here usefully call attention to some calculations, in reality based upon a false assumption, that I had made with a view to ascertaining approximately, from the observations, the limiting values of r, ρ, and R, that might be regarded as satisfactory evidence of dependence. I assumed that all coefficients obtained by correlating a crop with a period after it had been harvested, or before the seed had been put in the ground, were purely accidental: hence all such coefficients should be less than the required limiting values, and, being chance observations, should follow the normal law of error. Tabulating 116 such values of r, 84 values of ρ, and 42 values of R, I found, as was to be expected, that the average of r and ρ was practically 0; that of R was 0·265. Now in a normal distribution, practically the whole of the observations should fall within a value of three times the standard deviation on either side of the average. For r the standard deviation worked out at $\sigma = 0·22$; this gave a critical value of 0·66 as the practical end of the range of all chance values, *i.e.*, rather higher than the 0·58 found above. As a matter of fact, all the 116 coefficients lay between $\pm$ 0·5; which confirmed me in my supposition that I was safe in taking this quantity as my limiting value. The 84 partial coefficients yielded almost identically the same σ (viz., 0·21), with a range slightly smaller, for they all lay between $\pm$ 0·45. Hence I had already concluded that, for practical purposes, the probable error of ρ might be treated as the same as that of r, a supposition which Mr. Yule afterwards proved theoretically. The standard deviation of the coefficient of double correlation worked out at 0·15. As subsequent investigation showed that all periods prior to sowing the crop cannot be regarded as without influence, the above calculations can hardly be accepted as really throwing much light upon the point. I may remark, however, that it is precisely the largest of these coefficients that fall at periods when the seed is likely to be affected, and which can, therefore, be regarded as highly significant. This consideration is consequently a further confirmation of my opinion that the limiting values I have adopted are ample.

It will be remembered that the main problem of this paper is to determine the highest coefficients between each crop and the weather. But each coefficient, it must not be forgotten, is qualified by its probable error. I have not worked these out, because they can be so easily deduced from the formula; but they must not be overlooked. Any given correlation coefficient must only be regarded as the most probable value of that coefficient; and in making comparisons between any two the higher is as a rule in reality only more or less probably greater than the other. The degree of probability varies considerably: where the difference is slight, the probability is small, but it always exists. The paucity of observations is again unfortunate, as the probable error is so large that I am seldom able to state emphatically that any particular period is the most important. As an illustration, the probability that a coefficient of 0·6 really represents a degree of dependence greater than 0·5 is something like 3 to 1. With this reservation, which applies throughout, that period which yields the highest coefficient may be regarded as exercising the most influence* upon a crop. And it is always true to say that the actual coefficient found is an accurate measure of the amount of coincidence between the crop and the weather during the particular period under review; or that the difference between two coefficients measures the actual difference between the coincidences of the two periods in these years. The relationship found is therefore the relationship that has really existed during that period; but we are usually in a position to say only that the same relationship *probably* holds generally.

Two or three further cautions must be given concerning the data. First as regards the meteorological. All the calculations, and therefore all the deductions therefrom, relate solely to differences from the average. Differences from the average, however, may indicate very different meteorological conditions. A fall of 2 inches of rain in June, for instance, may be made up by a dull rather drizzly month, or it may be a single thunderstorm followed by a four weeks' drought. The effect upon a crop of these two sets of almost diametrically opposite conditions is probably entirely different. But I have perforce had to ignore such phenomena. Mere differences from averages, therefore, cannot tell the whole story of weather influences; all I have aimed at ascertaining is what story these do tell. The work on this has been very considerable, and I must, in regard to any other factor, adopt the ancient motto of this Society: *aliis exterendum* (let somebody else thresh it out).

* It would in many cases be truer to say that that period is more frequently than any other the dominant factor.

Secondly, as regards the crops, it must be borne in mind that the correlation coefficients relate solely to the quantity harvested, not the quality of the crop. I have unexpectedly, however, found evidence of the influence of the weather upon one quality of the seed. Finding, as already stated, that in certain cases some periods prior to sowing were important, it seemed possible that this might be due to the weather of the preceding harvest (or other) time having affected the ripening of the seed. This turned out to be the case, and it will be seen that a factor of great importance in some crops is the condition of the seed as harvested in the previous year. The figures have thus yielded evidence of the influence of the weather upon at least one quality of the seed. I shall use the word " condition " to denote this particular quality, and the term must be understood to mean solely " power of producing a bulky crop next season " (of grain, roots, &c., as the case may be) : in fact, quality from the seed merchant's point of view. The correlation coefficients with the *previous* growing season are therefore indicative of the conditions requisite for " condition " of a crop, and not quantity (except, of course, in the case of hay). I have no information regarding what is usually known as quality, from the consumer's point of view.

This distinction must be carefully borne in mind if some of my results appear unexpected. Indeed, I suspect that many of the factors required for quantity are injurious to quality (using the term in its ordinary sense, *i.e.,* milling, feeding, malting, &c., value). It does not therefore follow that the period which is most critical for the quantity of a crop is also the most critical so far as regards total value (quantity × quality). This is probably more especially the case as regards ripening of fruits, and perhaps also grain, for which sunlight (and consequently high temperature) during summer is generally regarded as necessary. For instance, I do not find a single crop that wants a hot summer to give a bulky yield ; yet the quality of many kinds of produce is injuriously affected by a cold wet summer. Sugar-beet, for instance, though possibly giving roots of large size in a wet season, would contain little sugar, and the feeding quality of mangolds is doubtless similarly affected. Having, therefore, no statistics of quality for consumptive purposes, this point is also *aliis exterendum ;* and nothing that follows can be taken as suggesting opinions contrary to those usually held upon this subject.

A consideration which may usefully be borne in mind is that, in investigations such as the present, a correlation coefficient zero is not necessarily an indication that there is no connection between the crop and the weather. The coefficient only tells us the degree of correspondence of the differences of the two variables from their respective averages (with a linear law). Imagine, for instance, a crop for which the average rainfall of the east of England is actually the most suitable; then any deviation, whether above or below, from this average should be the more detrimental according to the amount of the excess or deficiency, and the correlation coefficient would be, theoretically, zero. Similarly, if the optimum weather conditions were nearly, but not quite, the average, we should only have a small correlation coefficient. It is only when the optimum conditions differ materially from that of the district under review that we may expect to find significant coefficients, and be enabled to say that the crop does better in a different climate, or to specify the meteorological conditions that suit it. Hence, when we find no correlation between the weather and a crop, it by no means follows that the crop is indifferent to the weather. The correlation of data under such conditions is a very complex matter, and the question of whether a crop is indifferent to the meteorological changes or whether the actual meteorological conditions are the optimum, must be determined by other methods; the method of correlation is not adapted to this particular problem. I shall, however, have something to say in this connection later on.

It must further be remarked that the deductions drawn from coefficients other than the highest are qualified by the possibility of correlation between the weather of the two periods. How far the weather of one part of the year depends upon that of another is a big question that cannot be discussed within the limits of this paper. I am satisfied, however, that twenty-one years is much too short a period to allow of our ignoring random correlation (whether apparent or real). For instance, the average autumn rainfall in the first decade is much greater than in the second. I do not suppose the autumn is really getting dryer, but merely that the period is not long enough to yield a stable average. I have not had time to examine this possible connection except in one or two instances where the coincidence appeared striking. If there be correlation of the weather at any two periods, it may have the effect of reducing the coefficient between the crop and one (or possibly both) periods below the critical value. But the higher of the two coefficients, after this allowance has been made, will still remain the higher.

These cautions and limitations being premised, I now proceed to discuss the figures obtained for each of the individual crops.

Wheat (Seed gathered, August. Sown, mid-October to mid-November. Crop harvested, August).—The highest partial coefficient I have found for any eight-week period is − 0·62 with rain in the 37th—44th weeks—*i.e.*, at and just before the sowing period.

Absence of rain in September and October is therefore more important to the wheat crop than rain or temperature at any other period of the year. This is therefore the answer to the primary question arising out of the discussion on Dr. Shaw's paper, and may, I think, be accepted as strong evidence in favour of his contention. I observe, moreover, that the partial coefficient between wheat and *autumn* rain is only − 0·53 : it would therefore seem that the most critical period for wheat is shorter than three months. Of course, it is possible that a yet higher coefficient might be obtained by taking a slightly different eight weeks, or a somewhat longer or shorter period than that chosen.

The highest coefficient of all is − 0·69 for the cereal year as a whole. Naturally, the rainfall of the year is dependent upon that of the different seasons, but I think this means that a dry twelve months is (in so far as stress can be laid upon the difference between 0·69 and 0·62) rather more important than a dry autumn alone. But among the seasons a dry September-October ranks first among the wheat's requirements.

The most surprising feature at first sight, however, is its requirement of a dry warm winter. For the first eight weeks of the year $R = 0·68$, or just more than in the 37th—44th weeks ($R = 0·65$). The combined effect of rain and temperature in winter seems, therefore, at least as great as the autumn rainfall alone. The partial coefficient for rain in these first eight weeks is − 0·55 ; but this is largely due to the fact that the rainfall of 1st—8th weeks is highly correlated ($r = +0·60$) with the rainfall of the 37th—44th weeks. So large a coefficient indicates a real interdependence between the winter and autumn rainfall; still, even if the connection were accidental and due to insufficiency of the number of observations, its effect on the figures must be taken into account. Estimating the partial correlation coefficients between crop and rainfall of the two periods, we have − 0·48 for the autumnal eight weeks and − 0·31 only for the winter weeks (whereas r was − 0·66 and − 0·58 respectively). Hence the winter coefficient would seem to be partly adventitious, and the main connection to be with the autumn.

It is interesting to observe that Gilbert and Lawes noticed the detrimental effect of a wet winter[*] (November to February), but the importance of a dry seeding-time appears to have escaped them. My calculations indicate that this dependence upon a wet winter is largely due to correlation between the autumn and winter rainfalls ; but I have not the figures to enable me to determine whether the wheat

* Hall: "An Account of the Rothamsted Experiments," p. 60; also Gilbert and Lawes, Journal of the Royal Agricultural Society (1880), vol. xli, p. 173, *et seq.*

crops obtained at Rothamsted were correlated with the seed-time to the same degree as during the last two decades. Gilbert and Lawes dealt with a period almost immediately preceding mine; hence, if there were correlation - between crop and autumn rainfall, there would seem to have also probably [but by no means necessarily] been correlation between rainfall in winter and autumn. This would enormously increase the probability of a real connection between autumn and winter rain. Gilbert and Lawes concluded that the most critical period of the wheat's growth lay in the first four months, when the foundation of roots was being laid.* My calculations point to the foundation having been laid in a much shorter time, and I think a great deal of light could be thrown on the point if the Rothamsted figures were correlated for the much longer period at their disposal.

As regards the temperature, the matter is, I think, different. We find $\rho = + 0.57$ for the whole winter, indicating that wheat likes a mild winter. This is perhaps a little unexpected, but is, I think, borne out by a consideration of the experience of North America. In Great Britain, wheat is sown in autumn, and passes the winter in the ground; but in Canada and the northern wheat-growing districts of the United States, wheat is mostly a spring corn, comparatively little "fall wheat" being sown. In the southern portion of the wheat belt, and on the mild Pacific coast, on the other hand, the varieties grown are chiefly winter wheat. In other words, wheat is sown in America in the autumn in those States which have a relatively less rigorous winter. It would seem that experience has shown that a cold winter is detrimental.

No other partial coefficient during the period of growth amounts to 0.5; but there are two distinctly suggestive coefficients: the first ($- 0.44$ in the 17th—24th weeks) indicating that wheat likes a cold spring; the second ($- 0.46$ in the 25th—32nd weeks) pointing to a dry July.

As regards condition of the seed, we find two other important periods during the preceding year's growth. Partial coefficients of $- 0.49$ during the 21st—28th weeks (say about June) and of $+ 0.51$ during the 29th—36th weeks (covering August) indicate that absence of rain during the flowering period, and warmth at harvest time are wanted for good germinating seed. It seems clear, therefore, that in the case of wheat the condition of the seed is a very important factor, perhaps second only to the weather at the time of sowing, and during winter.

It would seem also that the temperature conditions during the summer affect the bulk and condition of the seed differently. All

* Hall: "An Account of the Rothamsted Experiments," p. 62.

through spring and summer of the harvest year there are a series of negative coefficients with bulk.   They do not quite attain, except in two instances, my criterion of suggestiveness, but I think the sequence is in itself suggestive that cool weather is a desideratum for a heavy yield.   For condition, on the other hand, the preceding summer should be warm.   Hence we might expect that the seed of a bulky crop would not usually be of good quality.   This consideration suggests a simple explanation of a phenomenon frequently observed, viz. : that a good crop is often succeeded by a poor one.

It may be said that farmers have always been quite aware that a wet autumn means a bad seed-bed for wheat.   In evidence of this I have correlated the rainfall of the 37—44th weeks with the area sown with wheat each year.   The coefficient works out to − 0·41,* thus showing that less land is put under wheat in a wet than in a dry autumn.   Further striking evidence of this will be found in a diagram in the Agricultural Statistics (Part I, p. 11) for 1906. This gives the area under wheat, barley and oats since 1867 ; and inspection will show that a fall in the wheat area is practically invariably followed by an increase in barley and oats, and *vice versâ.* I have correlated the successive annual changes in the figures in that diagram, and find that the coefficient between the wheat and barley areas of England is − 0·59, while that between the wheat and oat areas is as much as − 0·86, and between the wheat area and the whole area under barley or oats − 0·88.   This is an exceedingly high coefficient, indicating that the joint barley and oat area in any particular year is almost entirely dependent upon the area put under wheat five months earlier, and not upon the weather at the time of sowing.   In other words, the farmer proposes to devote a certain area to corn, and if the autumn prove too wet for wheat, he leaves a certain portion of that area unsown till the spring, when he puts in barley or oats.   Whether the farmer really knows that he is not likely to get a heavy yield with a wet seed-bed, as I believe is generally the case, or whether he merely refrains from tilling the land at that season on account of the mechanical difficulty of the operation, the result is the same : his practice agrees with what these statistics show to be the best. It may be thought that farmers might take greater advantage of the variations in the seasons, but this is not always possible ; they may want a certain amount of wheat straw, or a serious disturbance in the rotation might nullify any saving in this direction by loss on subsequent crops.

* Since the area under wheat has fallen largely during the period, I have correlated successive annual changes in the wheat area and the rainfall (*cf. Journal,* vol. lxviii, p. 696).

Before leaving the subject of the effect of autumn rainfall upon the wheat crop, mention may be made of another important factor pointed out by Dr. Shaw.* This is the periodicity in the yield of wheat. Dr. Shaw showed that there has been a very remarkable periodicity in the yield during the past twenty years, and has found an eleven year period; the actual harvests, as recorded by the Board of Agriculture, being in remarkable agreement with the results obtained from calculations based upon this theory. It so happens that 1906 forms, to a certain extent, a test of the relative importance of the autumn rainfall and periodicity factors. The autumn rainfall in 1905 was deficient, amounting to but 6·05 inches, and according to the formula given by Dr. Shaw as best applicable to the east of England,† W = 46 − 2·2 R, a yield of 32·7 bushels per acre, or well above the average, might be anticipated. On the other hand, the probable figure indicated for 1906 by the periodic curve is practically equal to a yield as low as any during the past twenty years—say about 27 bushels per acre. Hence the two factors are, for almost the first time in twenty years, in direct opposition, and it is accordingly of peculiar interest to see which wins. The yield actually recorded is 34·3 bushels per acre, which is in fair agreement with that forecasted from a study of the autumn rainfall. That it is 1½ bushels higher is due to practically all the other seasons being also favourable; the previous harvest time was very warm, the winter was warm : April to June was cool, and July and August were dry.‡ I observe that 1895-96 is mentioned by

* " Proc. Roy. Soc." A. vol. 78, 1906, p. 69.

† Proc. Roy. Soc. A. 1906, p. 76. Dr. Shaw's district is not absolutely identical with mine, but the difference is not sufficiently great to materially modify the formula.

‡ It is of some interest to compare Dr. Shaw's equation with the regression equation given by my data for the 37—44th weeks. The formula for this is

$$w = r \frac{\sigma_w}{\sigma_i} i$$ where w and i are the differences of the wheat yield and of the rainfall from their means, and σ_w and σ_i are the standard deviations of these two variables. The yield deduced for 1906 by this equation from the rainfall of the 37—44th week is therefore—

$$w = - 0.66 \times \frac{3.04}{1.90} \times (- 0.61) = + 0.64 \text{ bushels above average,}$$

indicating a total yield of 32 05 bushels per acre. But the autumn, although favourable, was not exceptionally so, and other factors have affected the crop of 1906 to a greater degree, particularly the period when the seed of the 1905 crop was being harvested. Forming the regression equation with the accumulated temperature of the 29—36th week of the preceding year, we get—

$$w = + 0 52 \times \frac{3.04}{89.0} \times 100 = 1.78 \text{ bushels above the average,}$$

corresponding to a yield of 33·19 bushels per acre. The bountiful wheat harvest of 1906 appears, in fact, to be mainly attributable to the condition of

Dr. Shaw as a nodal period, perhaps he can tell us whether we ought to have anticipated that at the next nodal period (eleven years later, *i.e.*, 1906-07) the forecast might not be reliable ?

Barley (Seed gathered, August. Sown, mid-March to mid-April. Crop harvested, August).—The chief, and very important, requisite for the barley crop appears to be a cool summer. No less than four successive (overlapping) periods show a coefficient greater than − 0·5 with temperature, indicating cool weather from May till the commencement of September, apparently from the time of flowering till harvest; the highest coefficient of all being − 0·70 in the 25— 32nd weeks (say mid-June to mid-August). At this period also there is a large negative coefficient (− 0·55) with rain ; barley would there- fore seem to prefer the somewhat unusual combination of a cool dry summer. There is also a suggestive coefficient indicating dry weather in January and February. This is perhaps in accordance with *à priori* expectations ; it is well known that barley seed should be sown in a fine tilth, and this can hardly be secured with a wet clogged soil. A rainfall above the average does not seem to be a necessity at any time. The preceding season also does not seem to have any very marked effect upon the condition of the seed ; a warm dry summer is probably preferable, for though none of the coefficients are large, the long sequence of positive coefficients with warmth, and of negative with rain, may be significant.

In connection with barley, it may be as well to recall that my figures can take no account of consumptive quality, whether for brewing or feeding. Brewing quality in this crop is, practically, recognised to be closely connected with early sowing ; and it is pretty generally known that, at the Brewers' Exhibitions, the prize samples of malting barley prove to be the earliest sown.* Barley is essentially a crop of which the profits depend on quality—the difference in price between a malting and a feeding sample being exceedingly great. I am afraid that my figures can therefore be of no assistance in determining what weather conditions most affect the profitableness of the crop.

the seed. There is probably some correlation between the figures measuring the weather at these two periods ; but if it were permissible to ignore this, we could say, with some degree of approximation, that the seed-time and condition of the seed together accounted for some 2·4 bushels (it is of course really some- thing less) of the total observed increase of 2·9 above the average. Some smaller additions are, as above noticed, due to the favourable weather at other periods of the year. As the coefficients for the various periods of the year show, there are several seasons which exercise an important influence on the wheat crop ; still, as might be expected, a better forecast is obtained by taking account of more than one season than by utilising only the principal period.

* *Cf.* Journal of the Board of Agriculture, vol. iii, p. 394.

Attention may perhaps be called to the different deductions which might be drawn from the total and partial correlation coefficients. The total coefficients are suggestive of the desirability of rain in the spring, but they are largely reduced when the connection between rain and temperature is taken into account; and their relative largeness becomes more apparent than real. On the other hand, in the 25—32nd week r is nearly 0, whereas the effect of rain is at that time really considerable, judged by ρ.

Oats (Seed gathered, August. Sown, mid-March to mid-April. Crop harvested, August).—Oats are similar to barley inasmuch as they urgently require a cool summer : the partial coefficients between oats and temperature being almost identical with those of barley in the 17—36th weeks. But they differ from barley in requiring rain in the spring; in fact for the spring (season) the coefficient with rainfall (+ 0·70) is just above the summer coefficient with temperature (– 0·69). Before harvest (25—32nd week), however, they would seem to like dry weather. There are some suggestive negative coefficients with rainfall during autumn; can they mean that oat seed does not keep well during a damp autumn ? The coefficients with the preceding summer all seem insignificant.

Comparing the three cereals, it is noteworthy that with barley and oats spring and summer are of preponderating importance, seed-time being relatively unimportant : with wheat, on the other hand, there are several different periods which may materially affect the crop, the seed-time being the most influential.

Beans (Seed gathered, mid-September to mid-October. Sown mid-October to mid-November.* Crop harvested, mid-September to mid-October).—These very much resemble wheat in their require-ments. They want a dry seed-time, but the coefficients are not quite so high as with the cereal. It would also seem that they like the temperature then to be low, whereas there was no such indica-tion with wheat. The most important point with beans, however, would seem to be the condition of the seed sown, for I find the highest coefficient in the 33rd—40th weeks, covering the period of the previous season's harvest. We may therefore infer that a previous dry summer, with warmth during the latest ripening period, is of more importance to the subsequent bean crop than the weather at sowing time.† With wheat, on the other hand, the reverse seemed to hold.

---

* The bulk of the crop in the eastern counties may be taken to be winter beans.

† This is of course subject to the qualification, to which attention has already been generally directed, that the probability of this coefficient (R = 0·57) being really higher than the next (R = 0·56 in the 17—24th weeks) is very small.

Of the other periods of the year, the figures suggest that beans like a warm winter, a wet spring and summer (the coefficients, though small, are worth a certain weight on account of their persistence), and cold weather about May. It must be borne in mind that considerable quantities of beans are sown in the spring: hence if the spring crop is affected by conditions to which the winter crop is indifferent, we might get a correlation coefficient (probably small) at that time without our being able to say which of the two crops was affected. It may be surmised, however, that the wet spring is required chiefly for the main (autumn-sown) crop, since we found that crop to prefer a dry seeding-time.

Peas (Seed gathered, August. Sown, mid-February to mid-March. Crop harvested, August).—Like beans, the chief factor (coefficient – 0·47) suggested is condition of the seed: for this the previous summer should be dry, and apparently not hot. There are also suggestions of a cool time about May in the season of growth; and the condition of the seed is perhaps favoured by a wet spring. The calculations with this crop (like the next) have yielded hardly any coefficients of importance, and their chief interest is the confirmation they give to the deductions regarding the other leguminous crop. The balance in favour of the condition of the seed being more important for beans than the seed time was, as we saw, slight; but the evidence of the peas lends additional force to the argument that this is the principal factor with these two allied plants.

Potatoes ("Seed" gathered, mid-August to mid-September. "Sown," March—April. Crop harvested, mid-August to mid-September).—Here also I get comparatively little information; as with peas, no coefficient reaches 0·5. A dry summer, from about May to August, seems to be required, and possibly a dry spell just before planting. Whether the dry summer would be directly required for a great weight of tubers in healthy conditions may possibly be doubted; it is very likely on account of drought retarding potato disease, which fungus spreads most rapidly in warm wet weather and is detrimental to the size of the tubers. As regards the condition of the "seed" (sets), also, but little information is forthcoming, though possibly the fact that the coefficients with temperature are all negative may indicate a preference for cool weather. (See also the footnote on p. 22.)

Turnips and **Swedes** (Seed gathered, second half of July. Sown, June—July. Crop harvested, November).—The highest coefficient, + 0·55, indicates rain in June and July, *i.e.*, the sowing season, as the chief necessity. This is no doubt, partly at least, required on account of the turnip fly, which, as is well known, will eat off

a young crop as soon as it shows above ground in a dry season,
to such an extent that a turnip field is frequently re-sown more
than once. Oddly enough, after this period I find no significant
correlation with rainfall, the partial coefficients indicating that the
real connection is with a cool temperature from Midsummer to
Michaelmas. In other words, rainy weather appears to suit turnips
because such weather is cool. The coefficient with rainfall for the
year as a whole is, curiously, higher than for any particular period
(except the eight weeks already mentioned), although not equal to
that with temperature. This latter coefficient for the whole cereal
year is also larger than that for any shorter period, but this
is natural in view of the whole series of negative coefficients
throughout absolutely the entire twelve months.

The absence of any large coefficients with rainfall in the late
summer seems rather remarkable ; indeed in the 33rd—44th weeks
(say mid-August to October) the coefficient is actually just negative.
Considering how farmers look to rain at this period to swell out the
roots when a dry summer has left them backward, such coefficients
are unexpected. I take the explanation to be partly that the
English climate usually furnishes a sufficiency of wet at some time
or another of the plant's growth. Autumn rainfall in fact is
perhaps only useful if the earlier part of the season has been dry.
Nevertheless, it may almost be doubted whether a wet summer is
vital for roots ; there are certainly some striking exceptions : the
exceedingly wet year of 1903 gave a turnip crop below the average,
while the dry season of 1906 has given practically an average yield.

There are a remarkable series of suggestive coefficients in the
autumn, pointing to the desirability of cool weather throughout the
whole autumn and winter previous to sowing. None of the coefficients attain the critical 0·5, but the regularity of the sequence of
figures cannot be ignored. It would almost seem that, as with oats,
we have here another case of the keeping quality of the seed
being affected, but in this case the requirement seems to be cold.
The winter coefficients may indicate the desirability of frosty
weather to secure a good tilth, but this explanation can hardly
apply to the coefficients in the early autumn. The highest of these
negative coefficients occur after the seed harvest, which would be
covered by the 25th—32nd weekly period.

Altogether, the connection between the turnips and the weather
seems the most curious, and most difficult to interpret.

Mangold (Seed gathered, end of August to beginning of
September. Sown, mid-April to mid-May. Crop harvested,
October).—This seems to require a cold spell from at least the
beginning of March to the end of June, and probably throughout

the summer. A rainfall above average also seems desirable in the spring. Mangolds require a fine tilth, and the explanation of the high coefficient with the temperature of the late winter —long before the seed is sown—may perhaps be that frosts are desirable for the proper mellowing of a good seed bed. The whole of the preceding summer should be dry, indicating that condition of the seed may be nearly as important as weather conditions during the season of growth.

Attention may perhaps be drawn to the comparatively high (negative) coefficient with accumulated temperature below 42° in the 37—44th week. A similar coefficient is found with turnips and swedes, and also with one or two other crops of which the harvest is completed by that date, so that too much stress cannot be laid upon these suggestive figures, especially as they have not been taken into account in calculating the more reliable partial coefficients. But it is well known that mangolds are seriously injured by frosts, and in the case of roots the figures may therefore be significant. They do not, I presume, mean that cold weather reduces the size of the roots, but that if cold weather sets in early the roots are lifted at once instead of being left to grow a little longer, as may occur in a warmer season.

Hay.—With this crop we get the highest coefficients of all ; the essential requirement being, as will appear strange to no one, a heavy precipitation during spring.

In the case of hay from clover and rotation grasses,* which I shall abbreviate to " seeds' hay," the partial correlation coefficient reaches its maximum, + 0·76 with the spring rainfall, the double coefficient, with " weather," being 0·80. Consideration of the eight-weekly periods shows that the critical period is much shorter than with most other crops, from mid-April to mid-June at latest evidently being the extreme limits for useful rains. There are also indications of the desirability of cool weather (irrespective of rain) in spring and summer. Unexpectedly high coefficients may be noticed in the autumn after sowing, indicating dry cool weather from August to October as desirable, the coefficient with temperature being as much as − 0·54, and with rain − 0·5. I am not sure how to translate this, perhaps I may venture to suggest that removal of the corn crop, and consequent exposure of the young crop to the heavens may in some way affect it. Probably the shelter it has enjoyed from hot

---

* Clover seed is gathered in September, grass seed in July. It is sown with the corn crop in the following spring (mid-March to mid-April) and the crop is harvested in June of the following year. My figures in the case of this crop, therefore, go back only as far as seed-time. A large proportion of the clovers and rotation grasses are, however, left down for two or three years.

sun is beneficial and the plant misses it at first; cool weather mitigating the shock which the young plants experience on the removal of the cereal crop that has previously nursed them. The crop perhaps also likes a dry winter.

Another unexpectedly high coefficient is the +0.51 found with the rainfall of the 9—16th weeks of the preceding season. Rain is evidently desirable then—probably with warmth—but is not required again until twelve months afterwards. The 9—16th weeks cover exactly the period of sowing. It may be remembered that neither barley nor oats, with which the clovers are usually sown, showed any special predilection for rain at this time.

The hay from permanent grass, or meadow hay (harvested mid-June to mid-July), exhibits some small differences from the seeds' hay which may nevertheless have a meaning. The coefficient with spring rainfall is slightly lower (+ 0.71). But the coefficients with temperature are all suggestive that the meadow hay requires cool weather throughout the spring and summer (the latest month doubtless affecting the second cut). I do not know whether these results indicate so much a real difference between the two classes of hay, as that a larger proportion of the permanent grass is low-lying, on damper land less suitable for arable culture, and in many cases irrigated. Such portions being rather better supplied with water, may be rather more indifferent to precipitation, and hence the correlation of the whole crop with the rainfall may be smaller, while the effects of temperature are able to show themselves. It is conceivable that the smaller demand of the seeds' hay for cooler weather is more apparent than real, and that its requirements in this respect are masked by the more urgent necessity for moisture.

With the permanent grass also there is some evidence that cool dry weather in the preceding autumn is an advantage; though the coefficients are not quite so high as in the case of the seeds' hay. This may indicate that my suggestion—that the removal of the sheltering crops is of importance—is wrong, or that permanent grass also really requires the same conditions at that period, and should not make too much growth. It is, however, quite likely that the connection may be only apparent, since the yields of the two kinds of hay are themselves so very closely correlated that, if one is connected with the autumn, the other will also show some correlation with it. Similarly, I imagine that the apparent requirements of the permanent grass, in the way of rain, in the 9—16th weeks of the preceding year are due to the correlation between the two hay crops. I may call attention to the fact that, although the differences in the coefficients for the two classes of hay are comparatively slight, they are all remarkably consistent in bearing out the suggestions I give as regards the behaviour of these crops.

The desirability of a cool spring before hay-making was hardly to be expected. Generally, farmers look to warm wet weather at this time of the year to bring the crops along, more especially grass : indeed, with warm rains, we can almost "see the plants " growing." But according to these figures such warmth is not wanted : cold rains seem to suit grass better than warm ones.

Regarding more generally the influence of the weather upon the crops, the statistics in most cases tell us little that we did not know before. But one feature stands out with—to me—quite unexpected prominence, and that is the advantage of cool weather during spring and summer for the great majority of the crops. Indeed, there is no coefficient, with the exception of those with potatoes, that even seems to suggest the possibility of warmth at that period being other than detrimental. The coefficients do not in all cases reach the critical 0·5 which I have adopted as the index to practical certainty, but potatoes and turnips are the only two that do not show at least a suggestive figure between April and June. Taking the 17th—24th weeks, or say the period from the end of April to mid-June, we have the following five partial correlation coefficients between temperature and the corn and pulse crops : $-0·44$, $-0·51$, $-0·60$, $-0·45$, and $-0·40$; and this cool weather should in most cases last considerably longer, generally throughout the summer. What is to be noticed more particularly, however, is that it is not because cool weather usually accompanies a wet May and June : the calculations I have made practically eliminate the influence of the rain, and show that it is really with cool weather, irrespective of rain, that the relationship exists. If rain comes also, it is as a rule acceptable, and in the case of oats especially rain is required, more particularly somewhat earlier.

The interpretation of this result I must leave to botanists, but to one who has no knowledge of that science it may perhaps be permitted to ask whether it means that, to secure a bulky yield, the grain should mature slowly. As already mentioned, other conditions may be desired for quality. In this connection the different behaviour of the grass crop may be noticed. Consideration of the coefficients prior to April point to the desirability of weather conditions which do not allow it to make much progress before then (once the seeds have had a good start), and the greatest bulk seemed to be secured when the grass can respond with sudden growth to the spring rains.

Root crops also appear to want cool weather throughout the summer—not rain : they want rain in the late spring and early summer only. In their case the evidence, although the different crops corroborate each other, is not so strong as with cereals ; still it seems probable that a good start, and cool weather to follow (? to allow of persistent uninterrupted growth), are the optimum conditions.

With hay, on the other hand, moisture is overwhelmingly important, temperature taking a secondary place. This is also, no doubt, as is generally known from practical observation, the case with the stalks and foliage of the cereal crops (straw) and of roots.

The second important point, which is perhaps only clearly realised among the more educated farmers, is that the condition of the seed sown may be quite as important as the weather during any period of growth. With the pulse crops, the figures indicate that it is the primary factor, while it is also a very weighty consideration in the case of wheat, mangolds, and possibly other roots.

This raises a nice point of practical importance. With many crops it is a not infrequent practice to import seed from a different part of the country. "Change of seed," as it is called, is often looked upon with favour. There seems for instance to be a growing practice among certain English farmers to import potato seed from Scotland ; while large quantities of clover and grass seed are imported from abroad, notably from warmer climates where it may be assumed to have ripened better (from the seedsman's point of view). My figures indicate—though feebly—cool weather as desirable for condition in potato seed : is this a theoretical reason (besides exhaustion of the stock) why Scotch seed, coming from a cooler climate, should be better than English grown ?* Dr. Somerville also informs me that much of the wheat and barley sown in Scotland and the north of England is not home-grown : my figures decidedly support this practice by showing the greater production from seed

---

* Since this was written, I have come across a booklet entitled "Potato Demonstration," by Messrs. Sutton. Experiments have been conducted by them which seem to answer this question in the affirmative, as Scotch and Irish seed yielded much better than English, particularly south English. They conclude that the chief requirement for the production of good seed potatoes is an equable climate, so that the plants can develop and the tubers form gradually without check, spells of hot dry weather being prejudicial. But another experiment in the same booklet is also of great interest, as indicating (what my statistics could not possibly show) that the Scotch and Irish seed is more productive *because* it is immature, not because the Scotch climate enables the seed to mature better. *Cf.* "Why potatoes vary in cropping power," by D. A. Gilchrist ("Journal of the Newcastle Farmers' Club," 1906) ; also Cambridge University, "Farmers' Bulletin, No. 4." (1905) and "Guide to Experiments" (1905 and 1906).

which has ripened under warmer skies. He also adds that clover and mangold seed are practically never saved in Scotland or the north of England; turnip and rye grass, on the other hand, are. I have not been able to carry my figures back to the harvest period of the grass and clover seeds; but the coefficients with the root crops suggest that the practice with both is correct in so far as they are dependent on the weather (unless the coefficient + 0·25 between turnips and temperature be as a matter of fact significant). If any practical deductions may be drawn under this head, it would seem that it is to the pulse seeds that most attention should be given: they should apparently be drawn from the driest districts of England. Possibly this is the case now.

The preparation of this paper has necessitated the use of a considerable amount of statistical material, and the calculation of some quantities to which but little attention has hitherto been devoted. It seemed to me a pity to leave these data unexplored in various directions when a few further simple calculations only were required to elicit certain points of interest. I make, therefore, no further apology for travelling beyond the original scope of the paper, and discussing briefly as a sort of addendum a few questions for which these figures form the necessary basis.

A question of economic interest is: What practical progress has been made during recent years in raising more produce from the land? We have now reliable data of the amount extracted from a given area of land since 1885. Of recent years considerable endeavours have been made to encourage the spread of agricultural education: County Council instruction in agriculture, now provided in some form or other, and in greater or less degree, in almost every county of England, has been a growth entirely since that date. Has there been any increased yield? It is doubtless too early to expect it, but I have in Table II taken out the average yield of each crop—in the district under review—for the first and last ten of the twenty years 1886-1905. I have also taken out similar figures for Scotland for comparison. [I had at first thought of comparing the earliest ten years (1885-94) with the latest, but the yields of 1885 were markedly high in the case of corn, and very bad indeed in the case of pulse; in fact, the crops of that year were on the whole considerably more abnormal than those of 1895, which comes in in its place.]

Before commenting upon these figures, a few of the exceptionally abnormal crops may be mentioned, as influencing the averages for the decades. In Eastern England 1893 and 1904 were both bad years for cereals, particularly the former; these, however, tend to

balance each other in a comparison of the two decades, except as
regards oats, for which 1893 was by far the worse. The comparison
as regards beans is completely vitiated by there being two bad years
(1891 and 1892, with deficiencies from the average of 8 bushels per
acre) in the first decade; the apparent increase here is therefore
quite illusory. Peas had only one abnormally bad year (1885, as
also beans) which fortunately does not come into account. 1893
was, moreover, an abnormally bad year for mangolds and both
classes of hay, and in these cases also the changes noted are somewhat discounted. It will not escape notice that, apart from the
wheat and barley, these exceptional years all fall in the first of the
two decades. In Scotland there do not appear to have been so
many abnormal years to vitiate comparisons, but very low yields of
beans and peas were recorded in 1888, and distinctly poor yields of
hay in 1891 and 1895. These again are in the first decade, but on
the whole they were not so extremely deficient as the years named
in England, and I think the Scottish comparison rather the more
trustworthy of the two. I have not had time to work out any
Scottish weather statistics, so am unable to give any meteorological
explanations in their case.

In Eastern England, only five crops show an increase, chief
among them being wheat and beans. But both these are largely
dependent upon autumn rain. Considering the 37th—44th weeks,
which are the most important period for wheat, I find that the
average rainfall in the first decade was as much as 5·0 inches; in
the second only 3·8 inches. Hence the conditions have been much
more favourable during the second decade, and so great a difference
is much more than sufficient to account for the comparatively small
increase found. Dr. Shaw gave the formula $W = 46 - 2·2\ R$ as
applicable for ascertaining approximately the yield of wheat in the
east of England, where R is the autumn rainfall. This amounted
to 7·7 and 6·1 inches respectively; hence the average yields of
wheat should be approximately 29·1 and 32·6 bushels in the two
decades, an increase of $3\frac{1}{2}$ bushels. The same factor has also
affected beans. Hence, when weather is taken into account, the
two material increases are transformed into decreases. I regret to
conclude therefore that there has been no progress, but rather the
reverse, in extracting more produce from the soil during the past
twenty years in this district of England.

Very probably the twenty years under review are insufficient
to justify any conclusions as to causes; the only cause that
suggests itself to me is, that, arable land being relatively so
unprofitable that much of it has been turned into pasture,
less attention has been given to it than formerly, and, with

the increase in dairying, more attention has been paid to the stock. In connection with this it is just possibly significant, although the changes are exceedingly slight, that the yield of seeds' hay (arable) is smaller and that of meadow hay larger. [The average rainfall during the most closely correlated period—spring—was 4·9 inches in both decades.] It does not follow, however, that the efficiency of the British farmer has diminished, for, if there has been no increase in the production, the labour expended thereon, and the cost of production generally—doubtless owing to the commoner use of machinery—has been much less. There are some very interesting diagrams in a report recently issued by the Board of Agriculture on the Decline in the Agricultural Population,* showing that the number of labourers on the land (in England as a whole) has decreased very much more rapidly than the arable land. Hence it is extremely probable that the production per person engaged in farming has increased during the twenty years.

Looking at the Scottish figures, a complete contrast is presented. The yield of the whole ten crops is greater in the second decade. As already mentioned I am quite unable to say whether any or all of these increases are due to the meteorological conditions. But we have seen that there were fewer abnormal years during the earlier decade, so I do not think it likely, or at least not to the same extent as in England. This result may lend a little support to the suggestion that the increase in stock raising has rendered the farmer of Eastern England somewhat apathetic towards his arable land. Turning again to the diagrams in the Report on the Decline of the Agricultural Population, it will be seen that Scotland has nearly maintained its arable area, and that the increase in stock is comparatively slight. Possibly, the Scotchman still continues therefore to devote most of his attention to the arable side of his farm. But, as already indicated, the probability is that the time has not been long enough to permit of any theories in this connection.

This possible connection between a diminished yield per acre from a diminished area leads directly to another point of economic interest. It is often said, for instance, that the high yield per acre of wheat in Scotland and Holland is due to the small area placed under the crop, and that districts can be found of equal area in England yielding an equal amount, since, theoretically, so small a proportion being placed under the crop, farmers select the land most suited to it. This is no doubt largely true, as in Scotland the great bulk of the wheat is grown in a very few counties where the soil and climate are specially favourable, and probably the same holds with the rich alluvial lands of Holland. It had occurred to me

* [Cd –3273], p. 12.

accordingly that the considerable reductions in the areas under certain crops during the past twenty years might have resulted in improved yields, apart from other causes. The figures already referred to, however, show no evidence in favour of such a theory : it may possibly be counterbalanced by relative indolence towards the less profitable crops where the difference in proportionate area is one of time and not of geography. It is to be remembered, moreover, that in any case it is not necessarily the most unsuitable area of the district which would go out of cultivation, but only the most unsuitable portions of each farm; considerations of rotation, &c., keeping much land under wheat that a farmer might otherwise wish to put under a more intrinsically profitable crop.

Another addendum which may perhaps find a place here is the actual change that has taken place in the utilisation of the land of these Eastern Counties as a district. The wheat area has been reduced from 863,152 acres in 1885 to 736,969 acres in 1905, with a minimum of 573,036 acres in the preceding year. Barley has fallen off rather more than wheat, viz., from 837,984 to 679,374 acres, or by 169,296 acres. The yield per acre has also been somewhat reduced, but the most important period of the year has been less favourable. Oats have increased their acreage from 299,296 to 444,245 acres (the area was 500,473 acres in 1904); the diminution in their yield is the same in amount (but less in percentage) as barley, in spite of less favourable conditions. Beans and peas have also reduced their acreage.

The potato area has largely increased, viz., from 89,358 to 156,286 acres, and the yield per acre has considerably diminished. As found above, it is not easy to decide which is the most important period of the year. Possibly the decline may be due to the planting of unsuitable lands, but possibly also exhaustion of the stock has something to do with it. The area of turnips has declined, that of mangolds shows no change.

Rotation hay has fallen off somewhat—by 28,722 acres from the 444,638 of 1886, while the area of meadow hay was identical in 1905 and 1886. Grass, naturally, is cut on the better lands, and frequently a meadow intended for cutting is left for grazing if the season prove dry; the hay figures thus hardly lend themselves to comparison.

Which is the most variable crop? The test of variability I take to be the standard deviation*; and in Table III I have given the average, the maximum, and the minimum, yield per acre, and the standard deviation, of each crop for the twenty-one years 1885-1905.

---

* Though, from the pecuniary point of view, it is quite arguable that the mean deviation is the better guide in practice.

There is one other crop the production of which is recorded in our Annual Returns, namely, hops. And this is, as is well known, the most uncertain and speculative of all our English crops. None, however, are grown in the district under review, and I have therefore inserted in this table similar particulars regarding the Kentish hop crop for comparison. It will be observed that the produce of this per acre has varied from 4·63 to 14·47 cwts. per acre (much lower yields have been noted in earlier years), with a standard deviation of as much as 27·8 per cent. of the average.

Apart from hops, the most uncertain are hay and beans—thanks mainly as regards the latter to the three very low years already mentioned. It may be remarked, however, that 1906, by giving a record yield per acre of beans, has still further increased its standard deviation. Meadow hay, as appears from the figures, has an even larger standard deviation (compared with the average), and the seeds' hay somewhat less. I suspect, moreover, that these figures under-estimate the real variability of this crop, inasmuch as, when the season is bad, considerable areas of the poorer grass are left for pasture, hence the yield of the portions cut in such years is somewhat higher than would otherwise be the case.* Other crops of course do not lend themselves to such treatment in poor seasons. This great variability of the grass crop is unfortunate when it is remembered that its total value is greater than that of any other crop in Great Britain.

The least variable crop is oats, followed closely by barley. The roots are more variable than the corn crops, and peas are very little more uncertain than wheat.

In Table III I have included similar data for Scotland, and, so far as the statistics permit, for France. The possibility of these being useful occurred to me in connection with the point raised on pp. 9 and 10, viz., that we could not expect to obtain significant correlation coefficients where a crop was grown in a country presenting the optimum weather conditions. If, therefore, the average temperature of Eastern England were very suitable for, let us say, potatoes, we might expect to find the correlation coefficient between temperature and potatoes to be nearly zero; but to obtain a negative coefficient in a warmer district like France, and a positive coefficient in a colder country like Scotland. To work out these coefficients would, of course, take just as long as the English figures; moreover, France is too large an area for such a purpose.

---

* The correlation coefficient between the area of permanent grass cut for hay and the yield per acre, in Eastern England, during the twenty years 1886-1905, is as much as +0·52.

But another comparison occurred to me. If a climate is suitable for a plant, and the plant does not mind moderate deviations from the average, we might, other things being equal, expect theoretically to find that the yield per acre was greatest in that district, and the standard deviation least. Now we can, owing to differences of soil, methods of cultivation, individual energy, variety of seed sown, &c., not expect to find the average production growing less according as we move further from the district of optimum climate; as between Scotland, England, and France, the other causes indicated are probably of much greater importance than the difference in climate. But I do not quite see why the standard deviation ought not to be a guide: this should only depend upon changes within the country. I hoped accordingly that this would admit of a practical application. Wheat we found to be highly correlated with dryness: might we not then expect to find the standard deviation of wheat to be less in France than in England? Oats are correlated with rain and cold; may we not then expect to find a smaller standard deviation in Scotland? And as regards crops which have not yielded significant coefficients, might we not assume that that country is most suitable which shows the smallest standard deviation? This was a theoretical consideration which seemed worth testing to the small extent that I have indicated.

Examination of Table III shows that it is useless for the purpose. With the single exception of potatoes, the whole of the crops are less variable—in most cases largely so—in Scotland than in Eastern England; while the mangold (*betterave fourragère*) and the hay crops alone are less variable in France than in England. I doubt whether France as an entity, however, could be considered as a reliable guide in this connection, the area is so large that the crops vary much from one district to another; the hay crops, moreover, are hardly comparable with ours.

Although the table has not yielded the information I desired, I have let the figures stand, as they present some points of interest. It will be observed that the majority of the crops show a heavier yield in Scotland than in Eastern England. To some extent this may be due to Scotchmen being better farmers than their southern brethren; to some extent to the above-mentioned greater apathy towards crops that are going out of cultivation (it has already been observed that the arable area in Scotland has diminished but little, as compared with the English), and to some extent to the fact that the great bulk of the crops in Scotland are grown in counties peculiarly suited to them. One great exception may be noted, and that is oats, the staple cereal of Scotland, and grown wherever a cereal is wanted. Of this the Englishman produces over 25 per cent. more than the Scotchman, in spite of the climate, judging by the correlation coefficients, being more favourable in the north. In this connection, however, the straw is of importance; the Scotch farmer puts far more value on the straw of the oat crop than does the English. As regards the hay crops, these are favoured by the rainier north, but different farmers may have entirely different notions as to whether a given quantity of grass in an area is worth saving as hay or not, and I think no comparisons can be made regarding this crop. On the whole, I am inclined to think that the main reason of the larger crops is probably the more suitable soil on which the bulk of the crops is grown, combined with the lower temperatures which we found to be so significant a factor with many of the crops, more especially as the Scotch appear to take care not to use home-grown seed in the case of those crops which mature their seeds best in a warmer climate.

That the standard deviations should practically throughout be less is also possibly due to similar reasons. In so far as the temperature affects each crop, the cooler districts of the north would tend to lower the standard deviation, and the same would apply as regards such crops as prefer a greater rainfall. But this does not explain why the standard deviation should be less in the case of wheat, unless it be that it is only grown in such suitable soil as to render it less dependent on the rainfall. Nor is it easy to understand why potatoes alone should be a more variable crop in Scotland; the average production, it will be noticed, is identical in the two districts.

Finally, I have not given the standard deviations, &c., of the various meteorological data. Useful as these would be for many purposes, the twenty-one years under review are insufficient to give more than an approximation to the true values. Many more years' data are available, and a nearer approach to the reality should be made by calculating such data from as long a series of observations as possible. For the particular purpose of this paper I have been obliged to use exactly the same period as for the crops; and I have given in Table IV the actual correlation coefficients required for this paper between rainfall and accumulated temperature above 42° F. These values, however, apply solely to the particular years specified, and should not be quoted as necessarily holding generally, since a more accurate guide to the interdependence of rain and temperature can be obtained from a longer series of years. Doubtless the same objection holds as regards these latter; but there is this difference, that with the meteorological statistics more accurate measures are obtainable; the produce statistics, on the other hand, are the best we have got, and so I have done my best with them.

Explanatory Note to Table I.

In Table I, r at the head of the first three columns denotes the *total* correlation coefficient between the crop and the meteorological data, ρ the *partial* coefficient, and R the double coefficient.

The suffixes to r and ρ denote the particular data correlated; the first is the initial of the crop named at the head of the table, while r = rainfall, a = accumulated temperature above 42° F., b = accumulated temperature below 42° F.

The double coefficient represents the joint effect on the crop of rainfall and accumulated temperature above 42° F.

The actual calculations of the partial coefficients were performed by using three places of decimals and a slide-rule. If calculated from the two places here given, slightly different figures may possibly be obtained.

TABLE I.—CORRELATION COEFFICIENTS BETWEEN WEATHER
AND CROPS.

(a) **Wheat.**

Period.	r_{wr}	r_{wa}	r_{wb}	ρ_{wr}	ρ_{wa}	R.
9—16th weeks	+0·02	+0·00	−0·18	+0·02	+0·01	+0·02
13—20th ,,	− ·21	+ ·12	− ·22	− ·17	+ ·01	+ ·21
17—24th ,,	− ·27	+ ·23	− ·13	− ·22	+ ·13	+ ·31
21—28th ,,	− ·49	+ ·12	....	− ·49	− ·11	+ ·50
25—32nd ,,	− ·23	+ ·31	....	− ·07	+ ·22	+ ·31
29—36th ,,	− ·15	+ ·52	....	+ ·08	+ ·51	+ ·53
33—40th ,,	− ·55	+ ·42	....	− ·44	+ ·21	+ ·56
37—44th ,,	− ·66	+ ·36	−0·07	− ·62	− ·00	+ ·66
41—48th ,,	− ·47	+ ·20	+ ·01	− ·44	+ ·09	+ ·47
45—52nd ,,	+ ·21	+ ·24	− ·07	+ ·19	+ ·22	+ ·31
49— 4th ,,	+ ·01	+ ·46	− ·32	− ·01	+ ·46	+ ·46
1— 8th ,,	− ·58	+ ·52	− ·39	− ·55	+ ·49	+ ·68
5—12th ,,	− ·30	+ ·17	− ·24	− ·31	+ ·18	+ ·34
9—16th ,,	+ ·32	− ·12	− ·15	+ ·32	+ ·01	+ ·32
13—20th ,,	+ ·36	− ·41	+ ·10	+ ·19	− ·28	+ ·45
17—24th ,,	+ ·26	− ·49	+ ·26	+ ·09	− ·44	+ ·50
21—28th ,,	+ ·01	− ·16	....	− ·04	− ·16	+ ·16
25—32nd ,,	− ·37	− ·01	....	− ·46	− ·30	+ ·47
29—36th ,,	− ·31	− ·07	....	− ·39	− ·25	+ ·39
33—40th ,,	+ ·01	+ ·02	....	+ ·03	+ ·03	+ ·03
37—44th ,,	+ ·19	− ·05	+ ·21	+ ·19	+ ·06	+ ·20
Seasons :—						
Previous Spring	− ·25	+ ·14	− ·27	− ·21	− ·00	+ ·25
,, Summer	− ·34	+ ·37	....	− ·15	+ ·21	+ ·39
,, Autumn	− ·61	+ ·36	− ·01	− ·53	+ ·14	+ ·61
Winter	− ·38	+ ·53	− ·39	− ·44	+ ·57	+ ·67
Spring	+ ·52	− ·51	+ ·02	+ ·32	− ·30	+ ·59
Summer	− ·28	− ·06	....	− ·40	− ·31	+ ·40
Cereal year	− ·65	+ ·10	− ·30	− ·69	− ·33	+ ·69

The first eleven rows (9—16th weeks through 45—52nd) are braced as *Previous year.*

Table I (*Contd.*).—(*b*) **Barley.**

Period.	r_{br}	r_{ba}	r_{bb}	ρ_{br}	ρ_{ba}	R.
9—16th weeks	−0·17	+0·07	−0·33	−0·16	−0·01	+0.17
13—20th ,,	− ·12	+ ·09	− ·12	− ·09	+ ·03	+ ·13
17—24th ,,	− ·04	+ ·25	− ·10	+ ·06	+ ·26	+ ·26
21—28th ,,	− ·37	+ ·28	....	− ·29	+ ·16	+ ·39
25—32nd ,,	− ·29	+ ·32	....	− ·15	+ ·19	+ ·35
29—36th ,,	− ·11	+ ·22	....	− ·02	+ ·20	+ ·23
33—40th ,,	− ·23	+ ·19	....	− ·16	+ ·09	+ ·25
37—44th ,,	− ·30	+ ·09	+ ·00	− ·30	− ·10	+ ·31
41—48th ,,	− ·12	− ·18	+ ·37	− ·18	− ·23	+ ·25
45—52nd ,,	+ ·22	− ·08	+ ·19	+ ·23	− ·11	+ ·24
49—4th ,,	− ·00	+ ·27	− ·06	− ·02	+ ·27	+ ·27
1—8th ,,	− ·41	+ ·31	− ·13	− ·35	+ ·24	+ ·45
5—12th ,,	− ·16	− ·04	+ ·01	− ·15	− ·03	+ ·16
9—16th ,,	+ ·27	− ·24	+ ·20	+ ·20	− ·16	+ ·25
13—20th ,,	+ ·30	− ·40	+ ·30	+ ·12	− ·30	+ ·42
17—24th ,,	+ ·27	− ·57	+ ·58	+ ·06	− ·51	+ ·57
21—28th ,,	+ ·32	− ·55	....	+ ·19	− ·50	+ ·57
25—32nd ,,	− ·07	− ·52	....	− ·55	− ·70	+ ·70
29—36th ,,	− ·02	− ·49	....	− ·32	− ·56	+ ·56
33—40th ,,	+ ·29	− ·14	....	+ ·26	+ ·02	+ ·29
37—44th ,,	+ ·40	− ·07	+ ·16	+ ·41	+ ·15	+ ·41
Seasons :—						
Previous Spring	− ·09	+ ·11	− ·29	− ·03	+ ·08	+ ·12
,, Summer	− ·33	+ ·30	....	− ·19	+ ·12	+ ·35
,, Autumn	− ·20	+ ·04	+ ·34	− ·21	+ ·05	+ ·21
Winter	− ·30	+ ·28	− ·10	− ·31	+ ·29	+ ·41
Spring	+ ·53	− ·49	+ ·34	+ ·35	− ·26	+ ·57
Summer	+ ·06	− ·57	....	− ·43	− ·67	+ ·67
Cereal year	− ·04	− ·38	+ ·10	− ·29	− ·46	+ ·52

(Previous year — bracket spanning 9—16th weeks through 45—52nd)

TABLE I (*Contd.*).—(*c*) **Oats.**

Period.	r_{or}.	r_{oa}.	r_{ob}.	ρ_{or}.	ρ_{oa}.	R.
Previous year. 9—16th weeks	+0·13	−0·03	−0·35	+0·13	+0·04	+0·13
Previous year. 13—20th ,, ...	− ·00	− ·11	+ ·07	− ·06	− ·12	+ ·12
Previous year. 17—24th ,, ...	+ ·03	+ ·15	+ ·05	+ ·10	+ ·18	+ ·18
Previous year. 21—28th ,, ...	− ·18	+ ·16	....	− ·13	+ ·10	+ ·20
Previous year. 25—32nd ,, ...	− ·29	+ ·25	....	− ·19	+ ·10	+ ·29
Previous year. 29—36th ,, ...	− ·20	+ ·07	....	− ·19	− ·09	+ ·20
Previous year. 33—40th ,, ...	− ·23	− ·05	....	− ·29	− ·20	+ ·30
Previous year. 37—44th ,, ...	− ·32	+ ·04	− ·04	− ·36	− ·17	+ ·36
Previous year. 41—48th ,, ...	− ·29	− ·12	+ ·28	− ·34	− ·22	+ ·36
Previous year. 45—52nd ,, ...	+ ·08	− ·11	+ ·14	+ ·09	− ·12	+ ·14
49— 4th ,, ...	− ·06	+ ·33	− ·15	− ·08	+ ·33	+ ·33
1— 8th ,, ...	− ·40	+ ·36	− ·19	− ·35	+ ·29	+ ·49
5—12th ,, ...	− ·20	− ·06	+ ·02	− ·20	− ·06	+ ·21
9—16th ,, ...	+ ·13	− ·32	+ ·23	+ ·01	− ·29	+ ·32
13—20th ,, ...	+ ·64	− ·52	+ ·25	+ ·52	− ·27	+ ·68
17—24th ,, ...	+ ·62	− ·68	+ ·46	+ ·52	− ·60	+ ·78
21—28th ,, ...	+ ·53	− ·65	....	+ ·45	− ·60	+ ·73
25—32nd ,, ...	+ ·09	− ·59	....	− ·41	− ·68	+ ·68
29—36th ,, ...	+ ·13	− ·53	....	− ·15	− ·53	+ ·54
33—40th ,, ...	+ ·17	− ·16	....	+ ·10	− ·08	+ ·18
37—44th ,, ...	+ ·22	+ ·07	− ·24	+ ·30	+ ·24	+ ·30
Seasons :—						
Previous Spring	+ ·05	− ·02	− ·26	+ ·04	+ ·00	+ ·05
,, Summer ...	− ·26	+ ·13	....	− ·24	− ·05	+ ·27
,, Autumn	− ·23	− ·04	+ ·32	− ·33	− ·18	+ ·33
Winter	− ·28	+ ·31	− ·16	− ·29	+ ·32	+ ·41
Spring	+ ·74	− ·52	+ ·29	+ ·70	− ·17	+ ·79
Summer	+ ·27	− ·70	....	− ·24	− ·69	+ ·72
Cereal year	+ ·10	− ·49	+ ·04	− ·19	− ·52	+ ·52

TABLE I (*Contd.*).—(*d*) **Beans.**

Period.	r_{br}.	r_{ba}.	r_{bb}.	ρ_{br}.	ρ_{ba}.	R.
Previous year. 9—16th weeks ...	+0·17	+0·06	−0·15	+0·22	+0·15	+0·23
Previous year. 13—20th ,, ...	− ·02	+ ·11	− ·25	+ ·04	+ ·11	+ ·11
Previous year. 17—24th ,, ...	− ·04	+ ·33	− ·32	+ ·09	+ ·34	+ ·34
Previous year. 21—28th ,, ...	− ·17	+ ·25	....	− ·08	+ ·20	+ ·26
Previous year. 25—32nd ,, ...	− ·33	+ ·26	....	− ·23	+ ·09	+ ·34
Previous year. 29—36th ,, ...	− ·52	+ ·25	....	− ·48	+ ·05	+ ·52
Previous year. 33—40th ,, ...	− ·39	− ·17	....	− ·56	− ·46	+ ·57
Previous year. 37—44th ,, ...	− ·30	− ·16	+ ·09	− ·47	− ·39	+ ·49
Previous year. 41—48th ,, ...	− ·47	+ ·06	+ ·16	− ·48	− ·10	+ ·48
Previous year. 45—52nd ,, ...	− ·21	− ·02	+ ·11	− ·20	+ ·01	+ ·20
49—4th ,, ...	− ·17	+ ·38	− ·26	− ·20	+ ·39	+ ·42
1—8th ,, ...	− ·36	+ ·44	− ·37	− ·30	+ ·40	+ ·52
5—12th ,, ...	− ·13	+ ·09	− ·13	− ·14	+ ·12	+ ·17
9—16th ,, ...	+ ·39	− ·10	− ·28	+ ·39	+ ·06	+ ·40
13—20th ,, ...	+ ·43	− ·31	− ·23	+ ·32	− ·11	+ ·44
17—24th ,, ...	+ ·38	− ·54	− ·06	+ ·22	− ·45	+ ·56
21—28th ,, ...	+ ·32	− ·35	....	+ ·23	− ·28	+ ·41
25—32nd ,, ...	+ ·20	− ·01	....	+ ·24	+ ·13	+ ·24
29—36th ,, ...	+ ·25	− ·02	....	+ ·27	+ ·12	+ ·27
33—40th ,, ...	− ·21	+ ·14	....	− ·17	+ ·04	+ ·22
37—44th ,, ...	− ·40	+ ·35	− ·18	− ·27	+ ·20	+ ·43
Seasons:—						
Previous Spring	+ ·07	+ ·12	− ·27	+ ·17	+ ·19	+ ·20
,, Summer	− ·39	+ ·23	....	− ·33	− ·03	+ ·49
,, Autumn ...	− ·45	− ·08	+ ·18	− ·53	− ·33	+ ·54
Winter	− ·36	+ ·27	− ·22	− ·37	+ ·29	+ ·45
Spring	+ ·46	− ·31	− ·30	+ ·37	− ·06	+ ·46
Summer	+ ·37	− ·16	....	+ ·34	+ ·07	+ ·38
Cereal year	− ·05	− ·17	− ·22	− ·15	− ·22	+ ·22

TABLE I (*Contd.*).—(*e*) **Peas.**

Period.	r_{pr}	r_{pa}	r_{pb}	ρ_{pr}	ρ_{pa}	R.
9—16th weeks ...	+0·31	−0·28	+0·15	+0·21	−0·17	+0·34
13—20th ,, ...	+·20	−·24	+·08	+·09	−·16	+·26
17—24th ,, ...	+·16	+·22	+·26	+·27	+·31	+·35
21—28th ,, ...	+·07	+·11	....	+·12	+·15	+·16
25—32nd ,, ...	−·15	−·12	....	−·27	−·26	+·30
29—36th ,, ...	−·40	−·07	....	−·47	−·28	+·47
33—40th ,, ...	−·13	−·13	....	−·22	−·22	+·26
37—44th ,, ...	+·14	−·10	+·10	+·10	−·03	+·14
41—48th ,, ...	−·02	−·04	+·02	−·03	−·05	+·05
45—52nd ,, ...	−·12	−·03	+·16	−·12	−·02	+·14
49—4th ,, ...	−·18	+·22	−·07	−·19	+·23	+·29
1—8th ,, ...	−·29	+·18	−·13	−·26	+·12	+·31
5—12th ,, ...	−·20	−·22	+·16	−·20	−·22	+·30
9—16th ,, ...	+·24	−·10	+·09	+·22	−·01	+·24
13—24th ,, ...	+·21	−·16	−·11	+·15	−·06	+·22
17—20th ,, ...	−·05	−·35	+·06	−·21	−·40	+·40
21—28th ,, ...	+·06	−·24	....	−·03	−·23	+·24
25—32nd ,, ...	+·24	−·11	....	+·22	+·04	+·24
29—36th ,, ...	+·14	+·07	....	+·19	+·15	+·21
33—40th ,, ...	−·18	+·31	....	−·02	+·25	+·31
37—44th ,, ...	−·39	+·49	−·34	−·20	+·38	+·52
Seasons :—						
Previous Spring........	+·42	−·21	+·13	+·38	+·03	+·42
,, Summer..	−·18	−·11	....	−·32	−·29	+·34
,, Autumn....	−·04	−·01	+·03	−·05	−·03	+·05
Winter	−·34	+·03	+·03	−·34	+·03	+·34
Spring.	+·17	−·16	+·00	+·10	−·07	+·19
Summer	+·22	−·13	....	+·19	+·01	+·22
Cereal year............... .	+·04	−·12	+·03	−·02	−·12	+·13

The left margin shows "Previous year." applied as a bracket to the first group of rows (9—16th weeks through 45—52nd).

TABLE I (*Contd.*).—(*f*) **Potatoes.**

Period.	r_{pr}	r_{pa}	r_{pb}	ρ_{pr}	ρ_{pa}	R.
9—16th weeks	−0 ·17	+0 ·06	+0 ·10	−0 ·16	−0 ·02	+0 ·16
13—20th ,, ...	− ·18	+ ·10	+ ·12	− ·15	− ·00	+ ·18
17—24th ,, ...	+ ·14	− ·10	+ ·21	+ ·11	− ·05	+ ·14
21—28th ,, ...	+ ·24	− ·31	....	+ ·13	− ·24	+ ·33
25—32nd ,, ...	+ ·24	− ·35	....	+ ·05	− ·27	+ ·35
29—36th ,, ...	+ ·28	− ·25	....	+ ·20	− ·16	+ ·31
33—40th ,, ...	+ ·03	+ ·07	....	+ ·08	+ ·10	+ ·10
37—44th ,, ...	+ ·05	+ ·12	+0 ·04	+ ·14	+ ·17	+ ·18
41—48th ,, ...	+ ·38	+ ·03	− ·20	+ ·41	+ ·16	+ ·41
45—52nd ,, ...	+ ·24	+ ·29	− ·21	+ ·22	+ ·27	+ ·36
49—4th ,, ...	+ ·06	+ ·04	+ ·18	+ ·06	+ ·03	+ ·08
1—8th ,, ...	− ·02	− ·26	+ ·38	− ·09	− ·27	+ ·27
5—12th ,, ...	− ·34	− ·07	+ ·32	− ·34	− ·07	+ ·35
9—16th ,, ...	− ·22	+ ·14	+ ·30	− ·18	+ ·05	+ ·22
13—20th ,, ...	− ·18	+ ·40	− ·05	+ ·04	+ ·36	+ ·40
17—24th ,, ...	− ·41	+ ·33	− ·04	− ·32	+ ·19	+ ·45
21—28th ,, ...	− ·43	+ ·09	....	− ·42	− ·05	+ ·43
25—32nd ,, ...	− ·13	− ·07	....	− ·21	− ·18	+ ·22
29—36th ,, ...	− ·32	+ ·19	....	− ·26	+ ·05	+ ·32
33—40th ,, ...	+ ·00	+ ·27	....	+ ·18	+ ·32	+ ·32
37—44th ,, ...	+ ·36	− ·10	+ ·31	+ ·36	+ ·09	+ ·37
Seasons :—						
Previous Spring	− ·04	+ ·04	+ ·14	− ·02	+ ·02	+ ·06
,, Summer	+ ·27	− ·25	....	+ ·15	− ·10	+ ·29
,, Autumn	+ ·23	+ ·08	− ·21	+ ·29	+ ·20	+ ·30
Winter	− ·12	− ·00	+ ·25	− ·12	− ·00	+ ·12
Spring	− ·15	+ ·21	+ ·27	− ·04	+ ·15	+ ·22
Summer	− ·46	+ ·13	....	− ·48	− ·18	+ ·49
Cereal year	− ·29	+ ·19	+ ·23	− ·23	+ ·05	+ ·29

The word "Previous year" appears vertically alongside the first ten period rows.

TABLE I (*Contd.*).—(*g*) **Turnips** and **Swedes.**

Period.	r_{tr}	r_{ta}	r	ρ_{tr}	ρ_{ta}	R.
9—16th weeks ...	+0 ·24	−0 ·06	−0 ·05	+0 ·24	+0 ·06	+0 ·25
13—20th ,, ...	− ·15	+ ·07	+ ·07	− ·14	− ·02	+ ·15
17—24th ,, ...	− ·30	+ ·36	− ·11	− ·19	+ ·25	+ ·40
21—28th ,, ...	− ·10	+ ·25	....	− ·01	+ ·23	+ 26
25—32nd ,, ...	− ·06	+ ·19	....	+ ·06	+ ·19	+ ·20
29—36th ,, ...	− ·18	− ·12	....	− ·25	− ·22	+ ·28
33—40th ,, ...	+ ·26	− ·38	. ....	+ ·08	− ·30	+ ·39
37—44th ,, ...	+ ·25	− ·45	+0 ·46	+ ·00	− ·39	+ ·45
41—48th ,, ...	+ ·09	− ·46	+ ·48	− ·04	− ·45	+ ·46
45—52nd ,, ...	− ·12	− ·41	+ ·42	− ·09	− ·40	+ ·42
49— 4th ,, ...	− ·26	− ·29	+ ·30	− ·26	− ·29	+ ·38
1— 8th ,, ...	+ ·03	− ·31	+ ·28	− ·05	− ·31	+ ·31
5—12th ,, ...	+ ·16	− ·26	+ ·21	+ ·17	− ·27	+ ·29
9—16th ,, ...	+ ·08	− ·11	+ ·04	+ ·04	− ·09	+ ·12
13—20th ,, ...	− ·06	− ·10	+ ·18	− ·13	− ·16	+ ·17
17—24th ,, ...	+ ·25	− ·13	+ ·35	+ ·21	− ·04	+ ·25
21—28th ,, ...	+ ·60	− ·32	....	+ ·55	− ·17	+ ·61
25—32nd ,, ...	+ ·39	− ·49	....	+ ·14	− ·36	+ ·50
29—36th ,, ...	+ ·34	− ·47	....	+ ·16	− ·37	+ ·49
33—40th ,, ...	+ ·03	− ·09	....	− ·02	− ·09	+ ·10
37—44th ,, ...	− ·13	+ ·20	− ·32	− ·04	+ ·16	+ ·20
Seasons :—						
Previous Spring	− ·08	+ ·03	+ ·01	− ·07	− ·02	+ ·08
,, Summer ...	− ·14	+ 0 ·7	....	− ·12	− ·02	+ ·14
,, Autumn	+ ·23	− ·44	+ ·53	+ ·06	− ·39	+ ·45
Winter	− ·10	− ·41	+ ·39	− ·11	− ·41	+ ·42
Spring	+ ·18	− ·04	+ ·07	+ ·19	+ ·07	+ ·19
Summer	+ ·50	− ·52	....	+ ·28	− ·32	+ ·57
Cereal year	+ ·57	− ·62	+ ·44	+ ·39	− ·47	+ ·69

Previous year. (bracket spanning the 9—16th through 45—52nd week rows)

TABLE I (*Contd.*).—(*h*) **Mangolds.**

	Period.	r_{mr}.	r_{ma}.	r_{mb}.	ρ_{mr}.	ρ_{ma}.	R.
Previous year.	9—16th weeks	+0·21	−0·12	−0·27	+0·18	−0·02	+0·21
	13—20th „	+ ·03	− ·10	− ·12	− ·03	− ·10	+ ·10
	17—24th „	− ·16	+ ·09	− ·18	− ·14	+ ·03	+ ·16
	21—28th „	− ·34	+ ·07	....	− ·33	− ·07	+ ·34
	25—32nd „	− ·38	+ ·44	....	− ·17	+ ·30	+ ·47
	29—36th „	− ·43	+ ·28	....	− ·37	+ ·12	+ ·45
	33—40th „	− ·22	− ·05	....	− ·25	− ·19	+ ·26
	37—44th „	− ·12	+ ·04	+ ·01	− ·12	− ·03	+ ·13
	41—48th „	− ·09	− ·03	+ ·17	− ·11	− ·06	+ ·11
	45—52nd „	+ ·12	− ·11	+ ·13	+ ·13	− ·12	+ ·17
	49— 4th „	+ ·06	+ ·09	− ·08	+ ·06	+ ·09	+ ·11
	1— 8th „	− ·09	− ·10	+ ·08	− ·12	− ·13	+ ·15
	5—12th „	− ·13	− ·45	+ ·27	− ·13	− ·45	+ ·47
	9—16th „	+ ·26	− ·47	+ ·16	+ ·09	− ·41	+ ·47
	13—20th „	+ ·50	− ·59	+ ·14	+ ·28	− ·45	+ ·63
	17—24th „	+ ·37	− ·56	+ ·44	+ ·20	− ·49	+ ·59
	21—28th „	+ ·36	− ·34	....	+ ·28	− ·26	+ ·52
	25—32nd „	+ ·01	− ·25	....	− ·19	− ·32	+ ·32
	29—36th „	+ ·05	− ·18	....	− ·04	− ·18	+ ·19
	33—40th „	− ·01	+ ·05	....	+ ·02	+ ·05	+ ·07
	37—44th „	− ·09	+ ·21	− ·34	+ ·01	+ ·17	+ ·21
	Seasons:—						
	Previous Spring	+ ·04	− ·21	− ·19	− ·10	− ·23	+ ·24
	„ Summer	− ·48	+ ·28	....	− ·41	− ·03	+ ·48
	„ Autumn	− ·08	+ ·01	+ ·20	− ·08	− ·02	+ ·08
	Winter	− ·06	− ·09	+ ·09	− ·06	− ·09	+ ·10
	Spring	+ ·60	− ·59	+ ·23	+ ·39	− ·38	+ ·67
	Summer	+ ·14	− ·36	....	− ·10	− ·34	+ ·37
	Cereal year	+ ·25	− ·54	+ ·18	− ·02	− ·49	+ ·54

TABLE I (*Contd.*).—(*i*) **Hay** from **Clover** and **Rotation Grass**.

Period.	r_{hr}	r_{ha}	r_{hb}	ρ_{hr}	ρ_{ha}	R.
9—16th weeks	+ 0 ·44	+ 0 ·05	− 0 ·41	+ 0 ·51	+ 0 ·30	+ 0 ·51
13—20th ,, ...	+ ·07	− ·06	− ·09	+ ·05	− ·03	+ ·08
17—24th ,, ...	+ ·11	− ·09	+ ·01	+ ·08	− ·05	+ ·12
21—28th ,, ...	+ ·05	− ·23	....	− ·05	− ·23	+ ·23
25—32nd ,, ...	− ·11	+ ·08	....	− ·09	+ ·02	+ ·12
29—36th ,, ...	− ·06	− ·11	....	− ·12	− ·15	+ ·16
33—40th ,, ...	− ·23	− ·32	....	− ·50	− ·54	+ ·57
37—44th ,, ...	− ·39	+ ·00	− ·01	− ·45	− ·26	+ ·45
41—48th ,, ...	− ·32	+ ·16	− ·03	− ·29	+ ·08	+ ·32
45—52nd ,, ...	+ ·12	+ ·08	− ·10	+ ·11	+ ·06	+ ·14
49—4th ,, ...	+ ·00	+ ·16	− ·20	− ·05	+ ·16	+ ·16
1—8th ,, ...	− ·31	+ ·13	− ·00	− ·29	+ ·05	+ ·32
5—12th ,, ...	− ·32	− ·14	+ ·19	− ·32	− ·15	+ ·35
9—16th ,, ...	+ ·04	− ·38	+ ·15	− ·14	− ·40	+ ·40
13—20th ,, ...	+ ·78	− ·48	− ·03	+ ·70	− ·13	+ ·78
17—24th ,, ...	+ ·73	− ·41	+ ·04	+ ·68	− ·19	+ ·75
21—28th ,, ...	+ ·37	− ·31	....	+ ·30	− ·22	·42
25—32nd ,, ...	+ ·09	− ·35	....	− ·22	− ·40	+ ·41
29—36th ,, ...	+ ·29	− ·27	....	+ ·17	− ·16	+ ·32
Seasons :—						
Previous Spring	+ ·18	− ·06	− ·36	+ ·18	+ ·05	+ ·18
,, Summer ...	− ·04	− ·13	....	− ·16	− ·20	+ ·21
,, Autumn	− ·29	− ·01	+ ·08	− ·32	− ·15	+ ·32
Winter	− ·24	+ ·09	− ·04	− ·24	− ·07	+ ·25
Spring......................	+ ·80	− ·40	+ ·04	+ ·76	+ ·10	+ ·80
Summer	+ ·31	− ·42	....	+ ·03	− ·30	+ ·42
Cereal year	+ ·20	− ·34	+ ·00	+ ·03	− ·28	+ ·35

The lefthand brace spanning the first ten rows (9—16th weeks through 45—52nd) is labelled **Previous year.**

TABLE I (*Contd.*).—(*j*) **Hay** from **Permanent Grass.**

Period.	r_{hr}	r_{ha}	r_{hb}	ρ_{hr}	ρ_{ha}	R.
9—16th weeks	+ 0·36	+ 0·04	− 0·33	+ 0·42	+ 0·22	+ 0·42
13—20th ,, ...	+ ·06	− ·11	− ·01	− ·00	− ·09	+ ·11
17—24th ,, ...	+ ·05	+ ·04	+ ·02	+ ·08	+ ·07	+ ·09
21—28th ,, ...	− ·18	+ ·04	....	− ·17	− 03	+ ·18
25—32nd ,, ...	− ·33	+ ·21	....	− ·27	+ ·04	+ ·34
29—36th ,, ...	− ·21	+ ·08	....	− ·19	− ·01	+ ·21
33—40th ,, ...	− ·16	− ·30	....	− ·40	− ·45	+ ·49
37—44th ,, ...	− ·25	− ·17	+ ·15	− ·40	− ·36	+ ·43
41—48th ,, ...	− ·29	− ·07	+ ·24	− ·32	− ·16	+ ·33
45—52nd ,, ...	+ ·01	− ·15	+ ·04	+ ·02	− ·15	+ ·15
49—4th ,, ...	− ·08	+ ·13	− ·12	− ·09	+ ·14	+ ·17
1—8th ,, ...	− ·28	+ ·20	− ·17	− ·24	+ ·14	+ ·31
5—12th ,, ...	− ·14	− ·14	+ ·09	− ·11	− ·11	+ ·20
9—16th ,, ...	+ ·15	− ·38	+ ·16	− ·01	− ·35	+ ·38
13—20th ,, ...	+ ·74	− ·50	− ·03	+ ·64	− ·19	+ ·75
17—24th ,, ...	+ ·68	− ·54	+ ·15	+ ·61	− ·41	+ ·74
21—28th ,, ...	+ ·42	− ·49	....	+ ·31	− ·42	+ ·56
25—32nd ,, ...	+ ·13	− ·38	....	− ·21	− ·41	+ ·43
29—36th ,, ...	+ ·25	− ·31	....	+ ·10	− ·22	+ ·33
Seasons :—						
Previous Spring........	+ ·12	− ·05	− ·27	+ ·11	+ ·02	+ ·12
,, Summer ...	− ·26	+ ·07	....	− ·26	− ·12	+ ·27
,, Autumn	− ·21	− ·17	+ ·32	− ·31	− ·29	+ ·35
Winter	− ·23	+ ·09	− ·13	− ·22	+ ·06	+ ·23
Spring	+ ·79	− ·49	+ ·07	+ ·71	− ·09	+ ·79
Summer	+ ·33	− ·49	....	− ·03	− ·38	+ ·48
Cereal year.................	+ ·27	− ·49	− ·01	+ ·03	− ·43	+ ·50

(Left margin bracket spanning rows 1–10: "Previous year.")

TABLE II.—AVERAGE ACREAGE AND YIELD OF CROPS, 1886-95
AND 1896-1905.

(a) **Eastern England** (*as defined on p.* 2).

Crop.	Area.		Yield per Acre.		
	1886-1895	1896-1905.	1886-95.	1896-1905.	Increase or Decrease.
	Acres.	Acres.	Bushels.	Bushels.	Bushels.
Wheat	845,136	713,219	30 ·4	32 ·1	+ 1 ·7
Barley	801,346	749,306	33 ·6	33 ·1	− 0 ·5
Oats	340,750	410,948	46 ·5	46 ·0	− 0 ·5
Beans	149,579	128,670	27 ·3	29 ·1	+ 1 ·8
Peas	95,979	82,341	26 ·9	27 ·2	+ 0 ·3
			Tons.	Tons.	Tons.
Potatoes	100,267	134,524	6 ·0	5 ·5	− 0 ·5
Turnips and swedes	397,164	346,489	12 ·0	11 ·3	− 0 ·7
Mangolds	161,348	162,749	16 ·9	17 ·3	+ 0 ·4
			Cwts.	Cwts.	Cwts.
Seeds' hay	450,209	463,528	28 ·1	27 ·9	− 0 ·2
Meadow hay	516,631	476,003	22 ·6	22 ·7	+ 0 ·1

(b) **Scotland.**

Crop.	Acres.	Acres.	Bushels.	Bushels.	Bushels.
Wheat	53,404	45,044	35 ·2	38 ·7	+ 3 ·5
Barley	217,116	226,120	35 ·3	36 ·1	+ 0 ·8
Oats	1,020,811	966,707	36 ·0	36 ·5	+ 0 ·5
Beans	15,544	12,354	30 ·4	33 ·8	+ 3 ·4
Peas	1,229	1,046	23 ·6	25 ·8	+ 2 ·2
			Tons.	Tons.	Tons.
Potatoes	143,392	130,751	5 ·7	6 ·0	+ 0 ·3
Turnips and swedes	481,037	462,116	15 ·0	15 ·2	+ 0 ·2
Mangolds	1,208	2,476	16 ·4	17 ·4	+ 1 ·0
			Cwts.	Cwts.	Cwts.
Seeds' hay	411,073	409,600	30 ·2	32 ·2	+ 2 ·0
Meadow hay	157,238	139,280	28 ·2	29 ·4	+ 1 ·2

TABLE III.—AVERAGE RANGE, AND STANDARD DEVIATION OF CERTAIN CROPS IN EASTERN ENGLAND, SCOTLAND AND FRANCE, 1885–1905.

Crop and District.	Period.	Average Yield per Acre.	Range.		Standard Deviation.	
			Maximum.	Minimum.	Actual per Acre.	Per Cent. of Average Yield.
		Bushels.	Bushels.	Bushels.	Bushels.	
Wheat, E. England	1885–1905	31 ·41	36 ·84	25 ·86	3 ·04	9 ·7
„ Scotland	„	36 ·81	42 ·47	31 ·12	2 ·67	7 ·3
„ France	„	18 ·20	22 ·05	14 ·68	1 ·93	10 ·6
Barley, E. England	„	33 ·57	38 ·17	27 ·77	2 ·57	7 ·7
„ Scotland	„	35 ·63	39 ·07	33 ·29	1 ·37	3 ·8
„ France	„	21 ·09	24 ·39	15 ·57	1 ·85	8 ·8
Oats, E. England	„	46 ·48	50 ·94	36 ·99	3 ·48	7 ·5
„ Scotland	„	36 ·05	39 ·43	31 ·93	1 ·63	4 ·5
„ France	„	25 ·88	30 ·64	18 ·12	2 ·62	10 ·1
Beans, E. England	„	27 ·78	33 ·58	19 ·38	4 ·48	16 ·1
„ Scotland	„	32 ·04	36 ·76	24 ·31	2 ·85	8 ·9
Peas, E. England	„	26 ·66	30 ·67	17 ·36	2 ·80	10 ·5
„ Scotland	„	24 ·54	27 ·16	18 ·79	1 ·99	8 ·1
		Tons.	Tons.	Tons.	Tons.	
Potatoes, E. England	„	5 ·81	7 ·06	4 ·63	0 ·69	11 ·9
„ Scotland	„	5 ·81	7 ·13	4 ·54	0 ·79	13 ·6
„ France	1885–1904	3 ·15	3 ·58	2 ·86	0 ·54	17 ·1
Turnips and swedes, E. England	1885–1905	11 ·59	13 ·77	7 ·82	1 ·70	14 ·7
Turnips and swedes, Scotland	„	15 ·05	17 ·25	12 ·23	1 ·35	9 ·0
Mangold, E. England	„	17 ·14	21 ·16	14 ·83	2 ·03	11 ·8
„ Scotland	„	16 ·83	20 ·95	13 ·21	1 ·82	10 ·8
„ France*	1885–1904	9 ·92	12 ·29	7 ·89	0 ·89	9 ·0
		Cwts.	Cwts.	Cwts.	Cwts.	
Hay from clover and rotation grass } E. England	1886–1905	28 ·02	36 ·74	14 ·97	4 ·42	15 ·8
Scotland	„	31 ·22	35 ·14	25 · 55	2 ·64	8 ·5
Clover hay, France	1885–1904	29 ·88	35 ·00	14 ·80	4 ·22	14 ·1
Hay from permanent grass } E. England	1886–1905	22 ·68	28 ·77	9 ·89	4 ·46	19 ·7
Scotland	„	28 ·84	31 ·65	22 ·61	2 ·34	8 ·1
France	1885–1904	25 ·05	28 ·80	11 ·20	3 ·93	15 ·7
Hops, Kent	1885–1905	8 ·84	14 ·47	4 ·63	2 ·46	27 ·8

* Betteraves fourragères.

TABLE IV.—CORRELATION COEFFICIENTS BETWEEN RAINFALL
AND ACCUMULATED TEMPERATURE ABOVE 42° F.

Period.	Twenty-one Years. 1884-1904.	Twenty-one Years. 1885-1905.	Twenty Years. 1885-1904.	Twenty Years. 1886-1905.
1—8th weeks	....	−0 ·24	....	−0 ·25
5 ,, ...	....	+ ·02	....	− ·00
9 ,, ...	−0 ·46	− ·41	−0 ·43	− ·42
13 ,, ...	− ·53	− ·53	− ·53	− ·53
17 ,, ...	− ·38	− ·39	− ·39	− ·39
21 ,, ...	−. ·39	− ·31	− ·40	− ·32
25 ,, ...	− ·57	− ·59	− ·54	− ·70
29 ,, ...	− ·40	− ·46	− ·44	− ·56
33 ,, ...	− ·50	− ·54	− ·54	....
37 ,, ...	− ·54	− ·48	− ·53	....
41 ,, ...	− ·29	....	− ·27	....
45 ,, ...	+ ·10	....	+ ·11	....
49—4th ,, ...	+ ·05	....	+ ·05	....
Seasons :—				
Winter	....	− ·06	....	− ·11
Spring	− ·57	− ·57	− ·57	− ·56
Summer ....:	− ·63	− ·59	− ·63	− ·71
Autumn	− ·42	....	− ·42	....
Cereal year	....	− ·50	....	− ·51

DISCUSSION on MR. R. H. HOOKER'S PAPER.

DR. SHAW said they were much indebted to Mr. Hooker for the
great labour he had bestowed on calculating the correlation
coefficients between the rainfall and warmth at different times of
the year and the various crops. The relation between the crops
and those conditions was in this way formulated for those who were
acquainted with the matter practically. It was a great advantage
to have these results put into a numerical form, because they were
very much shorter than the practical expression of the memory
of practical man, and much more easy to put into a table. He
would suggest that in the discussion they might have a pronouncement from some one acquainted with correlation coefficients and
their application to phenomena of different kinds, as to the meaning
which could be attached to correlation coefficients of comparatively
small values. There was no doubt that if you got them between
0·75 and 1, the indication of association was very close; but if
it fell below 0·75 or below 0·5, the precise application of the
correlation coefficients was more dubious. And he should like
to have from some expert illustrations of the extent to which
such a matter could be regarded as indicating a definite relation.
For instance, in the table relating to peas there was a correlation
coefficient of 0·49 between the crop of peas and the warmth of the
subsequent autumn. No doubt there might be or must be some
correlation between the crop and what happened afterwards—it

might be between the subsequent accumulated temperatures and the crop of peas. And that being so, whether o·5 was the proper critical point was worth examination. That particular correlation suggested to his mind an old-fashioned method of forecasting the weather, which he thought had rather gone out of fashion, namely, that if you got a large crop of hips and haws you would have a cold winter. Mr. Hooker had not touched on that particular correlation coefficient, but between the peas and the subsequent autumn he had given at least a suggestive coefficient which rehabilitated to a certain extent the possibilities of such a method ; and it added force to the conclusion that the question of correlation between different seasons was extraordinarily interesting. It was so particularly in connection with wheat. In a paper which he (the speaker) contributed lately to the *Cambridge Agricultural Journal*, he put in a table showing the accumulated temperatures and the rainfall for the different seasons corresponding to the yield of wheat for the last twenty years; and, to his great astonishment—he would not say that there was a correlation—there was an indication of a relation of the following kind. In sixteen years out of twenty-one years a wet autumn had a winter with a rainfall above the average ; or *vice versâ*, when it was below the average in one case it was below in the other. The two seasons ran parallel in 16 cases out of 21 ; but between the autumn and the spring they ran opposite. This did not show that the correlation coefficient would come very high, because there was no sort of proportionality between the amounts by which the autumn rainfall was increased or decreased, and the amount by which the corresponding spring rainfall was in defect or excess. As long as Mr. Hooker was speaking of the correlation coefficients he dealt with them strictly, taking them for better or worse, as he thought himself bound to do ; but in the latter part of the paper, where he proceeded to some speculations not based on the strict method of correlation coefficients, he referred to abnormal seasons, and he seemed to indicate that under certain circumstances he might reject data as having somehow or another gone wrong. He took it that in calculating the correlation coefficients you did not reject anything, but took them for better or worse. In a matter of this kind it did not seem to him to be necessarily an advantage to find correlation coefficients always between the " brut " data and the crop. For example, if you set out to find the correlation coefficient between the yield of wheat and the accumulated temperature in the year, as a rule you had to deal with a small variation in the one corresponding with a small variation in the other. But there was one year, 1879, when there really was not enough warmth to grow a wheat crop at all in this country. Practically, the experiment failed, and to bring in a failure of that kind, when the accumulated temperature was only numerically low, into association with other data where there was more or less proportionality, seemed to require a certain amount of justification. Therefore, he should once more like to ask experts whether it would be feasible in computing the coefficients to leave out of account some of the specially exceptional cases, as Mr. Hooker seemed disposed to do in the last few paragraphs. A very high coefficient of correlation, obtained for all years with one or two exceptions, might have a very definite meaning. Again, he should like to ask whether, if one calculated the combined correlation coefficient between the crop and several elements of the weather, say the spring rainfall and the autumn rainfall, or other different elements for which the partial correlation coefficients were high, one would get a very high correlation coefficient which would be an obvious indication of a close relationship. If that could be done it might be possible to get an indication for some crops of what in combination were the vitally important elements.

There was one little criticism he might venture to offer. Mr. Hooker had compiled a fresh district in the British Isles in order to find the relation between one thing and another. His impression was that there were already too many different groupings into districts. Probably it was not a matter of vital importance whether you included Lincolnshire when dealing with a question of this kind. As regards the relation between the yield of wheat and the rainfall, it was closer for the whole of England than for the Eastern counties taken as a district. He thought it would not be desirable not to introduce another scheme for classification of English counties into districts.

Mr. Hooker had challenged him to say something about the triumph of the autumn rainfall over the indication of the eleven-year periodicity. He had not yet seen the crop values for the individual counties, and he did not know whether the Board of Agriculture had yet issued them; but, supposing the triumph was as complete as it appeared to be, he might reply to Mr. Hooker that the occurrence of a node gave no particular reason for the relation kicking up its heels and bolting. A node was not specially the point where one would expect such things to occur.

Professor EDGEWORTH remarked that the statisticians who dealt with meteorology in relation to agriculture were fortunate in the stability of their subject. "O fortunatos!" he would say, if he might add "sua si *mala* norint;" for the condition of success in such investigations was to be aware of their difficulty. Mr. Hooker gave us confidence in his results by making ample allowance for the unavoidable deficiencies in his data. Not only was the number of observations, viz., 21, rather small, but also, as Mr. Hooker intimated when speaking of cycles in crops, there might be some correlation between those observations. Accordingly, in the computation of probable errors, the denominator proper to the case of independent observations, viz., $\sqrt{21}$, must be taken *cum grano*. The error to be apprehended might really be a little greater than appeared. He hoped that Mr. Hooker would confirm his theories by dealing with additional materials. Some trouble might perhaps be saved by a slight variation in the procedure. He referred to the " coefficients of double correlation " which Mr. Hooker had employed to exhibit the correlation between abundance of crop on the one hand, and on the other hand a pair of (mutually correlated) attributes, temperature and (deficiency of) rainfall—the pair happily subsumed by Mr. Hooker under the description "weather." To form the combination of temperature and rainfall constituting "weather," it would be agreed that the compound attribute, say z, should be related in the simplest manner to the two components, say x_1 and x_2; that z should be a linear function of x_1 and x_2. But there might be a difference of opinion as to the proper species of this genus. Mr. Yule, whom Mr. Hooker had followed, would determine the linear function by the condition that the correlation between the third attribute x_1, and the compound of x_1 and x_2, should be a maximum. It was as if we suspected complicity between an accused pair and a third party, and it was thought best to employ that form of trial or ordeal which would make the complicity appear greatest. He (Professor Edgeworth) thought that the purpose of an impartial inquiry might perhaps be as well served by some other arrangement. He would therefore propose as a variant method for coupling x_1 and x_2 the plan which he had suggested in the *Journal of the Royal Statistical Society** for the identification of criminals in cases where two attributes used for this purpose proved to be highly correlated. Take as the unit, in terms of which x_1 is measured, the corresponding *standards deviation*, and let x_1 be likewise measured by σ_2; then put $z = \dfrac{1}{\sqrt{2}}(x_1 + x_2)$; x_1 and x_2 being positively correlated. Thus, if each couple of concurrent observations of the type x'_1, x'_2 is represented by a dot on the plane of x_1, x_2, these dots being disposed in (a series of concentric and coaxal) elliptical rings—curves of equal probability—then z is to be measured along (a parallel) to the major axis of the ellipse (from the minor axis). The "weather" thus defined would be independent of the crop with which it was compared. The correlation between z thus defined and any third attribute x_1 might be used as a coefficient of double correlation. Its form was very simple. It was such as to become negative if there proved to be a negative coefficient of correlation—a repugnancy—between the "weather" at any period and the abundance of a certain crop.

Major CRAIGIE said he had listened to the paper with great interest, because he thought it was the beginning of a series of papers in which the practical knowledge of agriculturalists and the theoretical methods of arithmetical expression might be brought together. The agriculturalist had a storehouse of information; and a great many farmers if they examined the results of Mr. Hooker's conclusions would be, no doubt, somewhat startled. He was himself a little alarmed at the conclusion drawn as to the effect of the weather at certain periods on permanent grass; and he was very much surprised at certain figures. He hoped he was too much of a statistician to say that the figures were wrong, but, at any rate, they gave cause for thought. He did not feel quite sure whether the results were not obtained from possibly insufficient data. He must

---

* Vol. lix, 1896, "Supplementary Notes on Statistics," IV, p. 534 *sqq.*

join in congratulating Mr. Hooker on the first paper he had produced in his new position he held as Head of the Statistical Branch
of the Board of Agriculture. The connection of mathematical
knowledge and agricultural data promised a great deal in the future,
for they were now only making a beginning. He was not sure that
it might not be worth the consideration of the Council at some
future time whether a mixed Committee should be formed of
practical agriculturists and statisticians to go into some of these
points, which apparently wanted thrashing out across the table
rather than in a public discussion.

He should like, again, to consider what was the real meaning of
the want of progress to which Mr. Hooker pointed very forcibly in
the latter part of his paper. Why was it that, as regards England,
there was no progress, but rather the reverse, in the yield per acre
of crops since the great depression set in ? In a paper read in 1883
he had dealt with the older records of production, somewhat
scattered as they were, and his conclusion was that there had been
a distinct tendency to progress since 1883, as the area of wheat had
been reduced. But how was it with regard to other crops ? The
area under oats, for instance, had extended, but whether, with all
the advantages of the further knowledge, they were obtaining better
results than before, was a serious question, and he only hoped it
could be answered satisfactorily.

He agreed with Dr. Shaw that there were certain abnormal
years, such as 1879, that one always felt inclined to omit, as having
gone so far beyond the ordinary swing of the pendulum as to be
like a cataclysm of nature, which they could not expect to recur.
It was evident that this paper, and the previous one of Dr. Shaw,
were the opening of a new and very promising field of investigation.

Mr. YULE said that generally when a speaker rose late in a discussion the majority of his points had been already dealt with ; but,
during the present discussion, a large number of additional points
had been raised, and he found himself in some difficulty in dealing
both with the points of the paper and those raised by previous
speakers, particularly as he had been so interested in listening to
the remarks that he had not made any notes.

As to the question of probable errors raised by Dr. Shaw, and
the meaning to be attached to very small correlation coefficients,
one could not lay down any definite law. If you wrote down
certain numbers at random on tickets, and drew them by pairs out
of a bag, and treated the pairs as representing the wheat record
and the rainfall record, there ought not to be any connection at all
between the two numbers ; but, inevitably, you would find greater
or less correlation coefficients, sometimes positive, sometimes negative, and sometimes nearly zero. The values of the correlation
coefficients so obtained would fluctuate round zero, and large figures
of either sign would be very rare—but there was no absolute or
definite limit. Mr. Hooker had taken a fairly high limit, beyond
which he considered the coefficient as being significant of a definite
physical relationship. A more rash statistician might have taken a

lower limit; but it was largely a point of personal taste what limit one would take in any actual case.

As Mr. Hooker had referred to him in connection with the question of the probable error of the partial coefficient, he should say that he hoped to justify the formula given (p. 6) very shortly. The coefficient of double correlation, R, on which Mr. Hooker and himself presented a short note recently (*Journal*, 1906), was, however, a very troublesome quantity as regarded the effect of errors of sampling. It was not only subject to fluctuation round the true value, but was also subject to biassed error. In the formula for R, the positive sign was always to be attached to the square root, and, consequently, if the two coefficients, r_{12} and ρ_{13}, had any values whatever, due to fluctuations of sampling or otherwise, R would have a positive value. On averaging, consequently, a series of values of R obtained from cases where the variables were really independent, the mean would not approximate to zero, but to a sensible value which he estimated at $\sqrt{(v-1)/N}$ for the root-mean-square average, v being the number of variables and N the number of observations. This formula gave the value 0·31 cited by Mr. Hooker.

Passing to another point, also raised by Dr. Shaw, the question as to the form of relationship between the weather and the crop, and its influence on the coefficient of correlation, the value of r was most easily interpreted when there was a linear relation between the average value of the crop and the weather. If the relationship was of the kind which could only be expressed by a curve, say of such a kind that the greatest value of the crop corresponded with certain optimum weather conditions and was less for a deviation in either direction, you would obtain much lower values of the correlation. Unfortunately, with so small a number of observations it would be very difficult to be certain whether there were a relationship of that kind or no, unless it were extremely well marked.

He would like to emphasize two points which seemed to him to be of great importance in the conclusions which Mr. Hooker had reached. First, with regard to the importance of a cool spring and summer: if one looked through the signs of the partial correlation coefficients between the crops and the temperature in all the tables, during the period between the ninth and twenty-eighth weeks (which included four correlations), they were *all* negative in the cases of barley, oats, peas, turnips and swedes, mangolds, and both the hay crops. That was an extraordinarily sweeping uniformity of sign. In the case of wheat there was only one positive coefficient; and in beans only one. Potatoes was the only crop in which there were three positive coefficients to one negative. This conclusion, it seemed to him, was one of considerable practical importance. The second very important point was the apparent opposition indicated between the conditions requisite for good seed-quality and the conditions requisite for a bulky crop. He had tried to summarise Mr. Hooker's figures somewhat hastily in a different way in order to see if such opposition was more clearly indicated thereby. He found in the case of temperature that in all the weeks of the year between the ninth and the thirty-sixth (from early spring to early autumn) there were, out of six coefficients, with wheat, one positive in the harvest year, and five positive in the year in which the seeds were grown. In the case of barley it was the same thing : there were no positive coefficients in the harvest year, but five in the seed year. With oats, again, there were no positive coefficients in the harvest year, and four in the seed year. In the case of the rainfall, the opposition was not quite so marked. For wheat there were three positives in the harvest year to two in the seed year. But for barley there were four positives in the harvest year, and only one positive in the seed year. For oats, four positive in the harvest year, and two in the seed year. In the case of beans, again, there was a somewhat similar opposition. In all these cases of " seed crops," in which the seed was not only used as such but also for the food, there was a marked opposition between conditions requisite for the two qualities, good seed and a bulky crop. This fact bore on that curious tendency to alternation of good and bad crops to which Dr. Shaw had alluded. That tendency was well marked in the case of the years 1885 to 1905 ; they gave fourteen pairs of years in which a deviation of the crop in one direction from the average was followed by a deviation of the other sign; and only six pairs of years in which a deviation of one sign was followed again the next year by a deviation of the same sign. If the crop were above the average one year, the odds were therefore 7 to 3 that it would deviate in the other direction the next year.

As a corollary to the conclusions respecting the opposition between good seed qualities and bulky crop, he would like to raise the question whether there ought not to be greater specialization in growing a crop for seed and a crop for food, specialization either in districts or in the mode of growth, manuring, &c. ? In the case of potatoes there did seem to be some such specialization ; and he would like to know how far it was recognised as desirable, from a practical standpoint, in the case of other crops. He would like, in conclusion, to point out, as one who knew something of the matter, what an enormous labour must have been devoted by the author to his paper. Most statisticians knew the amount of calculation needed even to obtain many averages; but to calculate a correlation co-efficient required a great deal more, and in the present paper there were something like 700 total correlation coefficients, together with the partial correlations calculated therefrom by a not very handy formula. However, the labour had been well repaid, as it led to many con-clusions and speculations of a far-reaching and important kind.

Mr. SYDNEY YOUNG said he would like to say a word or two on the practical side of the question. It had been said that an abundant harvest was most likely to produce bad seed. But he should say that an abundant harvest produced good seed, but was often followed by a poor harvest owing to the fact that although the seed was good it was put into the ground in bad weather ; he thought that was really the reason why they sometimes got first a good crop and then a bad one—not that they got bad seed from a full harvest. It had also been said that the most critical time for the farmer in wheat harvest was the seed time. But wheat seed was very hardy indeed; it would stand a very large amount of rough treatment, so long as it was sown in dry weather. When the farmer had to sow it in wet weather, there was no doubt the chances were that he would get a bad result. In his opinion, the most critical time was the flowering time, which was about June. According to a great French scientist, M. Bidard, for a period of about fourteen days in the month of June the wheat was prepared to flower; and, as long as the temperature was within the region of 70° F. there would be a good flowering season, provided there was no rain or wind. If there were rain or wind, the flowers were spoilt; or directly they flowered the bloom withered. When you saw the withered flower you could tell whether you were going to get a good or a bad harvest as regards quantity. At other times you could only form an uncertain estimate. As long as the wheat germinated in the ground it did not matter whether it was frozen off or eaten off at a certain time, it would still grow up and produce good straw; and from that you would get a harvest; but the flowering time was the most important. With regard to the period of eleven years of cycle good and bad crops, he could not see that that was borne out by the statistics; the averages had remained between 26 and 34 bushels for a great number of years; but they did not go regularly from 34 downwards, or from 26 upwards and then down again; they were very irregular in sequence, and therefore he did not think there was that periodicity of good and bad crops which had been suggested.

Mr. REW said that if he wished to criticise this paper he had other opportunities of doing so, while if he eulogised it, it might possibly be thought that he was not altogether disinterested. He should, however, like to say that it was of the greatest importance and interest from the point of view of the Society that questions of this sort should be taken up by statisticians of the ability, industry and thoroughness of Mr. Hooker. Everyone must realise the enormous amount of work which had been put into this paper, and although Mr. Hooker had perhaps left one or two of his conclusions at rather a loose end, they would well repay further consideration. He had done work of great value to those interested in agricultural subjects in having opened a new field—or in extending the area of investigation which Dr. Shaw had opened up—in regard to the actual relationship between the weather and the crops. He hoped the suggestions made in the paper would be further followed up.

The CHAIRMAN conveyed to Mr. Hooker the cordial thanks of the meeting for his paper.

Mr. R. H. HOOKER, in reply, said that he was glad to find, from Professor Edgeworth's and Mr. Yule's remarks, that they regarded his critical value of 0·5 as sufficiently safe to justify conclusions being drawn from it. He would refer Dr. Shaw to p. 7 *sqq.* of his paper, in which he had dealt at some length with the theoretical considerations that led him to adopt this figure. As mentioned, the odds against there being no dependence, when such a coefficient was obtained with 21 observations, were something like 1 in 15,000 —of course, there was that one odd chance that the twenty-one years were so peculiar that the connection was adventitious. He had himself noted the coefficient of 0·49 between peas and temperature after harvest, and had concluded that it was a chance value, because the weather then could have no obvious connection with the crop. He would observe two things as regards this value : first, that by correcting for rainfall the net coefficient was reduced to 0·38 ; and, secondly, that he had specifically treated coefficients between 0·3 and 0·5, as suggestive only, not as proof, of dependency ; in fact, this particular coefficient—the largest of all those between any crop and a period with which it could apparently have no connection—had largely guided him in determining what might safely be regarded as the lowest limit of "proof." There was also the possibility that the weather after harvest was correlated with the weather of some other period that did affect the crop.

Dr. Shaw had mentioned the importance of correlation between one part of a year and another as affecting the figures : this was discussed on p. 3, and, with regard to autumn and winter rainfall in particular, on p. 11. Dr. Shaw found 16 cases in which the rainfall of these two periods corresponded in direction, and 5 when it did not, but that the amounts did not seem to correspond. The amounts for the eight weekly periods compared on p. 12 seemed to correspond to a considerable degree (in the last twenty-one years), and the big coefficient there given indicated a real connection between those two periods. He hoped accordingly that Dr. Shaw and his assistants would investigate possible connections between various seasons from the longer series of data at their disposal.

Dr. Shaw asked whether he could combine the effects of two seasons upon a crop so as to estimate their total effect. He saw no reason why the net and double correlation coefficients should not be formed between a crop and any two seasons, in exactly the same way as he had formed them for two other factors, viz., rainfall and temperature at one season. To find the joint effect of more than two seasons was much more complicated : correlation of three variables such as he had performed was comparatively simple, but with four variables the work, although similar in theory, became very complex, and with more than four the labour would be enormous, if not prohibitive.

Dr. Shaw also asked why abnormal seasons were not rejected. Simply because he was dealing solely with averages. He was not quite sure that the nature of the problem dealt with was clearly grasped. He (Mr. Hooker) was trying to obtain some idea of the *average* effect of deviations from the mean rainfall and temperature upon the crops. Dr. Shaw seemed inclined to think that a peculiar year like 1879 ought to be omitted. But it ought not, any more than Dr. Shaw should omit it in estimating, say, the average rainfall of 1870-1900. He wished he had the yields of 1879 in order that the effect of the weather of that year might be taken into account, and its relative influence on our crops in a long series of years estimated. When, however, he (Mr. Hooker) got to his little excursus at the end, he mentioned the abnormal years, because here he was no longer comparing crops with the weather affecting them, but the crops of different years *inter se*, and abnormal years would very seriously affect the average of so small a number as ten years. A crop 10 per cent. below the average, for instance, would lower the average of the decade by 1 per cent. The distribution of the crops during the period, in fact, and doubtless the weather also, was not normal ; and sufficient time had not elapsed to nullify the effect of abnormal years on the average. It is, on the other hand, quite permissible to correlate variables of which the distribution is not normal.[2]

Dr. Shaw had seemed rather to reproach him for including Lincolnshire. It would no doubt have been easier to take simply one recognised agricultural district, but Lincolnshire was the most important county for certain crops, and he could hardly omit it without largely reducing the acreage of these. He was not, of course, suggesting that his district should be taken for any other purpose, or by anybody else.

On the question of the frequent alternation of a good and bad wheat crop, he still thought this was due partly to the summer weather having a different effect upon the bulk and condition of the seed. It must be remembered that the summer weather was not the primary factor in the wheat yield ; other times were more important, hence a heavy crop, due, say, to a previous favourable seedtime, might sometimes give good seed, the summer, while favouring the quality, not being sufficiently detrimental to quantity as to overbalance previous development of the bulk. As regards a hot June being necessary for wheat, of course, other factors besides the weather affected the crop, but so far as regarded the differences from the averages, the figures clearly showed that, during the past twenty-one years, good crops had resulted when the temperature at that period was below the mean, not when the weather was hot.

Mr. Yule had asked whether growers specialised for seed : he believed that was largely done, more particularly by seed merchants. He had recently made some inquiries regarding the time of the harvest, and with regard to the dates mentioned for wheat on p. 12, one correspondent mentioned a much narrower period, viz., seed gathered in 19–25th August ; crop harvested 9–12th August. In eastern England, therefore, the wheat intended for seed was left standing for ten days or a fortnight later than that intended for consumption. Attention to the same point was, he had no doubt, generally paid in the case of other crops.

The following were elected Fellows of the Society :—

Andersson, Thor Erik Engelbrekt.] Gemmill, William.
Simon, André L.

---

[2] See " Proceedings of the Royal Society," vol. 60, p. 477.

STATISTICS *of* PRODUCTION *and* *the* CENSUS *of* PRODUCTION ACT
(1906).   *By* G. UDNY YULE.

[Read before the Royal Statistical Society, 19th February, 1907.
Sir RICHARD BIDDULPH MARTIN, Bart., President, in the Chair.]

Introductory.

As the passing of the Census of Production Act is a very important
event in the history of British statistics, it seemed that an opportunity for a discussion of the scope, purpose, and special features of
the Act by the Fellows of this Society might be of value. The
following notes have, accordingly, been put together as an
introduction to such a discussion.

The term production is used in economics in the general sense
of production of wealth, *i.e.*, of the useful qualities or utilities of
commodities.   Production may, therefore, be defined as the
rendering of a commodity, material or immaterial, available for use
or consumption in the widest sense of that term. Every act by
which a commodity is won for the use of man is therefore an act of
production, whether man did not interfere with the creation of the
commodity, as in the mining of coal or of ores, and the cutting of
natural forest timber, or did interfere, as in the growing of crops ;
and every act by which such raw commodities are further transformed into new and different commodities, as in the smelting of
ores, the working of timber, the milling of wheat, the making of
cloth into clothing, or the combining of iron, timber, and stone
into railways, is also an act of production.

It is the purpose of statistics of production, I take it, to exhibit,
one may almost say to measure, the activities of a nation or
community in the various fields of production and to show how the
activities are changing in magnitude and in kind. In the absence
of such statistics, writers on the subject are reduced to a system of
more or less biassed guesswork such as the recent controversy on
the state of our trade has only too often exhibited.

In order that a summary view may be obtained as to the total
production at any given time, it is necessary that the productions
of different commodities should be in some way added together.
But in order to do this the output of every commodity must be
measured in the same units. When quantities are stated, this is
not generally the case ; we have to deal with, say, bushels of corn,

tons of pig-iron, square feet of timber, yards of cloth, and so on. To avoid the difficulty, it is usual to reduce the statement of productions of all commodities to the common standard of money value. Statistics of production, therefore, not only usually include values, but sometimes values only and not quantities. The statement in terms of value has not only the convenience of expression by a common unit, but also of assigning to each commodity its proper importance in the scale of exchange. It clearly, however, introduces difficulties when such statistics are collected over a long period of time, owing to the changes in the standard of value. If a nation produces 1,100*l.* worth of commodities now where only 1,000*l.* worth was produced ten years before, this may be due solely to a rise of prices, and in order to correct for the rise of prices the values returned for each commodity would have to be reduced to the prices of a standard period.

Further, the addition of the values of commodities produced is a process that must be conducted with great caution, if the results obtained are to be susceptible of any ready interpretation, for it is only too easy to add in the value of many productions two or three times over. This may occur in two ways that are distinct from the commercial standpoint, though they really amount to the same. (1) Values may be duplicated by certain work being given out to a sub-contractor and the value returned by both chief contractor and sub-contractor. A builder, *A*, erects houses and contracts for the stonework with *B*, the ironwork with *C*, and so on. *A* returns the complete value of the house, and *B* and *C* both return the values of their jobs. The stonework and ironwork is counted twice over.[1] A manufacturer of cotton goods sends his cloth to the dyer and finisher : the value of the dyeing and finishing enters into the total value at which he returns his production, but the dyer also returns the value of the dyeing-finishing as his production. The dyeing and finishing is counted twice. A census of production must, therefore, in order to make some correction or allowance for this, demand particulars as to work given out on contract. (2) Similar duplication arises owing to the different stages in the production of a finished commodity being carried out by different establishments. This not only leads to error, but may lead to errors which vary with the scope of the census, and which gradually change over a long period of time, owing

[1] After the U.S.A. Census of 1900 special reports were obtained from the officials of a number of cities as to the estimated value of buildings erected during the census year. The total estimated cost was $325,000 ; the value of products returned at the census for building trades $405,000, although the census canvass was notoriously defective. Census, vol. vii, p. ccxlvi.

to alterations in the organisation of industry. Take the case of a basket-maker who buys osiers from a grower. The grower returns say, 500*l.* as the value of his production, if the census include agriculture, otherwise no return is made; the basket-maker, 1,500*l.* as the value of his productions. As the cost of the osiers is part of this value, they have been counted twice in the first case, once in the second. But the basket-maker finds it pays to purchase osier beds and grow his own. The value of the osiers is then no longer returned in either case. Similarly in textile manufactures : if the spinning and weaving industries are separated, the yarn gets counted twice; and the wool, if produced in the same country, and if the census include agriculture, three times. If the spinning and weaving are done by the same firm, the wool is the only commodity that gets counted twice. This is evidently not different from the last case in essentials, for the weaver may be regarded as letting out the yarn-making to the spinner as sub-contractor, and the spinner as letting out the growing of the wool. But the two cases are distinct in practice, and a schedule for a census of production must therefore ask two questions : (1) as to materials purchased and (2) as to work given out on contract, in addition to the inquiry as to total value of products.

The problem of duplication is discussed in some detail in the introduction to the "U.S.A. Census of Manufactures of 1900" (census, vol. vii, chap. xxvii, p. cxxxix), a new method of elimination having been attempted. At the censuses of 1870, 1880, and 1890, the "total cost of materials" was deducted from the "gross value "of products," and the result termed the "net value of products." " By this process the net value of the products for the United " States was made to appear less than the cost of the materials " consumed in the manufacture of these products, which is a " statistical absurdity." In 1900 the matter was approached from another point of view. The net value of products is made up of (1) the value of all raw materials (materials which have never been treated in any factory) entering into the output, (2) the entire value added to these raw materials by all manufacturing processes through which they have passed. At the 1900 census manufacturers were required to state the value of materials consumed under the two heads (1) "purchased in a raw state," (2) "purchased " in a partially manufactured form." As the partially manufactured materials should have been already returned separately, the net value will be given by deducting from the gross value the total value of "partially manufactured materials" (if the census be a census of manufactures only). Thus, take the case of clothing manufacture in four stages. The argument is that the returns, say,

from a comber, spinner, and weaver would have the fóllowing form
as regards the chief material only :—

| | Value in £1,000's. | | |
	Raw Materials.	Partially Manufactured Materials.	Products.
1. Wool comber	5	—	10
2. Spinner	—	10	15
- 3. Weaver	—	15	20
4. Clothier	—	20	25
			70
Totals	5	45	45
Net value	—	—	25

If the returns of all the firms were added together the total,
70,000*l.*, would include the wool four times, the yarn three times,
and the weaving twice. But, deducting the total of "partially
" manufactured materials," which are all duplicated, the right total
is given, viz., 25,000*l.* Evidently, had the census included raw
materials as well as manufactures, the total value of both raw and
partially manufactured materials would have to have been deducted
from the total value of products.

But this process is open to several objections and difficulties,
and, as it seems to me, the difficulty of the first method is partly
imaginary—due merely to an incorrect phraseology—and partly to
the fact that the census of manufactures apparently took no account
of the other portions of the census dealing with raw materials. In
the first place there is no rigid line between raw and partially
manufactured materials—*e.g.*, scrap iron is often classed as both—
and the demand for the division of "materials purchased" into the
two classes consequently gives rise to much additional trouble
In the second place—a much more serious objection—the value
returned by a producer for his product is the net value at the
factory; the value returned by a producer for his raw materials
includes intermediate profits and freight as well. Hence, in
deducting the cost of partially manufactured materials, much too
large a deduction has been made. Even greater difficulties arise if
it is attempted to apply the method to the products of a single
industry or of a single State or County. In the first case, partially
manufactured materials produced by another industry must not
be deducted, as they have not been counted into the gross total
of that industry. In the second case the cost of partially manufactured materials made in another State or County must not

be deducted, for they have not been counted into the gross total for the State or County, and there are no data as to exports and imports of single States or Counties.

To return to the first method then, if we deduct value of materials from the value of the products for any one manufacturer's schedule, it is certainly misleading to term the balance "net value of *products*" in the material sense, but it is the *net contribution of that producer to the value*, or the *net value of his production* (not of the objective product that leaves his hands, but of that which he has added to it, *i.e.*, of production in the economic sense). It is termed in the Massachusetts census the "industry product."[2] Hence, if value of materials be deducted from value of products, the resulting total, for any group, will give the value of the production of that group. The sum of the productions for all groups included in the census is their total production, and it will be equal to the value of the material products if (but only if) the census extends over the whole field of production, including raw materials. Value of work done by contractors should be treated precisely like value of materials, and deducted from value of products. This method seems to me better and more straightforward than the method used in the U.S.A. census of 1900, and the results easier to comprehend. Moreover, the method applies without any difficulty or ambiguity to single industries or single States, and it does not render it necessary to trouble the worried manufacturer with ambiguous classifications of the materials which he purchases.

In any practical attempt to measure production, the determination of the field to be covered must be a matter for grave consideration. In the first place, questions of limitation arise, as a complete census is almost an impossibility, not merely from its cost but from the difficulty of obtaining any data on certain forms of production. It is no use making the answering of a census question compulsory, and assigning heavy penalties for misstatements when it is impossible for a producer, with the best will in the world, to be sure that he is telling you the truth. Thus, for the reason mainly of cost, small areas are usually omitted from agricultural returns, the British figures, *e.g.*, taking no account of areas less than 1 acre under crops. For both reasons, in statistics of manufactures, it is common to limit the scope of investigation by excluding shops employing less than 4 or 5 hands (*e.g.*, Canada, Australia), or the product under a certain value (U.S.A. 1905 and some earlier censuses : Cape Colony). This not only enormously lessens labour and cost, but also avoids certain difficulties due to the

2 See table reproduced below, p. 70.

quite different organisation of small trades, or retail work even on a large scale, from the making of standardised products—difficulties that render true returns in the former case almost impossible (*see* below, p. 68).   At the same time such limitations are also open to objection if rigidly applied, for they exclude some industries altogether, and hence exceptions are generally made to the rule. The census may also be confined to special branches of production, *e.g.*, manufactures and agriculture, ignoring mining (U.S.A., 1900) or manufactures alone (Massachusetts).   Or, while the census covers a large extent of the field of production, it may tacitly ignore certain branches, which the reader may not immediately discover, *e.g.*, civil engineering works (U.S.A., Canada).

In the second place, questions of extension must also be considered. The prime object is the collection of statistics of production, the production of utilities or value, and in this collection statistics showing quantities or values actually produced naturally take the first place.   But the means of production come a close second, and most inquiries take into account such matters as capital, horse-power available, number of hands employed, wages, and regularity of employment (time worked in the year).   With the extension into such fields and allied branches of inquiry, the investigation begins to partake more and more of the character of an industrial census rather than a census of production.

II.—*Existing Statistics of Production.*

Such statistics of production as exist in Europe are only organised in any complete form for two branches of production, agriculture and mining : practically all civilised countries of the world, I believe, offer data on these heads.   Outside this limited field statistics are only available for certain definite industries, either because they are subject to special taxation (alcohol, tobacco), or to regulation by special laws, or because they are highly organised trades which desire the information for their own ends and are glad to supply it without compulsion.   In view of the limited character of such statistics (and of the time at my disposal), I have not thought it necessary to attempt to review them in detail, but have taken the statistics of the United Kingdom, which it was necessary to review, for consideration in connection with the Act, as sufficiently typical.[3]   After these, I have passed to the very detailed statistics

[3] There was a Census of Production, including returns (very detailed) of quantity and value of products, in France in 1845 ; another commenced in 1860, of which the results were only issued in 1873, and a third (less complete apparently) commenced in that year.   The industrial censuses of France in 1896 and in 1901, and the industrial censuses of other European countries appear to cover the instruments of production only.

of Australasia ; collected annually in Australia, quinquennially at the census in New Zealand.   Next I have taken the voluminous census of the United States, the modest but admirable census of manufactures of Massachusetts, the census of Canada, and the census of Cape Colony.   These will serve as examples with which to compare the present Act.

THE UNITED KINGDOM.—The principal statistics of production of the United Kingdom are those issued by the Home Office, the Board of Trade, the Board of Agriculture and Fisheries, and the Commissioners of Customs.

The most important Home Office statistics relate to the output and value of the minerals raised in the United Kingdom, and are issued annually.[4]   The collection of the statistics is in part authorised under (1) the Coal Mines Regulation Act (1887), (2) the Metalliferous Mines Regulation Act (1875), and (3) the Quarries Act (1894), which applies only to quarries over 20 feet deep. Under each of these Acts a return is required, *inter alia*, of the quantity of minerals wrought; but this statutory information is supplemented by voluntary returns.   In the case of the more important trades, *e.g.*, coal and iron, the information given is very complete.   Thus, for coal, tables are given showing quantities raised, total value at the pit's mouth, and average price per ton for each county and for each coalfield, with particulars as to amounts of other minerals, chiefly ironstone and fireclay, raised from coal mines.   For pig-iron, details are given for each county as to the number of works in operation, the number of furnaces built and the average number in blast, the quantity of pig-iron made, and the number of tons of coal and iron ore used.   A detailed table is also given showing for each individual works the total number of furnaces and average number in blast.   The statistics cover all minerals; to cite only a few in the alphabetical order in which they are given : Chalk, coal, copper, gypsum, igneous rocks, iron, lead, limestone, salt, sandstone, slate, tin, and zinc, and give us data, which are probably very reliable, over the major part of this important field of production.   The returns are most incomplete in the case of clay and brick earth where the workings are generally less than 20 feet deep, and consequently do not come under any of the Acts.   The tables issued annually by the Board of Trade on iron and steel and coal, giving international statistics of production, may be cited in this connection.[5]   Reference may also be made to certain returns which have been issued by the

---

[4] "Mines and Quarries." General Report and Statistics, pt. iii, Output.

[5] "Coal Tables, 1905" (1906), No. 321. "Iron and Steel, 1905" (1906), No. 322.

Home Office bearing on the capacity for production in the textile trades,[6] but not giving the actual production.

The annual statements of the navigation and shipping of the United Kingdom, issued by the Board of Trade, give statistics of shipbuilding for the Merchant Service, and these are collected, with other statistics as to production, in the "Annual Abstract of Labour "Statistics." The figures show tonnage launched in each district for the Merchant Service, and in each dockyard or district for the Admiralty, and the total tonnage for sailing vessels and steam vessels divided under the heads steel, iron, wood and composite. Annual returns are issued showing for all authorised gas undertakings, under local authorities and otherwise, the tons of coal carbonised and cubic feet of gas made, with numerous details as to finance, &c. [Returns, 393 and 394, 1906.] Similar returns are not, unfortunately, issued regularly for authorised electricity supply undertakings; returns were issued some years since giving, *inter alia*, the units generated, but have not been repeated. [343 and 344 of 1899, and 310, 311 of 1900.] For some of the more highly organised trades there are privately compiled statistics issued in trade journals or circulars, and these are occasionally reproduced in the official returns. A table showing production of steel ingots and puddled iron bars given in the "Annual Abstract of Labour Statistics," is based on statistics of the British Iron Trade Association published in the "Iron and Coal Trades Review." Tables showing estimated consumption of raw cotton and of wool (a guide, of course, to the productions of the corresponding trades) in the first Blue Book on British and Foreign Trade and Industrial Conditions[7] were similarly based on Ellison's "Annual Review of the Cotton Trade," and Messrs. Helmuth, Schwartze and Co.'s "Annual Report on Wool."

The Board of Agriculture and Fisheries have given statistics of production of the principal crops since 1885. The yield per acre is assessed by estimation, as the result of special enquiries in over 13,000 parishes of Great Britain. These estimates are collated with the parochial areas returned under each crop (voluntary returns), and hence the estimated total yield is obtained. The crops for which returns are given include wheat, barley, oats, beans, peas, potatoes, turnips and swedes, mangold, hay and hops. Areas under one acre are not reported. The statistics of animals include

---

[6] "Cotton Factories. Return of the Number of Spindles and Looms," No. 289, 1903. "Flax, Linen, Hemp and Jute Factories." Ditto, No. 290, 1905. "Woollen Worsted and Shoddy Factories." Ditto, No. 293, 1904.

[7] "Memoranda Statistical Tables and Charts . . . with reference to . . . "British Foreign Trade and Industrial Conditions." Cd-1761. (1903).

returns of numbers and value of cattle, sheep and pigs, and of supply at certain markets, but no statistics of production of animal products such as meat, milk or cheese.[8] Somewhat similar statistics for Ireland are issued by the Department of Agriculture, &c., for Ireland, but in certain branches they are more detailed ;[9] statistics are given of bee-keeping and forestry (number and ages of trees felled, &c.). The Sea-Fishery Reports[10] of the Board of Agriculture give detailed data as to quantities and values of each kind of sea fish landed. The similar reports on freshwater fisheries do not appear to contain any data as to production, except an occasional figure as to the takings of a salmon fishery.

The annual reports of the Commissioners of Customs give the annual production of beer, wines and spirits in the United Kingdom. Summary tables of international statistics have been issued from time to time on the same subject by the Board of Trade.[11]

The student will find abstracts of foreign statistics in several British publications. We have referred above to the Iron and Steel Tables and Coal Tables giving summaries of foreign statistics which are issued annually by the Board of Trade. Part IV of the Mines and Quarries Report of the Home Office is devoted entirely to colonial and foreign statistics. Abstracts of foreign statistics of agricultural production are included in the Board of Agriculture's annual returns, and much miscellaneous information in the Statistical Abstracts (Foreign and Colonial).

AUSTRALASIA.—The several States of Australia now collect very complete annual statistics of production in agriculture, mining and manufactures.[12] The details of the latter are published for all trades of sufficient magnitude, but, manufactures being still at an early stage of development, the necessity of not disclosing details as regards individual businesses imposes considerable restrictions on the scope of publication for single industries. Conferences have been held from time to time between the chief statisticians of the

---

[8] *Cf.* "The Report on the Production and Consumption of Meat and Milk," in the *Journal of the Royal Statistical Society* for 1904.

[9] "Agricultural Statistics of Ireland." (Annual.)

[10] "Annual Report of Proceedings under Acts relating to Sea Fisheries."

[11] "Alcoholic Beverages, 1903 " (1904). No. 345. The preceding return was No. 335 (1901).

[12] A very useful abstract of the statistics is given also in "Statistics of the " Six States of Australia and New Zealand, 1861-1904," by W. H. Hall, Acting Statistician, N.S.W. *See* also the "Statistical Account of Australia and New ".Zealand," 11th issue, 1903.04, by the Hon. T. A. Coghlan, to whom I am much indebted for information and correction on some of the points in the following notes.

States with a view to the co-ordination of the returns, and these conferences have been attended by the representative of New Zealand. All the States of Australia agreed, at the conference of 1901, to come into line, as regards statistics of production, with New South Wales : Victoria and Western Australia have done so, but the other States, though they have improved their statistics, do not collect information in the same detail as the larger States.   The statistics of New Zealand are generally similar in form to those of the Australian States, but are only collected quinquennially, at the census.   Under an Act of the Commonwealth of Australia, passed on 5th December, 1905, a Commonwealth statistician has been appointed, and it is enacted that (Section 16, Census and Statistics Act): "The " Statistician shall, subject to the regulations and the directions of " the Minister, collect annually statistics in relation to all or any " of the following matters :—(a) Population, (b) vital social and " industrial matters, (c) employment and non-employment, (d) " imports and exports, (e) inter State trade, (f) postal and " telegraphic matters, (g) factories, mines, and productive industries " generally, (h) agricultural, horticultural, viticultural, dairying, " and pastoral industries, (i) banking, insurance, and finance, (j) " railways, tramways, shipping, and transport, (k) land tenure and " occupancy, and (l) any other prescribed matters."   It is to be hoped that this Act will create a completely unified and co-ordinated system of returns for the Commonwealth.

The following notes give a few particulars respecting publications of the separate States of the Australian Commonwealth and New Zealand :—

New South Wales.[13]—Authority to collect statistics of any kind desired by the Government was given by an Order in Council long before responsible government (1856), and this was supplemented by decennial Census Acts.   In 1891 an Industrial Census Act was passed which enabled the statistician to collect statistics and other particulars on any subject upon which the Minister desires information.   Under this authority the most complete details were obtained in regard to land, crops, stock, labour, wages, manufactures, mining, banking, insurance, &c., and published in the form of census bulletins.   This census was put on a permanent footing by the Act of 1901, which re-enacted the provisions of the previous Industrial

---

[13] "Official Year Book of New South Wales, 1904.05."   "Statistical "Register for 1904" and previous years: Part v, Manufactories and Works; Part ix, Agriculture and Mining.   "Annual Report of the Department of " Mines for the year 1905."   It may be mentioned that the Statistical Registers of the Australian States are the primary returns, not secondary compilations like our " Statistical Abstract."

Census Act. In New South Wales therefore the statistical department is in a position to ask for any information it desires, provided the forms used are approved by the responsible Minister and gazetted. Collectors call every year at every holding (over 1 acre), mine, factory, or other establishment from which information is required. Particulars of the operations of factories and works are readily given, as the department treats all information as confidential. No prosecutions have been necessary since the Acts have been in operation. When a person from whom information is desired is ignorant and unable to make up his returns, the collector or experts of the department help him.

Tables are given in the "Statistical Register," part vi, showing for all industries number of establishments, hands employed (with considerable detail), wages paid, power of engines, and value of machinery and plant. At the census of 1901 information was obtained as to the value of land and buildings also, so that for that year the amount of fixed capital can be ascertained. The active capital was apparently estimated. Details are only given as to amount of production for the more important individual manufactures—soap and candles, bricks, flour, ale, beer, &c., sugar, tobacco, textiles, and gas—but a table is given showing the total value of materials used and of goods manufactured in each of nineteen classes. Establishments where no machinery is used are excluded from consideration unless at least four persons are engaged. Prior to 1896 the minimum was five hands; the change was made to secure uniformity throughout the Commonwealth. Data are given in the mineral statistics for the quantity and value of the output of gold, silver, coal, and the principal minerals, and value of machinery and plant. As regards the pastoral industry, particulars are given, *inter alia,* for the quantity and value of the wool-clip and for stock slaughtered and meat exported. In the dairying industry there are figures showing number of dairy cows in milk, production of milk, butter made and cheese made. Returns are also shown for bacon and hams and for honey. The agricultural statistics, which extend back to 1822, give annual returns for the quantity and value of all the principal crops with details for counties and divisions.

Victoria.[14]—As mentioned, the statistics are similar to those of New South Wales. For manufactories, tables are given showing under industries the number of factories, number using machinery, actual horse-power of engines (distinguishing kind), average number of

---

[14] " Statistical register of the State of Victoria for the year 1904 " (1905). Part viii : Production. " Annual Report of the Secretary for Mines and Water " Supplies for the year 1904."

persons employed, total salaries and wages paid, and approximate value of plant, land and buildings. For the more important industries we have the quantity of output, and for certain groups of industries the amount of wages paid, the value of fuel and light used, materials used and articles produced or work done. Under the agricultural statistics the usual data (annual) are given with respect to produce of crops (total and yield per acre, the data for several crops going back to 1839), and returns are also given as to quantity of milk, butter, cheese and honey, and stock slaughtered, as in New South Wales. As regards the milk produced, there is a footnote to the effect that many of the farmers could not supply the information. In the mineral statistics, figures are given for the yield of gold, metals other than gold, coal and stone.

Queensland.[15]—In Queensland systematic statistics relating to manufactories have been taken only since 1892. Figures are given for the number of factories and hands employed, value of machinery and plant, and output of " certain manufacturers in the State " for the year. This heading leaves one in some uncertainty as to the completeness of the returns. Area under and produce of crops, and output of gold and minerals are shewn in much the usual form.

South Australia.[16]—The returns appear to be much less complete than for the former States. The tables under the heading Manufactories only shew the power used (total horse-power and kind) and the number of hands employed (male and female under or over 16). There do not appear to be any figures shewing production. The tables under Mining give only a list of the mines. The only statistics of production shewn are for wheat, wool, spirits, wine and beer, and copper.

Western Australia.[17]—Part iv. of the Statistical Register shews the statistics of industrial establishments, part vii. of mining, and part v. of agriculture. In part vi., in addition to various industrial statistics, statistics of production are given for soap and candle works, brickwork and potteries, lime works, forest saw-mills cutting native timber, flour mills, aerated water, etc., factories, breweries, tobacco and cigar works, boot factories, electric light works, gas works and guano. The tables include horse-power and kind of engines and approximate value of land and buildings, plant and machinery. In certain cases the quantities of the raw materials

---

[15] " Statistics of Queensland."

[16] " Statistical Register for the State of South Australia for the year 1904." (1905). Part iii. Reduction. " Agricultural and live stock statistics for the year ending March 31st, 1905."

[17] " Western Australia. Statistical Register for the year 1905-06." " Report of the Department of Mines for the year 1904."

used are also stated.   The statistics of agriculture and mining do not seem to require special notice.

Tasmania.—In the statistics of Tasmania[18] figures are given shewing the number of manufactories using or not using machinery, the average number of persons employed under several heads, the horse-power and kind of engines, the approximate value of land and buildings, plant and machinery and the amount paid in salaries and wages.   Data respecting output are given for the aggregate of saw-mills, brickyards and potteries, tanneries, etc., flour mills, woollen mills, bark mills and jam factories.   For the minerals gold, silver, iron, tin, coal and stone there are annual returns of quantities and values.   In the agricultural statistics there are the usual returns for the yield of the various crops, and the total wool clip is given. Returns are also shewn for livestock slaughtered.   There do not appear to be any dairying returns.

New   Zealand.[19]—Information   respecting   manufactories and works is collected only once every five years at the census.   The definition of factory was changed for the 1901 census; previously, a factory was held to mean an establishment where manufacture was carried on wholesale, where machinery was employed, and where several hands worked together.   In the 1901 returns it was interpreted to mean any concern where two or more persons worked together in making articles for disposal, wholesale or retail, and without reference to machinery being used or not.[20]   The 1901 census accordingly covered all the minor industries to a greater or less extent. For all the principal industries, tables are given showing number of establishments, hands employed, wages paid, horse-power, value of all materials used, and value of all manufactures and produce, including repairs (for the year 1900), and approximate value of land, buildings, machinery and plant.   In the mining statistics there are returns as to the output of gold and coal, with details as to hands employed, wages paid, motive power, &c.   In the agricultural returns there are particulars of acreage and produce of crops, which appear to be cited from the statistics of the Department of Agriculture, upon which the duty of collecting returns devolved under the Agricultural and Pastoral Statistics Act, 1895.   The quantity of wool exported and produced is given, but I am unable to find any figures for dairying except exports, and the returns from butter and cheese factories.

UNITED STATES.—The first census of the United States was held in 1790, owing to the requirement of the Constitution that

---

[18] " Statistics of the State of Tasmania fór the year 1904.5 " (1906).

[19] "Statistics of the Colony of New Zealand for the year 1904" (1905). "Official Year-Book of New Zealand, 1906."

[20] " Year-Book," p. 335.

representatives and taxes should be apportioned amongst the States on a basis of population.[21] The census was held decennially up till 1900. Certain information as regards manufactures appears to have been obtained in 1810 and in 1820; in 1830 there were no questions on the subject, but from 1840 to 1870 there was a gradually increasing number of inquiries as regards manufactories, agriculture, mining, &c. In 1880, the investigation was made very much more detailed, as is shown by the fact that the number of inquiries or details relating to manufactures alone was raised from 18 to 29. In 1890 the number was again raised to 88. A census office was established for the 12th census of 1900 and subsequent censuses by an Act of 3rd March, 1899, and as the arrangements under this Act differ somewhat from those of previous censuses, some of the provisions may be mentioned. The Act deals in great detail with the staff and salaries (even the salaries of the messenger boys and charwomen are fixed). The inquiries of the census are restricted to four groups of subjects only:—(1) population; (2) mortality; (3) products of agriculture; (4) products of manufacturing and mechanical establishments. While the form and arrangement of the Schedule and the specific questions necessary to secure the information required are left to the discretion of the director, the subjects of the questions are specified in detail in each case. Thus (Section 7) " The schedules of inquiries relating to the products of " manufacturing and mechanical establishments shall embrace the " name and location of each establishment; character of organisa- " tion; whether individual, co-operative or other form; date of " commencement of operations; character of business or kind of " goods manufactured; amount of capital invested; number of " proprietors, firm members, co-partners, or officers, and the amount " of their salaries; number of employees, and the amount " of their wages; quantity and cost of materials used in manu- " factures; amount of miscellaneous expenses; quantity and value of " products; time in operation during the census year[22]; character " and quantity of power used, and character and number of " machines employed." For agriculture, information is demanded as to name and colour of occupant of each farm, tenure, acreage, value of farm and improvements, acreage of different products, quantity and value of products (for the calendar year preceding the census year) and number and value of live stock.

The census, it will be noted, does not cover mining. After the

---

[21] " History and Growth of the U.S. Census, 1790–1890." C. D. Wright and W. C. Hunt. Washington (1900).

[22] The fiscal year of such corporations or establishments having its termination nearest to and preceding June 1st, 1900.

completion and return of the enumeration and of the tabulation of the schedules relating to the products of agriculture and to manufactures, the Director of the Census is, however, authorised to collect statistics on special subjects, and amongst these special subjects are included electric light and power, telephone and telegraph business, transportation and mining.

In Section 7 of the Act it is also provided that "whenever he " shall deem it expedient, the Director of the Census may withhold " the schedules for said manufacturing and mechanical statistics " from the enumerators . . . and may charge the collection of these " statistics upon special agents, to be employed without respect to " locality." This provision was first incorporated in the Census Act of 1879, as a result of experience at the ninth census. The collection of manufacturing statistics is attended by peculiar difficulties, which have been greatly augmented by the general increase in the size and complexity of individual establishments. At the census of 1900 the number of cities and towns canvassed by special agents was 1,340, 1,891 such special agents being appointed. The cities and towns so canvassed furnished more than half of all the schedules tabulated in the census of manufactures (more than 350,000 out of 640,000), and the establishments covered by these schedules represented 79 per cent. of the capital invested in manufacturing and 81 per cent. of the total value of products.[23]

The census covers all trades, with the single exception that no hand trades were to be canvassed which were not carried on in a shop of some character,[24] but the more important hand work seems to have been well covered, *e.g.*, cycle repairing, blacksmithing, boot and shoe work (retail), clothing (retail), dyeing and cleaning, furniture, &c., making, lock and gun smithing, millinery (retail), sewing machine, typewriter, watch, clock and jewellery repairing. The building trades were also classed as hand trades.

Some particulars are given as regards difficulties in procuring statistics, more particularly from large industrial combinations. Some were only formed during or after the census year, and consequently it was not possible to obtain the complete returns required. Again, many of the combinations had plants in different States or in different counties or cities of the same State, and did not keep distinct accounts for such different plants. In such cases, the outputs of the separate plants had to be estimated in order to credit each locality with its proper output. The difficulty was still greater in the matter of capital, and it was stated in this case that much trouble was encountered in

[23] "12th Census U.S.A." (1900), VII (Manufactures, Part I), p. xxii.
[24] *Ibid.*, p. xxxix.

inducing the managers of such combinations to make returns in conformity with the schedules of inquiry.[25]

I have already dealt above with the difficult question of the mode of arriving at the net value of products, and need not refer to the matter again.

The statistics are discussed in very great detail. For the individual industries in each separate State the main headings are as shown below :—

States and Territories.	Average Number of Wage Earners, and Total Wages.							
	Total.		Men 16 Years and Over.		Women 16 Years and Over.		Children Under 16 Years.	
	Average Number.	Wages.	Average Number.	Wages.	Average Number.	Wages.	Average Number.	Wages.

Miscellaneous Expenses.				
Total.	Rent of Works.	Taxes, not including Internal Revenue.	Rent of Offices, Interest, &c.	Contract Work.

Cost of Materials used.								
Aggregate.	Principal Materials.			Fuel.	Rent of Power and Heat.	Mill Supplies.	Freight.	Products, including Custom Work and Repairing.
	Total.	Purchased in Raw State.	Purchased in Partially Manufactured Form (including "All Other Materials").					

It may be as well to mention a warning of the Director in a later report that the census data should not " be used to compute " profits on the year's business. There are many items of expense, " such as allowances for depreciation of plant, for bad debts, &c., " that are not considered in the Census Schedule; therefore, the " difference between the sum of the salaries, wages, miscellaneous " expenses, and cost of materials on the one hand, and the value of " products on the other, does not represent the gain or loss in the " business." [26] This warning applies to all similar censuses.

The reports on the census of manufactures fill four large quarto volumes of about 1,000 pages each (vols. vii to x of the Census).

I do not think I need give details with respect to the Census of Agriculture, as there do not appear to be any features of special importance. The data are contained in vols. v and vi of the Census.

[25] "12th Census U.S.A." (1900), VII (Manufactures, Part I), p. lxxvii.
[26] " U.S.A. Census of Manufactures, 1905." Bulletin 57, pp. 11 and 12.

In all censuses prior to the 12th the inquiry as regards mining formed part of the census. As mentioned above, it was excluded from the 12th census, but special inquiry was authorised. It was decided to undertake this special inquiry as for the year 1902, field work being commenced in conjunction with the Geological Survey in 1903, and the volume (Special Reports, Mines and Quarries) was published in 1905. In addition to quantity and value of output, data are given as regards numbers of mines, quarries, &c., in the different States, number of operators, officials, &c., number and salaries, wage earners (numbers and wages, distinguishing those above ground and below ground), contract work, miscellaneous expenses, and cost of supplies. There is also a good deal of purely descriptive matter. The Director expresses regret that mining was excluded from the scope of the ordinary census, and points out that this rendered it impossible to give a general view of production for the same year, and that as mining industries are frequently carried on by establishments engaged in both mining and manu-facturing, the separation led to difficulties.[27]

In the introductory report to the Census of Manufactures, 1900, the Director commented strongly on the difficulties of a hand trade canvass. He pointed out that the expense per schedule is as high as for factories, that it is almost impossible to keep such a canvass uniform, not only from census to census, but also from district to district (many agents misunderstanding their instructions as to what was to be included or excluded), and that much of the information naturally demanded on a schedule of manufactures could not apply to hand trades. For example, many large stores carry on work, say dressmaking and boot repairing. A separate schedule ought to be filled up for each of these branches, but it is impossible to assign a capital value for the "lands, buildings, etc." occupied, as the work people will be accommodated in one or two rooms. It will also be difficult, if not impossible, to determine the value of products for each such branch. The chief statistician accordingly strongly recommended the abandonment of all enquiries of this character at future censuses. This recommendation was in so far anticipated by Congress that in the Act providing for a permanent census it ruled that an intermediate or five year census of manufactures under that Act should be confined to factory manufactures, exclusive of the hand trades.[28] The reports on this census have very recently been issued. The census covered the calendar year, 1904, and to secure comparable figures the published statistics of 1900 were recompiled so as to eliminate, as far as possible, the

---

[27] See the Letter of Transmittal at commencement of volume on Mines.

[28] "12th Census, U.S.A." Vol. vii., p. xl., 1900. (1902).

minor non-factory industries, a process which involved considerable
·difficulty.   Reports were not secured, at the census of 1905, from
.small establishments in which manufacturing was incidental to
mercantile or other business; or from establishments in which the
·value of the products for the year amounted to less than $500 ; or
from educational, eleemosynary and penal institutions; or from
Government establishments.   The census was not confined, however,
to an enumeration of large factories.   The reports are being issued
·in separate bulletins for each State.   It does not seem necessary
to give further details as regards this intermediate census, seeing
that, apart from the exclusion of hand trades, it seems to have been
conducted on the general lines of the census of manufactures at
the twelfth census.

In concluding this general statement as regards the statistics of
production of the United States, it should be mentioned that annual
crop returns have also been given by the Department of Agriculture,
founded in 1866-7, since 1866, these showing area under crops,
.estimated produce, and number of live stock.[29]

MASSACHUSETTS.—A very remarkable Census of Manufactures
has been conducted annually by the Bureau of Statistics of labour
of the Commonwealth of Massachusetts since 1886.[30]   The annual
reports do not pretend to supply aggregates covering the entire
productive industry of the Commonwealth, but each report deals
with.two years, and includes only firms making returns for both
years; they thus render comparisons possible between identical
establishments sufficient in number to be typical of the state of the
different industries.   More detailed figures are supplied by the
Federal census.   It should be stated, however, that according to the
nineteenth report on statistics of manufactures for 1903-04 the *value*
represented by the annual returns is about 90 per cent. of the output of the State as determined by the census.   The tables are
arranged under five main heads, as follows : I. *Establishments and
their management.*   These tables show the form of management of
the establishments making returns, whether private firms, corporations, or industrial combinations, with the number of partners and
stockholders. II. *Investment, materials used, and products.*   These
tables cover the amount of capital *devoted to production*, cost value of
stock and materials used, and selling value of the goods made and
work done.   The limiting words " devoted to production " exclude
certain items which are included under " capital invested " in the
Federal census, and this renders comparisons impossible.   III. *Labour
and its compensation.*   Average, smallest and greatest numbers of
persons employed, total wages paid, classified weekly wages paid to

[29] Year Book of the Department. See also to " Crop Reporter."
[30] " The Annual Statistics of Manufactures." Boston, Mass.

adult males and females and to young persons for leading industries, &c.
IV. *Working time and proportion of business done*, the latter being based
on a maximum production of 100 per cent. V. *General Summary*.

Thus under II we have general tables for all industries of the
form :—

Capital Invested.

Industries.	Number of Establishments Considered.	Amount of Capital Invested.		Increase (+) or Decrease (−).	
		1899.	1900.	Amount.	Percentage.
Agricultural implements ....}	9	$ 1,068,986	$ 1,010,121	$ − 58,865	− 5·51

Stock Used.

Industries.	Number of Establishments Considered.	Value of Stock Used.		Increase (+) or Decrease (−)	
		1899.	1900.	Amount.	Per Cent.
Agricultural implements ....}	9	$ 508,881	$ 616,577	$ + 107,696	+ 21·16

Goods Made.

Industries.	Number of Establishments Considered.	Value of Goods Made and Work Done.		Increase (+) or Decrease (−)	
		1899.	1900.	Amount.	Per Cent.
Agricultural implements ....}	9	$ 1,219,811	$ 1,308,292	$ + 88,481	+ 7·25

In the " general summary " (V) interesting tables are given for
the nine leading industries individually, in the following form :—

Boots and Shoes.
[Comparison for 673 establishments.]

Classification.	1899.	1900.
	$	$
Amount of capital invested..........	27,182,381	26,716,110
Value of goods made and work done } (gross product)	127,427,884	129,189,130
Value of stock used and other materials } consumed in production .... }	80,829,679	80,966,554
Industry product (gross product less } value of stock and materials consumed) . ... }	46,598,205	48,222,576
Wages (labor's direct share of product)	27,648,530	27,476,207
Profit and minor expense fund (industry } product less wages) .... }	18,949,675	20,746,369
Percentage of industry product paid } on wages.... .... }	59·33	56·98
Percentage of industry product devoted } to profit and minor expenses .. .. }	40·67	43·02
Percentage of profit and minor expense } fund of capital invested .... }	69·71	77·65

The returns appear to be issued, without any delay, in the year following, *e.g.*, the letter of transmittal of the report for 1899-1900 is dated 15th July, 1901. I have only taken an earlier report as an example, since in that for 1903-04,[31] some comparisons are rendered impossible, the classification for 1904 having been changed to conform with the requirements of the intermediate Federal Census.

CANADA.—The Census of Canada includes a very complete census of production. The scope of the enquiries has, speaking generally, been extended from census to census, and I accordingly take the fourth and last (1901) for description[32]. The census is decennial.

Of the four volumes of the Report it is the second and third alone which concerns us, vol. ii dealing with natural products and vol. iii with manufactures.

The Statistics of Natural Products fall under five main heads. I, Agriculture; II, Dairying (butter, cheese and condensed milk factories); III, Forest Products; IV, Minerals; V, Fisheries. In the agricultural returns, farms (over 5 acres) are distinguished from lots (under 5 acres). Particulars are given as to area under and total yield of all field crops, fruit trees (including numbers bearing and non-bearing), small fruit and vineyards. The yields per acre of the more important crops are also worked out, returns referring in all cases to the census year from 1st April, 1900, to 31st March, 1901. The return of numbers of live stock are distinguished under twelve heads, and the numbers are given of cattle, sheep, swine and poultry sold for slaughter or export, the number of pounds of fine and coarse wool, the number of pounds of home made butter, of honey, and the number of dozens of eggs. As regards capital invested, there are data for the values of land, buildings, implements, and live stock. For the dairying industry under the factory system figures are given for number of factories, employees, salaries and wages, value of buildings and plant, and values of products of butter, cheese and condensed milk factories together, and in somewhat greater detail for butter and cheese factories separately. As regards forest products, there are data for cubic feet and value of ash, birch, elm, maple, oak pine and "all other" timber, square feet and value of logs for lumber, and quantities and values of miscellaneous products (bark for tanning, wood for pulp, fence posts, railroad ties, &c.). The value of furs is also given under this head. Minerals are classed under the six main heads—metallic ores and products, abrasive products, fuel and light materials, pigments, structural materials, and miscellaneous, each of these being again subdivided, and for each subdivision are given values of real estate and plant, numbers of offices and workmen, salaries and wages, and quantities and value of products. In the section on fisheries, in addition to particulars as to vessels and boats, fishing gear and curing and canning stations, quantities and values are given for all fish and fish products.

The results of the Census of Manufactures are given in vol. iii. In this census (1901) the instructions to enumerators provided that "no manufacturing establishment or factory will be recognised for census purposes which does not employ at least five persons, either in the establishment itself or as pieceworkers employed out of it" (p. vi), with the exception that the limitation should not apply to cheese and butter factories (vol. ii), or to certain mineral products, in which industries large operations may be carried on with less than five employees. The limitation probably resulted in the insufficient enumeration of certain industries, but it served the desired purpose of eliminating statistics of the hand and domestic trades. This limitation was not employed at the census of 1891, but the schedules of that census have been recompiled, according to the number of employees, so as to render comparisons possible. At the census of 1891 the total value of products of works employing less than five hands was $101,000,000, for works employing five hands and over $369,000,000, and the numbers of hands employed were 98,000 and 272,000 respectively.

In "factories" thus defined information was obtained as to (1) values of real estate, plant and working capital ; (2) salaries and wages of persons employed ; (3) working time of employees, including aggregate number of days worked, average number of hours that operatives are employed in the week, and number of months in the year that the establishment is kept in operation ; (4) miscellaneous expenses, including rent of works, offices, power and heat, fuel, light, taxes, interest and contract work ; (5) cost of materials and value of products ; (6) mechanical power employed.

The schedules used were approved and endorsed by the Canadian Manufacturers' Association (vol. iii, p. vii), and in a circular letter issued to manufacturers, that Association stated that it was a matter of the greatest importance that accurate information on the manufacturing industries of Canada should be obtained, and that to this end they had urged upon the Government the desirability of appointing special agents for the census of manufactures. Such special agents were employed in the larger and more important centres of industry, but elsewhere the work was done by the regular enumerators.

The following table headings may be given as showing the classification of some of the more important factors in the census of manufactures. In the tables giving a classification by provinces :—

TABLE 1 (p. x).—*Fixed and Working Capital.*

Province.	Establish- ments (Number).	Lands.	Buildings.	Machinery and Motive Power.	Tools and Implements.	Total Capital.

TABLE 2 (p. xi).—*Persons Employed on Salaries.*

Province.	Owners and Firm Members.		Salaried Officers, Managers, Salesmen, &c.			
	Men (No.).	Salaries.	Men (No.).	Salaries.	Women (No.).	Salaries.

TABLE 3 (p. xii).—*Persons Employed on Wages.*

Province.	In Establishments						Out of Establishments.	
	Men 16 Years and Over.	Wages.	Women 16 Years and Over.	Wages.	Children Under 16.	Wages.	Piece Workers.	Wages.

TABLE 5 (p. xiii).—*Working Time of Wage Earners.*

Province.	Aggregate Working Days in Year of			Average Hours and Working Time Per Week.
	Men 16 Years and Over.	Women 16 Years and Over.	Children Under 16.	

TABLE 11 (p. xvii).—*Cost of Materials and Value of Products.*

Province.	Crude Materials.	Partly Manu- factured Materials.	Total Cost of Materials.	Goods Manu- factured.	Custom* Work and Repairs.	Total Products.

The power employed (Tables 13, 14, and 15) is classed according to kind (steam, gas or gasoline, water, electric, other), the number of motors and the total of horse-power being given for each province. The total power supplied to and by other establishments is also stated.

Passing from the classification by provinces to the classification by industries, tables are given (16—31) for groups of industries and individual industries under the following general headings :—

Name or Kind of Industry.	Establish- ments. (No.)	Total Capital.	Wage Earners. (No.)	Wages for Labour. (Total.)	Cost of Materials.	Value of Products.

* "The true criterion for manufactures as opposed to the hand trades is "found in the standardisation of the process .... In the hand trades there can "be no standardisation, for these operations are all custom work ; that is, work "upon order from the customer."—"U.S.A. 12th Census" (1900), vii, p. xxxvi.

It will be noticed that values only, not quantities, are given for all manufactures.

In addition to the decennial figures of the census there are annual agricultural returns for certain of the Canadian provinces, and fishery statistics are issued annually by the Department of Marine.

CAPE COLONY.[33]—The issue of a special industrial schedule at the census of 1891, by which trustworthy data were obtained as to the state of the Colonial industries for the first time, was sufficiently successful to warrant a repetition of the experiment at the census of 1904, and the Census Act (1903) made provision accordingly. It is stated that "whilst in most other Colonies . . . the persons connected with industrial undertakings appear to emulate one another in assisting to obtain a successful result. Far other has been my experience during the present census in this colony, public-spirited action of this kind having been singularly lacking. Many examples of reluctance to impart information, even under the strictest precautions to ensure secrecy, might be given."[34] There was, however, only one prosecution owing to persistent refusal to render a return. The schedule covered all establishments where goods were manufactured of the total value of 100*l.* per annum and upwards, and in which gas, horse and water power was used, stone quarries and salt pans. A general table is given for all industries under the headings:—number of industrial institutions, number employing different sources of power (steam, gas, electric, water, &c.), number of workers usually employed (males and females, European and other), horse-power employed, approximate values of materials used and articles produced, and approximate value of land, buildings and improvements, machinery and plant. Additional particulars as to quantities of materials consumed and produced are given for certain industries (flour mills, breweries, tobacco, soap and candle works, distilleries, brickyards, fish-curing establishments, tanneries, wagon and cart works). Similar particulars are given for "mines, alluvial "diggings and quarries," of which, of course, the diamond mines are by far the most important, the output accounting for 4,800,000*l.* out of 5,400,000*l.*

The census also included a census of agriculture. The particulars collected were partly furnished on the ordinary householders schedules, but a supplementary form was issued asking for details as to different breeds of sheep, to deaths of stock from disease, and particulars as to certain crops, fruit and vines. Allotments under half a morgen were excluded from consideration.

[33] Census 1904. "Statistical Register," 1905.
[34] "Census," p. clxxxvii.

III.—*The Census of Production Act.*

The Bill was introduced by the President of the Board of Trade on 6th May of last year, under the ten minutes rule, when speeches are usually limited to one from the introducer and one from an opponent of the Bill. But on this occasion no one rose to oppose, and the explanatory statement of the President of the Board of Trade was followed by a speech from Mr. Joseph Chamberlain warmly supporting the proposals. The Bill was referred to the Standing Committee on Trade, by whom it was amended in several important respects, and some further amendments were introduced subsequently. No amendments were made by the Lords, and the Act received the royal assent on 21st December.

The complete text of the Act is printed as an appendix to this paper, but the following outline may be given of its provisions. The references are to the sections. (1) A census of production shall be taken in the year 1908, and subsequently at such intervals as the Board of Trade may determine by order laid before Parliament. (2) The Board of Trade shall superintend the taking of the census. The expenses incurred with the approval of the Treasury shall be paid out of money provided by Parliament. (3) Forms shall be filled up, by the persons specified in the schedule to the Act, with such of the following particulars as may be specified, in respect of the calendar year preceding the census :—Nature of trade or business, particulars of output, number of days on which work was carried on, number of persons employed, power used or generated, and "such other matters of a like nature, except the " amount of wages, as may be found to be necessary for the purpose " of enabling the quantity and value of production to be ascertained." The Board may vary the period for which the return is made, and may demand particulars of materials used and of work given out so as to avoid duplication. They may not, on the other hand, demand particulars as to quantity of output, except in the case of articles for which such particulars are required when exported or imported, nor may they demand information in greater detail than is then required. Every person must fill in his form, on receiving notice from the Board in writing, within three months of receipt. (4) The Board is to present, as soon as possible after any census, a report and summary of statistics. (5) The Home Office may issue and collect forms in lieu of the Board in certain cases. (6) All individual returns are confidential. The Board must not issue statistics in such a form that the figures for any individual firm can be recognised, and must avoid disclosing trade secrets or profits. (7) The exercise of the powers and duties of a local authority shall be treated as its trade or business. (8) In addition to doing anything necessary for

the carrying out of the Act, the Board may exempt any prescribed
class of persons from the obligation to make returns.   (9) The
Board is to appoint Advisory Committees, to advise regarding
schedules, &c.   (10) The intervals between returns under the
Factory Act may be brought into accord with returns under the
present Act.   (11) The Board may ask for voluntary information,
in addition to the information under the Act.   (12) Penalties are
assigned for refusing to make, or making false, returns.

The schedule shows the persons required to make returns, but
it must be remembered that this must be read in conjunction with
Section 8 (*b*) of the Act which enables the Board to exempt:—(*a*)
Occupiers of factories and workshops; (*b*) Owners, &c., of mines
and quarries; (*c*) Builders; (*d*) Persons who execute other works
of construction or repair (rail and tramways and other works of
civil engineering, gas and water mains, or electric lines, &c.); (*e*)
Persons who give out work to be executed by way of trade or
business; (*f*) Persons carrying on any other trade or business
which the Board may specify.

The scope of the Act may be indicated by a summary comparison
with the censuses of the United States and of Canada.   Taking
first certain important classes of products, the following tabular
statement shows how far they are included under the two censuses
and the Act.

Class of Production.	United States (1900 and 1905).	Canada (1901).	Census of Production Act (1906).
Agriculture	Included 1900 Excluded 1905 } Included		*Excluded.*
Mining, &c.	*Excluded*	,,	Included.
Wholesale manufactures	Included	,,	,,
Retail manufactures	Included 1900 Excluded 1905 } *Excluded*		,,
Building	Included 1900 Excluded 1905 }	,,	,,
Civil engineering	*Excluded*	,,	,,

It will be seen that, apart from the exclusion of agriculture, the
possible scope of the Act as regards branches of production included,
is distinctly wider than that of either the United States or Canadian
censuses, and this without taking account of the general Clause (F)
of the schedule.   Mining and civil engineering were both excluded
from the United States' census of 1900, and mining, civil engineering, retail manufactures (hand trades), and building, from the intermediate census of 1905.   Retail manufactures, building, and civil
engineering were all excluded from the Canadian census.   But all
these branches of production fall within the scope of the present

census Act, and the Board of Trade have power to collect statistics thereon. Some criticism was levelled, during the debates, at the " proposal " to include retail trades (*e.g.*, under (A) and (C) and (E) of the schedule)[35] with ironical references to bespoke bootmakers and jobbing decorators, and the words " repair or decoration " after " alteration " in (C) of the schedule of the Bill were omitted on an amendment moved by Lord R. Cecil.[36] But the Act generally gives an option, not compulsion, to the Board, who can exémpt small traders under Section 8 (*b*), and they can be trusted to exercise a wise discretion in the matter. If for no other reason, it is to the interest of the Board itself to avoid unnecessary friction and expense. The number of exceptions will probably, I should imagine, be large, especially at the first census, but I think it would have been regrettable if, say, " workshop " had been omitted from Clause (A) of the schedule, or if (C) and (E) had been dropped because there might be difficulty with employers in a small way of business. As regard the exclusion—or rather non-inclusion— of agriculture, a question was put in the House, by Mr. Beck, asking the President of the Board of Trade to consider the advisability of including the subject within the scope of the bill. He replied, pointing out that the ground was already covered by the Board of Agriculture.[37] The decision to exclude was, I think, judicious. The present system, based partly on the work of paid estimators and partly on voluntary returns, works with a complete absence of friction, and the returns probably possess quite sufficient accuracy for practical purposes. Even compulsory returns from farmers would be unlikely to possess any high degree of accuracy, and compulsion might consequently merely introduce friction with no corresponding gain. The Board of Agriculture are well aware of the deficiency of statistics as regards meat and dairy produce, and may be trusted to supply them if and when possible; but it will be generally recognised that these subjects present much greater difficulties than crops. If one may venture on a suggestion, made in some ignorance of possible practical difficulties, our statistics of meat supply might perhaps be improved by bringing slaughterhouses under the general Clause (F) of the schedule. Slaughterhouses are now required to be licensed, and this will facilitate their inclusion.

Passing from the consideration of the branches of production that fall under the Act, to the subjects on which information can be obtained as regards each several industry, the following tabular-

[35] " Parliamentary Debates," vol. 165, col. 1071 ; vol. 167, col. 909.

[36] *Ibid.*, vol. 167, col. 909.

[37] *Ibid.*, vol. 159, col. 1,140.

statement again exhibits the scope of the Act as compared with the censuses of the United States and of Canada.

Subject.	United States of America.	Canada.	Census of Production Act.
Value of materials purchased raw	Included	Included	Included
Value of materials partly manufactured	„	„	
Quantity of materials	,,	„	*Partially included*
Value of products.	„	„	Included
Quantity of products	„	„	*Partially included*
Numbers employed	„	„	Included
Days worked	„	,,	„
Horse-power and kind of engine	„	,,	„
Wages and salaries	„	,,	*Excluded*
Miscellaneous expenses ...	„	„	,,
Capital	,,	„	,,

In this respect our Act is distinctly narrower than the two censuses taken for comparison. In the first place no distinction is required between "raw" and "partially" manufactured materials used. The Board are only authorised to obtain "the aggregate "estimated value of the materials used." This seems to me to be little loss; the division is not, in my opinion, worth the considerable additional trouble which it gives. As I have already indicated above, the figures for partially manufactured materials do not appear to be essential for the interpretation of results.[38]

In the second place information as to *quantities* of materials and output (as distinct from values), can only be obtained in certain cases under the Act. (Section 3 (*c*)) :—

"Particulars as to the quantity of output shall not be required "except in the case of articles, the quantity of which is on their "importation into or exportation from the United Kingdom "required by the official import or export list to be entered, nor "shall such particulars be required in greater detail than in those "lists."

This limitation was inserted by the Standing Committee, presumably with the view of saving trouble or friction. It is obvious that the statistics of internal production should be in the same general form as statistics of foreign trade, in order to render collation possible. At the same time the statutory limitation introduces fresh difficulties. The export and import lists cannot be written on a half sheet of notepaper; they are lengthy documents, covering, with indices, some fifty pages foolscap apiece, or more. Are copies of these to be circulated with the schedules to every

[38] p. 55.

manufacturer ?   If not how is a demand for statutory information
as to quantities under the Act to be distinguished from a demand for
voluntary information as to quantities under Section 11 ?   Even if this
distinction can be made by the use of different schedules for different
classes of manufactures, what will happen if a manufacturer makes a
number of articles, some included in the lists for quantities and some
not ?   There are four-and-twenty chemicals, or classes of chemicals,
specified in the lists, for which quantities have to be given ;
unenumerated chemicals are returned by value only.   Is it not
extremely probable that a manufacturer may make both ?   I confess
to not understanding entirely why a return of value should be
preferred by a manufacturer to a return of quantities; I should
have thought the latter the least trouble to make up in most cases ;
it is quantities, not values, that are required by the various Acts
under which the mineral statistics of the Home office are issued.   It
would almost seem better to have left the demand for quantities to
the discretion of the Board, who could have exempted trades where
necessary.

In the Bill, as introduced, "wages paid" were specifically
included (Section 3) as one of the items on which information
might be demanded.   The words were simply omitted by the
Standing Committee "as the result of an agreement between
"both parties."[39]   The present definitely exclusive words "except
"the amount of wages," were inserted by an amendment moved
by Sir E. Carson on Report,[40] and accepted by the President of
the Board of Trade, who made a definite promise of a wage
census, apart from the Bill.[41]   Under these circumstances, the
omission may be regarded with equanimity.   To have obtained
the full information proper to a wage census under the Act, would
have entailed asking for a great deal more than the aggregate amount
of wages, and would have very much complicated the schedules.

Again, in the Bill introduced, Clause 3 (1) terminated with a
general phrase "and such other particulars as may be prescribed,"
which would no doubt have covered questions on capital.   For
these words, the Standing Committee substituted, "particulars
". . . . relating to such other matters of a like nature . . . . as
"may be found to be necessary for the purpose of enabling the
"quantity and value of production to be ascertained," words which
cannot cover capital.   An amendment, moved by Mr. Chiozza-Money,
to insert the words "capital employed" was, after some discussion
as to practical difficulties, withdrawn.   The general effect of this

[39] "Parliamentary Debates," vol. 167, col. 897.

[40] *Ibid.*, vol. 167, col. 898.

[41] *Ibid.*, vol. 167. col. 897 and 898.

and the preceding alteration in the Bill is to render the census much more purely a census of production, and not of means of production or of industry in general, and to simplify the possible schedule of compulsory questions greatly. All such simplifications are of course *per se* a gain, lessening the burden on those who have to make returns, and facilitating the smooth working of the Act.

With regard to any limitations of the Act, it must not be forgotten that section 11 gives the Board authority to obtain voluntary information either through the mechanism of the census or otherwise. The mass of such voluntary information is a feature of our statistics not always sufficiently remembered. The agricultural statistics are furnished without any compulsion ; the same thing holds of · the statistics issued by the Labour Department, and the figures issued by the Home Office as to the values of minerals raised are, as already mentioned, not required under the Acts. It is not likely, to judge from these precedents, that this section of the Act will be allowed to become a dead letter.

The intervals at which the census shall be repeated have, it will have been noted, not been determined ; it is desired first to obtain some experience as to the working of the Act. As soon as possible after the taking of the first census the period is to be fixed by an order of the Board of Trade laid before Parliament, so that the final decision will rest with the House. An amendment making the census annual was moved on report, by Sir George Doughty, and strongly supported by Mr. Chiozza-Money, who argued that the whole object of the census was to trace the course of trade, and that inquiries at long intervals might not be comparable owing to the one occurring during a boom in trade, and the other at a period of depression. The President of the Board expressed sympathy with the proposal, did not wish the opinion to prevail that the census would be quinquennial, and suggested that it might become biennial. He objected to the amendment, which was finally rejected, because he had the Treasury to deal with. Obviously this question of period is a most important one and will have to be carefully considered in connection with the scope of the census and the cost. The time, period, and classification of the population-census will also have to be taken into account if figures are to be obtained that may be reduced to a basis of population and treated in connection with the occupation returns. The needs of the census of production should, in fact, be specially considered in settling the lines of the occupation statistics. If the population census were made quinquennial—and it will be difficult to resist this reform if the junior census is to be taken at intervals that are certainly not longer—I am inclined to think that the same period would almost suffice for the census of production.   Personally, I regard the chief function of such a census as the exhibition of the slower secular movements in industry, rather than the rapid periodic movements, and would, therefore, favour a complete census at longer intervals rather than a less complete annual enquiry.   I have no doubt that this is a point on which opinions will be expressed during the discussion.   The intercensal interval is now five years in the United States.

The question of cost is a most important one, but it seems impossible to obtain any real basis for estimates, and the actual cost must depend very largely on the scope which the Board of Trade finally decide to give the census (as regards small trades, &c.), the mode of collection, and the amount of detail given in the report.   No data appear to be available for the cost of the Canadian census, which would appear to be fairly comparable with the English census.   (It includes agriculture, but excludes small trades.)   The United States census is costly, owing to the great detail of its inquiries.   During the financial years 1903-07, the cost of the permanent Census Office appears to have averaged about $1,500,000 (300,000*l.*), the actual appropriations for the fiscal year 1905 being as follows :—[42]

	$
Salaries, 1905	711,760
Collecting statistics, 1905	438,400
Tabulating statistics, 1905	50,000
Stationery, 1905	10,000
Library, 1905	2,500
Rent, 1905	26,600
Miscellaneous expenses, 1905	15,000
Printing, 1905	170,000
Expenses, 12th census	102,445
Total	1,526,705

The population of the United States and the United Kingdom being about 84 and 42 millions respectively, this would correspond to a cost of about 150,000*l.* for a *similar* census under a similar organisation here.   But the British census (so far as I can judge probabilities from the Act and from the questions of the United States schedules) is only likely to ask one question to about ten in the States schedule, and the relative cost would be proportionately reduced.   Further, the greater simplicity of the inquiry would seem to render the employment of special agents unnecessary, and inquiry by special agents is an expensive matter.   At the United States

[42] " Annual Report of the Secretary of Commerce and Labour, 1905," and " Annual Report of the Director of the Census, 1905."

census of 1900 the cost of schedules collected by special agents was
1 dollar, against 25 cents (the statutory payment) for schedules
collected by the ordinary enumerators.[43] No mechanism of
collection of any sort is specified in the Act, and the Board is
therefore free to adopt whatever method may be judged most
economical.

I have given, in the preceding sketch of the Act, references to
some of the alterations that were made at different stages in the
Bill. The following clause, section 5 (3), stood in the original Bill,
and was left by the Standing Committee, but omitted subsequently
on an amendment :—

" The Board of Trade may, if they think fit, make arrangements
" with the Secretary of State and any other department for the
" transfer to the Secretary of State, or that other department of
" any of their powers and duties under this Act as respects any
" particular industries or class of industries, and the Board of Trade
" and the Secretary of State, and any other department authorised
" under any enactment to collect statistical returns, may delegate
" to a committee containing representatives of the departments
" concerned, all or any of their powers and duties in relation to any
" such statistical returns under this Act or such other enactment,
" as the case may be."

A clause that proposed to create what would have been
practically a centralised statistical bureau, under an inter-departmental committee, is worthy, I think, of mention.

Whilst, no doubt, some of us may regret this or that limitation
in the present Act, or may wish that some clause or section had
been drafted otherwise, these, after all, are minor points, and I
think all statisticians will feel grateful to the originators of the
Bill for so valuable an addition to the statistical organisations
of the United Kingdom as that authorised under the Act. We
have suffered for long under the dearth of information as to the
real state of the industry and internal trade of the Kingdom, and
will await with keen interest the first report of the Director of the
new census.

I must not conclude these notes without expressing my great
indebtedness to the Board of Trade for the most cordial assistance
which was rendered me in their preparation ; without the aid given
by the supply of references to foreign and colonial publications,
and the books placed at my disposal, it would have been quite
impossible to complete the work in the time at my command.

---

[43] " Census, U.S.A," vol. vii., p. xxii.

APPENDIX.

Census of Production Act, 1906.

[6 Edw. 7.   Ch. 49.]

ARRANGEMENT OF SECTIONS.   A.D. 1906

Section.
1. Periodical census.
2. Central authority for and expenses of census.
3. Preparing and filling up of schedules.
4. Report to Parliament.
5. Inter-departmental arrangements.
6. Prohibition against publishing individual returns.
7. Returns by local and other authorities.
8. Power of Board of Trade to make rules.
9. Power to appoint advisory committees.
10. Intervals for making returns under 1 Edw. 7. c. 21. s. 130.
11. Voluntary information.
12. Penalty for offences.
13. Short title.
    SCHEDULE.

CHAPTER 49.

An Act to provide for taking a Census of Production.

[21st December 1906.]

BE it enacted by the King's most Excellent Majesty, by and with the advice and consent of the Lords Spiritual and Temporal, and Commons, in this present Parliament assembled, and by the authority of the same, as follows :—

1. A census of production shall be taken in the year one thousand nine hundred and eight, and subsequently at such intervals as may be determined by an order made by the Board of Trade as soon as practicable after the taking of the first census and laid before Parliament. *Periodical census.*

2.—(1) The Board of Trade shall superintend the taking of the census, and shall, subject to the provisions of this Act, prepare and issue such forms and instructions as they deem necessary for the taking of the census. *Central authority for, and expenses of census.*

(2) The expenses incurred, with the approval of the Treasury, for the purpose of the census shall be paid out of money provided by Parliament.

3.—(1) Forms shall be prepared for the purpose of being filled up by the persons specified in the schedule to this Act with such of the following particulars in respect of the calendar year next preceding the date of the census, or any prescribed part of that year, as may be prescribed; that is to say, the nature of the trade or business, and particulars relating to the output, the number of days on which work was carried on, the number of persons employed, and the power used *Preparing and filling up of schedules.*

or generated, and relating to such other matters of a like nature, except the amount of wages, as may be found to be necessary for the purpose of enabling the quantity and value of production to be ascertained : Provided that—

(a) If in any case it is found inconvenient to furnish such particulars as respects the calendar year, the Board of Trade may allow the particulars to be furnished as respects some other period of twelve months or prescribed part thereof ;

(b) In order to enable the Board of Trade to compile, as far as practicable, statistics of the net value of production without duplication, the prescribed particulars as to output may include particulars as to the aggregate estimated value of the materials used and the total amount paid to contractors for work given out to them ; and

(c) Particulars as to the quantity of output shall not be required except in the case of articles the quantity of which is on their importation into or exportation from the United Kingdom required by the official import or export list to be entered, nor shall such particulars be required in greater detail than in those lists.

(2) It shall be the duty of every person specified in the schedule to this Act, upon receiving notice in writing from the Board of Trade to that effect, to fill up, and sign, and to deliver in such manner as may be prescribed, on or before the prescribed date, such date not to be less than three months after the issue of the forms, the form appropriate to his trade or business.

(3) The Board of Trade shall issue to every person required to make a return under this Act the form to be filled up by him.

Report to Parliament. **4.** As soon as practicable after any census is complete the Board of Trade shall present to Parliament a report of their proceedings under this Act, and a summary of the statistics compiled from the returns under this Act, and from such other information as the Board are able to obtain; such summary shall include a separate statement of the statistics obtained in Ireland, and a similar separate statement for Scotland.

Inter-departmental arrangements. **5.**—(1) The Secretary of State may, as respects any factory, workshop, mine, or quarry, issue and collect any of the forms under this Act by arrangement with the Board of Trade, and in such case shall have the same powers and duties for the purpose as are by this Act conferred on the Board of Trade : Provided that the Board of Trade shall not transfer its powers to make rules under section eight.

(2) The Secretary of State may, if he thinks fit, by arrangement with the Board of Trade, cause any statistical returns, which under any other enactment he is authorised to obtain with respect to factories. workshops, mines, or quarries, to be collected at the same time, and, if convenient, on the same forms as returns under this Act.

Prohibition against publishing individual returns. **6.**—(1) No individual return, and no part of an individual return, made, and no answer to any question put, for the purposes of this Act shall, without the previous consent in writing of the owner for the time being of the undertaking in relation to which the return or-answer was made or given, be published, nor, except for the purposes of a prosecution under this Act, shall any person not engaged in connexion with the census be permitted to see any such individual return or any such part of an individual return, and every person engaged in connexion with the census shall be required to make a declaration in the prescribed form that he will not disclose or, except for the purposes of this Act, make use of the contents of any such individual return or any such part of an individual return, or any such answer as aforesaid, and any person who knowingly acts in contravention of any declaration which he has so made shall be - guilty of a misdemeanour and on conviction be liable to imprisonment, with or without hard labour, for a term not exceeding two years, or to a fine, or to both imprisonment and a fine.

(2) It shall be the duty of the Board of Trade in preparing forms, instructions, or rules under this Act, to have due regard to the circumstances of various trades and industries, and in particular to the importance of avoiding the disclosure in any return of any trade secret or of trading profits, or of any other information the disclosure of which would be likely to tend to the prejudice of the person making the return.

(3) In compiling any report, summary of statistics, or other publication under this Act, the Board of Trade shall not disclose in any manner whatever any of the particulars comprised in any individual return, or arrange them in any way which would enable any person to identify any particulars so published as being particulars relating to any individual person or business.

(4) Where it is shown to the satisfaction of the Board of Trade that any trade or business is carried on by any company in whole or in part by means of any one or more subsidiary companies, any aggregate of two or more returns relating to the trade or business so carried on shall for the purposes of this Act be treated as an individual return.

A company shall be treated as subsidiary to another company for the purposes of this provision if not less than three-fourths of its ordinary share capital is held by that other company.

(5) If any person, having possession of any information which to his knowledge has been disclosed in contravention of the provisions of this section, publishes or communicates to any other person any such information, he shall be guilty of a misdemeanour and shall on conviction be liable to imprisonment, with or without hard labour, for a term not exceeding two years, or to a fine, or to both imprisonment and a fine.

7. For the purposes of this Act the exercise and performance by a local or other public authority of the powers and duties of that authority shall be treated as the trade or business of that authority. *Returns by local and other authorities.*

8. The Board of Trade may, after consultation with the Secretary of State, make rules under this Act— *Power of Board of Trade to make rules.*

    (*a*) for prescribing, either generally or as respects any particular industry or class of industries, anything which, under this Act, is to be prescribed ; and

    (*b*) for exempting from the obligation to make returns under this Act, either wholly or to the prescribed extent, and either unconditionally or subject to the prescribed conditions, any persons or any prescribed class of persons; and

(c) generally for carrying this Act into effect.

All rules made in pursuance of this Act shall be laid before Parliament.

Power to appoint advisory committees. 9.—(1) The Board of Trade shall appoint one or more committees, including persons conversant with the conditions of and engaged in various trades and industries, for the purpose of advising them when considering the preparation of the forms and instructions necessary for the taking of the census and the making of any rules under this Act, and in particular such of those rules as prescribe the details of the particulars relating to output and other matters to be filled in in the several forms.

(2) There may be paid to the members of any such committee, as part of the expenses incurred for the purpose of the census, such travelling and other allowances as the Board of Trade fix. with the consent of the Treasury.

(3) Committees may be appointed under this section to advise the Board of Trade specially as regards any special forms, instructions, or rules, or generally as regards any class or classes of forms, instructions, or rules which the Board may assign to them.

(4) A member of an advisory committee shall not as such be permitted to see any individual return or any part thereof or to be made acquainted with any information contained in any answer to any question put for the purposes of this Act.

Intervals for making returns under 1 Edw. 7. c. 21. s. 130. 10. If the Secretary of State so directs, the intervals at which returns are to be made under section one hundred and thirty of the Factory and Workshop Act, 1901, may, notwithstanding anything in that section, be the same as the intervals at which a census is directed under this Act to be taken.

Voluntary information. 11. Nothing in this Act shall be construed as preventing the Board of Trade or the Secretary of State from obtaining such additional statistical or other information as any person may be willing to supply either by the insertion of additional particulars in the forms under this Act, or by the circulation of separate forms in any censal or inter-censal year : Provided that such particulars, if inserted in forms under this Act, shall be clearly distinguished from the particulars required under this Act to be filled in.

Penalty for offences. 12. If any person required to make a return under this Act—

(a) wilfully refuses or without lawful excuse neglects to fill up a form to the best of his knowledge and belief, or to sign and deliver it as required by this Act; or

(b) wilfully makes, signs, or delivers, or causes to be made, signed, or delivered, any false return in respect of any matter specified in the form ; or

(c) refuses to answer, or wilfully gives a false answer to, any question necessary for obtaining the information required to be furnished under this Act,

he shall for each offence be liable on conviction under the Summary Jurisdiction Acts to a fine not exceeding ten pounds and in the case of a continuing offence to a further fine not exceeding five pounds for each day during which the offence continues, and in respect of false

returns and answers the offence shall be deemed to continue until a
true return or answer has been made or given.

13. This Act may be cited as the Census of Production Act, 1906.   Short title:.

SCHEDULE.

LIST OF PERSONS REQUIRED TO MAKE RETURNS.   Section 3..

(A) The occupier of every factory or workshop within the meaning
of the Factory and Workshop Act, 1901.

(B) The owner, agent, or manager of every mine and quarry.

(C) Every builder, that is to say, a person who, by way of trade or
business, undertakes the construction or alteration of a building or
any part thereof.

(D) Every person who by way of trade or business executes works
of construction, alteration, or repair of railroads, tramroads, harbours,
docks, canals, sewers, roads, embankments, reservoirs or wells, or of
laying or altering gas or water pipes, or telegraphic, telephonic, or
electric lines or works, or any other prescribed works.

(E) Every person who by way of trade or business gives out work
to be done elsewhere than on his own premises.

(F) Every person carrying on any other trade or business which
may be prescribed.

DISCUSSION on MR. G. UDNY YULE'S PAPER.

SIR PHILIP MAGNUS, M.P., said that he had the opportunity of
hearing this subject considered in the House of Commons, but
owing to the weariness resulting from constant attendance on the
Education Bill, he had absented himself during the whole time
it was before the House, and consequently he had only become
acquainted with its main objects through this Paper. He congratulated the reader on the very able review he had given not
only of the Act but of the conditions under which trade statistics
were taken in the United States and in the principal British
Colonies. They must all agree that the time had now come when
a similar census should be taken of the industrial products of our
own country. Such a census would be of considerable value in
helping to solve this difficult fiscal problem which had recently
agitated the country. It was most desirable that they should be
well informed as to the products of industry in this country, and
be able to compare them with similar products in other countries
in order to arrive at any trustworthy conclusion on any of the
difficult questions now under consideration. He had been struck
with the difficulty of the problem which would meet those who
were responsible for taking the census. The first difficulty was
that it was not easy to obtain a correct estimate of the products of
industry owing to the fact that the figures were so liable to be

duplicated, and he did not see how that was to be got over. The mere deduction of the quantity and value of the raw material from the value of the manufactured products did not seem to him to afford a complete account of the value of the products. Another difficulty which occurred to him was with regard to the small industries; if they were excluded, and only factories in which at least five workmen were employed were included, the estimate of the product would not be very accurate. On the other hand, they might be able to compare their own statistics with those of other countries if the returns were arranged in the same form. But there again a difficulty presented itself, because it did not appear from this Paper that in any of the Colonies the statistics were arranged under the same headings, and therefore the difficulties of comparison would be very great. In Australasia many things were included which were not mentioned in this Census Act. He did not quite understand how the particulars relating to the output could be asked for, whilst demand could not be made for the quantity of the output. And it seemed to him that the quantity would probably be more useful than the value. He agreed heartily with the conclusion that we had suffered too long from a dearth of such information, and they would all await with keen interest the first Report under this Act.

Mr. D. F. SCHLOSS said that he could not usefully add very much to this extremely clear and complete Paper. In the brief account given of the Act it was not, of course, possible to explain all its provisions in full, and he was not in any way imputing any omission to the compiler if he ventured to draw attention to certain of these provisions which seemed to him of very great importance. Mr. Yule had noted that all individual returns were confidential; and he might have added, by reference to sub-section 4 of section 6, that, where any business is carried on by one company by means of subsidiary companies, any aggregate of two or more returns relating to the business is to be treated as an individual return. That was a provision of great practical importance with regard to a large section of some of our most important trades. What he particularly wished to direct attention to was sub-section 2 of section 6, which declared it to be the duty of the Board of Trade, in preparing forms and instructions, to have due regard to the circumstances of the various trades and industries. That corresponded with what was done in Canada, where the schedules were prepared by agreement with the Canadian Manufacturers' Association. This Act provided for similar consultation with different classes of manufacturers, so that the information required should be asked for in a form which would be adequate to yield the results required with a minimum of friction and trouble to the employers; that could only be done by consultation with them. Coming to the general question of the difficulties to be encountered and the benefit to be derived from the operations of the Census Office, he should like to mention some remarks made in his presence by a distinguished French economist. While the Bill was before the House there was a discussion, in which this gentleman took part, in which it was pointed out that it would be a very difficult Act to carry out; that the results would be difficult to obtain, and would be far from complete. The answer made by this French professor was as follows: "You either want this Bill or another Bill. You can get this Bill, but you cannot get the other. The Bill you want, if you do not pass this, is a law that will make it a penal offence—perhaps a capital offence—for people to put forward estimates of home production to suit their own views, without any basis whatever. However bad the figures produced under this -Census Act might be, they would be better than that."

Mr. H. BIRCHENOUGH desired to thank Mr. Yule for this Paper, and for his very clear and masterly description of the work of a similar character done in other countries. He had really come there to learn, not to offer any criticisms. The President of the Board of Trade had asked him to be a member of a small committee, consisting of men of business and economists, to advise on the preliminary arrangements for carrying out the Act, and he came there that afternoon to begin his own education, and he was glad to say that he had learned a good deal. Whatever criticisms might be directed against the shortcomings of this Act, it should be remembered that the important thing was to get any census of production at all. They owed a great debt of gratitude to Mr. Lloyd George for his courage in presenting to Parliament a measure of this kind. Inquiries into the details of business always aroused a large amount of jealousy and opposition ; and, however imperfect the Act might be, they had every reason to be gratified at getting it at all. He thought the difficulties in the way would speedily disappear. The results of the first census would not probably give general satisfaction, because people would be puzzled how to fill up the forms, and they might be reluctant to give all the details asked for ; they might fear lest their confidence should not be altogether respected. But those feelings would rapidly disappear, and each succeeding census would be of increasing value. One of the great difficulties foreshadowed was with the small trades—and there were also many trades large in their collective output which were carried on mainly by small producers. For instance, in Sheffield, although the bulk of the business was done by large firms, the certain important branches were carried on by small undertakers who were called "little mesters." And the trade of Sheffield was not exceptional in that respect. At first there might be great difficulty in obtaining details from these small producers ; but such difficulties would in time be removed, and they would get details from the small traders, who were collectively of great importance. Generally, he thought they should be satisfied with the Act even as it stood, not expecting too much at first, but looking forward to amending it after the results of each census were made known. With regard to the periods at which it should be taken, he was absolutely opposed to an annual census, which he thought would be a great waste of time and money, and rather tend to confuse that view of large results which they all desired. It would have been out of the question to introduce the Act on the basis of an annual census; and even when some time had elapsed and they had some practical experience of it, he thought they would have to give a sufficient length of time between each census to enable them to ascertain and appreciate those developments and changes which did not take place annually but only in the course of a few years. If the general census of population were to be taken every five years, he personally, for practical reasons, should approve of the census of production being taken at the same date; though he should prefer a less period, say, three or four years; because now-a-days changes in productive industries were taking place far more rapidly than formerly, owing to the strikes and continuous applications of science to industry. He thought five years was rather a long period; at the same time, they must look at this question from the practical and administrative side; and, on the whole, a five years' period would probably meet with approval of both men of business and economists.

Mr. T. A. COGHLAN thought he had probably some advantage over other gentlemen present in having administered a Statistical Department for more than twenty years, and having carried out many censuses of production. Of course, the difference between England, where manufactures were very highly organized, and Australia, where they were in their infancy, was so great, that Australian experience was only valuable up to a certain point. He quite agreed there would be enormous practical difficulties in carrying out the Act; but he did not think they would come from the manufacturers, who would, after the first return or two, be found willing to assist the department to the utmost. The difficulty would be in making sense out of the returns when they were obtained. However willing the smaller manufacturers might be, their returns would want watching. The great difficulties experienced in Australia had been those in connection with the examination of the returns after their collection, and before they were collated and published. If the returns were not examined by experts in the department, he was afraid no census of production would be entirely satisfactory. The United States census, which was sometimes held up as a model, was very defective in various respects, the returns being put together apparently just as they were received, and sometimes containing a good deal of contradiction. And the only way in which such a census could be made of value was to subject the returns of the manufacturers to expert scrutiny, so that when the final returns were presented to the public they would not require explaining or explaining away. He thought that a period of five years would be too long between the censuses. Trade in this country was subject to considerable vicissitudes. They had all observed the dishonesty with which men approached the examination of economical questions, affecting controversial politics, such as those affecting Free Trade and Protection; and how, for the purposes of political argument or illustration, certain periods were taken for comparison with other periods which gave a very false idea of the condition of trade and industry. He did not know or care which particular political party was responsible; but it is a matter of common knowledge that in order to establish certain conclusions, different years were taken as the point of comparison, one year to show progress and another to show depression, as it suited the arguments sought to be enforced. If the returns were every five years, or a longer period, it might by chance happen that they would be taken on the crest of a wave, or just the opposite; and, by that means a false idea would be pre- sented of the progress or otherwise of industry. To avoid this, they would probably be compelled to adopt shorter periods. In Australia they took their industrial census every year, and they were able to do so by means of the large force of State officers at the disposal of the central Government. It was different here; nevertheless, he did not think it would be desirable, even on the score of expense, to allow five years to pass before taking a second census. Coming to the details of the information to be collected, he was rather disposed to think there was a defect in the new Act with regard to the information required concerning wages. It was most essential that the amount of the wages should be obtained, and the returns would be deprived of a great deal of their value to students so long as this information was absent. It was something gained to obtain the value of the raw material and finished product, and the amount of the capital; but most important of all was the amount of wages paid, and this would not be obtained. It was idle to say that there would be returns of the rates of wages in different trades; these did not carry one very far. What they wanted to know was the amount paid, and its relation to the other factors of production. Given the number of persons employed, or said to be employed, and the weekly or daily rates of pay, students would undoubtedly be tempted to multiply the one by the other, and claim that the result was the amount of wages paid, which might, or might not, be right. The amount of wage, &c., paid was the easiest possible thing for the manufacturers to give; it was in their books. So far as he could see, the only thing the department would have really trouble over was a matter referred to by several gentlemen, namely, the quantities produced. To require quantities was to ask for something that could not be given. The only thing you could get satisfactorily was the amount produced. You might go to an engineering establishment, which produced a thousand different articles of different sizes and varying values. You could not say that a certain place produced 500 boilers and think you had any information, because each boiler might represent a different value and a different amount of material and work. You might as well say that you had produced 500 ships, when one ship might be 200 tons and another 10,000 tons. The only satisfactory way of obtaining information with regard to the total production was by values. In certain industries, such as spirits, beer, or cloth, you could get the quantities, but as regards industry generally it would be quite impossible. On that point he spoke with confidence, because he had handled many thousands of returns, and had found out how impossible it was to present anything satisfactory from those returns in regard to quantities of most manufactures. He rather differed from Mr. Yule as to the non-necessity of maintaining a distinction between raw materials and partially made-up materials; it was essential this distinction should be preserved. The raw material was sometimes a predominating factor in the total value. It was desirable to know the value of the raw material in British manufactures· in order to read the trade returns aright. They struggled to get an accurate statement of the value of the British manufactures exported, . and in the trade returns they showed British manufactures worth so much. But, as a matter of fact, they were not British manufactures at all; they represented a certain amount of imported raw material to which British capital, labour, and machinery had been applied. The great point was not the total export, but the export representing the products of British labour and capital. As everyone knows, the value added to some raw material might amount to 20 per cent.; but there were other raw materials to which the value added might amount to 500 per cent. So that the distinction between raw material and that partly made-up was very important. In any amendment of the Act he hoped that some of these points brought out by practical experience would be attended to.

Mr. S. ROSENBAUM thought it would have been better if this discussion had taken place upon the measure while it was still a Bill and before it became an Act; it might have been possible to make some useful suggestions in the direction of improving it and of eliminating some of the blemishes which the Act contains. Although they would all agree that the Act marked a very important period in the statistical history of the country, they would all agree also that not all the promises which had been held out for the census by the President of the Board of Trade were likely to be fulfilled. They would not be able to get a measure of the whole production of the country by means of this Act, for the very simple reason that it did not cover the whole area of production, and the corners of the field which were omitted from its scope were so extensive and so indeterminate that it would be impossible to use the figures obtained as any measure of the production of the country. In another way also the fact that it did not cover the whole area was a serious blemish because the organisation of industry was rapidly and constantly altering. Mr. Yule appeared to have satisfied himself that it was the intention to exclude small manufacturers, and it was suggested that it would be impossible to apply the Act to small factories containing less than five employés, but it should be noted that those factories were being gradually eliminated and becoming absorbed by larger factories. It followed, therefore, that the next time a census was taken the field covered would be larger than the present field. The figures would not be comparable unless there was some measure of the amount of that absorption which had taken place. Again, he was sorry that agriculture had been excluded; it had been said that was dealt with by the Board of Agriculture, but it was not from the point of view of the Census of Production. The Board of Agriculture told you the quantity of the products of different. classes, but, though these quantities might be translated into values, it would be impossible to add the values to obtain the aggregate agricultural output. It was exceedingly difficult, statistically, to add together grain products, meat products, and dairy products. It was a problem of the same kind, although infinitely more complex, which this Act, or rather the executive officials in charge of the Act, attempted to solve. Another objection was that a limited census could not, in his opinion, entirely eliminate duplication. Take, for instance, a man producing 10,000*l*. worth of coal; by the time it next appeared in any schedule it might have increased in value to 20,000*l*., owing to an enhancement in its value caused by carriage commissions and so on, and it might help to make the goods worth, say, 50,000*l*. But the enhancement of value between 10,000*l*. and 20,000*l*. did not appear in any of the schedules which would come before the census officers. To that extent the result would be defective, and they would not be able to compare the results obtained in successive censuses in this country, and certainly not with those obtained by simultaneous censuses. in other countries, where the relation of industries to one another is entirely different.

Another difficulty was raised by Mr. Yule, and a very important one, which he hoped the Department would try to solve as one of the incidental issues which they might tackle, namely, the question of determining some standard of prices for various goods, which would enable one to correct the value of products at different times. in order to get a measure of the change in quantities. The census. officials would be in intimate contact with all the manufacturers. throughout the country, and it would be for them a comparatively simple matter, and one possessing the utmost possible value, to determine from time to time the change in the average price of commodities. No one would suggest that this was an Act designed to obtain materials only for a census of production. Else, why was the number of employees included, and why should they ask that wages should be included? These were extremely important from the point of view of an industrial census; but if it was desired to simplify the operation of the Act as far as possible, why not confine oneself to the cost of material and value of the output? That raised another question. What was to be regarded as the value of the output? This problem was not met anywhere, he believed, certainly not in the United States elaborate census. How did they insure that the measure of value was the same at different censuses and by different people? One would say ordinarily the value of the output meant at the gate of the factory. But one could never be certain that at different censuses, and in different countries, the factory gates were always at the same distance from the centre of gravity of the factory's work. Further, by the time the same product appeared again in another schedule—as a partially manufactured material—

it had increased in value, and that increase was not accounted for by any of the schedules. Again, was it understood that municipal remunerative undertakings were to be included; and, if so, how were they going to measure the output of a tramway undertaking which was owned by the London County Council; or of a gas or electricity works; and, if not, how could they make allowance for changes of ownership which took place between different censuses?

He did not make these criticisms for the purpose of underrating the value of the census, but because he hoped that in a short time the Act would be amended. The object to be attained was the actual measure of the total production of the country, and he did not think they could obtain that under the present Act.

Mrs. J. RAMSAY MACDONALD said there was a special reason for getting the Australian statistics as full as possible, because they had there a special system of industry, which it was very interesting to follow out. They called it the New Protection; and, roughly, it was that the worker got his wages regulated, and very often raised, by law; the employer got his goods protected by high tariff duties, which in many cases were raised from time to time; and, recently, another factor was coming in, the consumer, who was naturally asking for his share in the arrangement; and a recent Act had fixed the prices at which harvesters so protected were to be sold to the consumer. When she and her husband were out there recently, there was a good deal of talk about this, and it appeared that the statistics of production were not sufficiently detailed or correlated to give the information they would like to have on this very interesting movement in industry. With regard to the period at which the British returns should be given, they had to remember the awful warning they had in the statistics of persons employed in factories and workshops. They used to be given annually; but the factory inspectors found it interfered with the practical work of their department, and they got a Bill introduced to make them returnable at a vague period. If she remembered rightly, that Society protested, and said that the returns would be of more value if they could be had annually; but the objection was ineffectual. The result was that they got very spasmodic and incomplete returns. The first return gave only the persons employed in factories; and a few days ago they had had one given of persons employed in workshops and laundries, which was the first for ten years nearly. Such sort of returns would be of very little use. They ought to insist on having a proper definite period at which the return should be given; and, in connection with that, she hoped they might get a more satisfactory arrangement of the return of persons employed in factories and workshops.

Dr. CANNAN deprecated all attempts to make the census furnish what was called a net aggregate value of production. He believed that those who discussed the elimination of duplicate entries believed that the process was going to bring out the total income of the country, though they did not actually use the word

income.   The census of production would have been better named
a census of products.   He expected it to tell him the amount of
each product.   He was quite content with agricultural returns
which gave the quantities of wheat, oats, and hay produced without
adding them together or attempting to say how much of the oats
were eaten by horses and how much by human beings.   If we made
the chimerical attempt to get income figures from these returns,
the turnips eaten by cattle would have to be "eliminated," leaving
only those eaten by human beings.   In dealing with quantities like
these we found little temptation to try to get aggregates and net
aggregates.   We did not try to add the wheat, the hay, and the
turnips into one jumble, and then deduct something.   We should
avoid the slightly greater temptation in those cases where we were
obliged to estimate quantities roughly by value.   We ought not,
for example, to deduct the value of the nails used in making boxes
from the value of the boxes, any more than we should deduct the
nails, measured by number or weight, from the boxes, measured by
capacity.   Of course, the aggregate value of all products would have
about as much relation to the national income as the Bankers'
Clearing House figures, and it would be about as easy to get the
national income by a proper system of elimination from the one as
from the other.   He hoped the Board of Trade would follow no such
will-o'-the-wisp as a "net aggregate production."   If that term
meant anything at all, it meant aggregate income, which was
properly ascertained by a much less cumbrous and uncertain
process.

Mr. REW desired, on behalf of the Council, as well as on his
own behalf, to say how much the Society was indebted to Mr. Yule
for the preparation of this Paper under very considerable difficulties
arising from a conspiracy of circumstances for which the influenza
fiend was mainly responsible.   At that late hour, he would not
attempt to discuss the Paper, although when the word "Agriculture"
was mentioned, it was naturally a little tempting.   He would only
say that he was glad to gather from Mr. Cannan that he, at any
rate, was satisfied with the present position with regard to
agriculture.   And he would point out to Mr. Rosenbaum that,
although he himself was, professionally, merciless with regard to
the collection of statistics, there were limits to the endurance of the
people.   They ought to be thankful that the nation was making a
very substantial step forward in acquiring statistical information.
They could not expect to get everything at once; and it was certain
they could not obtain more at the present time than was embodied
in the Act which Mr. Yule had so kindly explained.

THE CHAIRMAN, in proposing a vote of thanks to Mr. Yule,
said the difficulties of getting at the real result must be enormous;
but they did not want to eliminate from the total result all the
subsidiary trades, such as the woolcomber, the spinner, and the
weaver, until they got to the clothier.   They wanted to know
what those different trades were doing; what proportion they bore

to the whole trade, and how they were progressing in themselves. He thought the most promising course was to make the returns as full as possible at first, and find out later on how they could be diminished, rather than begin with a limited number and extend them afterwards.

Mr. YULE, in reply, said he might point out that many of the criticisms made were criticisms of the Act, and many of the questions were addressed rather to the President of the Board of Trade than to himself; and those he could not answer. Several speakers touched on the question of period, and the general sense was clearly against his view that five years would suffice. Mr. Birchenough preferred a shorter period; Mr. Coghlan also, and so did other speakers. He need hardly say that he fully appreciated the advantages of a full census carried out more frequently. It was the importance of collation with the population census which had impressed itself on his mind, that led him to suggest the five years' period. No doubt, however, a quinquennial population census would come soon, and even if there were a different interval in the case of the census of production, this difference of period would not then be of so much consequence, as they could estimate the population during the intercensal period with greater accuracy.

The inclusion of small trades, and the general question of the completeness of the census, was touched on by several speakers. On that point he agreed with Mr. Rew, that a complete census of production in the full economical sense of the word was an impossibility; you could not do it, simply from the expense, apart from the practical difficulties. He should attach a much higher value than he judged Mr. Rosenbaum did to such a partial census as that which was possible under this Act. He did not know from what passage of the paper Mr. Rosenbaum concluded that "he had satisfied himself that it was the intention to exclude small manufacturers"; he had no knowledge how far the Board of Trade would carry out their powers as regarded small trades; he only laid stress on their power of exemption, because he thought that rendered the extreme criticism as to the absurdity of including small trades unjustifiable. Those small trades could be omitted from which it was practically impossible to get reliable data; but any trades the total production of which was of importance could be included, if it were possible to obtain good returns. He fully recognized that in many trades you could not ask for quantities; the demand would be meaningless in the case, say, cited by Mr. Coghlan, of an engineering firm turning out all kinds of miscellaneous goods. Then you could only ask for values. But in many cases there was not that objection; even in the case of shipbuilding they did give the quantities in certain returns; not the number of ships, but the total tonnage. His point was that the system of exemption from stating quantities, as set up by the Act, was cumbrous, and that such exemptions would have been better left to the Board. He had cited as an illustration the case of chemicals, where those enumerated had to be returned by quantity, and those unenumerated by value only.   Such an arrangement seemed hardly logical.

Mr. Rosenbaum drew attention to the difficulty introduced by the varying value at which a commodity was returned when it appeared first of all as a final product, and later on at an enhanced value, including intermediate profits and freight, as a raw material in another industry.   The point was referred to near the beginning of his paper, in dealing with the method of correction adopted in the United States census of 1900 (p. 55).   It was an important question whether the census could cover freight and transport under any section of the Act.

He was inclined to dissent from the views expressed by Mr. Cannan.   It did not seem to him to be a question of getting at income at all, but of assessing output, and avoiding stating the values of produce in a way which would make the return of values enormously different according to the organization of industry.   If one did simply add together (and *pace*, Mr. Cannan, you must, in some way, merely to get a general view) the values of the actual commodities produced by the woolcomber, the spinner, the weaver, and the clothier, you got a total which would be quite different according as those processes were carried on by different firms or were all carried on by one large firm which did its own woolcombing, spinning, and weaving.   It was surely desirable to use some process which would eliminate the effect of changes in the organization of industry, which might bring the different processes under one head.   He did not regard a return under such a census in any way as a return of the income of the country, but as a return of total production in a certain sense which was easily comprehended. True, in the case of the farmer, one did not add the quantity of the turnips to the quantity of wheat and the quantity of stock, and so forth ; but he saw no objection to adding the value of the turnips to the value of the wheat, and, if necessary, to making a correction for such portion of the crops as might be used for feeding the cattle. He fully agreed with Mr. Coghlan with regard to the practical difficulties of the census—the serious practical difficulties which no doubt the office would meet with in collating and judging the individual returns, and seeing that they were made sufficiently clear and satisfactory to convey a definite meaning.   They must all wish the Director success in the interesting but onerous duties of his new office.

———————

The following communication was received from Mr. G. G. Chisholm :—

I am extremely sorry that another engagement will prevent me from being present at the reading of the valuable paper on Statistics of Production and the Census of Production which Mr. Yule has prepared for the Society in rather difficult circumstances, but I should like to be allowed to contribute a few observations on points in or connected with that paper.   First, I would say that I entirely agree with Mr. Yule in thinking that of the two methods he expounds for estimating the value of the total production, that of estimating for each producer the value of the utility which he adds to an article and adding together these utility values is "the better and more straightforward." There is one utility, however, for which it will be extremely difficult, perhaps impossible, to obtain a value, namely, that added by transport. It might perhaps be practicable to ask for a return not merely of the spot value of goods, but also their value in leading local markets; but, seeing that nearly all goods have to be transported a greater or less distance for consumption, I should think it likely that the cost of transport is tacitly included in the estimate of the value of the goods at the place of production. It is customary, however, to ask for f.o.b. prices, and, with reference to our export trade, there would be an advantage in obtaining these (at certain convenient ports differing in different cases) as well as factory values.

Mr. Yule indicates regret that quantities are not to be asked for in all cases in which that would be practicable, and therein I feel with him strongly. It is not merely desirable to have quantities, but wherever possible, quantities of the same unit, and that a unit of weight; and I still hope that this is amongst the information which may be collected under the authority conferred on the Board to obtain voluntary information. What makes this information so important is the indirect effect which quantity has on trade generally. One of the most striking features of modern trade is the degree in which the trade in bulky goods of low value cheapens the transport of the less bulky and more valuable goods. Professor Jevons emphasised this in the case of coal, but it is similarly true of many other bulky commodities. There is no doubt whatever that the great extent of our trade, both outward and inward, in bulky commodities is one of the main factors contributing to the growth of our shipping, and that similarly the rapid growth of such trade in Germany in recent years has helped greatly in promoting the growth of German shipping. It is this bulky trade that plays an important part in maintaining the value of our *entrepôt* trade, which is almost entirely in articles of relatively small value in proportion to their bulk. Under the Census of Production Act it appears that quantities are to be asked for only where they are asked for on their importation and exportation, and the quantities asked for will, of course, be of the same nature as those demanded in connection with our external commerce. As the quantities of all tissues are returned in yards, not by weight, few people can have any idea of the very small proportion of our shipping that is required for the carriage of the most valuable of our exports, cotton piece goods. I would suggest that in the case of those articles, the quantity of which by weight is not required, voluntary returns might be asked for as to the equivalence in weight of given quantities expressed in other terms, as to whether the goods are carried by sea as measurement goods or goods charged by weight, as to the addition that packing for sea transport makes to the quantity of goods, and the equivalence in measurement tons of a ton weight of different classes of goods, including packing, and the equivalence in weight of a measurement ton of goods carried by measurement. Such information would add greatly to the significance of our import and export tables.

The only other point on which I want to say anything is as to the collection of information, under the third clause of the Act, as to "power used or generated." Formerly we used to get such information in Returns under the Factory Acts. On pp. 522—528 of vol. xxxiv of the Society's *Journal* summaries under that head are given according to the returns of 1856, 1861, 1868, and 1870. I am not aware whether similar information is given under any more recent returns. In those days the power was distinguished simply as steam and water, and at that time that sufficed; but it seems to me that at the present day a more complicated schedule will be required to collect the important information. Since 1870 the development of electricity has given a new importance to water-power and has placed the value of fuel under a new point of view, and the development of internal combustion engines has altered the values of certain kinds of fuel. The coal-testing plant of the United States Geological Survey at St. Louis showed "that a higher grade of producer gas may be obtained from lignite than can be made from bituminous or anthracite coal or coke."[1] That is of little importance to us except indirectly, in view of the enormous stores of lignite in Germany and other Continental countries; but to us it is of more immediate consequence that peat also is said to be a very good fuel for the same purpose. In view of these considerations, therefore, it seems to me that it would be important to have a schedule like this :—

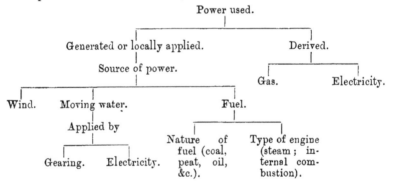

Where gas or power is supplied from a central station the source of power would be ascertained from the returns of that station, and to arrive at the total amount of power used or generated it would be necessary to obtain from the central stations the total amount of gas or power sold, and deduct that from the totals generated. The amount thus deducted would, however, be in excess of the amount entered as "derived" at the factories returning power us used, seeing that much of the power of central factories goes to small consumers who might not come within the scope of the Act.

[1] United States Geological Survey, "The Production of Coal in 1904," p. 180.

MISCELLANEA.

CONTENTS :

PAGE

I.—The late Viscount Goschen
(President, 1886-88)· 100

II.—On the Representation of
Statistical Frequency by
a Series. By Professor
F. Y. EDGEWORTH 102

PAGE

III.—Prices of Commodities in
1906. By A. SAUERBECK 107

IV.—Roumania's Forty Years'
Progress, 1866-1906. By
LEON GASTER ....: 122

V.—Correspondence.................... 129

I.—*The late Viscount Goschen* (*President* 1886-88).

THE Royal Statistical Society has lost in Lord Goschen one of its most distinguished Fellows, and one whose services have been recognised alike in the fields of practical statesmanship, of financial affairs, of literature, and of economic study. After a membership of all but forty years of our Society, testifying to his staunch appreciation of the value of its work, the sudden loss of so renowned a name from our roll of honour, where it has long stood, has evoked a real sorrow among all ranks of statisticians and economists. Born in 1831, George Joachim Goschen, after a distinguished career at Oxford, entered the active life of the City of London as a partner in his father's house of Frühling and Goschen, and by his authorship of "The Theory of Foreign Exchanges," he secured a reputation of no common order, followed by repeated proof of the confidence of his fellow citizens. As a Director of the Bank of England, as Member of Parliament for the City, and as selected to hold high office in the Ministry of the day, after but three years' service in the House of Commons, Mr. Goschen had achieved a political position of remarkable prominence for so young a man by the year 1866. Two years later, as President of the Poor Law Board in Mr. Gladstone's first Government, his opportunity of administrative work was extended, and from the same year, 1868, up to the time of his death on the 7th of February, 1907, his interest in the labours of the Royal Statistical Society is well known to have been continuous. Reaching the Chair in 1886, he signalised his tenure of office by the delivery in December, 1887, of a Presidential Address replete with matter of economic value, and presenting, for dissection and discussion, a more or less novel statistical thesis respecting the changes in the successive processes of wealth accumulation in the United Kingdom, indicated by the growth of what are called moderate fortunes. His data thus presented, strikingly showed

the multiplication of small investors and the increasing importance
in the political and economic structure of the State of the "smaller
middle class," as well as the development, to which he pointed in
the direction of an automatic socialism, due to the broadening of
the area of the distribution of wealth.   The effective ventilation
of this subject by so high an authority as the actual occupant
of the post of Chancellor of the Exchequer—for Mr. Goschen, after
a temporary withdrawal from active political life, had acceded
to that high office—proved notable in many ways.   By his action
he attracted to the study of statistics many of those who had not
previously recognised their great value as applied to the practical
questions of political administration and the adjustment of taxation.
The occupancy by the Finance Minister of the State of the Chair
of the Statistical Society was itself unique, and furnished a lesson
which, it may be permitted to hope, will not be forgotten by future
statesmen who may be distrustful of the advantage of combining
the authoritative explanation and defence of financial and fiscal
questions in Parliament itself with an exchange of views and a
direct consultation with those who, in the academic shade of
societies like our own, have made, under less polemic conditions, a
study of the methods of statistical analysis and deduction.

The detailed incidents of Lord Goschen's long and distinguished
public career have been told more fully by other and abler pens
in organs of wider circulation than our *Journal* can command.
But it is fitting that its pages should contain at least a short
tribute of admiration from the followers of the statistical craft to
one who, in and out of office, was at once a political leader and a
keen statistical inquirer.   The firmness of Lord Goschen's political
convictions, which was evidenced by his resolute independence
of decision amid the wavering breezes of party politics, may be
claimed as in some degree the product of that careful, cautious and
balanced judgment which the deliberate study of figures "from
both sides" may secure.   Alike as a statistician and as a politician,
Lord Goschen was always a fighter, and a hard hitter in debate, yet
one who never resented criticism, but took it in good part when
offered.   While, therefore, it may be admitted that controversy was
more than once aroused, both by some of his earlier and later
administrative actions, it has never been asserted that his conclusions, whether statistical or economic, were ever based on hasty
or casual impression, or even influenced by merely opportunist
expediency like so much of the political labour of our time.   Among
the monuments of his official work in the presentation and grouping
of facts, the famous report which he prepared in 1870 on the
incidence of local rates in the early stages of the local taxation
question, will ever be regarded as the precursor of later inquiries.
In this work Lord Goschen's ability was conspicuous, whether we
agree with him or venture to differ from some of his conclusions;
and he was well seconded, as he readily acknowledged, by the
indefatigable research and ingenuity of another President of our
Society—Sir Robert Giffen—who was so closely associated with
him in his task.

These pages are not the place for any record of Lord Goschen's Parliamentary successes, his brilliant endeavours, his masterly schemes, or his occasional failures, for in a career of such length and varied spheres he would not himself have refused to admit that some failures must be counted in the Budget schemes for which he was responsible. But whether at the Exchequer, or at the Board of Admiralty, whether dealing with local government or re-adjusting the items of national taxation, whether in the Governments of Mr. Gladstone or those of Lord Salisbury, the one feature of Lord Goschen's labours was that of courage in conception, and stout defence of principle. Greatest of all his administrative work will stand his conversion of the National Debt in 1888, which afforded scope both for his grasp of detail and his acute financial knowledge. To enumerate the many distinctions which Lord Goschen enjoyed as a testimony to the trust reposed in him by his fellow countrymen, would be a task beyond the space here at command, but no obituary of so distinguished a statesman could be complete which failed to take note of his Presidency of the Royal Economic Society from its institution in 1888 till within a few months of his death—a post so singularly suited to his temperament; and, last of all, of his unanimous promotion to the Chancellorship of the University of Oxford, to which he acceded on the death of Lord Salisbury, and which fitly crowned the academic distinctions of our deeply-regretted colleague.

P. G. CRAIGIE.

II.—On the Representation of Statistical Frequency by a Series.

By Professor F. Y. EDGEWORTH, D.C.L.

AN important contribution is made to this subject by Professor Bruns,[*] of the Leipsic University, in a recently published work which deals with the "doctrine of collective quantities." The series here employed to represent the frequency with which the different values of such quantities respectively occur, is not now propounded for the first time. It had been broached by Professor Bruns himself[†] in a paper published some nine years ago. Professor Charlier, of the Lund University, had reached the same result by a different route in a study[‡] "on the representation of arbitrary functions," published in 1905. Again, Professor Thiele,[§] of the

[*] *Wahrscheinlichkeitsrechnung und Kollektivmasslehre.* Von Dr. Heinrich Bruns. Leipzig: Teubner, 1906.
[†] *Zur Collectiv-Masslehre.* Wundt's *Philosophische Studien.* Band XIV.
[‡] *Über die Darstellung willkürlicher Funktionen.* Von C. V. L. Charlier. *Archiv för Matematick* . . . Band 2, No. 20. Stockholm.
[§] *Theory of Observations.* By T. N. Thiele. London: Layton, 1903.

Copenhagen University, from still a different point of view, had, writing in 1903, considered the same formula "as a most general functional form of a continuous law of error."

But to enumerate and compare all the authors who may have inspired, or have been inspired by, those whom we have named is not attempted here. It would exceed the knowledge of the present writer, and the interest of the statistical reader, to trace the genial conception of functional development to its sources in pure mathematics. It is in that high region that the discoveries of Professors Bruns and Charlier have been achieved. It is true that they have mostly in view a statistical problem, the construction of frequency-curves. But they do not define this problem in such wise as to limit seriously the generality of their conclusions. Thus, Professor Charlier postulates only of the function $F(x)$, which he seeks to develop in the form of a series, that it should vanish when $x = \pm \infty$. Considered thus, the proposed development may seem to be comparable with Taylor's Theorem in respect of its generality.

The way in which Professor Charlier attacks the problem recalls the earlier proofs of Taylor's Theorem. He posits the identity $F(x) = A_0 f(x) + A_1 f'(x) + A_2 f''(x) + \ldots$; where f is a subsidiary function such that the function itself and each of its derivatives vanishes when $x = \pm \infty$; $A_0, A_1, A_2 \ldots$ are constants (depending on the forms of F and f). Then $A_0, A_1, A_2 \ldots$ are determined by multiplying each side of the above identity successively by $1, x_1 x^2 \ldots$ and integrating between limits $\pm \infty$. There is thus obtained a formula suited, in the words of the author, to "represent in a very general manner real functions by series." This general formula is then narrowed by assigning to f a particular form, namely, that of the error-function, say, $\dfrac{1}{\sigma \sqrt{2\pi}} e^{-\frac{(x-b)^2}{2\sigma^2}}$; where σ is,

in Professor Pearson's terminology, the *standard deviation*, $A_0, A_1, A_2 \ldots$ are linear functions of the *moments* of $F(x)$, say, $\mu_0, \mu_1, \mu_2 \ldots$ It may be arranged without loss of generality that A_1 and A_2 should each be zero. We can then exhibit the first few of the constants in terms of the moments, as follows :— *

$$A = \mu_0. \qquad A_1 = 0. \qquad A_2 = 0.$$

$$A_3 = \frac{1}{3!}(- \mu_3)$$

$$A_4 = \frac{1}{4!}(\mu_4 - 3\sigma^4\mu_0)$$

$$A_5 = \frac{1}{5!}(- \mu_5 + 10\sigma^2\mu_3)$$

$$A_6 = \frac{1}{6!}(\mu_6 - 15\sigma^2\mu_4 + 15\sigma^6\mu_0).$$

We may put $\mu_0 = 1$ without serious loss of generality.

---

* Cf. Charlier, *loc. cit.*, p. 17.

Professor Bruns obtains a substantially identical result by a quite different route. He expands the (indefinite) integral of the assigned function, F (x) in the notation above employed, by an ingenious use of a certain definite integral associated with the name of Lejeune-Dirichlet.

The consilience between results obtained by methods so independent is calculated to inspire complete confidence in the accuracy of the formula common to both. But for the purpose of computation it is requisite that the expression should not only be formally true, but also practically available, if not in general, at least for the values of the variable with which we are concerned. But to ascertain the conditions by which the requisite approximation is secured, is, in the words of Professor Charlier, a "very far-reaching (*umfassende*), and probably also difficult problem," which he confesses that he has not fully solved. While this problem remains unsolved, the mathematical purist will probably object to the use of the series. But the statistician will observe that certain tests of approximation with which he is specially concerned are adequately fulfilled. It has been secured by the construction that the moments of the A_6 representative and of the represented locus should coincide up to the power designated by the subscript of the highest A coefficient that is utilised. For example, the mean fourth power of deviation from the average is for the actual locus μ_4; for the rerepresentative (referred to the centre of gravity as origin) it is the integral between extreme limits of the ordinate multiplied by the mean fourth power of the abscissa, *i.e.*, $\int_{-\infty}^{+\infty} x^4(1 + A_3D_3 + A_4D_4)\phi dx$; where the symbols have the meanings above assigned. This integral is $3\sigma^2 + 4!A_4$. Which reduces to μ_4, when there is substituted for A_4 its value above assigned, viz., $\frac{1}{4!}(\mu_4 - 3\sigma^4)$; μ_0 being equated to unity. In like manner the values above assigned to A_3, A_5, and A_6 may be employed to show that the mean third, fifth, and sixth powers coincide for the actual and the representative locus. The theorem is quite general. Professor Bruns devotes much attention to the question of convergency, and he seems to have attained considerable success in proving the availability of his formula. We have been deterred from following the difficult investigation by a preliminary doubt which occurs when we compare the Bruns-Charlier with a certain other series which purports to represent statistical frequency.

The series proposed for comparison is that which has been set forth in this *Journal* as the generalised law of error, or law of great numbers,[*] deduced from the hypothesis that the quantity under consideration depends upon a number of independent elements (each a collective magnitude in Professor Bruns's sense). It is this series, we submit, and not as Professor Charlier suggests,[†] the one which he obtained without utilising the fact of aggregation,

---

[*] *Journal of the Royal Statistical Society*, September, 1906.

[†] *Das Fehler-gesetz*, p. 9, *loc. cit.*, Band II., No. 8.

that constitutes the generalisation of Laplace's *Law of Error*.[*]
The Bruns-Charlier law, unlike the generalised law of error, does
not comply with the conditions required for the frequency-locus
of an aggregate. It does not satisfy the partial differential
equation, given by Professor Morgan-Crofton, which expresses
the condition that when a new element is taken on, the form of
the frequency-locus for the aggregate remains the same, while the
constants are altered.[†] The condition that the curve should be
" reproductive " is also unfulfilled : [‡] if P and Q are two collective
magnitudes obeying that law, it does not follow, as it ought, that
R, a quantity formed by putting together a value of P and a value
of Q, each taken at random, will also obey that law.

The two series may also be contrasted in respect of an attribute
which has been taken as the criterion of consilience between the
representative and the concrete locus of frequency : viz., that the
mean powers of deviation from the average (the moments) should
be the same—up to some fairly high power—for the two loci.[§]
Take first the case of a quantity not formed by aggregation. By
construction the criterion is satisfied both by the Bruns-Charlier
series and by the generalized law of error. In the case of aggregates
—a common case, it is submitted, in statistics—both series still
satisfy the criterion; but the generalized law of error satisfies it
better, because sooner—with a fewer number of terms.

The contrast may be exhibited by writing the Bruns-Charlier
formula $(1 + A_3D^3 + A_4D^4 + \ldots)\phi$, and the contrasted formula
$C^{B_3D^3 + B_4D^4 + \ldots}\phi$; where $A_3, A_4 \ldots$ are the constants of which
the values are given above;[||] D stands for the operator $\dfrac{d}{dx}$; ϕ is
that normal law of error, which, having the same mean square
of deviation as the frequency-locus which it is sought to represent,
forms the first approximation. Whereas $B_3 = A_3$; the second
approximation is the same for both systems. But though $B_4 = A_4$,
yet the third approximation is not the same for both systems.
According to the generalised law of error the third approximation
is formed by adding to the second $(A_4D_4 + \frac{1}{2}A_2^2D^6)\phi$. Not only
the sixth moments but many higher moments of the frequency-locus
thus designated will in general coincide with those of the given
concrete locus. But with the Bruns-Charlier series, it is necessary
to proceed to a later term. It is necessary to take in A_6, in order
to secure the coincidence between the sixth moment of the real
and that of the representative locus.

Thus the Bruns-Charlier series, in the case of aggregate quantities, seems to be at a disadvantage as compared with the series
formed by the generalised law of error. But even that series ceases

---

[*] As shown by the present writer in Sect. III. of the *Law of Error* in the
Cambridge Philosophical Transactions, vol. xx. (1905).

[†] *Loc. cit.*, sect. II.

[‡] *Loc. cit.*, sect. IV.

[§] *Loc. cit.*, sect. I.

[||] Above p. 103.

to be available when x, the distance from the centre, becomes considerable, when we are handling what has been called the "tail" of the curve.* Much more, then, does the other series cease to be available beyond a certain distance from the central region.

The difference between the two kinds of series must be noticed if they are to be judged fairly. Mr. Elderton, in an otherwise excellent work on *Frequency Curves*, has not attended to this distinction. Accordingly he has neither done justice to the *a priori* claims of the generalised law of error which are based on its genesis nor yet to the *a posteriori* evidence of its fitting concrete observations. It is not surprising perhaps that the evidence on the ground of origin should be ignored by one who is identified with a method which does not derive much support from that sort of claim. The prestige of birth is commonly not much dwelt on by those who have not that advantage. But even if we are to consider only what each formula is, not whence it is deduced, the two kinds of series ought not to be put in the same class. It ought to be noticed that, as shown above, the one formula admits only first powers of moments, the other admits also higher powers thereof. Accordingly the trial of the third approximation made by Mr. Elderton at his p. 162 relates only to the Bruns-Charlier series. Mr. Elderton confounds, under the common designation of "alternative systems," two methods which agree in differing from the one which he advocates—like "the Pagan magistrate who," according to Gibbon, "possessed neither leisure nor abilities to discern the almost imperceptible line which divides orthodox faith from heretical pravity." Perhaps we may seem to imitate what the same author describes as the "imprudent defence of the Christians," who explained that the horrid practices falsely ascribed to the orthodox were in reality committed by some heretical sectaries. We are not concerned to deny that some series as handled by some authors may be open to Mr. Elderton's criticism: "the neglect of later terms may involve considerable error."† But this criticism is not applicable to a series which it is not proposed to employ beyond the limits of safety, which is confined to the "body" as distinguished from the "tail"‡ of the locus under consideration. All that can be said against such a series is that it appears somewhat awkward and halting, as compared with a curve which, whole and smooth, keeps due on to the furthest extremities. An explanation, which accounts for a large class of facts, is in some respects less satisfactory than a description which is applicable not only to that body of facts, but also to some outlying phenomena.

---

* *Loc. cit.*, Appendix 2.

† See Appendix to the "Generalised Law of Error," *Journal of the Royal Statistical Society*, June, 1906.

‡ "Generalised Law," *loc. cit.*, p. 512.

III.—*Prices of Commodities in* 1906. By A. SAUERBECK.

THE following table shows the course of prices of forty-five commodities during the last twenty years as compared with the standard period of eleven years, 1867-77, which in the aggregate is equivalent to the average of the twenty-five years 1853-77 (see the Society's *Journal*, 1886, pp. 592 and 648, and 1893, pp. 220 and 247).

Summary of Index Numbers. Groups of Articles, 1867-77 = 100.

	Vegetable Food (Corn, &c.).	Animal Food (Meat, &c.).	Sugar, Coffee, and Tea.	Total Food.	Minerals.	Textiles.	Sundry Materials.	Total Materials.	Grand Total.	Silver.*	Wheat Harvest.†	Average Price of Consols.‡	Average Bank of England Rate
'87	64	79	67	70	69	65	67	67	68	73·3	110	101¾	3
'88	67	82	65	72	78	64	67	69	70	70·4	96	101	3
'89	65	86	75	75	75	70	68	70	72	70·2	103	98	3
'90	65	82	70	73	80	66	69	71	72	78·4	106	96½	4
'91	75	81	71	77	76	59	69	68	72	74·1	108	95¾	3
'92	65	84	69	73	71	57	67	65	68	65·4	91	96¾	2
'93	59	85	75	72	68	59	68	65	68	58·6	90	98¼	3
'94	55	80	65	66	64	53	64	60	63	47·6	106	101	2
'95	54	78	62	64	62	52	65	60	62	49·1	91	106¼	2
'96	53	73	59	62	63	54	63	60	61	50·5	116	111	2 1/16
'97	60	79	52	65	66	51	62	59	62	45·3	100	112¼	2⅞
'98	67	77	51	68	70	51	63	61	64	44·3	120	111	3¼
'99	60	79	53	65	92	58	65	70	68	45·1	113	107	3¾
'00	62	85	54	69	108	66	71	80	75	46·4	99	99½	4
'01	62	85	46	67	89	60	71	72	70	44·7	106	94	3¾
'02	63	87	41	67	82	61	71	71	69	39·6	113	94½	3⅓
'03	62	84	44	66	82	66	69	72	69	40·7	104	90¾	3¾
'04	63	83	50	68	81	71	67	72	70	43·4	93	88¼	3⅓
'05	63	87	52	69	87	72	68	75	72	45·7	113	89¾	3
'06	62	89	46	69	101	80	74	83	77	50·7	116	88¼	4¾
Average 97-1906	62	84	49	67	86	64	68	72	70	44·6	108	97¼	3 7/16
88-97....	62	81	66	70	70	59	66	65	67	61·0	101	101¾	2⅔
87-96....	62	81	68	70	71	60	67	66	68	63·8	122	100½	3
78-87....	79	95	76	84	73	71	81	76	79	82·1	97	99½	3 1/16

* Silver 60·84*d*. per oz. = 100.

† Wheat harvest in the United Kingdom, 29 bushels = 100.

‡ Consols and bank rate actual figures, not index numbers; consols 2¾ per cent. from 1888; per cent. from April, 1903.

The index number of all commodities was 77 last year, or five points higher than in 1905. It was 23 per cent. *below* the standard period 1867-77, but 10 per cent. *above* the average of the last to be available when x, the distance from the centre, becomes considerable, when we are handling what has been called the "tail" of the curve.* Much more, then, does the other series cease to be available beyond a certain distance from the central region.

The difference between the two kinds of series must be noticed if they are to be judged fairly. Mr. Elderton, in an otherwise excellent work on *Frequency Curves*, has not attended to this distinction. Accordingly he has neither done justice to the *a priori* claims of the generalised law of error which are based on its genesis nor yet to the *a posteriori* evidence of its fitting concrete observations. It is not surprising perhaps that the evidence on the ground of origin should be ignored by one who is identified with a method which does not derive much support from that sort of claim. The prestige of birth is commonly not much dwelt on by those who have not that advantage. But even if we are to consider only what each formula is, not whence it is deduced, the two kinds of series ought not to be put in the same class. It ought to be noticed that, as shown above, the one formula admits only first powers of moments, the other admits also higher powers thereof. Accordingly the trial of the third approximation made by Mr. Elderton at his p. 162 relates only to the Bruns-Charlier series. Mr. Elderton confounds, under the common designation of "alternative systems," two methods which agree in differing from the one which he advocates—like "the Pagan magistrate who," according to Gibbon, "possessed neither leisure nor abilities to discern the almost imperceptible line which divides orthodox faith from heretical pravity." Perhaps we may seem to imitate what the same author describes as the "imprudent defence of the Christians," who explained that the horrid practices falsely ascribed to the orthodox were in reality committed by some heretical sectaries. We are not concerned to deny that some series as handled by some authors may be open to Mr. Elderton's criticism: "the neglect of later terms may involve considerable error."† But this criticism is not applicable to a series which it is not proposed to employ beyond the limits of safety, which is confined to the "body" as distinguished from the "tail" ‡ of the locus under consideration. All that can be said against such a series is that it appears somewhat awkward and halting, as compared with a curve which, whole and smooth, keeps due on to the furthest extremities. An explanation, which accounts for a large class of facts, is in some respects less satisfactory than a description which is applicable not only to that body of facts, but also to some outlying phenomena.

---

* *Loc. cit.*, Appendix 2.

† See Appendix to the "Generalised Law of Error," *Journal of the Royal Statistical Society*, June, 1906.

‡ "Generalised Law," *loc. cit.*, p. 512.

III.—*Prices of Commodities in* 1906. By A. SAUERBECK.

THE following table shows the course of prices of forty-five commodities during the last twenty years as compared with the standard period of eleven years, 1867-77, which in the aggregate is equivalent to the average of the twenty-five years 1853-77 (see the Society's *Journal*, 1886, pp. 592 and 648, and 1893, pp. 220 and 247).

Summary of Index Numbers. Groups of Articles, 1867-77 = 100.

	Vegetable Food (Corn, &c.).	Animal Food (Meat, &c.).	Sugar, Coffee, and Tea.	Total Food.	Minerals.	Textiles.	Sundry Materials.	Total Materials.	Grand Total.	Silver.*	Wheat Harvest.†	Average Price of Consols.‡	Average Bank of England Rate.‡
1887	64	79	67	70	69	65	67	67	**68**	73·3	110	101¾	3 3/10
'88	67	82	65	72	78	64	67	69	**70**	70·4	96	101	3 3/10
'89	65	86	75	75	75	70	68	70	**72**	70·2	103	98	3 6/10
'90	65	82	70	73	80	66	69	71	**72**	78·4	106	96½	4 5/10
'91	75	81	71	77	76	59	69	68	**72**	74·1	108	95¾	3 3/10
1892	65	84	69	73	71	57	67	65	**68**	65·4	91	96¾	2 5/10
'93	59	85	75	72	68	59	68	65	**68**	58·6	90	98½	3 1/10
'94	55	80	65	66	64	53	64	60	**63**	47·6	106	101	2 1/10
'95	54	78	62	64	62	52	65	60	**62**	49·1	91	106¼	2
'96	53	73	59	62	63	54	63	60	**61**	50·5	116	111	2 5/10
1897	60	79	52	65	66	51	62	59	**62**	45·3	100	112¼	2 6/10
'98	67	77	51	68	70	51	63	61	**64**	44·3	120	111	3¼
'99	60	79	53	65	92	58	65	70	**68**	45·1	113	107	3¾
1900	62	85	54	69	108	66	71	80	**75**	46·4	99	99½	4
'01	62	85	46	67	89	60	71	72	**70**	44·7	106	94	3¾
1902	63	87	41	67	82	61	71	71	**69**	39·6	113	94½	3 3/10
'03	62	84	44	66	82	66	69	72	**69**	40·7	104	90¾	3¾
'04	63	83	50	68	81	71	67	72	**70**	43·4	93	88¼	3 3/10
'05	63	87	52	69	87	72	68	75	**72**	45·7	113	89¾	3
'06	62	89	46	69	101	80	74	83	**77**	50 7	116	88¼	4¼
Average 1897-1906	62	84	49	67	86	64	68	72	**70**	44 6	108	97½	3 5/10
'88-97....	62	81	66	70	70	59	66	65	**67**	61·0	101	101¾	2 9/10
'87-96....	62	81	68	70	71	60	67	66	**68**	63·8	102	100½	3
'78-87....	79	95	76	84	73	71	81	76	**79**	82·1	97	99½	3 2/10

* Silver 60·84*d.* per oz. = 100.

† Wheat harvest in the United Kingdom, 29 bushels = 100.

‡ Consols and bank rate actual figures, not index numbers; consols 2¾ per cent. from 1889 ½ per cent. from April, 1903.

The index number of all commodities was 77 last year, or five points higher than in 1905. It was 23 per cent. *below* the standard period 1867-77, but 10 per cent. *above* the average of the last

ten years and 17 per cent. *above* the average of the lowest decade
on record, 1890-99 (average index number 66).

Corn and sugar and coffee were on the *average* rather lower last
year, but all the other groups were higher than in 1905.

The monthly fluctuations were as follows :—

December, 1889....	73·7	December, 1904....	70·9	June,	1906....	76·9
February, '95....	60·0	„ '05....	74·9	July,	„	76·4
July, '96....	59·2	January, '06....	75·2	August,	„ ...	76·7
„ 1900....	76·2	February, „	75·0	September, „		77·5
December, 1901....	68·4	March, „	75·7	October, „		78·5
„ '02....	69·1	April, „	76·5	November, „		78·6
„ '03....	70·0	May, „	77·0	December, „		79·7

These figures show, as in the year before, a fairly steady
improvement, and the December figure is fully 6 per cent. higher
than at the end of 1905.[1]

Taking articles of food and materials separately, the index
numbers compare thus (1867-77 = 100) :—

	Average.			Dec., 1889.	Feb., 1895.	July, 1896.	Feb , 1900.	Dec., 1904.	Dec., 1905.	Dec., 1906.
	1878-87.	1887-96.	1897-1906.							
Food	84	70	67	73·1	63·8	60·0	65·8	69·1	68·7	68·4
Materials	76	66	72	74·2	57·0	58·6	81·9	72·3	79·4	87·9

Articles of food were slightly lower than a year ago, but the
rise for materials amounted to 10½ per cent., and their index
number is the highest since the early part of 1880, when it stood
at 89. As compared with the average of 1897-1906, the rise has
scarcely affected articles of food, which are only 2 per cent. dearer,
but materials stand 22 per cent. above that average, while the rise
from the lowest point in 1895 amounts to as much as 54 per cent.

The position of the six separate groups of commodities at the
end of the last three years in comparison with whole periods is
illustrated by the following index numbers (1867-77 = 100) :—

	Average.			Dec., 1904.	Dec., 1905.	Dec., 1906.	Last Year, per Cent.
	1878-87.	1887-96.	1897-1906.				
Vegetable food, corn, &c.	79	62	62	63·1	62·5	62·0	fall 1
Animal food (meat and butter)	95	81	84	82·6	89·1	88·1	„ 1
Sugar, coffee, and tea	76	68	49	57·5	45·5	46·7	rise 2½
Minerals	73	71	86	85·6	96·3	112·7	„ 17
Textiles.....................	71	60	64	66·6	75·9	80·8	„ 6
Sundry materials........	81	67	68	67·9	71·2	77·3	„ 8½

---

[1] In January, 1907, the index number was 80·0, and in February, 80·7.

Most sorts of corn had only moderate prices during the past year, and closed slightly lower than at the end of 1905, but potatoes and rice were higher. Beef, mutton, and butter experienced a very small improvement, but pork, after the rise in 1905, was distinctly lower at the close of 1906. Sugar and tea were somewhat higher at the end, coffee declined.

In the group of minerals Cleveland iron rose from 54*s*. per ton to 62*s*., hematite from 72*s*. to 80*s*. Standard copper was worth 79½*l*. at the end of 1905, touched 107¾*l*. in December, and closed at 105¼*l*. Tin started from 161*l*. per ton and touched 215*l*. in May, a quotation unprecedented in the history of prices ; it dropped to 164*l*. in July, and stood at 193½*l*. at the end. Lead went from 17¾*l*. per ton to 20¼*l*. House coal had moderate prices almost throughout the year, but jumped to 19*s*. 6*d*. per ton at the close against 16*s*. 6*d*. in December, 1905. The average export value of coal comes out at only 10*s*. 11*d*. per ton against 10*s*. 7*d*. in 1905 and 16*s*. 9*d*. in 1900, but Newcastle steam improved from 9*s*. 9*d*. per ton to 12*s*. 6*d*., Welsh from 12*s*. 6*d*. to 16*s*. 9*d*.

Among textiles, American cotton was worth 6·24*d*. per lb. at the end of 1905, and closed at 5·60*d*. in view of a very large crop. Flax was slightly lower, hemp and wool were a little higher, silk, and particularly jute, considerably higher than at the end of 1905.

In the group of "sundry materials," hides, leather, tallow, palm oil, nitrate, and timber had a good rise ; linseed oil was only slightly higher, petroleum a little lower.

In a comparison with former periods it will be observed that the groups of minerals and textiles stand very much higher than the average of the last twenty-nine years, while the value of articles of food is either normal or moderate.

The quarterly numbers show the average of three monthly figures, and by thus eliminating minor fluctuations they give a more reliable comparison of the gradual changes of the various groups of commodities. Last year's figures indicate a fairly steady level for articles of food, only animal food being appreciably higher during the first three quarters. Materials, on the other hand, show a generally rising course for minerals and sundry materials. Textiles improved in the first and second quarters but hardly maintained their prices later on, though their level is also considerably higher than for many years past, being in fact the highest since 1880.

Quarterly Movements of Prices.*

Summary of Index Numbers, 1867-77 = 100.

Years.	Quarters.	Vegetable Food (Corn, &c.).	Animal Food (Meat, &c).	Sugar, Coffee, and Tea.	Total Food.	Minerals.	Textiles.	Sundry Materials.	Total Materials.	Grand Total.	Silver.†
1899...	IV	59·6	77·4	53·6	64·8	98·8	68·7	68·7	76·8	71·8	44·5
1900 {	I	60·2	80·2	53·4	66·2	107·9	70·6	72·1	81·3	74·9	45·3
	II	62·3	87·5	55·0	70·0	108·6	65·4	71·4	79·6	75·6	45·6
	III	64·0	86·1	55·9	70·5	111·0	64·5	71·1	79·8	75·9	47·0
	IV	63·7	85·3	52·3	69·3	105·5	60·9	71·5	77·4	74·0	48·8
'01 {	I	62·5	87·4	48·6	68·7	94·0	60·3	70·6	73·7	71·6	45·7
	II	63·4	85·2	46·5	67·9	88·5	59·5	70·9	72·1	70·3	44·9
	III	61·5	85·8	43·8	66·7	86·7	59·6	71·1	71·7	69·6	44·3
	IV	62·3	84·1	42·3	66·1	83·9	58·2	72·2	71·0	69·0	42·6
'02 {	I	62·0	84·3	41·3	65·8	82·2	59·6	72·8	71·3	69·0	41·5
	II	63·5	90·5	39·6	68·5	83·2	60·3	72·7	71·7	70·3	39·2
	III	63·2	89·2	39·2	67·7	82·6	61·7	70·3	71·0	69·6	39·6
	IV	61·9	84·9	41·7	66·1	82·3	61·7	70·1	70·8	68·8	37·0
'03 {	I	61·6	86·9	42·6	67·0	85·7	63·7	70·2	72·4	70·0	36·6
	II	62·5	84·1	42·9	66·4	82·9	65·6	69·2	71·8	69·5	40·1
	III	64·0	85·0	43·2	67·3	81·0	65·9	68·7	71·2	69·5	43·6
	IV	61·7	81·7	45·1	65·6	80·3	67·9	69·9	72·1	69·3	43·3
'04 {	I	63·7	79·9	45·3	65·8	82·0	74·0	69·5	74·2	70·7	42·8
	II	62·9	84·7	48·1	67·8	79·9	70·2	66·9	71·4	69·9	42·0
	III	63·5	85·8	50·1	68·9	79·5	70·5	66·8	71·3	70·3	43·7
	IV	63·4	83·4	55·3	69·1	84·7	68·4	67·6	72·5	71·0	45·2
'05 {	I	62·6	85·7	58·6	70·3	85·6	67·9	67·0	72·3	71·5	44·6
	II	63·1	88·4	53·0	70·3	83·9	69·7	68·5	73·0	71·9	43·8
	III	61·9	87·9	47·9	68·6	87·0	74·9	67·9	75·2	72·4	45·8
	IV	62·9	86·6	46·1	68·1	94·1	75·5	70·8	78·5	74·1	48·8
'06 {	I	62.1	89·6	45·3	68·7	96·7	76·5	72·1	80·1	75·3	49·7
	II	63·8	89·0	45·1	69·2	99·1	81·3	72·7	82·5	76·8	50·3
	III	61·3	89·3	46·5	68·5	101·4	80·1	73·3	83·0	76·9	50·7
	IV	61·7	87·9	47·0	68·1	110·5	80·4	76·6	86·9	78·9	53·0

* The four quarterly figures of each year do not in all cases exactly (in the decimals) agree with the annual averages, as the latter are partly calculated from revised figures. See also the Society's *Journal*, 1893, p. 221; 1895, p. 144; and 1901, p. 90.

† Silver 60·84*d*. per oz. = 100.

The following figures show in each case the average index numbers of all the forty-five commodities for ten years (see the dotted line in the diagram of the *Journal*, 1886, and also the *Journal*, 1893, p. 220); they give the best picture of the gradual movement of the *average* prices of *whole periods*, as the ordinary fluctuations are still further obliterated :—

1818-27 = 111	1884-93 = 71	1891-1900 = 66
'28-37 = 93	'85-94 = 69	'92- '01 = 66
'38-47 = 93	'86-95 = 68	'93- '02 = 66
'48-57 = 89	'87-96 = 68	'94- '03 = 66
'58-67 = 99	'88-97 = 67	'95- '04 = 67
'68-77 = 100	'89-98 = 66	'96- '05 = 68
'78-87 = 79	'90-99 = 66	'97- '06 = 70

From the decade 1889-98 to the decade 1894-1903 the average of ten years had remained 66, the really lowest decade more closely calculated being 1890-99 ; the average for the last ten years has advanced to 70.

Silver was again required for India, and the quantity shipped from here was the largest on record (valued at 15,000,000*l*.), though the total value may have been a little higher in 1857 and 1859, when the price of the metal was double as high as last year (nearly 62*d*. per oz.). Purchases were also made by the United States and France. The price touched 33⅛*d*. per oz. in November, the highest since 1893. The prices and index numbers compare as follows (60·84*d*. per. oz. being the parity of 1 gold to 15½ silver = 100) :—

	Price.	Index Number.		Price.	Index Number.
	d.			*d.*	
Average 1887-96	38¾	= 63·8	End Dec., 1900	29$\frac{9}{16}$	= 48·6
,, '97-1906	27½	= 44·6	*Lowest* Nov., 1902	21$\frac{11}{10}$	= 35·6
,, '93	35⅜	= 58·8	End Dec., 1904 ...	28⅜	= 46·6
,, 1902 ....:	24$\frac{1}{16}$	= 39·6	,, Mar. '05 ..	25$\frac{13}{10}$	= 42·4
,, '05	27$\frac{13}{16}$	= 45·7	,, Dec. '05	30	= 49·3
,, '06	30⅜	= 50·7	,, Dec. '06 ...	32$\frac{5}{16}$	= 53·1

Gold.—The production was estimated in 1902 at 61,000,000*l*., in 1903 at 67,300,000*l*., in 1904 at 71,300,000, and in 1905 at 77,500,000*l*. Last year there was an increase of 4,500,000*l*. in South Africa, and also an increase in the United States, but a decrease in Australia and in some other countries ; the total, however, will probably have been over 81,000,000*l*.

The *Rate of Discount* in the three principal markets is shown in the following table :—

[Per cent. and two decimals.]

	London.		Paris.		Berlin.		Average of the Three Markets.	
	Bank Rate.	Market Rate.	Bank Rate.	Market Rate.	Bank Rate.	Market Rate.	Bank Rate.	Market Rate.
	Per cnt.	Per cnt.	Per cnt.	Per cnt.	Per cnt.	Per cnt.	Per cnt.	Per cnt.
1895	2·00	0·80	2·10	1·59	3·14	2·02	2·41	1·47
'99	3·75	3·25	3·06	2·96	5·04	4·45	3·95	3·55
1900	4·00	3·70	3·25	3·17	5·33	4·41	4·19	3·76
'01	3·75	3·14	3·00	2·48	4·10	3·06	3·62	2·89
'02	3·30	2·96	3·00	2·43	3·32	2·19	3·21	2·53
'03	3·75	3·24	3·00	2·78	3·84	3·01	3·53	3·01
'04	3·50	2·65	3·00	2·19	4·22	3·14	3·51	2·66
'05	3·00	2·61	3·00	2·10	3·82	2·85	3·27	2·52
'06	4·25	3·98	3·00	2·70	5·15	4·04	4·13	3·57

The average rates in 1895 were the lowest on record, those in 1900 were the highest since 1873. Last year's average was 1 per cent. above the preceding year, and very nearly as high as in the year 1900.

Review of the past year.—The past year was, no doubt, a very remarkable one in general trade. The recovery noticed in the previous year made not only further progress, but became almost universal. Wherever we look, whether to European countries— even much-disturbed Russia not excepted—or to America, North and South, to India and the Far East, or to Australia, we have evidence of rapid development and partly enormous prosperity. In this country, though certainly there may be some branches that had a hard fight against the rising prices of raw materials, it will be difficult to find industries of any importance rendering unsatisfactory reports. The cotton trade gave a splendid account, the ship building yards turned out a larger tonnage than ever before, the iron and engineering industries and the wool trade were all satisfactory. The external trade again topped the records of the three preceding years with a fresh advance of 96,000,000*l.*, of which about 50,000,000*l.*, or 5 per cent., was due to higher values, and 46,000,000*l.*, or over 4½ per cent., to larger quantities, and the total reached 1,068,000,000*l.* (exclusive of 124,000,000*l.* bullion and specie).

In Germany there was a very great expansion of industrial activity, and the great briskness in business and the general prosperity in the United States continued unabated.

The cereal crops were good in most countries (except in Russia), those of the United States bigger than ever before; the sugar production remains large, while the coffee crop is almost excessive; the American cotton crop is a very bulky one, and the world's wool production is gradually increasing. The output of iron is greater than ever, and last year the production of the United States exceeded 25,000,000 tons, that of Germany exceeded 12,000,000 tons, and that of Great Britain 10,000,000 tons, against 13,800,000, 8,300,000, and 9,000,000 tons, respectively, in the year of high prices, 1900. The world's production of iron was estimated at 60,000,000 tons, against 40,000,000 in 1900.

Gilt-edged securities had a bad time, owing to the great demand for capital for more profitable employment, the special demand for gold, and the consequently high money rates. Consols averaged 1½ per cent. less than in the previous year (88¼ against 89¾).

With reference to the prospects, we must not forget that the level of many raw materials is now a high one—in some instances possibly due to speculation—and that a reaction may easily occur. But looking at the conditions all over the world, there are certainly no signs of immediate danger. The industries everywhere are still well employed, and, if reports can be trusted, the production in many branches is sold forward for the better part of the year. It is, therefore, quite possible that we are only in the middle of a great movement, and that activity will still continue for some time to come.

————

The arithmetical mean of the forty-five index numbers, which is 77 in 1906 against 72 in 1905, has, as in former years, again been subjected to two tests :—

Firstly, by using the same index numbers of the separate articles, but calculating each article according to its importance in the United Kingdom on the average of the three years 1899-1901, when the mean for 1906 is 73·3, against 70·6 in 1905 and 70·4 in 1904.

Secondly, by calculating the quantities in the United Kingdom at their actual values (the production on the basis of my price tables, the imports at Board of Trade values, and consequently a considerable portion according to a different set of prices) and at the nominal values on the basis of the average prices from 1867-77. In this case the mean is 74·2 in 1906, against 70·7 in 1905, and 70·6 in 1904.

Both calculations make the rise again smaller than the ordinary index numbers, and the general level in 1906 and 1905 comes out somewhat lower than the arithmetical mean. The reason is that for some very large articles, viz., coal and wool, there was but a moderate rise on the average, while meat showed little change; wheat was even lower, and sugar considerably lower; only for cotton and iron the improvement was more important. On the other hand, there were very high prices for copper, tin, and jute, which are of smaller importance. But while it may be admitted that the ordinary index number gives a slightly exaggerated view of the advance during the last two years, it must also be remembered that in the second calculation, Board of Trade values are included which in a rising or falling market must naturally move more slowly than market quotations.

The following table gives the figures which have served for the second test (see also the Society's *Journal*, 1886, pp. 613—19) :—

Movements of Forty-five Commodities in the United Kingdom (Production and Imports).

	Estimated Actual Value in each Period.	Nominal Values at Average Prices of 1867-77, showing Increase in Quantities.	Movement of Quantities.		Movement of Quantities from Period to Period.	Ratio of Prices according to this Table, 1867-77 = 100.
			1848-50 = 100.	1871-75 = 100.		
	Mln. £'s and dec.	Mln. £'s and dec.				
Avge. 1848-50...	219·8	294·8	100	56	—	74·6
„ '59-61....	350·1	382·7	130	73	30% over 1849	91·5
„ '69-71....	456·6	484·6	164	92	27% „ '60	94·2
„ '71-75....	548·8	526·3	178	100	—	104·3
„ '74-76....	537·8	538·4	183	102	—	99·9
„ '79-81....	489·7	578·5	196	110	19% over 1870	84·6
„ '84-86....	445·7	610·1	207	116	—	73·0
„ '89-91....	504·1	685·2	233	130	18% over 1880	73·6
„ '94-96 ...	453·7	723·5	245	137	—	62·7
„ '99-1901..	562·2	775·5	263	147	13% over 1890	72·5
1903	558·0	785·3	266	149	—	71·0
'04...................	560·6	794·0	269	151	—	70·6
'05...................	570·9	808·0	274	153	} 5% over {	70·7
'06*	611·6	824·3	280	157	} 1900 {	74·2

* 1906, subject to correction after publication of the complete mineral produce returns.

The nominal values at the uniform prices of 1867-77 (second column) show the exact movements of *quantities* in the aggregate. Last year's total was about 2 per cent. larger than in the preceding year. The increase is 57 per cent. on 1871-75, and 180 per cent. on 1848-50.

The price movements of the external trade of this country— total imports into the United Kingdom and exports of British and Irish produce—were as follows, 1873 called 111 in accordance with my index number (see the Society's *Journal*. 1905, p. 146) :—

	Total Imports into United Kingdom and Exports of British and Irish Produce.			Ratio of Values. 1873 = 111.	
	Declared Value.	Value at Prices of Preceding Year.	Values at Prices in 1873.	British Trade.	My Arithmetical Index Numbers.
	Mln. £'s.	Mln. £'s.	Mln. £'s.		
1873	626·0	—	626	111·0	111
'89	675·3	664·5	1,005	74·6	72
'99	749·7	724·7	1,241	67·1	68
1900	815·1	739·1	1,224	73·9	75
'01	802·7	836·9	1,256	70·9	70
'02	812·4	831·9	1,302	69·3	69
'03	833·8	826·5	1,323	69·9	69
'04	852·2	847·0	1,345	70·3	70
'05	895·3	889·6	1,408	70·6	72
'06 ...	983·7	940·9	1,480	73·8	77

The third column at uniform prices shows the movements of quantities, and it will be seen that since 1873, a year in which the external trade was already unusually heavy, the total quantities have increased by about 136 per cent. The ratio of prices in this calculation is 73·8, against my index-number of 77. The advance on 1905 is 4½ per cent.

Construction of the Tables.

The Table of *Index Numbers* is based on the average prices of the eleven years 1867-77, and the index numbers have been calculated in the ordinary arithmetical way ; for instance, English wheat :—

		s.	*d.*	
Average, 1867-77....		54	6 = 100, average point.	
,,	'55	74	8 = 137, or 37 per cent. above the average point.	
,,	1906	28	3 = 52, ,, 48 ,, below ,,	

The index numbers therefore represent simple percentages of the average point.

Certain articles which appear to have something in common have been grouped together, with the following result :—

		Example for 1906.	
		Total Numbers.	Average.
1. Vegetable food, corn, &c. (wheat, flour, barley, oats, maize, potatoes, and rice)	With 8 Index Nos	498	62
2. Animal food (beef, mutton, pork, bacon, and butter)............................	,, 7 ,,	622	89
3. Sugar, coffee, and tea	,, 4 ,,	184	46
1—3. *Food*	,, 19 ,,	1,304	69
4. Minerals (iron, copper, tin, lead, and coal)	,, 7 ,,	710	101
5. Textiles (cotton, flax, hemp, jute, wool, and silk)	,, 8 ,,	643	80
6. Sundry materials (hides, leather, tallow, oils, soda, nitrate, indigo, and timber)	,, 11 ,,	815	74
4—6. *Materials*.....	,, 26 ,,	2,168	83
General average	,, 45 ,,	3,472	77

The *general average* is drawn from all forty-five descriptions, which are treated as of equal value, and is the simple arithmetical mean as shown above.

*Average Prices of Commodities.**

No. of Article	0	1	2	3	4	5	6	7	8	1—8	9	10
		Wheat.		Flour.	Barley.	Oats.	Maize.	Potatoes.*	Rice.	Vegetable Food.	Beef.‡	
Year.	Silver.†	English Gazette.	American.	Town Made White.	English Gazette.	English Gazette.	American Mixed.	Good English.	Rangoon Cargoes to Arrive.	Total	Prime.	Middling
	d. per oz.	*s.* and *d.* per qr.	*s.* and *d.* per qr.	*s.* per sack (280 lbs.).	*s.* and *d.* per qr.	*s.* and *d.* per qr.	*s.* per qr.	*s.* per ton	*s.* and *d.* per cwt.		*d.* per 8 lbs.	*d.* per 8 lbs
92	39 13/16	30·3	33	28	26·2	19·10	21¾	70	7·8	—	47	38
'93	35⅝	26·4	27·6	26	25·7	18·9	20	65	6·2	—	48	39
'94	28 15/16	22·10	23·6	22	24·6	17·1	20	70	5·10	—	47	37
'95	29⅞	23·1	25·6	23	21·11	14·6	19½	80	5·6	—	47	37
'96	30¾	26·2	29	25	22·11	14·9	15	55	6·2	—	45	34
97	27 9/16	30·2	34·6	30	23·6	16·11	14¾	70	6·9	—	47	36
98	26 15/16	34	37	33	27·2	18·5	17¾	82	7·2	—	46	36
99	27 7/16	25·8	30	26½	25·7	17	18	70	7·2	—	49	40
00	28¼	26·11	31·6	27½	24·11	17·7	20¼	78	7·4	—	51	42
01	27 3/16	26·9	30	26½	25·2	18·5	22¼	78	6·7	—	49	42
02	24 1/16	28·1	30·6	26	25·8	20·2	25	69	6·2	—	54	47
'03	24¾	26·9	31	27	22·8	17·2	22	84	7·3	—	48	42
'04	26⅜	28·4	33·6	28½	22·4	16·4	21½	90	6·7	—	48	42
'05	27 13/16	29·8	34	28½	24·4	17·4	23	65	6·9	—	47	40
'06	30⅞	28·3	32·6	26½	24·2	18·4	22	67	7·3	—	47	40
verage....												
97–1906	27⅛	28½	32½	28	24½	17¾	20¾	75	6⅞	—	48½	40
'88–97....	37	29	32	27½	25½	17½	20¼	73	6¾	—	47	37
'78–87....	50	40	43½	34½	31½	21	25	102	8	—	55½	46
'67–77 .	58½	54½	56	46	39	26	32½	117	10	—	59	50

Index Numbers (or Percentages) of Prices, the Average of 1867-77 being 100.

Year	0	1	2	3	4	5	6	7	8	1—8	9	10
92	65·4	56	59	61	67	76	67	60	77	523	80	76
'93	58·6	48	50	54	66	72	61	56	62	469	81	78
'94	47·6	41	42	48	63	66	61	60	58	439	80	74
'95	49·1	42	46	50	56	56	60	68	55	433	80	74
'96	50·5	48	52	54	59	57	46	47	62	425	76	68
97	45·3	55	62	65	60	65	45	61	67	480	80	72
98	44·3	62	66	72	70	71	55	70	72	538	78	72
99	45·1	47	54	58	66	65	55	60	72	477	83	80
00	46·4	49	56	60	64	68	62	67	73	499	86	84
01	44·7	49	54	58	65	71	68	67	66	498	83	84
02	39·6	52	54	56	66	78	77	59	62	504	92	94
03	40·7	49	55	59	59	66	67	72	72	499	81	84
04	43·4	52	60	62	57	63	66	77	66	503	81	84
05	45·7	55	61	62	62	67	71	56	67	501	80	80
06	50·7	52	58	58	62	70	68	57	73	498	80	80

* The annual prices are the averages of twelve monthly or fifty-two weekly quotations tatoes of eight monthly quotations, January to April and September to December.

† Index numbers of silver as compared with 60·84*d.* per ounce being the parity between gol d silver at 1 : 15½; not included in the general average.

‡ Meat (9—13), by the carcase, in the London meat market.

Average Prices of Commodities—Contd.

No. of Article	11	12	13	14	15	9—15	16A	16B	17	18A*	18B*	18
	Mutton.		Pork.	Bacon.	Butter.		Sugar.			Coffee.		
Year.	Prime. *d.* per 8 lbs.	Middling. *d.* per 8 lbs.	Large and Small, Average. *d.* per 8 lbs.	Waterford. *s.* per cwt.	Friesland, Fine to Finest. *s.* per cwt.	Animal Food. Total.	British West Indian Refining. *s.* per cwt.	Beet, German, 88 p. c., f.o.b. *s.* per cwt.	Java, Floating Cargoes. *s.* per cwt.	Ceylon Plantation, Low Middling. *s.* per cwt.	Rio, Good Channel. *s.* per cwt.	Mean of 18A and 18B.
892	53	42	48	68	108	—	13½	13¾	16	104	68	—
'93	53	42	50	68	106	—	14¼	15	17¼	103	81	—
'94	55	42	44	59	98	—	11¼	11¼	13¾	102	75	—
'95	58	44	37	54	93	—	10	10	12	98	74	—
'96	53	39	35	50	98	—	10¾	10½	12½	95	58	—
897	55	41	44	59	94	—	9¼	8⅞	11	95	40	—
'98	52	37	45	58	95	—	9½	9½	11¾	92	32	—
'99	54	41	40	51	103	—	10½	10	12¼	90	31	—
900	59	45	44	60	102	—	11¼	10½	12¾	75	40	—
'01	54	44	49	63	105	—	9¼	8½	10¾	70	35	—
902	55	44	48	63	102	—	7¼	6¾	8½	70	31	—
'03	58	47	44	60	100	—	8½	8¼	9¾	70	30	—
'04	59	50	39	57	102	—	10¼	10¼	11½	75	37	—
'05	59	51	46	65	107	—	11	11¼	12¾	75	40	—
'06	60	53	49	65	110	—	8½	8⅝	10	75	39	—
verage 897-1906	56½	45½	45	60	102	—	9½	9¼	11	79	35½	—
'88-97....	56	43½	42	61	100	—	12½	12½	14¾	97	70	—
'78-87....	64½	53	49	71	116	—	17	18	21½	78	52	—
'67-77....	63	55	52	74	125	—	23	24	28½	87	64	—

Index Numbers (or Percentages) of Prices, the Average of 1867-77 being 100.

Year	11	12	13	14	15	9—15	16A and 16B	17	18A*	18B*	18
892	84	76	92	92	86	586	58	56	120	106	113
'93	84	76	96	92	85	592	62	61	118	127	123
'94	87	76	85	80	78	560	48	48	117	117	117
'95	92	80	71	73	74	544	43	42	113	116	115
'96	84	71	67	68	78	512	46	44	109	91	100
897	87	75	85	80	75	554	39	39	109	64	86
'98	84	67	87	78	76	542	40	41	106	50	78
'99	86	75	77	69	82	552	44	43	103	48	75
900	94	82	85	81	82	594	46	45	86	63	74
'01	86	80	94	85	84	596	38	38	80	55	67
902	87	80	92	85	82	612	30	30	80	48	64
'03	92	85	85	81	80	588	36	34	80	47	63
'04	94	91	75	77	82	584	44	40	86	58	72
'05	94	93	88	88	86	609	47	45	86	62	74
'06	95	96	94	88	89	622	36	35	86	61	73

* Index numbers not included in the general average.

Average Prices of Commodities—Contd.

No. of Article }	19A*	19C*	19B*	19	16—19	1—19	20A	20B	21	22	—	23
	Tea.				Sugar,		Iron.			Copper.		Tin
Year.	Congou, Common.	Indian Good Medium	Average Import Price.	Mean of 19A and 19B.	Coffee, and Tea.	Food.	Scotch Pig.	Cleveland (Middlesbrough) Pig.	Bars, Common.	Chili Bars.	English Tough Cake.	Strait
	d. per lb.	l. per lb.	d. and dec. per lb.		Total.	Total.	s. and d. per ton	s. and d. per ton	£ per ton	£ per ton	£ per ton	£ per t
1892	4⅞	7	10·07	—	—	—	41·10	38·6	5¼	45	48	93
'93	5¾	7½	9·74	—	—	—	42·4	34·10	5	44	47	85
'94	4¼	7⅛	9·59	—	—	—	42·8	35·9	4⅞	40	43	68
'95	4⅝	7⅞	9·63	—	—	—	44·5	36·1	4⅞	43	46	63
'96	4	7½	9·55	—	—	—	46·10	38·2	5	47	50	60
1897	4	7¾	9·36	—	—	—	45·4	40·7	5¼	49	52	62
'98	4¼	6½	9·13	—	—	—	47·2	42·2	5½	52	55	72
'99	5½	7¼	8·82	—	—	—	63·9	60·1	7¼	74	78	123
1900	5¼	6¾	8·58	—	—	—	69·4	69·3	9	73	77	134
'01	4	5¾	7·67	—	—	—	53·9	45·5	6½	66	71	118
1902	3¾	5¾	7·20	—	—	—	54·6	49·3	6⅛	53	57	121
'03	4¼	6½	7·71	—	—	—	52·3	46·3	6¼	58	62	127
'04	5	6⅝	7·24	—	—	—	51·5	43·3	6⅜	59	63	127
'05	4¼	5¾	7·24	—	—	—	53·6	49·6	6⅜	70	74	143
'06	4	5¾	7·41	—	—	—	58·9	52·0	7¼	88	92	181
Average...												
1897–1906	4½	6¾	8	—	—	—	55	50	6⅝	64	68	121
'88–97...	4½	8	10¼	—	—	—	45	38½	5¾	50	53	83
'78–87...	6¼	—	12¾	—	—	—	46	38	5¼	55	60	89
'67–77...	11¼	—	17¼	—	—	—	69	60	8¼	75	81	105

Index Numbers (or Percentages) of Prices, the Average of 1867-77 being 100.

	*		*									
1892	43	—	59	51	278	1,387	61	—	66	60	—	89
'93	48	—	57	53	299	1,360	61	—	61	59	—	81
'94	38	—	56	47	260	1,259	62	—	59	53	—	65
'95	37	—	56	47	247	1,224	64	—	59	57	—	60
'96	36	—	56	46	236	1,173	68	—	61	63	—	57
1897	36	—	54	45	209	1,243	66	—	64	65	—	59
'98	40	—	53	46	205	1,285	68	—	67	69	—	69
'99	49	—	51	50	212	1,241	92	—	88	99	—	117
1900	47	—	50	49	214	1,307	100	—	109	97	—	128
'01	36	—	44	40	183	1,277	78	—	79	88	—	112
1902	33	—	42	38	162	1,278	79	—	74	71	—	115
'03	38	—	44	41	174	1,261	76	—	76	77	—	121
'04	44	—	42	43	199	1,286	74	—	74	79	—	121
'05	38	—	42	40	206	1,316	—	80	79	93	—	136
'06	36	—	43	40	184	1,304	—	86	88	117	—	172

* Index numbers not included in the general average.

Average Prices of Commodities—Contd.

No. of Article	24	25A	25B	26	20—26	27	28	29A	29B	30A	30B	31
	Lead.	Coal.				Cotton.		Flax.		Hemp.		Jute.
Year.	English Pig.	Wallsend Hetton in London.	New-castle Steam.	Average Export Price.	Mine-rals. Total.	Midd-ling Ameri-can.	Fair Dhollerah	St. Peters-burg.	Russian, Average Import.	Manila Fair Roping.	St. Pe-ters-burg Clean.	Good Medium
–	£ per ton	*s.* per ton	*s.* per ton	*s.* and dec. per ton		*d.* per lb.	*d.* per lb.	£ per ton	£ per ton	£ per ton	£ per ton	£ per ton
92	$10\frac{5}{8}$	$18\frac{1}{2}$	10	11·04	—	$4\frac{3}{16}$	3	28	26	28	24	15
93	$9\frac{3}{4}$	$19\frac{1}{2}$	$10\frac{1}{2}$	9·90	—	$4\frac{5}{8}$	$3\frac{9}{16}$	34	$31\frac{1}{2}$	26	24	13
94	$9\frac{5}{8}$	$16\frac{1}{2}$	10	10·50	—	$3\frac{13}{16}$	$2\frac{5}{8}$	32	33	22	24	$12\frac{1}{2}$
95	$10\frac{3}{4}$	15	$8\frac{1}{2}$	9·33	—	$3\frac{27}{32}$	$2\frac{3}{4}$	26	28	19	25	11
96	$11\frac{1}{2}$	15	8	8·85	—	$4\frac{11}{32}$	$3\frac{3}{32}$	26	27	$17\frac{1}{2}$	25	$12\frac{1}{4}$
97	$12\frac{5}{8}$	$15\frac{3}{4}$	$8\frac{1}{4}$	8·98	—	$3\frac{29}{32}$	$3\frac{1}{32}$	$24\frac{1}{2}$	27	16	25	11
98	$13\frac{1}{4}$	$16\frac{3}{4}$	$10\frac{3}{4}$	9·92	—	$3\frac{5}{16}$	$2\frac{1}{2}$	24	$25\frac{1}{2}$	27	25	11
99	$15\frac{3}{8}$	$18\frac{1}{2}$	12	10·72	—	$3\frac{9}{16}$	$2\frac{3}{4}$	23	$24\frac{1}{2}$	41	27	$12\frac{1}{2}$
00	$17\frac{1}{4}$	$23\frac{1}{2}$	$17\frac{1}{2}$	16·75	—	$5\frac{15}{32}$	$4\frac{3}{16}$	35	30	39	28	$14\frac{1}{4}$
01	$12\frac{3}{4}$	20	$12\frac{1}{2}$	13·86	—	$4\frac{3}{4}$	$3\frac{15}{32}$	38	$39\frac{1}{2}$	37	27	$12\frac{3}{4}$
02	$11\frac{3}{8}$	$18\frac{1}{2}$	$11\frac{1}{4}$	12·29	—	$4\frac{27}{32}$	$3\frac{11}{16}$	32	37	43	27	$12\frac{1}{4}$
03	$11\frac{3}{4}$	$16\frac{1}{2}$	$10\frac{1}{2}$	11·70	—	6·03	$4\frac{1}{8}$	32	36	36	27	$13\frac{1}{2}$
04	$12\frac{1}{4}$	$16\frac{1}{4}$	$9\frac{1}{2}$	11·13	—	6·60	5	36	$38\frac{1}{2}$	38	28	14
05	$14\frac{1}{4}$	$15\frac{1}{2}$	$9\frac{1}{4}$	10·56	—	5·09	$4\frac{5}{32}$	32	35	$39\frac{1}{2}$	29	$18\frac{1}{2}$
06	$17\frac{1}{2}$	$16\frac{1}{2}$	$10\frac{1}{2}$	10·90	—	5·95	$4\frac{13}{16}$	33	37	$41\frac{1}{2}$	31	$23\frac{1}{2}$
verage....												
97-1906	$13\frac{7}{8}$	$17\frac{3}{4}$	$11\frac{1}{4}$	$11\frac{7}{8}$	—	$4\frac{15}{16}$	$3\frac{3}{4}$	31	33	36	$27\frac{1}{2}$	$14\frac{1}{2}$
88-97....	12	$17\frac{1}{4}$	$9\frac{7}{8}$	$10\frac{1}{4}$	—	$4\frac{11}{16}$	$3\frac{5}{16}$	28	28	$28\frac{1}{2}$	25	13
78-87....	14	$16\frac{3}{4}$	$8\frac{5}{8}$	9	—	6	$4\frac{1}{4}$	33	34	$35\frac{1}{2}$	$26\frac{1}{2}$	15
67-77....	$20\frac{1}{2}$	22	$12\frac{1}{2}$	$12\frac{1}{2}$	—	9	$6\frac{3}{4}$	46	48	43	35	19

Index Numbers (or Percentages) of Prices, the Average of 1867-77 being 100.

Year	24	25A	25B	26	20—26	27	28	29A–29B (Flax)		30A–30B (Hemp)		31
92	52	84	—	88	500	46	45	57		67		79
93	48	89	—	80	479	51	53	70		64		68
94	47	75	—	84	445	42	39	69		59		66
95	52	68	—	75	435	43	41	57		56		58
96	56	68	—	71	444	48	46	56		55		64
97	62	72	—	72	460	43	45	55		53		58
98	65	76	—	79	493	37	37	52		67		58
99	75	84	—	86	641	40	41	51		87		66
00	84	107	—	134	759	61	62	69		86		75
01	62	91	—	111	621	53	51	82		82		67
02	55	84	—	98	576	54	55	74		90		64
03	57	75	—	94	576	67	61	72		81		71
04	60	74	—	89	571	73	74	79		85		74
05	70	70	—	84	612	57	62	71		88		97
06	85	75	—	87	710	66	71	74		93		124

Average Prices of Commodities—Contd.

No. of Article	32A	32B	33	34	27—34	35A	35B	35C	36A	36B	37A	37B
	Wool.			Silk.		Hides.			Leather.		Tallow.	
Year.	Merino, Port Phillip, Average Fleece.	Merino, Adelaide, Average Grease.	English, Lincoln Half Hogs.	Tsatlee.	Textiles. Total.	River Plate, Dry.	River Plate, Salted.	Average Import.	Crop Hides	Average Import.	St. Petersburg, Y.C.	Town.
	*d.** per lb.	*d.* per lb.	*d.* per lb.	*s.* per lb.		*d.* per lb.	*d.* per lb.	*d.* and dec. per lb.	*d.* per lb.	*d.* per lb.	*s.* percwt.	*s.* per cwt.
1892	13	6	8¾	12¼	—	5½	4⅝	4·91	13	14⅛	45	27
'93	12¾	6	10¼	12½	—	5½	4⅞	4·94	13	13⅞	48	30½
'94	11¾	5⅜	10⅛	10	—	5½	4¾	4·65	12½	13⅜	48	25½
'95	12	5⅝	12	10	—	7⅛	6¼	4·76	13½	13⅝	48	23
'96	13	6⅜	11½	10½	—	6¾	5½	4·89	13½	13⅛	48	21
1897	12¼	6	9⅝	10¼	—	6½	5½	4·93	13½	12¾	40	20
'98	13¼	6⅝	8¾	10½	—	7	6⅛	5·04	13½	13⅜	40	22
'99	17¼	8½	8¼	13	—	7⅜	6¼	4·94	13½	13½	—	25
1900	15¾	7⅞	7⅞	13	—	8⅛	6¼	5·31	14	13⅜	—	27½
'01	13	6⅜	6⅞	10½	—	7½	6	5·34	14	13½	—	28
1902	15	7⅝	6¼	11	—	7⅝	6⅜	5·52	14	14½	—	32½
'03	16	8¼	7¼	13½	—	8	6½	5·75	14	15½	—	29½
'04	16	8	10⅛	12½	—	8¼	6¾	5·66	14	15	—	26½
'05	17¼	8¾	12⅜	12¾	—	9	7¼	5·98	14	15¼	—	26½
'06	18	9¼	13⅜	13¾	—	10	7¾	6·52	16½	16	—	30½
Average 1897–1906	15⅜	7¾	9⅛	12	—	7⅞	6½	5½	14	14¼	—	27
'88–97....	14	6½	10½	12	—	6⅛	5¼	5	13½	14¼	43	25½
'78–87 ...	18½	8⅜	11¾	15	—	8⅝	6¾	6½	15	17	41	35½
'67–77....	21¼	9⅞	19¾	23	—	9	7	6⅞	16	18¾	45	45

Index Numbers (or Percentages) of Prices, the Average of 1867-77 being 100.

Year	32A–32B	33	34	27—34	35A–35B	35C	36A	36B	37A–37B
1892	61	44	53	452	63	—	81	—	80
'93	60	52	54	472	65	—	81	—	87
'94	55	51	43	424	64	—	78	—	82
'95	57	61	43	416	84	—	84	—	79
'96	62	58	46	435	77	—	84	—	77
1897	59	49	45	407	75	—	84	—	67
'98	64	44	46	405	82	—	84	—	69
'99	83	42	57	467	85	—	84	—	56
1900	76	40	57	526	90	—	87	—	61
'01	62	35	46	478	84	—	87	—	62
1902	72	32	48	489	87	—	87	—	72
'03	78	37	59	526	91	—	87	—	65
'04	77	51	54	567	94	—	87	—	59
					35A–35C		36A–36B		
'05	84	63	55	577	95		84		59
'06	87	68	60	643	103		94		68

* Port Phillip fleece washed nominal since 1895, exactly in proportion with the value of clean wool

Average Prices of Commodities—Contd.

No. of Article }	38	39	40A	40B	41	42	43	44	45A	45B	35—45	20—45	1—45
	Oil.			Seeds	Petro-leum.*	Soda.	Nitrate of Soda.	Indigo.	Timber.		Sundry Mate-rials. Total.	Mate-rials. Total.	Grand Total.
Year.	Palm	Olive.	Lin-seed.	Lin-seed.	Refined.	Crystals.		Bengal, Good Con-suming.	Hewn, Average Import.	Sawn or Split, Average Import.			
	£ per ton.	£ per tun.	£ per ton.	s. per qr.	d. per gall.	s per ton	s. per cwt.	s. per lb.	s. per load.	s. per load.			
892	24	36	18½	39	5	66	8¾	4½	40	44	—	—	—
'93	28	36	20½	42	4	58	9¼	5½	38	43	—	—	—
'94	24½	35	20¼	38	3⅞	42	9¼	5	36	44	—	—	—
'95	23	36	20¼	37	6	39	8¼	4¼	37	42	—	—	—
'96	22	30	17½	33	5½	42	8	4¼	40	44	—	—	—
897	22	31	15	33	4¾	51	7¾	4	41	47	—	—	—
'98	23	32	16¾	36	5⅛	54	7¼	3½	42	47	—	—	—
'99	25	33	20	40	6¼	56	7¾	3½	40	49	—	—	—
900	27½	36	30½	54	6¼	62	8	3½	41	56	—	—	—
'01	26	38	30	53	6½	65	9	3⅜	39	52	—	—	—
902	27½	34	28	50	6¼	64	9¾	3¼	39	51	—	—	—
'03	28	33	21	39	6¼	64	9¾	3¼	39	54	—	—	—
'04	27½	32	16	33	6⅜	64	10¼	2⅞	36	51	—	—	—
'05	27	36	18	39	5⅝	64	11	2⅞	38	51	—	—	—
'06	30½	39	20¾	43	6⅛	64	11¼	3	40	55	—	—	—
verage 897-1906	26½	34½	21¼	42	6	61	9¼	3 5/16	39½	51½	—	—	—
'88-97	24½	36	19½	39	5¼	52	8¾	4½	40½	44½	—	—	—
'78-87	32½	40	23	46	6⅞	62	12½	6	47	47	—	—	—
'67-77	39	50	30	60	12½*	92	14	7¼	60	54	—	—	—

Index Numbers (or Percentages) of Prices, the Average of 1867-77 being 100.

	Palm	Olive	Seeds	Petro-leum*	Crystals	Nitrate	Indigo	Timber	Sundry	Materials	Grand
892	61	72	64	40	72	63	62	74	732	1,684	3,071
'93	72	72	69	32	62	66	76	71	753	1,704	3,064
'94	63	70	65	31	46	66	69	70	704	1,573	2,832
'95	59	72	64	48	42	59	59	69	719	1,570	2,794
'96	56	60	56	44	46	57	59	74	690	1,569	2,742
897	56	62	53	38	56	55	55	77	678	1,545	2,788
'98	59	64	59	41	59	55	48	78	698	1,596	2,881
'99	64	66	67	50	61	55	48	78	714	1,822	3,063
900	71	72	94	54	67	57	48	85	786	2,071	3,378
'01	67	76	92	52	71	64	47	80	782	1,881	3,158
902	71	68	87	50	70	70	45	79	786	1,851	3,129
'03	72	66	67	50	70	70	45	82	765	1,867	3,128
'04	71	64	54	49	70	73	40	76	737	1,875	3,161
'05	69	72	63	45	70	79	40	78	754	1,943	3,259
'06	78	78	71	49	70	80	41	83	815	2,168	3,472

* Petroleum as compared with the average from 1873-77 only.

IV.—*Roumania's Forty Years' Progress*, 1866-1906. By LEON GASTER.

THE present area of Roumania is about 130,177 square kilometres, and from the climatological point of view it is one of the countries which has extreme temperatures well pronounced. In the summer the heat rises to 35° Centigrade (95° F.), and exceptionally to 40° (104° F.). In the winter it falls to 25° below zero (– 13° F.), and in exceptional cases even as low as 30° (– 22° F.). The winters are long and cold, but as a rule abundant in snow. The spring is short, and subject to occasional frosts; the summers are warm, and often very dry, the pleasantest season being the autumn. The physico-chemical composition of the Roumanian soil is very suitable for pasture and agricultural pursuits, the north of Moldavia being more fertile than that of Muntenia.

Population.—The population of Roumania in December, 1899, at the last census, was about 5,956,900 inhabitants, but it is now estimated to exceed 6,500,000. The average excess of births over deaths is about 1·2 per cent., and under ordinary circumstances it is expected that the population may be doubled in about sixty-five years. The number of inhabitants per square kilometre of inhabitable area is estimated at 50. The urban population of Roumania is estimated to exceed 1,250,000. The principal towns are : Bucharest, with over 300,000 inhabitants ; Iassy, with 79,000 ; Galatzi, with 65,000 ; Braila, with 59,000, &c., and the rest, of 5,250,000, form the rural population.

The principal occupation is agriculture, in which about 60 per cent. are employed; about 10 per cent. are engaged in the manufacturing industries, about 5 per cent. in commerce, about 7 per cent. are Government employees and pensioners, and the rest are represented by the liberal professions and the people without any occupation. The arable area over which agricultural pursuits has been extended exceeded, in the year 1905, 15,500,000 acres; and, adding to this the area of the forests and gardens, it approaches 76 per cent. of the whole area of the country.

Among the cereals grown, *wheat* and *maize* have the most prominent places. In 1905, wheat was sown over an area extending 5,000,000 acres, with an average yield of a little over 7 hectolitres per acre (a hectolitre = 2 bushels 3·35 pecks). In the last forty years the area over which wheat was sown has increased by 150 per cent., and the yield by 461 per cent. The export of wheat in 1866 was about 238,360 tons, representing a value of 2,200,000*l.* ; in 1905 the export exceeded 1,716,000 tons, valued at 10,043,000*l.* The area on which maize was grown in 1905 exceeded 5,000,000 acres; the average production, however, has fallen considerably during the last few years. Amongst other cereals of importance grown in the country are oats, barley, rye, &c. The total export of cereals in 1866 amounted to 547,608 tons, and in the year 1905 it exceeded 2,650,000 tons.

In 1905, the vineyards extended over an area of 225,000 acres, from which over 1,800,000 hectolitres of wine have been obtained.

Prunes and plums grow over an extensive area, and they are mostly used for the manufacture of a national drink called " *tzuica.*" Of the whole arable area, about 34 per cent. is in the hands of farmers owning above 250 acres, and the rest has been exploited by small farmers; 50 per cent. of the wheat is cultivated by the big farmers, but 80 per cent. of the production of maize is in the hands of the small farmers. The value of the annual agricultural produce for the year 1905, which is considered as a good year, was approximately 36,000,000*l*.

Live Stock.—The live stock and trade connected therewith does not present to-day, for Roumania, the same importance as in the past, the value of the stock being estimated to-day at a little over 18,000,000*l*. On account of the prohibition of export of live stock over the frontiers of Austria-Hungary, this important industry was almost stopped, but a new impetus was given by granting a concession to an English Syndicate for exporting meat to this country, and much good is expected to be derived to the country by the proper working of this undertaking. With the decrease of this industry, attention has been given to a better utilisation of the available fisheries, and from the exploitation of these the Government now obtains a revenue exceeding 100,000*l*. per annum, which is increasing.

Forest Exploitation.—One of the important natural resources of Roumania is the extensive forests which cover the whole mountainous region and extend over an area of 6,250,000 acres, and of which 38 per cent. belong to the Government, $4\frac{1}{2}$ per cent. to charitable institutions, a little over $2\frac{1}{2}$ per cent. to the Crown Lands, and 54 per cent. belong to private owners. The exploitation of the forests is regulated by special legislation. The revenue derived by the State from the exploitation of the forests is constantly increasing, and last year exceeded 260,000*l*. The commerce and trade with timber is also considerably extending, amounting to over 1,200,000*l*. in the year 1905.

Petroleum Industry.—Another of the most important natural sources of wealth of the country is the oil fields. The sub-soil of Roumania is considered very rich in petroleum, but there are not as yet any data available for determining its true value, some estimating it to exceed 300,000,000*l*. The present exploitation, however, is limited to four districts only, of which the district of Prahova produces about 90 per cent. of the total output. Next in order are Bacau, Buzeu, and Dambovitza. The production has grown enormously. In the year 1866 only about 5,370 tons of crude oil were produced, in 1905 it exceeded 600,000 tons, and for the first six months of last year over 380,000 tons have been obtained. The capital invested in the petroleum industry exceeds 6,000,000*l*, of which the largest part has been imported the last year or two, mostly being German, Dutch, French, Italian, American, &c., and a small proportion English. Apart from the exploitation of the oil fields, there are also a few large refineries being erected, equipped with the most up-to-date apparatus. It is expected from the development of this industry that a large number of other auxiliary industries will be created, giving employment to a considerable number of the native population. The Roumanian Government owns a large area of petroliferous land, and endeavours have been made in the last few years to regulate this exploitation ; but, unfortunately, no practical solution has as yet been given. The matter is receiving, however, the most earnest attention of the Government and the country generally.

Roumanian Industries.—Opinions are divided as to whether it is possible for large industries to be developed in Roumania. The result of the statistical inquiry made in the year 1901-02 showed, however, that Roumania had then 62,188 industrial establishments, of which 625 belonged to the big industries, 54,405 to the medium and small ones. The total number of persons employed in this manufacturing industry is represented by 170,000, of which 40,000 are employed in the big industries and the rest in the medium and smaller ones. The capital involved exceeds 20,000,000*l.* The situation has, however, been somewhat altered of late.

According to latest statistics (see *Bursa*, 3rd-16th December, 1906, Dr. N. Paianu's Statistics) the big industrial establishments can be divided in three categories: Firstly, those establishments which benefit from the law of 1887 for the encouragement of home industries, representing over 64 per cent. of the total number ; secondly, those industrial establishments, like the flour mills and the breweries, which, on account of the abundance of the raw material they are using, which is found in the country, do not require particular privileges to be granted to them by the Government, forming about 25 per cent.; and thirdly, the industrial establishments owned by the State, forming about 10 per cent. of the total number.

The principal centres for the development of industries are the capital, Bucharest, after which follow the district Prahova, with the enormous petroliferous oil fields, Bacau and Neamtzu, with the timber trade, and Covurlui, mostly on account of the port Galatzi on the Danube.

In the *first-mentioned category* are to be found over 170 factories, comprising the saw mills, works connected with the metallurgical industries, glass manufacture, brick and cement. In these factories 10,990 persons are employed, and machinery is used with a rated capacity of over 8,310 h.p. The capital invested is 1,700,000*l.*, and the working capital about 1,360,000*l*, the value of the annual production exceeding 1,229,200*l.*

Next in order is the *textile* and *clothing* industry, comprising 49 factories, giving employment to over 5,500 workmen, using over 2,500 h.p. machinery. The capital invested is 561,800*l.*, the working capital 375,021*l.*, and the value of the annual production being 747,294*l.*

Third in order is the *food industry*, comprising 35 factories, employing 2,770 workmen and using machinery of 4,610 h.p. The capital invested is 1,064,189*l.*, the working capital 544,625*l.*, the value of the annual production being 770,212*l.*

Next is the *paper* and *paper pulp* industry; comprising 21 factories, giving employment to 2,587 workmen and using machinery of

4,783 h.p. The invested capital is 537,744*l.*, the working capital 226,848*l.*, and the value of the annual production is about 309,556*l.*

Last in this category is the *chemical industry,* comprising 51 factories, amongst which 23 are refineries for petroleum, employing over 2,260 workmen, and using machinery of 2,025 h.p. The capital invested is 657,750*l.*, and the working capital 771,600*l.*; the annual production, which is on the increase, is now exceeding 1,024,800*l.*

In the *second category* are those big industrial concerns which do not require to be encouraged by the State, like the flour mills, spirit refineries, and breweries. The flour-milling industry comprises 86 establishments, employing 2,218 workmen, using 11,027 h.p. The invested capital is 1,302,080*l.*, the working capital 805,040*l.*, and the yearly production 3,047,620*l.*

There are 28 spirit refineries employing 1,355 workmen, with 1,420 h.p. The capital invested is 510,644*l.*, the working capital 355,280*l.*, and the value of the annual production is 209,720*l.* There are 12 breweries employing 858 workmen, and using machinery of 1,426 h.p. The capital invested is 376,800*l.*, the working capital 168,320*l.*, and the annual production 194,620*l.*

In the *third category* the industrial establishments belonging to the State are 52 in number, in which 1,943,315*l.* are invested, employing 9,742 persons, and using 9,230 h.p., the annual production exceeding 3,368,960*l.*

In the aggregate the big industries utilise more than 50,000 h.p. The invested capital exceeds 8,574,310*l.*, and the working capital 5,702,510*l.*

The Government gives considerable encouragement for the establishment and development of industrial concerns, exempting manufacturers from many heavy duties for the importation of raw materials, machinery, &c., allowing also a great reduction on the rates for railway transport, &c.

Trade and Commerce of the Country.—The progress made in the trade of the country for the last forty years can very well be gauged by examining the import and export figures which are given for each consecutive five years since 1866 :—

Years.	Imports.	Exports.	Years.	Imports.	Exports.
	£	£		£	£
1866	2,857,170	4,660,014	1891......	17,467,307	10,986,483
'71 ...	3,317,089	7,107,311	'96 .	13,516,917	12,962,266
'76	6,637,340	9,410,251	1901.....	11,697,430	14,153,235
'81.......	10,990,298	8,260,732	'05 ...	13,501,519	18,284,055
'86...	11,859,894	10,221,890			

It is true that the commercial activity of Roumania for the years 1904-05 has been very great. The value of the exports was the biggest ever registered, the imports gradually decreasing. The value of the exports exceeded the imports in the year 1905 by nearly 4,800,000*l.*

Roumania imported in the year 1904-05 principally from the following countries : Austria-Hungary contributed with 25 per cent., Germany with 27 per cent., England with 15 per cent., France with 5 per cent., Italy with 4 per cent., Turkey with 4 per cent., Belgium with 2 per cent., and Holland with 1½ per cent. Fifteen years ago the imports were as follows : Germany stood at the head with 32 per cent., England came second with 26 per cent., Austria-Hungary came third with 16 per cent., France with 10 per cent., &c.

In examining the exports, we find that for the year 1905, Belgium took 32 per cent., Holland 18 per cent., Italy 10 per cent., Austria-Hungary 9 per cent., Germany 7½ per cent., England 7 per cent., and France 4 per cent. Comparing these results with those of fifteen years ago, the following change is noticed. In the year 1891, England stood at the head of all the countries with no less than 52 per cent., Belgium with 15 per cent , Germany with 11 per cent., and Austria-Hungary with 8 per cent. It must, however, be borne in mind that although Belgium heads the list, this is only on account of the fact that Belgium acts as a country of transit, from which the goods are afterwards distributed to Germany, Switzerland, &c.

The imports of Roumania consist mostly of textiles and all kinds of metals and machinery. The principal products of export are cereals, which represent more than three-quarters of the total value of exports from Roumania.

Railway Extension.—Parallel with the development of the different industries, the means of communication have also been gradually improved and extended. The first railway erected in Roumania was in the year 1869, about 43·5 miles in length, connecting Bucharest with Giurgiu; in 1876 it extended over 597 miles, and to-day the net of railway lines exceed 1,975 miles. The railway belongs to the State, and the cost of same is estimated to exceed 35,400,000*l.* There are 338 stations, and about 20,000 to 21,000 officials and labourers are employed. In the year 1876 the passenger traffic was about 742,000, in 1905 the number exceeded 5,500,000. The gross revenue of the railways for the financial year 1904-05 was 2,840,000*l.*; the expenses being 1,500,000*l.*, leaves a net revenue of 492*l.* per kilometre of line. In 1876 the revenue was only 153*l.* per kilometre.

Ports.—Attached to the railway service there are also large docks erected at the ports at Braila and Galatzi, and new docks are in the course of erection at the port of Constanza on the Black Sea, where, on account of the extended export of petroleum, large petroleum tanks are also being erected by the Government. On account of this port Roumania becomes accessible the whole year round.

Maritime Service.—Among the means of transport belonging to the State, mention must be made of the maritime service, consisting of 10 steamers, of which 5 are used for the transport of goods, running between Braila and Rotterdam, and 5 are used for the transport of passengers and goods, running between Constanza and

Constantinople, which route is now to be extended to Smyrna, and Alexandria in Egypt. The cost of the steamers is estimated at 600,000*l*.

Postal, Telegraph, and Telephone Extensions.—The postal service, which is maintained by the State, has also received considerable extension. In the year 1904-05 28,400,000 letters, 9,000,000 official stamped envelopes, 26,000,000 post cards, and 40,000,000 packets of printed matter were circulated. The length of the telegraph wires, which in the year 1856 was only 3,790 miles, had increased to 4,412 miles in 1876, and in the year 1905 exceeded 11,530 miles. The number of telegrams, internal and foreign, for the same year exceeded 2,250,000. The telephone service is spread all over the country, and direct communication between Bucharest, Braila and Budapest is now established. A submarine cable has been laid connecting Constanza with Constantinople, and this is to be extended to Bagdad and Basorah, forming the shortest route between Berlin and the Orient. A wireless telegraphy station has also been installed at the seaport Constanza.

Revenues and Expenditure.—The economic progress of Roumania stands in very close relation to the State finances. At five-yearly intervals the income and expenditure were as follows :—

Years.	Income.	Expenditure.	Years.	Income.	Expenditure.
	£	£		£	£
1866	2,362,139	2,731,457	1891......	6,814,151	6,484,674
'71.....	2,640,367	2,969,410	'96	7,923,409	8,589,619
'76........	3,245,787	3,961,870	1901......	8,101,710	9,471,734
'81........	6,171,182	5,122,097	'06.......	12,321,877	10,504,016
'86.......	4,979,135	5,198,865			

For the financial year closing on the 30th September, 1906, the income had exceeded the expenditure by 1,800,000*l*., which is the best on record.

In examining the revenues derived from the direct and indirect taxation, and that obtained from the manufacture and sale of tobacco, salt, matches, playing-cards, cigar papers, and gunpowder, which are Government monopolies, the taxation per head of population is estimated at 17*s*. 6*d*., or per head of family 3*l*. 18*s*. 2*d*.

Among other sources of Government revenue, apart from the above-mentioned taxations, there may be mentioned those derived from the lease of the Government lands, which are on an increase, and those from the working of the State railways, post, maritime service, &c.

The financial state of Roumania seems to be greatly improving lately. The budgets for the last five years ending 30th September, 1906, have been closed with considerable surpluses :

Years.	Surplus.	Years.	Surplus.
	£		£
1901–02..................	848,600	1904–05..................	259,000
'02–03..................	1,193,000	'05–06, up to 30th Sept.	1,800,000
'03–04	1,146,000		

which for the five years mentioned exceeds 5,350,000*l.* The surplus is, as a rule, used for carrying out works declared of special public utility, and requiring immediate attention. It is quite true that the Roumanian finances have not always been so prosperous, the income being mostly dependent on the results obtained from the harvest, and which is very variable, as can be seen from the consideration of the last eighteen years' budgets. In five years out of the eighteen the budgets were closed with heavy losses, and these years correspond with those of bad harvest. In particular this fact is noticeable for the financial year 1899-1900 when the deficit exceeded by 1,400,000*l.*

The next important items of expense are those of the Ministry of War, which come up to 1,800,000*l.*, representing about 18 per cent. of the total expenditure. It must be remarked that in this year there has been spent another 740,000*l.* to improve the armament, which money was obtained from the reserve fund derived from the surpluses. Next is the Finance Ministry, spending 1,500,000*l.*, representing about 16 per cent. of the total expenditure. For education and religious instruction, as well as religious service, 1,040,000*l.* is spent, representing 11 per cent. For extra school requirements and church expenditure there are special funds provided, from which large sums are drawn as necessity arises. In the year 1904-05, 240,000*l.* was separately spent from the Church fund. The Home Office service costs 800,000*l.*, the maintenance of school buildings and other dependencies of the Ministry of Public Works requires an expenditure of 180,000*l.*, the Ministry of Justice 215,200*l.*, the Ministry of Agriculture, Commerce, and Industry, 169,000*l.*, and the Foreign Office 71,440*l.* These items naturally vary yearly, but on the whole represents a fair average of distribution of expenditure.

National Debt.—In order to achieve the great progress referred above, the national debt had to be increased. In the following table figures are given showing for the ten-yearly periods the increase of the debt, and the rate at which the repayment of annuities has to be made :—

Years.	National Debt.	Annuities.		
		Interest on Loan.	Amortisation.	Total.
	£	£	£	£
1866	3,210,000	380,000	69,000	449,000
'76.......	20,621,000	1,054,000	560,000	1,614,000
'86	28,960,000	1,773,000	400,000	2,173,000
'96........	47,320,000	2,640,000	440,000	3,080,000
1906	57,742,800	2,446,200	869,800	3,316,000

Last year's repayment of 3,316,000*l.* represents about 38 per cent. of the total budget expenditure.

The interest paid on the capital borrowed varied at different periods, exceeding in some cases even 8 per cent. ; but now the greatest part of the loan has been converted into "*rentes*" of 4 per cent., with the exception of only 13 per cent. of the total debt, which is still rated at 5 per cent. interest.

The national debt has to be extinguished in a very short period, and in some of the years it will be extraordinarily heavy. In forty years, according to the present arrangement, over 50,000,000*l.* will have to be repaid. The present Finance Minister, Mr. Tache Ionescu, is therefore endeavouring to put the finances of the country on a sounder basis.

It may be interesting to know that there are several financial institutions in Roumania, among which, in the first place, may be mentioned the National Bank, an institution placed under the control of the Government, founded twenty-five years ago with a capital of only 418,000*l.*; now it has a reserve in gold exceeding 4,000,000*l.*, which represents 33 per cent. of the nominal value of the issued papers. There are other important financial institutions like the "Credit Rural," the "Credit Urban," &c., and also other banking houses, amongst which the "Bank of Roumania, Ltd.," may be mentioned as an English institution.

There is a growing tendency to develop industries in Roumania, for which purpose foreign capital and experience was, and is still, needed to be introduced. Special mining laws had to be framed for safeguarding the interest of the would-be investors, and a patent law was passed last year for protecting inventors. Amongst other reforms necessary the Roumanian Government ought to settle the position of its large Jewish population, which will have far-reaching consequence for the development of the trade and commerce of the country. With the administration of the law more independent of political influences, Roumania will be able to show continuous progress in the future.

For most of the data contained in this article I am indebted to Dr. L. Colescu, the head of the Statistical Department of the Ministry of Domains, who, it may be mentioned, has also prepared two figurative tables showing at a glance the progress made during the forty years, in ten-yearly intervals.

V.—CORRESPONDENCE.

To the Editors of the Journal.

SIRS,—The result arrived at in the paper by Mr. Harris and the Rev. Kenneth Lake, on the "Estimates of the Realisable Wealth of the United Kingdom, based mostly on the Estate Duty Returns,"[1] is so erroneous, in consequence of the wrong principle adopted with the Estate Duty Returns, that some notice upon the subject seems to be needful.

[1] *Journal*, vol. lxix, p. 709 *sqq.*

In the year 1905-06 the duty was imposed upon 62,845 estates, of the total value of 272,172,947*l*. The average value of each of these estates was therefore 4,331*l*. And as their owners must have been persons of all ages above 21, and possessors of property of all differences of value, this sum may be taken to represent a fair average. The question then is, what is the number in the United Kingdom whose estates will be subject to duty at their death? The answer to this is to be obtained, not from the duration of inheritance, or from the average duration of life, but from the rate of the annual mortality of the class. Among the general population this rate is about 17 per 1,000; but, as of course this includes all ages under 21, it may be considered to be unsuitable for the present purpose. A suitable rate may, however, be obtained from a paper published in the *Journal* of the Society (vol. xxix, year 1863) on the "Mortality in the Nineteenth Century in the Peerage Families." From the statistics given in that paper it will be found that the rate of the annual mortality among the Peerage families between the ages 21 and 95 was 18·391 per 1,000, or 1 in 54·289. Adopting this ratio, it will be found that the number of the class now under consideration at the beginning of the year out of whom the 62,845 deaths arose was 3,411,812, and the total value of their property, 272,172,947*l*. × 54·289 = 14,776,560,000*l*.

Or the same result will be arrived at by multiplying the total number of owners, 3,411,812, by 4,331*l*., the average of each property.

In the paper the value is given as 7,687,992,684*l*.

Yours faithfully,

A. H. BAILEY.

This letter has been submitted to the Authors of the Paper referred to, who make the following rejoinder :—

If we knew the total private wealth of the United Kingdom, we should only have to divide it by the amount passing at death in one average year, to ascertain the multiplier sought for, which multiplier would also convert one year's returns into the total private wealth.

We *do* know the private wealth in one or two forms of fixed property; and the principle that applies to the whole applies equally to a part.

Thus the total value of realty in land in Scotland may be ascertained by multiplying the averaged gross assessed annual value by the number of years' purchase used for computing the capital for death duties. This is within a fraction of 19 years. We take the statistics of Scotch land because it is more free from necessary deductions for mortmain than English.

The assessed income (average of eight years) is 5,928,000*l*., and thus the capital value is 112,600,000*l*.

But part of this capitalised value belongs to interests not coming to probate, and therefore not private property, such as religious, educational, and charity endowments, farms belonging to Royalty (where let), public parks, land belonging to proprietary companies, local authorities, &c., &c. Deducting from 7 to 8 millions from the whole for the value of the above, we have 105,000,000*l.* as the private wealth in Scotch land.

Turning now to estate duty gross realty statistics, and adding 2 per cent. for some Scotch landed property belonging to Englishmen, and included in the English returns, the total value in the annual returns (averaging eight years) is 3,656,600*l.* Dividing 105,000,000 by this sum we get 28·7 as our multiplier.

A similar calculation for England is more complicated because the deductions for mortmain (and for some Irish returns wrongly included) would be about 20 per cent. instead of only about 7 per cent. The larger amount lends itself more easily to error. Nevertheless we have calculated it, and it comes approximately to the same result. It will be found that if the above be read with our paper of the 18th December, each will prove the other.

If Mr. Bailey will examine the tables he will find that out of 100 insured lives 14 per cent. die between the ages of 21 and 40, whereas 43 per cent. die between the ages of 56 and 75 (equal periods). The average property of each of the latter is certainly more than twice that of the former. Between the ages he gives (21 to 95), the same property must often come to probate three or four times.

W.J.H.
K.A.L.

NOTES ON ECONOMIC AND STATISTICAL WORKS.

CONTENTS:

	PAGE		PAGE
1.—Edgeworth F. Y., Theory and		7.—Bastable A., Assurance Sys-	
practice of statistics	145	tems	147
2.—Bowley A. G. and Fax		8.—Sanger E. P., Inter-	
E., Employment statistics		pretation in economics	148
from the census	145		
3.—Flux A. W., Methods of		9.—Avebury Lord, Municipal	
statistics	145	and private trading	144
4.—Jevons W. S. and Fox		10.—Meyer H. R., Municipal	
A., Census	145	ownership in Great Britain	145
5.—Thompson E., Population		11.—Ashley P., Local and	
and its growth	145	central government	148
6.—Aston A., The census		12.—Page A., Protective and	
statistics of densities of pop-		preferential import duties	150
	146	13.—Other new publications	153

1.—*Theory and practice of statistics*, by F. Y. Edgeworth, reprinted in the Journal of Statistics.

The main object of the present volume may be regarded as being to give a detailed description of the basis and practical application of those modern statistical methods that are associated with the name of correlation and related.

NOTES ON ECONOMIC AND STATISTICAL WORKS.

CONTENTS :

PAGE

1.—Elderton (W. P.). Frequency curves and correlation............ 132
2.—Spencer (M. G.) and Falk (H. J.). Employment pictures from the Census 134
3.—Prinzing (F.). Handbuch d. Medizin. Statistik...................... 135
4.—Burkett (C. W.) and Poe (C. H.). Cotton 136
5.—Thompson (H.). From cotton field to cotton mill 136
6.—Lescure (J.). Des crises générales et périodiques de surproduction............................ 138

PAGE

7.—Sachet (A.). Assistance des vieillards 141
8.—Seager (H. R.). Introduction to economics. 3rd edit. 143
9.—Avebury (Lord). Municipal and national trading 144
10.—Meyer (H. R.). Municipal ownership in Great Britain ʀ.... 146
11.—Ashley (P.). Local and central government..................... 148
12.—Pigou (A. C.). Protective and preferential import duties 150
13.—Other new publications 153

1.—*Frequency-Curves and Correlation.* By W. Palin Elderton. Published for the Institute of Actuaries by C. and E. Layton, London, 1906. Price 7s. 6d.

" The main object of the present volume may be regarded as being to give a detailed description of the basis and practical application of those modern statistical methods that are associated with the name of Professor Karl Pearson." This sentence from the preface adequately describes the work before us. There must be many who have been deterred by the difficulty, inaccessibility, cost, and multitude of the papers in scientific journals relating to the mathematical treatment of statistics, from pursuing a subject which can be made useful, simple, and attractive in the hands of an exponent, who has mastered the originals and has the gifts of clearness and conciseness. So far as the family of curves,

$$\frac{1}{y} \cdot \frac{dy}{dx} = \frac{a + x}{b_0 + b_1 x + b_2 x^2},$$ is concerned, Mr. Elderton is such an

exponent. He explains the general idea of frequency distributions, describes with numerical detail the method of fitting by moments, follows Professor Pearson's analysis of the seven types to which the family of curves just named belong, and gives fully worked examples (drawn exclusively from actuarial data) of fitting each type to a statistical table. This occupies the first and largest part of the book.

Apart from the convenience of the book, the most notable achievement in Part I is this selection of practical examples from well known statistical sources to illustrate the use and meaning of the curves. The fitting, as is shown on p. 144, is remarkably close. We should, however, have been glad to know whether the examples are the survival of the fittest, resulting from the rejection

of other less amenable groups.   Is this family of curves all-sufficing ?
Quite rightly, in accordance with the intention of the book, no
theoretic justification of the equation is given, and the short analysis
(pp. 36 and 37) leading to the "hypergeometrical series" is very thin.
These equations are allowed to rest on a frankly empirical basis;
as a fact, with four constants at disposal, the curves of this family
do fit closely very many and diverse statistical groups, they serve
as graduation formulæ, and the constants can be chosen and the
numerical values calculated on a systematic and not very laborious
basis.

Part II deals with correlation, probable errors, and tests of
goodness of fit.   The author warns us that it is more difficult than
Part I, and we regret that it has not either been simplified by
omitting proofs throughout but explaining applications, or been
completed by more systematic and rigorous analysis with less
appeal to authority.   Readers who are able to follow the analysis
of the formula for the correlation coefficient, reproduced from
Professor Karl Pearson's third communication, will not be satisfied
with such a statement as "it is often sufficient to assume that the
probable error by the [formula based on four partitions] will be
three times that by the formula $\cdot 67449 \dfrac{1 - r^2}{\sigma n}$"; while others would
be easily satisfied by Mr. Yule's analysis (*Journal of the Royal
Statistical Society*, vol. lx), which is also reproduced in a modified
form.   This is, however, a matter of opinion, and need not prevent
any judicious reader from tackling the whole book; nor will the
fact that the applications and to some extent the language are
based on actuarial ideas prevent students with other statistical
interests deriving great profit from the clear presentment of
difficult formulæ.

It is to be regretted that the author has confined himself so
exclusively to one family of curves and one method, without more
acknowledgment of the many important and practical methods of
analysing and testing the significance of statistics, which are based
on the pure theory of chance and cannot be reached on the lines of
this book.   A short descriptive chapter would have been enough
to show that the "hypergeometric series" was not the only contribution of mathematics to statistics, and to direct the student to
other paths of analysis.   As it is "Alternative Systems of Frequency-Curves" are relegated to a somewhat unsatisfactory
appendix of three pages.   Here Professor Edgeworth's method of
translation is not quite correctly described, and the curves given
by Professors Charlier and Edgeworth (which are not the same)
are confounded; while the fact that the theoretical basis of the
generalised law of error assigns the limits within which successive
approximations may be expected to hold is lost sight of.   Again,
the "median," which has many practical uses, is dismissed very
summarily in the Introduction (p. viii).

To speak of some matters of detail :—We are sorry not to see
Professor Charlier's useful method of calculating moments with
tests of accuracy reproduced rather than Mr. Hardy's (p. 20).   On

pp. 30—33 a means of fitting parabolic formulæ by moments is given, which will be of use in smoothing a short range of values. Mr. Sheppard's adjustments are given considerable prominence, but the proof of them is not complete, for it depends on an unverified assumption on p. 25. There is not much discussion of the method of dealing with statistics which are known over only part of their actual range, a very difficult and important problem. We are not inclined to admit, as is implied on p. 132, that a deviation of two or three times the probable error is sufficient evidence that a particular case does not belong to a given group ; three times the modulus, or six times the probable error, is a more reasonable exaction. In the excellent chapter on the goodness of fit, we miss the rough test of percentage misfit. The refined method, reproduced from Professor Karl Pearson's well known paper, is not applicable to many of the crude cases which actually occur, when the observations or items are not independent of each other. An equation may be a very useful summary of a table, and have a correct theoretical basis, even though the test discussed would lead to its rejection.

Though we are not in complete agreement with the author on all points, yet these remarks must not be taken in depreciation of the value of the book. There can be nothing but praise for the work within the limits that it is intended to cover.   A.L.B.

2.—*Employment Pictures from the Census.* By M. G. Spencer and H. J. Falk, M.A., with a Preface by Professor C. S. Loch, D.C.L. London : P. S. King and Son. Price 2*s.* 6*d.*

It is not to be supposed that people in general will ever take more than a perfunctory interest in the results of the census, but there are no doubt many persons who have occasion to consider the relative importance of places and industries, without possessing the time and knowledge necessary for reference to the census volumes. To these this admirable little book will be a welcome aid. The main facts of occupation and sex and age-distribution are set forth in tabular and graphical form for each of the boroughs of London. One series of diagrams shows the relative importance of occupations in each metropolitan borough, another the relative numerical importance of the borough to each occupation, so that at a glance it can be seen, for example, that workers in precious metals are concentrated in Islington and St. Pancras, while furniture makers are distributed in Stepney, Shoreditch, Bethnal Green, Hackney, Islington and St. Pancras, but form a larger proportion of the population of Stepney than of the other boroughs. The roughness of the census classification must, however, be borne in mind. Diagrams need very careful interpretation ; thus in Diagram LIX it appears that 72 per cent. of "retired and unoccupied" males are between 10 and 20 years of age, but only 22 per cent. of similarly described females are in that age-group ; if readers can see that this follows from the greater proportion of females than males of all ages that are unoccupied, they are probably safe from the more obvious pitfalls.

The graphic presentation is wonderfully clear considering the small size of the figures and the multitude of detail; but two methods of elucidation have been ignored. Three colours, red, blue and black (each combined with white), are used, but apparently at haphazard. Why was not the black used for absolute numbers, and red and blue reserved for relative proportions, the former for males and the latter for females? Circles are used extensively and correctly for relative proportions, but they are all of the same size. It would have been possible in many, but not in all, cases to have made the areas of the circles proportional to the absolute numbers, at the same time that the sectional divisions were kept for the proportions. The authors of the booklet are respectively secretary and treasurer of the Central Bureau for the Employment of Women.

A.L.B.

3.—*Handbuch der Medizinischen Statistik.* Von Dr. Med. Friedrich Prinzing. 559 pp. Jena: Gustav Fischer, 1906. Price 15 marks.

This is a systematic treatise, giving the more important methods and results of medical statistics, or what is more usually known in this country as vital statistics. An introductory chapter deals with the materials and methods employed. There is nothing specially novel in this chapter; and the author, although he rightly emphasises the importance of subdividing death-rates, &c., into groups according to age, does not describe the methods of obtaining comparable "corrected" death-rates for all ages together, with which we have been made familiar by the Annual Summaries of the Registrar-General of England.

In the first section birth statistics are considered; and it does not increase one's pride in English statistics to find that for many of the problems connected with natality English data are entirely lacking. In nearly every European country except the United Kingdom the percentage which still-births form of total births can be given. It varies from 2·2 in Hungary and 2·5 in Sweden to 4·5 in Belgium and 4·6 in France. It has to be noted, however, that the methods and extent of registration of still-births differ in various countries. Statistics as to multiple births are similarly absent from English returns. In other countries they vary from 8·7 per cent. of the total births up to 14·7 per cent. in Finland.

In the second section valuable statistics are given as to sickness and accidents in different occupations, among school children, &c., while elaborate chapters deal with the statistics of insanity, blindness, prostitution, and many other forms of disability and vice.

The third section is concerned with mortality statistics. Death-rates at different ages are considered, infantile mortality receiving very full consideration. Then the chief causes of death are enumerated, and international comparisons made respecting each of these. Mortality in relation to occupation is fully discussed, and the influence of various social conditions on mortality is passed under review. Thus, on page 449 is given a table taken from the Berlin Year Book, giving the proportion of deaths from phthisis, according to the storey of the house in which the patients died. In cellars the deaths from this disease formed 5·2 per cent. of all deaths, on the ground floor 15·1 per cent., first floor 19·0 per cent., second floor 22·0 per cent., third floor 20·3 per cent., fourth floor 18·4 per cent. It would be absurd to argue from these results that cellar dwellings are particularly good for phthisis. Before the crude figures can be accepted, one needs to know more about the conditions of occupation of each storey, and particularly as to the age and sex-constitution of the populations in each storey.

In the preceding brief survey we have merely indicated the lines on which the book runs. We venture to think it will be most valuable for reference for all those who wish to make international comparisons of vital statistics without requiring to trouble to refer to the original reports for each country. The work of international comparison is well done, and will save the student of medical statistics much time and trouble. A.N.

4.—*Cotton: Its Cultivation, Marketing, Manufacture, and the Problems of the Cotton World.* By Charles William Burkett and Clarence Hamilton Poe. xii + 331 pp. London : Archibald Constable and Co., 1906.

As one of the authors is Professor of Agriculture at the North Carolina College of Agriculture and Mechanical Arts, the reader will be prepared to find this work strongest on the agricultural side, and his expectations will be realised. Taken as a whole, it is a useful popular manual, largely descriptive, relating to all that concerns cotton from its growing to ultimate use, though manufacture is only just noticed, and occupies less than twenty pages out of a total of 331. The introduction is "Hail, the King"; Section I is entitled "King Cotton: His Realm and his Subjects"; Section II, "The Cotton Plant: How it Grows and is Grown"; Section III, "Marketing and Prices"; and Section IV, "Manufactures and By-products." The insertion of some account of the by-products is to be welcomed. The range of this part of the book may be suitably indicated by the headings of the chapters, which run as follows :—"Cotton Seed: Once an Outcast, now a Prince—Cotton Oil: The King Feeds as well as Clothes his Subjects—Meal and Hulls: King Cotton also Feeds our Flocks and Herds." In Section III the economic analysis of commercial functions is hardly more than skin deep: closer scrutiny is requisite before right judgments can be framed on the difficult question of the effect of "Futures." The book is made attractive by numerous illustrations and is full of descriptive detail, and escapes the dullness which such a work so rarely succeeds in avoiding. S.J.C.

5.—*From the Cotton Field to the Cotton Mill; a Study of the Industrial Transition in North Carolina.* By Holland Thompson. xii + 284 pp. New York: The Macmillan Company, 1906.

The group of phenomena examined by Mr. Thompson constitutes part of one of the most interesting events of recent times. The American cotton industry has of late experienced prodigious expansion, and the remarkable feature of the expansion is that it has been quite independently localised. The New England States were pre-eminently the Lancashire of America, but now North and South Carolina, Georgia, and Alabama possess an industry which dwarfs in magnitude those of many countries whose activities in the cotton manufacture are by no means contemptible. In 1880 the four States mentioned contained half a million spindles : to-day they hold, say, eight and a half millions, that is about as many as Germany and more than the whole of France, Russia, or India. In addition, the number of Southern American looms may be estimated at 200,000 ; that is again nearly as many as Germany possesses, and many more than are to be counted in Russia or France. This magnificent industry shot up hundreds of miles away from its ancient origins in the United States; and yet it is certain that if the same rate of growth had taken place in England, Lancashire and the vicinity would have held the whole of the new creation. The explanation is manifold. In Lancashire the industry is more organic, its parts being held in relation by the marketing centres of Manchester and Liverpool. A mill far away from these markets would labour under a severe handicap. In America the individual business is more self-contained : the geographical area covered by the industry has been too wide for the specialised commercial centre to evolve and thereby afford ground for the differentiation of the industry. Hence there was no absolute necessity for the new factories to appear in the New England States. The Southern States offered a comparatively virgin labour market, a local market to sell in (which owing to cost of transport could be almost monopolised) and proximity to supplies of cotton.

Mr. Thompson, who is well equipped for his work as a Fellow of Columbia University, has scientifically depicted in a most instructive volume the exploitation of one of these virgin fields, namely, that of North Carolina. Beginning with times before the war, he traces industrialism through domestic manufacturers to the present time. But the centre of gravity of his book is recent phenomena, and particularly its social aspects. " Social, religious, and political ideas are undergoing change. The gregarious instinct develops rapidly, and solitude, once no hardship, becomes unendurable. The religious ideas and organisation which served the rural inhabitant seem not so satisfactory to the factory worker . . . . Political unrest is not yet general, but in a few localities the workers are slowly becoming conscious of themselves. Feeble attempts to organise a Socialist propaganda may be seen. The labour agitator is at work. Those left on the farms are affected by the withdrawal of population, a part of which goes to the towns for employment in the various industries, and another part to invest its capital in trade or manufacturing rather than in agriculture. Both the Churches and the schools feel the loss. Neighbourhoods once attractive from a social standpoint are now lonely. On the other hand, the establishment of little towns in the fields and woods around the widely distributed mills affords new markets for farm produce. The wages for farm labour—for a long time either stationary or decreasing—rise because of the increased demand and the smaller supply, and improved machinery and more intensive farming are necessarily introduced" (pp. 5 and 6). Our author's conclusions are classified by himself into those relating to (1) the industry itself; (2) the employer; (3) the operatives and their dependents, and (4) the State as a whole. As regards those of group (1), a closer analysis would be possible, but in the space at his disposal, with his centre of interest otherwise placed, our author cannot be charged with remissness. "The manufacturers are not yet economic entrepreneurs. In most cases they were not trained in cotton mills, but entered the business after succeeding in something else. Some are shrewd and far-sighted, few are harsh and despotic. Their success has been due more largely to general business experience, and to tact in the management of their employees, than to wide knowledge of the cotton business" (pp. 272 and 273). As regards the operatives, we cannot venture to reduce Mr. Thompson's wealth of detail to a few phrases. The reader must be referred to the book, with the assurance that he will find in it lights to illumine the history of our own industrial revolution, "The State has not yet found itself; has not yet adjusted its agricultural philosophy to industrial conditions" (p. 278).   S.J.C.

6.—*Des Crises Générales et Périodiques de Surproduction.* Par Jean Lescure. 652 pp. Paris: L. Larose et Forcel, 1907.

This elaborate treatise is a valuable addition to French economic literature. The subject which Dr. Lescure handles with masterly ease and comprehensiveness is, as he states in his Introduction, both vast and complex. It involves, in effect, the study, from the commencement of the nineteenth century to our own day, of the economic history, not only of France, but also of England and of the United States, and, more recently, of Germany, in addition. It is a topic equalled by few and surpassed by none in social interest. A crisis, according to the felicitous definition given in this book, is the point of intersection between a period of excitement and a period of depression. Of the value of a full discussion of the causes, nature, and effects of crises, no doubt could be entertained by the scientific student; and Dr. Lescure has contrived by his skilful mode of treatment to render his essay attractive to the statesman and the man of business.

Nor is its appearance at this moment inopportune. Some twenty years have now elapsed since the publication of the well-known works of M. Juglar; and, as Dr. Lescure shows, that recognised authority was inclined to fix his attention too narrowly on a single special feature, which was a common or regular accompaniment rather than a cause of the phenomena to which he devoted his attention. The best contemporaneous work upon the subject is the product of the pen of a Russian writer, M. Tugan-Baranowsky, and to this book our author makes frequent reference, although he does not agree with all of its conclusions. The Russian savant, however, by contrast with M. Juglar, and others, has sought rightly for the cause of crises, not in the circumscribed area of currency and credit, but in the larger region of production. His history of English crises was based on original documents, and he has created a school of followers in Germany. But he confined his study to those English crises, and his book was published in Russian in 1894, and translated into German in 1900: while a considerable portion of the present volume is occupied with an account of the crisis which occurred in Germany in the latter year, and with the lessons both new and old to be deduced from the rich abundance of fresh evidence available in this connection.

As Dr. Lescure argues instructively in his full and exact history of the crises of the past, with the lapse of time the observation of such phenomena in England alone has required to be supplemented by the study of similar movements in the United States and in Germany in addition to those in his own country. And the significant circumstance that since 1893 America has been practically immune from the disturbing effects of crises, while Germany suffered in an especial degree from one which occurred in 1900, serves as a basis for the very interesting suggestion that in the development of Trusts an effective remedy may possibly be found for a malady for which the rudimentary imperfect form of combination offered by the German Cartels has proved an inadequate preventive. For this opinion some of Dr. Lescure's readers may think that he has furnished forcible rather than conclusive reasons ; but they will not dispute the originality of the idea, evoked by the marked prominence of certain novel features in the modern business world. If indeed his point be finally established, he has disclosed an unexpected beneficial consequence of developments which many observers have regarded as ill-omened and unwelcome, if they were not to be treated as the abnormal unnecessary results of exceptional local conditions.

Dr. Lescure's book is divided into an introduction, three chapters, and a conclusion. In the first of these three chapters a full review is attempted of the phenomena. After a historical study of the crises of the past from 1810 to the so-called "Baring crisis" of 1890, the crisis of 1900, which had not previously been examined systematically, is submitted to very close inspection ; and the significant conclusion noted above is drawn respecting the comparative effects of the German Cartels and the American Trusts. The consequence of the former apparently was to shift the burden of the depression following the period of exuberant prosperity from the shoulders of the stronger to the weaker. The Cartels themselves have not prevented the depression, and the movement towards closer combination in lieu of their looser kind of union has, on the whole, been stimulated. In the United States, on the contrary, the recurrence of alternating periods of excitement and depression, which looked like an established law of the business world, has seemingly been broken, and the action of the Trusts, steadily lowering the expenses of production, is, in Dr. Lescure's opinion, mainly, if not wholly, responsible for this welcome departure from old routine. For, according to his view, the "vera causa" of the depression consequent on the excitement is the impossibility of meeting a decreased demand by lowered costs of production without a diminution of profit which business enterprise organised on the older lines is unwilling or unable to sustain.

This ingenious theory is propounded in the second of his three chapters, where he examines with the same exhaustive pains as that bestowed on the historical investigation of the past the different causes suggested by different writers for the over-production which marks these crises. With a mind singularly open and alert he reviews the various theories advanced. He pronounces on their sufficiency or inadequacy with judicial calm; and, while he recognises the merits of the contributions they may make to the full solution of the problem, he is keen to detect and prompt to disclose their shortcomings or mistakes. Rejecting first the group of views which has attached exclusive importance to the phenomena of the circulation, whether in the form of the crude theory which fastened on the variations of the stock of metallic money in the world, or in the shape of the larger and yet inadequate notions associated with the advocates of the "currency" as opposed to the "banking" principle, or of the more comprehensive though still unsatisfactory ideas which would fix the scrutiny of the observer on the fluctuations of credit, he then proceeds to investigate the theories which have sought more correctly for an explanation in the phenomena of production, consumption and distribution.

Here what he distinguishes as "inorganic" theories have advanced a multiplicity of causes, while the "more organic" theories have, by contrast, been inspired by certain general guiding ideas, such as the tendency, emphasised by Ricardo, and afterwards, more extravagantly, by Henry George, of profits to fall as rent rises, or the notion of under-consumption on the part of capitalist or workman, or the more subtle conceptions propounded by Marx, or, lastly, the theory which finds anarchy and irregularity in the production of the "means of production." In some of these theories he discovers ingredients of truth mixed with preponderating additions of error, and especially in the case of the explanation mentioned last. He himself would here state the position differently. He would represent crises as due to the fact that a rise in the cost of production is unable to obtain compensation either in an extension of consumption or in an increase of price. This conclusion may perhaps appear to readers who have followed with care his minute criticism of other views unsatisfying, and he may seem to resolve the problem by describing the resulting position rather than by discovering the antecedent cause. But, as in other instances, so in this, the search for a satisfactory answer to a perplexing question may be an illuminating process, which becomes its own reward, by suggesting new points of view and revealing unsuspected difficulties in older tenets.

In the third chapter, where Dr. Lescure examines remedies, he certainly offers rich material for fresh consideration in his novel hint of the beneficial possibilities of trusts; although, apart from that stimulating suggestion, the other palliatives or preventives which he puts forward, such as the execution of public works, or the raising of the rate of discount, or the suspension of the currency principle, are familiar commonplace. In his conclusion he inquires carefully into the means of forecasting the approach of crises. His treatise, as a whole, is, we think, likely for some time to be considered the authoritative discussion of the subject ; and the pains with which the abundant material has been collected, the skill and care with which it has been arranged, and the freshness and lucidity with which it is presented to the reader, should secure for it this deserved position.   L.L.P.

7.—*Assistance des Vieillards, Infirmes et Incurables. Commentaire de la Loi du 14 Juillet, 1905, et des Règlements d'administration publique qui en assurent l'application. Contenant, en outre, les instructions ministérielles et les circulaires des 16 Avril et 18 Août, 1906. Par* Adrien Sachet, Président du Tribunal civil de Vienne.   vi + 327 pp. Paris : Librairie de la Société du Recueil J. B. Sirey et du Journal du Palais (L. Larose et L. Tenin, directeurs), 1907.   Price 7 frs.

The French Legislature enacted on 14th July, 1905, a law by which every Frenchman deprived of resources, incapable of providing the necessaries of existence by his labour, and either aged more than 70 years, or suffering from an infirmity or a malady ascertained to be incurable, should under certain conditions be entitled to assistance.   The bureau of assistance in each municipality is to prepare an annual list of the persons resident there who are entitled to assistance, and to specify the kind of assistance those persons require, and where it is an allowance in money, the amount per month.   An appeal against the decision of the municipal council on that list is given to any claimant or to any inhabitant ; with a final resort to the Minister of the Interior.   The monthly allowance in ordinary cases is from 5 frs. to 20 frs., but the assistance may take the form of maintenance in an hospice.   Charitable gifts may be received in aid of the revenue, and the State grants a considerable subvention.   Documents used for the purpose of the law are exempt from stamp duty and registration fees.

The present work of M. Sachet, whose previous treatise on the legislation relating to accidents to workmen has reached a fourth edition, is a commentary upon the above-mentioned law, designed to facilitate the task of those who have to administer it, and to illustrate the position held by it in social economics.   His own attitude towards it is one of admiration as an instrument of social progress, which will be honourable alike to the legislature and to the administration.   In an introductory chapter, he discusses the foundation and limitations of the right to assistance, the history of past legislation on the subject in France, its present position in England and other countries, and the preliminary proceedings which led to the passing of the present law.   The account given of the English system is very brief, occupying only a single page.

The body of the work is arranged under similar headings to those of the law itself.   The first heading relates to the organisation of the assistance, and defines the requisite conditions, the body granting it, the precautions as to residence, the legal remedies, and the departmental arrangements. The second relates to the admission of the claim for assistance; upon the application of the aged, infirm or incurable person to the local office, which reports to the municipal council, from whom there is an appeal to a cantonal commission at the instance of the Prefect, some of whose functions are transferred to a departmental commission; the final determination resting with the Minister of the Interior, on the advice of a central commission. The third relates to the methods of assistance, in public or private establishments, or at the homes of the persons assisted, to the monthly allowance, the manner of payment, the keeping of accounts, the selection of the hospital or other institution, the control of its administration, the selection of the inmates, and the method of meeting the expenses. The fourth relates to ways and means. The fifth to the competence of the respective authorities. It will be seen that a commentary on these complicated provisions was a matter of necessity, and that such a commentary, well executed, could not fail to be very useful.

As bearing upon the prospects of legislation in this country, there are one or two points which it is interesting to note. The first is, the smallness of the ordinary allowance. From 4s. 2d. to 16s. 8d. per month appears a very inadequate provision. A municipal council is not to fix an allowance exceeding the latter amount otherwise than in exceptional circumstances. Where it fixes an allowance between 16s. 8d. and 25s. per month, the grounds upon which the proposal is made are to be stated in writing, and the Minister of the Interior is not to sanction it without consulting the Superior Council of Public Assistance. The conditions of life are, however, it is explained, so variable, that the legislature has not fixed any maximum; but it has imposed on any municipal council which resolves upon an allowance exceeding 25s. per month the obligation of finding the money itself, without the assistance of any subvention from the department or from the State. The allowance, therefore, in all ordinary cases will probably range from the equivalent of 1s. to 4s. per week, and in exceptional cases may reach 6s. It is reducible by the amount of the private resources of the claimant, except that where those resources are derived from saving, as by the purchase of a deferred annuity, and do not exceed 2l. 8s. 4d., the reduction is not to be made; and where resources derived from saving do not exceed 4l. 16s. 8d., and the claimant has maintained at least 3 children until the age of 16 years, the reduction is not to be made. Where the private resources derived from saving do not exceed 19l. 4s., the reduction is to be one-half only. M. Sachet observes that the privilege granted to those who have maintained children extends to both the father and the mother, and to illegitimate as well as legitimate offspring. It would indeed extend to grandparents and adoptive parents, provided they had fulfilled the condition of maintaining the children during their first sixteen years of life. It works out as follows:—In a commune where the allocation of assistance is fixed at an annual sum of 60 frs., a person who, having maintained 3 children, had an income of 200 frs. derived from his own savings, would be entitled to an allowance of 20 frs.; for the first 120 frs. of his income would not be taken into account, and of the remaining 80 frs., only half, or 40 frs., would be deducted.

The law came into operation on the 1st January, 1907, and its working will be watched with great interest. It introduces two novel elements—the discrimination in favour of property acquired by saving, and the reward for maintenance of children. E.B.

8.—*Introduction to Economics.* By Henry Rogers Seager, Professor of Political Economy in Columbia University. Third edition, revised and enlarged. New York: Henry Holt and Co., 1906. (London : George Bell and Sons.)

The fact that this treatise has reached a third edition in less than two years is at once evidence of its popularity and practical utility, and a reason for not noticing it here at great length. Its general scheme comprises short descriptions of the growth of the modern industrial system in England and the United States (the chapter dealing with the latter being of special value to students here), a careful and detailed analysis of the abstract theory of consumption, production, distribution and value, and a series of thirteen chapters dealing with applied economics, *e.g.*, with money, tariffs and trusts. The whole is copiously illustrated with descriptions of existing methods and institutions, and the student will feel from the beginning that political economy is a practical science, with immediate application to everyday industrial life. None the less the treatment is thorough, modern, and (at any rate in general) orthodox. Perhaps one of the most masterly sections is that which deals with the productivity and exchange theories of interest, and shows that they are complementary, not contradictory. This "Introduction" is a very valuable first text-book for a mature student; for the treatment is not so diffuse or complicated as to cause danger of losing the main thread of the argument, which is frequently summarised, while at the end of each chapter are bibliographical references for collateral reading. Perhaps the principal value which English readers, acquainted with ordinary theory, will glean is in the chapters dealing with existing problems and conditions in the United States.

Statistics are used little, and in the one case where the argument rests on them, statisticians will not agree with the author. A cursory description is given of the method of index-numbers, and Falkner's and Sauerbeck's numbers are shown from 1860 to 1891 and 1899 respectively. The author remarks that "It would be unsafe to base any exact conclusions upon the price fluctuations indicated by the chart, because neither of the investigations whose results it records is free from errors. In fact, it is doubtful whether the statistical method has yet been perfected to a point which makes the exact measurement of the general level of prices, or the value of money, possible. All that is claimed for these investigations is that they reflect those general tendencies which were so marked as to overcome any possible margin of error in the calculations themselves." This is to damn the method with faint praise. The author appears not to have realised the extreme accuracy which can be obtained from the

the legi.
second ''
the appli
office, wl.
an appe.i
some of
mission :
Interior,
to the m
at the hon
manner (
hospital o
selection (
The fourtl
of the re-
on these
such a con
   As be;
there are (
first is, th
16s. 8d.
municipal
amount ot.
fixes an all
upon whicl
the Ministe
the Superi
are, howeve
not fixed (
council whi
the obligati
of any sub?
allowance. t
the equivale
reach 6s. It
claimant, ex.
as by the pu-
the reduction
saving do not
least 3 childre
made. Where
19l. 4s., the 1
the privilege
to both the 1
legitimate off-
adoptive pare.
maintaining tl
It works out ...
assistance is fix
maintained ^
own

...rable to the financi.. ...ospects of municipalities than
...ed by Lord Avebury. ...growth of municipal indebted-
...ulated to arouse m... ...ug in the breasts of much less
...iers; and it is diffi.ul: ...lieve that the credit of munici-
...rs has not already be. ...versely affected by the opinions
their financial wisdo.. ...ong those shrewd frequenters
whose hab... ...work it is to gauge the relative
..i investments. Th... ...rd ground, on which Lord
...ondemns municipal t... ...g. also suggests a real danger;
...es that "it will invol. ...nicipalities in labour disputes."
...e exerted at ele.ti... ...r electors who are themselves
...es of the publi. l... ...r or against the candidates for
..., of which they re... ...ir votes, has been for some
...monplace with cr... ...of State Socialism; and in
...fairs the peril is r... ...mminent, because the relation
...governors and the ... ...ed, who are also respectively
...s and the employe... ...ose
...ebury's fourth poi.t ...no in a sense a commonplace;
t and g... It is at any rate probable
attention will not be so
constant in a ty as in private business,
consequence " will be a loss, or the service
re." It is tr. the growth of companies of
...bility it becom. to say that in private
guarantee for red which is absent in
dertakings; and the m.re justifiable comparison must
de between salaried nd official bureaucrats.
illors may comman ces of experts no less
than shareholders or d.ctors; and yet it still seems
t the opportunity f. .eakage will be larger in the
.nd that the "working .sses" will, in Lord Avebury's
the greatest sufferers. b the relaxation of the stimulus
and attention. Nor lastly, is his fifth criticism
although here, once m.e, he may mistake what may
bly accompany for w.t must necessarily attend
.ndertakings. He say. hat this development, which
...ed or has occurred, is a .rious check to progress and
There is obviously .. .is inertiæ" characteristic of
which is often a hi... .e to innovation; and, while
..ev sometimes mean ...gression, it usually implies
.or is it only adheren.. ..old routine or fixed tradition
..e the obstacle; the ..icipality may itself be com-
...me method of produ. .n which is menaced by a new
may have embarked .. .me industry large quantities
..ich would be rende. .nremunerative or useless, if
.ndustry were allowe. ..ome into the field.
..i, are the five reasons w..h Lord Avebury advances for
.. believes that the ho... . of the working classes has on
.. delayed rather than ... .oted by municipal enterprise;
..he correctness of the l.. .keeping of municipal authori-
...nks that a profit i. .cen shown which would be

ratio of weighted averages, of which index-numbers are a conspicuous example. They reflect small and short-period fluctuations as certainly and with probably more numerical accuracy than long-period and great movements. It is true that they are not an exact measure of (the reciprocal of) the value of money, for they do not rest on the basis of all the goods on which money is spent; but they form a very sensitive and accurate barometer of price changes over the range to which they apply. Further references might well be given in the bibliographical note to more recent English writers than Jevons on the method and accuracy of index-numbers; and the figures should be brought up to date.

We notice that the item "Definition of Statistics" occurs in the index, and we are surprised on turning to the page indicated to find merely: "Where the phenomena to be observed are as numerous as they are in economics, induction may take the form of *statistics*. Individual instances of the same phenomenon are counted and the result given in numerical form." The book is not, however, a treatise on statistics, and we will not criticise this definition.

A.L.B.

9.—*On Municipal and National Trading.* By the Right Hon. Lord Avebury. vi + 176 pp 8vo. London: Macmillan and Co., 1907.

Within the compass of 170 pages Lord Avebury states the case against municipal trading with forcible directness. He makes no secret of the strong convictions which he entertains; and it is possible that opponents or bystanders may consider that in his anxiety to disclose defects and emphasise extravagance he may occasionally have strained his argument. He may seem unwilling to admit any qualification in the severe comprehensive censure which he bestows on developments in the direction of " commercial undertakings " essayed or contemplated by municipal authorities. Yet not a few of his most serious strictures seem deserved; and if he has overlooked the "pros," it is possibly not amiss that the " cons " should be set forth thus plainly and incisively before any further large extension of municipal trading becomes an irretrievably accomplished fact. There is, at any rate, no concealment in this book of the grounds on which Lord Avebury bases his assault ; and, should his readers think that he has established his main contention, they will not, we believe, pronounce the separate counts of the indictment trivial or irrelevant.

"The undertaking by municipalities of commercial business is," he says, "undesirable mainly on five grounds." Firstly, their present "legitimate" functions and duties tax their whole energies, and fully occupy their time. The description, furnished of the agenda paper of the London County Council, certainly affords a significant illustration of the mass and variety of work to which a conscientious councillor must perforce give his attention. Secondly, such trading will involve an "immense" increase of municipal debt. Even, when the distinction has been drawn between "remunerative" and "unremunerative" expenditure on lines more favourable to the financial prospects of municipalities than those adopted by Lord Avebury, the growth of municipal indebtedness is calculated to arouse misgiving in the breasts of much less strict financiers; and it is difficult to believe that the credit of municipal borrowers has not already been adversely affected by the opinions formed of their financial wisdom among those shrewd frequenters of the money market whose habitual work it is to gauge the relative security of investments. The third ground, on which Lord Avebury condemns municipal trading, also suggests a real danger; for he argues that " it will involve municipalities in labour disputes." The pressure exerted at elections by electors who are themselves the employees of the public body, for or against the candidates for membership of which they record their votes, has been for some time a commonplace with critics of State Socialism; and in municipal affairs the peril is more imminent, because the relation between the governors and the governed, who are also respectively the employers and the employed, is closer.

Lord Avebury's fourth point is also in a sense a commonplace; but it is both pertinent and grave. It is at any rate probable that the stimulus to economy and attention will not be so keen and constant in a municipality as in private business, and that in consequence " either there will be a loss, or the service will cost more." It is true that with the growth of companies of limited liability it becomes less possible to say that in private business a guarantee for economy is secured which is absent in municipal undertakings; and the more justifiable comparison must now be made between salaried managers and official bureaucrats. Town councillors may command the services of experts no less successfully than shareholders or directors; and yet it still seems probable that the opportunity for leakage will be larger in the former case, and that the " working classes " will, in Lord Avebury's words, " be the greatest sufferers " by the relaxation of the stimulus to economy and attention. Nor, lastly, is his fifth criticism inapplicable, although here, once more, he may mistake what may not improbably accompany for what must necessarily attend municipal undertakings. He says that this development, which is threatened or has occurred, is a serious check to progress and discovery. There is obviously a " vis inertiæ " characteristic of officialdom, which is often a hindrance to innovation; and, while change may sometimes mean retrogression, it usually implies advance. Nor is it only adherence to old routine or fixed tradition which may be the obstacle; the municipality may itself be committed to some method of production which is menaced by a new invention, or may have embarked in some industry large quantities of capital which would be rendered unremunerative or useless, if a competing industry were allowed to come into the field.

Such, then, are the five reasons which Lord Avebury advances for his view. He believes that the housing of the working classes has on the whole been delayed rather than promoted by municipal enterprise; he questions the correctness of the book-keeping of municipal authorities, and thinks that a profit is often shown which would be converted into a loss, if the particular undertaking were debited with its due share of the general expenses of administration, or full allowance had been made for depreciation; he maintains that railways under private management in this country compare favourably in facilities and enterprise with the State-managed railways of Continental nations; he argues that the departure from the approved maxim that "taxation should accompany representation" is made in municipal finance and is of serious omen. He does not wish indeed, as he states at the conclusion of his book, to be considered hostile to municipalities; but he is a convinced opponent of "municipal trading." There is perhaps a difficulty in settling the exact point at which the forbidden limits are transgressed, and it might be argued that in some cases at least the actual developments, which Lord Avebury deprecates, have been the result of a gradual extension along a course which has been proved secure by successive experience. But in other instances the pace may have been unduly precipitate; and the dangers which Lord Avebury announces have been forgotten or ignored. He has certainly made a contribution to the discussion which, coming from the source from which it proceeds, and expressed with the clearness and vigour displayed, was bound to command attention. L.L.P.

10.—*Municipal Ownership in Great Britain.* By Hugo Robert Meyer. xii + 340 pp., 8vo. New York: The Macmillan Company, 1906.

This book, the author states in his preface, is the second of a series of four. The general object of the series is to present the results of an examination into the "actual working" of the "public regulation and the Government ownership and operation of the so-called public service industries." These embrace the "railway, the telegraph, the street railway, the electric light, the electric power plant, and the telephone." The field of investigation has included the United States, Great Britain, Germany and Australia; and the period of time occupied in the inquiry has extended from the autumn of 1892. In the volume now before us special attention has been devoted to Great Britain, and in successive chapters the influence of legislation on the development of tramways and the application of electricity to industry is forcibly portrayed. The large opportunity for obstruction, which has been placed by the Legislature in the power of the municipal authorities, is demonstrated by abundant illustration, and the great influence wielded over Parliament by the organised combination of those authorities is shown by numerous and striking examples.

The author may not, of course, be free from bias; but he has spared no pains to acquaint himself with the facts which he sets forth, and he occupies the detached position of the external observer who is anxious to discern the true significance of what he is examining. His book consists, in the main, of detailed evidence collected with praiseworthy diligence and arranged in lucid order. The facts themselves do not seem open to dispute; and they spontaneously suggest the conclusion which is drawn. It is noticeable that Lord Avebury in a book upon Municipal Trading, also reviewed in the present number of this Journal, makes frequent reference to Professor Meyer's writings in support of his own argument; and certainly the plain unvarnished narrative related in this volume is not favourable to municipal enterprise.

It is, at any rate, not easy to dispute the thesis that legislation in Great Britain has hindered the development of street railways, and checked the progress of the electrical industry. A comparison of the means of locomotion provided in the cities of the United States and in those of the United Kingdom shows how far we are behind; and it is now generally acknowledged that the Electric Lighting Act of 1882 proved so serious a barrier to enterprise in that direction that in a very real sense electric lighting was brought to a "standstill" in this country. The Act of 1888, by extending the duration of the charters to be granted to electrical companies from the short period permitted in the earlier Act, did something to remove an obstacle which had proved, in fact, prohibitive of private enterprise; but it may be doubted whether the means still taken to safeguard the powers of purchase by the local authorities were not unnecessarily restrictive. Actual experience has unquestionably shown that the public interest may be injured, and not served, by imposing conditions to which private initiative will not willingly submit; and legislation may, with the most excellent intentions, defeat its object, if it extinguishes the possibility of earning a sufficient profit to induce the supply of the requisite capital, and to encourage the continued application of the desirable business capacity and inventive power. Professor Meyer shows that the drift of legislation in Great Britain has been in the direction of allowing local authorities opportunities, not merely of effecting an early purchase on advantageous terms, but of imposing onerous and costly conditions at the very outset; and he argues that the discretion given nominally to the Board of Trade by legislative enactment is in practice subject to the real interference of municipalities.

The result, he contends, has been prejudicial to the public interest. Progress has been delayed, enterprise has been diverted into channels where the impediments presented are less serious and frequent, the United Kingdom has fallen notoriously behind other countries, and the English people have been deprived unnecessarily of facilities they might under other conditions have enjoyed at an earlier date. In support of his thesis Professor Meyer quotes chapter and verse; and he who runs may read the moral of his treatise. For it can be seen between the lines of every page; and the cumulative force of the indictment is noteworthy. If useful knowledge is gained by "seeing ourselves as others see us," Professor Meyer's book will furnish Englishmen with the means of securing this advantage in connection with municipal ownership. Under the guidance of an acute and trained observer they are enabled to study the authoritative history of recorded fact. They may not in every case agree with the views formed by their investigator, but he possesses the strong recommendation that he is neither town councillor nor municipal elector. He does not conceal the character of his conclusions; but he reaches them by independent observation. If he be not credited with entire impartiality, he can hardly with justice be accused of being a blind or ignorant partisan. 　　　　　　　　　　　L.L.P.

11.—*Local and Central Government.* By Percy Ashley.

Students of the science of local government will probably find this book of considerable utility. Its chief value lies in its graphic description of the systems of local government existing in England, France, and Prussia, and their relations to the central government in each country. This description is followed by a history of local administration in each country, an arrangement which, while transgressing chronological order, will probably be found advantageous by the student. There is a chapter on the government of American cities; but the accounts of the European systems are more complete and more easily comparable, and will doubtless prove more attractive to English readers. The danger which besets any book of this kind—of lapsing into a mere enumeration of duties performed and services administered—is avoided with consummate literary skill, and throughout the author has succeeded in lending interest to a subject which is invariably considered an especially dry one.

In discussing the difference between the three systems, and endeavouring to trace their causes, the author has a more congenial task. National characteristics and traditions are well exemplified in the comparison he has instituted as to the relations of local governing authorities to the central government. He claims for England the greatest development of local self-government and the greatest freedom of local authorities from central control, though he does not regard this as an unmixed advantage. His description of the position and functions of the French prefects and the Prussian presidents, landraths, and burgomasters goes to the root of the national differences. All these officials nominally possess greater power and have to carry heavier responsibilities than the average local government official in England. But they probably exercise less real influence than the town clerks of the great English municipalities, and Mr. Ashley perhaps attaches too great importance to the office of mayor in this connection and too little to the office of town clerk. The difficulties of the prefects, presidents, &c., are due to the fact that they are officials of the central government as well as responsible for local administration, and it is always a difficult matter to steer a course between local opinion and central control. "No man can serve two masters," notwithstanding the superior method of the French and Prussian systems. There can be no doubt that the English plan begets far more public confidence. Instead of one great official, weighed down with manifold, diverse and even conflicting duties, we have in England part of those duties (viz., those in relation to the central government) omitted, and the remainder divided between the mayor on the one hand and the town clerk on the other, the mayor supplying the representative and the town clerk the official element. The prefect of the French

" Department" is, strictly speaking, more analogous to the chairman and clerk of the County Council than to the mayor and town clerk of an English municipal borough, but county councils, being bodies of recent creation, have not yet secured that hold on public imagination possessed by the older municipal authorities. There can be no doubt that the power, retained in so many instances by the central government in France and Prussia, to appoint and dismiss the officials responsible for local administration, must tend to minimise public interest in local matters. The extent of this interference on the part of the central government is probably greater in Prussia than in France.

Yet there is something to be said on the other side, and Mr. Ashley says it well. The central government in Prussia, knowing its power over local administration, has been able to grant to local authorities much wider and more general powers than those possessed by local authorities in England. Under the influence of enlightened and energetic officials, some Prussian municipalities have succeeded in raising local administration to a high pitch of excellence; and in the department of what is commonly, but not quite correctly, called "municipal trading" they are in advance of many English towns.

Perhaps the greatest difference between English and Continental local government is to be found in what Mr. Ashley calls "administrative law." In France and Prussia there are judicial tribunals appointed specially to deal with public administration, and in many respects public officials are amenable only to the jurisdiction of those tribunals. No tribunal of this character can be said to exist in England, where the law is administered by the same series of tribunals whether it affects a public official or a private individual. The nearest approach in England to the administrative courts of France and Prussia may be found in the Local Government Board, which in certain cases is empowered to determine disputes as to the powers and duties of local authorities.

Special sections are devoted to London and Paris, each of which is in many respects an exception to the general system. In the case of London, Mr. Ashley says: "It is not that the problems are different in kind, for the needs of the vast urban populations are everywhere the same, but their larger extent renders it practically impossible for all the administrative details to be dealt with adequately by a single authority." In the case of Paris, he ascribes the difference of treatment to the fact that "the French Government has always considered itself bound to pay special attention to the capital city and to spend money lavishly upon it; and, further, the history of the revolutions of Paris has made every government anxious to keep it under the closest possible control." It may be doubted whether either of these arguments is adequate as a reason for the unique treatment of these two capitals. The similarity of the problems to be dealt with being admitted, their larger extent only involves a larger organisation; and there is the greatest possible difference in principle between an arbitrary subdivision of a single community, however large, and the delegation (or "deconcentration," as Mr. Ashley calls it) of administrative powers and duties. The Municipal Council of Paris, subjected as it is to what is almost a veto possessed by the prefect, cannot obviously compare in authority or standing with the London County Council.

Much light is thrown upon many local government problems by a consideration of the system of " deconcentration," which Mr. Ashley describes as existing in France and Prussia, as compared with the decentralisation which is more the fashion in England. When a public body is overburdened with work in England, it is usual to transfer some of its duties to another body ; but in the French and Prussian systems the central authority meets the difficulty by delegation (and, if necessary, redelegation) of its powers, retaining the power of final decision in its own hands. In the great majority of cases it has no need to exercise it, reposing confidence in the action of subordinates. While we should not like to see a complete system of this kind set up among the many and widely differing communities of England, Mr. Ashley is more than justified in hinting at the utility of some " deconcentration " as a help to the solution of those local government problems which owe their difficulty rather to volume than to complexity. Decentralisation—the English system—as applied to London, has given us separate central authorities for (1) police, (2) fever hospitals and imbecile asylums, (3) water, (4) poor law administration, and (5) general local administration, without any practicable machinery for co-ordination or co-operation.

The book confines itself rigidly to its own subject. Local taxation and finance are not dealt with except incidentally, and as they directly concern the relations between the local and central authorities. It is, however, necessary to point out that the English Local Government Board has not such complete control of the work of the boards of guardians as might be supposed from the statements made in Chapter I. Boards of Guardians act on their own responsibility in many matters, including such an important point as the adminstration of out-door relief. The description of the metropolitan common poor fund, in the same chapter, also leaves much to be desired. Minor blemishes of this character are, however, almost inevitable in first editions of a work covering so wide a field. In a revised and extended form, this book will no doubt become the accepted text-book on the special subject with which it deals.

E. J. H.

12.—*Protective and Preferential Import Duties.* By A. C. Pigou, M.A., F.S.S. xiv + 117 pp., crown 8vo. London : Macmillan and Co., 1906.

In this small volume Mr. Pigou has, as he states in his Preface, " incorporated considerable portions " of two anonymous contributions to the *Edinburgh Review*, and of a signed article published originally in the *Fortnightly*. The readers of those papers will gladly renew their acquaintance with the subtle argument, which was their distinguishing characteristic, in the more permanent shape of the present book; and whether they agree or do not agree with the pronouncements on practical politics, from which the author does not refrain, they will allow that the theoretical exercises of so skilful a manipulator of the most modern elaborations of mathematico-economic analysis have deserved to be thus rescued from the ephemeral literature of the fiscal debate.

Mr. Pigou indeed is, perhaps, unduly sanguine when he declares that between the leading controversialists on both sides of that vexed discussion "there is no disagreement on broad economic matters"; and it may on the contrary, we suspect, be held by not a few, that it is by pushing down to the fundamental assumptions taken as granted by him and by other writers, that it is possible to throw grave doubt on the security of their conclusions. An illustration may be given. At the very opening of his argument, in the second paragraph of his first chapter, Mr. Pigou tells us that "presumably, if people prefer the roundabout process of obtaining certain goods by national production *plus* international exchange," they "expect by resort to it, to obtain more of the goods they want by a given expenditure of productive power." "In general," he says a little later, "what a person chooses as his immediate material interest is more likely really to be so than anything that a distant official, by means of a general rule, can hope to press upon him. Each person, therefore, if allowed to exchange as he will, may be expected to obtain a larger modicum of dividend than he would obtain if "managed" from above. The National Dividend is, however, the sum of the private dividends of the members of the nation. Hence it follows that the dividend of the whole community is, *prima facie*, larger when exchange is free than where it is subjected to impediments." A hostile critic would probably object to the employment in this reasoning of epithets or expressions which, he might contend, beg or at any rate prejudice the question. The plain man might fail to understand some of the terminology employed; but many modern thinkers upon politics would be likely to dispute the validity of the broad assumptions which, they would urge, lie beneath the surface of this kind of argument. The virtual identification of "freedom" with "administrative nihilism," the conception of government as an extraneous force coercing or compelling individuals who can emancipate themselves, if they please, from its disturbing influence, the notion that a community as a whole, whether in economics or in politics, is no more than the sum of the "members" of which it is composed, are at any rate alien to much recent thought. And it is not incorrect to say that such fundamental differences of view as these sever the reasoning protectionist from the reasonable free trader.

From the vulgar misconceptions and the crude ill-informed ideas, which are the exclusive product of the noisy ignorant adherents of neither side alone, Mr. Pigou is, as we should expect, immune; but he does not, we think, succeed in preserving even throughout the limited space of this little brochure a clear or strict distinction between economic theory and political practice. His strong political leanings appear to us at any rate to win an easy victory in the end over the laudable aim, with which apparently he starts, to hold the scales even between opposing views. He sometimes mixes what

belongs more suitably to occasional controversy with reasoning
which might be regarded rightly as of a more enduring nature.
His strictures, for example, upon certain statistical contentions may
not be undeserved, but they seem to be dragged by the heels into
the book rather than take an appropriate place in a continuous
argument.

An unfriendly reviewer, again, might detect a discrepancy between
the nice equipoise of the fine conclusions which Mr. Pigou reaches
as the result of a prolonged comparison of the different weights to
be attached to opposite considerations, and the large emphatic
inferences which he at once proceeds to draw respecting the entire
invalidity of certain particular opinions. He might be surprised,
for instance, to discover that Mr. Pigou allows a small balance of
advantage to result from preferential dealing with the Colonies on
the basis even of existing trade; but his gratification, if he were a
tariff reformer, would be immediately alloyed when he found that
straightway Mr. Pigou produced from a stock of weapons in reserve
the unqualified rejection of such proposals on other grounds. And
he might be disposed to agree more fully with the author in his
earlier than in his later mood when he noticed, among other reasons,
that to meet the expressed wishes of Colonial statesmen was considered more likely to promote dissension, and to cause disunion, than
to decline to give a favourable hearing to proposals thus put forward;
that the bonds of sentiment would, it appeared, be strengthened
and not weakened by disregarding aspirations which had been
avowed; and that the possibilities of the future could be satisfactorily dismissed with scant consideration. Mr. Pigou sometimes,
or even frequently, is prepared to make large concessions to his
opponents on what he styles the "formal" statement of an
argument, but in nearly every instance he proceeds without delay
to cancel these concessions by the commentary that in practice the
conditions necessary to the applicability of the reasoning have not
been, and are not likely to be, realised. These quick transitions
from one standpoint to another are calculated to confuse or even
to mislead; and with some justification may be disliked, or at any
rate suspected, by the ordinary reader.

He may, however, find more serious reason for complaint in the
severe nature of the discipline to which Mr. Pigou would ask him to
submit. For, when Mr. Pigou speaks of the "technical" statement
of a proposition, he generally means its expression in mathematical
language, and some of his reasoning is hard to follow. Mathematical economics, such as he favours, is, we fear, likely to remain
"caviare to the general"; and the plain citizen will continue to
doubt whether such refined discussions can contribute much to the
satisfactory solution of practical problems. It is, however, from this
high standpoint in the main that Mr. Pigou considers, firstly, whether
protective duties would injure the "national dividend," and, if the
answer be, as he thinks, returned in the affirmative, whether the
"national welfare" can nevertheless be promoted by such a policy.
These questions form the subject of his first two chapters. In the
third and fourth he deals with preferential duties, first with regard

to what he calls the " direct business question " of the advantage
or disadvantage which would result, and secondly, with respect to
the more general question which arises when, setting economics
aside, we turn to political and moral considerations. In this second
portion of his work he is necessarily less " technical "; but even
here he does not spare his readers. The professional economist
accordingly, we believe, is more likely to be interested in such
reasoning than the average citizen; and he will admire, without
reserve, Mr. Pigou's rare capacity for handling complex argument.
But even he perhaps may sometimes think that the smallness of
the final result could hardly be deemed a satisfactory outcome of so
much ability and pains, unless Mr. Pigou had sought, illegitimately
it would appear, compensation from other quarters than those
belonging strictly to the passionless realm of theory.   L.L.P.

13.—*Other New Publications.*

Avebury (Rt. Hon. Lord). Representation. Revised Edition.
90 pp., 8vo. London : Swan, Sonnenschein and Co., 1906. 1s.
  [1st edit., 1885; recommends a single transferable vote as a means for
  securing proportional representation.]

Baden-Powell (B. H.). A short account of the land revenue and its
administration in British India ; with a sketch of the land
tenures. 2nd edit. revised by T. W. Holderness, C.S.I. 262 pp.,
8vo. Oxford : Clarendon Press, 1907.

Bartholomew (J. G.). Atlas of the world's commerce. A new
series of maps, with descriptive text and diagrams, showing
products, imports, exports, commercial conditions, and economic
statistics of the countries of the world ; compiled from the latest
official returns at the Edinburgh Geographical Institute. Fol.
London : George Newnes, 1906-07.
  [Contains a " Description and distribution of commercial commodities " by
  W. A. Taylor.]

Bertillon (Dr. Jacques). Fréquence des principales causes de décès à
Paris pendant la seconde moitié du 19ᵉ siècle, et notamment
pendant 1886-1905. 8vo. Paris : Imprimerie Municipale, 1906.
  [Extracted from the " Annuaire Statistique de la Ville de Paris.]

Foster (Frank). Engineering in the United States. [Gartside
Report. University of Manchester]. 8vo. Manchester : Sherratt
and Hughes, 1906.
  [A practical description of mechanical and electrical engineering undertakings.]

Foville (A. de). La monnaie. 240 pp., sm. 8vo. Paris : Lecoffre,
1907.

Gonnard (R.). L'émigration européenne au 19ᵉ siècle. Angleterre,
Allemagne, Italie, Autriche, Hongrie, Russie. 8vo. Paris :
Armand Colin, 1906.

Guyot (Yves). Le commerce extérieur de la France en 1905, 56 pp.
8vo. 1907.

Heath (H. Llewellyn). The infant, the parent, and the State. A social study and review. xv + 191 pp., 8vo. London : P. S. King and Son, 1907. 3*s*. 6*d*. net.
[Advocates the systematic care of infants.]

Helguero (Fernando de). Per la risoluzione delle curve dimorfiche. 45 pp., diagrams, 4to. Roma : R. Accademia dei Lincei, 1906.

Kebbel (T. E.). The agricultural labourer : a summary of his position. 4th edition abridged, with a new preface. 8vo. London : Swan, Sonnenschein and Co., 1907. 2*s*. 6*d*.
[1st edit., 1870 : Now abridged in parts, but with amplified tables of wages, &c.]

[Kenny (P. D.).] Economics for Irishmen, by "Pat." 164 pp., 8vo. Dublin : Maunsel, 1906.
[An attack on Irish peasant proprietors.]

Lethbridge (Sir Roper). India and Imperial preference, with statistical tables. 8vo. London : Longmans, 1907.
[Recommends meeting the " Swadeshi " movement by Imperial preference.]

Martinez (Albert B.) and *Lewandowski (Maurice).* L'Argentine au 20e siècle. 2e édit. 8vo. Paris : Armand Colin, 1906.

Mayr (D. G. von). Die Bevölkerung Britisch-Indiens nach dem Zensus von 1901. 22 pp., maps, &c., 8vo. Halle a. S.: Gebauer-Schwetschke Druckerei, 1907.

Mombert (Dr. Paul). Studien zur Bevölkerungsbewegung in Deutschland in den letzten Jahrzehnten, mit besonderer Berücksichtigung der ehelichen Fruchtbarkeit. 8vo. Karlsruhe : M. G. Braun, 1907.

Moore (Harold E.). Our heritage in the land, with introduction, and scheme to provide work on the land for the unemployed, and to assist the creation of small holdings by State aid, by Sir William Mather. 2nd Edit. 8vo. London : P. S. King and Son, 1906. 1*s*. net.

Nicolaï (Edmond). Les valeurs mobilières. 40 pp., 4to. Bruxelles : Hayet, 1906.
[Enlarged from a paper contributed to the Bulletin of the International Statistical Institute, xi, 2, 1899.]

Pierce (Franklin). The tariff and the trusts. 8vo. London : Macmillan, 1907. 6*s*. 6*d*. net.
[A statement of the " flagrant wrongs " imposed by the Dingley tariff.]

Popplewell (Frank). Some modern conditions and recent developments in iron and steel production in America. . . . [Gartside Report. University of Manchester.] 8vo. Manchester : Sherratt and Hughes, 1906.

Pratt (Edwin A.). German *v.* British railways, with special reference to owner's risk and trader's claims. 64 pp., 8vo. London : P. S. King and Son, 1907.
[Discusses owners' liability in Germany, and declares the German system unsuited to England.]

Pratt (Edwin A.). Licensing and temperance in Sweden, Norway and Denmark. 8vo. London: Murray, 1907. 2s. 6d. net.

[Examines the Gothenburg system at work, and claims that it is ineffective.]

Schooling (John Holt). London County Council finance, from the beginning down to 31st March, 1907, made clear to ratepayers. 8vo. London: Murray, 1907. 2s. 6d. net.

Strachey (J. St. Loe). The manufacture of paupers; a protest and a policy. With an introduction by J. St. Loe Strachey. 8vo. London: Murray, 1907.

[Papers by various writers reprinted mostly from *The Spectator.*]

Sutherland (William). The colonisation of Scotland. 94 pp., 8vo. London: D. J. Rider, 1907.

[Shows the advantages of the Scottish model of land settlement.]

Wagner (Henry R.). Irish economics: 1700-83. A bibliography, with notes. 95 pp., 8vo. London: Davy, 1907.

Yermoloff (Alexis). La Russie agricole devant la crise agraire. 8vo. Paris: Hachette, 1907.

STATISTICAL AND ECONOMIC ARTICLES IN RECENT PERIODICALS.

United Kingdom—

Accountants' Magazine, 1907—

January—Some Points in Ranking: *Watts (James)*.

February.—Bankruptcy Reform: *Morton (W. Kinniburgh)*. Capital and Revenue Accounts: their Origin and Nature: the Genesis of the Double Account System: *Macdonald (James B.)*.

March—The Capital Expenditure of British Railways: its Conditions and its Critics: *Spens (Nathaniel)*. Machinery—Heritable or Moveable: *Scott (James)*.

Bankers' Magazine, 1907—

January—The Progress of Banking in Great Britain and Ireland during 1906: No. 1. Capital and Reserve Funds. Bank Reserves and how they may be Augmented (I): *Gibson (A.H.)*. Our Gold Reserves: *Schuster (Sir Felix*, Bart.). Stock Exchange Values for the past month and year.

February—Progress of Banking in Great Britain and Ireland during 1906: No. 2. The Increase in the number of Banking Offices opened. Credit and Trade. Banking Superannuation and Pension Funds. Cash Banking and Credit Banking. Bank Reserves and how they may be Augmented (11): *Gibson (A. H.)*. Gold Reserves: Speech by Mr. E. H. Holden, M.P. Australasian Banking Returns.

March—Bankers and the Gold Reserve Question. Bank Balance Sheets. Bank Reserves and how they may be Augmented (III): *Gibson (A. H.)*. Leading Bankers on Gold Reserves.

Economic Journal. March, 1907—The Congress of the Royal Economic Society. Inaugural Address to the Congress: *Haldane (Rt. Hon. R. B.*, M.P.). The Social Possibilities of Economic Chivalry: *Marshall (Prof. A.)*. Land Value Taxation and the Use of Land: *Trevelyan (Charles*, M.P.). The Proposed Relief of Buildings from Local Rates: *Cannan (Edwin)*. India's Present Monetary Condition. Cotton Supplies: *Chapman (Prof. S. J.)*, and *McFarlane (J.)*. Labour Exchanges and the Unemployed: *Beveridge (W. H.)*. The Economic Legislation of the Year: *Barlow (M.)*. The State and Small Holdings: *Winfrey (R.*, M.P.). Rural Housing: *Bray (Reginald A.)*. The Report of the Viceregal Commission on the Irish Poor Law: *Eason (Charles)*. Insurance against want of employment in Norway and Denmark: *Trier (Sven)*. Obituary—Lord Goschen: *Giffen (Sir R.)*.

Economic Review. January, 1907—Christian Education in Elementary Schools: *Temple (W.)*. Bournville: *Dale (J. A.)*. Economic Crises and some Aspects of Trusts: *Neurath (The Late Prof. W.)*. The Poplar Workhouse Inquiry: *Crosse (Gordon)*. Imprisonment for Debt: *Landa (M. J.)*. The Economic Position: *Fleming (Owen)*.

UNITED KINGDOM—*Contd.*
Journal of the Board of Agriculture, 1906-07—
December—The Decline in the Agricultural Population. Wheat Cultivation in Russia.
January—Report of the Small Holdings Committee. Imports of Agricultural Produce in 1906.
February—Agricultural Education in England and Wales. Cost of Producing Farm Products.
March—The Value of Poultry Manure.
Journal of the Department of Agriculture, &c., for Ireland. January, 1907—Irish Seed Potatoes in England. Flax Experiments, 1905.
Journal of the Institute of Actuaries. January, 1907—Opening Address by the President: *Wyatt (Frank B.)*. Model Office Reserves for Endowment Assurances: *Buchanan (James)*. Note on the Report of the Registrar of the Land Registry for 1902-05: *Hart (James R.)*. On the Error introduced into Mortality Tables by Summation Formulas of Graduation: *King (George)*.
Journal of the Institute of Bankers, 1907—
January—Our Gold Reserves: *Schuster (Sir F., Bart.)*. Bankers' Advances upon Title Deeds to Landed Property: *Campion (Bernard)*.
February—Bankers' Advances upon Title Deeds to Landed Property: *Campion (Bernard)*. Notice of Suspension of Payment as an act of Bankruptcy: *Barchard (E. H.)*. The work of the London Bankers' Clearing House during 1906.
March—Bank Balance Sheets: *Palgrave (R. H. I.)*. Bankers' Advances on Title Deeds to Landed Property: *Campion (B.)*. Stamping of Securities: *Perry (S. E.)*.
Journal of the Royal Colonial Institute, 1907—
January—"The Colonial Press": *A'Beckett (A. W.)*. "St. Helena": *Melliss (J. C.)*.
February—"Federal Tendencies in Education": *Sargant (E. B.)*. "A Link of Empire: The Royal Colonial Institute": *Colquhoun (Archibald R.)*.
March—Some Reflections on Modern India: *Robertson (Lieut.-Col. Sir Donald)*. "Rhodesia and its Resources": *Miller (Edward H.)*.
Journal of Statistical and Social Inquiry Society of Ireland. December, 1906—The Commercial Court: *Stanuell (Charles A.)*. Canals and Waterways at Home and Abroad: *Morris (E. A. M.)*. The Land Purchase Problem: *Johnston (W. J.)*. Proposals for a New Labourers Bill; an attempt to solve the Rural Housing Question in Ireland: *Synnott (Nicholas J.)*. Suggested Substitutes for the Present Poor Law System: *Dawson (Charles)*.
Surveyors' Institution. Transactions. Session 1906-07—
Part 3—The Improvement of our Woodlands: *Wood (Leslie S.)*.
Part 4—Some Notes on Sanitary Law: *Blake (E. H.)*.
Part 6—On the Ventilation of London: *Hudson (A. A.)*.
Part 7—On the Agricultural Holdings Act, 1906: *Spencer (Aubrey J.)*.

UNITED STATES—
American Journal of Sociology. January, 1907.—Industrial Insurance : *Henderson (Charles R.).* Factory inspection in the United States : *Herron (Belva M.).*
Bankers' Magazine (New York), 1907—
  December—Private Corporation Securities; Corporate Bond Types : *Deusen (Edgar van).* The Plans for Currency Reform : *Conant (Charles A.).* A Practical Treatise on Banking and Commerce; Security and Securities in General : *Hague (George).*
  January—Private Corporation Securities — Corporate Bond Types : *Deusen (Edgar van).* A Practical Treatise on Banking and Commerce—Security and Securities in General : *Hague (George).*
  February—Farm Mortgage Loans as Investments : *Deusen (Edgar van).* Trust Companies : their Organisation, Growth and Management : *Herrick (Clay).*
Bulletin of Bureau of Labor. January, 1907.—Free Public employment offices in the United States : *Conner (J. E.).* Laws of foreign countries relating to employees on railroads : *Clark (Lindley D.).*
Journal of Political Economy, 1907—
  January—Employment of Women in Industries: Cigarmaking : its History and Present Tendencies : *Abbott (Edith).* The Quantitative Theory of Prices : *Bolles (Albert S.).* Women in Manufactures : A Criticism : *Rubinow (I. M.).*
  February—Secretary Shaw and Precedents as to Treasury Control over the Money Market : *Patton (Eugene B.).* Labor in the Packing Industry : *Thompson (Carl William).* Ricardo and Marx : *Bell (Spurgeon).*
Political Science Quarterly, 1907—
  March—British Colonial Policy, 1754-65 : *Beer (George L.).* The Alien Contract Labor Law : *Orth (Samuel P.).* The Variability of Wages : *Moore (Henry L.).* Inflation and Prices : *Howard (Ernest).* Concentration of German Banking : *Schumacher (H. A.).* Philippines and the Filipinos.—A Reply : *Willis (H. Parker)*; A Rejoinder : *Le Roy (James A.).*
Quarterly Journal of Economics. February, 1907—The Taxation of Corporations in Massachusetts : *Bullock (Charles J.).* Capital and Interest once more : II. A Relapse to the Productivity Theory : *Böhm-Bawerk (E.).* Constant and Variable Railroad Expenditures and the Distance Tariff : *Lorenz (M. O.).* The Socialist Economics of Karl Marx and his followers ; II : *Veblen (Thorstein).* Labour Organisation and Labour Politics, 1827-37 : *Commons (John R.).* An Assize of Bread at Mobile, Alabama : *Scroggs (William O.).* The German Imperial Inheritance Tax : *Fetter (Frank A.).*
Yale Review. February, 1907—Government and Liberty : *Garner (James W.).* A German Solution of the Slaughter - house Problem : *Brooks (Robert C.).* Corrupt Practices connected with

UNITED STATES—*Contd.*
Yale Review. February, 1907—*Contd.*
the Building and Operation of the State Works of Pennsylvania : *Bishop (Avard L.).* Industrial Arbitration in New York State : *Groat (George Gorham).* British Legislation in 1906 : *Porritt (Annie G.).*

AUSTRIA—
Statistische Monatschrift, 1906-07—
November, December—Die stichprobenweisen Viehschätzungen : *Pfaundler (Richard)* und *Weyr (Franz).* Studentenstiftungen im Jahre 1905 : *Lorenz (Dr. Alfred).* Bericht über die Tätigkeit des Statistischen Seminars an der Universität in Wien, 1905-06.
January—Über eine bisher übersehene Quelle für agrarstatistische Forschungen : *Schullern-Schrattenhofen (Dr. Hermann).* Die Wiener Personentransportmittel in den letzten Jahren : *Bratassevic (Ed.).* Ansiedlungsverhältnisse und Viehstand : *Weyr (Dr.).*

FRANCE—
Annales des Sciences Politiques. January, 1907—A propos de " la question du sud " en Italie ; la Basilicate : *St. Piot.* Le commerce britannique en temps de guerre : *Savary (H.-R.).* Le cadastre et les livres fonciers : *Chaise (J. de la).* Les vicissitudes du peuple allemand (1848-70) : *Matter (Paul).* Chronique des questions industrielles (1906) : *Bellet (D.).*
Bulletin de Statistique, Ministère des Finances, 1907—
January—Les fabriques de sucre et leurs procédés de fabrication en 1905-06. L'exploitation du monopole des allumettes chimiques en 1905. L'exploitation du monopole des tabacs en 1905. Les revenus de l'État.
February—Le Budget de 1907. Loi portant fixation du budget général des dépenses et des recettes de l'exercice 1907. Projet de loi portant suppression des contributions directes et établissement d'un impôt général sur les revenus et d'un impôt complémentaire sur l'ensemble du revenu.
Journal des Économistes, 1907—
January—1906 : *Molinari (G. de).* Le marché financier en 1906 : *Raffalovich (A.).* Le mouvement colonial en 1906 : *Bellet (Daniel).* La mutualité agricole : *Bonnaud (Paul).* Contrat politique et contrat économique : *Rouxel (M.).* Une exposition internationale en faveur de la paix à La Haye : *Bolt (J. C.).*
February—La banque-route du socialisme scientifique : *Guyot (Yves).* Une industrie mal protégée : l'industrie de la soie en Italie : *Giretti (Edoardo).* L'entrepreneur, est-il un quatrième facteur de la production :. *Bellom (Maurice).* Mouvement agricole : *Molinari (Maurice).* Revue des principales publications économiques en langue française : *Rouxel (M.).* Lettre des États-Unis : *Tricoche (George N.).*

FRANCE—*Contd.*

Journal des Économistes, 1907—*Contd.*

March—Théorie de l'évolution : *Molinari (G.).* Le rachat des chemins de fer : *Nouvion (Georges).* L'impôt sur le revenu et liberté individuelle : *Revillon (Albert).* Mouvement scientifique et industriel : *Bellet (Daniel).* Revue de l'Académie des sciences morales et politiques : *Lefort (J.).* Travaux des chambres de commerce : *Rouxel (M.).* Lettre de Pologne : *Domanski (Ladislas).* Correspondance. Contrat économique et contrat politique.

Journal de la Société de Statistique de Paris, 1907—

January—L'apprentissage dans les métiers de l'ameublement : *Barrat (M.).* Rapport du Ministre de l'intérieur sur les résultats du recensement du 4 Mars, 1906.

February—Révision de la loi sur les pensions civiles : *Malzac (M.).* Les progrès de l'île de Formose sous la domination japonaise : *Meuriot (Paul).*

March—Mémoires sur les pensions civiles : *Malzac (M.)* and *Barriol (A.).* Chronique de statistique judiciaire : *Yvernès (Maurice).*

La Réforme Sociale, 1907—

1st January—Les " Jaunes " et les questions sociales : *Biétry (Pierre).* Le droit électoral féminin, en Languedoc, au moyen âge : *Roque-Ferrier (Alphonse).* Les jardins ouvriers de Beaune en 1906 : *Fontaine (A.).*

16th January—L'Anerbenrecht en Allemagne : *Fischer (Dr. Otto).* Les retraites ouvrières et le socialisme.—Réflexions d'un contribuable à propos d'un livre récent : *Kérallain (René).* L'école de La Paix Sociale.—La vie, ses œuvres : *Auburtin (F.).* Chronique du mouvement social.—Pays de langue anglaise : *Angot des Rotours (Baron J.).*

1st February—Patrons et ouvriers : *Roguenant (Arthur).* Les warrants agricoles d'après les lois des 30 Avril 1906 et 18 Juillet 1898 : *Hans (Pierre).* Le rachat du Chemin de fer de l'Ouest : *Rivière (Louis).* A propos de la dépopulation des campagnes et des logements ouvriers : *Blondel (Georges).* Chronique du mouvement social.—France, Belgique et Suisse : *Béchaux (Auguste).*

16th February—La supériorité de l'Asie antique et moderne dans la doctrine et dans les applications de la liberté de conscience : *Luzzatti (Luigi).* Les retraites ouvrières et le socialisme chrétien. Dernières réflexions d'un contribuable : *Kerallain (René de).* Une enquête sur les retraites ouvrières.—Questionnaire de la commission sénatoriale. Un peuple peut-il avoir une vie morale saine si l'État en élimine les religions ? : *Rostand (Eugène).* L'école-atelier d'apprentissage de la rue Vercingetorix : *Vovard (André).*

1st March—De l'origine paternelle du Pouvoir.—Une vieille controverse : *Etcheverry (L.).* La peur de l'enfant : *Bayard (M.).* Les sociétés anonymes et les réformes nécessaires : *Baugas (Paul).* Chronique du mouvement social.—France : *Béchaux (Auguste).*

FRANCE—*Contd.*

La Réforme Sociale, 1907—*Contd.*

16*th March*—Le Play et le Christianisme : *Imbart de la Tour (P.).*
Une enquête sur la Belgique : *Rivière (Louis).* Chronique
du mouvement social.—Pays de langue anglaise : *Angot des
Rotours (Baron J.).*

Revue d'Économie Politique. December, 1906—Une campagne
syndicaliste : les sous-agents des postes : *Girard (Pierre).* Les
grèves en Italie : *François (G.).* Le mercantilisme libéral à la
fin du XVIIe siècle. Les idées économiques et politiques de
M. de Belesbat : *Schatz (Albert)* et *Caillemer (Robert).* Chronique
ouvrière : *Rist (Charles).* Chronique législative : Documents
officiels : *Villey (Edmond).*

GERMANY—

Archiv für Rassen- und Gesellschafts-Biologie. January, February,
1907—Beweise für die Vererbung erworbener Eigenschaften ;
ein Beitrag zur Kritik der Keimplasmatheorie : *Semon
(Dr. Richard).* Die Sterblichkeit der Juden in Wien und
die Ursachen der jüdischen Mindersterblichkeit : *Rosenfeld
(Dr. Siegfried).* Normalität und Abnormität in der Sozial-
ökonomie : *Nordenholz (Dr. A.).* Die Abgrenzung der Begriffe :
Rassen- und Gesellschaftshygiene (und - biologie), Soziale
Hygiene und Soziale Medizin : *Elster (Dr. A.).* Die Militär-
tauglichkeit des russischen Volkes 1874-1901, auf Grund einer
amtlichen Statistik des Jahres 1903 : *Claassen (Dr. Walter).*

Archiv für Sozialwissenschaft und Sozialpolitik, 1907—
January—Der Untergang des englischen Bauernstandes in
neuer Beleuchtung : *Hasbach (Wilhelm).* Arbeiterbewegung
und Arbeiterpolitik in Australasien von 1890 bis 1905 :
Lux (Käthe). Der Entwurf eines Gesetzes betreffend gewerb-
liche Berufsvereine und seine erste Lesung im Reichstage :
Schulz (M. von). Stammlers "Ueberwindung" der materialistischen Geschichtsauffassung : *Weber (Max).*

March—Zur sozialwissenschaftlichen Begriffsbildung. II. Der
Stoff der Sozialwissenschaft : *Gottl (Friedrich).* Heimstätten-
rechts-Bestrebungen in Frankreich : *Grünberg (Carl).* Arbeiterbewegung und Arbeiterpolitik in Australasien von
1890 bis 1905 (Schluss) : *Lux (Käthe).*

*Jahrbuch für Gesetzgebung, Verwaltung und Volkswirtschaft
(G. Schmoller), Heft* 1, 1907—Ernst Abbes Sozialpolitische
Schriften. Ein Beitrag zur Lehre vom Wesen und Gewinn der
modernen Grossunternehmung und von der Stellung der
Arbeiter in ihr : *Schmoller (G.).* Das Rentenprinzip in der
Verteilungslehre. I. : *Schumpeter (J.).* Organisation, Lage und
Zukunft des deutschen Buchhandels : *Koppel (A.).* Wie kann
die Börse mehr der Allgemeinheit dienstbar gemacht werden ?
Von einem Praktiker. Organisation des amerikanischen
Bankwesens : *Stubbe (A.).* Über die Aktienform der Unter-
nehmung : *Gottschewski (A.).* Ulpianus als Statistiker : *Seute-
mann (Karl).* Bericht über die 26. Jahresversammlung des

GERMANY—*Contd.*

Jahrbuch für Gesetzgebung, Verwaltung und Volkswirtschaft—*Contd.*
deutschen Vereins für Armenpflege und Wohltätigkeit : *Munster-berg (E.).* Über Arbeitslosenversicherung und Arbeitsnachweis : *Oldenberg (K.).* Die Aussichten der vom Verbrauch ausgehenden Ordnung der Volkswirtschaft : *Gunther (E.).* Ethik und materialische Geschichtsauffassung : *Koppel (A.).*

Jahrbücher für Nationalökonomie und Statistik (Conrad's), 1907—
January—Ist die Grundrente in der Peripherie der Stadt eine "allgemeine Monopolrente" ? : *Pabst (Fritz).* Der Berliner Getreidehandel unter dem deutschen Börsengesetz : *Ruesch (H.).* England's wirtschaftliche Gesetzgebung im Jahre 1905 : *Brodnitz (Georg).* Die Entlastung der öffentlichen Armenpflege durch die Arbeiterversicherung : *Grunspecht (David).* Der Tarifvertrag im Deutschen Reich : *Neve (Oscar).* Ergebnisse der Volkszählung in Preussen.

February—Der Berliner Getreidehandel unter dem deutschen Börsengesetz (Fortsetzung und Schluss) : *Ruesch (H.).* Frankreichs wirtschaftliche Gesetzgebung im Jahre 1905 : *Gehrig (Hans).* Die notwendigen Aenderungen unseres Etats-, Kassen- und Rechnungswesens : *Loeffler (—).* Das Postbankwesen : *Kräiner (G.).*

March—Der Stand der Statistik der Bevölkerungsbewegung im Deutschen Reiche und die Hauptzüge der Bevölkerungsentwickelung in den letzten 15 Jahren : *Seutemann (Karl).* Zur Methode der Wirtschaftswissenschaft bei D. Ricardo : *Lifschitz (F.).* Die heutige amerikanische Trustform und ihre Anwendbarkeit in Deutschland : *Liefmann (Robert).* Die wirtschaftliche Gesetzgebung des Deutschen Reiches im Jahre 1906 : *Hesse (Albert).* Die Entlastung der öffentlichen Armenpflege durch die Arbeiterversicherung (Fortsetzung und Schluss) : *Grunspecht (David).* Preisaufgaben der Rubenow-Stiftung. Die "Partei der Nichtwähler" : *Wurzburger (Eugen).* Sind die Einkommen- und Ergänzungssteuern richtig verteilt ? : *Bönisch (—).* Das indische Geldwesen unter besonderer Berücksichtigung seiner Reformen seit 1893 : *Arnold (A.).*

Vierteljahrshefte zur Statistik des Deutschen Reichs. Heft 1, 1907—
Anordnungen für die Reichsstatistik bis zum Schluss des Jahres 1906. Erntestatistik für 1906. Zur Statistik der Preise. Nachtrag zur Statistik der Reichstagswahlen, 1903. Die Ersatzwahlen. Die Selbstmorde in 1902 bis 1905. Seereisen deutscher Schiffe, 1905. Seeverkehr in deutschen Hafenplätzen, 1905. Die überseeische Auswanderung, 1906. Weinmost-Ernte, 1906. Eheschliessungen, Geburten und Sterbefälle, 1905. Volkszählung, 1. Dezember 1906.

Zeitschrift für Socialwissenschaft, 1907—
Heft 1—Zur Lehre vom Tarifvertrag : *Oertmann (Paul).* Bevölkerungstheoretische Probleme : *Prinzing (Friedrich).* Die Stadtgemeinschaft in ihren kulturellen Beziehungen. I : *Jastrow (Dr. J.).*

GERMANY—*Contd.*
Zeitschrift für Socialwissenschaft, 1907—*Contd.*
  Heft 2—Die religiöse Sanktionierung des Eigentums auf tieferen
    Kulturstufen : *Westermarck* (*Eduard*). Die Stadtgemein-
    schaft in ihren kulturellen Beziehungen. II : *Jastrow* (*J.*).
Zeitschrift für die gesamte Staatswissenschaft. Heft 1, 1907—
    Wirtschaft und Verbrechen : *Herz* (*H.*). Die Analphabeten in
    den Vereinigten Staaten : *Schultze* (*E.*). Die Entwicklung der
    Oberschwäbischen Zementindustrie : *Kehm* (*O.*). Die Organisa-
    tion des Medizinalwesens im früheren Herzogtum Nassau und
    deren moderne Fortsetzungen : *Seidel* (—.) Zur Reform der
    Volksversicherung : *Zwiedineck-Sudenhorst* (*O. von*). Ernst Abbe
    als Sozialpolitiker : *Hahn* (*G.*). Die Zukunft der deutschen
    Müllerei und die in Anregung gebrachte Umsatzsteuer für
    Grossmühlen : *Hempel* (—). Zur Frage : Haushaltungsbudgets
    oder Wirtschaftsrechnungen ? : *Bucher* (*K.*).
Zeitschrift für die gesamte Versicherungs-Wissenschaft. January,
    1907—Dr. Ferdinand Hahn. [Obituary Notice.] Die Bedeu-
    tung der beiden Berliner Internat. Kongr. für Versicherungs-
    Wissenschaft : *Emminghaus* (*Prof.*). Der IV. Internat. Kongress
    für Versicherungs-Medizin : *Florschütz* (*Dr.*). Der versicherungs-
    rechtliche Interessebegriff : *Hagen* (—). Die Gewinnbetei-
    ligung der Mitglieder grösserer deutscher Feuerversicherungs-
    Vereine auf Gegenseitigkeit : *Domizlaff* (*Dr.*). Das neue
    preussische Knappschaftsgesetz : *Hahn* (—). Das neue
    Versicherungsgesetz des Staates New York : *Broecker* (*Dr.*).
    Bedenken gegen die Haftpflichtgarantie - Versicherung :
    Serini (*Dr.*).

ITALY—
  Giornale degli Economisti, 1906-07—
    October—Per la difesa di un testo : La teoria del costo di
      reproduzione e la critica : *Berardi* (*D.*). Della obbiettività
      dell' economia politica come scienza : *Cossa* (*E.*). Statistiche
      agrarie; studio di metodologia statistica : *Fornasari di Verce*
      (*E.*). Cronaca (Le convenzioni marittime) : *Papafava* (*F.*).
    November—Applicazioni della matematica all' economia politica
      del prof. Vilfredo Pareto (Traduzione dal tedesco) :
      Sensini (*G.*). La statistica del movimento migratorio e il
      calcolo dell' aumento della popolazione : *Contento* (*A.*). Il
      patrimonio minerario dei comuni e la loro attivita economica :
      Tenerelli (*F. G.*). La periodicità nei fenomeni collettivi :
      Corridore (*Fr.*). Cronaca (Il nuovo fiasco degli sgravi) :
      Papafava (*F.*).
    December—Nuove polemiche sullo zucchero : *Giretti* (*E.*). L' au-
      mento di poplazione delle grandi agglomerazioni urbane in
      Italia durante il secolo XIX : *Raseri* (*E.*). Le popolazioni
      delle grandi città Italiane secondo il sesso e l' età dei loro
      componenti : *Mortara* (*E.*). I coniugati sotto l' età legale e il
      censimento 10 Febbraio 1901 : *Coletti* (*F.*). Cronaca (Per
      l'esercito e per la riforma tributaria) : *Papafava* (*F.*).

ITALY—*Contd.*

Giornale degli Economisti, 1906-07—*Contd.*

January—Sull' interpretazione e comparazione di seriazioni di redditi o di patrimoni : *Bresciani (C.).* L' inesistenza di plus-valore nel-lavoro e la fonte del profitto : *Cossa (E.).* La tensione monetaria in Europa, negli Stati Uniti d'America e l'organizzazione delle banche : *Spillmann (U.).* Il fenomeno migratorio e l' intervento delle stato : *Montemartini (G.).*

La Riforma Sociale, 1907—

January—La distribuzione della ricchezza secondo le antiche e le recenti dottrine economiche : *Tivaroni (Jacopo).* Trasformazione e riscatto del debito vitalizio dei comuni : *Gennaro (Giovanni De).* Per la verità sulle condizione degli ufficiali inferiori : *Alfiere.* Le condizioni di lavoro nelle risaie : *Spectator.* La previdenza all' esposizione di Milano : *Schiavi (Alessandro).* La riforma dell' imposta di ricchezza mobile : *Rocca (Eugenio Paolo).*

February—L' emigrazione interna e gli uffici governativi di collocamento : *Cabiati (Attilio).* Giovanni Botero, statistico ed economista : *Prato (Guiseppe).* La previdenza all' esposizione di Milano : *Schiavi (Alessandro).* La vittoria dei conservatori nelle elezioni germaniche nel 1907 : *Michels (Robert).* Il mercato finanziario nel 1906 : *Raffalovitch (A.).*

Rivista Italiana di Sociologia. September-December, 1906.—L' opera scientifica di Augusta Bosco : *Bodio (L.).* Origine e vicende dei popoli dell' Asia centrale : *Puini (C.).* Sociologia e storia : *Xénopol (A. D.).* Parallelismi psicu-demologici : *Marpillero (G.).* I movimenti migratorii nella popolazione italiana : *Raseri (E.).* Il metodo negli studi di etnologia giuridica : *Mazzarella (G.).*

SWITZERLAND—

Journal de Statistique Suisse. Lieferung 1, 1907—

Die Tilgungshypothek im Dienst der Landwirtschaft : *Näf (Ed.).* Mitteilungen über die Preise der wichtigsten Lebensmittel und anderer Bedarfsartikel, Nov. 1906 : *Zuppinger (C.).* Die geschichtliche Entwicklung der appenzellischen Gebäudeversicherung : *Merz (J.).* Vergleichung der Fleischpreise in 1893-1906 : *Zuppinger (C.).*

QUARTERLY LIST OF ADDITIONS TO THE LIBRARY.

During the Quarter ended 15th March, 1907, the Society has received the publications enumerated below. The titles are arranged alphabetically under the following heads:—(a) Foreign Countries; (b) India and Colonial Possessions; (c) United Kingdom and its Divisions; (d) Authors, &c.; (e) Societies, &c. (British); (f) Periodicals, &c. (British).

(a) Foreign Countries.

Argentine Republic—

Agricultura. Ministerio de. Boletin mensual de Estadistica y Comercio. (Current numbers). 1907
Agricultura. Plano indicativo de las Tarifas del Trigo, lino y maiz en las lineas de ferro-carriles ... 1906. Sheet .... } The Ministry of Agriculture

Bulletin démographique argentin. (Current numbers.) Fol. 1907 .... } The Oficina Demografica Nacional

Buenos Ayres (Province). Direccion General de Estadistica. Boletin mensual. (Current numbers.) 1907 .... } The Provincial Statistical Bureau

Buenos Ayres (City). Annuaire Statistique de la ville de Buénos-Ayres. 15ᵉ Année, 1905. 8vo. 1906 .... } The Municipal Statistical Bureau

Cordoba (Province). Anuario de la Direccion general de estadistica, año 1905. (Campaña agricola, 1905-06.) 8vo. 1906 .... } The Provincial Statistical Bureau

Austria-Hungary—

Ackerbau-Ministeriums. Statistisches Jahrbuch des k.k., fur 1906. (Current numbers.) 8vo. 1907 .... } The Government of Austria-Hungary

Arbeitsstatistischen Amtes im Handelsministerium. Mitteilungen des k.k. (Current numbers.) 8vo. 1907 ....
Arbeitseinstellungen und Aussperrungen in Österreich während 1905. 8vo. 1906 ....
Arbeiterverhaltnisse im Ostrau-Karwiner Steinkohlen-reviere ... Teil 2, Lebens- und Wohnungsverhält-nisse. 4to. 1906 ....
Arbeit. Bleivergiftungen in hüttenmännischen und gewerblichen Betrieben. Ursachen und Bekämpfung. Teil 5. 4to. 1907 .... } The Austrian Labour Department

Eisenbahnstatistik, Österreichische, fur 1905. Teil 1, Hauptbahnen und Lokalbahnen. La. fol. 1906 ... } The I. and R. Ministry of Railways

Mittheilungen des k.k. Finanzministeriums. (Current numbers.) La. 8vo. 1907 .... } The Ministry of Finance

Österreichisches Wirtschaftspolitisches Archiv (vormals "Austria"). (Current numbers.) 8vo. 1907
Post- und Telegraphenwesens. Statistik des Österreichischen, im Jahre 1905. 8vo. 1906 . ... } The Ministry of Commerce

Bewegung der Bevölkerung im Jahre 1903. Fol. 1906
Rechtspflege. Statistische Nachweisungen über das zivilgerichtliche Depositenwesen, &c., im Jahre 1904. Fol. 1906 ....
Rechtspflege. Ergebnisse der Zivilrechtspflege im Jahre 1904. Fol. 1906 ....
Sparkassen. Statistik der, für 1904. Fol. 1906 ... } The Central Statistical Commission

(a) Foreign Countries—*Contd.*

Austria-Hungary—*Contd.*

Unterrichtsanstalten.   Statistik   der,   für   1903-04.⎫
Fol. 1906 ....   ⎪   The Central Sta͵is-
Statistische Monatschrift. (Current numbers.) 1907 ⎬   tical Commission
Statistische Nachrichten aus dem Gesammtgebiete der ⎪
Landwirtschaft. (Current numbers.) 1907.............⎭

Bericht über die Tätigkeit des Statistischen Seminars ⎫   Dr. Franz   Ritter
an der k.k. Universität in Wien, 1905-06. 8vo. 1906 ⎭   von Juraschek

Bohemia.   Mitteilungen des Statistischen Landes- ⎫   The Statistical Bu-
amtes. Band 8, Heft 2, Band 10, Heft 1.   2 vols., ⎬   reau
8vo. 1906-07 ....⎭

Budapest.   Monatshefte des Budapester Communal- ⎫   The Municipal Sta-
Statistischen Bureaus. (Current numbers.) 1907 ⎭   tistical Bureau.

Belgium—

Annales des Mines. (Current numbers.) 8vo. 1907 ⎰   The Administration
                                                    ⎱   of Mines

Statistique médicale de l'Armée belge.   Année 1905. ⎫   The Belgian Govern-
La. 8vo. 1906 .... ⎭   ment

Tableau général du Commerce avec les Pays étrangers ⎫   The   Bureau   of
pendant 1904. La. fol. 1905 ....⎭   General Statistics

Travail.   Conseil Supérieur du Travail.   8ᵉ Session, ⎫
1906. Fasc. 1.   Travail des ouvriers dans les ports. ⎪
4to. 1906 .... ⎪
Travail.   Industries à domicile en Belgique. Vol. 8. ⎪
8vo. 1907 .... ⎬   The Belgian Labour
Travail.   Monographies industrielles. 14. Industries ⎪   Department
du papier. Fabrication et mise en œuvre du papier ⎪
et du carton. 8vo. 1906.............................. ⎪
Travail.   Rapports annuels de l'Inspection du Travail. ⎪
11ᵉ Année (1905). 8vo. 1906 ....⎭

Brussels. Rapport annuel. Démographie-Statistique, ⎫   The Department of
&c. Anneé 1905. 8vo. 1906.............................⎭   Health

Académie Royale de Belgique—
Bulletin de la classe des lettres... 1906. (Current ⎫
numbers.)... ⎬   The Academy
Annuaire. 73ᵉ Année, 1907.   8vo.   1907 ....⎭

Bulgaria—

Causes des décès dans les villes de la Principauté ⎫
pendant 1900. Statistique des. 4to. 1906 .... ⎪
Recensement des bâtiments dans la Principauté au 31 ⎪   The Statistical Bu-
Décembre 1900. Résultats du. 4to. 1906........... ⎬   reau
Recensement des Industries encouragées par l'Etat. ⎪
(31 Dec. 1904.) 4to. 1906 ....⎭

Statistique décennale du commerce extérieur de la ⎫   The Registrar-Gene-
Bulgarie, 1886-95.   La. fol. 1906 ....⎭   ral of England

Chile—

Estadistica criminal, año 1905. 4to. 1906 ....⎰   The Registrar-Gene-
                                                         ⎱   ral of England

China—

Customs Gazette. (Current numbers.) 4to. 1907....⎫   The   Inspectorate-
List of Lighthouses, &c., for 1907. 4to. 1907 ....⎬   General of Cus-
                                                         ⎭   toms, Shanghai

Cuba—

Boletin oficial de la Secretaria de Agricultura, In- ⎫
dustria y Comercio. (Current numbers.) 8vo. 1907 ⎪   The National Library
Provincia de Oriente. Memoria sobre el estado de la ⎬
Provincia ... durante 1904-05.   La. 8vo. 1906 ...⎭

Boletin oficial de la Camara de Comercio, &c. Año 1. ⎫   The Chamber
8 parts, 8vo. 1906..⎭

(a) **Foreign Countries**—*Contd.*

Denmark—

Annuaire Statistique. 11ᵈ Année, 1906. La. 8vo. ⎫
1906 .... ⎪
Causes des décès dans les villes de Danemark en 1892, ⎬ The State Statistical
1904 et 1905. 3 vols, 4to. 1893-1906 .... ⎪ Bureau
Marine marchande et navigation en 1905. 4to. 1906 ⎭

Egypt—

Comité de conservation des monuments de l'art arabe. ⎫
Exercice 1905. Fasc. 22. Rapports, &c. 8vo. 1906 ⎬ The Committee

Postal Guide. No. 30. 1907. 8vo. 1907 .... ⎰ The   Postal   Ad-
⎱   ministration

Navigation in Ports of Egypt and the Suez Canal. ⎫ The Statistical De-
Quarterly Returns. (Current numbers.) 8vo. ⎬ partment, Ministry
1906-07............ ⎭ of Finance

France—

Annuaire Statistique. 25ᵉ volume. 1905. 8vo. 1906 ⎰ The French Labour
⎱ Department

Agriculture. Ministère de l'. Bulletin mensuel de ⎫
l'Office de Renseignements agricoles. (Current ⎬ The   Ministry   of
numbers.) 8vo. 1907 . ... ⎭ Agriculture

Chemins de fer français. Statistique au 31 Déc., 1904. ⎫
Documents divers. 1ᵉ Partie. Intérêt général. ⎪
France. Algérie et Tunisie. 4to. 1906 .... ⎬ The   Ministry   of
Chemins de fer français. Statistique au 31 Décembre, ⎪ Public Works
1904. Documents principaux. 4to. 1906 .... ⎭

Commerce de la France. Documents statistiques ⎫
[mensuels] sur le. Janvier, 1907. 8vo. 1907........ ⎬ The Director-Gene-
Tableau Général du Commerce et de la Navigation. ⎪ ral of Customs
Année 1905. Vol. 1. La. 4to. 1906............ ⎭

Finances. Ministère des. Bulletin de Statistique et ⎫
de Législation comparée. (Current numbers.) ⎬ The   Ministry   of
1907 ... . ⎭ Finance

Monnaies et Médailles, Administration des. Rapport ⎫
au Ministre des Finances. 11ᵉ Année, 1906. 8vo. ⎬ The French Mint
1906 .... ⎭

Minérale, Statistique de l'Industrie, et des appareils à ⎫
vapeur en France et en Algérie pour 1905. 4to. ⎪
1906 .... ⎬ The   Ministry   of
Navigation intérieure. Statistique de la. Relevé ⎪ Public Works
général du Tonnage des Marchandises. Année ⎪
1905. Fol. 1906 .... ⎭

Recensement, 24 Mars 1901. Résultats Statistiques ⎫ The Registrar-Gene-
du. Tome 4. Population présente, Résultats géné- ⎬ ral of England
raux. 4to. 1906 . . .. ⎭

Banque de France. Assemblée générale des Action- ⎫
naires, 31 Janvier 1907. Compte rendu . . . 4to. ⎬ The Bank of France
1907 .... ⎭

Société de Statistique de Paris. Annuaire de 1907. ⎫ The Society
12mo. 1907 .... ⎬

L'Expansion française. 1ᵉʳᵉ Année. No. 1. Janvier ⎫ The Publisher
1907. 4to. 1907 .... ⎬

Germany—

Amtliche Nachrichten des Reichs-Versicherungs ⎫
amts. 23 Jahrgang. No. 1. Jan. 1907. 4to. 1907 ⎬ The Imperial In-
[Contains the Reports on Accident and Sickness In- ⎪ surance Office
surance for 1905.] ⎭

Binnen-Schiffahrt im Jahre 1905. 4to. 1907 .... ⎰ The Imperial Sta-
⎱ tistical Bureau

(a) Foreign Countries—*Contd.*

Germany—*Contd.*

Gesundheitsamtes. Veröffentlichungen des Kaiser- } The Imperial Health
lichen. (Current numbers.) 8vo. 1907 ... ... } Bureau

Handel. Auswärtiger, des deutschen Zollgebiets im
  Jahre 1905 Teil 1. Verkehr mit den einzelnen
  Ländern. Hefte 1—24. Teil 2. Darstellung nach
  Warengattungen. Hefte 1—6. 4to. 1906 .... }
Kriminalstatistik für 1904. 4to. 1906 .... } The Imperial Sta-
Seeschiffahrt im Jahre 1905. Teil 2, Schiffsunfälle, } tistical Bureau
  &c. 4to. 1907 ......
Vierteljahrshefte zur Statistik des Deutschen Reichs.
  (Current numbers.) 4to. 1907 ......

Bavaria. Gemeinde-Verzeichnis f. d. Königreich } The Registrar-Gene-
Bayern nach der Volkszählung 1 Dec. 1905. 4to. } ral of England
1906 ......

Prussia—

Zeitschrift des K. Preussischen Statistischen Landes-
  amts. (Current numbers.) Fol. 1907 ....
Brände. Statistik der, im preussischen Staate für
  1895-98. (Pr. Stat. 174.) Fol. 1906 ....
Heilanstalten im preussischen Staate während 1904. } The Royal Prussian
  (Pr. Stat. 198.) Fol. 1906 .... } Statistical Bureau
Ländliche Verschuldung in Preussen. Teil 2. (Pr.
  Stat. 191.) Fol. 1906 ....
Viehzählung 1 Dec. 1902. Ergebnisse der ausseror-
  dentlichen. (Pr. Stat. 185.) Fol. 1906 ....

Saxony. Zeitschrift des K. Sächsischen Statistischen } The Statistical Bu-
  Landesamts. (Current numbers.) 4to. 1907 ...... } reau of Saxony

Hamburg. Bericht des Medicinalrates u. d. Medicini- } The Registrar-Gene-
  sche Statistik des Hamburgischen Staates für 1905. } ral of England
4to. 1906..............

Almanach de Gotha. 1907...... .... Purchased

Deutscher Verein für Versicherungs-Wissenschaft zu
  Berlin. Satzungen, Bericht über das Jahr 1906, } The Society
  &c. 8vo. 1907 ....

Metallgesellschaft und Metallurgische Gesellschaft
  A.G. Comparative statistics of lead, copper, &c. } „
  12th annual issue 1895-1904. 4to. 1905 ....

Italy—

Cause di Morte. Statistica delle, nell' anno 1904. } The Director-Gene-
  Introduzione. 8vo. 1907 .... } ral of Statistics

Emigrazione e Colonie. Raccolta di Rapporti dei R.R. } The Commissioner of
  Agenti diplomatici e consolari. Vol. 2. Asia, } Emigration
  Africa, Oceania. 8vo. 1906 ....

Statistica giudiziaria penale per l'anno 1903. 8vo. 1907 } The Director-Gene-
Statistica industriale. Riassunto delle notizie sulle con- } ral of Statistics
  dizioni industriali del Regno. Parte 1. 8vo. 1906

Japan—

Sanitary Bureau of Department of Home Affairs. } The Registrar-Gene-
  Annual Report of Central, for 1902. 4to. 1906.... } ral of England

Mexico—

Anuario estadistico de la Republica Mexicana, 1904. }
  8vo. 1906 ...... }
Boletin de Estadistica fiscal. 1er y 2 Semestres del } The Statistical Bu-
  año fiscal de 1904-05. 2 vols. Fol. 1906 .... } reau
Censo y division territorial, 1900. Jalisco, Tepic, y }
  Baja California. 3 vols. La. 8vo. 1905.............. }

(a) Foreign Countries—*Contd.*

Mexico—*Contd.*
Boletin de Estadistica fiscal. (Current numbers.) ⎫
Fol. 1907 .... ⎪ The Director-Gene-
Estadistica fiscal. Datos relativos. (Current numbers.) ⎬ ral of Statistics
Fol. 1907 .... ⎭

Netherlands—
Crimineele Statistiek over het jaar 1904. 4to. 1906 ⎫
Jaarcijfers. Rijk in Europa. 1905. 8vo. 1906 .... ⎪
Loop der bevolking in Nederland over 1905. Sta- ⎪
tistiek van den. 8vo. 1906.............................. ⎪
Maandcijfers. No. 16. 1ᵉ maanden van 1906. 8vo. ⎪
1906 .... ⎪ The Central Statis-
Revue mensuelle du Bureau Central de Statistique. ⎬ tical Bureau
(Current numbers.) 8vo. 1907 .... ⎪
Sterfte. Statistiek van de, naar den Leeftijd en naar ⎪
de oorzaken van den Dood, 1905. 4to. 1906 . ⎪
Travail. Statistique du jugement des contraventions ⎪
des lois sur le travail et la sûreté des ouvriers en ⎪
1905. 8vo. 1906 .... ⎭

Norway—
Annuaire Statistique de la Norvège. 26ᵉ Année. ⎫
1906. 8vo. 1906 .... ⎪
Journal du Bureau central de Statistique. 23ᵉ Année. ⎪
1905. 8vo. 1906 .... ⎪
Aliénés. Statistique des hospices d'aliénés pour 1904. ⎪
8vo. 1906. (V—1) .... ⎪
Assistance publique. Statistique pour 1903 et 1904. ⎪
8vo. 1906. (V—20) .... ⎪
Assurance. Statistique de l'institution générale des ⎪
assurances des bâtiments contre l'incendie pour ⎪
1900-1904. 8vo. 1906. (V—11) .... ⎪
Assurances contre les accidents du travail. Statistique ⎪
pour 1895-99. 8vo. 1906. (V—16) .... ⎪
Banques privées par actions. Statistique pour 1905. ⎪
(V—14). 8vo. 1906 .... ⎪
Caisses d'epargne. Statistique pour 1905. (V—18). ⎪
8vo. 1906 .... ⎪
Commerce. Statistique du Commerce de la Norvège ⎬ The Central Statisti-
en 1905. (V—9). 8vo. 1906 .... ⎪ cal Bureau
Divorces et séparations de corps (IV—130). 8vo. ⎪
1905 .... ⎪
Ecoles professionnelles, 1902-05. (V-6). 8vo. 1906 ⎪
Etat économique des préfectures. Rapports pour la ⎪
période 1896-1900. (IV—106). 8vo. 1905 ...... ⎪
Finances des communes pendant 1902 et 1903. 8vo. ⎪
1905-06. (IV—127 and V—12) .... ⎪
Instruction publique. Statistique pour 1903. 8vo. ⎪
1906. (V—5).. ⎪
Justice criminelle. Statistique pour 1901 et 1902. ⎪
(IV—126, V—3). 8vo. 1905-06 .... ⎪
Navigation. Statistique pour 1904 avec appendice ⎪
pour 1905. (V—13). 8vo. 1906 .... ⎪
Péches. Grandes pêches maritimes pendant 1905. ⎪
(V—19). 8vo. 1906 .... ⎪
Population. Mouvement de la population pendant ⎪
1901 et 1902. (V—2). 8vo. 1906 .... ⎪
Postes. Statistique postale pour 1905. (V—17). ⎪
8vo. 1906 .... ⎭

(a) Foreign Countries—*Contd.*

Norway—*Contd.*

Prisons. Annuaire de l'administration générale des⎫
prisons, 1902-03. (V—7). 8vo. 1906 ....⎪
Recensement. 3 Dec. 1900. Aperçu général. (V—⎪
4.) 8vo. 1906 ....⎪
Recrutement. Statistique pour 1905. (V—10.)⎪
8vo. 1906 ....⎪
Sanitaire, Etat, et Médical. Rapport pour 1903.⎪ The Central Statisti-
(IV—128.) 8vo. 1905 ....⎬ cal Bureau
Télégraphes et Téléphones de l'Etat. Statistique⎪
pour 1904-05. (IV—129). 8vo. 1905 ....⎪
Travail. Situation économique et sociale des cou-⎪
turières à Kristiania, et salaires d'autres ouvrières⎪
en Norvège. 8vo. 1906. (IV—8) ....⎪
Vétérinaire, Service, et inspection de viande, 1904.⎪
(V—15). 8vo. 1906 ....⎭

Paraguay—
Direccion General de Estadistica. Boletin trimestral.⎫ The Statistical Bu-
Año 1. No. 2. 8vo. 1906 ....⎬ reau

Portugal—
Colonies. Estatistica do Commercio e Navegação da⎫
India, Macau e Timor, &c., ncs. 1901-03 e Resumos⎪ The Statistical Bu-
do movimento commercial dos 1890-1904. 2 vols.,⎬ reau
la. 8vo. 1906 ....⎭

Roumania—
Bulletin Statistique. (Current numbers.) 8vo. 1907⎫
Commerce extérieur. 1ᵉʳ trimestre de 1906. 8vo.⎪ The Statistical Bu-
1907 ....⎬ reau
Finances. Rapport à M. le Ministre des Finances sur⎪
le recensement fiscal de 1905. 4to. 1906...............⎭
Statistica . . . Anul 1. No. 4. Dec. 1906. 8vo.⎫ Mr. R. H. Rew
1906 ....⎬

Russia—
Annuaire du Ministère des Finances, 1905. La. 8vo.⎫ The Ministry of
1906 ....⎬ Finance
Agriculture. Récolte des céréales et pommes de terre⎫ The Central Statisti-
en 1906. Résultats généraux. 6 pp., fol. 1906....⎬ cal Committee
Agriculture. Year-Book of Department, for 1906.⎫ The Department
Part 5. 8vo. 1906 ....⎬
Prices of Grain at Ports. Return of (in Russian).⎫ The Ministry of
Sheets. (Current numbers.) 1907...............⎬ Finance
Kazan University. Bulletin of the. (Current⎫ The University
numbers.) (In Russian.) 8vo. 1907 ....⎬
Finland—
Annuaire Statistique de Finlande. Nouvelle Série.⎫
4ᵉ Année, 1906. La. 8vo. 1906...............⎪ The Central Statis-
Emigration pendant 1903 et 1904. La. 8vo. 1906⎬ tical Bureau
Mouvement de la Population de Finlande en 1903⎪
et 1904. La. 8vo. 1906 ....⎭
Eleven vols. of Statistical Returns dealing with⎫
Agriculture, Assurance, Monts-de-piété, Public⎬ The Registrar-Gene-
Health, Industries, Emigration. 8vo. 1905-06⎭ ral of England
Fennia. Bulletin de la Société de Géographie de⎫
Finlande. Vols. 19—22. 1902-03—1904-05.⎪ The Society
[With separate vol. of maps and diagrams.]⎬
5 vols., 8vo. 1903-05...............⎭

(a) **Foreign Countries—***Contd.*

Salvador—
Boletin del Consejo Superior de Salubridad. (Current numbers.) 8vo. 1907 .... } The Board

Servia—
Prix. Statistique des prix des produits agricoles et autres dans le royaume. 3ᵉ vol. La période de 1901–1905. 4to. 1906 .... } The Statistical Bureau

Spain—
Estadística del Impuesto de Transportes por Mar. (Current numbers.) 8vo. 1907............................ } The Director-General of Customs

Sweden—
Bidrag till Sveriges Officiella Statistik. 4to. 1906—
  A. Befolkningsstatistik, 1900. (Census) ....
  F. Handel, 1905. (Trade) ....
  G. Fångvården, 1905. (Prisons) ....
  I. Telegrafväsendet, 1905. (Telegraphs) ....
  L. Statens Järnvägstrafik, 1905. (Railways) ....
  M. Postverket, 1905. (Postal) ....
  N. Jordbruk och Boskapsskötsel, 1906. (Agri-
    culture) ....
  P. Undervisningsväsendet, 1903–4. (Education)....
  S. Allmänna Arbeten, 1905. (Public Works) ....
  V. Brännvins Tillverkning, &c., 1904–5. (Dis-
    tilleries, &c.) ....
  Y. Sparbanksstatistik, 1904–1905. (Savings Banks)
In- och utvandring år 1904. 15 pp., 4to. 1906 ....
} The Central Statistical Bureau

Meddelanden fran k. Kommerskollegii afdelning for Arbetsstatistik. (Current numbers.) 8vo. 1907.... } The University of Upsala

Rikets In-, och Utforsel. (Current numbers.) 1907....
Sammandrag af de enskilda sedelutgifvande bankernas. (Current numbers.) 1907............................
Sammandrag af Riksbankens Ställning. (Current numbers.) 1907.................
Statistisk Tidskrift. (Current numbers.) 8vo. 1907
} The Central Statistical Bureau

Yrkesinspektionens verksamhet, år 1905. 8vo. 1906.... { The University of Upsala

Stockholm—Bulletin mensuel du Bureau de Statistique de la ville. (Current numbers.) 8vo. 1907 .... } The Municipal Statistical Bureau

Switzerland—
Alcools. Régie des. Rapport sur la gestion et le compte de la Régie pour 1905. 8vo. 1906 ....
Données statistiques concernant la gestion de la Régie en 1905. Fol. 1906 ....
} The "Régie"

Commerce Spécial de la Suisse en 1906. Tableau provisoire du. La. fol. 1907 .... } The Director-General of Customs

Résultats du recensement fédéral des entreprises agricoles, &c. 9 août, 1905. Vol. 1. Les entreprises et nombre des personnes actives dans ces entreprises. Fasc. 1. Canton Zurich. 4to. 1906.... } The Federal Statistical Bureau

United States—
Agriculture. Report of Secretary of Agriculture, 1906. 94 pp., 8vo. 1906...
Crop Reporter. (Current numbers.) Fol. 1907........
} The Department of Agriculture

(a) Foreign Countries— *Contd.*

United States— *Contd.*

Census Bureau Bulletins—

52-56 and 58-60. Census of Manufactures, 1905, for different States. 8 parts, 4to. 1906 . ...

57. Census of Manufactures, 1905. United States. 4to. 1906 ....

61. Census of Manufactures, 1905. Canning and Preserving, Rice Cleaning and Polishing and Manufacture of Beet Sugar. 4to. 1906 .... } The Bureau of Census

62. Census of Manufactures, 1905. Glass and Clay Products. 4to. 1907 ....

63. Supply and Distribution of Cotton for year 1905-06. 4to. 1906 ....

Commerce and Finance. Monthly Summary. (Current numbers.) 4to. 1907 .... } Department of Commerce and Labour

Commercial Philippines in 1906. 4to. Jan., 1907 ...

Debt. Monthly Statements of the Public, and of Cash in Treasury. (Current numbers.) Sheets. 1907 } The Secretary of the Treasury

Gold, Silver, and Notes, &c., in Circulation. Monthly Statements. (Current numbers.) Sheets. 1907 ..

Education. Report of Commissioner of Education for year ending 30th June, 1904. Vol. 2, 8vo. 1906 } The Bureau of Education

Finance. Annual Report of Comptroller of Currency. 3rd Dec., 1906. 8vo. 1906 .... } The Comptroller

Immigration. Annual Report of Commissioner-General of Immigration for fiscal year ended 30th June, 1906. 8vo. 1906 .... } The Bureau of Immigration

Library of Congress. Report of Librarian, &c., for year 1905-06. 8vo. 1906 .... } The Library

Mineral Products of the United States. Calendar Years 1896 to 1905. Sheet. 1907 .... } The United States Geological Survey

Naval Observatory. Synopsis of report of Superintendent of, for 1905-06. 10 pp., 8vo. 1906............ } The Superintendent

Navigation. Annual Report of Commissioner of Navigation. 20th Nov., 1906. 8vo. 1906 .... } The Bureau of Navigation

California—

State Board of Health. Monthly Bulletins. 8vo. 1907. (Current numbers) ....

19th Biennial Report of State Board of Health for fiscal years from 1st July, 1904, to 30th June, 1906. 8vo. 1906 .... } The Board

12th Biennial Report of Bureau of Labor Statistics, 1905-06. 8vo. 1906 .... } The Bureau

Iowa. Bureau of Labor Statistics. 12th Report for 1905. 8vo. 1907 .... }   ''

Maine. Bureau of Industrial and Labor Statistics. 20th Annual Report for 1906. 8vo. 1907 .... }   ''

Massachusetts. Labor Bulletin. (Current numbers.) 8vo. 1907 .... } The Bureau of Labor Statistics

Nebraska. Crop Statistics of Nebraska. 1906. Bulletin of State Bureau of Statistics. No. 10. Nov., 1906. 8vo. 1906 ....,..... } The Bureau

New York State—

Bureau of Labor Statistics. 23rd Annual Report for year ended 30th Sept., 1905. 8vo. 1906 ....

Labor. 5th Annual Report of Commissioner of Labor for year 1904-05. 20th Annual Report on Factory Inspection for 1904-05. 19th Annual Report of Board of Mediation and Arbitration for 1904-05. 1 vol., 8vo. 1906 .... } The State Department of Labor

Labor. 6th Annual Report of Commissioner of Labor for year 1905-06. 8vo. 1907 ....

(a) Foreign Countries—*Contd.*
United States—*Contd.*

Pennsylvania. Bureau of Industrial Statistics. Report of, for 1905. 8vo. 1906 .... } The Bureau

Boston—
Monthly Bulletin of the Statistics Department. (Current numbers.) 4to. 1907 .... The Municipal Statistical Bureau
Receipts and Expenditures of ordinary Revenue. 1901-05. 4to. 1906 ....

New York (City). Public Library. Bulletin. (Current numbers) 8vo. 1907 .... } The Library

Commercial America. Published monthly. (Current numbers.) Fol. 1906 .... } Philadelphia Commercial Museum

Dun's Review. (Current numbers.) Fol. 1907........ { Messrs. R. G. Dun and Co.

Actuarial Society of America. Transactions. Vol. ix, No. 36, 8vo. 1906. With Title page and Index to Vol. 9 .... } The Society

American Philosophical Society. Record of the celebration of the 200th anniversary of the birth of Benjamin Franklin, under the auspices of the Society, 17th–20th April, 1906. 8vo. 1906........... ”

Columbia University Studies. Vol. 25, No. 1. Municipal control of public utilities: *O. L. Pond.* 8vo. 1906 .... } The University, per Messrs. P. S. King and Son

Johns Hopkins University Studies. Series 24, Nos. 3-4, Finances of American Trade Unions: *A. M. Sakolski.* Nos. 5-6, Early diplomatic negotiations of the United States with Russia: *John C. Hildt.* Nos. 7-8, State rights and political parties in N. Carolina, 1776-1861: *H. M. Wagstaff.* Nos. 9-10, National Labor Federations in the United States: *W. Kirk.* 8vo. 1906 .... } The Johns Hopkins University Press

Smithsonian Institution. Annual Report of Board of Regents for year ended 30th June, 1905. 8vo. 1906 .... } The Institution

International—
Bulletin International des Douanes. (Current numbers.) 8vo. 1907 .... } The Board of Trade

Berichte, Denkschriften und Verhandlungen des 5. Internationalen Kongresses für Versicherungs-Wissenschaft, Berlin, Sept., 1906. 8vo. 1906 .... } Messrs. E. S. Mittler und Sohn

(b) India and Colonial Possessions.
India, British—
Forest Bulletins, Nos. 7 and 9. 2 parts, 8vo. 1906 ... { The Indian Government

Cotton Spinning and Weaving. Monthly Statistics of. (Current numbers.) 8vo. 1907.... .. ..
Indian Trade Journal. (Current numbers.) 4to. 1907 .... The Director-General of Commercial Intelligence
Mint and Coinage. Advance pages of Statistics for 1905-06 and earlier years. Fol. 1906 ....
Trade and Navigation. Annual Statement of Seaborne, for year ended 31st March, 1906. Vols. 1 and 2. La. 4to. 1907 ....}

(b) **India and Colonial Possessions**—*Contd.*
India, British—*Contd.*

Review of Trade of India in 1905-06. [Cd-3272.]⎫
1906 .... ⎪
Trade. Tables relating to Trade of British India for ⎪
1901-02 to 1905-06. [Cd-3356.] 1907 .... ⎪
Bengal. District Gazetteers. Cuttack and Gaya. ⎪
2 vols., 8vo. 1906 .... ⎪
Central Provinces. District Gazetteers. Districts of ⎪
Damoh, Narsinghpur, Wardha. 3 vols., 8vo. 1906 ⎪
Madras— ⎬ The India Office
District Gazetteers. Statistical Appendix for ⎪
Ganjam, Nellore, and Salem Districts. 3 vols., ⎪
8vo. 1905-06 .... ⎪
District Gazetteers. Districts of Malabar, Tanjore, ⎪
and Vizagapatam. 4 vols., 8vo. 1905-06 .... ⎪
Punjab. District Gazetteers. Vol. 13. A. Jhelum ⎪
District Gazetteer. Supplement. 1905. Fol. 1905 ⎪
United Provinces of Agra and Oudh. Vol. 20 of ⎪
District Gazetteers. Fatehpur. 8vo. 1906. ....⎭

Australia, Commonwealth of—
Parliamentary Debates. Session 1906. (Current ⎫
numbers.) 8vo. 1907 .... ⎬ The Commonwealth

Canada, Dominion of—
Banks. Monthly Reports on Chartered. (Current ⎫ The Deputy Minister
numbers.) 4to. 1907 .... ⎭ of Finance
Budget Speech by Hon. W. S. Fielding, M.P., ⎫ The Hon. W. S.
Minister of Finance, in House of Commons, 29th ⎬ Fielding, M.P.
Nov., 1906. 66 pp., 8vo. 1906 .... ⎭
Canada Year-Book, 1905. Second series. 8vo. ⎫ The Census and Sta-
1906 .... ⎭ tistics Office
Debates of House of Commons. Session 1906. ⎫ The Clerk of House
Vols. 1-4. 4 vols., 8vo. 1906.... .... ⎭ of Commons
Estimates for fiscal year ending 31st Mar., 1908. ⎫
8vo. 1906 . ... ⎪
Public Accounts for year ended 30th June, 1906. ⎬ The Finance De-
8vo. 1906 .... ⎪ partment
Insurance. Report of Superintendent of Insurance ⎪
for 1905. 8vo. 1906 ....⎭
Manitoba. Journals and Sessional Papers of the ⎫ The King's Printer,
Legislature, 1906. 8vo. 1906 .. .. ⎭ Winnipeg
North West Provinces. Census of North West ⎫
Provinces, Manitoba, Saskatchewan, Alberta. 1906. ⎪
1, Population of 1906 compared with 1901. 2, ⎬ The Census Office,
Summary Statistics of Field Crops and Live Stock. ⎪ Ottawa
8vo. 1907 ....⎭
Ontario—
Department of Agriculture. Bulletins. (Current ⎫ The Ontario Depart-
numbers.) 8vo. 1907 .... ⎭ ment of Agriculture
Bureau of Industries. Annual Report for 1905. ⎫ The Bureau
Parts 1 and 2, 8vo. 1906...... .... ⎭
Canadian Life and Resources. (Current numbers.) ⎧ The Assistant Super-
Fol. 1907 .... ⎨ intendent of Emi-
  ⎩ gration

Cape of Good Hope—
Acts of Parliament. Session of 1906. 8vo. 1906....⎰ The Colonial Secre-
  ⎱ tary
Births, Marriages and Deaths. Report of Registrar- ⎫ The Registrar-Gene-
General of, for 1905. Fol. 1906 .... ⎭ ral

(b) **India and Colonial Possessions**—*Contd.*
Cape of Good Hope—*Contd.*

Votes and Proceedings of Parliament. Session 1906.
1 vol., fol. 1906 ....
Appendix I to Votes and Proceedings. 7 vols., fol. } The Colonial Secre-
1906 .... tary
Appendix II to Votes and Proceedings. 4 vols., 8vo.
1906 ....

Ceylon—

Ceylon Government Railway. Annual Report for } The General Mana-
1905. Fol. 1906 .... ger
Papers laid before the Legislative Council of Ceylon } The Ceylon Govern-
during Session 1905-06. Fol. 1906 .... ment

New South Wales—

Census of New South Wales. Life Assurance. 4to. } The Registrar-Gene-
1904 .... ral of England
Financial Statement of the Premier and Colonial } The Agent-General
Treasurer. Sept., 1906. 8vo. 1906 .... for N. S. Wales
Report of Registrar of Friendly Societies for 1905.
Fol. 1906. ....
Statistical View of progress of New South Wales. } The Registrar
Sheet. 1906 ....
Statistical Register for 1905. Part 7, Hospitals and } The Bureau of Sta-
Charities. Part 9, Land Settlement. 8vo. 1906.... tistics
Year-Book of New South Wales. 8vo. 1907 .... { The Agent-General
for N. S. Wales

New Zealand—

Official Year-book, 1906. 15th year of issue. 8vo. } The Registrar-Gene-
1906. 2 copies .... ral
Wellington Harbour Board. Statement of Accounts, } The Board
with Reports for year 1905-06. Fol. 1907 ....

Queensland—

Vital Statistics, 1905. 46th Annual Report of } The   Government
Government Statistician. Fol. 1906 .... Statistician

Rhodesia—

Chamber of Mines. Monthly Reports of Executive
Committee, and Returns of Output of Gold, &c. } The Chamber
(Current numbers.) Sheets. 1907 ....

South Australia—

Public Library, Museum, &c. Report of the } The Principal Li-
Governors for 1905–06. Fol. 1906 . ... brarian

Straits Settlements—

Supplements to the Perak Government Gazette, 1906. } The   Government
(Current numbers.) Fol. 1907 .... Secretary

Tasmania—

Railways. Report on Government Railways for } The General Mana-
1905–06. Fol. 1906 .... ger

Transvaal—

Agricultural Journal. (Current numbers.) 8vo. } The   Agricultural
1907 . ... Department
Mines Department, Transvaal. Monthly Statistics. } The Department
(Current numbers.) Obl. 4to. 1907 ....

(b) **India and Colonial Possessions**—*Contd.*
Transvaal—*Contd.*

Johannesburg. Statistics. (Current numbers.) Fol. } The Town Statis-
1907 .... } tician

Transvaal Chamber of Mines. Monthly Analysis of }
Gold Production in Transvaal. (Current numbers.) } The Chamber
1907 .... }

Victoria—

Friendly Societies. Report of Registrar of, for 1905. } The Registrar
10 pp., fol. 1906 .... }

Statistical Register of the State for 1905. Part 9, } The   Government
Production. Part 10, Interchange. Fol. 1906 .... } Statistician

Western Australia—

Monthly Statistical Abstract. (Current numbers.) ⌉
Fol. 1907 .... |
Supplements to Government Gazette, containing | The Registrar-Gene-
Monthly Mining Statistics. (Current numbers.) } ral and Govern-
1907 .... | ment Statistician
Statistical Register for 1905. Part 10. Education, &c. |
Fol. 1907 .... ⌋

Western Australian Year-book for 1902-04. 13th Edit. } The Agent-General
8vo. 1906 .... } for W. Australia

(c) **United Kingdom and its several Divisions.**
United Kingdom—

Army Medical Department. Report for 1905. 8vo. } The Army Medical
1906 .... } Department

Board of Trade Journal. (Current numbers.) 1907.... The Board

Building Societies. 11th Annual Report for 1905. } The Chief Registrar
Part 1. Report. (56.) 1907 .... } of Friendly Societies

Canal Boats Acts, 1877 and 1884. Extract from⌉
Report of Local Government Board for 1905-06. |
8vo. 1906 .... } Purchased
Casualties to Ships on Navy List. (319.) 1906 .... |
Coal (Export Duty). (355.) 1906 .. ..) ⌋

Coal Tables, 1905. (321.) 1906 .... The Board of Trade

Colonial Reports. Annual. No. 511, Sierra Leone. ⌉
513, Basutoland. 2 parts, 8vo. 1906 .... |
Criminal Appeal Bills. (201.) 1906 .... |
Customs Tariffs of the United Kingdom from 1897-98 |
to 1906-07. [Cd-3198.] 1907 ... . |
Education. Board of. Report for 1905-06. [Cd-3270] |
8vo. 1906 .... |
Education Rates. Report of Departmental Com- |
mittee, with Appendices. [Cd-3313] 1907 .... } Purchased
Education. Return. Higher Education. England |
and Wales. Application of funds by local authori- |
ties during 1904-5. (391.) 1906 .... |
Education. Statistics of Public Education in England |
and Wales, 1904-5-6. [Cd-3255.] 1906.............. |
Electric Lighting Acts, 1882 to 1902. Applications |
and Appeals. (341.) 1906.................. ... . ⌋

Factory and Workshop Act, 1901. Preliminary Tables⌉
of Cases of industrial poisoning and fatal accidents |
in factories. &c , during 1906. 8 pp. Fol. 1907 .... |
Factories and Workshops. Supplement to Annual } The Home Office
Report of Chief Inspector for 1905. Return of |
persons employed in 1904 in workshops and laun- |
dries. [Cd-3323.] 1907.......................... ......,⌋

(c) **United Kingdom and its Divisions**—*Contd.*
United Kingdom—*Contd.*

Gas Undertakings. (Local Authorities) Return for
year 1905-6. (394.) 1906 ... .
Gas Undertakings. Return for 1905. (393.) 1906.
Housing of Working Classes Acts Amendment Bill.
Report and Special Report from Select Committee.
(376.) 1906 ....
Inclosures. Number of, in different Counties.
6 parts. 1906.............................. ....
Income Tax. Report of Select Committee, with
Minutes of Evidence and Appendix. (365.) 1906.
India. Excise Committee, 1905-06. Report. } Purchased
[Cd-3327.] 1907 ....
International Sugar Commission, Autumn Session,
1906. Report of Proceedings. [Cd-3301.] 1907.
Labour Regulation. Memorandum on International
Conference on, Berne. Sept.,1906. [Cd-3271.] 1906.
Land Values Taxation, &c (Scotland), Bill. Report
and Special Report from Select Committee. (379.)
1906 ....
London Livery Companies Commission. Report and
Appendix. Vols. 1 and 2. Fol. 1884 ....

Mines and Quarries. General Report and Statistics
for 1906. Advance proofs of Tables of Fatal } The Home Office
Accidents and of Output of Minerals and Numbers
Employed in 1906. Fol. 1907 ....

Navy (Health). Statistical Report of Health of } The Medical Depart-
Navy for 1905. 8vo. (318.) 1906 .... } ment of Navy

Pauper Children. Boarding out of. Report by
Miss M. H. Mason. 8vo. 1906.............................
Poor Relief (England and Wales). Statement for
half-year ended Lady-day, 1906. (315.) 1906 ....
Public General Acts, 6th Edward VII. 1906. 8vo.
1906 .... } Purchased
Railway and Canal Traffic Act, 1888. 9th Report by
Board of Trade. (367.) 1906.................................
Small Holdings in Great Britain. Report of Depart-
mental Committee and Minutes of Evidence.
[Cd-3277 and 3278.] 1906 ....

Statistical Abstract for the British Colonies, Possessions, } The Commercial De-
&c., 1891 to 1905. 43rd No. 8vo. 1906. [Cd-3253.] } partment, Board
Statistical Abstract for Foreign Countries, 1894 to } of Trade
1903-4. 32nd No. 8vo. 1906. [Cd-3136.] ....

Trade Returns, 1905. Supplement to Vols. 1 and 2.
Tables showing countries of consignment of im- } Mr. A. J. Wood,
ports, and countries of ultimate destination of } Custom House
exports. [Cd-3282.] 1906........... ....
[Another copy presented by The Board of Trade.]
Tramways and Light Railways (Street and Road).
(298.) 1906 ....
Tuberculosis (Human and bovine). 2nd Interim
report of Royal Commission. Part 1, Report. } Purchased
[Cd-3322.] 1907 ....
Unemployed Workmen's Act, 1905. (Proceedings of
distress committees.) (392.) 1906 ....

Tariff Commission. Import and Export Trade of
United Kingdom in 1905 and 1906. 8 pp., 4to.
1906 .... } The Commission
The New Canadian Tariff and Preferential Trade
within the Empire. 24 pp., 4to. 1906 ....

(c) United Kingdom and its Divisions—*Contd.*

Great Britain—

Board of Agriculture and Fisheries—

Agricultural Statistics, 1906. Vol. 41, Part 1, ⎤
Acreage and live stock returns. [Cd-3281.] ⎟
8vo. 1906 .... ⎟
Journal of the Board. (Current numbers.) 8vo. ⎟
1907 .... ⎬ The Board
Leaflets. (Current numbers.) 8vo. 1907 .... ⎟
Weekly Returns of Market Prices (of Cattle, Dead ⎟
Meat, Provisions, Fruit, and Vegetables, Hay and ⎟
Straw). (Current numbers.) Fol. 1907............. ⎦

England and Wales

British Museum. Subject Index of modern works ⎤
added to library of the British Museum in 1881- ⎟
1900. 3 vols., la. 8vo. 1902-03 .... ⎬ The Trustees
British Museum. Subject Index of modern works ⎟
added to library of the British Museum in 1901-05. ⎟
La. 8vo. 1906 .... ⎦

Births, Deaths, and Marriages in England and Wales. ⎤ The Registrar-Gene-
68th Annual Report of Registrar-General for 1905. ⎬ ral
[Cd-3279.] 8vo. 1907 .... ⎦

Judicial Statistics, England and Wales, 1905. Part 1, ⎤ The Home Office
Criminal Statistics. [Cd-3315.] 4to. 1907 .... ⎦

Local Taxation Returns. Year 1904-05. Part 1 ⎤ The Local Govern-
(311), 1906. Part 2 (311-1), 1906.................... ⎦ ment Board

London County Council. Expenses incurred in pro- ⎤
moting Bills in Parliament, 1903-06. (386.) ⎟
1906 .... ⎬ Purchased
Metropolitan Borough Councils. (Bills in Parlia- ⎟
ment.) (385.) 1906.. ⎦

London County Council—

Statistical Abstract for London, 1906. Vol. 9. 8vo. ⎤
1906 .... ⎟
Report of Education Committee submitting report ⎟
of the Medical Officer (Education) for year ended ⎟
31st March, 1906. 8vo. 1906............................. ⎬ The London County
Education. Report on higher education for year ⎟ Council
ended 31st March, 1906. Fol. 1907.................. ⎟
Report of Public Health Committee, submitting ⎟
report of Medical Officer for 1905. Fol. 1906.... ⎟
[Another copy presented by the Medical Officer.] ⎦

Comparison of rates levied, 1901-02 to 1906-07. ⎤
8vo. 1906 .... ⎟
Fair wages and hours of labour. Fol. 1907 .... ⎬ Purchased
Rates of pay and hours of labour. Fol. 1907....... ⎦

London County Council Gazette. (Current num- ⎤ The London County
bers.) Fol. 1906 .... ⎦ Council

Wandsworth. Report of Council of Metropolitan ⎤
Borough of, for 1905-06, with Report of Medical ⎬ The Town Clerk
Officer of Health for 1905. 8vo. 1906................ ⎦

Manchester—

Abstract of Treasurer's Accounts for year 1905-06. ⎤
8vo. 1906 .... ⎟
Estimates for year ending 31st March, 1907. 8vo. ⎟
1906 .... ⎬ The City Treasurer
Education Committee. Fourth Annual Report for ⎟
1905-06. 8vo. 1906... ⎟
Poor. Abstract of Accounts of Guardians for 1905- ⎟
06. 8vo. 1906 .... ⎦

(c) **United Kingdom and its Divisions**—*Contd.*

Ireland—
Department of Agriculture and Technical Instruction.
Journal of the. (Current numbers.) 8vo. 1907....
Congestion in Ireland. First and Second Reports,
with Appendices, of Royal Commission. [Cd–3266]. } Purchased
[Cd–3267]. 1906. [Cd–3318]. [Cd–3319]. 1907 ...
Housing of Working Classes Acts. Return (337).
1907 ....

Scotland—
Burgh Trusts (Scotland). Return. (328.) 1907 ....
Judicial Statistics of Scotland for 1905. Report and
Statistics. [Cd–3226.] 4to. 1906 .... } Purchased
Land Values, Taxation, &c. (Scotland) Bill. Report
and Special Report from Select Committee. (379.)
1906 ....
Edinburgh. Accounts published in the year 1906. } The City Chamber-
Fol. 1907 ....   lain
Aberdeen. Report of Medical Officer of Health for } The Medical Officer
1905. 4to. 1906 ....   of Health

(d) **Authors, &c.**
Avebury (Lord) (*Sir John Lubbock, Bart.*, M.P.). } Messrs. Swan, Son-
Representation. Revised Edition. 8vo. 1906 ....   nenschein and Co.
Bartholomew (J. G.). Atlas of the World's Commerce. } Purchased
22 parts. Fol. 1906-07 ....
Bertillon (Dr. Jacques). Fréquence des principales
causes de décès à Paris pendant la seconde moitié du } The Author
19e siècle et notamment pendant 1886-1905. 8vo.
1906 ......
Boyd (William K.). Ecclesiastical Edicts of the } Columbia University
Theodosian Code. 8vo. 1905 ....   Library
Burk (Addison B.). Golden Jubilee of the Republican } The Hon. William
Party. [United States.] The Celebration in   Barnes, Senr.
Philadelphia, June 17-19, 1906. 8vo. 1906...........
Cosenza (Mario Emilio). Official positions after the
time of Constantine. 8vo. 1905..................... } Columbia University
Davis (Michael M.). Gabriel Tarde. An Essay in   Library
Sociological Theory. 8vo. 1906........ ....
Elderton (W. Palin). Frequency-Curves and Correla- } Messrs. C. and E.
tion. 8vo. 1906 ....   Layton
Ferraris (Carlo F.)—
Economisti tedeschi contemporanei. Adolfo Wagner.
20 pp. 8vo. 1906........... ...   } The Author
Gli Inscritti nelle Università, &c., Italiani. 1893-94
al 1905.06. 15 pp. 8vo. 1907............
Fornasari di Verce (E.). Statistiche agrarie. Studio } "
di metodologia statistica. 63 pp. 8vo. 1906 ....
Foster (Frank). Engineering in the United States. } Messrs. Sherratt and
[Gartside Report. University of Manchester]. 8vo.   Hughes
1906 ......
Foville (A. de). La Monnaie. Sm. 8vo. 1907 .... The Author
Gonnard (R.). L'Emigration européenne au 19e
siècle. Angleterre, Allemagne, Italie, Autriche, } M. Armand Colin
Hongrie, Russie. 8vo. 1906 ....
Guyot (Yves). Le commerce extérieur de la France en } The Author
1905. 56 pp., 8vo. 1907.....................
Hain (Joseph). Handbuch der Statistik des Osterrei- } Purchased
chischen Kaiserstaates. 2 vols., 8vo. 1852-53............

N 2

(d) **Authors, &c.**—*Contd.*

Hamilton (*J. G. de Roulhac*). Reconstruction in North Carolina. 8vo. 1906 ...... } Columbia University Library

Hatch (*Leonard W.*). Government Industrial Arbitration. 8vo. 1905 } Columbia University Library

Heath (*H. Llewellyn*). The Infant, the Parent, and the State. A Social Study and Review. 8vo. 1907 } Messrs. P. S. King and Son

Helguero (*Fernando de*). Per la risoluzione delle curve dimorfiche. 45 pp., diagrams, 4to. 1906. } The Author

Hishida (*Seiji G.*). The international position of Japan as a great power. 8vo. 1905 } Columbia University Library

Hodding, King and Co. (*Messrs.*). American Railways Traffic Book. 22nd year of issue. 8vo. London, 1907 } Messrs. Hodding, King and Co.

Hooper (*Frederick*). Statistics relating to Woollen and Worsted Trades of United Kingdom, including the year 1906. 8vo. 1907 } The Author

Kautsky (*Karl*). The Social Revolution and on the morrow of the social revolution. Translated from the German by J. B. Askew. 8vo. 1903 } Purchased

Kebbel (*T. E.*). The Agricultural Labourer : a summary of his position. 4th edition. 8vo. 1907 } Messrs. Swan, Sonnenschein and Co.

[*Kenny* (*P. D.*)]. Economics for Irishmen, by "Pat." 8vo. 1906 } Purchased

Lawson (*Thomas W.*). Frenzied Finance, The Crime of Amalgamated. 8vo. 1906 } „

Lescure (*Jean*). Des Crises générales et périodiques de Surproduction. La. 8vo. 1907 } Messrs. Larose and Tenin, Paris

Lethbridge (*Sir Roper*). India and Imperial Preference, with statistical tables. 8vo. 1907 } Messrs. Longmans

McCleary (*G. F.*), *M.D.* Infantile Mortality and Infants' Milk Depôts. 8vo. 1905 } Purchased

Martinez (*Albert B.*) and *Lewandowski* (*Maurice*). L'Argentine au 20e siècle. 2e édit. 8vo. 1906 } M. Armand Colin

Maseres (*Francis*). The Doctrine of Permutations and Combinations, being an essential and fundamental part of the doctrine of chances... 8vo. 1795 } Mr. G. U. Yule

Mayr (*D. G. von*). Die Bevölkerung Britisch-Indiens nach dem Zensus von 1901. 22 pp. Maps, &c. 8vo. 1907 } The Author

Meyer (*Hugo Richard*). Municipal Ownership in Great Britain. 8vo. 1906 } Messrs. Macmillan and Co.

Mombert (*Dr. Paul*). Studien zur Bevölkerungsbewegung in Deutschland in den letzten Jahrzehnten, mit besonderer Berücksichtigung der ehelichen Fruchtbarkeit. 8vo. 1907 } M. G. Braun, Karlsruhe

Moore (*Harold E.*). Our heritage in the land. 2nd Edit. 8vo. 1906 } Messrs. P. S. King and Son

Nicolai (*Edmond*)—
La dépopulation des campagnes et l'accroissement de la population des villes ... 70 pp., 8vo. 1903 ...... |
Notice sur la repercussion des droits de douane. 14 pp., 8vo. 1903 ...... } The Author
Les Tribunaux de Commerce en Belgique. 40 pp., 8vo. 1904 ...... |
Les valeurs mobilières. 40 pp., 4to. 1906 ...... |

Pierce (*Franklin*). The Tariff and the Trusts. 8vo. 1907 } Messrs. Macmillan and Co.

Pigou (*A. C.*). The Riddle of the Tariff. 2nd impression. 107 pp., 8vo. 1904 } Purchased

Popplewell (*Frank*). Some modern conditions and recent developments in Iron and Steel Production in America.... [Gartside Report. University of Manchester.] 8vo. 1906... } Messrs. Sherratt and Hughes, Manchester

(d) Authors, &c.—*Contd.*

Pratt (Edwin A.)—

German *v.* British Railways, with special reference to owner's risk and trader's claims. 64 pp., 8vo. 1907 — Messrs. P. S. King and Son

Licensing and Temperance in Sweden, Norway, and Denmark. 8vo. 1907 .... — The Author

Rozenraad (C.). Table comparing Gold and Silver Stock of principal European Banks of Issue, their Bank Rate, &c., at end Dec., 1906 and 1905. Sheet — The Compiler

Sachet (Adrien). Assistance des vieillards, infirmes, et incurables. Commentaire de la loi du 14 Juillet, 1905 ... 8vo. Paris, 1907. .... — Messrs. Larose and Tenin

Schooling (John Holt). London County Council Finance from the beginning down to 31st Mar., 1907, made clear to Ratepayers. 8vo. 1907 .... — Mr. John Murray

Seager (Henry Rogers). Introduction to Economics. 3rd Edit. 8vo. 1906 .... — Purchased

Seyd (Richard). Statistics of Failures in United Kingdom during 1906. Sheet. 1907......................... — The Compiler

Simpson (Thomas). The nature and laws of chance ... Sm. 4to. 1740 .... — Mr. G. U. Yule

Spencer (M. G.) and *Falk (H. J.).* Employment pictures from the Census. With preface by Prof. C. S. Loch. 8vo. 1906 .... — Messrs. P. S. King and Son

Strachey (J. St. Loe). The Manufacture of Paupers; a protest and a policy. With an introduction by, 8vo. 1907 .... — Mr. John Murray

Sutherland (William). The Colonisation of Scotland. 94 pp., 8vo. 1907 .... — Mr. D. J. Rider

Wagner (Henry R.). Irish Economics: 1700—1783. A bibliography, with notes. 95 pp, 8vo. 1907 .... — The Author

Yermoloff (Alexis). La Russie agricole devant la crise agraire. 8vo. 1907 .... — Messrs. Hachette and Co.

Yusuf-Ali (A.). The Indian Mohammedans: their past, present, and future. 19 pp., 8vo., 1907 .... — Messrs. P. S. King and Son

---

(e) Societies, &c. (British).

Actuaries, Institute of. Journal. Vol. xli. Part. I. Jan., 1907. 8vo.................................... — The Institute

Anthropological Institute. Journal. Jan.-June, 1906. La. 8vo. 1906..................................... — :

Civil Engineers, Institution of. Minutes of Proceedings. Vol. 166. 8vo. 1906 .... — —

Corporation of Foreign Bondholders. 33rd Annual Report of the Council for 1905-06. 8vo. 1907 .... — The Council

Edinburgh, Royal Society of—
Proceedings. Session 1905-06. Vol. 21. No. 6. 8vo. 1907 ....
Transactions. Vol. xli, Part 3. Session 1904-5. Vol. xlv, Part 1. Session 1905-6. 2 vols. 4to. 1906 .... — The Society

Glasgow, Royal Philosophical Society of. Proceedings. Vol. 37. 1905-06. 8vo 1906 .... — „

Iron and Steel Institute. Journal. Nos. 3 and 4. 8vo. 1906 .... — The Institute

London School of Economics and Political Science. (University of London.) Calendar, 1906-07. 8vo. 1907 .... — The School

National Liberal Club. Political and Economical Circle. Transactions. Vol. 4, and Parts 1—6, 8—14, of Vol. 5. 8vo. [1903-06] .... — The Secretary, National Liberal Club

(e) Societies, &c. (British)—*Contd.*

Royal College of Physicians. Catalogue of Accessions ⎫
  to Library during year ending July, 1906 ... 8vo. ⎬ The College
  1906 .... ⎭

Royal Society of London. Year-book, 1907. 8vo. 1907 The Society

Society of Comparative Legislation. Journal. New ⎫
  Series. No. 16. 8vo. 1906 .... ⎬   ..

Statistical and Social Inquiry Society of Ireland. Journal, ⎫
  Dec., 1906. (Part 86, Vol. xi.) 8vo. 1906 .... ⎬   ,,

Surveyors' Institution. Professional Notes. Vol. xiv. ⎫
  Part 1 and Scottish Supplement. No. 24. 8vo. 1906 ⎬ The Institution

Woolwich Equitable Building Society. 59th Annual ⎫ Mr. Geo. Bishop,
  Report for year 1905-06. Fol. 1906 .... ⎬   Secretary

---

(f) Periodicals, &c., and Miscellaneous (British).

African Monthly. Vol. I. No. 1. Dec., 1906. 8vo. ⎫ Messrs. W. Dawson
  1906 .... ⎬   and Sons, Ltd.

Biometrika. Vol. V. Part 3. Feb., 1907. 8vo. ⎫
  1907 .... ⎬
"The Times" Monthly Index for Jan. and Feb., 1907. ⎬ Purchased
  8vo. 1907................ ⎭

Licensed Victuallers' Official Annual for 1907. 8vo. ⎫ Mr. A. B. Deane
  1907 .... ⎭

Newspaper Press Directory. 62nd Annual Issue. 1907 { Messrs. C. Mitchell
                                                       and Co.

Vivian, Younger and Bond (Messrs.). Metal Price ⎫
  Current. Prices of certain metals in London on 1st of ⎬ The Firm
  month of 1887-1906. Sheet. 1907................ ⎭

Weddel (W. and Co.). 19th Annual Review of the ⎫
  Frozen Meat Trade, 1906, with chart. 4to. 1907 .... ⎬   ,,

Banking Almanack for 1907 .... ⎫
British Almanack for 1907 .... ⎪
Burdett's Hospitals and Charities, 1907 .... ⎪
Co-operative Wholesale Societies. Annual for 1907 .... ⎪
Daily Mail Year-Book for 1907................ ⎬ Purchased
Medical Directory for 1907 .... ⎪
Municipal Year-Book of the United Kingdom for 1907 ⎪
Official Year-Book of Church of England for 1907 .... ⎪
Shipping World Year-Book for 1907. 8vo. 1907 .... ⎪
Willing's Press Guide. 1907 .... ⎭

The weekly, monthly, or quarterly issues of the following returns have also been received during the past quarter :—

Consular Reports—From United States and United Kingdom.

Labour Reports, &c.—From Austria-Hungary, Belgium, France, Germany, Italy, United States, Massachusetts and New York States, Canada, New Zealand, and United Kingdom.

Trade Returns—From Argentina, Austria-Hungary, Belgium, Bulgaria, China, Denmark, Egypt, France, Germany, Greece, Italy, Mexico, Netherlands, Norway, Roumania, Russia, Spain, Sweden, Switzerland, United States, India, and United Kingdom.

Vital Statistics—From Argentina, Egypt, Germany, Italy, Netherlands, Roumania, Switzerland, United States (Connecticut and Michigan only), Queensland, South Australia, and United Kingdom.

Vital Statistics of following Towns—Buenos Ayres, Buda-Pesth, Brünn, Prague, Brussels, Copenhagen, Berlin, Bucharest, Moscow, Madrid, Stockholm, London, Manchester, Dublin, Edinburgh, and Aberdeen.

The weekly, monthly, or quarterly issues of the following periodicals, &c., have also been received during the past quarter. They are arranged under the countries in which they are published:—

Denmark—Nationalökonomisk Tidsskrift.

France—Annales des Sciences Politiques. Économiste Français. Journal des Économistes. Monde Économique. Polybiblion, Parties Littéraire et Technique. Réforme Sociale. Le Rentier. Revue d'Économie Politique. Revue de Statistique. Journal de la Société de Statistique de Paris.

Germany—Allgemeines Statistisches Archiv. Archiv für Rassen- und Gesellschafts-Biologie. Archiv für Sozialwissenschaft und Sozialpolitik. Jahrbuch für Gesetzgebung, Verwaltung, und Volkswirtschaft. Jahrbücher für Nationalökonomie und Statistik. Kritische Blätter für die gesamten Socialwissenschaften. Zeitschrift für die gesamte Staatswissenschaft. Zeitschrift für die gesamte Versicherungs-Wissenschaft. Zeitschrift für Socialwissenschaft. Mittheilungen aus der Handelskammer Frankfurt a. M.

Italy—L'Economista. Giornale degli Economisti. Rivista Italiana di Sociologia. Riforma Sociale. Societa Umanitaria, Bollettino mensile.

Sweden—Ekonomisk Tidskrift.

Switzerland—Journal de Statistique suisse.

United States—Bankers' Magazine. Bradstreet's. Commercial and Financial Chronicle, with supplements. Duns' Review. Journal of Political Economy. Political Science Quarterly. Quarterly Journal of Economics. Yale Review. American Academy of Political and Social Science, Annals. American Economic Association, Publications. American Geographical Society, Bulletin. American Statistical Association, Quarterly Publications. American Philosophical Society, Proceedings and Transactions. Columbia University, Studies in History, &c.

Canada—The Chronicle: Insurance and Finance.

India—Indian Engineering.

New Zealand—Government Insurance Recorder. Trade Review and Price Current.

United Kingdom—The Accountant. Accountants' Magazine. Athenæum. Australian Trading World. Bankers' Magazine. Broomhalls' Corn Trade News. Browne's Export List. Colliery Guardian. Commercial World. Economic Journal. Economic Review. Economist. Fireman. Incorporated Accountants' Journal. Insurance Record. Investors' Monthly Manual. Investors' Review. Joint Stock Companies' Journal. Labour Co-partnership. Licensing World. Local Government Journal. Machinery Market. Nature. Navy League, Journal. Policy-Holder. Post Magazine. Produce Markets' Review. Public Health. Publishers' Circular. Sanitary Record. Shipping World. Statist. The Times. Anthropological Institute, Journal. Cobden Club, Leaflets. East India Association, Journal. Howard Association, Leaflets, &c. Institute of Actuaries, Journal. Institute of Bankers, Journal. Institution of Civil Engineers, Minutes of Proceedings. Iron and Steel Institute, Journal. Lloyd's Register of British and Foreign Shipping, Statistical Tables. London Chamber of Commerce, Journal. London University Gazette. Manchester Literary and Philosophical Society, Memoirs and Proceedings. Royal Agricultural Society, Journal. Royal Colonial Institute, Proceedings and Journal. Royal Geographical Society, Geographical Journal. Royal Irish Academy, Proceedings and Transactions. Royal Meteorological Society, Meteorological Record and Quarterly Journal. Royal Society, Proceedings. Royal United Service Institution, Journal. Sanitary Institute, Journal. Society of Arts, Journal. Statistical and Social Inquiry Society of Ireland, Journal. Surveyors' Institution, Professional Notes and Transactions. Trade Circulars.

PERIODICAL RETURNS.

REGISTRATION OF THE UNITED KINGDOM.
No. I.—ENGLAND AND WALES.
MARRIAGES—To 30th September, 1906.
BIRTHS and DEATHS—To 31st December, 1906.

A.—*Serial Table of* Marriages, Births, *and* Deaths, *returned in the Years* 1906-1900, *and in the* Quarters *of those Years.*

Calendar Years, 1906-1900:—*Numbers.*

Years	1906.	'05.	'04.	'03.	'02.	'01.	'00.
Marriages No.	—	260,489	257,524	260,710	261,750	259,400	257,480
Births ,,	934,391	929,457	944,703	917,949	940,509	929,807	927,062
Deaths .... ,,	530,715	519,939	549,393	514,450	535,538	551,585	587,830

Quarters *of each Calendar Year,* 1906-1900.
(I.) Marriages:—*Numbers.*

Qrs. ended last day of	1906.	'05.	'04.	'03.	'02.	'01.	'00.
March...... No.	45,432	45,130	44,914	45,584	54,056	43,862	43,917
June .... ,,	74,326	70,927	71,430	73,096	62,463	72,173	71,518
September ,,	75,882	72,726	71,215	71,958	71,511	72,201	69,772
December ,,	—	71,706	69,965	70,465	73,720	71,164	72,273

(II.) Births:—*Numbers.*

Qrs. ended last day of	1906.	'05.	'04.	'03.	'02.	'01.	'00.
March...... No.	237,396	238,100	240,117	235,165	231,169	231,161	239,987
June .... ,,	237,187	236,767	238,891	241,652	237,522	233,548	234,644
September ,,	234,684	235,205	237,282	241,125	241,488	235,580	232,579
December ,,	225,124	219,385	228,413	230,007	230,330	229,518	219,852

(III.) Deaths:—*Numbers.*

Qrs. ended last day of	1906.	'05.	'04.	'03.	'02.	'01.	'00.
March...... No.	140,462	148,360	153,255	138,275	150,554	146,137	181,290
June .... ,,	125,387	123,041	124,222	123,594	132,518	128,570	141,563
September ,,	129,421	120,792	133,511	116,607	115,410	139,615	133,074
December ,,	135,445	127,746	138,405	135,974	137,056	137,263	131,903

Annual Rates of MARRIAGES, BIRTHS, *and* DEATHS, *per* 1,000 PERSONS
LIVING *in the Years* 1906-1900, *and in the* QUARTERS *of those Years.*

Calendar YEARS, 1906-1900 :—*General Ratios.*

YEARS	1906.	Mean '96-1905.	1905.	'04.	'03.	'02	'01.	'00.
Estmtd. Popln. of England and Wales *in thousands* in middle of each Year....	34,547,	—	34,153,	33,763,	33,378,	32,998,	32,621,	32,249,
Persons Married	—	15·8	15·3	15·2	15 6	15·9	15·9	16·0
Births ,...............	27·0	28·7	27·2	27·9	28·4	28·5	28·5	28·7
Deaths...............	15·4	16·8	15·2	16·2	15·4	16·2	16·9	18·2

QUARTERS *of each Calendar Year,* 1905-1899.

(I.) PERSONS MARRIED :—*Ratio per* 1,000.

Qrs. ended last day of	1906.	Mean '96-1905	1905.	'04.	'03.	'02.	'01.	'00.
March	10·7	11·4	10·7	10·7	11·1	13·3	10·9	11·0
June..................	17·3	17·3	16·7	17·0	17·6	15·2	17·7	17·8
September	17·4	17·1	16·9	16·7	17·1	17·2	17·6	17·2
December	—	17·5	16·7	16·4	16·7	17·7	17·3	17·8

(II.) BIRTHS:—*Ratio per* 1,000.

Qrs. ended last day of	1906.	Mean '96-1905.	1905.	'04.	'03.	'02.	'01.	'00.
March	27·9	29·2	28·3	28·5	28·6	28·4	28·7	30·2
June..................	27·5	29·1	27·8	28·4	29·0	28·9	28·7	29·2
September	27·0	28·8	27·3	27·9	28·7	29·0	28·7	28·6
December	25·9	27·8	25:5	26·8	27·3	27·7	27·9	27·0

(III.) DEATHS:—*Ratio per* 1,000.

Qrs. ended last day of	1906.	Mean '96-1905.	1905.	'04.	'03.	'02.	'01.	'00.
March	16·5	18·7	17·6	18·2	16·8	18·5	18·2	22·8
June..................	14·6	15·9	14·4	14·8	14·9	16·1	15·8	17·6
September	14·9	16·2	14·0	15·7	13·9	13·9	17·0	16·4
December	15·6	16·7	14·8	16·3	16·2	16·5	16·7	16·2

.—*Special Town Table:*—Population; Birth-Rate *and* Death-Rate *in each Quarter of* 1906, *in the* Seventy-Six *Large Towns.*

ties and Boroughs.	Estimated Population in the Middle of the Year 1906.	Annual Rate to 1,000 Living during the Thirteen Weeks ending							
		31st March,1906. (1st Quarter.)		30th June, 1906. (2nd Quarter.)		30th Sept., 1906. (3rd Quarter.)		29th Dec , 1906. (4th Quarter.)	
		Births.	Deaths.	Births.	Deaths.	Births.	Deaths.	Births.	Deaths.
venty-six towns	15,818,360	28·7	16·6	28·3	14·9	27·9	16·2	26·5	16·2
cluding—									
London*	4,721,217	27·8	16·6	27·0	14·8	26·5	15·4	25·5	16·0
West Ham	301,617	32·5	14·2	30·3	12·1	29·9	16·4	29·8	15·8
Croydon	151,011	25·4	13·5	26·8	11·3	27·0	14·2	23·5	12·8
Brighton	128,095	23·4	17·8	22·9	12·9	22·1	13·7	20·9	14·3
Portsmouth	205,118	29·1	14·8	28·8	13·3	28·8	16·2	28·1	15·3
Plymouth	118,014	24·0	18·8	25·2	15·1	23·5	14·5	23·2	16·6
Bristol	363,223	27·2	16·7	25·9	13·5	26·1	13·0	24·4	14·7
Cardiff	183,823	27·8	14·7	27·4	13·9	28·1	12·5	25·8	14·9
Swansea..............	96,848	33·4	20·0	33·3	15·9	34·5	17·4	31·0	19·9
Wolverhampton	100,729	27·9	17·2	28·4	12·4	27·2	15·3	26·4	14·3
Birmingham	548,022	30·8	17·9	29·6	16·1	30·2	17·4	26·9	15·8
Norwich	117,958	27·0	16·5	27·3	15·9	26·4	19·0	24·2	19·4
Leicester	232,111	25·8	15·4	26·0	12·5	24·8	14·4	24·1	13·5
Nottingham	254,563	27·3	18·8	27·6	12·9	26·8	17·2	24·8	15·4
Derby	123,981	25·3	14·3	26·2	14·1	24·4	12·5	24·6	16·0
Birkenhead	117,292	33·0	16·0	33·5	16·2	31·7	19·9	29·2	17·0
Liverpool†	739,180	33·4	21·3	33·7	20·5	32·6	21·0	31·2	19·7
Bolton	180,502	25·0	14·6	27·0	14·8	25·4	15·4	24·2	15·9
Manchester	637,126	29·6	17·9	29·8	19·0	29·3	20·2	28·6	19·6
Salford	234,077	31·2	16·6	31·6	18·4	29·0	19·2	29·2	18·8
Oldham	140,969	26·3	17·5	26·8	17·3	27·5	18·1	27·1	22·1
Burnley..............	102,808	29·3	18·5	28·0	18·5	28·4	20·7	25·4	20·5
Blackburn..........	134,015	25·1	18·0	25·6	14·9	26·0	14·9	24·6	16·3
Preston	116,399	29·3	22·5	31·7	15·7	27·6	18·1	26·1	20·4
Huddersfield	94,851	26·3	16·5	23·4	16·5	24·2	18·6	23·4	17·7
Halifax†	109,272	19·2	17·0	18·6	15·2	19·7	11·9	18·0	15·5
Bradford	288,544	20·8	16·1	21·6	17·4	21·3	15·8	18·8	15·1
Leeds	463,495	26·9	17·3	25·9	15·3	26·9	15·4	24·9	14·5
Sheffield	447,951	30·3	15·3	29·0	14·6	30·4	18·9	29·7	16·9
Hull	262,426	30·6	16·2	29·7	14·8	30·7	19·6	28·3	17·2
Sunderland	154,385	34·4	19·1	35·3	16·8	37·1	18·1	32·8	20·3
Gateshead..........	123,191	34·9	16·3	30·9	14·2	30·9	17·1	30·9	17·7
Newcastle - on - ⎫ Tyne ....⎭	268,721	31·7	17·3	31·2	16·7	30·1	17·3	29·5	17·2

* Including deaths of Londoners in the Metropolitan workhouses, hospitals, and
natic asylums outside the County of London, but excluding deaths of non-Londoners
the London Fever Hospital, the Metropolitan Asylums Hospitals, and the Middlesex
unty Lunatic Asylum, within the County of London. The deaths in the other towns
ve been similarly corrected.

† As extended in 1902.

Divisional Table:—Marriages *in the Year ending 30th September; and* Births *nd* Deaths *in the Year ending 31st December,* 1906, *as Registered Quarterly.*

	2	3	4	5	6	7
			Marriages in Quarters ending			
DIVISIONS. England and Wales.)	Area in Statute Acres.	Enumerated Population, 1901.	31st December, 1905.	31st March, 1906.	30th June, 1906.	30th September, 1906.
		No.	No.	No.	No.	No.
ᴅᴅ. & Wales ...Totals	37,327,479	32,527,843	71,706	45,432	74,326	75,882
London	74,839	4,536,429	10,849	6,461	10,727	12,271
South-Eastern	3,994,374	3,311,617	7,172	4,108	6,867	7,159
South Midland	3,247,169	2,181,174	4,609	2,431	4,601	4,919
Eastern	3,126,517	1,892,299	4,326	2,157	3,580	3,888
South-Western	5,023,292	1,913,393	3,949	2,592	4,043	3,581
West Midland	4,051,707	3,679,594	8,272	4,850	8,506	8,296
North Midland	3,495,711	2,042,406	4,627	2,715	5,156	4,540
North-Western	1,911,104	5,212,156	10,895	8,114	12,681	13,616
Yorkshire	3,721,094	3,596,325	7,829	5,215	8,583	8,365
Northern	3,536,522	2,129,051	4,502	3,515	5,230	4,897
Monmthsh. & Wales	5,145,150	2,033,287	4,676	3,274	4,352	4,350

	9	10	11	12	13	14	15	16
	Births in each Quarter of 1906 ending				Deaths in each Quarter of 1906 ending			
DIVISIONS. England and Wales.)	31st March.	30th June.	30th September.	31st December.	31st March.	30th June.	30th September.	31st December.
	No.	No.	No.	No.	No	No.	No.	No.
ᴅ. & Wales....Totals	237,396	237,187	234,684	225,124	140,462	125,387	129,421	135,445
London	32,670	31,760	31,233	29,989	18,910	16,967	17,743	18,292
South-Eastern	21,184	21,455	21,153	20,401	13,130	11,254	11,615	11,839
South Midland	15,125	15,534	15,497	14,630	8,586	7,183	7,844	7,887
Eastern	13,932	13,864	13,532	13,315	7,710	6,659	7,311	7,352
South-Western	11,268	11,208	11,139	10,726	7,995	6,949	5,860	7,068
West Midland	27,969	27,921	27,244	25,796	16,454	14,253	14,185	14,789
North Midland	15,072	15,450	15,186	14,680	8,779	7,104	7,849	8,034
North-Western	38,577	38,925	38,504	37,010	23,870	22,792	23,826	25,207
Yorkshire	26,090	25,790	25,937	25,118	15,715	14,548	15,532	15,598
Northern	18,535	18,539	18,244	17,718	9,901	9,037	9,645	10,295
Monmthsh. & Wales	16,974	16,741	16,955	15,714	9,412	8,641	7,973	9,084

D.—*Comparative Table of* CONSOLS, PROVISIONS, COAL, *and* PAUPERISM *in each* QUARTER *of* 1904-05-06.

Cols...	1			2	3		4						5			
	Average Prices of															
Quarter ended	CONSOLS (for Money) per 100*l*. Stock.*			Average Minimum Rate per Cent. of DISCOUNT Charged by the Bank of England.*	WHEAT per Quarter.†		Price per Pound at the Metropolitan Cattle Market (Sinking the Offal).‡ Beef.			Mutton.			Average Price of Seaborne COAL per Ton in the London Market §		Average Number of PAUPERS Relieved on the *Last Day* of each Week.	
							Inferior Quality.	Second Quality.	First Quality.	Inferior Quality.	Second Quality.	First Quality.			In-door.	Out-d
1904	£	*s.*	*d.*	£	*s.*	*d.*	*d.*	*d.*	*d.*	*d.*	*d.*	*d.*	*s.*	*d.*		
Mar. 31	86	16	7	4·00	27	5	3⅝	5¼	6½	5¾	7⅝	8⅞	16	8‖	247,013	521,6
June 30	89	9	9	3·18	27	1	4⅛	5⅜	6¾	5⅞	7¾	8¾	14	10‖	232,658	509,0
Sept. 30	88	11	10	3·00	28	5	4¼	5½	7⅛	5⅞	7⅝	8¾	14	4¶	227,411	506,9
Dec. 31	88	3	8	3·00	30	3	4¼	5¼	6⅞	5⅝	8	9	14	9‖	247,345	536,0
1905																
Mar. 31	89	17	0	2·87	30	6	4¼	5¼	7⅛	5⅞	8	9	14	11‖	256,537	562,6
June 30	90	9	6	2·50	30	11	4⅜	5¼	6⅞	5¾	7⅞	8¾	No quotation.		241,520	531,2
Sept. 30	90	3	4	2·66	29	5	4⅜	5½	7	6	7⅝	8¾			234,713	522,3
Dec. 31	88	17	0	4·00	27	11	4¼	5¼	6⅞	5⅞	7¼	8¾			253,742	537,6
1906																
Mar. 31	90	2	8	4·00	28	6	4¼	5¼	6¾	7	8¼	9⅜	15	8**	261,475	554,5
June 30	89	11	2	3·65	29	10	4¼	5¼	6¾	5⅞	7⅜	8⅝	15	2**	242,777	527,2
Sept. 30	87	6	4	3·60	28	5	4⅛	5¼	6¾	6¾	7⅞	8⅞	15	4**	236,139	515,0
Dec. 31	86	5	9	5·70	26	3	4	5¼	7¼	7⅛	8⅜	9⅜	16	8**	255,324	524,2

* The prices of Consols and the Rate of Discount are furnished by the Chief Cashier of t
Bank of England. The prices of Consols relate to stock bearing 2½*l*. per cent. interest.

† As published by the Board of Agriculture.

‡ Furnished by the Board of Agriculture.

§ Furnished by the Mineral Statistics Department of the Home Office.

‖ Newcastle and Hartlepool coal only.

¶ Hartlepool coal only.

** Sunderland coal only.

Cols.......	1	2	3	4	5	6	7	8	9	10	1
	Births.	Deaths.	Principal Epidemic Diseases, Cols 4—10.	Small-Pox.	Measles.	Scarlet Fever.	Diphtheria.	Whooping Cough.	Fever.	Diarrhœa.	Dea unc 1 Y t 1, Bi
England and Wales ...	25·9	15·6	1·49	0·00	0·28	0·10	0·23	0·14	0·15	0·59	
76 great towns	26·5	16·2	1·72	0·00	0·34	0·13	0·24	0·15	0·15	0·71	13
142 smaller towns	25·6	14·7	1·59	—	0·34	0·09	0·22	0·14	0·17	0·63	13
England and Wales, less the 218 towns	25·2	15·1	1·21	0·00	0·20	0·08	0·22	0·13	0·15	0·43	11

No. II.—SCOTLAND.

BIRTHS, DEATHS, AND MARRIAGES, IN THE YEAR
ENDED 31ST DECEMBER, 1906.

Serial Table :—Number of BIRTHS, DEATHS, *and* MARRIAGES *in Scotland, and their Proportion to the Population estimated to the Middle of each Year, during each Quarter of the Years* 1906-1902 *inclusive.*

	1906.		1905.		1904.		1903.		1902.	
	Number.	Per 1,000.	Number.	Per 1,000	Number.	Per 1,000.	Number.	Per 1,000.	Number.	Per 1,000.
Quarter—										
Births	32,976	28·3	32,004	27·8	32,894	28·5	32,109	28·4	31,801	28·5
Deaths........	20,488	17·6	20,820	18·1	22,240	19·3	20,931	18·5	22,218	19·9
Marriages ..	7,302	6·3	6,867	6·0	7,619	6·6	7,727	6·8	7,043	6·3
Mean Temperature	37°·9		40°·2		37°·9		39°·9		37°·9	
d Quarter—										
Births	34,960	29.7	35,476	33·4	35,082	30·4	36,377	31·9	34,697	30·7
Deaths........	19,306	16·4	18,763	16·1	19,519	16·9	19,020	16·7	20,771	18·4
Marriages ..	8,699	7·4	8,153	7·0	8,347	7·2	8,515	7·5	8,575	7·6
Mean Temperature	48°·7		49°·2		49°·3		47°·9		47°·4	
d Quarter—										
Births	32,109	27·0	33,044	28·1	32,967	28·3	32,928	28·5	33,263	29·1
Deaths.......	16,439	13·8	16,412	13·9	16,882	14·5	16,609	14·4	16,022	14·0
Marriages ..	8,576	7·2	8,178	6·9	8,118	7·0	8,235	7·2	8,021	7·0
Mean Temperature	56°·0		55°·6		55°·4		54°·2		53°·8	
Quarter—										
Births	31,875	26·8	30,857	26·2	31,627	27·1	32,085	27·8	32,489	28·4
Deaths........	19,352	16·3	18,531	15·7	19,320	16·6	19,413	16·8	18,935	16·6
Marriages ..	8,546	7·2	8,045	6·8	8,169	7·0	7,843	6·8	8,239	7·2
Mean Temperature	43°·2		41°·9		42°·5		41°·7		43°·3	
ar—										
Population .	4,726,070		4,676,603		4,627,656		4,579,223		4,531,299	
Births	131,920	27·9	131,381	28·1	132,570	28·6	133,499	29·2	132,250	29·2
Deaths........	75,585	16·0	74,526	15·9	77,961	16·8	75,973	16·6	77,946	17·2
Marriages ..	33,123	7·0	31,243	6·7	32,253	7·0	32,320	7·1	31,878	7·0

II.—*Special Average Table:—Number of Births, Deaths, and Marriages in Scotland
and in the Town and Country Districts for each Quarter of the Year ending
31st December, 1906, and their Proportion to the Population; also the Number
of Illegitimate Births, and their Proportion to the Total Births.*

Registration Groups of Districts.	Total Births.		Illegitimate Births.		Deaths.		Marriages.	
	Number.	Annual Rate per Cent.	Number.	Per Cent. of Total Births	Number.	Annual Rate per Cent.	Number.	Annual Rate per Cent.
1st Quarter—								
SCOTLAND	32,976	2·83	2,204	6·7	20,488	1·76	7,302	0·63
Principal towns	15,030	2·85	1,000	6·7	9,511	1·80	3,931	0·74
Large ,, ...	4,646	3·16	235	5·1	2,685	1·83	1,004	0·68
Small ,, ...	6,862	2 92	403	5·9	3,982	1·69	1,326	0·56
Mainland rural	5,890	2·60	535	9·1	3,855	1·70	917	0·40
Insular ,, ...	548	1·96	31	5·7	455	1·63	124	0·44
2nd Quarter—								
SCOTLAND	34,960	2·97	2,261	6·5	19,306	1·64	8,699	0·74
Principal towns ...	16,160	3·03	1,014	6·3	8,984	1·68	4,782	0·90
Large ,, ...	4,916	3·31	270	5·5	2,603	1·75	1,108	0·75
Small ,, ...	7,332	3·09	427	5·8	3,664	1·54	1,551	0·65
Mainland rural	6,026	2·63	510	8·5	3,581	1·56	1,193	0·52
Insular ,, ...	526	1·86	40	7·6	474	1·68	65	0·23
3rd Quarter—								
SCOTLAND	32,109	2·70	2,291	7·1	16,439	1·38	8,576	0·72
Principal towns ...	14,594	2·70	1,043	7·1	7,659	1·42	4,928	0·91
Large ,, ...	4,448	2·96	254	5·7	2,179	1·45	1,214	0·81
Small ,, ...	6,768	2·82	439	6·5	3,241	1·35	1,519	0·63
Mainland rural ...	5,686	2·45	522	9·2	2,956	1·28	864	0·37
Insular ,, ...	613	2·15	33	5·4	404	1·42	51	0·18
4th Quarter—								
SCOTLAND	31,875	2·68	2,139	6·7	19,352	1·63	8,546	0·72
Principal towns ...	14,702	2·72	1,023	7·0	9,359	1·73	4,448	0·82
Large ,, ...	4,422	2·94	219	5·0	2,585	1·72	1,046	0 70
Small ,, ..	6,684	2·78	418	6·3	3,560	1·48	1,562	0·65
Mainland rural ...	5,447	2·35	449	8·2	3,466	1·50	1,372	0·59
Insular ,, ...	620	2·17	30	4·8	382	1·34	118	0·41

Population of Scotland.

Population.	Scotland.	Principal Towns.	Large Towns.	Small Towns.	Mainland Rural.	Insular Rural.
By Census of 1901	4,472,103	1,956,561	577,273	896,490	925,110	116,669
Estimated to the middle of 1906	4,726,070	2,143,052	596,193	953,517	920,018	113,290

III.—*Divisional Table:*—Marriages, Births, *and* Deaths *Registered in the Year ended 31st December,* 1906.

(Compiled from the Registrar-General's Quarterly Returns.)

1	2	3	4	5	6
DIVISIONS. (Scotland.)	Area in Statute Acres.	Population, 1901. (*Persons.*)	Marriages.	Births.	Deaths.
		No.	No.	No.	No.
Scotland .... *Totals*	19,069,500	4,472,103	33,123	131,920	75,585
I. Northern	2,330,092	112,175	503	2,315	1,724
II. North-Western........	4,671,744	162,728	732	3,483	2,543
III. North-Eastern	2,317,773	460,371	2,958	12,680	6,778
IV. East Midland	2,565,126	665,215	4,536	13,609	10,832
V. West Midland	2,576,404	352,981	2,176	10,552	6,118
VI. South-Western........	1,440,676	1,862,775	15,811	62,924	33,572
VII. South-Eastern	1,168,149	662,415	5,197	17,980	10,914
VIII. Southern	1,999,536	193,443	1,210	4,377	3,104

No. III.—GREAT BRITAIN AND IRELAND.

Summary *of* Marriages, *in the Year ended 30th September,* 1906; *and of* Births *and* Deaths, *in the Year ended 31st December,* 1906.

(Compiled from the Quarterly Returns of the respective Registrars-General.)

COUNTRIES.	[000's omitted.]		Marriages.	Per 1,000 of Population.	Births.	Per 1,000 of Population.	Deaths.	Per 1,000 of Population.
	Area in Statute Acres.	Population Middle 1906. Estimated.						
		No.	No.	Ratio.	No.	Ratio.	No.	Ratio.
England and Wales	37,327,	34,547,	267,346	7·8	934,391	27·1	530,715	15·4
Scotland	19,070,	4,726,	32,622	7·1	131,920	27·9	75,585	16·0
Ireland	20,228,	4,386,	22,566	5·2	103,459	23·6	74,425	17·0
Great Britain and Ireland	76,625,	43,659,	322,534	7·4	1,169,770	26·7	680,725	15·5

Trade of United Kingdom, 1906-1905-1904.—*Distribution of* **Exports** *of British and Irish Produce and Manufactures from United Kingdom, according to their Declared Real Value; and the Declared Real Value (Ex-duty) of* **Imports** *at Port of Entry, and therefore including Freight and Importer's Profit.*

Merchandise (*excluding Gold and Silver* Imported from, and Exported to, the following Foreign Countries, &c.	1906.		1905.		1904.	
	Imports from	Exports to	Imports from	Exports to	Imports from	Exports to
	£	£	£	£	£	£
Russia { Northern ports	20,820,	7,871,	19,784,	7,053,	17,682,	6,849,
Russia { Southern „	9,233,	818,	13,584,	1,095,	13,721,	1,381,
Sweden	10,727,	5,600,	9,828,	5,226,	9,707,	4,770,
Norway	6,907,	3,725,	5,959,	3,305,	5,644,	2,963,
Denmark	16,433,	4,670,	15,416,	4,004,	15,912,	3,580,
Germany	38,033,	33,627,	35,826,	29,712,	33,944,	25,103,
Holland	36,652,	11,615,	35,482,	9,703,	34,690,	8,200,
Belgium	29,098,	11,592,	27,746,	10,069,	27,536,	9,052,
France	53,816,	20,495,	53,097,	16,051,	51.107,	15,254,
Portugal	3,343,	2,605,	2,932,	2,238,	2,864,	2,068,
Spain	15,842,	4,641,	13,871,	4,249,	13,672,	4,338,
Italy	3,611,	11,185,	3,313,	8,892,	3,325,	8.371,
Austria-Hungary	1,214,	2,369,	1,488,	1,845,	1,817,	1,894,
Greece	2,223,	1,411,	1,345,	1,172,	1,264,	1,478,
Roumania	3,613,	1,591,	1,690,	1,235,	3,137,	1,056,
Turkey (European and Asiatic) and Crete }	6,079,	8,099,	5,511,	6,687,	5,754,	7,347,
Egypt	16,857,	8,936,	14,977,	7,843,	14,302,	8.273,
Java	537,	2,922,	1,890,	2,992,	1,187,	2,909,
Philippine and Guam	1,658,	1,527,	1,889,	2,276,	2,338,	1,415,
China, excluding Hong Kong	3,304,	12,237,	2,346,	13,153,	2,762,	8,809,
Japan	2.953,	12,913,	1,860,	9,684,	2,349,	4,889,
United States { Atlantic	127,738,	27,142,	113,632,	23,461,	116,025,	19.844,
United States { Pacific	3,367,	647,	2,051,	446,	3,202,	353,
Peru	1,681,	1,344,	2,369,	1,215,	2,372,	1,146,
Chile	6,295,	6,084,	6,062,	4,451,	5,423,	3,259,
Brazil	9,115,	7.653,	8,114,	6,634,	6,238,	5,988,
Argentine Republic	23,809,	19,430,	25,034,	12,979,	23,035,	10.847,
Other countries	10,844,	21,660,	10,283,	18,773,	10,011,	17,337,
Total—Foreign Countries...	465,802,	254,409,	437,379,	216,443,	431,020,	188,773,
BRITISH POSSESSIONS.						
Channel Isles	1,559,	1,140,	1,669,	1,103,	1,586,	1,105,
Niger Protectorate	1,556,	920,	1,341,	948,	1,430,	872,
Cape of Good Hope	5,541,	10,501,	4,909,	10,514,	4,933,	12,049,
India	35,486,	41,582,	33,671,	39,785,	34,244,	37,061,
Burmah	2,344,	3,569,	2,402,	3,235,	2,229,	3,580,
Straits Settlements	8,903,	5,521,	6,838,	3,298,	6,284,	3,120,
Ceylon	4,448,	1,575,	4,486,	1,379,	4,135,	1,411,
Australia	29,143,	20.230,	26,968,	17,023,	23,569,	17,336,
New Zealand	15,605,	7,391,	13,391,	6,467,	12,742,	6,315,
Canada	30,331,	13,647,	25,685,	11,910,	22,621,	10,624,
British West Indies*	2,109,	2,188,	1,976,	2,003,	1,895,	2,025,
Other Possessions	5,161,	13,000,	4,557,	15,915,	4,350,	16,431,
Total—British Possessions	142,186,	121,264,	127,893,	113,580,	120,018,	111,938,
Total — Foreign Countries and British Possessions .... }	607,988,	375,673,	565,272,	330,023,	551,039,	300,711,

* Including Bahamas.

Trade of United Kingdom, for the Years 1906-1901.—*Declared Value of the Total Exports of* Foreign *and* Colonial *Produce and Manufactures to each Foreign Country and British Possession.*

Merchandise Exported to the following Foreign Countries, &c.	[000's omitted.]					
	1906.	1905.	1904.	1903.	1902.	1901.
	£	£	£	£	£	£
Russia { Northern ports	6,675,	6,248,	6,705,	6,825,	4,943,	5,094,
Russia { Southern „	418,	467,	350,	225,	315,	443,
Sweden and Norway {	1,066, 485,	} 1,193,	1,118,	1,282,	1,183,	1,580,
Denmark*	514,	483,	363,	415,	421,	557,
Germany	14,729,	13,060,	11,325,	10,967,	10,244,	10,647,
Holland	5,228,	4,845,	4,709,	5,354,	4,625,	4,655,
Belgium	5,220,	4,755,	4,423,	3,949,	4,210,	4,468,
France	8,293,	7,091,	6,448,	7,347,	6,688,	7,229,
Portugal	657,	575,	607,	421,	417,	383,
Spain	703,	599,	573,	671,	581,	628,
Italy	1,319,	897,	851,	671,	684,	681,
Austria-Hungary	809,	746,	674,	672,	588,	698,
Greece	103,	81,	82,	83,	69,	66,
Roumania	76,	67,	96,	53,	128,	73,
Turkey (European and Asiatic) and Crete	329,	289,	240,	243,	286,	321,
Egypt	214,	212,	158,	120,	107,	104,
Java	16,	19,	103,	13,	14,	25,
Philippine Islands and Guam†	36,	298,	119,	43,	41,	51,
China ‡	107,	162,	81,	57,	47,	54,
Japan §	207,	135,	154,	126,	211,	77,
United States	25,483,	23,378,	19,075,	19,001,	19,320,	19,257,
Peru	109,	121,	141,	127,	102,	133,
Chile	320,	321,	273,	323,	224,	196,
Brazil	305,	296,	245,	230,	260,	288,
Argentine Republic	481,	379,	727,	592,	251,	221,
Other countries	1,896,	1,627,	1,819,	1,316,	1,369,	1,579,
Total to Foreign Countries	75,798,	68,544,	61,459,	61,236,	57,328,	59,508,
BRITISH POSSESSIONS.						
Channel Islands	226,	215,	216,	229,	223,	228,
Nigerian Protectorates	107,	115,	131,	129,	139,	132,
Cape of Good Hope	1,078,	986,	1,039,	1,221,	1,420,	1,193,
India (including Burmah)	1,233,	1,363,	903,	844,	810,	768,
Straits Settlements (including Malay States)	68,	57,	54,	74,	60,	79,
Ceylon	92,	68,	55,	72,	63,	60,
Australia	2,551,	2,486,	2,505,	1,985,	2,000,	2,157,
New Zealand	656,	571,	582,	593,	481,	469,
Canada	1,779,	1,854,	1,624,	1,631,	1,650,	1,545,
British West Indies (including Bahamas)	321,	302,	309,	239,	225,	334,
Other Possessions	1,195,	1,238,	1,428,	1,320,	1,416,	1,369,
Total to British Possessions	9,306,	9,255,	8,846,	8,337,	8,487,	8,334,
Total to British Possessions and Foreign Countries	85,104,	77,799,	70,304,	69,574,	65,815,	67,842,

* Including Iceland and Greenland.　　　† Included Ladrone Islands before 1905.
‡ Excluding Hong Kong, Weihaiwei and Macao.　§ Including Formosa.

Values of Imports *into the United Kingdom for the Years* 1904-05-06.*

[From the Monthly Trade Returns, December, 1906.]

	Year ended 31st December,			Increase (+) or Decrease(−) in 1906 as Compared with 1905.	Increase (+) or Decrease(−) in 1906 as Compared with 1904.
	1904.	1905.	1906.		
I. FOOD, DRINK, AND TOBACCO—	£	£	£	£	£
A. Grain and flour	68,796,597	69,200,285	67,879,948	−1,320,337	− 916,649
B. Meat, including animals for food	48,666,315	49,431,748	52,044,106	+2,612,358	+3,377,791
C. Other food and drink—					
(1.) Non-dutiable	66,387,599	63,023,140	68,837,005	+5,813,865	+5,449,406
(2.) Dutiable	45,282,096	45,922,482	44,734,345	−1,188,137	− 547,751
D. Tobacco.................. ..	4,512,378	3,721,920	4,734,062	+1,012,142	+ 221,684
Total, Class I.................	230,644,985	231,299,575	238,229,466	+6,929,891	+7,584,481
II. RAW MATERIALS AND ARTICLES MAINLY UNMANUFACTURED—					
A. Coal, coke, and manufactured fuel....................	2,689	42,582	47,100	+ 4,518	+ 44,411
B. Iron ore, scrap iron, and steel	4,599,200	5,525,575	6,766,763	+1,241,188	+2,167,563
C. Other metallic ores	6,597,702	7,610,990	9,040,766	+1,429,766	+2,443,064
D. Wood and timber	23,637,985	23,274,020	27,511,279	+4,237,259	+3,873,294
E. Cotton	55,024,825	52,370,878	56,125,204	+3,754,326	+1,100,379
F. Wool	23,316,455	26,648,737	30,540,421	+3,891,684	+7,223,966
G. Other textile materials	13,030,669	14,511,978	17,026,320	+2,514,342	+3,995,651
H. Oil seeds, nuts, oils, fats, and gums	25,290,505	23,600,927	25,644,240	+2,043,313	+ 353,735
I. Hides and undressed skins ...	6,576,310	8,084,793	10,699,293	+2,614,500	+4,122,983
J. Materials for paper making ...	3,554,133	3,802,501	3,935,570	+ 133,069	+ 381,437
K. Miscellaneous	20,582,340	22,633,578	24,172,245	+1,538,667	+3,589,905
Total, Class II.	182,212,813	188,106,559	211,509,201	+23,402,642	+29,296,388
III. ARTICLES WHOLLY OR MAINLY MANUFACTURED—					
A. Iron and steel and manufactures thereof	8,216,772	8,589,405	8,360,135	− 229,270	+ 143,363
B. Other metals and manufactures thereof	20,953,877	21,840,696	28,229,260	+6,388,564	+7,275,383
C. Cutlery, hardware, implements, and instruments...	3,814,587	3,615,107	3,771,646	+ 156,539	− 42,941
D. Electrical goods and apparatus (other than machinery and telegraph and telephone wire).....................	845,873	1,010,304	1,187,565	+ 177,261	+ 341,692
E. Machinery	4,312,440	4,537,871	5,127,187	+ 589,316	+ 814,747
F. Ships (new)	26,196	32,623	28,400	− 4,223	+ 2,204
G. Manufactures of wood and timber (including furniture)	2,083,306	1,968,196	2,016,918	+ 48,722	− 66,388
H. Yarns and textile fabrics—					
(1.) Cotton	6,648,062	7,920,252	9,326,527	+1,406,275	+2,678,465
(2.) Wool	11,428,539	12,524,037	12,075,874	− 448,163	+ 647,335
(3.) Other materials	19,385,895	19,244,139	20,081,042	+ 836,903	+ 695,147
I. Apparel ....:	3,512,904	3,952,693	3,785,167	− 167,526	+ 272,263
J. Chemicals, drugs, dyes, and colours	9,211,770	9,624,638	10,102,490	+ 477,852	+ 890,720
K. Leather and manufactures thereof (including boots and shoes, and gloves) ...	10,893,182	11,037,983	12,745,138	+1,707,155	+1,851,956
L. Earthenware and glass	4,337,273	4,312,218	4,219,291	− 92,927	− 117,982
M. Paper.........................	4,940,619	5,256,065	5,728,520	+ 472,455	+ 787,901
N. Miscellaneous	25,359,965	27,930,680	29,021,088	+1,090,408	+3,661,123
Total, Class III...............	135,971,260	143,396,907	155,806,248	+12,409,341	+19,834,988
IV. MISCELLANEOUS AND UNCLASSIFIED (including parcel post)	2,209,570	2,216,876	2,442,978	+ 226,102	+ 233,408
Total	551,038,628	565,019,917	607,987,893	+42,967,976	+56,949,265

* The values of the imports represent the cost, insurance, and freight; or, when goods are consigned for sale, the latest sale value of such goods.

Values of **Exports** *of British and Irish Produce and Manufactures for the Years* **1904-05-06.***

[From the Monthly Trade Returns, December, 1906.]

	Year ended 31st December,			Increase (+) or Decrease(−) in 1906 as Compared with 1905.	Increase (+) or Decrease(−) in 1906 as Compared with 1904.
	1904.	1905.	1906.		
I. FOOD, DRINK, AND TOBACCO—	£	£	£	£	£
A. Grain and flour	1,804,503	2,768,937	2,582,092	− 186,845	+ 777,589
B. Meat, including animals for food	745,197	924,365	1,339,686	+ 415,321	+ 594,489
C. Other food and drink	13,538,705	14,724,557	16,145,652	+1,421,095	+ 2,606,947
D. Tobacco	776,045	981,774	1,061,395	+ 79,621	+ 285,350
Total, Class I.	16,864,450	19,399,633	21,128,825	+1,729,192	+ 4,264,375
II. RAW MATERIALS AND ARTICLES MAINLY UNMANUFACTURED—					
A. Coal, coke, and manufactured fuel	26,862,386	26,061,120	31,504,291	+5,443,171	+ 4,641,905
B. Iron ore, scrap iron, and steel	500,621	473,326	596,474	+ 123,148	+ 95,853
C. Other metallic ores	130,630	114,465	176,091	+ 61,626	+ 45,461
D. Wood and timber	67,593	77,056	91,710	+ 14,654	+ 24,117
E. Cotton	..	...	...	...	...
F. Wool	2,164,823	2,511,711	2,901,726	+ 390,015	+ 736,903
G. Other textile materials	179,672	155,477	164,455	+ 8,978	− 15,217
H. Oil seeds, nuts, oils, fats, and gums	2,759,019	2,592,538	2,826,521	+ 233,983	+ 67,502
I. Hides and undressed skins	1,428,041	1,853,885	2,210,850	+ 356,965	+ 782,809
J. Materials for paper making	428,481	535,840	714,293	+ 178,453	+ 285,812
K. Miscellaneous	1,709,446	1,936,543	2,084,838	+ 148,295	+ 375,392
Total, Class II.	36,230,712	36,311,961	43,271,249	+6,959,288	+ 7,040,537
III. ARTICLES WHOLLY OR MAINLY MANUFACTURED—					
A. Iron and steel and manufactures thereof	28,066,671	31,826,438	39,880,563	+8,054,125	+11,813,892
B. Other metals and manufactures thereof	6,991,421	8,920,533	10,127,102	+1,206,569	+ 3,135,681
C. Cutlery, hardware, implements, and instruments	4,891,191	5,115,316	5,882,385	+ 767,069	+ 991,194
D. Electrical goods and apparatus (other than machinery, and telegraph and telephone wire)	1,607,316	2,431,744	2,381,691	− 50,053	+ 774,375
E. Machinery	21,065,191	23,260,326	26,732,693	+3,472,367	+ 5,667,502
F. Ships (new)	4,455,151	5,431,298	8,685,240	+3,253,942	+ 4,230,089
G. Manufactures of wood and timber (including furniture)	1,281,678	1,214,039	1,305,569	+ 91,530	+ 23,891
H. Yarns and textile fabrics—					
(1.) Cotton	83,873,746	92,010,985	99,602,535	+7,591,550	+15,728 789
(2.) Wool	26,923,563	29,150,610	31,844,608	+2,693,998	+ 4,921,045
(3.) Other materials	12,414,591	13,204,899	14,979,559	+1,774,660	+ 2,564,968
I. Apparel	5,745,368	6,021,242	6,818,136	+ 796,894	+ 1,072,768
J. Chemicals, drugs, dyes, and colours	13,647,449	14,536,857	15,526,782	+ 989,925	+ 1,879,333
K. Leather and manufactures thereof (including boots and shoes, and gloves)	4,758,999	5,660,494	6,390,980	+ 730,486	+ 1,631,981
L. Earthenware and glass	3,116,223	3,205,552	3,661,605	+ 456,053	+ 545,382
M. Paper	1,876,797	1,939,767	2,062,611	+ 122,844	+ 185,814
N. Miscellaneous	22,621,588	25,143,114	29,726,652	+4,583,538	+ 7,105,064
Total, Class III.	243,336,943	269,073,214	305,608,711	+36,535,497	+62,271,768
IV. MISCELLANEOUS AND UNCLASSIFIED (including parcel post)	4,278,935	5,031,806	5,664,128	+ 632,322	+ 1,385,193
Total	300,711,040	329,816,614	375,672,913	+45,856,299	+74,961,873

* The values of the exports represent the cost and the charges of delivering the goods on board the ship, and are known as the "free on board" values.

PING.—(United Kingdom.)—*Account of Tonnage of Vessels Entered and Cleared Cargoes, from and to Various Countries, during the* **Years** *ended Dec.*, **1906-05-04.**

Countries from whence Entered and to which Cleared.	Total British and Foreign.					
	1906.		1905.		1904.	
	Entered.	Cleared.	Entered.	Cleared.	Entered.	Cleared.
	Tons.	Tons.	Tons.	Tons.	Tons.	Tons.
REIGN COUNTRIES.						
⎰ Northern ports ...	2,293,975	1,880,022	2,171,572	1,809,207	⎫	
a ⎨ Southern ,, ...	780,788	277,699	1,072,154	248,338	⎬3,434,179	2,142,150
⎱ Pacific ,, ...	—	12,766	—	1,899	⎭	
en	1,805,742	2,228,759	1,672,701	2,063,769	1,741,107	2,040,632
ay	1,566,923	1,232,893	1,489,257	1,206,985	1,443,646	1,176,801
ark.....................	492,941	1,838,687	474,356	1,711,686	480,192	1,690,885
any....................	2,842,042	5,448,404	2,615,509	5,451,824	2,612,675	4,868,559
rlands	2,775,614	3,348,841	2,640,007	2,955,058	2,621,858	2,574,667
m	2,332,566	2,894,110	2,161,223	2,445,494	2,114,168	2,381,372
e	2,789,166	6,116,142	2,762,645	4,909,993	2,752,477	4,879,812
....	3,706,301	1,816,609	3,595,410	1,708,513	3,104,635	1,781,428
gal	250,497	647,568	210,890	590,640	264,217	596,372
....	265,172	4,270,357	265,641	3,611,284	242,719	3,519,188
ia-Hungary	103,142	463,629	115,602	362,606	153,674	395.389
e	214,086	230,739	193,808	201,334	205,904	248,073
y	296,249	354,139	253,390	351,621	345,988	372,735
ania	307,144	146,168	158,018	146,161	318,337	130,249
, ...	420,052	1,504,532	449,764	1,336,616	401,957	1,326,622
ia	259,235	454,816	248,103	417,626	232,062	296,326
guese East Africa ...	77,474	323,999	74,993	340,126	69,852	286,494
d States of America ...	7,546,987	5,767,874	6,921,386	5,565,869	6,871,316	5,373,701
o, Foreign W. Indies, ⎱ Central America ....⎰	320,327	548,241	312,202	486,834	231,738	324,463
bia	82,649	159,447	40,513	166,254	81,541	290,369
....	220,758	903,929	207,450	893,842	182,864	815,579
....	108,861	92,841	99,063	79,515	137,333	96,475
....	188,893	522,404	192,959	549,485	197,720	461,258
ay	7,612	485,296	21,834	317,436	10,501	340,287
tine Republic	1,628,751	1,976,961	1,585,741	1,512,022	1,623,527	1,309,302
....	21,309	110,659	32,983	221,769	26,851	278,511
....	48,755	203,345	123,197	194,246	77,470	252,319
....	400,072	558,750	283,259	449,730	260,763	313,953
countries	456,714	569,113	440,439	537,146	454,153	572,877
l, Foreign Countries.	34,610,797	47,389,739	32,886,069	42,844,928	32,695,424	41,136,848
ITISH POSSESSIONS.						
American Colonies ...	2,493,336	1,868,507	2,141,354	1,689,521	2,143,543	1,525,321
h India	1,752,371	1,508,600	1,875,972	1,495,604	1,941,457	1,496,873
itius, Ceylon, Straits⎱ ements, & Hong Kong⎰	68,659	359,274	53,378	379,824	53,746	607,264
alia.....................	936,587	755,708	1,049,129	736,582	⎱1,318,961	1,122,897
Zealand	353,961	420,051	285,192	345,850	⎰	
Indies	194,685	162,431	208,849	190,206	212,443	185,523
nel Islands.	406,149	321,380	418,059	315,227	420,463	315,209
ltar and Malta........	88,340	366,691	32,203	369,652	85,014	472,188
h South Africa...........	728,046	713.112	738,374	863,480	822,078	1,161,766
possessions	326,220	432,864	307,647	392,249	248,768	442,475
al, British Possessions	7,348,354	6,908,618	7,110,657	6,778,195	7,246,473	7,329,516
FOREIGN COUNTRIES RITISH POSSESSIONS.						
e Months ⎰ 1906........	41,959,151	54,298,357	—	—	—	—
ided ⎨ '05	--	—	39,996,726	49,623,123	—	—
ember, ⎱ '04.......	—	—	—	—	39,941,897	48,466,364

GOLD AND SILVER BULLION AND SPECIE. —(United Kingdom.)
—*Declared Real Value of*, IMPORTED AND EXPORTED, *for the* Years
1906-05-04.

[000's omitted.]

Countries.	1906. Gold.	1906. Silver.	1905. Gold.	1905. Silver.	1904. Gold.	1904. Silver.
Imported from—	£	£	£	£	£	£
Australasia	6,901,	81,	4,047,	205,	4,687,	274,
S. America, Brazil, Mexico, W.Indies	1,514,	535,	1,279,	351,	1,234,	176,
United States	71,	14,891,	25,	9,785,	26,	8,413,
	8,486,	15,507,	5,351,	10,341,	5,947,	8,863,
France	3,400,	422,	366,	321,	472,	284,
Germany, Holland, and Belgium	3,006,	536,	3,266,	511,	2,441,	523,
Portugal, Spain, and Gibraltar	129,	61,	144,	53,	202,	128,
Malta and Egypt	504,	70,	310,	34,	33,	52,
China, with Hong Kong and Japan	—	327,	—	—	10,	86,
West Coast of Africa	797,	50,	594,	160,	344,	90,
British Possessions in South Africa	25,714,	72,	21,286,	22,	16,342,	14,
British East Indies	3,228,	—	7,067,	—	7,956,	676,
All other Countries	779,	243,	184,	1,550,	130,	971,
Totals Imported	46,043,	17,288,	38,568,	12,992,	33,877,	11,687,
Exported to—						
France	4,621,	1,292,	12,442,	693,	5,607,	653,
Germany, Holland, Belg.,and Sweden	1,091,	386,	1,151,	451,	9,910,	407,
Russia	1,695,	110,	--	3,954,	73,	825,
Portugal, Spain, and Gibraltar	243,	76,	161,	74,	57,	58,
Malta and Egypt	6,380,	192,	2,156,	167,	4,419	348,
	14,030,	2,056,	15,910,	5,339,	20,066,	2,291,
B. India, China, Hong Kong, and Japan	4,681,	15,498,	3,930,	8,723,	4,121,	10,038,
United States	14,188,	—	1,817,	—	697,	198,
South Africa	55,	8,	65,	12,	1,	10,
S. America, Mexico, W. Indies	7,789,	277,	7,314,	122,	6,322,	139,
All other Countries	1,874,	1,026,	1,794,	366,	1,832,	588,
Totals Exported	42,617,	18,865,	30,830,	14,562,	33,039,	13,264,
Excess of imports	3,426,	—	7,738,	—	838,	—
„ exports	—	1,577,	—	1,570,	—	1,577,

BANK OF ENGLAN

Pursuant to the Act 7th and 8th Victoria, cap. 32 (1844

[0,000's omitted.]

	2	3	4	5		
		ISSUE DEPARTMENT.				
Liabilities.			Assets.		Notes	Minimum Rates
	DATES.			Gold Coin	in Hands of Public.	of Discount at
Notes Issued	(Wednesdays)	Government Debt.	Other Securities.	and Bullion.	(Col. 1 minus col. 16.)	Bank of England.
£ Mlns.	1906.	£ Mlns.	£ Mlns.	£ Mlns.	£ Mlns.	Per cnt.
45,87	Jan. 3	11,02	7,43	27,42	29,35	4
46,94	,, 10	11,02	7,43	28,49	29,43	
48,02	,, 17	11,02	7,43	29,57	28,41	
49,37	,, 24	11,02	7,43	30,92	28,28	
49,60	,, 31	11,02	7,43	31,15	28,47	
50,41	Feb. 7	11,02	7,43	31,96	28,23	
50,89	,, 14	11,02	7,43	32,44	28,06	
52,71	,, 21	11,02	7,43	34,26	27,91	
53,94	,, 28	11,02	7,43	35,49	28,27	
54,85	Mar. 7	11,02	7,43	35,90	28,29	
54,76	,, 14	11,02	7,43	36,31	27,93	
55,28	,, 21	11,02	7,43	36,83	28,09	
55,08	,, 28	11,02	7,43	36,63	28,50	
53,86	April 4	11,02	7,43	35,41	29,18	3½
51,81	,, 11	11,02	7,43	33,63	29,26	
50,68	,, 18	11,02	7,43	32,23	28,88	
50,06	,, 25	11,02	7,43	31,61	28,71	
49,56	May 2	11,02	7,43	31,11	29,06	4
48,36	,, 9	11,02	7,43	29,91	28,81	
48,68	,, 16	11,02	7,43	30,23	28,66	
50,46	,, 23	11,02	7,43	32,01	28,62	
50,73	,, 30	11,02	7,43	32,28	28,95	
50,71	June 6	11,02	7,43	32,26	28,99	
51,80	,, 13	11,02	7,43	33,35	28,63	
54,17	,, 20	11,02	7,43	35,72	28,96	3½
54,59	,, 27	11,02	7,43	36,14	29,37	
53,84	July 4	11,02	7,43	35,89	30,28	
54,36	,, 11	11,02	7,43	35,91	30,07	
54,37	,, 18	11,02	7,43	35,92	29,91	
54,29	,, 25	11,02	7,43	35,84	29,95	
53,82	Aug. 1	11,02	7,43	35,37	30,58	
53,37	,, 8	11,02	7,43	34,92	30,03	
54,10	,, 15	11,02	7,43	35,65	29,60	
54,83	,, 22	11,02	7,43	36,38	29,33	
55,57	,, 29	11,02	7,43	37,12	29,21	
55,07	Sept. 5	11,02	7,43	36,62	29,09	
52,09	,, 12	11,02	7,43	33,64	28,73	
51,76	,, 19	11,02	7,43	33,31	28,38	4
51,18	,, 26	11,02	7,43	32,73	29,09	
48,78	Oct. 3	11,02	7,43	30,33	29,67	
46,18	,, 10	11,02	7,43	27,73	29,28	5
46,15	,, 17	11,02	7,43	27,70	28,76	6
45,49	,, 24	11,02	7,43	27,04	28,69	
45,64	,, 31	11,02	7,43	27,19	28,84	
46,42	Nov. 7	11,02	7,43	27,97	28,56	
46,89	,, 14	11,02	7,43	28,44	28,23	
48,35	,, 21	11,02	7,43	29,90	28,22	
50,42	,, 28	11,02	7,43	31,97	28,10	
50,06	Dec. 5	11,02	7,43	31,63	28,41	
50,04	,, 12	11,02	7,43	31,59	28,50	
47,22	,, 19	11,02	7,43	28,77	28,73	
46,49	,, 26	11,02	7,43	28,04	28,80	

—WEEKLY RETURN.

for Wednesday in each Week, during the Year **1906.**

[0,000's omitted.]

	Liabilities.				DATES.	Assets.				T.
Capital and Rest.		Deposits.		Seven Day and other Bills.	(Wednesdys.)	Securities		Reserve.		Li t ɛ As
Capital.	Rest.	Public.	Private.			Government.	Other.	Notes.	Gold and Silver Coin.	
£ Mlns.	£ Mlns.	£ Mlns.	£ Mlns.	£ Mlns.	1906.	£ Mlns.	£ Mlns.	£ Mlns.	£ Mlns.	M
14,55	3,33	9,56	50,11	,9	Jan. 3	17,39	42,40	16,52	1,33	77
14,55	3,46	8,09	47,97	,10	,, 10	18,34	37,02	17,51	1,30	74
14,55	3,51	7,73	41,14	,12	,, 17	12,84	33,20	19,61	1,40	67
14,55	3,53	7,81	47,29	,9	,, 24	13,44	37,22	21,09	1,52	7?
14,55	3,54	8,02	45,34	,10	,, 31	13,94	34,88	21,12	1,61	7?
14,55	3,58	9,64	41,79	,12	Feb. 7	12,58	33,31	22,17	1,62	6?
14,55	3,61	13,66	39,55	,12	,, 14	12,68	34,33	22,83	1,66	7?
14,55	3,63	16,81	42,53	,10	,, 21	15,23	35,84	24,80	1,76	77
14,55	3,68	18,10	45,45	,9	,, 28	16,39	38,03	25,67	1,78	81
14,55	3,69	17,40	41,74	,8	Mar. 7	16,38	33,25	26,05	1,77	77
14,55	3,70	19,12	41,01	,8	,, 14	16,11	33,72	26,83	1,80	7?
14,55	3,71	19,37	42,70	,9	,, 21	16,11	35,32	27,19	1,80	8?
14,55	3,78	19,26	43,62	,6	,, 28	16,11	36,75	26,58	1,82	81
14,55	3,16	15,59	42,75	,7	April 4	16,11	33,55	24,68	1,77	76
14,55	3,19	10,15	44,66	,7	,, 11	16,11	32,31	22,55	1,65	72
14,55	3,21	9,89	43,50	,7	,, 18	15,98	31,88	21,80	1,57	71
14,55	3,23	9,54	48,50	,7	,, 25	15,98	37,06	21,36	1,49	75
14,55	3,24	8,33	48,08	,6	May 2	15,98	36,39	20,50	1,39	74
14,55	3,25	8,21	44,79	,6	,, 9	15,98	34,00	19,55	1,33	7?
14,55	3,27	9,42	42,10	,7	,, 16	15,98	32,04	20,02	1,37	69
14,55	3,28	10,33	42,12	,11	,, 23	15,98	31,23	21,84	1,35	7?
14,55	3,26	10,05	42,68	,10	,, 30	15,98	31,48	21,79	1,39	7?
14,55	3,24	8,58	44,58	,8	June 6	15,98	32,04	21,72	1,30	71
14,55	3,25	9,05	42,74	,9	,, 13	15,98	29,13	23,17	1,41	69
14,55	3,26	11,53	42,73	,11	,, 20	15,98	29,54	25,21	1,46	72
14,55	3,27	11,41	44,64	,12	,, 27	15,98	31,36	25,22	1,43	73
14,55	3,38	12,09	48,87	,9	July 4	16,98	36,55	23,56	1,41	78
14,55	3,44	7,17	45,90	,9	,, 11	15,98	29,41	24,29	1,46	71
14,55	3,48	9,04	43,50	,7	,, 18	15,98	28,80	24,46	1,42	7?
14,55	3,49	9,73	43,58	,7	,, 25	15,98	29,76	24,34	1,35	71
14,55	3,53	9,49	42,39	,6	Aug. 1	15,98	29,42	23,24	1,39	7?
14,55	3,53	8,46	42,24	,5	,, 8	15,97	28,13	23,35	1,39	68
14,55	3,57	9,52	42,11	,6	,, 15	15,97	27,96	24,49	1,39	69
14,55	3,62	11,15	42,24	,6	,, 22	15,97	28,72	25,50	1,42	71
14,55	3,55	10,57	43,75	,5	,, 29	15,97	28,74	26,36	1,40	72
14,55	3,68	8,91	45,66	,5	Sept. 5	15,96	29,53	25,97	1,39	72
14,55	3,69	9,22	42,48	,5	,, 12	15,96	29,27	23,35	1,41	69
14,55	3,71	11,15	40,89	,7	,, 19	15,96	29,63	23,88	1,40	70
14,55	3,78	11,33	43,20	,7	,, 26	15,96	33,58	22,09	1,29	72
14,55	3,80	9,73	43,19	,6	Oct. 3	15,96	34,97	19,10	1,30	71
14,55	3,23	6,17	45,36	,5	,, 10	15,96	35,12	16,90	1,39	69
14,55	3,24	7,59	42,39	,6	,, 17	15,96	33,02	17,39	1,47	67
14,55	3,25	8,90	40,78	,5	,, 24	15,96	33,39	16,80	1,39	67
14,55	3,25	9,60	40,09	,4	,, 31	15,96	33,42	16,80	1,36	67
14,55	3,28	8,84	40,88	,4	Nov. 7	15,96	32,55	17,86	1,22	67
14,55	3,30	9,31	40,36	,5	,, 14	15,46	32,10	18,67	1,36	67
14,55	3,32	10,58	42,34	,6	,, 21	15,46	34,03	20,12	1,24	70
14,55	3,32	8,31	44,22	,4	,, 28	15,46	31,37	22,83	1,29	70
14,55	3,28	6,13	44,98	,5	Dec. 5	15,46	30,59	21,67	1,27	68
14,55	3,29	6,57	41,76	,4	,, 12	15,46	28,02	21,54	1,21	66
14,55	3,33	7,00	44,07	,7	,, 19	15,46	33,86	18,49	1,22	69
14,55	3,34	6,43	43,41	,7	,, 26	15,46	34,12	17,70	1,02	68

REVENUE of the United Kingdom.

Calendar Years.

Net Produce in Quarters *and* Years *ended 31st* Dec., **1906-05-04-03.**

[000's omitted.]

QUARTERS, ended 31st Dec.	1906.	1905.	1906. Less.	1906. More.	Corresponding Quarters. 1904.	Corresponding Quarters. 1903.
	£	£	£	£	£	£
*Customs	8,708,	9,389,	681,	—	9,628,	8,717,
*Excise	8,790,	8,550,	—	240,	8,760,	8,870,
*Stamps and estate, &c., duties	5,720,	5,380,	—	340,	5,450,	5,260,
Taxes (Land Tax and House Duty)	90,	110,	20,	—	110,	40,
Post Office	4,450,	4,470,	20,	—	4,270,	4,100,
Telegraph Service	1,070,	1,070,	—	—	970,	920,
	28,828,	28,969,	721,	580,	29,188,	27,907,
Property and Income Tax	2.200,	2,230,	30,	—	2,190,	2,060,
	31,028,	31,199,	751,	580,	31,378,	29,967,
Crown Lands	170,	180,	10,	—	180,	180,
Interest on Advances	13,	1,	—	12,	1,	3,
Miscellaneous	571,	367,	—	204,	290,	344,
Totals	31,782,	31,747,	761,	796,	31,849,	30,494,

Net Incr. £35,

YEARS, ended 31st Dec.	1906.	1905.	1906. Less.	1906. More.	Corresponding Years. 1904.	Corresponding Years. 1903.
	£	£	£	£	£	£
*Customs	33,731,	34,415,	684,	—	35,646,	33,998,
*Excise	30,327,	30,220,	—	107,	31,120,	31,290,
*Stamps and estate, &c., duties	22,611,	21,310,	—	1,301,	19,450,	21,100,
Taxes (Land Tax and House Duty)	2,560,	2,630,	70,	—	2,680,	2,510,
Post Office	16,830,	16,600,	—	230,	15,850,	15,070,
Telegraph Service	4,160,	4,060,	—	100,	3,760,	3,670,
	110,219,	109,235,	754,	1,738,	108,506,	107,638,
Property and Income Tax	31,197,	31,030,	—	167,	28,510,	37,150,
	141,416,	140,265,	754,	1,905,	137,016,	144,788,
Crown Lands	490,	470,	—	10,	460,	455,
Interest on Advances	1,100,	1,084,	—	16,	1,010,	960,
Miscellaneous	1,776,	1,475,	—	301,	1,416,	1,650,
Totals	144,782,	143,294,	754,	2,232,	139,902,	147,853,

Net Incr. £1,478,

* Exclusive of transfers to local taxation account.

REVENUE OF THE UNITED KINGDOM.

FINANCIAL YEARS.

Net Produce in Quarters in 1906, and in Financial Years ended 31st March, 1905-06, 1904-05, 1903-04, 1902-03.

[000's omitted.]

QUARTERS, ended	31st March, 1906.	30th June, 1906.	30th September, 1906.	31st December, 1906.	31st March, 1907.
	£	£	£	£	£
*Customs	8,430,	8,453,	8,210,	8,708,	—
*Excise	7,240,	6,887,	7,420,	8,790,	—
*Stamps and estate, &c., duties	5,420,	5,721,	5,590,	5,720,	—
Taxes (Land Tax and House Duty)	2,160,	330,	20,	90,	—
Post Office	5,580,	3,100,	3,980,	4,450,	—
Telegraph Service	980,	1,000,	1,180,	1,070,	—
	29,810,	25,491,	26,400,	28,828,	—
Property and Income Tax	23,860,	3,837,	1,620,	2,200,	—
	53,670,	29,328,	28,020,	31,028,	—
Crown Lands	110,	110,	110,	170,	—
Interest on Advances	419,	5,	677,	13,	—
Miscellaneous	441,	539,	264,	571,	—
Totals	54,640,	29,982,	29,071,	31,782,	—

YEARS, ended 31st March,	1905-06.	1904-05.	1904-05. Less.	1904-05. More.	Corresponding Years. 1903-04.	Corresponding Years. 1902-03.
	£	£	£	£	£	£
*Customs	34,475,	35,730,	1,255,	—	33,850,	34,433,
*Excise	30,230,	30,750,	520,	—	31,550,	32,100,
*Stamps and estate, &c., duties	21,150,	20,050,	—	1,100,	20,500,	22,050,
Taxes (Land Tax and House Duty)	2,670,	2,750,	80,	—	2,650,	2,550,
Post Office	16,880,	16,100,	—	780,	15,450,	14,750,
Telegraph Service	4,130,	3,830,	—	300,	3,700,	3,630,
	109,535,	109,210,	1,855,	2,180,	107,700,	109,513,
Property and Income Tax	31,350,	31,250,	—	100,	30,800,	38,800,
	140,885,	140,460,	1,855,	2,280,	138,500,	148,313,
Crown Lands	480,	470,	—	10,	460,	455,
Interest on Advances	1,099,	1,014,	—	84,	982,	958,
Miscellaneous	1,514,	1,426,	—	88,	1,603,	1,826,
Totals	143,978,	143,370,	1,855,	2,462,	141,545,	151,552,

NET INCR. £1,825.

* Exclusive of transfers to local taxation account.

FOREIGN EXCHANGES.—*Quotations as under,* LONDON *on Paris, Hamburg, Calcutta;—and New York and Hong Kong, on* LONDON, *for* **1906.**

1	2	3	4	5	6	7	8	9
			Calcutta.				Price per Ounce.	
DATES. (Tuesdays or nearest Dates.)	London on Paris. 3 m.d.	London on Hamburg 3 m. d.	London on Calcutta. Demand.	Indian Council Bills. Minimum Price per Rupee.*	New York on London. 60 d. s.†	Hong Kong on London. 4 m. d.†	Gold Bars (Fine).	Standard Silver in Bars.
1906.			*s.* *d.*	*s.* *d.*	$	*s.* *d.*	*s.* *d.*	*d.*
Jan. 2	25·31 1/4	20·66	1 4 1/32	1 4 1/32	4·82	2 0 9/16	77 10 7/8	30 1/16
,, 16	25·31 1/4	20·67	1 4 1/32	1 4 1/16	4·85 1/2	2 0 5/8	77 10 1/8	30 3/16
,, 30	25·30	20·68	1 4 1/32	1 4 1/16	4·83 7/8	2 0 1/4	77 9 1/2	30 3/16
Feb. 13	25·32 1/2	20·69	1 4 1/32	1 4 1/16	4·83 1/8	2 0 3/4	77 9 1/2	30 9/16
,, 27	25·33 3/4	20·69	1 4 1/32	1 4 1/32	4·82 5/8	2 0 13/16	77 9 3/8	30 13/16
Mar. 13	25·33 3/4	20·70	1 4 1/32	1 4	4·82 1/2	2 0 7/16	77 9 7/8	29 3/16
,, 27	25·33 3/4	20·70	1 4 1/32	1 3 15/16	4·82 3/8	2 0 5/8	77 10	30 1/8
Apl. 10 ...	25·31 1/4	20·67	1 3 31/32	1 3 15/16	4·80 3/4	2 0 1/2	77 11 1/8	29 5/8
,, 24	25·32 1/2	20·68	1 3 31/32	1 3 31/32	4·81 1/4	2 0 7/8	77 11 1/2	30 1/4
May 8	25·35	20·71	1 3 31/32	1 4	4·82 1/4	2 1 3/8	77 10 5/8	30 7/8
,, 22	25·36 3/4	20·70	1 3 31/32	1 4	4·82 1/8	2 1 1/2	77 9	31 3/16
June 5	25·36 1/4	20·70	1 4	1 3 31/32	4·82 5/8	2 1 1/8	77 9	30 1/2
,, 19	25·35	20·69	1 3 31/32	1 3 31/32	4·82 1/4	2 1 3/8	77 9	30 3/8
July 3	25·33 3/4	20·68	1 4	1 3 31/32	4·82	2 1 1/2	77 9 5/8	29 15/16
,, 17	25·33 3/4	20·66	1 4	1 3 31/32	4·81 3/4	2 1 5/16	77 10 5/8	30 1/4
,, 31	25·32 1/2	20·66	1 3 31/32	1 3 31/32	4·82 1/4	2 1 1/4	77 9 5/8	30 1/16
Aug. 14	25·33 1/4	20·67	1 4	1 4.	4·81 7/8	2 1 1/2	77 10 1/4	30 7/16
,, 28	25·35	20·66	1 4 1/32	1 4 1/32	4·80 1/8	2 1 7/8	77 10	30 7/8
Sept. 11	25·36 1/4	20·68	1 4 1/32	1 4 1/32	4·80 3/8	2 2 7/16	78 0 5/8	31 5/8
,, 25	25·37 1/2	20·70	1 4 1/32	1 4 1/16	4·79 5/8	2 2 3/8	77 11 5/8	31 11/16
Oct. 9	25·37 1/2	20·71	1 4 1/32	1 4 1/32	4·81 1/8	2 2 3/4	77 11 1/4	31 3/4
,, 23	25·48 3/4	20·80	1 4 1/32	1 4	4·80 3/4	2 3 1/4	77 10	32 7/16
Nov. 6	25·45	20·82	1 4	1 4	4·80 5/8	2 3 7/16	77 9	32 3/4
,, 20	25·48 3/4	20·82	1 3 7/8	1 4 1/16	4·84 1/2	2 3 5/16	77 9	32 13/16
Dec. 4 ...	25·45	20·79	1 4 1/16	1 4 1/16	4·79 3/4	2 2 7/8	77 9	31 15/16
,, 18 ...	25·45	20·81	1 4 1/16	1 4 3/32	4·77 7/8	2 2 7/8	77 9	32 3/16

* Wednesdays following. † Fridays following.

Vol. LXX.]   [Part II.

JOURNAL

OF THE ROYAL STATISTICAL SOCIETY.

JUNE, 1907.

The ALLEGED INCREASE of INSANITY.

By NOEL A. HUMPHREYS, I.S.O.

[Read before the Royal Statistical Society, 19th March, 1907.
SIR RICHARD BIDDULPH MARTIN, Bart., President, in the Chair.]

IN submitting for the consideration of the Royal Statistical Society
a further paper on this subject, after a lapse of seventeen years,
it is disappointing to have to admit that, notwithstanding the
valuable and much improved statistics recently issued by the
Lunacy Commissioners, thoroughly satisfactory materials are still
wanting for solving the question whether the prevalence of insanity,
as a physical disease, is or is not increasing. The importance of the
problem, however, especially in its bearing on the persistently urged
theory of progressive physical deterioration, and its undoubted
statistical interest, has overcome my hesitation to submit the
question for the further consideration of the Society.

The statistical interest in this problem arises mainly from the
fact that there has been, since the formation of the Lunacy
Commission in 1859, a constant increase in the number of the
registered insane in England and Wales; that the rate of this
increase has considerably exceeded the rate of increase of the
English population; and that these facts are very generally held
to afford unquestionable proof of the increase of occurring insanity.
If, however, reasonable doubt can be thrown on this somewhat
natural inference that the prevalence of insanity, as a disease, is
actually increasing, it will afford a very useful object lesson of the
danger of accepting, without the fullest and most careful examination, an apparently obvious conclusion based on figures, the accuracy
of which is beyond question.

If, as appears to be the case, only a variable and increasing
proportion of the mentally unsound have yet been certified or

registered as insane; if the rates, both of mortality and discharge, among the certified insane have declined; and if there is an increasing tendency to certify, as insane, cases that were not so certified in years past, then very considerable doubt is thrown on the inference that this increase in the number and proportion of the certified insane must necessarily signify the increased prevalence of insanity as an occurring physical disease.

The *Times* recently published three interesting articles, from a correspondent, containing an urgent appeal for a systematic application of the resources of medical science to the investigation of the causes of insanity as a physical disease. These articles, with a view, as it would appear, of accentuating the urgency of the important and useful object they were intended to promote, unhesitatingly asserted that the actual increase of insanity as a disease was proved by the simple facts of the case, and further asserted as an "admitted fact" that the insane under restraint are surrounded by a *constantly growing* fringe of borderland cases without reference to any proof of this "admitted fact." The articles referred in disparaging terms to "the many estimable people who like to " amuse themselves with hypotheses, while they close their minds " firmly against unpleasant facts, and urge that the constantly " growing number of the permanent inmates of lunatic asylums " does not indicate any actual increase of the diseases for which " seclusion is enforced." With a view to meet some of the arguments advanced against the acceptance of this large and constant increase in the number of the certified insane as trustworthy and conclusive proof of an increase of occurring insanity, the *Times* correspondent asserted that " the effect of the mere " sweeping up and incarceration of the harmless so-called 'naturals' " of country villages was exhausted within a few years of the " passing of the Lunacy Acts of 1845 "; he further stated that the " total number of insane persons of all ranks discovered in England " and Wales by a careful official inquiry, in 1844, was 21,788," equal to a proportion of 1,320 per million of the population. He further compared this number with the most recent figures published by the Lunacy Commissioners, which show that on the 1st January, 1906, the number of the insane under their control was 121,979, equal to 3,531 per million of the population. The figures for 1844 were based upon a report of the Metropolitan Commissioners in Lunacy to the Lord Chancellor in that year; but the Commissioners in this report only claimed that their figures, undoubtedly obtained with much care and difficulty, should be accepted as affording some approximation to the total numbers of the insane at the time. For instance, they state with regard to private cases that " a large class

" of insane persons *under certificate* exists, in respect to whose number
" there are no materials for calculation ; and as regards also those
" of whom returns ought to be made it is believed that in a very
" small proportion of instances is the law complied with." They
further stated that even if the returns of these private cases under
certificate were complete "there would still remain a considerable
" class of insane persons, of all ranks of life, under the care of
" guardians or relatives, *without certificate*, of whose probable number
" there are no means of forming an estimate." Any comparison
between the admittedly incomplete return of 1844 and the recent
figures issued by the Lunacy Commissioners (still far from showing
the total number of the insane), with a view to prove the alleged
increase of insanity among the English population could therefore
answer no useful purpose, as the deficiency in the 1844 return
of persons of unsound mind was obviously far greater than that
at the present time. It is, moreover, necessary to refer to a few
facts bearing on the assertion by the *Times* correspondent that
the mere sweeping up and incarceration of the harmless so-called
"naturals" was exhausted "within a few years of the passing of
"the Lunacy Acts of 1845." It is easy to prove that at the present
time, more than sixty years since the passing of the Acts referred
to, there still exists a very considerable aggregate number of persons
of unsound mind in England and Wales, constituting a reserve of
uncertified cases of insanity. A certain varying proportion of
cases from this reserve is from time to time brought within the
knowledge of the Commissioners, counting as new cases of
insanity, thus increasing the aggregate number and the proportion of the registered and certified insane to the population. The
Lunacy Commissioners, admittedly indeed, have never had official
cognizance of more than a varying and constantly increasing proportion of the whole number of cases of mental unsoundness. A
variety of causes have tended in recent years to accelerate certification of an increasing proportion of the cases from this reserve ;
and there is good ground for asserting that year by year the figures
published by the Lunacy Commissioners more nearly approach the
true aggregate numbers of the insane among the English population,
and that consequently the aggregate of the reserve is decreasing.
The reports on the last four census enumerations throw much light
upon the varying number of this reserve of the uncertified insane
in the English population.

The first English census at which provision was made in the
householders' schedule for the statement and collection of information relating to mental unsoundness, including all those various
forms loosely described as lunacy, idiocy and imbecility, was the

Seventh National Census in 1871.   The result of this enumeration was a return of 39,567 persons described as lunatic, and 29,452 as idiot ˈor imbecile; in all, 69,019 were returned as insane or mentally unsound.   Precisely similar information was required in the schedules used at the two following censuses in 1881 and 1891 ; and the numbers of the mentally unsound enumerated in those years rose successively to 84,503 in 1881 and to 97,383 in 1891. In the reports on each of these censuses the opinion was expressed that the enumerated numbers of the mentally unsound were most probably understated, but that there was good ground for presuming that a nearer approximation to the true number was returned at each successive enumeration.   This obviously suggests that, at any rate, part of the enumerated increase between 1871 and 1891 was due to greater accuracy of the returns in the census schedules, rather than to any real increase of insanity.

When the householders' or occupiers' schedule, to be used at the census in 1901 was under discussion, the desirability of substituting the term "feeble-minded" for "idiot" was urged upon the Registrar-General by persons officially connected with the care of the insane, on the ground that such substitution would lead to greater accuracy in the returns.   It was urged that householders who would hesitate to return a member of their family or household as "lunatic" or "idiot," might not object to describe such member as "feeble-minded."

This suggested substitution of terms was, in view of the source from which it emanated, adopted in the census schedule used in 1901, and resulted, as was expected, in a very marked increase in the number of persons returned in the schedules as insane, or of unsound mind.   The number returned which had been 97,383 in 1891, rose to 132,654 in 1901.   The adoption of "feeble-minded" in place of "idiot" at the last census very possibly caused the return in 1901 to represent more accurately the number of the English population (more especially of children) that were then mentally unsound; but there can be no doubt that this substitution has entirely destroyed the value of the figures in 1901 for comparison with the returns at the three previous censuses.

The number of persons returned as insane at the censuses in 1871, 1881, and 1891 were in the proportion of 3,039, 3,253, and 3,358 per million of the total population respectively.   These rates showed an increase of 7·04 per cent. in the ten years 1871-81 ; whereas in the succeeding ten years, 1881-91, the increase declined to 3·23 per cent.   Under the influence of the change of nomenclature, however, the insanity rate based upon the census returns in 1901 further rose to 4,078 per million, and showed an increase of no less than 21·4 per cent. upon the rate in 1891 ; a percentage of increase in the ten years more than double the percentage of increase in the twenty years, 1871-91, which was only 10·5.

Bearing in mind that these census figures are derived from schedules filled up, in 1901, by more than seven millions of separate occupiers, a very large proportion of whom had had but limited educational advantages, and recognising the real difficulty in the way of defining and differentiating the true import of the mental conditions they were required to describe in the schedules as lunatic, idiot, imbecile, or feeble-minded, it is impossible to attach scientific value to these returns of mental unsoundness. The figures, however, at any rate, conclusively prove that there has always existed, and that there still exists, a large reserve of mental unsoundness, in excess of the constantly increasing number of the certified insane.

It may or may not be true that the use of the term "feeble-minded " gave in 1901 a nearer approximation to the true extent of this reserve of mental unsoundness, but it cannot be doubted that this reserve includes a very considerable proportion of so-called "borderland " cases, from which the number of the certified insane is and will be constantly recruited. A really important question naturally arises whether there has been any continuing and really scientific uniformity in the system of certifying insanity, and whether it be a fact, as seems more than probable, that cases are now being certified that formerly would not have been certified. This branch of the subject demands further notice.

TABLE A.—*Aggregate Numbers of the Insane enumerated at the four Censuses, 1871-1901, and those reported to the Lunacy Commissioners on 1st January in each of those Years ; and Percentage of Deficiency in the Lunacy Commissioners' Numbers.*

Years.	Persons.		Males.		Females.		Deficiency per Cent. of Lunacy Commissioners' Numbers.		
	Census.	Lunacy Commis-sioners.	Census.	Lunacy Commis-sioners.	Census.	Lunacy Commis-sioners.	Persons	Males.	Females.
1871	69,019	56,755	32,874	26,009	36,145	30,746	17·8	20·9	14·9
'81	84,503	73,113	39,789	32,973	44,714	40,140	13·5	17·1	10·2
'91	97,383	86,795	45,392	39,162	51,991	47,633	10·9	13·7	8·4
1901	132,654	107,944	62,063	49,188	70,591	58,756	18·6	20·7	16·8

The accompanying table shows the numbers of persons enumerated as of unsound mind in England and Wales at each of the last four censuses in 1871–1901, side by side with the numbers of the insane known to and under the control of the Lunacy Commissioners on the 1st of January in each of those four years. It is there shown that 17·8 per cent. of the cases of mental unsoundness enumerated at the census in 1871 were not under the control of the Lunacy Commissioners. This percentage of deficiency in the numbers of the insane reported on by the Commissioners declined successively to 13·5 and 10·9 in 1881 and 1891. The proportion of this reserve of uncertified insanity, however, influenced undoubtedly by the adoption of the term " feeble-minded " in substitution for " idiot," showed a marked increase in 1901, when the percentage of deficiency in the number returned by the Lunacy Commissioners rose to 18·6, and exceeded that shown thirty years before, in 1871, when it was 17·8. This deficiency in the Commissioners' figures in each of the four census years has invariably been much larger among males than among females, but the influence of the change of nomenclature in 1901, upon the amount of the deficiency, was far greater among females than among males.

There is, unfortunately, no satisfactory method for deciding to what precise extent the increased proportion of the mentally unsound returned at the last census in 1901 was due to greater accuracy in filling up the schedules and how much to the change made in the schedule at that census. It will be well, however, to note some remarkable changes in the relative proportions of the mentally unsound, enumerated at different groups of ages, since 1871.

TABLE B.—*Incidence Rate of Insanity per Million of the Population at each of the four Censuses, 1871-1901, on Five Groups of Ages; and Increase or Decrease of the Rate in each Intercensal Period.*

Ages.	Insanity Rate per Million Living at each of the Last Four Censuses.				Increase or Decrease per Cent. of Insanity Rate in Intercensal Periods.		
	1871.	1881.	1891.	1901.	1871-81.	1881-91.	1891-1901.
All ages	3,039	3,253	3,358	4,078	+ 7·04	+ 3·23	+ 21·44
Under 15	583	581	509	629	− 0·34	−12·39	+ 23·58
15—25	2,298	2,161	2,002	2,388	− 5·96	− 7·36	+ 19·28
25—45	4,498	4,789	4,756	5,263	+ 6·47	− 0·69	+ 10·66
45—65	6,158	7,205	7,831	9,087	+17·00	+ 8·69	+ 16·04
65 and upwards	6,950	8,000	8,612	11,922	+15·09	+ 7·65	+ 38·43

During the ten years 1871-81 the rate of insanity to population showed a decline of 6 per cent. among persons aged under 25 years, whereas it increased more than 6 per cent. among those aged 25—45, 17 per cent. in the age group 45—65, and 15 per cent. among persons aged upwards of 65 years. During the following decade, 1881-91, the insanity rate showed a further marked decline under the age of 25, and a slight decline (instead of the increase in 1871-81) between the ages of 25 and 45; an increase (far smaller than that in the preceding decade) being alone shown in the two age groups, 45—65 and 65 and upwards. The substitution of "feeble-minded" for "idiot" in 1901, makes it impossible usefully to continue this comparison, as regards the figures returned at that census. It is obvious that large numbers of persons at all ages were in 1901 returned as "feeble-minded" who would not have been returned as "idiot." For instance, the rate of children under the age of 15 years, returned as of unsound mind, showed a decline of 12 per cent. in the ten years, 1881-91, whereas it showed an increase of 24 per cent. during the ten years, 1891-01. A marked increase of the insanity rate was also shown by the census figures in 1901 at each of the subsequent age periods; it was 19 per cent. at 15—25, 11 per cent. at 25—45, 16 per cent. at 45—65, and 38 per cent. at the ages above 65. It is evident, therefore, that the term "feeble-minded" was extensively used in the census schedules at all ages, although probably in the largest proportions among children aged under 15, and among persons aged upwards of 65 years.

This change of nomenclature naturally did not affect the census returns from public or private lunatic asylums, but its effect on the workhouse returns was very striking. It is well known, from the reports of the Lunacy Commissioners, that the number and proportion of the insane returned in workhouses has constantly declined during the last 50 years; but in consequence of the adoption of the term "feeble-minded," 14,972 inmates of workhouses were recorded as of unsound mind in the census returns for 1901, against but 10,592 at the census in 1891, although the Lunacy Commissioners' report showed that the number of insane inmates of workhouses on the 1st of January in that year did not exceed 11,389. Thus it appears that 23·9 per cent. of the inmates of workhouses returned in the census schedules in 1901 as of unsound mind (including those described as feeble-minded) were not included in the Lunacy Commissioners' report on the insane in workhouses for that year. The census returns of the insane in workhouses in 1901 showed an increase of 41·4 per cent. upon the number so returned in 1891, and the increase among the insane not located in any public institution was equal to no less than 57·1 per cent.

It seems clear that the value of census returns of the mentally unsound, beyond proving the existence of a large reserve of cases that have not yet come within the control of the Lunacy Commissioners may now be practically disregarded as trustworthy evidence of the actual amount of existing insanity, or of its increasing or decreasing rate of prevalence from census to census. The change of terms used in the schedules having destroyed the value of these returns for comparative purposes, the question of their maintenance, or further modification, will require very careful consideration when arrangements are made for the next census enumeration.

STATISTICS OF THE LUNACY COMMISSIONERS.

It is now desirable to examine the statistics issued by the Lunacy Commissioners bearing upon the constantly increasing numbers and proportion to population of the registered and certified insane coming under their control, with special reference to the rates of admissions and discharges (including deaths) in recent years.

The following table shows the mean annual rate of the certified insane (persons, males and females) reported on by the Commissioners in each quinquennial period since 1859, to a million of persons, and of each sex, with the percentage of increase shown by such mean rates between each period :—

TABLE C.—*Mean Annual Ratio of Certified Cases of Insanity (Reported on by Lunacy Commissioners), in Quinquennial Periods, per Million of Population; and Increase per Cent. between the several Periods.*

Quinquennial Periods.	Mean Annual Ratio of Insane reported by Lunacy Commissioners per Million of Population.			Increase per Cent. between Quinquennial Periods.		
	Persons.	Males.	Females.	Persons.	Males.	Females.
1859–63 ...	1,972	1,840	2,097			
				12·9	13·2	12·7
'64–68	2,226	2,083	2,363			
				11·7	12·2	11·2
'69–73 ..	2,486	2,337	2,627			
				7·5	6·5	8·5
'74–78 ...	2,673	2,488	2,849			
				5·2	4·8	5·4
'79–83 ...	2,811	2,607	3,004			
				3·9	4·1	3·7
'84–88 ...	2,920	2,714	3,116			
				2·4	2·9	1·8
'89–93 ...	2,989	2,793	3,173			
				5·1	5·7	4·6
'94–98	3,141	2,952	3,318			
				6·2	6·5	6·0
'99–1903	3,336	3,143	3,517			
				5·0	6·1	4·1
1904–06 (3 years)	3,504	3,336	3,660			

This table shows that the mean annual proportion of the certified insane of both sexes, reported upon by the Commissioners, increased from 1,972 per million of the population in the five years 1859-63, to 3,336 per million in the five years 1899-1903; and the reported mean annual proportion on the 1st January in the three years 1904-06 had further increased to 3,504 per million. It further appears from the table that this mean annual rate of certified insanity in the population of England and Wales showed an increase of 12·9 per cent. in the five years 1864-68 compared with that in the preceding five years 1859-63; in the five succeeding five-year periods (1869-93) this percentage of increase successively declined to 11·7, 7·5, 5·2, 3·9 and 2·4 respectively. This declining percentage of increase changed to an increasing percentage during the five years 1894-98, when the mean annual rate of certified insanity exceeded that which prevailed in the preceding five years (1889-93) by 5·1 per cent. This rise in the percentage of increase was maintained in 1899-1903 when it was 6·2; and has been fully maintained during the last three years 1904-06.

It may further be noted that the mean annual proportion of the certified insane, to a million of the population, in the last three years (1904-06) exceeded the annual proportion in the five years, 1859-63, by 77·8 per cent. among persons; by 81·3 per cent. among males; and by 74·5 per cent. among females. Thus while the proportion of the certified insane among the female population has since 1859 continuously exceeded that among the male population, the difference between the sex proportions of the rate during that period has lessened; as in equal numbers living of both sexes, the number of the female certified insane to 100 of the male insane, which was 113 in 1859-63, declined to 109 in 1904-06. The rate of increase among the male certified insane has since 1859, almost continuously, exceeded that among the female insane.

It is clear, however, from these figures that the rate of increase of the certified insane, after due allowance for increase of population, has recently been less than half that which prevailed during the ten years, 1859-68. Having regard to the still large reserve of mental unsoundness existing outside the control of the Lunacy Commissioners, it is necessary to inquire whether the increasing proportion of the certified insane is due to increased certification from this reserve, or to a real increase of occurring insanity. The Commissioners' statistics of admissions do not, unfortunately, throw much light on this point.

In the reports of the Commissioners a table has long been given showing the number of pauper and private patients admitted to county, borough, and other asylums, hospitals, and licensed houses (exclusive of transfer cases), and their proportion to population; but until recently no successful attempt appears to have been made to differentiate between first admissions and re-admissions; and without this information the number and proportion of admissions is practically useless as evidence of the growth of insanity. The figures for the eight years 1898-1905, however, show that the annual proportion of first admissions, to a million of the population, was 503 in the four years 1898-1901, and rose to 547 in the four years 1902-05. It is noteworthy, however, that while the ratio to population of these first admissions steadily increased each year from 492 per million in 1898 (the earliest year for which this information is available) to 576 in 1902, it has since as steadily declined each year to 521 in 1905. The actual number of first admissions, to all classes of lunatic asylums, declined year by year from 18,992 in 1902 to 17,796 in 1905, a fact which in itself is strong evidence against the assertion that the prevalence of insanity is now increasing. The value of these figures, however, much depends upon the circumstances under which these first admissions occur. If, as seems probable, a considerable proportion of these first admissions occur among those persons of unsound mind in workhouses or residing with relatives or others, the numbers of first admissions to asylums just referred to, in such case, overstate the annual number of new occurring cases of insanity. To throw light on this point it would be necessary to have tabulated facts relating to the previous history of the about 18,000 first cases admitted annually to the asylums, showing in the first place the numbers that had previously been reported on by the Commissioners as residing in workhouses or with relatives or others, and the numbers admitted from the reserve of mentally unsound cases not previously within the knowledge and control of the Commissioners.

ACCUMULATION OF THE INSANE.

The constant increase in the number and proportion of the insane within the cognizance of the Lunacy Commissioners is practically the sole basis of the somewhat natural assertion of the progressive increase of insanity as a physical disease. On the other hand, those, who refuse to accept the figures of the Commissioners as actual proof of this alleged increase of insanity assert that, apart from the growing tendency to treat increasing proportions of cases of mental unsoundness in asylums, the reduction of the rate of mortality and of the rate of discharge among the insane under treatment in asylums has caused, and is still causing, a very considerable accumulation of cases under observation that, deceptively, implies an increase of occurring insanity. The reports of the Commissioners have long shown the annual rate of mortality among the inmates of asylums, but, unfortunately, they contain no information as to the rate of mortality among the insane retained in workhouses, or residing with relatives or others. In 1859 only 62 per cent. of the insane within the knowledge of the Commissioners were under treatment in asylums, hospitals, or licensed houses; but in 1906 the proportion of the insane located in such institutions, had increased to 86 per cent. of the number dealt with by the Commissioners. Any change, therefore, in the rate of mortality among this large proportion of the registered insane must necessarily have a considerable effect upon the aggregate number of existing cases of insanity from year to year. Dr. William Farr, in his " Report on the Mortality of Lunatics," read before this Society in 1841, stated that "There may be ten times as many lunatics in " civilised as in barbarous countries and times ; not because the ten- " dency to insanity is greater, but because the lunatics live ten times " as many months or years." This axiom shows the importance of considering the mortality statistics relating to the certified insane issued by the Lunacy Commissioners since 1859. The figures in the accompanying Table are derived from successive reports of the Commissioners :—

TABLE D.—*Annual Rates of Mortality in County and Borough Asylums, Hospitals and Licensed Houses in Ten-Year and Five-Year Periods, during the Forty-Seven Years, 1859-1905.*

Years.	Annual Death-rate per 1,000 of Average Number Resident.			Years.	Annual Death-rate per 1,000 of Average Number Resident		
	Persons.	Males.	Females.		Persons.	Males.	Females.
10-year periods—				5-year periods —contd.			
1859–68.	103·1	—	—				
'69–78	101·7	122·0	83·6	1869–73	101·2	120·6	83·7
'79–88 ...	95·5	114·0	79·6	'74–78	102·2	123·3	83·4
'89–98.... ...	96·6	114·7	81·3	'79–83	94·7	114·4	77·7
'99–1905 (7 years)	99·4	113·6	87·3	'84–88 . .	96·3	113·6	81·5
				'89–93	98·7	116·8	83·3
5-year periods—				'94–98	94·5	112·7	79·2
1859–63	102·2	—	—	'99–1903 .	100·0	114·6	87·6
'64–68	103·9	—	—	1904–05 (2 years)	98·0	111·2	86·6

Note.—The reports did not show the sex mortality of the inmates of asylums, &c., prior to 1869.

The table shows that the mean annual rate of mortality among the inmates of the various lunatic asylums, hospitals, and licensed houses was equal to 103·1 per 1,000 during the ten years 1859-68, and successively declined to 101·7 and 95·5 per 1,000 in the two following periods of ten years 1869-78 and 1879-88. The decline in the asylum death-rate during these thirty years has not, however, been fully maintained, as the mean annual rate rose slightly to 96·6 in the ten years 1889-98, and further rose to 99·4 during the seven years 1899-1905. The mean annual death rate in the ten years 1889-98 was, however, 6·5 per 1,000 lower than that which prevailed thirty years earlier—in 1859-68. The number of inmates of the asylums dealt with in the Commissioners' reports averaged 70,859 during the ten years 1889–98; and this decline of 6·5 in the annual rate of mortality among this asylum population, during these ten years, implies that 4,605 inmates survived during this period who would have died had the death-rate been equal to that which prevailed during the ten years 1859-68. To this extent the increase in the number of the asylum population during the ten years 1889-98 may, therefore, be attributed to accumulation due to the decline in the death-rate of the asylum inmates, and not to any real increased prevalence of insanity. The slight increase in the rate of mortality among asylum inmates during the last seven years, 1899-1905, may be partly attributed to the marked increase of the proportion of the asylum population now aged over 60 years, to which further reference will be made, as the rate of mortality of the insane, as well as that of the general population, naturally increases with age.

Accumulation in asylums, hospitals, and licensed houses, beyond that due to the decline in the death-rate, is moreover caused by a similar decline in the rate of discharge on recovery, which decline has been continuous in recent years. A table in the last report of the Commissioners shows that the annual proportion per 1,000 of discharge on recovery, to the average daily number resident, which averaged 115·4 during the five years 1873-77, steadily declined, in successive five-year periods, to 92·5 per 1,000 in 1898-1902, and further fell to 88·0 in the three years 1903-05. Having regard to the decline of the death-rate in asylums it seems more reasonable to attribute this decline of discharge on recovery to the increasing inability or unwillingness of relatives to resume the personal care of the insane, on their attainment of a harmless condition, than to any decrease of success in the treatment of the insane in asylums. It cannot, however, be questioned that this decline in the rate of discharges on recovery is a still more influential factor in the production of accumulation in asylums, than the reduction of the death-rate.

In order to test the reality and full extent of accumulation on the increase in the number of inmates of asylums, hospitals, and licensed houses, it is necessary, however, to deal with the total discharge rate, including deaths. This mean annual total discharge rate from all asylums and hospitals, according to a table in the last report of the Commissioners, was equal to 218·0 per 1,000 of the average daily number resident during the five years 1873-77 ; whereas it steadily declined during the five succeeding five-year periods to 191·2 per 1,000 in the five years 1898-1902, and further fell to 186·9 in the three years 1903-05. Thus the total annual discharge-rate in the last three years was 31·1 per 1,000 lower than that which prevailed among the asylum population nearly thirty years earlier, in the five years 1873-77. On the 1st January, 1903, the inmates of these asylums numbered 90,855 ; while on the 1st January, 1906, the number returned in these asylums was 98,091, showing an increase of 7,236 in the three years. The mean of these two numbers (94,473) may be assumed to approximately represent the average annual number of asylum inmates during these three years. If, therefore, the total discharge rate (including deaths) during these three years had been as high as was the rate that prevailed during the five years 1873-77, an additional discharge rate of 31·1 per 1,000 would have occurred, and the number of inmates would thereby have been reduced by 2,938 per annum, or by 8,814 in the three years. Thus, instead of the recorded increase of 7,236 in the number of asylum inmates during the three years, there would have been an actual decline of 1,578, if the total discharge rate of 1873-77 had prevailed during the three recent years, 1903-05. This is not the time and place to discuss the advantage or disadvantage, in the public interest, of this remarkable and steady decline in the proportion of discharges on recovery, it is sufficient for the purposes of this paper to call attention to its effect upon the number of our asylum population in the causation of accumulation. It is hardly necessary to pursue the subject by calculating what the present number of asylum inmates would have been if the total discharge rate prevailing in 1873-77 had since been constantly maintained. It may, however, be pointed out that the higher rate of discharge on recovery would, on the other hand, have probably to some extent increased the number of re-admissions caused by the relapse of so-called recoveries.

AGE DISTRIBUTION OF THE INMATES OF ASYLUMS.

In my former paper I called the attention of the Society to certain marked changes in the proportional age distribution of the insane enumerated in lunatic asylums at the four census enumera-

tions in 1851, 1861, 1871 and 1881, as affording evidence of
accumulation. A table given in that paper, which is here reproduced,

TABLE E.—*Proportional Age-Distribution of the Enumerated Inmates of Lunatic
Asylums at each of the Four Censuses, 1851-81.*

Ages.	Proportion per 1,000 at All Ages.											
	Persons.				Males.				Females.			
	1851.	1861.	1871.	1881.	1851.	1861.	1871.	1881.	1851.	1861.	1871.	1881.
All ages	1,000	1,000	1,000	1,000	1,000	1,000	1,000	1,000	1,000	1,000	1,000	1,000
0—15	9	6	3	1	13	8	5	2	6	4	2	1
15—25......	75	78	67	55	86	85	71	60	66	72	65	52
25—45......	465	458	438	429	497	490	464	462	436	431	414	399
45—65........	368	365	382	398	333	338	364	376	399	388	397	417
65 and upwards }	83	93	110	117	71	79	96	100	93	105	122	131

shows that during the thirty years 1851-81 there was a marked and
steady increase .in the proportions of inmates at the later age
periods, implying a distinct increase in the mean age of the inmates.
Of 1,000 inmates of asylums there were, in 1851, 549 aged under
45 years, while at the three following censuses this proportional
number steadily declined to 542, 508, and 485. On the other
hand, the proportion per 1,000 of inmates aged upwards of
45 years steadily increased from 451 in 1851, to 515 in 1881.
Between the ages of 45 and 65 the proportional increase in the
thirty years was from 368 to 398, equal to 8·2 per cent. ; above the
age of 65 years the increase in this period was from 83 to 117,
equal to 41·0 per cent. Measured by the proportion of asylum
inmates to the general population at similar age-groups, we find
that the increase of the rate of insanity in asylums during this
thirty years was 80 per cent. between 25 and 45, 102 per cent.
between 45 and 65, and no less than 173 per cent. among inmates
aged upwards of 65 years. Unless it could be proved that insanity
now attacks persons at a later age than was formerly the case, it
seems impossible to doubt that this marked increase in the proportion of insane patients in asylums at advanced ages is mainly
the result of accumulation, due to the decline of the death-rate and
of the rate of discharge on recovery.

Tables published in recent reports of the Lunacy Commissioners
show that the proportions of the inmates of asylums at advanced
ages continues to increase. Comparison of the age distribution of
the inmates in 1894 and 1904 shows that of 1,000 in 1894 the
proportional number at ages under 45 was 498, and had declined to

480 in 1904 ; while the number aged above 45 years increased from 502 in 1894 to 520 in 1904.

TABLE F.—*Proportional Age-Distribution of the Inmates of Lunatic Asylums, Hospitals and Licensed Houses in 1894 and 1904, based on Tables in the Reports of the Lunacy Commissioners.*

Ages.	Proportional Distribution at Several Age-Periods.					
	Persons.		Males.		Females.	
	1894.	1904.	1894.	1904.	1894.	1904.
All ages...............	1,000	1,000	1,000	1,000	1,000	1,000
0—15	14	14	20	19	9	9
15—25	73	70	87	84	62	59
25—45	411	396	434	423	391	373
45—65	384	394	359	369	405	415
65 and upwards	118	126	100	105	133	144

The above table shows the age distribution of persons, males and females in asylums, hospitals and licensed houses in 1894 and 1904, at five groups of ages. It should, however, be noted that these more recent figures include the inmates of idiot asylums, which considerably raised the proportion of inmates under 15 years of age, compared with the proportions given in the table relating to the years 1851-81, when but few congenital idiots were included. The increased proportion of inmates at advanced ages shown in the more recent table is thereby somewhat understated.

In the following table the rate of incidence of asylum insanity upon a million of the general population at the several age-groups in 1894 and 1904 is shown for persons, males and females :—

TABLE G.—*Ratio of Incidence of Inmates of Lunatic Asylums, Hospitals and Licensed Houses on Population, on Five Groups of Ages, in 1894 and 1904, calculated from Tables in Reports of the Lunacy Commissioners.*

Ages.	Rate per Million of Population.					
	Persons.		Males.		Females.	
	1894.	1904.	1894.	1904.	1894.	1904.
All ages	2,354	2,827	2,234	2,731	2,467	2,945
0—15	99	121	123	158	70	85
15—25	890	1,025	1,000	1,170	788	863
25—45	3,562	3,959	3,616	4,111	3,512	3,819
45—65	6,228	7,512	5,652	6,878	6,746	8,085
65 and upwards	5,885	7,656	5,213	6,829	6,413	8,294

The ratio of the asylum population to a million of the general population (persons) at all ages increased from 2,354 in 1894 to 2,827 in 1904; equal to an increase of 20 per cent. in the ten years. The increase of this insanity rate during the ten years was 12·2 per cent. at ages under 45 years, and 30·1 per cent. among persons aged upwards of 65 years. While it is probable that this marked increase in the rate of asylum insanity among the population aged upwards of 65 years is partly due to the increasing proportion of cases of senile dementia transferred from workhouses to asylums in recent years, it is undoubtedly incumbent on those who ignore the effect of accumulation on the increase of the number of inmates of asylums to suggest some other explanation, than accumulation, of the marked changes in the age distribution of the asylum population during the past fifty years, such as proof that first attacks of insanity now occur at a later age than was formerly the case.

AGE DISTRIBUTION OF PATIENTS ON ADMISSION TO ASYLUMS, HOSPITALS, AND LICENSED HOUSES FOR THE INSANE.

With a view to test the effect of changes in the ages of patients on admission to asylums, &c., upon the age distribution of the inmates of these institutions in recent years, the following table, showing the mean ages of patients admitted during the two five-year periods 1890-94 and 1900-04, has been derived from tables in the 50th and 60th Reports of the Lunacy Commissioners :—

TABLE H.—*Average Annual Admissions to Lunatic Asylums, Hospitals, and Licensed Houses; Proportional Age-Distribution of Admissions; and Rate of Admissions to 10,000 Population; at Five Age-Groups; in Five-Year Periods 1890-94 and 1900-04.*

Ages.	Average Annual Number of Admissions.		Proportion in each Age-group to 1,000 Admissions at all Ages.		Annual Rate of Admissions to 10,000 Population.	
	1890-94.	1900-04.	1890-94.	1900-04.	1890-94.	1900-04.
All ages....................	17,086	21,298	1,000	1,000	5·9	6·5
0—15	262	266	15	12	0·3	0·3
15—25	2,520	2,903	148	136	4·5	4·6
25—45	7,822	9,488	457	446	10·1	10·3
45—65	4,879	6,389	286	300	11·8	13·2
65 and upwards	1,603	2,252	94	106	11·7	14·8

The figures in this table show that, during the period dealt with, there was a large proportional decline of admissions, under the age of 45, and a corresponding proportional increase above that age.

Of 1,000 admissions the number under the age of 45 years declined from 620 in 1890-94 to 594 in 1900-04; while the proportion of the admissions above the age of 45 increased from 380 to 406. More-over, it appears that while in 1890-04 the proportional number admitted to asylums above the age of 65 did not exceed 94 per 1,000, it had increased to 106 in the five years 1900-04. This marked increase in the number and proportion of elderly patients admitted to asylums in recent years has been much commented on in recent reports of the Commissioners. It was pointed out in the report for 1905 that during the five years 1884-88 the average annual number of admissions of persons aged upwards of 65 years was equal to 99 per 100,000 of the population living at those ages; whereas fifteen years later (in 1899-1903) the annual rate of admissions at these ages had increased to 143 per 100,000. Thus the rate of admissions above 65 years of age, to population, at those ages showed an increase of no less than 44 per cent. during the fifteen years 1886-1901. The average annual number of admissions above the age of 65 years which did not exceed 1,267 in the five years 1884-88, had increased to 2,145 in the period 1899-1903, showing an annual increase in the latter period of 878 admissions at these advanced ages. These statistics of admissions to the asylums, above the age of 65 years, of course relate to the total admissions, whether transferred directly from home or from workhouses. The same report, however, contains much interesting information relating to 1,455 cases of admissions of persons aged upwards of 70 years, to 83 asylums in England and Wales, during the years 1903 and 1904, directly from 393 union workhouses; of these 1,455 cases, 690 were transferred from workhouses to asylums in 1903 and 765 in 1904. The Commissioners reported that of these 1,455 cases of admission, 1,141 were of persons aged between 70 and 80 years, and 314 of persons aged upwards of 80 years (equal to 21·5 per cent. of the whole) including 18 whose ages exceeded 90 years. The Commissioners discussed in their report the desira-bility, or otherwise, of this increasing tendency to transfer these cases of senile dementia from workhouses to asylums, which often appears to prejudicially affect the patients, as well as giving a false impression of the increase of insanity. They point out that of these 1,455 cases of senile dementia transferred from workhouses to asylums, in 1903 and 1904, 37, or 2·5 per cent., died within a week of their transfer; 175, or 12·0 per cent., died within a month; 502, or 34·5 per cent., within six months; and 666, or 45·7 per cent., within one year of their transfer. It is reported that a considerable proportion of the medical superintendents of the asylums, in reply to inquiry, expressed the opinion that many of these transferred senile cases were really unsuitable for ordinary work-house treatment.   The high rate of mortality among the transferred patients seems, however, to throw doubt on the beneficial result of the transfer, while there is still more doubt whether such cases should be classed among those suffering from what is generally understood as insanity.   This gives added weight to the importance of a scientific definition of the term insanity as a physical disease.

Before leaving this branch of the subject it seems desirable to refer to some statistics referring to the admission of aged patients to the London County asylums, published in the last issued annual report of the Asylums Committee of the London County Council. It appears that during the eighteen months ending on the 30th September, 1905, no fewer than 462 patients (189 males and 273 females) aged over 65 years were admitted to the London County asylums, representing more than 9 per cent. of the total admissions during that period.   Of these 462 cases, 216 were aged between 65 and 70 years, 131 between 70 and 75, 83 between 75 and 80, and 32 were aged above 80 years; 12·1 per cent. of these aged patients died within three months of their admission to the asylums.   The Asylums Committee express the opinion in this report that "the " certification of old people is a very important factor in the " recorded increase of lunacy," and further state that "the great " majority of old persons who are received in asylums are in such a " condition that it is possible to certify them as not of sound mind, " *i.e.*, not in enjoyment of all their faculties ; but at the same time " it is right to point out that in many instances this condition is the " consequence only of natural decay through advance of years, " and in many cases it is their physical rather than their mental " condition which calls for most attention.   This circumstance may " explain why boards of guardians are so ready to send old persons " who become troublesome in their infirmaries to asylums."   It may be noted that the number of the insane known to and under the control of the London County Council on the 1st January, 1906, was 24,957, showing an increase of 305 upon the number at the beginning of the previous year.   These were equal to 5,310 per million of the estimated population of the county against 3,531, the mean ratio in the whole of England and Wales, at the same date. Of these 24,957 London insane, 72·7 per cent. were in asylums or licensed houses, 25·7 per cent. in the imbecile asylums of the Metropolitan Asylums Board, 1·1 per cent. in ordinary workhouses, and only 152, or 0·5 per cent., were known to be residing with relations or others ; the mean proportion of these cases known to be so residing with relatives or others was equal to 9·1 per cent. in the whole of England and Wales.   In order to secure asylum treatment for practically the whole of the London insane, the amount of asylum accommodation provided by the County Council, and by the Metropolitan Asylums Board, has been increased from 12,930 on the 1st January, 1890, to 23,941 on the 1st January, 1906. A still further addition of about 4,617 beds is now in course of provision, in order fully to provide for the 1,547 London insane patients accommodated, under contract, in out-county asylums and at a licensed house, on the 1st January, 1906, and for any further increase in the number of the certified insane belonging to the County of London.

There can be no doubt that the statutory grant-in-aid of 4s. per week for pauper lunatics treated in asylums has much accelerated the transfer of mentally unsound inmates of workhouses to lunatic asylums, including a large proportion of harmless, chronic and imbecile cases not really requiring the expensive treatment provided in these asylums. The Royal Commission on Local Taxation recommended that the financial objection to this grant-in-aid should be removed by extending the present grant so as to be payable, not only for pauper lunatics maintained in county and borough asylums, but also for all pauper lunatics, epileptics and imbeciles *properly* maintained in other institutions and separated from other workhouse inmates. As regards London, however, it should be noted, that under the provisions of the Common Poor Fund the whole cost of lunatics is centralised, while the centralisation of the cost of ordinary paupers is only partial. This arrangement offers to the metropolitan guardians a strong inducement to transfer as many paupers as possible from the workhouse or workhouse infirmary to the county asylums, or to the asylums of the Metropolitan Asylums Board, the expenses of which are also wholly centralised. It has been estimated that each pauper so transferred causes a reduction in the local rates of about 15*l.* per annum. This inducement naturally appeals most strongly to the Guardians of those Unions in which deficiency of workhouse accommodation renders it necessary to board out some of their paupers, in which cases the whole cost of maintenance and accommodation (about 35*l.* per annum) would apparently be saved by the transfer. It has been pointed out, however, that while individual unions undoubtedly derive financial gain by such transfer, each transfer adds to the financial burden of London as a whole, as the cost of maintenance and accommodation is considerably higher in asylums than in workhouses. It is estimated that the average annual cost of an insane patient in the County of London asylums is about 42*l.*, and in the imbecile asylums of the Metropolitan Asylums Board about 44*l.* ; while, as stated above, the average annual cost of an ordinary indoor pauper in London does not exceed about 35*l.* It may be hoped that this financial question and its effects upon the alleged increase of insanity will be fully considered in the forth-coming report of the Royal Commission on the Feeble-minded, as it unquestionably throws much light on the exceptionally high rate of so-called insanity in the County of London, and, as has been pointed out, has indeed a very general bearing on the whole question of this alleged increase of insanity.

The Effect of Insanity upon the Rate of Mortality.

Dr. William Farr, a former President of this Society, in the paper read by him in 1841, to which reference has already been made, called attention to the then recent case of an action brought by the executors of a clergyman, who died insane, to recover 2,000*l.*, the amount of a policy of insurance on his life. The medical evidence as to the effect of insanity on life was of a conflicting character, and the judge, in charging the jury, instructed them to consider whether insanity had a tendency to shorten life, pointing out that if, in their opinion, insanity had that tendency, they must find for the defendants, whereas if they came to the opposite conclusion, they must find for the plaintiffs. The jury, it is said, after a short deliberation, gave a verdict for the plaintiffs on the ground that insanity had no tendency to shorten life. In explanation of this remarkable verdict, it must be remembered that at that time very little was known of the science of vital statistics, which Dr. Farr may be said to have founded on the basis of the civil registration of births, deaths, and marriages, enacted in 1837. Seventy years ago the mere knowledge that a considerable number of the insane lived to advanced ages was sufficient to convince many minds that insanity was not a fatal disease. Dr. Farr, however, in the paper referred to, showed that the mean age of the insane in asylums at that time was between 35 and 40 (it is now more), and that whereas the annual rate of mortality in England and Wales at this age did not exceed 13 per 1,000, it averaged 90 per 1,000 in the Bethlem Asylum during the years 1827-39, although from this institution dangerous cases were carefully excluded. Dr. Farr wrote, " The mortality of severe cases of insanity cannot, I think, in " favourable circumstances, be less than 60 per 1,000, so that the " mortality is three times greater among lunatics than among the " general population at the same age."

At the present time, however, we may fairly expect to know more definitely the true effect of insanity upon the mean rate of mortality at different ages and under different treatment. Tables published in recent reports of the Lunacy Commissioners afford the means for comparing the rate of mortality among the inmates of lunatic asylums, hospitals and licensed houses, with the rates prevailing among the general population, at several groups of ages, and thus to ascertain more precisely the effect of insanity on mortality at different age periods. These tables show the ages, in twelve groups, of the inmates of these asylums in the year to which they relate, as well as the ages, in the same groups, of the inmates whose deaths occurred during the year. The last published report of the Commissioners contains these statistics relating to the year 1904, and to a certified insane population of 95,940 inmates of these institutions.

TABLE I.—*Annual Rate of Mortality per 1,000 among the Certified Insane, at Five Age-Groups, compared with the Rate of Mortality in the General Population at the same Age-Groups, in 1904.*

Ages.	Annual Rate of Mortality per 1,000.		Death-Rate of the Certified Insane, the Death-Rate in the General Population taken as 100.
	England and Wales.	Inmates of Lunatic Asylums, &c.	
PERSONS.			
Above 15.....................	14·5	97·9	675
15—25	3·4	69·0	2,030
25—45	6·8	73·1	1,075
45—65	20·8	90·8	437
65 and upwards............	87·5	214·5	245
MALES.			
Above 15.....................	15·2	111·9	736
15—25.....................	3·7	71·7	1,907
25—45.................	7·5	86·5	1,153
45—65...........	23·4	108·7	465
65 and upwards	92·7	252·6	272
FEMALES.			
Above 15.....................	13·8	85·9	622
15—25.....................	3·1	65·7	2,119
25—45.....................	6·2	59·8	965
45—65.................	18·4	76·0	413
65 and upwards	83·6	190·4	228

In this comparison of the rate of mortality among the inmates of asylums, &c., with that in the general population, it is, of course, necessary to restrict the comparison to ages above 15 years as the proportional number of the insane below that age is very small. The annual rate of mortality in England and Wales in 1904 among the general population aged above 15 years was equal to 14·5 per 1,000; among the 94,612 certified insane at the same ages, dealt with in the table referred to, it ·was equal to 97·9 per 1,000. Thus, in equal numbers living, of both sexes at similar ages, the mortality of these certified insane was nearly seven times as high as the mean mortality among the general population; it was equal to 675, the mortality among the general population being taken as 100. Among the male patients in these asylums above the age of 15, the rate of mortality in 1904 was equal to 111·9 per 1,000, whereas among the female patients it did not exceed 85·9; among the general population the mean mortality of males above the age of 15, in 1904 was equal to 15·2, and of females not more than 13·8 per 1,000. Thus, taking 100 to represent the mortality of each sex above the age of 15, the mortality of the male patients in the asylums in 1904 was equal to 736, and that of the female patients to 622.

Examination of a similar table in the Lunacy Commissioners' Report for 1896, shows that the rate of mortality among the inmates (persons) of asylums in 1894 above the age of 15 was somewhat lower than the rate in 1904; it was 92·5 per 1,000 in 1894 against 97·9 in 1904, and compared with the death-rate in the general population taken as 100, the mortality in asylums was equal to 634 in 1894, against 675 in 1904. The figures in the above table may, however, be accepted as fairly representing the approximate effect of certified insanity on mortality at all ages above 15, and at each of the four age-groups dealt with therein. These figures (as well as those for 1894) show clearly that the excess of mortality due to insanity is heaviest at the earlier ages when. the proportion of acute cases is obviously greatest, although the rate of mortality among the certified insane increases with age, as in the general population, but at a very different ratio. Thus among persons of both sexes in the age-group 15—25, the death-rate of the inmates of asylums in 1904 was equal to 69·0 per 1,000, and more than twenty times the rate in the general population, which was only 3·4 per 1,000; between 25 and 45 years of age the death-rate in asylums was 73·1 per 1,000, and more than ten times the general rate at those ages, which was 6·8 per 1,000; at the age-group 45—65 the death-rate of the insane patients was 90·8 and was equal to 437, the rate in the general population being taken as 100; and among the certified insane aged over 65 years the death-rate was 214·5 per 1,000, against 87·5 among the general population, equal to 245, taking 100 to represent the general rate. With reference to the excess of mortality in the two sexes due to insanity, it may be noted that in the earliest age-group 15—25, the mortality among the certified female insane was 2,119 to 100 in the general population, whereas among males the proportion did not exceed 1,907 to 100 ; at each of the three subsequent age-groups, however, the proportional excess of mortality due to insanity among males considerably exceeded the excess among females. In the general population, the rate of mortality at each of the four age-groups shown in the table was considerably lower among females than among males ; and the smaller proportional excess due to insanity among females (except between the ages 15—25) would appear to point to the fact that the type of insanity certified for admission to asylums is milder, or at any rate less fatal, than that of males certified for admission.

Referring to the conclusions drawn by Dr. Farr from the statistics of Bethlem Asylum, in his paper read in 1841, it would appear that the mean mortality of the certified insane at the present time does not widely differ from the rate in that asylum during the years 1827-39. It must be remembered, however, that all so-called dangerous cases were at that time carefully excluded from Bethlem Asylum, whereas all classes of cases are now included in the asylum statistics of the Lunacy Commissioners ; and further that the higher mean age of the inmates of asylums at the present time must tend to raise the annual death-rate. It is, however, clear that Dr. Farr under-estimated the effect of insanity on human mortality when he stated that the mortality is " three times greater " among lunatics than among the general population at the same " age," although he apparently meant that it was four times as great. The Commissioners' statistics, on which the above table was constructed, show that the asylum mortality in 1904 was nearly seven times, and in 1894 more than six times, the mortality among the general population at the same ages.

METROPOLITAN ASYLUMS BOARD STATISTICS.

In my last paper on this subject I dealt, in some detail, with the excellent statistics issued by the Metropolitan Asylums Board relating to the asylums for idiots and imbeciles under their control, and, having been favoured by that Board with recent statistics concerning their institutions, they call for some further consideration. The earliest of these asylums were established in 1870 at Leavesden and Caterham, and several other asylums have since been added. The average annual numbers of residents in these asylums have steadily increased from 2,901 in 1871, to 6,652 in 1906. In the first five years of their existence, 1871-75, the annual

rate of mortality among the inmates of these asylums averaged
133·4 per 1,000.

TABLE J.—*Average Annual Death-Rate in the Metropolitan Asylums for
Idiots and Imbeciles in Seven Quinquennial Periods,* 1871-1905.

Quinquennial Periods.	Average Annual Death-Rate per 1,000 of the Average Annual Number of Residents.		
	Persons.	Males.	Females.
1871–75	133·4 ·	160·1	112·4
'76–80	83·2	105·1	66·5
'81–85	77·3	80·2	75·1
'86–90	89·4	90·3	82·6
'91–95	92·8	98·4	87·0
'96–1900	77·2	82·4	73·0
1901–05	71·3	73·4	69·8

If we except a temporary increase during the ten years 1886-95,
the rate of mortality in these institutions, as is shown by the above
table, has steadily declined, and in the most recent quinquennial
period, 1901-05, it fell to 71·3. The male rate during the seven
five-year periods declined from 160·1 to 73·4, and the female rate
from 112·4 to 69·8. In the five years 1871-75 the annual death-
rate of persons (male and female) in these asylums exceeded by 32·0
per 1,000 the average annual rate that prevailed in the county,
borough, and other lunatic asylums under the control of the Lunacy
Commissioners. In the recent five years 1901-05, however, the
mean annual rate in the metropolitan asylums was 28·1 per 1,000
below the mean rate in the county, borough, and other lunatic
asylums. There can be no doubt that this marked decline in the
death-rate in these institutions has caused a considerable accumulation of inmates. We have seen that the transfer, of aged paupers
suffering from senile dementia, from workhouses to asylums appears
to cause very high death-rates among those transferred, and the
high death-rates in the metropolitan asylums during the early years
of those institutions may probably be thus explained. That the
death-rate in these asylums in recent years is so far below that
which prevails in ordinary lunatic asylums is most probably due to
the fact that the inmates consist almost entirely of harmless chronic
cases, no cases of acute mania being received therein.

The Managers of the Metropolitan Asylums Board, as well as
the Lunacy Commissioners and the Asylum Committee of the
London County Council, have recently protested against the
" increasing practice of certifying as lunatics quiet, harmless, and
" mostly senile cases," which in their opinion might well be retained
in the workhouse infirmaries. · The result of this practice has been

to fill the Tooting Bec Asylum with such cases, whereas that asylum was provided, in a great measure, for the reception of infirmary cases from the old asylums at Leavesden and Caterham. The Managers, moreover, expressed the opinion that the retention of these harmless senile cases in the workhouse infirmaries, "on "humanitarian grounds alone, seemed to be the proper course, as "it involved neither the removal of the patients to distances, which "rendered visitation by friends a matter of some difficulty (not to "speak of expense), nor the possible injury to family connections "by the slur of insanity."

The following table affords a comparison between the annual rates of mortality prevailing among the inmates of these Metropolitan asylums aged upwards of 20 years at four age-groups during the three years 1904-05-06, and the mean annual death-rates at the same ages in the general population of London in the same three years.

TABLE K.—*Average Annual Death-Rate in the Metropolitan Asylums for Idiots and Imbeciles during the Three Years, 1904-05-06, at Four Age-Periods, compared with the Death-Rate in the General London Population at the same Ages and in the same Years.*

Populations dealt with.	Annual Rate of Mortality per 1,000 at each Age-Period.			
	Age-Periods.			
	20—40.	40—60.	60—80.	80 and Upwards.
Metropolitan Asylums (1904-05-06)	57·0	60·3	177·9	348·7
General London Population (1904-05-06)	5·3	17·2	58·8	199·7
In equal numbers living, deaths in Metropolitan Asylums to 100 in London General Population...	1,075	351	303	174

The mean annual death-rate in the Metropolitan asylums was, as is shown in the table, 57·0 per 1,000 at the ages 20—40, and 60·3 at the succeeding age group 40—60; at the earlier of these groups the rate was more than ten times as high as that among the general London population at the same ages, while at the ages 40—60 the Metropolitan asylum rate did not exceed 351 compared with the rate in the London population taken as 100. Between 60 and 80 years the asylum rate was 177·9 per 1,000—about three times the general London rate: and among the inmates over 80 years the rate was 348·7 per 1,000, and equal to 174 compared with 100, taken to represent the general London rate at the same ages. It may be noted that, as in the case of lunatic asylums, the rate of mortality among the inmates of the Metropolitan asylums showed far the largest excess at the earliest age period, 20—40, although no acute cases are received in these asylums; it is, however, probable that a large proportion of the admissions occur at these ages, and it has been pointed out that the rate of mortality is generally high among new cases during their early period of asylum treatment. Compared with a somewhat similar table given in my former paper, the excess of mortality in 1904-05-06, due to that form of insanity treated in the Metropolitan asylums, somewhat exceeded that which prevailed in 1886-87-88 between the ages of 20 and 80, while it showed a decline above the age of 80 years. The increase of this calculated excess of mortality among the inmates of these asylums is partly due to the decline in the general death-rate in London during the last eighteen years, and partly to a recent increase in the death-rate of the inmates of the asylums at the earlier age-groups. There can, moreover, be no doubt that the rate of mortality in an asylum is considerably affected by changes in the proportion of new cases admitted, and it is not easy to over-estimate the value of carefully prepared statistics relating to the different classes of the insane, including the necessary information relating to the ages of the inmates, of the patients on admission to asylums, and of the patients dying therein.

CONCLUSION.

It must once more be admitted, in drawing conclusions from the statistics thus submitted for the consideration of this Society, that many of the arguments based upon them, with a view to discredit the assertion that the prevalence of insanity is steadily increasing, are more or less of a negative character. The object of the paper has been mainly to establish the fallacy of the assertion that the long-continued increase in the numbers of the certified and registered insane affords conclusive proof of the increasing prevalence of insanity as a physical disease. If it could be proved that there had been no change, since 1859, in the standard of mental unsoundness calling for registration and certification, then the numbers of the registered and certified insane might possibly be accepted as affording proof of the increase of prevailing insanity. The evidence of the Lunacy Commissioners, of the Asylums Committee of the London County Council, of the Metropolitan Asylums Board, and indeed of most experts in lunacy, affirms, however, without doubt, that the standard of mental unsoundness calling for special asylum treatment is constantly undergoing change, and that a large proportion of cases are now certified for such treatment, which would not have been so certified twenty, forty, or sixty years ago.

Then it is equally beyond doubt that there exists, over and above the numbers of the registered and certified insane, a very considerable reserve of more or less harmless borderland cases, constituting a reserve of the mentally unsound, from which the numbers of the registered and certified insane is being constantly recruited, without affording any proof of the increasing prevalence of insanity. Public confidence in the advantage of asylum treatment has undoubtedly increased in recent years, together with an increasing inability or disinclination to bear the trouble and expense involved in the private care of aged and infirm relatives.

The census returns in 1871, 1881, and 1891 showed a marked decline in the aggregate of this reserve of unregistered cases; and it seems very doubtful whether the large increase in the numbers of this reserve enumerated at the census in 1901, the result of the substitution of the term "feeble-minded" for "idiot" in the occupiers' schedule then used, really indicated any increase in the proportional numbers of the mentally unsound in the English population between 1891 and 1901. The change of nomenclature in 1901 without doubt entirely destroyed the value of comparison with the returns at previous censuses. We know, however, that 17·8 per cent. of the mentally unsound returned at the census in 1871 were not registered or certified by the Lunacy Commissioners; and that this deficiency in the number of the insane dealt with by the Commissioners had declined to 13·5 per cent. in 1881, and further to 10·9 per cent. in 1891, although the opinion was expressed in the census reports that the returns of the mentally unsound showed increased accuracy at successive censuses, and therefore a nearer approximation to the true aggregate of cases of insanity in the English population.

The probability that the numbers of the registered and certified insane (reported upon from year to year by the Lunacy Commissioners), constantly shows an increasing proportion of the aggregate total of the insane in England and Wales, is supported by the marked decline in the annual rate of increase in the ratio of the registered insane to population, which was (see Table C) 12·9 per cent. in the five years 1864-68, and fell to 2·4 per cent. in the five years 1889-93, since which it has only increased to 6·2 per cent. in the five years 1899-03.

The value of statistics of admissions to asylums is very generally vitiated by the absence of information as to the previous history of the cases, whether admitted from among cases under treatment in workhouses, or from pauper cases residing with relatives, or from the large reserve of unregistered cases. It appears from recent reports of the Commissioners, however, that the ratio to population of first admissions to asylums, &c., which increased from 4·92 per 10,000 in 1898 to 5·76 in 1902, steadily declined again in three following years to 5·21 in 1905.

The marked changes in the proportional age-distribution of the inmates of lunatic asylums, hospitals, and licensed houses, in the absence of any conclusive proof that insanity, as a disease, now attacks at a later age than formerly, afford the strongest evidence of accumulation, which causes an increase of existing cases of insanity, not due to the increase of occurring lunacy. In 1851, the earliest date for which this information is available, of 1,000 inmates of public institutions for the treatment of the insane, 549 were aged under 45 years and 451 above that age : in 1904 the proportion under 45 years had declined to 480, while that above 45 years had increased to 520. As an explanation of this change in the age proportions of the inmates of asylums, involving a considerable increase in the mean age of the insane, it has been pointed out that there has been a persistent decline in the discharge-rate (including deaths) of the insane in asylums since 1873.

On the basis of a table published in the last issued report of the Lunacy Commissioners, it has been shown that if the annual discharge-rate (including deaths), from asylums, hospitals, and licensed houses for the treatment of the certified insane, had been, in the three years 1903-04-05, as high as it was in the five years 1873-77, the number of the inmates of these asylums would have shown an actual decline of 1,578, whereas there was a recorded increase of 7,236 in the number of inmates during these three years. This recorded increase in the asylum population during 1903-04-05 seems clearly to have resulted from accumulation due to the decline in the discharge-rate.

There is, moreover, abundant evidence, acknowledged by the Lunacy Commissioners, the Asylums Committee of the London County Council, and the Metropolitan Asylums Board, that in recent years there has been an increasing tendency to certify, in great measure, on financial grounds, simple cases of senile dementia for treatment in lunatic asylums. This raises, in connection with the subject under discussion, the very urgent necessity for a scientific definition of insanity as a disease. This is, indeed, a need which should receive the fullest consideration of the Royal Commission on the Care and Control of the Feeble-minded, under their extended Reference, as it is obvious that, before we can furnish a satisfactory answer to the question whether the prevalence of insanity, as a disease, is or is not increasing, we must make up our minds as to what is meant by insanity. It may or may not be desirable that pauper cases of senile dementia should be treated in special institutions, other than Workhouse Infirmaries, but the statistics and observations on this point, of the Lunacy Commissioners, and of other authorities charged with the care of the insane, deserve more serious consideration than they have yet received on at least three grounds :—(*a*) the effect of the certification of these cases on the alleged increase of insanity; (*b*) the high rate of mortality among the recently transferred cases; and (*c*) the taint of insanity which is thus imposed upon the relatives of the deceased inmates of asylums suffering from senile dementia.

It further seems especially desirable that there should be a well-considered and scientific classification of the cases of so-called insanity, with a view at any rate to throw light upon the increase or decrease of the several forms of mental unsoundness which are, in the aggregate, now treated in asylums.

The *Times* correspondent in his articles points out :—" We do " not even know whether the varieties of insanity, in the so-called " 'classification' of which much labour has been wasted, are the " consequences of a single noxious agent applied in varying " quantities and under varying conditions to brains of varying " structure or organisation, or the consequences of noxious agents of " different kinds."   In connection with the desirable claim for the application of exact methods of chemical and physical research to the scientific study of insanity, as a physical disease, one of the first necessary steps would appear to be to adopt some uniform classification of the cases treated in public institutions, based upon expert knowledge, in order to establish a basis for calculating the increase or decrease of new cases of the several forms of mental unsoundness admitted for asylum treatment.

The tables of the Lunacy Commissioners are of little use for this purpose.   It is true that in the last few reports of the Commissioners there is a table showing the average numbers of patients admitted to lunatic asylums, hospitals and licensed houses during recent five-year periods, from nine "forms of mental disorder," including four forms of "dementia"; but as these tables are obviously based upon returns furnished from a large number of separate institutions, the degree of uniformity in the system of the present classification is doubtful.   Moreover, while the five-year average is useful in showing the mean proportions of admissions from the several forms of mental disorder, this table affords no means for testing the increase or decrease in the proportions of the several forms from year to year, even of general paralysis of the insane, for instance, which now appears as one of the forms of mental disorder.   On referring to the report for 1896, moreover, the classification is found to include only six forms of insanity, among which general paralysis of the insane finds no place. Dr. T. Clifford Allbutt, formerly a Lunacy Commissioner, in a recent letter to the *Times*, wrote: " Asylum segregation is not pathological but legal; in respect of " pathology it is segregation by chance, and the name 'insanity' " is a vague and abstract title which covers a vast medley of " diseased persons, no two of whose cases were ever identical, and " between the extremes of which there lies an enormous distance " both of extent and kind."

My further careful study of existing statistics on this subject, after a lapse of seventeen years, justifies me in expressing a decided opinion that there is no absolute proof of actual increase of occurring insanity in England and Wales, and further strengthens the conviction expressed in my former paper, that the continued increase in the number and proportion of the registered and certified insane, reported on from time to time by the Lunacy Commissioners, is mainly, if not entirely, due (*a*) to changes in the degree and nature of mental unsoundness for which asylum treatment is considered necessary or desirable; and (*b*) to the marked decline in the rate of discharge (including deaths) from asylums. In fact that this increase of the registered and certified insane is not really the result of increased prevalence of insanity as a physical disease.

The importance of the subject, however, induces me to hope that it may be found possible to organize an improved system of statistics on the subject, which will afford the means for throwing more light on this important social and statistical problem.

Such statistics should include more precise information concerning the previous history of all the new cases coming under observation during each year, combined with an expert and uniform system of classifying the form of mental unsoundness in each case. In view of the conclusions that have been drawn from the fact that the number of private patients among the certified insane has long been practically stationary, and that the ratio of so-called discharges-on-recovery among private patients so largely exceeds those among pauper patients, it is most desirable that information should be available as to the number of private patients who subsequently become pauper patients. It should, moreover, be possible to classify, on the same uniform system, the inmates of institutions for the treatment of the certified insane suffering from each of the more distinct forms of mental unsoundness. I may in conclusion repeat what I said in my previous paper :—" It is even still more essential to the definite " solution of the problem under discussion, that provision should at " once be made for obtaining trustworthy statistics concerning the

" annual admissions, transfers, discharges, and deaths occurring
" among the pauper insane retained in workhouses; and similar
" information relating to insane paupers in receipt of outdoor relief."
There does not appear to be any insuperable difficulty in the way
of obtaining this information, and the responsibility for its collection
and utilization seems to rest between the Local Government Board
and the Lunacy Commissioners.

When these additional statistics are available, some Fellow of
the Royal Statistical Society will probably be able to furnish a
more conclusive refutation of the alleged increase of insanity than
now seems possible.

DISCUSSION *on* MR. NOEL A. HUMPHREYS' PAPER.

DR. R. DUDFIELD said that he agreed so entirely with what
Mr. Humphreys had written that his remarks were more in the
nature of an endorsement of the opinions enunciated than a
criticism. In the tables of ages of lunatics quoted by Mr. Humphreys
there were no returns for the last Census, an omission which it was
desirable should be rectified. At p. 157 of the General Report of
the Census of 1901, there was a table showing the proportions of
the insane in lunatic asylums, workhouses, &c. Although there
had been since 1891 an increase of 36·2 per cent. in the total
number of lunatics, yet the proportion of all lunatics in public
asylums had decreased from 66·6 per cent. in 1891 to 65·4 per cent.
in 1901. Similarly there had been a decline from 4·7 to 2·8 per
cent. in private asylums. The increase in workhouses was 0·4 per
cent. only, but that "elsewhere" 2·7. Having regard to the
changes in the custody of lunatics indicated by those figures, the
ages at the last Census might be expected to throw some light on
the subject under discussion. His own opinion was that the bulk of
increase recorded at the last Census was among the very young and
the very old, especially the latter.

Table C of the paper showed a steady decline in the rate of
increase of the mean annual ratio of insane reported by the Lunacy
Commissioners down to the period of 1889-93, when it was
2·4 per cent., while during the next period it rose to 5·1. It was
a little curious that the creation of the administrative counties took
place in 1889, and that the transfer of the public lunatic asylums
to the Council should coincide with a change in the rate of increase.
He suggested that possibly some increase in the public confidence
in administration by popularly elected bodies might have had

something to do with the increase in the proportion of lunatics in such institutions. It was also noteworthy that a check in the rate of increase was recorded in the last period included in the table. Another factor which he thought had no small share in the increased number of lunatics under the jurisdiction of the Commissioners, was the great growth of "flat life" which had taken place within the last ten or fifteen years. Living in what may be described as barracks people had neither the accommodation nor the privacy for retaining in their homes members of their families mentally afflicted. Further, the standard of living was much higher now, and therefore more expensive. By getting afflicted relatives into asylums more scope was left for show and personal comfort. It cost less to keep the afflicted in safety in an asylum than in the home.

The question of the transfer of the old folk (cases of senile dementia) from workhouses to asylums was, he thought, to some extent influenced by considerations of policy. The guardians were feeling the strain of finding accommodation sufficient to satisfy all applications for relief, especially in those districts where out-relief was largely refused. It was cheaper to transfer the senile dementia cases to asylums and thus make room for other paupers than to keep the former in the workhouses and provide new buildings to keep pace with the demand for admission.

Mr. Humphreys' hope for an improved system of statistics on the subject of lunacy endorsed the suggestion made by the speaker in a communication presented to the Society two years previously, urging the creation of a central statistical bureau to co-ordinate the work of such different and independent bodies as the Lunacy Commissioners, the Census Commissioners, &c., and to indicate the lines on which it was desirable that statistical inquiries and reports should be formulated.

Dr. FORBES WINSLOW congratulated the author on having dealt with this subject in every aspect. The Paper had raised certain important points for discussion, but he was afraid time would not allow for them to be fully discussed. When Carlyle, some forty-five or fifty years ago, probably suffering from an attack of irritation due to indigestion, pronounced the community to be mostly a nation of fools, he must have foreseen the increase of insanity at the present day. If he could have known that, whilst in 1859 there was but one insane person in every 536 of the population, and that in the present day there was one in 285, it would not have taken him long to have calculated the year when there would be more insane people in the world than sane. He objected to a person suffering from an acute form of insanity, who might have been ill but a few hours, perhaps raving mad, with the delirium of pneumonia, and who might under ordinary circumstances get well in forty-eight hours, being removed to an asylum as a "person of unsound mind," and thus branded for his life with the stigma of lunacy because he had been registered as a lunatic on the Commissioners' list. In whatever calling of life he might be, in whatever occupation he might be engaged, the fact of his once having been registered as a lunatic stands out as a hideous nightmare.

What was required was a half-way house, where persons suffering from an acute form of insanity might be placed and treated, and not placed with the ordinary classes of unsound mind; and he hoped that would soon be brought about. He could not agree with the remark that it was now-a-days easier to get people certified as of unsound mind than it was in days gone by. Many years ago it was illegal to take into a house a person of unsound mind for profit; without the legal documents the same law exists to-day, but with this exception, that before an action can be brought against a person who has charge of an individual, it must be proved that the individual is certifiably insane; whereas in the old days any form of insanity, certifiable or not, was included.

There is no such thing as a harmless lunatic. He had often heard it stated that the reason why there were so many pauper lunatics in asylums was that there were so many old cases who ought to be in the infirmaries of the workhouses. Some years ago he went to see a patient at Claybury, London and County Asylum, and in course of conversation with Dr. Jones, the Medical Superintendent, he was informed that the Guardians were constantly interfering with these cases, and that a few days ago an old lady patient whom they considered perfectly harmless was, at their suggestion, taken back to the workhouse. Within twenty-four hours of this the so-called harmless lunatic threw herself out of window and committed suicide. You never can tell when a harmless lunatic might develop dangerous symptoms. With regard to the increase of insanity in civilised countries, it is a well-known fact that where education exists to a greater extent and where stress and strain enter into competition, insanity is bound to be on the increase, whereas among the nomadic savages, who only have their wigwams and hunting to amuse themselves, lunacy is rarely, if ever, seen.

Dr. W. D. MORRISON said, as an old member of a Board of Guardians, he must question the statement made by the last speaker. He thought the last thing Boards of Guardians wanted to do was to get lunatics into the union, and, once they got them away they were only too glad to keep them away; so that the case referred to must have been a very exceptional one.

He thought this was one of the best papers on comparative statistics which had been read for many years; it pointed out very truly that comparisons between the present day and a certain number of years ago were useless, and that it was on the basis of those useless comparisons that the public had been unduly alarmed as to the alleged increase of insanity. He agreed that when the figures were carefully examined there was no proof whatever that insanity had increased at all. It was sometimes very difficult to say when a man was insane and when not. For many years he was connected with our prison service, and he had seen men under examination as to whether they were insane or not, and in many cases it was just a toss up whether they should be certified or no. It depended to a very large extent upon the particular ideas of the medical officer with regard to insanity. And again, after the medical officer had come to a decision, it-ultimately depended on the ideas of the magistrates who were to certify. His own experience led him to think that the present tendency was both for medical officers and magistrates to be much more ready to certify that a man was insane than it was, say, twenty years ago ; and, if that were so, that one fact led to considerably more persons being sent to asylums now than before, although there was no increase of insanity in the population as a whole. It had been said that the increased pressure of life on the community might have some effect in leading to a loss of mental balance. But, on the other hand, it must be recollected that at the present time people were better fed and better housed than they used to be; and the one fact might counterbalance the other. It was quite evident that the apparent increase of insanity, as derived from the statistics, was not to be accepted as a proof that insanity was really on the increase, and Mr. Humphreys had rendered valuable service in bringing this fact before the public.

The Right Hon. Sir JOHN DORINGTON, Bart., congratulated Mr. Noel Humphreys on his Paper. He had had to consider the question whether insanity was on the increase or not, because in his county the numbers in the asylum were growing, and that was taken as being a *primâ facie* proof that insanity was on the increase. He rather doubted the fact, and he thought it was rather the number taken care of that was increasing, which was quite a different matter. One cause of the apparent increase was the confidence which the public now had in the management of asylums ; there was no longer the belief that was entertained in the Valentine Vox days. The poorer classes now, where they had an aged relative who had got into a state of senile decay, were much too ready to ask for the intervention of the doctor and the magistrates to send him to an asylum. Two or three such cases had come under his personal observation, where he had been called in, and, more than once, he had refused to certify, and told the people they ought not to send away their old mother or father simply because they had passed the age of 80 and wanted constant watching. In one or two of these cases in a short time death supervened, and it could not have been right to move those aged people away to an asylum—in fact—they would very possibly have died on the road there. The asylum authorities had often to complain of the condition in which aged persons were sent to the asylums ; they were not sent until the last moment, when nothing could be done for them, and this only led to suffering on the part of the patient, and an increase of the number of deaths in the asylum. The number of the insane treated in the public institutions was certainly always increasing, but it was remarkable that the number under private treatment was constantly diminishing. Why was this ? It seemed to prove that taking those classes which originally were fully and adequately provided with asylum accommodation where all the cases that could not be controlled at home were sent, and in which originally there was no reserve of lunacy, there were not now so many cases to treat as formerly, and that in fact lunacy was diminishing in those classes at all events. The fact that the average number per 10,000 of private patients had fallen from 57 to 28, seemed to prove that in the class on which a great deal of the modern stress and strain of life fell, lunacy was diminishing, and, therefore, why should they suppose there was an increase in the class lower down, which had to resort to public institutions? The increase there was, in his opinion, due to many causes; to increased confidence on the part of the public, and perhaps to an increased disinclination on the part of the poor to retain the charge of their aged relatives, and not necessarily to an increase of lunacy. It was impossible quite to satisfy oneself what was the real cause, but, in his view, the increase in the number of the certified insane was not a proof of the increase of insanity.

Dr. SCOTT TEBB said it might be rather presumptuous on his part as an analyst to speak on a question of this kind, but his profession induced a critical and inquiring state of mind, and it so happened that an investigation which he undertook for the borough of Southwark actually brought him into close contact with this subject. He thought that Society was the one above all others which should undertake an investigation of that kind. As Dr. Farr had said many years ago, the Royal Statistical Society, as a body, was quite disinterested, and probably better qualified than any other to collect information on this subject and to submit the results to the public. He was afraid he could not altogether follow the statistical intricacies of this very important and valuable Paper, but one matter did seem to him to be clear. According to Table C, in 1904-06, the number of certified cases was 3,504 to the million of population, or 1 to 285; therefore, whether insanity was increasing or not, that was a very important fact which they could not get away from. And, he believed, whether insanity was increasing or not in this country, there was no doubt whatever that it was increasing in the sister isle. He should like to quote from the Report of the Inter-Departmental Committee on Physical Deterioration, which was signed by the statistical expert of the Registrar-General, Dr. Tatham. It stated that insanity was on the increase in Ireland. According to the published returns, the number of lunatics under care in 1880 was 250 per 100,000, or 1 in 400; and in 1902 it was 499 per 100,000, or 1 in 200. If the number of lunatics and idiots at large were added, the whole number would be 58 per cent. per 100,000, or 1 in 170, whereas some fifty years ago the number is said not to have exceeded 1 in 730. That report quoted the opinion of the Bishop of Ross, who said that lunacy had become so common it was practically no longer a disgrace, and he found that the number of families affected was so great that the apprehension based on the risk of inter-marriage had ceased to operate. He had serious difficulties in that way, because according to the Canon law a bishop ought not to admit amongst the clergy any person whose relations within certain degrees were affected with insanity, and if he drew the line very strictly he should have to refuse practically all the applicants. From the table comparing the death-rate amongst the insane with that amongst the general population, it appeared that in 1904 it was seven times, and in 1894 six times, as great; and, according to some earlier figures of Dr. Farr's, the mortality at that time amongst the insane was only about three times as great as amongst the general population. Mr. Humphreys thought that if Dr. Farr had made out his figures to the present day he would have made some corrections, but he could not think that the difference between three and seven times had been accounted for.

Table I, comparing the death-rate of the insane with the general mortality at different ages, was a very interesting table; at the ages of 15 to 25 the figure was " 2030," or twenty times as great as the general mortality at these ages, which was a very serious matter. As to the cause, they must look not only at the habits and customs of the people, such as alcoholism, tea drinking, the use of tobacco, &c., but to heredity. If insanity was on the increase, there must, in addition, be some cause operating during the period of pregnancy. It seemed to him also there must be some important cause operating during young life after birth, and he would suggest that one was the universal case of brain irritation in young life owing to the system of compulsory education in this country. The point to be considered was whether they had not gone crazy on this question. Personally, he was of opinion that it was much more important, especially for the labouring classes, that they should have good eyesight and good physique, and that their intellects should be stimulated by natural objects, rather than that they should be able to read and write a little better than they would otherwise do. Only the other night Sir Shirley Murphy read a valuable Paper before the Epidemiological Society, in which he proved to demonstration that the increasing incidence from diphtheria in this country was partly due to the number of young children aggregated at school ages. Another question was whether short-sightedness, or myopia, was not becoming more common than formerly, and from the evidence of several important authorities it appeared that there was some ground for believing it had been increased by the system of compulsory education. Other things might be factors : one was alcoholism, though he did not think there was a very strong case for that, as the nation's drink bill for recent years had decreased from 186,000,000*l.* in 1899 to 164,000,000*l.* in 1905.

Dr. MERCIER expressed his great satisfaction that this exceedingly important subject was being taken up by a gentleman who was a competent expert and an eminent statistician, by whom alone such problems could be properly investigated. It had been before him for many years, and they all knew the great increase in the number of persons in asylums, but he had always held a strong opinion that that increase did not represent any real increase of mental disease in the community. What he was concerned about was the last paragraph, namely, "The urgent desirability of an expert and scientific definition of what constitutes so called insanity in order to facilitate the solution of the problem of the alleged increase of insanity as a disease," and he should like to make some contribution to that definition. As a matter of fact, insanity was not a disease; there was a thing called "insanity," but it was not a disease, it was but a portion of a very much larger malady. It consisted of a certain number of cases separated off from an enormously larger number of cases of mental disorder. It only became insanity when the individual affected by mental disorder was so affected as to become dangerous or noxious or a nuisance to the community or to himself so that he had to be placed under control. But there was an enormous amount of mental disorder which did not amount to insanity; it might be considerably greater in degree than insanity, or it might be less, but it was not insanity, because it did not require the seclusion of the patient in an asylum. Practically, insanity was a legal entity, not a medical entity at all; it consisted of those cases of the disease which it was necessary to place under control. There were a vast number of persons who suffered from many forms of mental disorder, morbid fears, morbid hesitation, morbid depression, morbid desire, and mental disorder of many kinds which one was in the habit of seeing constantly but were never considered to be insanity. It was manifest, therefore, that the spread of insanity or the extent of that section of mental disorder would depend on the view people took of the desirability or otherwise of placing persons under control. There were, no doubt, a large number whom it was now considered desirable to place under control, who in former times would not have been thought to come within the definition of insanity, although the medical aspect of the case would not have been altered in the least. It might be thought to be for the patients' benefit in many ways, or for the benefit of the public, as, for instance, that he should not be able to propagate his kind. But there were a number of patients now placed under control, not because they were dangerous to others or themselves, but in order that they might receive skilled treatment and have a better chance of recovery. In times when there was no skilled treatment and when asylums were not carried on in the humane manner they now were, there was every motive for the friends of a patient to keep him out of the institutions, but now-a-days there was every motive to send him in. Amongst the motives might be the shirking of his maintenance, and shirking the trouble involved, but thirdly, much more often the motive was to place the patient under skilled treatment and facilitate his recovery, and for all those reasons the asylums went on filling. The numbers confined in the asylums depended on the view taken partly as to their being dangerous and partly also on the view taken by the physician of their prospects of recovery. He did not know that he should have agreed with Sir John Dorington in refusing to make an order in the cases he referred to; he had admitted that they died within a few days, and it seemed to him that if they had been sent to the asylum, in all probability their lives would have been considerably prolonged, which might or might not be a desirable result, but it tended to show how the asylums did get filled and how much the committal of a person to an asylum depends on the view taken of his case.

The PRESIDENT then proposed a cordial vote of thanks to Mr. Noel Humphreys for his valuable Paper, which had produced a most interesting discussion; it showed on the one hand the value of scientific statistics in checking crude figures, and on the other that questions of this sort should be thoroughly investigated before results could be published as facts. Mere figures did not really satisfy the case. It had also tended to show how difficult it was to say what was lunacy; he reminded his audience of the old adage that at one time or another we all were mad. *Semel insanivimus omnes.* The border line was so very close between the action of a brain which rendered a person liable for his actions, and the action that would make him not responsible, that it would be highly desirable if the amount of derangement which carried the brain action of any man on one or other side of this narrow line could be brought within some scientific definition which would enable people who took up statistics of this kind to draw an accurate line and scientifically define sanity, lunacy, idiocy, or feeble-mindedness.

Mr. NOEL HUMPHREYS, in reply, said there were just one or two points on which it seemed desirable to say a word. With regard to the decrease among pauper patients of discharges from, and the increase of admissions to, asylums, a partial explanation had been suggested which seemed to him to possess a considerable amount of probability, namely, the decline of home industries. Our census returns showed that there had been in recent years a large decrease of home industries throughout the country, and it seemed more than probable that this considerably increased the difficulty of retaining at home imbecile or feeble-minded members of the family who required constant personal attention. Dr. Scott Tebb had referred to the undoubted increase in the proportion of the insane in Ireland, and that raised an interesting point in connection with lunacy statistics. There used to be a very general idea that insanity was more prevalent in rural than in urban districts. It was a fact that in rural districts the proportion of the certified insane to the general population was, speaking generally, much larger than in towns, and it was also true that the ratio of insanity to population was actually higher in Ireland than in England and Wales or in Scotland. But what was the explanation? In all places where there is a decreasing population the most healthy and vigorous young people migrate to the towns or emigrate—from Ireland to all parts of the world—leaving their older or more or less feeble members of the family at home. This migration caused a very high rate of insanity among the residuum of the population, but it did not necessarily signify that the Irish people were exceptionally liable to insanity any more than it did in rural districts, where migration of young people causes an apparently high rate of insanity among the resident population.   With regard to the mortality of the insane, the calculations he had referred to, he might venture to say, were reliable; but it must be remembered that Dr. Farr's paper was written nearly seventy years ago, when he had not the advantage of the statistics now available.   His figures were based solely on the statistics of Bethlem Hospital, to which acute and serious cases were never admitted.   There was, however, a little vagueness in the expression used in his paper.   He said "three times more numerous," which was probably intended to signify "four times as numerous."   Moreover, as a very large proportion of acute and serious cases were now admitted to all asylums, that would in a great measure account for the difference between Dr. Farr's statistics, relating to the Bethlem Hospital, and those of the Lunacy Commissioners.   There was no doubt that the calculated mortality was extraordinarily high among the cases under 25 years of age—it was, indeed, at those ages twenty times as great as amongst the general population.   This was, however, probably in great measure due to the fact that comparatively few cases were certified at these ages unless they were of an acute or serious nature.

The following were elected Fellows of the Society :—

à Ababrelton, Robert R. de R. | Denman, The Hon. Richard Douglas.

The HERRING FISHERY. *By* ALBERT E. LARK, F.C.A.

[Read before the Royal Statistical Society, 16th April, 1907.
SIR RICHARD BIDDULPH MARTIN, Bart., President, in the Chair.]

IT has been suggested to me by Mr. R. H. Inglis Palgrave that, in consequence of the very large development in recent years of this industry, a paper embodying some of the facts may be of interest to the members of the Society, and to that section of the population interested in the trade.

The fisheries, as a whole, present a branch of national industry of great importance, but I desire to deal only with that of the herring, and have in consequence collected the statistics which enable me to separate this from the whole industry.

The fact that Yarmouth is the most important centre of the herring fishery in England and Wales has given me the opportunity of being intimately acquainted with the practical side of the subject.

The Antiquity of the Herring Fishery.

Though not much is known of the methods of fishing generally on our coasts in very early times, the records as to the size of the boats and of the nets render it extremely improbable that, until sixty or seventy years ago, any great alteration or improvement in the ancient modes of the herring fishing had taken place.

It is probably of the herring fishing that we have the oldest records, and of the Yarmouth herring fishing the most authentic. Precise records of other fisheries do not go back as far as those relating to the herring. Undoubtedly the fishing for herrings originated along the shores of Norfolk and Suffolk.

Swinden, in his "History of Great Yarmouth" published in 1772, expresses his belief that the herring fishery began there soon after the year 495.

From Domesday Book we find that Yarmouth was a place of considerable importance owing to its herring fishery. From the same record we find that numerous manors in Suffolk yielded rents of herrings. Yarmouth itself, when erected into a burgh by Henry I in 1108, annually paid for this privilege " ten milliers of herrings."

In the reign of Edward the Confessor the lordship of Beccles yielded 30,000 herrings yearly to the abbey of Bury St. Edmunds.

The annals of the monastery of Barking in Essex, which was founded in 670, inform us that a tax was then levied on herrings, and was known as " herring-silver."

In the records of the monastery of Evesham, which was founded in 709, there are several references to the herring fishery, showing that even to a long distance inland the herring was known and prized as an article of food.

The plentifulness of the herring made it an easy medium of exchange when coin was scarce. Thus we find that the Abbott of St. Bennett-at-Holme in 1240 agreed to pay 1,000 herrings yearly in Lent to the provost of Carrow for certain rights of fishing at Carrow, Norfolk. The Abbott and Monks of Ely were entitled to an annual contribution of 24,000 herrings from the men of Dunwich. An oblation of this fish was made annually to the minister of Great Yarmouth, called Christ's half-dole; a certain quantity was allowed annually to the chief magistrate, and a considerable portion went towards the discharge of municipal expenses; all these payments were in course of time commuted for coin.

England and Wales.

The coasts on which herrings are principally landed are divided by the Board of Agriculture and Fisheries into :—

(*a*.) Northern District, including ports from Berwick to Whitby.

(*b*.) North-eastern, from Scarborough to Boston.

(*c*.) Eastern, from Sheringham to Brightlingsea.

(*d*.) South-eastern, from Queensborough to Worthing

(*e*.) Southern, from Beer to Plymouth.

(*f*.) South-western, from Looe to Ilfracombe.

(*g*.) South Wales.

(*h*.) North Wales.

(*i*.) North-western, from Liverpool to Maryport.

(*j*.) The Isle of Man.

A dissection of the total catch over these districts was completed for the first time in 1903.

Table showing Percentage to Total Catch of the Quantities Landed at the Various Districts and the Principal Month.

Coast.	Number of Principal Ports.	Percentage to Total Catch.			Principal Month.
		1905.	1904.	1903.	
(a.) Northern District..........	5	11·49	8 85	9 38	August.
(b.) North-eastern ,, ...	2	13·05	17·7	16·55	September.
(c.) Eastern ,, ...	2	72 18	70 7	69·25	November.
(d.) South-eastern ,, ...	Nil	0·49	0·25	0·26	November.
(e.) Southern ,, ...	1	0 76	0·87	1·74	December.
(f.) South-western ,, ...	2	1·29	1·95	1·86	December.
(g.) South Wales ,, ...	Nil	0 12	0 07	0·16	May.
(h.) North Wales ,, ...	Nil	0·06	0·08	0·06	December.
(i.) North-western ,, ...	Nil	0 08	0·12	0·03	July.
(j.) Isle of Man ,, ...	1	0·48	0·67	0·71	July.
		100	100	100	

It is generally admitted that the herrings caught in the month of November are the finest in quality, as at that period of the year they are fully matured.

Scotland.

The districts in which the herrings are landed in Scotland are :—

(a.) The East Coast, with the principal ports of Fraserburgh, Peterhead, Wick, Aberdeen, Anstruther and Eyemouth.

(b.) Orkney and Shetland Isles.

(c.) West Coast, with principal ports, Stornoway, Loch Broom, Barra and Campbeltown.

Table showing Total Quantities Landed in Scotland for the Ten Years, 1896-1905, Divided over the Districts.

	1896.	1897.	1898.	1899.	1900.	1901.	1902.	1903.	1904.	1905.
	Cwts.	Cwts.	Cwts.	Cwts.	Cwts.	Cwts.	Cwts.	Cwts.	Cwts.	Cwts.
East coast..........	2,824,977	1,503,693	3,047,434	1,522,351	1,528,006	1,926,317	2,740,585	2,381,666	2,736,602	2,313,253
Orkney and Shetland....	540,880	658,429	782,144	929,346	1,155,826	1,701,878	1,199,424	1,185,131	2,045,613	2,409,862
West coast	594,424	803,843	874,063	755,381	836,384	710,440	813,935	712,688	650,279	619,662
	3,960,281	2,965,965	4,703,641	3,207,078	3,520,216	4,338,635	4,753,944	4,279,485	5,432,494	5,342,777

Percentage of Total Quantities Landed in the Three Districts for the Ten Years, 1896-1905.

	1896.	1897.	1898.	1899.	1900.	1901.	1902.	1903.	1904.	1905.
East coast...	71·3	50·7	64·8	47·5	43·4	44·4	57·7	55·7	50·4	43·3
Orkney and Shetland....	13·7	22·2	16·6	29·0	32·8	39·2	25·2	27·7	37·6	45·1
West coast	15·0	27·1	18·6	23·5	23·8	16·4	17·1	16·6	12·0	11·6
	100	100	100	100	100	100	100	100	100	100

ENGLAND AND WALES.—*Quantities Landed at the Various Stations and also the Three Coasts during the Ten Years 1896-1905.*

Port.	1905.	1904.	1903.	1902.	1901.	1900.	1899.	1898.	1897.	1896.
	Cwts.	Cwts.	Cwts.	Cwts.	Cwts.	Cwts.	Cwts.	Cwts.	Cwts.	Cwts.
Yarmouth	1,272,919	1,421,597	1,227,020	1,520,025	989,805	982,663	912,525	634,524	776,284	623,587
Lowestoft	935,017	827,477	889,900	1,154,232	751,134	699,073	654,016	393,472	466,543	282,589
Grimsby	300,675	391,819	342,820							
Scarborough	97,430	138,041	159,100							
North Shields	184,408	127,880	130,980							
North Sunderland	69,264	49,121	67,480	658,447	521,318	584,627	456,304	637,549	385,954	475,743
Hartlepool	53,885	60,411	43,900							
Berwick	25,221	28,844	19,920							
Whitby	4,024	—	7,920							
Total, principal east coast ports	2,942,843	3,045,190	2,889,040							
Other stations on east coast	18,040	18,560	24,631							
Total for east coast	2,960,883	3,063,750	2,913,671	3,332,704	2,262,287	2,266,363	2,022,845	1,665,545	1,628,781	1,381,919
Plymouth	13,708	22,600	49,580							
St. Ives	19,690	47,979	24,260							
Newlyn	15,251	8,223	23,560	150,032	190,561	158,894	216,331	166,878	186,984	144,194
Peel	9,675	12,859	13,480							
Other stations, south and west coast	42,858	29,161	34,460							
Total quantity landed, England and Wales	3,062,065	3,184,581	3,059,011	3,482,736	2,452,848	2,425,247	2,239,176	1,832,423	1,815,765	1,526,113
East coast	2,960,883	3,063,750	2,913,671	3,332,704	2,262,287	2,266,363	2,022,845	1,665,545	1,628,781	1,381,919
South coast	54,889	42,191	83,887	69,940	109,399	41,580	73,231	41,432	50,050	53,264
West coast	46,293	78,640	61,453	80,092	81,162	117,304	143,100	125,446	136,934	90,930
Total quantity landed, England and Wales, as above, divided over the three coasts	3,062,065	3,184,581	3,059,011	3,482,736	2,452,848	2,425,247	2,239,176	1,832,423	1,815,765	1,526,113

Notes on the Quantities Landed at the Various Stations.

England and Wales.

From this table we see how enormously the catch has increased during the ten years from 1896 to 1905.

The figures with regard to Yarmouth show that the catch in 1905 was more than double that of 1896; whilst the catch at Lowestoft in 1905 was more than treble that of 1896.

The catch of the other stations on the East Coast during the same period has also advanced materially.

The table shows conclusively that it is the East Coast herring fishery which is of predominant importance, and the figures ascertained, show that it is to Yarmouth and Lowestoft that we look on the average for 70 per cent. of the total catch for England and Wales. The fact, therefore, that we have to lump together the figures for the other ports on the East Coast does not affect the remaining statistics.

If we refer to the table of percentages of the total catch for 1905, we see that the quantity landed on the East coast is no less than 96 per cent. of the total for the whole country, and we may therefore assume that the records of these ports form a sufficient basis for the study of the herring fishery.

The figures for 1903 to 1905 showing the quantities landed at the various stations, are taken from the report of the Board of Agriculture and Fisheries; but 1903 was the first time such a dissection was published. For the previous years, I have, therefore, ascertained the total catches at Yarmouth and Lowestoft respectively, and converted the last to cwts. at 30 cwts. to one last, which is, I think, a fair average to take. The "last" is a measure of "*number*," there being 13,200 fish in the "last," and therefore the weight must necessarily vary according to the size, condition, &c., of the fish.

Of late years the Scotch measure the "cran" has been largely employed at Yarmouth and Lowestoft, as it is a more expeditious and—what perhaps appeals to the Scottish element—a less costly method of delivering the fish to the buyers. The development of the practice of delivery of herrings by the cran in England has undoubtedly led to an increase in the quantity of fish landed, as the boats are enabled to clear their cargoes more expeditiously and get to sea again.

The "cran" is a measure of "*quantity*," and is equal to about $37\frac{1}{2}$ gallons. Ten crans are usually considered equal to one last; hence, although the official total catches at Yarmouth and Lowestoft are given in cwts., it is made up of returns arrived at sometimes by actual counting, *i.e.*, the "last," and sometimes by measure, *i.e.*, the "cran."

Taking into consideration the above factors, I am of opinion that the conversion at 30 cwt. to the last in order to arrive at the comparison necessary, is a fair average.

But for 1903 (the first year, as I have before stated, in which official dissection over the ports is made), I find that the figures of the total catches at Yarmouth and Lowestoft respectively, obtained locally, if converted from lasts, in which they are given, to cwts. at 30 cwt. to the last, do not equal the Board of Agriculture and Fisheries' figures as given in cwts. by about 15 per cent. I am not cognizant of the manner in which the figures in the Board of Agriculture and Fisheries' Report are arrived at, and this variation of 15 per cent. I have therefore taken into account in the years for which the official dissection is not obtainable.

Notes on Percentage of Total Catch Table. England and Wales.

From this table it will appear that the percentage attributable to Yarmouth of the total catch landed in England and Wales during the ten years from 1896 to 1905, has remained fairly constant at about 40 per cent. of the total, whilst Lowestoft during the same period has increased its percentage very materially.

As will be seen from the table, Yarmouth and Lowestoft between them annually account for 70 per cent. of the total catch of herrings for England and Wales.

Aggregation of the Annual Values of Herrings Landed in the United Kingdom of Great Britain and Ireland for the Ten Years 1896-1905.

Year.	England and Wales.	Scotland.	Ireland.	Total.
	£	£	£	£
1896	380,377	673,687	63,092	1,117,156
'97...	529,866	707,555	61,602	1,299,023
'98.	432,638	952,402	69,537	1,454,577
'99	798,874	1,143,296	97,096	2,039,266
1900	934,429	1,243,407	83,956	2,261,792
'01...... .	892,637	1,061,034	97,868	2,051,539
'02........... ..	1,094,963	1,360,492	76,537	2,531,992
'03	891,251	1,244,656	84,446	2,220,353
'04....	759,674	1,017,541	93,004	1,870,219
'05............	1,164,422	1,343,080	121,846	2,629,348

ENGLAND AND WALES.—*Percentages of the Total Catch Landed at the Various Stations, 1896-1905.*

Port.	Order of Importance.	1905.	1904.	1903.	1902.	1901.	1900.	1899.	1898.	1897.	1896.
Yarmouth	1	41·5	44·6	40·1	43·6	40·3	40·5	40·7	34·6	42·7	40·8
Lowestoft	2	30·6	26·0	29·1	33·1	30·6	28·8	29·2	21·4	25·6	18·5
Grimsby	3	9·8	12·3	11·0							
Scarborough	4	3·2	4·3	5·2							
North Shields	5	6·0	4·0	4·3							
„ Sunderland	6	2·3	1·5	2·2	19·0	21·3	24·1	20·3	34·8	21·2	31·1
Hartlepool	8	1·7	2·2	1·4							
Berwick	11	0·9	0·9	0·7							
Whitby	13	0·1	—	0·3							
Other stations on East coast	—	0·6	0·5	—							
Total for East coast	—	96·7	96·3	94·3	95·7	92·2	93·4	90·2	90·8	89·5	90·4
Plymouth, Newlyn, St. Ives, Peel and 79 other stations	7, 9, 10 and 12	3·3	3·7	5·7	4·3	7·8	6·6	9·8	9·2	10·5	9·6
	—	100	100	100	100	100	100	100	100	100	100

Extract from the Board of Agriculture and Fisheries' Report.

" It must be understood that all the foregoing figures represent
" the values at the time of landing only, nothing being included for
" the earnings of other fishing industries connected with curing and
" like operations . . . . . . by which the value of the fish is
" frequently much enhanced before it reaches even the wholesale
" markets. In comparing these figures with estimate of the value of
" the fishing industry of the United Kingdom in which other items
" are included, the difference in the basis should always be borne in
" mind, for if the value of the fish were to be taken at a late stage
" of the industry the annual value . . . . . . might well
" amount to double that total."

*Table showing the Total Catch and Value of Herrings Landed in England
and Wales, Scotland, and Ireland for each of the Years 1896-1905.*

Year.	England and Wales.		Scotland.		Ireland.		Year.
	Cwts.	Value.	Cwts.	Value.	Cwts.	Value.	
		£		£		£	
1896 ..	1,526,113	380,377	3,960,281	673,687	244,328	63,092	1896
'97....	1,815,765	529,866	2,965,965	707,555	287,678	61,602	'97
'98...	1,832,423	432,638	4,703,641	952,402	464,318	69,537	'98
'99...	2,239,176	798,874	3,207,078	1,143,296	427,382	97,096	'99
1900...	2,425,247	934,429	3,520,216	1,243,407	284,251	83,956	1900
'01....	2,452,848	892,637	4,338,635	1,061,034	347,605	97,868	'01
'02....	3,482,736	1,094,963	4,753,944	1,360,492	201,187	76,537	'02
'03....	3,060,000	891,251	4,279,485	1,244,656	232,980	84,446	'03
'04....	3,184,581	759,674	5,432,494	1,017,541	286,496	93,004	'04
'05 ..	3,062,065	1,164,422	5,342,777	1,343,080	354,144	121,846	'05

*Table showing the Total Catch and Value of Herrings Landed in England
and Wales, Scotland, and Ireland for each of the Years 1896-1905,
taking the Figures of 1896 as Equivalent to 100.*

Year.	England and Wales.		Scotland.		Ireland.		Year.
	Cwts.	Value.	Cwts.	Value.	Cwts.	Value.	
		£		£		£	
1896....	100	100	100	100	100	100	1896
'97...	118	139	74	105	117	97	'97
'98...	120	113	118	141	190	110	'98
'99	146	210	80	169	174	153	'99
1900 ..	158	245	88	184	116	133	1900
'01....	160	234	109	157	142	155	'01
'02...	227	287	120	204	82	120	'02
'03....	200	234	108	184	95	134	'03
'04...	208	199	137	151	117	147	'04
'05....	200	306	134	199	144	193	'05

Conclusions to be drawn :—

That since 1896 the disparity between the volume of the herring trade (both "*quantities*" and "*values*") in Scotland as compared with England and Wales has rapidly lessened.

Export of Herrings.

The following tables show the exports of herrings in barrels from the United Kingdom in each of the years 1896 to 1905 :—

Quantity.

Year.	Russia.		Germany.		Other Countries.		Total Barrels.
	Barrels.	Per Cent. of Total.	Barrels.	Per Cent. of Total.	Barrels.	Per Cent. of Total.	
1896	264,364	19	860,587	63	248,876	18	1,373,827
'97	180,770	16	693,210	62	245,274	22	1,319,254
'98	310,585	18	1,175,828	67	256,622	15	1,743,035
'99	185,170	14	956,897	68	262,406	18	1,404,473
1900	234,693	15	1,060,022	69	246,160	16	1,540,875
'01	296,263	16	1,303,552	69	278,837	15	1,878,652
'02	356,147	16	1,570,632	70	314,197	14	2,249,976
'03	414,068	20	1,299,544	63	320,370	17	2,033,982
'04	526,050	20	1,649,144	66	368,679	14	2,543,873
'05	485,640	18	1,740,893	66	417,655	16	2,644,188

Value.

Year.	Russia.		Germany.		Other Countries.		Total.
	Value.	Per Cent. of Total.	Value.	Per Cent. of Total.	Value.	Per Cent. of Total.	
	£		£		£		£
1896	244,781	18	793,064	60	290,817	22	1,328,662
'97	195,026	14	882,812	65	286,536	21	1,364,374
'98	360,080	19	1,233,872	65	305,265	16	1,899,217
'99	349,239	16	1,526,274	69	329,704	15	2,205,217
1900	367,505	15	1,651,441	71	318,876	14	2,337,822
'01	407,819	17	1,636,272	69	332,249	14	2,376,340
'02	484,929	16	2,057,686	71	391,249	13	2,933,864
'03	527,079	22	1,523,214	62	405,571	16	2,455,864
'04	547,417	21	1,656,921	63	430,081	16	2,634,419
'05	576,093	19	2,042,483	65	515,313	16	3,133,889

The export trade may be divided into :—

    (*a*.) Exports of "red" herrings.

    (*b*.) Exports of pickled herrings.

    (*c*.) Exports of herrings in ice.

With regard to (*a*), the export of red herrings from Yarmouth to Roman Catholic countries has always been extensive (especially as a provision for Lent).

The mode of curing is for the herring to be hung entire on rods passed through the mouth and gills, and smoked above smouldering oak logs. This treatment gives them a dark brown appearance, and enables them to be kept for a long period before being eaten.

According to the antiquary Palmer, although since the Reformation the fishing merchants at Yarmouth have usually been staunch Protestants, they did not object to drink as a toast:—

> " The health of the Pope, and his triple crown ;
> May the price of red herrings never come down."

The chief country of export of this branch is Italy.

(*b.*) Manner of curing:—The fresh fish are "gutted" by women, and packed in brine in well-made barrels.

This branch of the trade is assuming more and more importance. By reference to the table it is seen that Germany leads the way as the principal importing country, but it must not be inferred that Germany herself consumes the whole of this quantity. A large proportion of the German import is subsequently despatched to Russia and Austria-Hungary overland, and also by river and canal, the magnificent waterways of these countries being utilised for the employment of huge barges. As a matter of fact, Russia is undoubtedly our best customer for pickled herrings, and the figures of the table are, therefore, very misleading in that respect.

According to the Scottish Fishery Report for 1905, the prospects of a still further development of this trade are very bright, as herrings are now on sale and consumed in places in the interior of Russia, whose inhabitants had, until the last year or two, never seen a herring.

The competition between the foreign distributing merchants is very keen, and I have heard it stated that many are content to obtain for their profit the value of the empty barrel.

The export of barrels to America is increasing, and is expected to develop rapidly in the near future, owing to the large influx into the American States during recent years of Russians, Germans, &c.

(*c.*) For this trade the herrings are packed in ice and salt in barrels or flat boxes and despatched by steamer, the herrings arriving in time to be sold in the fresh state.

Germany admits fresh fish free to her markets, and the employment of ice and salt enables the United Kingdom to export herrings in such a state. This trade has proved to be a remunerative and expanding one.

A report by the Vice-Consul at Bremerhaven (Mr. F. A. Oliver) to the Foreign Office, issued in August, 1905, states that of the total import of fresh fish into Germany in 1903, the comparative share supplied by the United Kingdom was 40 per cent. of the weight and 27 per cent. of the value, and that while there was at present no question of fish becoming a staple article of food for the masses of the inland population, active steps are being taken to popularise the use of it. These efforts were being greatly assisted by the high price of meat, and the expectation that, in view of the increased tariff which would come into operation in 1906, the price would be appreciably enhanced and thus materially increase the consumption of fish.

Number of Barrels Despatched Over-Sea from Yarmouth, 1896-1905.

1896	26,882	1901	171,273
'97	77,007	'02	296,025
'98	56,512	'03	266,049
'99	126,304	'04	323,038
1900	167,024	'05	317,013

The trade in pickled herrings is of recent growth at Yarmouth, and the above shows the enormous increase in ten years.

Fish Traffic by Railways.

The figures relating to Yarmouth would be practically wholly in respect to herrings : but those of Lowestoft would include a large quantity of trawl fish. It is therefore rather difficult to draw a safe conclusion therefrom ; but it would appear that the amount of herrings despatched both from Yarmouth and Lowestoft by rail has practically remained stationary during the ten years 1896 to 1905, and that any increase may be taken to be trawl fish, and not herrings.

We therefore see from these figures, what undoubtedly is the fact, that whereas the quantity of herrings, landed at these two stations during the ten years has increased at Yarmouth 100 per cent., and at Lowestoft 200 per cent., the despatch has not been by rail, but by oversea traffic.

This fact is also to be established by viewing the table showing the exports of herrings in barrels, from which it will be seen that both in quantity and value this branch of the trade has practically doubled in ten years.

Quantity of Fish of All Kinds carried by Railway from the Ports of the United Kingdom in Each Year, 1896 to 1905.

Year.	England.	Scotland.	Ireland.	Year.	England.	Scotland.	Ireland.
	Tons.	Tons.	Tons.		Tons.	Tons.	Tons.
1896...	356,214	107,202	12,959	1901	398,424	130,022	15,272
'97....	353,889	105,001	13,772	'02	465,821	142,904	12,691
'98...	374,457	101,135	16,017	'03 ..	468,574	141,153	14,215
'99 ..	371,718	103,317	17,445	'04 .	486,575	151,271	18,408
1900....	385,694	115,104	15,815	'05	468,518	146,895	18,341

Corresponding Figures for Yarmouth and Lowestoft.

	Yarmouth.	Lowestoft.		Yarmouth.	Lowestoft.		Yarmouth.	Lowestoft.
	Tons.	Tons.		Tons.	Tons.		Tons.	Tons
1894 ..	27,641	29,210	1898....	24,359	30,042	1902....	29,122	40,461
'95....	28,805	29,456	'99..	23,540	31,249	'03 .	32,812	36,748
'96....	26,736	26,972	1900....	25,710	37,282	'04 ·	28,987	35,583
'97...	25,809	36,196	'01 ..	25,934	37,974	'05 ·	26,123	32,185

Imports of Herrings.

The total quantity and value of herrings imported during each of the five years 1901-05 were as follows:—

	Quantity.	Value		Quantity.	Value.
	Cwts.	£		Cwts.	£
1901	444,140	154,782	1904	544,607	180,183
'02	414,998	151,398	'05	602,422	205,530
'03 ...	520,583	198,762			

95 per cent. of the total came from Norway.

The average value of herrings landed in England and Wales, Scotland and Ireland, in each of the years 1896 to 1905, was as follows:—

Year.	England and Wales.		Scotland.		Ireland.	
	Per cwt.		Per cwt.		Per cwt.	
	s.	*d.*	*s.*	*d.*	*s.*	*d.*
1896	4	11¾	3	4¾	5	2
'97.....	5	10	4	9¼	4	3½
'98	4	8¾	4	–½	3	–
'99....	7	1¾	7	1	4	6½
1900......	7	8½	7	–¾	5	11
'01	7	3¼	4	10¾	5	7½
'02...........	6	3½	5	8¾	7	7¼
'03...........	5	10	5	9¾	7	3
'04...........	4	9	3	9	6	6
'05...........	7	7	5	–	6	10½

A comparison of the total yearly catches and the average prices reveals some curious results.

The total quantities landed in Scotland during the ten years 1896 to 1905, show an increase of 34 per cent., whereas the total value shows an increase of 100 per cent. The average price in 1896 was 3*s.* 4¾*d.* per cwt., and in 1905 5*s.* per cwt.

It will be noticed that in those years in which there was a shortage in the catch, there was a corresponding increase in the average price. This was especially apparent in the years 1899 and

1900, when the average price in each of these years was 7s. 1d. per cwt., the previous year being only 4s., and the succeeding year only 4s. 10¾d.

The average price in England and Wales has remained fairly constant, the exceptions being 1899 and 1900, when, as was the case in Scotland, the prices were very high, namely, 7s. 1¾d. and 7s. 8½d. respectively.

In 1905 the average was very high, and for 1906 the figure will undoubtedly be higher still.

The total quantities landed in England and Wales during the years 1896 and 1905 show the somewhat remarkable increase of 100 per cent., the total value showing an increase of 200 per cent.

Ireland, although hampered by lack of means of getting the fish to the markets, has also shared in this activity, the total quantity landed and the value having increased in the same ratio as Scotland. The high price, of course, works to the advantage of the catcher, *i.e.*, the fisherman, and the owner of boats and gear, and to the disadvantage of the merchant or curer; but on the other hand, if a low price is rather hard on the fisherman, a large quantity landed proves an immense boon to the workers ashore, who are thus kept in constant employment. It does not always happen that a "glut" (large delivery) forces down prices, for in some years, just as many herrings as could be caught would be sold at a remunerative price to the catcher. Such a season would be satisfactory to the catchers and the workers ashore. The merchant and exporter, however, would have to give a big price for his herrings, but would get no more for them on the Continent. His profits are therefore cut. Thus we see how rarely can the markets work in such a manner as to be satisfactory to all the varied branches of the industry.

As to the Inexhaustibility of Our Fisheries and the Alleged Damage to Spawn.

For more than fifty years the cry has been that our fisheries are being ruined; that they are being carried on in such a manner as to cause more destruction of fish life than could be compensated for by the vast reproductive powers of those fishes which escape the nets and hooks of the fishermen.

The general complaint has been of the wasteful destruction of spawn and very young fish by beam-trawling and sean nets. This outcry culminated in the Royal Commission of 1863, which would probably have never come into existence had the facts then been known which have since come to light about the spawning habits of most of our edible fishes.

The testimonies of Professors Huxley and Allman in 1867 before a select committee of the House of Commons, and the investigations of Professors G. O. Sars, of Christiania, and M. A. W. Malm, of Gothenburg, are to the effect that, with the possible exception of the herring, all the important kinds of fish taken by our line fishermen and beam-trawlers may be reasonably included among the species whose spawn floats at or near the surface of the sea, and their ova cannot, therefore, be liable to the slightest injury by any method of fishing which is carried on, upon, or near the ground.

With regard to the apparent exception of the herring, whose spawn it has been alleged has been destroyed by the beam-trawlers, it is certain that, to avoid injury to their nets, the trawlers must work where the ground is smooth, and in the few precise localities where it has been positively ascertained that the herring does spawn, the general character of the bottom is rough ; and even if knocked about, the spawn of the herring, as shown by the experiments of Professor Allman and Dr. M'Bain, does not readily lose its vitality, and may even be hatched after having been exposed to most unnatural conditions.

Professor Huxley, in the course of a memorable address delivered at the Fishery Exhibition in June, 1883, remarked :—

" The Royal Commission, of which I was a member in 1864 and
" 1865, was appointed chiefly on account of the allegation by the
" line fishermen that the trawlers destroyed the spawn of the white
" fish—cod, haddock, whiting, and the like. But in point of fact
" the 'spawn' which was produced in support of this allegation,
" consisted of all sorts of soft marine organisms, except fish. And
" if the men of practice had then known what the men of science
" have since discovered, that the eggs of cod, haddock, and plaice
" float at the top of the sea, they would have spared themselves and
" their fellow fishermen the trawlers, a great deal of unnecessary
" trouble and irritation."

In the course of his address he also said :—

" I believe it may be affirmed with confidence that, in relation
" to our present modes of fishing, a number of the most important
" sea fisheries, such as the cod fishery, the herring fishery, and the
" mackerel fishery, are inexhaustible, and I base this conviction on
" two grounds ; first, that the multitude of these fishes is so incon-
" ceivably great that the number we catch is relatively insignificant ;
" and secondly, that the magnitude of the destructive agencies at
" work upon them is so prodigious that the destruction effected by
" the fishermen cannot sensibly increase their death-rate."

Since those words were spoken greater interest has been taken in the scientific study of marine life, with a special regard to its bearing on the prosecution of the fisheries. In connection with the researches of the International Council for the investigation of the North Sea, the Scottish Fishery Board and the Marine Biological Association have in recent years been prosecuting inquiries, with the aid of substantial subsidies from the Government. The Lancashire and North Western Sea Fisheries Committee and other voluntary associations have also been actively engaged in similar investigations. The Committee on Ichthyological Research, which reported in 1901, laid down very explicitly the lines upon which investigation should proceed, and the steps which it was desirable to take to provide for the due prosecution of inquiries. Although the recommendations of that Committee have not been fully carried out some progress has been made, and undoubtedly our knowledge of the essential facts connected with the sea fisheries is being gradually extended.

Splendid work is done at the laboratory and hatchery at the Bay of Nigg, near Aberdeen, and in the "Scotch Fishery Report for 1904" Mr. J. T. Cunningham contributes a paper of great importance on the age and growth of fishes. This particular branch of study in marine life is of momentous consequence; it envolves the elucidation of various problems bearing on the regulations which should govern sea fishing round our coasts.

The result of the researches in regard to plaice and cod is to show generally that they do not grow so fast or reach maturity so soon as is commonly supposed.

Number and Value of Boats and Gear, and Numbers of Fishermen and Others Engaged in the Industry.

In searching for any precise information on the above points, I am necessarily limited by the fact that no exact dissection is attempted between the herring and other fisheries. One fact, however, is clear that a steady increase may be noted in the capital employed and the numbers engaged. On this point the Scottish Fishery Report for 1902 contains the following :—

" A remarkable feature is the steady decrease in the number of " fishing vessels concurrently with the increase in the value of the " capital employed as well as in the resulting catch. As explained " in previous reports, this is an indication of the general and " constant tendency of the Scottish fishing industry towards con- " centration. The movement is an economic one—the resultant of " many causes. No doubt the more immediately predisposing " causes are the accumulation of capital through successful fishings ; " the frugality and enterprise of the best class of Scottish fishermen ;

" and possibly also the necessity for proceeding farther to sea
" to meet the ever-increasing demands upon the fish supply.
" These and the application of steam power to propulsion and to
" other operations incident to the work of fishing are the main
" causes of this concentration of fishermen into fewer boats of
" greater value and efficiency.

" It is also gratifying to know that this concentration is not
" attended with displacement of fishermen.   In fact, there has
" been for the last five years a steady increase in the total number
" of men and boys who man and work the fishing fleet."

From data which I have been enabled to gather, I have arrived
at the conclusion that not less than 3,000,000*l.* is invested in the
boats and gear of the fleets prosecuting the herring fisheries of the
United Kingdom.   The numbers engaged regularly and occasionally
in manning the fleet are not less than 50,000, while at least the
same number are engaged ashore in the various operations of
herring-curing.

As an example of " this concentration of fishermen into fewer
" boats of greater value and efficiency," it may be mentioned that
on the East Coast of England the building of wooden sailing boats or
" drifters" as they are termed locally, has practically ceased.   In their
place we have wooden or iron steam-propelled boats.   The sailing
drifters used to cost, equipped for sea, between 600*l.* and 700*l.*
The wooden steam-drifters cost from 2,200*l.* to 2,400*l.*, and the
iron boats from 2,700*l.* to 2,800*l.*   The steam-propelled boats, in
consequence of more frequent incursions to the fishing grounds
than the sailing boats, cause a greater wear and tear of nets and
gear.   This latter item of gear has to be maintained and renewed
constantly, and the average value attaching to each vessel in respect
thereto is between 700*l.* and 900*l.*

*The Fishing Fleet as an Assistance to National Prosperity and an Aid
to the Navy.*

The importance to a maritime nation like Great Britain of an
industry which is the finest and most economical school for seamen
and a nursery for its navy, must be generally recognized.

Not only does the industry produce seamen, but able pilots,
since the successful exercise of their occupation depends upon an
intimate knowledge of the nature of the ground surface, the situation
of banks and channels, with the particular direction and forces of
tides and currents.

The aid furnished to the naval power by the fishing industry in
time of war is of long standing, for we learn from the " Roll of the
Huge Fleet of Edward III before Calais," extant in the Public

Record Office, that in 1347, at the taking of Calais, Great Yarmouth assisted the King with forty-three ships, on board of which were 1,075 mariners, being a larger number than even London supplied.

During the seventeenth and eighteenth century, the importance of the fisheries as a source of supply for the Navy was always recognised, and strenuous efforts were made to stimulate and encourage them.

The link connecting the regular maritime forces with the fisheries is furnished at the present time by the Naval Reserve training which provides an occupation for the fishermen for a month every year, and being usually taken in the month of January, fills up on the East Coast the period of inactivity between the Yarmouth fishing and the commencement of the West of England mackerel fishing.

DISCUSSION on MR. A. E. LARK'S PAPER.

MR. HENDRIKS said that Mr. Lark had contributed a most interesting and instructive Paper, in which there were three points of great statistical importance in enabling them to form an accurate judgment: first, as to the magnitude of the herring fishery of Yarmouth and its neighbour Lowestoft, the two being generally taken together as they were so closely connected. Although the weight of their catch was given, its value was not stated so distinctly, but the author observed that 70 per cent. of the whole catch of England and Wales was not too high an estimate for those two ports, so that it would appear that as the value of the catch in England and Wales in ten years from 1896 to 1905 was about 7,879,000*l.*; then 70 per cent. of that sum gave a little more than 5,500,000*l.* as the share of Yarmouth and Lowestoft, a very handsome amount indeed for those two ports, giving an average per annum of 550,000*l.*, an amount which seemed likely to increase very largely in the future if anything like the present rate of progress was maintained. The next point was the extent of the whole catch of the United Kingdom, and its value. By adding together the figures in the Paper for the ten years, it would be found that this catch represented nearly 19½ millions sterling in value, and that the total weight was about 70,718,000 cwts.; therefore, the average price comes out at 5*s.* 5½*d.* per cwt. for 1896-1905.

The next point was the export trade in herrings. The table gave the export in barrels, but the author had not stated the relation of the barrel to the cwt., and, therefore, it was difficult to make a calculation of the exact quantity exported. The value of this was of course also important, because it was the cured herring which was mostly exported, and the proportion of cured herrings to pickled herrings was not stated. Probably the cured herrings bore a much higher price than the pickled herrings, but the official value of the two sorts together appears on the basis of the figures in Mr. Lark's Paper to come out at an average of 1*l*. 4*s*. 5¼*d*. per barrel.

One other point he might mention, which was of less importance, namely, the antiquity of the herring trade. The author quoted Swinden's History of Yarmouth, published in 1772, in which he said that he believed the industry began soon after the year 495. He remembered that their distinguished Member, Dr. Cunningham, of Cambridge, in his book on the Early Commerce of England, mentioned the herring fishing as being well known to the Romans; and there was very little doubt that such good judges of food, and such epicures as the ancient Romans were, would be as well acquainted with the merits of the Yarmouth herring as they were with those of the South Coast oyster, and, as they had a very important fortress called Garianonum, now known as Burgh Castle, near Yarmouth, no doubt the garrison there participated in the Yarmouth herring fishery at a much earlier period than 495.

Mr. WRENCH TOWSE thought Mr. Lark had made a slight error in saying that the red herring was hung entire on rods. He always understood that they were first gutted; in fact, in all curing operations, gutting was the first step. He believed that early in the year 1905 the herring fishery season was bad, but it improved as the season advanced. Herrings were cured principally on shore, though he believed the Norwegians had now adopted the plan of gutting and cleaning the fish before landing, which was a practise to be commended, as it gave the means of keeping the fish in a good condition for a much longer time than if they remained ungutted. There were various forms of cured herrings: some were pickled ungutted, which was not desirable, then kippered and packed in boxes; and, again, herrings were put in tins after being boiled up to a certain point to get all the air out, and then hermetically sealed, and in that way they were exported and largely dealt in abroad. Again, they were cured as "reds" and "bloaters," the last being very much esteemed by the public in general. Germany had large centres of tinning factories and curing stations, and he had heard that large quantities were smoked, somewhat in the style of bloaters, and packed in boxes containing about 30, which presented a most appetising appearance. He did not recollect seeing anything of that description in England, but they might, perhaps, advantageously follow the Germans in that direction. Again, herrings were usually exported to Hamburg merely sprinkled with salt. Those interested in the curing of herrings had, he believed, benefited very materially by their increased price; and he rather differed from Mr. Lark in saying that the merchants had not, because he thought they also had benefited.

Mr. J. M. TABOR said this was a most excellent Paper as might
be expected from the author, who had a thorough knowledge of the
subject, but he thought he was slightly incorrect in the weight of
the last, and he would have been more accurate if he had taken the
Board of Agriculture Returns. A "last" of herrings was usually
split up into 20 barrels, and each barrel weighed 2 cwts. From
that, the weight of the barrel, 28 lbs. each, has to be deducted,
so that the actual weight of a last of herrings, instead of being
30 cwts., was 35 cwts. If the extra percentage was added
the figures would practically agree with the figures of the
Board of Agriculture. As to the reason for the large increase
in the value of herrings during the last ten years, it should be
noticed that the greater part of that increase was during the last
two years : and, as the English Consul in Germany mentioned, the
reason was that, owing to the German Tariff, meat there was
extremely dear, so that what would in England cost 1s. would
there cost 1s. 10d., and the result was that the demand for herrings
in that country increased very rapidly. And as the German fishing
fleet, although it increased rapidly, could not keep pace with the
demand, the result was that they drew more largely on the English
herrings. The table on p. 248 showed that from 1904 to 1905 there
was an increase of 33 per cent. on the value of herrings landed in
England and Wales. With regard to a continuance of that high
value, although the Scotch Fishery Report mentioned that the
prospects were very bright of a still further increase, he thought in
that respect they had gone astray, and had been carried away on
the wave of prosperity, and that before long there would be the
inevitable re-action. As a matter of fact, the German herring fleet
was increasing very rapidly, as also was the Dutch. On the other
hand, there was always the possibility that the German people
would force their Government to reduce the tariff on imported
meat, and, if that were done, the price of meat would naturally go
down and the price of and the demand for herrings would fall
off. Remembering that the demand in England was practically
stationary, he thought it would be found that, with a slackening in
the German demand, a larger quantity would be thrown on the
English markets than could be absorbed, and then the price would
go down. That would be the result, even if there were no reduction
of the German tariff, from the rapid increase in the Dutch and
German fishing fleets.

With regard to the competition between the foreign distributing
merchants, as a matter of fact, it was very keen; and this year
practically the whole of the exporters of pickled herrings had lost
money because, owing to the great demand for fresh herrings for the
foreign market, the curers had paid higher prices in England than
were actually realised in Germany. The whole of the factors in
Yarmouth, rather than lose more money by not employing their
workpeople, were forced to buy at a higher price than they could
really afford. The greater part of the increase in the export of
herrings to Germany had been in fresh fish, iced and salted, mainly
because that went in free of duty, whereas pickled herrings paid

duty. The best thing for everybody was moderate values. Very high prices might be good for the fishermen, but were extremely bad for the merchants and exporters. Even London merchants suffered from high prices. The demand in London was not much affected by the demand in Germany; and when English buyers were forced to pay higher prices it made a bad season for them. The number of British boats was increasing every year, and had been doing so for fifty years, and there had been the usual outcry about the destruction of the fisheries. This, he thought, was based more on imagination than actual facts. Although there had been that increase in the means of catching, there was no notable diminution in the supply, in fact it was larger, and there were no signs that the shoals became smaller. Looking at it from a broad point of view, and remembering that every fish produced an enormous number of eggs, it depended on the supply of food and other conditions in the neighbourhood where the eggs were hatched out whether they could live or not. You might catch almost any number of fish, but every one which was left spawned an enormous number of eggs, and, if there was sufficient food in their neighbourhood, there was no limit to their multiplication.

Mr. FRYER said it was rather refreshing to hear a gentleman of such great practical experience say a good word for the statistics of the Board of Agriculture and Fisheries, and express a preference for the returns of that department over the local returns. Mr. Lark said he had "taken into account" a difference of about 15 per cent. between the local returns based on the number of fish landed and the official returns based on the weights. But it was not clear in which way he had allowed the 15 per cent.—whether he had given Yarmouth and Lowestoft the benefit of the extra 15 per cent. or had adhered throughout to the local figures. The calculation of 30 cwts. to the last of 13,200 fish, would work out at an average of 4 oz. per herring. That was very small, and he should imagine that if the figures of the Board of Agriculture and Fisheries erred at all, they erred on the side of defect rather than of excess. He had lately seen herrings weighing nearer 1 lb. a piece than 4 oz. landed on the English coast. That brought him to a point to which attention was not called in the Paper, namely, the great development which had taken place recently in the use of the trawl for the capture of herrings. It was quite possible that the development of the Otter trawl in this fishery might result in a considerable alteration in the figures for different parts of the coast, and that the supremacy of Yarmouth and Lowestoft might possibly be challenged by other ports, even on the southern and western coasts unless they adopted more generally the new method.

Some very serious considerations were suggested by this fact, and it would have been interesting if that matter had been more fully discussed in the Paper, though no doubt the author felt himself limited by having Yarmouth mainly in view.

With regard to the export of herrings from Yarmouth and Lowestoft, over-sea rather than by rail, that seemed to suggest an enquiry whether it was in any way due to the supply of herrings on other parts of the coast being sufficient to meet the demands inland, thus compelling the East Coast ports to get rid of their surplus fish over-sea rather than by sending them to English centres.

He would not follow Mr. Tabor into the very serious question of alleged over-fishing, because that did not arise so much in connection with a fish like the herring as it did in connection with fish of more sedentary habits, such as flat fish. Of all the fisheries, the herring fisheries were the most noted for fluctuation. There were records of fisheries being established and towns built, as it were, on herring bones, and then suddenly disappearing—first the industry and then the town. These fluctuations, though very marked, were owing to purely natural causes.

Some curious points arose out of the table of the comparative values and quantities of herrings landed on different parts of the coast. With regard to England and Wales, the weights showed, with the exception of the years 1903, 1904 and 1905, a steady increase, while the values showed very marked fluctuations; whereas in Scotland the fluctuations in weight were, apparently, greater than the fluctuations in value. In Ireland, the figures were not so large, and the differences not so noticeable. But an interesting subject of enquiry arose as to what caused the differences between the relative values and weights in the two most important herring-producing countries. The steady increase shown in the quantity landed on the English coasts might possibly be due partly to increased effectiveness in the collection of the returns ; but it was certainly not entirely due to that. As regards the fact, alluded to in this Paper, of the statistics in Scotland being much more complete than in England, it was pretty well known that Scotland had always fostered its fisheries, particularly the herring fishery, and that the machinery for the collection of statistics had been in operation a very long time as one of the necessary and recognised means of obtaining information necessary for the development of that industry. The importance of fishery statistics was being more and more recognised in this country ; and it was becoming still more necessary that the herring statistics should be placed on as complete a basis as possible, in view of the development of the fishery not only on the old lines by drift-nets and Seine-nets, but more particularly by the trawl.

Mr. REW congratulated the author of the Paper on being the first to bring the subject of Fisheries before the Society, although, as Mr. Lark was well aware, he was only touching the fringe of a great and complicated subject. The importance of the fisheries as bearing on the food supply had, no doubt, been recognised from very early times, but it was probably not until about the time of the Royal Commission of 1863 that people began seriously to consider problems connected with the fisheries and their future. Scientists —if he might use a rather barbarous word—had since that time paid some attention to the various questions which cropped up ;

but, speaking for himself, he was not sure that they had yet carried the solution of practical problems very far, although no doubt they had done a great deal of very useful work. In late years, statisticians had begun to have their opportunity, although, so far as England and Wales was concerned, it was only very recently that the application of statistics to fisheries had been allowed anything like a reasonable chance. The Society would note with interest the opinion of Mr. Fryer, who spoke as an expert, that from statistical enquiries properly undertaken, in the sense of having an efficient method of collection, and also efficient means of dealing with the. data when obtained, they might hope to solve the practical problems which were of so much interest to the fishing industry and the country at large. The primary problem could. be crudely stated by adapting the proverbial phrase—" Are there as good fish in the sea, and as many of them as there were ? " It was very easy to say that there were as many fish taken out of the sea as ever. because the figures of the total catch landed showed a great increase in the last fifteen years. There was no doubt that a much larger quantity of fish had been landed, but, at the same time, the fishing power applied had greatly increased and the area over which fishing took place had been enormously extended. The limits might be now said to be from the White Sea to the coast of Morocco, as being the range of the boats which supplied our markets. It followed, put in the simplest way one could, that they wanted to discover to what extent the increased supply was due to the application of the increased power and greater area over which the fishing extended. That was the direction in which statistics, if properly collected for a sufficient length of time, would give great help. It was desirable to remember that any student of statistics who addressed the statistical sphinx must have, for the first of all his virtues, patience. Nowadays, many people seemed to think it possible to set up a system of statistical enquiry and to obtain an answer immediately, but nothing was more fallacious than to expect that any statistical deductions could be drawn unless a reasonable time were allowed to elapse before one began to draw conclusions from the data collected. As indicating the growing attention which statisticians were giving to the subject of fisheries, he might mention that it would, for the first time, be brought before the International Statistical Institute at its meeting at Copenhagen in August next. It had also engaged the attention of the International Council for the Investigation of the North Sea, and also the Congress which arose out of the Fishery Congress of Vienna a year or two ago—all tending to show that the importance of applying statistics to fishery problems was becoming more and more recognised, not only in this country, but in other countries concerned.

The CHAIRMAN said he was sure all the members would wish to pass a hearty vote of thanks to Mr. Lark for this Paper, which was a very valuable one. It almost went without saying that the question of fisheries had very considerably increased in importance during the last few years. The very fact that the Board of Agriculture was now the Board of Agriculture and Fisheries, and that the Minister bore the same title, would sufficiently indicate that.

He might also remind them that a great deal of practical interest was taken by the nations bordering on the North Sea, whose fishing territory was comprised in the North Sea, in the question of the destruction or non-destruction of fish. On that point he would not attempt to enter, but he could not but think that the trawls used nowadays, dragging every atom from the bottom of the Dogger Bank, must affect the supply of fish more or less, even if it did not drive them away altogether, especially as they heard that in other parts of England the mere practice with big guns had affected the fishing interest. There were a good many points like that which required to be investigated, all of which would naturally affect the statistics of fishing, and give a reason for either the falling off or the increase in the amount of the total catch.

It was always supposed that herrings were practically inexhaustible, but if they took to migrating to where they could not be easily caught, or, if caught, could not be easily brought to market, it would seriously affect the total supply of fish landed, and which total represented a considerable item in the food of the people. Mr. Rew was quite right in saying that the fishing grounds of English fishermen now extended from the White Sea to the coast of Morocco; they now went all the way round Iceland, whereas only a few years ago only its south-eastern corner was fished. A great many important points were raised about that, and especially what was the sea-limit within which any one Power could prevent another fishing.

He did not propose to make any comment on the Paper itself, beyond saying that a town he knew very well was mentioned in it, namely, Evesham. He did not know whether in the early days, when there was a monastery there, it was at all likely to have got its fish from Yarmouth, or whether they would not have been more likely to come from Bristol; but, wherever they came from, it was interesting to find that the herring was known in such a midland situation.

Mr. LARK, in reply, said he was much obliged to the Fellows for the interest they had taken in his Paper. The method by which he arrived at the weights landed at the various stations on the East Coast of England was as follows:—The figures for the years 1903 to 1905 were those shown in the returns of the Board of Agriculture and Fisheries, but no official dissection existed for the previous years. He therefore obtained locally the quantities landed at Yarmouth and Lowestoft for these previous years as given in "lasts" and converted them from lasts to cwts., at 30 cwts. to the last.

Pursuing the same plan with the years 1903 to 1905, in order to check the manner of conversion, he found that the lasts landed at Yarmouth and Lowestoft from 1903 to 1905 converted to cwts., at 30 cwt. to the last, did not amount to the total as given in the Board of Agriculture and Fisheries report by about 15 per cent.

He therefore added 15 per cent. in each of the years 1896-1902 to the total arrived at by converting the local figures of lasts to cwts. at 30 cwt. to the last.

As for the point raised by Mr. Fryer in regard to the fact that fluctuations in weight were greater than fluctuations in value in Scotland, whereas there were marked fluctuations in value in England, it might be pointed out that the merchants commenced buying in the early part of the year in the North of Scotland, and if the markets were not to their liking and against them they only bought lightly there. When they got south to Yarmouth and Lowestoft, in order to fulfil their contracts, they had to buy whatever the price.

As would be seen, this procedure might cause fluctuations in the price in England. There was also the fact that the greater quantity of herrings caught on the East Coast of England were landed in November, when they were of better quality and usually commanded a higher price.

He believed the Dutch were now building boats to enable them to perform the process of pickling on board, but at Yarmouth they had only one boat built in that way. It had not been followed by other fishermen, and was not likely to come into vogue as it was considered cumbersome. He must contradict the statement that fish were not cured " whole," because red herrings were. It was generally known that when one purchased a red herring it had the roe and other interior inside it. The herrings which went to Italy and Greece were almost wholly of this class. They were lightly cured over smoking oak logs, which gave them a brown appearance. For home consumption, they were smoked for a slightly longer period. Kippering was another process, in which all the interior was first extracted, but the export of this branch was small compared to red herrings. The bloater was quite different; that was a lightly-cured herring principally for home consumption. The bloater was cured entire, and only remained fit for consumption for a few days, whereas the red herring remained fit, if hard smoked, for a year.

He quite agreed that the German tariff had done a great deal for the herring trade. Notwithstanding, Russia was the great customer, because of its vast population. He had been told the one article which assisted that very dry compound, rye bread, to become palatable was the herring, because of its greasy nature.

The following were elected Fellows of the Society :—

Bailey, Walter. | Cleaver, Edgar John, F.A.A.
Tebb, William Scott, M.A., M.D., F.I.C.

The Decline in Number of Agricultural Labourers in Great Britain.

By Lord Eversley.

[Read before the Royal Statistical Society, 14th May, 1907.
Sir Richard Biddulph Martin, Bart., President, in the Chair.]

Two years ago, when the fiscal controversy was at its height, and when it was not unfrequently alleged that the great reduction in the number of agricultural labourers in Great Britain during the last forty years was due mainly, if not wholly, to the admission of corn and other agricultural products free of duty, and the consequent fall of prices,[1] I raised a discussion on the subject at the Political Economy Club. I endeavoured to distinguish how far the reduction of labourers was due to changes in the system of farming, such as the laying down of arable land in grass, and the increased cultivation of temporary grasses in lieu of corn on arable land, which could be directly attributable to the low price of corn since 1880, and how far to other causes, such as the economy of labour effected by the use of machinery and improved methods, which were in no way connected with the fiscal policy of Free Imports. The discussion which took place in the Club was of a private character, and was not reported in the Press. Towards the end of last year (1906), Major Craigie, your late President, suggested that I should expand my address into one for this Society. Since I undertook to do so, a report of a most able and interesting character on the same topic—" The Decline in the Agricultural Population "—has been issued by the Board of Agriculture. It is the work of Mr. Rew, the assistant-secretary in charge of the Land and Statistical Division of that Board, who also so ably fills the position of honorary secretary of this Society. In view of this report, it would seem to be a work of superfluity to proceed with my present Paper. The report, however, of Mr. Rew deals only with the twenty years from the census of 1881 to that of 1901, during which time alone it can be alleged that the decline in the number of agricultural labourers has been due to the great fall in prices of agricultural produce and the consequent depression of agriculture. By far the larger amount of the reduction of labourers took place in the previous twenty years, from 1861 to 1881, when prices were at a high level, when agriculture was prospering, and rents were on the rise. As the distinction between these periods is not borne in mind by many, and the whole of the reduction of labourers in the forty years is often attributed to

the same cause, namely, the low prices of produce and the consequent
changes in cultivation, it has seemed to me to be worth while to
consider the subject in its larger view, that is, over the forty years.
There are other differences in treatment of the subject, and in the
grouping of the statistics, which may make my address of some value,
not in any way as in conflict with, but rather as a supplement to the
official report, and such that the two together may form the subject
of consideration and discussion by the members of this Society.

That the reduction in the number of agricultural labourers
during the forty years from 1861 to 1901 has been of serious
import in its bearing on the economic condition of the country
admits of no doubt.   There has, however, been some exaggeration
on the subject, due in part to a table included in the Memorandum
issued by the Board of Trade three years ago giving a mass of
statistics bearing on the Fiscal question.   The table, founded on
the census returns, gave the number of persons employed in agriculture in England and Wales at the decennial censuses from 1851
to 1901, as follows :—

1851	1,904,600	1881	1,199,800
'61	1,803,000	'91	1,099,500
'71	1,423,800	1901	988,300

These figures showed a reduction in the fifty years of nearly one
million, or of about 50 per cent.   It formed the text for a
good many speeches on different features of the question of agricultural depression, and the land system of England.   It was, I doubt
not, the authority for the statement made by the eminent leader of
Tariff Reform in an oft-quoted speech at Luton, in which he said
that a reduction had taken place in the number of persons employed
in agriculture in England and Wales since the repeal of the Corn
Laws of nearly one million.   " What," he added, " has become of this
" million of persons ?   The oldest, for whom there was no change
" of employers, have gone to the workhouse.   Others have broken
" up their homes, have gone to foreign countries, and have contri-
" buted to their prosperity, when they might have remained to
" contribute to ours.   Many of them have migrated to the towns,
" and what have they done there ?   Crowded the courts and alleys of
" our great cities, lowered the standard of health and strength of the
" people, and flooded the market with a surplus of underpaid labour."

This statement not unfairly represents the views prevalent in
many quarters as to the causes, extent and effect of the migration of
rural labourers.   Some part of it might have been dispelled or
mitigated by a consideration of the following fuller table, given later
in the Memorandum of the Board of Trade to which I have referred,
and showing in detail from the census returns the numbers of persons
of different sex and different age included in the earlier table :—

Number of Persons in England and Wales Employed in Agriculture.

Year.	Adults Aged 20 Years and Upwards.			Persons Under 20 Years of Age.			Total of All Ages.		
	Males.	Females.	Total.	Males.	Females.	Total.	Males.	Females.	Total.
1851........	1,140,900	336,230	1,477,130	327,620	99,950	427,560	1,468,510	436,170	1,904,690
'61........	1,119,000	301,030	1,420,030	323,100	59,920	383,020	1,442,110	360,942	1,863,040
'71........	972,000	122,440	1,094,440	277,180	52,210	329,420	1,249,180	174,080	1,423,860
'81........	884,270	50,050	934,320	254,480	11,020	265,500	1,138,750	61,070	1,199,820
'91......	816,460	39,730	856,290	237,110	6,240	243,350	1,053,570	46,000	1,099,570
1901.......	749,800	43,390	793,190	186,070	9,060	195,130	935,880	52,460	982,340

U 2

It will be seen from this table how very largely the numbers of women and of persons under the age of 20 entered into the enumeration. Of the 1,904,600 persons counted in 1851 as employed in agriculture, 436,100 were women, and 327,600 were males under the age of 20. Deducting these, the number of males above 20 in that year was 1,140,000. Of the total of 935,800 employed in 1901, 52,400 only were women, and 186,000 were males under the age of 20. Deducting these, the number of males above 20 in 1901 was 749,800, to compare with 1,140,000 in 1851, a difference of 390,200, or about 35 per cent. This figure, from which I shall presently show that considerable deductions must be made, is that on which we must mainly concentrate our attention. The number represents so many heads of families. Those below the age of 20 are for the most part the sons of labourers or others employed in agriculture. With respect to the enormous reduction in the number of women alleged to be employed in agriculture, namely, from 436,200 in 1851 to 52,400 in 1901, the greater part of this is altogether misleading. In the census returns of 1851 and 1861 there were subheads of " wives of farmers " and of " daughters and " other female relatives living with farmers," in the class of persons employed in agriculture, and 163,500 wives and 85,000 daughters, &c., were enumerated under these heads in 1861. In the later returns wives and daughters, &c., of farmers were transferred to another class. These numbers, therefore, ought to be excluded from the figures for 1861, for the purpose of comparison. Deducting these, there remain about 112,442 women of all ages employed in agriculture in 1861. This number was reduced to 61,000 in 1881, and 52,400 in 1901. The number of women farmers included in the census returns for the three periods were 22,700, 20,500 and 21,500. Making these deductions, it would seem that there were 164,800 women employed as labourers in 1861, 40,000 in 1881, and 31,000 in 1901. As agriculture was very prosperous during the years 1861 to 1881, this great alleged reduction in the employment of women during this period cannot be attributed to any cause connected with changes in the system of cultivation. After careful consideration of the figures, I feel very sceptical as to them, so far as the first three decades are concerned. I have difficulty in believing that in 1861 164,000 women, above and below the age of 20, were employed in farm work. I think it probable that large numbers were so enumerated who were only employed at certain periods of the year, in such seasonable work as the picking of fruit and hops, in haymaking and harvesting. Women so employed were certainly not included in the class of labourers in 1881 and 1901.

The census for 1901 gives the number of women above the age of 20 employed in agriculture as 43,393, and below that age 9,065. Of the first of these figures, 21,500 were women farmers. Deducting these, there remain only 22,000 above the age of 20. This is probably not more than the number of dairymaids permanently employed on farms. To whatever extent the census figures are to be relied on as showing a great reduction in the employment of women on the land, they must be considered as satisfactory rather than the reverse; they must show that women were withdrawn by their husbands and parents from field work. It may be that this change was one of the first results of the improved condition of agricultural labourers, which undoubtedly occurred between 1861 and 1881.

It is clear from the above that, in comparing the conditions of employment in agriculture at the different censuses, it is safer to omit all reference to women.

With respect also to the reduction in the number of males under the age of 20, it must be recollected that the Education Acts of recent years, requiring the attendance of boys at school, had the effect of withdrawing large numbers of children below the age of 15 from work in the fields. What numbers were so withdrawn we have no means of computing. But here, again, any reduction due to this cause is matter for satisfaction. In comparing the numbers employed at the different periods, it would seem to be safer to omit those under 20, and to confine our attention mainly to those above that age.

Omitting reference to the census figures of 1851—which, except as regards women, show no material difference with those of 1861 —we find that the census returns as tabled in the Memorandum of the Board of Trade for the three periods of 1861, 1881, and 1901 show a reduction in the forty years of 369,200 males above the age of 20 employed in agriculture, of which 234,800 occurred in the first half of the period, and 134,400 in the second half from 1881 to 1901.

There are, however, several points on which these figures must be further corrected.

In the census of 1881 a change was made in the classification of persons no longer able to work by reason of old age. In previous returns, farmers and labourers unable to work on the land, and either retired or in workhouses and asylums, were still included in the class of persons employed in agriculture. In 1881 and subsequent years they were enumerated in another class. This accounted for a reduction in 1881 (as shown in a separate return) of 27,000 males, viz., 13,000 farmers and 14,000 labourers. For

the purpose of a fair comparison, these numbers, and probably a
somewhat larger number as regards labourers, should be deducted'
from the figures of the census of 1861.

Correction ought also to be made for the figure given in the
census of 1861, under the head of "farmers' sons and relatives."'
In that census it was assumed that all such persons were engaged'
in agriculture. The figure for that year was 60,046 (over 20).
In the census of 1871 only those were enumerated under this head
who declared that they were employed on the farms. The figure
for 1881 is 47,120, the reduction, as compared with 1861, being
largely due to the above qualification. But in 1901 the figure
again rose to 55,600, the number of farmers remaining about the
same. It is difficult to account for this. I have not felt justified
in making a correction in this respect, but the figures are open to·
great doubt.

It should again be recollected that the census of 1901 was taken·
in the middle of the war in South Africa, when all the Army·
Reserve men, about 80,000 in number, were called out and were·
employed in South Africa, and when nearly all the Militia regiments·
were enrolled, and were employed either in Africa or in military·
posts abroad and at home, and when large numbers of Yeomanry·
and Volunteers were also employed in the war. It cannot be
doubted that the absence of these men accounted for a large
reduction in the number of agricultural labourers and of farmers'
sons at the census of 1901. It was well known that farmers were
in great difficulty at the time as regards labour. The War Office
are unable to supply any figures showing the number of men
ordinarily employed in agriculture who are in the Army Reserve or
Militia. The only light they can throw on the· subject is that
15 per cent. of the men enlisted for the army describe themselves
as agricultural labourers. On this basis, I think that, on a very
low estimate, 20,000 should be added to the number of persons
employed in agriculture in England and Wales, who were tempo-
rarily withdrawn from their work for the Army Reserve, Militia,.
and Volunteers.

Lastly, there is a yet larger correction to be made of the table
in the Board of Trade Memorandum. It includes only farmers,
farmers' sons and relatives working on the farms, bailiffs, shepherds,.
labourers, and woodmen. It does not include the very large and
growing class of gardeners, other than domestics, including market'
and nursery gardeners, florists, seedsmen, and fruit growers. All
these are employed on the land. They represent "intense"'
cultivation as distinct from ordinary farm cultivation. The·
labourers so employed are generally paid rather higher wages than

ordinary farm labourers. There seems to me to be no good reason for the exclusion of this class when comparing the number of persons employed in agriculture at different periods. The increase of this class has been very great of late years.

The census returns for the earlier years under review mix up the number of these non-domestic gardeners with those of domestic gardeners in a most imperfect and confusing manner, as the following figures show :—

	1851.	1861.	1871.	1881.	1891.	1901.
Seedsmen, florists, &c. ..	2,400	2,800	5,100	7,000		123,100
Gardeners, non-domestic	69,600	76,700	95,800	63,600	174,000	
„ domestic	4,500	14,600	18,700	74,600		87,900
Total	76,500	94,100	119,600	145,200	174,000	211,000

It is evident from these figures that very grave errors of enumeration were made in the first three decades, and that very large numbers of domestic gardeners must have been included in the list of non-domestic gardeners. It is impossible to believe that the numbers of domestic gardeners at the three periods were so low as 4,500, 14,600, and 18,700, and that they then jumped up to 74,600 in 1881. It is equally impossible to believe that the number of non-domestic gardeners fell from 95,800 in 1871 to 63,600 in 1881. We are justified, I think, in assuming that the figures for 1881 and 1901 are correct, and that there was the same relative increase of numbers of domestic and non-domestic gardeners in the first three decades. On this assumption I have re-formed the table as follows —maintaining the same totals :—

	1851.	1861.	1871.	1881.	1891.	1901.
Gardeners, non-domestic, nursery gardeners, seedsmen, &c.	22,000	33,100	51,700	70,600	93,000	123,100
Domestic gardeners	54,500	61,000	67,900	74,800	81,000	87,900
Total	76,500	94,100	119,600	145,200	174,000	211,000

On this assumption the non-domestic gardeners increased in number from 33,100 in 1861 to 123,100 in 1901, and the domestic gardeners from 61,000 to 87,900. I have included the numbers of non-domestic gardeners in my revised list of persons employed in agriculture. The census returns do not distinguish between the numbers under this head who are employers and those who are labourers. Nor can we ascertain what is the area of land thus cultivated.[1]

This great increase of non-domestic gardeners has been very unevenly spread over the different counties of England. It has been very great in the counties round London, in Middlesex, Herts, Kent, Surrey, Sussex, and Essex, and also in Norfolk, Suffolk, Leicester, Cambridge, Lancashire, Cheshire, and Worcester. In Dorsetshire, Wiltshire, Salop, Cumberland, Northumberland, and in the whole of Wales, the increase has been small.

Making these various corrections in the census returns for the years 1861, 1881, and 1901, I have constructed the following table,—omitting women, and giving males above and below 20 separately, except in the cases of farmers, bailiffs, and woodmen, where the numbers under 20 are very small, and not worth distinguishing.

---

[1] The "Report of the Tariff Commission on Agriculture" describes the recent development of market gardening in the Evesham district of Worcestershire: "The acreage," it says, "under fruit and vegetable cultivation has " much increased since 1879 on lands formerly under corn. The methods " of California and Canada have been copied; cultivation is greatly improved, " and made more scientific and uniform than formerly. Very heavy clay land, " not worth 5s. per acre for wheat-growing, is adapted for fruit and vegetables, " especially asparagus, of which hundreds of acres have been put down. In " 1870 small holders held 2,000 acres within 8 miles of Evesham; now 2,400 " cultivate 15,000, averaging 1 to 10 acres each, and these holdings increase " every year. . . . Land practically derelict twenty years ago was taken by " labouring men at 1l. per acre. Many now hold 6 acres. They own their " houses, and some of them have sufficient means to support them for life. " A Ledbury (Worcestershire) witness puts the culture and market gardening " cost of labour at 11l. 15s. per acre, as against 25s. for ordinary farm labour " —that is, nearly ten times the amount. It is further stated in the evidence that 1,150 acres are now under glass in England for fruit cultivation, employing 7,000 labourers.

ENGLAND AND WALES.

Male Persons Employed in Agriculture.

	1861.		1881.		1901.	
	Over 20.	Under 20.	Over 20.	Under 20.	Over 20.	Under 20.
Farmers	226,960	—	203,430	—	202,760	—
Corrected figure	*213,960*	—	—	—	—	—
(Women farmers)	*(22,750)*	—	*(20,520)*	—	*(21,550)*	—
Sons and relatives of farmers working on the farms	60,040	32,280	47,120	28,080	55,680	33,480
Bailiffs and foremen	15,700	—	19,370	—	22,610	—
Shepherds	20,660	4,200	20,090	2,750	22,230	3,100
Labourers, out-door and in-door..................	788,760	283,940	585,960	221,650	435,750	148,030
Corrected figure............. ..	*774,760*	—	—	—	*455,750*	—
Woodmen	7,910	990	7,600	640	11,210	820
Gardeners (non-domestic), florists, seedsmen, &c..	28,200	5,600	58,900	11,700	105,400	17,720
Totals	1,147,840	327,010	942,370	264,820	855,640	203,150
Corrected figures	*1,120,840*	*327,010*	*942,370*	*264,820*	*875,720*	*203,150*

Reduction of all male persons above 20 employed in agriculture from 1861 to 1881 (corrected figure)	*178,470*	
Reduction of male persons above 20 from 1881 to 1901 (corrected figure)............	66,650	
	245,120	22 per cent.
Reduction of farm labourers above 20, exclusive of those employed in nursery or other gardens, from 1861 to 1881 (corrected figure)	188,800	
Reduction of farm labourers above 20, only, from 1881 to 1901 (corrected figure)	130,200	
	319,000	41 per cent.

It will be seen that there has been a reduction of farmers of about 12,000. This occurred between 1861 and 1881, and was doubtless due to the amalgamation of farms during a period when farming on a large scale was very profitable.

The corresponding figures for Scotland are as follows :—

Male Persons Employed in Agriculture.

	1861.		1881.		1901.	
	Over 20.	Under 20.	Over 20.	Under 20	Over 20.	Under 20.
Farmers	54,670	—	48,120	—	45,550	—
Corrected figure..........	*51,400*	—	—	—	—	—
(Women farmers).....	(6,410)	—	(7,060)	—	(7,820)	—
Sons and relatives of farmers working on the farms	11,300	6,400	10,720	5,470	11,160	6,360
Bailiffs	3,150	—	3,520	—	4,650	—
Shepherds	6,540	730	9,260	1,020	8,670	960
Labourers	89,330	38,890	61,730	30,050	51,050	27,740
Corrected figure...............	*87,580*	—	—	—	*53,550*	
Foresters	2,600	220	2,860	246	3,750	370
Totals....................	167,990	46,240	136,210	36,780	124,830	35,430
Corrected figures	*162,920*	*46,240*	*136,210*	*36,780*	*122,330*	*35,430*

Reduction of all male persons above 20 employed in agriculture from 1861 to 1881 (corrected figures)	26,710	
Reduction of all male persons above 20 employed in agriculture from 1881 to 1901.....................	13,910	
	40,620	25 per cent.
Reduction of farm labourers above 20 from 1861 to 1881 (corrected figures)	25,800	
Reduction of farm labourers above 20 from 1881 to 1901 (corrected figures)	8,180	
	33,980	38 per cent.

It appears that the total reduction of males employed in agriculture above 20 has been 40,600, or 25 per cent., compared with 22 per cent. in England, the difference being due to the fact that there has not been the same increase of non-domestic gardeners in Scotland. The reduction of agricultural labourers above 20 has been about 34,000, or 38 per cent., as compared with 41 per cent. in England.

The above tables show that the number of farmers in England and Wales in 1901 was 202,700 men and 21,500 women, a total of 223,500. To this must be added the number of bailiffs presumably holding farms, 22,400, making a total of 243,900 persons.

In Scotland the figures are : 45,800 male farmers, 7,800 women farmers, 4,650 bailiffs, a total of 58,000 persons.[2] It may be worth while to consider how many of these persons returning themselves as farmers can really be considered as such.

A return of the Board of Agriculture in 1895 gave the following figures as regards the occupation of land :—

[2] It is probable that many of the 23,400 bailiffs enumerated in England and Wales, and 4,600 in Scotland, do not hold farms. On the other hand, a large number of farms are held by landowners and other persons not enumerated in the census as farmers. The numbers may be considered as balancing one another.

England.

	5 to 20 Acres.	20 to 50 Acres.	50 to 100 Acres.	100 to 300 Acres.	300 to 500 Acres.	500 to 1,000 Acres.	Over 1,000 Acres.	Total.
Number of holdings	108,145	62,446	46,574	60,381	11,112	3,942	524	293,130
Acreage	1,210,716	2,077,950	3,403,760	10,434,130	4,188,650	2,570,680	693,510	24,579,420

Wales.

	5 to 20 Acres.	20 to 50 Acres.	50 to 100 Acres.	100 to 300 Acres.	300 to 500 Acres.	500 to 1,000 Acres.	Over 1,000 Acres.	Total.
Number of holdings	18,570	12,400	10,217	7,896	386	54	3	49,525
Acreage	211,260	423,750	749,460	1,238,570	142,906	32,810	3,920	2,802,670

Scotland.

	5 to 20 Acres.	20 to 50 Acres.	50 to 100 Acres.	100 to 300 Acres.	300 to 500 Acres.	500 to 1,000 Acres.	Over 1,000 Acres.	Total.
Number of holdings	23,104	10,817	9,834	12,968	2,070	620	76	59,489
Acreage	245,666	363,260	732,090	2,203,300	782,370	397,686	104,410	4,828,370

These figures show that in England and Wales there are 216,000 holdings of land of over 20 acres, and in Scotland, 36,350; as compared with 244,000 farmers and bailiffs in England and Wales, and 58,000 in Scotland.

It appears probable, then, that of 126,700 holders of land of from 5 to 20 acres in England and Wales, about 27,000 return themselves as farmers, and that in Scotland of 23,000 holders of between 5 and 20 acres, 21,700 return themselves as farmers. It should be recollected that the small holders of land in Scotland have generally large grazing rights over the neighbouring moors and mountains. Of the holdings of land between 5 and 20 acres, by far the greater proportion in England and Wales is in the occupation of persons not in the position of farmers, who hold it in connection with their residences, or of persons engaged in other local industries.

If we reckon only holdings of 20 acres and over as farms in the ordinary sense of the term, the 185,000 farm holdings in England average 127 acres, those in Wales, 31,000, average 83 acres, and the 36,400 in Scotland average 133 acres.

It will be seen from my corrected tables that if we include all persons above 20 engaged in agriculture in England and Wales, including those employed in intense cultivation of fruit, &c., there was a reduction in the number of 178,400 in the twenty years from 1861 to 1881, and of 66,500 in the second period of twenty years from 1881 to 1901. The total reduction, therefore, in the forty years of males above 20 was at the rate of 24 per cent., and about three-fourths occurred in the first period and one-fourth in the second period. If, however, we confine ourselves only to agricultural labourers above 20 employed on farms, excluding those engaged in intense cultivation, the proportion works out differently— the numbers reduced in the first period from 1861 to 1881 was 188,800, and in the second period was 130,200; and the total reduction in the forty years was 41 per cent.

It need not, however, be pointed out that the reductions which were effected between the years 1861 and 1881 were in no way connected with agricultural depression, or with the great fall of prices resulting from free import of foreign produce.

The twenty years, 1861 to 1881, with the exception of the last two years, were a period of great prosperity to the agricultural interest in Great Britain. Though corn and other agricultural produce were admitted free of duty (save the 1s. registration duty on corn up to 1871), prices of corn, and still more of meat, wool and other produce, were remunerative.

The price of wheat, which had been 58s. 4d. in the three years before the repeal of the Corn Laws, fell to 44s. from 1849 to 1852, but rose again during the war with Russia to 58*s*. or 60*s*. It fell again in 1860 to slightly over 50*s*., and for the twenty years, 1861 to 1881, the price averaged 51*s*. a quarter. It was not till very near the end of this period that the price began to fall. It then fell continuously and rapidly for some years till it reached the average of 28*s*. in 1901, a point at which it has since remained nearly stationary. The following table shows the average price during the whole of the period from 1840 to 1900.

1840-47.	1848-52.	1853-60.	1861-70.	1870-80.	1881-99.	1891-1900.
s. *d.*	*s.*	*s.* *d.*	*s.*	*s.*	*s.* *d.*	*s.* *d.*
58 1	44	58 4	51	51	35 9	28 2

The prices of meat, and of other agricultural produce such as wool, butter, cheese, &c., rose considerably during the years 1861 to 1881, and especially during the years 1870 to 1875, and they attained a much higher level than they had ever done before. It was not till after 1881 that the prices of these products fell. The result was that, in spite of free imports, agriculture prospered greatly during the twenty years 1861 to 1881. Farmers made good profits; there was a great demand for farms; rents rose considerably. The increase of the assessments of land for Income Tax during this period is good proof of this. For England and Wales the assessment rose from 44,650,000*l.* to 51,182,000*l.*, and for Scotland from 6,675,000*l.* to 7,648,000*l.*

During this period of agricultural prosperity, the great reduction of the number of agricultural labourers in farms took place, in England amounting to 188,800 above the age of 20, 62,000 below that age, and in Scotland to 26,000 above 20, and 8,000 below 20. This was to a very small extent connected with any change in the system of cultivation, such as the laying down of arable land in grass. The agricultural returns of the relative areas of arable and pasture do not go back to the year 1861. There is no reason to believe that any change in this respect took place before 1861 and 1871. Between 1871 and 1881 the returns show a reduction of arable land of about 1,000,000 acres, and an increase of permanent pasture of about 2,400,000 acres, due in part to the reclamation of land from mere and waste, and in part, perhaps, to more accurate returns by farmers.

The reduction of arable land took place, not in the most arable parts of England, but mainly in the more pastoral districts. Whatever the cause of this, there was nothing in it to account for the

great reduction in the number of labourers in the laying down of
arable land in grass. This conversion of arable to grass was effected
almost equally in the five years between 1871 and 1876, when prices
were at their best, as between 1879 and 1881, as the following
figures show :—

Great Britain.

	Arable Land.	Permanent Pasture.
	Acres.	Acres.
1871	18,403,400	12,435,400
'76	18,035,600	13,515,900
'81	17,568,000	14,643,600
1901	15,590,100	16,827,200

The explanation of the great exodus of labourers from rural
districts during the twenty years 1861 to 1881 was undoubtedly to
be found in the great prosperity, and the general rise of wages of
the manufacturing and mining districts; in the fact that labourers
were tempted by the higher wages in the towns, and on work on the
railways, and in the rural police, to give up farm work. It was
also in part due to a growing disinclination to farm work among
labourers in rural districts, to the absence of opportunities to them
of rising in their vocation, and to a desire for the greater independence and freedom of life in towns.

As a result of this exodus, wages rose considerably in rural
districts. The following table from the Board of Trade Memorandum
shows the course of weekly wages of agricultural labourers in
England and Wales during the last fifty years :—

1850.	1851-60.	1861-70.	1871-80.	1881-90.	1891-1900.	1901-03.
s d.	s. d.	s. d.	s. d.	s.	s. d.	s. d.
9 4	10 4	11 5	13 4	13	13 4	14 7

It will be seen that money wages rose nearly 30 per cent.
between 1860 and 1880, from the miserably low rate which prevailed
before 1850, a rate at which, having regard to the high price of
wheat and other requisites, it is difficult to understand how agricultural labourers contrived to exist and bring up their families.
Farmers were compelled during this period to meet this rise of
wages by economising labour, and adopting machinery and other
improved methods.

This reduction in the number of labourers took place over the
whole of England and Scotland in not very unequal proportions.

In Scotland the reduction was 30 per cent., in Wales 32 per cent. and in England 25 per cent.

It was not till nearly the close of these twenty years that a turn occurred in the tide of agricultural prosperity. In the year 1879 the harvest was one of the worst ever experienced in this country. The produce of corn was extremely small. The pastures were seriously damaged by incessant rain through the summer and autumn. Cattle and sheep suffered in consequence. The price of corn, for the first time almost in this country, did not rise in some proportion to the deficient produce. In the years beginning with 1881, the prices of wheat, barley, and oats fell continuously, and in 1884 the price of meat, wool, butter, and other agricultural produce also began to fall. In the fourteen years from 1881 to 1894 the price of wheat fell 50 per cent.; barley, 32 per cent. ; oats, 30 per cent.; meat from 15 to 20 per cent. ; wool, 32 per cent.; and dairy produce from 10 to 15 per cent. I will not enter upon the causes of the great fall of prices. Whatever they were the effect on agriculture in this country was most serious. Farmers experienced great losses. The fall of prices affected the different parts of the country very unequally. The reduction of the price of wheat was relatively greater than that of other corn or other agricultural produce. That of dairy produce was the least. The wheat-growing districts of the East of England suffered most. Oats were substituted for wheat in many parts. A great extent of land previously under the plough was laid down as pasture, or was allowed to fall back into very indifferent grass. Many arable farms became derelict. In many parts of the arable districts the system of rotation of crops was altered, and green crops were substituted for corn crops.

Rents gradually fell, to the extent of 50 per cent. in the purely arable districts, 25 per cent. in those of mixed husbandry, and 10 to 15 per cent. in the purely pastoral districts. Farmers had the benefit of lower rates in consequence of the reduction of their assessments, and the Agricultural Rating Act of 1896 relieved them of one-half the rates previously paid. They also benefited by lower prices for all their requirements, for feeding stuffs for their cattle, for artificial manures, for their machinery and implements, and for most of their family requirements. If the money wages of labour had fallen in the same ratio as the price of agricultural produce, and as rents and rates, farmers would have been sooner able to adjust themselves to the new range of prices. The money wages, however, of labourers were not only maintained, but rose to a somewhat higher point, as the table already given shows. Labourers, therefore, as compared with their condition between the years 1861-81, and still more as compared with anterior times, had the benefit, not only of higher wages, but of lower prices for their food, for their bread and meat, for their tea and sugar, for their clothing and every other requirement. This great reduction in the cost of living was equivalent to a further rise in the money value of their wages of from 30 to 40 per cent. Taking into account wages and the price of food, they were certainly twice as well off in the decade 1891-1901 as in the times before 1861. In spite of this improvement in their condition, the exodus of labourers continued, though not in the same proportions. Farmers were again compelled to economise labour as far as possible by the increased use of machinery, by laying down arable land in grass, or by changing the rotation of crops. It is not uncommonly believed that the reduction of the area of land under the plough accounts for the whole of the reduced number of labourers in the twenty years from 1881 to 1901. This was certainly not the case. It can be shown very clearly that the larger part of the reduction of labourers employed in agriculture was not due to this cause, but to those other causes which resulted in the still greater reduction in the previous twenty years.

The late Mr. William Little, a great authority on agricultural subjects, who reported in 1894 to the Royal Commission on Labour on the condition of agricultural labourers, stated in his report : " It " is undoubtedly the opinion of many persons that want of employ- " ment was the cause of the labourers' emigration to the towns, but " I venture to maintain that the reduction of the working staff of " farms was the consequence of, and not the cause of, the emigration."

He reported that out of thirty-eight typical districts inquired into there were twenty-seven in which the supply of labour was about equal to the demand. In seven districts the supply was in excess of the demand, and in only three districts was the demand in excess of the supply. He added : " There was universal agreement " that if the system of farming had remained what it was there " would have been a difficulty in finding the necessary hands." In a further passage he said : " It is no exaggeration to say that in the " last quarter of a century a great economic revolution, accomplished " with little aid from legislation, has transferred to the labourers " from one-third to one-fourth of the profit which the landowners " and farmers previously received from the cultivation of the " land."

The meaning of this was that the money wages of the labourers having increased and the price of their food being very greatly reduced, the wages paid on a farm bore a far higher proportion to the farmer's profits and to rent than they had ever done before.

There is further proof of the above in the fact that the reduction in the purely pastoral parts of England, Wales, and Scotland has been as great, if not greater than, in the arable districts; and that in those few parts of England and Scotland, where there has been no change whatever in the system of cultivation, there has been as great a reduction in the number of labourers as in the districts which have suffered most from depression, and where a large extent of land under the plough has been laid down in grass.

In 1881 the area of arable land in Great Britain, as shown by the figures already quoted, was 17,568,000 acres, and that of permanent pasture 14,643,000 acres. In 1901 the proportion was nearly reversed; the arable land was reduced to 15,590,000 acres, or by nearly 2,000,000 acres, and the permanent pasture was increased to 16,827,000, or by 2,184,000 acres. In other words, somewhat less than one-eighth of the land under the plough was laid down in grass. By this change in the proportion of arable to pasture a considerable reduction was effected in the employment of labour. Much of the land so laid down became very indifferent pasture. But the change thus affected accounts for only a part of the reduction of labourers.

With the object of throwing light on the subject, and especially on the comparative number of persons employed on farms, as distinct from intense cultivation, in the two periods of twenty years ending in 1881 and 1901, in different parts of the country, distinguishing the arable districts from the pastoral districts, I have separated the English counties into six groups. Of these, the first consists of three purely pastoral counties, Derbyshire, Westmoreland, and Monmouth, where the proportion of arable land in 1901 was less than 20 per cent. of the total cultivated area, and the last of six counties in the East of England, Norfolk, Suffolk, Essex, Lincoln, Cambridge, Herts, and York (East Riding), where the arable land was over 60 per cent. of the total cultivated area. The other four groups are intermediate between these two. I have also shown separately the Welsh and the Scotch counties. I have compared these eight groups for the years 1861, 1881, and 1901 as regards the numbers of male persons above or below 20 employed in the cultivation of farms as distinct from nursery, market, and other gardens. In the following table (C) I have shown the percentage reduction of all males employed and of labourers employed, and also the number of persons above 20 and of labourers above 20 employed, and in Table D I have compared the number of persons employed per 100 acres in these different groups.

TABLE C.—*Percentage Reduction of Males above* 20 *Employed on Farms from* 1861 *to* 1901, *distinguishing all Persons so Employed from Labourers, and excluding those engaged as Gardeners in Intense Cultivation.*

	1861 to 1881.		1881 to 1901.		1861 to 1901.	
	All Males Employed.	Labourers only.	All Males Employed.	Labourers only.	All Males Employed	Labourers only.
	Per cent.	Per cent.	Per cent.	Per cent.	Per cent.	Per cent.
Group 1	22	20	6	20	28	47
,, 2 ...	26	32	20	30	40	53
., 3 ....'	20	25	16	28	34	46
,, 4	19	22	16	30	33	45
,, 5 ...	16	19	27	33	38	46
,, 6	11	14	13	22	22	33
Wales	20	33	9	23	27	47
Scotland	20	30	9	16	27	43

TABLE D.—*Number of Males above* 20 *and under* 20 *Employed on Farms per* 100 *Acres in* 1861, 1881 *and* 1901 (*including Farmers, Farmers' Sons, Bailiffs, Shepherds, and Labourers*).

	1861.		1881.		1901.	
	Above 20.	Under 20.	Above 20.	Under 20.	Above 20.	Under 20.
Group 1 .	3·3	0·7	2·4	0·5	2·1	0·5
,, 2 ...	5·3	1·3	3·7	0 8	3·0	0·5
,, 3 . ..	3·9	1·0	3·0	0·8	2·5	0·7
,, 4	4·1	1·1	3·3	0·8	2·8	0·6
,, 5	4·3	1·5	3·6	0·9	2·7	0·6
,, 6	4·1	1·3	3·6	1·0	3·2	0·8
Wales	3·5	0·8	2·5	0·5	2·3	0·4
Scotland ..	3·6	1·0	2·8	0·8	2·5	0·7

It should be pointed out that in these tables, and in those in the Appendix for the various groups of counties, I have not made the corrections I have adverted to in my aggregate of numbers for England, Wales and Scotland, due to the changes of classification in the census returns of 1881 and 1901, and to the absence of reservists, &c., in South Africa during the census of 1901. If made, they would result in a difference in the reductions of numbers, whether of all persons employed or labourers only, between 1861 and 1901, of about 3 per cent., and this difference would be divided between the two periods of 1861 to 1881 and 1881 to 1901.

I have also not thought it worth while to distinguish between the numbers of males employed above and under 20, except in the cases of labourers and of the sons and relatives of farmers. The numbers of farmers, bailiffs, and shepherds under 20 years of age are so small that it is not necessary to distinguish them. In the case of several counties the census returns for 1881 and 1901 do not distinguish persons above or under 20 for the sub-heads of labourers or farmers' sons, and I have, therefore, taken them at the same proportion as the census returns show for the whole country.

The two tables giving the percentages of reductions and the number of males employed per 100 acres for the different groups show clearly how evenly spread the reductions have been over the whole of England, Wales, and Scotland irrespective of any difference in the systems of cultivation. The reduction has been greatest in Group 2, where the arable land is only between 20 and 30 per cent. of the total cultivated area. The reduction of all males above 20 employed has been 40 per cent., and of labourers 53 per cent. The reduction has been least in the six most arable counties in the East of England—namely, 22 per cent. for all persons employed, and 33 per cent. for labourers only.

In Wales, which is mainly pastoral, the reduction of all males employed has been 27 per cent., and of labourers 47 per cent. This almost exactly tallies with the reduction in the three most pastoral counties of England. It is to be noted that the great difference in these districts between the reduction of all persons employed and of labourers only is due to the very small proportion of labourers to farmers and their sons. In Wales the labourers above 20 were, in 1901, little more than half the number of farmers and farmers' sons or relatives—to wit: Farmers, 29,800; women farmers, 5,200; farmers' sons (above 20), 9,560; labourers, 23,550. In the three most pastoral counties of England the numbers are: Farmers, 9,700; farmers' sons, 2,750; labourers, 9,200. For the whole of Scotland the farmers number 45,500, women farmers, 7,800, their sons above 20, 11,100, and the labourers above 20, 53,500 only. It is only in the more arable parts of England that the labourers now bear a large proportion to the numbers of farmers and farmers' sons. In the six most arable counties of England the proportions are: Farmers, 35,100; women farmers, 2,000; farmers' sons above 20, 7,800; labourers above 20, 121,900. The proportion of labourers to farmers is, therefore, a little over 3 to 1. In Wales and in the pastoral parts of England and Scotland where the farms are small, a large part of the manual work is done by the farmers themselves.

The table giving the number of persons above and under 20 employed per 100 acres is also of interest. It shows that the difference in employment of all persons, including farmers or farmers' sons as well as labourers, between the most pastoral and the most arable parts of England is only slightly more than 1 male above 20, and 0·2 below 20 per 100 acres. In Wales the reduction in the forty years has been from 3·5 males above 20, and 0·8 under 20 per 100 acres to 2·3 above 20 and 0·4 under 20. There is little in the change of cultivation to account for this. It must be due to economy of labour and the use of machinery and improved methods.

There are three counties in England where there was practically no change in the system of cultivation in the forty years between 1861 and 1901. They are Cheshire, Lancashire and Cornwall.

In Cheshire the area of arable land in 1901 was slightly above that in 1871, but the reduction since 1861 of all persons employed has been 21 per cent., and of labourers nearly 40 per cent., very slightly below the average of other counties. The assessment of land has been reduced between 1881 and 1901 by less than 10 per cent., and in the later year was about the same as in 1861. It cannot be said, then, that there has been serious depression in that county.

The same may be said of Lancashire. The area of arable land increased between 1881 and 1901 by about 10 per cent., from 227,000 acres to 243,000, and was only 5,000 acres below that of 1871. The area of permanent pasture also slightly increased, doubtless from reclamation of moor and waste land. There has, therefore, been no change in the system of cultivation, but the number of persons employed has been reduced by 40 per cent, and the number of labourers (above 20) by 53 per cent.—a larger reduction than in any other county in England. There has been a considerable reduction in the number of farmers, from 16,000 to 12,170. The farms even now are of small average—those above 20 acres average 71 acres, or considerably less than one-half the size of farms in the arable districts in the East of England.

In Cornwall also the arable land has remained nearly stationary, viz., 375,000 acres 1871, 363,000 acres 1881, and 361,000 acres 1901. The permanent pasture has, according to the return, increased from 132,000 acres in 1871 to 245,000 in 1901. How much of this is due to reclamation and how much to more accurate returns does not appear. Farms are small and average only 90 acres. The number of labourers has been reduced by one-half since 1861— namely 12,400 in 1861, 10,200 in 1881, and 6,300 in 1901. The greatest reduction has here taken place in the twenty years from 1881 to 1901, viz., 40 per cent. The number of labourers is 25 per cent. less than that of farmers. The assessment of land has been reduced by about one-ninth since 1881, but is greater by one-seventh than it was in 1861.

In Scotland, also, there are some counties where little or no change has been made since 1861 in the proportion of arable land to pasture.

The county of Aberdeen is the most arable district in Great Britain. Five per cent. only of its area is in permanent pasture. There has been an increase of arable land, as the following figures show :—1861, arable, 548,000 acres; pasture, 31,000; 1881, arable land, 572,000 acres; pasture, 27,000 acres; 1901, arable, 597,000 acres; pasture, 33,000. The area of corn cultivation has remained unchanged, 212,000 acres. The reduction of labourers above 20 has been at the rate of 33 per cent., of which the larger amount was between 1881 and 1901 :—1861, 11,700; 1881, 10,100; 1901, 7,940. The number of farmers has been reduced from 8,700 in 1861 to 7,000 in 1901. The farms are small in area, those above 20 acres averaging 92 acres. It will be seen that the reduction of persons employed—22 per cent.—is considerably less than the average of Scotland as a whole. This is doubtless due to the fact that the farms are worked by the farmers and their families, who number more than the labourers.

An interesting comparison may be made between this county of small arable farms, and the three counties of large arable farms in the south-east of Scotland—Berwick, Roxburgh, and Edinburgh. In these three counties the arable land remains much as it was twenty and forty years ago, viz. :—380,000 acres, 1861; 385,000 acres, 1881; 374,000 acres, 1901. The permanent pasture has increased from 111,000 acres to 132,000 acres.

The number of labourers above 20 has been reduced by 40 per cent., from 7,400 in 1861 to 6,000 in 1881, and 4,400 in 1901. The cultivation in these counties is of a very high order. The average of farms above 20 acres is 256 acres, the proportion of persons above 20 per 100 acres is lower than in any other part of Great Britain. It is only 1·7, and the proportion of those under 20 is only 0·5 per 100 acres. Taking the two classes together, they are about one-half the percentage of arable counties in the East of England in Group 6.

The comparison between these three counties and Aberdeenshire affords a striking illustration of the difference between the systems of large and small holdings of arable land, as the following table shows :—

	Number of Agricultural Holdings				Area of Holdings above 300 Acres.	Total Area of Cultivated Land.
	1 to 20 Acres.	20 to 100 Acres.	100 to 300 Acres.	Above 300 Acres		
Aberdeen	5,230	4,280	1,910	124	50,690	630,300
Berwick, Edinburgh, and Roxburgh	1,210	580	780	571	324,650	505,000

	Number of Farmers, including Women and Bailiffs.	Sons, &c., of Farmers Working on Farms.	Labourers and Shepherds over 20.	Total Persons Employed over 20.	Reduction of Males Employed from 1861 to 1901.	Assessment of Land for Income Tax, per Acre.
					Per cent.	*s.*
Aberdeen	8,750	1,680	8,400	18,820	20	20
Berwick, Edinburgh, and Roxburgh	2,315	380	5,760	8,450	27	28

It appears from these figures that Aberdeen, with a cultivated area only 25 per cent. more than the three South-Eastern Counties, has nearly four times the number of farmers and bailiffs, and 50 per cent. more labourers and shepherds (over 20). The total number of persons employed on its land is more than twice as large. The reduction in the last forty years has been less by one-fifth. On the other hand, judging from the assessment of land, the owners of land in Aberdeenshire receive 8s. per acre less rent, or 30 per cent., and must have far greater outgoings or deductions from rent for the maintenance of farm buildings for their tenants. I am told that this higher rent of the three South-Eastern Counties is mainly due to the better average quality and position of their land. This makes it the more remarkable that so much larger a community of farmers and labourers should be able to make a good living out of the land of the more northern country. It may well be a question which is the soundest and best system, looked at from the interest of the country as a whole, which is concerned not so much in the amount of the surplus rent as in the maintenance of a vigorous and independent population. It is to be noted that a consolidation of holdings has been proceeding in Aberdeenshire, the number of farmers having been reduced by 1,700 from 1861 to 1901.

Comparing again the three South-Eastern Counties with the two pastoral counties of Ayrshire and Lanarkshire, we find in the latter that there has been a small reduction of arable land from 327,000 acres in 1861 to 311,000 in 1881, and 308,000 acres in 1901, and an increase of permanent pasture from 218,000 acres in 1861 to 268,000 in 1901. There has been in the forty years a reduction of 40 per cent. in the numbers of all persons above 20 employed, and of 60 per cent. in the number of labourers above 20, a greater reduction than in any other part of Great Britain. Of this, three-fourths took place between 1881 and 1901. The number of farmers has been reduced by one-fifth, from 5,200 to 4,150. The number of persons employed per 100 acres is slightly above that in the three arable counties, viz., 2·0 of persons above 20, and 0·45 of persons under 20. The proportion of persons employed per 100 acres is less than in any of the pastoral parts of England.

In view of those cases where there has been no change in the system of cultivation, and where in spite of this there has been a large reduction in the number of persons employed on the farms, and in view also of the percentage reduction of labour in the pastoral districts as compared with the arable districts, it is quite clear that a very large proportion of the reduction of labour between 1881 and 1901 was due to other causes than the laying down of arable land in grass. The same causes which were in operation in the period from 1861 to 1881 must have continued. Labourers were again tempted by better wages in other employments to give up work on the land; farmers were again compelled to economise labour by the greater use of machinery and improved methods.

How many, then, of the 130,000 fewer farm labourers in England and Wales, and 10,000 in Scotland, above the age of 20, who were employed in 1901 as compared with 1881, were reduced owing to the laying down of arable land in grass? The question is not an easy one to answer. The reduction of arable land in the twenty years amounted to about 2,000,000 acres. On a review of all the figures and the facts I have been able to gather, I don't think that the reduction of labour due to the laying down of the arable land has been more than 2 males per 100 acres, of whom three-fourths were above 20 and one-fourth under that age. Undoubtedly in some cases the reduction has been greater, as, for instance, where arable farms became derelict for a time, or where land of a very bad quality, such as the chalk downs, was allowed to go back into poor pasture; but these are exceptional cases. The derelict farms have now been let and are again cultivated—not to the same extent as arable land, but under a mixed system of agriculture, in which dairying takes a large part. The question is, what is the difference in the employment of labour on an average arable farm with some 30 or 40 per cent. of pasture and a farm where the proportions are reversed?

On this point I have consulted, among others, a farmer who was one of those Scotchmen who were tempted to farm in Essex by the very low rent, and who have introduced there the more economical system which they followed in Scotland. This gentleman farms 500 acres of stiff clay land, of which 150 acres are under the plough. The remainder is in grass. He tells me that he employs 10 labourers only. With himself and two sons that makes 13 men, of whom two are under 20. He keeps 80 cows, and this necessitates a larger number of men than he would otherwise employ. He says that many of his neighbours who are Scotchmen, and who have twice the proportion of arable land, employ even fewer men per 100 acres than he does. " The extension of dairying," he said, " means the employment of more men here in Essex; it is dairying " that has saved Essex. There is no derelict land now as there " was twelve years ago. Two years ago I could not get a farm " when I wanted a change, and I had to raise money on a mortgage " to buy the farm I now have."

It would be very desirable to pursue this enquiry further, and to determine what is the number of men employed per 100 acres on an average arable and an average pastoral farm from which skilful farmers succeed in making a profit. On this will depend the answer to the question whether the reduction of farm labourers effected between 1801 and 1901 will be carried yet further in the future, on the assumption that no further change will be made in the system of cultivation by the laying down of more arable land in grass.

The above cases and the great differences in different parts of the country, and especially the small number of labourers employed in the arable counties of Scotland, and the success of the immigrating farmers from Scotland to Essex and some others of the Southern Counties, would tend to show that we have not yet reached the limit of economies of labour in many parts of England. As the result of enquiries made by the Board of Agriculture, Mr. Rew is of opinion that during the past six years there has been a further reduction in the number of labourers employed on farms in England, though not in the same ratio as between 1881 and 1901. It may be that extended use of petroleum engines will in the future dispense to a large extent with horse labour on the land, and in such case may yet further economise labour. At all events, one may safely predict that there will be no increased employment for labour in England and Wales on farms cultivated on the ordinary systems now in use on comparatively large farms.

The hope for increased employment for labour will be in the direction of intense cultivation of comparatively small holdings for fruit, vegetables, &c. I showed in the early part of this paper that the increase in this direction in England and Wales has been very great of late years, from 33,000 persons in

1861 to 74,000 in 1881, and 123,000 in 1901.[3] There is reason to
believe that this increase has been carried further in the last six
years. It is unfortunate that the census is not taken at five years'
interval in lieu of ten years, so that we might know what is the
progress made in this important direction. I do not propose to
discuss the question whether Parliament should stimulate progress
in this direction by facilities for creating small holdings. I will
only express my own belief that there is room for a great extension of
intense cultivation, and for a consequent increase of employment of
labour on the land.

The question arises whether this great economy of labour has
been effected at the expense of a reduction of products other than
that resulting from the laying down of arable land in grass, or from
the alteration of the rotation of crops in the direction of a less area
of corn in proportion to green crops. As regards the pasture land
of Great Britain, which constitutes considerably more than half its
area, there seems to be no ground for the suggestion. On the contrary,
it is certain that, owing to the low prices of feeding stuffs and of
artificial manure, these districts carry a greater stock of cows and
cattle than they did. There is distinct proof of this in the statistics
of the pastoral counties already referred to, in which there has been
no change in the system of agriculture, as the following figures
show :—

1881.

	Cows.	Other Cattle.	Sheep.	Horses.
Lancashire	122,100	99,900	318,100	38,300
Cheshire	91,100	60,700	97,800	23,000
Ayrshire and Lanarkshire	75,300	77,400	579,600	16,500
Wales	261,300	393,600	2,718,200	134,800

1901.

	Cows.	Other Cattle.	Sheep.	Horses.
Lancashire	139,000	101,400	335,400	44,900
Cheshire	106,400	73,000	102,400	27,100
Ayrshire and Lanarkshire	90,000	86,900	624,100	16,700
Wales	280,900	462,100	3,427,700	154,600

The figures show in nearly all cases a considerable increase.
The same increase of cows and cattle is shown by the statistics
of more arable counties where there has been little or no change in
the proportion of arable land to pasture :—

[3] A deduction should be made from these figures for "seedsmen," if under
this head are enumerated the vendors of seeds living in towns, and also for
florists under the same conditions.

1881.

	Cows.	Other Cattle.	Sheep.	Horses.
Cornwall	55,100	108,500	426,500	31,500
Aberdeen	41,300	110,800	137,600	26,800
Berwick, Roxburgh, and Edinburgh	18,700	33,600	945,000	13,900

1901.

	Cows.	Other Cattle.	Sheep.	Horses.
Cornwall	70,400	134,600	394,300	31,000
Aberdeen	44,310	136,600	226,600	30,700
Berwick, Roxburgh, and Edinburgh	19,000	35,700	1,050,700	14,100

Whether arable land as a rule is worse cultivated and produces less owing to the less employment of labour is more difficult to determine. The agricultural statistics show that, on the average of the last few years, compared with previous years, there has been an increased production of wheat of rather over three bushels per acre.[4] But this is stated to be due to inferior land having been laid down in grass, and the consequent improvement in the average of what remains under wheat cultivation. On the other hand, there is a general impression that labour has been somewhat stinted on arable farms, and that the cultivation has not been as neat as it used to be. To what extent this has reduced the production it is impossible to determine. The difference, in any case, cannot be large.

With respect to the 130,000 labourers above 20 who have been withdrawn in England and Wales from farm cultivation in the twenty years from 1881 to 1901, I have shown that 46,000 of them found employment at better wages in intense cultivation of gardens (non-domestic). A further 10,000 represents the increase of domestic gardens taken doubtless from the same class of agricultural labourers. The remaining 74,000 doubtless found employment at higher wages than they were getting as agricultural labourers, in the numerous avocations and industries where physical strength is necessary—on the railways, in the rural police, as carmen, and labourers in towns. Many of them also emigrated. It is not the fact that the older men were compelled to go to the workhouse, or that those who found employment in towns lowered the standard of health and strength there, or

[4] The average yield of wheat in England was, till a few years ago, reckoned to be about 28 bushels per acre. For the last ten years, since 1895, the average yield has been 31·26 bushels per acre. There has been a somewhat less corresponding increase in the yield of other cereals per acre.

that they flooded the market with a surplus of underpaid labour. If this were the case we should find that the worst men left the rural districts and that the best remained there. We should find that the wages of labour were lowered in rural districts. With lower wages some of the difficulties of farmers in the last twenty years would have been overcome, and they would have been sooner able to make the two ends meet. Exactly the reverse has occurred. Money wages rose ; wages as measured in what can be got for the money in bread, meat, tea, sugar, clothing, and all articles of necessity were very greatly increased. The labourers were induced to leave the rural districts—tempted by yet higher wages in the towns in other employments. The best, and not the worst, men went. This was the main cause that wages in rural districts, when measured by the price of food, rose during the last twenty years. It compelled the farmers to resort to new means of economising labour by the use of machinery and improved methods. As a result it would seem that adjustment has been made by most farmers to the new conditions. There is no part of Great Britain at the present time where there is any difficulty in letting farms at the present rents. In many districts there is keen competition for farms, and it is very difficult for any outsider to find one. However much we may deplore the reduction in rural districts of the number of labourers who constitute the reserve of physical wealth and strength of the country, we must recognise the economic causes which have been at work and the material advantages obtained by the labourers who left the land and by those who remained. There is no reason to believe that any rise in price of agricultural produce will reverse what has taken place, or will induce farmers to forego the economies they have already effected. There must be a very large rise in the price of corn to induce farmers to break up again on a large scale the land which has been laid down as pasture. A rise in price may add to the profits of farmers and raise rents, but only on condition that wages will not be increased. If wages are not increased in proportion to the rise in price of bread and meat and other requisites, the condition of the labourer will be worsened in the same proportion, and the inducement to leave the rural districts will be increased rather than reduced.

In conclusion, I must repeat that it is in the direction of intense cultivation in connection with small holdings, under the stimulus of ownership, or of security of tenure different from that of yearly tenancy, which is the rule with larger farms under the system of British agriculture, that we must look forward to a greater employment of labour on the land, and to the increase of a vigorous and independent rural population.

APPENDIX.

TABLE I.—*Three Counties where the Arable Land is Under 20 per Cent. of the Total Cultivated Area :* — DERBYSHIRE, WESTMORLAND, MONMOUTH.

Male Persons Employed on Farms.

	1861.		1881.		1901.	
	Over 20.	Under 20.	Over 20.	Under 20.	Over 20.	Under 20.
Farmers	10,120	—	9,790	—	9,710	—
(Women farmers)	(*1,310*)	—	(*1,230*)	—	(*1,230*)	—
Sons and relatives of farmers employed on farms	2,860	1,520	1,920	1,200	2,750	1,430
Bailiffs	390	—	470	—	540	...
Shepherds	340	—	350	—	330	—
Farm labourers	17,370	5,520	11,550	3,860	9,200	3,030
Total males	31,080	7,040	24,080	5,060	22,530	4,460

Reduction of males above 20 from 1861 to 1901 8,550   28 per cent.

„   labourers   „   „   ....   —   47   „.

	1871.	1881.	1901.
Arable land .... acres	311,800	225,300	175,700
Permanent pasture........ „	642,000	770,100	808,800
Total cultivated area........	953,800	995,400	984,500
	1861.		
Assessment of land for income tax............................	£1,491,800	£1,708,600	£1,465,300
Number of men above 20 per 100 acres	3·3	2·4	2·1
Number of men below 20 per 100 acres	0·7	0·5	0·7

Number of farms in 1895 above 20 acres, 10,220; average, 90 acres.

TABLE II.—*Five Counties where the Arable Land is between 20 and 30 per Cent. of the Total Area of Cultivated Land:*—LANCASHIRE, LEICESTER MIDDLESEX, SOMERSET, STAFFORDSHIRE.

Male Persons Employed on Farms.

	1861.		1881.		1891.	
	Over 20.	Under 20.	Over 20.	Under 20.	Over 20.	Under 20.
Farmers	33,330	—	31,280	—	28,040	—
(Women farmers)	*(3,830)*	—	*(3,350)*	—	*(2,995)*	—
Sons, &c., of farmers	9,079	5,160	6,330	3,270	8,870	4,460
Bailiffs	1,160	—	1,780	—	1,770	—
Farm labourers	98,320	28,780	65,660	21,890	46,350	15,420
Shepherds	1,830	—	1,330	--	1,320	—
Total males	143,710	33,940	106,380	25,160	86,350	19,880

Reduction of males above 20 from 1861 to 1901 57,366   40 per cent.

    „   labourers   „   „   52,000   53   „

	1871.	1881.	1901.
Arable land .... acres	995,100	881,300	749,600
Permanent pasture .... „	1,729,400	1,955,400	2,097,000
Total cultivated area	2,724,500	2,836,700	2,846,600
Assessment of land for income tax	1861. £6,018,800	£6,677,500	£5,194,000
Number of men above 20 per 100 acres	5·3	3·7	3·0
Number of men below 20 per 100 acres	1·2	0·8	0·5

Number of farms in 1895 above 20 acres, 27,496; average, 95 acres.

TABLE III.—*Twelve Counties where the Arable Land is between* 30 *and*
40 *per Cent. of the Total Cultivated Area :*—BUCKS, CHESHIRE, DORSET,.
DURHAM, GLOUCESTER, HEREFORD, NORTHANTS, NORTHUMBERLAND,
RUTLAND, SALOP, WARWICK, WORCESTER.

Male Persons Employed on Farms.

	1861.		1881.		1901.	
	Over 20.	Under 20.	Over 20.	Under 20.	Over 20.	Under 20.
Farmers	42,430	—	38,460	—	40,530	—
(Women farmers)	(*3,950*)	—	(*3,960*)	—	(*3,996*)	—
Sons, &c., of farmers	10,820	6,100	9,720	4,860	11,660	5,820
Bailiffs	3,380	—	3,660	—	3,800	—
Shepherds	6,180	—	4,830	—	5,570	—
Farm labourers	160,700	56,720	121,050	40,350	86,760	28,910
Total males	223,510	62,820	177,720	45,210	148,320	34,730

Reduction of males above 20 from 1861 to 1901 75,198   34 per cent.

„   labourers   „   „   73,990   46   „

	1871.	1881.	1901.
Arable land .... acres	2,889,000	2,569,100	2,131,800
Permanent pasture .... „	2,811,400	3,313,200	3,812,500
Total cultivated area	5,690,400	5,882,300	5,954,300
Assessment of land for income tax....	£10,003,700	£11,460,900	£8,274,200
Number of men above 20 per 100 acres.	3·9	3·0	2·5
Number of men below 20 per 100 acres	1·0	0·8	0·7

Number of farms in 1895 above 20 acres, 42,844; average, 132 acres.

TABLE IV.—*Eight Counties where the Arable Land is between* 40 *and* 50 *per Cent. of the Total Cultivated Area:*—CUMBERLAND, DEVON, KENT, SURREY, SUSSEX, WILTS, YORK (N.R.), YORK (W.R.).

Male Persons Employed on Farms.

	1861.		1881.		1901.	
	Over 20.	Under 20.	Over 20.	Under 20.	Over 20.	Under 20.
Farmers	53,300	—	47,280	—	47,710	—
(Women farmers)	(*4,590*)	—	(*3,060*)	—	(*3,170*)	—
Sons, &c., of farmers ...	14,670	7,480	11,740	5,860	17,790	8,890
Bailiffs	4,340	—	4,770	—	4,540	—
Shepherds....................	5,530	—	4,590	—	5,610	—
Farm labourers	177,450	62,090	138,200	46,060	97,590	32,530
Total males	255,290	69,570	206,580	51,920	173,240	41,420

Reduction of males above 20 from 1861 to 1901 82,162   33 per cent.

„ labourers „ „ 79,800   45 „

	1871.	1881.	1901.
Arable land .... acres	3,313,200	3,068,600	2,535,400
Permanent pasture........ „	2,640,300	3,227,600	3,738,900
Total cultivated area........	5,953,500	6,296,200	6,274,300
	1861.		
Assessment of land for income tax	£6,441,400	£7,615,300	£5,243,000
Number of men above 20 per 100 acres	4·1	3·3	2·8
Number of men below 20 per 100 acres	1·1	0·8	0·6

Number of farms in 1895 above 20 acres, 49,632 ; average, 122 acres.

TABLE V.—*Seven Counties where the Arable Land is between* 50 *and* 60 *per Cent. of the Total Cultivated Area:*—BEDFORD, BERKS, CORNWALL, HANTS, HUNTINGDON, NOTTS, OXFORD.

Male Persons Employed on Farms.

	1861.		1881.		1901.	
	Over 20.	Under 20.	Over 20.	Under 20.	Over 20.	Under 20.
Farmers	21,260	—	19,260	—	19,140	—
(Women farmers)	(*1,926*)	—	(*1,300*)	—	(*2,370*)	—
Sons, &c., of farmers	4,890	2,980	4,420	2,210	5,050	2,520
Bailiffs	1,760	—	2,140	—	2,380	—
Shepherds	3,880	—	3,120	—	3,080	—
Farm labourers	98,540	42,880	80,360	27,780	52,670	17,560
Total males	130,330	45,860	109,300	29,990	80,320	20,080

Reduction of males above 20 from 1861 to 1901 50,010   38 per cent.

„   labourers   „   „   45,870   46   „

	1871.	1881.	1901.
Arable land .... acres	1,967,400	2,002,300	1,706,300
Permanent pasture .... „	811,500	955,100	1,296,600
Total cultivated area.......	2,778,900	2,957,400	3,002,900

	1861.		
Assessment of land for income tax...................... }	£4,687,600	£5,239,600	£3,680,100
Number of men above 20 per 100 acres .... }	4·3	3·6	2·7
Number of men below 20 per 100 acres .... }	1·5	0·9	0·6

Number of farms in 1895 above 20 acres, 21,043 ; average, 135 acres.

TABLE VI.—*Seven Counties where the Arable Land is over* 60 *per Cent. of the Total Cultivated Area:*—CAMBRIDGE (76·3), ESSEX (62·2), HERTS (63·5), LINCOLN (67·1), NORFOLK (73), SUFFOLK (75·8), YORK, E.R. (68·5).

Male Persons Employed on Farms.

	1861.		1861.		1901.	
	Over 20.	Under 20.	Over 20.	Under 20.	Over 20.	Under 20
Farmers	34,870	—	32,470	—	35,160	—
(Women farmers)	(2,708)	—	(2,250)	—	(2,000)	—
Sons, &c., of farmers	7,080	4,090	5,890	2,940	7,800	3,900
Bailiffs	5,700	—	8,830	—	11,700	—
Shepherds	5,920	—	5,180	—	5,980	—
Farm labourers	181,400	71,320	156,310	52,100	121,890	40,630
Total males	234,970	75,410	208,680	55,040	182,530	44,530

Reduction of males above 20 from 1861 to 1901 52,440   22 per cent.

,,   labourers   ,,   ,, ... 59,900   33   ,,

	1871.	1881.	1901.
Arable land .... acres	4,294,100	4,258,400	3,938,200
Permanent pasture ... ... ,,	1,255,100	1,444,900	1,688,400
Total cultivated area........	5,548,300	5,703,300	5,626,600
	1861.		
Assessment of land for income tax................	£8,947,600	£10,138,300	£5,989,000
Number of men above 20 per 100 acres	4·1	3·6	3·2
Number of men below 20 per 100 acres	1·3	1·0	0·8

Number of holdings in 1901 above 20 acres, 33,920; average, 163 acres.

Table VII.—Wales.

Male Persons Employed on Farms.

	1861.		1881.		1901.	
	Above 20.	Under 20.	Above 20.	Under 20.	Above 20.	Under 20.
Farmers	32,700	—	30,100	—	29,800	—
(Women farmers)	(*4,860*)	—	(*5,200*)	—	(*5,286*)	—
Sons, &c., of farmers....	10,510	5,290	9,370	4,630	9,560	4,730
Bailiffs	1,000	—	800	—	1,200	—
Shepherds	1,030	—	830	—	1,240	—
Farm labourers	45,070	16,320	30,600	10,300	23,550	7,850
Total males	90,210	21,610	71,700	14,630	65,350	12,580

Reduction of males above 20 from 1861 to 1901 24,860   27 per cent.

„   labourers   „   „   21,450   47   „

	1871.	1881.	1901.
Arable land.................... acres	1,111,040	969,500	831,700
Permanent pasture......... „	1,494,400	1,815,400	1,941,300
Total cultivated area.......	2,604,800	2,784,900	2,823,000
	1861.		
Assessment for income tax	£2,650,700	£3,248,400	£3,000,700
Number of men above 20 per 100 acres	3·5	2·5	2·3
Number of men below 20 per 100 acres	0·8	0·5	0·4

Number of holdings in 1901 above 20 acres, 30,950; average, 83 acres.

TABLE VIII.—*Showing the Number of Males Employed in Agriculture in Three English Counties where there has been little or no change in the System of Cultivation.*

CORNWALL.

Male Persons Employed on Farms.

	1861.		1881.		1901.	
	Over 20.	Under 20.	Over 20.	Under 20.	Over 20.	Under 20.
Farmers	7,780	—	7,720	—	7,550	—
(Women farmers)	*(450)*	—	*(420)*	—	*(430)*	—
Sons, &c., of farmers	1,780	1,230	1,840	1,250	1,900	1,290
Bailiffs	160	—	190	—	380	—
Labourers	12,470	6,320	10,260	5,130	6,360	3,320
Shepherds	230	—	70	—	90	—
Total males	22,420	7,550	19,080	6,380	16,280	4,610

Reduction of males above 20 from 1861 to 1901 6,140   28 per cent.

„   labourers   „   ..   ....   —   50   „

	1871.	1881.	1901.
Arable land .... acres	375,300	363,500	361,400
Permanent pasture .... „	132,000	195,200	245,000
Total cultivated area	510,300	558,700	606,400
	1861.		
Assessment for income tax	£746,400	£951,100	£850,300
Number of males above 20 per 100 acres	4·6	3·5	2·7
Number of males below 20 per 100 acres	1·5	1·1	0·8

Number of holdings in 1895 above 20 acres, 6,270 ; average, 88 acres.

CHESHIRE.

Male Persons Employed on Farms.

	1861.		1881.		1901.	
	Over 20.	Under 20.	Over 20.	Under 20.	Over 20.	Under 20.
Farmers	6,500	—	6,280	—	5,950	—
Women farmers	930	—	960	—	990	—
Sons, &c., of farmers....	2,150	1,110	1,850	970	2,130	1,060
Bailiffs	170	—	270	—	370	—
Labourers	17,800	5,430	12,400	4,140	10,600	3,530
Shepherds	80	—	170	—	160	—
Total males	26,700	6,540	20,970	5,110	19,210	4,590

Reduction of males above 20 from 1861 to 1901 5,730   21 per cent.

,,   labourers   ,, ...   —   40   ..

	1871.	1881.	1901.
Arable land .... acres	193,400	174,500	196,700
Permanent pasture .... ,,	314,800	362,200	339,300
Total cultivated area........	508,200	536,700	536,000
Assessment for income tax	1861. £1,069,300	£1,195,300	£1,105,800
Number of men above 20 } per 100 acres .... }	5·0	4·0	3·6
Number of men below 20 } per 100 acres .... }	1·2	1·0	0·9

Number of holdings in 1895 above 20 acres, 5,520; average, 88 acres.

LANCASTER.

Male Persons Employed on Farms.

	1861.		1881.		1901.	
	Over 20.	Under 20.	Over 20.	Under 20.	Over 20.	Under 20.
Farmers	16,090	—	14,820	—	12,170	—
(Women farmers)	*(2,080)*	—	*(1,680)*	—	*(1,400)*	—
Sons, &c., of farmers	4,930	2,610	2,680	1,340	4,390	2,190
Bailiffs	240	—	590	—	590	—
Labourers	32,310	7,460	19,710	6,570	15,130	5,040
Shepherds	200	—	110	—	110	—
Total males	53,770	10,070	37,910	7,910	32,380	7,230

Reduction of males above 20 from 1861 to 1901........ 21,390   40 per cent.

„   labourers   „   „   17,186   53   „

	1871.	1881.	1901.
Arable land .... acres	250,600	227,500	245,800
Permanent pasture .... „	485,300	560,100	576,300
Total cultivated area	735,900	787,600	822,100
	1861.		
Assessment for income tax	£1,661,000	£1,855,200	£1,570,000
Number of males above 20 per 100 acres	6·8	4·8	4·0
Number of males below 20 per 100 acres	1·3	1·0	0·9

Number of farms in 1895 above 20 acres, 10,262; average, 71 acres.

TABLE IX.—*Showing Numbers of Males Employed on Farms in Five Counties in Scotland where there has been little or no change in the System of Cultivation.*

AYRSHIRE AND LANARKSHIRE.

Male Persons Employed in Agriculture.

	1861.		1881.		1901.	
	Over 20.	Under 20.	Over 20.	Under 20.	Over 20.	Under 20.
Farmers	5,220	—	4,340	—	4,150	—
(Women farmers)	(*450*)	—	(*420*)	—	(*400*)	—
Sons, &c., of farmers	1,420	790	1,410	770	1,340	670
Bailiffs	160	—	240	—	270	—
Labourers	10,840	3,610	5,820	1,950	4,360	1,840
Shepherds	420	—	520	—	680	—
Total males	18,060	4,400	12,430	2,720	10,800	2,510

Reduction of males above 20 from 1861 to 1881........   5,630

     ..   ..   ..   '81 „ 1901........   1,630

     „   '61 „ '01........   7,260   40 per cent.

   „ labourers „ '61 „ '01   6,480   60   „

	1871.	1881.	1901.
Arable land .... acres	327,400	311,000	308,000
Permanent pasture .... „	219,300	253,000	268,000
Total cultivated area........	546,700	564,000	576,000
	1861.		
Number of men above 20 per 100 acres	3·3	2·2	2·0
Number of men below 20 per 100 acres	0·8	0·5	0·45

Number of farms in 1895 above 20 acres, 4,635 ; average, 120 acres.

ROXBURGH, BERWICK, *and* EDINBURGH.

Male Persons Employed in Agriculture.

	1861.		1881.		1901.	
	Over 20.	Under 20.	Over 20.	Under 20.	Over 20.	Under 20.
Farmers	1,790	—	1,500	—	1,580	—
(Women farmers)........	(90)	—	(80)	—	(85)	—
Sons, &c., of farmers....	400	200	360	150	380	170
Bailiffs	550	—	500	—	650	—
Shepherds	1,210	—	1,360	—	1,350	—
Labourers	7,430	3,720	6,070	2,530	4,410	2,300
Total males	11,380	3,920	9,790	2,680	8,370	2,470

Reduction of males above 20 from 1861 to 1881............ 1,590

           ..   '81 ,, 1901............ 1,420

           '61 ,, '01............ 3,010   27 per cent.

     ,,   labourers   ,,   '61 ,, '01............ 3,020   40   ,,

	1871.	1881.	1901.
Arable land.................... acres	380,000	385,300	374,000
Permanent pasture........ ,,	111,200	124,100	132,000
Total cultivated area........	491,200	509,400	506,000
	1861.		
Assessment for income tax	£833,000	£988,000	£695,000
Number of. men above 20 } per 100 acres .... }	2·3	1·9	1·7
Number of men below 20 } per 100 acres .... }	0·8	0·5	0·5

Number of farms in 1895 above 20 acres, 1,920; average, 256 acres.

ABERDEENSHIRE.

Male Persons Employed on Farms.

	1861.		1881.		1901.	
	Over 20.	Under 20.	Over 20.	Under 20.	Over 20.	Under 20.
Farmers	8'730	—	7,680	—	7,022	—
(Women farmers)	(950)	—	(900)	—	(1,038)	—
Sons, &c., of farmers....	1,410	790	1,510	800	1,680	1,030
Bailiffs	430	—	350	—	690	—
Shepherds	320	—	380	—	460	—
Labourers	11,710	3,900	10,180	3,390	7,940	3,360
Total males	22,200	4,690	20,100	4,190	17,790	4,390

Reduction of males above 20 from 1861 to 1901 4,410   20 per cent.

„   labourers   „   „   3,770   33   „

	1871.	1881.	1901.
Arable land ....acres	548,300	572,500	597,300
„ under corn „	(212,400)	(212,400)	(214,300)
Permanent pasture........ „	31,200	27,400	33,000
Total cultivated area	579,500	599,900	630,300
	1861.		
Assessment of land for income tax................................ }	£542,100	£682,000	£619,400
Number of men below 20 per 100 acres .... }	3·9	3·3	2·8
Number of men above 20 per 100 acres .... }	0·8	0·7	0·7

Number of farms in 1895 above 20 acres, 7,336; average, 80 acres.

DISCUSSION *on* LORD EVERSLEY'S PAPER.

THE CHAIRMAN, in opening the proceedings, much regretted to announce that Lord Eversley was unable to be present, having met with a slight accident, and was forbidden by his medical attendant to leave the house. He was sure the meeting would wish to convey to Lord Eversley their regret, and hope that he would be soon restored to perfect health.

The Paper was then read by Sir ATHELSTANE BAINES.

The Rt. Hon. JESSE COLLINGS, M.P., much regretted that he should not be able to remain to hear the discussion on this very interesting Paper, which went into great detail and required much examination and consideration. It was said very truly that from 1861 to 1881 agriculture was prosperous and rents were rising, but it must be remembered that during that period the agricultural labourer's wages were very low. It always had been so; high prices and prosperous agriculture had in the past been accompanied by very low wages. He did not attach much importance to what Lord Eversley said as to the enormous rise of wages up to 1901. If he remembered rightly, the average wages rose from 10s. 4d. to 13s. 4d. But, so long as wages were inside the starvation circle, as 13s. 4d. was, they need go no further to account for the labourer wishing to get away from such a state of things. Then it was said that the reduction in the cost of food was equal to a further 40 per cent. rise, so that altogether the labourers were twice as well off. He disputed that the reduction in the cost of living was anything like that named. Take the old state of things in what were called "the hungry forties": the labourer, as far as the necessaries of life were concerned, was then far and away better off than he was afterwards. Butter, cheese, milk, bacon, pork, rent, coal, and fuel, all those things were much lower than in the brilliant times which were described; and it was of no use attempting to disguise that fact. They ought not to keep on talking about the agricultural labourer having such a large share of agricultural prosperity and therefore being so much better off. So long as he had only 13s. 4d. or even 15s. or 16s. a week on which to keep himself, wife and family, there was no need for further discussion as to his condition. It was little better than starvation; and it was not right to cover it up by saying how much the wage had increased. If you started at zero, you could easily show an immense increase. Again, in the old times what were called "perquisites" were far greater than in later days, and employment was more regular and continuous. In the old-fashioned days the farmers kept their hands on all the year round; whereas now, when they were day labourers, they were often sent home on wet days. Nothing of that sort was known in the early decades of the last century. By consulting the writings of almost any agricultural author, it would be found that farmers had nearly twice the force on their farms in the old days. The question was not how many men were engaged on the land, but how many ought to be. There was now a great deal less land under cultivation, and consequently less labour and a diminished production. Further, besides the low wages, what did they find? That there was no time at which the labourer had any prospect whatever on the land, none to speak of; one here and there got on, but there was not, as there was in every other occupation, a possibility of his rising in his profession. He called it a "profession" because the old agricultural labourer was one of the ablest men to be found as a technical skilled labourer. If he had not science, he had observation, and came to a conclusion from his experience and observation on matters in connection with the weather, the soil, the habits of animals, and so on, almost as correct as the scientific man came to to-day. They had yet to learn what they had lost in the splendid *personnel* of the old agricultural labourer. It was about three o'clock in the afternoon with England unless they got that class of man back again; but how was it to be done? That was the question of the day, a question on which their safety depended in the future, and with regard to which all statements about increasing wealth might be disregarded. He was glad to see how this question was coming forward. There were two sentences in the Paper which he thought of more practical value than all the rest of it put together: one was at p. 290, which said that "the hope for increased employment would be in the direction of intense cultivation of comparatively small holdings for fruit, vegetables, &c." The other, which was still more conclusive, was the sentence on p. 293, which stated that for an increase of a vigorous and independent rural population we must look to the stimulus of ownership or a security of tenure different from that of yearly tenancy. "Security of tenure" was a very vague term which no one had yet been able to define, and though they, parrot-like, constantly repeated it, nobody knew how to secure it except by ownership. He would ask his friend Major Craigie's special attention to these two paragraphs, and ask him to put from his mind all those financial considerations, which were of small importance in the face of what they wanted to secure. It was a question of life and death for this nation. What was wanted was, to restore the old class of yeoman-ownerships and peasant proprietors owning the land they tilled. That did not mean that all the country was to be cut up in that way; there should be every kind of tenure and holding; but ownership must be the basis of the system, not a mere incident in it. Our system of land tenure had thoroughly broken down, not only in England, but had been discarded by every other country in Europe. Great Britain remained the only country that had not yet found out (though it was rapidly finding out) that a system based on three separate castes, landlord, tenant, and labourer, was a rotten one. What they wanted to do was to restore those great classes which originally made England what it was. They could be restored: there was a land-hunger, not only among the rural population, but there were thousands of good and suitable men in the towns who would be only too glad to get back to the country on fair and proper conditions.

Mr. RICHARDS said that as one who took part in the Royal Commission of 1892, he might say that the Commissioners were absolutely united in the conclusions they came to as to the vastly improved condition of the labouring classes, and they were all extremely careful to give the figures and facts on which they formed those conclusions. He was, therefore, somewhat surprised to find a gentleman of the eminence of the last speaker setting up his own imagination against facts which were beyond dispute. They were all agreed that it was very desirable, if possible, to retain the population on the land, and the question was as to the best method of keeping them there. They could not be kept there by artificial means. He entirely agreed with Lord Eversley, that much might be done by increasing the facilities for small holdings; but that was a matter which could not be forced, and, whatever Parliament might do, it could only be successful so far as it coincided with natural economic methods. He believed that agriculture would have to develop very much as other industries. He would take, for instance, one with which he was best acquainted, that of cotton spinning. Many years ago a mill with 100,000 spindles would have been thought an enormous undertaking, but to-day a man would be thought very foolish who built a mill containing less than 700,000 or 800,000. Side by side with facilities for small holdings would have to be placed the conditions of natural economic development. When on the Royal Commission, it fell to his lot to examine a district which was about the best in England, and the only one in which the farmsteading had been laid out with a view to economising the employment of labour—he referred to Lord Tollemache's estate—and he found that the same amount of land might be worked as well with less labour. Some people deplored the use of these economic methods as tending to a still greater depopulating of the rural districts, and that might appear to be the first effect. But the first thing to do was to establish a prosperous agriculture. When you had done that, you would soon get an abundant supply of labour. Mr. Collings had spoken of the vagueness of the term "security of tenure," but he thought it was understood, in a broad sense, to mean that the man who farmed the land should have the whole benefit of the brains and material he put into it. Before there could be anything like intense farming in England, there must be greater security of tenure than there exists to-day. It was said that as between landlord and tenant, if a tenant took a farm for twenty-one years on certain terms and conditions, he had no complaint to make when he surrendered the farm at the end. But on the other hand, the interest of the nation should always be paramount in the contract. Under existing conditions, an intelligent, scientific farmer during the earlier years of his tenancy brought his land to a high pitch of cultivation, and during the last three or four years he put nitrate of soda on it to force out the good qualities which made the farm productive. That was the natural process by which the tenant recouped himself, but the nation suffered. Absolute security of tenure was required, so that at the end of the tenant's term the land should be left in as good a state of cultivation as when he took it. He saw no reason why small holdings and large holdings should not go on side by side in the neighbourhood of large towns, such as Liverpool, Manchester, and London. The ground would be made rich, because of the proximity of a favourable market; intense cultivation would take place, and huge crops be raised. On the other hand, there were certain districts where the natural development would be in a different direction, fences would be broken down and steam ploughs introduced, and successful agriculture brought about by economising labour.

Dr. LONGSTAFF said it was only natural that politicians should be led astray by the charms of rhetoric. It had been a great disappointment to him not to have had the opportunity of meeting his friend and former colleague, Lord Eversley; but he thought he, too, had been carried away to some extent by the eloquence of a politician when he wrote that " it might well be a question which was the soundest and best system, looked at from the interests of the country as a whole, which was concerned not so much in the securing of a maximum rent as in the maintenance of a vigorous and independent population." He could very well imagine an able advocate of Tariff Reform making great fun of that sentence, and paraphrasing it by saying that it was a question whether a minimum price really was the greatest hope of the nation. It was the duty of their Society to prepare dry facts on which the flowers of rhetoric might be expended, but not to indulge in them themselves. Lord Eversley seemed to think that because all were glad that women were not employed on the land to the same extent as formerly, and that children were in school instead of working in the fields, they were not to be counted among agricultural labourers; but that seemed to him to be wrong. Whatever might be the desirability or otherwise of the change, if there had been a reduction in the number of adult labourers and also of women and child labourers, it showed that the question of total reduction was all the more serious. As a matter of fact, there were so many fewer people deriving their living from the land. Some years ago, in a paper on Rural Depopulation, he (the speaker) called attention to a point which was not alluded to in this Paper, but was not without importance, though it was impossible to state it numerically; that was, the substitution of the town tradesman for the agricultural labourer in a great many occupations. There was a time when, at all events over the corn-growing portions of England, buildings were mainly roofed with thatch, and the thatchers were to a great extent agricultural labourers, since they did not spend the whole of their time in thatching. That trade had almost died out, and buildings were now covered with slates or tiles by tradesmen coming from towns. In the same way the introduction, first, of

wire-fencing and, secondly, of barbed-wire fencing, greatly diminished
the work of the hedger and ditcher, and was mainly done by contractors in towns. Again, a great deal that used to be done by the
local blacksmith was now done by the manufacturer at Wolverhampton or Birmingham; and in those parts of the country where
suitable stone could be obtained, stone-drains used to be made; but
pipe-drains were now substituted, the pipes being manufactured
outside the place altogether by a different set of men; and the work
was often done by contractors, and much less by labourers on the
spot than used to be the case. In the same way, the threshing on
the farms was almost entirely done by contractors who came from
outside, and only very little local labour was employed in connection
therewith. Again, there was a tendency, only incipient at present,
for a great deal of butter-making to be done as a matter of trade by
persons . outside the farm altogether. To his mind, the most
interesting fact brought out in this Paper was the evenness of
the diminution of agricultural labour over the different parts
of the country. It was a curious thing that no one had yet
mentioned a factor which probably had as much to do with
the migration of farm labourers as anything, and that was
education; it made people more familiar with the towns, and showed
the labourer that there was another life besides that which their
fathers and grandfathers lived; finally, the improved means of
communication afforded facilities for migration. He thought
Lord Eversley was wrong in denying that the influx of country
labourers into towns deteriorated the health of the towns and overcrowded the slums. That was one of those flowers of rhetoric, and
several steps were missed out. No doubt the agricultural labourer
going into the towns did tend, not to deteriorate the health of the
towns, but to deteriorate the average health of the nation, by the
fact that his children and grandchildren would be brought up in
the town and not in the country, and he for one did not believe you
could permanently keep a town population as vigorous as a country
population. Those vigorous men coming from the country displaced
the ineffective and feeble men, and pushed them to the wall. It
was not the strong man who came to London and joined the police
who went into the slums; but he pushed a man, who pushed
another, and in that way the slums got overcrowded. He should
like to hear from Major Craigie to what extent the changes in the
accuracy of the returns affected that argument, alluding especially
to the second part of the Paper, which had relation to the product.
He was a small landowner, and had a small amount of land in hand;
sometimes he feared that he filled up his return wrongly, and sometimes forgot to fill it up at all. It seemed to him possible that his
tenants might not be much more accurate, and he very often
wondered whether Major Craigie was really analysing sound
material. It was sometimes said that the more enlightened the
person who filled up the return the worse the result, and possibly
that might be so. No doubt Lord Eversley intended to say, though
he omitted it, that in Lancashire and Cheshire the question was very
much governed by the large industries affording ample means of

employment in those districts. Mr. Collings had said that if you began at zero it was easy to show a great percentage of increase, and, in the same way, in diminishing from a fixed number down-wards, there was a limit to which you could go. The smaller diminution of agricultural labourers in the second period of twenty years was largely due to the fact that you had a smaller number to diminish, and, for the same reason, he anticipated in the next twenty years a still smaller decrease.

Major CRAIGIE said they must all deeply regret the absence of Lord Eversley, and especially the cause of it. Although nearly twenty years had passed since their senior ex-President had filled the Chair, many of them had experience of his continued interest in statistical inquiry, and they recognised the value of his services and advice. The question placed before them that day was statistical and not political. When he heard his friend Mr. Jesse Collings make the interesting remarks he had just offered, he began to be afraid that the Society might be led off from the true ground they were asked to discuss by more fascinating topics of general agrarian politics. The real question to-night was one of the truth and sufficiency of the figures relied on to demonstrate and to measure the decline of agricultural labour, where and when the decline had taken place, and what particular forms of labour were those which had declined most. This investigation would allow them to see what were the causes pointed to by the recorded movements of the population, and it was to this close attention should be given, and not so much what might be the alleged advantage of one or other of the various political schemes or methods for rejuvenating agriculture, or keeping people on the land in the future. The comparative value and the accuracy of the census returns was the first thing one thought of. By some misfortune each succeeding census, particularly as regarded the occupations of the people, differed more or less in form from that which had preceded it, and a good deal of Lord Eversley's work had consisted, therefore, in trying to disentangle the meaning of the figures from the obscurity which hindered recognition of the real situation. He had dissected the large totals from which political arguments were often drawn, and the result so carefully arrived at reduced the exaggerated totals which, perhaps naturally enough, without close examination of the census figures, many people had accepted at their face value. Even if it was permissible to talk of the "million" who had left the land, Lord Eversley had made it quite clear that the greater reduction of numbers took place in the twenty years before 1881, and but only a smaller proportion since that date, and only the latter period coincided in any way with what was called agricultural depression. He had not dealt, as he probably would if the inquiry had been carried further, with the parallel movements of the agricultural population in other countries, under conditions different from our own; but they were also very striking. Anyone who would take in detail the German or French censuses would see that the movement of agricultural labour was not wholly a British phenomenon. He

agreed with Dr. Longstaff that the loss of women from the fields
was a distinct loss of labour, and in this respect there was a
striking difference apparent if you compared the position with
that of other countries.   Some American statisticians, dealing
with the effect on labour of new forms of machinery, had pointed
out that in one or two classes of farms female labour was
actually increasing.   Again, if you went to Denmark, where so
much attention was given to dairy-farming, there was a tendency
to maintain and develop the employment of women on the
land.   Unless that kind of labour was employed, it would be very
difficult to carry out with any economic success any of these
schemes of small holdings to which allusion had been made.   He
did not share the feeling that women were entirely unsuited for
some kinds of agricultural labour.   With reference to the figures
before them, he should like to have seen a further explanation of
the effect of the change made in the second item of the occupation
schedule in bringing into the category of the agricultural workers
in 1901 the female relatives of the farmer who were assisting in
agriculture.   This appeared for the first time in recent years in the
census of 1901, and may suggest a correction in the opposite
direction to some of those made in the Paper.   He still thought it
was a necessary extension, but it affected certain of the figures
when they came to compare them with his other records.   He
thought the tables now presented would prove most useful as a
starting point for local examinations in detail, and he would
suggest as a future sphere of inquiry that they should apply to
the bare figures of numbers of persons employed the calculations they had had on former occasions before the Society with
regard to wages.   An endeavour to discover what was the relative
saving in farmers' outlay or in the cost of production, if any, by the
diminution of manual force employed on the farm would be quite
worth maturing.   They must also take account in any inquiry as to
more economic production of the number of working horses.   So
far as the agricultural returns might be accepted on this point, the
apparent diminution in the number of acres under the plough had
not been reflected in the number of horses kept for ploughing,
and it would seem that whatever gain in labour outlay was effected
by the farmers having fewer ploughmen to pay, might be lost if too
many working horses are retained.   Dr. Longstaff had asked how
far they might trust the figures with regard to areas and crops now
issued by the Board of Agriculture.   On the whole, he thought
they had every reason to believe in the approximate accuracy of
their general result.   There might be an error and an omission here
and there, but such errors, where they had, as in this case, a solid
basis of half a million returns filled up by different individuals,
the *minus* and the *plus* errors cancelled each other.   It might be
interesting to Dr. Longstaff to know that up to quite a recent date
the total percentage of returns not sent in was as low as 3 per cent.
He did not say all the returns received were accurate in every
detail, but they supplied a statistical basis of a much wider and
better character than statisticians often had to deal with, and these

agricultural returns, maintained annually as they had been in so nearly uniform a shape for forty years, were a more valuable and more consistent source of information than, he feared, could be found in the occupation tables of the census.

Mr. JESSE ARGYLE, after remarking on the general interest of the Paper, said it would be interesting to know how many people had been misled by the great change in the method of compiling the census which took place in 1871. He remembered the very point referred to by Lord Eversley of the removal of the wives and daughters of farmers from the agricultural class so puzzled such a careful paper as "The Economist" that it propounded various theories to account for what was in reality an imaginary decrease of nearly 250,000 in the number of women employed in agriculture in a single decade. He agreed that it was much the best to entirely exclude women engaged in agriculture in making comparisons with previous years; there being another reason for this not mentioned by the author. While the censuses of 1851 and 1861 included all the wives and daughters of farmers, and while those of 1871, 1881 and 1891 carefully excluded them so far as they could, in 1901 they were again to some extent introduced. Whilst in previous returns there was the line, "Farmers' sons, grandsons and other male relatives," in 1901 this was altered to read "Sons, *daughters*, &c.," and, in that way, about 18,000 women were re-introduced. He could not say whether these were previously returned as farm-servants; possibly they were, but there was nothing to show it. Another point which might easily mislead was that in the earlier censuses landowners were returned as being engaged in agriculture; whilst in the more recent ones they were all relegated to the "independent" or "unoccupied" class. In 1861 there were more than 30,000 of these landowners returned under the head of "agriculture." With regard to the greater employment of machinery in farming, the census figures were interesting. In 1871 there were only 1,500 persons returned as agricultural machine proprietors and attendants, whilst in the last census there were 6,600. There was one point which he had not heard mentioned anywhere, but which seemed to be of some importance. To a considerable extent, the transfer from agriculture to a town occupation was not direct, but indirect. A number of small industries, other than agriculture, had been started in the villages, and the agricultural labourers had put their sons to those trades, instead of putting them on to the land. No doubt education had a good deal to do with that; but what had, be believed, largely happened was, not that the young men had gone direct to the industrial centres, but had learnt their trades in the villages, and then, as opportunity occurred, went to the towns. As a young man, he lived two or three years in a tiny agricultural town in the West of England, and he saw this process going on. Whilst he was there, there was a great dispute in the printing trade, and two or three young men, sons of agricultural labourers, who were working in the rural printing office, seized the opportunity and went straight to London, where they were soon, he was told, earning 4*l.* or 5*l.* a week on a morning newspaper, instead of the 1*l.* they got in the country. And he knew that they had been the means of bringing up others from the same parts of the country. You could not really wonder at it, for in that place there was absolutely no amusement of any kind whatever for the young fellows in winter, apart from the public-house—no concerts, no reading-room, and no discussion-class ; there was nothing for them to do in the long evenings but to loaf about the·unlit street, or, if they could afford it, go into the tap-room of the local beer-house. With such a state of things, it was no wonder that a young man seized the first opportunity of going to a great town. He agreed with the view that agricultural depression had little to do with the change that was going on ; it was mainly due to other causes. In the neighbourhood he had referred to, there was, save possibly amongst a very few aged people, no actual distress ; though wages were low, they were sufficient to provide for actual needs, and there was nobody out of work ; but there was an absence of future prospects. Another thing was, the practical absence of social liberty and privacy ; you could not do anything whatever but what it was known to everybody else for miles round.

Mr. WILLIS BUND said Lord Eversley had done very valuable service in showing the fallacies which lay in some of the census tables, but he was not quite sure he had not, in his zeal for small holdings, rather fallen into a fallacy himself. In the next census, probably there would be a number of additional persons returned as connected with land, and the public would·be told in glowing terms that small holdings were a wonderful success. He might give a little experience of his own with reference to small holdings. In a district not far from Bromsgrove, there was a number of persons who used to follow the occupation of nailers, they had now taken small holdings, and they spent so many days working in their nail shops, and so many days on the land, and they would now all be returned as having come on the land as small holders, but they had not come from the towns, they were the same people who were in the village before. Great care would, therefore, have to be taken in making out these statistics to avoid mistakes and prevent people speaking in glowing terms of what small holdings were to bring people back to the land, when in fact they were there already.

Mr. B. SANSOME said he should like to call attention to one point referred to in the Paper, namely, the cost of living. In the book mentioned by Mr. Collings, "The Hungry Forties," written by a daughter of Cobden, it was stated that in 1845, the cost of a loaf was 5*d.*, butter 7*d.* lb., cheese 2*d.*, bacon 3*d.*, and beef 4*d.*, a score of potatoes 2*d.*, and new-laid eggs 30 a 1*s.* The total of those figures comes to 2*s.* 11*d.* Under present prices, the loaf was 5½*d.*, butter 1*s.*, cheese 6*d.*, bacon 8*d.*, beef 8*d.*, potatoes 9*d.*, eggs 1*s.* 6*d.*, thus making 5*s.* 6½*d.* There was, therefore, 3*s.* more payable by the labourers than it cost them sixty years ago. That being so, the wages mentioned by Lord Eversley, 13s. compared with 10s., had not, it was plain, improved the condition of the labourers. It was entirely wrong to say that the price of food, taking the leading articles, had gone down, it was, in fact, 40 or 50 per cent. higher.

Mr. JOHN LLOYD desired to call attention to the many charges on the land which militated very much against the progress of agriculture. He referred especially to the burden of the tithe rent charge, which was very heavy on the best corn-growing land, often amounting to 4s. per acre. Then there was the land-tax, the interference of sanitary inspectors, who would not allow people to keep pigs, a tax on the farmer's trap, and many other things. The main burden, however, was that of tithes; there were thousands of acres of beautiful arable and pasture land which were not cultivated on account of that impost.

Mr. W. R. LAWSON said Major Craigie had advised the speakers to stick to hard-and-fast figures; but he did not indorse that. On the contrary, he did not see what was to be made of mere figures, especially when you got such variations and contradictions in them as they had seen in this discussion. It seemed to him that the effect of this Paper was, to show that they could not have the slightest faith in any of the census returns, as they so seldom agreed with each other. It was often thrown in their faces that anything could be proved by statistics: but Lord Eversley had shown them that anything could be explained away by statistics. If the Paper had any practical meaning, it was that there had been no disappearance of farm labourers worth speaking of. But supposing it had established that, how far did that carry them in solving what they all knew to be the fundamental problem before the nation at the present time? The question was, not simply whether there were now 100,000 fewer agricultural labourers than there were sixty years ago, but what proportion the rural population bore to the town population. During those sixty years, the proportion of urban population had increased to a very unhealthy extent; and, with all respect to Major Craigie, he could not see how the urban population was going to maintain the health of the country as the rural population would do. Nowadays, there were slum suburbs close to London nearly as bad as Whitechapel used to be. There was another fallacy in this Paper which showed what a very short distance you could go if you stuck to hard and dry figures. Apparently, it did not occur to Lord Eversley that for fifty years previous to 1846, when this depopulation was supposed to have commenced, agriculture in England had been growing at a very rapid rate, the rural population had been increasing almost as rapidly as that of towns, and its condition was better in many respects. They ought to take the period when agriculture was growing, and compare it with the recent period when it had been decreasing. That was more important than merely figuring up how many labourers there were in one census or in another, and then confessing, when you had done with them, that none of the returns were to be relied upon. He had been several times in Canada, and had learnt many things there, some of them bearing on this question. The Canadians had a type of provincial town which, he believed, we should ultimately have to adopt. He knew one or two such towns in Ontario, with a population of 8,000 or 10,000, situated in agricultural districts, but not wholly dependent on agriculture. In their early days they were blessed with citizens with brains, who had business-like ideas of developing them. They offered free sites for factories with freedom from taxes for twenty years, and thus induced people to come in with considerable capital and build factories. Some of these employed 300 or 400 people right in the heart of the country. That was what we should probably have to come to. Such towns did not lose their rural character; the town and the country elements being successfully combined in them.

The CHAIRMAN said he should confine himself to proposing a hearty vote of thanks to Lord Eversley for his very interesting Paper, for the discussion had ranged over such a variety of subjects that it was impossible to deal with them at the moment. He was sure the Fellows would criticise the Paper carefully and accurately, and would give to economists, politicians, and statesmen the benefit of those dry statistical facts at which they arrived.

——————

The following communication has since been received from Lord Eversley :—

I hope I may be permitted in the *Journal* of the Society to add a few words by way of comment on the discussion which took place after the reading of my Paper in my enforced absence. In the first place I must emphasize that my object, as Major Craigie well pointed out, was to determine the real reduction which has taken place in the forty years, from 1861 to 1901, in the number of persons employed in agriculture, to disentangle the facts and figures from the intricate confusion created by the different classifications adopted in successive census returns, and to dispel many exaggerated statements which have been founded on them. Secondly, having determined the figures, my object was to show how far the reduction was due to changes in the system of cultivation, such as the laying of arable land in grass, and how far to other causes, such as the economy of labour effected by the use of machinery and other improved methods. It was not my intention to enter upon the subject discussed by several speakers, whether an increase of rural population could be effected by multiplying small holdings. Having, however, shown that there is no reason to expect a larger employment of labour on the land under the existing system of large farms, but rather the reverse, I incidentally expressed the hope and belief that it is in the direction of intense cultivation on small holdings, there is room for a greatly increased employment of labour on the land. With respect to the reduction of agricultural labourers in the forty years under review, I showed that by far the greater part of it took place in the first half between 1861 and 1881, when agriculture was prosperous, when prices were high and when money wages were largely increased, and that much the smaller part took place between 1881 and 1901, when prices of produce were continually falling, when grave depression of agriculture existed, and when, in spite of this, wages, measured in what could be obtained for them in food and other requirements of labourers, were again largely increased.

As a conclusion from this I showed how very much improved has been the condition of agricultural labourers in the forty years. On this point I must entirely dissent from the statements made by Mr. Jesse Collings to the effect that " agricultural labourers, as far as the necessaries of life were concerned, were far away better off in what have been called the hungry forties than in more recent years "; that " butter, cheese, milk, bacon, pork, rent, coal and fuel were all much lower " in these good old times. No one who has really studied the figures of prices and of wages can possibly come to these conclusions. I am not able to state what the average rate of agricultural labourers' wages was between 1840 and 1850. It is certain, however, that it was no higher than in 1850. The Board of Trade memorandum, which I quoted, gave the average weekly wage for that year as 9s. 4d. It showed how this gradually rose till in 1901-3 it was 14s. 7d., an increase of 5s. 3d., or more than 50 per cent. As regards what could be got for these money wages there is an interesting statement by the late Mr. William Little, in his report to the Royal Commission on Labour of 1894, to the effect that the average price of a sufficiency of flour, butter, cheese, tea and sugar for a week's consumption of an adult male labourer gradually fell during the period under review from 50·4d. to 29·2d., a reduction of more than 40 per cent. To this extent, independent of the rise of money wages, the labourers of late years have been better off. All the other requirements of labourers — clothes, boots, petroleum, fuel, &c., have fallen in about the same ratio. Meat alone has not fallen in price in the same proportion. But nothing is more certain than that agricultural labourers in the days of dear bread were never able to afford the luxury of butchers' meat, while at the present time they are generally able to do so. The further statement of Mr. Collings that " in old-fashioned days farmers kept their hands on all the year round, whereas now the men were day labourers, and were often sent home on wet days " is one which cannot be sustained. It is a matter of common knowledge that in the days of protection and high prices, there was a great redundancy of labour in rural districts. Large numbers of men were discharged by farmers in the winter, and were thrown upon the rates for outdoor relief. Of late years there has been a deficiency of labour rather than the reverse in rural districts. Pauperism has largely decreased. There are as a rule no men out of work at any period of the year.

I quite agree with Dr. Longstaff, that in considering the reduction in the number of labourers, account should be taken of the many ways in which labour has been dispensed with in rural districts by such changes as the substitution of wire fencing for hedges, and of slates and tiles for thatching. If I did not mention these altered methods, I had them in my mind when I referred to the economy of labour which has been effected of late years. I would also observe, with reference to his remarks, that when I controverted the statement " that the migration of rural labourers had resulted in lowering the standard of health and strength of the people of the towns, and flooded the market with a surplus of underpaid labour," I was not unmindful of the effect of this migration on the lowest classes of workers in towns, by adding to the competition for work, and in many cases by increasing the difficulties of over-crowding. It is for this reason, among others, that I should welcome any measures which, by increasing the inducements and facilities for intense cultivation and small holdings, will give greater employment for labour in rural districts, and stem this tendency to concentrate population in urban districts. I have only to conclude by thanking the many speakers for their kindly personal references to me.

The following were elected Fellows of the Society :—

Marius Taudin Chabot. | Samuel Lord, A.S.A.A.

William Palin Elderton, F.I.A.

REPORT OF THE COUNCIL

For the FINANCIAL YEAR *ended* 31*st December,* 1906, *and for the*
SESSIONAL YEAR *ending* 18*th June,* 1907, *presented at the*
SEVENTY-THIRD ANNUAL GENERAL MEETING *of the* ROYAL
STATISTICAL SOCIETY, *held at the Society's Rooms,* 9, *Adelphi*
Terrace, Strand, W.C., London, on the 18*th of June,* 1907.

THE Council have the honour to submit their Seventy-third
Annual Report.

The roll of Fellows on the 31st December last as compared with
the average of the previous ten years was as follows :—

Particulars	1906.	Average of the previous Ten Years.
Number of Fellows on 31st December	891	913
Life Fellows included in the above	177	178
Number lost by death, withdrawal, or default	63	51
New Fellows elected	43	49

Since the 1st January last, 16 new Fellows have been elected,
and the Society has lost 36 by death, resignation, or default, so
that the number on the list, excluding Honorary Fellows, on
18th June, 1907, is 871.

The Society has to deplore the death since June last year of its
past President, Viscount Goschen, and of the other undermentioned
Fellows :—

Deaths of Fellows since June, 1906.

		Date of Election.
	Bevan, Thomas	1875
	*Burdett-Coutts, Right Hon. The Baroness	1873
d	*Bushill, Thomas W.	1893
	*Carillon, J. Wilson	1872
	Carr, Ebenezer	1888
d	Doyle, Patrick	1878
d	*Finnemore, R. I.	1884
	Goodsall, D. H.	1885
c d p	GOSCHEN, Right Hon. Viscount, Hon. Vice-President	1868
	Groves, Dr. Joseph	1903
	Herring, George	1898
	Hyde, H. Barry	1887
d	Murray, Adam	1878
	*Oelsner, Isidore	1880
	Power, Edward	1871
d	Praschkauer, Maximilian	1877
	*Radcliffe, Sir David	1888
	Rhens, Robert	1886
	Saunders, Cecil R.	1893
d	Seyd, Richard	1873
	Wahrmann, Ernest	1902
d	Whiteley, William	1884

Deaths of Honorary Fellows since June, 1906.

d p	Körösy, Joseph	1893
d	Olanesco, Grégoire P.	1896

During the same period the following new Fellows have been elected :—

à Ababrelton, R. R. de R.
Andersson, T. E. E., Ph.D.
Archer, Walter E.
Bailey, Walter.
Baldwin-Wiseman, W. R.
Bernard, Major Francis T. H.
Bush. Joseph H.
Chabot, Marius Taudin.
Choles, Herbert J.
Cleaver, Edgar J., F.A.A.
Clements, Major Harry Charles.
Contractor, Burjorjee C.
Cornish, G. F.
Denman, Hon. R. D.
Elderton, W. Palin, F.I.A.
Gemmill, William, F.I.A.
Graham, Major J. R. D.
Hannon, Patrick J. H.

Heron, David, M.A.
Hind, Robert, J.P.
Hooper, Frederick.
Khras, Minocher J. S.
Knibbs, George H.
Lempfert, R. J. K., M.A.
Lord, Samuel, A.S.A.A.
Magnus, Sir Philip, M.P.
Rutter, Frank Roy.
Simon, André L.
Stanley of Alderley, Lord.
Stock, Edward J., A.I.A.
Tebb, W. Scott, M.A., M.D.
Templeton, Col. J. Montgomery, C.M.G., V.D., F.I.A.
Wilson, Walter.
Wyldbore-Smith, E. C.

Two Honorary Fellows also were elected :—

Raseri, Professor Enrico. | Westergaard, Professor Harald.

---

* Life Fellow.
c Ex-Member of the Council.
d Donor to the Library.
p Contributed a Paper to the Society's Transactions.

The financial condition of the Society is shown in the Auditors' report [*vide* Appendices A(i), A(ii)]. In the estimate of assets [A(ii)], the values of the invested stocks held by the Society have been taken at current prices. On 1st January, 1906, there was a balance from 1905 of 653*l.* 17*s.* ; the receipts of the year were 2,274*l.* 2*s.* 9*d.*, and the expenditure was 1,988*l.* 13*s.* 3*d.*, leaving a balance of 939*l.* 6*s.* 6*d.* on 31st December, an increase of 285*l.* 9*s.* 6*d.* from that of 1905. Details for the last twenty-five years are given in Appendix B. The cordial thanks of the Council have been tendered to the Auditors for their honorary services in auditing the Treasurer's accounts for the past year.

The excess of income over expenditure during the year was mainly due to the receipts from the Guy Bequest, which have enabled the Council to increase their invested funds by 600*l.* The question of the best means of utilising the additional funds now available is still under consideration, but in the meantime the financial position of the Society is being strengthened by the accumulation of dividends.

The contributions to the Society's transactions presented at the Ordinary Meetings of the Session, 1906-07, have been as follows :—

1906.

I.—20th November .... MARTIN, Sir Richard Biddulph, Bart. Presidential Address : "The Electoral Swing of the Pendulum."

II.—18th December .... HARRIS, Wm. J., and the Rev. Kenneth A. LAKE. Estimates of the Realizable Wealth of the United Kingdom, based mostly in the Estate Duty Returns.

1907.

III.—15th January .... HOOKER, R. H. Correlation of the Weather and Crops.

IV.—19th February .... YULE, G. Udny. Statistics of Production and the "Census of Production Act (1906)."

V.—19th March ... . HUMPHREYS, Noel A. The Alleged Increase of Insanity.

VI.—16th April .... LARK, Albert E. The Herring Fishery.

VII.—14th May .... EVERSLEY, Right Hon. Lord. The Decline in Number of Agricultural Labourers in Great Britain.

VIII.—18th June .... ADAMS, W. G. S. Some Considerations Relating to the Position of the Small Holding in the United Kingdom.

The attendance at the ordinary meetings has been generally satisfactory, and the thanks of the Society are due to those Fellows who have contributed so largely, by the reading of papers, to the maintenance of public interest in the Society's proceedings.

The growth of the Society's Library, and the extent to which it is used by Fellows of the Society and others, are shown in Appendix C. The monthly average number of books lent during 1906 was 55, and that of borrowers 31. The total number of Fellows and others using the Library during the year was 699, or an average of 58 persons per month.

The printing of the new Catalogue of the Library has been commenced, and it is hoped that the work will be published during the present year. In connection therewith, a complete index of the Society's *Journal* is in course of preparation, and will be issued as a separate volume.

In response to a request made by the International Statistical Institute at its last meeting, a bibliography of works dealing with the prices of grain has been prepared by the Librarian under the direction of the Hon. Foreign Secretary, and will be presented to the Institute at its meeting in Copenhagen in August next.

The Council appointed Dr. Dudfield and Mr. G. Udny Yule to represent the Society on a deputation to the Prime Minister in February last, to urge the desirability of the institution by Government of an Anthropometric Survey.

The Council have appointed Sir Shirley Murphy and Dr. Dudfield as delegates to the Second International Congress on School Hygiene, to be held in London in August next.

The thanks of the Society are due to Mr. G. Udny Yule for the gift of a valuable collection of books relating to the theory of statistics which he has presented to the Library.

Under the conditions laid down in the regulations for the award of the Guy Medal, the Council have awarded a medal in gold to Professor Edgeworth, M.A., D.C.L., for his extraordinary services to statistical science, and for his many important and valuable contributions to the transactions of the Society. They have also awarded a medal in silver to Mr. Noel A. Humphreys, I.S.O., for his paper on "The Alleged Increase of Insanity," which was read before the Society on 19th March.

The subject selected for essays in competition for the Howard Medal in 1907-08 is "The Cost, Conditions, and Results of Hospital "Relief in London."

The following Fellows (nominated in accordance with Bye-law 14) are recommended for election as President, Council, and Officers of the Society for the Session 1907-08 :—

PRESIDENT.
The Right Hon. Sir Charles Wentworth Dilke, Bart., M.P.

COUNCIL.

William M. Acworth, M.A.
Sir J. Athelstane Baines, C.S.I.
*James Bonar, M.A., LL.D.
*Edward Bond.
Arthur L. Bowley, M.A.
Sir Edward W. Brabrook, C.B., F.S.A.
George G. Chisholm, M.A., B.Sc., F.R.G.S.
Sir Ernest Clarke, M.A., F.L.S., F.S.A.
Timothy A. Coghlan, I.S.O.
Nathaniel L. Cohen.
Richard F. Crawford.
Reginald Dudfield, M.A., M.B.
Sir William C. Dunbar, Bart., C.B.
Prof. F. Y. Edgeworth, M.A., D.C.L.

A. Wilson Fox, C.B.
*Sir John Glover, J.P.
Frederick Hendriks, F.I.A.
*Noel A. Humphreys, I.S.O.
Arthur W. Waterlow King.
Prof. C. S. Loch, D.C.L.
Bernard Mallet.
*Theodore Morison, M.A.
Sir Shirley F. Murphy, M.R.C.S.
Francis G. P. Neison, F.I.A.
*George Paish.
L. L. Price, M.A.
Sir Lesley C. Probyn, K.C.V.O.
R. Henry Rew.
David A. Thomas, M.A., M.P.
G. Udny Yule.

Those marked * are new Members of Council.

TREASURER.
Sir Richard Biddulph Martin, Bart.

HONORARY SECRETARIES.
R. H. Rew.   A. Wilson Fox, C.B.   G. Udny Yule.

HONORARY FOREIGN SECRETARY.
Sir J. Athelstane Baines, C.S.I.

The abstract of receipts and payments, and the estimate of assets and liabilities on 31st December, 1906, together with the report of the Auditors on the accounts for the year 1906, are appended.

Signed on behalf of the Council,

RICHARD B. MARTIN,
President.

J. ATHELSTANE BAINES, ⎫
R. H. REW, ⎬ *Hon. Secretaries.*
A. WILSON FOX, ⎭

J. H. MAGEE,
Assistant Secretary.

APPENDICES TO ANNUAL REPORT.

A (i).—ABSTRACT *of* RECEIPTS *and* PAYMENTS *for the* YEAR *ending* 31*st* DECEMBER, 1906.

RECEIPTS.	£ s. d.		PAYMENTS.	£
Balance in Bank on Deposit, 31st December, 1905 ...... £300 – –			Rent and Taxes:—	
			Rent ... £356 5 –	
Balance in Bank on Current Account, 31st December, 1905 .... 333 14 6			Taxes 56 6 2	
			—————— £412 11 2	
			Less sublet ...... 12 10 –	
Balance of Petty Cash Account...... 15 11 7			——————	400
,, Postage Account 4 10 11			Fire, Lights, and Water	47 1
			Furniture and Repairs	24
	653 17 –		Salaries, Wages, and Pension ...	554
			Journal, Printing...... £565 12 3	
			,, Shorthand Reporting 26 10 8	
Dividends on Consols 305 – 8			,, Literary Services 52 18 2	
,, on G.N.R. Stock 15 4 –			——————	645
Interest on Deposit ... 13 3 1			Ordinary Meeting Expenses	21
	333 7 9		Advertising	29 1
			Postage and delivery of Journals..	60 1
			Stationery and Sundry Printing...	57
			Library	95
Annual Subscriptions:—			Incidental Expenses	51
58 Arrears .... 121 16 –			Guy Medal	1 1
623 for 1906 .... 1,308 6 –				
16 in Advance ...... 33 12 –				
——	1,463 14 –		Balance on Deposit at Bank, 31st December, 1906...... £500 – –	
697			Balance on Current Account at Bank, 31st December, 1906 .... 431 14 8	
Compositions .... 81 18 –			Balance of Petty Cash 5 15 8	
Journal Sales .... 225 1 –			,, Postage Account............ 1 16 2	
Advertisements in Journal .... 44 2 –				939
Sale of Surplus Books .... 126 – –				
Total £2,927 19 9			Total £2,927 1	

(Signed)

" CHAS. ATKINSON,		
" A. H. BAILEY,	}	*Auditor*
" S. CHAPMAN,		

" 31*st January,* 1907.

A (ii).—ESTIMATE *of* ASSETS *and* LIABILITIES *on* 31*st* DECEMBER, 1906.

LIABILITIES.	£	s.	d.
Harrison and Sons, for December "Journal"	123	4	8
Miscellaneous Accounts	162	8	7
16 Subscriptions received in advance	33	12	–
	319	5	3
Balance in favour of the Society (Exclusive of (1) Books in Library; (2) Journals, &c., in Stock; and (3) Pictures, Furniture, and Fixtures)	12,160	14	7
	£12,479	19	10

ASSETS.		£	
Balance on Deposit Account £500 – –			
Cash Balances 439 6 6		939	
3,000*l.* Consols		2,580	
Guy Bequest, 9,843*l.* 7*s.* 10*d.*, Consols		8,465	
400*l.* G.N.R. Preferred Converted Ordinary Stock		404	
Arrears of Subscriptions recoverable .... estimated		84	
Sundry debtors			
		£	

(Signed) " CHAS. ATKINSON,

" A. H. BAILEY, }*Auditors*

" 31*st January*, 1907. " S. CHAPMAN,

A (iii).—BUILDING FUND (ESTABLISHED 10*th July*, 1873), BALANCE SHEET, *on* 31*st* DECEMBER, 1906.

This Fund is invested in Metropolitan Consolidated 3*l.* 10*s.* per Cent. Stock. On 31st December, 1905, the Fund was invested in 345*l.* 1*s.* 5*d.* Stock. With dividends received during 1906, additional Stock to the amount of 11*l.* 3*s.* 2*d.* purchased by the Bank of England for the Society. Accordingly, on the December, 1906, the total investment amounted to 356*l.* 4*s.* 7*d.* Stock.

A (iv).—"REPORT OF THE AUDITORS FOR 1906.

"*The Auditors appointed to examine the Treasurer's Accounts of the Society for the Year* 1906,

"REPORT :—

"*That they have compared the Entries in the Books with the several Vouchers for the same, from the* 1st *January to* 31st *December,* 1906, *and find them correct, showing the Receipts (including a Balance of* 653l. 17s. *from* 1905) *to have been* 2,927l. 19s. 9d., *and the Payments* 1,988l. 13s. 3d., *leaving a Balance in favour of the Society of* 939l. 6s. 6d. *at the* 31st *December,* 1906.

"*They have also had before them an Estimate of the Assets and Liabilities of the Society at the same date, leaving an excess of Assets over Liabilities of* 12,160l. 14s. 7d., *exclusive of* (1) *Books in the Library ;* (2) *Journals, &c., in Stock ; and* (3) *Pictures, Furniture, and Fixtures.*

"*The Building Fund at the end of the year* 1905 *was invested in* 345l. 1s. 5d. *Metropolitan Consolidated Three and a Half per Cent. Stock, and, with the Dividends received during* 1906, *additional Stock to the amount of* 11l. 3s. 2d. *was purchased by the Bank of England for the Society. Accordingly, on the* 31st *December,* 1906, *the total investment amounted to* 356l. 4s. 7d. *Stock.*

"*They have verified the Investments of the Society's General Funds and of the Building Fund, and also the Banker's Balance, all of which were found correct.*

"*They further find that at the end of the year* 1905 *the number of Fellows on the list was* 911, *which number was diminished in the course of the year to the extent of* 63, *by Death, Resignation, or Default and that* 43 *new Fellows were elected or restored to the list, leaving on the list on the* 31st *December,* 1906, 891 *Fellows of the Society.*

(Signed)   " CHAS. ATKINSON, ⎫
              " A. H. BAILEY,   ⎬ *Auditors.*"
              " S. CHAPMAN,   ⎭

" 31st *January,* 1907.

B.—Statement of the Condition of the Society in the last Twenty-five Years 1882-1906.

Year.	Number of Fellows on 31st December.	Number of Life Fellows included therein.	Losses during Year by Deaths, &c.	Gains by Election, &c., during Year.	Income from					Expenditure.			Amount Invested on 31st December.	Year.
					Annual Subscriptions.	Compositions.	Journal Sales.	Investments and other Sources.	All Sources.	Total.	On Journal.	On Library.		
					£	£	£	£	£	£	£	£	£	
1882	786	135	63	42	1,291	189	227	131	1,838	1,782 a	553	60	3,200	1882
'83	860	139	41	115	1,361	126	150	141	1,778	1,943 a	585	49	3,500	'83
'84	909	150	57	106	1,447	294	207	1,198	3,146 b	3,088 c	645	38	2,500	'84
'85	928	148	55	74	1,462	63	188	349	2,062 d	2,070 e	625	27	2,500	'85
'86	943	156	70	85	1,583	231	180	92	2,086	2,106 e	735	32	2,500	'86
'87	977	160	59	93	1,621	126	188	94	2,029	2,135 f	609	87	2,500	'87
'88	1,059	172	58	140	1,686	334	171	101	2,292	2,003	711	58	2,500	'88
'89	1,060	175	69	70	1,678	126	229	82	2,115	2,003 g	623	146	2,500	'89
1890	1,063	177	65	68	1,764	84	155	94	2,097	2,096 a	567	68	2,900	1890
'91	1,019	172	80	36	1,707	42	146	181	2,076 h	1,957 i	582	172	2,900	'91
'92	994	171	70	45	1,634	84	158	104	1,980	1,883 j	539	94	2,900	'92
'93	964	176	66	36	1,560	124	128	92	1,904	1,921	578	63	2,900	'93
'94	933	180	67	36	1,491	105	152	82	1,830	1,904	649	75	2,900	'94
'95	928	180	59	54	1,468	63	180	82	1,793	1,823 k	576	56	2,900	'95
'96	910	181	48	30	1,478	42	168	84	1,772	1,787	571	44	2,900	'96
'97	892	182	58	40	1,472	145	157	83	1,857	1,986 l	650	50	2,900	'97
'98	878	180	57	43	1,451	115	182	105	1,853	1,825	609	55	3,300 m	'98
'99	896	181	44	62	1,432	95	167	127	1,821	1,805	564	33	3,300	'99
1900	923	179	36	63	1,514	21	189	148	1,872	1,817	521	53	3,300	1900
'01	926	177	49	52	1,464	63	211	129	1,867	1,823	518	42	3,300	'01
'02	932	177	52	58	1,504	21	255	152	1,932	1,839	543	73	3,300	'02
'03	939	174	49	56	1,517	84	293	151	2,045	1,875	593	91	3,300	'03
'04	925	175	58	44	1,407	124	253	152	1,936	1,931 a	521	92	3,400	'04
'05	911	178	59	45	1,465	168	220	220	2,073	2,074 n	665	67	11,975 o	'05
'06	891	177	63	43	1,464	82	225	408	2,274 p	1,988	645	95	11,449	'06

a Includes purchase of Government stock.　　b Includes sale of 1,000l. stock.　　c Includes expense of moving to new premises.
d Includes Dr. Guy's legacy of 250l.　　e Includes cost of Jubilee Volume.　　f Includes cost of Catalogue and Index, and of Charter.
g Includes cost of part iv of Index to Journal.　　h Includes Mrs. Lovegrove's legacy of 100l.

C.—*Numbers of Books Added to the Library and Lent, and Numbers of Borrowers from the Library in 1905, 1906, and part of 1907.*

Months.	Works Received.*			Books Lent.						Borrowers.			Fellows and Visitors using the Library.		
	1905.	1906.	1907.	1905.		1906.		1907.		1905.	1906.	1907.	1905.	1906.	1907.
				Works.	Vols.	Works.	Vols.	Works.	Vols.						
January	396	320	429	55	67	49	62	54	68	37	30	37	76	53	55
February				81	120	.62	71	86	94	44	42	37	80	70	60
March	363	368	—	53	74	45	55	57	62	34	30	36	70	72	80
April				74	95	32	43	41	55	32	23	27	56	43	71
May	342	359	—	54	71	60	76	80	86	38	41	44	72	56	68
June				59	72	36	39	—	—	36	30	—	61	58	—
July				38	47	32	37	—	—	20	19	—	50	41	—
August	384	370	—	38	43	65	69	—	—	23	36	—	53	29	—
September				35	37	36	46	—	—	25	26	—	104	67	—
October				36	48	50	64	—	—	23	30	—	85	70	—
November				52	63	59	60	—	—	28	40	—	68	74	—
December				44	51	37	43	—	—	29	27	—	51	66	—
Year	1,485	1,417	—	619	788	563	665	—	—	369	374	—	826	699	—
Monthly average	124	118	—	52	65	47	55	—	—	31	31	—	69	58	—

* These are the numbers of entries in the quarterly *Journal* under "Additions to Library," and do not represent volumes; they are also exclusive of about 170 periodicals received yearly.

Proceedings *of the* Seventy-third Annual General Meeting, held on 18th June, 1907.

Sir Richard Biddulph Martin, Bart., President, in the Chair.

Sir J. Athelstane Baines, C.S.I. (Honorary Secretary), read the notice convening the meeting, and the Minutes of the last Ordinary Meeting were read and confirmed.

The President announced that under Rule III of the rules for the award of the Guy Medal, the Council had awarded the Guy Medal in gold to Professor F. Y. Edgeworth, M.A., D.C.L., for his extraordinary services to statistical science, and for his many important and valuable contributions to the transactions of the Society ; and that they had also awarded a medal in silver to Mr. Noel A. Humphreys, I.S.O., for his paper entitled "The Alleged Increase of Insanity," which was read before the Society on 19th March.

The Report of the Council was taken as read.

The President moved "that the Report of the Council, the Abstract of Receipts and Payments, the Estimate of Assets and Liabilities, and the Report of the Auditors be adopted, entered on the Minutes, and printed in the *Journal.*"

The Right Hon. Lord Eversley seconded the motion, which was carried unanimously.

The Honorary Secretary having read out the list of defaulters, the President declared that they had ceased to be Fellows of the Society.

The ballot was then taken, and the Scrutineers (Messrs. Jesse Argyle and Sydney Young) reported that the proposed President, Council, and Honorary Officers for the ensuing session had been duly elected.

The President moved a cordial vote of thanks to the Scrutineers, which was carried unanimously.

The President announced that the subject appointed for the Howard Medal Essay Competition, session 1907-08, was "The Cost, Conditions, and Results of Hospital Relief in London."

Sir WILLIAM C. PLOWDEN, K.C.S.I., moved a cordial vote of thanks to the President, Council and Officers for their services during the past year. He remarked that these offices, like many others of the highest importance in this country, were entirely unpaid; and the only acknowledgment which they could make for the great services rendered to the Society was to pass a very hearty vote of thanks to them.

Mr. J. W. SOWREY seconded the motion, which was carried unanimously.

The PRESIDENT, in response, said it was a great pleasure to him to occupy the Chair, and thus be in a position to return thanks for the Council and Officers. He had felt it a great honour to be allowed to occupy for one year a chair which had been filled by so many eminent men, whose names stood high in the history of the country. They were much indebted to the Honorary Secretaries, without whose assiduity and zeal he did not know how the Society could exist.

The Right Hon. Sir CHARLES W. DILKE, Bart., M.P., said that he felt that the honour conferred upon him in electing him as President was very great, because he was not a scientific statistician, but simply a user of statistics. The amateurishness of the amateur became more evident in all the sciences every day as the sciences deepened and became more scientific. There was one subject in which he had practical experience and which he thought he might promote by bringing it before the Society, namely, the question of the official statistics in this country, the imperfections of which seemed to him to be conspicuous, and had been illustrated on more than one occasion in papers read there. The matter had never been dealt with as a whole, and compared with the systems which existed, for instance, in the Colonies, or compared with ideal systems which might be devised. He was afraid that an over-worked member of Parliament could not attend at all the Ordinary Meetings of the Society, and that had made him somewhat reluctant to accept the office, but he had been told that it would not be necessary for him always to attend. He should of course feel it his duty to give all the time necessary, apart from such formal attendances, to attend elsewhere to the business of the Council. He proposed to devote his energy mainly to the consideration of that problem, which eminently deserved consideration, the official statistics of this country.

The PRESIDENT said they might all congratulate the Society on having elected so distinguished a President, and if he carried out what he had foreshadowed, the Society would be indebted to him for information of permanent value.

MISCELLANEA.

Dr. Joseph Körösy—M. G. Olanesco.

WE regret to have to record the loss of two Hon. Fellows of the Society of great distinction in the branches of statistics to which they had respectively devoted their attention.

Dr. Joseph Körösy is well known not only for his remarkable industry in connection with municipal vital statistics but also for his unremitting efforts to secure uniformity of returns at the census of the different States represented in the International Statistical Institute. Beginning life as a journalist, at the age of 25, he was induced by the Municipality of Pest to harness his imagination to the comparatively jog-trot career of urban statistics, in preference to allowing it the untrammelled freedom it might have enjoyed in the record of general history from day to day. He practically created the municipal department over which he presided for nearly thirty-seven years and at the head of which he died last summer. It was here he began to collect the vast amount of detailed information upon which he based his well-known studies of birth-rates and fecundity, published in English, French, and German, for he was an excellent linguist. So far as his work related to the great city with which he was so intimately connected, he had reason to be proud of its results, since upon it was founded the greater part of the sanitary administration which has effected a remarkable improvement in the hygienic conditions of that crowded and partially-oriental population. The inferences he deduced from his data, however, were occasionally apt to be extended beyond the sphere to which they legitimately belonged, for Dr. Körösy was a stalwart advocate of the system of "type-studies," under which the results of minute researches amongst a restricted community are assumed to be established for the population at large. It is permissible to conjecture that the tendency thus induced underlay the intense importance attached by Dr. Körösy to international uniformity in census details which others are inclined to place outside the category of subjects susceptible of useful international comparison, an importance which he attached, also, to the adoption of synchronism in the enumeration of all civilised countries. His enthusiasm in advocating his cherished schemes or conclusions, his unfailing good humour, and the amusing resourcefulness with which he parried all attacks or brought forward amended suggestions, not to mention the real statistical genius he brought to bear upon complicated investigations, all tended to make him welcome in any discussion in which he could be induced to participate. He was unable to attend the Institute's Congress in London in 1905, but on several previous occasions he has been here and taken part in the proceedings of the Society.

The untimely death of M. Olanesco was due to a railway accident, in which both he and his wife perished. They both belonged to old and distinguished Roumanian families, and had interested themselves in educational and charitable work amongst their fellow countrymen. M. Olanesco studied in Paris as well as in Bucharest, and, after taking his degree, entered the Civil Service, where he filled successively the posts of Director of Customs and Chief Secretary in the Ministry of Finance. In the former capacity he published an important work on the Geography of Customs Duties. In 1889 he took to political life, on the Conservative side, and, after several years of active work as deputy, he became Vice-President of the Senate, a post which he held until 1901. He was an assiduous member of the International Statistical Institute, to the records of which his last noteworthy contribution was a report upon "La Statistique internationale de prêts hypothécaïres." He was elected an Hon. Fellow of this Society in 1896.   J.A.B.

NOTES ON ECONOMIC AND STATISTICAL WORKS.

CONTENTS:

PAGE

1.—Jacquart (C.). Statistique et science sociale 334
2.—Galton (F.). Probability:.. 335
3.—Annuario statistico della città italiane 335
4.—Schuster (E.). Inheritance of ability 336
5.—Bertillon (J.). Fréquence des causes de décès à Paris........ 337
6.—Pearson (K.). Statistics of pulmonary tuberculosis 338
7.—Macrosty (H. W.). Trust movement 338
8.—Macgregor (D. H.). Industrial combination 340
9.—Condizioni della classe operaia in Milano 344
10.—Child labor in the United States.................. 346
11.—Gainsborough Commission. Life and labour in Germany 347
12. —Black (Clementina). Sweated industry 349
13.—Fisher (Irving). Capital and income 351

PAGE

14.—Wolff (H. W.). Co-operative banking 353
15.—Holt (B. W.). Gold supply and prosperity 356
16.—Lauterbach (E.). Staats u. Kommunal-Besteuerung......... ... 358
17.—Halle (E. von). Die Weltwirtschaft 359
18.—Yermoloff (A.). La Russie agricole 360
19.—Martinez (A. B.) Argentine au 20e siècle 363
20.—Morison (T.). · Industrial organisation of an Indian province 364
21.—Lethbridge (Sir R.). India and preference... 366
22. —Ballard (A.). Domesday inquest 368
23.—Collings (Jesse). Land reform 370
24.—Slater (G.). The English peasantry 372
25.—Other new publications......... 375

1.—*Statistique et Science sociale : aperçus généraux. Conférences données à l'Institut supérieur de Philosophie de Louvain.* Par Camille Jacquart. 120 pp., 8vo. Bruxelles : Desclée, de Brouwer et Cie, 1907.

This little volume is based on a short course of lectures by M. Jacquart, who is the author of several tracts on the vital statistics of Belgium which are in the Society's library. After a short introduction, four chapters follow on statistical administration, statistics as science, statistical method, and some difficulties of interpretation of statistics. A brief historical sketch is given of the rise and growth of official statistics and an outline of the different methods of organisation (in connection with the separate Government departments, under a centralised bureau and so forth). In the next chapter, the question is debated whether there is a statistical science, a question which the author— rightly we think—inclines to answer in the negative : " Je considère la statistique comme une excellente méthode d'observation des faits collectifs, mais ce n'est qu'une méthode." " Statistical method " is usually held to cover a great deal more than a method of observation, but, following his somewhat narrow definition,.

M. Jacquart's chapter on method deals solely with such fundamental matters as the facts suitable for investigation, the
questionnaire, &c.; mathematical method is ignored, except for a
passing reference to elementary arithmetic (p. 81). Stress is laid
on the necessity for a critical study of the original data and for
careful and unbiassed investigation, and in the last chapter a few
examples (statistics of illiteracy, marriage and longevity, &c.)
are discussed as illustrations. The treatment is fair and lucid,
but we should like to carry some of the discussion a little further.

If we might make a small criticism, it is that the style seems at
times unduly flippant. The candidate for initiation should approach
La Statistique with respect; M. Jacquart merely beseeches him to
greet her with his least ironical smile . . . . Surely this is not the
best way to begin ?   G.U.Y.

2.—*Probability, the Foundation of Eugenics.* (*The Herbert Spencer
Lecture.*) By Francis Galton, F.R.S. 30 pp., 8vo. Oxford:
Clarendon Press, 1907. Price 1s. net.

We regret to notice, from *The Times* report, that Mr. Galton,
owing to a slight accident, was unable to deliver the Herbert Spencer
lecture, which was read in his absence on June 5th by Mr. Arthur
Galton. The author gives a short sketch of the history of "eugenics,"
with references to his own papers on the subject and the work of
Professor Pearson and the late Professor Weldon. In connection
with the application of the theory of probability to the subject, an
interesting outline is given of a short course of object-lessons in the
methods of biometry. In concluding the lecture, Mr. Galton points
out that human action is guided "less by certainty and by probability than by assurance to a greater or less degree," and assurance
is largely dependent on custom, prejudice, and other unreasonable
influences; but "whenever public opinion is strongly moved it will
lead to action, however contradictory it may be to previous custom
and sentiment," and "it is reasonable to expect that it will be
strongly exerted in favour of eugenics when a sufficiency of evidence
shall have been collected to make the truths on which it rests plain
to all."   G.U.Y.

3.—*Annuario Statistico della Città Italiane.* Anno I, 1906.
300 pp., 4to. Firenze: Alfani e Venturi, 1906.

At a conference of the mayors of the principal Italian towns,
held on the 25th March, 1905, at Florence, on the invitation and
under the presidency of Senator Niccolini, Syndic of that city, it
was unanimously agreed to proceed with the publication of a Year-
book of Statistics relating to the population, hygiene, public services,
and finances of the larger municipalities of Italy. The plan for this
work was drawn up by Professor Ugo Giusti, Principal of the
Statistical Department of the Municipal Council of Florence, who
was subsequently entrusted with the task of collecting and editing
the material for the first volume. The participating municipalities
contributed towards the cost of the scheme in proportion to their

population, and agreed to purchase a certain number of copies of the Annual when published.

Schedules of questions were issued by Professor Giusti to 116 councils of towns with over 20,000 inhabitants, and after much correspondence and solicitation these were returned with more or less complete answers in 88 cases. The material thus collected was supplemented by information furnished by the Directors of the Meteorological Observatories; tables of births, deaths, and marriages, and causes of death, compiled by the General Bureau of Statistics; postal and telegraph statistics, prepared by the Ministry of Posts and Telegraphs; a table of the contributions to lotteries, by the Ministry of Finance; and a report on municipal trading, by the Ministry of the Interior. The principal official publications were also consulted and utilised for certain tables.

From these various sources the first volume of the statistical Year-book now before us has been compiled. It contains seventeen chapters dealing with (1) meteorology; (2) area and population, births, deaths, marriages, causes of death, occupations of heads of families, migration; (3) prices of land, rents, and building statistics; (4) roads and highways, public cleansing, gardens and open spaces; (5) water and lighting: cost of water, gas, and electricity; (6) markets and abattoirs; (7) public instruction; (8) libraries, museums, municipal theatres, orchestras, and bands; (9) relief of the poor and sick, charitable organisations, municipal pawnshops, hospitals, mutual aid societies; (10) police and public safety; (11) municipal expenditure; (12) local rates; (13) local indebtedness; (14) municipal employees and pensioners; (15) commercial activity and means of communication: inns, hotels, cafés, theatres, music halls: public and private conveyances: automobiles and bicycles: number of horses, mules, asses, oxen, and dogs: railways, tramways, and shipping; postal, telegraph, and telephone statistics; (16) municipal trading; and (17) lotteries.

Professor Giusti is to be congratulated on the compilation of an interesting and comprehensive volume, in spite of the many difficulties he experienced at the outset. He hopes that future issues of this Year-book will eventually present a complete statistical review of urban life in Italy, and he therefore regards it as essential to secure the effective collaboration of the local authorities of all towns with a population of at least 20,000 inhabitants.   R.F.C.

4.—*The Inheritance of Ability.* (*Eugenics Laboratory Memoirs, I.*) By Edgar Schuster, M.A., and Ethel M. Elderton. 42 pp., 4to. London: Dulau, 1907. Price 4s.

In the last volume of the *Journal* (p. 590) we gave a notice of the volume on "Noteworthy Families" (Modern Science), by Mr. Galton and Mr. Schuster, which was the first of the publications of the "Eugenics Record Office of the University of London," founded by Mr. Galton. The office has now been reorganised, and it has been decided to "provide the workers associated with it with a direct channel of publication of their own," the memoirs being issued from time to time through Messrs. Dulau and Co. The present memoir is of high interest. The data are derived from the Oxford class lists and the school lists of Harrow and Charterhouse; the former give material for the discussion of inheritance (father and son) and resemblance between brothers, the latter for resemblance between brothers only. The results are striking. Thus, taking the Oxford lists for sons who took (or should have taken) their degree between 1860 and 1892, the percentages of fathers with first or second class honours were:—For sons who took a first class, 36·2 per cent.; sons with second class, 32·2 per cent.; sons with third class, 29·4 per cent.; sons with fourth class, 24·7 per cent.; sons with pass degree, 13·8 per cent.; sons with no degree, 12·8 per cent. Of course, only those cases are included in which the father as well as one son at least was at Oxford.   G.U.Y.

5.—*De la Fréquence des Principales Causes de Décès à Paris pendant la Seconde Moitié du XIXe Siècle et notamment pendant la Période* 1886-1905. Par Le Dr. Jacques Bertillon, Chef des Travaux Statistiques de la Ville de Paris. 346 pp., la. 8vo. (with numerous illustrations). Paris: Imprimerie Municipale, 1906.

This admirable review was undertaken by Dr. Jacques Bertillon to indicate under what diseases has occurred the fall of mortality which in his statistical report for 1903 he showed to have taken place during the 19th century, especially in its last twenty years. In 1821-25 the general death-rate of Paris per 1,000 inhabitants was 32, in 1901-05 it had fallen to 17·9. The death-rate at ages under 5 is not much more than a third, that at ages 5—10 only one-fourth, and that at ages 5—15 only a third of the rate holding good in 1821-25. The rate of infant mortality, measured in proportion to the living births, has declined from about 158 to 110. One has some hesitation in comparing this figure with the English figure of 128 per 1,000 births, owing to the possibility of differences in the system of registration of births. It would be a most useful piece of work to make comparable infantile death-rate for the great cities of different countries, in which allowance would be made where practicable for differences of methods of registration of births and deaths, especially as bearing on what is meant by "live-born" and "still-born."

The death-rate from typhoid fever in Paris has declined from 88 per 100,000 of population in 1881-85 to 12 in 1901-05, a very great reduction, though the death-rate from this admirable index of sanitation or its deficiencies is still higher than in London, in which it was 9 in 1901-04, and in Berlin 5 in 1896-1900, and in Vienna 6 in 1896-1900.

Measles, as in London, shows no continuous decline, and this disease remains untouched by the methods of preventive medicine hitherto employed. In London the death-rate from this disease is nearly twice as high as in Paris, but much of this excess is owing to the fact that measles as a fatal disease is especially a disease of childhood.

Scarlet fever appears to have never been so formidable a cause of mortality in Paris as in London, and the death-rate in the latter in

1901-04 was 10, as compared with 4 per 100,000 in the former. On the other hand, in the past diphtheria has been more constantly epidemic and a heavier cause of mortality in Paris than in London. Since the introduction of treatment by antitoxin, the death-rate from diphtheria in Paris has become slightly lower than that in London, in which this treatment is not utilised so systematically.

The statistics of tuberculosis form an important section of Dr. Bertillon's report. There is only a small decline in the death-rate from all forms of this disease, viz., from 499 per 100,000 inhabitants in 1886-90 to 456 in 1901-05.

The death-rate from pulmonary tuberculosis was 441 per 100,000 in 1881-85, 436 in 1886-90, 408 in 1891-95, 377 in 1896-1900, and 358 in 1901-05. In London the death-rate from this disease has declined in fifty years from 286 to 161 per 100,000 of population ; in Berlin from 353 in 1871-80 to 211 in 1901-04.

It is not necessary to quote from the figures relating to cancer, alcoholism, and the many other causes of death which Dr. Bertillon in succession passes under review. We know of no summary of international vital statistics giving so much valuable information in a readily available form ; and the gratitude of all statisticians is due to Dr. Bertillon for having accomplished so laborious and so useful a work. A.N.

6.—*A First Study of the Statistics of Pulmonary Tuberculosis.* (*Drapers' Company Research Memoirs : Studies on National Deterioration, II.*) By Karl Pearson, F.R.S. 26 pp., 4to. London : Dulau, 1907. Price 3s.

The title of this memoir is somewhat misleading. It is almost solely a study of certain statistics placed at the disposal of Professor Pearson by Dr. W. C. Rivers, of the Crossley Sanatorium, Frodsham, and affording data for the discussion of inheritance. It is concluded that "the diathesis of pulmonary tuberculosis is certainly inherited," "there is no reduced fertility in the case of tuberculous stocks," and "the elder offspring . . . appear subject to tuberculosis at a very much higher rate than the younger members " (pp. 24-25). "There is an anti-social disregard for natural eugenics in the conduct of medical men who can write to the public press that the marriage, or even inter-marriage, of members of tuberculous stocks is of no social detriment, provided they live with a good supply of fresh air " (p. 14). G.U.Y.

7.—*The Trust Movement in British Industry.* By Henry W. Macrosty, B.A. 398 pp., 8vo. London : Longmans, Green and Co., 1907.

Mr. Macrosty has conferred a great benefit upon the student of the course of modern industrial combinations by the publication of this careful record of the developments that have taken place in the United Kingdom during recent years.

His object has not been to construct a critical treatise—the development being probably of too recent occurrence to enable a balanced judgment to be formed—but "to detail, with as little bias

.as possible, as many facts as could be ascertained in relation to the modern organisation of (British) industry."

His choice of the United Kingdom as the best field for studying the growth of combination was apparently dictated by the fact that "this problem is being worked out in Britain free from complications of tariffs or secret railway agreements." "Where trust methods have been obviously illegal, or where they flourish behind an oppressive tariff," says Mr. Macrosty, "what to do is plain. But the case is different in the United Kingdom, where the continuance of amalgamations and associations depends solely upon their efficiency as instruments of production and distribution. Too little attention has hitherto been given to this normal development of combination, and it has too often been lumped in the same condemnation with the most oppressive American trust or German Kartell." . . . "The point cannot be too much emphasized that we have not in this country to face the American problem or the German problem, but a problem of our own."

Mr. Macrosty therefore proceeds to analyse the recent history of industrial combination in the different British industries, grouping them under general headings of (*a*) the iron and steel industries, (*b*) the extractive industries, (*c*) the textile industries, (*d*) the chemical industries, (*e*) grain and milling, (*f*) the tobacco and liquor trades, (*g*) the retail trades, (*h*) the transport industries, and (*i*) miscellaneous industries.

The story—as the book is read through—leaves an impression upon the mind that the process that has been in operation in nearly all these industries during recent years has been curiously unscientific. Probably each step forward seemed at the moment inevitable, but looking from afar on the whole field of action, the record is one of sanguine anticipation, disappointing realisation, and final reconstruction ; the principal agents in this career of distress being not amateurs but the shrewdest business men of the nation.

The truth seems to be that these men are, perforce, the pioneers in a new field of civilisation, and as they meet with new forces, different in character from those to which they have been accustomed, they are compelled to recede with a broken and discredited organisation. It would be easy, however, to take too despondent a view from the history of these failures. The process of squeezing water out of a combination is an exceedingly painful one, but it need not necessarily destroy the essential soundness of the concern. The error was the permeation of the original structure with water and the formulation of theories of expansive properties that the organisation did not possess and never could have possessed.

The history of the Calico Printers' Association may be cited—among many given by Mr. Macrosty with an illustrative wealth of detail—as typical of a very usual course of procedure. The project was an ambitious one. The combination included 46 firms of printers and 13 merchants—59 firms and companies in all. The plant included 830 printing machines, 277,264 cotton spindles, and 6,656 power looms. The prospectus, issued in December, 1899, stated that the business acquired comprised about 85 per cent. of the calico printing industry in Great Britain. The Association included nearly every leading house in the trade, and the directors "emphasized their opinion that as the outcome of the amalgamation far different and more profitable results may be confidently expected in the near future than have been realised for many years past."

At the first annual meeting, the Chairman was discouraging. "It took many months before they fully realised the magnitude of the task of organising so large a company on suitable lines." . . . . "In plain English (the directors) were not equal to the task" . . . . "The situation created . . . . was so novel that . . . . serious mistakes had been made." Finally, the results became so bad that a committee of investigation was appointed, and a new board of directors was elected to carry out their drastic recommendation of reform. Thenceforward the organisation for three years paid $2\frac{1}{2}$ per cent. on its ordinary capital and 4 per cent. in 1905-06. "It must not be concluded," says Mr. Macrosty, "that the higher dividend is proof of an essentially stronger position. . . . The works in the Association have to bear the burden of practically paying the closed works not to compete."

On the other hand, there are organisations, such as those of Messrs. S. and P. Coats, who seem to have followed a particularly judicious policy from the beginning. They combined only the strong competitors, and trusted to their superior efficiency and to the economies of concentrated manufacture to reduce the competition of outsiders to a negligible quantity." Their system of working enabled "every half-penny stamp to be traced," and under the circumstances it is scarcely surprising to read of net profits approaching 3,000,000*l.* on a capital of 12,000,000*l.*, and of a reserve fund of 4,500,000*l.*

The problem of the relationship of the State to these strong combinations is one that Mr. Macrosty considers not yet to be ripe for treatment, and his view is probably accurate, though it would be well perhaps for the State to hold a watching brief, and at all events to be familiar with every turn in the affairs of these industrial organisations. "The position of the British combination in regard to the interests of the community may be summed up as not at present dangerous, but containing, like every new development, great and unknown possibilities alike for good and evil."

Altogether Mr. Macrosty is to be cordially congratulated on the noteworthy contribution to historical knowledge that he has made. Much discrimination has been shown in the choice of material, which has evidently been collected with indomitable industry. But Mr. Macrosty has probably quite enjoyed the task, for he tells us "hunting down an association is quite an exhilarating sport: there is no cover so unlikely in which the game may not be started." O.F.

8.—*Industrial Combination.* By D. H. Macgregor, M.A. 245 pp., 8vo. London: George Bell and Sons, 1906.

From the detached ground of English soil "where trusts and cartels have not yet become a matter of public agitation," from the still more detached atmosphere of Trinity College, Cambridge, where the fierce shouts of the conflict of the world's industrial armies can only distantly be heard, comes this calm and acutely reasoned analysis of the present situation.

Industrial combination — in Mr. Macgregor's view — is not monopolistic. To allege that combination has superseded competition, urges Mr. Macgregor, is "untrue both in fact and in analysis." The strongest industrial combination, in order to hold its position, "requires to maintain the strongest competitive force within its own structure," and "in the external market it employs against its rivals competitive methods of exceptional severity. There is no competition like that between one or two great organisations."

Moreover, it is pointed out that combination does not necessarily affect the ethical duties of man to man. As in independent competition, such practices as rebates, boycotts, and discriminated prices flourish, and combination—or as it might perhaps more accurately be termed, associated competition—tends to accentuate these practices. Combination is not necessarily more moral nor less moral than individual action. It is only more powerful either for moralisation or for extortion. This is in a sense true, but perhaps gives hardly sufficient allowance to the spirit of comradeship and human sympathy which grows up between the workers in all large industrial organisations that sometimes tends to modify for a time the strict scientific working of the law of economic necessity.

Mr. Macgregor rightly insists on the view that industrial combination is not a new form of organisation that has sprung up and supplanted the "natural system of competition." Competition, he urges, is the essence of any and every economic system. It has various methods of working—"the independent or the combined method or mixtures of the two." "Industrial competition . . . is a competitive method based on that foresight by which the Darwinian Law is qualified in the sphere of human activity . . . The type which survives and is representative of its period owes its position to its strength as a competitor, on its power to take as well as on its power to give advantage."

The factors of competing strength are analysed under the heads of "productive efficiency," "risk," "bargaining strength," and "resource," in four carefully argued chapters.

The causes which operate in the formation of trusts and cartels are then examined, and it is pointed out that in over-capitalised industries the absence of agreement among the producers will, under conditions of decreasing cost, lead to a price-war in which business is conducted by many firms at a loss ; . . . or, again, in a rising market, each individual firm may be afraid to raise its prices lest the others do not follow. . . . The ups and downs, the fluctuations and uncertainties so created, will suggest to producers the remedy of agreement or association to regulate price and output, and avoid wasteful competition.

To form an effective trust or cartel the following conditions are thought to be necessary :—

1. The parties should be few enough in number to come to terms readily.
2. They should be near one another.
3. There shall not be great differences in the competing strength of the firms which combine.
4. There should be some degree of uniformity in the products of the firms.
5. Previous opportunities for communication between the combining parties ' are held to facilitate the process of formation.
6. In early stages the help of capital is required.

A good deal of attention is given to the question of the influence of tariffs on industrial combination. He distinguishes between a protective tariff and an over-protective tariff. A tariff is held to be simply protective when it does no more than enable the protected country to become the producer of certain goods. It is held to become over-protective when it does more than establish these producers and affords them a margin for raising their prices above full cost price. He is inclined to the view that "simple protection" is comparatively harmless, but through economies peculiar to the protected parties it may result in over-protection, which does not always conduce to the benefit of a country. "Although it is important not to exaggerate the influence of tariffs," holds Mr. Macgregor, "yet they have a strong influence whose theoretical basis is plain, and which spreads further than is at once apparent. . . . Combination which is based on the tariff, or on objective conditions created by human institutions, is liable to be rendered unstable as these institutions are continually modified and revised."

In these days of steadily-increasing prices of commodities, it is interesting to read Mr. Macgregor's views of the effect of these industrial combinations upon prices. When the causes contributing to the combinations are reasons of defence or aggression, the effect will appear in a *régime* of higher prices. "Prices will rule high, not only in relation to the abnormally low prices due to excessive competition, but with reference to normal conditions."

But high prices, even if steady, are not necessarily an advantage. To ascertain their real effect it becomes necessary to trace their effects on industry generally. Their effect is to reduce the consumer's purchasing power for other foods, and to lead elsewhere to crisis from under-consumption. In such a condition of affairs the "other industries" may cartel themselves and make their prices in turn higher and steadier. The result is a higher level all over the market. Mr. Macgregor shows how, by the interplay of forces, this result is almost inevitable. He holds, however, that it should be within the power of combination to steady prices without the quite inconsequent operation of putting them up. Steadiness is thought to have little economic meaning if it goes with a higher level of prices.

Mr. Macgregor goes on to discuss the economic effect upon the producer of the policy of selling in foreign markets at a loss, and he concludes that this may not be good if, in a national market controlled by strong combinations, the point of greatest profit is reached before the full tariff is made effective on price. "But if the limit allowed by the tariff is reached first, so that prices cannot vary upwards, the consumers may possibly gain, as well as the combination, by this policy if pursued under conditions of decreasing cost."

In so thoughtful a book as this, especial interest attaches to the author's analysis of the relationship of the State to industrial combinations.

He is impressed with the evident dangers. "A strong combination for the production of a staple commodity gives to a few men, who may have no other motive than private interest, an invidious power over national life and work." "It is an evil thing when trade influences creep into the legislature, and private interests are made cumulatively stronger by their power to obtain secret or open protection or concession." "The domination of industrial magnates is felt to endanger the virility of social life, and to relax the standards of every-day morality." Public opinion is not an adequate safeguard, and a new measure of active attention is required from the State.

The State may act as consumer, producer and legislator. As consumer, its powers of regulation are held to be only slight. On the question of organised State production, he does not admit the public ownership of commodities like water, gas and electricity constitutes a precedent, as these goods, though theoretically transferable in character, actually are non-transferable, as they need " a prepared way to be laid out over the whole area supplied," which way "is of no use to carry any commodity except one, so that its whole cost falls on the producer of that commodity." This condition of things "leads to narrow markets, and a strong tendency to decreasing cost within those markets." "The price of gas in Bristol would have to rise very high before it would be worth while to pack it in cylinders and send it from London." The whole market becomes, therefore, split up into local and non-competing monopolies.

These special considerations are held not to apply to goods which move freely over national or international markets. With regard to their industries, he finds himself confronted with a dilemma, "either the State must take them over one by one as economic forces consolidate them, but in this case the dangers of municipal trade, the influencing of public officials on behalf of private interests affected, will appear on a national scale—or it must wait until the industry least liable to combination is combined." This he feels to be impracticable. Grave difficulties would, in his judgment, ensue, if public policy were to regard combination as antecedent to socialisation, but it is from the foreign relations of governments that his final attitude towards a socialist development of economic combination is derived. " There is no time, so long as the international stress lasts, and occupies the best energies of legislatures, for industrial socialism." The burden of government would be intolerably increased if new officials were answerable to the legislature for all the complications of the conduct of national industries." He submits finally that "neither inductive nor deductive reasoning can be used fairly to assimilate the industries in which the problems of combination are pressing to those which already have silently come into the hands of public authorities."

He then considers what measures, short of ownership, the State can take, and, after consideration of the arguments, concludes that the State cannot without danger either forbid, or circumscribe, or by special inquisitorial registration sanction, the combination movement. "There is then left for it only the duty of ensuring that the movement will owe its success or failure to the action of the openest competition with other methods," and the author closes a book— wherein nearly every word has a measured value—with the following opinion: "If the combination movement comes to realise itself fully in time, so that industry concentrates to a high degree its strength, its risks, its powers for good, and its powers for harm, then, to revert to the metaphor of leadership, a nation's best hope is 'that a better conception of the place and dignity of industry may induce the best men of the nation to become captains in this war.'" O.F.

9.—*Le Condizioni Generali della Classe Operaia in Milano: Salari, Giornate di Lavoro, Reddito, ecc.* (Pubblicazioni dell' Ufficio del Lavoro della Società Umanitaria, Numero 15). 254 pp., 4to. Milano, 1907.

This volume contains the belated results of an investigation, instituted in the summer of 1903, into the general conditions of the working classes of Milan. This inquiry was undertaken by the Labour Department of the Humanitarian Society, at the instigation of the Trades Council, who desired to obtain statistical details as to wages, hours of labour, piece work, &c., for the use of the various labour organisations represented on the Council, while the Humanitarian Society sought at the same time to procure precise information as to the extent of the dearth of employment as a guide in the adoption of measures for the relief of the unemployed. As the Municipal Council of Milan had also decided to make an inquiry into the housing and sanitary accommodation, arrangements were made for the simultaneous delivery and collection of the schedules of questions relating to both inquiries. The persons to whom the schedules were distributed were asked to make their answers relate to 1st July, 1903. At the end of June meetings were held in the working class districts to explain the objects of the investigations, and circulars were issued intimating that authorised persons would attend on certain evenings at the local schools to complete the schedules for those who were unable to understand them.

The schedule issued by the Labour Department contained sixteen questions, in which the worker was asked, *inter alia*, to state his

name and the date and place of his birth ; how long he had lived in
Milan ; his trade ; whether he worked at home, and if so, on his own
account or not; on how many days he worked in the year and his
daily wages; whether he was out of employment; how long he had
been unemployed ; and to what agency he applied for work. It was
found that many persons refused to furnish details as to their
daily wages, on the ground that the demand for this information
was an encroachment upon their private affairs. Of an even more
inquisitive character were two questions inviting the worker to give
the name and address of the firm or person by whom he was
employed, but the results do not show to what extent answers were
given on this point. The inquiry extended to all wage earners, and
included also persons working at their homes on their own account,
itinerant vendors, and cabmen ; but professional persons, officials,
shopkeepers, and proprietors of businesses were excluded.

The total number of individuals included in the inquiry was
340,354 ; but in 32,988 cases the forms were returned blank, and after
deducting a further 23,016 which related to professional persons or
officials, and 3,851 incomplete returns, the total number of persons
represented by the remaining useful schedules was 280,519, or about
57 per cent. of the entire population of Milan as ascertained at the
census of February, 1901. The results of the inquiry are tabulated
with somewhat excessive elaboration in eighty-five tables, accompanied by explanatory observations, with occasional diagrams, and
grouped under eight chapters relating to the composition of working
class families, immigration, family incomes and expenditures, occupations, unemployed, and wages and number of days of work.

Excluding persons living singly, there were 264,428 persons
enumerated in 68,255 working class families (an average of 3·87 to
the family), and of these 143,229, viz., 91,199 males and 52,030
females, were returned as employed wage earners, and 5,615 (4,129
males and 1,486 females) as unemployed. Particulars as to incomes
were forthcoming in 46,867 cases. There were 33,625 families, or
71·7 per cent., with incomes ranging from 11s. to 28s. a week ; of
the remainder 7,642 received less than 11s. weekly, and 5,600 had
incomes in excess of 28s. In 1,640 cases these figures included
wages in kind as well as money ; but 2,929 families had free
lodgings, the value of which was not estimated. Details as to cash
wages, which are minutely analysed in 130 pages of the volume,
were obtained in 132,397 cases, 87,069 males and 45,328 females.
In round numbers, 30,000 workers earned in cash less than $9\frac{1}{2}d.$ a
day, 53,500 from $9\frac{1}{2}d.$ to 1s. 7d., 33,000 from 1s. 7d. to 3s. 2d., and
17,500 more than 3s. 2d. In the two lowest paid groups were
41,000 of the female workers whose daily wages were less than
1s. 2d. a day. In 9,698 cases the wages were supplemented by free
board and lodgings, and other emoluments, the value of which was
not ascertained. Numerous tables are given showing in much detail
the wages paid in relation to the ages of the workers, daily rates
and piece-work rates, the number of days worked in each trade, and
other statistical aspects of the information collected as to wages.

R.F.C.

10.—*Child Labor in the United States.* No. 69 of the Bulletin of the Labor Department of the U.S.A. Census Bureau, Washington, 1907.

Not only literature and pamphlets of a kind dubbed "sensational," but the reports of scientific academies have recently shown that the conditions under which children are employed for money in the United States constitute a serious peril for the future of society in that great nation. The Census Bureau was therefore requested to compile a statistical account of the extent of child-employment and its distribution according to age, sex, and occupation. The report shows that 1,750,000 children between 10 and 15 years were returned at the twelfth census as having a gainful occupation. It is not, however, to be supposed that these are all working in factory, mine or sweat-shop, for 1,060,000 are engaged in agricultural pursuits, two-thirds of the total child-breadwinners being employed on the farm, and most of these children being members of farmers' families. It is also pointed out, as some qualification of the evil, that when grouped according to age, the percentage of children occupied is highest in the higher ages, being only 8·1 at 10 years old, and 31·6 at 15. Almost one-third of the child-workers are thus 15 years old, and more than one-half are 14 or 15. Of the younger children, aged 10 to 13 years, 186,000 are engaged in occupations other than agricultural, very nearly the same number, by the way, as the workers aged 10 and under 14 in England and Wales. (*Labour Abstract*, 1902-04, p. 208.) The difference in the distribution according to occupation in the two countries is worth notice. Textiles occupy in the United States 27,000 children under 14, about half the number so employed in England. On the other hand, it is somewhat surprising to find nearly 50,000 servants, waiters and waitresses of that age-group in the States as against 25,000 here (p. 8.)

A very interesting table on p. 11 shows the percentage of bread-winning children of different races :—

Percentages of Children, 10 to 15, who are Breadwinners.

	All Occupations.	Agricultural	All Others.
Native white, both parents native	15·1	10·2	4·9
„ one or both parents foreign-born	12·4	3·2	9·2
Foreign-born white	24·8	2·9	21·9
Negro	40·0	31·5	8·5

As might be expected, the highest percentage occurs among the negro race, and the foreign-born white children, being mostly those of immigrant alien families, with a standard of life lower than the white natives', but higher than the negroes', occupy an intermediate position. The families in which the parents are native Americans no doubt represent a higher level of prosperity than the immigrants. There is a slight apparent discrepancy between this theory and the above figures, which show that the native white children of native parents are relatively more numerously occupied than those of families more recently arrived, in which the children, but not the parents, or not both parents, are native born. The explanation given is (p. 12) that the immigrant population is almost exclusively urban, while the native population is largely rural and agricultural. In the industrial occupations chiefly carried on in cities, in which the objection to child labour is greatest, the percentage occupied is lowest among the families which have been longest settled in America and presumably attained a higher social level than have the more recent arrivals. When we come to consider the manufacturing industries in greater detail, it appears that, " to a greater extent than any other manufacturing or mechanical industry, the cotton mill furnishes employment to children " (p. 42). Some of the evil effects of child labour are strikingly illustrated by the fact also brought out, (p. 39), that the greatest degree of illiteracy is that which is shown for the children in cotton mills. In the Northern States, in most of which there is some degree of State inspection and control of factories, both the number and percentage of children in cotton mills is, as might be expected, less than in the South, where industry is still mostly unregulated, and in some districts disgraced by terrible abuses of long hours and insanitary conditions of work. It is significant in this connection to note that the greater number and proportion of children employed is associated with a smaller total of workers.

Cotton Operatives.

	All Over 10.	10 to 15 Years.	
		Number.	Per Cent.
United States of America	246,391	44,427	18·0
Northern and Western States	147,724	16,404	11·1
Southern States......................	96,467	28,023	29·0

Mr. North appears to have proved his case that child-employment in injurious and exhausting occupations is relatively of less extent than was supposed. There are, however, among children under 14, besides textile-workers, 1,400 glass-workers, 49,000 labourers not specified, nearly 10,000 messengers (an occupation known to be very demoralising and exhausting for children), nearly 2,500 metal-workers, and 9,000 miners. The numbers are considerable enough to constitute a serious problem in the absence of effective control and inspection by some external authority.   B.L.H.

11.—*Life and Labour in Germany.* With an Appendix : *Infirmity and Old Age Pensions in Germany.* Reports of the Gainsborough Commission. London : Simpkin, Marshall, Hamilton, Kent and Co., 1907. Price 2*s.* net.
It appears that Germany is behind England at any rate in one respect, that is, in the official study of wages, hours of labour,

and even of retail prices. From the sporadic accounts which are accessible to English readers, it is exceedingly difficult to obtain anything approaching an accurate statistical view of the German working classes; whereas we are already able to give a reasonably complete account of the numbers and wages in our own country. The main difficulty that lies behind a comparison of money wages in the two countries is in connection with the relative proportions between skilled and unskilled, town and country labour. Whatever a fiscal system may or may not do, it is almost certain to act unevenly on these classes; a system designed to benefit manufacturers is likely to injure agriculturists and *vice versâ*; and no comparative study bearing on the fiscal question is complete in its essentials till this is taken into account. The group of workmen who were sent by Mr. Moreing from Gainsborough in 1905, and guided through parts of Germany by Mr. J. L. Bashford, made no attempt to strike this balance, and, in fact, confined their attention to the towns and manufacturing villages: in consequence, their reports, which are contained in the volume before us, do not afford any complete comparison between the economic positions of German and English workpeople as a whole. For what they profess to do, they are nevertheless of the greatest value; thus the men's mission was to see with their own eyes the condition of the German workmen, and to prove or dispel the assertion (stated to have been frequently made in 1905) that their condition was one of abject poverty. They appear to have been studiously unbiassed, and to have described exactly what they saw. They quote, almost without comment, statements by Germans in favour of and against protection, and they give cases where prices are and where they are not higher in Germany because of or in spite of protection. The result is that their accounts are of the greatest interest, and their statistics, though quite uncollated and incomplete, have a considerable value for comparison with other accounts. It seems probable that the actual factories they inspected were above the average in respect of comfort and paternal arrangements for the welfare of the employees, but they heard the other side, if any, from the socialist and other working-class representatives to whom they had easy access.

It is hardly necessary to say that they at once and completely destroyed the one-sided idea of general German poverty, and found all the signs of prosperous and contented industrial conditions and of very great progress during the past thirty years. The impression obtained from their reports is that given by Hasbach and other careful observers, that the German artisan works distinctly longer hours for distinctly lower rates of pay than persons of similar occupations in England, though rates vary considerably from place to place, and that the German unskilled man is relatively to the artisan better off than his English contemporary. The question— how far the one nation is more prosperous than the other?—is thus removed from the arena of *à priori* political speeches, and relegated to the delicate measurements of statistics, measurements for which, as yet, the data do not exist.

A considerable part of the reports is devoted to the arrangements made by employers and by the government for the housing, pensioning, nursing and insuring the working classes. The official schemes have long been familiar to those who have cared to study them; but most readers will be surprised at the prevalence and development of the paternal system, at the arrangements for boarding and lodging unmarried men, and for housing others, at the dining-rooms, libraries, baths and recreation-rooms which were so frequently found at the factories the Commission visited. Connected no doubt with these is the long tenure of work for one employer; very many men qualify for the bonuses given for long-continued service. The tractability of the German workmen is evident throughout the account.

We are told a great deal about rents and prices, but the extreme difficulties of the problems of retail purchasing power are not handled seriously. There is much good description of how the German workman lives, and it is abundantly clear that he spends his wages on different commodities in different proportions from the Englishman in similar circumstances. But we are left completely in doubt as to whether a man earning 30 marks in Dortmund is better off or not than one earning 30s. in Manchester. A careful account is given of the price of bread, and it seems established that rye bread in Germany costs, weight for weight, the same as wheaten bread in England, and that the Germans prefer the former. A great deal of stress is laid on this equality, but nothing is said about the nutritive value of the two, nor is the price of rye or of wheat in the two countries compared. It appears from other sources (Cd–2337, p. 227, and *Statistical Abstract for the United Kingdom*) that rye in Prussia costs about 7s. per cwt., while rye imported into Great Britain averages about 5s. 6d. per cwt.

The book is not very well compiled or printed; it is digressive and often irrelevant, and contains sentences of which the following is an exaggerated specimen: " It is to be regretted that our newspapers have not earlier given us some reliable information . . . instead of throwing sand into our eyes in the form of anecdotes that do not hold water."

It is rather odd to find English workmen, who have obtained a 54 hours' week and a Saturday half-holiday, reporting that the German, with 60 hours work a week " has ample facilities for healthy recreation for himself and family."   A.L.B.

12.—*Sweated Industry and the Minimum Wage.* By Clementina Black, with an Introduction by A. G. Gardiner. xxiv + 281 pp., crown 8vo. London: Duckworth and Co., 1907. Price 3s. 6d.

Miss Clementina Black has borne an active share in the efforts made for many years to raise the status of women workers by means of combination in trade unions. Her qualifications for the task attempted in this new volume will not be questioned, and to the final conclusion reached the weight of informed and mature experience attaches. She first presents in successive chapters a general survey of labour underpaid in various kinds of industry.

From workers in factories and workshops she passes to shop assistants, to clerks and waitresses, and to traffic workers, and finally to wage-earning children. Part I of her book, which is entitled "Sweated Industry," deals thus with the conditions on which labour is conducted in such employments, and ends with an endeavour to explain the real causes of this calamitous situation. It is a heart-rending tale of misery which is here unfolded; although Miss Black may have selected of deliberate purpose the worst characteristics of the industrial life which she portrays, drawn from that portion of the whole area covered by the particular trades in question where they are found in their most distressing intensity. The title of her opening chapter, styled the "poorest of all," might arouse in some hostile critics a suspicion that she was availing herself of the well-known artifices of the special pleader anxious to enlist the sympathies of a compassionate jury. Yet it would not be easy to deny the prevalence in many different quarters of the deplorable evils which she describes, or to question the substantial validity of the reasoning by which she urges that without the decisive applica-tion of remedial treatment such hopeless and degrading misery must be pronounced inevitable.

Of the existence in modern communities of a large mass of "sweated industry" there can unfortunately be no doubt, although a hasty impression gathered from these vivid chapters might produce an exaggerated notion of its magnitude and even of its misery. The life of many shop assistants, for example, combines, according to Miss Black's graphic language, the "disagreeables of boarding school with those of domestic service, while failing to afford the pleasant features of either." The confidence, which will be felt in her general verdict that the evil is "not confined to women, nor to home workers, nor to any class or trade," nor indeed to any special "country," is strengthened by the circumstance that she does not fail to indicate her disagreement with some exaggerated views accepted too readily by certain critics. Like other observers, she shows that the workers in factories and workshops are, on the whole, better situated in respect of hours than the home workers; she contends that accusations freely made of immorality among the employers of shop assistants lack substantiation, and she admits that the condi-tions of child-labour to-day in the United States, especially in the South, are happily without a parallel in the existing circumstances of this country. But, after making such deductions, sufficient misery remains to prompt an imperative demand for effective remedies, and to banish the hard conception that labour can safely, left to itself, be considered as a mere commodity.

In the second section of her book Miss Black proceeds to the examination of remedial measures. She notes that co-operation and trade unionism, as voluntary agencies, and the coercive interference of factory laws, ever extending the range of their application, and raising the scale of their requirements, do in this country at the present moment operate as checks on sweating. But, on the other hand, she does not set much value on "supposed remedies" of the nature of emigration. She questions the assumed improvidence of early marriages among the poor ; she doubts the real wisdom of thrift on their part save in certain specified directions. She does not believe that drunkenness is the cause of *general* poverty or that Consumers' Leagues can cover more than a portion of the field of action which is small compared with that left unaffected. She is led by the observation of what has happened in the cotton trade of England in the past, and of what is now occurring under systems of compulsory arbitration and wages boards in our Australasian Colonies, to the significant conclusion that the enforcement of a "minimum wage" by legislative action is at once a feasible remedy, and the only effectual cure, for the evils of underpaid employment. She thinks that no serious apprehension need be felt in this matter on account of foreign competition. It is possible that many of her readers will dissent from her conclusion, but they will not deny that she presents a powerful case for their consideration. Her opinion has evidently not been formed in haste or in ignorance of the actual situation. It is on the contrary the outcome of an experience which has extended over so long a period as twenty years, during which she has been brought into the closest contact with the hard realities of the industrial life of women workers. Her pages are alive with knowledge, and she must, we suspect, have learnt by now to discriminate between imaginary possibility and genuine necessity. Her diagnosis at least of the disease cannot be set aside without grave risk ; and the medicine which she recommends would seem on these grounds to deserve a trial. It need not, perhaps, be added that such is the firm opinion stated with emphasis in Mr. Gardiner's Preface.   L.L.P.

13.—*The Nature of Capital and Income.* By Irving Fisher, Ph.D. xxi + 427 pp., 8vo. New York : The Macmillan Company, 1906. Price 12s. 6d. net.

Professor Irving Fisher remarks in his Preface that his "whole book" may be said to be the "elaboration" of "ideas outlined some years ago in the *Economic Journal*." Those ideas are summarily stated in the definitions of Capital and Income given on page 52 of the present volume. "A *stock of wealth* existing at an *instant* of time is called *capital*. A *flow of services* through a *period* of time is called *income*." These definitions may perhaps appear to be open to the charge often brought against definitions, whether in Economics or in other inquiries, that they are in some sense arbitrary, and lend themselves easily to the support of the particular thesis which the author is anxious to enforce. Nor, in spite of the censure which Professor Fisher bestows, not undeservedly, on the unsatisfactory character of the previous treatment of his subject by authoritative writers, who, in some instances, he maintains, have taken refuge from formidable difficulty in studied obscurity or unconscious ambiguity, and, in others, in an illusive search for exaggerated precision have been misled into an unreal phraseology removed by an excessive distance from the ordinary usage of common parlance, does he himself fail to admit frankly that his handling of capital and income might be shortly described as a new exposition of the ancient text that "capital is what yields an income." The ideas expressed in his definitions, and outlined in the articles in the *Economic Journal,* are indeed so simple in essence, when stated without note or comment, that they should commend themselves to the favourable reception of most of his readers. Yet the full, lucid and forcible exposition they have now received in the important treatise before us was, we think, needed to exhibit their far-reaching significance, and Professor Fisher may congratulate himself on having made a substantial and permanent addition alike to the scientific and to the practical study of Economics.

No professional student who possesses a tolerable acquaintance with text-books on principles would, we imagine, be disposed to deny that the conception of capital has been the occasion of a vast amount of difficult discussion ; and it would require considerable boldness to affirm that the results hitherto attained have been commensurate with the trouble and ingenuity applied by a multitude of able and instructed writers. Professor Fisher shows how some of the most scrupulous and competent of those writers have attempted without complete satisfaction to fit their ideas to facts by drawing distinctions which it has become hard or impossible to justify in the end ; while with the acceptance of his suggested definitions many of the rough places become smooth, and not a few awkward corners are easily turned. His book enjoys the additional advantage—or perhaps, we should more correctly say, possesses the peculiar merit—of harmonising the theoretical reasonings of economic science with the commonsense *raison d'être* of practical accounting. By his felicitous interpretation of the terms "capital" and "income" he succeeds in demonstrating the existence of the same fundamental philosophy below that system of book-keeping by double entry which is well-nigh universal in actual business, and also beneath the conception of the functions of capital, and its relations to income, which forms part of the familiar apparatus of economic speculation. He ends in this important department at least the divorce between theory and practice which is the bane of so much economic writing of the highest quality ; for his chapters on economic theory with convincing appropriateness alternate with chapters in which he illustrates and proves his contentions by examples of business accounting.

He does not, however, sacrifice the legitimate claims of scientific precision to the imperative exigencies of intelligible commercial practice. For the most part, it is true, he removes to appendices the technical mathematical treatment of economic formulæ ; but characteristic geometrical curves are not absent from the pages of the main body of his text, and he does not spare his readers the hard thinking which is necessary to grasp the complete significance of his contentions. As students of his previous writings are aware, he is fully equipped with the fine weapons of modern mathematical economists ; and yet his admirable lucidity will, we believe, enable the general reader, for whom his book is partly intended, to follow his reasoning, especially if he omits, in accordance with the author's own suggestions, the "technical portions," or, following his advice, returns for a second perusal to chapters which on a first reading may not be entirely plain. There are, it may be noticed, many observations made by the way which deserve attention, and the cumulative strength of the chief thesis enforced is not likely to be fully appreciated until the concluding chapters have been reached, and brought into explicit connection with their predecessors. The book therefore is one which needs careful reading; but we are sure that professional economists will feel that their knowledge has been corrected and enlarged by acquaintance with Professor Irving Fisher's arguments, and we have little doubt that many practical accountants and actuaries in particular, and not a few ordinary business men in general, will be keenly interested by the skilful exposition here supplied of the "philosophy of economic accounting." We ourselves have in the end felt compelled to accept without reserve his definitions of capital and income; for they seem to us to illuminate the obscure and to disentangle the confused.   L.L.P.

14.—*Co-operative Banking: its Principles and Practice; with a Chapter on Co-operative Mortgage Credit.* By Henry W. Wolff. xv + 301 pp. London: P. S. King and Son, 1907. Price 7*s.* 6*d.* net.

Mr. Wolff brings to the discussion of this subject not merely an intimate knowledge of it, and a well-trained literary faculty, but a long practical acquaintance with the working of co-operative banks at home and abroad, and the experience gained by much active work in the promotion of the movement. It is trite to say that this is a form of co-operation which has made less headway in our own country than in Germany, Italy, and elsewhere on the Continent. In excellent works on "People's Banks: a record of Social and Economic Success," and "Agricultural Banks, their Object and their Work," Mr. Wolff has powerfully advocated the movement. He has also furnished those interested in it with materials in the way of model rules, &c., for the launching of a co-operative bank, and has had some success in that direction.

Taking as his motto a saying of M. Jules Simon, that the greatest banker in the world is the one who deals with the pence of the people, he states that his object in the present book is to set forth the causes which have produced the magnificent results secured by the co-operative banks of foreign countries, to explain the mechanism and rationale of the institution, and to give the why and wherefore of each of its parts. He draws two curious parallels, on which, however, it would not be right to lay too much stress: that the 950 Schultze-Delitzsch banks in Germany keep in circulation for the enrichment of the nation the very 100 millions sterling that Mr. Chamberlain thought he might raise by tariff reform; and that co-operation in Germany, directly supported by the co-operative banks, manages to raise the price of corn to the producer by just that 2*s.* per quarter which Mr. Chamberlain suggested as proper. Such coincidences as these strike the imagination, and assist it to realise the true fructifying power of the industry and thrift of the people, when directed to the fuller development of their own resources in the locality where they reside. It is this which constitutes the special note of all the various systems of co-operative banking in distinction from ordinary banking.

The problem which a co-operative bank has to solve, in one form or another, is how to transmute character into security—how to ensure that a poor man to whom a loan is made, whether it be for the purpose of buying tools or implements for his labour, goods, or means of conveyance for his trade, or of developing a small agricultural holding or the like, shall really so employ that loan that the desired result may be obtained, and shall honestly repay it out of the proceeds of the improvement thus effected. He has no other security to offer; if that fails, how is the loss to be met? The answer is, in general terms, that in practice it does not fail.

We do not find any reference in Mr. Wolff's book to a body which has, in a modest but effectual way, anticipated some of the work which he desires to effect by means of his co-operative banks. The district committees of the Charity Organisation Society have long been engaged in working out the plan of making relief in distress effectual and productive by granting a sum for a specific purpose by way of loan repayable in a given time. Many poor persons of both sexes have by this means been enabled entirely to retrieve their position, and to become self-reliant and relatively prosperous.

A similar illustration of the effectiveness of a loan, when made with a definite object and after a thorough investigation into character, is afforded by the proceedings of the Central (Unemployed) Body for London, and other similar bodies, with regard to emigration. Those only are selected to be emigrants who will make good use of the opportunities afforded them, and will repay the loan made to them as soon as they find themselves able to do so. The results have, we understand, been favourable in this respect.

These are not matters which commend themselves to Mr. Wolff. The broad principle of the institutions advocated by him is that of collective credit. It implies and renders necessary the same knowledge of character that is the motive of the investigations set on foot by bodies granting relief; but that knowledge is not acquired in the same way. The free vote of the members declares whether a candidate is worthy to join them, whether he is one for whose honesty they are willing to be collectively responsible.

The methods of making that collective security available are twofold, and are widely different. The first is the method of the Schultze-Delitzsch banks, that of raising a capital by shares. The founder of this system laid it down that the shares should be large. He was anxious that the members should be placed under an obligation to exercise thrift and to lay by money. As Mr. Wolff points out, this can as easily be done by encouraging the member to take a number of small shares as by requiring him to take one large one; and the advantages of a small share are obvious.

Mr. Wolff states, but not with precise accuracy, the varieties of
liability that are contemplated by the British Companies Acts.
These are—

1. Unlimited liability.
2. Liability limited by shares.
3. Liability limited by guarantee, the capital being divided into
   shares.
4. Liability limited by guarantee, the capital not being divided
   into shares.

The second and third methods are those which are applicable to
the class of bank which places its main dependence upon the savings
of its members. The first and fourth are more applicable to the
class of banks associated with the name of Raiffeisen, which places
its main dependence upon credit, and has for a fundamental principle
unlimited liability. If, therefore, the promoters of these banks had
been content to avail themselves of the provisions of the Companies
Acts, they would have found something to meet their case in one
or other of the four varieties of company we have enumerated. But
registering a company is an expensive formality, and they have
therefore been anxious to obtain a legal constitution under some of
the Acts specially devised to meet the case of societies of working
men, as the Industrial and Provident Societies Act or the Friendly
Societies Act. As Mr. Wolff points out, however, neither of these
Acts by itself offers the same variety of constitution that is allowed
by the Companies Acts, nor indeed would they do so if it were
possible to work them in combination with each other.

In the year 1875, we urged in this *Journal* (vol. xxxviii, p. 185)
that the right principle of legislation with regard to societies is
that the general provisions of the law should be made applicable
to them rather with regard to the form of their organisation
than to its purpose. Mr. Wolff's experience confirms this view.
Sir Horace Plunkett's is also in point. He had established a
number of agricultural banks in Ireland under a special authority
pursuant to the Friendly Societies Act, and was desirous that some
of these banks should obtain assistance from the Congested Districts
Board, which that Board was willing to grant. The Friendly
Societies Acts did not contemplate borrowing or receiving deposits,
except from a society's own members, and accordingly a short Act
had to be passed through Parliament in 1898 enabling such societies
to borrow from persons or corporations other than their members,
in the case where the society has rules expressly providing (*a*) that
no part of the funds shall be divided by way of profit, bonus,
dividend, or otherwise among the members; (*b*) that all money
lent to members by the society shall be applied to such purpose
as the society or its committee of management may approve.

Mr. Wolff has an interesting chapter on the functions of the
co-operative bank as a bank for savings, and renews the attack
he has elsewhere made on the present savings bank system of
investment, exclusively in the public funds or government
securities. This raises a question of great complexity and difficulty.

Undoubtedly, if the Government had more freedom of investment, it might both earn more interest and promote many laudable undertakings; but it is open to grave doubt whether the proceeding would not be accompanied with some risks and some disadvantage. At any rate, we need not dissent from Mr. Wolff's conclusion that, by the side of the old and useful savings banks, "we want free, unbound, co-operative banks, to receive savings to be employed in a very different manner, returning into productive use, stimulating employment, housing, settling, financing working folk, and fructifying largely."

Mr. Wolff has some good suggestions on union for purposes of inspection. It is clear that the small local banks will require aid in various ways if they are not to fall into mistakes and incur losses, and some central body has therefore to be constituted to supply this requirement. At the same time, "co-operative banks, to be useful, can be formed only by their own members, and must stand independently, each upon its own solid foundation." Its own members must manage it.

An index would have added to the value of this excellent book.

E.B.

15.—*The Gold Supply and Prosperity.* Compiled and edited by Byron W. Holt. 262 pp., sm. 8vo. New York: Moody Corporation, 1907.

The interest of this book lies in the compilation it contains of the brief opinions of a number of prominent representatives of commerce and of economic thought in the United States on two, just now, burning questions, which were, perhaps, also two of the most discussed theories of economics of the past century. It is a reproduction (a) of seven articles on "the Quantity Theory of Money," which appeared last autumn in an American magazine, and (b) of thirteen articles on "the Increasing Supply of Gold, and its effects on Prices of Commodities, Interest, Wages, Prices of Securities, &c.," which were published in the same journal in December, 1905. The contributors are mostly men of affairs, and this frees the pages from the pedantry so abundant as a rule in books and articles on this subject. To the above are added an introduction and conclusion—not very valuable—by the Editor of the magazine, and part of an article—of still less value—by a writer from Los Angeles.

Of (a) the Quantity Theory Professor Irving Fisher truly says (p. 35) "much has been written both by the wise and the foolish on the quantity theory of money," and the statement finds some confirmation within the pages of the book itself. If the quantity theory is to be anything more than a shadow, "money" must be restricted to gold (held in bank reserves and in circulation, or either), with or without bank notes and paper money of various kinds, but it cannot be extended to include bank deposits, cheques, bills of exchange, &c. If so, the theory evaporates, and the only residuum is the indisputable statement that prices are determined by the demand for, and supply of commodities.

It is very noticeable that all the contributors agree on the vital point that the quantity theory of money is only tenable if "money" includes paper currency (redeemable and irredeemable), "bank checks," "drafts," "token coins," "individual deposits" in national and state banks, "fiat money," "all substitute forms" for money. Yet in spite of the concensus of opinion, in spite of the modifications in the theory which successive writers have been compelled to make in their efforts to retain it, the Editor advances it in its crudest form, thus :—" In view of the facts, it is reasonably safe to conclude, even against the authority of many leading economists, and with the full sanction of but few of our living economists, that the quantity theory of money—*gold alone being real money*— is substantially true and that prices are affected *in direct ratio as to the quantity of gold.*" This is an extraordinary statement at this time of day, but it is not quite so bad as the fustian about the sphericity of the earth on page 19, or as this, "nor is it necessary that the standard of value should possess utility or even tangibility . . . . The distance from here to the sun could be made the standard. Suppose we assume that distance to be 100,000,000 miles, that we issue that many paper notes, each representing one mile, each note called a dollar, and declare them legal tender. Prices would adjust themselves, &c." This is some of the foolishness which Professor Irving Fisher tells us is written, but there is not much of it.

In the short statements of the six writers whose opinions were sought by the Editor there is much that is worthy of attention from every one sufficiently interested in the subject to deal seriously with them, and something worth quoting in this *Journal*, e.g., Mr. Muhleman's opening sentence (p. 39), "In the application of the quantity theory of money and prices to certain phenomena, such as the concurrence of low prices and an over supply of money as was the case in 1897 [he should have said from 1894 to 1897], it appears that another factor must be considered. This seems to be the relative activity or inactivity of capital . . . . without this the extent to which the money supply affects prices is indeterminable." This factor is of importance, and has not, up to the present, had the attention, in any of the literature of the subject, which it deserves.

Concerning (*b*), the thirteen articles on the Supply of Gold and its effects, *tot homines quot sententiæ.* Coming as they do from writers of the standing of Horace White, M. L. Muhleman, Professor Irving Fisher, F. A. Vanderlip, they cannot be otherwise than weighty, and there is much in them which will appeal to business men as well as to students. On the whole, there is a decided expression of opinion that prices of commodities will rise owing to the increased output of gold which seems assured, and that various effects, many of them easy to predict, will follow. Several of the writers, however, are wise enough to commit themselves no further than this. "I think everyone will accept, *subject to important modifying conditions*, the statement that the monetary supply has a *tendency* to advance prices. . . . I do not believe we are

facing any economic revolution as a result of this influx of gold."
(Vanderlip.)

The introduction and conclusion as well as some of the contributions, particularly those parts dealing with the rate of interest,
contain much contentious matter which it is impossible to notice
here.

The Editor writes, one would think, to alarm men as to the
prospective value of their investments and the changes which they
should hasten to make in them, having regard to the coming rise
in commodity prices. If it be admitted, as it is assumed throughout, that the rise will be general and great, the advice given may be
sound. It is, however, a commonplace of business, and especially
of the trafficking in commodities and stocks and shares, that the
effects of foreseen events are rapidly discounted, and it is a
matter for reflection whether in forcing up prices of copper from
48*l.* to 105*l.* per ton, of tin from 62*l.* to 192*l.*, of lead from 11*l.*
to 20*l.*, of cotton from 7·2 cents. to 10·75 cents. per lb., of wool
from 7½*d.* to 11½*d.* per lb., in ten years, our American friends
have not "sliced the melon" so avidiously as to leave little or
nothing for their children. Admitting a great and continued
gold supply, he would be a bold man indeed who would act on
the opinion (see p. XI) that the price of copper (say) may be
300*l.* per ton or wheat 5*l.* a quarter ten years hence.

The wise investor is told (p. 257) to "study the gold factor."
If he is wise he will do nothing of the kind unless he is drawn
to it by something more than a desire to well invest his savings.
The whole subject lies in that region of economics which is most
difficult to enter and most harassing to traverse. He will be better
advised if he takes care to carry from this book the wisdom of
Mr. E. H. Roberts (p. 140), "He who will study these subjects most
closely and deeply will be least dogmatic in his predictions." In
his contribution the Editor seems to have been too much absorbed
in the contemplation of the maleficent effects of the coming rise in
prices—"unrest, discontent, agitation, strikes, riots, rebellion, wars,"
"complete ruin as the final goal for many industries," are some of
his words. There is no warrant for this in the collected articles,
and he might with advantage read what has been said on the other
side, *e.g.*, by Mr. L. L. Price, in the latter part of his excellent little
book on "Money and its relation to Prices."   J.S.

16.—*Die Staats- und Kommunal-Besteuerung in Deutschland,
England, den Vereinigten Staaten von Nordamerika und den englischen
Kolonien.* Von Dr. jur. Eugen Lauterbach. Berlin: Verlag von
Franz Vahlen, 1906. Price 7 marks.

This book is only of indirect use to statisticians. It is occupied
with a very careful and detailed comparative account of the systems
of taxation in the countries named, and is a very handy book of
reference for students of public finance. It further supplies
accurate definitions of the amounts included under different
categories; thus a foreigner, wishing to know exactly what was
meant by the gross assessment for income-tax in the United

Kingdom, would find a historical and practical description here. Since so much turns on questions of definition, or rather of delimitation, in comparative statistics, and since it is in general so difficult to know exactly what is included under a simple designation in unfamiliar statistics, it is clear that the book has some use for a wide field of readers. It is to be regretted that neither the actual budgets nor tables of the yield of separate taxes are included. The discussion of local taxes only occupies 29 pages, all the several States of the United States of America being dismissed in four ; this treatment is clearly inadequate.

A.L.B.

17.—*Die Weltwirthschaft : ein Jahr- und Lesebuch : unter Mitwirkung zahlreicher Fachleute.* Herausgegeben von Dr. Ernst von Halle, Professor an der Universität Berlin. I. Jahrgang 1906. I. Teil : *Internationale Uebersichten*, viii + 366 pp. II. Teil : *Deutschland*, vi + 253 pp. III. Teil : *Das Ausland*, vi + 281 pp. Imperial 8vo. Berlin : Teubner, 1906. Price 12 marks.

It is the intention of the editor of this year book to provide a general survey of the industry, trade, and commerce of the world. By a careful selection and co-ordination of the more important facts and figures, the endeavour has been made to make the volume, not a mere statistical almanac, but readable and interesting. It is intended to exhibit the relations between the facts described, and to give "a picture of the entire web which the labour of millions has woven during the past year on the roaring loom of Time."

Such a survey can be carried out on two plans, according to countries, or according to the different divisions of industry. A survey on the former plan is necessary to exhibit the varying development of each separate nation, whilst the second is essential in order to bring out the relations between the different states. As the latter type of survey gives the wider and more general view, it is rightly given in the first Part of the volume; Part II gives the special survey for Germany, and Part III the similar surveys for other countries of the world. The data, for the most part, refer to 1905.

The international surveys in the first part are carried out in nineteen articles or chapters by different authors having special knowledge of each subject. The three introductory chapters are on politics — "Weltpolitik," "Weltwirthschaftspolitik" . (tariffs, treaties and agreements affecting trade, &c.), and "Weltsocial-politik" (movements affecting the working classes, housing and temperance reform, &c.). These are followed by two chapters on agricultural production and the production of the raw materials of industry, and four on the money market. We have then a brief survey of international trade, and three articles on transport and communications, the remainder dealing with insurance, the finances of the European and principal extra-European states, technology the industrial arts, the poor (legislation and movements affecting the poor, charitable organisations, the problem of unemployment, &c.), and "Wirthschaftsrecht," *i.e.*, the legislation affecting the internal trade of each country, as distinct from that affecting the international trade which was dealt with in the earlier article on " Weltwirthschaftspolitik." We have read several of the articles with considerable interest, and they appear to us to give useful summaries. It would be very desirable, however, especially in a year book intended for those who are not specialists, to do something towards a conversion of the tables to a uniform system of units. It is bewildering, for example, in the article on agricultural production, to keep passing from hectares to acres and from bushels and quarters to metric tons. Very few references are given in most chapters, and these might in future be made a little more complete for the sake of those who wish to refer to original sources.

The second part of the year book is, as we have stated, devoted entirely to Germany, with chapters on politics, agriculture, manufactures (treated in considerable detail, with chapters on each of the more important industries by specialists), building trades, internal waterways, banking and the money market, the labour market, industrial organisations, and foreign trade. Other countries are treated in less detail in Part III. Mr. Hewins has been entrusted with the article on the British Empire, and gives, wherever possible, comparative statistics for a series of years ; the article is, in fact, of distinctly a more historical tone than most. In general this is an advantage, but it is carrying the historical principle too far to give in such an article an introduction attributing the imperfections of our statistical organisation to the influence of "theoretical" conceptions and of the doctrine of *laissez faire.* The United States are treated very briefly but clearly in a series of curt summaries with an introduction by Dr. H. C. Emery. Each of the larger States of Europe has a chapter to itself, and the volume concludes with chapters on the Balkan States and Turkey, East Asia, and South America. The articles seem to vary a good deal in scope and arrangement, and it would be well if greater uniformity could be secured in this respect. Each part is paged separately and provided with an index.

Our general impression of the work is that the first part is likely to prove by far the most useful to the student. It is not a very difficult matter, if one has to do it, to obtain such information as is given in Parts II and III concerning the majority of the States there dealt with, but the international comparisons of the first part and the survey there given of the industrial movement of the world have not, so far as we are aware, their counterpart in any other volume. If the work could be lightened and rendered somewhat less costly by a compression of the last two parts, we believe it would be an advantage.　　　　　　　　　　　　　　　　　　G.U.Y.

18.—*La Russie Agricole devant la crise agraire.* Par Alexis Yermoloff. 350 pp., sm. 4to. Paris : Hachett and Co., 1907.

When ex-Ministers of Agriculture write an exposition on the agricultural position and agrarian politics of their own countries their labours command an attention among ordinary agricultural literature second only to that of an authoritative document of State. M. Méline's recent work on the French situation as regards the landed classes of the Republic, which was reviewed in this *Journal* (Dec., 1906), is now followed by the work which M. Yermoloff has published in French, and primarily for French readers, respecting the special characteristics of Russian agriculture, and their bearing both on the sad events lately witnessed in that Empire, and on the possibilities of agrarian reform. M. Yermoloff, whose personality is already favourably known to agriculturists far beyond his own country, and whose participation in the International Statistical Congress of 1897 at St. Petersburg will be remembered by some of our Fellows, held for upwards of twelve years the post of Minister of Agriculture and of the Domains of the Russian State from the foundation of that Ministry in 1893 by Alexander III, and he has played a considerable part in the efforts made to improve the very defective organisation of agriculture in Russia. Occupying, as he also does, the position of a practical agriculturist of reputation, owning and farming estates of considerable extent both on the south-east and near the centre of the Empire, and with further interests in the Caucasian littoral of the Black Sea, he is qualified to give a very reliable opinion. In a short preface to the present work, M. Henri Sagnier introduces to his brother agriculturists of France the Russian ex-Minister, and commends the skill in which he traces the evils of a grave situation without exaggeration and without passion, pointing out the true causes of the evils under which the peasantry of Russia labour, and the inevitable failure of the revolutionary and socialistic remedies sometimes recommended as likely to improve their future. While he equally opposes the wicked obstinacy of the classes who struggle to maintain the abuses of the present system, he unfolds in the several chapters of this volume a series of practical steps which may give hopes of reasonable reforms.

The work before us cannot take rank as a statistical treatise, nor does it lend itself to the criticism of statistical reviewers. The larger facts and figures of the vast Russian territory, its crops, its herds and flocks must be sought elsewhere in official publications. But these "studies," as M. Yermoloff names his several essays, are none the less to be recommended to the attention of the statistical student who would read aright the lessons of the huge and complex agricultural system of an Empire which at the same time as it exhibits a large exporting industry in primary agricultural products displays recurrent famines and distress at home, and a seething mass of agrarian tumult reflecting the chronic difficulties and misfortunes of the Russian producers.

Of the essential facts, we may remind the student that agriculture is the business of 80 per cent. of the 130,000,000 of inhabitants credited to this great State—even the workers engaged in other industries to a large extent retain their interest in the soil and return periodically to their country homes where their plots of land are tended by their wives and families. It might be hoped that here is realised that close relation to the soil—which some land reformers tell us would cure our own agricultural ills—for the greater part of the inhabitants of the country are described as "proprietaires terriens"—with plots varying from 2½ to 10 acres or more to each male. These may in the communes of the west actually belong to themselves—but in the provinces of the centre, north and east, the ownership falls rather to the "Mir," or commune, the land so held being only saleable under recent laws to members of the same commune or to other peasants with the authority of the "Mir," and not to persons of other classes. But the bad working of the communal system of land-working is clearly traced by the writer with all the local variations of condition to be found in the Empire. The want of labour at proper seasons leads to the migration of bands of workmen and the emigration of others towards new and less occupied territories in Siberia, in the north and east, and even towards Turkestan and the Caucasus. In many passages M. Yermoloff traces the hopeless impediments towards effective agricultural cultivation offered by the communal system of ownership, the changing allocation of the strips of peasant land everywhere, and the need of legislation tending to the establishment of the individual and responsible, rather than collective ownership with its hindrances to the proper culture of the soil. For the methods by which this may be accomplished, the reader must be referred to the chapters of this volume, as well as for the exposure which M. Yermoloff offers of the utopian schemes of a wholesale expropriation of such proprietors as now exist in certain provinces. Where they do so, they maintain a level of production which no peasant lands approach. The vaunted right of each person to the land, however attractive in theory, leads solely and inevitably, as he shows, to a "right to die on a plot of worn-out uncultivated soil unable to maintain a man." The vastness of the issues involved in the Russian agrarian system is evidenced by such figures as are here quoted.

While the peasant land at present covers 157,000,000 hectares, the extent of the proprietary estates is here quoted as nearly 117,000,000 hectares. The estates of the Crown and the Imperial family are put at a still higher figure, or 167,000,000 hectares, but these include 105,000,000 hectares of forest and 50,000,000 more of wastes impossible of cultivation. Of the arable land of Russia in Europe—129,000,000 hectares—two-thirds are in the hands of the peasants, 38,000,000 are in the hands of proprietors, and only 5,000,000 are left to be accounted for as owned by the State, or the "propriété de main-morte." It is interesting to note also in passing that 68 per cent. of the grain crops are grown on peasant land. The production on the peasant land is, as might be expected in all cases, below that of the owned land—ranging from 82 to 88 per cent. of the latter. Taking the four principal cereals which collectively yield to-day 476,000,000 of quintals, M. Yermoloff thinks the concentration of land in the peasants' hands would mean a loss of from 15 to 18 per cent in the aggregate production of the State.　　　　　　　　　　P.G.C.

19.—*L'Argentine au XXe Siècle.*   Par Albert B. Martinez et Maurice Lewandowski. 2nd Edition. 429 pp., 8vo. Paris : Librarie Armand Colin, 1907.   Price 5 fr.

Yet another publication respecting the character and industries of a State, prepared and issued by writers recently holding office, makes a claim to be noticed as offering a more or less authoritative exposition of the national position and outlook.   This time it is the Argentine Republic which is the subject of a treatise thus vouched for as at least semi-official, for not only is the first of the two authors above named himself a former Under-Secretary, but the volume is prefaced by an introduction from the pen of a late President of this South American State, M. Charles Pellegrini.   The position which Argentina has come to occupy and the growing volume of the business which its citizens transact with the Old World makes the pacific development of this country well deserving of attention, both as a field towards which a considerable stream of European emigration has been directed, and as one in which European, and more especially English, capital has been largely and successfully invested.   Indeed, it is here suggested that the successful invasion of Argentina by English capitalists was something in the nature of a pacific revenge for the failure of some military efforts to place our flag on Argentine soil early in the nineteenth century.   The writers of the present work are anxious that statisticians, economists, and commercial men here should learn more clearly the conditions which mark off the Argentine from the less stable neighbouring republics, such as Paraguay and Uruguay.   The satisfactory settlement of the dispute with Chili, by the arbitration which our own monarch undertook, has left the country free to develop its productive soil without the drawbacks and alarms which for fifty years threatened the republic.   After a preliminary chapter dealing with the country from the geographical and economic point of view, its railway system and mode of colonisation, the second part of the work treats of the agricultural conditions, the third of the commerce, and the last of the financial aspect in the Argentine.   To the numerous and interesting statements regarding the growth of the country in recent years the reader must be referred, and he will have no hesitation in agreeing with the writers that to secure a career of such development Argentina needs only to make more secure order and peace within its own borders and to improve its political administration. The authors claim for their country that its territories cover an area as large as all Europe, omitting Russia, but with a population of just over 5,000,000 persons.   Whether they have quite sufficient evidence for the assertion that its vast pampas afford room enough for 100,000,000 residents may of course be open to discussion, but the mere suggestion affords reason for thought as to its future.   Be this as it may, the wealth of Argentina rests, as the authors point out, on its agriculture, with its extending growth of cereals, and its breeding of live stock, and increasing exportation of their products. The maps attached to the volume give indication of the widely varying density of the agricultural production of wheat, of maize, of flax, and so on, and suggest that the extreme variety of physical and climatic conditions existing on Argentine territory must not be overlooked in any estimate of the ultimate development of the future of the country.   P.G.C.

20.—*The Industrial. Organisation of an Indian Province.* By Theodore Morison. vi + 327 pp., 8vo. London : John Murray, 1906. Price 10s. 6d. net.

Mr. Morison's interesting study was, he tells us in his Preface, " intended primarily for Indian students." His main object was to " review the principal economic facts in the society with which Indian students are familiar, and to show the relations of those facts to the abstract economics which they read in their text-books." He thus sought to substitute for illustrations of economic theories drawn from European industry examples less remote from actual Indian experience.   But, in the pursuit of this aim, which was directly practical, and specially appropriate to a teacher instructing pupils, he has contrived to produce a book which, we have no doubt, will fulfil the additional hope to which he has simultaneously given expression in his Preface.   It will, we are confident, also prove " interesting " to European readers, who " desire to study the industrial organisation of India for the purpose of comparative economics."   It is likely to be specially useful for this second object, with which the readers of the *Journal of the Royal Statistical Society* are more immediately concerned, because the author has taken great pains to show that the competitive forces, which are characteristic of modern European business, can be detected by careful scrutiny exerting an appreciable and persistent, if gradual, influence in the direction of change beneath a customary order of society which apparently remains on the surface unchanged.   He admits indeed a marked difference of environment, modifying the pace and affecting the results of the movement; but his mode of treatment of the particular subject he has chosen for close investigation tends to lessen and not to accentuate the sharp contrast often drawn between the Oriental and the Western world in economic affairs.   In this respect at any rate his book is unquestionably written from a standpoint which possesses the great interest of being new.

He himself, with justice, claims special novelty for the attempt here made to " consider the economic phenomena of an Indian province *as one whole*."   Studies of " particular industrial problems " are, he says, " scattered through the official literature " of the Government of India, and many experts have dealt previously in exhaustive fulness with technical subjects " like settlement, irrigation," and " famine relief."   He considers these last matters " only so far as is necessary to show their economic bearing "; and they thus take their fitting place in a detailed review of the whole industrial organisation of the province which he describes.   Not a few important considerations, however, connected with them arise in the natural course of his narrative, and they will, we suspect, be fresh to many of his readers.   The success in fact of his book, which, we believe, will be generally acknowledged, is largely due to the admirable skill with which he contrives to mingle suggestive apercus of future possibilities with faithful description of past and present fact. In recording what has been accomplished he does not neglect what may be achieved. The most important difference noted by him between India and Europe is the circumstance that in the former country the labourer works usually on his own account, and the rate of wages is accordingly of slight concern to the working class. On the other hand, in a society where industry is not directed, as in Europe, by men possessing "technical skill, commercial knowledge and administrative ability," the "national dividend" is likely to be small, and the share of each individual worker is much less than that of the ordinary English workman hired by a superior employer. Nor can division of labour be carried very far in such an environment, and the many small agricultural villages, in which the mass of the people are dispersed, constitute in the main self-sufficing industrial units. Agriculture indeed is still the chief industry with which an Indian province is familiar; and a survey of the industrial organisation of such a region is therefore necessarily for the most part a description of the economic conditions which govern agriculture.

Mr. Morison is careful here to distinguish what he calls the true "Indian" conception of landed property, which has only gradually gained recognition, from the "economic" theory which regards land as belonging to the State, and the land tax strictly as rent, and from the "English" view which has sought to discover or to create in India individuals who were or would become analagous to English landlords. According to the "Indian" conception, by contrast, the State does not seek to appropriate all the increment arising from the land, but, taking a considerable portion, it endeavours to protect the rights of subordinate tenants from the undue encroachments of the landlords whom it recognises. By the irony of fate, as Mr. Morison instructively argues, the establishment of settled order by the British Government has tended to remove the security against bad treatment by their landlords which the subordinate tenants previously obtained from the unsettled conditions that prevailed; and the interference of the State on their behalf has been required with increasing urgency and accorded in fuller and fuller measure. The pervasive business of the money-lender has seemed to demand no less careful attention from a government anxious for the welfare of the governed, and here again the caprice of destiny has afforded larger facilities for the practice of this opprobrious trade *pari passu* with the spread of civilised order and peaceful rule. For the danger is imminent that the peasant will use with avidity every opportunity given for extended credit; and in India a problem of perplexing difficulty in this connection has to be faced and overcome similar to that found in Europe wherever peasant proprietorship prevails. There the solution has been discovered in credit banks of the "Raiffeisen" type; and there unrestricted liberty of mortgage has proved a misfortune or curse rather than a benefit. Acts regulating the power of alienation, and encouraging Co-operative Credit Societies, have, for similar reasons, been recent features of Indian Legislation.

Such are a sample of the interesting questions which Mr. Morison discusses in his lucid narrative ; and the summary account we have given of his earlier chapters will suffice to show the independence and acumen with which he pronounces an opinion on the vexed points which arise. The careful investigation he has made in his final chapters on Indian prices will be of special interest to the readers of this *Journal*, and they will note that he confirms the conclusions advanced by Mr. F. J. Atkinson in a paper submitted to the Society in 1897. For he holds that the evidence of inland prices, so far as they can be ascertained, does not corroborate the inference commonly drawn from the prices of certain selected exports, that silver was a more stable measure of value than gold, because, while gold prices had fallen in Europe, silver prices had apparently not risen in India. On the contrary, he argues, three conclusions may be established by a study of charts of Indian prices of grain. Those conclusions are, firstly, that the prices of agricultural produce fluctuated violently before 1850 and attained comparative stability after 1860 ; secondly, that prices before 1850 were low and after 1860 were high, with a rising tendency ; and, thirdly, that before 1850 prices in different localities moved independently of each other, and that after 1860 they were linked together and fluctuated simultaneously. For the detailed arguments brought forward in support of these conclusions we would refer readers to Mr. Morison's book ; and we are certain that, if they once take it in their hands, they will not lay it down without entertaining a genuine appreciation of its absorbing interest. They will share with us a feeling of sincere and abiding gratitude to its competent and careful author.

L.L.P.

21.—*India and Imperial Preference*; with Statistical Tables. By Sir Roper Lethbridge, K.C.I.E., M.A. xiv + 105 pp., crown 8vo. London: Longmans, Green and Co., 1907. Price 2s. 6d. net.

In the vigorous discussion upon fiscal reform which has occupied so large a share of the attention of the British public during the last few years the position occupied by India in a scheme of Imperial Preference has, as we might expect, received some notice. The official opinion of the Government of India was stated at an early stage of the controversy in a Despatch which was naturally interpreted both by convinced free traders and by ardent tariff reformers as hostile to Mr. Chamberlain's propaganda. At the recent Colonial Conference Sir James Mackay reiterated the views expressed in that despatch. Yet it may be the case that these official declarations rested on a conception of the economic situation which can be shown to be narrow or mistaken ; and, when the examination of the present facts of Indian trade is pressed home, and a searching investigation made into the possibilities of the future, the final conclusion may be different. It may even be established that the interests of India in the substitution of Imperial Preference for the existing fiscal system are greater and more immediate than those of the self-governing Colonies, and that, more obviously than they, she stands to gain and not to lose by such a change. At any rate this is the thesis to which Sir Roper Lethbridge addresses himself in the interesting and important brochure which he has opportunely published; and no candid reader will rise from its perusal without feeling that, whether he agrees or does not agree with the issue of the argument, he must reckon with a very powerful statement of the case.

Sir Roper Lethbridge writes with the double advantage of a first-hand acquaintance with the circumstances of India, and of a professional knowledge of systematic Economics; and it is not uninstructive to note that he derives reasons for questioning those contentions of the Despatch of the Government of India, which were repeated the other day by Sir James Mackay, from considerations put forward authoritatively by Sir Edward Law, then Finance Minister of India, in a Minute appended to the Despatch. As was remarked at the time of the original publication of that despatch by the advocates of fiscal change, some inconsistency was apparent between the Despatch and the Minute. Free Traders may perhaps observe with suspicion that Sir Roper Lethbridge, like most Tariff Reformers, does not conceal an impatience with the hard dogmatic manner in which the free trade position has been stated by unyielding orthodoxy; nor does he refrain from the frank application of scornful epithets to some at least of the arguments of his opponents. He is avowedly a firm believer in the advantage and necessity of the cause which he champions. But he adduces substantial reasons for the faith that is in him, and he appeals to the solid evidence of recorded facts.

With the discretion of a robust courage founded on sure conviction he makes his way directly to the central position; for he scrutinises at close quarters the plausible argument that India has to fear dangerous reprisals from those foreign nations to which she now sends the bulk of the exports, on the continuance of which she confessedly depends largely for abiding prosperity, should she be joined with England and the self-governing Colonies in a system of Imperial Preference. Both on general grounds of reasonable policy, and on the basis of a detailed examination made seriatim of the different exports of India and of the circumstances of her trade with each separate country to which those exports go, he adduces forcible considerations in favour of his view that the fear of retaliation is unsubstantial. Modern tariffs are, he urges, deliberately framed to encourage the importation of raw materials, and the exports of India to foreign countries consist for the most part of raw materials which those countries need. It is improbable that they should, in the homely language of a well-known proverb, "cut off their nose to spite their face." Such an unlikely assumption rests only on the insecure foundation of the vulgar conviction that protectionists are ignorant fools. We think that, if Sir Roper Lethbridge be considered to have succeeded in this portion of his case, he has won more than half the battle; and we therefore commend the chapters in which he discusses this crucial question to the special notice of his readers. For our own part we have no doubt that he has shown that the matter had not hitherto received the full examination which it required, and that the conclusions of advocates of the *status quo* had been accepted on insufficient scrutiny.

But, if Sir Roper Lethbridge's criticisms in this respect, supported as they are by statistical fact, and by the arguments of Sir Edward Law in his Minute, be endorsed, his plea for Imperial Preference on the other grounds which he brings forward becomes of great, perhaps of irresistible, strength. That India can supply what England needs, and England furnish what India requires, in the way of trade, and that the two, united by preference, can make a further advance towards the goal of a self-contained sufficient business unit than the other constituent portions of the Empire, that special encouragement given to exports from India to the United Kingdom would be in itself of great economic advantage to the former country, would facilitate its moral and material welfare, and would simplify the problem of its finance, and that the political benefits to be derived from diverting the movement for native protection into the channel of mutual preference, and from securing as a *quid pro quo* from the self-governing Colonies that recognition of Imperial Citizenship for Indian-born subjects, which they now withhold, would be worth obtaining—are weighty considerations which might of themselves turn the scale in favour of Imperial Preference. In our opinion they are subordinate to that to which we previously directed attention, although they are advanced by Sir Roper Lethbridge with persuasive pains. His book is a notable contribution to the fiscal controversy, and deserves, and we feel sure that it will receive, the careful study of friends and foes alike. It may perhaps be fittingly read as a supplement to the official report of the proceedings at the recent Colonial Conference; for, while the Colonial Premiers had an opportunity of making some reply to the arguments adduced against the views which they had put forward on behalf of the self-governing Colonies, the case against preference seems alone to have been stated with reference to India. Sir Roper Lethbridge has shown that another view is possible, and it is well that view should be published. L.L.P.

22.—*The Domesday Inquest.* By Adolphus Ballard, B.A., LL.B., Town Clerk of Woodstock. 283 pp., 8vo. London: Methuen, 1907. Price 7*s.* 6*d.* net.

In the days when questions of valuation are again impending in the Legislature any fresh commentary on the monumental Valuation List of William the Conqueror may claim attention here, both on historical grounds and as a specimen of the statistical work of the eleventh century. The bulky volume appearing under the above title, with many illustrations and plates of intrinsic merit, aims, as its author tells us, at a careful presentation of the scope of the great survey of England in 1086, and an explanation in very full detail of the various terms employed. It is admitted that much has already been written on Domesday problems, but it is equally true that commentators not infrequently differ, and certain that much of the literature of the subject is scattered, and that some of

the most valuable treatises are hidden away in the transactions of
local archæological societies. Mr. Ballard naturally makes due
acknowledgment of the writings of earlier scholars, and quotes fully
such investigators as Professors Maitland and Vinogradoff and
Mr. Round, but the volume now before us makes a praiseworthy
endeavour to bring together and elucidate the mass of technical
information embodied in the original statistics as illustrating the
condition of rural England in the latter half of the eleventh
century, making, so far as may be, the phrases of the Domesday
book their own interpreter. The "questions" accidentally preserved at the Ely Inquest, or occasionally the several groups of
these questions, are taken in Mr. Ballard's work as texts for the
successive chapters, and the contents thus cover in successive
sections the questions of the Hide and the Teamland, the Vill and
the Manor, the Hundred and the Shire, while the condition of the
"Magnates" and that of "Humbler folk" is discussed in separate
chapters. On the Domesday evidence here collected, Mr. Ballard
ranges the latter in five categories—as freeholders, sokesmen,
villans, cottars and slaves. The methods of eleventh century
farming are deduced from the records in other chapters, and a
picture of a typical English village is constructed from the details
forthcoming in the description of Islip in Oxfordshire. A good
deal of space is occupied with the method and arrangement of the
original Domesday volumes with their varying degree of exhaustive-
ness, and it is shown how the smaller of the two original volumes—
that which contains the results for Essex, Norfolk and Suffolk—is
much the most complete, with its descriptions of the stock, the
encroachments, and even, in the last-named county, the names of
individual freemen. The balder statistics of the larger volume
confirm the idea that the East Anglian section was the first
compiled, and that its bulk deterred the later editors from
attempting again so lavish a use, and such a direct transcription
of the original returns, even if the "inquest" itself, as it proceeded,
was equally exhaustive in the particulars demanded.

Mr. Ballard insists on the advantage of studying the Domesday
book from William the Conqueror's own view of his position as
direct successor of Edward the Confessor, with whose reign, it is to
be remembered, the later data are contrasted in the twenty year
comparisons of 1066 with 1086; Harold's name, when it occurs
in the Domesday volume, it is noteworthy to remember, is
carefully suppressed or his rank reduced to that of "earl." The
fiscal uses and general purposes of the great inquiry and its
statistical methods and results, with their local variations, and
the pictures which these present, are carefully discussed in this
treatise into which so much scattered information is compressed.

In the statistical tables quoted, the possessions of landowners
of various grades and the number of teams employed on the King's
and other estates are shown county by county. The church lands
also are distinguished in some detail, and the last table furnished
brings together the relative numbers of tenants in capite, mesne
tenants having agriculturists under them, villans, bordars and

cottars, slaves, sokesmen, freemen, burgesses, and others. So far
as it goes, therefore, we have here an abstract of the population
dealt with almost in the manner of a census, for the Domesday
inquiry was not of course limited to the assessment area and the
values of the several properties. The King required to know also
the person liable to pay "geld," and this section of the work
provides some means of estimating the classes interested in the land
in their relative proportions.

Accepting Sir Henry Ellis's figures of 1,400 tenants in chief, and
7,871 mesne tenants, together regarded as making up the richer
class, and reckoning the recorded men of the lower class to represent
263,000 families, an estimate is made of the area of land sown with
corn south of Chester and Yorkshire. The net production of no
more than four bushels of grain per acre testifies to the low level
of agriculture in these distant times, and founding on that figure
and assuming 40 bushels per annum to suffice for the maintenance
of a man and his family, Mr. Ballard calculates that 3,900,000
acres would be required to provide this quota, together with the
tithes and dues exacted, whereas some 1,560,000 acres more would
represent the proportion of the demesne land under corn—making,
with an allowance for the area required to grow the food of working
oxen—a total of 6,000,000 acres.

The King himself comes first on the roll of landowners, and,
like the Czar of to-day, he was the largest individual landowner
of his kingdom. The proportion of the cultivated land held by
King William in 1086 was over 15 per cent., and a like proportion
of the teams were employed on his lands. The King's largest
estates lay, it would seem, in Devon, many of them forfeited
lands. In Middlesex he had only about $12\frac{1}{2}$ acres of "no man's
land," and, according to these Domesday figures, the land, on
which dwelt 32 cottagers, yielding him an income of $1l.\ 7s.\ 6\frac{1}{4}d.$
Omitting the three counties of Cheshire, Yorkshire and Suffolk,
on the ground of the extreme complexity of their statistics,
Mr. Ballard calculates that one-fourth of the whole assessment
of the country in the year 1066 was in the possession of the
church and its officers, and that $26\frac{1}{2}$ per cent. of its cultivated
area was so held twenty years later. South of the Thames, indeed,
$38\frac{3}{4}$ per cent. of the geld was paid by the church in 1066, and $31\frac{1}{4}$
per cent. of the cultivated land was so held in 1086, while north
of the Thames at this period only $18\frac{1}{2}$ per cent. of the geld was
paid by the church and 22 per cent. of the cultivated area owned.
The references to local questions and the variations of the record
for different districts is facilitated by a copious index.   P.G.C.

23.—*Land Reform, Occupying Ownership, Peasant Proprietary, and
Rural Education.* By the Right Hon. Jesse Collings, J.P., M.P.
443 pp., 8vo. London: Longmans, Green and Co., 1906.
Price 12s. 6d. net.

It is difficult to review, within the scope and under the limitations
of this *Journal*, what is more a library of political essays than a
treatise of an economic type, but it would be invidious to deny a

notice of his latest work to so honest and consistent a champion of "occupying ownership" as Mr. Jesse Collings is on all hands acknowledged to be. Even those who have not found him a convincing antagonist are ready to accord a cordial tribute to the sincerity of his advocacy in pressing in and out of season on all parties and on all Governments the views which he has made his own. Nevertheless, it may be forgiven to the reviewer if he expresses some regret that a more convenient arrangement had not been followed than the sequence adopted in these pages affords. For the reader is taken first over the detailed provisions of Mr. Collings' two measures, the Land Purchase Bill and that for promoting Agricultural Education and Nature Study in Public Elementary Schools, and only at the seventh chapter carried back to the origin and history of our present land system in England. Dealing with that history from the point of view of the peasant and the yeoman, the writer insists on the ills attributed to the policy of enclosures, and traces the successive " peasant revolts " from the days of Wat Tyler to those of Joseph Arch. It is surely by inadvertence, however, that the heading of "revolts"—even if the title be allowed to cover the story of the unsuccessful efforts of the Agricultural Labourers' Unions in 1872—is continued over the chapter, which reverts again to modern legislative efforts, and records the passing of the recent Allotment Acts and the Parliamentary history of the period which followed the carrying of Mr. Collings' Amendment to the Address in 1886. From this point the volume passes to a comparison of the English agricultural system, with the prevalence of occupying ownership in France. Arguments follow designed to meet the assertion that there is "no land hunger in England," and the comparative success of the Worcestershire County Council in working the otherwise unsuccessful Small Holdings Act of 1892, with a map and illustrations of the cottages erected, carries us to the close of the first half of the volume. With Chapter XVI come the answers offered to the objections raised to a land purchase scheme on Mr. Collings' scale and with the aid of State credit in the Irish fashion, while other schemes of land reform than those of the author are passed in review, special attention being drawn to the course of German land legislation begun by Stein and Hardenburg, which is contrasted with the policy of the territorial party in England, here regarded as depriving the rural population of all interest in the soil they cultivated.

A different class of arguments are then entered upon, and Mr. Collings may claim to be reaching statistical ground in asserting the too frequently overlooked importance of the "home market," and the losses which affect the industrial and commercial classes from the reduced profits of British agriculture in the last thirty years. Quoting the estimates of recent losses by the agriculturists of Britain as estimated by various authorities at figures running into many millions annually, the writer is brought to the general question of agricultural depression, the reduced supplies of native wheat, and to the dangers attending the food supply of the country in time of war. The report of the late Royal Commission

on this question is condemned as unsatisfactory, and it is suggested that they should have given greater attention to a development of the area under wheat in these islands. This area Mr. Collings still thinks could be wisely increased if only "cultivating ownership" were made more general, and some stimulus by bounties given either to wheat growing or wheat storing. It is interesting to note that he thinks that, instead of 2,000,000 acres under this cereal, 7,000,000 acres could be easily provided, and with that surface he assumes a supply sufficient, with the aid of Indian and Colonial imports, to guarantee the inhabitants of the United Kingdom against having to resort to the foreigner for any part of their bread. Neither, however, in the feasibility of this calculation with its attendant changes in the distribution of crops, nor in the estimates as to the development of employment can we follow the writer, and it would be useful to refer on this point to Mr. Crawford's cogent figures in his paper on Food Supply in this *Journal* in 1899 (vol. lxii). Some greater change than a scheme of land purchase would obviously be needed, and it is therefore not without significance that Mr. Collings passes from this point to deal with the relations of agriculture and fiscal policy in Great Britain; and it may be granted that he here touches a question which, if the analogies of foreign States are considered, bears probably more closely than any other on the conditions of extending profitable production. But there are other considerations introduced by this reference, on which it is not here possible to embark, if it were desirable in this place, even with the prospect of learning how to revive a great industry which suffers from low prices. Nor need we here do more than allude to the passages of this work which deal with rural depopulation and the relative density of the population carried on other than urban areas. The tables which are designed to show what room there is yet even in England for a denser agricultural population may well furnish matter for examination, but light is thrown on this question in the last discussion on Lord Eversley's paper on the decline of agricultural labourers, in which Mr. Collings himself took part; and, whatever gain there may be on hygienic and political grounds in that closer "repeopling of the country sides," for which Mr. Collings pleads, we notice with some regret his incidental use of this argument to condemn emigration, even where that is directed to the wide areas of food supply which, although they lie outside the narrow acreage of these islands, are nevertheless within the oversea regions of the British Empire. P.G.C.

24.—*The English Peasantry and the Enclosure of Common Fields.* By George Slater, M.A., D.Sc. 337 pp., 8vo. London: Constable and Co., 1907. 10s. 6d. net.

Noted as No. 14 of the "Studies in Economics and Political Science" of the London School of Economics, Dr. Slater's book has the advantage of coming before the public with an introduction by the present holder of the Presidency of the Board of Agriculture— Earl Carrington. It thus may be said to form one, therefore, of a series of treatises which have almost simultaneously appeared dealing with the past or present agrarian conditions of different States under the more or less direct official commendation. Among the additions of this type to the Library of the Royal Statistical Society we may include what M. Méline says of France, M. Yermoloff of Russia, and M. Pellegrini of Argentina. Apart, however, from this introduction, any re-statement of the history of the English peasantry and the exchange of collective for individual ownership of land demands a hearing in a time when both in political and statistical circles renewed attention is directed to agrarian policy. Lord Carrington, indeed, expressly points to this circumstance as justifying a closer study of the movement which altered the status of the English peasant, and he voices the reaction which is evident in the literature of the day from the old attitude of comparative neglect of matters agricultural attributed, not without reason, to a nation of town dwellers like the English. However much the decay of the village community may be in certain aspects a matter for regret, the hard logic of facts rendered the changes which brought this about, as Lord Carrington himself here very clearly admits, "inevitable." That being so, the interest which attaches to the history of enclosure in its varying forms in the sixteenth, seventeenth, and eighteenth centuries, at all events, is in a sense more academic than practical to-day ; and even the continued process in the first half of the nineteenth century, as it is chronicled in these pages, bears but indirectly on the problems of the agricultural situation of Great Britain in the twentieth century of our era.

Dr. Slater's work is avowedly and primarily academic in so far as it summarises the result of a painstaking series of researches into local and official records which he has been pursuing since 1894, and which formed the groundwork of a thesis approved by the University of London for the degree of Doctor of Science in Economics. One part of his labours can only be indicated here, for the valuable series of detailed county maps on which the author displayed the local distribution of "Common Field Enclosure" are to be sought for and consulted at the School of Economics by any students who desire to pursue this branch of investigation. Some of the reductions of the maps exhibited on the plates included in this volume suggest how interesting these geographical representations must be.

How far the record of the past and the picture of comparatively recent survivals of the old common field system may contain a lesson for new developments may indeed be open to question, but it is clear that the author himself hopes even yet to see a future in collective as opposed to individual ownership. Despite his efforts at impartial historical inquiry, one cannot get rid of the impression that in the marshalling of the facts he fails to appreciate at their true value the existing evidence in favour of enclosing. The admitted improvements of agriculture, which were aimed at by the enclosers, resulted in something rather more important than a mere "enhancement of rents," and justified and indeed required a new departure. The wasteful cultivation and arcadian simplicity of the old common field life of the peasant could not have continued unless the progress of the nation was to be checked. The pages of the work unconsciously breathe the author's own aspiration that even yet the agricultural policy of the twentieth century may be, as he describes it, "democratised" by the re-establishment of some revived principle of collective ownership. Ready as many of us may be to agree with Dr. Slater in desiring more facilities for modern types of co-operation and for opening a career of individual advance to each competent worker, the hard economic facts of agricultural production under twentieth century conditions forbid any confident hope that this goal may be reached by a recognised "right" of independent access to the soil for every single tiller of the land. The school and the railway have by themselves obliterated most of the old conditions under which the isolated village culture of the past survived, and it is a fortunate coincidence to find in another column of this *Journal* a timely warning in the condemnation by the *R*ussian Minister of Agriculture of the practical results of collective owner-ship and communal tillage in hindering the welfare and checking the production of the agriculturists of the east of Europe.

Apart, however, from the controversial side of the arguments here embodied, it is impossible not to award a high meed of praise to the industry of the writer and a welcome for this renewed presentation of the history, the progress, and the transformation of the land system of our country. The extracts from the General Report on Enclosures of 1808 are full of picturesque and signifi-cant detail. From a purely statistical standpoint, Dr. Slater has unearthed and grouped a mass of most interesting data respecting the local distribution and extent of the common field lands of England. The full lists of enclosures and the distinc-tion between parliamentary and non-parliamentary action represent much elaborate research and furnish very useful and com-pendious references for the student. The local reports of the condition of the country as respects the different forms of enclosure, made to the old Board of Agriculture more than a hundred years ago, are here subjected to careful analysis. Certain Parliamentary Returns, and notably that of 1873 (which it is a pity is not quoted by its official reference number), come in for criticism which is quite cogent and valuable. Those who have had occasion to study the history of enclosure well know the pitfalls which attend the examination of such records of area, and Dr. Slater's contention is that the estimate of still existing common fields, as distinct from common or waste officially given a generation ago, was exaggerated in the light of local facts here reproduced. To attempt to explain in detail the reduced and corrected estimates which are given would be a task beyond the scope of these notes. Both the tabular matter and the numerous local examples which are here so fully set out may well be recom-mended for study. But it must be clearly impressed on those who employ the looser arguments on the effect of enclosure that Dr. Slater's clear distinction between the effect of enclosure of waste—leading to the extended use of land for cultivation and arable production—and the minor process of enclosing arable common fields, with a view to a more profitable use of the land as pasture, must always be observed. The direct connection between certain forms of enclosure and depopulation which is here treated of may not be accepted in its entirety. In the face of more important factors governing the movement of population under the most diverse system of land tenure, this particular issue, which has been the subject of so much debate, is at the present day dead, as is indeed admitted here. The last words of the author point to the economic results of "the whole mass of little village revolutions" herein dealt with as increased population, increased production, increased national resources for taxation and for war—and so far we may agree with his conclusions, even if we find not quite proved the indictment that this was everywhere accompanied by a moral degradation of the quality as distinct from the quantity of human life. P.G.C.

25.—*Other New Publications.*

Alden (Percy) and *Hayward (Edward E.).* Housing. 2nd edit. [Social service handbooks. Edited by Percy Alden, M.P. No. 1.] 176 pp., 8vo. London: Headley Brothers, 1907. 1*s.* net.

Archer (J. A.). Compound interest, annuity and sinking fund tables. xvi + 180 pp., la. 8vo. Shaw and Sons, 1907.

"Artifex" and "Opifex." Causes of decay in a British industry. xvi + 296 pp., 8vo. London: Longmans, 1907. 7*s.* 6*d.* net. [Shows the injurious effect of legislation during 50 years on the fire-arms industry of Birmingham.]

Baden-Powell (B. H.). A short account of land revenue and its administration in British India: with sketch of land tenures. 2nd edit. 8vo. Oxford University Press, 1907.

Cadbury (Edward) and *Shann (George).* Sweating. [Social service handbooks. Edited by Percy Alden, M.P. No. 5.] 145 pp., 8vo. London: Headley Brothers, 1907. 1*s.* net.

Chorlton (J. D.). The rating of land values. 177 pp., 8vo. Manchester: University Press, 1907. 3*s.* 6*d.* net. [A review of various schemes in England and abroad, which involve the separate assessment of lands and buildings.]

Clark (Victor S.). The labour movement in Australasia. A study in social democracy. 8vo. London: Constable, 1907. 6*s.* net. [A history of the political labour party in Australia, by an American.]

Devas (Charles S.). Political economy. [Stonyhurst Philosophical Series.] 3rd edit. 8vo. London: Longmans, 1907. 7*s.* 6*d.* [1st edit., 1891, published in the series "Manuals of Catholic Philosophy."]

Evans (Samuel). Certain aspects of Transvaal taxation. Paper read before the Statistical Society of South Africa, March, 1907. 18 pp., 4to. Johannesburg, 1907. [The first publication of this newly formed Society.]

Fisher (Irving). Effect of diet on endurance based on an experiment, 1906. 46 pp., 8vo. Yale University Publications, 1907.

—— A graphic method in practical dietetics. 24 pp., 8vo. New Haven, Conn., 1907.

Fisher (Irving). Influence of flesh-eating on endurance. 16 pp., 8vo. New Haven, Conn., 1907.
[Three pamphlets giving the statistical results of experiments.]

Gannett (Henry). Statistical abstract of the world. viii + 84 pp., 24mo. New York: John Wiley and Sons, 1907.

Guyot (Yves). La science économique: ses lois inductives. [Bibliothèque des sciences contemporaines.] 3ᵉ édit. entièrement refondue. [1st edit., 1881.] xi + 531 pp., 8vo. Paris: Schleicher Frères. 1907. 5 frs.

Hall (Bolton). Three acres and liberty. Introduction by George T. Powell. 8vo. New York: Macmillan, 1907. 7s. 6d. net.
[Shows the possibilities of intense cultivation.]

Haynes (Thomas H.). Survey of Canadian imports and the results of preference. 16 pp., 8vo. London: *Daily Chronicle,* 1907. 2d.
[A continuation of a paper on Australian imports which appeared in the *Journal,* March, 1906, showing the difficulties of fixing a standard by which to test British exports for preferential treatment.]

Jacquart (Camille). La mortalité infantile dans les Flandres. Étude de démographie belge. 8vo. Bruxelles: Albert Dewit, 1907.

Joly (Henri). La Belgique criminelle. 8vo. Paris: J. Gabalda and Cie, 1907.

Julin (A.). De quoi se compose le commerce extérieur de la Belgique? [Études sur la statistique du commerce extérieur.] 50 pp., 8vo. Bruxelles: *Revue économique internationale.* 1907.

Mills (J. Saxon). Landmarks of British fiscal history. 123 pp., 8vo. London: A. and C. Black, 1907.
[Traces preferential policy in past British fiscal history.]

Pearce (A. James), A.C.A. Municipal rating and the collection of rates. 110 pp., 8vo. London: Gee, 1907.
[A practical handbook, giving form of rate book, &c.]

Pratt (Edwin A.). The licensed trade: an independent survey. 330 pp., 8vo. London: Murray, 1907. 5s. net.
[Deals with the problem from the point of view of actual traders.]

——— State Railways: object lessons from other lands. With translation of M. Marcel Peschaud's articles on " Les Chemins de fer de l'État Belge." 107 pp., 8vo. London: P. S. King and Son, 1907.

Punnett (R. C.). Mendelism. 2nd edit. 84 pp., 16mo. Cambridge: Macmillan and Bowes, 1907. 2s. net.
[An account of recent developments of Mendel's discoveries in heredity.]

Raseri (E.). Aumento di popolazione delle grandi agglomerazioni urbane in Italia durante il Secolo XIX. 20 pp., 8vo. 1907.

Spicer (A. Dykes). The paper trade. A descriptive and historical survey of the paper trade from the commencement of the 19th century. 282 pp., 8vo. London: Methuen, 1907. 12s. 6d. net.

Statistisches Handbuch für das deutsche Reich. Herausgegeben vom K. Statistischen Amt. 1. Teil. 750 pp., la. 8vo. Berlin: Carl Heymans Verlag, 1907. 7 Marks.

STATISTICAL AND ECONOMIC ARTICLES IN
RECENT PERIODICALS.

UNITED KINGDOM—

Accountants' Magazine, 1907—

April—The high bank rate: *Clark (Arch. B.).* Bankruptcy Reform: Private arrangements: *Morton (W. Kinniburgh).*

May—Economic causes as affecting the political history of the United States: *Daniels (Prof. W. M.).* The law of Agency: *Gloag (W. M.).*

June—The law of Agency: *Gloag (W. M.).* Parish council accounts: *Tod (Frederick).*

Bankers' Magazine, 1907—

April—Progress of Banking in Great Britain and Ireland during 1906: No. 3. Balance-sheets of banks in the United Kingdom. The gold reserve problem: *Revis (G. W.).* The latest American currency schemes: *Lawson (W. R.).*

May—Progress of Banking in Great Britain and Ireland during 1906: No. 4. Proportion of cash to deposits. How to strengthen the National Gold Reserve.

June—Progress of Banking in Great Britain and Ireland during 1906: No. 5. Proportion of capital and reserve to deposits. How prosperous trade affects the money market: *Lawson (W. R.).*

Economic Journal. June, 1907—The Budget of 1907 considered with special reference to the Income Tax: *Bastable (C. F.).* The English aspect of the small holding question: *Jebb (Miss L.).* Government and *laissez faire: Cohn (Gustav).* Economic literature in France at the beginning of the twentieth century: *Gide (Charles).* The influence of the rate of interest on prices: *Wicksell (Knut).* Appreciations of mathematical theories: *Edgeworth (F. Y.).* A letter of Malthus to Ricardo: *Foxwell (H. S.).* The Canadian tariff revision: *Flux (A. W.).* Commandite in France: *Saint-Léon (Et. Martin).* "Polish Labour" in the Scottish mines: *Maclauchlan (Francis).* The incidence of import duties: *Pigou (A. C.).*

Economic Review. April, 1907—First impressions of India: *Carter (Rev. J.).* Immigration and transmigration: *Dearle (N. B.).* L'Abbé Rambaud: *Raikes (Elizabeth).* Unemployment. I: *Mercer (A.).* Infant mortality: *McCracken (L. A. M. Priestley).* The economic position: *Fleming (Owen).* Legislation, parliamentary inquiries, and official returns: *Gough (G. W.).*

Journal of the Board of Agriculture, 1907—

April—A new method of treating meteorological statistics: *Lempfert (R. G. K.).* Maize as a fodder and silage crop: *Russell (Edward J.).*

May—Problems in potato-growing: *Bear (William E.).* Australian dairy legislation.

June—Agricultural arbitration in Scotland: *Connell (Isaac).* Utilisation of Peat land on the Continent.

UNITED KINGDOM—*Contd.*

Journal of the Department of Agriculture, &c., for Ireland. April, 1907—Field experiments, 1906. Barley, meadow hay, potatoes, mangels, oats and turnips. Technical instruction in Ireland : City of Belfast. Marketing of Irish eggs, poultry and fruit in 1906.

Journal of the Institute of Actuaries. April, 1907—Further notes on some legal aspects of life assurance practice : *Barrand (Arthur Rhys).* An investigation into the mortality among Scandinavian emigrants to the Congo : *Bergholm (Paul).*

Journal of the Institute of Bankers, 1907—
   April—The international money market : *Rozenraad (Cornelius).* Gilbart lectures, 1907. I and II : *Paget (Sir John, Bart.).* Clearing House returns of the United States.
   May—Bankers' advances on title deeds to landed property. Lecture IN : *Campion (Bernard).* Gilbart lectures, 1907. III and IV : *Paget (Sir John, Bart.).*
   June—Report of the council and proceedings at the annual general meeting. Bankrupts, and after acquired property : *Paget (Sir John, Bart.).*

Journal of the Royal Colonial Institute, 1907—
   April—The resources of Western Australia : *Rason (Hon. C. H.).*
   May—Some federal tendencies in Australia : *Hackett (Hon. J. W.).* The commercial possibilities of West Africa : *Mountmorres (Rt. Hon. Viscount).*
   June—Some phases of Canada's development : *Griffith (W. L.).* Agricultural possibilities in the Transvaal : *Burtt-Davy (J.).*

Surveyors' Institution. Transactions. Session 1906-07—
   Part 9—Underground Water. A discussion of certain recent enactments affecting water rights : *Graham (W. Vaux) and Bidder (Harold F.).*
   Part 11—The Prevention of Corruption Act, 1906 : *Gwyer (Maurice L.).*
   Part 12—Some features of the position of Scottish Agriculture, including the live stock industry : *Wallace (Robert).* The valuation roll in Scotland and the proposal to enter land values upon it : *Murray (David).* Notes on the Small Land-holders (Scotland) Bill, 1907 : *Mather (James).*

UNITED STATES—

American Journal of Sociology. 1907—
   March—The American Sociological Society. The establishment of sociology : *Ward (Lester F.).* How should sociology be taught as a college or university subject ? *Ellwood (Charles A.).* Western civilization and the birth-rate : *Ross (Edward A.).* Points of agreements among sociologists : *Small (Albion W.).*
   May—Sociology and the other social sciences : A rejoinder : *Hoxie (Robert F.).* Industrial insurance : *Henderson (Charles Richmond).* Progress as a sociological concept : *Woods (Erville Bartlett).*

UNITED STATES—*Contd.*

Bankers' Magazine (New York), 1907—*May*—The economic benefits of investments abroad : *Conant (Chas. A.).* Stock shares of private corporations : *Van Deuson (Edgar).* Frauds, forgeries and defalcations : *Hague (George).*

Bulletin of Bureau of Labor. March, 1907.—Wholesale prices, 1890 to 1906. Digest of recent reports of State bureaus of labor statistics : Kansas, Louisiana, Maryland, and West Virginia. Digest of recent foreign statistical publications. Decisions of courts affecting labor. Laws of various States relating to labor, enacted since January 1, 1904.

Journal of Political Economy, 1907—

March—The nature of capital and income : *Fetter (Frank A.).* The trade union programme of "enlightened selfishness" : *Cummings (John).* A statistical point in the Ricardian theory of Gold : *Bell (Spurgeon).*

April—The tendency of modern combination. I : *Youngman (Anna).* Economic problems in agriculture by irrigation : *Taylor (Henry C.).*

May—The commercial policy of Germany : *Lotz (Walther).* The tendency of modern combination. II : *Youngman (Anna).* The Prussian railway department and the milk supply of Berlin : *Meyer (Hugo R.).*

Political Science Quarterly. June, 1907—Iron and steel bounties in Canada : *Porritt (Edward).* Influences affecting thrift : *Johnson (A. S.).* Radical democracy in France. III : *Sloane (W. M.).* Formosa : Japan's first colony : *Hishida (Seiji).* Frederick William Maitland. Recent reports on taxation : *Seligman (E. R. A.).*

Quarterly Journal of Economics. May, 1907—Concerning the nature of capital : a reply : *Clark (John Bates).* The street-railway question in Chicago : *Fairlie (John A.).* The re-adjustment of San Domingo's finances : *Hollander (Jacob H.).* The concept of an economic quantity : *Carver (T. N.).* Bank reserves in the United States, Canada, and England : *Mead (F. S.).* English finances under the Long Parliament : *Scroggs (William O.).* Laws regulating the migration of Russians through Germany : *Goldenweiser (E. A.).* The Wisconsin Tax decisions of 1906 : *Adams (T. S.).*

Yale Review. May, 1907—The agrarian movement in Russia : *Simkhovitch (Wladimir G.).* The recent reforms in the consular service of the United States : *Bishop (Avard L.).* Our currency reform proplem : *Fairchild (Fred Rogers).* The basis of rate-making as affected by competition *versus* combination of railroads : *Brown (Harry G.).*

Annals of the American Academy of Political and Social Science, 1907—

January—Child labor; Papers by various writers. (Supplement.) Child labor legislation : *Goldmark (Josephine C.).*

March—Railway and traffic problems ; Papers by various writers. (Supplement.) Our State constitutions : *Dealey (James Quayle).*

UNITED STATES—*Contd.*
Annals of American Academy of Political and Social Science—Contd.
May—Tariffs reciprocity and foreign trade ; Papers by various
writers.

AUSTRIA-HUNGARY—
Statistische Monatschrift, 1907—
February—Die Methoden der medizinischen Statistik : *Winkler*
(*Dr. Ferdinand*). Österreichs Sparkassen im Jahre 1905 :
Ehrenberger (*H.*). Aufnahmen in den Staatsverband der im
Reichsrate vertretenen Königreiche und Länder und Entlas-
sungen aus demselben in den Jahren 1901-05 : *Rom* (*Adalbert*).
Der Verkehr auf den österreichischen Binnenwasserstrassen
und dessen Bedeutung für den Inlandsverkehr und den
Aussenhandel : *Krickl* (*Rudolf*).
March—Das österreichische Strassenwesen 1891-1904 : *Weyr*
(*Dr. Franz*). Die zeitliche Verteilung der Verunglückungen
im österreichischen Bergbau : *Rosenfeld* (*Dr. Siegfried*). Die
Pester öffentlichen Volksschulen in den Jahren 1871-1900 :
Bunzel (*Julius*). Die Ergebnisse der Viehzählung in Russland
1906 : *Pfaundler* (*Dr. Richard*). Die Bewegung der Be-
völkerung im Jahre 1905.
April—Gesellschaften mit beschränkter Haftung : *Herber*
(*Dr. Johann v.*). Österreichs Sparkassen im Jahre 1905.
Fortsetzung) : *Ehrenberger* (*H.*). Österreichs Banken im
Jahre 1905 : *Lowe* (*A. K.*).

FRANCE—
Annales des Sciences Politiques, 1907—
March—L'intérieur du gouvernement consulaire (1800) :
Vandal (*Albert*). Questions ouvrières et industrielles en
France depuis 1870 : *Levasseur* (*Émile*). Le parti du centre
en Allemagne et les élections de janvier-février 1907 :
Isambert (*G.*). Les débuts de l'expansion coloniale de la
France moderne : *Lavagne* (*Paul*). Chronique des questions
ouvrières (1906) : *Festy* (*O.*).
May—La politique douanière de l'Espagne (1816-1906) :
Marvaud (*A.*). Les voies de pénétration et de communication
en Afrique occidentale française (avec cartes) I : *Ferry* (*R.*).
Les " Études politiques " de M. E. Boutmy : *Caudel* (*M.*).
Chronique budgétaire et législative (1906) : *Lavergne* (*de*).
Bulletin de Statistique, Ministère des Finances, 1907—
March—Projet de loi portant suppression des contributions
directes et établissement d'un impôt général sur les revenus
et d'un impôt complémentaire sur l'ensemble du revenu. Les
revenus de l'État. Angleterre—La dette nationale en 1905-06.
April—Recettes et dépenses comparées des exercices 1896 à
1905. Les monnaies fabriquées à la Monnaie de Paris et la
circulation monétaire en 1906. Angleterre — L'exposé
financier du Chancelier de l'Échiquier. Russie—Le projet
de budget pour 1907.

France—*Contd.*
  Bulletin de Statistique, Ministère des Finances, 1907—*Contd.*
    May—Le projet de budget pour l'exercice 1908. Les revenus
    de l'État. Pays divers—Les émissions publiques en 1906.
    Angleterre—L'income-tax de 1895-96 à 1905-06.
  Journal des Économistes, 1907—
    April—Lettres inédites de Du Pont de Nemours au Comte
    Chreptowicz : *Schelle (G.).* Théorie de l'évolution : Progrès
    nécessités par la fondation des états : *Molinari (G. de).* Le
    mouvement financier et commercial : *Zablet (Maurice).* Revue
    des principales publications économiques de l'étranger : *Breton
    (René).* La ligne souterraine nord-sud de Paris : *Letourneur
    (E.).* Lord Goschen (1831-1907) : *Raffalovich (A.).*
    May—La banqueroute du socialisme de la chaire : *Guyot (Yves).*
    Le service des transports en commun : *Mossé (Armand).*
    Mouvement agricole : *Molinari (Maurice de).* Revue des
    principales publications économiques en langue française :
    Rouxel (M.). Les mesures d'interventionnisme contre le
    chômage en Grande-Bretagne : *Bellet (Daniel).* Le developpe-
    ment économique de l'Empire Allemand : *Huart (Albin).*
    Lettre des États-Unis : *Nestler-Tricoche (George).*
    June—La théorie de l'évolution : *Molinari (G. de).* L'indé-
    pendance fiscale des pouvoirs locaux et la liberté individuelle :
    Goy (Louis de). La municipalisation du service des pompes
    funèbres : *Letourneur (E.).* Mouvement scientifique et
    industriel : *Bellet (Daniel).* Revue de l'académie des sciences
    morales et politiques (du 15 février au 15 mai 1907) : *Lefort
    (J.).* Travaux des chambres de commerce : *Rouxel (M.).*
    Quelques conséquences de l'impôt sur le revenu : *X . . .*
  Journal de la Société de Statistique de Paris, 1907—
    April—Le peuple algérien. Essais de démographie algérienne :
    Demontès (V.). La répartition des industries aux États-Unis
    d'après le Census de 1900 : *Guyot (Yves).* Les émissions et
    remboursements d'obligations des six grandes compagnies de
    chemins de fer en 1906 : *Neymarck (Alfred).* Les pensions
    civiles : *Malzac (M.).*
    May—La répartition des industries en France, d'après les
    résultats statistiques du recensement de 1901 : *Guyot (Yves).*
    La population et la représentation parlementaire en Angle-
    terre : *Meuriot (Paul).* Composition et importance de la
    fortune de l'État, en France : *Colonjon (F.).*
    June—La répartition des industries en Belgique : *Guyot (Yves).*
    Composition et importance de la fortune de l'État, en France :
    Colonjon (F. de).
  La Réforme Sociale, 1907—
    1st April—Les institutions locales de l'Angleterre—I. Autrefois :
    Auburtin (F.). Études de vie rurale. Un bon placement,
    lettre ouverte à un archi-millionnaire : *Vidal (Victorin).* La
    situation générale de l'Allemagne et son rôle dans la politique
    universelle : *Combes de Lestrade (Vicomte),* &c. La société
    pour l'assistance paternelle aux enfants employés dans les

FRANCE—*Contd.*

La Réforme Sociale, 1907—*Contd.*

1*st April—Contd—*
industries des fleurs et des plumes : *Voyard* (André). Le
problème des habitations ouvrières à Venise : *Lepelletier* (F.).

16*th April*—La réunion annuelle de 1907 sur le rôle des institutions patronales dans la vie industrielle contemporaine :
Auburtin (*Fernand*). L'impôt sur le revenu à l'étranger et en
France (premier article) : *Hubert-Valleroux* (M.). L'action
sociale des catholiques belges : *Rivière* (*Louis*). Les com-
munautés de famille en Auvergne : *Achalme* (*Lucie*).

1*st May*—Le taudis, ses dangers, ses remèdes : *Cheysson* (E.).
L'impôt sur le revenu (dernier article) : *Hubert-Valleroux* (M.).
Le faux libéralisme, à propos d'un livre recent : *Cilleuls*
(Alfred des). L'œuvre de "L'ouvrière au grand air" à
Chambéry : *d'Oncieu de Chaffardon* (*Marquis*). Chronique du
mouvement social—Italie et Espagne : *Lepelletier* (F.).

16*th May*—Comment travaillait Le Play (Souvenirs personnels) :
Escard (*François*). Les institutions locales de l'Angleterre—
II. Aujourd'hui : *Auburtin* (*Fernand*). Positivisme et
anarchie : *Cottin* (*Paul*). L'assurance contre le chômage :
Las Cases (*Philippe de*), &c. Études de vie rurale. Une
terrienne modèle : *Vidal* (*Victorin*).

1*st June*—La défense patronale en cas de grèves : *Gigot* (Albert).
La situation de l'ouvrière isolée : *Lebrun* (P.). L'assurance
contre le chômage : *Las Cases* (*Philippe de*). Les fidéicommis
en Allemagne : *Blondel* (*Georges*). Les jardins ouvriers de
l'Oise et de Compiègne : *Escard* (*Paul*). Le coût de retraites
ouvrières dans les deux systèmes de l'assurance obligatoire
et de la liberté subsidiée : *Cheysson* (E.) and *Rostand* (*Eugène*).

16*th June*—La famille détruite par le code civil. L'agonie des
Mélouga : *Bayard* (M.). La petite bourgeoisie en Belgique :
Pyfferoen (*Oscar*). Les institutions locales de l'Angleterre.
III. Aujourd'hui (dernier article) : *Auburtin* (*Fernand*).
L'Éducation sociale à Amsterdam : *Rivière* (*Louis*).

GERMANY—

Allgemeines Statistisches Archiv. Band 7. *Halbband* 1. 1907—
Die Berechtigung der "Moralstatistik" : *Mayr* (*Georg v.*). Die
Ursachen der Totgeburt : *Prinzing* (*Dr. Fr.*). Ueber den Anteil
germanischer Völker an der Entwicklung der Statistik : *Behre*
(*Otto*). Methodologisches zur Verwertung der Einkommen-
steuerstatistik. Ueber die Notwendigkeit systematischer Arbeits-
teilung auf dem Gebiete der Bevölkerungs- (Sozial-) Statistik
(Schluss) : *Bleicher* (H.). Zur Methodik und Tecknik statisti-
scher Karten : *Mayr* (*Georg v.*). Kartographische Darstellung der
Volksdichtigkeit : *Schmidt* (*Dr. G. H.*). Rückläufige Gebürt-
lichkeit und Säuglingssterblichkeit in Neu-Südwales : *Most*
(*Dr. Otto*). Zur Geschlechtsgliederung der städtischen und
ländlichen Bevölkerung : *Feld* (*Dr. W.*). Ueber die spezifische
Sterblichkeit der beiden Geschlechter : *Knöpfel* (L.). Die

GERMANY—*Contd.*
Allgemeines Statistisches Archiv. *Band* 7. *Halbband* 1. 1907—*Contd.*
  wirtschaftliche und soziale Struktur Oesterreichs : *Fehlinger (H.)*.
  Die britisch-indische Bevölkerung nach den Ergebnissen der
  Volkszählung von 1901 : *Mayr (Georg v.)*.   Der Zensus von
  1903 auf den Philippinen : *Fehlinger (H.)*.
Archiv für Rassen- und Gesellschafts-Biologie, 1907—
  March-April—Untersuchung über den Erfolg und die zweckmäs-
    sigste Art der Durchführung von Veredelungs-Auslese-Züch-
    tung bei Pflanzen mit Selbstbefruchtung. [Completed in next
    issue] : *Fruwirth (Dr. C.)*.   Über Dolichocephalie und Brachy-
    cephalie. Zur Kritik der Indexangaben : *Johannsen (Dr. W.)*.
    Die Sterblichkeit der Juden in Wien und die Ursachen der
    jüdischen Mindersterblichkeit (Schluss) : *Rosenfeld (Dr. S.)*.
    Kritik und Antikritik der Mneme : *Semon (Dr. R.)*.
  May-June—Entwicklungsgeschichtliche Gedanken zur Frage
    der Kurzsichtigkeit und Weitsichtigkeit : *Steiger (Dr. A.)*.
    Die jüdische Rassenfrage : *Auerbach (Dr. E.)*.   Offener Brief
    an Herrn Dr. Elias Auerbach : *Luschan (Dr. F. von)*.   Zwei
    historische Geburtenkurven fürstlicher und ritterschaftlicher
    Geschlechter.   Ein Beitrag zur Lorenz'schen Generationen-
    lehre : *Strohmayer (Dr. W.)*.
Archiv für Sozialwissenschaft und Sozialpolitik, May, 1907—Sozio-
  logie der Über- und Unterordnung : *Simmel (Prof. G.)*.   Die
  Verschuldungsgrenze für Bauerngüter in Deutschland : *Mauer
  (Dr. H.)*.   Zur Lage der Kellnerinnen im Grossherzogthum
  Baden : *Peter (Dr. H.)*.   Kellnerinnenelend : *Jellinck (Camilla)*.
  Die genossenschaftliche Kreditorganisation des Kleingewerbes
  und Kleingrundbesitzes in Oesterreich : *Gaertner (F.)*.   Arbeiter,
  Unternehmer und Staat in Japan : *Schachner (R.)*.
*Jahrbuch   für   Gesetzgebung,   Verwaltung   und   Volkswirtschaft
  (G. Schmoller), Heft* 2, 1907—Zur Philosophie der Herrschaft :
  Simmel (G.).   Spinoza in der deutschen Staatslehre der Gegen-
  wart : *Menzel (A.)*.   Zur naturwissenschaftlichen Gesellschafts-
  lehre, IV. Eine Replik : *Tönnies (F.)*.   Emil Steinbach als
  Sozialphilosoph : *Wittmayer (L.)*.   Klima, Boden und Mensch :
  Penck (A.).   Das Rentenprinzip in der Verteilungslehre, II :
  Schumpeter (J.).   Das Geldsystem des Grossherzogthums Luxem-
  burg : *Calmes (A.)*.   Organisation, Lage und Zukunft des
  deutschen Buchhandels.   Zugleich ein Beitrage zur Kartell-
  frage, II : *Koppel (A.)*.   Über Arbeitslosenversicherung und
  Arbeitsnachweis, II : *Oldenberg (K.)*.   Die Ertartungsfrage in
  England : *Herkner (H.)*.
Jahrbücher für Nationalökonomie und Statistik (Conrad's), 1907—
  April—Die Böhm-Bawerksche Kapitalzinstheorie: *Schaposchnicoff
  (N.)*.   Gutszertrümmerungen und die braunschweigische
  Statistik über dieselben : *Zimmermann (F. W. R.)*.   Der
  preussische Sparkassengesetzentwurf vom Standpunkte städt-
  ischer Finanzpolitik : *Zahn (F.)*.   Die wirtschaftliche Gesetz-
  gebung der deutschen Bundestaaten im Jahre 1906. [Contd.
  in June No.] : *Hesse (A.)*

GERMANY—*Contd.*

Jahrbücher für Nationalökonomie und Statistik (Conrad's), 1907—*Contd.*
May—Über die Methoden der Einkommenverteilungsstatistik :
Bresciani (C.). Über die Kursnotierung an der Börse, ihre
Schäden und die Mittel zur Schaffung der Kurszettelwahrheit :
Wermert (G.). Die finanzstatistische Arbeit in deutschen
Städten, erläutert an dem Material über die Kostensteigerung
der höheren Schulen in Barmen : *Seutemann (K.).* Die
Baumwollfrage : *Koch (Hans).*
June—Die Grossstadt als Standort der Gewerbe : *Schwarzschild*
(O.). Die Auskünfte der Arbeitgeber für Steuerzwecke und
ihre Verwendung für die Einkommen- und Lohnstatistik :
Hesse (A.). Zur Versicherung der Privatbeamten :
Wagner (M.).
Vierteljahrshefte zur Statistik des Deutschen Reichs. Heft 2, 1907—
Die Finanzen des Reichs. Zur Statistik der Preise. Kriminal-
statistik (Heer und Marine), 1906. Krankenversicherung
(1905, and 1901-05). Schlachtvieh- und Fleischbeschau, 1906.
Zeitschrift für Socialwissenschaft, 1907—
Heft 3—Die Stellung der Frau in der Urgeschichte der
Zivilisation : *Westermarck (Prof. E.).* Der Gegensatz der
Japaner und der Nord-Amerikaner im Stillen Ozean : *Brandt*
(M. von). Die schwedische Eisenerzfrage : *Fahlbeck (Prof. P.).*
Der Entwurf der schweizerischen Kranken- und Unfallver-
sicherung : *Mugdan (Dr. O.).*
Heft 4—Die Verstaatlichungsfrage beim Kalibergbau : *Strutz*
(Dr.). Der weltwirtschaftliche Ausgleich zwischen Landwirt-
schaft u. Industrie : *Schilder (S.).* Heiratsbeschränkungen,
I : *Marcuse (Max).* Der Sklavenhandel im mittelalterlichen
Italien : *Schneider (K.).* .
Heft 5—Die Gebiete der offenen Tür in der Weltwirtschaft :
Schilder (Sigmund). Heiratsbeschränkungen, II (Schluss) :
Marcuse (Max). Der Selbstmord bei den afrikanischen
Naturvölkern, I : *Steinmetz (S. R.).* Die Arbeiterversicher-
ungsgesetze in der russischen Montanindustrie : *Martell (P.).*
Heft 6—Die Tropen in der Weltwirtschaft : *Schilder (S.).* Die
Zukunft des Kupfers : *Schmidt (A.).* Methoden des gewerb-
lichen Einigungswesens : *Harms (B.).* Der Selbstmord bei
den africanischen Naturvölkern, II (Schluss) : *Steinmetz (S. R.).*
Zeitschrift für die gesamte Staatswissenschaft. Heft 2, 1907—
Wege und Abwege der Steuerpolitik : *Mayr (G. von).* Die
Reform der direkten Steuern in Frankreich : *Hoffmann (P. G.).*
Die geschichtliche Entwicklung der deutschen Arbeitgeber-
organisation : *Kessler (G.).* Volks- und Pensionsversicherung
und die Vereinsversicherungsbank für Deutschland : *Seidel (—).*
Ergebnisse des V. Internat. Kongresses für Versicherungs-
wissenschaft : *Worner (G.).*
Zeitschrift für die gesamte Versicherungs-Wissenschaft. April, 1907—
Die Bedeutung der drahtlosen Telegraphie für die Versicherung,
insbesondere die Seeversicherung : *Lodemann (Lieut.).* Über
die traumatische Neurose : *Müller (F. C.).* Der Einfluss der

GERMANY—*Contd.*
Zeitschrift für die gesamte Versicherungs-Wissenschaft—Contd.
Dimensionen des Feuerrisikos auf den Prämiensatz: *Savitsche*
(*S. von*). Die deutsche Viehversicherung in ihren Haupt-
formen: *Ehrlich* (*H.*). Die englische Arbeiter-Unfallver-
sicherung nach der Novelle zum Haftpflichtgesetz: *Wolff*
(*H. W.*). Der Einfluss des künftigen Reichsgesetzes über den
Versicherungs-Vertrag auf die bestehenden Versicherungs-
bedingungen: *Gerhard* (*S.*). Beitrag zur Zinstheorie:
Pexider (*I. V.*). Zur Verteidigung der Haftpflichtgarantie-
Versicherung: *Kohl* (*H.*).

ITALY—
Giornale degli Economisti, 1907—
  February—Appunti sui metodi per la rilevazione dell' anda-
    mento del mercato del lavoro: *Bachi* (*R.*). Due recenti libri
    sul commercio internazionale e la politica commerciale:
    Graziani (*A.*). Sulla funzione revisoria della corte dei conti:
    Nicario (*F.*). Nota su di un problema d'annualità: *Broggi*
    (*U.*). Rassegna del movimento scientifico: *Ricci* (*U.*) and
    Flora (*F.*).
  March—I lavoratori della terra in provincia di Bari (condizioni
    economiche): *Ragone* (*G.*). Sulla funzione revisoria della
    corte dei conti: *Nicario* (*F.*). Note alla statistica metodo-
    logica del Prof. Benini: *Broggi* (*U.*). Principii fondamentali
    di economia: *Menger* (*C.*). [Translation continued.]
  April—Appunti sui metodi per la rilevazione del mercato del
    lavoro: *Bachi* (*R.*). Il problema delle assicurazioni operaie
    in Italia: *Bagni* (*T.*). Rapport au Ministère des finances par
    l'Administration des monnaies et des médailles: *Salvioni* (*B.*).
    I coniugati sotto l'età legale e il censimento 10 Febbraio
    1901: *Mortara* (*G.*). Rassegna del movimento scientifico:
    Ricci (*U.*) and *Bresciani* (*C.*). A proposito di una recensione:
    Natoli (*F.*).
  May—L'interpolazione per la ricerca delle leggi economiche:
    Pareio (*N.*). Appunti sui metodi per la rilevazione dell'
    andamento del mercato del lavoro: *Bachi* (*R.*). Se l'arbitrato
    obbligatorio sia oggi possibile nell' agricoltura: *Coletti* (**F.**).
    Rassegna del movimento scientifico: *Ricci* (*U.*).
La Riforma Sociale, 1907—
  March—La determinazione della durata della generazione e il
    calcolo della ricchezza privata di un paese: *Coletti* (*Francesco*).
    Gli enti locali e le spese di stato: *Garelli* (*Alessandro*). Il
    Ministero di agricoltura. (Discorso pronunciato il 15 Febbraio
    alla Camera dei Deputati): *Nitti* (*F.*). Conti culturali e
    dazio sul grano: *Cabiati* (*Attilio*). Un' inchiesta sul riposo
    festivo: *Regis* (*A.*). Il demanio forestale dei comuni e la
    loro attività economica: *Tenerelli* (*F. C.*)
  April—La determinazione della durata della generazione e il
    calcolo della ricchezza privata di un paese: *Coletti* (*Francesco*).
    La previdenza all' esposizione di Milano: *Schiavi* (*Alessandro*).

ITALY—*Contd.*

La *Riforma Sociale*, 1907—*Contd.*

April—*Contd.*

Per una storia giuridico-sociale di Roma: P*rato* (*Giuseppe*). Piccola polemica.: *Mosca* (*Gaetano*). Milano benefica e previdente: *Spectator.* Il debito ipotecario fruttifero al 31 Dicembre 1903: *Spectator.*

May—Sulla disoccupazione operaia: *Graziani* (*Augusto*). La basilicata: *Vita* (*Alfredo*). Appunti sull' emigrazione dalla Calabria: *Nobili* (*Leonello de*). Una questione grave per i pubblici impiegati e la legge per la cedibilità del quinto: *Gabriel.* L'imposta sulle aree fabbricabili e il nuovo progetto di legge per Roma: *Geisser* (*Alberto*).

Rivista Italiana di Sociologia, 1907—

January-February—La concezione naturalistica dell' universo e la sociologia: *Gumplowicz* (*L.*). Tendenze socialistiche nella Persia del Medio Evo: *Pizzi* (*I.*). Lotta di classe e pensiero moderno: *Vaccaro* (*M. A.*). La forza di attrazione delle grandi città: *Mortara* (*G.*). Dati statistici sulla composizione delle famiglie in Piemonte nel 1621: *Ottolenghi* (*C.*). Intorno alla popolazione del Piemonte nel secolo XVII: *Prato* (*G.*).

March-April—Il costo della vita e la classe operaia in Francia: *Levasseur* (*E.*). Il fattore economico dell' espansione coloniale: *Fanno* (*M.*). Intorno alla costituzione politica e sociale dei popoli oceanici: *Savorgnan* (*F.*). La teoria della conoscenza e la sue attinenze con lo studio della società: *Pagano* (*A.*).

SWITZERLAND—

Journal de Statistique Suisse. Lieferung 2, 1907—Das Armenwesen in Oberitalien: *Schmid* (*Dr. C. A.*). La Suisse et la question des langues: *Henry* (*René*). Die Selektionssterbetafeln, die Unkostendeckung und die Verrechnung von Abschlusskosten der Versicherungen auf den Todesfall: *Riem* (*J.*). Die Versicherungswissenschaften im Unterrichtswesen der Schweiz: *Bohren* (*Dr. A.*). Die Verbreitung der Lungentuberkulose im Kanton Basellandschaft: *Bollag* (*Dr. M.*). Mitteilungen uber die Preise der wichtigsten Lebensmittel und anderer Bedarfsartikel im Januar 1907: *Zuppinger* (*C.*). Verbrauch von Nahrungsmitteln im kantonalen Frauenspital in Bern im Jahre 1906: *Herzig* (*Ernst*). Die Rentenversicherung in verschiedenen Ländern: *Kihm* (*C.*).

QUARTERLY LIST OF ADDITIONS TO THE LIBRARY.

During the Quarter ended 15th June, 1907, the Society has received the publications enumerated below. The titles are arranged alphabetically under the following heads:—(a) Foreign Countries; (b) India and Colonial Possessions; (c) United Kingdom and its Divisions; (d) Authors, &c.; (e) Societies, &c. (British); - (f) Periodicals, &c. (British).

(a) Foreign Countries.

Argentine Republic—

Agricultura. Ministerio de, Boletin mensual de Estadística y Comercio. (Current numbers). 1907 Estadística Agricola, año 1906. 8vo. 1907 .... } The Ministry of Agriculture

Bulletin démographique argentin. (Current numbers.) Fol. 1907 .... } The Oficina Demografica Nacional

Buenos Ayres (Province). Direccion General de Estadística. Boletin mensual. (Current numbers.) 1907 .... } The Provincial Statistical Bureau

Córdoba (City). Boletín mensual de estadística municipal. Año ii, No. 14. Fol. Feb., 1907. .. ... } The Municipal Statistical Bureau

Austria-Hungary—

Ackerbau-Ministeriums, Statistisches Jahrbuch des k.k., für 1906. (Current numbers.) 8vo. 1907 ... } The Government of Austria-Hungary

Arbeitsstatistischen Amtes im Handelsministerium. Mitteilungen des k.k., (Current numbers.) 8vo. 1907 .... Arbeit. Bericht über die Tätigkeit des k. k. Arbeitsstatistischen Amtes während 1906. 8vo. 1907 .. } The Austrian Labour Department

Eisenbahnstatistik für 1905, Österreichische, Teil 2, Kleinbahnen und diesen gleichzuhaltende Bahnen sowie Schleppbahnen. Fol. 1907 .... } The I. and R. Ministry of Railways

Landwirtschaftlichen Betriebszählung, 3. Juni 1902. Vorläufige Ergebnisse der, Summarische Daten für das Reich, die Länder und die Verwaltungsgebiete. Fol. 1907 .... } The Central Statistical Commission

Mittheilungen des k.k. Finanzministeriums. (Current numbers.) La. 8vo. 1907 .... } The Ministry of Finance

Österreichisches Wirtschaftspolitisches Archiv (vormals "Austria"). (Current numbers.) 8vo. 1907 } The Ministry of Commerce

Rechtspflege. Ergebnisse der Strafrechtspflege im Jahre 1904. Fol. 1907 .... Sanitätswesens, Statistik des, für 1903. Fol. 1907 Statistische Monatschrift. (Current numbers.) 1907 Statistische Nachrichten aus dem Gesammtgebiete der Landwirtschaft. (Current numbers.) 1907............ } The Central Statistical Commission

Hungary—

Annuaire Statistique Hongrois. Nouveau cours, xiii, 1905. La. 8vo. 1907 .... Dénombrement de la population en 1900. 5e partie. Quelques autres détails concernant la profession de la population et Statistique des entreprises. 7e partie. Données professionnelles combinées avec les principales données démographiques. 2 vols., la. 8vo. 1906 .... } The Central Statistical Bureau

(a) **Foreign Countries**—*Contd.*

Hungary—Contd.

Table de Mortalité, sur la base des données du
recensement de 1900 et sur celle des données
relatives uu mouvement de la population de 1900
et 1901. La. 8vo. 1906 .... } The Central Statisti-
cal Bureau

Budapest. Monatshefte des Budapester Communal-
Statistischen Bureaus. (Current numbers.) 1907 } The Municipal Sta-
tistical Bureau

Compass. Finanzielles Jahrbuch für Oesterreich-
Ungarn. 1907. 40er Jahrgang. 2 vols. 8vo. 1906 } The Editor

Belgium—

Annales des Mines. (Current numbers.) 8vo. 1907 { The Administration
of Mines

Budgets des recettes et des dépenses du Royaume
pour l'exercice 1907. Fol. 1906 ....
Chemins de fer, postes, télégraphes, téléphones et } Dr. J. S. Keltic
marine. Compte rendu des opérations pendant 1904.
Fol. 1905 ....

Travail. Monographies Industrielles. Aperçu écono-
mique, technologique et commercial. Groupe iv.
Industries céramiques. 8vo. 1907.. .... } The Belgian Labour
Travail. Statistique des grèves en Belgique, 1901-05. } Department
8vo. 1907 ....

Hasselt. Exposé de l'administration et de la situation } The Burgomaster
des affaires communales pendant 1905-06. 8vo. 1907

Académie Royale de Belgique. Bulletin de la classe des } The Academy
lettres... 1906.07. (Current numbers.) 8vo. 1907

Bolivia—

Estadística comercial de 1905. 8vo. 1906 .... Dr. J. S. Keltie

Brazil—

Importação e Exportação. Movimento maritimo, } The Statistical Bu-
cambial e do café . . . em 1905. 4to. 1907 . ... } reau

Brazilian Review. Vol. x. No. 18. 30 April, 1907, } The Editor
and later issues. Fol. 1907 ... .

Bulgaria—

Causes des décès dans les villes. Statistique pour
l'année 1901. 4to. 1907.............................
Écoles primaires. Statistique des, dans la Principauté
pendant 1900-01 à 1902-03. 3 vols., 4to. 1906
Écoles secondaires, &c. Statistique des, dans la } The Statistical Bu-
Principauté pendant 1900.01 à 1902-03. 3 vols, } reau
4to. 1906 ... .
Mouvement de la Population pendant 1902. 2e
Partie. 4to. 1906 ....
Recrutement militaire régulier. Statistique pendant
1900. 4to. 1907 ....

Chile—

Movimiento de poblacion en 1903. 8vo. 1905 ... ... } Dr. J. S. Keltie
Sinópsis estadística i jeográfica en 1903. Parte 1 and 2. }
8vo. 1904-5 ....

China—

Customs Gazette. (Current numbers.) 4to. 1907.... } The   Inspectorate-
Returns of Trade and Trade Reports, 1906. Part 1. } General of Cus-
4to. 1907 . ... } toms, Shanghai

(a) **Foreign Countries—***Contd.*

Colombia—
Estadística general de la Republica de Colombia. 8vo. 1905 .... } Dr. J. S. Keltie

Costa Rica—
Censo de la ciudad de San José, 1904. Obl. fol. 1906 .... } Dr. J. S. Keltie

Cuba—
Boletin oficial de la Secretaria de Agricultura, Industria y Comercio. (Current numbers.) 8vo. 1907
Beneficencia y correccion. Quinta conferencia nacional de Cuba, 1906. Memoria oficial. 8vo. 1906 .... } The National Library

Estadística general. Consumo é importación de Ganado. Quinquenio de 1901–05. Requeza pecuaria, 1905. Fol. 1906 .... } The Secretaria de Haeienda

Industria Azucarera y sus derividas Zafra de 1904-05. 4to. 1907 ....
Los asientos antiguos de gravamenes y las menciones de derechos vigentes en los registros de la propiedad . . . . 23 pp., 8vo. 1907 ....
Havannah. Asociacion de dependientes del comercio de la Habana. Relacion de los trabajos efectuados por la directiva en el 4° tremestre de 1906. 8vo. 1907 .... } The National Library

Denmark—
Communications Statistiques. 4ᵉ Série. Tome 22. 8vo. 1907 .... } The State Statistical Bureau

Egypt—
Commerce extérieur de l'Égypte pendant 1906. 8vo. 1907 .... } The Director-General of Customs
Dette publique. Compte rendu des travaux de la commission pendant 1906. 8vo. 1907 .... } The Caisse de la Dette
Postes d'Égypte. Rapport de l'Administration sur l'exercice 1906. 8vo. 1907 .... } The Postal Administration
Navigation in Ports of Egypt and the Suez Canal. Quarterly Returns. (Current numbers.) 8vo. 1907 ....
Suez Canal. Statistical Return of Navigation through the Suez Canal for 1906. Fol. 1907 .... } The Statistical Department, Ministry of Finance

France—
Annuaire Statistique. 25ᵉ volume, 1905. 8vo. 1906 { The French Labour Department
Agriculture. Ministère de l'. Bulletin mensuel de l'Office de Renseignements agricoles. (Current numbers.) 8vo. 1907 . ... } The Ministry of Agriculture
Agriculture. Statistique agricole annuelle, 1903— 1905. 8vo. 1905-07 ....
Budget général de l'exercice 1906. 16 parts, 4to. 1905 ....
Budget général de l'exercice 1907. 14 parts, 4to. 1906 .... } Dr. J. S. Keltie
Commerce de la France. Documents statistiques [mensuels]. (Current numbers.) 8vo. 1907 .... } The Director-General of Customs
Finances. Ministère des. Bulletin de Statistique et de Législation comparée. (Current numbers.) 1907 .... } The Ministry of Finance

(a) Foreign Countries—*Contd.*

France—*Contd.*

Pêches maritimes. Statistique des, année 1903. 8vo. 1906	Mr. R. J. Thompson
Recensement général de la Population 24 Mars, 1901. Tome 4, Résultats généraux. 4to. 1906 .... Travail. Notes sur la journée de huit heures dans les établissements industriels de l'État. 8vo. 1906 ...	The French Labour Department
Colonies. Annuaire de la Guadeloupe et Dépendances pour 1904. 8vo. 1904........	Dr. J. S. Keltie

Germany—

Amtliche Nachrichten des Reichs-Versicherungs-amts. No. 4. 15 April, 1907. 4to. 1907 .... [Contains the Report of the Department for 1906.]	The Imperial Insurance Office
Deutsches Handels-Archiv. Jahrgang 1906. Jan.—Dec. 4to. 1906	Dr. J. S. Keltie
Eisenbahnen Deutschlands, Statistik der im Betriebe befindlichen, nach den Angaben der Eisenbahn-Verwaltungen ... Rechnungsjahr 1905. La. fol. 1907	Purchased
Gesundheitsamtes, Veroffentlichungen des Kaiserlichen. (Current numbers.) 8vo. 1907	The Imperial Health Bureau
Krankenversicherung im Jahre 1904. 4to. 1907 ... Reichstagswahlen von 1907. Statistik der. Teil 1, Vergleichende Übersicht der Reichstagswahlen von 1903 und 1907. 4to. 1907 .... Seeschiffahrt im Jahre 1905. 3er und 4er Teil. Seeverkehr in den deutschen Hafenplatzen. Seereisen deutscher Schiffe. 4to. 1907 .... Statistisches Handbuch fur das Deutsche Reich. Teil 1. 8vo. 1907 ....: .... Stromgebiete das Deutschen Reichs. Teil 3b. Gebiet der Donau. 4to. 1907....... Vierteljahrshefte zur Statistik des Deutschen Reichs. (Current numbers.) 4to. 1907	The Imperial Statistical Bureau

Prussia—

Zeitschrift des K. Preussischen Statistischen Landes-amts. (Current numbers.) Fol. 1907...............	The Royal Prussian Statistical Bureau
Preussische Central-Genossenschafts-Kasse. Mitteilungen zur deutschen Genossenschaftsstatistik für 1905. Fol. 1907	Dr. A. Petersilie
Statistisches Jahrbuch für den Preussischen Staat 1905-06. 2 vols., 8vo. 1906-07	Purchased

Saxony—

Zeitschrift des K. Sachsischen Statistischen Landesamts. (Current numbers.) 4to. 1907 .. Statistisches Jahrbuch für das Konigreich Sachsen. 35. Jahrgang 1907. 8vo. 1907	The Statistical Bureau of Saxony

Wurttemberg—

Statistisches Handbuch für das Königreich Württemberg. Jahrgang 1904 und 1905. 1 vol., la. 8vo. 1906 .... Württembergische Jahrbücher für Statistik und Landeskunde. Jahrgang 1905, Heft 2, und Jahrgang 1906, Heft 1. 2 vols., 4to. 1906	Dr. J. S. Keltie

Berlin—

Statistisches Jahrbuch der Stadt Berlin. 30. Jahrgang, enthaltend die Statistik das Jahres 1905. 8vo. . 1907 .... Tabellen ü. die Bevölkerungsvorgänge Berlins und die Bautätigkeit 1905, sowie über den Wohnungsmarkt, 1906. Fol. 1907	The Municipal Statistical Bureau

(a) Foreign Countries—*Contd.*

Germany—*Contd.*

Frankfort. Frankfurter Verein für Geographie und Statistik. Jahresbericht. 60er Jahrgang 1905-06. 8vo. 1907 .... } The Society

Wiesbaden. Statistische Monatsberichte der Stadt Wiesbaden 1. Jahrgang Nr. 1—3, Jan.-Mär. 1907. Fol. 1907 .... } The Municipal Statistical Bureau

Allgemeines statistisches Archiv. Herausgegeben von Dr. Georg von Mayr. Band 7. Halbband 1. 8vo. 1907 .... } The Editor

Rheinische Creditbank. Geschäfts-Bericht für 1906. 4to. 1907 .... } The Bank

Verein für Socialpolitik—
Verfassung und Verwaltungsorganisation der Städte. Band 4. Heft 5. Die Hansestädte. Mit Beiträgen von Geert Seelig und Johannes Bollmann. 8vo. 1907 ....
Verfassung und Verwaltungsorganisation der Städte. Band 6. Österreich. 8vo. 1907 .... } Purchased

Greece—
Bulletin trimestriel du commerce special de la Grèce avec les pays étrangers. 4e Trimestre de 1906. 4to. 1906 } The Bureau of Statistics

Italy—
Annali di Statistica. S. 4, No. 109. Atti della commissione per la statistica giudiziaria e notarile. Sessione del Marzo 1906. 8vo. 1907.................... } The Director-General of Statistics

Annuario Statistico delle Città italiane, anno 1, 1906. La. 8vo. 1906 .... } The Compiler, Professor Ugo Giusti

Bollettino di statistica e di legislazione comparata, anno vi. Fasc: 2—4. 1905-06. 8vo. 1906-07.... } Dr. J. S. Keltie

Movimento Commerciale del Regno d'Italia nell' anno 1905. 4 vols., fol. 1906 ....
Movimento della Navigazione, anno 1905. 4 vols. Fol. 1906 ....
Statistica dei debiti comunali e provinciali per mutui al 31 Dicembre degli anni 1896, 1899 e 1900. La. 8vo. 1905 ....
} The Director-General of Statistics

Statistica del debito ipotecario fruttifero esistente al 31 Dicembre 1903. Risultati del primo accertamento. Fol. 1906 ....
Statistica delle forze motrici impiegate al 1° Gennaio 1904, nell'agricoltura e nelle industrie del Regno con notizie sulle forze motrici impiegate in alcuni stati esteri. La. 8vo. 1906..... } Dr. J. S. Keltie

Turin. Annuario del Municipio di Torino 1905-06. 8vo. 1906 .... } The Municipal Statistical Bureau

Società Umanitaria, Milano. Pubblicazioni dell' Ufficio del lavoro. No. 15, 1907. Le condizioni generali della classe operaia in Milano. Salari, Giornate di lavoro, Reddito, ecc. 253 pp., la. 8vo. 1907 ...... } The Society

Japan—
Department of Agriculture and Commerce. 22nd Statistical Report for 1905. 8vo. 1907.................... } The Department

État de la population de l'Empire du Japon au 31 Décembre 1903. Fol. 1906 .... } Dr. J. S. Keltie

(a) Foreign Countries—*Contd.*

Japan—*Contd.*

Mouvement de la population de l'Empire du Japon pendant 1904. Tableaux. Fol. 1907	The Bureau of General Statistics

Mexico—

Boletin de Estadistica fiscal. (Current numbers.) Fol. 1907 .... Estadistica fiscal. Datos relativos. (Current numbers.) Fol. 1907	The Director-General of Statistics

Netherlands—

Faillites dans les Pays-Bas pour l'année 1905. Statistique de. 4to. 1907 .... Maandcijfers en andere periodieke opgaven betreffende Nederland en de Koloniën. Nieuwe volgreeks. No. 17. Jaar 1906 en de eerste maanden van 1907. 8vo. 1907 .... Pénitentiaire, Statistique, des Pays-Bas pour 1905. 4to. 1907 .... Revue mensuelle du Bureau Central de Statistique. (Current numbers.) 8vo. 1907 .... Travail. Aperçu des salaires et des heures du travail aux travaux de l'État en 1905. 4to. 1906	The Central Statistical Bureau
Zeescheepvaart over het jaar 1905. Statistiek van de, Sm. fol. 1907......	Ministry of "Laudbouw," &c.

Norway—

Journal du Bureau central de Statistique. (Current numbers.) 8vo. 1907	The Central Statistical Bureau

Roumania—

Bulletin Statistique. (Current numbers.) 8vo. 1907	The Statistical Bureau
Rapport sur le recensement fiscal de l'année 1905. Fol. 1906	Dr. J. S. Keltie

Russia—

Commerce extérieur de la Russie par la frontière d'Europe. Exercice du mois de Décembre mis en regard avec celui de toute l'année 1906. 4to. 1907	The Customs Department
Justice. Annuaire Statistique du Ministère de la Justice pour 1905. 1re Partie, Russie d'Europe. 2e Partie, Russie d'Asie. 2 vols., la. fol. 1907 ... . [Another copy presented by Mr. R. H. Rew.]	Major P. G. Craigie, C.B.
Prices of Grain at Ports. Return of (in Russian). Sheets. (Current numbers.) 1907....	The Ministry of Finance
Kazan University. Bulletin of the. (Current numbers.) (In Russian.) 8vo. 1907	The University
Moscow. Bulletin récapitulatif de la ville de Moscou. Année 1906. 8vo. 1907	The Municipal Statistical Bureau

Salvador—

Boletin del Consejo Superior de Salubridad. (Current numbers.) 8vo. 1907	The Board

Spain—

Estadística general del comercio de cabotaje en 1905. Fol. 1907 .... Estadística del impuesto de transportes por mar y á la entrada y salida por las fronteras. Primer trimestre de 1907. 8vo. 1907	The Director-General of Customs

(a) Foreign Countries—*Contd.*

Spain—*Contd.*

Madrid.   Estadística demografica.   Resumen del ⎱ The Ayuntamiento
año 1905. Fol. 1907 .... ⎰ de Madrid

Sweden—
Bidrag till Sveriges Officiella Statistik. 4to. 1907—⎤
  D. Fabriker och Handtverk, 1905. (Factories) ....
  E. Sjöfart, 1905. (Shipping) ....
  K. Hälso- och Sjukvården, 1905. (Lunacy)...........
  . N. Jordbruk och Boskapsskötsel, 1905. (Agri-
     culture) ....
  P. Undervisningsväsendet, 1904 ....
  U. Kommunernas Fattigvård och Finanser, 1904. ⎱ The Central Statis-
Extrait du rapport sur la situation et gestion de la ⎰ tical Bureau
  Caisse d'épargne postale de Suède pendant 1905.
  4to. 1907 ....
Kapital- Konto till Riks- Hufvud- Boken for 1905.
  Fol. 1906 ....
In- och utvandring år 1905. 15 pp., 4to. 1907 ....
Öfversikt af Sveriges Riksbanks Ställning. 1906 .....
Riksstat for år 1907. Sm. 4to. 1907 ....⎦
Meddelanden fran k. Kommerskollegii afdelning for ⎤ The University of
  Arbetsstatistik. (Current numbers.) 8vo. 1907... ⎰ Upsala
Rikets In-, och Utforsel. (Current numbers.) 1907....⎤
Sammandrag af de enskilda sedelutgifvande bankernas.
  (Current numbers.) 1907.................................
Sammandrag af Riksbankens Ställning. (Current
  numbers.) 1907 .....
Statistisk Tidskrift. (Current numbers.) 8vo. 1907 ⎬ The Central Statis-
Sveriges Utförsel och Införsel, ar 1906 . . . 2 parts., ⎰ tical Bureau
  8vo. 1907 ....
Uppgift å Folkmängden inom kvarje Kommun, Härad,
  Tingslag, Domsaga, Stad och Län, 31 December,
  1906. 17 pp., 4to. 1907 ....⎦
Stockholm—
  Bulletin mensuel du Bureau de Statistique de la⎤
    ville. (Current numbers.) 8vo. 1907............. ⎮
  Stockholms stads statistik. iii. Hälso- och sjuk- ⎬ The Municipal Sta-
    vård.   Hälsovårdsnämndens berattelse jamte ⎰ tistical Bureau
    öfvessikt af Stockholms sanitära statistik för
    1905. 4to. 1906 ....⎦

Switzerland—
Annuaire Statistique de la Suisse. 15ᵉ année 1906.⎤
  8vo. 1907 .... ⎮
Mouvement de la Population de la Suisse pendant ⎮
  1905. 4to. 1907 . ... ⎮
Résultats du recensement fédéral du 1 Dec. 1900. ⎬ The Federal Sta-
  Vol. 3. Population d'après les Professions. 4to. ⎰ tistical Bureau
  1907 ....
Résultats du recensement fédéral des entreprises
  agricoles, &c., du 9 août, 1905. Les entreprises
  et le nombre des personnes actives dans ces entreprises. Fasc. 2 and 3. 4to. 1907 ....⎦

Turkey—
Ottoman public debt. Annual report of council of⎤
  administration for twenty-third financial period ⎮
  (14th March, 1904, to 13th March, 1905), with ⎬ Dr. J. S. Keltie
  special report on the history of the Ottoman Public ⎮
  Debt. 8vo. 1905 ....⎦

(a) **Foreign Countries**—*Contd.*

United States—

Agriculture, Department of. Report of Chief of ⎫
Bureau of Statistics for 1906. 15 pp., 8vo. 1906 ⎪

Agriculture. Department of. Bulletins—

  42. Russia's wheat surplus; conditions under which
    it is produced. 8vo. 1906 ... .

  48. Cost of producing farm products. Methods of
    investigation. Cost of growing Minnesota field ⎬ The Department of
    crops, 1902, 1903, 1904. 8vo. 1906 .... ⎪   Agriculture

  49. Cost of hauling crops from farms to shipping
    points. 8vo. 1907 .. ..

  50. Hops in principal countries . . . with statistics
    of beer brewing. 8vo. 1907 ....

  130. Egyptian Irrigation. 8vo. 1903 ....

Crop Reporter. (Current numbers.) Fol. 1907........⎭

Census Bureau Bulletins—

  64. Census of Manufactures, 1905. Butter, ⎫
    Cheese, Milk, &c. 4to. 1907 .... ⎪

  65. Census of Manufactures, 1905. Coke. 4to.
    1907 ....

  66. Census of Manufactures, 1905. Automobiles, ⎪ The Bureau of Cen-
    Bicycles, &c. 4to. 1907 .... ⎬   sus

  67. Census of Manufactures, 1905. Metal-working ⎪
    Machinery. 4to. 1907 ....

  69. Child labor in United States. 4to. 1907 . ...

  70. Census of Manufactures, 1905. Petroleum
    Refining. 4to. 1907.................................⎭

Commerce and Finance. Monthly Summary. (Current ⎫
numbers.) 4to. 1907 ....

Exports of Manufactures from the United States, and ⎪ The Bureau of Sta-
their distribution by articles and countries. 1800 ⎬   tistics,   Depart-
to 1906. 4to. 1907 .... ⎪   ment of Commerce

Foreign Commerce and Navigation of the United ⎪ and Labor
States for year ended 30th June, 1906. 4to.
1907 ....⎭

Debt. Monthly Statements of the Public, and of ⎫
Cash in Treasury. (Current numbers.) Sheets. 1907 ⎪ The Secretary of the

Gold, Silver, and Notes, &c., in Circulation. Monthly ⎬   Treasury
Statements. (Current numbers.) Sheets. 1907....⎭

Interstate Commerce Commission. 20th Annual ⎫
Report, 19th December, 1906. 8vo. 1907.............. ⎪

Interstate Commerce Commission. 18th Annual ⎬ The Commission
Report on Statistics of Railways for year ending ⎪
30th June, 1905. 8vo. 1906 ....⎭

Mineral Resources of the United States. Calendar ⎱ The United States
year 1905. 8vo. 1906 ....⎰   Geological Survey

Mint. Annual Report of Director of Mint for year ⎫
ended 30th June, 1906. 8vo.. 1906 .... ⎪ The Director

Report of Director of Mint on production of precious ⎬
metals in United States during 1905. 8vo. 1906....⎭

Statistical Abstract of the United States, 1906. 29th ⎧ The Department of
Number. 8vo. 1907 .... ⎨   Commerce   and
                                  ⎩   Labor

California. State Board of Health. Monthly ⎱ The Board
Bulletins. 8vo. 1907. (Current numbers) ....⎰

Connecticut—

  Bureau of Labor Statistics. 22nd Annual Report ⎱ The Bureau
  for 1905-06. 8vo. 1906 ....⎰

  State Board of Health. 29th Annual Report for ⎫
  1906, with Registration Report for 1905. 8vo. ⎬ The Board
  1907 ....⎭

(a) **Foreign Countries**—*Contd.*

United States—*Contd.*

Maryland. Bureau of Statistics and Information. 15th Annual Report for 1906. 8vo. 1907 ....} The Bureau

Massachusetts—
Annual Report of State Board of Conciliation and Arbitration for 1906. 8vo. 1907 ....} The Board

Labor Bulletin. (Current numbers.) 8vo. 1907
Labor and Industrial Chronology for year ending 30th Sept., 1906. Part 6, pp. 389—644. 8vo. 1907 ....} The Bureau of Statistics of Labor

Nebraska. Annual Bulletin of the State Bureau of Statistics. No. V, Dec., 1906. Part I, Summary of Nebraska Counties. Part II, Freight Rates and Shipments in Nebraska. 8vo. 1907 .... } The Bureau

New York State—
Education Department. 1st and 2nd Annual Reports of the Department for years 1903.04 and 1904-05, with supplemental volume to 1st report. 3 vols., 8vo. 1905-06 ... .
Library. 87th Annual Report for 1904. 2 vols., 8vo. 1906 ... .
Library. Bulletins, Nos. 98 and 99. 2 parts, 8vo. 1905 ....
Library. Year-book of Legislation, 1904, 1905. 2 vols., 8vo. 1905-06 ....
Museum. 57th Annual Report, 1903. 3 vols., 8vo. 1905 ....
Museum. Bulletins. Nos. 83—92, 94—98, 100, 102—105. 8vo. 1905-06 ... .} The New York State Library

Ohio. Bureau of Labor Statistics. 30th Annual Report for 1906. 8vo. 1907 ....} The Bureau

Boston. Monthly Bulletin of the Statistics Department. (Current numbers.) 4to. 1907 ....} The Municipal Statistical Bureau

New York (City). Public Library. Bulletin. (Current numbers.) 8vo. 1907 ....} The Library

San Francisco. Relief and Red Cross Funds. (A Corporation.) Department Reports as submitted to the Board of Directors at their meeting, 19 Mar., 1907. 8vo. 1907 ....} The Secretary

Commercial America. Published monthly. (Current numbers.) Fol. 1906 ....} Philadelphia Commercial Museum

Dun's Review. (Current numbers.) Fol. 1907........ { Messrs. R. G. Dun and Co.

American Academy. Supplement to Annals. Mar., 1907. Our State Constitutions : *J. G. Dealey.* 8vo. 1907 ....} The Academy

American Economic Association. Publications. 3rd Series. Vol. 8, No. 1. Papers and Discussions of 19th Annual Meeting, Dec., 1906. 8vo. 1907 ....} The Association

American Philosophical Society. Proceedings, Oct.-Dec., 1906. 8vo. 1907 ....} The Society

Columbia University Studies. Vol. **xxv**, No. 2. The Budget in American Commonwealths : *Eugene E. Agger.* 8vo. 1907 ....} The University, per Messrs. P. S. King and Son

John Crerar Library. 12th Annual Report for 1906. 8vo. Chicago. 1907 ... ...} The Library

Smithsonian Institution—
Annual Report of Board of Regents for years ending 30th June, 1905 and 1906. (National Museum.) 2 vols., 8vo. 1906.... ....} The Institution

(a) **Foreign Countries**—*Contd.*
United States—*Contd.*
Smithsonian Institution—*Contd.*
Smithsonian Miscellaneous Collections. Vol. 3,⎫
  part 3. 8vo. 1907 ... .⎬ The Institution
Remarks on the type of the fossil cetacean agoro-⎪
  phius pygmæus (Müller). 8 pp., 4to. 1907 ....⎭

International—
Bulletin International des Douanes. (Current⎫
  numbers.) 8vo. 1907 ....⎬ The Board of Trade
Institut International de Statistique. Bulletin.⎫
  Tome 16. Livr. 1. 161·pp., 4to. 1907 .. ..⎬ The Institute
Internationaler Kongress fur Hygiene und⎫
  Demographie, Berlin, Sept., 1907. Programme of⎬ The Secretary
  Proceedings, &c. 4to. 1907 ....⎭

(b) **India and Colonies.**
India, British—
Cotton Spinning and Weaving. Monthly Statistics⎫ The Director-Gene-
  of, (Current numbers.) 8vo. 1907...... .. ..⎪ ral of Commercial
Indian Trade Journal. (Current numbers.) 4to.⎬ Intelligence
  1907 ....⎭
Imperial Gazetteer of India. The Indian Empire.⎫
  Vol. I, Descriptive. Vol. 3, Economic. Vol. 4,⎪ The Oxford Univer-
  Administrative. New edition. 3 vols., 8vo.⎬ sity Press
  Oxford, 1907 ....⎭
Moral and material progress and condition of India⎫
  during 1905-06. Statement exhibiting the, 42nd⎬ The India Office
  No. (149.) 1907.............................. ....⎭
Trade carried by rail and river in India in 1905-06⎫ The Director-Gene-
  and four preceding years. Accounts of, 18th⎬ ral of Commercial
  issue. Fol. 1907 . ...⎭ Intelligence
Assam District Gazetteers. Vol. x. 8vo. 1906 ......⎫
Bengal—⎬ The India Office
  District Gazetteers. Muzaffarpur. 8vo. 1907 ... ⎭
Report on public instruction in Bengal for 1905-06.⎫ The Lieutenant-Go-
  Fol. 19 6 ....⎬ vernor of Bengal
Madras District Gazetteers. Madura and Vizaga-⎫ The India Office
  patam. 2 vols., 8vo. 1906-07 ....⎭
East Indian Railway Company. 122nd (Half-yearly)⎫
  Report, 1906, and Diagrams of Traffic audited⎬ The Company
  2nd half of 1906. Fol. 1907 . ...⎭

Australia, Commonwealth of*—
Nomenclature of Diseases and of Causes of Death ...⎫
  [Dr. Bertillon's Classification] for use of Registrars,⎪
  &c. 8vo. 1907 ....⎪
Population and Vital Statistics. Bulletin No. 1, De-⎪
  termination of the population of Australia for each⎬ The Commonwealth
  quarter from 31st December, 1900, to 31st Decem-⎪ Statistician
  ber, 1906. Fol. 1907 ....⎪
Trade, Shipping, and oversea Migration of the Com-⎪
  monwealth. Official Bulletins for Jan. - March,⎪
  1907. Fol. 1907 ....⎭
Parliamentary Debates. Session 1907. (Current⎫ The Commonwealth
  numbers.) 8vo. 1907.......................................⎭

* See also the several divisions of Australia.

(b) **India and Colonies**—*Contd.*

Canada, Dominion of—

Analytical index to official report of debates of House of Commons of the Dominion. Second Session— Tenth Parliament. 6. Edward VII. 1906. 8vo. 1906 .... *— The Clerk of the House of Commons*

Auditor-General. Report of, for year ended 30th June, 1906. 3 vols., 8vo. 1906 .. .. *— The Auditor-General for Canada*

Banks. Monthly Reports on Chartered. (Current numbers.) 4to. 1907 .... *— The Deputy Minister of Finance*

List of shareholders in chartered Banks of the Dominion as on 31 December, 1906. 8v.. 1907 .... *— The Finance Department*

Manitoba. Public buildings erected and improved by the Government of Manitoba during 1900-06. Obl. 8vo. 1906 .... *— The King's Printer, Winnipeg*

Ontario—

Agricultural College and Experimental Farm. 32nd Annual Report, 1906. 8vo. 1907............ .... Department of Agriculture. Bulletins. (Current numbers.) 8vo. 1907 .... *— The Ontario Department of Agriculture*

Canadian Life and Resources. (Current numbers.) Fol. 1907 .... *— The Assistant Superintendent of Emigration*

Royal Bank of Canada. 37th Annual Report, 1906. 4to. 1907 .... *— The Bank*

Cape of Good Hope—

Civil Service List and Calendar, 1907. 21st publication. 8vo. 1907 .... *— The Colonial Secretary*

Ceylon—

Administration Reports, 1905. Vols. 1 and 2. 2 vols., fol. 1906................. .... *— The Government of Ceylon*

Jamaica—

Annual Report of Registrar-General for year ended 31st March, 1906. Fol. 1907 ... . *— The Registrar-General*

Natal—

Immigration Restriction Department. Annual Report for 1906. Fol. 1907 .... *— Mr. G. W. Dick*

New South Wales—

Public Works. Report of Department of, for year ended 30th June, 1906. 8vo. 1906 .... *— The Agent-General for N. S. Wales*

Returns under the several Acts of Parliament administered by the Registrar-General for 1906. Fol. 1907 .... *— The Registrar-General*

Statistics. Six States of Australia and New Zealand, 1861-1905. 8vo. 1907 .... Statistical Register for 1905 and previous years. Parts 8, Shipping and Commerce. 10, Agriculture, &c. 11, Law and Crime. 12, Private Finance. 13, Industrial Wages. 8vo. 1907... .... Vital Statistics for 1905 and previous years. 8vo. 1907 .... *— The Director, Bureau of Statistics*

New Zealand—

Statistics of the Colony of New Zealand for 1905. 2 vols., fol. 1906 ....,.................... ... . *— The Registrar-General*

(b) India and Colonies—*Contd.*

Queensland—

Vital Statistics, 1905. 46th Annual Report of ⎱ The Agent-General
Government Statistician. Fol. 1906 .... ⎰ for Queensland

Rhodesia—

Chamber of Mines. Monthly Reports of Executive ⎫
Committee, and Returns of Output of Gold, &c. ⎬ The Chamber
(Current numbers.) Sheets. 1907........ .... ⎭

South Australia—

Agricultural and Live Stock Statistics for the year ⎰ The Under Secretary
ended 31st March, 1906. Fol. 1907.................. ⎱ and Government Statistician

Statistical Register, 1905. Fol. 1906 .... The Chief Secretary

Straits Settlements—

Supplements to the Perak Government Gazette, 1907. ⎱ The Government
(Current numbers.) Fol. 1907 .... ⎰ Secretary

Tasmania—

Complete Guide to Tasmania . . . 8vo. 1906 ....⎰ The General Manager, Government Railways

Transvaal—

Agricultural Journal. (Current numbers.) 8vo. ⎫
1907 .... ⎬ The Agricultural Department
Agricultural Department. Annual Report, 1905-06. ⎭
8vo. 1907 ....

Customs. Return showing quantity and value (and ⎫
duty received) of all imports and exports in 1905. ⎬ Dr. J. S. Keltie
Fol. 1906 .... ⎭

Mines Department. Annual Report of Government ⎫
Mining Engineer for year ended 30th June, 1906. ⎬ The Engineer
Fol. 1906 .... ⎭

Mines Department, Transvaal. Monthly Statistics. ⎱ The Department
(Current numbers.) Obl. 4to. 1907 .... ⎰

Johannesburg. Statistics. (Current numbers.) Fol. ⎱ The Town Statistician
1907 .... ⎰

Johannesburg Chamber of Commerce. Annual Report ⎫ The Chamber of
for year ended 28th February, 1907. 17th Year. ⎬ Commerce
8vo. 1907 .... ⎭

Transvaal Chamber of Mines. 17th Annual Report ⎱ The London Secretary
for 1906, with Map. 4to. 1907 ... . ⎰

Transvaal Chamber of Mines. Monthly Analysis of ⎱ The Chamber
Gold Production. (Current numbers.) 1907 .... ⎰

Statistical Society of South Africa. Certain Aspects ⎫ The Statistical
of Transvaal Taxation by *Samuel Evans.* 18 pp., ⎬ Society of South
8vo. 1907 . ... ⎭ Africa

Victoria—

Friendly Societies. 28th Annual Report. Report of ⎱ The Actuary for
Actuary for 1905. Fol. 1907................. .... ⎰ Friendly Societies

Western Australia—

Friendly Societies. Report of proceedings by the ⎫
Registrar [under certain Acts] for 1905. Fol. ⎬ Mr. Edgar T. Owen
1906 .... ⎭

Monthly Statistical Abstract. (Current numbers.) ⎫
Fol. 1907 .... ⎪ The Registrar-General and Government Statistician
Supplements to Government Gazette, containing ⎬
Monthly Mining Statistics. (Current numbers.) ⎪
1907 .... ⎭

(b) India and Colonies—*Contd.*
Western Australia—*Contd.*

Statistical Register for 1904. Part 7. Mineral
  Statistics and Water Conservation. Fol. 1907 ....
Statistical Register for 1905. Parts 3. Accumulation.
  4. Interchange. 5. Land Settlement, Agriculture,
  Live Stock. 6. Industrial Establishments. 8. Law,
  Crime, &c. 9. Religion, &c. 11. Local Govern-
  ment. Fol. 1907 ....
Statistical Register for 1906. Part 2. Public
  Finance. Fol. 1907.................

The Registrar-General and Government Statistician

(c) United Kingdom and its several Divisions.
United Kingdom—

Aliens Act, 1905. Part 1, First Annual Report.
  Part 2, Statement with regard to expulsion of aliens
  for 1906. [Cd–3473.] 1907 ....
Allotments and Small Holdings. Memorandum as to
  difficulty of obtaining land. [Cd–3468.] 1907 ....
Army. General Annual Report on the British Army
  for 1905-06. [Cd–3365.] 8vo. 1907 ....
Australia. Customs Tariff (British Preference) 1906
  Reserved Act, with despatch thereon. [Cd–3339.]
  1907 ....
Australia. Report of Royal Commission on Old Age
  Pensions. [Cd–3341.] 1907 ....

> Purchased

Board of Trade Journal. (Current numbers.) 1907.... The Board
Brewers' Licences. (14.) 1907................. Purchased
Building Societies. Annual Report for 1905. Part 2,
  Abstract of Accounts. (56–1.) Fol. 1906 ....

The Chief Registrar of Friendly Societies

Coal Exports, &c. (94.) 1907 ....
Coal. Prices of exported coal. (90.) 1907 ....
Colonial Reports. Annual. No. 516, Northern
  Nigeria. Report for 1905-06. 8vo. 1907 ....
Colonial Reports. 40, Northern Nigeria. Memo-
  randum on Taxation of Natives. [Cd–3309.] 8vo.
  1907 ....
Colonial Reports. Annual. No. 519, East Africa
  Protectorate. Report for 1905-06. 8vo. 1907 ....
Commercial. No. 3 (1907). Return of most-favoured
  nation clauses in existing treaties of commerce
  between Great Britain and Foreign Powers on
  1st Jan., 1907. [Cd–3395.] 1907 ....
Commercial. No. 4 (1907). Return of National
  Treatment Clauses in existing treaties of commerce
  between Great Britain and Foreign Powers on
  1st Jan., 1907. [Cd–3396.] 1907 ....
East India. Accounts and Estimates, 1907-08.
  [Cd–3479.] 1907 ....
East India. Income and Expenditure, 1895-96 to
  1905-06. (119.) 1907 ....
Ecclesiastical Commissioners. 59th Report for
  1905-06, with Appendix. [Cd–3377.] 8vo. 1907
Education Act, 1902. (Rates raised under Section 18.)
  83. 1907 ....
Emigrants' Information Office. Memorandum on.
  [Cd–3407.] 1907 ....
Egypt. No. 1 (1907). Reports on Finances, Ad-
  ministration, and Condition of Egypt and the
  Soudan in 1906. [Cd–3394.] 1907 ....

> Purchased

(c) **United Kingdom and its Divisions**—*Contd.*
United Kingdom—*Contd.*

Egypt. No. 2 (1907). Despatch from Earl of Cromer ⎫
respecting Water Supply of Egypt. [Cd-3397.] |
1907 .... ⎬ Purchased
Financial Statement (1907-08). (115.) 1907 .... |
Foreign Office Reports. Annual Series and Miscel- |
laneous Series. Current numbers. 8vo. 1907 .. ⎭

Friendly Societies, &c. Reports of Chief Registrar of ⎫
Friendly Societies for 1905. Part B, Industrial and |
Provident Societies. Part C, Trade Unions. ⎬ The Registrar
(55—II, III.) 1906 .... ⎭

Gas Companies. (Metropolis) Accounts for 1906. ⎫
(98.) 1907 .... |
Housing of Working Classes Acts Amendment Bill. |
Session 1906. Index and digest of evidence to ⎬ Purchased
Reports from Select Committee. (376.) 1907 |
Imports and Exports at prices of 1900. [Cd-3446.] |
1907 .... |
Licensing Statistics, 1906. [Cd-3419.] 1907 .... ⎭

Life Assurance Companies Return for 1906. (58.) ⎫ The Board of Trade
1907 .... ⎭

Local Option (Colonies). Return. (47.) 1907 ...... Purchased

London Traffic. Royal Commission on, Vol 4. ⎫ Sir Francis S. Powell,
Appendices to Report, with Index. [Cd-2987.] ⎬   Bart., M.P.
1906 .... ⎭

Metropolitan Water Board. Annual Report, &c, ⎫
for year 1905-06. (399.) 8vo. 1906 .... |
Miners' Eight Hour Day Committee. First Report of ⎬ Purchased
the Departmental Committee. Parts 1—3. |
[Cd-3426—7—8.] 1907 .... ⎭

Mines and Quarries : General Report and Statistics for ⎫ The Home Office
1906. Part 1. District Statistics. [Cd-3478.] 1907 ⎭

Municipal employees. Numbers of, 1906. (136.) ⎫
1907 ... . |
National Debt. [Cd-3476.] 1907................. .... |
Naval expenditure (principal Naval Powers). (310.) |
1906 ... . |
"Options" and "Futures" in Food Stuffs. Legisla- |
tion (respecting). Reports. [Cd-3280.] 1907 .... ⎬ Purchased
Parliamentary Constituencies (Electors, &c.) (United |
Kingdom). (22.) 1907 .. .. |
Parliamentary Papers. Numerical List and Index for |
Session 1905. (339.) 1905 .... |
Railway und Canal Traffic Acts, 1854-94. 18th |
Annual Report of Commission for 1906. [Cd-3399.] |
1907 .... ⎭

Railway Returns (Preliminary Statement) for the ⎫ The Board of Trade
year 1906. [Cd-3485.] 1907 .... ⎭

Rateable Hereditaments, &c. (including Railways). ⎫
(183.) 1906 .. .. ⎬ Purchased
Reformatory and Industrial Schools. 50th Report for |
1906. Part 1. [Cd-3438.] 1907 .... ⎭

Statistical Abstract for British Empire from 1891 to ⎫ The Board of Trade
1905. 3rd number. [Cd-3328.] 8vo. 1907. ...... ⎭

Trade. Annual Statement of Trade of United King- ⎫ Mr. A. J. Wood,
dom with Foreign Countries and British Possessions, | Custom House
1906. Vols. 1 and 2. [Cd-3466] and [Cd-3529]. ⎬
1907 .... ⎭
   [Another copy presented by Board of Trade.]

Transvaal. Annual Report of Foriegn Labour Depart- ⎫ Purchased
ment, Johannesburg. 1905-06. [Cd-3338.] 1907 ⎭

(c) **United Kingdom and its Divisions**—*Contd.*
United Kingdom—*Contd.*

Trustee Savings Banks. Report for 1906. (19.) 1907
Tuberculosis (Human and Animal). 2nd Interim report of Royal Commission. Part 2, Appendix, Vol. 4. [Cd-3378.] 1907 ....
Volunteer corps of Great Britain. Annual Return for 1906. [Cd-3367.] 8vo. 1907.................... } Purchased
Warlike operations (Killed and Wounded), 1898.1903. (25.) 1907 ....
Youthful offenders. Treatment of. (84.) 1907........

Tariff Commission—

Calculations bearing upon various schemes of Reciprocal Tariff Preference. 8 pp., 4to. 1907
Report. Vol. 5. The Pottery Industries, with } The Commission
analysis and summary of evidence and statistical tables. 4to. 1907 ....

Great Britain—

Board of Agriculture and Fisheries—

Agricultural Statistics, 1906. Vol. xli, Part 2, Produce of Crops. [Cd-3372.] 8vo. 1907........
Agricultural Holdings. Number of, in 1890, 1895, 1903 and 1906. [Cd-3408.] 1907.. . ...
Annual Reports of Proceedings under the Diseases of Animals Acts, the Markets and Fairs (Weighing of Cattle) Acts, for 1906. [Cd-3415.] } The Board
8vo. 1907 . ...
Journal of the Board. (Current numbers.) 8vo. 1907
Leaflets. (Current numbers.) 8vo. 1907 ....
Weekly Returns of Market Prices (of Cattle, Dead Meat, Provisions, Fruit, and Vegetables, Hay and Straw). (Current numbers.) Fol. 1907......... ..

England and Wales—

Births, Deaths, and Causes of Death in England and Wales, and in London and other large towns. } The Registrar-General
Annual Summary for 1906. 8vo. 1907 ... .
Charity Commissioners. 54th Report for 1906. [Cd-3389.] 8vo. 1907 .... } Purchased
Judicial Statistics, England and Wales, 1905. Part II, Civil Judicial Statistics. 4to. [Cd-3477.] 1907 } The Home Office
Poor Relief (England and Wales). Statement for half-year ended Michaelmas, 1906. 1907 .... } The Local Government Board
Poor Relief (England and Wales). (315-I.) 1907....

London County Council—

Education. Conference of Teachers, 1907. Report of Proceedings. Fol. 1907 ....
Education Department (Executive). Handbook containing Examination Papers set in the Elementary School Leaving Examination, 1906, with results. Fol. 1907 ....
Education. Report on accommodation and attendance in Elementary Schools for year ended 31st } The London County Council
March, 1906. Fol. 1907..... .. ..
Education. Report on Industrial and Reformatory Schools for year ended 31st March, 1906. Fol. 1907 ....
Education. Report of Education Committee submitting Report and Returns relating to Public Elementary Day Schools for year ended 31st March, 1906. Parts 1 and 2. Fol. 1907 ....

(c) United Kingdom and its Divisions—*Contd.*
England and Wales--*Contd.*
  London County Council—*Contd.*

Fire Brigade. Report of Chief Officer of the ⎫
  Brigade for 1906. Fol. 1907. .... ⎪
Licensed premises acquired by the Council. 4 pp. ⎪
  1907 .... ⎬ The London County
    [Estimated premium value of the sites of these pre- ⎪   Council
    mises, the licences of which have been allowed to ⎪
    lapse, 344,000*l*.] ⎪
London County Council Gazette. (Current num- ⎪
  bers.) Fol. 1907 .... ⎭

Metropolitan Asylums Board. Annual Report for ⎫ The Board
  1906. 9th year of issue. 8vo. 1907...................... ⎬
Paddington. Report of the Medical Officer of Health ⎫ Dr. Reginald Dud-
  for 1906. Fol. 1907 .... ⎬   field
Bristol. Port Sanitary District. Annual Report of ⎫
  Medical Officers of Health, and Chief Port Inspector ⎬ The Medical Officer
  of Nuisances, for 1906. 8vo. 1907 .... ⎪   of Health
Cardiff. Annual Report of Medical Officer of Health ⎭
  for 1906. Fol. 1907 ....
Newcastle-on-Tyne. Tuberculosis : its casualties, ⎫
  causes and control. Report by the Medical Officer ⎬
  of Health. 56 pp., 8vo. 1907 .... ⎭
Norwich. Annual Report upon Healthiness of ⎫
  Citizens and Sanitary Condition of Norwich, for ⎬
  1906. 8vo. 1907 .... ⎭
Wigan. Annual Report on Health of Wigan in ⎫
  1906. 8vo. 1907 .... ⎭

Ireland—

Agricultural Statistics, 1906. Extent in statute acres, ⎫
  produce of crops and numbers of live stock for ⎪
  1906. [Cd-3412.] 8vo. 1907 .... ⎪ The Department of
Agricultural Statistics, 1906. Report and Tables ⎬   Agriculture and
  relating to Irish Migratory Agricultural Labourers, ⎪   Technical In-
  for 1906. [Cd-3481.] 8vo. 1907 .... ⎪   struction
Department of Agriculture and Technical Instruction. ⎪
  Journal of the. (Current numbers.) 8vo. 1907.... ⎭
Congestion in Ireland. Third Report and Appendix ⎫
  to Third Report of Royal Commission. [Cd-3413 ⎪
  and 3414.] 1907 .... ⎬ Purchased
Local Taxation (Ireland) Returns for 1905-06. ⎪
  [Cd-3422.] 1907 ... :................................. ⎪
Local Taxation (Ireland) Account. (15.) 1907 .... ⎭

Scotland—

Area, Population, and Valuation of Counties, &c., ⎫
  1906-07. [Cd-3432.] 1907.................................... ⎪
Births, Deaths, and Marriages. Report for 1906. ⎪
  [Cd-3417.] 8vo. 1907 . ... ⎪
Congested Districts Board. 9th Report for year ⎪
  1906-07. [Cd-3471.] 1907............................ ⎪
Crofter's Commission. Report for 1906. [Cd-3418.] ⎪
  1907 .... ⎬ Purchased
Ecclesiastical Assessments (Scotland). (45.) 1907 .. ⎪
Local Taxation Returns (Scotland) for 1904-05. (2.) ⎪
  1907 ... . ⎪
Occupiers of Farms (Scotland). (127.) 1907........ .. ⎪
Parish Trusts (Scotland). No. 1. (326.) 1907........ ⎪
Technical Education (Scotland), 1905-06. Return. ⎪
  (107.) 1907 .... ⎪
Unemployed Workmen Act, 1905. Report on Distress ⎪
  Committees in Scotland. [Cd-3431.] 1907............ ⎭

(c) **United Kingdom and its Divisions**—*Contd.*
Scotland—*Contd.*
  Scotch Education Department—
    Code of regulations for continuation classes. 1907.
      [Cd-3482.] 1907 ....
    Code of Regulations (1907) for day schools, with
      appendices. [Cd-3388.] 8vo. 1907
    Memorandum on teaching of English in Scotch
      Primary Schools. [Cd-3410.] 8vo. 1907 ....
    Memorandum on the teaching of arithmetic in ⎫ The Scotch Educa-
      primary schools. [Cd-3448.] 8vo. 1907 .... ⎬ tion Department
    Memorandum on the study of languages. [Cd- ⎩
      3546.] 8vo. 1907...
    Minute . . . for distribution of general aid grant.
      [Cd-3387.] 1907 ....
    Regulations (1907) for preliminary education, train-
      ing, &c., of teachers for various grades of schools.
      [Cd-3390.] 8vo. 1907 ....
  Aberdeen. Report of the Chief Sanitary Inspector ⎫ The Inspector
    for 1906. 8vo. 1907 .... ⎭

(d) **Authors, &c.**

Deparcieux (Antoine). Essai sur les probabilités de la ⎫
  durée de la vie humaine ; d'où l'on déduit la manière │
  de déterminer les rentes viagères, tant simples qu'en │
  tontines. Précédé d'une courte explication sur les │
  rentes à terme ou annuités et accompagné d'un grand │
  nombre de tables. 4to. Paris, 1746 .... │
Derham (W.). Physico-Theology or a demonstration │
  of the Being and Attributes of God from His works │
  of Creation . . . 7th Edit. 8vo. 1727 .... │
Franklin (Benjamin). The interest of Great Britain, │
  considered with regard to her Colonies, and the │
  acquisition of Canada and Guadaloupe, to which is │
  added observations concerning the increase of man- │
  kind, peopling of Countries, &c. 58 pp., 8vo. 1760 │
Graunt (John). Natural and political observations │
  mentioned in a following index, and made upon the │
  bills of mortality. 16 + 85 pp., sm. 4to. 1662 ...... │
Nieuwentyt (Dr.). The Religious philosopher, or the │
  right use of comtemplating the works of the Creator. │
  I. In the wonderful structure of animal bodies, and ⎬ Mr. G. U. Yule
  in particular man. II. In the no less wonderful and │
  wise formation of the elements, and their various effects │
  upon animal and vegetable bodies ; and, III. In the │
  most amazing structure of the heavens, with all its │
  furniture. Designed for the conviction of atheists and │
  infidels. 2 vols. 3rd Edit. Sm. 4to. 1724 .... │
Playfair (William)— │
  For the use of the enemies of England. A real statement │
  of the finances and resources of Great Britain, illus- │
  trated by two copper-plate charts. 32 pp., 8vo. 1796 │
  Lineal arithmetic applied to shew the progress of the │
  commerce and revenue of England during the │
  present century, which is represented and illustrated │
  by 33 copper-plate charts . . . 8vo. 1798 .... │
  The commercial and political atlas, representing, by │
  means of stained copper-plate charts, the progress of │
  the commerce, revenues, expenditure, and debts of │
  England during the whole of the eighteenth century. │
  The 3rd edit. 16 + 97 pp., 8vo. 1801 .... ⎭

(d) **Authors, &c.**—*Contd.*

Playfair (William).—*Contd.*

The statistical breviary, shewing, on a principle entirely
new, the resources of every state and kingdom in
Europe, illustrated with stained copper-plate charts
representing the physical powers of each distinct
nation with ease and perspicuity . . . 64 pp., 8vo.
1801 ....
An inquiry into the permanent causes of the decline
and fall of powerful and wealthy nations, illustrated
by four engraved charts. 2nd edit. 4to. 1807 ....   } Mr. G. U. Yule
A letter on our agricultural distresses, their causes and
remedies, accompanied with tables and copper-plate
charts shewing and comparing the prices of wheat,
bread, and labour from 1565 to 1821. 72 pp., 8vo.
1821 ....

Süssmilch (Johann Peter). Der Königl. Residenz Berlin
schneller Wachsthum und Erbauung. 80 pp., sm.
4to. Berlin, 1752 ....

Miscellanea Curiosa. Being a Collection of some of
the principal Phænomena in Nature . . . with
several Discourses read before the Royal Society
. . . 8vo. London, 1705 ....

"*Akaroa.*" Dangers ahead! Essays by. 64 pp., 8vo.
1907 ....   } The Author

Alden (Percy), M.P., and Hayward (Edward E.).
Housing. (Social Service Handbooks. No. 1.) 2nd   } Messrs. Headley
edition. 176 pp., 8vo. 1907 ....   Brothers

Archer (J. A.). Compound Interest, Annuity and }   Messrs. Shaw and
Sinking Fund Tables. xvi + 180 pp., la. 8vo. 1907 }   Sons

"*Artifex*" and "*Opifex.*" Causes of Decay in a British
Industry. xvi + 296 pp., 8vo. 1907 ....

Avenel (Vicomte G. d'). Histoire économique de la propriété, des salaires, des denrées et de tous les prix   } Purchased
en général depuis 1200 jusqu'à 1800. 2 vols., la. 8vo.
1898 ....

Baden-Powell (B. H.). Short Account of Land Revenue
and its administration in British India : with sketch   } The Oxford Univer-
of land tenures. 2nd Edit. 8vo. 1907 ....   sity Press

Barthe y Barthe (Andrés)—

Cuáles son los medios que podrian ponerse en practica
para mejorar nuestra circulacion monetaria. 15 pp.,
8vo. 1893 ... ...
Le Salaire des Ouvriers en Espagne. 63 pp., 8vo. 1896
Influencia de los transportes en los Mercados y en la
baja de los precios. Memoria. ... 110 pp., 8vo. 1899 } The Author
Reformas en los Presupuestos. 64 pp., 8vo. 1902 ....
Estudio crítico de la Crisis Monetaria. Memoria.
105 pp., 8vo. 1905 ....
El aumento de la riqueza en España desda 1795.
46 pp., 8vo. 1907 ....

Black (Miss Clementina). Sweated Industry and the
Minimum Wage. With introduction by A. G.   } Messrs. Duckworth
Gardiner. 281 pp., 8vo. 1907 ....   and Co.

Cadbury (Edward) and Shann (George). Sweating.
(Social Service Handbooks. No. 5.) 145 pp., 8vo.   } Messrs. Headley
1907 ... .   Bros.

Chorlton (J. D.). The Rating of Land Values. 177 pp., } Purchased
8vo. 1907 ....

Clark (Victor S.). The Labour Movement in Austral-   } Messrs. A. Constable
asia. A Study in Social Democracy. 8vo. 1907 ....   and Co.

(d) **Authors, &c.**—*Contd.*

Devas (*Charles S.*).   Political Economy.   3rd Edit. ⎫ Messrs. Longmans
8vo. 1907 ....⎭

Fisher (*Irving*)—
Effect of diet on endurance based on an experiment, in ⎫
thorough mastication, with nine healthy students of ⎪
Yale University, January to June, 1906. 8vo. 1907 ⎪
A Graphic Method in Practical Dietetics.   24 pp., ⎬ The Author
8vo. 1907 .... ⎪
Influence of Flesh-eating on endurance.   16 pp., 8vo. ⎪
1907 ....⎭

Galton (*Francis*).   Probability, the foundation of ⎫ Clarendon   Press,
Eugenics. The Herbert Spencer lecture, delivered on ⎬ Oxford
5th June, 1907. 30 pp., 8vo. 1907 ....⎭

Gannett (*Henry*).   Statistical Abstract of the World. ⎫ Messrs. John Wiley
1st edit. viii + 84 pp., 24mo. 1907 .... ⎭ and Sons

Grangel (*D. Villar*).   El problema de los cambios. ⎫ Dr. J. S. Keltie
109 pp., 8vo. 1906........... ....⎭

Guyot (*Yves*)—
La Grève des Électriciens. 19 pp., 8vo. 1907........ ... ⎫
La Science économique : ses lois inductives. 3rd edit. ⎬ The Author
xi + 531 pp., 8vo. 1907 ....⎭

Haggard (*F. T.*).   Our National Balance-sheet. Freight ⎫ ,,
an Important Asset. 3 pp. 1907 ....⎭

Hall (*Bolton*).   Three Acres and Liberty. 8vo. 1907 ⎰ Messrs. Macmillan
                                                          ⎱ and Co.

Halle (*E. von*).   Die Weltwirtschaft.   Ein Jahr- und ⎫ Mr. B. G. Teubner,
Lesebuch.   Herausgegeben von, 1. Jahrgang 1906. ⎬ Leipzig
La. 8vo. 1906...⎭

Haynes (*Thomas H.*).   Survey of Canadian Imports and ⎫ The Author
the results of Preference. 16 pp., 8vo. 1907 .... ⎭

Holt (*Byron W.*).   The Gold Supply and Prosperity. ⎫ The Moody Corpora-
Compiled and Edited by. 261 pp., 8vo. 1907.......... ⎭ tion

Jacquart (*Camille*)—
La Mortalité Infantile dans les Flandres.   Étude de ⎫ The Author
Démographie Belge. 8vo. 1907 .... ⎭
Statistique et Science Sociale.   Aperçus Généraux. ⎫ Messrs. Desclée, De
121 pp., 12mo. 1907 ....⎭ Brouwer & Co.

Jagger (*J. W.*).   The Trade of South Africa and Cape ⎫ The Author
Colony. 26 pp., 8vo. 1907 ....⎭

Joly (*Henri*).   La Belgique Criminelle.   8vo. 1907 . ⎰ Messrs. J. Gabalda
                                                          ⎱ and Co.

Julin (*A.*).   De quoi se compose le commerce extérieur ⎫
de la Belgique ? (Études sur la Statistique du com- ⎬ The Author
merce extérieur.) 50 pp., 8vo. 1907...... ....⎭

Lampertico.   Fedele Lampertico.   VI Aprile 1907. ⎫ MM. D. and O.
1. Anniversario dalla sua morte. 550 pp., 8vo. 1907 ⎭ Lampertico

Leake (*P. D.*).   The question of depreciation and the ⎫
measurement of expired outlay on productive plant ; a ⎬ The Author
plea for the study and use of better methods. 44 pp., ⎪
8vo. 1907 ....⎭

Lee (*Arthur*).   The Bank rate and our gold reserves. ⎫
Memoranda . . . 24 pp., 8vo. 1907.... ....⎭

Macrosty (*Henry W.*).   The Trust Movement in British ⎫
Industry ; a study of business organisation. 8vo. ⎬ Messrs. Longmans
1907 ....⎭

Mills (*J. Saxon*).   Landmarks of British Fiscal History. ⎫ Messrs. A. and C.
123 pp., 8vo. .... ⎭ Black

Mortara (*Giorgio*).   La forza di attrazione delle grandi ⎫ The Author
città. 30 pp., 8vo. 1907 ....⎭

Patton (*Jacob Harris*).   Natural resources of the ⎫ Purchased
United States. xv + 530 pp., 8vo. 1888 . ...⎭

Societies, &c. (British)—

(d) Authors, &c.—*Contd.*

Pearce (A. James). Municipal Rating and the collection of rates. 8vo. 1907 .. .. } Messrs Gee and Co.

Pinkus (Prof. Dr. N.). Workmen's Insurance in Germany. (In Russian.) 157 pp., 8vo. 1903 ..... } The Author

Porter (S. Lowry). The Education Bill of 1906. 8vo. 1907 .... } Purchased

Pratt (Edwin A.).—
    The licensed trade : an independent survey. 8vo. 1907 .. . . } The Author
    State Railways : object lessons from other lands. With translation of M. Marcel Peschaud's articles on " Les Chemins de fer de l'État Belge." 107 pp., 8vo. 1907 .... } Messrs. P. S. King and Son

Prost (Eug.). La Belgique agricole industrielle et commerciale. Étude économique. 8vo. 1904 .... } Dr. J. S. Keltie

Punnett (R. C.). Mendelism. 2nd Edit. 84 pp., 16mo. 1907 .... } Messrs. Macmillan and Bowes

Raseri (E.)—
    Movimenti migratorii nella popolazione Italiana. 18 pp., 8vo. 1906 ....
    Aumento di popolazione delle grandi agglomerazioni urbane in Italia durante il Secolo XIX. 20 pp., 8vo. 1907 .... } The Author

Seeber (Francisco). Great Argentina. Comparative studies between Argentina, Brazil, Chile, Peru, Uruguay, Bolivia, and Paraguay. 8vo. 1904 ... . } Dr. J. S. Keltie

Slater (Gilbert). The English peasantry and the enclosure of common fields. With introduction by the Right Hon. the Earl of Carrington, K.G., &c. Plates, &c., 8vo. 1907 ... . } Messrs. A. Constable and Co., Ltd.

Smith (Goldwin). Labour and Capital, a letter to a labour friend. 38 pp., 8vo. 1907 ... ... } Purchased

Spicer (A. Dykes). The Paper Trade. A descriptive and historical survey of the paper trade from the commencement of the 19th century. 8vo. 1907 .. } Messrs. Methuen and Co.

Wolff (Henry W.). Co-operative Banking : its principles and practice with a chapter on Co-operative Mortgage Credit. 8vo. 1907 .... } Messrs. P. S. King and Son

---

(e) Societies, &c. (British).

Actuaries, Institute of—
    British Offices Life Tables. (1893.) Valuation Tables deduced from the graduated experience of whole-life participating assurances on male lives (O^m Table) at $2\frac{1}{2}$, $2\frac{3}{4}$, 3, $3\frac{1}{2}$, 4 and $4\frac{1}{2}$ per cent. 8vo. 1907 ....
    British Offices Life Tables. (1893.) Values of temporary annuities . . . at $2\frac{3}{4}$ per cent. interest according to the O^m and O$^{m\ (5)}$ mortality tables. 24 pp., 8vo. 1907 .... } The Institute
    Journal. Vol. XLI. Part 2. (No. 228) April, 1907 ....
Actuaries, Institute of, and Faculty of Actuaries in Scotland. British Offices Life Tables. (1893.) Select Tables deduced from the graduated experience of Whole-Life Assurances on Male Lives. xiv + 432 pp., 8vo. 1907.. .... }

Agricultural Society, Journal of the Royal. Vol. 67. 8vo. 1906 .... } The Society

(e) **Societies, &c. (British)**—*Contd.*

Anthropological Institute. Journal. July–Dec., 1906. } The Institute
8vo. 1907 ....

British Association. Report of 66th meeting of British ⎫
Association for Advancement of Science. York.. ⎪
August, 1906. 8vo. 1907 .... ⎪
British Iron Trade Association. Annual Statistical ⎪
Report on the home and foreign iron and allied ⎬ The Association
industries for 1906. 8vo. 1907 .... ⎪
British Weights and Measures Association. British *v.* ⎪
Metric Weights and Measures. Reports of the Con- ⎪
ference of Representatives of the Cotton and Allied ⎪
Trades . . . 62 pp., 8vo. 1907 ....⎭

Channel Tunnel. Reports by British and French En- ⎫
gineers. Papers on National Defence. 56 pp., 4to. ⎬ The Channel Tunnel
1907. Also several Pamphlets and Leaflets on the ⎪ Company
Channel Tunnel ....⎭

Civil Engineers, Institution of. Minutes of Proceedings. } The Institute
Vol. clxvii. 8vo. 1907.......... ....

Gainsborough Commission. Reports. Life and Labour ⎫ Messrs.   Simpkin,
in Germany. With an Appendix : Infirmity and Old ⎬ Marshall and Co.
Age pensions in Germany. 286 pp., 8vo. 1907 ... .⎭

Jews. 37th Annual Report and Accounts of the United ⎫
and Constituent Synagogues for 1906 and Estimates ⎬ The Secretary
for 1907. Fol. 1907 ....⎭

Liverpool University. Institute of Commercial Research
in the Tropics—
  Maize, Cocoa, and Rubber. Hints on their pro- ⎫
  duction in West Africa. By Viscount Mount- ⎪
  morres. 44 pp., 8vo. 1907 .... ⎬ The University
  Quarterly Journal. Vol. ii. No. 4. April, 1907. ⎪
  8vo. 1907 ....⎭

Peabody Donation Fund. 42nd Annual Report of } The Secretary
Governors for 1906. 4to. 1907 ....

Poor. Central Poor Law Conference. Report of pro- ⎫ Messrs. P. S. King
ceedings . . . February, 1907. No. 11 of 1906-07. ⎬ and Son
8vo. 1907 ....⎭

Royal Society of Edinburgh. Proceedings. Session } The Society
1906-07. Vol. 27. Nos. 1 and 2. 8vo. 1907 ....

Royal United Service Institution. Index to Subjects ⎫
and Names of Authors appearing in " Journal," ⎬ The Institution
1887-1906. 8vo. 1907........ ....⎭

Surveyors' Institution. Professional Notes. Vol. xiv. ⎫
Part 2. Mar., 1907. 8vo. 1807 ....⎭   ..

(f) **Periodicals, &c., and Miscellaneous (British).**

"The Times " Monthly Index. 8vo. 1907 . ... Purchased
Brewers' Almanack for 1907 .... Mr. P. C. Morgan
Motor, Motor-cycle, and Cycle Trades Directory for } The Lancashire Pub-
1905-06. 8vo. 1905 .... lishing Company
National Telephone Journal. Vol. I. No. 10. Jan., } The Editor
1907 ....
Post Magazine Almanack, Insurance Directory, Refer- } Mr. T. J. W. Buckley
ence and Year-Book for 1907. 8vo. 1907 ... .
Statesman's Year-Book for 1907. Edited by J. Scott } The Editor
Keltie, LL.D. 8vo. 1907 ....
Stock Exchange Official Intelligence for 1907. 4to. } The Stock Exchange
1907 ....
Thom's official directory of the United Kingdom of ⎫
Great Britain and Ireland for the year 1906. 8vo. ⎬ Dr. J. S. Keltie
1906 ....⎭

The weekly, monthly, or quarterly issues of the following returns have also been received during the past quarter :—

Consular Reports—From United States and United Kingdom.

Labour Reports, &c.—From Austria-Hungary, Belgium, France, Germany, Italy, United States, Massachusetts and New York States, Canada, New Zealand, and United Kingdom.

Trade Returns—From Argentina, Austria-Hungary, Belgium, Bulgaria, China, Denmark, Egypt, France, Germany, Greece, Italy, Mexico, Netherlands, Norway, Roumania, Russia, Spain, Sweden, Switzerland, United States, India, and United Kingdom.

Vital Statistics—From Argentina, Egypt, Germany, Italy, Netherlands, Roumania, Switzerland, United States (Connecticut and Michigan only), Queensland, South Australia, and United Kingdom.

Vital Statistics of following Towns—Buenos Ayres, Buda-Pesth, Brunn, Prague, Brussels, Copenhagen, Berlin, Bucharest, Moscow, Madrid, Stockholm, London, Manchester, Dublin, Edinburgh, and Aberdeen.

The weekly, monthly, or quarterly issues of the following periodicals, &c., have also been received during the past quarter. They are arranged under the countries in which they are published :—

Denmark—Nationalökonomisk Tidsskrift.

France—Annales des Sciences Politiques. Économiste Français. Journal des Économistes. Monde Économique. Polybiblion, Parties Littéraire et Technique. Réforme Sociale. Le Rentier. Revue d'Économie Politique. Revue de Statistique. Journal de la Société de Statistique de Paris.

Germany—Allgemeines Statistisches Archiv. Archiv für Rassen- und Gesellschafts-Biologie. Archiv für Sozialwissenschaft und Sozialpolitik. Jahrbuch für Gesetzgebung, Verwaltung, und Volkswirtschaft. Jahrbücher für Nationalökonomie und Statistik. Kritische Blätter für die gesamten Socialwissenschaften. Zeitschrift für die gesamte Staatswissenschaft. Zeitschrift für die gesamte Versicherungs-Wissenschaft. Zeitschrift für Socialwissenschaft. Mittheilungen aus der Handelskammer Frankfurt a. M.

Italy—L'Economista. Giornale degli Economisti. Rivista Italiana di Sociologia. Riforma Sociale. Societa Umanitaria, Bollettino mensile.

Sweden—Ekonomisk Tidskrift.

Switzerland—Journal de Statistique suisse.

United States—Bankers' Magazine. Bradstreet's. Commercial and Financial Chronicle, with supplements Duns' Review. Journal of Political Economy. Political Science Quarterly. Quarterly Journal of Economics. Yale Review. American Academy of Political and Social Science, Annals. American Economic Association, Publications. American Geographical Society, Bulletin. American Statistical Association, Quarterly Publications. American Philosophical Society, Proceedings and Transactions. Columbia University, Studies in History, &c.

Canada—The Chronicle : Insurance and Finance.

India—Indian Engineering.

New Zealand—Government Insurance Recorder. Trade Review and Price Current.

United Kingdom—The Accountant. Accountants' Magazine. Athenæum.
Australian Trading World. Bankers' Magazine. Broomhalls' Corn
Trade News. Browne's Export List. Colliery Guardian. Commercial
World. Economic Journal. Economic Review. Economist. Fireman.
Incorporated Accountants' Journal. Insurance Record. Investors'
Monthly Manual. Investors' Review. Joint Stock Companies' Journal.
Labour Co-partnership. Licensing World. Local Government Journal.
Machinery Market. Nature. Navy League, Journal. Policy-Holder.
Post Magazine. Produce Markets' Review. Public Health. Publishers'
Circular. Sanitary Record. Shipping World. Statist. The Times.
Anthropological Institute, Journal. Cobden Club, Leaflets. East India
Association, Journal. Howard Association, Leaflets, &c. Institute
of Actuaries, Journal. Institute of Bankers, Journal. Institution of
Civil Engineers, Minutes of Proceedings. Iron and Steel Institute,
Journal. Lloyd's Register of British and Foreign Shipping, Statistical
Tables. London Chamber of Commerce, Journal. London University
Gazette. Manchester Literary and Philosophical Society, Memoirs and
Proceedings. Royal Agricultural Society, Journal. Royal Colonial
Institute, Proceedings and Journal. Royal Geographical Society, Geo-
graphical Journal. Royal Irish Academy, Proceedings and Transactions.
Royal Meteorological Society, Meteorological Record and Quarterly Journal.
Royal Society, Proceedings. Royal United Service Institution, Journal.
Sanitary Institute, Journal. Society of Arts, Journal. Statistical and Social
Inquiry Society of Ireland, Journal. Surveyors' Institution, Professional
Notes and Transactions. Trade Circulars.

Vol. LXX.]   [Part III.

JOURNAL

OF THE ROYAL STATISTICAL SOCIETY.

SEPTEMBER, 1907.

SOME CONSIDERATIONS *relating to the* POSITION *of the* SMALL
HOLDING *in the* UNITED KINGDOM.

By W. G. S. ADAMS, M.A.

[Read before the Royal Statistical Society, 18th June, 1907.
SIR RICHARD BIDDULPH MARTIN, Bart., President, in the Chair.]

THE several inquiries into the small holdings question, while they
have brought together a great deal of valuable information, have
still left the data very incomplete whereon to determine the
economic position of the small holding. At the present time there
is difficulty even in ascertaining the number and size of small
holdings in the United Kingdom, while information is still more
imperfect as regards the cropping and stocking of these holdings,
their expenditure and receipts, and the general economic strength
and efficiency of the small holding in relation to the medium and the
large-sized holdings. Viewed from the point of view of the national
balance of population, and from the standpoint of general social
economics, the case for small holdings has received a wide provisional
acceptance. But there is not yet ripe conviction on the matter, and
this cannot come until there has been a thorough examination and
settlement of the agricultural economics of the question. This
Paper does not lead us much nearer to the end in view, but a step
forward will be made if the discussion helps to indicate the lines of
future investigation and if attention is directed not only to existing
statistics and their interpretation but to the need of fresh statistics.
     Before proceeding, it may be well for the purposes of discussion
to recall the definition of a small holding and to exclude certain
classes of small holdings from present consideration. The Small
Holdings Act of 1892 defines a small holding as " land which does
" exceed one acre and either does not exceed 50 acres, or if exceed-
" ing 50 acres is of an annual value for the purpose of income tax
" not exceeding 50*l.*" The present Small Holdings and Allotments
Bill for England defines a small holding as from 5 to 50 acres, and

places allotments at from 1 to 5 acres—a desirable limitation in the definition of a small holding. Though, therefore, in the statistical tables herewith submitted, holdings of from 1 to 5 acres are included, it is holdings of a size larger than this which I have in mind. But it is desirable, in view of the very wide range of the type of small holdings, to define the scope of the present discussion still more particularly. Accordingly, I do not consider here holdings, whether under or over 5 acres, existing under conditions of soil and situation whereby a very specialised culture, such as bulbs, flowers, fruit and vegetables, is carried out on a highly intensive scale. These are types to which everyone interested in the development of small holdings must attach great importance. But the problem which I raise for discussion is the small farm holding with average land and average facilities as regards markets, on which the holder is earning his whole livelihood. What is the economic position and outlook of this type of holding? The question of the small economic farm holding, I venture to think, is the main small holding question. At present it affects a large class of the community, for, apart from new holdings of this order which may be brought into being, there are hundreds of thousands of such holdings existing in the United Kingdom. In this connection, therefore, I wish to consider the following points :—

(1.) The statistical evidence as to the number and size of small holdings in Great Britain and Ireland.

(2.) Certain changes in agricultural economic conditions affecting the small holding problem, especially (*a*) the shrinkage of the area of tillage, (*b*) the increase in agricultural imports, and (*c*) the changes in agricultural prices.

(3.) Conditions essential to the economic development of a small farm holding.

I should like to explain that I have drawn largely on Irish evidence and statistics, partly because they are more familiar to me, and partly because Ireland is pre-eminently a country of small holdings.

Size and Number of Holdings in the United Kingdom.

In considering the number and size of holdings in the United Kingdom, it will be remembered that the statistics of the number and size of holdings in Great Britain deal only with the areas of cultivatable land, *i.e.*, the area under crops and under pasture, excluding rough and mountain grazing, whereas in the case of the statistics of the size and number of holdings in Ireland the total area of the holding is included, whether that area be of cultivatable land, rough grazing, waste mountain, or the area occupied by buildings. As a result the contrast between the number and size of holdings in Great Britain and in Ireland is more marked than would appear from the published statistics. It is necessary that this point should be kept in mind, and while in certain cases I have been able to put the Irish statistics on a basis comparable with the English returns, in other cases it is not possible to reduce the available information to a similar form. The following summary, taken from Table 6 of the Agricultural Statistics of 1905, will recall the number and size of agricultural holdings in Great Britain in 1905, together with the average size of holding :—

	Above 1 and not exceeding 5 Acres.	Above 5 and not exceeding 50 Acres.	Above 50 and not exceeding 300 Acres.	Above 300 Acres.	Total.	Average Size of Holdings.
						Acres.
Total for Great Britain	110,259	232,966	150,561	17,918	511,704	63·1
England	81,232	166,622	109,498	14,792	372,144	66·1
Wales	10,342	31,671	18,008	408	60,429	46·2
Scotland	18,685	34,683	23,055	2,718	79,131	61·7

From this it will be seen that out of 401,445 holdings exceeding 5 acres in Great Britain, no less than 232,966 had a cultivatable area of between 5 and 50 acres. If even a considerable allowance is made for farms consisting largely of mountain and rough pasture, it is evident that the number of small holdings in Great Britain is very large, and that the question of the economic position and the extension of these holdings is one of wide interest. A further insight into the differentiation of these large classes of holdings in the year 1895 is obtained from the following return handed in by Mr. Rew to the Departmental Committee on Small Holdings. As no marked change has taken place in the relation of the different classes of holdings since 1895, the return may be considered to represent substantially the position in 1905 : —

	Number.	Percentage of Number.	Acreage.	Percentage of Acreage.	Average Size of Holding.
		Per cent	Acres.	Per cent	Acres.
Above 1 and not exceeding 5 acres	117,968	22·68	366,792	1·13	3
,, 5 ,, 20 ,,	149,818	28·80	1,667,647	5·12	11
,, 20 ,, 50 ,,	85,663	16·47	2,864,976	8·79	33
,, 50 ,, 100 ,,	66,625	12·81	4,885,203	15·00	73
,, 100 ,, 300 ,,	81,245	15·62	13,875,914	42·59	171
,, 300 ,, 500 ,,	13,568	2·61	5,113,945	15·70	377
,, 500 ,, 1,000 ,,	4,616	0·89	3,001,184	9·21	650
Above 1,000 acres	603	0·12	801,852	2·46	1,330
Total	520,106	100·00	32,577,513	100·00	63

From this table it appears that, of the holders between 5 and 50 acres, much the largest proportion consists of holdings between 5 and 20 acres cultivatable land. Again, as regards the percentage of acreage in holdings of 50 acres or under—a point of great interest—it appears from the table that 6·25 per cent. of the land was in holdings of from 1 to 20 acres, and 15·04 per cent. of the land in holdings of from 1 to 50 acres. It will also be noticed that the average size of all holdings in Great Britain in 1895 was 63 acres, and from the figures of the Agricultural Statistics in 1905, it appears that the average size of holding in Great Britain, cultivatable land, was 63·1—the average size in England being 66·1, in Scotland 61·7, and in Wales 46·2. It is further of interest to note that if the figures are taken by counties, the only counties in England in which the average was 50 acres or under were, in descending order, the following :—

	Acres.		Acres.
Stafford	49·3	Chester	44·0
Worcester	47·2	Derby	42·2
Middlesex	45·3	Lancashire	40·8
Cornwall	44·8	London	31·9
West Riding of Yorkshire	44·2		

London, however, may be excluded as abnormal, inasmuch as there were but 505 agricultural holdings, of which 115 were under 5 acres. What is chiefly of interest is the fact that, roughly speaking, small holdings are mainly in counties of a strong industrial as well as agricultural life. In Wales, the average size of holdings was as follows :—

	Acres.		Acres.
Montgomery	49.7	Anglesey	36·2
Glamorgan	47·3	Flint	35·6
Denbigh	47·3	Carnarvon	27·3
Cardigan	41·0		

The low average acreage of holding is, it will be seen, most marked in the counties of Northern Wales.

In Scotland only the following counties had an average size of holdings under 50 acres :—

	Acres.		Acres.
Bute	45·0	Inverness	20·5
Banff	44·2	Ross and Cromarty	19·7
Argyll	41·5	Shetland	16·1
Caithness	40·5	Sunderland	12·3
Orkney	32·2		

Thus, whereas in England small holdings are largely to be seen in the central and industrial counties, in Scotland small holdings exist in the outer and what are known as the Highland counties. In these counties the proportion of mountain pasture to agricultural land is large, and in consequence the number of small holdings appears greater than it really is. But it is also in these counties that many holdings are to be found small in size and uneconomic in character comparable to the holdings in the Irish congested districts.

Turning to the Irish statistics, the total area of Ireland is returned as 20,710,589 acres, of which amount in 1905 15,262,749 acres represented the area under crops and grass—a figure comparable with the cultivated area shown in the statistics of Great Britain. The following table shows the total number of holdings in 1905 exceeding 1 acre, the number of holdings in each class, and the total extent of land occupied by each class of holding. It will be remembered that in this table mountain land, rough grazing, building land, &c., are included :—

Holdings, 1905.—Statement showing the Number of Holdings above 1 Acre in extent in Ireland in 1905, classified according to Acreage, the Percentage of the Total Number of each Class to the Total Number above 1 Acre in extent, the estimated Total Area of each Class, and the Percentage of the Total Area of each Class to the Total Area of Ireland.

Holdings Classified According to Acreage.	Number of Holdings Above 1 Acre.	Percentage of Total Number of Holdings Above 1 Acre	Estimated Total Acreage of Each Class.	Percentage of Total Acreage of Ireland.
	Number.	Per cent.	Acres.	Per cent.
Above 1 and not exceeding 5 acres	62,126	12·0	224,000	1·1
,, 5 ,, 15 ,,	154,560	30·0	1,623,000	8 0
,, 15 ,, 30 ,,	134,370	26·0	3,008,000	14·8
,, 30 ,, 50 ,,	74,611	14·5	3,024,000	14·8
,, 50 ,, 100 ,,	57,707	11·2	4,257,000	20·9
,, 100 ,, 200 ,,	22,857	4·4	3,447,000	16·9
,, 200 ,, 500 ,,	8,046	1·6	2,764,000	13 6
,, 500 acres	1,526	0·3	1,967,000	9·7
Total	515,803	100·0	20,314,000	99·8

From this table it will be seen (1) that of a total number of 453,677 holdings exceeding 5 acres, no less than 363,541 were between 5 and 50 acres in extent ; (2) that taking the total number of holdings exceeding 1 acre, 82·5 per cent. were of 50 acres or under ; and (3) that the percentage of the total acreage of Ireland occupied by holdings of 50 acres or under, was 38·7. These figures bring out clearly the preponderance of small holdings in Ireland. It will be noticed that the largest classes of holdings are, respectively, those between 5 and 15 and between 15 and 30 acres.

As regards the average size of holding, taking the total area of Ireland, viz., 20,350,725 acres, and subtracting barren mountain, turf bog, building land, &c., and allowing also for the land in the possession of holdings under 1 acre, we have a round figure amounting to 17,020,000 acres representing the area of land which is under crops, grass, rough grazing, woods and plantations. The actual number of complete holdings in 1906 is somewhat less than 516,651, the figure shown in the following table, owing to the fact that in the case of certain classes of holdings extending into two enumeration divisions the parts are recorded separately and are regarded as holdings; but the exact figure cannot be ascertained from existing information. Dividing 516,651 holdings into 17,020,000 acres, the average holding works out at approximately 33 acres. But if, as in the Agricultural Statistics of Great Britain, mountain land and the woods and plantations are excluded, the average holding works out at 28·6 acres.

These figures indicate a striking contrast between the size of holding respectively in Great Britain and in Ireland. The average Irish holding works out at less than half the average holding in Great Britain. In order to afford some further comparison of the size of holdings in Ireland as compared with Great Britain, a table is submitted showing the average size of holding in each county in Ireland, allowing, as in the case of the statistics of Great Britain, for cultivatable land only.

Holdings, 1906.

	Total Number of Holdings exceeding 1 Acre.	Total Extent under Crops and Pasture.	Average Extent under Crops and Pasture on Holdings exceeding 1 Acre.
Carlow	4 590	195,033	42·5
Dublin	6,001	192,638	32·1
Kildare	7,285	355.032	48·7
Kilkenny	11,909	452,748	38·0
King's	9,341	351,644	37·6
Longford	8,025	205.721	25·6
Louth	6,564	172,380	26·3
Meath	10,186	531,732	52·2
Queen's	9,275	351,000	37·8
Westmeath	9,524	364,330	38·3
Wexford	14,494	514,780	35·5
Wicklow	7,006	323,331	46·2
Total of Leinster	104,200	4,010,369	38·5

Holdings, 1906 —*Contd.*

	Total Number of Holdings exceeding 1 Acre.	Total Extent under Crops and Pasture.	Average Extent under Crops and Pasture on Holdings exceeding 1 Acre.
Clare	17,416	598,296	34·4
Cork	32,666	1.387,111	42·5
Kerry	19,538	652,162	33·4
Limerick	14,402	587,474	40·8
Tipperary	21,479	869,012	40·5
Waterford	8,074	322,580	40·0
Total of Munster	113,575	4,416,635	38·9
Antrim	20,202	536,676	26·6
Armagh	18,211	270,949	14·9
Cavan	18,901	388,356	20·5
Donegal	30,541	527,514	17·3
Down	24,244	507,424	20·9
Fermanagh	12,769	336,115	26·3
Londonderry	15,278	369,478	24·2
Monaghan	16,246	277,820	17·1
Tyrone	25,315	557,632	22·0
Total of Ulster	181,707	3,771,964	20·8
Galway	34,029	881,103	25·9
Leitrim	14,012	285,744	20·4
Mayo	34,564	635,380	18·4
Roscommon	20,339	480,083	23·6
Sligo	14,225	309,996	21.8
Total of Connaught	117,169	2,592,306	22·1
Total of Ireland	516,651	14,791,274	28·6

From this table it will be seen that Ulster and Connaught are pre-eminently the provinces of small holdings. The agricultural statistics for Ireland show that in 1905 in Ulster altogether only 19,488 holdings exceeded 50 acres in extent, whereas there were 162,206 holdings between 1 and 50 acres. In Connaught there were 11,322 holdings of over 50 acres, and 111,980 holdings between 1 and 50 acres.

Before passing from the statistics of number and size of small holdings in Ireland, the following table, showing the number and proportion of each class of holding in Ireland since 1841, is of considerable interest :—

Year.	Number of Holdings.					Total Number of Holdings above 1 Acre in extent.	Decrease in Number of Holdings per Decade.
	Above 1 Acre and not exceeding 5 Acres.	Above 5 Acres and not exceeding 15 Acres.	Above 15 Acres and not exceeding 30 Acres.	Above 30 Acres and not exceeding 50 Acres.	Above 50 Acres.		
1841—							
Number	310,436	252,799	79,342	48,625		691,202	—
Per cent.	44·9	36·6	11·5	7·0		100·0	—
1851—							
Number	88,083	191,854	141,311	70,093	78,997	570,338	120,864
Per cent.	15·5	33·6	24·8	12·3	13·8	100·0	17·5
1861—							
Number	85,469	183,931	141,251	72,449	85,384	568,484	1,854
Per cent.	15·0	32·4	24·8	12·8	15·0	100·0	0·3
1871—							
Number	74,809	171,383	138,647	72,787	86,516	544,142	24,342
Per cent.	13·7	31·5	25·5	13·4	15·9	100·0	4·3
1881—							
Number	67,071	164,045	135,793	72,385	87,449	526,743	17,399
Per cent.	12·7	31·1	25·8	13·8	16·6	100·0	3·2
1891—							
Number	63,464	156,661	133,947	73,921	89,019	517,012	9,731
Per cent.	12·3	30·3	25·9	14·3	17·2	100·0	1·8
1901—							
Number	62,855	154,418	134,091	74,255	90,228	515,847	1,165
Per cent.	12·2	29·9	26·0	14·4	17·5	100·0	0·2
1905—							
Number	62,126	154,560	134,370	74,611	90,136	515,803	—
Per cent.	12·0	30·0	26·0	14·5	17·5	100·0	—

It will be seen that, broadly speaking as regards the changes in the size and distribution of holdings in Ireland, three periods may be distinguished during the past sixty years. The first, in which change was catastrophic, closed before the census of 1851. The number of holdings between 1 and 15 acres was reduced by half, while the holdings exceeding 50 acres accordingly increased. The second period, extending for thirty to forty years from 1851, marked a still further decline in the number of holdings not exceeding 15 acres, with a corresponding increase in the larger classes of holdings ; in the third period, that of the past twenty years, there has been a comparative absence of change. In recent years, the Government, through the Congested Districts Board and the Estates Commissioners, has been enlarging some of the very small and uneconomic holdings, and in order to provide the additional land required a number of the larger holdings and estates have been broken up. It is recognised that much work in this direction remains still to be done, and there is thus likely to be a slow but steady increase in the number of medium-sized small holdings in Ireland. The problem in Ireland is not the creation of small holdings but the making of them economic.

Changes in Agricultural Economic Conditions.

This brings me to the second question, namely, certain changes in agricultural economic conditions affecting the small holding problem. There are a number of such changes which it is not now possible to enter on, but three main lines of evidence must be referred to :—(1) the changes in the area under tillage and in the numbers of live stock ; (2) the increase in agricultural imports ; and (3) the movements of agricultural prices. These three points are intimately connected with one another, and bear jointly and severally on the small holdings question. For a good system of small holdings involves an increase in tillage, and the development of agricultural imports and the changes in agricultural prices are among the best tests as to the state of supply and demand in regard to the classes of produce which must be the staple of the small holder. With regard to (1) the decrease in the area of tillage, this has been common to all parts of the United Kingdom. The following table shows the changes which have taken place respectively in the area under corn and green crops in England, Wales, Scotland, and Ireland since 1867, from which year comparisons can be made between the statistics of Great Britain and Ireland :—

	1867.	1871.	1881.	1891.	1901.	1904.	1905.
	Acres.	Acres.	Acres.	Acres.	Acres.	Acres.	Acres.
			England (area 32,550,882 acres).				
Corn crops	7,399,347	7,683,692	6,960,958	6,214,882	5,524,082	5,369,862	5,467,123
Green ,,	2,691,734	2,897,545	2,681,953	2,530,450	2,401,265	2,310,018	2,352,530
Flax	—*	15,949	6,410	1,787	630	551	437
Hops	64,273	60,022	64,943	56,145	51,127	47,799	48,967
			Wales (area 4,777,132 acres).				
Corn crops	521,404	560,700	482,315	417,249	361,970	347,105	346,508
Green ,,	138,387	136,541	124,550	122,185	110,479	107,421	106,571
Flax	—*	175	13	4	6	3	—
			Scotland (area 19,458,727 acres).				
Corn crops	1,364,029	1,430.869	1,404,703	1,292,692	1,247,656	1,236,067	1,240,601
Green ,,	668,042	704,094	704,065	644,934	617,486	618,587	617,941
Flax	—*	1,242	111	10	4	9	4
			Ireland (area 20,350,725 acres).				
Corn crops	2,115,700	2,124,034	1,777,175	1,492,763	1,317,574	1,279,189	1,271,190
Green ,,	1,432,410	1,511,689	1,270,026	1,191,424	1,079,443	1,050,483	1,044,373
Flax	253,257	156,670	147,145	74,665	55.442	44,293	46,158

* Not distinguished in Returns for 1867.

The decrease, it will be seen, has taken place chiefly in cereals, but also, though to a less extent, in green crops, a much more serious feature. It will be noticed that the shrinkage in corn and green crops has been more marked in Ireland than in Great Britain, and that in Great Britain it has been less in Scotland than in either England or Wales. The agricultural statistics for 1905 show also that in Great Britain—including land for hay and not for hay— there were 4,477,518 acres of grass under rotation, and 17,200,494 acres permanent pasture, whereas the corresponding figures in Ireland were 1,255,113 acres under rotation and 11,637,387 permanent pasture. The proportion of tillage to pasture is thus very much lower in Ireland than it is in Great Britain. But the contrast between Ireland and Great Britain, which, striking in itself, does not afford any evidence as to the relation between small holdings and the prevalence of tillage. It is a matter for regret that there are no recent statistics which show the respective percentages of tillage in the various classes of holdings, but the following tables, respectively, for the years 1864 and 1874 are of considerable interest, even at the present time, the distribution of small holdings since 1874 not having seriously changed :—

Return of the Number, Size, and Percentage of Crops, &c., in each Class of Holding in Ireland.

In 1864.

Classification of Holdings.	Proportion per Cent. of Holdings in Each Class.	Under Crops.	Grass.	Fallow.	Woods and Plantations.	Bog and Waste.	Total.	Average Extent of the Holdings in Each Class. A. R. P.
Holdings not exceeding 1 acre	8·2	84·7	6·1	0·2	0·9	8·1	100	0 2 4
above 1 and not exceeding 5 acres	13·6	63·6	26·7	0·2	1·0	8·5	100	3 2 3
„ 5 „ 15 „	29·2	48·1	41·6	0·1	0·6	9·6	100	10 1 26
„ 15 „ 30 „	22·6	41·0	46·3	0·2	0·5	12·0	100	22 1 15
„ 30 „ 50 „	11·9	35·8	49·2	0·2	0·7	14·1	100	40 1 22
„ 50 „ 90 „	9·1	29·2	52·4	0·2	1·1	17·1	100	73 1 30
„ 100 „ 200 „	3·7	21·4	51·7	0·2	2·0	21·7	100	150 0 38
„ 200 „ 500 „	1·4	12·3	51·5	0·1	3·3	32·8	100	344 2 33
„ „ 500 acres	0·3	3·5	31·0	0·1	3·1	62·3	100	1,315 1 35
Total	100·0	27·9	47·7	0·2	1·6	22·6	100	—

In 1874.

Classification of Holdings.	Proportion per Cent. of Holdings in Each Class.	Under Crops.	Grass.	Fallow.	Woods and Plantations.	Bog and Waste.	Total.	Average Extent of the Holdings in Each Class. A. R. P.
Holdings not exceeding 1 acre	8·6	84·7	6·6	0·2	0·8	7·7	100	0 1 34
above 1 but not exceeding 5 acres	12·0	59·6	31·1	0·1	1·0	8·2	100	3 2 18
„ 5 „ 15 „	28·6	44·8	45·6	0·1	0·6	8·9	100	10 2 0
„ 15 „ 30 „	23·5	38·5	50·3	0·1	0·5	10·6	100	22 1 22
„ 30 „ 50 „	12·5	33·4	53·1	0·1	0·7	12·7	100	40 1 29
„ 50 „ 100 „	9·5	27·2	56·7	0·1	1·1	14·9	100	73 2 11
„ 100 „ 200 „	3·7	19·5	58·9	0·1	2·0	19·5	100	150 3 8
„ 200 „ 500 „	1·4	11·5	54·1	0·1	3·4	30·9	100	343 1 38
„ „ 500 acres	0·2	2·9	33·4	0·0	3·2	60·5	100	1,373 3 23
Total	100·0	25·9	51·5	0·1	1·6	20·9	100	—

These tables indicate (1) the much larger proportion under crops as compared with grass in the holdings up to 50 acres, and (2) the decline in the area of tillage not only in the large farms but also in the small holdings. This year information is being collected along similar lines, and it will be of great interest to see how the proportion of tillage to grass now stands in the various classes of farms, and whether, over a period of thirty years in which there has been a great decline in tillage, the small holding has maintained tillage to a much greater extent than the large holding. For from the economics of the situation it is clear that the small holding can only effectively survive as a tillage holding. As regards the number of live stock, the following table shows the figures respectively for Great Britain and Ireland from 1867 :—

	1867.	1871.	1881.	1891.	1901.	1904.
	Number.	Number.	Number.	Number.	Number.	Number.
England (area 32,550,882 acres).						
Horses	—*	962,840	1,094,103	1,143,050	1,161,914	1,204,124
Cattle	3,469,026	3,671,064	4,160,085	4,870,215	4,791,535	5,020,936
Sheep	19,798,337	17,530,407	15,382,856	17,874,722	15,548,057	14,698,018
Pigs	2,548,755	2,078,504	1,733,280	2,461,185	1,842,133	2,083,226
Wales (area 4,777,132 acres).						
Horses	—*	117,176	137,767	150,186	154,624	161,923
Cattle	544,538	596,588	655,345	759,309	743,078	738,789
Sheep	2,227,161	2,706,415	2,466,945	3,233,936	3,427,734	3,534,967
Pigs. ..	229,917	225,456	191,792	270,082	212,971	211,479
Scotland (area 19,458,727 acres).						
Horses	—*	177,434	193,068	195,167	194,893	206,386
Cattle	979,470	1,070,107	1,096,212	1,223,297	1.229,281	1,227,295
Sheep	6,893,603	6,882,747	6,731,252	7,623,900	7,401,409	7,024,211
Pigs ...	188,307	195,642	123,018	157,506	124,821	130,214
Ireland (area 20,350,725 acres).						
Horses	524,180	538,095	548,354	592,819	564,916	608,994
Cattle	3,707,803	3,976,372	3,956,595	4,448,511	4 673,323	4,645,215
Sheep	4,835,519	4,233,435	3,256,185	4,722,613	4,378,750	3,749,352
Pigs	1,235,191	1,621,423	1,095,830	1,367,712	1,219,135	1,164,316

* Statistics not collected until 1869.

There has thus been an increase in the number of live stock, but this can hardly be set off as any compensation for the decline in tillage. A tillage country can support a very much larger stock, both of men and beasts, than a country which is going or has nearly gone into grass.

This brings us to the consideration of the increase in agricultural imports and the changes in agricultural prices, questions which are closely related. In connection, however, with the records of agricultural prices, there is a technical consideration which should not be overlooked. The collection of agricultural price statistics and the making of reliable comparisons present very great difficulties. With the differentiation of modern markets and the introduction of the system of grading into so many classes of articles, prices have become very varied in character. This, while it calls for greater organisation with regard to the collection of price statistics, simplifies the problem of obtaining a satisfactory record of present-day prices, but it complicates the problem of making comparisons with the past. It will be admitted that our best records of prices are very limited in their character, and for this reason comparisons stretching over a wide range of years are of considerable difficulty. This is more the case in certain articles than in others ; for example, the difficulty is greater in the case of dairy produce and of poultry and eggs than in the case of beef, and greater as regards beef than as regards cereals. But allowing for the conditions which existed in the past, the data of agricultural prices, such as they are, remain of the greatest value in considering the economic position of the small holder. Moreover, the limitations which exist in our records are, from the practical point of view, not of such serious consequence as may at first appear, because the existing records indicate in a broad way the trend of development ; and so far as comparisons with several decades past are concerned, this is sufficient, while as regards recent years the records now available, being much more detailed in character and collected in a more scientific manner, enable reliable comparisons to be made between one year and another, and so indicate the tendencies which present-day prices have—a question of great importance as regards the future of the small holder. Within the scope of this Paper it is only possible to refer to the broad changes as regards imports and prices of agricultural produce which affect the economic position of the small holder. The following table shows the total estimated value of the imports of the main classes of agricultural produce since 1871 :—

Table showing the Total Value of certain Agricultural Produce Imported into the United Kingdom in each of the Years 1871, 1876, 1881, 1886, 1891, 1896, 1901, 1906.

	1871.	1876.	1881.	1886.	1891.	1896.	1901.	1906.
	£	£	£	£	£	£	£	£
Wheat and flour	26,816,891	27,919,526	40,736,754	26,137,681	39,633,091	30,906,862	33,422,891	39, 3498
Other cereals	15,874,573	23,892,912	20,120,014	17,410,498	22,389,318	21,893,221	27,752,399	24,657,928
Horses	78,495	1,198,779	221,696	189,901	432,268	1,027,736	1,095,683	535,532
Cattle	3,582,501	4,860,440	6,251,577	5,068,846	8,581,574	9,305,055	8,810,664	9,732,180
Sheep and lambs	1,789,826	2,226,952	2,191,762	2,010,194	663,015	1,133,634	586,139	156,947
Poultry and game	174,518	297,018	457,553	639,704	456,979	705,478	980,757	985,457
Rabbits					286,981	401,614	618,826	110,786
Bacon and hams	2,725,909	8,611,329	10,729,945	8,402,828	9,441,761	10,990,604	18,118,564	1 5209
All other meat	2,098,543	2,923,184	5,499,173	5,496,843	10,419,134	13,359,852	21,214,828	22,015,374
Butter	6,939,040	9,718,226	10,866,151	8,141,438	11,591,183	15,344,364	19,297,396	23,460,196
Eggs	1,263,612	2,620,306	2,322,390	2,884,063	3,505,522	4,184,656	5,495,767	7, 8022
Cheese	3,341,496	4,237,763	5,245,115	3,871,359	4,813,404	4,900,342	6,227,135	7,607,641
Fruit	1,242,471	1,987,667	2,450,298	2,843,190	3,856,671	3,739,410	3,155,131	4,770,530
Flax	5,030,431	3,052,546	2,803,479	2,081,124	2,581,054	2,779,451	2,606,565	3, 4046
Wool	17,442,906	23,244,554	25,842,311	22,388,028	27,856,546	24,058,346	21,504,577	27,146,133
	88,401,212	116,791,292	135,828,218	107,565,697	146,508,501	145,630,625	170,947,322	189,860,679

This table indicates (1) the enormous annual value of imports of agricultural produce; and (2) the rapid increase in these imports in recent years, especially as regards meat, bacon and hams, dairy produce and eggs. What has been the influence of such large imports on agricultural prices, and what is the outlook for home production as regards the small holder? It is only possible to indicate some of the main changes which affect the problem at present under consideration. The conclusions as regards prices are based chiefly on a study of the returns issued by the Board of Agriculture. Also I have had before me the prices in Ireland as issued by the Department of Agriculture and Technical Instruction for Ireland. The evidence presented in these reports points to the fact that as regards cereals, prices during the past twenty years have fluctuated but have not seriously fallen, the heavy fall, especially in the case of wheat, having taken place earlier. In view, however, of the foreign and colonial area now available for the cultivation of the cereals, and of the economy of production which machinery and transport facilities have brought about, it would not be wise to build hopes on the extension to any great extent of the area of corn crops in the United Kingdom. In this connection I may refer to Bulletin 48 recently issued by the United States Department of Agriculture, where, in a most careful statistical investigation, the very low cost of producing grain crops in America is demonstrated. While therefore for the purpose of home feeding both of man and beast it is desirable to see the area of cereals increased in the United Kingdom—considering prices and the development of foreign and colonial production—the hope for home agriculture does not lie in growing grain crops to sell.

With regard to roots and green crops, the conditions of production are more favourable to the home producer and the small farmer. The element of labour is more important, both in the cultivation and in the saving and storing of these crops, and while machinery has done much for the economic management of root crops, manual labour will remain a more important factor here than in the case of corn crops. It is partly for this reason, and partly owing to climatic conditions, that the production of green and root crops in the United States seems, from the evidence in Bulletin 48, to cost more than in the United Kingdom. And as the small holder must look mainly to animal produce for his receipts, the growing of roots, green crops, and feeding stuffs is of cardinal importance to him. At the same time, the growing of potatoes for marketing purposes, where the soil is suitable and where improved varieties are grown and the cultivation properly carried out, allows a margin of profit sufficient to make it a crop of great value to the small holder. It is not easy to obtain satisfactory data regarding the changes in the value of crops other than the cereals, but in the official prices of agricultural produce in Ireland, there is a record for the past twenty years of the prices of potatoes, hay, grass seed, and flax. all of which are crops of considerable importance to the small farmer in Ireland, while there is also evidence in the *Report* of the Board of Trade on wholesale and retail prices in the United Kingdom in 1902. &c.

The main question, however, for the home farmer is the development in the supplies and changes in the prices of animal produce, of beef. mutton, pork, dairy produce, eggs and poultry. If the evidence of values of imported produce is taken it would appear (1) that there has been a fall in the prices of beef. mutton, and pork during the past twenty years, the fall being greatest in the case of beef : (2) that in recent years the prices of fresh pork, and still more of bacon and hams. have been better maintained than the prices of beef and mutton : and (3) that the prices of butter, cheese, and eggs, while fluctuating, cannot be said to have fallen. From the evidence of import values it is not, however, legitimate to draw more than broad deductions. But it may be said that on the whole the records of home prices confirm the conclusion that the trend of prices has been favouring the production of pig meat, butter, cheese, eggs and poultry as compared with beef. The fall in the price of beef has, however, been less than the import values suggest, and if the prices of first, second, and inferior beef at the Metropolitan market are examined, or the returns of prices in the Dublin fat stock market, it will be seen that while there have been considerable fluctuations from year to year, the fall in the prices of beef in the past twenty years has not been great.

Again, as regards the store stock trade, which is one of much importance to the small holder, whether the record of the Teviotdale Farmers' Club is taken, or the prices collected by the Land Commission and subsequently the Department of Agriculture and Technical Instruction in Ireland, the evidence points to the fluctuations of prices rather than a general fall in the past twenty years.

Further. in considering the prices of beef, it will be remembered that they vary widely according to quality from an average of $7d.$ per lb. first quality home grown to $2\frac{3}{4}d.$ for Argentine frozen fore quarters. and if an examination of the detailed prices of beef in recent years is made. what appears is the fact that prices of the highest qualities have neither fluctuated nor fallen to the same extent as those of the lower grades of beef. The best qualities of home-grown and home-fed beef have advantages over port-killed beef, and still more over the chilled and frozen imports. At the same time the promise of development not only in the quantity but in the quality of the output of beef from new countries, especially the Argentine, makes the future uncertain. With the abundance of cheap pasture and the large amount of capital and organisation which has now been invested in the raising of beef in new countries, prices may go still lower. The home producer will only be able to meet this competition by himself growing an abundant supply of feeding stuffs, especially of green crops and roots, by hand-feeding live stock, and by producing for the market the first quality of beef.

As regards the prices of pork, bacon and hams, these have fluctuated greatly, but on the whole the tendency has been upwards. And with the enormous home market for this line of produce there is room for a very considerable increase in the number of pigs in the United Kingdom. Economically the extension of pig-breeding works in with the development of tillage and the production of milk and dairy produce, and it is a factor of great importance in the development of agricultural small holdings.

With regard to butter, the value of the annual imports shows the enormous field which there is for development in the United Kingdom. This, however, involves, if to be profitably carried out, the improvement of the milk production of our cows—as has been the case in Denmark—and, with an extended crop area, an increase in the number of cows. With regard to the prices of butter, while it is very difficult to compare present-day prices with those of past years, owing to the much greater differentiation which has taken place in agricultural produce, it is clear that the good qualities of butter are realising remunerative prices, and that, for the higher grades of butter, prices have been rising in recent years. There are creameries which are obtaining 1s. per lb. for their butter the year round, and, at the same time, there are butters which are only realising half this amount. Anyone who has looked into the question of the prices obtained for butter in different parts of the country, and the astonishing difference there is in the quality of the butter and the causes of this difference, must feel that there is room for great improvement in the butter production of the United Kingdom. But in order to supply to a large extent our own demand, and to obtain more remunerative prices, winter dairying must be developed, and this again depends on the extension of the area of winter-feeding crops.

To a somewhat less extent than in the case of butter, grading has affected the comparison of the prices of eggs, but whether one regards the import figures of the past twenty years or whether one looks to the record of home prices, there is evidence

of an upward tendency in the price of eggs. Every year since 1902 has shown better prices being obtained for Irish eggs. Again, it is plain that the output of eggs in the United Kingdom could be enormously increased. So far as Ireland is concerned, there is evidence that it is at the present time steadily advancing, and the export in the year 1904 exceeded a value of 2,000,000*l*. What is true of eggs is true of poultry, and, in general, of all classes of fresh produce. The system of grading has led to better prices.

Considering, therefore, on the one hand the demand for agricultural produce, as shown by the quantity imported and by the range of prices, and on the other hand the economic conditions which determine production as amongst the various competing countries of to-day and of the immediate future, the conclusion to which one is forced is that the future of agriculture in the United Kingdom, especially in the case of the small holder, must depend to an increasing extent on dairy produce, eggs and poultry, fruit, vegetables, and perishable produce, as well as on the production of the best grades of beef. Behind all this the fundamental question is the growing of grain, roots, and green crops, which are the raw material of all the animal produce.

Conditions Essential to the Economic Development of a Small Farm Holding.

The further question which remains for consideration is that of the capacity of the small holder as a producer and the essential conditions for him of economic production. It is a matter of considerable difficulty either to ascertain what might be regarded as the present average productive capacity of an agricultural small holding or to set up what may be considered a high but nevertheless attainable standard of production. If this is to be done it is necessary to define the size and type of small holding and then to obtain as complete a balance sheet as possible of expenditure and income. Inquiries which have been made in Ireland into the average productive capacity of, for example, the 20-acre farm, show how difficult it is to obtain correct and complete information regarding the average production and cost of such farms. In some cases, reckoning up the various items of expenditure and income, the small holder of 20 acres of average land appears to have only a balance of 30*l.*—40*l.*—plus a house, as net income—after interest on capital has been deducted. In other cases the net income runs from 60*l.*—70*l.* The small holding is thus a business in which both industry and wise management are essential to success, and the more one studies the economic position of the small holder and sees the forces with which he has to compete and the limited income which he can realise, the clearer does it become that the problem of the success of the small holder is largely the question of the man.   We require the small farmer who has got into his head the sense of comparative values.   For the economy of the small holder depends on whether you are going to have the man who sees to it that he has cows and feeds them to give him 800 gallons of milk rather than 400, that he keeps only those hens which give him 140 eggs and not 80, that he gets 10 tons of potatoes to his acre instead of 5, that he joins with others to buy and sell on the most economic lines, that he grows to a large extent his own food and his beasts' food, that he feeds his cattle and pigs rationally, and, in a word, that he is alive as an individual to all the small economies, as well as the larger ones, which contribute to prosperity.   This question of the man is absolutely at the root of the whole question of success or failure.   And it is for this reason that, in view of the remarkable changes and advances in the scientific and the economic conditions of present-day farming, a thorough system of rural education and organisation must accompany the providing of facilities of land and capital for small holdings.

In order to make the economic situation as concrete as possible I attach a statement furnished by a farmer who has a wide experience of Irish holdings as to the capacity of the 20-acre farm, if worked on the lines which appear to him most productive.   It is postulated that the small holder is a man of industry and knowledge, that he farms with his head as well as with his hands, that he has capital to thoroughly stock and equip his holding, that he has the assistance and co-operation with other farmers in regard to the disposal of his milk, eggs, poultry, and in the purchasing of his manures, seeds, &c., that he is able also to have at certain times the help of a neighbour farmer in return for like services, and that he has some one to look after his house and attend to the milking of the cows and help in the management of the pigs and poultry.   It is assumed also that the land is good average land, but without any special suitability for the growing of crops of high value, such as early potatoes. The yields of crops may in certain cases appear high, but they are yields which are actually being obtained by good farmers on the class of land which is assumed, and the prices of stock are also prices which farmers who know their business are realising.   In addition to the net revenue of 84*l*. the farmer has house and garden free, and obtains for his household such food stuffs as the farm produces at the rate at which he sells them and not at ordinary retail cost. Such a statement gives a concrete view—whether one agrees with it or not—of the capacity for production on the one hand, and on the other hand of the real income of the small holder—the two

main aspects of the position of the small holder. It is not intended
to present what exists, but to indicate what is possible.

Regarding the general economic conditions essential to small
holdings, reference may briefly be made to four factors of great
importance : (1) the tenure of land ; (2) the equipment and stocking
of the holding ; (3) the general organisation of the agricultural
small-holding community ; and (4) the provision of agricultural
education.

As regards tenure and rent, whatever view one may take on the
question of ownership versus tenancy, it will be admitted that if
small holdings are to be successful, one condition is that the small
holder should have every inducement to improve his land, and
should be assured that the benefits of these improvements will accrue
to him. The final verdict on the comparative advantages of different
forms of tenure has not yet been given, and it will be felt by at
least many students of economic and statistical matters that considerably more data are yet required before this verdict can be
given. But whether by individual and unrestricted ownership, or
by a system of restricted ownership with the public retaining a lein,
or a residual claim on the property, or whether through a system of
fixity of tenure and fair rent, in one direction or another, the
security of the small holder has to be assured. Granted this, then
more important even that the particular form of tenure which may
be adopted, is the weight of rent, instalment, or interest—as the
case may be—which falls on the small holder. This is a serious
item in his cost of production, and affects directly his economic
stability and power of survival. It is therefore necessary that the
most powerful assistance which the economic organisation of credit,
public and private, can give, should be, under satisfactory conditions
of control, at the disposal of the small holder, and that the burden
of rent, instalment, or interest, should be made as light as possible.
Hence, in the experiments which have been and are being carried
out on so large a scale as regards the system of fair rent fixing and
of land purchase in Ireland, the fact that public credit has been
brought to the assistance of the farmer as regards rent is a step of
the greatest importance, and is one of the most justifiable and
economic uses of organised national credit.

With regard to the second point, the stocking and equipment of
holdings, this is in the closest relationship with what has been said
regarding rent. It is not enough that the small holder should have
his land on as good terms as possible. It is necessary that he should
have the means of properly equipping and stocking that land. This
is a very serious aspect of the small holdings question, and one
which the advocates of small holdings must be prepared to meet, for

the small holder has serious disadvantages as well as advantages in his economic situation, and the chance is that if he is to start with little or no capital the struggle for existence will be extremely hard; and the very objects, mental and moral as well as material, which are in view in the promotion of small holdings will be defeated. In short, the small holder must be helped to obtain on the best terms which the money market will permit the capital necessary for the proper stocking and equipment of his holding.

This brings us immediately to the machinery by which this is to be done, and to the third and larger question of the organisation of agriculture in the small holding community. This organisation must be co-operative. The essence of co-operation is that men join together to manage their common interests, on a system of voluntary action and self-government which avoids the incurring of any heavy expenses of administration. It brings to the small holder much of the economic strength of the large holder. Now, as has been so well brought out in the thought and practice of co-operation in France, the co-operative idea and spirit is the source of life in the whole organisation. But looking at the forms in which the idea embodies itself, the most important fact is that the true centre of the co-operative system of agriculture is co-operative credit. Capital is the great need of the farmer, and to give the farmer as elastic and economic a system of credit as possible is the greatest assistance which can be given him. This has been the great strength of the movement in Germany, where on the 1st March, 1906, of the total number of registered agricultural co-operative societies amounting to 19,763, no less than 13,452 represented savings and loan societies. The fact, however, that co-operative credit is the heart of the co-operative system will be most clearly realised by briefly referring to the various sides of co-operative activity, all of which enter into the making of the economic small holder. Co-operative societies may be classed in three groups : (1) purchasing, (2) producing and marketing societies, (3) provident societies.

The purchasing societies have sprung up and developed chiefly in connection with the buying of seeds and manures. But while these have been the main articles of their trade, these societies, through a central agency, can advantageously supply the small farmer with other agricultural requirements, such as implements and machinery, or feeding-stuffs. The evidence of various countries shows that the development of these societies has led to a considerable reduction in the prices of the materials of production to the small farmer, and a consequent increase in the capacity of the small farmers to purchase. At the same time not only has the price been improved, but the security of the farmer regarding the quality and standard of his article has been increased, for the system of requiring standard quality, especially in the case of artificial manures, and of providing a system of testing consignments has been made possible by means of combined purchase.

Co-operation is no less necessary for the small holder in the producing and marketing of his goods. The small holder in Europe and in the United Kingdom must depend largely on the production of dairy produce, butter, cheese, milk, &c., eggs and poultry, fruit and vegetables. Especially in the production of butter combined action has become necessary. Modern market conditions require supplies which are large in quantity and regular in quality, and the creamery is the natural consequence of this demand. Hence the remarkable creamery development of butter-producing countries—Denmark on the one hand and Ireland on the other. The production of butter is the best example of the necessity of combination amongst small holders for production and marketing, and co-operation has had its great extension in this field. But the small holder requires to combine for the marketing of his other small produce, whether eggs, poultry, fruit or vegetables, if he is to receive the benefits of grading his produce and of securing connections with the market which capacity to supply a regular standard alone insures.

The third main sphere for co-operative action is in connection with provident societies. It is necessary that the small holder should not only be able to purchase and to produce cheaply, but that he should be able to provide against loss. Here the principle of insurance meets his requirements, and co-operation is admirably adapted to the work of insurance. Most important in this direction is the insurance of live stock, and while certain developments have been, and are being made in this country, they are small compared with the enormous extension of co-operative live-stock insurance in foreign countries. But in other matters as well as live stock the small holder must take precaution to insure. The larger small holders will themselves employ labour, and here they must insure against liability under the Workmen's Compensation Act—a practice far less extended among the small farmers employing labour than among the larger employers. Already in Ireland an interesting experiment has been made in this direction by the Irish Agricultural Organisation Society, which has arranged with the Yorkshire Insurance Company a scheme whereby a number of small holders can take out a joint policy on favourable terms. Similarly in other matters, such as the question of insurance against fire, the small holder must safeguard himself. In all these spheres of co-operative action, whether purchasing, producing, or provident, the centre is the system of credit which enables these various activities to be adequately financed and economically carried out.   What is required thus for the small holder is a complete system of organisation, and any policy dealing with the small holding problem must secure this.   The development of co-operation in the United Kingdom has been much more slower than in the leading agricultural countries of continental Europe, and the cause of this is no doubt in large measure due to the more limited number of small holdings in Great Britain.   In Ireland, on the other hand, where small holdings abound, co-operation has found more congenial soil, and the co-operative movement has within the past twenty years struck firm root.   The following table shows the number of various co-operative societies according to the last report of the Irish Agricultural Organisation Society :—

Creameries	275	Bee-keepers' societies	18
,, (unregistered)	56	Bacon-curing societies	2
Agricultural societies	151	Miscellaneous societies	13
Credit societies	232	Federations	4
Poultry societies	25		
Flax societies	9	Total	835
Industries societies	50		

But co-operation even in Ireland is only in its early stages, and there must be a great advance in co-operative action if the Irish small holder is to hold his own in the home market.   The same is true of Great Britain if the small holder is to become a force in agriculture.

The fourth factor in the economy of the small holder is agricultural education.   It has been said that the problem of the small holding is the problem of the man.   The small holder, if he is to reach a real standard of comfort, must make the most of his limited resources, and to do this he must have economic methods of work and be kept informed of the advances in agricultural science.   Also he has to be kept in touch with the changing condition of markets. All this involves a liberal practical education, and the opportunities of obtaining reliable advice regarding his work.   The problem is, therefore, to bring within the reach of the small-holding class a scheme of education suited to its requirements and resources, which will provide not simply for the training of a young generation of small holders, but will help the existing generation of small farmers to make the most of their position.   Hence it is not a question which can be solved by provision in our elementary schools, though such provision is a matter, in my opinion, of great urgency. The information must be brought to the small holder on the farm, and at times which will allow him to carry on his regular daily work.   Such is the problem in Ireland, where there are a large number of small holders, and where within recent years considerable developments have taken place in agricultural education. First, there was itinerant instruction to awaken interest — this being the pioneer work of the earlier years. Second, winter classes have been established—work which is rapidly extending. These are local classes for men working on their farms held during fifteen to twenty weeks in the winter for two or three days of the week. At them the young farmer is given an all-round practical course of instruction in the developments of modern farming. The number at a centre is limited to 24, so that the instruction may be as individual as possible. This work has proved practical in its results, and is capable of meeting to a large extent the needs of the small holders. Third, there are residential agricultural school stations, at which young men who have had experience of farm work, who can spare the necessary time and money, and who intend to go back into farming, receive one year's training in scientific and practical work. Similarly for women there are special facilities for education and training in rural economy. By such agencies, as well as by other means, as, for example, experimental stations, and supplemental to the experimental stations, demonstration plots on the farms of small holders, the work of education can be advanced and the small holder enabled to make his agricultural position as economically strong as the case will allow. Thus properly established as regards land tenure, provided with facilities for adequately stocking and equipping his farm, organised for purchase, for production and marketing, and for insurance against loss, educated and informed as to the best methods, the small holder can prove himself to be " economically sound." And while his standard of comfort will be simple he will have a life which has security of employment, variety of interest, and a measure of independence far greater than that of millions of the working classes to-day. The small holding must not be judged too much in the light of the large or even the medium-sized farm. One must think, when considering the general economic and social position of the small holder, of the agricultural and of the industrial labourer.

Further, not one type but a wide variety of small holdings is required. There is no stereotyped pattern which can be manufactured as long as there is land to carve up. There are holdings which are practically allotments, there are holdings where a man gives the greater part of his time to his own land but also has some labour to dispose of, there are holdings where a man can find an outlet for all his labour and energy without employing any labour, such as the case to which we have specially referred ; and all these may well be economic holdings.

These are some considerations which bear on the question of the present and the future of small holdings, but the main work of investigation has yet to be done. For if the economic position of the various classes of agricultural holders is to be realised, and if there is to be a clear and conscious State policy in promoting the growth of economic small holdings, there is need of a great deal more statistical inquiry and of a much fuller presentation of co-ordinated statistical data.

APPENDIX.

Statement regarding a 20 Acre Farm of Good Average Land, Well Cultivated.

Distribution of land.   8 course rotation.

2½ acres after lea	⌠ 1 acre of oats. ⎨ 1 ,, and peas. ⌡ ½ ,, ,, vetches.
2½ ,, manured land	⌠ 1½ acres of potatoes. ⎨ ½ acre of mangels. ⌡ ½ ,, beans.
2½ ,, grain crops	⌠ 2 acres of oats. ⌡ ½ acre of wheat.
2½ ,, manured land	⌠ 2 acres of turnips. ⌡ ½ acre of cabbages.
2½ ,, grain crops	⌠ 2 acres of oats. ⌡ ½ acre of barley.
2½ ,, "seeds" hay.	
5 ,, grazing.	

Statement Showing Acreage of Different Crops.

			Acres.	Acres.
Grain crops	⌠	Oats	5	
	⎨	Wheat	½	
	⌡	Barley	½	6
Feeding crops	⌠	Oats and peas	1	
	⎨	Vetches and oats	½	
	⌡	Beans	½	2
Green crops	⌠	Potatoes	1½	
	⎨	Turnips	2	
	⎨	Mangels	½	
	⌡	Cabbage	½	4½
Hay crop				2½
Grazing				5

20

Estimated Average Yields from the Different Crops.

			Tons.	Cwts.
5 acres of oats	{ Grain		5	–
	Straw		9	–
½ acre of wheat	{ Grain		–	10
	Straw		1	5
½ „ barley	{ Grain ·		–	9
	Straw		–	18
1 „ oats and peas	{ Oats and peas		1	–
	Straw		1	10
½ „ vetches............	Green feed............	8 to 10	–
½ „ beans	{ Beans		–	10
	Straw		–	12½
1½ „ potatoes	(Large and small)		15	··
2 acres of turnips			45	–
½ acre of mangels			15	–
½ „ cabbage			12	–
2½ acres of hay			6	–

Number of Stock Proposed to be Kept.

1 horse.	1 sow.
3 cows.	16 pigs reared and sold as
3 young cattle (21 months).	pork.
3 calves.	40 fowl.
2 bought-in stores run over winter (October-May).	

Value of Stock

	£	s.	d.		£	s.	d.
1 horse	22	10	–	1 sow	4	–	–
3 cows	52	10	–	8 pigs......	16	–	–
3 cattle (14 months)	27	–	–				
3 calves (6 months)........	13	10	–		138	10	–
Poultry	3	–	–				

Value of Dead Stock under Wear.

	£	s.	d.		£	s.	d.
1 cart............	5	··	–	1 thresher	20	–	–
1 wheelbarrow	–	10	–	Winnower.........................	3	–	–
1 chill plough	2	–	–	Pulper	2	··	–
Harrows...............	1	10	–	Boiler..............................	1	10	–
1 drill plough	1	10	–	Reaper and mower	8	–	–
1 light grubber............. ..	2	–	–	Harness	1	5	–
Saddle harrow	1	–	–	Sundry articles......	2	10	–
1 hunter hoe....................	–	15	–				
1 roller	2	–	–		54	10	–

Amount of Food Requisite for Consumption by Stock (chiefly Home Raised,
but some Purchased).

1 horse will require { 20 cwts. oats, 4 cwts. beans, 5 cwts. maize and bran, 50 cwts. hay.

3 cows will require { 19½ cwts. oats, 19½ cwts. decorticated cotton cake, 9¾ cwts. bran, 5 tons 12 cwts. straw, 34 tons turnips and green feed.

3 young cattle raised to 21 months old will require { 165 gallons whole milk, 14½ cwts. oats, 2¾ cwts. maize, 9 stones linseed, 8¼ cwts. cake, 18¾ tons turnips and green food, 60 cwts. straw, 7½ cwts. hay.

2 stores (October—May) will require { 6 cwts. oats, 3 cwts. linseed cake, 10 tons turnips, 50 cwts. straw.

1 sow will require .... { 1 ton potatoes, 3 cwts. peas and oats, 3 cwts. barley, 5 cwts. maize, 4 cwts. wheat for sow and young.

16 pigs raised to 6 months old will require .... { 85 gallons whole milk, 3 tons potatoes, 38 cwts. mixture, peas, barley, and oats, crushed with 22 cwts. maize.

40 head of fowl will require .... { 25 cwts. potatoes, 5 cwts. maize, with tail corn, wheat refuse, &c.

Disposal of Live Stock and Surplus Produce.

	£	s.	d.
Milk, 2,000 gallons at 4d.	33	6	8
Eggs, 400 dozen at 8d.	13	6	8
3 cattle 21 months old......................	36	—	—
Profit on 2 stores wintered.................	10	—	—
16 pigs at 3l. 15s.	60	—	—
33 cwts. oats at 5s. 6d. per cwt.	9	1	6
6 cwts. wheat at 6s.	1	16	—
8¼ tons potatoes at 2l.	16	10	—
62½ cwts. hay at 3s. per cwt.	9	7	6
	189	8	4

Statement of Expenses.

	£	s.	d.		£	s.	d.
Rent	15	—	—	Veterinary surgeon	1	—	—
Interest on tenant right at 4 per cent. .... }	14	—	—	Smith	1	—	—
				Upkeep of tools	3	—	—
Feeding stuffs	27	9	3	,, buildings	2	—	—
Manures and lime	12	—	—	Insurance of buildings....	1	10	—
Seed oats, 14 stone	—	11	8	,, cattle	3	10	—
5 cwts. seed potatoes	1	—	—	Crushing of feeding stuffs	2	8	—
Grass and clover seeds....	2	15	—	Marketing expenses	2	—	—
Turnip seed	—	8	—	Rates	3	—	—
Mangel seed	—	4	—	Interest on stock and implements .... }	8	—	—
Vetch seed, beans, and peas .... }	1	12	—	Potato boxes	—	9	—
Spraying potatoes...........	—	15	—				
Service of cows	—	15	—		104	11	11
,, sow	—	5	—				

Annual Balance on Working Account.

	£	s.	d.
To proceeds of live stock and produce sold	189	8	4
By working expenses.....................	104	11	11
	84	16	5

DISCUSSION *on* MR. W. G. S. ADAMS'S PAPER.

LORD EVERSLEY expressed his regret at not being able to be present last month when his own Paper was read, and desired to thank those who took part in the discussion on that occasion for their kind references to himself. Mr. Adams's Paper formed a very proper sequel to his own, though written from a different point of view. He had then dealt with the conditions of land holdings in England, and endeavoured to show how far the reduction of population in the rural districts during the last forty years was due to the fall of prices or to other causes. Mr. Adams had carried the matter further and dealt with the question of small holdings, laying down the conditions under which he thought they might be made profitable, no doubt with an eye to legislation now in prospect. He thought Mr. Adams had somewhat over-estimated the number of small holdings in Great Britain. What they understood generally by that term were those holdings of land which were cultivated by owners or tenants by their own hands, and by which they lived either wholly or partly in combination with some other rural occupation. Beyond this, however, there were a large number of small holdings included in the agricultural returns quoted by Mr. Adams which were held in connection with residential property or occupation of land by village tradesmen and so forth. As an illustration, he might say that in his own parish in Hampshire he did not know of a single case of a small holding in the sense in which Mr. Adams understood that term; but there were, perhaps, 8 or 10 of the other character he had referred to. Again, in another large parish in Kent in which he was interested, consisting of 2,500 acres, a purely rural district, there was not, to his knowledge, a single small-holder in the true sense; but there were several small holdings included in the returns belonging to landowners in the parish and connected with their residences, and also other small holdings held by village tradespeople by way of occupation land, sometimes by the village publican and people of that class. What, then, was the real number of small holdings in England, Wales, and Scotland, for the purpose of that discussion? He found that in Great Britain, according to the census returns, there were 277,000 persons, male and female, who called themselves farmers; and 166,000 of those held farms of above 50 acres in extent. Subtracting the latter, we find only 111,000 persons who could possibly be called small holders in the defined sense, or something less than one half the number given by Mr. Adams as taken from the agricultural returns. There were practically very few small holdings, in the true sense of this term, in the south or east of England. What there were, between 5 and 50 acres, were in the main in pastoral parts of England, in Wales, and in Lancashire, Cheshire, Yorkshire, and so forth. There was a small community in Lincolnshire, in the Isle of Axholme, which had been there from very ancient times, and there was a community of small holders in Worcestershire occupied with the cultivation of fruit; but in the arable parts of England and Scotland there were very few small holdings. It was, of course, different in Ireland. Mr. Adams had given the number as something over 500,000, but that included a large number of cottier tenants in the south and west, cultivating small patches of potato land, who could not be called small holders in the sense in which they used that term. Many of them were rather migratory labourers who lived in the congested districts, coming over to England and Scotland in harvest time and returning home in the winter. They constituted a large proportion of those included in the census in Connaught and Munster. At the same time, in the rest of Ireland there were a large body of men who lived on the land entirely, cultivating it themselves with their families, who had built their own houses, or whose predecessors had, and who some years ago were merely tenants at will of the landlord, but who, by legislation of late years, had been invested with some of the attributes of ownership under the Land Act of 1881, and were now being rapidly converted into full owners under more recent legislation. Though he had questioned some of Mr. Adams' statistics, he agreed with the general tenor of this Paper, especially the latter part, which dealt with the conditions under which small holdings were possible and profitable. Small holdings in England and Wales were almost wholly in the pastoral districts, and it was not easy to find out the exact conditions under which they could be made profitable in arable districts. Mr. Adams had given a sort of hypothetical balance-sheet, derived from some gentleman in Ireland, suggesting what was the best condition of cultivation in which 20 acres could be made profitable. There was a good illustration of this to be found in the evidence before the recent committee appointed by the Board of Agriculture. It was the case of a small tenant who had a farm in Cheshire of only 20 acres paying a rent of 2*l*. 15*s*. per acre per annum. Of that 20 acres, one half was permanent pasture, 6 acres clover and temporary grasses, 1½ acres oats, 1½ acres potatoes, and 1 acre vegetables; and on the land thus cultivated the tenant worked himself and employed a young man as servant under him, so that there were two men employed on the 20 acres and making their living upon it. The holding was seven miles distant from a market; there was one horse employed, either in ploughing the land or in conveying produce to the market. Out of that land the man, his wife, and family were maintained; and he had been told that he made a very good living, and laid by money. It was interesting to compare that farm, which he was told was average land in the district, with other large farms in the country. It would seem that if the rest of Cheshire were cultivated in the same way as the holding he referred to, there would be exactly double the number of persons getting their living on the land in the county, and something like double the amount of produce. That man kept nine cows and some pigs, of which he sold a considerable number, and actually spent 132*l*. a year on feeding stuffs. That result was, of course, only brought about by intense labour, and no doubt partly by the security which he had in the good faith of his landlord; so that he was induced to devote to the cultivation of the holding more labour and energy than was given by the ordinary tenant farmer on a larger scale. That was a good illustration of what could be done on a small holding. There was a part of Scotland, to which he called attention in his own Paper, in which there was a large community of small holders cultivating arable land in the county of Aberdeenshire—there were something like 7,000 tenants cultivating land between 5 and 50 acres—and he ventured to make a comparison between that and the counties of Roxburgh, Berwick, and Edinburgh, which were counties of very large farms, averaging 280 acres, whereas in Aberdeen the average acreage was only 80. The result of that comparison was that in Aberdeen there were five times the number of farmers and twice the number of hands employed on the land; and, as far as he could make out from the agricultural returns, the number of cows and cattle was very much greater. On the other hand, it was true that the rent in the three southern counties was 8*s.* per acre more than in Aberdeen, but he was told that the land in Aberdeen was not so good. There we have an illustration of a large community of small holders, with the result that Aberdeenshire, which had much the same area as the other three counties, contained more than double the number of persons employed in agriculture, and a proportionally larger amount of produce.

Amongst the conditions to which Mr. Adams adverted as being important, and which seemed to him to be almost essential to prosperity in the long run on a large scale of small holdings, was that of security of tenure. His own belief was that only the impulse of ownership, or a security of tenure infinitely greater than that which prevailed generally, would give an impulse to cultivation by small-holders such as would induce them to embark on the enterprise with the energy, zeal, and labour which were necessary if they were to make small holdings pay.

Sir HORACE PLUNKETT said the problem of Ireland at the present moment was the small holdings problem. As Lord Eversley had pointed out, it was very different from that which confronted them in the other parts of the United Kingdom. What Irishmen called a small holding, Englishmen, as he understood Lord Eversley, would not call a holding at all. The most interesting aspect of the Irish small holding problem at the moment was the search for what was called the "economic holding." Probably some 250,000 people, at the lowest computation, were living on holdings in Ireland on which they could not possibly maintain a decent standard of comfort. On the other hand, there were large tracts of grazing land (although not nearly enough to adjust matters) which the Estates Commissioners had power to acquire voluntarily, and might possibly be given power to acquire compulsorily in the near future. In any case, some of those lands had been acquired and were being re-distributed in, what were called, economic holdings. There were a great many men thinking about this problem in Ireland, but he doubted whether there were two men

who were agreed as to what an economic holding was. He
agreed with Mr. Adams that it was more a question of the man
than of the land. Indeed, he could not decide what an economic
holding was, while they had got neither an economic system nor,
indeed, very many economic men to put upon small holdings.
Perhaps there were a few interesting specimens in England, such
as the Cheshire farmer, about whom they had heard, who was able
to maintain 9 cows upon an area of land which was only entitled,
according to the usual English computation, to maintain 6⅔. But,
speaking generally, until the co-operative system had gone a great
deal further, and, still more, until they had made a great advance in
agricultural education, they would not be in a condition to say
what sized holding would be permanent in Ireland. Personally,
he was strongly against stereotyping any size for holdings at
the present stage, though he was in great hopes that when the
Royal Commission on Congestion, which was making an exhaustive
inquiry in Ireland at the present time, had issued its report, the
Government would come to the conclusion that it was vitally
important, before any large re-distribution of land was undertaken,
that a great many experiments should be tried. He was inclined to
think that even in England a great many experiments would have
to be tried before they could determine the best policy in this
vitally important question of providing holdings which would
maintain the largest possible rural population in comfortable
permanence. His own view was that an immense amount of
thought would still have to be given even outside the scope of
Mr. Adams' Paper. From his own studies of rural life in Ireland,
and from what he knew of it in this country, which was mostly at
second hand, and in the United States, where he had a fair amount
of first-hand knowledge, he was convinced that even when material
comfort had been provided for by all that administration and
legislation could do, it would still remain for social and intellectual
movements to provide some counterpart for the movements to
which towns owed so much of their progress. If they want to
get the best elements of the country to remain there and to put
up with, what must necessarily be, a modest standard of physical
comfort with little luxury, and certainly a more toilsome existence
than was provided in the modern town, every side of country life
must be brought up to the newer standards of physical and social
requirements. The only criticism he would make on the Paper
was, that of the four factors on which the author relied, he should
put education first instead of last. Until they had dealt with the
rural schools and given the country population a new and brighter
outlook, and a higher appreciation of the interests and enjoyment
of the country—until they had greatly improved the domestic
economy of the people which seemed to him to have fallen sadly
since the days of our forefathers, when the home was self-supporting
—it would be very hard to build up rural life. But his chief con-
structive suggestion was that holdings, whether they were called
" small " or " economic," ought to be considered and practically
dealt with, not so much individually or separately, as in groups.

An association of such holdings might be entirely different, both economically and socially, and had much higher possibilities than could the isolated holding. He should like to see some experimental colonies actually planted by the State with the distinct object of testing the possibilities of communities of small holders. It was to him a true paradox, that while the isolated peasant proprietor was, under present circumstances, almost an economic absurdity, a peasant proprietary co-operatively organised, combining the closer attention, deeper interest, and more strenuous labours of the family, working for hearth and home, with the advantages of the larger operations within the power of combination, furnishes the best means of producing the utmost return from the land. And, what is more important, given a proper system of rural education, you may rebuild a rural society which will resist the call of the town.

Mr. JESSE ARGYLE said he did not feel qualified to discuss the general questions raised by this interesting Paper, but, bearing in mind the qualifications which were laid down as essential in order to successfully manage a small holding, he would venture to suggest that successful small-holders, like poets, were born and not made. He felt devoutly thankful that in our large towns it was possible to get a living without having to be such an agglomeration of virtue and knowledge as seemed to be necessary when you were a small-holder. There was one point in the Paper on which he wished to say a word, and that was in regard to the success of co-operative agriculture in foreign countries. He happened to be present a few weeks ago at the Co-operative Congress at Preston, where he was much interested in the remarks made by the foreign delegates as to the success of co-operation, particularly in Denmark, where the delegates said that the co-operative movement commenced in 1886, and was modelled entirely on the Rochdale system; in fact, most of the foreign representatives expressed their indebtedness to England for having set the example in this matter. They had now in Denmark 1,200 shops with 180,000 members, and yearly sales of over two and a half millions sterling. It was almost entirely agricultural co-operation. The first co-operative dairy started in 1882, but now they had 1,076, with 158,000 members, delivering last year to dairies milk to the value of about 8,000,000l. They started in 1895 the exportation of eggs, and in 1906 their total sales were 250,000l. They had also founded co-operative sanatoria, with the object of helping the poor. The Swiss delegates reported similar success, there being over 160,000 members in their societies. It struck him that there was an important lesson to be learned from these results. If other and much smaller countries, copying what had been initiated in Great Britain, could do so much, there must be very great possibilities for co-operative farming in this country.

. Mr. R. WINFREY, M.P., said that, having had some practical experience in putting small holders on the land, his own feeling was that the first thing to do, in England at any rate, was to get the land to put the men upon. There were a good many thousand men at the present time who were desirous of having small holdings, and the first thing to do was to get them on to the land. When they were there, he believed the co-operative societies and all the other good things would follow. So far as the conditions under which they should be put there were concerned, he had no hesitation in saying that he was in favour of tenancy rather than ownership. He had had a good deal to do with the small freeholder in this country who had gone into the open market and bought land at more than its value, borrowing four-fifths of the money. The mortgage was generally shifted periodically every few years, and it seemed to him that that was not the type of man they wanted. He believed a tenant paying a fair rent, with reasonable fixity of tenure, was preferable. He said "reasonable fixity," because he believed it was an advantage to any association or public body which might have the duty of providing small holdings that they should have some control over such tenants. If they had, as he had under his control, some 200 or 300 small holding tenants, it was a great advantage, if a man was found to be not farming properly, to be able to say to him, "If you do not farm properly, you must go out." It was no advantage to the community or to the man that he should be permitted to farm in an unhusband-like manner. With respect to purchase, perhaps Lord Eversley did not know that the Cambridge County Council were the first County Council to put into force the Small Holdings Act of 1892. They made purchases, and they sold the land to a number of men. He had just seen a recent report showing that there were only two or three of the original purchasers on the land, that in one way or another they had got rid of their holdings, which showed pretty clearly, in the first instance, that the Cambridge County Council would have done better to have retained the control in their own hands. This was now the opinion of the Council. With regard to co-operation, there was one matter which Mr. Adams had not mentioned : where an association managed the land, rather than single individuals, there was great advantage in the rating question. In England, directly you divided a farm up into small holdings and each man stood on his own basis, a new assessment was made, and the assessment was generally put up by 50 per cent., so that you had the small holder paying 50 per cent. more rates and taxes than the large farmer. They obviated that in the Lincolnshire and Norfolk Small Holdings Association by keeping the farms which were divided up rated as one, paying the rates in a lump and dividing it according to acreage amongst the tenants. There, they had co-operation in paying the rates—not compounding—and they had their land at the fair average rating of the district, and did not have it put up. Only three weeks ago they had the satisfaction of letting a farm to tenants, owing to the death of the farmer, and his widow not being able to carry the farm on. They took it over at twenty-four hours' notice, and it was let within three weeks to some 16 or 17 working men living in that immediate neighbourhood. It was not in a village nor even in a hamlet, but in the scattered Fens district of Lincolnshire, and they had no difficulty in getting men from the surrounding districts to take the land. A neighbouring farmer had told him that they had taken five of his best men, and made small holders of them, but he said he did not mind, though he did not want to lose them, and he should have to look out for five other men and bring them into his locality. That showed the advantage of establishing small holdings, and especially of creating tenants, as none of those men had been in a position to purchase: they required all their little capital to farm with. He congratulated Mr. Adams upon the able way in which he had placed the subject before them.

Major CRAIGIE said this Paper, and the discussion upon it, fully justified the Council in putting that opportune subject before them as a sequel to their last month's Paper. It presented so many different points—educational, statistical and economical—which really still required exhaustive discussion, that he was sure all would endorse the note of caution that had been apparent throughout Mr. Adams's Paper, and which was again emphasised in Sir Horace Plunkett's speech. Certainly the Legislature would need to exercise great circumspection if they were seriously to enter on a policy of artificially creating a number of new small holdings elsewhere than in the districts where small farms had maintained a successful existence under the economic conditions of the day. Many of the difficulties which impeded the profitable use of small areas of land had not yet been experimentally settled, and this ought to be done before they could feel confident that they were on the right lines. Lord Eversley had given them an impression that statistics overstated the number of small farms in existence. He told them that in many parts of the country there were really no small holdings to be found of the type which they were considering, but he happened to be living now not very far from the same neighbourhood as Lord Eversley, and his own experience was not exactly the same. All round him on the edge of the New Forest there were numerous and fairly successful small holders already.

Lord EVERSLEY said that he ought to have made an exception with regard to the New Forest, because, in consequence of the rights of turning out cattle, a considerable number of small holdings had been preserved there.

Major CRAIGIE, continuing, said that it was not only in these conditions that the small farm still survived. In several of his Papers, particularly in one which he read to the Society some twenty years ago, on the size of agricultural holdings in England and abroad, he gave his reasons for saying that there were, if you looked about for them, very good examples both of success and of failure to be met with in this country. In his Paper of 1887, he had quoted a certain parish in the Isle of Ely, consisting of 11,000 acres, where the soil was owned by no less than 179 different persons, 65 of whom were farmers or gardeners, 41 were engaged in trade or commerce, and 32 were agricultural labourers holding little bits of land.   There were 243 separate holdings or occupations, 47 of which were under 1 acre, while in 68 cases in this single parish the properties were occupied by their owners.   He hoped that the immediate and most valuable effect of any fresh legislation would be to increase the number of such examples by careful and prolonged experiments, at the public cost if necessary.   He had been for some two years sitting on a Departmental Committee of Inquiry, which naturally had a great many types before it; but the effect of the evidence on their minds, as was reflected in their report, was the relatively heavy cost of equipment, the great difficulty of finding the right type of man, and of deciding on the right type of holding. He thought Mr. Adams was quite right in saying that local conditions were so diverse that holdings must be of various types. It was no use beginning elaborate and costly schemes to purchase or hire large areas of land and so burdening either the rates and taxes until they were surer than they now were of getting the capable men.   He doubted if these men could be found quite as easily as Mr. Winfrey imagined.   They must not generalise too rapidly from exceptional cases.   Nor was it enough to say that small holdings prevailed largely abroad.   A mistake was frequently made when comparing our own statistics on this point with those of foreign countries, by overlooking the initial point or unit at which the statistics of the different countries began.   When they heard it said we had less than half a million agricultural holdings in England as against $5\frac{1}{2}$ millions in Germany, they should remember that in Germany the statistics began at zero, while our returns began at 1 acre.   If we were to add, in the German fashion, all the scraps of garden and allotment holdings, outside the Agricultural Returns in this country and under the acre limit, there would then be a great apparent augmentation of the units of holdings, and something like 90 per cent. of the holdings in England would appear to stand below 50 acres, as against 94 per cent. in Germany.   The Paper before them that evening was not directed to the tenure of petty plots and allotments, but rather to small farms of 20 acres, and a very interesting example of one of these was given in the appendix.   Recurring to that estimate, he asked Mr. Adams if he would give a little more information as to this typical farm?   They well knew that in Ireland it was "the pig that paid the rent"; but, obviously, here, with 60*l.* from pigs alone kept on those 20 acres, the pig was far and away the most important contributor to the income.   There were some other figures which, he confessed, struck him as very remarkable.   From a farm on which Mr. Adams's hypothetical farmer kept 3 cows in milk this lucky farmer sold annually 2,000 gallons, which seemed to him an extraordinary proportion after allowing for what was required for calves, &c. Those cows must be of a most excellent breed and character, and their keep must be correspondingly good.   Really, had this statement not been given on so good an authority as Mr. Adams quoted he would hardly have imagined the result possible.

The figures for the yield of hay and potatoes was also very large; though he quite understood that Mr. Adams put that forward not as what was being done to-day but as what was conceivable; but it seemed to him that, in order to accomplish such superlative results, they would require not only to induce the farmers to keep their pigs on the Irish scale, but also to have a very specially trained breed of farmers, and a reformed and highly-developed breed of cows.

Mr. WILLIS BUND said that he should like to emphasise what Sir Horace Plunkett and Mr. Adams had said, that no one type of farm would be successful in this country. He could point to two instances within his own experience to show that one type alone would be a failure. In the parish of Bromsgrove, years ago, small holdings were tried by Fergus O'Connor, but as they were ordinary agricultural holdings they were a miserable failure, and everybody connected with them lost money, But, almost adjoining this failure, the Worcestershire County Council established some small holdings for growing strawberries, and they had been a very great success. The persons who cultivated them were persons who gave only part of their time to the small holdings, and worked at other trades during the other part of their time. So here the attempt to set up whole-time small holders had been a complete failure, while part-time was a success. The other case that he wished to mention was one on the other side of the county, where, in response to a great appeal for land, the County Council started small holdings. A good many were taken, but they had some left on their hands; and, although they were told there was a tremendous demand for small holdings and petitions were largely signed, it was found very difficult to get the small holdings taken when the land was purchased. A gentleman who resided in that parish let out a good deal of his land in small lots, ranging from 5 to 50 acres; some of those were cultivated for fruit, but most of them in the ordinary course. He was a man of considerable means, and was rather careless about collecting his rents. On his death the executors desired to sell the property, and they came to the County Council to ask them to buy the land to prevent these men being turned out. He was much taken with that idea, and he made some inquiries. But he found that every one of those men was more or less in arrear with his rent, and some as much as five years; so that it was impossible, under the circumstances, to buy the land, and at the present time those persons who had been carrying on those small holdings for some years were all practically bankrupt.

With regard to agricultural education, it was impossible in our elementary schools at present to carry on successfully anything beyond the existing course of education. The managers of county schools were, for the most part, the parson and the farmers. The farmers said they must keep down the rates, and they objected to any special subjects being taught. They said: "All a man wants to learn about agriculture is how to grow potatoes, a few turnips, and onions, and he can do that without education." As long as they had that class of managers, anything like a proper system of agricultural education in elementary schools was impossible.

Mr. HISCOCK said there was one sentence in the Paper which had struck him particularly, namely, that which referred to the proper cultivation of suitable and improved varieties of potatoes for market. This crop might be of great value to the small-holder. The Jersey farmer had just been blessed with a very great crop of potatoes, and, fearful of disease, he was now unloading them so rapidly as to overstock the market and reduce prices. The consequence was, that at the present time, prices were suffering from this over-production. They wanted not only the strong individuality and experience in necessarily small holdings, for which the Jersey farmers were noted, but also co-operation in the matter of distributing produce, which did not appear to exist at present.

Mr. ADAMS, in reply, said the largeness of the subject must be his excuse for the very fragmentary treatment he was able to give to it. His object was to bring forward the great need there was for further investigation. He could only now meet one or two remarks which had been made on the points raised in the Paper. With regard to Lord Eversley's comments on the number of small holdings, he thought there had been some misunderstanding as to what was said in the Paper. He was fully aware that, especially with regard to holdings of between 1 and 5 acres, and still more in the Irish statistics which included holdings under 1 acre, a large number of these holdings were residential houses with pieces of land attached. But, when you went above 5 acres and up to 50 acres, most of the holdings in the English statistics, and certainly most of those in the Irish statistics, were small farm holdings. As regards the case of the congestion in the west, there were, according to the official returns, some 25,000 agricultural migratory labourers living in Ireland, but they included the women and the farmers' sons who migrated. There were only something over 3,000 of the migratory labourers who were returned as landholders, and if this number was deducted from the total of holdings in Ireland exceeding 5 acres in extent, it made but a very slight difference. He respectfully submitted that Lord Eversley's remarks conveyed a wrong impression as to the number of small farm holdings. Most of the existing small holdings were uneconomical under present management, but they were there, and the only way to meet the problem was to make them as economic as possible.

The other point which had been raised was as to the hypothetical holding. While it was hypothetical, still it was put forward as a type or an ideal, something which could be criticised and approximated to. The problem everybody had to face was, that there was such an infinite variety of types that if you started to make budgets of small holdings, you would have a stock which even the compass of the *Journal of the Royal Statistical Society* would not admit. The type set out in the Paper was put forward somewhat as an ideal small holding—a concrete view of what was possible. There were many wonderful things there, no doubt, and the cow seemed to be a cause of stumbling to both Mr. Winfrey and Major Craigie. But, if he remembered rightly, it was something like 750 gallons a year which each of these cows was expected to give, and he knew of records of cows giving 1,000 gallons a year in Ireland. The Danish statistics showed that the record for milk production had steadily gone up, and the yield assumed in the Paper was by no means impossible, provided you had the right man, who knew how to select his cows, and how to feed them rationally.

With regard to the yield of hay or potatoes, he could show returns of from 14 to 20 tons of potatoes to the acre instead of 10 tons. Those were extreme cases, but there was no reason why, with good land, careful choosing of seed, proper cultivation and spraying, the small holder should not get 10 tons to the acre. In the same way with regard to hay, the figures seemed to be high, but the hay crop in Ireland was most remarkable. He had seen "weighed" returns as high as 3 tons and over to the acre. The hay in the case they were considering was not old meadow hay, it was "rotation" hay. He must repeat that it was an ideal, but a realisable ideal, which was being put forward.

The following were elected Fellows of the Society :—

Clements, Major Harry Charles. | Rutter, Frank Roy.
Stanley of Alderley, The Lord.

MISCELLANEA.

CONTENTS :

PAGE

I.—Congress of the International
Statistical Institute 449
II.—Note on the Mortality from
Tuberculosis, 1851-1905.
By R. DUDFIELD, M A.,
M.B. 454

PAGE

III.—Meeting of the British
Association. Discussion
on Modern Methods of
treating Observations 471
IV.—Agricultural Returns of
Great Britain, 1907 477

I.—*Congress of the International Statistical Institute.*

THE eleventh of these gatherings was held at Copenhagen between the 26th and the 31st of August, upon the invitation of the Government of Denmark. Considering all we have gone through this year, it is worth recording, at the outset, that the weather generously seconded the efforts of the Organisation Committee in making the Congress eminently successful. As in the case of the Congress of London, the Heir to the Throne did the Institute the honour of accepting the post of Honorary President for the occasion, and in this capacity delivered the address of welcome, and honoured the members by presiding at the concluding banquet. H.M. the King of Denmark also showed his interest in the proceedings by attending throughout one of the earlier sittings. The only interruption to the diurnal business of the Congress was that of a full day's excursion to Elsinore and other places north of the capital, and even on that occasion, members were called upon to attend a short sitting of their Sections before starting upon their frolics.

The attendance reached 102 in all. Of those present, 69 were members of the Institute, and 33, visitors specially invited for the occasion. No less than 38 were officially delegated by their respective Governments, 10 from France, 11 from Austria-Hungary, and 2, Major Craigie and Mr. Rew, from this country. It was, unfortunately, again the case that the United Kingdom was distinguished by the small proportion present of the members it contributes to the roll of the Institute. In addition to the two mentioned above, only Messrs. Hendriks, Baines, and Dudfield attended. Sir E. Brabrook, however, was amongst those specially invited, and Mr. Balleine, also in the capacity of visitor, was enlisted to perform in Copenhagen the same secretarial duties he so efficiently carried out for this Society, when it received the Institute in London. Much regret was expressed on all sides at the absence of so well-known and popular members as Vice-

President Levasseur and ex-Secretary Bodio, whose advanced age makes their attendance at long distances from home uncertain. Possibly the selection, on the invitation of the French Government, of La Ville Lumière for the next Congress, may be an inducement to the Elders of Statistical science to rally round the standard they helped to erect. In regard to the officers of the Institute, the President, Vice-Presidents, and Treasurer, were re-elected. Major Craigie, who has undertaken the work of Secretary for the last two years, as a temporary measure, did not seek re-election, to the regret of his colleagues, so the onerous duties of that post were imposed at the last sitting of the Congress upon the younger shoulders of Dr. Verrijn Stuart, of the Hague. There were 17 nationalities represented at the meeting. The largest contingent was from France, 18. Germans numbered 13, and Danes, including the visitors, the same. Russians and Austrians also reached double figures. There was no election of Fellows, so that this, one of the most fruitful sources of international differentiation, being absent, the discussions, where not concentrated upon the proposals of an individual, were unusually cosmopolitan in their general lines, and business-like and well sustained accordingly. The Congress, in fact, was one of ventilation, so to speak, rather than of construction or initiative. The work done during the last two years, in pursuance of resolutions passed at previous meetings, was set forth by the chairmen of the respective sub-committees, and, so far as time allowed, was examined and discussed in the main sections of Demography and Economics. In the end, further inquiry, sometimes on slightly different lines, were usually recommended. Herein is found one of the most useful functions of the Institute, since it often appears advisable to modify the scope of special statistical inquiries after they have proceeded a certain distance, and experience has shown that in some directions further investigation is not likely to turn out fruitful, whilst in others the field may be advantageously extended. For instance, the compilation of the returns of different countries into one table for international comparison sometimes gets no further than the presentation of the figures for each unit separately, the investigator then finding that combination is impracticable by reason of the intrinsic variations in the scope and basis of the originals, regarding which, therefore, he appends full explanatory notes and comment. Such is the case with an exposition of municipal finance, or the subdivisions of landed property, both of which came under review. Another is the enumeration of population in countries where no census has yet been taken. Considerable progress has been made in regard to this by various Governments since the subject was first brought before the Institute by Director Kiær, as, for instance, in British tracts in Africa. It has been decided, however, that the matter has now gone as far as the Institute can promote it, so further measures have been left to the joint consideration of geographers, who have taken the question on to their programme for their International Congress. Then, again, it was proposed by some that statistics should be obtained of the number, cost, and circulation of newspapers in different countries; but it was found that the full information suggested might, perhaps, be procurable in Germany and Austria, but that elsewhere it would be either refused or deliberately falsified. The resolutions of the Section, therefore, were shelved by the full sitting, or, in other words, "ordered to be read this time two years." On the other hand, several interesting inquiries and suggestions were materially advanced. Valuable statistics upon the movement of population in European countries have been recently published by M. L. March in a French official year-book, along with an excellent introduction on the whole subject; and though he is unable to continue the series annually, he was warmly thanked by the Congress for his promise to issue a quinquennial volume of the same nature. Such a publication cannot fail to be of the greatest convenience to inquirers, as it includes in a single set of tables matter which has otherwise to be sought over numbers of reports in different forms and in different languages. M. March deals only with the natural increase or decrease, and has found it beyond the scope of his scheme to incorporate such figures as are available on the subject of migration, but he includes, with the absolute figures of marriages, births, and deaths, the most recent tables of mortality, and, where rates are given, explains as far as possible the method and basis on which they are calculated. Progress has been made, too, since 1905 in the elaboration of the system of obtaining international statistics of railway transport, entrusted by the Institute to the capable hands of General de Wendrich. His general proposals have been adopted by the International Congress of Tramways and Local Railways, held last year at Milan, and, in his own country, the "way-bill" devised by him is now in force for the large through traffic in butter on the Siberian lines, forming the basis of a very comprehensive tabulation of cost, time, distance, direction, and truck-accommodation involved in the trade in question. A concrete form was given to the proposal made by Professor Mandello at the London meeting, for the preparation of some authoritative glossary of general statistical terms, by the nomination of a committee to consider the method upon which such a publication should be based. On this committee Messrs. Rew and Yule are the British representatives, and Mr. Mandello has been appointed secretary. A committee was also formed, on the proposal of M. March, to decide whether it was practicable to compile a comprehensive glossary of technical terms and names of processes required for a census of industries, to be prepared in English, French and German, so that the results of the respective inquiries might be accurately compared. The preparation of such a work is necessarily a heavy task, but the specimens circulated by M. March in support of his proposal show how useful it would be for the purpose indicated. Messrs. Llewelyn Smith and Wilson Fox were nominated to represent this country on the committee, whilst Dr. Willcox, of the United States Census Department, was proposed for the almost equally onerous task across the Atlantic. In connection, too, with the enumeration of professions and industries, a short paper was contributed by Dr. van der Borght, descriptive of the methods of the census shortly to be taken in Germany. The inquiry is here to include both breadwinners and dependents in every branch of livelihood, professional, agricultural and mechanical. It includes, also, information in reference to workmen's insurance, as well as to the movement of labour from one part of the Empire to another, so far as details of birthplace form an indication of this last. In other respects, the operations are on much the same lines as the enumeration of 1895. The inquiry into the statistics of Tuberculosis cannot be said to have got far beyond the stage in which they were discussed in London two years ago. Dr. Bertillon contributed a paper showing the need of greater discrimination in the terminology used in the returns of deaths from the causes included under one main head, and Professor Lexis produced some statistics based upon returns from hospitals in various parts of Germany, the bearings of which were the subject of considerable controversy. In the end, the scheme of inquiry proposed by Dr. Bertillon was approved. It expressly distinguishes between the two separate objects in view, to ascertain, first, the prevalence of the disease, and secondly, the nature and duration of the latter, and its amenability to hospital treatment. For the former, an enumeration by age, sex, occupation and locality is necessary; whilst the returns of institutions should be organised with special reference to the latter points. The name of Dr. Dudfield was added to the sub-committee dealing with the whole subject. The detailed reports upon the values of shares and other negotiable securities, of which M. Neymarck is in charge, are kept up to date, and a brief review of the facts of the last two years was presented by the author. The fecundity of marriage and the fertility of wives is another hardy biennial which blooms at every Congress, but has lost one of its staunchest advocates in Dr. J. Körösi. On the present occasion, the Congress approved of various proposed additions to registers of death and marriage and to Census schedules, recommended by Director Kiær and others, in order to get information, in the case of wives past the child-bearing age, of the age at marriage and the total number of children born, surviving or deceased. A special inquiry into similar facts within areas taken as representative was recommended, mainly with reference to the fertility of different social grades. After adopting the above suggestions, the Congress accepted the suggestion of Dr. Raseri that wherever population-registers are sufficiently well organised, they should be made use of in the extension of this inquiry, rather than that the census and registration of vital statistics should be overburdened with additional questions. An interesting paper was presented by M. March on statistics of families in France, compared with others previously published for Norway, New South Wales and certain large cities of Europe. The inquiry now being instituted under his supervision into the family-composition of the vast army of State and Municipal functionaries serving the Republic, should be still more valuable; but there is much need for data procured from a wider field than those as yet explored, and M. March considers, apparently with reason, that more can be got from the birth, death and marriage registers than from the census. He judiciously deprecated any attempt to prescribe fixed forms for universal adoption, but would indicate the line of inquiry and the sort of returns essential to its prosecution, leaving each country to devise its own means of securing the results. The *Bibliography of the Prices of Cereals*, which it was suggested in London should be prepared by this Society, was duly compiled, with considerable trouble and research, by Mr. Mackenzie, the Librarian, and was formally presented by the Hon. Foreign Secretary, with the request that he might be furnished within the next few months with the titles of any works published abroad which may have been omitted. It is almost impossible, without such supplementary aid, to get together a complete bibliography on so wide a subject, and already some of the lacunæ have been supplied. The inquiry into the prices of cereals, in connection with which this publication was prepared, was placed in the hands of Professor Béla Földes, with the object of organising a system of tabulating these prices on uniform lines. Certain general features were proposed by the Section, and adopted by the Congress, but the question is so intricate that no doubt it will be long before the desired end is attained. Messrs. Rew and Baines are the British members nominated in the first instance, but the experience and leisure of Major Craigie form an anchorage not to be passed over.

Amongst the subjects brought to the notice of the Institute for the first time, was an inquiry into bounties and subsidies in aid of trade, etc., by M. Raffalovich. There was some discussion as to whether indirect aid should not be included, but the proposer stuck to his guns, and the inquiry was finally limited to the direct. M. Raffalovich, like our Guy medallist, M. Yves Guyot, is a member of the Cobden Club, and no doubt, with "sugars" on his mind, wishes, like his distinguished colleague, that the Club had given to their efforts for the suppression of bounties on the Continent "un appui moins platonique!" The produce of salt and fresh-water fishing in various countries, brought forward by M. Hoek, was considered to need investigation, and the question as to how the matter could be best treated statistically was made over to a sub-committee, under Mr. Rew as chairman. The paper by M. Yves Guyot, on the alleged tendency towards concentration in modern industrial enterprise, dealt with the statistics furnished by the industrial census in the United States, France and Belgium. According to his review, so far from indicating concentration, the figures show that the number of separate establishments was keeping pace with the increased amount of business. He proposed that the term concentration should be used only for a decrease in the number of establishments concomitant with the increase of the aggregate of the enterprise, a suggestion which was referred to the new committee on statistical terms. The only paper dealing with statistics in general was that of M. de Foville, who, in his own lucid and diverting manner, showed up the exaggerated reverence demanded by Quetelet and some of his successors for the "mean," as exemplified by "homo Medius," a being as alien to practical experience as the "homo economicus," his predecessor, affiliated by the author of the paper on the British economists, but now fossilised in the classics of that science. M. de Foville, after dwelling on the difference between the mean and the normal man, showed that the former notion may be a good servant, but a bad ideal, considering that a person in whom beauty and ugliness, vice and virtue, wisdom and the reverse, were all so combined as to neutralise each other, would turn out to be only "un piètre sire," to whom those inferior to his mediocrity might perhaps look up, to their advantage no doubt, but whose pedestal should not be made high enough to raise him above the superior qualifications of others, on whom his position was equally dependent. The paper of Professor Westergäard, on a Horoscope of the Twentieth Century, dealt with the decline in the birth-rates and in mortality, the tendencies of which, assuming them to continue in their present direction, indicated to him the approach of a stationary stage amongst the most advanced civilisations. The paper, however, was not printed during the sittings of the Congress, and, like that of Professor Béla Földes, on the statistics of "Condamnability," must await comment until the appearance of the volumes of Proceedings.

Taken as a whole, the Congress of Copenhagen was distinguished for the hospitality and friendliness of its hosts, the efficiency of the arrangements made by them for the conduct of business and printing the current documents essential thereto, and for the range and quality of the sectional discussions.   J.A.B.

II.—*Note on the Mortality from Tuberculosis from* 1851-1905.
By REGINALD DUDFIELD, M.A., M.B., F.S.S.

I.—Although certain data relating to the causes of death are to be found in the Reports from 1838 onwards, the tabulation of deaths according to the sex and age of the deceased and cause of death was not commenced until 1847. From 1843 to 1846 inclusive, the causes of death in the whole country were not taken out. It has, therefore, been thought desirable to take the year 1851 as the commencement of the appended series of statistics.

II.—The designations given to the four divisions of tuberculosis in this note are those first used by the Registrar-General. The titles used in later Reports are indicated below :—

Phthisis.—Since 1901 the single entry has been divided into " Pulmonary Tuberculosis " and " *Phthisis.*"[1]

Tabes Mesenterica.—Since 1901 described as " Tuberculous Peritonitis, *Tabes Mesenterica.*"

---

[1] Italics are used in the Reports to indicate terms which are no longer recognised by the official nomenclature. The use of such designations is discouraged.

Hydrocephalus.—In 1881 altered to "Tubercular Meningitis (Acute Hydrocephalus)," and in 1901 to "Tuberculous Meningitis."

Scrofula.—Altered in 1891 to "Other Forms of Tuberculosis, Scrofula," and in 1901 divided under four entries, viz., "Lupus," "Tubercle of other Organs," "General Tuberculosis," and "Scrofula."

In the text, "tuberculosis" is used to cover all the above forms, and "other forms" all forms excluding phthisis.

III.—The statistics are based on the particulars entered in the Registrar-General's Reports under the respective heads, irrespective of corrections, which are probably necessary for changes in diagnosis and classification and for transferences of deaths from the tubercular to other diseases. In the first decennium the deaths from certain forms of the disease at ages 15— and 20— have been obtained by splitting up the numbers given in the annual reports for the single age-groups, 15—25. The rates based on the calculated numbers are indicated in the tables by italic figures.

A. Mortality at All Ages : Persons.

1. *England and Wales.*—In 1851 the deaths from tuberculosis numbered 64,075, equal to 16·2 per cent. of all deaths, comprising 49,166 from phthisis and 14,909 from other forms; the mortality rates[2] being, tuberculosis, 3·56; phthisis, 2·73; other forms, 0·83.

In 1905 the deaths from tuberculosis numbered 55,837, equal to 10·7 per cent. of all deaths, comprising 38,950 from phthisis and 16,887 from other forms; the mortality rates being, tuberculosis, 1·63; phthisis, 1·14; other forms, 0·49.

2. *London.*—In 1851 the deaths from tuberculosis numbered 9,770, equal to 17·6 per cent. of all deaths, comprising 7,047 from phthisis and 2,723 from other forms; the mortality rates being, tuberculosis, 4·13; phthisis, 2·97; other forms, 1·16.

In 1905 the deaths from tuberculosis numbered 9,036, equal to 12·7 per cent. of all deaths, comprising 6,536 from phthisis and 2,500 from other forms : the mortality rates being, tuberculosis, 1·93; phthisis, 1·39; other forms, 0·53.

The foregoing figures, although apparently satisfactory, showing reductions (per cent. of mortalities in 1851) as below :—

	Tuberculosis.	Phthisis.	Other Forms.
England and Wales	54	58	41
London	53	53	54

cannot be received without reservation. Apart from all questions as to changes in diagnosis, &c., there remain the errors arising from a comparison of single years and from changes in the sex-age composition of the populations.

---

[2] All rates are calculated per 1,000 individuals of each age-group.

3. In Table 1 the mean rates for the quinquennia and decennia which have elapsed since 1851 are set out, together with (in the lower half of the table) the relative mortalities, that of the first period being in each case taken as 100.

Examining the decennial rates, as the more trustworthy, it will be found—

(*a*) That there has been an apparently permanent increase in the mortality from scrofula ; [3]

(*b*) That where decreases have been recorded, such decreases have not only not been in every case uniform, but have been in some cases interrupted by temporary increases ; and

(*c*) That the rates of decreases are themselves decreasing quantities.

To this last conclusion the rates from hydrocephalus in the Metropolis form an exception. The decreasing rate of fall of mortality is made clear for the varieties of tuberculosis other than scrofula by the appended statement, which shows the changes that have taken place during each period, stated as percentages of the rate for the first decennium (1851-60) :—

Rate of Change in Successive Decennia.

	England and Wales.				London.			
	Phthisis.	Tabes.	Hydro-cephalus.	Scrofula.	Phthisis.	Tabes.	Hydro-cephalus.	Scrofula.
1851-60 ....⎫ '61-70 ....⎬	− 8	− 13	+ 13	− 4	− 1	− 14	+ 5	− 5
1861-70 ....⎫ '71-80 ....⎬	− 27	− 7	+ 9	− 10	− 11	− 15	+ 11	+ 6
1871-80 ....⎫ '81-90 ....⎬	− 15	− 17	− 16	+ 29	− 16	− 26	− 14	+ 40
1881-90 ....⎫ '91-1900 ⎬	− 12	− 9	− 26	+ 11	− 9	− 9	− 29	+ 6
1891-1900 ⎫ 1901-05 ....⎬	− 7	− 8	− 16	− 10	− 9	− 6	− 31	− 16

It will be of interest to note that the deaths from tuberculosis in England and Wales during 1851-60 constituted 15·71 per cent. of all deaths, the percentage falling in the four succeeding decennia to 14·53, 13·53, 12·68, and 9·23. In London the percentages have been 16·74, 15·87, 15·59, 14·63, and 12·98.

B. Mortality at Different Ages : Two Sexes.

4. In Tables 2 and 2A, an attempt has been made to show the changes in the mortality from the four divisions of the disease for each age-group of the two sexes, while in Tables 3 and 3A the relative mortalities are set out, the rates for 1851-60 being taken, for each sex-age-group as 100.

[3] The decrease noted in 1901-05 must be accepted under reservation.

Phthisis.

England and Wales.—The first point to note is that, whereas in the two first decennia the mortality (at all ages) for females was greater than that for males, the position has been reversed since 1871. The Table (Table 2) shows clearly how the mortality falls on the adults, both male and female, and that the reduction in the mortality already noted has taken place among females rather than males and at the younger ages of life. This will be better seen from Table 3. The check in the rate of decrease in recent times is also manifest.

London.—The mortality (all ages) for males has always exceeded that for females, the difference being greater than in the case of the whole country. At certain ages the contrast between the sexes is very marked, notably at ages exceeding 25 years. The decrease which has taken place in the mortality among females is greater than that among males, and on the whole the differences in the mortalities among the two sexes are greater now than they were. (Is it permissible to suggest that the better results among the females are due to better housing, and to the fact that women, as a whole, spend more of their time in their homes?) With but one or two exceptions, the reductions in the mortalities at the different ages have been less in the Metropolis than in the country as a whole.

Tabes Mesenterica.

England and Wales.—The mortality has throughout been heavier among males than females, but at certain ages near the middle of life the position is reversed. The whole of the reduction in the mortality at all ages, already noted, has taken place at ages under 15 years; above that age the mortality has increased, in some cases notably so.

London.—The incidence of mortality has been much the same as in the whole country, but the actual rate in most cases lower. While the reduction in the mortality at the younger ages has been greater (Table 3A), that at the higher ages has been less, the contrast at certain of the old-age groups being very great.

Hydrocephalus.

England and Wales.—At all ages the mortality among males has always been higher than that among females. Although there has been a very satisfactory reduction in the all-ages group, there has been a very considerable increase in the mortality at the middle ages of life—from 15 to 65 years. It is noteworthy that at those ages the mortality among females is greatly in excess of that among males.

London.—The great differences in the mortalities (all ages) among males and females recorded in the earlier periods has disappeared, the two being now nearly equal, and not much in excess of the rates for the whole country. Further, the reduction in the mortality (Table 3A) has been greater in the Metropolis than in the whole country. The great diminution in the mortality at all ages has taken place in spite of the very great—they may in some cases be called enormous—increases at certain ages.

Scrofula.

England and Wales.—In this case an increase in the mortality at all ages, both sexes, has been recorded, such increase following diminutions in the second and third decennia. Many of the age-groups show diminutions, but great increases have taken place at the youngest ages (0—5 years). The increase has been generally greater among females than males.

London.—Increased mortality (all ages) is again recorded, but, with one exception (males, second decennium), there has been no diminution in the mortality. The greatest increase in any age-group is that for the group 0—5 years, the increase being, however, lower than that for the whole country. The mortality among young adult males has been higher than that for females at corresponding ages, therein differing from the country as a whole.

The foregoing paragraphs may be summed up by saying that where decreases in the mortality (all ages) have been recorded, the greater part thereof has taken place at ages under 15 years, and that, with the exception of phthisis, there has been in every case increased mortality from all forms of tuberculosis at the working and most useful ages of life (15—65 years). Even as regards phthisis, the reductions in the mortality at those ages cannot be considered as altogether satisfactory.

It has also to be noted that the check in the rate of decrease already referred to is to be found at nearly every age.

TABLE 1.—*Mortality at All Ages.*
MEAN MORTALITY RATES PER 1,000 PERSONS.

Period.	England and Wales.				London.			
	Phthisis.	Tabes Mes-enterica.	Hydro-cephalus.	Scrofula.	Phthisis.	Tabes Mes-enterica.	Hydro-cephalus.	Scrofula.
1838-40*	3·836	0·053	0·503	0·077	4·007	0·137	1·006	0·060
Quinquennia—								
1841-45†	3·708	0·073	0·499	0·078	3·619	0·205	0·897	0·070
'46-50‡	2·893	0·249	0·434	0·143	2·966	0·388	0·694	0·145
'51-55	2·806	0·267	0·426	0·146	2·958	0·386	0·645	0·154
'56-60	2·575	0·255	0·373	0·149	2·802	0·312	0·551	0·154
'61-65	2·528	0·285	0·364	0·157	2·818	0·348	0·555	0·176
'66-70	2·449	0·307	0·333	0·129	2·885	0·376	0·471	0·120
'71-75	2·219	0·307	0·314	0·118	2·582	0·380	0·408	0·138
'76-80	2·042	0·331	0·324	0·137	2·466	0·422	0·436	0·174
'81-85	1·831	0·289	0·264	0·157	2·222	0·368	0·354	0·209
'86-90	1·636	0·266	0·241	0·181	1·961	0·339	0·298	0·229
'91-95	1·463	0·238	0·226	0·194	1·842	0·288	0·281	0·233
'96-1900 ...	1·323	0·196	0·207	0·179	1·758	0·217	0·270	0·217
1901-05	1·215	0·166	0·184	0·171	1·548	0·146	0·236	0·202
Decennia—								
1841-50§	3·165	0·191	0·456	0·121	3·292	0 296	0·795	0·107
'51-60	2·667	0·260	0 397	0·147	2·864	0·345	0·593	0·154
'61-70	2·472	0·295	0·346	0 142	2·842	0·362	0·509	0·146
'71-80	2·117	0·318	0·317	0·127	2·510	0·401	0·421	0·156
'81-90	1·725	0·276	0·251	0 169	2·078	0·351	0·324	0·218
'91-1900 ...	1·385	0·209	0·215	0·186	1·795	0·251	0·275	0·227

RELATIVE MORTALITIES.

Period.	England and Wales.				London.			
Quinquennia—								
1851-55	100	100	100	100	100	100	100	100
'56-60	92	95	87	102	95	81	85	100
'61-65	90	107	85	107	95	90	86	114
'66-70	87	115	78	88	97	97	73	78
'71-75	79	115	74	81	87	98	63	90
'76-80	73	124	76	94	83	109	67	113
'81-85	65	103	62	107	75	95	55	136
'86-90	58	100	56	124	66	88	46	149
'91-95	52	89	53	133	62	75	43	151
'96-1900	47	73	48	122	59	56	42	141
1901-05	43	62	43	117	52	38	36	131
Decennia—								
1851-60	100	100	100	100	100	100	100	100
'61-70	92	113	87	96	99	105	86	95
'71-80	79	122	80	86	88	116	71	101
'81-90	64	106	63	115	72	102	55	141
'91-1900 ...	52	80	54	126	63	73	46	147
1901-05 (5 years).... }	45	64	46	116	54	42	40	131

* For three years (1838-40), England and Wales. For 1840 only, London.
† For 1841 and 1842, England and Wales. For whole period, London.
‡ For 1841-50, England and Wales. For whole period, London.
§ For five years only, England and Wales. For whole period, London.

TABLE 2.—ENGLAND AND WALES. PHTHISIS. *Mean Rates per Mille.*

Ages	0—	5—	10—	15—	20—	25—	35—	45—	55—	65—	75—	All Ages.
Males.												
1851-60	1·329	0·525	0·763	2·397	4·055	4·034	4·005	3·830	3·333	2·389	0·927	2·580
'61-70	0·990	0·431	0·605	2·188	3·884	4·092	4·165	3·860	3·298	2·023	0·660	2·467
'71-80	0·783	0·340	0·481	1·676	3·093	3·698	4·118	3·861	3·195	1·924	0·603	2·209
'81-90	0·553	0·253	0·342	1·287	2·333	3·024	3·562	3·488	2·916	1·815	0·688	1·846
'91-1900	0·441	0·173	0·233	0·992	1·875	2·353	3·074	3·125	2·602	1·581	0·554	1·572
1901-05	0·363	0·149	0·173	0·765	1·573	2·101	2·691	3·042	2·506	1·581	0·492	1·193
Females.												
1851-60	1·281	0·619	1·292	3·515	4·288	4·575	4·175	3·120	2·883	1·634	0·716	2·774
'61-70	0·947	0·476	1·045	3·110	3·966	4·378	3·900	2·850	2·065	1·239	0·446	2·482
'71-80	0·750	0·375	0·847	2·397	3·140	3·544	3·399	2·463	1·777	1·093	0·407	2·027
'81-90	0·518	0·327	0·699	1·800	2·315	2·787	2·730	2·053	1·512	0·974	0·396	1·608
'91-1900	0·385	0·238	0·501	1·286	1·581	1·909	2·106	1·633	1·232	0·804	0·349	1·209
1901-05	0·314	0·196	0·400	0·975	1·223	1·524	1·727	1·439	1·104	0·777	0·366	1·009

TABLE 2 (*Contd.*).—ENGLAND AND WALES. TABES MESENTERICA. *Mean Rates per Mille.*

Ages.	0—	5—	10—	15—	20—	25—	35—	45—	55—	65—	75—	All Ages.
Males.												
1851–60	1·752	0·168	0·086	0·046	0·016	0·015	0·011	0·015	0·020	0·023	0·008	0·282
'61–70	1·993	0·155	0·080	0·049	0·034	0·018	0·016	0·020	0·025	0·018	0·005	0·320
'71–80	2·198	0·141	0·076	0·051	0·031	0·018	0·018	0·018	0·021	0·021	0·008	0·347
'81–90	2·008	0·120	0·066	0·047	0·033	0·023	0·020	0·019	0·024	0·021	0·010	0·304
'91–1900	1·611	0·102	0·062	0·049	0·037	0·029	0·026	0·029	0·027	0·022	0·011	0·235
1901–05	1·177	0·102	0·065	0·047	0·039	0·033	0·034	0·035	0·039	0·025	0·010	0·181
Females.												
1851–60	1·498	0·146	0·096	0·056	0·034	0·026	0·018	0·022	0·019	0·017	0·008	0·239
'61–70	1·718	0·124	0·082	0·070	0·042	0·034	0·025	0·025	0·028	0·021	0·006	0·271
'71–80	1·857	0·117	0·080	0·068	0·038	0·033	0·025	0·024	0·025	0·026	0·009	0·290
'81–90	1·613	0·122	0·084	0·064	0·044	0·035	0·029	0·025	0·024	0·025	0·012	0·249
'91–1900	1·303	0·101	0·074	0·065	0·052	0·044	0·040	0·030	0·026	0·020	0·007	0·197
1901–05	0·936	0·107	0·074	0·065	0·048	0·053	0·043	0·038	0·028	0·019	0·011	0·153

TABLE 2 (*Contd.*).—ENGLAND AND WALES. HYDROCEPHALUS. *Mean Rates per Mille.*

Ages.	0—	5—	10—	15—	20—	25—	35—	45—	55—	65—	75—	All Ages.
Males.												
1851-60	2·914	0·396	0·105	0·031	0·012	0·007	0·007	0·007	0·008	0·008	0·010	0·464
'61-70	2·578	0·326	0·093	0·020	0·008	0·005	0·003	0·002	0·002	0·003	0·001	0·412
'71-80	2·241	0·331	0·119	0·048	0·025	0·017	0·012	0·006	0·004	0·002	0·001	0·377
'81-90	1·690	0·319	0·114	0·055	0·033	0·021	0·012	0·010	0·004	0·002	0·002	0·289
'91-1900	1·479	0·283	0·110	0·059	0·036	0·025	0·018	0·010	0·007	0·003	0·001	0·241
1901-05	1·175	0·275	0·114	0·060	0·038	0·028	0·022	0·016	0·009	0·006	0·001	0·200
Females.												
1851-60	2·161	0·331	0·098	0·030	0·008	0·006	0·004	0·005	0·005	0·007	0·007	0·334
'61-70	1·847	0·256	0·085	0·022	0·008	0·004	0·003	0·002	0·002	0·002	0·001	0·285
'71-80	1·558	0·272	0·116	0·049	0·023	0·015	0·010	0·005	0·004	0·002	0·001	0·261
'81-90	1·227	0·295	0·127	0·061	0·030	0·019	0·012	0·006	0·003	0·002	—	0·215
'91-1900	1·160	0·269	0·120	0·062	0·037	0·024	0·014	0·009	0·005	0·003	0·000	0·191
1901-05	1·024	0·261	0·122	0·064	0·037	0·023	0·019	0·012	0·007	0·002	0·002	0·170

TABLE 2 (*Contd.*).—ENGLAND AND WALES.   SCROFULA.   *Mean Rates per Mille.*

Ages	0—	5—	10—	15—	20—	25—	35—	45—	55—	65—	75—	All Ages.
Males.												
1851-60	0·314	0·144	0·164	0·192	0·174	0·145	0·104	0·110	0·123	0·162	0·111	0·168
'61-70	0·436	0·123	0·138	0·142	0·134	0·109	0·081	0·087	0·115	0·138	0·086	0·161
'71-80	0·558	0·095	0·085	0·094	0·084	0·065	0·050	0·058	0·079	0·090	0·044	0·143
'81-90	0·759	0·124	0·104	0·114	0·108	0·082	0·076	0·078	0·079	0·067	0·030	0·182
'91-1900	0·811	0·146	0·115	0·130	0·140	0·117	0·112	0·111	0·115	0·096	0·060	0·205
1901-05	0·662	0·127	0·160	0·119	0·135	0·128	0·129	0·128	0·144	0·118	0·067	0·189
Females.												
1851-60	0·275	0·107	0·118	0·138	0·097	0·094	0·088	0·087	0·117	0·129	0·113	0·127
'61-70	0·405	0·090	0·087	0·098	0·082	0·069	0·070	0·078	0·090	0·096	0·081	0·125
'71-80	0·485	0·069	0·060	0·064	0·048	0·044	0·044	0·051	0·066	0·087	0·050	0·112
'81-90	0·633	0·128	0·116	0·118	0·093	0·076	0·065	0·052	0·055	0·051	0·041	0·156
'91-1900	0·665	0·132	0·122	0·136	0·106	0·094	0·088	0·071	0·074	0·076	0·067	0·167
1901-05	0·566	0·125	0·107	0·123	0·101	0·101	0·096	0·083	0·096	0·093	0·092	0·155

TABLE 2A.—LONDON. PHTHISIS.   *Mean Rates per Mille.*

Ages	0—	5—	10—	15—	20—	25—	35—	45—	55—	65—	75—	All Ages.
Males.												
1851-60	1·489	0·593	0·692	2·724	3·586	4·529	5·953	6·096	5·116	3·565	1·952	3·290
'61-70	1·491	0·570	0·491	1·983	3·812	4·792	6·183	6·379	5·314	3·200	1·493	3·350
'71-80	1·028	0·400	0·444	1·569	3·008	4·404	6·166	6·114	4·958	2·734	0·891	3·002
'81-90	0·723	0·251	0·290	1·170	2·261	3·801	5·298	5·474	4·637	2·706	1·187	2·547
'91-1900	0·623	0·187	0·200	0·961	1·967	3·07	4·790	5·116	4·333	2·759	1·100	2·233
1901-05	0·531	0·157	0·167	0·806	1·624	2·157	3·955	4·892	4·101	2·647	1·017	2·037
Females.												
1851-60	1·458	0·686	0·864	2·009	2·888	3·682	4·121	3·295	2·411	1·556	0·917	2·492
'61-70	1·400	0·601	0·803	1·962	2·668	3·698	4·097	3·203	2·299	1·354	0·669	2·307
'71-80	1·094	0·434	0·672	1·622	2·235	3·241	3·862	3·014	2·069	1·177	0·433	2·076
'81-90	0·670	0·339	0·534	1·200	1·619	2·595	3·240	2·582	1·819	1·060	0·528	1·659
'91-1900	0·553	0·236	0·416	0·961	1·167	1·841	2·731	2·281	1·586	1·041	0·549	1·350
1901-05	0·467	0·222	0·316	0·767	668·0	1·388	2·131	1·257	1·450	1·059	0·672	1·112

TABLE 2A (*Contd.*).--LONDON. TABES MESENTERICA. *Mean Rates per Mille.*

Ages	0—	5—	10—	15—	20—	25—	35—	45—	55—	65—	75—	All Ages.
Males.												
1851-60	2·614	0·222	0·087	0·027	0·013	0·007	0·009	0·008	0·013	0·032	—	0·396
'61-70	2·753	0·179	0·061	0·033	0·023	0·014	0·009	0·012	0·017	0·006	0·010	0·418
'71-80	3·119	0·155	0·065	0·032	0·014	0·011	0·009	0·011	0·013	0·015	0·017	0·466
'81-90	2·904	0·122	0·054	0·029	0·018	0·014	0·015	0·014	0·010	0·004	0·007	0·412
'91-1900	2·112	0·097	0·050	0·034	0·023	0·022	0·020	0·028	0·023	0·021	0·012	0·286
1901-05	1·157	0·089	0·049	0·035	0·030	0·027	0·029	0·027	0·046	0·022	0·011	0·168
Females.												
1851-60	2·254	0·163	0·075	0·035	0·011	0·010	0·009	0·013	0·013	0·012	0·025	0·302
'61-70	2·304	0·142	0·064	0·030	0·016	0·014	0·014	0·012	0·009	0·022	0·011	0·312
'71-80	2·571	0·127	0·057	0·029	0·012	0·011	0·009	0·013	0·016	0·012	—	0·343
'81-90	2·265	0·106	0·059	0·032	0·022	0·020	0·015	0·016	0·009	0·024	0·007	0·298
'91-1900	1·725	0·098	0·062	0·036	0·026	0·028	0·029	0·021	0·019	0·015	0·006	0·220
1901-05	0·868	0·107	0·053	0·047	0·028	0·025	0·027	0·032	0·021	0·012	0·011	0·125

TABLE 2A (*Contd.*).—LONDON. HYDROCEPHALUS. *Mean Rates per Mille.*

Ages	0—	5—	10—	15—	20—	25—	35—	45—	55—	65—	75—	All Ages.
Males.												
1851–60	4·831	0·465	0·069	0·013	0·021	0·010	0·004	0·015	0·007	0·003	0·044	0·722
'61–70	4·009	0·398	0·080	0·021	0·013	0·013	0·004	0·003	0·003	0·006	0·010	0·627
'71–80	3·225	0·390	0·103	0·044	0·018	0·016	0·017	0·008	0·006	—	—	0·513
'81–90	2·421	0·368	0·088	0·042	0·024	0·020	0·015	0·013	0·007	0·004	0·007	0·382
'91–1900	2·112	0·338	0·107	0·050	0·040	0·024	0·021	0·009	0·005	0·006	0·006	0·318
1901–05	1·695	0·328	0·103	0·059	0·039	0·027	0·024	0·016	0·002	0·018	—	0·231
Females.												
1851–60	3·644	0·354	0·053	0·019	0·009	0·005	0·005	0·006	0·004	0·002	0·013	0·480
'61–70	2·692	0·300	0·077	0·022	0·010	0·004	0·003	0·003	0·001	0·002	—	0·406
'71–80	2·353	0·321	0·102	0·030	0·016	0·010	0·008	0·008	0·002	0·005	—	0·339
'81–90	1·882	0·299	0·079	0·040	0·019	0·013	0·011	0·006	0·004	0·006	—	0·271
'91–1900	1·690	0·320	0·099	0·044	0·026	0·018	0·012	0·006	0·004	0·004	—	0·236
1901–05	1·549	0·327	0·118	0·047	0·021	0·015	0·016	0·009	0·005	0·003	—	0·214

TABLE 2A (*Contd.*).—LONDON. SCROFULA. *Mean Rates per Mille.*

Ages	0—	5—	10—	15—	20—	25—	35—	45—	55—	65—	75—	All Ages.
Males.												
1851-60	0·570	0·205	0·165	0·087	0·105	0·090	0·074	0·074	0·110	0·121	0·133	0·184
'61-70	0·645	0·145	0·118	0·106	0·088	0·061	0·062	0·072	0·095	0·106	0·038	0·167
'71-80	0·890	0·136	0·091	0·089	0·039	0·040	0·037	0·046	0·080	0·091	0·042	0·183
'81-90	1·261	0·165	0·106	0·110	0·085	0·085	0·099	0·088	0·076	0·067	0·042	0·254
'91-1900	1·234	0·210	0·145	0·124	0·115	0·114	0·126	0·127	0·114	0·121	0·105	0·266
1901-05	0·996	0·164	0·117	0·112	0·113	0·117	0·115	0·156	0·147	0·136	0·136	0·229
Females.												
1851-60	0·449	0·154	0·132	0·100	0·072	0·060	0·061	0·049	0·077	0·082	0·102	0·127
'61-70	0·578	0·106	0·094	0·069	0·037	0·048	0·052	0·058	0·083	0·075	0·075	0·128
'71-80	0·756	0·093	0·058	0·044	0·028	0·029	0·030	0·014	0·049	0·030	0·031	0·133
'81-90	1·040	0·159	0·104	0·080	0·064	0·050	0·051	0·034	0·046	0·048	0·042	0·186
'91-1900	1·004	0·174	0·123	0·105	0·078	0·075	0·070	0·059	0·064	0·088	0·093	0·191
1901-05	0·866	0·153	0·119	0·105	0·068	0·078	0·090	0·066	0·089	0·144	0·185	0·177

TABLE 3.—ENGLAND AND WALES. *Relative Mortalities.*

Ages	0—	5—	10—	15—	20—	25—	35—	45—	55—	65—	75—	All Ages.
						PHTHISIS.						
Males.												
1851-60 ...	100	100	100	100	100	100	100	100	100	100	100	100
'61-70 ...	74	82	79	91	96	101	104	101	99	85	71	96
'71-80 ...	59	55	63	70	76	92	103	101	96	80	65	86
'81-90	42	48	45	54	57	75	89	91	87	76	74	71
'91-1900...	33	33	30	41	46	58	77	81	78	66	60	61
1901-05 ...	27	28	23	32	39	52	67	79	75	66	53	46
Females.												
1851-60	100	100	100	100	100	100	100	100	100	100	100	100
'61-70........	74	77	81	88	92	96	93	91	72	76	62	89
'71 80....	58	60	65	68	73	77	81	79	62	67	57	73
'81-90	40	53	54	51	54	61	65	66	52	60	55	58
'91-1900 .	30	38	39	36	37	42	50	52	42	49	49	43
1901-05.	24	32	31	28	28	33	41	46	40	47	51	36
						TABES MESENTERICA.						
Males.												
1851-60......	100	100	100	100	100	100	100	100	100	100	100	100
'61-70	114	92	93	106	131	120	145	133	125	78	62	113
'71-80 .	125	84	88	111	119	120	174	120	105	91	100	123
'81-90 . ..	115	71	77	102	127	153	182	127	120	91	125	108
'91-1900 .	92	61	72	106	142	193	236	193	135	96	137	83
1901-05 ..	67	61	75	102	150	220	309	233	195	108	125	68
Females.												
1851-60	100	100	100	100	100	100	100	100	100	100	100	100
'61-70 ..	115	85	85	125	123	131	139	114	147	123	75	113
'71-80 .	124	80	83	121	112	127	139	110	131	153	112	121
'81-90.....	108	83	87	114	129	135	161	114	126	147	150	104
'91-1900.	87	71	77	116	153	169	222	136	137	118	87	82
1901-05...	62	73	77	116	141	204	239	173	147	112	137	64
						HYDROCEPHALUS.						
Males.												
1851-60......	100	100	100	100	100	100	100	100	100	100	100	100
'61-70 ..	88	82	88	64	67	71	43	28	25	37	10	89
'71-80......	77	83	113	155	208	243	171	85	50	25	10	81
'81-90........	57	80	108	177	275	300	171	144	50	25	20	62
'91-1900	51	71	105	190	300	357	257	144	87	37	10	52
1901-05........	40	69	108	193	317	400	314	228	125	75	10	43
Females.												
1851-60	100	100	100	100	100	100	100	100	100	100	100	100
'61-70 ..	85	77	87	73	100	66	75	40	40	28	14	85
'71-80	72	82	118	163	287	250	250	100	80	28	14	78
'81-90 . .	57	89	129	203	375	316	300	120	60	28	—	64
'91-1900 .	54	81	122	207	462	400	350	180	100	43	—	57
1901-05 . .	47	79	124	213	462	383	475	240	140	28	28	51

TABLE 3 (*Contd.*).—ENGLAND AND WALES. *Relative Mortalities.*

SCROFULA.

Ages ...	0—	5—	10—	15—	20—	25—	35—	45—	55—	65—	75—	All Ages
Males.												
1851-60........	100	100	100	100	100	100	100	100	100	100	100	100
'61-70... ...	139	85	84	74	77	75	78	79	93	85	77	96
'71-80 ...	178	66	52	49	48	45	48	53	64	55	40	85
'81-90	142	86	63	59	62	56	73	71	64	41	27	108
'91-1900..	258	101	70	68	80	81	108	100	93	59	54	122
1901-05	211	88	97	62	77	88	124	116	117	73	60	112
Females.												
1851-60 ....:	100	100	100	100	100	100	100	100	100	100	100	100
'61-70.......	147	84	74	71	84	73	79	90	77	74	72	98
'71-80	176	64	51	46	49	47	50	59	56	67	44	88
'81-90 ..	230	120	98	85	96	81	74	60	47	39	36	123
'91-1900	242	123	103	98	109	100	100	82	63	59	59	131
1901-05 .	206	117	91	89	104	107	109	95	82	72	81	122

TABLE 3A.—LONDON. *Relative Mortalities.*

PHTHISIS.

Ages......	0—	5—	10—	15—	20—	25—	35—	45—	55—	65—	75—	All Ages
Males.												
1851-60 ...	100	100	100	100	100	100	100	100	100	100	100	100
'61-70 ..	100	96	82	93	106	106	104	105	104	90	76	102
'71-80 ..	69	67	74	74	84	99	103	100	97	77	46	91
'81-90 .	48	42	48	55	63	84	89	90	91	76	58	77
'91-1900	42	31	33	45	55	66	80	84	85	77	56	70
1901-05..... .	36	26	28	38	45	54	66	81	80	74	52	62
Females.												
1851-60	100	100	100	100	100	100	100	100	100	100	100	100
'61-70 ...	96	88	93	93	92	100	99	97	95	87	72	96
'71-80	69	63	78	81	77	88	94	91	86	76	47	83
'81-90 .	46	45	62	60	56	70	79	78	75	68	57	66
'91-1900..	38	34	48	48	40	50	68	69	66	67	60	54
1901-05.......	32	32	36	38	31	38	52	59	60	68	73	45

TABLE 3A (*Contd.*).—LONDON. *Relative Mortalities.*

Ages......	0—	5—	10—	15—	20—	25—	35—	45—	55—	65—	75—	All Ages.
					TABES MESENTERICA							
Males.												
1851–60.......	100	100	100	100	100	100	100	100	100	100	—	100
'61–70......	105	81	70	122	177	200	100	150	131	19	100	105
'71–80.......	119	70	75	118	108	157	100	125	100	47	170	117
'81–90.......	111	55	62	107	138	200	166	175	77	12	70	104
'91–1900 .	81	44	57	126	177	314	222	350	177	66	120	72
1901–05	44	40	56	130	231	385	322	337	354	69	110	42
Females.												
1851–60.......	100	100	100	100	100	100	100	100	100	100	100	100
'61–70.......	102	87	85	86	145	140	155	92	69	191	44	103
'71–80.......	114	78	76	83	109	110	100	100	123	100	—	113
'81–90	100	65	79	91	200	200	166	123	69	200	28	99
'91–1900....	76	60	83	103	236	230	322	161	146	125	24	73
1901–05........	38	66	71	134	254	250	300	246	161	100	44	41
					HYDROCEPHALUS.							
Males.												
1851–60.......	100	100	100	100	100	100	100	100	100	100	100	100
'61–70	85	85	116	161	62	130	100	20	43	200	23	87
'71–80	67	84	149	338	86	160	425	53	86	—	—	71
'81–90	50	79	127	323	114	200	375	87	100	133	16	53
'91–1900 ..	44	73	155	385	194	240	525	60	72	200	41	44
1901–05	35	70	149	454	186	270	600	107	29	600	—	36
Females.												
1851–60........	100	100	100	100	100	100	100	100	100	100	100	100
'61–70........	79	87	145	116	111	80	60	33	25	100	—	84
'71–80......	64	91	192	158	178	200	160	50	50	250	—	71
'81–90	52	84	150	210	211	260	220	100	100	300	—	56
'91–1900 ...	46	90	187	231	289	360	240	100	100	200	—	49
1901–05........	42	92	123	247	233	300	320	150	125	150	—	44
					SCROFULA.							
Males.												
1851–60........	100	100	100	100	100	100	100	100	100	100	100	100
'61–70	113	71	71	57	85	68	84	97	86	88	28	91
'71–80........	158	66	55	47	37	44	50	62	73	75	31	100
'81–90........	221	80	64	59	81	95	134	119	70	55	31	138
'91–1900 ...	216	100	88	66	109	127	170	172	104	100	79	144
1901–05	175	80	71	60	108	130	155	211	134	112	102	124
Females.												
1851–60.......	100	100	100	100	100	100	100	100	100	100	100	100
'61–70	128	69	71	69	51	80	85	118	108	91	73	101
'71–80........	168	60	44	44	39	48	49	90	64	97	30	105
'81–90	232	103	79	80	89	83	84	69	60	58	41	146
'91–1900. ..	224	113	93	105	110	125	115	118	83	107	91	150
1901–05........	193	100	90	105	94	130	147	135	115	176	181	130

III.—*The meeting of the British Association.   Discussion on Modern
Methods of Treating Observations.*

THE British Association met at Leicester this year, from 31st
July to 7th August, under the Presidency of Sir David Gill, F.R.S.
Professor W. J. Ashley was President of Section F (Economics and
Statistics), and delivered a very able and interesting address on the
history and present position of economics in this country. The
address of Mr. G. G. Chisholm to Section E (Geography) on
"Geography and Commerce" also deserves especial mention; and
we may note the discussion on "Anthropometry in Schools," in
Sections H (Anthropology) and L (Education) meeting conjointly,
which was introduced by papers by Mr. J. Gray and Dr. Shrubsall.
The majority of the papers read before Section F were of an
economic rather than a statistical character, and the chief statistical
event of the meeting was a discussion before Section A (Mathematical
and Physical Science), in which several Fellows of the Society took
part, on "Modern Methods of Treating Observations, with especial
reference to Meteorology." It should be stated that the time
allowed for the discussion was brief, and several speakers had to
curtail their remarks somewhat unduly.

The discussion was inaugurated by Mr. W. PALIN ELDERTON,
whose communication dealt with the application of recognised
statistical processes to meteorological statistics. It was pointed out
that the questions naturally arising from, say, rainfall statistics
were :—(1.) What is the average rainfall? (2.) Where should we
make the division between wet weeks and dry weeks? (3.) What
is the most likely rainfall in any week? (4.) Are there many very
wet weeks and some quite dry weeks, or is the rainfall fairly
uniform? The answers to the first three of these questions by the
calculation of the mean, median and mode were explained, and the
methods of calculating the values were given for rainfall statistics
drawn from a paper by Dr. W. N. Shaw, F.R.S.[1]

The "Method of Moments" was described and, after the
necessity of using a general method of fitting curves had been
mentioned, an example of the application of the method was given
by fitting a parabolic curve to statistics of rainfall in East England,
also drawn from Dr. Shaw's paper.

The standard deviation was then explained, and it was pointed
out that this function, by measuring the way observations are
scattered about their mean, supplies an answer to the fourth
question indicated above.

The importance of calculating a "standard deviation" or a
"probable error" corresponding with means was then insisted on, and
it was pointed out that the mere statement of a mean is statistically
insufficient, and is of no use for comparative purposes until we
know what deviations from the calculated value may arise.

[1] "Seasons in the British Isles from 1878," *Journal of the Royal Statistical
Society*, June, 1905.

Numerical examples were given to show the practical uses of this measure of accuracy.

The remainder of the communication dealt mainly with correlation. It is frequently important to decide whether two functions are related to one another. or not, and if they are related to find a measure of the relationship. The coefficient of correlation gives a satisfactory measure, in the majority of cases, and its meaning and use were explained. As a numerical example the rainfall in the east of England was compared with that in the north of Scotland and in the Channel Islands (Dr. Shaw's statistics), and the coefficient of correlation in the former case was shown to be very small in comparison with that brought out in the latter. In the case of correlation as well as that of means it is especially important to calculate the probable errors of the coefficients used, as it is not till such calculations have been made that it is possible to assert that a correlation is significant, or that there is in reality a closer connection in one case than in another. In the case of the rainfall statistics already mentioned, the coefficient between East England and North Scotland was ·07, and as its probable error was ± ·07 the coefficient was not significant. In the other case the coefficient was shown to be ·374 ± ·065, indicating that the rainfall in East England is correlated with that in the Channel Islands. Another example taken was the correlation between rainfall and typhoid cases in Surrey districts, the water supply of which is obtained from river sources. The statistics were furnished by Dr. E. C. Seaton, the medical officer of health, and the author expressed his indebtedness for permission to use them. The coefficient of correlation was found to be ·116 with a probable error of ·073, so that it is impossible to assert definitely that there is any relation between rainfall and typhoid, at any rate on the evidence afforded by these statistics. It was remarked that the matter seemed well worth further investigation with other statistics.

Reference was also made to work that had already been done in meteorology with modern statistical methods, and a paper by Professor Karl Pearson, F.R.S., and Miss Alice Lee[2] was briefly summarised. It was also pointed out that Dr. Gilbert T. Walker, F.R.S., in his interesting memoranda on the meteorology of India[3] had made use of the coefficient of correlation for measuring the correlation between sunspots and the precipitation in December to March, and had given a table of coefficients showing the correlation between various pressures, rainfall and snowfall connected with Indian meteorology. This table was reproduced, and it was remarked that Dr. Walker used his results for foretelling the weather for the following year.

[2] "On the Distribution of Frequency of the Barometric Height at Divers Stations," *Philosophical Transactions*, A, vol. 190, pp. 423—469.

[3] Memorandum on the Meteorology of India: (i) .before the advance of S.W. Monsoon of 1906; (ii) during October and November, 1906; (iii) before the advance of the S.W. Monsoon of 1907. Simla: Government Printing Office, 1906 and 1907.

The communication concluded with an appeal for the more scientific treatment of statistics with the help of modern methods.

Dr. W. N. SHAW expressed the thanks of meteorologists to Mr. Elderton for his Paper, and hoped that it might be printed *in extenso*, so that the details which could not be introduced in the discussion might be available for reference.

From the point of view of meteorology, it was a very appropriate time for a discussion of the methods of dealing with observations. Sufficient observations had now been obtained for the preparation of mean values, if not for the whole world, at least for the greater part of it; and the next stage in the scientific process was the consideration of departures from the mean.

In other quarters a great amount of attention had been paid to the development of methods of observation, and it was very desirable that students of meteorology should be acquainted with these new methods. Not only had Professor Karl Pearson introduced the method of computing the "coefficient of correlation," of which Mr. Elderton had spoken, but advances had been made in other directions. The method of harmonic analysis had been known for a long time, but Professor Schuster[4] had developed it by suggesting the construction of a "periodogram," which indicated the prominence of any particular periodic variation in the complex changes of a quantity in a manner analogous to the resolution of the complex vibration of a ray of light of mixed colours into its constituents by spectrum analysis. Professor Chrystal,[5] in discussing the component periods of oscillation of the seiches of Scottish lochs, had introduced a "method of residuation," which had to do with the effect produced upon the components of various periods by adding consecutive ordinates with specified intervals. The consideration of this method was specially important for meteorologists, in order that they might realise what was the effect upon the various periodic components, due to the "smoothing" by adding consecutive values according to Bloxam's rule or in some other manner.

The study of all these methods was of such importance that meteorologists were under an obligation to the Committee of Section A for arranging the discussion and to Mr. Elderton for opening it.

A very slight study of meteorological values was sufficient to show the necessity of dealing with them in some other manner than by merely taking arithmetic means. He was able to exhibit some diagrams prepared in the Meteorological Office which illustrated the relation of the mean to the frequency of occurrence of the various values. The curves showed the mean weekly values of accumulated temperature, sunshine, and rainfall, and the limits of the weekly values above and below the mean, which would include, on the

---

[4] *Proceedings of the Royal Society*, Ser. A, vol. 77, pp. 136 *sqq.* (1906), and earlier papers.

[5] *Transactions of the Royal Society of Edinburgh*, vol. xlv, part ii (No. 14) p. 385 (1906).

average, one-third of the whole number of occurrences; also the limits that were exceeded in either direction only once in twelve times. The limits had been computed from the *Weekly Weather Report*, so that the character of a season might be satisfactorily represented by correcting the number of weeks of specified character included in it.

Mr. G. U. YULE stated that he felt the same diffidence as Mr. Elderton in speaking on the application of statistical methods to meteorology, as he had practically no knowledge of that subject, but only of statistical method. Statistical methods, however—the methods of dealing with observations affected by a plurality of causes—were the same from whatever field of science the observations were drawn. For such simple comparisons—*e.g.*, of the meteorological conditions in two localities—as were made without any afterthought of discussing hypotheses as to causation, the arithmetic mean—or some other form of average—was practically the only constant used. To do this was to neglect all the other characters in which two frequency distributions might differ; and of such characters, as had been already pointed out, scatter or dispersion was the most important. The standard deviation (root-mean-square deviation from the mean) was the most convenient measure of dispersion algebraically, but the "interquartile range," or difference between the two values which were just exceeded by one-quarter and three-quarters of the observations respectively, was the most readily calculated. Where the problem was more complex and it was desired to discuss the relation between two variables, various methods were available, but that of the correlation coefficient was the most important. In the cases with which the physicist dealt, the form of the function relating the two variables was the chief point of interest, but in the cases most typical of statistics —as in Mr. Elderton's diagrams—the observations were, in general, so scattered that a simple straight line served almost as well as any more elaborate curve, marked divergence from linearity occurring in a smaller proportion of cases than might be expected. The correlation coefficient was a measure of the approach towards such a simple linear relation between the two variables, and the method could be extended to cover those cases—numerous in practice—in which it was necessary to deal with more than two variables—say three or four. Referring to Dr. Shaw's remarks, he would suggest that such methods as harmonic analysis, while of service in certain cases, hardly came within the scope of methods of statistics proper; the method had no special applicability to observations affected by a plurality of causes.

Mr. A. R. HINKS said that a recent paper,[6] published under the auspices of Professor Karl Pearson, had raised in his mind certain misgivings as to the advantages of discussing astronomical statistics by the theory of correlation. An attempt was made to find the correlation between the parallax and the photometric magnitude

[6] "Some considerations regarding the number of the stars." Winifred Gibson. *Monthly Notices R.A.S.*, vol. lxvi, p. 445.

of stars. He would like to call attention to two points in this paper. The first was a question of theory. Suppose that the stars were uniform in size and brilliancy, so that parallax and magnitud were rigidly connected—the relation between them would be expressed by a logarithmic curve, and consequently the coefficient of correlation would not be unity, but something less, depending upon the distribution of the stars in space. In this case it seemed to him that the coefficient of correlation between parallax and magnitude would tell us little about the closeness of the actual relation between them. He understood that in such a case it was proper to use correlation ratios, but not correlation coefficients. If that was so, he would ask the exponents of modern statistical methods to erect a very large and conspicuous danger signal, to keep astronomical statisticians from falling into such a trap.

His second point concerned the material discussed in the above paper, which contained a diagrammatic representation of the relation between parallax and magnitude derived from 72 stars. The curve was complex, with three peaks. It was suggested in a footnote that a quartic curve might be made to fit it. But anyone who knew anything of stellar parallax work could explain at once the existence of these peaks. The first belonged to stars of the first magnitude, which had all been investigated *because they were of the first magnitude.* A few of them had large parallaxes. The second peak belongs to stars of the fourth and fifth magnitudes. They were not representative of the average star of that magnitude, but had been chosen *because of their exceptionally large proper motion,* and the consequent presumption of a measurable parallax. The third peak belonged to a few faint stars which had been investigated for the same reason—that they had large proper motion. The material under discussion was not, therefore, representative of the stars in general, but was hopelessly biassed, and he would like to express the conviction that no good was done in discussing astronomical results by any method of statistics that overlooked such considerations as those which he had ventured to bring forward.

Mr. R. H. HOOKER thought that he could best serve the purpose of the discussion by giving one or two examples of the practical use that could be made of the method of correlation. Dr. Shaw had shown that there was an important connection between the autumn rainfall and the following wheat harvest. By correlating the weather of different seasons with the crop, he had been able to go further[7] and show that the connection was closer with the autumn rainfall than with either rain or temperature at any other time of the year. Moreover, by the use of the method of partial correlation, he had been able to separate the effects of rainfall or temperature on the crops, finding, for instance, that cool weather during spring and early summer was very important as conducive to bulk in practically all agricultural crops.

Professor H. H. TURNER drew attention to the need for caution in interpreting statistics, as illustrated by a letter in the *Times* of

[7] *Journal of the Royal Statistical Society,* March, 1907.

the preceding day.[8]　It had been asked by a Member of Parliament how it was that the death-rate from plague in India " was highest where inoculation was greatest." In the letter it was pointed out that the death-rate was much lower amongst the inoculated than amongst the non-inoculated, but that too small a number was inoculated to sensibly influence the total mortality. The relation noticed was simply due to the fact that most inoculations were made in the districts where plague was worst and the mortality consequently highest.

Professor EDGEWORTH said that the remarks of the preceding speakers fell under three heads—law, chance, and a mixture of the two. To the first head belonged Dr. Shaw's attempt to trace periodicity in meteorological phenomena. The extension of mathematical law to new regions was a triumph familiar to Section A; a brilliant example had lately been given by the President of the Section. He (Professor Edgeworth) would follow Mr. Yule in limiting the present discussion to Statistics in a narrow sense, covering only the last two of the three heads specified. The hypothesis, proper to the second head, of numerous independent causes seemed to account for a greater proportion of actual frequency-distributions than was commonly supposed. No doubt the hypothesis was often not adequately fulfilled; some one or two agencies were unduly preponderant. The statistics out of which life-tables were constructed seemed to be of this character—belonging to the third, rather than the second head. Professor Pearson's method of representing frequency-distributions was appropriate to this head. It was not based on an antecedently probable hypothesis, but was rather an empirical formula apt to represent the data given by observation. We ought, no doubt, to have regard to the data of observation, as Bacon, who had been mentioned, was always insisting. We ought also, like philosophers before and after him, to seek for explanations of observed phenomena. A formula was more valid when it rested, not only on empirical verification, but also on an *à priori* hypothesis. It might be hoped that a reason would be forthcoming for the wide applicability of Mr. Yule's method of treating correlation in general, according to the rule proper to " normal " distribution of frequency.

In replying briefly to the discussion, Mr. ELDERTON pointed out to Mr. Hinks that it was very seldom that the regression curve deviated much from a straight line in ordinary statistical work; but if Mr. Hinks found that in certain astronomical statistics it was impossible to use a straight line, he would have to work out a coefficient (correlation ratio) different from that dealt with in the opening communication. Of course he, Mr. Elderton, quite agreed with Professor Turner, that in all statistical work it was easy to misinterpret one's results, and many difficulties of interpretation would remain even if modern methods were used.[9]

---

[8] Letter from Professor W. J. Simpson. *Times*, 5th August, 1907.

[9] A letter from Professor Karl Pearson, with reference to the remarks of Mr. Hinks, was published in *Nature*, 19th September.

IV.—*Agricultural Returns of Great Britain*, 1907.

PRELIMINARY statement for 1907, compiled from the returns collected on the 4th June; and comparison with 1906:—

CROPS.

Distribution.	1907.	1906.	Increase.		Decrease.	
	Acres	Acres.	Acres.	Per cnt.	Acres.	Per cnt.
Total area (excluding water)	56,201,418	56,201,418	—	—	—	—
Total acreage under all crops and grass*	32,244,110	32,266,755	—	—	22,645	0·1
Wheat	1,625,488	1,755,696	—	—	130,208	7·4
Barley	1,712,166	1,751,238	—	—	39,072	2·2
Oats	3,122,936	3,042,926	80,010	2·6	—	—
Rye	61,211	64,808	—	—	3,597	5·6
Beans	309,761	288,891	20,870	7·2	—	—
Peas	166,138	153,979	12,159	7·9	—	—
Potatoes	548,921	565,921	—	—	17,000	3·0
Turnips and swedes....	1,563,031	1,590,920	—	—	27,889	1·8
Mangold	450,063	431,458	18,605	4·3	—	—
Cabbage	74,897	70,368	4,529	6·4	—	—
Kohl-rabi	20,687	17,714	2,973	16·8	—	—
Rape	91,273	93,830	—	—	2,557	2·7
Vetches or tares	154,058	142,047	12,011	8·5	—	—
Lucerne	63,796	55,734	8,062	14·5	—	—
Other crops	121,499	113,997	7,502	6·6	—	—
Clover and rotation grasses—						
For hay..............	2,250,371	2,191,587	58,784	2·7	—	—
Not for hay	2,240,657	2,249,159	—	—	8,502	0·4
Total	4,491,028	4,440,746	50,282	1·1	—	—
Permanent grass—*						
For hay........	4,936,823	4,784,895	151,928	3·2	—	—
Not for hay	12,341,420	12,459,839	—	—	118,419	1·0
Total................ ...	17,278,243	17,244,734	33,509	0·2	—	—
Flax	372	263	109	41·4	—	—
Hops..........................	44,938	46,722	—	—	1,784	3·8
Small fruit	82,167	80,226	1,941	2·4	—	—
Bare fallow	261,437	314,537	—	—	53,100	16·9
Orchards†	250,172	247,687	2,485	1·0	—	—

* Excluding 12,742,779 acres returned as mountain and heath land used for grazing in 1907, and 12,748,364 acres in 1906.

† The acreage of any crop or grass grown under the trees in orchards is also returned under its proper heading.

LIVE STOCK.

Distribution.	1907.	1906.	Increase.		Decrease.	
	No.	No.	No.	Per cnt.	No.	Per cnt.
Horses used for agricultural purposes* }	1,115,962	1,116,505	—	—	543	0·0
Unbroken horses—						
1 year and above....	313,961	315,235	—	—	1,274	0·4
Under 1 year	126,484	136,941	—	—	10,457	7·6
Total of horses....	1,556,407	1,568,681	—	—	12,274	0·8
Cows and heifers in milk or in calf .... }	2,759,318	2,738,411	20,907	0·8	—	—
Other cattle—						
2 years and above	1,389,282	1,426,754	—	—	37,472	2·6
1 year and under 2	1,440,433	1,494,795	—	—	54,362	3·6
Under 1 year	1,323,486	1,350,896	—	—	27,410	2·0
Total of cattle	6,912,519	7,010,856	—	—	98,337	1·4
Ewes kept for breeding	10,277,428	10,061,104	216,324	2·2	—	—
Other sheep—						
1 year and above	5,194,029	5,098,876	95,153	1·9	—	—
Under 1 year	10,645,046	10,260,380	384,666	3·7	—	—
Total of sheep ...	26,116,503	25,420,360	696,143	2·7	—	—
Sows kept for breeding	380,272	336,322	43,950	13·1	—	—
Other pigs	2,256,536	1,987,139	269,397	13·6	—	—
Total of pigs	2,636,808	2,323,461	313,347	13·5	—	—

* Including mares kept for breeding.

BOARD OF AGRICULTURE AND FISHERIES,
  26th August, 1907.

NOTES ON ECONOMIC AND STATISTICAL WORKS.

CONTENTS :

PAGE

1.—Registrar-General. Supplement to 65th Annual Report [Cd-2618], 1907 479

2.—Irish Imports and Exports, 1905 [Cd-3631], 1907 481

3.—Old Age Pensions. Tables [Cd-3618], 1907 483

4.—Mackenzie (W. L.). and Foster (A.). Physical condition of Glasgow school children [Cd-3637], 1907 485

5.—Canada. Census Bulletin I. Wage-earners by occupations ... 486

6.—France. Album graphique de la statistique générales 489

7.—Statistisches Handbuch für das Deutsche Reich. Teil I 490

8.—Berliner Statistik für 1905. Uebersichten, 1907 491

9.—Bailey (W. B.). Modern social conditions (U.S.A.) 491

10.—Chatterton-Hill (G.). Heredity and selection in sociology.... 492

11.—Punnett (R. C.). Mendelism 493

12.—Mombert (P.). Bevölkerungsbewegung in Deutschland 494

13.—Jacquart (C.). Mortalité infantile dans les Flandres 494

14.—Bray (R. A.). The town child 495

PAGE

15.—Dewsnup (E. R.). Housing problem in England............... 497

16.—Alden (P.) and Hayward (E. E.). Housing 498

17.—Turot (H.) aud Bellamy (H.). Surpeuplement et habitations à bon marché 499

18.—Boverat (R.). Socialisme municipal en Angleterre............ 499

19.—Porter (R. P.). Dangers of municipal trading 501

20.—Devas (C. S.). Political economy 504

21.—Guyot (Yves). Science économique. 3rd ed., 1907 505

22.—Martel (F.) and Grigaut (M.). Economie politique 507

23.—Simiand (F.). Salaire des ouvriers des mines de Charbon en France 508

24.—Welsford (J. W.). Strength of nations 509

25.—Jebb (L.). Small holdings in England ....:..... 512

26.—Barbour (J. S.). William Paterson and the Darien Co. 515

27.—Sociological Society. Papers, Vol. iii 517

28.—Other new publications 519

1.—*Supplement to the Sixty-fifth Annual Report of the Registrar-General of Births, Deaths, and Marriages in England and Wales,* 1891-1900. Part I, 1907. [Cd-2618.] 760 + cciv pp., 8vo. Price 4s. 3d.

The publication of Dr. Tatham's second decennial supplement to the Registrar-General's reports has been eagerly looked for by all interested in vital statistics, and we welcome its somewhat belated appearance. Part II of the supplement dealing with occupational mortality is, we are told, in an advanced stage of preparation, and will be issued " in due course." While admitting that accuracy and completeness of records are more important than early issue, it is nevertheless regrettable that the limited staff of the General Register Office does not enable these important decennial supplements to be issued at an earlier part of the decennium following that with which the supplements are concerned.

Having indulged in the grumble to which all Englishmen feel themselves entitled, we hasten to express our thanks for this last and most valuable, because most complete and accurate, of all the five decennial supplements which have appeared. The word " accurate " is used advisedly, because in this report we have for the first time death-rates corrected to a standard population for all the registration districts of England and Wales. The same table gives the infantile mortality for the same districts, the birth and marriage-rates, and the index of crowding. In regard to the last point, a great stride has been made, the old index of crowding—the number of persons per acre—having been replaced by two columns, giving for each district the percentage at the census of 1901 of tenements of fewer than five rooms and of such tenements with more than two persons to a room. As it was in a paper on the Vital Statistics of Peabody Buildings, published in the *Journal of the Royal Statistical Society* some years ago, that the number of persons per room was urged as the proper index of crowding instead of the older index used by Farr, it is especially satisfactory to find that these two columns have been added to Table I in the present report. They greatly enhance its value and accuracy. We cannot speak with equal approval of the column in the same table stating the birth-rate of each registration district per 1,000 females aged 15—45 years. Birth-rates are required for two purposes: (*a*) To give the ratio of increase by births of the population; (The birth-rate per 1,000 of that population is satisfactory in this respect. This is given in Table I.) (*b*) To give the number of births per 1,000 women of child-bearing ages who are living under marital conditions. This furnishes information as to the relation between the actual fertility of different populations. Now the birth-rate per 1,000 women aged 15—45 satisfies neither of these conditions, for we do not know how many of these women were married. Doubtless there were reasons rendering it impossible to obtain the number of married females aged 15—45 in each registration district. Failing these figures, we submit that the crude birth-rate per 1,000 of population is preferable to the birth-rate per 1,000 females aged 15—45.

This is not the only table in the report. Most of its bulk is occupied with tables giving the most important causes of death and death-rates for 1891-1900 for each of 45 counties, and for 631 registration districts. The male and female death-rates from each of the chief zymotic diseases, from cancer, phthisis and other tuberculous diseases, from diseases of the chief organs of the body, from puerperal fever, child-birth (female), and violence are given; and the number of deaths of persons at each single year under 5, at each quinquennial period 5—25, and decennial periods afterwards are set forth.

Table 2 is a most valuable table, to which attention should specially be called. It gives for each of the 631 registration districts the death-rate per 1,000,000 living under 5 years of age from all causes, and from the chief zymotic, tuberculous and respiratory diseases.   While expressing a wish (much wants more) that a column had been devoted to phthisis as well as to all tuberculous diseases, we think that this table is of great national importance.   Table 1 gives the infant mortality, Table 2 enables the comparisons to be pursued into the next four years of life, and by this means will give important clues to the causes of unsatisfactory child-life.

In Table 3 this valuable comparison can be carried further so far as counties are concerned.   For males and females separately the death-rates are given for those living at ages 5—10, 10—15, and at each subsequent period of life.

Table 5 is a familiar friend.   It gives the death-rates in the whole county at eleven groups of ages among persons, males and females, for four successive decennial periods from all causes, and from each of the chief causes of death.

In thus enumerating some of the statistical riches of this report, its wealth has been far from exhausted, for the very important preliminary letter by Dr. Tatham contains a series of tables, A to Z and A_1 to K_1, each of which possesses great interest for all who are interested in the medical and social problems of disease.

Mr. A. C. Waters has contributed a valuable section on estimates of population, which deserves careful study, in connection with the technical details of life-table construction given on pp. xvii-xix. We have left ourselves no space to discuss in detail the two new English life-tables given in this report for England and Wales and for selected healthy districts.   Their lessons are clearly stated by Dr. Tatham, whose report on this, as well as on the other vital statistics of the decennium, will be read with great interest and appreciation.   His remarks on tuberculosis and on cancer are especially worthy of study, but the whole of his report is a scholarly publication, worthy of the high traditions of Farr and Ogle.   Not only to the medical officer, but also to every social student, whether medical man or layman, this volume will be an indispensable guide, and Dr. Tatham and those who have collaborated with him are to be congratulated on its publication.   A.N.

2.—*Report on the Trade in Imports and Exports at Irish Ports in* 1905.   [Cd-3631.]   xxvi + 134 pp., 8vo.   Dublin : H.M. Stationery Office, 1907.

This is the second annual report which has been issued dealing with the external trade of Ireland in 1905.   The first report, for 1904, was dated 27th October, 1906, while the third report, for 1906, is promised to make its appearance shortly.   In time it may be expected, perhaps, that these reports will be published within a comparatively few months from the end of the year with which they purport to deal.

The report is prepared by the Department of Agriculture and Technical Instruction for Ireland, its value as an official document being affected to some extent, however, by the absence of any powers in the Department to compel returns by importers and exporters at Irish ports.   The returns have been collated from information voluntarily supplied by the various port authorities, customs officers, railways, shipping companies, private traders, and others.   It is not surprising, therefore, that, in respect to values, it is admitted "that the information given . . . cannot claim to be more than approximate;" while, as for the report as a whole, it "is, therefore, neither complete as regards quantities nor exact as regards values."

The principal object of the report is to obtain some measure of the external trade of Ireland with all countries, including Great Britain.   The only information at present officially available is that supplied by the customs authorities, giving the imports and exports direct from or to countries other than Great Britain.   This trade is estimated to amount only to one-eighth or one-ninth of the total which it is desired to investigate.   There is no information as to the direct trade in Great Britain, or the trade to all other countries *via* Great Britain; the data for the whole of this trade is covered at best by the ships "manifests"—documents which are about as useful and difficult to handle statistically as would be the delivery notes of any railway company.   They contain no information at all as to the values of the goods carried; while even, as regards the quantities, these are carelessly inscribed, and the goods are insufficiently described to be of much use.

In spite of these limitations the reports which have been issued are extremely valuable, and reveal a large amount of patience in overcoming the difficulties which beset them.   On the whole the figures given are probably not far removed from the truth, and as time goes on and the officials become more accustomed to the new work and the various authorities become better acquainted with their requirements, a larger amount of accurate information will become available from which still more valuable returns will be prepared.

It is interesting to note—and this merely illustrates the magnitude of the difficulties which have had to be faced—that whereas the figures for 1904 were put forward tentatively and were said to be much below the truth, yet a revision of the 1904 figures in the 1905 report has led to their reduction.   In 1904 the "imports" into Ireland were estimated at 55,100,000*l*. and the exports to 46,600,000*l*.; whereas in the 1905 report the revised estimates for 1904 are put at 53,300,000*l*. for imports and 49,200,000*l*. for exports.   Thus the imports in 1904 are now admitted to have been overestimated by 1,800,000*l*. and the exports to have been underestimated by 2,600,000*l*.   Until some finality is assumed for the figures published, it appears somewhat premature to speculate on the intricate question of the "balance of trade."

These reports of the Irish external trade are obviously of the greatest value in supplying some measure of the social and economic differences in Ireland from the rest of the United Kingdom.   In the case of articles like tea, coffee, tobacco, sugar, wine—the consumption of which coincides with the importation—we are enabled to measure the rate of consumption in Ireland and Great Britain.

Such information must form a very valuable contribution to the discussions on the Irish " financial relations " problem. Then, again, the data relating to the supplies to this country from Ireland of live-stock and important agricultural products, and to Ireland from this country for the necessary manufactures, are of the greatest interest in connection with current political questions. It comes somewhat as a surprise that whereas 9,666,000*l.* of live cattle were imported into the United Kingdom in 1905, the exports from Ireland, almost entirely to Great Britain, and not included in the above total, were 8,900,000*l.* The export of eggs from Ireland was estimated to have amounted to 2,500,000*l.*, while the total import into the United Kingdom, exclusive of Irish eggs, was 6,800,000*l.*

In order that these returns may become of greater value than they possess at present, it is desirable that they should separate the trade with Great Britain from all other countries. It should be possible to demand from exporters and importers at Irish ports the same full and detailed information respecting all cargoes entering or leaving the ports as are supplied when coming direct from or going direct to a foreign country. By placing the collection in the hands of one authority for the whole of the United Kingdom the value of the returns would be greatly enhanced, from the fact that uniformity would be established between the returns for Great Britain and Ireland respectively. The difficulty of dealing with 20 different measures for butter and 10 for lard would then not arise, as was the case with the voluntary returns with which the Irish officials had to deal.

In making the suggestions in the foregoing paragraph, no idea of criticism upon the capacity or industry of those who have compiled these reports is intended. With the limited powers which were available to them, and the general novelty of the work, they have carried out this self-imposed task in a manner at once admirable, and as complete as could be expected.   S.R.

3.—*Old Age Pensions. Tables which have been prepared in connection with the question of Old Age Pensions, with a preliminary memorandum.* Presented to both Houses of Parliament by command of His Majesty. [Cd–3618.]   54 pp., fol.   London : H.M. Stationery Office, 1907.   Price 5½*d.*

This very timely and useful official publication summarises and brings down to the present time the conclusions arrived at by a long series of Commissions and Committees, and will be found to be valuable by all those who have a real desire to make themselves acquainted with the question of Old Age Pensions, and with the difficulties that surround it. So far as it is possible to predict with any certainty the course of the future in legislation, that question will come up for determination in the next Session of Parliament, and this excellent blue book will furnish the combatants with a good supply of ammunition. Sir Samuel Provis, the Secretary of the Local Government Board, is the responsible and probably the actual author of the preliminary memorandum, and the public are much indebted to him for it.

The course of inquiry begins with Lord Aberdare's Commission of 1893 " to consider whether any alterations in the system of poor law relief are desirable in the case of persons whose destitution is occasioned by incapacity for work resulting from old age, or whether assistance could otherwise be afforded in those cases." The Commissioners reported in 1895 that they were unable to recommend the adoption of any of the schemes of Old Age Pensions that had been submitted to them.

In 1896 Lord Rothschild's Committee was appointed by the Treasury " to consider any schemes that may be submitted to them for encouraging the industrial population, by State aid or otherwise, to make provision for old· age." They came to the conclusion in June, 1898, that none of the schemes submitted to them would attain the objects in view, and that they could not devise one free from grave inherent disadvantages.

In 1899 Mr. Chaplin's Select Committee of the House of Commons sat and formulated a scheme. In the same year Sir Edward Hamilton's Committee, of which Sir Samuel Provis was an important member, was appointed to investigate the financial aspects of the scheme proposed by the Select Committee. Another Select Committee, appointed in 1903, adopted with certain modifications the scheme of Mr. Chaplin's Committee, but no legislation has as yet resulted from either Report.

Series A of the Tables relates to the population, and shows that the number of persons living in the middle of 1907 above 65 years of age was, according to one method of estimation, 2,116,267 ; according to another, 2,147,536. Taking the lower estimate, a pension of 6*s.* a week or 15*l.* 12*s.* a year to every individual would cost 33,013,765*l.* per annum, or, if 3 per cent. be added for expenses, more than 34,000,000*l.*

Series B of the Tables relates to the various disqualifications for pension that were formulated by Mr. Chaplin's Committee, and is based on the labours of Sir E. Hamilton's Committee, but brings down their figures to the year 1907. These disqualifications are estimated to reduce the number of pensionable persons from 2,116,267 to 686,456, and the consequent cost, including 3 per cent. for expenses, to 10,780,000*l.*

Series C of the Tables relates to the rates of mortality and increase in the expectation of life of the general population, as derived from returns furnished by the General Register Office, and contains some important information as to the average age at death of members of trade unions.

Series D relates to certain classes of persons at present in receipt of pensions and superannuation allowances. It includes a communication from Mr. Stuart Sim, F.S.S., Chief Registrar of Friendly Societies, to the effect that, in the year ending 31st December, 1905, 70 trade unions paid 256,754*l.* by way of superannuation allowances to 13,383 of their members. It also contains particulars relating to the pensioners of local authorities in England and Wales, and to pension and almshouse charities in certain counties, compiled from information given by the Charity Commissioners.

Series E relates to pauperism, and shows that the number of persons receiving poor law relief in the United Kingdom has diminished from 37 per 1,000 of the population in 1872 to 24 per 1,000 in 1902. Of persons aged 65 and upwards, about 187 per 1,000 were receiving poor law relief on 1st September, 1903. The cost of poor law relief was for 1903-04 15,891,348*l.*; for 1904-05 16,507,690*l.*

Series F gives the results of the test census which Sir E. Hamilton's Committee instituted to ascertain the incomes of persons 65 years of age and upwards. Forty per cent. of the persons who were visited and gave information on the question acknowledged that they had incomes exceeding 10*s.* a week.

Series G relates to membership and funds of friendly societies, trade unions, savings bank depositors, &c., and shows a very considerable increase, both in regard to number and amount.

Other important matters in relation to the provision of State pensions are discussed in the memorandum, as, for example, the question to what extent it would be possible to reduce poor law expenditure under a system of Old Age Pensions. It is shown that the cost of indoor relief would be practically unaffected; and that the only appreciable saving would be in that portion of the cost which relates to outdoor relief. The total amount distributed in outdoor relief in 1904-05 was about 4,014,000*l.* Sir E. Hamilton's Committee, in 1899, computed that about 1,858,000*l.* of outdoor relief was granted to persons above 65 years of age. This includes medical relief, which would still have to be provided. The margin for saving in poor law expenditure is, therefore, not large. E.B.

4.—*Report on a Collection of Statistics as to the Physical Condition of Children attending the Public Schools of the School Board for Glasgow.* By Dr. W. Leslie Mackenzie and Captain A. Foster (Scotch Education Department). [Cd–3637.] 57 pp., 3 plates. Price 10½*d.*

In 1905, the School Board for Glasgow decided to institute records of physical measurements of the children attending their Primary and Higher Grade Schools, and at the same time to ascertain particulars as to housing and home conditions of the children. The School Board provided the equipment, the teachers undertook the actual work of measurement and enquiry, and the data were classified and issued by the Scotch Education Department.

The present report deals with the data for stature and weight only, in conjunction with housing conditions. Comparisons are made of the average stature and weight of boys and girls from age 5 upwards, with the standard averages of the British Association Anthropometrical Committee. The data are also classified according to the social character of the district from which the school draws its pupils (the schools being graded in four groups), and according to the number of rooms in the house (tenement) in which the child lives. With hardly any exceptions, the averages obtained are lower than the British Association averages taken as standards, and

show a marked gradation according to the social class of the
district and the number of rooms occupied : these differences appear
most strikingly in the curves of height and weight at different ages,
for children in tenements of different numbers of rooms, given in
plates at the end of the volume.

Certain figures that were widely cited at the time of issue of the
Report are, however, very seriously vitiated by a fallacy so obvious
that we are surprised at its having escaped attention. "For all the
ages from 5 to 14," it is written, "the numbers examined are so
large that comparison between the different groups can legitimately
be made . . . . If we take all the children of ages from
5 to 18, we find that the average weight of the one-roomed boy
is 52·6 lbs. ; of the two-roomed, 56·1 lbs. ; of the three-roomed,
60·6 lbs. ; of the four-roomed and over, 64·3 lbs. The respective
heights are 46·6 inches, 48·1 inches, 50·0 inches and 51·3 inches."
Similar figures are given for the girls, and the results are enforced
in a later paragraph. It does not appear to have occurred to the
writers of the report, or to those responsible for its issue, that
averages based on children ranging from 5 to 18 years of age are
primarily dependent on the age-distributions. Now the percentages
of one, two, three and four-roomed boys, respectively, who were
8 years of age and less are, in round numbers, 44, 39, 31 and
27 per cent. ; while the percentages aged 12 or more are 20, 26, 33
and 39 per cent.—*i.e.*, the average age of two-roomed boys is greater
than that of one-roomed, that of three-roomed greater than two-
roomed, and so on. No wonder, then, that the average height and
weight are correspondingly greater! There is, it is true, a
significant difference between tenement-classes age for age, but—
roughly speaking—it is only half that given.

If one other criticism may be made, it is that the tables are
too detailed; data should not be published for single schools, as
they are practically worthless; 16 out of 32 so-called "averages,"
in Table 24, for instance, are based on single individuals. Apart
from these criticisms on individual points, we have, however, nothing
but admiration for the way in which the research has been initiated
and carried through by local effort, and with official recognition and
support. Scotland has set a good example.   G.U.Y.

5.—*Census and Statistics (Canada). Bulletin I. Wage-earners by
Occupations.* xxviii + 105 pp., 8vo. Ottawa : S. E. Dawson, 1907.

The first bulletin, supplementary to the reports of the Canadian
census of 1901, deals with the numbers and earnings of employees
over 16 years of age, except in manufactures, where the limit is
15 years. The data given are classified by occupations for Canada
as a whole, and the aggregates are compared by provinces in the
chief groups of occupations. The numbers for whom the record
obtained was complete were :—661,485 males and 153,445 females,
or about 40 per cent. of the male population between 15 and 65
years of age, and 10 per cent. of the female population of like age.
Partial returns relating to 75,064 males and 32,597 females were
secured, in addition to these complete returns.

We have, it is clear, not a record of all *occupied* persons, and the difference between *occupied* and *employed* in Canada is very important. It would be easy to misinterpret some of the results through neglect of this fundamental point. If the enumeration may be taken as approximately exhaustive, we might conclude that one-half, or thereabouts, of the adult males of Canada are self-employed. Even if a large allowance be made for those under (say) 20 years of age who are not yet at wage-earning employment, but will shortly be so occupied, the proportion of self-employed will remain very high. This is of especial importance in agriculture, and of very considerable moment in the professional class. Manufactures employ more than three times as many male wage-earners as agriculture, and the wages earned by the former are fully six times as great in the aggregate as those earned by the latter. But it would be an error of the first order to permit the impression produced by these figures to serve as the foundation of a judgment as to the relative importance of these two great divisions of industry in the Dominion. The reports of the Census Bureau still fail to provide the data necessary for this comparison.

So far as appears from the bulletin, no estimate of the value of payments in kind, of food or lodging provided in addition to money-wages, has been included in the figures set forth. There results, of necessity, an unfavourable comparison between different groups of occupations, possibly also between different provinces. Thus the earnings of the average male employee in manufactures are $403 yearly, in agriculture $207. The contrast between the economic situation of employees in these two great branches of industry is probably a good deal less than these figures imply. Similarly, the average female in domestic or personal service is stated to have earned $137, while in manufactures the average female earnings are given as $193, and, in the trade and transportation group, $238. How the comparison between domestic service and factory or office work would stand were an estimate of the value of board and lodging supplied to be included with earnings, we are at liberty to form our own opinion. It is easy to understand that the matter presents difficulties too great to be readily overcome.

But what is worthy of remark is that neither of the points here selected for comment is referred to in the introductory memorandum, though the low average of female servants' earnings is pointed out, and space is given to tables and remarks on the comparative earnings and working-time in the different groups of industries. Space is found, too, for comment on the way in which the results illustrate the subjects of division of labour and the competition of the sexes in industry. As to these comments, the number of occupations scheduled depends to a considerable extent on the taste of the maker of the schedules. On the first four pages of the detailed list of occupations, of about 130 classes of occupations listed, some 50 were followed by numbers expressed in units, and 36 of these had not more than three persons scheduled as employed in them. In this respect, the pages in question are not by any means exceptional. The exact value of the statement that: "Altogether there

are in the Dominion 1,621 kinds of occupations affording employment to wage-earners at their own trade or occupation, 1,494 of
which give employment to males and 487 to females," is, to say the
least, problematical. The 1,256 occupations of the manufacturing
class and the 23 of the agricultural class present a contrast, indeed,
but its force might be modified if a revision of the lists of occupations were made, though it is by no means impossible that the
contrast might be made more striking yet. The division of persons
employed in various mechanical industries into employees, apprentices, foremen, managers, superintendents, hardly seems to correspond
to that separation of tasks at which the use of the results would
suggest that the compiler·aimed. It makes, moreover, the same
number of occupations in industries where the principle of the
division of labour is applied in widely different degrees. This
point would not have provoked comment here, but for the remarks
of the introductory memorandum.

Attention is directed in this introduction to the low level of
remuneration secured by teachers in the eastern provinces of the
Dominion. The average for female teachers is four times as great
in British Columbia as in Quebec, while for male teachers it is but
50 per cent. higher. The fact that the ratio of female to male
teachers is nearly four times as great in Quebec as in the Pacific
province may be noted as not unrelated to these figures of earnings.

There are some points where the figures supplied are difficult to
accept without protest. Thus, the foreman of dyers, cleaners and
scourers in a cotton factory who is credited with a salary of $8,000
must be the result of a mistake in copying, just as the 14 firemen
apprentices whose average earnings of $20·28 result from an
aggregate earnings of $2,818 are clearly the subjects of an error,
not the only one of its kind we have noticed. How far the general
results may have been subjected to adequate checking, so as to be
unaffected by errors such as are here observed in small details, we
have no means of knowing, but trust we may assume that due
attention has been devoted to so important a matter.

The completeness and accuracy of one portion of the data, or
the representative character of that part which is complete, may be
doubted. It is that relating to professors, of whom 122 are recorded,
while 82 of them supply fuller details. The average earnings of
these 82 are returned at $674·46, or a trifle less than the average
of the males in the professional class, some $63 less than the
average of the four authors and literary men working for hire,
only $37 more than the average municipal clerk, and $171·45 less
than the remuneration of the average Government clerk. The
average journalist is credited with $798·38, while even the average
lithographer is reported to earn $672·93. Can it be that the 40
professors whose earnings are not reported include all those earning
over (say) $1,000 per annum, or is the list of professors curiously
deficient? The leading universities of Canada could account for
the number of professors scheduled, and, though the inadequacy of
professorial salaries has formed the subject of no little discussion
recently, an average of $675 per annum is very far below the worst

figures adduced. Even allowing for the cases of medical or legal professors receiving a merely nominal emolument from their universities, the figure is incredible. What is a professor in the view of this bulletin? It is certainly not going too far to assert that the earnings stated are not representative of the class. And if this be so, in how many other of the occupations do the figures supplied fail to be representative? While the motto, *ex pede Herculem*, may not be proper to apply in judging of the tables before us, some hesitation in accepting all they present cannot but be suggested by the occurrence of such figures as those cited.

As is pointed out in the introductory memorandum, the figures of this bulletin relating to employees in manufactures cannot be directly compared with those which were given in the second volume of the Census Report. These latter excluded records of all employees in works where less than five hands were employed, while the new bulletin refers to all wage-earners over 15 years of age, but excludes owners, piece-workers, and children, who were included in the Census Report. Omitting these latter from the census record, there remain 241,976 males, with an average wage of $365, as against 226,001, with an average wage of $403, in the present enumeration. For females, the older report similarly dealt with 63,371 with an average wage of $180, as against 49,662 with an average wage of $193 recorded in the bulletin before us. The schedules which have served as basis for this bulletin are thus, as is pointed out, less comprehensive than those used in the earlier report, and appear to present a larger proportion of the better-paid workers in manufacturing establishments.

One other feature of importance in the bulletin is a record of extra earnings secured by about 20,000 individuals outside their regular employment. If the earners of these extras secured, in their regular work, as much as the average wage-earner of the same sex, the supplement afforded by their outside work was important, fully 30 per cent. for males and over one-third for females (of whom but 952 are recorded as securing extra earnings). In relation to the aggregate of regular earnings, on the other hand, the extra earnings are almost insignificant, being less than 1 per cent. of their amount. A.W.F.

6.—*Album graphique de la Statistique générale de la France.* viii + 280 pp., 4to. Paris: Imprimerie Nationale, 1907.

The purpose of this volume, which consists almost entirely of shaded maps and diagrams, is to popularise the results of the Census of 1901 and of the contents of the Statistical Annual. The idea is admirably carried out, and it is possible by turning through these pages to see at a glance the main tendencies of French statistical history, and to pick out those problems which call for further study. To review the volume completely would be to review the whole body of the statistics of France; we can only notice a few points. The centre of gravity of the population has only moved 13 miles (N.N.E.) in a century—a very striking contrast to that of the U.S.A., for example. Since 1851 the age distribution has changed considerably, an excess of persons over 55 years conterbalancing a defect under 20; the maps showing the birth, marriage, and death rates, and the falling excess of births over deaths throw light on this. The trend of the population towards Paris is shown depart-ment by department for several occupations. Other maps show the distribution of foreign visitors, the location of each of the important industries, the massing of the army at the frontiers, the condition as to marriage of the various districts—in fact, almost everything that can be put in statistical form. The plan generally adopted is that of black and white hatchetting, the darker the shading the more pronounced the phenomenon in question. There are two important criticisms to be made on this method. First, the scale of shading is quite arbitrary; it differs from map to map, and the intervals are irregular: *e.g.*, for "veuves pour 10,000 françaises mariées" the shading changes at 431, 555, 680, and 870. Any user of Bartholomew's half-inch coloured contour maps will realize how confusing this makes the optical impression. No explanation is given of the principles by which these limits are determined. Secondly, the choice of the department as unit necessarily causes each department to appear homogeneous. Thus, to open the book at random, all the inhabitants of "Rhone" appear to be addicted to photography, because Lyon is included; this cannot be avoided without using a more elaborate and detailed method, but is a permanent weakness of shaded and coloured maps. An alternative method of placing small blocks of colour, proportional to the numbers occupied in each district, is used in some cases here with advantage. There is less obvious use in another large class of diagrams, in which the horizontal scale represents some phenomenon (*e.g.*, the amount of education), but the vertical scale represents nothing, occupations or districts being in arbitrary juxtaposition; a table of numbers is just as informing. A graver fault is the presence of many diagrams in which space is saved at the expense of the zero line, for in these cases the eye cannot judge the importance of the fluctuations without a troublesome reference to the numerical scale. It is much to be wished that the wealth of statistics which is collected annually in the United Kingdom should be presented in an accessible, attractive form, with as much ingenuity, clearness, and skill as in the example before us. A.L.B.

7.—*Statistisches Handbuch fur das Deutsche Reich.* Herausgegeben vom kaiserlichen Statistischen Amt. Teil 1. xii + 749 pp., 8vo. Berlin: Carl Heymann, 1907.

This volume is an important addition to the publications of the German Statistical Office. Each volume of the *Statistische Jahrbuch fur das Deutsche Reich*, published since 1880, can neces-sarily only cover a short period of years, and hence, for investigations of a historical character, it is necessary to refer to early issues—with the natural result that many have gone out of print. The *Handbuch* is intended to supplement the *Jahrbuch* by providing a convenient work of reference giving series of data from, as far as possible, the commencement of their collection, the arrangement being that of the *Jahrbuch.* The present "first part" covers everything except foreign trade, which will be included in a second part to be issued very shortly. Some of the tables would be the better for more explanatory footnotes; *e.g.*, in Table 17 certain population figures are given in two styles of type, but the meaning of these two styles is not explained.   G.U.Y.

8.—*Uebersichten aus der Berliner Statistik für das Jahr* 1905. Herausgegeben vom Stat. Amt der Stadt Berlin. 62 pp. Berlin : P. Stankiewicz, 1907.

This tiny pamphlet contains statistical tables abstracted from the *Statistical Yearbook* of Berlin. It is convenient, inexpensive and portable; but the professed statistician will probably require to refer to the original for explanation as to the meaning of many of the figures. Although issued in 1907, the data are only carried to 1905.   G.U.Y.

9.—*Modern Social Conditions. A Statistical Study of Birth, Marriage, Divorce, Death, Disease, Suicide, Immigration, &c., with Special Reference to the United States.* By Wm. B. Bailey, Assistant-Professor of Political Economy in Yale University. Size 9 in. × 6 in., 377 pp. New York: The Century Company, 1906.

The sub-title is more expressive of the character of this book than its chief title. It is, in fact, a guide to vital statistics, the first 66 pages of which are concerned with methods, and the rest with results. It is intended to meet the need of American students who are interested in the demography of their country, and there can be no doubt that for a limited time it will be valuable as a book of reference for those desiring information upon the topics enumerated above.

The first chapter deals briefly with the history of statistics. Schlözer's witty, but now scarcely sufficient, definition : "History is statistics in motion; statistics, history at rest," is quoted, but no definite reference is given. The definition occurs in Schlözer's note to Section 5 of Achenwall's "Statsverfassung," 6th ed., 1781 : "Statskunde ist eine stillstehende Statsgeschichte : so wie diese eine fortlaufende Statskunde." In his posthumously published "Theorie" (1804) Schlözer repeats the definition but recognises the existence of historical statistics : "Geschichte ist eine fortlaufende Statistik, und Statistik ist eine stillstehende Geschichte. Nun so lasse man sie stille stehen, wo man will und so lange man will. Warum nicht auch Statistiken der Vergangenheit ?" (p. 86 : cited from Lueder's "Geschichte," p. 99). The scope of questions embraced for discussion, which is all too brief, comprises a paragragh on statistics and freedom of the will. The view taken by the author is summed up in the dictum : "This regularity in the moral acts of man is not the result of blind fate which we are forced to obey, but of causes which can not only be determined but modified." A sound view is taken as to the desirability of limiting census questions, and especially of not asking questions which arouse suspicion in the subject. The importance of exact instructions is illustrated by Dr. Jacques Bertillon's story of the census in France, in which an attempt was made to classify houses according to the number of stories. One person wrote to ask whether a building which in one portion had five stories and in another four, should be included among those with nine stories?

The discussion of methods is not sufficiently detailed to obviate the necessity of consulting other works. Nor is any attempt made to illustrate and warn against the chief fallacies with which the history of even current vital statistics is strewn. The second part, dealing with results, is much more satisfactory, though here again it is unfortunate that, in a book having the year 1906 on its title page, the latest report of the English Registrar-General of Births and Deaths, which is quoted, is that for 1900 on p. 150, and that for 1901 on p. 295. Similarly, on p. 320, Dr. Hope is described as still Assistant Medical Officer of Health of Liverpool. Evidently the author has had very incomplete access to English data. Notwithstanding this fact, the chapters dealing with births, marriages, and deaths are full of interesting information derived from many countries. It is particularly useful also, to have the chief items of the bulky American census reports in this much more easily accessible form; and we have no doubt that the book will prove very useful for handy reference. We trust also that it may help in stimulating our American cousins to more complete and accurate registration of births and deaths than they have hitherto secured outside certain specially-favoured areas.   A.N.

10.—*Heredity and Selection in Sociology.* By George Chatterton-Hill. xxxii + 571 pp., 8vo. London: Adam and Charles Black, 1907. Price 12*s.* 6*d.* net.

This volume consists of three parts, Part I being an introduction on biology or "the theory of descent," Part II on "social pathology"—suicide and insanity, syphilis as a social factor, conflict and progress, and so forth—and Part III on "the actual conditions of social selection." The main argument of the book is in the last part, the conclusion being reached that religion is of vital importance in evolution as a factor of "social integration," *i.e.,* as making the individual feel that he is truly a member of the social body. The view differs from that of Mr. Benjamin Kidd, who regarded religion only as giving an "ultra-rational sanction" for the subordination of the interests of the individual to those of the society. Liberalism, it is argued, is bankrupt; socialism, "in so far as it aims at reducing the amount and intensity of conflict in the world," "infringes the primordial law of progress" and "diminishes the value of life"; and "science" will not serve as the force essential to the cohesion of the social organism, as it has no absolute sanction.

There are many points that might be traversed in the reasoning of Part III. Much of the familiar argument against socialism, for instance, was answered over ten years since by Professor Pearson in his article on "Socialism and Natural Selection" (*Fortnightly Review,* 1894; reprinted in "The Chances of Death," 1897). But Parts I and II occupy some three-quarters of the volume, and the character of these alone renders it impossible, we fear, to commend the author on his work. The first part, as we have said, is purely biological; but, unfortunately, the author appears to be quite unaware of much of the most important work of recent years in connection with heredity. To discuss the mechanism of heredity, to give a chapter on hybridisation, to describe in detail Weismann's ideal hierarchy of "ids," "determinants," and "biophors," without mentioning the name of Mendel or the work of his successors is, at the present day, misleading as to the state of knowledge. The work of Galton and Pearson is not so purely biological, but much of it is of the first importance from the sociological standpoint—*e.g.*, the work of the latter on reproductive selection—and both are completely ignored. We find the name of Galton mentioned once, it is true, in the text (P. 100), but neither name finds a place in the index. The statistician will hardly be more satisfied with the first chapters of Part II. In discussing the increase of suicide, figures are given for absolute numbers without any reference to the rates on the population, or the increase in population, during the period (pp. 185-6). The same thing is done in the case of insanity (P. 267 *et seq.*), and figures (absolute figures) for *three* successive years are given as illustrating the increase (pp. 267, 270, 274), and to "permit of our judging of the constancy of its increase." Most even of these tables stop short at 1888, and, whatever they illustrate, do not illustrate present conditions. None of the causes of fallacy involved in the available data respecting insanity are mentioned; the author might do well to refer to the papers of Mr. Noel Humphreys. The same lack of avoidance of elementary fallacies is exhibited later (p. 346), when a table, comparing the figures for 1900 with those for the previous decade, 1890-99, is given to show that while the phthisis mortality of (male) children has decreased, that of men over 45 has increased —"the mortality of . . . the reproductive classes has been increased by the modern care for the child." If the writer had referred to the *Decennial Supplement*, and compared his figures by decades, he would have seen that on the average of years, the phthisis mortality of males has decreased at all age-groups. An unfamilarity with his subject is exhibited in a different way by Figs. 5 and 6, in which a "symmetrical frequency curve" is represented by a semicircle, and an "asymmetrical frequency curve" (these are the titles below the figures) by a segment of a circle greater than a semicircle! The volume raises seriously the question asked at the end of the notice of *Sociological Papers.*   G.U.Y.

11.—*Mendelism.* By R. C. Punnett. Second edition. viii + 86 pp., sm. 8vo. Cambridge: Macmillan and Bowes; London: Macmillan and Co., 1907. Price 2*s.* net.

As references to Mendelism are now so frequent in memoirs dealing with the biological aspects of sociology, we think it worth while to draw attention to this admirably simple exposition of the method and results. It will be found most useful for anyone who wishes to follow, for example, the references to the subject in the

first few papers of the volume just issued by the Sociological
Society. The little volume has reached its second edition within
two years, and has been brought up to date.   G.U.Y.

12.—*Studien zur Bevolkerungsbewegung in Deutschland.* Von
Dr. Paul Mombert. 280 pp., 8vo. Karlsruhe: G. Braun, 1907.

This is a statistical study of the recent changes in the birth-rate
and in the fertility of married women in Germany. The two first
chapters deal with mortality and with marriage, in so far as a
comprehension of these factors is necessary for interpreting the
meaning or estimating the effects of changes in fertility, and the
third and fourth chapters then proceed to the question of the birth-
rate. In Germany (as in England) the birth-rate has fallen more
or less continuously since about 1876, but this fall has, in Germany,
been accompanied by a rise in the proportion of married women to
the population, a fall in the mean age at marriage, and a rise in the
proportion of persons married at the most fertile ages. The whole
of the fall in the birth-rate appears to be due to the decrease in
fertility of married women. This fall, Dr. Mombert argues, is due
to the increasing welfare of the population and the concomitant
growth of prudence and foresight, and supports his arguments by
showing (1) that the most fertile districts in the great towns of
Germany are those with the greatest proportions of overcrowded or
low-rented tenements; (2) that those towns or districts with the
highest fertility (births per 1,000 married women aged 15–45) have
the lowest proportion of savings-bank accounts per 1,000 inhabitants; (3) that in those districts where the fertility has fallen most,
the proportion of savings-bank accounts has, on the whole, risen
most. The two last chapters contain, respectively, a short note on
the excess of births over deaths, and a critique of the doctrine of
Malthus indicating that the principal factors now operating were
neglected by him.

In the case of both marriages and births, we should like to have
seen an attempt at a more complete correction for age distribution,
though we do not think that the rougher methods used are likely
to lead to any serious error. Some rather disturbing slips have
unfortunately escaped correction, *e.g.*, " Eheschliessungen " for
" Eheschliessende Personen " in some of the tables of marriage-
rates, and a displacement of the decimal point in stating some
fertility-rates (*e.g.*, pp. 123 and 124): these will, however, be
obvious to the reader. The volume is a useful contribution to the
subject.   G.U.Y.

13.—*La Mortalité infantile dans les Flanders: Étude de Démographie Belge.* Par Camille Jacquart. 156 pp., 8vo., 1 map.
Bruxelles: A. Dewit, 53, Rue Royal, 1907.

In Belgium, as in other European countries, observers have
been struck by the coincidence between a falling general death-rate
and an infant mortality which is almost stationary; and the rapid
decline in the birth-rate has made this phenomenon still more
important. M. Jacquart has undertaken a statistical study of

the excessive infant mortality in the provinces of West and East Flanders in Belgium, the fruit of which is here presented. His first point, derived from a preliminary study of infant morality in different countries, is that this mortality varies with the intellectual and moral circumstances of the family, and with the degree of the culture of its members more than with their freedom from poverty. "Le milieu familial," which is disastrous to the infant, comprises artificial feeding, prejudice and ignorance of the parents leading to defective care of the infant.

Incidentally M. Jacquart dwells on the natural selection supposed by some to be exercised by a high infant mortality, and confirms, so far as Flanders is concerned, the opposition to this view furnished by the statistics of F. Prinzing. If a high infant mortality eliminated the weakest, the death-rate at ages 1—5 associated with it ought to be lower than that in communities with a lower infant mortality. This is found not to hold good.

From his elaborate study of the different communes of Flanders, M. Jacquart finds that the infant mortality increases with the size of the towns. He then shows the distribution of infant mortality according to the age in months, and follows this with a study for the same communes of the death-rate at ages 1—5. It is not necessary to follow M. Jacquart into his detailed examination of the chief medical causes of excessive infant mortality, but his results on this score may advantageously be compared with the fuller and more complete data given in the English Registrar-General's reports.

A.N.

14.—*The Town Child.* By Reginald A. Bray, L.C.C. viii + 332 pp. 8vo. London: T. Fisher Unwin, 1907. Price 7s. 6d. net.

Somebody is reported to have recently improved the old saying that "God made the country, and man made the town," by adding that the devil made the suburbs. All three are probably hasty generalisations. The beauties of nature do not redeem the deadly dulness of the country : the aggregation of people in towns is a necessary condition of progress; and the suburbs represent in their origin some justifiable pride in achievement. Mr. Bray is eloquent upon the effect of environment, and thinks that the forces now busy at work in enlarging the towns and impoverishing the villages are injurious to both, and ought not to be permitted to continue their influence without control. If these forces are not checked, then "in the villages the few remaining inhabitants will be blind to the wide expanse of heaven and to all the visions that it sends ; while, in the town, men's eyes will indeed be open, but there will be no visions to see." This he truly regards as a "dismal consummation."

His work bears evidence of genuine earnestness, practical study, sympathetic insight, and literary skill, but he rarely supports his arguments by statistical data, and his conclusions involve debatable political questions. Hence it is not easy to discuss them in this *Journal.* His general conclusion is that the principle of individualism has failed, and that the principle of collectivism must be resorted to. Indeed, he goes so far as to write of "the wild orgy of individualism into which the nineteenth century plunged with all the reckless abandonment of desperate and insensate folly." We confess we should be sorry to see in the twentieth century a reaction tending to a " wild orgy " of socialism.

Mr. Bray justly protests against the use of an expression like " socialism " to prejudice a proposal of reform. Let us see, therefore, what are his practical suggestions. One is that "the State must exact that, if a man is employed at all, he must receive an income sufficient to keep himself and his family in health and decency." He does not tell us how that income is to be ascertained. Surely, it must vary with the number of the family, the situation of the employment, the character of the man employed, and other circumstances; or it must be a merely empirical amount, arrived at by rule of thumb. But, supposing if once fixed, must not the necessary consequence be an increase in the price of commodities essential for " health and decency," including the rent of the dwelling; and must not that increase at once automatically render the fixed income insufficient, and so on, *ad infinitum?*

The result, as it seems to us, would be an endless succession of sumptuary laws, and those have never done any good, any more than the attempts in mediæval and Tudor times to limit the size of cities, which Mr. Bray would seem to wish to renew, as if their failure were not too apparent. Besides a minimum wage, he would give us improved housing conditions, State maintenance of widows, municipal schools, municipal dinners, municipal washhouses, municipal playing fields. Some of these we have already, others would be of very doubtful use. Notwithstanding Mr. Bray's disparagement of the individualism of the nineteenth century, it at any rate availed to greatly diminish pauperism, and largely to increase the prosperity of the country.

His statistics of infantile mortality show the result, which is not in itself unsatisfactory, that it did not increase between the years 1851-60 and 1891 to 1900; but other mortality decreased, and all must admit that a good deal of infantile mortality is preventible, and that any well-considered measures to limit it would be desirable. Mr. Bray is not yet prepared with a remedy that would "go to the root of the matter," but meanwhile suggests feeding the mother, municipally providing sterilised milk, and diseminating knowledge amongst the mothers. Now it is one of his principles, and a sound one, that what is provided for one should be provided for all; and the picture drawn in Huddersfield of visitation by ladies on the mothers of newly-born children, for the purpose of giving "suitable advice," strikes us as inappropriate to the general condition of such mothers, and as likely to be a feverish sort of proceeding. We doubt if it has yet been established that the sterilisation of milk is a safe process.

We agree with Mr. Bray's suggestions for an anthropometric survey, and for the organisation of voluntary workers.

His chapter on "The Child and the School" is eloquent and interesting, and as we read it we can almost forgive him the extravagance of some of the proposals it contains. We agree with him when he urges the formation of habits, the creation of interests, and the stimulation of imagination as the essential purposes of education; and when he says that "a child, who leaves school bearing in his satchel a goodly store of serviceable habits, bids fair to become an efficient member of society. If, in addition, he possess a many-sided interest and a strongly-developed faculty of imagination, he carries with him a magic wand, potent to transform the world by his experience." These define the sphere where the influence of the school is most beneficent.

The chapters on "The State and Religion" and "The Child and Religion" cannot be discussed here.   E.B.

15.—*The Housing Problem in England*, 1907.   By E. R. Dewsnup. 328 pp., 8vo.   Manchester: University Press, 1907.

The first of these works is the honest attempt of an onlooker to take a general view of the housing question in England; but it undoubtedly suffers from the author's lack of practical acquaintance with the conditions treated of.   Many valuable statistics of density of population and overcrowding have been disinterred from the census reports and brought into useful focus in Part I of this volume.   The marked decrease of overcrowding between 1891 and 1901—both in amount and as a proportion—is clearly brought out, but the very important bearing upon housing problems of the great movements of population, and of facilities for cheap and rapid travelling, has been almost disregarded, the subject of transit being disposed of in barely two pages.   Part II contains an account of English legislation on the subject, and of some of its results.   In this connection much is sometimes made of legislative provisions which have been found exceptionally difficult to apply in practice, such as the obstructive buildings clause, under which the owner of the property benefited by the demolition is made liable to contribute towards the cost.   This is notoriously a dead letter.   On the other hand, one of the most important points of the Act of 1903—the increased stringency of the limitation on compulsory displacements—is dismissed in a sentence, as if it were of small importance.   That Act made the displacement of thirty *persons* the test of the obligation to rehouse, whereas previously promoters had only to acquire less than twenty *houses* occupied by persons of the working class *in each parish* in order to escape that obligation altogether.   Thus astute promoters could, by spreading their displacements over a sufficient number of parishes, remove the dwellings of dozens, if not hundreds, of families without being compelled to make any provision for their rehousing.   These points are typical of the method of this work, and they naturally deprive it of any claim to be regarded as a practical text-book, although much conscientious research has evidently gone to its preparation.   The author's discussions of policy, in Part III, lead him to the conclusions that our existing powers to prevent the extension of improper housing conditions are not inadequate; that municipal building is undesirable save under exceptional conditions; and that rating reform is not likely to play any important part in the solution of housing difficulties.   E.J.H.

16.—*Housing*, 1907.   By P. Alden and E. E. Hayward.   Social Service Series.   2nd edition.   176 pp., 12mo.   London : Headley, 1907.   1s. net.

Messrs. Alden and Hayward, in what they modestly call "an introduction to the study of the problem," have not attempted to cover a wide field of statistics or to produce large total results. Their method is to quote individual facts in illustration of their arguments, so that the statistical student will need sundry blue books—particularly the census returns—in order to carry the inquiry forward.   The book is written from the practical point of view, and does not greatly concern itself with past legislation, but it contains a clear and succinct account of existing powers and a useful little summary of the recommendations of last year's Select Committee on the rural side of the question.   Appreciating the cardinal point that the first difficulty is financial, it devotes attention to the standard of rent.   Perhaps the most interesting chapter is that entitled "the Land Question and Taxation Reform," in which is shown the effect upon rents of the transfer of local taxation from land and buildings to land alone.   The importance of this branch of the subject is becoming more and more widely recognised, and further space might with advantage have been given to its exposition.   The dearth of houses has never been any serious difficulty. The root of the evil is, and has always been, the inability of the very poor to pay rents which shall yield a fair commercial return upon the accommodation they need in the interests of health and decency. Let this inability be removed and there will be an immediate competition among the house-builders to supply the demand thereby rendered effective.   If, therefore, as its advocates contend, the rating of land values will tend to reduce house rent and increase the opportunities of employment, nothing could be more efficacious as a remedy.   For it would thus, at one and the same time, increase the earnings and reduce the necessary expenditure of the poorer classes.   In other words, it would increase the ability to pay rent, while reducing the standard by which rent is estimated.

Another useful section of the inquiry is that as to the comparative suitability of different types of buildings.   Common lodging houses, family homes, block dwellings, tenement houses, cottage flats and single cottages are studied from all points of view, especially the financial.   A strong opinion is expressed against block dwellings, and this fact may be taken as a good indication of the progress made in the course of the last twenty-five years.   In 1880 "Peabody Buildings"—the typical block dwellings—were regarded as a wonderful advance upon the then existing conditions. Now we see them condemned (and on sanitary grounds mainly) by the advocates of healthy dwellings for the people.

The system of administration is also shown to have a material bearing upon the success or failure of housing schemes, the example of Miss Octavia Hill being warmly commended.   The question of transit forms the subject of a separate chapter, as also does the garden city movement.   In considering the province of private enterprise, it is to be regretted that neither Messrs. Alden and

Hayward nor Professor Dewsnup appear to have had access to the returns (published annually since 1900 by the London County Council) of the new working class accommodation provided in the County of London and the adjacent districts, showing the comparatively small part borne by public authorities, notwithstanding their recent activity, in the provision of house accommodation.   E.J.H.

17.—*Le Surpeuplement et les Habitations à Bon Marché,* 1907. Par H. Turot et H. Bellamy.   258 pp., 8vo.   Paris : Félix Alcan, 1907.

The chief interest of MM. Turot and Bellamy's work on overcrowding and cheap dwellings in France lies in the evidence it affords that, in this important branch of social reform, England is far ahead of her friend and neighbour south of the Channel.   It appears that overcrowding in Paris was greater in 1901 than 1891, notwithstanding an improvement which has been in progress since 1896.   The authors practically give up the idea of suburban dwellings for town workers on account of the cost of transit, and direct their energies mainly to advocating the removal of insanitary conditions, the abatement of overcrowding, and the provision of dwellings by public authorities.   They give a lucid account of French legislation on the question, and add for comparison short statements of the legislation of England, Germany, Italy, and Belgium.   Among the inducements offered to private enterprise by French authorities are the exemption of workmen's dwellings from certain items of taxation for a period of twelve years ; and societies formed to provide such dwellings are given special additional concessions, including borrowing facilities on very reasonable terms. The results achieved are not, however, considered satisfactory. Recently the Municipal Council of Paris has appointed a Special Commission to deal with the matter, and Lord Rothschild has given 400,000*l.* for the building of dwellings.   Parisian reformers, it may be noted, appear to share Messrs. Alden and Hayward's objections to block dwellings.   The book contains valuable overcrowding statistics, compiled by M. Bertillon.   E.J.H.

18.—*Le Socialisme Municipal en Angleterre et ses Resultats financiers.*   Par Raymond Boverat, docteur en droit, diplômé del' Ecole des Sciences politiques, Avocat à la Cour d'Appel.   687 pp., 8vo.   Paris : Arthur Rousseau, 1907.

Dr. Boverat adds to the qualifications set forth on his title page the hereditary interest that he is the grandson of the late M. Ernest Brelay, whose intimate acquaintance and genuine sympathy with English economic movements were well known.   A work of 687 pages on a question of English finance is in itself a testimony to the indefatigable industry of the author.   He opens his historical summary of municipal undertakings with a kind of apology for his title.   He holds that the French expression " municipal socialism" and the English "municipal trading" mean the same thing, but are neither of them adequate to express the whole meaning ; the one omitting to denote its industrial and commercial element, the other its social signification.

It is mainly to their financial bearing that the author devotes his study of the question of municipal undertakings, but he precedes it with a statement of the socialist or collectivist arguments by which they have been supported, and a brief discussion of the machinery of local government in England. Among the causes that have indirectly contributed to facilitate in England the development of municipal enterprise, he includes the tendency now shown to the unification and fusion of great industries, leading to monopoly, monopoly to abuse, abuse to control, and control to municipalisation. The last step is one easily taken, and M. Boverat's opinion is that it has often been taken without due consideration, and that the control of private monopolies would have been preferable. It is more likely, we think, that we have here an instance of the deception that lies in generalisations, and that no sound conclusion can be reached without inquiry into the circumstances of each case.

With regard to municipal waterworks, which M. Boverat admits to be a public service *par excellence*, and one of the most simple to manage, since it does not require any special commercial qualities, he yet thinks the results unsatisfactory, the supply being allowed to become manifestly insufficient before steps were taken to increase it, those steps having been unduly costly, and the tariff of rates insufficient to cover the expenses. Whether things would have been better under the administration of the water companies does not appear.

With regard to municipal gasworks, the author admits that some towns have made reasonable profits, but thinks that this of itself is not sufficient evidence that gasworks in general should be municipalised. The profits to be derived from the manufacture of gas are not as great as they have been in the past, and we do not know what the future of that illuminant will be. Hence, he holds, municipal gasworks should be avoided as speculative. Electricity, he thinks, would have paid better in private hands, but he gives his approval to the undertaking of a " refuse destructor."

On the subject of tramways, he makes the very excellence and cheapness of the service a ground of complaint, and urges that the municipality ought to have the same regard to financial considerations of capital expenditure and . profit margin that a private company would have. The existing policy, he says, can only be justified where public health, order, or morality are concerned, and not in a mere matter of locomotion.

The subject of workmen's dwellings is undoubtedly one that concerns these grave considerations, and here the course of events has forced the hands of the municipalities. M. Boverat has a good word for the municipal lodging houses, as having established interesting models, and furnished an example for private speculators.

Baths and washhouses, markets and abattoirs, cemeteries and the like, have so long been treated as municipal undertakings, that they offer no ground for special criticism.

The second part of the book is devoted to the relations of the municipal authorities in England with their workmen and other employees —their wages and hours of work, their right of voting, the establishment of a works department, and the formation of labour bureaus. To all these, M. Boverat sees grave economic objections.

The third part of the book is devoted to local finance—the great increase of local expenditure, local taxation, and local indebtedness, and the portion of that increase which is recovered by means of reproductive enterprise ; the system upon which money is borrowed, the sinking funds, the depreciation of capital, the audit of municipal accounts, the effect of local taxation upon industry, the weakening of the spirit of enterprise consequent upon municipal undertakings, the aggrandisement of the functions of the municipalities, its effect on the qualifications of the councillors, and its tendency towards a bureaucratic system, and the question of profit and loss. On all these, M. Boverat has much to say. The summary of his complaint against municipal socialism is :—

1. That the local expenses increase much faster than the rateable property.

2. That the local debt also increases much faster than the value of that property.

3. That the municipalities have to deal with the most difficult problems of labour.

4. That they conduct their enterprises profitably only when they possess a monopoly, and then in hardly any case except that of gasworks, where their profits are but small ; that their accounts are badly kept.

5. That municipal trading hinders and opposes the progress of private enterprise.

6. That it is alike imprudent and unjust to give the right to vote to persons who pay no rates and to deprive of it those who pay the larger portion.

He suggests as a programme of reform : 1. To hinder as much as possible the creation of new municipal enterprises. 2. To diminish the inconveniences inherent to their operation when they have been erected. 3. To arrange that the management of monopolies entrusted to private concerns shall answer the needs of the public in the future better than they now do.

It is in the third head of this programme that its weakness lies. If the sins of the municipalities have been great, those of the private monopolists have been greater. The power granted to them to interfere with the roads has been abused. There is no principle of individualism which requires us to allow irresponsible persons to deprive us of the benefit of property created for the use of all.

E.B.

19.—*The Dangers of Municipal Trading.* By Robert P. Porter. 320 pp., 8vo. London : George Routledge and Sons, 1907. Price 2*s.* 6*d.*

In the view of the author of this volume, the most important of the dangers which threaten to result from the expansion of the field of municipal enterprise would appear to be the aid and stimulus afforded to the spread of socialist doctrine and aspirations. The tone of Mr. Porter's book certainly supports the opinion that this, even more than the direct evils of municipal trading, inspired him in his presentation of a case whose strength must be admitted. The startling growth of municipal debts in Great Britain in recent times is a but too familiar fact, and the need for careful analysis of the accounts of municipal undertakings cannot be too much emphasized. The tendency of public representative bodies to over-burden themselves with the care of numerous enterprises, for conducting which they have often too little capacity, and the care of which hinders the performance of their more imperative public duties—these and like points have been often expounded, and to readers of this *Journal* they are familiar, so that it is sufficient to say that the book before us passes them in review, and once again insists on their fundamental importance. The volume is, in the main, a reprint of a book issued at the beginning of the year in New York, and the writer is largely concerned to combat the tendency which exists to argue from the success of municipal undertakings in Britain to the desirability of establishing like enterprises in American cities. He challenges the proofs of the alleged success in Britain, and further very properly urges that, were the success here demonstrated, the case for imitation would be very far from established, in view of the very great differences in conditions, especially political conditions, on the two sides of the Atlantic.

The branches of municipal enterprise particularly selected, as illustrations of failure, are tramways, electric supply, telephones, and housing, to each of which a separate chapter is devoted. Without entering into the discussion of the details presented, we may refer to the general principle, enunciated elsewhere in the volume, that Government control of such undertakings, conducted by joint-stock enterprise, is preferable in the public interest to Government operation. Our author seems somewhat optimistic as to the efficiency of such control by local governments. On both sides of the Atlantic a strong point in favour of public ownership has been the tendency of powerful public-service corporations to defy reasonable control in the interests of the general public which they serve. "The duty of private traders," says our author, "if they are to succeed in calling a halt to the advance of the municipalities in both countries, is clear. They must once and for all nail to the counter the lie that they extort unfair profits out of the public, and also fail to perform good service." This is sound doctrine, if it be not too late to drive it home. Were what is here called a lie actually, in general, an obvious untruth, not a few who are to-day discriminating supporters of extended municipal activities would be found advocating reliance on wisely conducted and reasonably controlled private enterprise.

In his eagerness to make a case, Mr. Porter has permitted himself to be somewhat less critical of certain statistical details of his proofs than might have been expected from a statistician of his experience. Thus (pp. 114 and 115), when the aggregate outstanding local debt of the United Kingdom, and its growth, are under discussion, the figures cited for 1890 are not those of the United Kingdom, but those of England and Wales, the growth to later dates being thus exaggerated. In assigning the increasing burden of local rates to the growth of indebtedness on so-called reproductive works, it is at least worthy of mention that debt incurred for other purposes is not negligible in comparison. Thus, of 195 millions sterling increase in outstanding local loans in England and Wales between 1890 and 1904, over 100 millions were on account of other than reproductive works, and a further 28 millions on account of waterworks, the conduct of which is admitted as not a part of the disputed functions of local authorities. The need for so great outlay on the more necessary work of local government might serve as an argument against straining the credit of the authorities on behalf of less vital undertakings, for which, moreover, commercial considerations might be trusted to provide. The complaint that the voting power is in the hands of those who pay no taxes, at least directly, and thus do not feel the pressure of heightened rates, is hardly consistent with the reference to the data of Mr. Charles Booth, cited to show that 80 per cent. of London's inhabitants below the middle class are the greatest sufferers from increase of local taxation. Allegations of improper increases of assessments as a means of increasing the yield of rates do not receive much support from an analysis of figures cited in this connection. Thus, if we accept the accuracy of the table quoted on p. 122 from Mr. Holt Schooling's article in the *Fortnightly Review* for August of last year, the average valuation per head in 1890 was about 5*l.* 6*s.* 6*d.*, and the increase to 1902 was but 6¼*d.*, or about 2½ per cent. In a community of growing wealth this hardly justifies anathemas of local authorities in general, on the ground of hiding growing levies by inflating the basis of the levy. Are the figures of the table in error, or is the condemnation lacking in discrimination?

One other point only can be noticed in the space at our disposal. It is the habit of the author, in common with others sharing his views, to refer to increased municipal debt as if it represented a net increase of liability. Only if the enterprises condemned were so lacking in reproductive capacity that they failed to provide any surplus over the cost of operation and depreciation charges would this be the case. If they fail to provide out of their revenue for the entire interest charge due to them, they are *to that extent* a net burden. One awful example is cited in the case of London. In the year 1904-05, of the total charge for interest and repayment on the net debt, "74 per cent. was met out of the taxes, and the balance, 26 per cent., from the 'earnings!' of revenue-producing services." Two pages later we find that, of the London County Council's net debt in 1906, some 15 per cent. "was remunerative or 'reproductive.'" It is not stated what part of the net debt of London is represented by the net debt of the London County Council, but the figures supplied are quite consistent with the view that if the revenue-producing services supplied the funds for 26 per cent. of the debt charge of London, they were no very great burden on the rates. Incidentally, it may be mentioned that the figures for the end of the year 1904-05 and the end of 1905-06 are not clearly distinguished. Further, we fail to be startled at the statement that London's debt is one-fifth of that of local authorities throughout the United Kingdom. In view of the proportion of London's population to that of the entire Kingdom, this proportion is not so surprising as our author appears to regard it, especially as the recent large outlay in acquiring water-works is included in the figures of the London debt.

In the preceding remarks we have endeavoured to treat Mr. Porter's book, not from a partisan standpoint, but from that of impartial criticism. We hold no brief for municipal traders, being, indeed, far more in sympathy with Mr. Porter than with the movement he attacks. We have endeavoured to apply the same standard of criticism to his book that we might apply to one written in defence of the views of which he desires to prove the unsoundness.

There are included in the volume three chapters to which attention should be called. They illustrate the view that the volume is one on the dangers of municipal socialism, with the emphasis on the " socialism " rather than on the municipal, a view presented earlier in this notice. These chapters are, the first, entitled " The Destruction of Individuality," dealing with Russian state enterprise ; the second on the Australian socialistic public works policy ; the third on Nationalisation of Railways. Only as illustrations of the same general principles as those which support the conclusion that municipal trading is full of dangers, can they be regarded as in place in a volume whose title implies that it is concerned with " municipal" as opposed to " state " enterprises. We fail, further, to appreciate the greater appropriateness of the chapter on railways in the English edition than in the American edition, in which it did not appear. All three chapters are interesting, but we abstain from further comment here, contenting ourselves with directing our readers' attention to their presence and importance. A.W.F.

20.—*Political Economy.* By Charles S. Devas. Third Edition. xxii + 672 + xxiv pp., crown 8vo. London : Longmans, Green and Co., 1907. Price 7*s.* 6*d.*

The publication of a third edition of this book has a melancholy interest ; for it was severed by only a brief interval from the death of its accomplished author. He had indeed, as he remarks in a new Preface, the satisfaction of knowing that with regard to some of the matters on which, in earlier editions, he had enunciated views opposed to those more commonly accepted by the prominent authoritative economic teaching of the time, public opinion had moved since in the direction of his "unorthodox" declarations, and this movement had even been reflected in professional circles. But his death was a serious loss to economic study ; for, as every chapter of this fresh edition shows, he had kept himself abreast of the latest developments of economic inquiry on all or most of its different sides ; and he never failed to form an independent judgment of his own, for which he was able to adduce grave reasons, on the precise value of the individual contributions made by various writers to the common advancement of economic knowledge.

This treatise belongs, it is true, to a special series known as the Stonyhurst Philosophical Series; and observant critics will. find traces of the influence of the religious faith which Mr. Devas held upon particular opinions stated in his exposition of economic principles. His views on the question of population, for example, are probably correct; and he would not shrink from testing them by fact; but the peculiar emphasis with which he explains those views accords with the common teaching of the official repre- sentatives of the Roman Catholic Church. His justification, again, of the medieval condemnation of usury testifies to the breadth and accuracy of his historical study, but it may also be considered to be partly influenced by a natural tenderness felt by him in approaching Canonist doctrine on that subject. His power- ful claim, lastly, for the recognition of the ethical side of economics is by no means destitute of support on other grounds; but it may be treated, not unjustly, as a characteristic outcome of his religious ardour. In any event, it is well that a treatise written under these auspices should be accessible to economic students.

But, apart from its particular origin, it demands on its merits alone a high position among systematic expositions of economic principles. In his general scheme, Mr. Devas has followed the main lines of traditional treatment, firstly, discussing production (and consumption); secondly, dealing with exchange; thirdly, handling distribution; and fourthly and finally, public finance. In the details, however, of this discussion he maintains throughout an independent attitude. He does not subscribe wholly to the teaching of the older writers, but makes considerable departures from their views. On the fiscal question, for example, he is no "convinced Free Frader"; and he extends the law of diminishing returns to manufacturing industry, and limits its application to agriculture. Yet on the other hand he does not adopt, without reserve, the more modern developments of the newer writers; and his criticisms in this connection are both numerous and pertinent. In fact it would, we believe, be difficult to find a greater abundance of suggestive commentary than is compressed within the limits of this book. On nearly every page, in the matter printed in smaller type, which is intended for the serious student as contrasted with the ordinary reader, there are plentiful stores of nutritious thought. Experienced teachers will, we are sure, rise from the perusal of this new edition with a renewed sense of their indebtedness to its acute and learned author; and they will share the deep regret we feel at the great loss occasioned to economic study by his decease.   L.L.P.

21.—*La Science Économique.* Par Yves Guyot. Troisième Édition. xi + 331 pp., crown 8vo. Paris: Schleicher Freres 1907.

M. Guyot tells us in the interesting and characteristic Preface to this new issue of his treatise that some years have passed since the second edition was exhausted, and that the book has been submitted to complete revision before its publication in its present form. Among the more important changes made we imagine that the incorporation in the chapter on interest of the conclusions reached by Dr. Böhm Bawerk should be reckoned ; but many improvements of detail have probably recommended themselves to an experienced pen, and add to the permanent value of an attractive work. M. Guyot's command of vivid writing has long been familiar to many readers in countries other than his own. The place given to statistical matter in this systematic exposition of economic science should be welcome to members of the Royal Statistical Society who will not be likely to consider inappropriate the attention thus bestowed by a distinguished statist, who is proud of being a Guy Medallist ; and the ease, directness and lucidity which characterise the treatment of the whole subject will enlist the favour of the general public which might be repelled by a less entertaining teacher. For M. Guyot is never tedious or obscure. He is always interesting and alive. His book is not indeed intended as a preparation for examinations, and in its arrangement of material, and in the assignment of proportions of the space to different topics, it departs from traditions commonly observed, and might perhaps be termed unsystematic. But on the other hand it reflects that close contact with living interests which has marked the busy career of its energetic author ; and it sets forth in plain definite language the very positive opinions he has formed in many an eager controversy of vital moment.

An interval of a quarter of a century, he informs us, separates this present third edition from the original appearance of the book ; and during the whole of that period he has been concerned with economic or financial questions, now as Deputy in the French Chamber, now as Minister of Public Works, now again as ordinary citizen, and lastly, as a member of important Commissions charged with inquiry into special questions. It may perhaps be doubted whether this full life, thus busied on a variety of concrete experiences, has brought any material change to the compact economic creed with which M. Guyot started on his career. But it may have led him to state on the title page of this treatise that he proposes to expound the "*inductive*" laws of Economic Science ; and the appropriation of a large section to the topic of money and prices, and other considerable portions to such subjects as population, and wages-systems, may be traced to a similar cause. And yet we think it possible that other critics besides those protectionists, bimetallists, and socialists, whom he embraces in emphatic condemnation in his final section as "les negateurs de la Science Économique," may regard him as more "orthodox" than the straitest exponents of "deductive" reasoning ; and he himself significantly describes the "inductive" laws which he explains as expressing the "*constant*" relations of economic phenomena.

Nor is he troubled by misgiving on the certainty, finality, or sufficiency of the conclusions which he reaches on debated problems. With pardonable egotism he enumerates in his Preface the successive occasions on which, as he holds, he has been shown to be right, and his opponents have been proved to be wrong, in vexed controversies; and this tone of easy confidence pervades the book. We are not sure that he is not betrayed in consequence into criticism, such, for instance, as that of the significance of index numbers, where he fails to appreciate fully the precise position of those from whom he differs. We are hardly convinced that his dogmatic statement of the necessary relations between fixed and circulating capital, for which he claims the novelty of a discovery, successfully unlocks every troublous riddle to which he would apply it. We think that his robust belief in the supreme efficacy of liberty in practice is in danger of blurring or ignoring awkward circumstances which would -arrest the attention of less convinced observers. But he has in abundant measure the qualities of his defects; and it is rare to find such power of attractive writing used on topics which can easily become repellent, or to see such dazzling illumination shed on obscure places by such vivid exposition.   L.L.P.

22.—*Économie Politique.* Par Felix Martel et M. Grigaut. 353 pp., crown 8vo. Paris : Ch. Delagrave, 1907. Price 3 frs.

This compendious manual forms a part of a series published under the direction of the Inspector-General of Public Instruction in France for use in Practical Schools of Commerce and Industry. In this particular volume M. Martel has sought the competent assistance of Professor Grigaut; and the attempt here made to present the elements of Economics in a plain attractive fashion for the benefit of students in these schools seems, so far as we can judge, to have been attended with a gratifying measure of success. In such a text-book a discussion of the nicer refinements of abstract reasoning would be out of place; but, on the other hand, we cannot see any traces of the narrow dogmatism into which, under such conditions, the adherents of a particular school of thought might easily have been betrayed.

The first section is devoted to a description of the part taken in production by the different agents—nature, labour, and capital. In the second section we pass to the consideration of the principles governing the distribution among them of their respective shares. In the third and fourth parts exchange and consumption are discussed. In simple language the outlines of the subject are presented, and at the close of several of the chapters passages are quoted from well-known writers which are calculated to awaken or intensify the interest taken by the student, while special stress is laid on the concrete embodiments of the various principles successively expounded. When the subject of consumption is reached, in the fourth section, a mention of the headings of the various chapters devoted to its treatment will suffice to show the "actuality" of the discussion. Population, emigration, and colonisation, luxury, alcoholism, saving, and insurance are handled in succession.

The subjects of the two remaining sections of the book are perhaps even more significant of the attitude of the writers and their manner of discussion. Association in the various forms of societies . of mutual aid, societies of popular credit, co-operative societies for production and consumption, and of those syndicates which are the counterparts in France of our employers' associations and workmen's trade unions, is described in detail in the fifth section, and the functions of the State form the topic of the sixth and final section. Those English students who have, with reason, been accustomed to regard the authoritative exposition of economic principles in France as unduly dominated by the orthodoxy of the straitest sect may be agreeably surprised to notice in this little book the liberality of tone with which such subjects as the "interference" of the State in industry is treated. They will be less astonished, perhaps, to read that the question of free trade and protection is considered to be difficult and complex. The discussion, we are told, is far from having ended; and an absolute general judgment cannot yet be framed. This balanced moderation is not unwelcome in this instance; and it is characteristic of the temper prevalent throughout the book. To its particular purpose, we repeat, this manual seems to have been skilfully adapted. L.L.P.

23.—*Le Salaire des Ouvriers des Mines de Charbon en France.* Contribution à la théorie économique du salaire. Par François Simiand. 520 pp., la. 8vo. Paris: Éd. Cornély et Cie., 1907. Price 10 frs.

"At a given moment the selling price of coal rises brusquely. At this moment also (*a*) the labour cost or average wage per ton rises (though relatively less); (*b*) the average production per day's work does not rise (or does not rise permanently), and even falls; (*c*) the average daily wage rises . . . For a short time after the selling price has begun to fall the labour cost per ton . . . continues to rise, and the average daily production still falls, the daily wage still rising or remaining stationary, according to the relative amplitude of these opposite variations. But these movements do not last. When the price of coal has fallen, it soon results that (*a*) the labour cost . . . falls equally (or perhaps a little less), but that, on the other hand, (*b*) the average daily production rises, and that (*c*) the daily wage rests at the same level without rising or falling, or falls less than the labour cost . . ." This (roughly translated) is the author's main thesis. He arrives at it by a careful and comprehensive study of the official French mineral statistics from 1844-1902, rejecting after analysis various alternative hypotheses, verifies it by consideration of the statistics of the separate districts, and finds an adequate explanation of all the apparent exceptions. He then proceeds to search for the causes of this recurring cycle of changes of price, production, and wage, and finds them in the natural desires of employers and workmen to avoid a fall of total profits or earnings and to minimise their efforts. Among other things, he notices that a fall of the wage rate stimulates the workman to increase his output till his former earnings are obtained, and *vice versâ*. Every point is made the subject of elaborate and systematic analysis, and, in fact, the main fault of the book is its undue length; it could have been reduced to one quarter of its size, without great loss, if the author had left a little more to the reader's intelligence. Apart from this pardonable fault of extension, we have nothing but praise for this systematic attempt to verify economic principles by an appeal to a very important group of facts. The statistical tables and graphic illustrations are well done, but in the latter we should have preferred to find the numerical scales on the face of the diagram, and not left to the explanatory legend.　　A.L.B.

24.—*The Strength of Nations: an Argument from History.* By J. W. Welsford, M.A.　x + 327 pp., crown 8vo. London: Longmans, Green and Co., 1907. Price 5s. net.

The fiscal controversy, which has engaged so large a measure of the attention of the English public during the last few years, has, among other notable effects, occasioned a close scrutiny of economic theory on the subject of dispute. The more temperate advocates on either side will probably allow that this pertinacious criticism has resulted in improvement in the expression of that theory, even if they are not ready to concede that it has wrought material change in its fundamental basis or its essential structure. It is natural that the powerful motive thus supplied for inspection and revision should extend its influence to the sphere of economic history; and impartial bystanders, if any such remain, will welcome, in the interests of complete and accurate information, those strenuous inquirers, who would investigate afresh the descriptions of past incidents, or the conceptions of the men and policies of previous times, which have been accepted hitherto in unquestioning reliance on confident authority. For we are wont to receive too readily on trust what we are not at the pains to examine for ourselves; and we often accumulate unconsciously a mass of ideas, which, we imagine, correspond to fact, though we have taken no effectual means to test their accord or disagreement. It is wholesome that this complacent acquiescence should be disturbed; and it is not inappropriate or incorrect to add that the salutary consequences of the process are often in proportion to its disregard of ceremony.

At any rate, in the book before us, Mr. Welsford does not waste his compliments on his opponents; and the suspicions of hostile critics may be excited by the vehemence of his denunciatory epithets. These are applied, not merely to the protagonist of the Anti-Corn-Law agitation, who, as an ardent controversialist, could hardly complain of receiving no milder treatment than that which he dealt habitually to his own adversaries, but also even to the respected character and time-honoured utterances of Adam Smith. We do not say that a portion of the censure thus pronounced on the author of the "Wealth of Nations," who was influenced by a strong bias in many of his views, is wrong or undeserved; and the very title of the present volume, we imagine, is designed to sound a note of bold defiance at the outset, and to set the old ideal of "power," cherished and pursued by the English statesmen of the past, in sharp and complimentary contrast with that new ideal of "plenty" which was emphasized and urged by Adam Smith. But, nevertheless, we think that the argument which Mr. Welsford draws from history might have gained in convincing force, had he omitted altogether, or modified in some degree, some at any rate of his damnatory judgments. He also, not unfrequently, intersperses in his narrative scornful observations by the way, which may tend to enliven the regular sequence of his story, and serve to rouse the lethargic reader from incipient somnolence; but they will, we have no doubt, be treated justly by unconvinced observers as signs of the appearance of the "cloven hoof." They disclose an animus which the author himself perhaps has no desire to conceal; and yet, necessarily, it must hinder the reception of his views. For, interpreted by this running commentary, his opinions are not likely to be treated by readers of an alien persuasion as the reflections of an impartial student, whose sole concern, manifestly, is to ascertain and to present the bare true significance of history.

Nor can we avoid entirely the conclusion that Mr. Welsford, like many other investigators, has been betrayed into the common error of attributing to a single cause, or set of causes, what is really due to the co-operating and conflicting influence of a variety of divers forces. For it is difficult to believe that the rise and fall of nations can be connected so exclusively with their fiscal policy as he seems to think. We are not indeed on that account prepared to deny the cogency or pertinence of his main contention that such policy may have exerted an amount of influence which had not previously been noted by historians, or perhaps suspected by the general public. It is refreshing to find economic forces (even in the special shape of those fiscal arrangements for which in our opinion Mr. Welsford tries to erect too arbitrary a separation from other influences) given an emphatic prominence; for, as he shows, until lately it had been the fashion with writers of authority to thrust them into the distant background, or to ignore them altogether.

Of the suggestiveness of this fresh examination of the course of history from the commencement of the Christian era to the present day there can, we consider, be no question. Of the combined novelty and power of the sustained argument here presented no careful candid reader of the separate chapters will, we are bold to affirm, fail to feel a genuine appreciation. Of its great importance, if it be admitted, as a controversial weapon in the present debate, it is in our opinion hardly possible to frame an exaggerated estimate. For what does Mr. Welsford endeavour to enunciate as the true lesson of past history? What he contends is that union and production furnish the only permanent basis of the "strength of nations." Trade without production, he maintains, is doomed to fail, when once the customers of a trade centre cease to be disunited. Protection is consequently the proper policy for countries to pursue in fiscal matters, if they would preserve their strength; and free trade, on the contrary, is likely to prove a mischievous illusion, viewed from a national standpoint, however amiable it may appear when regarded superficially through cosmopolitan spectacles.

The ancient method, by which Imperial Rome obtained through tribute the products of other lands for the consumption of her people, led eventually to her decline; but the system of tribute finds its modern counterpart, fraught with equal danger, in the receipt of interest drawn from the single source of foreign investment.   In the Middle Ages, Constantinople, the Italian cities, the German towns, and Holland, in turn, tried to become rich and strong through international trade.   They succeeded in each case as long as they could contrive, consciously or unconsciously, to keep their several customers apart; and Constantinople thus interposed between East and West during an Empire which lasted for more than eleven hundred years.   It was disunion which ruined Italy; and the Medici, mentioned with approbation by Cobden, were international traders, who destroyed the liberties of Florence. Holland also fell in consequence of disunion, although the Dutch acted at one time as the carriers for the whole European world.

By contrast, England steadily pursued, with success, the true ideal of a strong nation.   That consists in the "union of agricultural production, industry, commerce, and shipping, under central control." First, by protection, a monopoly of the raw material, wool, was effectively secured.   Then, by protection also, supremacy was gained in weaving, and in dressing and in dying, the manufacture, cloth. Lastly, on the basis of industrial production, by means of protection once again, commerce and shipping were permanently established. England thus triumphed over disunited European producers until the time when France became united, like herself, under the protectionist regime of Colbert.   But in the struggle which ensued the latter country failed in the end because at the suggestion of the Physiocrats she abandoned a protective policy.   And now, the free trade, adopted later by victorious England, in the fond belief of some of her statesmen that other nations would follow her example, and allow her thus to become the workshop of the world, competing to furnish her with raw material and to buy her finished goods, has, in consequence of the very different policy pursued, wisely for their own interests, by those other nations, been transformed into the dangerous and illusive substitute of free importation practised on one side alone.   A reversion, accordingly, to older methods is required by the circumstances of the times; and, in an economic union of the Empire, tropical raw material should now be linked to British industry.

Such is the thesis sketched in outline in Mr. Welsford's Preface, and in the foregoing remarks we have often quoted his own language. Such is the argument which he develops at length in the main body of his book, examining in turn the history of successive epochs, and describing the fiscal policies pursued, with corresponding failure or good fortune, by different nations in those periods.   Whether he does or does not win assent for his contentions, he has certainly made a fresh contribution of peculiar interest to the literature of the fiscal question.   It deserves, and we have no doubt that it will command, the careful notice of both parties to the debate.   Fiscal Reformers will utilise with gratitude his powerful support; convinced Free Traders can hardly afford to disregard this strenuous and clever onslaught on their position.   L.L.P.

25.—*The Small Holdings of England: a Survey of the Various Existing Systems.* By L. Jebb. 445 pp., 8vo. London: John Murray, 1907. Price 10s. 6d. net.

Miss Jebb's extensive review of the several conditions of success and of failure which attend the working of small holdings in England comes before the public at a very opportune time, for it deals with those holdings which modern enterprise has fostered into being, as well as those which still survive in certain districts. It has, moreover, this advantage over the hasty and partial pictures of the journalist, or the fragmentary rhetoric of the politician on this subject, that it presents a long and consistent and well-arranged series of ascertained facts and a carefully compiled collection of local opinion gathered on the spot. The laborious work of inquiry and of record was undertaken, as the authoress tells us in her preface, for the Co-operative Small Holdings Association, and congratulations are due both to the promoters of this detailed investigation and to the lady herself, who has, over a period of three years, travelled and watched and questioned and noted to such good effect. The result is the production of a work of reference on the subject of the existing conditions of the *petite culture* in England, as they appear just before the Legislature has decided to embark on a new career of artificial stimulation.

It is true that partial statements of Miss Jebb's reports and opinions have seen the light, in pamphlet form, before this volume issued from the press. But these are of sectional interest only, and are embodied in and covered by the contents of the large treatise now presented. Much, too, of this active lady's experiences have been extracted from her in the witness box when called before Lord Onslow's recent Departmental Committee, and may therefore be found in detail—and with the undoubted advantage of cross-examination on certain points—in the evidence of the bulky blue book issued last winter. For one person, however, outside of official circles, who reads this evidence in its Parliamentary form there will be ten who can turn to this more attractive volume, printed with a typography which no blue book is permitted to rival, and these readers may glean, with far less exertion to the eye and the brain, the features of the varying tale here exhibited. Whether a day will ever come when the stern economists of the Treasury can be induced to abandon their love of that intensely forbidding compression of type which is worshipped by the Stationery Office, and dress in less deterrent shape the costly piles of officially accumulated information, buried in the recesses of a gigantic blue book, may be doubted. But the readable appearance of Miss Jebb's work, even on so trite and dry a subject as small holdings, forces one to put the question whether English Government reports could not be made readable, even if a series of separate volumes were required to display the views and opinions of a selected group of eminently capable witnesses. Miss Jebb has, however, no need at this time to fear this sort of competition from any more artistic summary and purview of the complex and often contradictory evidence drawn by the Committee from an aggregate of 10,990 questions put to the group of 58 separate witnesses, of whom Miss Jebb herself was but a unit. That evidence must be left where it is marshalled, or rather immured, in the "rock-tomb" of the Departmental Report. The authoress of the present volume wisely eschews the loose rhetoric which is too often applied to questions of land tenure and land sub-division. She writes, it is true, with undoubted sympathy for the further multiplication of small holders, and she is occasionally perhaps a little unduly severe on the older reports which expose the hard facts of the economic struggle which the small holder has to face. Her plan is to analyse the various existing systems and their results, and this is done seriatim, without superfluous padding, and in terse and clearly worded sentences, which nevertheless embody many accurate pictures—some attractive and some forbidding—of real rural life. It is as a consecutive series of illustrations rather than as in any sense a statistical treatise this book finds notice here.

After introductory matter, in which a reference is made to the decline of small farming, Miss Jebb passes first in review those groups of small holdings which are of what she calls "natural occurrence." Two different and well-known Lincolnshire regions, one the Isle of Axholme, and another in the east around Boston, come under this class, with those at Evesham and elsewhere in Worcestershire, in Bedford, in Dorset, in Cornwall, as well as the fruit-growing farms near Wisbech and Cambridge and the seed-growing holdings at Tiptree, in Essex. Company promoted groups come next, such as those of the National Land Company, the Small Farm and Labourers' Land Company, and the Cudworth Small Holdings Association. These all contemplated some profit, but were more or less philanthropic in intention—although the criticism is offered that the philanthropy and the percentage are equally problematical. To these follow descriptions of the more purely commercial enterprises, including such schemes as those of "Homesteads, Limited," where many of the plots are purely residential, and hardly belong to the agricultural class. The groups which in Lincoln, Norfolk, and Bucks have been quite lately established by associations privately organised by enthusiastic individuals, and those by associations of more spontaneous origin, are next dealt with. In all these cases Miss Jebb endeavours to set out analytically what are the distinctive conditions as to soil and climate, markets, and external openings for labour, as well as the scale of prices and rents, under which they have flourished or failed. Most practical and effective of all the small holdings schemes of recent origin are those attributed to the direct action of landowners; and here Miss Jebb's account of the small holdings on Mr. Harris's estate at Halwill offers singularly useful lessons of what may be done, even in a country far from markets and purely agricultural, in establishing—mainly, it is true, on grass land and in a cattle-breeding district—a flourishing and active peasantry, who have turned the bleak moorlands lying 600 feet above the sea into valuable small farms. In all or nearly all cases here the occupier has the holding as an adjunct to some other work, and the transformation has been effected under the wise stimulation of a sympathetic landlord and without the cumbersome machinery attending the intervention of local authorities and public companies. Numerous precise details are offered throughout the volume of the cost of creating holdings and equipping them, and everywhere experience proves the dominant importance which attaches to the individual capacity of the men who have set their hands to the task. The extremely varied conditions in which small holdings flourish, whether as occasionally for a livelihood, or and much more commonly, as a useful supplement to some other occupation, are exhibited by the story of those on good land in Lincoln, and on poor land in Norfolk. Still more clearly is success denoted when the culture of the land is allied with grazing rights, such as in the district around the New Forest.

The warnings which are occasionally offered of "over capitalisation" in equipment in some of these pictures are not at all unneeded ; and Miss Jebb not only finds instances where heavy building outlays have proved deterrent factors, but also other cases, where by a change of farming system, large outlays are not infrequently speedily found obsolete or unneeded. Warnings, too, are suggested, as by some of the market gardeners at Upwey, in Dorset, as to the killing effect of extensive local competition, induced by rapid multiplication of smaller holders in adjoining areas, all aiming at success by cutting into each other's markets and lowering prices all round ; and these deserve more attention than they often receive at the hands of advocates of any indiscriminate promotion of small farms in particular areas by local authorities ready to risk their rates in the speculation.

In view of the controversy now in progress over the legislative proposals of this year, it is interesting to note concrete examples of the very different feelings which animate the smaller holders of different districts in two areas, which are alike distinguished in the utilisation of small farms for the growth of fruit. On the one hand Miss Jebb found in the Cambridgeshire districts which she visited the strongly prevalent desire to own the surface on which fruit trees were planted, on the other, among the fruit gardens at Evesham, in Worcestershire, few men wanted to buy, but all wanted to rent, land. The security offered by the "Evesham custom" may no doubt in some degree account for this variety of feeling. But on reading these reports one is tempted to wish that, long as Miss Jebb's travels have been, she had extended them yet further, and dealt with the experiences detailed in Lord Onslow's Committee's Report of the raspberry growers of Blairgowrie, in Scotland, where the difficulty of adjusting possible compensation claims for land newly planted with fruit led to the high rents offered or the desire to buy out the owners even at large acreage rates.

No inconsiderable space is devoted, of course, in this book to the genesis of the Act of 1892, and the disappointing reports of its working in all but a few counties, while the powers of the several grades of local authorities are fully and usefully discussed. On the other hand, we may complain that less scope is devoted to and less reference made to the important suggestions of the latest

Departmental Committee, whose labours are both more recent and whose conclusions bear far more directly on the present position than the far less systematised and less valuable Parliamentary inquiry of 1889-90. But it may not be uncharitable to suppose that Miss Jebb's volume was mainly written before the Committee of 1905-06 had reported, and that what is said of their doings is more by way of a postscript to the earlier notes than any serious comment.

With the conclusions ultimately reached, however, the reviewer of a work such as the present cannot find much fault, and for the form in which the facts are gathered he is grateful. For in these conclusions Miss Jebb again insists on the fact so often ignored by impatient reformers, that "England already possesses what might be called a definite small-holding system of her own, and that where the laws of supply and demand are allowed free play in land, there is a distinct tendency to the natural occurrence of small holdings under many and various conditions." She shows, also, that "certain schemes fostered by idealists and faddists, although valuable as affording distinct lessons, have not been generally successful when viewed from the standpoint of the object of their creation," although this failure does not afford an argument for predicting the failure of small holdings generally. On the other hand, where local knowledge and real understanding has been brought to bear, whether through private efforts, the formation of associations, or the action of individual landowners, the success is very marked. Like many another inquirer, Miss Jebb moreover concludes that, with whatever variations of failure and success in individual instances, small holdings serve a purpose "other than that of mere agricultural success in the economy of nations."   P.G.C.

26.—*A History of William Paterson and the Darien Company.* By James Samuel Barbour. x + 284 pp., crown 8vo. Edinburgh : William Blackwood and Sons, 1907. Price 6*s*. net.

The name of William Paterson's famous in the economic history of Great Britain as that of the original founder of the Bank of England, although he himself soon ceased to be a Director of the Company which he had started. The part which he played in the monetary affairs of Scotland at the same period was not less conspicuous; but his connection with the Northern district of the island was, unhappily for his own subsequent repute, as well as for the immediate fortunes of those associated with him in his venture, attended by disaster well-nigh as resounding as the great success that ultimately followed his shrewd notion of combining the provision of effective means for meeting the pecuniary requirements of the military policy of William III with the institution of the Bank of England. For that calamity indeed, or at any rate for its full extent, Paterson himself, as the writer of this volume shows, was not wholly, or perhaps mainly, responsible; for his advice on important details had been disregarded, and at one time his active co-operation was peremptorily thrust aside. And, while a long interval elapsed before he himself received any of that assistance from public sources to which, with the other shareholders in the Darien Company, he was entitled, his fellow-sufferers by the failure of his scheme were previously enabled, largely through his vigorous efforts on their behalf, to make the payment of ample compensaticn for their losses an accompanying condition of the measure uniting the parliaments of the two Kingdoms.

By supplying in narrative form, from the scattered documents and books in existence concerning the Darien Company, and the relations to it of its projector, an account of the initiation, course, and issue of that famous but disastrous venture—of the high hopes which it aroused in a wide circle of supporters, of the mistakes committed, and the obstacles encountered, in the attempt to give effect to those sanguine aspirations, of the complete failure following the large expenditure of money which the scheme involved, and of the ultimate recovery by the subscribers of the funds they had invested —Mr. Barbour has filled satisfactorily a gap in financial history. "The story," he remarks with justice, "forms an interesting episode," "which should not be allowed to sink into oblivion." In the text, and in a number of appendices, he quotes in detail from authentic documents, which he has carefully examined; and this authoritative evidence assists him to unravel the tangled circumstances of the conception and the execution of Paterson's seductive plan for enriching the adventurous.

He shows from correspondence which passed in the early stages of the project that the founder of the Bank of England wished, characteristically, to connect an issue of bank notes with the Darien Company, and that the new Bank of Scotland did not dare to offer active opposition to so powerful a rival. But this additional function was soon abandoned. Paterson himself evidently possessed, as his letters prove, no small measure of the apt and fertile ingenuity which subsequent promoters of companies have been accustomed to employ to induce the public to support their ventures. He used no illegitimate methods for this purpose; but he certainly displayed a shrewd knowledge of the weaknesses of human nature in the various suggestions which he put forward. The passing by the Scotch Parliament of the Darien Company's Act, granting very extensive powers of trade, roused an opposition in England, which was fanned by the East India Company, whose interests were directly threatened. This opposition checked the subscription, which had been contemplated, in the Southern portion of the island, and (perhaps in accordance with Paterson's latent design) stopped that East Indian trade which was comprised in the original announcement of the scheme. But it also put the inhabitants of the Northern portion of the island on their mettle, and enlisted jealous patriotism in its support. The project was greeted with wild enthusiasm in Scotland, and all classes of the people were eager to subscribe. It is to be noted that the roseate prospect which Paterson then held out of large fortunes to be made with rapid ease by the command of an entrepôt trade across the isthmus separating South from North America was in a sense no more than an anticipation of similar ideas entertained two centuries later respecting the construction of the Panama Canal; and those ideas apparently are destined to find an early practical fulfilment under the auspices of the Government of the United States. He was accordingly in this respect merely before his time; and in not a few of his views on other matters he seems to have been equally advanced.

The melancholy story of the first and second expeditions made to America are narrated in these pages with considerable detail; and we learn how mistakes about provisions at the beginning of the earlier voyage combined with the effects of an unhealthy climate and the lack of sufficient strong support from home to bring about disaster. The second expedition arrived only to find that the first party had already gone; and in the end a very large sum of money had been spent with no return. Mr. Barbour then proceeds to describe the course of the negotiations by which the subscribers to the Darien Company recovered their capital, with interest, from the English in return for the surrender of the extensive powers of trade originally conferred upon them. The last day on which the Scottish Parliament sat (the 25th March, 1707), saw also the passing of an Act for this particular purpose. In a final chapter we are told how Paterson himself, after long delay, and repeated disappointment of the promises made to him by others, received from the English Parliament indemnity for the serious losses he had personally sustained; and Mr. Barbour removes the doubt felt about the actual payment of this indemnity by reproducing in an Appendix a detailed official letter on the subject addressed to the "Scotsman" by the General Manager of the Royal Bank of Scotland. He thus concludes a most interesting account of a famous financial venture, and he draws an attractive portrait of its able but unfortunate projector. His authoritative narrative forms a valuable contribution to Scottish economic history. It affords a fresh example of the competent learning and unwearied industry now applied to that department of historical research.   L.L.P.

27.—*Sociological Papers.* Volume III. Published for the Sociological Society. 382 pp., la. 8vo. London: Macmillan and Co., 1907. Price 10s. 6d.

This volume contains the papers read before the Sociological Society during the third session of its existence (1905-06). The papers fall, roughly speaking, into three main groups: Miscellaneous papers on special subjects—amongst which we could specially mention an introduction by Mr. W. H. Beveridge to a discussion on the problem of the unemployed, one of the ablest and most lucid contributions to the volume — papers on the application of biological ideas to sociology, and on questions of scope and method respectively.

In the biological group, Dr. Archdall Reid contributes a characteristically clear and vigorous exposition of "the biological foundations of sociology," in which he emphasises his views as to the importance of selection in the evolution of the race and of nurture in the development of the individual, more especially as regards mental characteristics. Mr. McDougall follows with "a practicable eugenic suggestion," viz., that the salaries of civil servants should be graduated on a sliding scale, according to the number of their children; a post now paid 800*l.* being scaled at 500*l.*, say, for a bachelor, and 600*l.* for a married man, with an increment of 75*l.* for every surviving child.   The proposal met with a good deal of criticism during the discussion, but we think Mr. McDougall's argument that the present system constitutes a process of negative selection, as the State selects its servants with great care and the relatively low salaries offered are a positive inducement to late marriage or celibacy, is perfectly correct.   A memoir by Dr. Lionel Tayler urges that the study of the individual should precede the study of social groups, and Professor J. Arthur Thomson, on "the sociological appeal to biology," gives a useful warning as to the necessity of care in the application of biological formulæ to the study of human societies.

In the papers respecting scope and method, we may mention an interesting contribution from the American standpoint by Professor Wenley, of the University of Michigan, on "sociology as an academic subject," and a provocative paper by Mr. H. G. Wells on "the so-called science of sociology," which drew some vigorous replies. Discussions of this type are very reminiscent of the early history of statistics.   We may note a short article by Mrs. Sidney Webb on "methods of investigation," in which the function of statistical method in sociology is briefly discussed.   The author holds that this function is limited to prevention of the "fallacy of the individual instance," and in the discussion (given in abstract) it was stated that the difficulty with statistical method was that the facts were collected and classified by mathematicians whose competence as sociologists was not above question.   In replying, Mrs. Webb agreed with what had been said, and added the somewhat cryptic remark ·that the statistician "should never be allowed to collect his own data."   We are inclined to suspect from the context that this may mean "the statistician who collects sociological data should be trained in sociology"—a type of statement with which we should always be in agreement, *e.g.*, substituting for "sociological" and "sociology" "biological" and "biology" or "meteorological" and "meteorology"—though the meaning, as the phrase stands, is hardly clear.   But surely a sociologist, biologist, or meteorologist who handles the statistical data of his science in complete ignorance of statistical method is quite as bad as a statistician who deals with the data of a science of which he has no special knowledge ?   The hope for the future is, of course, that those who require to use statistical data will be trained in method, and the present distinction will pass away.   We notice that the volume only includes papers read up to April, 1906. It would be an advantage if arrangements could be made for earlier publication.   G.U.Y.

28.—*Other New Publications.*

Australasia. Unification of Australasian statistical methods and co-ordination of the work of the Commonwealth and State bureaux. Conference of Statisticians of the Commonwealth and States of Australia and Colony of New Zealand. Melbourne, Nov. and Dec., 1906. 73 pp., fol. Melbourne: J. Kemp, 1906.

Berglund (Abraham). The United States steel corporation. A study of the growth and influence of combination in the iron and steel industry. 178 pp., 8vo. New York: Columbia University Press, 1907. $1.50.

Brisco (Norris A.). The economic policy of Robert Walpole. 222 pp., 8vo. New York: Columbia University Press, 1907. $1.50.

Brown (Richard). History of accounting and accountants. Edited and partly written by Richard Brown, C.A. xvi + 459 pp., 8vo. Edinburgh: The Society of Accountants in Edinburgh, 1905.
> [An account of the origin and growth of the profession from the earliest times.]

Bullock (Charles J.). Historical sketch of the finances and financial policy of Massachusetts, from 1780 to 1905. 144 pp., 8vo. New York: American Economic Assoc., 1907. $1.00.

Crackanthorpe (Montague). Population and progress. 132 pp., 8vo. London: Chapman and Hall, 1907.
> [Essays in application of the " voluntary principle."]

Dykes (D. Oswald). Scottish local government. Lectures on the organisation and functions of local bodies. 160 pp., 8vo. Edinburgh and London: Oliphant, Anderson and Ferrier, 1907. 1s. net.

Easton (H. T.). Money, exchange and banking in their practical, theoretical, and legal aspects. A complete manual for bank officials, business men, and students of commerce. 2nd edition. 312 pp., 8vo. London: Sir Isaac Pitman and Sons, Ltd., 1907. 5s. net.

Friedman (Harry G.). The taxation of corporations in Massachusetts. 178 pp., 8vo. New York: Columbia University Press, 1907. $1.50.

Galton (Francis), F.R.S. Inquiries into human faculty and its development. 262 pp., 8vo. London: Dent, 1907.
> [1st ed. (Macmillan), 1883 : " The starting point of that recent movement in favour of national eugenics which has its home in University College, London."]

Gilbert (James Henry). Trade and currency in early Oregon. A study in the commercial and monetary history of the Pacific Northwest. 126 pp., 8vo. New York: Columbia University Press, 1907. $1.00.

Hord (John S.). Internal taxation in the Philippines. 45 pp., 8vo. Baltimore: Johns Hopkins Press, 1907.

Hull (Walter Henry). Practical problems in banking and currency. Being a number of selected addresses by prominent bankers, financiers and economists. Edited by W. H. Hull, with introduction by the Hon. Charles Francis Phillips. 8vo. New York: The Macmillan Co., 1907.
> [A special section deals with the trust company as a factor in finance.]

Jacobstein (Meyer). The tobacco industry in the United States. 208 pp., 8vo. New York: Columbia University Press, 1907. $1.50.

Knibbs (G. H.). The classification of disease and causes of death, from the standpoint of the statistician. An address given to the Victorian branch of the British Medical Association, 12th June, 1907. 24 pp., 8vo. Melbourne: Intercolonial Medical Journal, 1907.

Levasseur (E.). Questions ouvrières et industrielles en France sous la 3e République. lxxii + 968 pp., la. 8vo. 1907. 15 francs.
[The final volume of the series of works which began with the author's "Recherches historiques sur le système de Law," published in 1854.]

MacDonald (J. Ramsay). Socialism and society. (The Socialist Library. II.) 5th edition. 186 pp., 8vo. London: Independent Labour Party, 1907. 1s. net.

Pearson (Karl), F.R.S. Scope and importance to the state of the science of national eugenics. 45 pp., 8vo. London: Frowde, 1907.

———— A first study of the statistics of pulmonary tuberculosis. (Drapers' Company Research Memoirs, II.) 26 pp., 4to. London: Dulau, 1907. 3s.

Saint-Maurice (Comte de). La fortune publique et privée au Japon. 61 pp., 8vo. Paris: Georges Roustan, 1907.

Schuster (Edgar) and *Elderton (Ethel M.).* Inheritance of ability, being a statistical study of the Oxford class lists and of the school lists of Harrow and Charterhouse. (Eugenics Laboratory Memoirs. I). 42 pp., 4to. London: Dulau, 1907. 4s.

Simon (André L.). History of the wine trade in England. Vol. ii. Progress of the wine trade in England during 15th and 16th centuries. 340 pp., 8vo. London: Wyman, 1907.

Sundbärg (Gustav). Bevölkerungsstatistik Schwedens, 1750-1900. Einige Hauptresultate (XIV. Internationaler Kongress fur Hygiene und Demographie, Berlin, Sept. 1907). 170 pp., 8vo. Stockholm: P. A. Norstedt and Söner, 1907.

Supino (Camillo). Le crisi economiche. xi + 202 pp., 8vo. Milan: Ulrico Hoepli, 1907.

Tenney (Alvan A.). Social democracy and population. 90 pp., 8vo. New York: Columbia University Press, 1907. $0.75.

Waltershausen (A. Sartorius von). Das volkswirtschaftliche System der Kapitalanlage im Auslande. 442 pp., 8vo. Berlin: Georg Reimer, 1907. 10 M.

Williamson (Charles C). The finances of Cleveland. 266 pp., 8vo. New York: Columbia University Press, 1907. $2.00.

Yoxall (J. H.) and *Gray (Ernest).* The N.U.T. handbook of education, containing . . . particulars respecting the supply, organisation, and administration of elementary and secondary education in England and Wales, 1907. 590 pp., 8vo. London: The National Union of Teachers, 1907. 3s. 6d.

STATISTICAL AND ECONOMIC ARTICLES IN RECENT PERIODICALS.

UNITED KINGDOM—

Accountants' Magazine, 1907—

July—The law of agency (*continued in August number*): *Gloag* (*W. M.*). Trustee savings banks : *Howden* (*J. M.*).

Bankers' Magazine, 1907—

July—The production of gold. An Australian view of the London money market : *French* (*J. Russell*). Banking in Australasia.

August—Consols as a credit barometer. The treasury of the United States. The Bank of France. The Imperial Bank of · Germany.

September—Central and South America—A field for banking operations. The shrinkage in British securities : *Lawson* (*W. R.*). Australia's recovery : *Philps* (*F. J.*). National Bank of Belgium.

Biometrika. Vol. V. Part IV. June, 1907—Statistical observations on wasps and bees : *Edgeworth* (*F. Y.*). Grades and deviates : *Galton* (*Francis*). Statistical studies in immunity—A discussion of the means of estimating the severity of cases of acute disease : *Brownlee* (*John*). The calculation of the moments of a frequency-distribution : *Sheppard* (*W. F.*). On the inheritance of psychical characters. Being further statistical treatment of material collected and analysed by Messrs. Heymans and Wiersma : *Schuster* (*Edgar*) and *Elderton* (*Ethel M.*). Reply to certain criticisms of Mr. G. U. Yule : *Pearson* (*Karl*). Notices and bibliography.

Economic Journal. September, 1907—The Sugar Convention and the West Indies : *Cooke* (*E. Cozens*). The taxation of site values with reference to the distribution of population : *Darwin* (*Major Leonard*). The evolution of a modern industrial town : *Leppington* (*Miss C. H. E.*). Social improvement and modern biology : *Pigou* (*A. C.*). The wine crisis in south France : *Gide* (*Prof. Charles*). The income-tax in Holland : *Pierson* (*N. G.*). The textile industry in France : *Clapham* (*Prof. J. H.*). Arbitration in the corn trade in London : *Chattaway* (*C.*). Correspondence of Ricardo with Maria Edgeworth.

Economic Review. July, 1907—The " Inhabited house " duty : *Bonar* (*J.*). Free trade in India : *Beauclerk* (*F.*). Unemployment, II : *Lansbury* (*G.*). The land and the Bill : *Lewis* (*T. Preston*).

Journal of the Board of Agriculture, 1907—

July—Plant import regulations—Cape Colony, Argentina. Notes on the weather and the crops in June.

August — Co-operative horse insurance : *Charleton* (*W. L.*). Establishment of small holdings on Crown Lands.

UNITED KINGDOM—*Contd.*

Journal of the Department of Agriculture, &c., for Ireland. July, 1907—The cost of forest planting. The functions of the department in relation to rural industries: *Fletcher (G.).* Workmen's Compensation Act, 1906.

Journal of the Institute of Actuaries. July, 1907—On the rationale of formulæ for graduation by summation: *Lidstone (George J.).* Some illustrations of the employment of summation formulas in the graduation of mortality tables: *Spencer (John).* Frequency-curves and moments (Reprinted from the "Transactions of the Actuarial Society of America"): *Henderson (Robert).*

Journal of the Royal Colonial Institute. July, 1907—The trend of Victoria's progress: *Bent (Hon. Thomas).*

Sociological Papers. Vol. 3. 1907—The biological foundations of sociology: *Reid (Dr. G. Archdall).* A practicable eugenic suggestion: *McDougall (W.).* The study of individuals (individuology) and their natural groupings (sociology): *Tayler (Dr. J. Lionel).* The sociological appeal to biology: *Thomson (Prof. J. Arthur).* A suggested plan for a civic museum (or civic exhibition) and its associated studies: *Geddes (Prof. Patrick).* The origin and function of religion: *Crawley (A. E.).* Sociology as an academic subject: *Wenley (Prof. R. M.).* The Russian revolution: *Wesselitsky (G. de).* The problem of the unemployed: *Beveridge (W. H.).* Methods of investigation: *Webb (Mrs. Sidney).* The so-called science of sociology: *Wells (H. G.).*

Surveyors' Institution. Transactions. Session 1906-07. Part 13— Title page and contents, &c.

UNITED STATES—

American Journal of Sociology. July, 1907—Are the social sciences answerable to common principles of method?: *Small (Albion W.).* Industrial insurance, IV. The insurance of the fraternal societies: *Henderson (Charles Richmond).* The opium trade in the Dutch East Indies. I: *Scheltema (J. F.)*

Bankers' Magazine (New York), 1907—

June—Governmental bonds as investments: *Deusen (Edgar van).* A bankruptcy law: *Hague (George).* The international bureau of the American Republics. Latin-America as a field for U.S. capital and enterprise: *Barrett (John).*

July—The existing mechanism of the New York money market: *Conant (Charles A.).* Insurance in its relation to banking: *Hague (George).*

August—Trust companies.—Their organization, growth and management: *Herrick (Clay).* Canadian banking and commerce: *Eckardt (H. M. P.).*

Bulletin of Bureau of Labor. May, 1907.—The Italian on the land: a study in immigration: *Meade (Emily Fogg).* A short history of labor legislation in Great Britain: *Low (A. Maurice).* The British Workmen's Compensation Acts: *Packer (Launcelot).* British Workmen's Compensation Act of 1906.

UNITED STATES—*Contd.*

Journal of Political Economy, 1907—

June—Reciprocity with Germany, I : *Willis* (*H. Parker*). The trade-union point of view : *Hoxie* (*Robert F.*). Mortality statistics, 1905 : *Cummings* (*J.*).

July—Reciprocity with Germany, II : *Willis* (*H. Parker*). The standard of value and prices : *Hess* (*Ralph H.*). The municipal bridge and terminals commission of St. Louis : *Perkins* (*Albert T.*). Professor Fetter on capital and income : *Fisher* (*Irving*).

Quarterly Journal of Economics. August, 1907—The treasury and the banks under Secretary Shaw : *Andrew* (*A. P.*). The growth of the Union Pacific and its financial operations : *Mitchell* (*Thomas Warner*). Modes of constructing index-numbers : *Flux* (*A. W.*). Tax discrimination in the paper and pulp industry : *McCrea* (*Roswell C.*). Municipal owner-ship of telephones in Great Britain : *Holcombe* (*A. N.*). Industrial concentration as shown by the Census : *Ripley* (*William Z.*).

Yale Review. August, 1907—Rebates : *Newcomb* (*H. T.*). The Standard Oil Company and pipe lines : *Montague* (*Gilbert Holland*). The paradox of Governor Pennypacker : *Woodruff* (*Clinton Rogers*).

Annals of American Academy of Political and Social Science. July, 1907—The annual address : The development of a colonial policy for the United States : *Beveridge* (*Hon. Albert J.*). Some difficulties in colonial government encountered by Great Britain, and how they have been met : *Bryce* (*Right Hon. James*). Naturalization and citizenship in the insular posses-sions of the United States : *Charlton* (*Hon. Paul*). A bureau of information and report for the insular possessions : *Parsons* (*Hon. Herbert*).

AUSTRIA-HUNGARY—

Statistische Monatschrift, 1907—

May—Die statistischen Unterlagen der Wahlreform : *Rauchberg* (*Dr. H.*). Zum Gedächtnis an Josef v. Körösy : *Inama-Sternegg* (*K. T. von*).

June—Zur Kritik der „Moralstatistik" : *Inama-Sternegg* (*Karl Theodor v.*). Die statistischen Unterlagen der Wahlreform : *Rauchberg* (*Prof. Dr. H.*). Die österreichisch - ungarische Bank und die übrigen Wiener Aktienbanken im Jahre 1906 : *Lowe* (*A. K.*).

July—Die Grenzen der Kriminalstatistik : *Hoegel* (*Dr.*). Der Verkehr der Liegenschaften in Wien im Jahre 1906 : *Zwilling* (—).

August—Die Grenzen der Kriminalstatistik (Fortsetzung) : *Hoegel* (*Dr.*). Erhebungsarten der Blindheit und ihre Rückwirkungen auf die Statistik : *Wagner* (*Emil*).

DENMARK—

Statistiske Meddelelser. Vol. 23. 1907—Importation et exportation en 1906, production d'eau de vie, de bière, de sucre de betteraves et de beurre artificiel. Industries du Danemark le 12 juin 1906 ; compte-rendu préliminaire. Les hautes écoles des paysans et les écoles agronomiques du Danemark en 1904-05 et en 1905-06. Importation et exportation du Danemark au trimestre d'octobre 1906. Suicides et décès par accident 1896 (1897)-1905.

FRANCE—

Annales des Sciences Politiques. July, 1907 — Les primes à la marine marchande et la loi du 19 avril 1906 : *Lavergne (A. de).* Les canaux : Un instrument de transport du passé : *Bellet (D.)* Les voies de pénétration et de communication en Afrique occidentale française (avec 3 cartes) (suite) : *Ferry (R.).* Les finances locales du Canada : *Dewarrin* (—). Chronique coloniale (1906) : *Mourey (Charles).*

Bulletin de Statistique, Ministère des Finances, 1907—

June—Les dons et legs en faveur d'œuvres d'assistance et d'instruction. Les finances coloniales de 1895 à 1904. Les revenus de l'état.

July—Rapport sur les résultats de la reduction à 10 centimes du tarif des lettres. Production des alcools en 1906 et 1905. Statistique des fabriques, entrepôts, magasins de vente en gros et magasins de vente en détail, etc., soumis en 1906 aux exercices des agents des contributions indirectes. Les exemptions temporaires d'impôt foncier dans les départements phylloxérés pendant l'année 1906. Allemagne—L'impôt sur le revenu en Prusse. (Loi du 19 juin 1906.)

Journal des Économistes, 1907—

July—L'automobile est-elle une richesse ? *Molinari (G. de).* Rodbertus contre Bastiat : *Guyot (Yves).* Les réformes gratuites : *Rouxel* (—). Suprimons l'inscription maritime . . . et le protectionnisme : *Bellet (Daniel).* Mouvement financier et commercial : *Zablet (Maurice).* Revue des principales publications économiques de l'étranger : *Breton (René)* et *Castelot (E.).* Lettre de province : *Courcelle-Seneuil (J.).* Lettre de Pologne : *Domanski (Ladislas).*

August—Théorie de l'évolution : *Molinari (G. de).* La comptabilité des dépenses engagées : *Fontaine (Gabriel).* Le budget de la ville de Paris pour 1907 : *Letourneur (E.).* Mouvement agricole : *Molinari (Maurice de).* Revue des principales publications économiques en langue Française : *Rouxel* (—). Lettre des États-Unis : *Tricoche (Georges Nestler).* Un bon livre : *Passy (Frédéric).* Encore Rodbertus contre Bastiat : *Guyot (Yves).*

Journal de la Société de Statistique de Paris, 1907—

July—Statistique de la franc-maçonnerie : *Limousin (Ch.-M.).* Résultats pour les contribuables parisiens du projet d'impôt sur le revenu déposé par le gouvernement : *Desroys du Roure (M.).*

FRANCE—*Contd.*
Journal de la Société de Statistique de Paris, 1907—*Contd.*
 August—Résultats pour les contribuables parisiens du projet
 d'impôt sur le revenu déposé par le gouvernement : *Desroys
 du Roure (M.)*. Une nouvelle carte électorale de l'empire
 allemand, d'après les élections du Reichstag de 1907 :
 Meuriot (Paul). Chronique trimestrielle des banques, changes
 et métaux précieux : *Roulleau (M. G.)*.
La Réforme Sociale, 1907—
 1*st and* 16*th July*—Le patronage devant le syndicalisme et la
 coopération : *Beauregard (Paul)*. La fondation Commines de
 Marsilly et les pupilles de la Société D'Économie Sociale :
 Joly (Henri). Les œuvres sociales dans les chemins de fer :
 Noblemaire (M.). Les enseignements de La Play sur la
 famille : *Lacombe (Emmanuel)*.
 1*st and* 16*th August*—Les institutions patronales en France,
 leur nécessité et leur évolution : *Cheysson (E.)*. Les conseils
 d'usine ou comités ouvriers en Allemagne : *Brants (Victor)*.
 Les patrons et la mutualité : *Dédé (E.)*. Les patrons
 et l'apprentissage : *Roguenant (A.)*. L'habitation ouvrière
 agricole : *Pasquier (Is.)*. Un gentilhomme campagnard ; sa
 vie et ses travaux ; les résultats du métayage et du patronage
 rural : *X (—)*. Chronique du mouvement social : *Lepelletier
 (F.) and Angot des Rotours (Baron J.)*.
 1*st and* 16*th September*—L'organisation du patronage dans une
 grande ville industrielle : *Vanlaer (Maurice)*. L'épreuve
 Américaine d'après deux ouvrages récents : *Primbault (H.)*.
 Les institutions privées de conciliation et d'arbitrage en
 France et à l'étranger : *Boissieu (Henri de)*. Le système de
 l'assurance dans l'organisation des retraites ouvrières : *Olphe-
 Galliard (G.)*. Les commissions mixtes et la vie syndicale :
 Perrin (Alfred). Chronique du mouvement social : *Lepelletier
 (F.) et Blondel (Georges)*.

GERMANY—
 Archiv fur Rassen- und Gesellschafts-Biologie. July-August, 1907—
 Verwandtenehe und Geisteskrankheit : *Weinberg (W.)*. Die
 geistige Leistungsfähigkeit des Weibes im Lichte der neueren
 Forschung : *Alsberg (Moritz)*. Nordamerikanische Bevölkerungs-
 u. Rassenprobleme : *Heiderich (Hans)*.
 Archiv fur Sozialwissenschaft und Sozialpolitik, July, 1907—Der
 Begriff der Stadt und das Wesen der Städtebildung : *Sombart
 (Werner)*. Wertrechnung und Preisrechnung im Marx'schen
 System, II : *Bortkiewicz (Dr. L. v.)*. Der österreichisch-
 ungarische Ausgleich, I : *Gaertner (Friedrich)*. Die deutsche
 Sozialdemokratie im internationalen Verbande : eine kritische
 Untersuchung : *Michels (Robert)*. Kritische Beiträge zu Prof.
 M. Webers Abhandlung : „ Die protestantische Ethik und der
 Geist des Kapitalismus " : *Fischer (Karl)*. Kritische Bemer-
 kungen zu den vorstehenden „ Kritischen Beiträgen " : *Weber
 (Max)*. Die deutschen Volksbibliotheken : *Schultze (Dr. Ernst)*.

GERMANY—*Contd.*

Jahrbuch fur Gesetzgebung, Verwaltung und Volkswirtschaft (*G. Schmoller*), Heft 3, 1907—Die philosophischen Voraussetzungen der materialistischen Geschichtsauffassung : *Erdmann* (*Benno*). Geschichte des Ursprungs des modernen Patentwesens in England und der Streit um das Spielkartenmonopol bis zum englischen Patentgesetz von 1623 : *Damme* (—). Gemeinwirtschaft und Unternehmungsformen im Mormonenstaat : *Wilson* (*Albert Edgar*). Beiträge zur Frage der Bodenspekulation und ihrer Gewinne : *Mohr* (*Paul*). Englische Kartelle der Vergangenheit, I : *Levy* (*Hermann*). Weinbau und Winzer im Rheingau : ein Beitrag zu den Agrarverhältnissen des Rheingaues, I : *Kayser* (*Emanuel*). Der landwirtschaftliche Warrant : seine Entstehung, seine Resultate und die Gesetzgebung in Frankreich : *Rudloff* (*Hans L.*). Organisation des amerikanischen Bankwesens. II : *Stubbe* (*A.*). Zur Zinstheorie : I. Zuschrift : *Oswalt* (*H.*) ; II. Entgegnung : *Bortkiewicz* (*L. von*). Wie kann die Börse mehr der Allgemeinheit dienstbar gemacht werden ? "*Praktiker.*" Der Beruf des praktischen Volkswirts : seine Entstehung und seine Lage : *Krueger* (*Hermann Edwin*). Die Spekulation im modernen Städtebau : *Fuchs* (*Carl Johannes*).

Jahrbucher fur Nationalokonomie und Statistik (*Conrad's*), 1907—

July—Zivilprozessstatistik : *Hesse* (*Albert*). Das australische Sparkassawesen mit für das deutsche und österreichische öffentliche Sparwesen vorbildlichen Einrichtungen : *Schachner* (*Robert*). Kontinuierlicher Fabrikbetrieb : *Sternkopf* (*Jon.*). Die deutsche Literatur des Jahres 1906 über Kartelle und Trusts : *Liefmann* (*Robert*).

August—Zur Anschauung der Antike über Handel, Gewerbe und Landwirtschaft : *Neurath* (*Otto*). Das Problem der Altersversicherung der Kleingewerbetreibenden in Oesterreich : *Wokurek* (*Ludwig*). Untersuchungen über die Verhältnisse des deutschen Eichenschälwaldbetriebs : *Henze* (—). Die Generalaussperrung in der deutschen Holzindustrie : *Croner* (*Joh.*). Das Gothenburger System in Finnland : *Harmaja* (*Leo*). Die kleinen Güter in der neuesten Agrarstatistik Englands : *Levy* (*Hermann*).

Vierteljahrshefte zur Statistik des Deutschen Reichs. Heft 3, 1907— Dampfkessel-Explosionen 1906. (Mit 2 Tafeln.) Die Krankenversicherung in den Knappschaftskassen und -Vereinen 1905. Zur Statistik der Preise. Spielkarten-Fabrikation und -Versteuerung 1906. Schaumwein-Erzeugung und -Besteuerung. Die Volkszählung am 1. Dezember 1905. (Endgiltige Ergebnisse. 3. Mitteilung.) Herstellung und Besteuerung von Zigaretten, Zigarettentabak und Zigarettenhüllen im deutschen Zollgebiet in der Zeit vom 1. Juli 1906 bis 31. März 1907. Zollbegünstigungen der Weinhändler 1906. Tabakbau und Tabakernte 1906.

Zeitschrift fur Socialwissenschaft, Heft 7—8, 1907—Die Kolonien in der Weltwirtschaft : *Schilder* (*Sigmund*). Die moderne Bankenkonzentration : *Biermann* (*W. Ed.*). Das Grundproblem

GERMANY—*Contd.*

Zeitschrift für Socialwissenschaft, Heft 7—8, 1907—*Contd.*
der deutschen Verfassungsgeschichte : *Keutgen* (*F.*). Die
ersten drei Jahre des Mitteleuropäischen Wirtschaftsvereins :
Wolf (*Julius*). Der neue Stahlwerksverband : *Diepenhorst*
(*Franz*). Die Entwicklung des Kupferpreises während der
letzten 25 Jahre : *Burner* (*K.*). .
Zeitschrift für die gesamte Staatswissenschaft. Heft 3, 1907—
Das neugefundene Bruchstück eines römischen Berggesetzes :
Neuburg (*C.*). Die parlamentarische Redefreiheit und der
Schutz Dritter gegen den Missbrauch derselben : *Zimmermann*
(*F. W. R.*). Der Alkoholismus in Deutschland : *Seidel* (—).
Die Reform der Staatssteuern in Oldenburg : *Ephraim* (*Hugo*).
Das Unterstützungswesen der Gewerkschaften Deutschlands :
Fehlinger (*H.*). Das rechtliche Verhältnis der Vorschriften des
Reichsgesetzes vom 3. Juni 1906 über den Stempel von
Frachturkunden und Fahrkarten zu den Verträgen über die
internationalen Flüsse : *Wittmaack* (*H.*).
Zeitschrift für die gesamte Versicherungs-Wissenschaft. July, 1907—
Umbau und Ausbau der Arbeiterversicherung : *Stier-Somlo.*
Die Todesursachen beim land- und forstwirtschaftlichen
Personale : *Gollmer* (—). Glossen zur Haftpflichtversicherung :
Marcus (—).

ITALY—

Giornale degli Economisti, 1907—
June—La situazione del mercato monetario : *X.* L' imposta
sulle aree fabbricabili : *Gobbi* (*Ulisse*). Teoria dei cambi
esteri : *Sensini* (*Guido*). Travisamenti della teoria degli
scambi internazionali : *Ricci* (*Umberto*).
July—L'imposta sul reddito in Francia : *Flora* (*Federico*). A
proposito di "una serie di studii sulla vita economica e
sociale della Sardegna" : *Coletti* (*Francesco*). Curve delle
espropriazioni per cause fiscali in Sardegna : *Di Suni*
(*Francesco*). Rassegna del movimento scientifico. Economia :
Ricci (*Umberto*).
August—La scienza economica : *Guyot* (*Yves*). Della natalità e
della fecondità : *Beneduce* (*Alberto*). Il tasso di sconto della
banca di Francia : *François* (*G.*). La questione agraria nella
provincia di Ferrara : *Sitta* (*Pietro*).
La Riforma Sociale, 1907—
June—La determinazione della durata della generazione e il
calcolo della ricchezza privata di un paese : *Coletti* (*Francesco*).
Commercio internazionale e politica commerciale : *Natoli*
(*Fabrizio*). Il riscatto delle linee telefoniche : *Cavalieri*
(*Gastone*). L'industrializzazione della viticoltura francese :
Jarach (*Cesare*). Per la trasformazione industriale della
terra italiana : *Spectator* (—).
July—La colonizzazione, il movimento operaio e la questione
sociale : *Fanno* (*Marco*). La politica industriale delle
organizzazioni operaie.—A proposito di un contratto di

ITALY—*Contd.*
 La Riforma Sociale, 1907—*Contd.*
 July—*Contd.*
   lavoro in Italia : *Cabiati* (*Attilio*). La trasformazione delle
   opere pie di culto : *Virgilii* (*Filippo*). Come funziona la
   nostra imposta sulla ricchezza mobile : *Jarach* (*Cesare*). I
   primi risultati delle ispezioni sull' applicazione delle leggi
   sul lavoro in Italia : *Ottolenghi* (*Costantino*).
 August—Questioni controverse nella teoria del baratto :
   Jannaccone (*Pasquale*). La previdenza all' esposizione di
   Milano : *Schiavi* (*Alessandro*). Emigrazione e finanza :
   Carano-Donvito (*G.*).
Rivista Italiana di Sociologia, 1907. *May-June*—Lo svolgersi del
   formalismo nei vari istituti giuridico-sociali : *De la Grasserie*
   (*Raoul*). Sulla costituzione del Comune italiano nel medio evo :
   Solmi (*Arrigo*). Femminismo e condizioni sociali : *Miceli* (*V.*).

SWITZERLAND—
 Journal de Statistique Suisse, 1907—
   Lief. 3 — Die Simplonbahn : eine verkehrswirtschaftliche
   Studie : *Möhring* (*A.*). Einige kritische Bemerkungen und
   Vorschläge betreffend die schweizerischen Volkszählungen
   und die Berechnung der Säuglingssterblichkeit : *Vogt* (*Adolf*).
   St. Gallische Gesellschaft für Statistik und Staatswissen-
   schaft : Verzeichnis der in der Amtsdauer 1903-07 gehal-
   tenen Vorträge. Mitteilungen über die Preise der wichtig-
   sten Lebensmittel und anderer Bedarfsartikel im April 1907 :
   Zuppinger (*C.*). Schiffahrtswege der Schweiz : *Epper* (*Dr.*).
   Bewegung in den Anstalten für schwachsinnige Kinder im
   Jahre 1906. Allgemeine Ergebnisse der ärztlichen Untersuchung der in den Jahren 1900-06 ins schulpflichtige Alter
   gelangten Kinder.
   Lief. 4—Geschichte der Lebensversicherungswissenschaft in der
   Schweiz : *Kummer* (*J. J.*). Statistisch-Volkswirtschaftliche
   Gesellschaft zu Basel. Wintersession 1906-07. Die schwei-
   zerische Staatsaufsicht über das private Versicherungswesen
   und ihre Tätigkeit : *Stampfli* (*Walter*). Dienstbefreiungs-
   gründe : Mangelhafte Hörschärfe und andere Gehörleiden,
   Stottern, Rheumatismus, Gicht-Skrofulose, Rhachitis,
   Caries und deren Folgen. Enquete über die Arbeiterinnen
   im Kanton Appenzell A. Rh., aufgenommen im Sommer
   1905 : *Zinsli* (*Ph.*). Der Reduktionsfaktor in der Theorie
   der Krankenversicherung und die Besselschen Funktionen :
   Böschenstein (*Karl*). Vocabulaire français-allemand de termes
   techniques d'actuariat : *Straub-Robert* (*R.*). Nachtrag zu dem
   Artikel : Die Versicherungswissenschaften im Unterrichtswesen der Schweiz : *Bohren* (*A.*). Leistungen der Fisch-
   brutanstalten des Kantons Wallis.
   Lief. 5—Eidgenössische Betreibungsstatistik pro 1900.
   Schweizer in Russland. Verwendung des zur Bekämpfung
   des Alkoholismus bestimmten Alkoholzehntels im Kanton

SWITZERLAND—*Contd.*
  Journal de Statistique Suisse, 1907—*Contd.*
    Lief 5—*Contd.*
    Wallis in den Jahren 1891 bis und mit 1905 : *Hildebrand*
    (*Bruno*).   Die Ergebnisse der Strafstatistik des schweize-
    rischen Zentralpolizeibureaus für das Jahr 1905 : *Kaufmann*
    (*Joseph*).   Die Durchschnittsnoten der pädag. Rekrutenprüf-
    ungen in den 19 grössern Städten mit mehr als 10,000
    Einwohnern.   La taille humaine en Suisse : *Pittard* (*Eugène*)
    et *Karmin* (*Otto*).   Die geistige Beschränktheit : Geisteskrank-
    heit als Dienstbefreiungsgründe in den Jahren 1886-1905.
    Renseignements statistiques sur la maison de santé de
    Malévoz (Valais) : *Repond* (*Paul*).   Mitteilungen über die
    Preise der wichtigsten Lebensmittel und anderer Bedarfs-
    artikel im Juli 1907 : *Zuppinger* (*C.*).   Preise der wichtigsten
    landwirtschaftlichen Erzeugnisse (1885-1905).

INTERNATIONAL—
  Bulletin de l'Institut International de Statistique.   Tome xvi, livr. 1,
    1907—La statistique internationale des valeurs mobilières :
    Neymarck (*Alfred*).   Statistics of population and pauperism :
    Loch (*C. S.*).   Nécrologies ; Viscount Goschen, Augusto Bosco,
    Ernst Hirschberg, Max von Proebst, Joseph de Körösi, and
    Grégoire P. Olanesco.

QUARTERLY LIST OF ADDITIONS TO THE LIBRARY.

During the Quarter ended 15th September, 1907, the Society has received the publications enumerated below. The titles are arranged alphabetically under the following heads:—(a) Foreign Countries; (b) India and Colonial Possessions; (c) United Kingdom and its Divisions; (d) Authors, &c.; (e) Societies, &c. (British); (f) Periodicals, &c. (British).

(a) Foreign Countries.

Argentine Republic—

Anuario de la Dirección general de estadística correspondiente al año 1905. Tomo II. 8vo. 1906 — The Director-General of Statistics

Agricultura. Ministerio de, Boletín mensual de Estadística y Comercio. (Current numbers). 1907 — The Ministry of Agriculture

Bulletin démographique argentin. (Current numbers.) Fol. 1907 .... — The Oficina Demográfica Nacional

Buenos Ayres (Province). Dirección General de Estadística. Boletín mensual. (Current numbers.) 1907 .... — The Provincial Statistical Bureau

Córdoba (City). Boletín mensual de estadística municipal. (Current numbers.) Fol. 1907 .... *Santa Fé.* Boletín de estadística municipal, Abril, Mayo y Junio, 1907. Fol. 1907 .... — The Municipal Statistical Bureau

Austria-Hungary—

Ackerbau-Ministeriums. Statistisches Jahrbuch des k.k., für 1906. (Current numbers.) 8vo. 1907 .... — The Government of Austria-Hungary

Arbeit. Mitteilungen des k.k. Arbeitsstatistischen Amtes im Handelsministerium. (Current numbers.) 8vo. 1907 .... — The Austrian Labour Department

Binnen-Fischerei in Österreich, 1904. 8vo. 1907 .... — The Central Statistical Commission

Eisenbahnministerium. Bericht über die Betriebsergebnisse der Kaiser Ferdinands-Nordbahn im Jahre 1906. 4to. 1907 .... Eisenbahnministerium. Bericht über die Ergebnisse der k.k. Staatseisenbahn-Verwaltung für 1906' 4to. 1907 .... — The I. and R. Ministry of Railways

Ergebnisse der Gewerblichen Betriebszählung vom 3. Juni 1902. 1. Heft. 2. Abteilung. Reichsübersichten nach Gewerbearten. Fol. 1907 .... Getreide im Weltverkehr. Statistische Tabellen über Produktion, Handel, Konsum und Preise. Neue Folge. 8vo. 1905 .... — The Ministry of Commerce

Mittheilungen des k.k. Finanzministeriums. (Current numbers.) La. 8vo. 1907 .... — The Ministry of Finance

Österreichisches Wirtschaftspolitisches Archiv (vormals "Austria"). (Current numbers.) 8vo. 1907 — The Ministry of Commerce

Statistisches Jahrbuch der autonomen Landesverwaltung in den im Reichsrate vertretenen Königreichen und Ländern. Jahrg. 6. 8vo. 1907 . .... Statistische Monatschrift. (Current numbers.) 1907 Statistische Nachrichten aus dem Gesammtgebiete der Landwirtschaft. (Current numbers.) 1907.......... — The Central Statistical Commission

(a) Foreign Countries—*Contd.*

Austria-Hungary—*Contd.*

Hungary. Dénombrement de la population des pays de la Sainte Couronne Hongroise en 1900. 3ᵛ Partie. Démographie détaillée. 9ᵉ Partie. Conditions de la propriété bâtie et foncière. 2 vols 8vo. 1907 .... } The Central Statistical Bureau

Bosnia and Herzegovina. Hauptergebnisse des auswärtigen Warenverkehres Bosniens und der Hercegovina, 1906. 8vo. 1907 ....

Bukowina. Mitteilungen des statistischen Landesamtes. Heft 11. La. 8vo. 1907 ....

Agram. Monatliche statistische Mittheilungen Feb., 1907. 8vo. 1907 .... } The Statistical Bureau

Budapest. Monatshefte des Budapester Communal-Statistischen Bureaus. (Current numbers.) 1907

Krakow—
Bulletins mensuels de statistique municipale, Jan.-Dec., 1906. Fol. 1907 ....
Statystyka Miasta Krakowa. Zeszyt 9. Czesc. 1. 8vo. 1905 .... } The Municipal Statistical Bureau

Belgium—
Annales des Mines. (Current numbers.) 8vo. 1907 { The Administration of Mines

Annuaire statistique de la Belgique. 37ᵉ année, 1906. 8vo. 1907 ....
Bulletin de la Commission Centrale de Statistique. Tome xix, années 1902-06. 4to. 1906 .... } The Administration of General Statistics

Travail. Annuaire de la législation du travail. 10ᵉ année, 1906. 8vo. 1907 ....
Travail. Monographies industrielles. Aperçu économique, technologique et commercial. Groupe IV. Fabrication et travail du verre. 8vo. 1907 .... } The Belgian Labour Department

Tableau général du commerce avec les Pays Étrangers pendant 1906. Fol. 1907 .... { The Administration of General Statistics

Académie Royale de Belgique. Bulletin de la classe des lettres . . . (Current numbers.) 8vo. 1907 .... } The Academy

Chambre de commerce néerlandaise, Bruxelles. 4ᵉ rapport annuel 1906. 8vo. 1907 .... } The Chamber of Commerce

Brazil—
Boletim do serviço de estatística commercial. Jan.-Mar., 1907. 8vo. 1907 .... } The Statistical Bureau

Brazilian Review. (Current numbers.) Fol. 1907 . . The Editor

Bulgaria—
Mouvement commercial de la Bulgarie avec les pays étrangers, mouvement de la navigation par ports et prix moyens dans les principales villes pendant le 3ᵉ trimestre de 1906. 4to. 1907 .... } The Statistical Bureau

China—
Customs Gazette. (Current numbers.) 4to. 1907 . .
Trade. Returns of Trade and Trade Reports, 1906. Part 2, Port Trade Statistics and Reports (in 5 parts). Part 3, Analysis of Foreign Trade. Vol. 1. Imports. Vol. 2, Exports. 4to. 1907 ... . } The Inspectorate-General of Customs, Shanghai

(a) Foreign Countries—*Contd.*

Congo Free State—

An answer to Mark Twain. [Anon.]   48 pp., 8vo. } The Publishers
Brussels, 1907   ....

Cuba—

Boletín oficial de la Secretaria de Agricultura, Industria y Comercio. (Current numbers.) 8vo. 1907 } The National Library

Comercio exterior.   2ᵈᵒ Semestre de 1905 y Año de 1905.   4to.   1907 .... } The Statistical Bureau

Estadística general.   Presupuestos municipales.   Año fiscal de 1904-05.   Fol.   1906 .... } The "Secretaria de Hacienda"

Camara de Comercio, Industria y Navegacion.   Boletín oficial.   Año 1, Nos. 12, 13; Año 2, Nos. 1-3.   8vo. } The National Library
1906-07   ....

Denmark—

Communications Statistiques.   4ᵐᵉ Série.   Tome 23. 8vo.   1907 ....

Comptes communaux et de ports, 1900-1904-05.   4to. } The State Statistical Bureau
1907   ....

Précis de Statistique, 1907.   56 pp., 8vo.   1907 ... ...

Egypt—

Education.   Statistical return of pupils attending public and private schools in Egypt, 1906-07.   4to. 1907 ....

Navigation in Ports of Egypt and the Suez Canal. Quarterly Returns. (Current numbers.) 8vo.   1907 } The Statistical Department, Ministry of Finance, Cairo

Postal traffic in Egypt.   Comparative statistics for the years 1880-1906.   Fol.   1907 ....

Statistical return of navigation in ports of Egypt for 1906.   4to.   1907   ....

France—

Album graphique de la Statistique générale de France. Résultats statistiques du Recensement de 1901. Mouvement de la Population.   Résumé rétrospectif de l'Annuaire Statistique.   4to.   1907 .... } M. Lucien March

Agriculture.   Ministère de l'Agriculture.   Bulletin mensuel de l'Office de Renseignements agricoles. (Current numbers.) 8vo.   1907 .... } The Ministry of Agriculture

Commerce de la France.   Documents statistiques [mensuels].   (Current numbers.) 8vo.   1907 ... . } The Director-General of Customs

Commerce.   Tableau général du Commerce et de la Navigation.   Année 1905.   Vol. 2.   Navigation. Fol.   1906   .... } The French Government

Finances.   Ministère des Finances.   Bulletin de Statistique et de Législation comparée.   (Current numbers.)   1907... } The Ministry of Finance

Justice.   Compte général de l'administration de la justice civile et commercielle pendant 1904.   4to. 1907 ....

Justice.   Compte général de l'administration de la justice criminelle pendant 1905.   4to.   1907........ ... } The Ministry of Justice

Prisons.   Statistique pénitentiaire pour l'année 1905. 8vo.   1907   ...... } The French Government

Travail.   Conseil Supérieur du Travail.   L'Inspection du Travail.   Rapport.   4to.   1906........ .... } The French Labour Department

Travail.   Conseil Supérieur du Travail.   16ᵉ Session Novembre, 1906.   Compte rendu.   4to.   1907........

(a) Foreign Countries—*Contd.*

France—*Contd.*

Colonies—

Statistiques coloniales pour 1895-1904. Finances.
8vo. 1907 ....
Statistiques coloniales pour 1905. Commerce:
Tome 1. Statistiques générales — Colonies
d'Afrique. Tome 2. Colonies d'Asie et d'Océanie. } The French Colonial
2 vols. 8vo. 1907 .... Office
Statistiques coloniales pour 1905. Navigation. 8vo.
1907 ....
Madagascar. Statistiques générales. Situation de la
colonie au 1er Janvier, 1906. 4to. 1907 ....

Paris. Annuaire statistique de la ville de Paris.
25e Année, 1904, et principaux renseignements } Dr. Jacques Bertillon
pour 1905. 8vo. 1906 ....

L'Expansion Française. Revue des Intérêts Artisti-
ques, commerciaux et industriels à l'extérieur. } The Publishers
Juillet, 1907. 4to. 1907 ....

Germany—

Arbeit. Beiträge zur Arbeiterstatistik. No. 6, Rege-
lung des Arbeitsverhältnisses bei Vergebung öffent- } Purchased
licher Arbeiten. 8vo. 1907 ....
Arbeit. Streiks und Aussperrungen im Jahre 1906. } The Imperial Sta-
4to. 1907 .... tistical Bureau
Deutsche Flagge in den ausserdeutschen Häfen
(1905). 4to. 1907 ....
Handel. Monatliche Nachweise über den Auswärtigen
Handel Deutschlands. (Current numbers.) 8vo. 1907 } The Imperial Sta-
Kriminalstatistik für das Jahr 1905. 4to. 1907 . .. tistical Bureau
Statistisches Jahrbuch für das Deutsche Reich.
Jahrgang 28, 1907. 8vo. 1907 ......
Stromgebiete des Deutschen Reichs. Teile IIb and IIc,
and Teil IIIa. 3 vols., 4to. 1907 ..... .
Veröffentlichungen des Kaiserlichen Gesundheitsamtes. } The Imperial Health
(Current numbers.) 8vo. 1907 .... Bureau
Vierteljahrshefte zur Statistik des Deutschen Reichs. } The Imperial Sta-
(Current numbers.) 4to. 1907 .... tistical Bureau
Statistisches Jahrbuch Deutscher Städte. Jahrgang } Purchased
14. 8vo. 1907 ....
Prussia. Zeitschrift des K. Preussischen Statistischen } The Royal Prussian
Landesamts. (Current numbers.) Fol. 1907... . Statistical Bureau
Saxony. Zeitschrift des K. Sächsischen Statistischen } The Statistical Bu-
Landesamts. (Current numbers.) 4to. 1907 ... ... reau of Saxony
Württemberg. Württembergische Jahrbücher für
Statistik und Landeskunde. Jahrgang 1906. Heft 2. } Mr. I. P. A. Renwick
4to. 1907 ....

Berlin—

Mitteilungen des Statistischen Amts der Stadt
Berlin. No. 1. Fol. 1907.............
Übersichten aus der Berliner Statistik für das } The Municipal Sta-
Jahr 1905 (Auszug aus dem 30. Jahrgang des tistical Bureau
Statistischen Jahrbuchs der Stadt Berlin.) 62 pp.,
12 mo. 1907 ....
Frankfurt. Jahresbericht über die Verwaltung des
Medizinalwesens, die Krankenanstalten und die
öffentlichen Gesundheitsverhältnisse der Stadt } The Statistical Bu-
Frankfurt a.M. Jahrgang 1904. 8vo. 1907 .... reau
Hamburg. Statistik der Mieten in der Stadt Ham-
burg, 1906. 6 pp., fol. 1906 ....

(a) Foreign Countries—*Contd.*

Greece—

Bulletin trimestriel du commerce spécial de la Grèce avec les pays étrangers. 1ᵉʳ Trimestre de 1907. 4to. 1907	The Bureau of Statistics

Italy—

Annali di agricoltura, 1907. ˙L'azione del ministero in favore della pesca e dell' acquicoltura nel 1906. 8vo. 1907	The Ministry of Agriculture
Finanze. Relazione sull' amministrazione del demanio e delle tasse sugli affari per l'esercizio finanziario 1905-06. 4to. 1907	Mr. I. P. A. Renwick
Sanita Pubblica. Direzione Generale della. Bollettino Sanitario. Anno 1, No. 1. Jap., 1907. 8vo. 1907	The Department
Tabella indicante i valori delle merci nell' anno 1906 per le statistiche commerciali. 8vo. 1907	The Director-General of Statistics

Japan—

Résumé statistique de l'Empire du Japon. 21ᵉ Année. Sm. 4to. 1907	The Statistical Bureau
Seventh Financial and Economic Annual of Japan, 1907. Department of Finance. 8vo. 1907............	The Department of Finance

Mexico—

Boletín de Estadística fiscal. (Current numbers.) Fol. 1907	
Boletín de Estadística fiscal. Año fiscal de 1904-05, No. 285. Fol. 1907..........	The Director-General of Statistics
Estadística fiscal. Datos relativos. (Current numbers.) Fol. 1907	

Netherlands—

Grèves et lock-outs dans les Pays-Bas pendant 1906. 8vo. 1907	
Jaarcijfers voor het Koninkrijk der Nederlanden. Koloniën 1905. 8vo. 1907	The Central Statistical Bureau
Revue mensuelle du Bureau Central de Statistique. (Current numbers.) 8vo. 1907	
Statistiek van den in-, uit-, en doorvoer over het jaar 1906. Gedeelte I. Fol. 1907	Ministry of Finance
Statistiek der periodieke verkiezingen voor de Provinciale Staten gehouden in 1907. La. 8vo. 1907	The Central Statiscal Bureau

Norway—

Arbeidsmarkedet, udgivet af det Statistiske Central-bureau. 4. Aargang, 1906, 8vo. 1907	
Grèves et lock-outs en Norvège, 1903 à 1906. 20 pp., 8vo. 1907	The Central Statistical Bureau
Journal du Bureau central de Statistique. (Current numbers.) 8vo. 1907	
Statistique sociale. VI. Dénombrements du chômage en 1905 et 1906. 24 pp., 8vo. 1907	
Christiania. Beretning fra Kristiania sundhedskommission og kommunale sygehuse for 1906. 8vo. 1907	The Department of Health

Portugal—

Annuario estatistico de Portugal, 1900. 8vo. 1907	The Director-General of Statistics

Roumania—

Bulletin Statistique. (Current numbers.) 8vo. 1907	
Commerce extérieur de la Roumanie, dans le semestre Janvier-Juin 1906. Mouvement des ports pour le trimestre Avril-Juin 1906. 8vo. 1907	The Statistical Bureau

(a) Foreign Countries—*Contd.*

Russia—

Agriculture. Year-Book of Department of Agriculture. 1906, Part 6. 1907, Parts 1 and 2. (In Russian.) 8vo. 1906-07 .... } The Department of Agriculture

Prices of Grain at Ports. Return of (in Russian). Sheets. (Current numbers.) 1907.... .... } The Ministry of Finance

Trade Returns for 1905. (In Russian.) Fol. 1907 { The Department of Customs

Kazan University. Bulletin of the. (Current numbers.) (In Russian.) 8vo. 1907 .... } The University

Salvador—

Boletin del Consejo Superior de Salubridad. (Current numbers.) 8vo. 1907 .... } The Board

Servia—

Annuaire statistique du Royaume de Serbie. Tome 10, 1905. 8vo. 1907 .... } The Statistical Bureau

Spain—

Estadística del impuesto de transportes por mar y á la entrada y salida por las fronteras. Segundo trimestre de 1907. 8vo. 1907 ... . Memoria sobre el estado de la renta de aduanas en 1906. 8vo. 1907 .... } The Director-General of Customs

Junta de aranceles y de valoraciones. Tablas de valores para la importación y exportación de mercancias del Año de 1906. 8vo. 1907.... .... } The "Junta"

Movimiento natural de la poblacion de España, año 1902. 8vo. 1906 .... } The Geographical and Statistical Institute

Sweden—

Bidrag till Sveriges Officiella Statistik. 4to. 1907—
  A. Befolkningsstatistik, 1904. (Population.) 4to. 1907 .. ....
  B. Rattsväsendet, 1905. (Justice.) 4to. 1907 . .
  C. Bergshandteringen, 1906. (Mining.) 4to. 1907
  K. Hälso-och Sjukvården, 1905. (Public Health.) 4to. 1907 ....
  O. Landtmäteristyrelsens Underdåniga Berättelse, 1906. 4to. 1907 ... .
  R. Valstatistik, 1904 4to. 1907 ....
  T. Lots-och Fyrinrattningen, 1906. (Pilotage.) 4to. 1907 .. ..
  V. Brannvins tillverkning och försäljning samt Hvitbetsocker- och Maltdryckstillverkningen. 1905-06. 4to. 1907...... ....} The Central Statistical Bureau

Försäkringsvasendet i Riket år 1905. I. 8vo. 1907 .... } The University of Upsala

Meddelanden fran k. Kommerskollegii afdelning for Arbetsstatistik. (Current numbers.) 8vo. 1907....
In- och utvandring år 1906. 15 pp., 4to. 1907 ....
Riksstat för år 1908. 8vo. 1907 ....
Rikets In-, och Utforsel. (Current numbers.) 1907....
Sammandrag af de enskilda sedelutgifvande bankernas. (Current numbers.) 1907. ....
Sammandrag af Riksbankens Ställning. (Current numbers.) 1907 ....
Sparbanksstatistik. 1. Sparbanker och liknande penningenrättningar. 1905 ....
Statistisk Tidskrift. (Current numbers.) 8vo. 1907 } The Central Statistical Bureau

(a) **Foreign Countries**—*Contd.*
Sweden—*Contd.*
Stockholm—

Annuaire Statistique de la ville, année 1905, 4to.⎤
1907 ....⎟ The Municipal Sta-
Bulletin mensuel du Bureau de Statistique de la ⎬ tistical Bureau
ville. (Current numbers.) 8vo. 1907.. ....⎦

Switzerland—

Agriculture. Résultats du recensement fédéral des⎤
entreprises agricoles, industrielles et commerciales⎬ The Federal Sta-
du 9 août 1905. Vol. I. Fascicule 4. 4to. 1907⎦ tistical Bureau
Alcool. Données statistiques concernant la gestion⎤
de la Régie fédérale des alcools en 1906. Fol. ⎟ The " Régie fédérale
1907 ....⎬ des alcools "
Alcool. Rapport sur la gestion et le compte de la ⎟
Régie des alcools pour 1906. 8vo. 1907 ....⎦
Assurances. Rapport du Bureau Fédéral des Assur-⎤
ances sur les entreprises privées en matière d'assur-⎬ The Bureau
ances en 1905. 4to. 1907 ....⎦
Examen pédagogique des recrues en automne 1906.⎤ The Federal Sta-
4to. 1907................... ....⎦ tistical Bureau

Turkey—

Ottoman Public Debt. Special report on the debt,⎤
and translation of annual report of Council of⎬ Mr. I. P. A. Renwick
administration for twenty-fourth financial period, ⎟
1905-06. 8vo. 1906.. ... .⎦

United States—

Agriculture. Department of. Crop Reporter. (Cur-⎤ The Department of
rent numbers.) Fol. 1907 .... ⎦ Agriculture
Census Bureau Bulletins—.
71. Estimates of Population, 1904, 1905, 1906.⎤
  Including the census returns of States making an⎟
  intercensal enumeration. 4to. 1907 ....⎟
72. Census of Manufactures, 1905. Boots and ⎟
  Shoes, Leather, &c. 4to. 1907 ....⎟
73. Census of Manufactures, 1905. Electrical ⎟
  Machinery, &c. 4to. 1907 ....⎟
74. Census of Manufactures, 1905. Textiles. 4to.⎟
  1907 ....⎟
76. Cotton Production, 1906. 4to. 1907 ....⎬ The Bureau of Cen-
77. Census of Manufactures, 1905. Lumber and ⎟ sus
  timber products. 4to. 1907 ....⎟
78. Census of Manufactures. 1905. Iron and steel ⎟
  and tin and terne plate. 4to. 1907 . ...⎟
Census Bureau. Mortality statistics, 1905. Sixth ⎟
  annual report, with revised rates for intercensal ⎟
  years 1901 to 1904, based upon State censuses of ⎟
  1905. 4to. 1907 ....⎟
Census Office. Special Reports. Wealth, Debt, and ⎟
  Taxation. 4to. 1907 ....⎦
Commerce and Finance. Monthly Summary. (Current⎤
numbers.) 4to. 1907 ....⎟ The Bureau of Sta-
Commercial Porto Rico in 1906, showing commerce, ⎬ tistics, Depart-
production, transportation, finances, area, popula- ⎟ ment of Commerce
tion, and details of trade with United States and ⎟ and Labor
foreign countries during a term of years. 4to. 1907⎦
Education. Report of Commissioner of Education⎤
for year ending 30th June, 1905. Vols. 1 and 2. ⎬ The Board of Edu-
8vo. 1907 ....⎦ cation

(a) Foreign Countries—*Contd.*

United States—*Contd.*

Debt. Monthly Statements of the Public, and of Cash in Treasury. (Current numbers.) Sheets. 1907 .... } The Secretary of the Treasury

Gold, Silver, and Notes, &c., in Circulation. Monthly Statements. (Current numbers.) Sheets. 1907 ....

California. State Board of Health. Monthly Bulletins. 8vo. 1907. (Current numbers) .... } The Board

Illinois—

Bureau of Labor Statistics. 13th Biennial Report, 1904. 8vo. 1907 .... } The Bureau

University. University Studies. Vol. ii., No. 4, May, 1907. 8vo. 1907.................... } The University

Massachusetts—

Metropolitan Water and Sewerage Board. Sixth annual report. 1st Jan., 1907. 8vo. 1907 ... } The Board

Labor Bulletin. (Current numbers.) 8vo. 1907.... Strikes and Lockouts in Massachusetts, 1906. 48 pp., 8vo. 1907 .... } The Bureau of Statistics of Labor

Minnesota. Bureau of Labor. 10th Biennial Report, 1905-06. 8vo. 1907 .. .. } The Bureau

Nebraska. University Studies, Vol. 7, No. 1, containing: Statistical inquiry into the influence of credit upon the level of prices: *Minnie T. England.* 8vo. 1907 .... } The University

New York State—

Museum. 57th Annual Report, 1903. Vols. 3 and 4. 2 vols., 4to. 1905 .... New York State Library

Museum. 58th Annual Report. 1904. Vols. 1—5. 8vo. 1906 .. .. ..

Museum. Bulletins 106—109. 8vo. 1907 ....

Boston. Monthly Bulletin of the Statistics Department. (Current numbers.) 4to. 1907 .... } The Municipal Statistical Bureau

Chicago. 49th Annual Report of the Trade and Commerce of Chicago, 1906, [with section giving] Acts of Incorporation, rules, &c., of the Board of Trade of Chicago; also Rules governing the state inspection of grain. 8vo. 1907 .... } The Board of Trade

New York (City). Public Library. Bulletin. (Current numbers) 8vo. 1907.................... } The Library

Commercial America. Published monthly. (Current numbers.) Fol. 1906 .... } Philadelphia Commercial Museum

Dun's Review. (Current numbers.) Fol. 1907........ { Messrs. R. G. Dun and Co.

Mineral Industry, The, its Statistics, Technology and Trade during 1906. Vol. 15. 8vo. 1907 .... } The Editor

Actuarial Society of America. Transactions. Vol. x. No. 37. 16th and 17th May, 1907. 8vo. 1907 .... } The Society

American Economic Association Publications —

Historical sketch of the finances and financial policy of Massachusetts, from 1780 to 1905: *Charles J. Bullock,* Ph.D. 3rd Series. Vol. viii, No. 2, May. 8vo. 1907 .... The Association

Handbook of the American Economic Association. 3rd Series. Vol. viii, No. 2, Supplement, May. 8vo. 1907 . ...

American Statistical Association. Quarterly Publications. Vol. x, No. 77. Mar., 1907. 8vo. 1907 .... } „

(a) Foreign Countries—*Contd.*

United States—*Contd.*

Columbia University Studies—

Vol. xxv, No. 3. The Finances of Cleveland: Charles C. Williamson, Ph.D. 8vo. 1907 ....

Vol. xxvi, No. 1. Trade and currency in early Oregon. A study in the commercial and monetary history of the Pacific Northwest: James Henry Gilbert, Ph.D. 8vo. 1907 . ...

Vol. xxvi, No 2. Luther's table talk. A critical study: Preserved Smith, Ph.D. 8vo· 1907 ... ..

Vol. xxvi, No. 3. The tobacco industry in the United States: Meyer Jacobstein, Ph.D. 8vo. 1907 . ...

Vol. xxvi, No. 4. Social democracy and population: Alvan A. Tenney. Ph.D. 8vo. 1907 ....

Vol. xxvii, No. 1. The economic policy of Robert Walpole: Norris A. Brisco, Ph.D. 8vo. 1907 ....

Vol. xxvii, No. 2. The United States Steel Corporation. A study of the growth and influence of combination in the iron and steel industry: Abraham Berglund, Ph.D. 8vo. 1907 ....

Vol. xxvii, No. 3. The taxation of corporations in Massachusetts: Harry G. Friedman, A.B. 8vo. 1907 ....

Vol. xxviii, No. 1. De Witt Clinton and the origin of the spoils system in New York: Howard Lee McBain, Ph.D. 8vo. 1907 .....

} The University, per Messrs. P. S. King and Son

Johns Hopkins University Studies—

Series xxiv, Nos. 11–12. Maryland during the English civil wars. Part I: Bernard C. Steiner. 8vo. 1906 ......

Series xxv, No. 1. Internal taxation in the Philippines: John S. Hord. 8vo· 1907 ......

Series xxv, Nos. 2–3. The Monroe mission to France, 1794-1796: Beverly W. Bond, jun. 8vo. 1907 ... ...

Series xxv, Nos. 4–5. Maryland during the English civil wars. Part II: Bernard C. Steiner. 8vo. 1907 ......

} The Johns Hopkins Press

Smithsonian Institution—

Smithsonian Miscellaneous Collections. Quarterly issue. Vol. 3, part 4; vol. 4, part 1. 8vo. 1907 ....

Smithsonian Miscellaneous Collections. Nos. 1720 and 1721. 8vo. ·1907 ......

} The Institution

Uruguay—

Anuario estadístico de la República. Años 1904-06. Tomo 1. La. 8vo. 1907 . ... The Director-General of Statistics

Oficina de Crédito Público. Deuda Pública de la República, 1906. Obl. 4to. 1906 .... Mr. I. P. A. Renwick

Venezuela—

Boletín de estadística de los Estados Unidos de Venezuela. Año iii, Tomo iv, Núm. 33. Marzo de 1907. 8vo. 1907 .. .. The Director-General of Statistics

International—

Bulletin International des Douanes. (Current numbers.) 8vo· 1907 ...... The Board of Trade

(a) **Foreign Countries**—*Contd.*

International—*Contd.*

Institut International de Statistique. xi° Session à Copenhague, 1907. Compte - Rendu provisoire. 74 pp., 8vo· 1907 .... } The Institute

International Labour Office. Bulletin. Vol. 1, Nos. 1—3. 1906. 8vo. 1907.... ... . } Purchased

---

(b) **India and Colonies.**

India, British—

Coal. Note on the production of Coal in India, to 1906. 22 pp., fol. 1907 ....

Coffee. Note on production of Coffee in India in 1906. 9 pp., fol. 1907 ....

Cotton Spinning and Weaving. Monthly Statistics of. (Current numbers.) 8vo. 1907........... ....

Financial and Commercial Statistics of British India. 13th issue. La. fol. 1907 ....

Indian Trade Journal. (Current numbers.) 4to. 1907 ....

Judicial and Administrative Statistics of British India for 1905-06 and preceding years. 11th issue. Fol. 1907 ....

Tea. Production of tea in India, 1906. 23 pp., fol. 1907 ....

Trade. Review of Trade of India in 1906.07. Fol. 1907 ....

} The Director-General of Commercial Intelligence

Mines. Report of Chief Inspector of Mines in India for 1906. Fol. 1907 .... } The Department of Mines

Sanitary measures in India, Report on, in 1905-06. Vol. 39. [Cd-3559.] 1907.... . ...

Statistical abstract relating to British India from 1896-97 to 1905-06. 41st number. [Cd-3724.] 8vo. 1907 ....

Agra and Oudh. Basti: A Gazetteer, being Vol. 32 of the district gazetteer of the United Provinces. 8vo. 1907 ....

Bengal—

District Gazetteers. Darjeeling and Diarbhanga. 2 vols., 8vo. 1907 ....

} The India Office

Report on administration of Bengal, 1905-06. Fol. 1907 ....

Supplement to Report on Public Instruction in Bengal for 1905-06. 32 pp., fol. 1907 ....

} The Lieutenant-Governor of Bengal

Report on Maritime trade of Bengal for year 1906-07. Fol. 1907 .... } The Collector of Customs

Eastern Bengal and Assam. Report on Administration of E. Bengal and Assam, 1905-06. Fol. 1907 ... . } The Secretary, Judicial and General Department

Bombay. Gazetteer of Bombay Presidency. Vol. viii-B. Kathiawar. 8vo. 1907...............

Central Provinces. District Gazetteers. Sambalpur District. B Volume. Statistical Tables, 1891-1901. 8vo. 1905 ....

} The India Office

Punjab—

District Gazetteers. Vol. xix-B. Lahore District. Statistical Tables with maps, 1904. 8vo. 1905

Report on Sanitary Administration for 1906. Fol. 1907 .... } Lieut.-Col. C. J. Bamber

(b) **India and Colonies**—*Contd.*

Australia, Commonwealth of—

Population and Vital Statistics. Bulletin No. 1, Determination of population of Australia for each
quarter from 31st December, 1900, to 31st December, 1906. Fol. 1907 ....

Population and Vital Statistics. Bulletin No. 2,
Summary of Commonwealth Demography for
1901-06. Fol. 1907 ......

Trade and Customs and Excise Revenue of the
Commonwealth for 1906. Fol. 1907 .... } The Commonwealth Statistician

Trade, Shipping, and oversea Migration of the Commonwealth. Official Bulletins. (Current numbers.)
Fol. 1907 ....

Unification of Australasian statistical methods and
co-ordination of the work of the Commonwealth
and State bureaux. Conference of Statisticians of
the Commonwealth and States of Australia and
Colony of New Zealand. Melbourne, Nov. and
Dec., 1906. 73 pp., fol. 1906.. ....

Parliamentary Debates. Session 1907. (Current
numbers.) 8vo. 1907 .... } The Commonwealth

Canada, Dominion of—

Banks. Monthly Reports on Chartered. (Current
numbers.) 4to. 1907 .... } The Deputy Minister of Finance

Banks. Report of Dividends remaining unpaid,
unclaimed balances in chartered Banks as at
31st December, 1906. 8vo. 1907 ....
Building Societies, loan and trust companies. Report
for 1906. 8vo. 1907 .... } The Finance Department

Census and Statistics. Bulletin 1, Wage-earners by
Occupations. 8vo. 1907. (2 copies) .... } The High Commissioner for Canada

Debates of House of Commons of Canada. Official
Report. Session 1906-07. 4 vols., 8vo. 1906-07 } The Clerk of the House

British Columbia. Annual Report of Minister of
Mines for year ending 31st December, 1906. 8vo.
1907 .... } Provincial Mineralogist

Ontario—

Agricultural and Experimental Union. 28th
Annual Report, 1906. 8vo. 1907 .... } The Union

Bureau of Industries. Annual Report for 1905.
Part 1, Agricultural Statistics. Part 2,
Chattel Mortgages. 192 pp., 8vo. 1907 ....
Department of Agriculture. Bulletins 158, 159.
2 parts. 8vo. 1907 .... } The Department of Agriculture

Canadian Life and Resources. (Current numbers.)
Fol. 1907 .... } The Superintendent of Emigration

Commercial handbook of Canada : a year book,
edited by Ernest Heaton. 3rd year, 1907. 8vo.
1907 .... } Purchased

Royal Society of Canada. Proceedings and transactions. Second series. Vol. xii. Meeting of May,
1906. 8vo. 1906 .... } The Royal Society of Canada

Cape of Good Hope—

Births, Deaths and Marriages. Report of Registrar-
General for 1906. [With tabular statements.]
Fol. 1907 .. ..
Statistical register of the colony of the Cape of Good
Hope for 1906. (2 copies.) Fol. 1907 .... } The Colonial Secretary

(b) India and Colonies—*Contd.*

Ceylon—
Progress of the Colony of Ceylon, 1904-1907. A } The Colonial Secre-
Review by His Excellency Sir Henry Arthur Blake, } tary, Colombo
G.C.M.G. 58 pp., fol. 1907 .... }

Mauritius—
Blue-Book for the Colony of Mauritius, 1906. Fol. } The Colonial Secre-
1907 .... } tary

New South Wales—
Mines. Annual report of Department of Mines for } The Agent-General
1906. Fol. 1907 .... }
Vital Statistics. Preliminary report on vital statistics } The Bureau of Sta-
of New South Wales for 1906. Fol. 1907 .... } tistics

New Zealand, Dominion of—
Friendly Societies. Thirtieth annual report by the } The Registrar
Registrar for 1906. Fol. 1907 ... . }
Old-age Pensions Department. Ninth annual report }
for the year ended 31st March, 1907. 17 pp., fol. } The Department
1907 .... }

Queensland—
Agricultural and Pastoral Statistics. Report of } Government Statis-
Government Statistician for 1906. Fol. 1907 .... } tician

Rhodesia—
Chamber of Mines. Monthly Reports of Executive }
· Committee, and Returns of Output of Gold, &c. }
(Current numbers.) Sheets. 1907 . ... } The Chamber
Rhodesia Chamber of Mines, Buluwayo. Report of }
Executive Committee for year 1906-07. 4to. 1907 }

South Australia—
Friendly Societies. 5th Report of Public Actuary. }
Report for quinquennial period 1900.04, with }
third valuation of all Registered Societies, as at }
31st Dec., 1904; also mortality and sickness ex- }
perience during 1895-99 and 1900.04, and during } The Public Actuary
the combined period 1895-1904. Fol. 1907 .... }
South Australian School of Mines and Industries and }
Technological Museum. Annual Report for 1906. }
8vo. 1907 .... }

Tasmania—
Statistics of the State of Tasmania for 1905-06. Fol. } The Government of
1907 .... } Tasmania

Straits Settlements—
Supplements to the Perak Government Gazette, 1907. } The Government
(Current numbers.) Fol. 1907 .... } Secretary

Transvaal—
Agricultural Journal. (Current numbers.) 8vo. } The Agricultural
1907 .. .. } Department
Mines Department, Transvaal. Monthly Statistics. } The Department
(Current numbers.) Obl. 4to. 1907 ... ... }
Johannesburg. Statistics. (Current numbers.) Fol. } The Town Statis-
1907 .... } tician
Transvaal Chamber of Mines. Monthly Analysis of } The Chamber
Gold Production. (Current numbers.) 1907 .... }

(b) India and Colonies—*Contd.*
Transvaal and Orange River Colony—
Inter-Colonial Council—

Debates at 5th Ordinary Annual Meeting, May, 1907. 4to. 1907 .... Minutes 5th Ordinary Annual Meeting, May, 1907. Fol. 1907	The Secretary of the Council
Reports of Auditors-General on Loan Expenditure, 1905-06. Fol. 1907	The Auditor-General

Victoria—

Statistical Register of the State of Victoria for 1905. Fol. 1906 .... Statistical Register for 1906. Part 1, Blue-Book. Part 2, Finance. Fol. 1907	The Government Statist

Western Australia—

Finance. Report by Edgar T. Owen, Government Actuary, on proposals of Commonwealth Treasurer and recommendations of Interstate Conference held at Brisbane in May, 1907, containing an equitable solution of the Federal financial problem. 6 pp., fol. 1907..	Mr. E. T. Owen
Monthly Statistical Abstract. (Current numbers.) Fol. 1907 .... Supplements to Government Gazette, containing Monthly Mining Statistics. (Current numbers.) 1907 .... Statistical Register for 1904 and previous years. Fol. 1907 .... Statistical Register for 1906. Part 13, Summary of Statistics. Fol. 1907	The Registrar-General and Government Statistician

(c) United Kingdom and its several Divisions.
United Kingdom—

Accidents. General report upon accidents on railways during 1906. [Cd-3681.] 1907...............................	The Board of Trade
Bankruptcy, 1906. 24th General Annual Report. (295.) 1907	The Inspector-General in Bankruptcy
Board of Trade Journal. (Current numbers.) 1907 Companies (Winding up). 16th General Annual Report by the Board of Trade. (248.) 1907	The Board of Trade
Customs. 51st Report of Commissioners of Customs (for year ending 31st March, 1907). [Cd-3701.] 8vo. 1907	The Commissioners
Factories and Workshops. Annual Report of Chief Inspector for 1906. Reports and Statistics. [Cd-3586.] 1907	The Home Office
Friendly Societies, &c. Reports of Chief Registrar of Friendly Societies for 1905. Part A.—Appendix (N). Particulars of valuation returns. 55-I. 1906	Chief Registrar of Friendly Societies
Inland Revenue. 50th report of Commissioners for year ended 31st March, 1907. [Cd-3686.] 1907....	Secretary of Inland Revenue
Joint Stock Companies Return, June, 1907. Fol. 1907	Registrar of Joint Stock Companies
Mines and quarries : general report and statistics for 1905. Part IV—Colonial and foreign statistics. [Cd-3566.] 1907	The Home Office
Mint. 37th Annual Report of Deputy Master and Comptroller of the Mint, 1906. [Cd-3598.] 8vo. 1907	The Deputy Master

(c) **United Kingdom and its Divisions**—*Contd.*
United Kingdom—*Contd.*

Navigation and shipping of United Kingdom. Annual } The Board of Trade
Statement for 1906. [Cd-3545.] 1907. ... .}

Accounts of Local Authorities—
Report of Departmental Committee. Vol. i, Report.⌉
[Cd-3614.] 1907 ....
Minutes of evidence taken before Departmental
Committee. Vol. ii. [Cd-3615.] 1907 ... .
Allotments and Small Holdings. Copies of Acts.
(189.) 1907 ....
British and Foreign Trade and Industry. (190.) 1907
British Museum. Return, 1907. (105.) 1907 .. ....
Charity Commissioners. (Agricultural Land.) (148.)
1907 ....:........
China (No. 1, 1907). Report on journey through
provinces of Shantung and Kiangsu. [Cd-3500.]
1907 ....
Civil Service Commissioners. 51st Report. [Cd-3602.]
8vo. 1907 ....
Colonies. Papers relating to Brussels Sugar Conven-
tion. [Cd-3565.] 1907 ....
Colonial Merchant Shipping Conference, 1907.
Report. [Cd-3567.] 1907 . ...:
Colonial Reports. Annual. 534. Gold Coast, Report
for 1906. 8vo. 1907 ....
Commercial Attachés and Agents. Report on system
of British. [Cd-3610.] 1907 ....
Company laws in the British Empire. Comparative
analysis, with Memorandum. [Cd-3589.] 1907 ...
County Courts (Plaints and Sittings). Return, 1906.
(258.) 1907 ... .
Crown Agents. Return. (181.) 1907 ....
Crown Lands Act, 1906. 1st Report. (253.) 1907 ⎬ Purchased
Danube. Report on operations of the European Com-
mission during 1894-1906. [Cd-3646.] 1907 ....
East Africa Protectorate. Papers [158.] 1907 ..
East India. (Home Accounts.) (145.) 1907... ....
East India. (Textile Factories Labour Committee.)
Report. [Cd-3617.] 1907 ....
East India. (Punjab land colonisation bill) (202.)
1907 ....
Education Board. Special Reports. Vol. 17. Schools
in North of Europe. [Cd-3537.] 8vo. 1907 .. ....
Education. England and Wales. Voluntary Schools.
(231.) 1907 ....
Finance Accounts of United Kingdom for 1906-07.
(212.) 1907 ....
Fleets. (Great Britain and Foreign Countries.) (184.)
1907 ....
Foreshores. (Sales, &c.) (269.) 1907...................
Government Factories and Workshops Committee.
Report. [Cd-3626.] 1907 ....
Insurance under the Workmen's Compensation Acts.
Report of Departmental Committee. [Cd-3568-9.]
1907 ....
Inebriates Acts, 1879 to 1900. Report of Inspector
for 1905. [Cd-3246.] 1906 ....
Jamaica. Colonial Reports, Annual. No. 524, Report
for 1905-06. 8vo. 1907 ... .
Military Prisons. Report on, for 1906. [Cd-3368.]
8vo. 1907 ... .⌋

(c) United Kingdom and its Divisions—*Contd.*
United Kingdom—*Contd.*

Mines. Royal Commission. 1st Report. [Cd-3548.] 1907 ....

Municipal Representation Bill [H.L.]. Report of Select Committee. (132) 1907.......................

Old Age Pensions. Tables regarding, with Memorandum. [Cd-3618.] 1907 ....

Parliamentarv Debates. Report of Select Committee. (239.) 1907 ....

Patriotic Fund. 3rd Report, for 1906. [Cd-3583.] 1907 ....

Patents, Designs, and Trade Marks. 24th Report, for 1906. (164.) 1907 ....

Proportional Representation in Public Elections abroad. Reports. [Cd-3501.] 1907 ....

Public Income and Expenditure. Return. (254.) 1907

Publications. Report of Select Committee. (272.) 1907 ....

Post Office Servants. Report of Select Committee. (266.) 1907 .... } Purchased

Railway Accidents. (180.) 1907 ....

Revenue, Imperial. (Collection and Expenditure.) Great Britain and Ireland. (242.) 1907 ....

Revenue and Expenditure. (England, Scotland, and Ireland.) (245.) 1907... ....

Small Holdings and Allotments Bill. Report of Standing Committee C. (285.) 1907 ....

South Africa. Papers relating to a federation of the S.A. Colonies. [Cd-3564.] 1907 ....

Suez Canal. Returns of Shipping and Tonnage, 1904-06. [Cd-3579.] 1907.......................

Sugar Commission, International. Report, Spring Session, 1907. [Cd-3607.] 1907 ....

Trade with Australia. Report on conditions and prospects of British Trade in Australia. [Cd-3639.] 1907 ....

Transvaal Loan Act, 1907, and Papers respecting the Finances of the Colony. [Cd-3621.] 1907 ....

Tariff Commission—

Report. Vol. 6. The Glass Industry, with analysis and summary of evidence and statistical tables. 4to. 1907..... ...

Report. Vol. 7. Sugar and Confectionery, with } The Commission analysis and summary of evidence and statistical tables. 4to. 1907 ....

Great Britain—

Board of Agriculture and Fisheries—

Agricultural Statistics, 1906. Vol. xli, Part 3. Prices and Supplies of Corn, Live Stock, and other Agricultural Produce. [Cd-3653.] 8vo. 1907 ....

Agricultural Returns of Great Britain, 1907. Preliminary Statement for 1907. [Acreage and Live Stock] .... } The Board

Journal of the Board. (Current numbers.) 8vo. 1907

Leaflets. (Current numbers.) 8vo. 1907 ....

Weekly Returns of Market Prices (of Cattle, Dead Meat, Provisions, Fruit, and Vegetables, Hay and Straw). (Current numbers.) Fol. 1907...........

(c) **United Kingdom and its Divisions—***Contd.*

England and Wales—

Annual Summary of Births, Deaths, &c., in London and other large towns, 1904. 8vo. 1905 ....

Census of England and Wales, 1901. Instructions to Clerks employed in classifying the occupations and ages of the people. 4to. 1901 ....

Supplement to 65th Annual Report of Registrar-General of Births, Deaths, and Marriages in England and Wales. 1891-1900. Part 1. 8vo. [Cd–2618.] 1907 ....

} The Registrar-General.

Local Taxation Returns. Year 1904-05. Parts 3, 4, 5, and 6. 1906-07 ....

Pauperism (England and Wales). Half-yearly statement for 1st Jan., 1907. (108.) 1907 ....

} The Local Government Board

London County Council—

Debt of Great Towns, 1905-06. 8vo. 1907 ....

New Working-class accommodation, 1906. Fol. 1907 ....

} Purchased

Report of joint committee on underfed children for the season 1906-07. Fol. 1907 ....

Special Schools for blind, deaf, and defective children. Report for year ended 31st Mar., 1906. Fol. 1907 ....

London County Council Gazette. (Current numbers.) Fol. 1907 ....

} The London County Council

Metropolitan Water Board. 4th Annual Report for year ended 31st Mar., 1907. 8vo. 1907 ....

} The Board

Poplar. Annual Report for 1906 on the sanitary condition and vital statistics of Poplar. 8vo. 1907 ....

} The Medical Officer of Health

Birmingham—

Epitome of Blue-Book for year ended 31st March, 1907. 12 pp., la. 8vo. 1907 ....

Financial statement for year ended 31st March, 1907. La. 8vo. 1907 ....

} The Treasurer

Report of Medical Officer of Health on the health of Birmingham for 1906. 8vo. 1907 ....

} The Medical Officer of Health

Bradford. Report on public health of the City for 1906, by the Medical Officer of Health. 8vo. 1907 ....

Bristol. Annual Report of Medical Officer of Health for 1906. 8vo. 1907 .. ..

Derby. Annual Report of Medical Officer of Health, 1906. 8vo. 1907 ....

Halifax. Report of Medical Officer of Health for 1906. 8vo. 1907 ....

} "

Leicester. Abstract of accounts of the Corporation, 1st April, 1906, to 31st March, 1907. 8vo. 1907

} The Borough Treasurer

Liverpool. Report on health of the City of Liverpool during 1906. 8vo. 1907....

} The Medical Officer of Health

Manchester. Report on health of the City of Manchester for 1906. 8vo. 1907 ....

} "

Nottingham. Abstract of corporation accounts for year ending 31st March, 1907. 8vo. 1907 .. ....

} The City Accountant

Preston. Annual Report of Medical Officer of Health for 1906. 8vo. 1907 ....

} The Medical Officer of Health

Wolverhampton. Annual Report on health of Wolverhampton for 1906. 8vo. 1907 ....

} ..

Mersey. Report on the present state of the navigation of the River Mersey (1906). By Vice-Adm. Sir G. S. Nares, K.C.B., F.R.S. 22 pp., 8vo. 1907

} Mersey Conservancy

(c) United Kingdom and its Divisions—*Contd.*

Ireland—

Births, Deaths, and Marriages. 43rd detailed annual report of the Registrar General for Ireland for 1906. [Cd-3663.] 1907 .... } Registrar - General for Ireland

Banking and Railway Statistics, Ireland. December, 1906. [Cd-3533.] 8vo. 1907 ....

Department of Agriculture and Technical Instruction. Report of proceedings under the Diseases of Animals Acts for 1906. [Cd-3667.] 8vo. 1907....

Department of Agriculture and Technical Instruction. Journal of the. (Current numbers.) 8vo. 1907.... } The Department of Agriculture and Technical Instruction

Agriculture and Technical Instruction, Department of. Report of Departmental Committee of Inquiry. [Cd-3572.] 1907. Minority Report. [Cd-3575.] 1907 ....

Agricultural and Technical Instruction Schemes (Ireland). (174.) 1907 ....

Congestion in Ireland. Appendix to 4th Report of Royal Commission. [Cd-3509.] 1907.................

Education (Ireland) 1906. Annual Report of Commissioners for 1906. [Cd-3469.] 1907 ....

Education. Report of Intermediate Education Board for 1906. [Cd-3544.] 8vo. 1907 .... } Purchased

Judicial Statistics (Ireland). 1906. Part 2. Civil Statistics. [Cd-3616.] 1907 ....

Land Commission. Return of Advances, 1903.1905. [Cd-3447.] 1907 ....

Trade. Report on Trade in Imports and Exports at Irish Ports in 1905. [Cd-3631.] 8vo. 1907 ....

Dublin Metropolitan Police. Statistical Tables for 1906. [Cd-3551.] 1907 ....

Scotland—

Crofter's Holdings (Scotland) Acts. (296.) 1907 ...

Crofting parishes (Scotland) Population. (30.) 1907 ....

Education. Report on a collection of Statistics as to physical condition of school children in Glasgow. [Cd-3637.] 1907 ....

Land values taxation, &c. (Scotland) Bill. Index and Digest of Evidence to Report. (379, Ind.) 1907 } Purchased

Lunacy. 49th Report of General Board of Commissioners in Lunacy for Scotland. [Cd-3520.] 1907 ....

Small Landholders (Scotland) Bill. Report from Standing Committee. (278.) 1907 ....

Valuation of Lands (Scotland) Act. (284.) 1907 ...

51st detailed annual report of the Registrar-General of births, deaths and marriages in Scotland. (Abstracts of 1905.) [Cd-3650.] 8vo. 1907 .... } The Registrar-General for Scotland

Scotch Education Department—

Memorandum on the teaching of drawing. [Cd-3662.] 8vo. 1907...............................

Regulations as to grants to secondary schools, 1907. [Cd-3600.] 8vo. 1907 ....

Report of Committee of Council on Education in Scotland, with Appendix, 1906-07. [Cd-3522.] 8vo. 1907 .... } The Scotch Education Department

(d) **Authors, &c.**

"*Akaroa.*" Some writing on the wall. Specimen papers from a selection, now being prepared for publication. 28 pp., 8vo. 1907 .... } The Author

Babbage (Charles). Thoughts on the principles of taxation with reference to a property tax and its exceptions. 4th Edit. 16 pp., 8vo. 1907 .... } Major-Gen. H. P. Babbage

Bailey (William B.). Modern social conditions. A statistical study of birth, marriage, divorce, death, disease, suicide, immigration, &c., with special reference to the United States. 377 pp., 8vo. New York, 1906 .... } Purchased

Barbour (James Samuel). History of William Paterson and the Darien Company. 284 pp., 8vo. 1907 .... } Messrs. Wm. Blackwood and Sons

Boverat (Raymond). Le Socialisme municipal en Angleterre et ses résultats financiers. 8vo. 1907 .... } The Author

Bray (Reginald A.). The town child. 334 pp., 8vo. 1907 .... } Mr. T. Fisher Unwin

Brown (Richard). History of Accounting and Accountants. Edited and partly written by Richard Brown, C.A. xvi + 459 pp., 8vo. Edinb., 1905 ...... } The Society of Accountants in Edinburgh

Chatterton-Hill (George). Heredity and selection in sociology. 571 pp., 8vo. 1907 .... } Messrs. A. and C. Black

Collet (Collet Dobson). History of the taxes on knowledge : their origin and repeal. With an introduction by George Jacob Holyoake. Vols. 1 and 2, 8vo. 1899 .... } Purchased

Conant (Charles A.). History of modern banks of issue, with an account of the economic crises of the present century. 5th impression. xv + 595 pp., 8vo. New York, 1902 .... } "

Crackanthorpe (Montague). Population and progress. 132 pp., 8vo. 1907.... } Messrs. Chapman and Hall

De Caux (J. W.). The herring and the herring fishery, with chapters on fishes and fishing and our sea fisheries in the future. 160 pp., 8vo. 1881 ...... } Purchased

Dewsnup (Ernest Ritson). The housing problem in England : its statistics, legislation and policy. (University of Manchester. Economic series, 7). 328 pp., 8vo. 1907 .... } Messrs. Sherratt and Hughes

Dykes (D. Oswald). Scottish Local Government. Lectures on the Organisation and Functions of Local Bodies. 8vo. Edinb. and London, 1907............ } Messrs. Oliphant Anderson and Co.

Easton (H. T.). Money, exchange and banking in their practical, theoretical, and legal aspects. A complete manual for bank officials, business men, and students of commerce. 2nd Edit., 8vo. 1907 .... } Sir Isaac Pitman and Sons, Ltd.

Fahlbeck (Pontus). La constitution suédoise et le parlementarisme moderne. 8vo. 1905 .... } The Author

Galton (Francis), F.R.S. Inquiries into human faculty and its development. 2nd Edit. [1st Edit. 1883], 8vo. 1907............ } Purchased

Heckscher (Eli F.). The influence of railways upon the economic development of Sweden. [In Swedish.] 171 pp.. 8vo. Stockholm, 1907 .... } The Author

Hull (Walter Henry) (Editor). Practical problems in banking and currency. Being a number of selected addresses by prominent bankers, financiers and economists. With introduction by the Hon. Charles Francis Phillips. 8vo. 1907 .... } The Macmillan Co.

Jebb (L.). The small holdings of England. A survey of various existing systems. 8vo. 1907 .... } Mr. John Murray.

(d) **Authors, &c.**—*Contd.*

Johnston (R. M.). Reference list of various books and memoirs on scientific and social and economic subjects, written and published since 1873 by R. M. Johnston, I.S.O. 14 pp., 8vo. Hobart, 1907 .... } The Author

Juraschek (Dr. Franz von). Otto Hübner's geographisch-statistische Tabellen aller Länder der Erde, 1907. Obl. 8vo. 1907 .... } „

Kerr (Andrew William). History of Banking in Scotland. 2nd edit. 8vo. London, 1902 .... } Purchased

Knibbs (G. H.). The classification of disease and causes of death, from the standpoint of the statistician. An address given to the Victorian branch of the British Medical Association, 12th June, 1907. 24 pp., 8vo. 1907 .... } Commonwealth Bureau of Census and Statistics

Levasseur (E.). Questions ouvrières et industrielles en France sous la 3e République. lxxii + 968 pp., la. 8vo. 1907 .... } Mons. Arthur Rousseau, Paris

MacDonald (Arthur). \ Statistics of Child Suicide. 5 pp., 8vo. 1907 .... } The Author

MacDonald (J. Ramsay). Socialism and society. (The Socialist Library. II.) 5th Edit., 8vo. 1907 .... } Purchased

Martel (Félix) and *Grigaut (M.).* Economie politique (Bibliothèque des Écoles Pratiques de Commerce et d'industrie). 354 pp., sm. 8vo. 1907 .... } Librairie Ch. Delagrave, Paris

Martin (Benjamin). Biographia philosophica, being an account of the lives, writings, and inventions of the most eminent philosophers and mathematicians. 8vo. 1764 .... } Purchased

Pearson (Karl), F.R.S.—
Scope and importance to the State of the Science of National Eugenics . . . 45 pp., 8vo. 1907 ...... } Mr. Henry Frowde
A first study of the statistics of pulmonary tuberculosis. (Drapers' Company Research Memoirs, II.) 26 pp., 4to. 1907 .... } Purchased

Petty (Sir William). Essays on mankind and political arithmetic. [Cassell's National Library.] 12mo. 1888 .... } „

Porter (Robert P.). Dangers of municipal trading. xii + 320 pp., 8vo. 1907 .... } Messrs. G. Routledge and Sons

Raffalovich (Arthur). Année economique et financière, 1906-07. Le marché financier. 8vo. Paris, 1907 .... } The Author

Rozenraad (C.). Table comparing Gold and Silver Stock of principal European Banks of issue, their bank-rate, &c., &c. Sheet. 1907 .... } The Compiler

Saint-Maurice (Comte de). La fortune publique et privée au Japon. 61 pp., 8vo. Paris, 1907 .... } Purchased

Schuster (Edgar) and *Elderton (Ethel M.).* Inheritance of ability, being a statistical study of the Oxford class lists and of the school lists of Harrow and Charterhouse. (Eugenics Laboratory Memoirs. I). 42 pp., 4to. 1907 .... } „

Simiand (François). Le salaire des ouvrières des mines de charbon en France. Contribution à la théorie economique du salaire. 8vo. Paris, 1907.... .... } „

Simon (André L.). History of the Wine Trade in England. Vol. ii. Progress of the Wine Trade in England during 15th and 16th centuries. 8vo. 1907 } The Author

Simon (Sir John). English Sanitary Institutions, reviewed in their course of development, and in some of their political and social relations. 2nd edit. 8vo. 1897 .... } Purchased

(d) **Authors, &c.**—*Contd.*

Sundbärg (Gustav). Bevölkerungsstatistik Schwedens, 1750-1900. Einige Hauptresultate. (XIV. Internat. Kongr. fur Hygiene u. Demographie, Berlin, Sept., 1907.) 170 pp., 8vo. 1907 .... } The Author

Supino (Camillo). Le crisi economiche. xi + 202 pp., 8vo. Milano, 1907 .... } M. Ulrico Hoepli, Milan

Turot (Henri) and *Bellamy (Henri).* Le surpeuplement et les habitations à bon marché. 260 pp., 8vo. Paris, 1907 .... } Purchased

Waltershausen (A. Sartorius Freiherr von). Das volkswirtschaftliche System der Kapitalanlage im Auslande. 8vo. 1907 .... } M. Georg Reimer, Berlin

Welsford (J. W.). The Strength of Nations. An argument from history. x + 327 pp., 8vo. 1907 .... } Messrs. Longmans

Yoxall (J. H.) and *Gray (Ernest).* The handbook of education, containing particulars respecting the supply, organisation, and administration of elementary and secondary education in England and Wales. 1907. 8vo. 1907 .... } The National Union of Teachers

---

(e) **Societies, &c. (British).**

Institute of Actuaries. Catalogue of Library. 8vo. 1907
Institute of Chartered Accountants. List of Members, Charter and Bye-laws. 8vo. 1907.... } The Institute

Institution of Civil Engineers. Minutes of proceedings, with other selected and abstracted papers. Vol. 168. 8vo. 1907 .... } The Institution

Iron and Steel Institute. Journal. Vols. 73 and 74. 2 vols., 8vo. 1907 ......
Royal Colonial Institute. Proceedings. Vol. 38. 1906-07. 8vo. 1907 .... } The Institute

Scottish Automobile Club. Scottish Reliability Trial for touring cars, 25th-29th June, 1907. Official Report. La. fol. 1907.......... } Mr. R. G. Smith

Society of Comparative Legislation. Journal. New Series. Vol. vii, No. 17. 8vo. 1907.......... } The Society

Society for propagation of Gospel. Report for 1906. 8vo. 1907 .... } "

Sociological Society. Sociological papers. Volume iii. 382 pp., 8vo. 1907.......... } The Secretary

Surveyors' Institution. Professional Notes. Vol. 14, Part 3, and Scottish Supplement. No. 26. 8vo. 1907 .... } The Institution

---

(f) **Periodicals, &c., and Miscellaneous (British).**

Biometrika. Vol. 5. Part 4. June, 1907. 8vo. 1907
London Manual for 1907. 8vo. 1907 ....
"The Times." Annual Index, 1906. 8vo. 1907 ....
"The Times" Monthly Index. 8vo. 1907 .... } Purchased

Barnardo's (Dr.) Homes : National Incorporated Association. 41st Annual Report for 1906. 4to. 1907 .. } The Secretary

Channel Tunnel. Reports by British and French engineers. Papers on national defence, and other leaflets. 56 pp., 4to. 1907 .... } The Channel Tunnel Company

Lloyd's Register of British and Foreign Shipping. Statistical summary of vessels of all nations of 100 tons and upwards, totally lost, condemned, &c., during 1906. 8 pp., fol. 1907 .... } Lloyd's Register

The weekly, monthly, or quarterly issues of the following returns have also been received during the past quarter :—

Consular Reports—From United States and United Kingdom.

Labour Reports, &c.—From Austria-Hungary, Belgium, France, Germany, Italy, United States, Massachusetts and New York States, Canada, New Zealand, and United Kingdom.

Trade Returns—From Argentina, Austria-Hungary, Belgium, Bulgaria, China, Denmark, Egypt, France, Germany, Greece, Italy, Mexico, Netherlands, Norway, Roumania, Russia, Spain, Sweden, Switzerland, United States, India, and United Kingdom.

Vital Statistics—From Argentina, Egypt, Germany, Italy, Netherlands, Roumania, Switzerland, United States (Connecticut and Michigan only), Queensland, South Australia, and United Kingdom.

Vital Statistics of following Towns—Buenos Ayres, Buda-Pesth, Brünn, Prague, Brussels, Copenhagen, Berlin, Bucharest, Moscow, Madrid, Stockholm, London, Manchester, Dublin, Edinburgh, and Aberdeen.

The weekly, monthly, or quarterly issues of the following periodicals, &c., have also been received during the past quarter. They are arranged under the countries in which they are published :—

Denmark—Nationalökonomisk Tidsskrift.

France—Annales des Sciences Politiques. Économiste Français. Journal des Économistes. Monde Économique. Polybiblion, Parties Littéraire et Technique. Réforme Sociale. Le Rentier. Revue d'Économie Politique. Revue de Statistique. Journal de la Société de Statistique de Paris.

Germany—Allgemeines Statistisches Archiv. Archiv für Rassen- und Gesellschafts-Biologie. Archiv für Sozialwissenschaft und Sozialpolitik. Jahrbuch für Gesetzgebung, Verwaltung, und Volkswirtschaft. Jahrbücher für Nationalökonomie und Statistik. Kritische Blatter für die gesamten Socialwissenschaften. Zeitschrift für die gesamte Staatswissenschaft. Zeitschrift für die gesamte Versicherungs-Wissenschaft. Zeitschrift für Socialwissenschaft. Mittheilungen aus der Handelskammer Frankfurt a. M.

Italy—L'Economista. Giornale degli Economisti. Rivista Italiana di Sociologia. Riforma Sociale. Societa Umanitaria, Bollettino mensile.

Sweden—Ekonomisk Tidskrift.

Switzerland—Journal de Statistique suisse.

United States—Bankers' Magazine. Bradstreet's. Commercial and Financial Chronicle, with supplements. Duns' Review. Journal of Political Economy. Political Science Quarterly. Quarterly Journal of Economics. Yale Review. American Academy of Political and Social Science, Annals. American Economic Association, Publications. American Geographical Society, Bulletin. American Statistical Association, Quarterly Publications. American Philosophical Society, Proceedings and Transactions. Columbia University, Studies in History, &c.

Canada—The Chronicle: Insurance and Finance.

India—Indian Engineering.

New Zealand—Government Insurance Recorder. Trade Review and Price Current.

United Kingdom—The Accountant. Accountants' Magazine. Athenæum. Australian Trading World. Bankers' Magazine. Broomhalls' Corn Trade News. Browne's Export List. Colliery Guardian. Commercial World. Economic Journal. Economic Review. Economist. Fireman. Incorporated Accountants' Journal. Insurance Record. Investors' Monthly Manual. Investors' Review. Joint Stock Companies' Journal. Labour Co-partnership. Licensing World. Local Government Journal. Machinery Market. Nature. Navy League, Journal. Policy-Holder. Post Magazine. Produce Markets' Review. Public Health. Publishers' Circular. Sanitary Record. Shipping World. Statist. The Times. Anthropological Institute, Journal. Cobden Club, Leaflets. East India Association, Journal. Howard Association, Leaflets, &c. Institute of Actuaries, Journal. Institute of Bankers, Journal. Institution of Civil Engineers, Minutes of Proceedings. Iron and Steel Institute, Journal. Lloyd's Register of British and Foreign Shipping, Statistical Tables. London Chamber of Commerce, Journal. London University Gazette. Manchester Literary and Philosophical Society, Memoirs and Proceedings. Royal Agricultural Society, Journal. Royal Colonial Institute, Proceedings and Journal. Royal Geographical Society, Geographical Journal. Royal Irish Academy, Proceedings and Transactions. Royal Meteorological Society, Meteorological Record and Quarterly Journal. Royal Society, Proceedings. Royal United Service Institution, Journal. Sanitary Institute, Journal. Society of Arts, Journal. Statistical and Social Inquiry Society of Ireland, Journal. Surveyors' Institution, Professional Notes and Transactions. Trade Circulars.

Vol. LXX.]   [Part IV.

JOURNAL

OF THE ROYAL STATISTICAL SOCIETY.

DECEMBER, 1907.

The PRESIDENTIAL ADDRESS *of* THE RIGHT HON. SIR CHARLES W. DILKE, BART., M.P., *for the* SESSION 1907-08. DELIVERED *to the* ROYAL STATISTICAL SOCIETY, 19TH NOVEMBER, 1907.

I HAVE already expressed my deep sense of the honour done me in my election to the Presidency for the year.

Before proceeding to the subject of my address, a brief reference must be made, in conformity with what is, I understand, the general practice at the opening of a new Session, to the domestic affairs of the Society during the past year. We have to deplore the death of Lord Goschen, who had been a fellow since 1868, and filled the presidential chair in 1886-88, and of Dr. Körösy and M. Olanesco, two distinguished honorary fellows of the Society. At the eleventh session of the International Statistical Institute, held at Copenhagen in August last, the Society was represented by one of its past presidents, its honorary foreign secretary, one of its honorary secretaries, and two members of Council, in addition to one of its vice-presidents, who was present as a visitor. The Bibliography of Cereals, which was prepared by the Society at the request of the Institute, was duly presented by Sir Athelstane Baines. At the International Congress on School Hygiene, held in London in August, the Society was represented by Sir Shirley Murphy and Dr. Dudfield. The complete catalogue of the library, which has been for some time in preparation, is now passing through the press, and will, it is hoped, shortly be published, together with a continuation of the index to the Journal. The Papers read before the Society last Session, which it is not necessary to recapitulate, covered a wide range of subjects, and those already offered for the present Session give promise of important contributions to statistical discussion. The presentation of the Guy Medal in gold to Professor Edgeworth and in silver to Mr. Noel Humphreys, which would in the usual course have taken place at this meeting, has, unfortunately, to be deferred in consequence of the indisposition of both recipients as the result of accidents.

Parliament Street and its neighbourhood show that we are becoming bureaucratic. The War Office swells; the Local Government Board and the Board of Education display a stupendous growth. Scientific arrangement of the work of government did not precede, and has not accompanied, the change.

Rather more than a quarter of a century ago a distinguished member of the French Institute, formerly President of the Statistical Society of Paris, and still happily living, explained the organisation of Government statistics in various countries. He told us that the United Kingdom paid but little attention to the subject: "It is not "surprising to find a total absence of any central or general super-"vision over official statistics."[1] Each department, M. Cheysson wrote, collected and tabulated its own statistics; in the Board of Trade, however, as he admitted, we had something like a true statistical office.

Certain questions were put by me in the course of the Income Tax inquiry of 1906 on the absence of such statistics as my Committee had hoped to find. The base was the inquiry of 1878-79.[2] Mr. Bowley, Mr. Chiozza Money, and Mr. Coghlan[3] pointed out in their replies that there had been little improvement in the organisation of our statistics—unless it be within the Board of Trade—since the report signed by weighty names such as those of Childers, Ritchie, Welby, and Arthur Balfour.

The final Report of the Committee on Official Statistics had favoured the creation of a small central Statistical Department. The whole of the Blue Book of 1880 is of deep interest, and many of the general defects exposed by the late Lord Farrer, Lord Welby, and Sir Robert Giffen continue to this moment; while the determination of the Departments concerned to remedy the evils is less strong than it was when Mr. W. H. Smith, as Secretary of the Treasury, originally appointed the Committee in 1877. His Treasury minute was, perhaps, sounder than the ultimate recommendations, marked as they were by timidity. Sir Robert Giffen proposed a scientific system, to which the Committee offered the objection that it was hardly likely that the Registrar-General would concur. The whole controversy had arisen from a conflict between the Customs and the Board of Trade; and Sir Robert Giffen's warning that "there will be a natural tendency to this continual

---

[1] See Journal of the Statistical Society of Paris for September, 1882, and translation in our *Journal* for the same year.

[2] Official Statistics Committee Reports, 1880.

[3] Q. 487, 499, 1403, 1410—1415.

" splitting-off of statistical offices," such as " really ought to be
" restrained," although " endorsed " by the Committee, is even more
needed at the present moment than when it was written. To the
list of Departments given by Lord Farrer as those "which furnish
" more or less independently a considerable mass of Parliamentary
" statistics," must now be added the Education Department and the
Ministry of Agriculture as regards all their branches created since
1879. It is still true, as set forth in Appendix A, published in
1880, but drawn up in 1875, that since the institution of the
Statistical Department at the Board of Trade in 1832, statistical
offices have been created in connection with other departments,
" totally independent of each other," and " possessing but imperfect
" knowledge of the work upon which the other offices have been or
" are engaged." Even now, " with but few exceptions, the statistics
" of each Department are treated as having only an individual
" departmental significance," and "are often found to be perfectly
" useless on occasions of general inquiry." Few of the many
illustrative cases of defect pointed out in 1875, and again, by
Sir Robert Giffen in 1876, have been remedied, and fresh instances
of similar defects may be found by comparison of Census and Local
Government Returns with Returns under various recent statutes.

As our system of collating motions for Parliamentary Returns,
notably between England, Scotland, and Ireland, and of indexing
those returns when made, is as weak as are our official statistical
methods, it requires the industry and experience of a Giffen to
detect even one-tenth of those defects which now exist. It is still
almost as true as it was in 1871, when Mr. Purdy contributed
a paper to the Royal Statistical Society,[4] that Parliamentary
statistics are confused and frequently ill-prepared for the press,
by reason of defective supervision. Purdy, moreover, quoted on
departmental statistics an admirable speech by Goschen criticising
Local Taxation Returns, to which indeed the words of that
illustrious President of the Local Government Board are still
applicable. The fault is not entirely that of the departments, for
members of both Houses often move for Statistical Returns
without having first considered whether they desire them for
England and Wales, or Great Britain, or the United Kingdom.
Sometimes they intend the United Kingdom, but select words
applicable only to England under the Local Government Board,
and inapplicable to the Local Government of Scotland or of Ireland.
It is at present not the duty of anyone to find the general form of
words, or to point out difficulties which must arise after the
return is granted. As Mr. Cannan also shows, it is still as hard

---

[4] *Journal,* vol. xxxiv, pp. 21 *et seq.*

as it was in the Purdy-Goschen days to discover such apparently necessary statistical facts as the amount of the rates in an English rural parish. Averages of rates are officially published by the Local Government Board, but no one knows the highest or the lowest rated parish. In Scotland there are both statutory peculiarities and departmental "fads"; in Ireland also. Purdy's conclusions favoured supervision by a Statistical Department to point out if returns moved for are practicable in the shape proposed, and to see that the departments scrutinise the return in proof, with a view of ascertaining if the requirements of Parliament have been met on a uniform plan.

When an enquirer undertakes serious research into a matter concerning a Department of the State he finds the statistics crumble under his examination, where they are not (as is often the case) wanting. Parliament is an offender in making the year end for different purposes at different dates. But the departments are not, perhaps, exempt from reproach in sometimes allowing Parliament unwarned to show such levity.

It is a well known and perhaps inevitable difficulty that Revenue Returns relate to years ended 31st March, while trade, shipping, railway, post office, and most other statistics relate to years ended 31st December. Returns, however, for saving banks through the Post Office are for the latter or usual year, though returns for trustee saving banks are for years ended 20th November. Revenue returns are for the financial year, but the Income Tax year is not exactly the same. All figures for receipt of tax are for the financial year, but all figures relating to income assessed are for an Income Tax year ending 5th April. So too for inhabited house duty, with the exception of Scotland, where the House Duty year ends on 24th May. Excise licenses expire at varying dates. Statistics relating to the receipt of duty from these are for the financial year. The returns of brewers and brewing are for a Brewing year ending 30th September; though the tables relating to beer quantities falling under beer duty are for the financial year. As for the spirit licences, the tables relating to distilling follow a year ending 30th September. The Land Tax year ends on 25th March; but the figures of tax received follow the general principle that tables of receipt of duty are for the financial year, even where the periods covered by the charge or the assessment are for a different year. The Poor Rate years of the three kingdoms are all, I believe, still different from each other and also from the years just named, as was the case when Purdy wrote. The Board of Trade returns relating to gas undertakings refer to a year ending 25th March, and are not statistically comparable with the gas figures in the Local Taxation returns, relating as these do to a year ended 31st March. On the other hand, the Board of Trade returns for tramways and light railways are not for the Board of Trade gas year, but for the usual financial year. Difficulties of comparison are increased by the Board of Trade returns placing the county boroughs under their geographical counties.

The defects pointed out by Sir Robert Giffen more than thirty years ago in the classification of diseases, combined with the artificial nature of the areas chosen for statistics of population and of occupation, are assuming every day increasing importance. The science of sociology is making strides, but the statistics on which it should be based are misleading. In the Report from the Select Committee on Official Publications, 1906, it was recommended that Members of Parliament should be told of more economical plans for accomplishing their end. On this ground, "the minister responsible " should consult the Stationery Office before agreeing to the form." But surely the form should be scrutinised, not only for cheapness, but also, statistically, for suitability and effectiveness.

The Treasury is frightened of the men of science, regarded in the light of sturdy beggars ; but such is the amount of overlapping in our statistics, as well as of publication of statistics either wholly unnecessary or comparatively unimportant, that a Quetelet, or indeed any trained statistician, would save much money to the State if placed in command of the whole of our statistics with orders to make them as good as possible. In 1870 Mr. Shaw-Lefevre, now Lord Eversley, when Secretary to the Board of Trade, succeeded, by simplification of the Monthly Trade Returns, in bringing them out more usefully and promptly, at a saving, it is said, of 20,000*l.* a year.

It is enough for my historical case that the conclusive demonstration of waste and inefficiency made public in 1880 has been followed by no general improvement.

It seems hardly necessary to declare that the interest of the State should be considered rather than the rivalry of Departments ; but no one can read the reports and evidence published between 1877 and 1881 by the Official Statistics Committee without discovering that Departmental considerations, to which the Secretary of the Treasury and Sir Robert Giffen had risen superior, played a leading part in the paralysis which overtook the movement for improved national statistics.

At the time when M. Cheysson examined the condition of Government statistics in the principal countries, there was none, unless it were Prussia, which could be taken as an exemplar. The organisation of statistics in Prussia dated from 1805. Attached to the Central Department M. Cheysson found a school of Statistics of a highly scientific type and a magnificent statistical library. Since 1882 Germany has developed imperial statistics, especially as regards invalidity, old age, and accidents. The insurance legislation of Germany, and her rapidly increasing direct taxation, have both of them contributed to the progress of statistical science in that Empire. There has been improvement in Italy and in Austria, as well as in the federal work of the United States.

Although some prefer the Vienna Statistical Bureau, the Italian method is probably the most perfect in the old world. Mr. Labouchere is not usually thought of as a statistician : his writings and conversation are not of a dry description ; but he is known to his friends as the kindest of men. I have to thank him for obtaining, through the highest Italian authority, an account of the system which prevails in the Direction-General of Statistics under the Ministry of Agriculture, Industry and Commerce. Of the two Divisions in which the office under the Director-General of Statistics is arranged, the first deals with " Administrative and Judicial " Statistics," as well as with "General Statistical Affairs," while the second handles "Demographic, Economic and Educational " Statistics," and includes the Census and movements of population such as that by emigration. There is no other country in the world which has so large an annual outflow and return of her own working-people. Estimates of population (dangerous everywhere) are specially useless in the case of Italy, as compared with tangible proof of facts : births, deaths, emigration, and immigration. The Italian *Annuario Statistico*, or Year-Book, has not recently been published every year.

The Bureau of Statistics at Washington is under the Department of Commerce and Labour. It is not a central statistical office for the whole of the statistics of the United States, and there still exist those separate investigations by the Department of Agriculture and other offices which cause defects pointed out in an article of the Political Science Quarterly in 1896. Nevertheless, in 1903[5] the Division of Statistics of the Department of Agriculture of the United States, older by twenty years than the Department itself, received the more complete organisation of a Federal Bureau, and is now styled the Bureau of Statistics of the Department of Agriculture. It is still separate from the Bureau of the Census, permanently organised by an Act of 1902, and placed under the Department of Commerce and Labour. Thus the most important department in the United States from the statistical point of view is the Department of Commerce and Labour, with its Bureau of

[5] "Publications of the American Statistical Association," vol. ix, p. 149.

Statistics and its Bureau of the Census, both distinct from the Bureau of Statistics attached to the Department of Agriculture. Roughly it may be said that in the United States the Commerce and Labour Department has all the statistical work of our Board of Trade and of our Census. The Treasury Department of the United States produces some statistics, but less than in this country, much of the statistical work done through our Customs and Inland Revenue belonging at Washington to the Commerce and Labour Department.

In the Dominion of Canada, by the Census and Statistics Act of May, 1905, and the organisation of an office under the Act in October of that year, there is developed a system of collection and publication of general statistics for Canada which gives to the permanent office, under the direction of the Minister of Agriculture, commercial, educational, vital, manufacturing and criminal statistics.

Certain defects in American and Canadian statistics have been pointed out in notes contained in the September number of our *Journal.* Moreover, the difficulties of the newer countries are less considerable than those which surround our own Departments, or those of a highly-developed bureaucratic country such as France. This fact in part explains the excellence of the statistics of the Australasian colonies. It is not possible, however, to read without envy the evidence of Mr. H. H. Hayter in 1879, or that of Mr. Coghlan before the Income Tax Committee in 1906.

To return to the old world, already in 1882, as M. Cheysson showed, Sweden had a central statistical commission or permanent census office which had lasted for a century and a quarter. Switzerland had a federal office of a similar description. It now possesses a Federal Statistical Bureau which combines in one annual publication the statistics of the various departments. In many countries, small and great, such as Belgium (thanks to Quetelet), Russia, Italy, Spain, Austria, Hungary, and Norway, were to be found central statistical commissions, mainly representative of the various ministries, holding monthly or quarterly meetings, charged with the duty of co-ordinating the statistics of the departments and settling in advance all questions relating to the organisation of future statistical work.

The object of M. Cheysson was to secure a general supervision and a controlling authority, and so to bring about " harmony, " proportion, order and uniformity of arrangement in national " statistics." Although France has been since Richelieu and Colbert, and still more since the Consulate, a highly centralised country, he pointed out that there was no other country in which decentralisation of statistical activity was so marked, unless indeed it were

chaotic England. As a result of the labours of M. Cheysson there
was founded in 1885 a French Conseil Supérieur de Statistique
modelled on that of Belgium. M. Arthur Fontaine, the Directeur
du Travail—nominally permanent head of the new Ministry of
Labour, but in reality still the head of a separate Department in
close touch, as was also previously the case, with the Ministry
of Commerce—tells me that he separates administrative statistics
from those " drawn up for scientific observation in view of economic
" or social study without direct administrative interest. La
" Statistique Générale de la France, attached to the Ministry of
" Labour, co-ordinates and publishes, in a statistical *Annuaire*, the
" précis of the statistics of the other Departments. It helps them
" when necessary in the statistical treatment of their documents, and
" is responsible for the statistics of population, as well as for other
" statistics with which no special Department has been charged.
" Connected with the same Ministry is the Conseil Supérieur de
" Statistique, which has for its duty to advise Government on the
" undertaking and publishing of new statistics, and on statistical
" methods . . . . The Council consists of 29 members taken
" from Parliament and from learned bodies, and 35 delegates of
" Ministries." It has recently dealt with the difficult branch of
criminal statistics, in respect of which Sir John Macdonell has
rendered great, but partly as yet unsuccessful, service in this
country. La Statistique Générale de la France publishes " the
" statistical results of the Census, taken every five years." The
portion of the Census which has administrative importance as
regards the work of the Ministry of the Interior in its relations
with Local Authorities, is published, however, by that Ministry.
It will be seen that France has not yet obtained the statistical unity
at which M. Cheysson aimed. There results that perplexity from
which all suffer who investigate the state of France as well as of
the United Kingdom.

Examples of overlapping and even contradiction, waste and
confusion, as regards this country, have been given by many
Presidents, and in many papers read before the Royal Statistical
Society. It is perhaps safer to criticise another country than our
own, though I shall have to run the greater risk. M. Cheysson
called attention to the lack of facilities for training those who were
to conduct the Census, decennial with us, quinquennial in France
since 1801. He gave as his best example of overlapping, and of
sources of error, the failure in an agricultural country such as
France to produce by departmental treatment, uniform or intelligible
statistics even of the growth of crops. " The figures for cereals are
" set forth in different measures by the several Ministries concerned."

The Society has appointed a Census Committee, and we await their proposals. Mr. Bowley has already suggested, in connection with the last Census, improvement in the classifications of occupations. I believe that Mr. Cannan doubts whether occupation statistics obtained through Census investigations can ever be useful. In the case of the millions who have mixed occupations, it is difficult to describe these on a uniform plan. Mr. Cannan thinks that for occupations we must trust to the administrative statistics of those concerned with factory, workshop and home workers, seamen and so forth. Mr. Cannan and Mr. Bowley have joined in suggesting the remedy of much lack of uniformity between England, Scotland and Ireland, and correction of misleading estimates of population.[6] Mr. Cannan, in 1898, complained of the nature of our estimates of population. The Registrar-General informs the country how many are added by birth and lost by death, while the Board of Trade states the numbers who come in and go out. The so-called estimate is not, however, based upon these facts, but upon a rate of increase in a previous period ; except in Ireland, where account is taken of addition to and subtraction from the previously-existing population. Up to the Report of 1893, published in 1895, it was explained that the method followed " was not likely to lead to " serious error." The estimates are obviously not worth much, and may be made by anyone. When the estimated increases come to be (as we are told in the Annual Report of the Registrar-General for 1905, published this year) "distributed among the counties, " after making due allowance for their several rates of increase," there is further liability to error, the extent of which is illustrated by the intermediate numbering of the population in the case of London. The Kentish parishes of London in a period of Government activity in the manufacture of war stores, as compared with a period of reduction of staff, form an obvious case in point. To the confusion between the Registrar-General's figures and those of the Local Government Board it may be necessary for me to return. The Local Government Board can never be a satisfactory statistical Department for National purposes, if for no other reason, on account of its want of direct authority in Ireland and in Scotland. The same difficulty, to some extent, exists in the case of the Board of Agriculture, which also is represented in Ireland and partly in Scotland by separate bodies under different control.

By the modest reform he recommended, M. Cheysson desired to allay Departmental suspicion. Opposition is not aroused by mere co-ordination through a representative advisory Committee. It is,

[6] "Demographic Statistics of the United Kingdom," by Edwin Cannan, M.A., *Journal of the Royal Statistical Society*, 1898, vol. lxi, pp. 19 *seq.*

however, the fact that there exists a real reason, wholly apart from political or working difficulties, for continuing to collect some at least of our statistics through administrative departments in separate ministries. The occupier who is called upon by the Board of Agriculture to fill up some, to him, more or less unintelligible form, and those connected with the fishing industry who are similarly "worried" by the Fisheries Department, can hardly be induced to perform their task, and would retire into bankruptcy (or suicide) if asked to do it twice. They may, perhaps, be less unwilling to make their returns to a department from which they may hope for aid, than to a purely statistical office in whose machinations they would detect some lurking devilry. The owners of coal mines and of quarries, the occupiers of factories and workshops, must make their returns to the Home Office, as these are chiefly needed for the administrative purposes of the inspectors of that ministry. Military statistics are the immediate concern of the Director of Recruiting, of the Army Council, and of the Secretary of State for War. But there is no obvious reason why statistics departmentally collected should not be at once available for statistical, as contrasted with administrative, purposes, when shaped by a director of national statistics or a statistical office. Those, however, who desire to follow the line of least resistance are perhaps inclined to be content with the representative commission or meeting of Departments advocated for France by M. Cheysson.

Mr. Purdy was one of those who first pointed out in the paper already quoted the improvement which might be made even by the smaller scheme. Were there a Department which merely indexed and explained the statistical returns of other Departments, and the statistical part of the principal papers published by them, upon some intelligible system, it would for the first time be ascertained what information exists upon any given subject. Such investigation must lead to uniformity of plan in the reports of Medical Officers of Health, now most valuable locally, but affording no means of comparing district with district, or of giving a complete view of the country. This duty could not be undertaken by the Local Government Board on account of the Irish and Scotch difficulty already named. So, too, would gradually be co-ordinated such inquiries as those undertaken privately by Mr. Booth in London, Mr. Rowntree in York, Miss Jebb in Cambridge, and Miss Mona Wilson and others in Dundee and in West Ham. As has been shown by Mr. Coghlan, and in the valuable paper on "The Future of Statistics" by a Hungarian economist,[7] the money

[7] Mandello, *Journal of the Royal Statistical Society,* 1905, vol. lxviii, pp. 725 *seq.*

and energy saved by diminution of printing in the adoption of an orderly plan would be sufficient to transform our statistics. " Why " should busy people hunt in big volumes, ... compile, " calculate, making mistakes, and hardly ever finding what they " really want, if their requests . . . . . could be . . . . . " easily answered, or if they could be told that the figures looked " for are not known, or the question raised is not answerable " statistically ? "

In his Presidential Address to his Section of the British Association in 1906, and in his recent writings on our national position, Mr. Bowley has advocated the institution of a central statistical department. To obtain one will require a strong popular or Parliamentary demand, sufficient to overcome the hesitation of the Treasury and of all, or perhaps all but one, of the Government Offices. Of such popular or Parliamentary pressure there is little sign, although the Royal Commission on Local Taxation and the last two Committees on Income Tax, not to speak of the fiscal or tariff reform agitation, have all shown the need of co-ordination, re-arrangement, and simplification of our national statistics. An article, signed " B.M.," in the new volume of " The Dictionary of " Political Economy," quotes the evidence of Mr. Money, M.P., and refers to that of Mr. Coghlan before the last Income Tax Committee. The writer adds : " There is a quantity of valuable " statistical material in connection with the collection of the Income " Tax which might be utilised if . . . . . . a Central " Statistical Bureau . . . . . existed in this country." It may be as confidently asserted now as it was by William Newmarch in 1869,[8] that any Chancellor of the Exchequer desiring to reform our whole system of taxation would find himself without the necessary statistical equipment for his task. The alteration of relations between the national and municipal exchequers will also meet with unnecessary difficulties, by reason of the absence of organisation in our national statistics.

It is understood from some references in his speeches that Mr. Austen Chamberlain, when Chancellor of the Exchequer, was not satisfied with the statistical system of the country ; but it is perhaps best to base an allusion to the opinions of British Chancellors of the Exchequer on an addition made by Lord Goschen in an edition of " Essays and Addresses," published in 1905. The essay in question was, in its original form, a Presidential Address to the Royal Statistical Society in 1877, but the words that I shall quote are from the supplemental study annexed to it by Lord Goschen

[8] " The Progress and Present Condition of Statistical Inquiry." Presidential Address, *Journal of the Royal Statistical Society*, vol. xxxii, pp. 359 *seq.*

after the date of his last tenure of high ministerial office. At the
close of the essay on "The Increase of Moderate Incomes," he
explains that "The methods of the Inland Revenue Department do
" not contribute sufficiently to this class of research. Nor does
" there appear to be enough co-ordination between the various
" official centres which distribute statistical information." "The
" labours of the Inland Revenue Department have not been
" sufficiently utilised for statistical purposes." These last words
have been echoed in the evidence of Mr. Bowley before the Income
Tax Committee. Lord Goschen went on: "It has often occurred
" to me that our national statistics should be concentrated under
" one head." Goschen desired that there should be some person,
Committee, or Department "to take a wider survey than the mere
" tabulation of figures," and "consider scientifically what further
" materials . . . . . . throwing light on the economic con-
" dition of the country might be extracted from official records and
" made available . . . . . . for public use." He urged that
" the tedium" of his own examination of incomes, constantly stopped
at points "of great economic . . . . . . importance," should
induce others to "call attention in the proper quarters to the need
" of reforms." There could be no higher authority upon such a
subject than Lord Goschen, whose immense administrative experience
and whose carefulness of the public purse make him a safe guide.
Unfortunately, as was proved to me by my experience in the Chair
of the Income Tax Committee, his weighty advice has not been
followed.

No one can doubt the truth of Mr. Coghlan's strictures, or of
Mr. Bowley's words:[9] "Whenever a scientific enquirer endeavours
" to describe accurately some social or industrial development, or
" wishes to bring to the test of statistics the effect of some proposed
" reform, whether in taxation . . . . . . care of young
" children, or whatever it may be, some essential information is
" found lacking, for the reason that it has been no one's business to
" collect it . . . . . . We continue in our ignorance of the
" aggregate national income and of its distribution. We have no
' adequate knowledge of the age, physical condition, or former
" occupation of the persons who receive public relief. Illustrations
" such as these could be multiplied by everyone who has tried
" to use official statistics." One by Mr. Bowley has been the
obvious lack during the last three years of true statistics of unemployment. Credit is due to the Board of Trade for doing what
it can, and to the present President for undertaking the Census of

Production. Certain improvements, Mr. Bowley admits, we owe
" to the enterprise of the Board of Trade . . . . . . but
" there are as yet no signs of the consideration of the general
" question of what statistical measurements of the wealth, industry,
" occupations, and physical condition of the nation should
" . . . . . . be undertaken."

There is a good deal of matter bearing upon our topic of to-day
in the Report from the Select Committee on Official Publications
already named. It is pointed out that Government Departments
include " in their Annual Reports quantities of matter, not because
" it is instructive or interesting . . . . . . but because it
" shows how much work has been done during the year." A good
deal of that work itself has, in fact, been undertaken because
Government Bills have been improved by amendments impossible of
insertion in a direct or mandatory form. Matters are left to the
discretion of a Department, with the intention that action shall take
place universally or generally, as well as with promptitude. The
power once given to the Department, a different view prevails, and
each case becomes the subject of costly and prolonged inquiry, and
swells the huge fabric of unnecessary work. When a Government
draftsman, who thought that the English " Rural Parish " was rural,
and that the " Urban District " was urban in its character, drew a
sharp distinction between the two, it was at once shown and
admitted that no such distinction in fact exists, and that in many
cases the line is arbitrary. The central authorities at one time
adopted, for a moment, the fashion of conferring " urban powers "
upon purely rural parishes to give them control of roads. The
policy was reversed, but the result continues in the technically
" urban " nature of many of the most rural parishes in our most
rural counties. How was the difficulty to be overcome and the hard
and fast lines between municipalities of 2,000 people, urban districts
of 60,000, urban districts with 1,500 people living in vast agricultural or pastoral parishes, and other, or " rural," parishes to be
effaced ? Parliament, hampered by reference legislation without
consolidation, threw the decision on the Local Government Board.
The result is inquiry with all formalities in every case where
extension of local privilege is proposed, and often now double
inquiry, by the County and by the Central Authority of England.
Such inquiries in their turn swell false statistics and burden us with
cost, as well as disgust the politician who receives vast masses of
unnecessary printed matter. Thus do we kill true and valuable
statistics.

In " Plain Tales from the Hills " is to be found a little-known
story misnamed " Pig." It contains Kipling's admirable explanation

of how official statistics often grow. Let us hope that we are not as yet so bureaucratic as our Indian Empire ; no one can pretend that we are not more bureaucratic than we were.

The Select Committee on Publications of 1907, appointed in consequence of the Report of 1906 already named, in order to examine the publications presented through Public Departments from the point of view of "unnecessary expense," dealt at length with Local Government Board publications, though not from the statistical point of view. The only paragraph which it is necessary to quote refers to the Local Taxation Returns, and states that it is intended to simplify them in the future, while it is pointed out that "the set for 1903-04 was only completed in December, 1906."

There are statistical allusions in the Report of the Departmental Committee of 1907 on the Accounts of Local Authorities,[10] but it is to be remembered that the inquiry related to England and Wales only, and rather illustrated such difficulties as those which I have described than pointed towards a remedy. It is clear, as Mr. Runciman's Committee declared, that "The Statistical infor-"mation thus obtained is not uniform."

My reference just now to "Urban Districts" reminds me of the special difficulties of England and Wales, caused not only by over-lapping boundaries but also by differences of names. Nomenclature is as confusing to the inquirer in the special case of Local Government and Vital Statistics as it is in the indexing of official papers, where, for example, "Africa," "Egypt" and "South Africa" clash, and India has to be sought for as "East India." Dr. Tatham, when presenting his last decennial Report as Superintendent of Statistics in the General Register Office, used pathetic words to express "regret that the elaborate series of Tables . . . cannot, except "in a few instances, be utilised . . . because of the overlapping "and confusion of areas." He added a list of 109 Urban Districts of which the names differ from those of the Registration Districts in which they are wholly or partly situate. Such a word as "Liverpool" may refer to the city of Liverpool or to the Poor Law Union of that name, or even to some other area not existing as a Local Government unit. A further drawback is that Part I of the Supplement was only circulated at the end of June, 1907, while Part II is still promised "in due course." It is not denied that the returns of occupations clash with the vital statistics owing to the artificial nature of Registration Districts. In cases where the statistics do not clash the ordinary inquirer is, never-theless, unable to utilise them on account of the confusion in the names.

<hr>

[10] Cd. Paper 3614.

The complication of our legislation, and the absence of consolidation—due, generally, to overwork or, in a few cases, laziness—are responsible for many of the evils for which we have now to find palliatives on their statistical side. It is disagreeable for a statistician to have to snub unscientific though statistically-minded inquirers. In connection with the rival schools of advocates of women's franchise, we have been bombarded with imaginary statistics, and, when these were questioned, with requests for real ones. Unfortunately, such is our franchise legislation, that in this country true franchise statistics are unattainable. When asked the number of voters affected by a Plural Voting Bill, the total number of voters in the country, or the number of women who would be enfranchised by any form of limited franchise or extension to women of the male franchises, or even by the franchise of all grown women, unless accompanied by the abolition of the plural vote, Governments and Oppositions can make no reply. The estimates of skilled observers as to the number of plural voters differ by 10 to 1, and are insusceptible of statistical treatment. The absence of sufficient interest in statistics and of sufficient supervising authority vitiates even those statistics which can be given and are given, such as the Tables of the number of registered electors. The return of "Parliamentary Constituencies (Electors)," which, like most of our Parliamentary statistics, contains one or two obvious errors, detected at a glance by the skilled eye, is used in books of reference, and naturally taken to be authoritative and correct. The absence of supervision already named is sometimes shown in this Annual Return by such footnotes as "Excluding "duplicates," or "Including duplicates," phrases which reveal to the well-informed want of knowledge upon the real meaning of the Registers.

War Office statistics are usually left alone by statisticians, which accounts, perhaps, for the fact that that department for many years issued figures in which garrison artillery was contrasted with horse and field artillery in parallel columns, but in which the garrison artillery was over-stated by a very considerable number of thousands of men; the imaginary garrison gunners being, in fact, more numerous than the total garrison artillery of any other power on a peace footing.

Our one attempt at general statistical work for the United Kingdom and for the Empire is to be found in the Statistical Abstracts prepared by the Board of Trade. These compare unfavourably—even making allowance for the advantage in such respects possessed by the less populous new countries—with Mr. Coghlan's "Statistical Account of Australia and New Zealand."

There is a Colonial Abstract which included Protectorates under the Foreign Office, some of them now at last transferred to the Colonial Office, and an Abstract for the Empire, which includes India. In some respects they overlap, and they also do not exactly coincide with statistics of the Home Office, as, for example, in regard to coal production, or with the Inland Revenue publications as regards consumption of spirits.

One of our Vice-Presidents, Mr. Coghlan, organised the Statistical Department of the Commonwealth of Australia under the Act of 1905, relating to the census and to the statistics of the Commonwealth. By this Act was given leave to appoint a Commonwealth Statistician with enormous powers covering all the Departments. The Statistician was to be allowed to collect the statistics of the entire Commonwealth on population, employment, trade (foreign and inter-State), on posts and telegraphs, on factories, mines and industries, on agriculture, banking, insurance and finance, railways, shipping, land tenure and occupancy, and virtually on all matters.

Even before federation, the South Sea colonies had held conferences of statists, as, for example, in 1875, to settle the bases of a uniform system of statistics. Such gatherings continue, and we now possess a most valuable report on the unification of Australasian statistics, as the result of the conference held in December last in which the Commonwealth, the Australian States, and the Dominion of New Zealand took part. The result of past care may be seen by comparing Mr. Coghlan's " A Statistical Account of Australia " and New Zealand " with our Statistical Abstracts. The Australian document is not confined to bare figures, but contains elaborate essays of a really useful character; and the Australian vital statistics are immeasurably superior to our own. The Commonwealth gives to its people fuller information, made accessible by an excellent system of indexing, and provides explanations which both bring out the significance of the figures and enable inquirers to handle them with safety. In our Statistical Abstract for the United Kingdom those who are dealing with public finance, for example, are continually referred to other parliamentary papers and so referred by means of symbols which will not always help them to find the Blue Books wanted. If we compare Mr. Coghlan's " A Statistical Account of Australia and New Zealand " with our Abstract, in the matter of revenue and expenditure we find here a display of tables, many of which cannot be understood by an ordinary statistician, while the Australian volume contains an essay, the intention and the effect of which are to make the financial position of the Commonwealth plain to every reader. Were we able to produce such Abstracts for the United Kingdom and the

Empire as would correspond to the Australian volume, every elementary school in the United Kingdom might be supplied with a handbook, now lacking.   The defects and omissions of the Abstracts are not the fault of the present compilers so much as of the departmental figures which they have to use.

The Board of Trade, being allowed, in certain cases, to give us statistics of a general nature, but hampered by the statistical departments of other offices in other cases, often favours us with details as to some remote part of the Empire such as are not given for the United Kingdom.   It has, I think, been pointed out that we know the number of private schools in Fiji by our official statistical tables published here, but not the number of such schools in the United Kingdom.   So, too, we know officially, at the expense of the home taxpayer, the average prices of the principal commodities in each year in Fiji, but fewer in the United Kingdom.   For Fiji we receive the wages of labour, including that of house servants. There are no wage figures in the Statistical Abstract for the United Kingdom, published by the same Department.   The wage figures in the "Abstract of labour statistics" are avowedly so incomplete as to be misleading, and those published elsewhere are far from being scientific.   We receive from the Board of Trade banking statistics for the colonies, but not for the United Kingdom.

A reply may be made to the effect that it is not fair to compare the issue "Colonies, Statistical Tables," with the "Abstract" for the United Kingdom.   But there exists no comprehensive official volume of United Kingdom statistics.   In face of the excellent separate colonial statistics published in most colonies, we need one volume for the Colonies here, it would seem that we also require a volume containing the principal statistics of the United Kingdom, fuller and better than the present "Abstract."   The "Abstract" is far from dealing only with that part of the administrative figures obtained by the departments which is capable of scientific treatment.   For example, the tables which give the number of paupers in receipt of relief on "one day in winter and on one day in "summer," and base on these figures the tables of proportions, select a different day in winter and a different day in summer for each of the three kingdoms.   The "summer day" in Scotland is the 14th or 15th day of September.   No doubt, the variation of the harvests affects the summer proportion of paupers, but not in the same degree as the variation of the dates selected.   The difference between the 15th January and the 1st January as the winter day is also of disturbing importance as the 1st January (the date chosen in England) is far nearer to Boxing Day than is the 14th or 15th January to the similar festival of New Year's Day in Scotland.

One point in a comparison between colonial statistics officially published here and the volume compiled for the United Kingdom by the same department, suggests a further remark. The criminal statistics of the Fiji Islands are much more completely and elaborately given to us in the volume which receives general circulation than in the corresponding volume for the United Kingdom, where we find less classification of offences, trials, and convictions in superior and inferior courts.

As regards the full but unsatisfactory Criminal Judicial Statistics, published for England and Wales by the Home Office, and separately for Scotland, and at Dublin, enough might be written to furnish an interesting paper on the subject; such as was, indeed, contributed to the Society's *Journal* in 1867,[11] when those differences between the three Kingdoms had been reduced, which have now grown again to vitiate our statistics further.

Sir John Macdonell has more than once written introductions to the Criminal Judicial Statistics in which he has drawn attention to some of their anomalies and to the discrepancies between them and other official statistics. He has also, I understand, communicated with Local Authorities and with officials who collect criminal statistics, calling attention to differences and trying to ensure that the figures should be collected in different places in the same manner. There are some serious and, perhaps, insuperable obstacles to obtaining satisfactory judicial statistics; a remark which applies, not only to the criminal statistics, but also, and still more, to the Civil Judicial Statistics, statistically less important, because inevitably less clear. Not only are statutory powers to call for the right statistics wanting, but it would be difficult in any case to prevent the various Courts concerned from giving only such information as they might feel disposed to give. Criminal Courts fill up forms sent out by the Home Office, but it has often been found that there was a lack of the exact information desired. Where such information has been asked from Civil Courts, it has frequently been refused. It has sometimes been given in one year and refused in others. There is no adequate staff in many Courts which could collect and record statistics, a matter outside the ordinary work of the officials, to whom no payment is given for an expenditure of time which they look upon as being outside their duties. There is no paid editor of the Judicial Statistics, and the work which Sir John Macdonell has done has been a labour of love. Even the best foreign judicial statistics contain obvious defects; and there are points in which the English figures answer important questions upon which the corresponding foreign statistics

[11] Vol. xxx, p. 424.

fail to throw light. From the point of view of the lawyer the English statistics may possibly seem better, and seem good : by no means the same thing ; but from the statistician's point of view the case is different. To obtain such judicial statistics as exist in Prussia and other German States, or in Italy, would mean increased control.

The apparently transcendant criminality of the County Borough of Newport, as compared with Cardiff, and the apparent immunity from Crime (as compared with its rivals) of which Preston may boast, are, obviously, in whole or in part, imaginary. "Crimes known to the Police" mean different things in different places. Cumberland is probably not really twice as criminal as Cornwall, nor East Sussex twice as criminal as the North Riding.

In the Judicial Statistics also the figures affecting Reformatory Schools clash with those in the Report of the Inspector of Reformatory Schools. It is suggested that they may be reconciled by allowing for re-admissions, re-captures, and transfers. But our point here is only that statistics offered to the public as dealing with the same matter are compiled on varying principles, and spoil all investigation based upon them. Comparison of the two sets of figures in this case also reveals a bewildering difference in official nomenclature, maddening to all who require to refer to special cases. The order and grouping of the schools are different, and when the enquirer has had the patience to decipher the cryptogram, he finds at last that in the one case the Hampshire school is to be looked for under H, and in the other under S. Lastly, although the Judicial Statistics with which I am now dealing (unlike those in the Abstract of the Board of Trade) are issued by the Home Office in both cases, the children admitted to reformatories are grouped in steps of one year, where they are over 10 years of age, and in the Report of the Inspector of Reformatories, under the same Department, in steps of two years.

The ages of juvenile offenders are a fruitful source of statistical absurdities. If we turn to the Reports of the Commissioners of Prisons, we find odd titles and odd divisions. This Department has invented for the Home Office a class who in factories would be partly " M.Y.P.," " F.Y.P.," or " Adults, M. or F.," and styles them " Juvenile Adults." In the case of inquests on deceased persons the Judicial Statistics of the same Department describe as " Youths " all who are between 16 and 25, thus including as youths those four years older than the oldest of the " Juvenile Adults." As the ages, sexes, and other sub-divisions are again differently grouped in Scotland and Ireland, there are certainly not fewer than 30 different age-divisions, mostly with different titles or nicknames, in our Judicial Statistics and Home Office documents dealing with the same figures.

The tabulation of ages and the steps of graduation in separate sets of statistics may need to be different in some cases, on account of their use in statute and administration, but the differences are infinitely more numerous than can be accounted for by this obvious cause. If we take deaths, paupers, immigrants, and so forth, we find that all differ from the Judicial Statistics, and that Poor Law Statistics differ from those of the Registrar-General. In short, it may almost be said that all our statistics differ each from the other where they in the least degree cover the same ground.

The reason given for certain differences otherwise inexplicable is that a conference between the Home Office and Board of Trade with the Registrar-General before the last Census showed that revision would have broken the continuity of the occupational mortality statistics and made the statistics of one Census not comparable with those of previous decades. As for ages, the excuse given is that Census classification, being decennial, and in some degree quinquennial, cannot agree with factory statistics, where the critical ages are 12, 16, 18, and a few others. This latter explanation will not bear examination, and the statement that although Census and Factory Department " Classifications are not identical, they are very " readily comparable," cannot be accepted.

That educational statistics must deal with age-groups of a special kind may be admitted, but there seems no obvious reason why our education statistics should vary between themselves and should also vary as between England, Scotland and Ireland. Neither are things growing better, for in such simple matters as children on the register in England and in Scotland, or on the rolls in Ireland, we find the age-groups even more various now than they were when examined above thirty years ago.

One main reason of inconsistencies in our local statistics comes, as we have already learnt in Dr. Tatham's words, from the artificial choice of districts. The Census gives us statistics of vital conditions and occupations under administrative districts. Births and deaths are treated in detail by the Registrar-General under registration districts. It is difficult to work out the deaths, say, from potter's rot, or the special phthisis of any trade, for areas in the least resembling those of the particular employment. Enquirers are puzzled when they try to deal even with the great towns, separately treated though these are, in the annual summary of deaths, for administrative areas corresponding to the Census. Administrative Birmingham has more than twice as many inhabitants as registration " Birmingham," and administrative Liverpool nearly five times as many as registration "Liverpool." On the other hand, Blackburn registration district includes nearly 50 per cent. more people than administrative Blackburn. In the "Annual Report of the Registrar- "General" many towns besides "Blackburn," as, for example, "Ashton-under-Lyne," appear with a population far larger than that included in the area of the borough. Not only are the figures of births and deaths by unions misleading, but the "registration "counties" are in the same position. People are now familiar either with the administrative county and county borough or with the "ancient" or cricket county, but no one has ever known anything about the registration county. Although this striking discrepancy is in some degree remedied in the annual summary dealing with the large towns, sex is not distinguished, so that the figures are rendered useless for certain purposes, such as occupation-disease inquiry; while in the "Registrar-General's "Report" deaths are distinguished between male and female, but births only between legitimate and illegitimate.

Such is the confusion between the figures of different Departments concerning the same subjects that there are branches of enquiry in which no amount of research can reconcile the discrepancies or elucidate the facts. The mere difference of the year chosen in the tramways' accounts of the Board of Trade and of the Local Government Board respectively cannot explain the differences in the case of some towns. Revenue in the Local Taxation Returns sometimes exceeds gross receipts as given in the Board of Trade Returns, and occasionally exceeds fourfold the net receipts as stated in the latter figures. The "revenue" from tramways in the case of Burnley for the last year I have examined exceeds, in the Local Taxation Returns, the gross receipts, in the Board of Trade Returns, for a "Burnley," which includes another borough, two urban districts, and, again, a rural parish, all, of course, outside the borough of Burnley.

The differences between the figures of the Local Government Board in the Local Taxation Returns and those given by the Board of Trade in so far as they relate to gas and tramways (leaving aside electric light) are, of course, capable of explanation, though this does not meet our statistical case. The Local Taxation Returns aim at being a statement of cash receipts and of cash payments during a financial year, both arranged under the head of the purposes in respect of which local authorities possess powers. It is the cash finance of the local authority for the year that is in view, rather than the particular undertaking and its income and expenditure. On the other hand, the Board of Trade has a different point of view, and its Returns relate primarily to the undertakings of local authorities as trading concerns. Gross receipts and working expenditure are shown, and the difference—if it yields a surplus— is called "Net Receipts." The principle of the Local Government Board Returns seems to break down where a corporation, as in the case of Burnley, has undertakings beyond its boundaries ; Burnley, for example, paying rental to the borough of Nelson and to other local authorities for its tramways in their districts. Another cause of confusion is that where tramways and electric lighting have both been established by the same municipal corporations, the current supplied, which may work for the tramways, is sometimes differently treated by the two departments. The boroughs themselves annually publish an abstract of the accounts of their Treasurers, and a close scrutiny of these will no doubt explain the reason of the dis- crepancies in any particular case. Statistical confusion, however, remains. The Board of Trade themselves explain that "in many "cases the columns will not correspond with . . . . . the "municipal accounts." In the case of gasworks the different way in which expenditure for the purposes of public lighting is treated is another cause of statistical error.

Not only do Board of Trade and Local Government Board figures clash (with one another and) with figures of the Census and of the Registrar-General, but so also do Home Office figures in the case of Occupation. In the returns of persons employed, published as Supplements to the Report of the Chief Inspector of Factories, the classification of the trades does not agree with that of the Census ; as for instance in the cotton trade. The Board of Trade figures of employment are based on voluntary returns made monthly by the principal firms. Some do not report at all, and others only inter- mittently. The figures given are those from the firms which report continuously ; and in all cases new works are obviously excluded. Although not sharing their views I cannot wonder at some of the complaints made by members of the so-called Tariff Commission. The grouping of commodities has led to misconception as to the growth or decline of particular branches of trade. Change and finality are both difficult to procure. New trades develop and old trades are split up ; but statistical supervision would have lessened the difficulty by creating originally a sounder classification. The recent change officially effected which classifies imports as far as possible under the countries of origin instead of the countries from which they are shipped would have been made much sooner had there been a controlling or even an advisory official statistical department or council. The familiar example of the enormous import of Dutch beef occurs to us all. It is not easy to feel sure how much of the beef which now figures as either German or Dutch is in fact

Hungarian or of still more distant origin. But if we are not yet accurate in our facts we are at least far nearer to accuracy than was previously the case, and the fact that the change has been deferred now causes the mistaken impression of an increase of German imports more rapid than is the case.

Our trade returns are still imperfect as regards internal commerce and coasting trade. The coal trade is fairly known, but with the other exception of British-grown grain, general statistics of internal commerce are lacking, while apart from coal little information is available as to the nature of goods carried coast-wise from our ports. Attention has recently been called to the incompleteness of the returns of interchange by way of trade between Great Britain and Ireland. Figures of production are full for minerals, agriculture, and fisheries, but wanting for steel production and the textile industries. The iron trade and cotton trade publish their own statistics. The Census of Production will be un-necessarily complete for general purposes, but, on the other hand, the intervals will be too long for most inquirers. In our knowledge of the income of our people we still stand behind many other countries, and our legislation on unemployment and old-age pensions will have to be based chiefly on incomplete trade-union returns; while unorganised labour virtually escapes statistical treatment.

The most pressing need is that we should hand over to a Statistical Department those statistics which are collected by various Departments in the course of administrative work, and of which the publication is not necessary for the purposes of administration. This Statistical Department should arrange such statistics (except those purely administrative) as are collected by the other Departments.

The responsibility incurred by Census makers or compilers of official information sometimes extends like an earthquake wave over large portions of the surface of the globe. In most books of reference, for example, statistics will be found of "Catholics," affecting both the Kingdom of the Netherlands and the Canton of Geneva, in which there are added together Catholics of the faith officially known as "Catholic, Apostolic, Roman," "Old Catholics," and those of the Jansenists who claim to be Catholics rightly in communion with the Western Church under the authority of the Pope, but are rejected by that Church for holding doctrines which, as a fact, they may or may not hold. It is better to be without statistics than to gather them in such a way as to mislead the inquirers of the world.

It may perhaps be well to state my own opinion as the result of some experience and some recent inquiry. A mere meeting of statisticians from the various Departments, to constitute an advisory committee, would in my judgment be an insufficient result of our labours. A permanent statistical direction is, I think, required. The Treasury is the Department which ought to bring about reform, but it seems to shrink from creating an office to do work that should have been taken-up long ago. To advocate a true statistical direction of national statistics is doubtless a " counsel of " perfection," the object sought being important to the country, but, like most great ends, difficult of accomplishment. Want of co-ordination in the work of the various offices is obvious and is not denied, but, save for the efforts of the Board of Trade, now redoubled under Mr. Lloyd George as President, we do not adopt a remedy.

APPENDIX A.

In respect of certain alleged "discrepancies between Local Government Board Returns and Census or Registrar-General Returns," the following table shows for what kinds of areas information is published in recurring Returns of the Registrar-General and the Local Government Board.

'tatement as to the Classification of Areas in certain Periodical Statistical Returns mentioned below, which are issued (i) *by the Registrar-General, and* (ii) *by the Local Government Board.*

(i) *Returns issued by the Registrar-General.*

Titles of Returns, and Nature of Information Given.	Areas for which Information is Given.		Remarks.
	Registration Areas (*i.e.*, Divisions, Counties, Districts, and Sub-Districts).	Administrative Areas (*i e*, Counties, County Boroughs, Non-County Boroughs, other Urban Districts, and Rural Districts).	
Census, 1901. reas*..	Yes, and separately for each constituent parish	Yes, and separately for each constituent parish, Rural Districts excepted	Nil.
opulation	Do.	Do.	A table gives the population, &c., of parishes situate in one Registration County, but in another, Administrative ; and *vice versâ.*
'umber of houses	Do. ...	Do.	
'umber of tenements	Nil	Yes	Nil.
irths, Marriages and Deaths (1891-1901)	Yes, sub-districts excepted	Nil	Nil.
ges	Yes, sub-districts excepted	Yes	Nil.
'ondition as to Marriage	Yes, Counties only ..	Yes, for the Administrative County, for the aggregates of Urban and Rural Districts in each Administrative County, for each County Borough, and for each Urban District of over 50,000 population	Nil.

* See also part of General Report on Census of 1901 relating to " Areas," pp. 11 to 15.

Classification of Areas in certain Periodical Statistical Returns—Contd.
(i) *Returns issued by the Registrar-General—Contd.*

Titles of Returns, and Nature of Information Given.	Areas for which Information is Given.		Remarks.
	Registration Areas (*i.e.*, Divisions, Counties, Districts, and Sub-Districts).	Administrative Areas (*i.e.*, Counties, County Boroughs, Non-County Boroughs, other Urban Districts, and Rural Districts).	
Occupations	Nil	Yes, for the Administrative County, for the aggregates of Urban and Rural Districts in each Administrative County, for each County Borough, and for each Urban District of over 5,000 population	Nil.
Numbers of blind, deaf, dumb, and insane	Nil	Yes, Counties and County Boroughs only	Nil.
Birthplaces	Nil	Yes, only for residents in County Boroughs and for residents in Urban Districts of over 50,000 population; also for residents in Ancient (or Geographical) Counties	Nil.
Language spoken in Wales and in Monmouthshire	Nil	Yes, for the Administrative County and for each Urban and Rural District	Nil.
Persons enumerated in Workhouse Establishments, in Hospitals and Lunatic Asylums, in Prisons, and in certified Reformatory and Industrial Schools	Yes, divisions excepted	Nil	Nil.
Annual Report of Registrar-General (1905). Populations	Yes, corrected for alterations of boundaries subsequent to date of Census	Nil	An Index indicate the Registration are or areas in which each urban district i comprised. A note refers to Tables in the Census giving particulars as t the constitution o each registration and urban area. At the end of 1905 only 149 of the 1,16 urban districts were co-extensive with one or more registration areas (districts o sub-districts).
Areas	Do.	Nil	
Births	Yes	Nil	
Deaths	Do.	Nil	
Marriages	Yes, sub-districts excepted	Nil	
Causes of death	Do.	Nil	

Classification of Areas in certain Periodical Statistical Returns—Contd.
(i) *Returns issued by the Registrar-General—Contd.*

Titles of Returns, and Nature of Information given.	Areas for which Information is Given.		Remarks.
	Registration Areas (*i.e.*, Divisions, Counties, Districts, and Sub-Districts).	Administrative Areas (*i.e.*, Counties, County Boroughs, Non-County Boroughs, other Urban Districts, and Rural Districts).	
Annual Summary of Births, Deaths, &c. (1906).			
Estimated Population	Yes, Divisions and Counties only	Yes, limited to all towns, as at present constituted, with population of 20,000 and over at Census of 1901	Nil.
Births	Yes, Divisions, Counties, and London and suburban areas only	Do.	Nil.
Deaths (limited classification of causes)	Do.	Do.	Nil.
Marriages	Yes, Divisions and Counties only	Nil	Nil.
Notified cases of infectious disease	Nil	Yes, limited to towns with population of 20,000 and over at Census of 1901	Nil.
Quarterly Return of Marriages, Births and Deaths.			
Estimated Population	Yes, Divisions and Counties only	Yes, limited to all towns, as at present constituted, with population of 20,000 and over at Census of 1901	A table giv[...] population of areas tra[...] from one regi[...] area to anotl[...] ing the quart[...] Index indic[...] registration areas in whi[...] Urban Dist[...] situated.
Births	Yes	Do.	
Deaths (limited classification of causes)	Yes	Do.	
Notified cases of infectious disease	Nil	Yes, as regards certain large towns	
Marriages	Yes, except sub-districts	Nil	
Weekly Return.			
Estimated Population	Nil	Yes, for towns with more than 50,000 population in 1901	Nil.
Births	Yes, for London and Suburban areas	Do.	Nil.
Deaths (limited classification of causes)	Do.	Do.	Nil.
Notified cases of infectious disease	Nil	Yes, for Metropolitan Boroughs	Nil.

Classification of Areas in certain Periodical Statistical Returns—Contd.

(i) *Returns issued by the Registrar-General—Contd.*

Titles of Returns, and Nature of Information Given.	Areas for which Information is Given.		Remark
	Registration Areas (*i.e.*, Divisions, Counties, Districts, and Sub-Districts.	Administrative Areas (*i.e*, Counties, County Boroughs, Non-County Boroughs, other Urban Districts, and Rural Districts).	
Decennial Supplement. *Part I.*			
Estimated Population	Yes, for sexes and for separate ages in the ten · year period. Counties and Districts	Nil	Nil.
Births	Yes, Totals, Males and Females for ten years in Counties and Districts	Nil	Nil.
Marriages	Yes, Totals for ten years in Counties and districts	Nil	Nil.
Deaths (abridged classification of causes)	Yes, Totals at several age groups in ten years in Counties and Districts	Nil	Nil.
Life Tables...	For England and Wales and Selected Healthy Districts	Nil	Nil.
Part II.			
Deaths in Different Occupations (abridged classification of causes)	Yes, for England and Wales and groups of Selected Registration Areas	Nil	Nil.

Classification of Areas in certain Periodical Statistical Returns—Contd.

(ii) *Returns issued by the Local Government Board.*

Titles of Returns, and Nature of Information Given.	Areas for which Information is Given.		Remarks.
	Registration Areas.*	Administrative Areas.	
Pauperism Returns. Number of paupers on 1st January and 1st July. Cost of In-Mainten-ance and Out-Relief —half-years ended Lady Day and Michaelmas	Yes, for Poor Law Unions and Union Counties, *i.e.*, groups of entire Unions	Nil	The particula "Divisions" now given.
Monthly Returns of Numbers of Paupers	Yes, for Divisions only	Nil	Nil.
Local Taxation Returns. Part I (1905-06). Valuation	Yes, for Poor Law Unions, and Union Counties	Yes, limited to Counties and County Boroughs	Nil.
Accounts of Over-seers (exclusive of London)	Nil	Do.	Prior to 1905-accounts of Ov were also cl according to Law Unions.
Accounts of Boards of Guardians (exclu-sive of London)	Yes, for Poor Law Unions	Nil	A summary giv tain particula each Union and Division sive of Londo
Part IV (1904-05). Accounts of Boards of Guardians in London	Yes. for Poor Law Unions	Nil	The receipts a penditure o overseers of th for the paris City of London are shown in note.
Accounts of other authorities	Nil	Yes (generally)	Nil.
Parts II, III, V, and VI (1904-05)	Nil	Do.	Nil.

*In the Local Government Board Returns the Poor Law Unions represent, with exceptions, the same areas as the Registration Districts, and the Divisions and the Union C correspond with the Registration Divisions and Counties.

APPENDIX B.

The Melbourne Conference last December dealt with the "Unification of Australian Statistical Methods and Co-ordination "of the work of the Commonwealth and State Bureaux."

Australia has recommended to the Australian States, and is likely to obtain exactly that improvement and unity which we need as between, for example, England, and Scotland, and Ireland.

So also, the recommendations and improvements as regards inter-State trade closely resemble those still required as regards trade between Ireland and Great Britain.

The "Conference of Statisticians" included not only the Commonwealth and States of Australia, but New Zealand—now the Dominion of New Zealand.

The New Zealand system, as superior in certain points, was recommended for adoption in Australia in such cases. The conference inculcated the "Advantages of statistical uniformity"; "Uniformity in categories . . . . . in collection," and in settling districts. It made special reference, needed for these days, to finance : *i.e.*, to bases and possibilities of taxation, which it put high in its lists. We find recommendation of calendar year ; agreement to retain certain exceptional State bases of certain population estimates and other tables up to a fixed date before complete uniformity ; settlement of uniform forms of Returns ; valuable record of reasons for dissent of the State of Victoria on certain points.

PROCEEDINGS *on the* 19TH NOVEMBER, 1907.

AFTER the formal business of the Meeting had been disposed of,

The PRESIDENT announced that Professor Edgeworth and Mr. Noel A. Humphreys being prevented through accidents from attending this Meeting to receive the Guy Medals awarded to them, the presentation would be made at the Ordinary Meeting on 17th December.

The PRESIDENT announced that the subject of the Howard Medal Essay Competition for 1907-08 was "The Cost, Conditions and Results of Hospital Relief in London."

The PRESIDENT having delivered his Address,

Sir ALFRED E. BATEMAN said it was his privilege, having been connected with the Society in various ways for many years, to move a hearty vote of thanks to the new President for his excellent address; and he appreciated the privilege all the more because it gave him an opportunity of saying something of the work done by a gentleman with whom he had been associated nearly thirty years, who was one of the most conscientious users of statistics. He had seen so many members of both Houses of Parliament, especially the House of Commons, who wanted statistics made to order, and when the figures did not prove what they desired thought it was the fault of the statistics; but their President had never shown any inclination of that sort. It was a well understood rule in the Royal Statistical Society that the Presidential Address should not be discussed; no one was allowed to point out where they thought the President was wrong, or to criticise his statements adversely, but they might fairly show where he was right. He had this evening been listening to a number of criticisms about those official statistics, with which he had been connected so many years, when a few words of explanation on many of them would have thrown quite a different light. However, he should not attempt to transgress the rule. They were very much indebted to Sir Charles Dilke for this painstaking Paper, which would be of great use, and might supply steam for a movement in favour of a Central Statistical Commission, which had been going on for nearly thirty years, but owing to various causes, in great part to certain opposition in high quarters, had never yet succeeded. They had gone on doing the best they could with the statistics they were able to produce in their own departments, and considerable improvements had been effected in international statistics through the aid of the International Statistical Institute, founded in London twenty years ago, which had brought foreign criticism to bear on their work. It could not, however, be said that at any of their meetings abroad the official statistics of this country had received such severe criticism as had been forced on them by one of their own countrymen in the Presidential chair here! He did not draw any moral from that, but it had been very useful to have the aid of the International Institute in showing them what was being done by different departments in foreign countries. As to the practical proposal of the President there could be only one opinion, that it was very desirable. Almost every foreign country had such a Central Commission in one form or another; some went so far as to co-opt the statisticians of other countries, at any rate as corresponding members. He was himself a member of the Belgian Central Statistical Commission. He hoped that after this important Address something more might be heard of the movement; and they were much indebted to the President for having brought the matter forward.

Major P. G. CRAIGIE, in seconding the motion, said that those who had filled the chair of that Society, fully appreciated the responsibility and the opportunity afforded to each successive President for bringing before the members at the opening of each session some one particular subject which might hereafter and in detail be debated with advantage to statistical science. In this case there would be a special occasion for doing that which neither he nor Sir Alfred Bateman could, by the custom of the Society, do that evening, namely, in detail, criticising, objecting to, if need be, any specific proposals in the address. The Sessional Card told them that their friend, Mr. Bowley, whose authority was repeatedly appealed to in the address, was already sharpening his pen for the purpose of exposing the official defects in a form which might be expected to give the academic view of the possibilities of reform, and throw down the glove to those who practised the art of preparing official statistics, and offer them some opportunity of explaining anomalies which undoubtedly existed. They would all, however, unhesitatingly thank the President for rescuing from the apparent oblivion into which the topic had fallen in this country, the important question of the better concentration and co-ordination of statistics; for, whatever opinions they might hold on particular points, there were many undoubted faults which had hampered them all, time after time in their inquiries, faults which met them, however, even in the more logical arrangements of foreign countries. He was delighted to welcome there to-night his successor in the Secretariat of the International Statistical Institute—the distinguished President of the Central Statistical Council of the Netherlands. Even in the presence of that gentleman, it might be claimed that this country produced statistics which, in certain respects, and largely in respect of relative promptitude, were the envy of other States. As to the scope for improvement, there were some points beyond debate on which they were all agreed. First of all, a radical reform was necessary in the occupation statistics of the census, as for the classification of the population was at the base of all statistics.

In that connection, he might remind them that only a few months ago, at the Copenhagen meeting of the International Institute, there was a valuable paper by Dr. Van der Borght, of the German Imperial Statistical Office, explaining recent improvements made in the German system in this respect. The further question of the non-reconciliability of areas was another prominent cause of confusion in this country, but here the fault was not that of the statistician, but of the politician, and Parliament must bear the blame. No one could doubt that much might yet be done to make the statistics of this country more intelligible and more accurate, and their presentation more attractive; but a reform of procedure dominated by a desire for mere cheapness would hardly conduce to this end, and he could not help, as an old official, doubting whether it was from the Treasury, before which statistical reformers had quailed on many occasions in times past, they could look for any material improvement. All in that room would agree in thanking the President for his Address.

The motion was put to the meeting by Sir A. E. BATEMAN and carried unanimously.

The PRESIDENT, in acknowledging the vote of thanks, said that he should like to associate himself with what had been said as to the presence on that occasion of Dr. Verrijn Stuart. As regarded the agricultural statistics, he had guarded himself; and he could imagine one other class in which they, perhaps, set a good example. That in some classes they were better than the French or the United States, did not prove that they were good. He had shown in his Paper that he did not think the French shone in their official statistics as they did in many other departments of government. They could, undoubtedly, look to the possibility of having here a system which might easily be superior to that of any of our greatest rivals and neighbours, unless it were Germany.

One moral he should like to draw from the kind speeches which had been made about the Address. Sir Alfred Bateman, who had so long and honorable a connection with the Board of Trade, and Major Craigie similarly connected with the Agricultural Department, both fully admitted many points which he had brought forward; and they cordially accepted his main remedy. That being so, it was needless to quarrel about details. His object was, not to hammer this or that Department, but to get that done in which it appeared they all agreed.

He was most anxious that the Session should produce that criticism which, by some absurd *privilegium*, he was protected from that evening, and his earnest desire was, not that this should be a shot in the air, but, that there should be a prolonged, active, and even venomous criticism, if necessary. It would bring out the truth and tend to achieve the object they all had in view. The only other thing he might say was, that he had tried in this Paper to make full admission of all the difficulties that lay in their way. In this country they had many advantages; but statistical science was under a peculiar drawback. The differences between Irish, Scotch, and English legislation were enormous. Other special difficulties were caused by the fact that areas were chosen at the time of the new Poor Law, for one purpose, which were subsequently used for a wholly different purpose. They were originally justified on a principle which was fatal to their utility for the ultimate purpose. The object of the framer of the Poor Law was to bring rural and urban districts together. The idea in more recent times was to separate the urban from the rural. That change was the origin of a great deal of difficulty, and it affected the question of nomenclature. Major Craigie had suggested that it was chiefly the fault of Parliament. He had tried to be fair by blaming both Parliament and the Departments impartially. As regarded the adoption of new years and new areas for certain purposes, Parliament might no doubt be the chief offender; but the Departments, as the Address had put it, sometimes allowed Parliament, unwarned, to indulge such whims. With regard to the question of saving, he might refer any observer of this question to the documents published by one single Department alone, the Local Government Board for England and Wales. There was a great mass of statistics, and he asked if they were all necessary, and whether, along with a saving of money, it might not be possible to have more valuable statistics? That Department published a great mass of statistical matter, and he thought it was an obvious case in which co-ordination and examination might reform them. The most important case for improvement, probably, was that alluded to by Lord Goschen, namely, the income and financial statistics. The importance of those figures was so great that he thought they might be usefully improved by means of money saved out of some statistics issued by the Local Government Board.

As the result of the ballot the following Candidates were declared elected Fellows of the Society :—

Arthur Edwin Balleine.

Herbert Harry Bassett.

Henry Mitchell Boddy.

Lieut.-Col. Guillermo Rafael Calderón.

Herbert Stanley Jevons, M.A., B.Sc.

Professor Thomas Hudson Middleton, M.A.

Frederick William Mitchell.

Sir Nathaniel Nathan, K.C.

R. Stanley Osborne.

John Joyce Ryder.

James Edward Shimmell, A.I.A.

J. Penry Cyril Clutton Williams, B.A.

An INQUIRY *into the* RENT *of* AGRICULTURAL LAND *in*
ENGLAND *and* WALES *during the* NINETEENTH CENTURY.

By ROBERT J. THOMPSON.

[Read before the Royal Statistical Society, 17th December, 1907.
Major P. G. CRAIGIE, C.B., Hon. Vice-President, in the Chair.]

THE share of the produce taken by the landlord for the use of the
soil and for the equipment of the farm, which we call rent, has
formed the subject of much economic argument, but comparatively
few statistics exist to enable us to take a larger view of the general
rise and fall in agricultural rents than is afforded by the casual
records of individual estates. There is, in fact, but one general
statement referring to the country at large, viz., the Inland Revenue
return of the gross income derived from the ownership of "lands."
This dates from the year 1842-43, though there are the earlier
figures of the assessments under the Property and Income Tax Acts
for the years 1810-11 and 1814-15.

Besides these general statements, the reports of numerous Committees and Commissions which at various times inquired into the
"State of Agriculture," contain many scattered references to the
subject of rent, though until we come to the Royal Commission on
Agriculture of 1893-96 very little effort seems to have been made
to obtain actual records over a series of years. This Commission,
however, applied to a number of the principal landowners, and was
successful in obtaining detailed statements of rent and expenditure,
which form a valuable mine of information for the comparatively
short period which they cover. The Committee on Tithe Rent
Charge in 1890 also made inquiries, but the results were embodied
in general statements of the fall in rents in different counties.
Another official body which took evidence on the point was the Royal
Commission on the Depression in Trade in 1886. Sir James Caird
seems to have been the principal witness, and he based his
conclusions chiefly on the income tax figures. Apart from these
official statements, mention may be made of the estimate made by
Sir James Caird in his "English Agriculture in 1850-51," and of
his later statement in 1878. There is also the valuable record
of two of the Bedford estates given by the Duke of Bedford in his
book, "The Story of a Great Agricultural Estate," while the rents

received by certain Oxford Colleges have been given in several interesting papers read before this Society by Mr. L. L. Price. On the whole, however, the statistical evidence of the general trend of rents in the past century is very meagre.

The deficiency of information no doubt largely arises from the nature of the subject. The great diversity of soil and situation, of size of farms, of buildings, and of methods of cultivation causes wide variations in the rent paid per acre, and makes it difficult to arrive at an average which can be regarded as typical of the $27\frac{1}{2}$ million acres of cultivated land in England and Wales. Rents, however, necessarily tend to adjust themselves to prices, so that continuous returns from the same area ought to afford an approximately accurate indication of the average rise and fall of rents in the country as a whole.

It will easily be understood that the difficulty of obtaining returns covering any long period is considerable. Old account books may have been lost or destroyed, or may be practically inaccessible, or they may have been kept in such a way that the labour of extraction is prohibitive. Frequently estate accounts only deal with the estate as a whole, and it is practically impossible to separate the agricultural land from the villages, woods, moors, parks, and residential houses, which are included in it. It is difficult again to get returns which synchronize sufficiently with one another to be of much use.

I have been fortunate enough, however, to obtain more or less detailed statements from 16 estates, and in addition I have made use of the information given in the publications of the Royal Commission on Agriculture and in the Duke of Bedford's book. From these sources tables have been constructed showing the rent actually received for—

    (1.) 70,000 acres from 1801 to 1900.
    (2.) 120,000   ,,   '16 ,: '00.
    (3.) 400,000   ,,   '72 ,, '00·

The information has been supplied on the understanding that the particulars should not be published in such a way as to enable any particular estate to be identified. The tables, therefore, represent in every case a number of estates and are given without identification.

My sincere thanks are due to the following landowners who were good enough to allow certain particulars of their estates to be supplied to me : the Duke of Bedford, the Duke of Newcastle, the Marquess of Ripon, the Marquess of Northampton, the Earl of Jersey, Lord Carrington, Lord Onslow, Mr. Christopher Turnor, the Ecclesiastical Commissioners (through Sir Alfred de Bock Porter), and the Trustees of Guy's Hospital (through Mr. Cosmo H. Bonsor). I have also to express my thanks to the following gentlemen for the trouble they have taken in furnishing me with statements and other information : Mr. R. H. Inglis Palgrave, F.R.S.; Mr. L. L. Price, M.A. ; Mr. Alex. Goddard, Mr. H. Herbert Smith, Mr. D. T. Thring, Sir Francis Walker, Mr. W. Forrester Addie, Mr. Oswald H. Wade, Mr. Frank H. M. Savile, Mr. J. J. Done, Mr. Arthur E. Elliott, Mr. H. M. Jonas, Mr. Arthur H. Bowles, Mr. R. E. Prothero, Mr. C. P. Hall, Mr. W. D. Little, and to many other gentlemen who have assisted me in one way or another.

The information covers but a very small part of the actual agricultural area of England, and is open to the criticism that there is no guarantee of its representative character, but in so far as a general agreement is shown, the returns may, I think, be regarded as typical of the rise and fall in rents in England generally, though they cannot always be taken as an absolute indication of the average rent over the whole country.

Naturally, the main interest to us lies in the trend of rents in comparatively recent times, but it may be of some value if I give first of all the particulars available for earlier years, and so trace by gradual stages the various changes in agricultural rents during the past century.

Changes in Rent (a) 1801-20.

In the early years of the century many factors combined to favour a rise in rent : there was, first, the growth in the population and the increased demand for produce ; secondly, the high prices, resulting from bad crops, war taxes and a depreciated currency ; thirdly, the improved knowledge of agriculture, which enabled more produce to be obtained from the land; and, finally, the enclosure of common-fields. In the case of farms already enclosed, high prices and the consequent large profits of the farmers were alone sufficient to cause an increase in rent, while in the case of the enclosures the considerable outlay of capital required in buildings, drainage, fencing, and in legal expenses necessitated the promise of a substantial return. The rise in rent on newly enclosed land was estimated by Sir John Sinclair to average 9s. per acre.[1]

The only early statement of a general character is based on an inquiry made by the Board of Agriculture through their correspondents in 1804.[2] The result of this inquiry showed that the average increase in rent over the whole of England between 1790

---

[1] " Communications to the Board of Agriculture," 1797, vol. i, p. lviii.

[2] *Ibid.*, 1806, vol. v, p. 21.

and 1804 was 39¾ per cent. On the average of twenty-five counties, the rent per 100 acres in 1790 is put at 88*l.* 6*s.* (17*s.* 8*d.* per acre), and in 1803 at 121*l.* 2*s.* 7*d.* (24*s.* 3*d.* per acre). From an examination of publications of the time, however, I cannot but think that these figures (which merely represent the opinions of certain individuals) are unduly high if taken as an average. There is probably little doubt that insufficient allowance was made for the large areas of poor, low-rented land.

The figures which I have been able to obtain for the period 1801-20 (see Appendix A) represent the rental actually received from some 65,000 acres situated in Lincoln, Essex, Hereford, and North Wales. They are shown in the following table in five-year periods, but the area is too small and not sufficiently distributed to be really representative :—

TABLE I.

Years.	Acreage.	Average Rent per Acre.		Years.	Acreage.	Average Rent per Acre.	
		s.	*d.*			*s.*	*d.*
1801–05............	62,655	11	2	1811–15............	65,920	14	7
'06–10............	63,981	11	7	'16–20............	67,143	15	2

This table shows an increase from 11*s.* 2*d.* per acre in 1801-05 to 15*s.* 2*d.* per acre in 1816-20, or about 36 per cent. The extreme rise, however, was from 10*s.* 10*d.* in 1802 to 15*s.* 11*d.* in 1818, or about 47 per cent.

I have no means of estimating to what extent these figures represent the average tendency of rents in England during these years, but it seems certain that some such general rise actually took place. Contemporary records contain many references to the great increases which occurred in individual farms, and I give in Appendix E several cases showing the rent of separate farms over long periods. The only figures which can be quoted for comparison are those given by McCulloch,[3] which are based on the property tax. According to these estimates the average rent in England and Wales was 15*s.* 9½*d.* per acre in 1810-11, and 18*s.* 4½*d.* per acre in 1814-15 : a rise of 16 per cent. in four years. It will be seen that McCulloch's average for England and Wales is higher than that given in Appendix A. This is chiefly owing to the fact that the area included in the latter contains a large proportion of Welsh land which unduly depresses the average. In Appendix B, however, the proportion of English land is increased by the inclusion of additional areas from the year 1816, and it is interesting to notice that in that year the average is 18*s.* per acre or within 4½*d.* of the amount given by McCulloch for the preceding year.

[3] "Account of British Empire, 1854," vol. i. p. 551.

An important fact which should be borne in mind in speaking of this period is the suspension of specie payments,[4] owing to which the currency was depreciated above 18 per cent. during the five years ending 1815, though, as McCulloch points out, rents might not be raised in consequence by more than 10 per cent. because many long leases would not fall to be renewed.

(b) 1820-45.

Throughout the foregoing period prices kept at a high level, and farmers found consolation for bad seasons and deficient harvests in the enormous returns obtained for their produce.   In the next twenty-five years, however, prices were comparatively low, and farmers, accustomed to the high war prices, made loud complaints of the unremunerative character of their business.   Much of the distress was undoubtedly due to the disorganisation in values resulting from the currency being placed on a gold basis in 1819, while losses from sheep-rot and indifferent crops contributed to the distress in certain years.   That agriculture had ceased to flourish may be gathered from the Parliamentary inquiries of 1821, 1833, 1836 and 1837 into the depressed state of the industry and into "the Burdens on Land" in 1844, but the bulk of the distress after the country had begun to recover from the dislocation of prices caused by the resumption of cash payments was confined to the heavy clay lands, which at current prices would not bear the cost of growing grain, and were, it is stated, "allowed to run down and in many cases abandoned."[5]   The history of the lighter soils and grazing counties seems to have been less eventful, and it must not be forgotten that these represent the major part of the country.

The position in the earlier years of the period is probably well reflected in the observations of the Select Committee on the State of Agriculture of 1833, who state that "the landlords in every part "of the United Kingdom, though in different degrees, have met "the fall of price (since 1820) by a reduction of rent, except where "during the war the rents on their estates had not been raised, or "where, by a large expenditure of capital, permanent improvements "have enriched the nature of the soil itself.   The spread of the drill "system of husbandry, a better rotation of cropping, a more judi-"cious use of manures, especially of bones, improvement in the

---

[4] Porter notes that "owing to the depreciated state of our currency" the average price of wheat in 1810, viz., 103*s*. 3*d*., was not equal to more than about 90*s*. in gold.   He estimates 122*s*. as equal to 100*s*. in 1812, and 72*s*. 1*d*. as equal to 54*s*. in 1814.   ("Progress of the Nation," vol. i, 1836.)

[5] Committee of 1833.

"breed both of cattle and sheep, have all contributed to counter-
"balance the fall in price, and to sustain that surplus profit in the
"culture of the soil on which rent depends."

The later years of the period showed signs of a revival. The
Tithe Commutation Act was passed in 1836, and removed a source
of annoyance, as well as a hindrance to improvements, while the
value of drainage, of artificial manures, and of the application of
science to agricultural practice began to be more generally recognised.

Table II gives in quinquennial periods the rent of about
110,000 acres, from 1816 to 1845. The figures for each year
are given in Appendix B.

TABLE II.

Years.	Acreage.*	Average Rent per Acre.		Years.	Acreage.*	Average Rent per Acre.	
		s.	*d.*			*s.*	*d.*
1816–20 ..	110,476	18	8	1831–35....	113,945	18	5
'21–25 ..	111,255	17	11	'36–40 .	114,894	18	8
'26–30. ..	112,483	17	9	'41–45	118,371	20	1

* In Lincoln, Hereford, Bucks, Beds, Cambridge, Essex, and North Wales.

It will be seen that there was a downward tendency in the first
half of this period, followed by a recovery after 1830. The figures
for the individual years (Appendix B) show a decline from 19s. 5d.
in 1818 to 17s. 2d. in 1822, or 11½ per cent., corresponding to the
initial period of depression, followed by a number of fluctuations
up to 1830. There was little variation between 1830 and 1839,
from which date a steady upward movement is recorded. Over
the whole period the increase is only 7½ per. cent., but the extreme
variation was from 17s. 2d. per acre in 1822 to 20s. 6d. in 1845, or
nearly 20 per cent.

On the whole; these years represent, first, a decline, then a
period of adjustment and recovery, and then the beginning of an
upward tendency, which continued with little intermission until
1878.

McCulloch, by a calculation based on the Income Tax Returns,
puts the average rent in England and Wales in 1842-43 at 21s. 6¼d. per
acre. From this it would seem that the figures given in Appendix B
are still somewhat low, and comparing them with those for later years
I believe this to be the case, though they probably represent fairly
well the general trend of rents during the period. McCulloch's
figures, however, have no special significance, as they are arrived at
simply by dividing the total area of England and Wales into the
total value of the assessment.

(*c*) 1845-72.

This period is distinguished by the general advancement of the standard of farming throughout the country. The agricultural practices, which in 1845 were known and adopted here and there, came into general use. An indication of awakened interest may be found in the establishment of the Royal Agricultural Society in 1839, and the spirit in which that great Society was founded well reflects the new attitude taken up by farmers in this country. In the letter to Earl Spencer, which led to the formation of the Society, Mr. H. Handley, M.P., observes : " Farmers are at length convinced " that it is not in parliamentary interference that they must seek a " remedy (for low prices). Repeated inquiries have terminated in " repeated disappointments. It is to their own energies and their " own resources they must look, and by cheapening the cost and " increasing the amount of production pave the way to future " prosperity." [6]

The introduction of free trade in 1846 gave an emphasis to these words, although it did not for many years produce any effect on the price of corn. In fact throughout this period prices generally showed a steady tendency to rise, though not to any very marked degree until towards 1870. Sauerbeck's index-number for the two groups, "animal and vegetable food," averaged 87 for the five years 1846-50, 89 for 1851-55, 92 for 1856-60, 90 for 1861-65, 97 for 1866-70, and 99 for 1871-72.

There were two other factors which also operated to increase rents. The first was the outlay of capital in drainage and other improvements, and the second the development of the means of transit by railway.

The advantages of soil drainage were hardly recognised before 1840. In that year Philip Pusey, one of the foremost agriculturists of the day, says "its introduction is too new to be placed altogether " beyond the risk of disappointment," [7] but so rapidly did it advance in public favour that in 1846 the Government set aside a sum of 2,000,000*l.* to promote the improvement of land in Great Britain by drainage through the medium of loans to landowners, because, as the preamble to the Act states : " the productiveness and value " of much of the land in Great Britain and Ireland are capable of " being greatly increased by drainage." [8] In 1850 a further two millions were granted, the money being also applicable to other improvements. Under these and other Acts no less than 7,381,000*l.*

---

[6] A letter to Earl Spencer on the formation of a National Agricultural Institution, by Henry Handley, M.P., 1838.

[7] " Journal of the Royal Agricultural Society," vol. i, p. 6, 1840.

[8] 9 and 10 Vict., c. 101.

was expended on drainage between 1846 and 1872, and 2,797,000*l.* on other works, or in all 10,178,000*l.*, and up to 1906 the total outlay under these Acts was 18,000,000*l.* No record exists of the outlays out of private capital, apart from that mentioned under the Improvement of Lands Acts, but with the increasing recognition of the utility of drainage, the expenditure from this source must have been very large, and it may fairly be assumed that an important factor in the rise in rents in this period is to be found in the improvement in the soil by drainage, and of the farm by better buildings.

The third factor, to which I am inclined to attribute a greater influence than has been usually ascribed to it, was the development of railway communication. The network of railways which spread over the country after 1840 brought remote and inaccessible districts into touch with the Metropolis and the large towns, opened up new markets, and enabled farmers to send their produce distances which would have been impossible by road. The cost of production was cheapened, farming became more profitable, and the rent which farmers could afford to pay consequently increased.

In the next table I have included, in addition to the figures given in Appendix B, some 12,000 acres for which particulars have been supplied at five-year intervals only, but the average rent is practically unaffected.

TABLE III.

Years.	Acreage.*	Average Rent per Acre.		Years.	Acreage.*	Average Rent per Acre.	
		s.	*d.*			*s.*	*d.*
1846-50....	131,347	21	–	1861-65....	134,020	23	7
'51-55..	132,885	20	9	'66-71†	134,719	24	8
'56-60....	133,785	23	1				

* In Lincoln, Hereford, Bucks, Beds, Cambridge, Essex, Northampton, Warwick, and North Wales.

† Six years.

The increase shown in this table from 21*s.* in 1846-50 to 24*s.* 8*d.* in 1866-71 is equal to 17 per cent., but the extreme range was from 19*s.* 10*d.* in 1851, a year of great depression, to 24*s.* 10*d.* in 1869, or about 25 per cent. A comparison of prices with rents in this period will be made later.

There are two general estimates of rent at the beginning of this period with which the above figures may be compared. McCulloch, on the same basis as before, estimated the average rent of land in 1851-52 in England and Wales at 22*s.* per acre. Caird, on the other hand, as the result of his enquiry in 1850,[9] put the rent of "cultivated land" in England alone (32 counties) at 27*s.* 2*d.* per acre.

[9] *English Agriculture in* 1850-51.

It is probable, however, that he subsequently thought this figure too high, as in 1878 he put the average rent at 30s., an increase of only about 10 per cent. From the figures given in Appendix C, showing the rent of 400,000 acres from 1872, it would seem that the average rent given in the table above is still too low. The true average would probably be 2s. or 3s. higher.

(d) 1872-1900.

About midway between the seventies and the eighties, the country entered upon a remarkable and long-sustained period of agricultural depression. To sum it up briefly, it may be said to have had two distinct and separate causes : Unfavourable seasons and low prices. The witnesses before the Royal Commission on Agriculture of 1879-82 agreed in ascribing the depression at that time " mainly to a succession of unfavourable seasons," while the subsequent Commission of 1892-96 found a " concensus of opinion " that the chief cause of the existing depression is the progressive " and serious decline in the prices of farm produce."

It is interesting to notice that a new influence was at work. Hitherto, bad harvests and unfavourable seasons had always in the history of agriculture offered some compensation in the fact that owing to the scarcity the farmer obtained a higher price for his produce, though the quantity for disposal may have been small.[10] From this time, however, the harvests of distant climes began to be brought to our markets at little extra cost, and the English crops ceased to influence the market, which was controlled by the combined production of the world. The following table, based on Appendix C, shows the average rent in 1872-92 for the whole area for which I have particulars, but unfortunately I have not been able to continue it up to 1900.

TABLE IV.

Years.	Acreage.*	Average Rent per Acre.		Years.	Acreage.*	Average Rent per Acre.
		s.	d.			s.	d.
1872-74....	416,801	28	10	1884-86....	406,545	24 11
'75-77....	419,793	29	4	'87-89....	405,149	22 11
'78-80 ..	421,201	27	6	'90-92....	403,237	22 10
'81-83....	413,036	26	9			

* In Lincoln, Essex, Hereford, Beds, Bucks, Cambridge, Montgomery, Rutland, Norfolk, Suffolk, Gloucester, Northumberland, Devon, Sussex, Westmorland, Yorks, Cheshire, Oxford, Derby, Nottingham, Northampton, Kent, Worcester, Wilts, Somerset, and other counties.

Rents continued to rise until 1878, when a sharp fall occurred followed by a progressive decline which continued until the close of

[10] Address to Statistical Section of the British Association, by Mr. G. Shaw-Lefevre, M.P., 1879.

the century. For the twenty years shown in the above table, the fall from 29s. 4d. in 1875-77 to 22s. 10d. in 1890-92 represents 22 per cent., while the fall between 1877 and 1892 is equal to 25 per cent.

Although the figures on which the above table is based cannot be given beyond 1892 as regards some 300,000 acres, I have obtained another collection of returns representative of a very similar area and equally distributed over England, the figures in regard to which approximate so closely to the first series that no great error is likely to arise, if the two tables are regarded as continuous.

TABLE V.

Years.	Acreage.	Average Rent per Acre.		Years.	Acreage.	Average Rent per Acre.	
		s.	d.			s.	d.
1893-94....	377,234	21	8	1897-98....	390,263	20	6
'95-96....	385,750	21	1	'99-1900	399,043	20	-

On this assumption, which is obviously sufficiently accurate for the purposes of a broad statement, the average fall in rents between the early seventies and the end of the century was approximately 30 per cent. The average rental in 1900 was, roughly, about 20s. per acre. On the whole area of 482,000 acres for which I have particulars for that year, the average rent works out to 20s. 2d. per acre.

The majority report of the Royal Commission of Agriculture (1893-96) does not make any definite estimate of the average reduction in rent, apart from estimates based on the income-tax figures, but observes that rents in the most depressed parts of England have fallen by 50 per cent.; in less depressed districts the fall ranged from 20 to 30 per cent., and in some dairying and grazing districts it was not more than 15 per cent. Mr. G. Lambert, however, in his supplementary report, puts the average decrease between 1878 and 1892 in England alone at 18·7 per cent.

Comparison of Figures of Rent with Income Tax Returns and with Prices of Agricultural Produce, 1845-1900.

The second half of the nineteenth century covers a period of great agricultural interest, and it is worth while to examine it rather more closely than I have done in the foregoing general survey.

Four sets of figures are available for comparison :—

(1.) Returns of the net rent received for some 120,000 acres in Lincoln, Hereford, Bedford, Bucks, Essex, Cambridge, and North Wales for fifty-five years, 1845-1900. These furnish a continuous record over practically the whole period of the prosperity of British agriculture up to about 1878 and of the subsequent depression.

(2.) Returns of the net rent received from approximately 400,000 acres distributed over the whole of England and Wales from 1872 to 1900. As I have explained, there is a break in these figures between 1892 and 1893, but, for all practical purposes, I think they may be regarded as continuous.

(3.) The only official or other statements which afford any means of testing the accuracy of the two preceding sets of figures are the Inland Revenue Returns of the gross annual value of the property assessed for income tax (Schedule A), under the heading, " Lands, including tithes commuted under the Tithe Commutation " Acts."

The income tax figures have been relied upon by various writers and Royal Commissions as affording an indication of the rise and fall of rents, but they are subject to several qualifications, which it is well to bear in mind. In the first place, the figures refer to " lands " whether cultivated or uncultivated, including ornamental grounds, gardens attached to houses when exceeding one acre in extent, tithe rent charge, and farm-houses and farm-buildings. Secondly, the amount returned is to be the gross rent payable under the lease or agreement, and not the rent paid after deducting any temporary abatement or remission of rent allowed by the landlord. Thirdly, the valuation is only made every five years (formerly every three years), so that changes between each valuation are only made on appeal to the District Commissioners. Fourthly, the valuation of " lands " built on or appropriated to other uses is transferred to " houses."

It will be seen that the inclusion of ornamental gardens and grounds, and the non-deduction of abatements, would tend to keep the total valuation up; the triennial or quinquennial valuation tends to refer the bulk of the changes to years not necessarily those in which they were made, while the transfer of building land produces, as far as it operates, an artificial decline in the total, which is not attributable to any fall in " rents." It may be noted also that a rise in 1864-65 was stated to be due to improved administrative control.[11]

[11] The question of the validity of these figures is discussed at great length in the " Report of the Royal Commission on Land in Wales," p. 361. The " Final Report of the Royal Commission on Agriculture, 1896 " also deals with the subject. In this Report (p. 26) some importance is attached to the transfer to Schedule A, since 1842 of the uncommuted tithe amounting to 1,964,000*l*. So far as this has taken place, it would tend to keep up the assessment.

(4.) For the purpose of comparing these three sets of figures with the prices of agricultural produce, I have taken Mr. Sauerbeck's index number for the articles included by him under the headings "animal and vegetable food" (groups I and II), viz., wheat, flour, barley, oats; maize, potatoes and rice; beef, mutton, pork, bacon and butter. This list includes rice which does not affect the farmer and omits wool which does, but broadly it may be accepted as a fair indication of the course of agricultural prices. In the following table these four sets of figure are expressed as percentages. For the purpose of comparison with Sauerbeck's index number, the period 1867-77 has been taken as a base, except in the case of column 2, where the year 1872 has been chosen as the mean of 1867-77.

TABLE VI.—*Comparison of the Figures of Rent, Income Tax Returns, and Prices expressed as Percentages.*

Year.	1 Rent of 120,000 Acres. 1867-77 = 100.	2 Rent of 400,000 Acres. 1872 = 100.	3 Income Tax Returns. 1867-77 = 100.	4 Sauerbeck's Index Number. 1867-77 = 100.	Notes as to Seasons.
1846 .	83	—	84	93½	
'47	82	—	84	108½	
'48 ..	85	—	86	87½	
'49 .	81	—	86	75	
1850 .	82	—	86	70½	{ Bad season ; great agricultural distress.
'51 ..	79	—	84	70½	
'52 .	81	—	84	74½	
'53....	81	—	84	91	
'54 .	82	—	84	103½	
'55 .	84	—	84	103½	
'56	88	—	84	98½	
'57	92	—	87	97	
'58 .	93	—	87	85	
'59 .	93	—	88	85	
1860 .	92	—	88	95	Wet and cold ; crops deficient.
'61	94	—	91	96½	
'62 .	94	—	91	92	
'63 .	94	—	91	86	
'64	94	—	95	84	
'65 .	93	—	95	90½	
'66 .	94	—	95	95½	} Cattle plague.
'67....	95	—	97	102	
'68	99	—	97	100½	
'69 .	100	—	98	93½	

Table VI.—*Comparison of Figures expressed as Percentages—Contd.*

Year.	1 Rent of 120,000 Acres. 1867-77 = 100.	2 Rent of 400,000 Acres. 1872 = 100.	3 Income Tax Returns. 1867-77 = 100.	4 Sauerbeck's Index Number. 1867-77 = 100.	Notes as to Seasons.
1870 .	96	—	100	93	
'71 . .	98	—	100	97	
'72....	100	100	100	101	
'73 ..	101	101	102	107½	
'74....	102	102	102	104	Crops generally below the average.
'75....	102	102	103	100½	
'76....	102	102	106	100	
'77	105	104	106	100½	
'78 .	106	103	105	98	
'79....	79	93	106	80½	{ "The most disastrous season this century."
1880.	86	92	105	95	
'81 ..	82	91	104	92½	
'82 .	94	95	99	94	
'83 .	93	96	98	92½	
'84	90	93	97	84	
'85..	72	84	94	78	
'86....	84	85	93	76	
'87 .	68	79	91	71½	
'88 .	78	81	86	74½	
'89 ..	80	82	85	75½	
1890 ..	78	81	84	73½	
'91...	78	81	84	78	
'92	74	79	83	74½	
'93....	68	77	82	72	Prolonged drought; heavy losses.
'94....	64	75	81	67½	
'95 .	65	75	80	66	
'96	68	73	79	63	
'97 .	68	72	78	69½	
'98 ..	68	72	76	72	
'99 .	69	70	76	69½	
1900	69	70	75	73½	

Note.—Column 1 is based on Appendix B ; column 2 on Appendix C ; column 3 on Appendix D ; column 4 is the mean of the two groups—vegetable food (corn, &c.) and animal food (meat. &c.)—in Mr. Sauerbeck's tables.

Looking at this table (Table VI) and the diagram, it will be seen that the income-tax figures in column 3 start at practically the same level as the rent figures in column 1, and in 1851 showed a decline corresponding to the fall in column 1, which was the result of the short period of depression in prices which occurred in 1849-52. The influence of the decline in rents operated in the case of the income-tax returns until 1856, from which date a steady rise set in

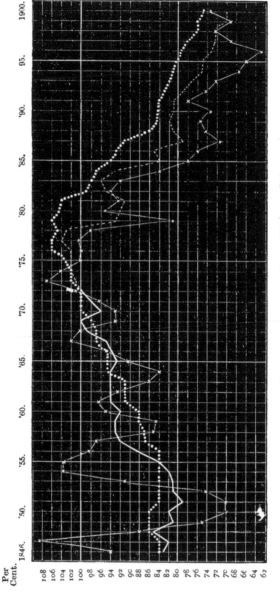

Diagram showing a Comparison between the Rent of Agricultural Land, the Income Tax Returns of Income from Land, and Sauerbeck's Prices of Animal and Vegetable Food (all expressed as Percentages, see Table VI).

Rent of 120,000 acres from 1846-72. (Column 1.)

Rent of 400,000 acres from 1873-1900. (Column 2.)

Income Tax Returns. (Column 3.)

Sauerbeck's Prices. (Column 4.)

and continued until 1879, though the influence of the triennial valuation is very well marked.

The income-tax figures moved much more slowly than the rent figures. It is interesting to notice that they stood several points above the figures for rent in each of the periods of depression, for instance in 1849-53, 1864-67, 1870-72, and 1879-1900, whereas, in prosperous times of rising rents they are usually a few points lower. This is only natural, as their adjustment must come subsequent to alterations in rent, but there is, I think, another reason why they should remain higher than a falling rent, viz., that, as explained above, abatements and deductions are not shown in the income-tax figures, which represent the gross rent payable under agreement. The rent-curve, on the other hand, shows only the rent actually received, and it must be remembered that the decline in the rent is very largely caused by abatements, which are called "temporary" for several years (and sometimes for long periods) before they are made permanent. It is natural, therefore, that the rent-curves should reach a lower point and reach it earlier than do the income-tax figures. The latter attained their lowest point in 1900, when they stood nine points below what they were fifty-four years earlier.

The figures in column 1 show the same general movement, though with more fluctuations and with a marked tendency to respond to changes in price. In 1872 the figures in columns 1, 2 and 3 are identical, and continue very close together up to 1878, when column 2 shows a fall of one point, followed in 1879 by a decline of 10 points. A much greater fall is shown in column 1, and from this year the fluctuations in this column are considerable, though they agree substantially with those of column 2, where the larger area tends to smooth out the curve. In the diagram the figures for column 1 are given up to 1872, and for column 2 subsequent to that date. The diagram also enables the rent curve to be compared with Sauerbeck's index number for food products, and shows fairly well the dependence of rent on prices. It will be seen that each of the periods of low prices, viz., 1848-52, 1858-9, 1863-64, 1869-71 found a corresponding check in rents a year or two later. Prices reached their maximum point in 1873, but rents continued to rise until 1877, four years after prices began to fall. This fact seems to lend some support to a contention which was strongly brought to the notice of the Royal Commission on Agriculture of 1882, to the effect that rents had not been reduced in time. I attribute this principally to the fact that prices, though falling, still remained very high, the depression in agriculture which was felt in 1879 being chiefly due to bad seasons, and not to exceptional prices. Another factor tending to keep up rents was that agriculture had, on the whole, been flourishing for nearly thirty years. Consequently, there was a very good demand for farms, and a succession of bad seasons, though disastrous for the sitting tenants, did not act as a deterrent to those who wished to take up land.

After 1879 every successive year saw prices fall lower and lower, a movement which it will be seen was closely followed by rents.

On the whole, the general agreement of all these figures constitutes a strong argument in favour of the substantial accuracy of the particulars as to rent given in columns 1 and 2. They show that the average rent of agricultural land in England and Wales in 1900 was 30 per cent. below the figure of 1872, 34 per cent. below the maximum of 1877, and 13 per cent. below the figure of 1846.

Estimate of the Proportion of the Gross Rent Expended in Repairs, Improvements, and other Out-goings.

Up to now we have been considering the gross rent paid for land in this country, but it has to be remembered that the gross rent is in part interest on capital expended in equipping the estate, and as such is subject to a number of deductions for repairs, insurance and expenses of management, as well as for the works executed from time to time under the heading of permanent improvements. These expenses amount in the aggregate to a substantial proportion of the gross rent, and, as this fact is not perhaps always borne in mind in discussions about rent, I have thought it worth while to tabulate the figures relating to certain estates, with a view to showing what may reasonably be regarded as the average deductions to which rent is subject in England.

The main outlay is naturally on repairs, fencing, gates, new buildings, drainage, and other so-called permanent improvements. I have not attempted to distinguish between "repairs" and "permanent improvements," because in many accounts the distinction is not made, and in any case it seems to me to be a purely artificial one. Repairs are intended to maintain the letting value of the farm, while new buildings and other permanent improvements are intended either to maintain or increase the letting value, and as such are reflected in the rent. It would not, of course, be justifiable to burden one year's rent with the whole cost of improvements, which may last for many years, but, taking the average of a number of estates and of a number of years, they may fairly be charged against income, as they are when money is borrowed under the Improvement of Land Acts, to be repaid, capital and interest, over a number of years.

The other outgoings include tithe (where payable), land tax, drainage and local rates paid by owner, expenses of management, and miscellaneous payments.

The figures given in the table below are compiled from certain estates of which particulars were furnished to the Royal Commission on Agriculture,[12] excluding, I may observe, those which, from any special circumstances, appear exceptional, or for which particulars are given for less than twenty years. It is for this reason that they do not agree with certain calculations put forward by the Commission itself, which were based on a somewhat larger number of estates, but which extended over only seven years, from 1886 to 1892.   The Commission observes : " if we take the average " of these seven years, we find from these accounts, which include " estates in some of the most favoured parts of the country, that " for every 100*l.* received during the seven years, 1886-92, by the " owners in England and Wales, 39*l.* 4*s.* was absorbed by ordinary " outgoings, and an additional sum of 15*l.* 12*s.* was spent upon " improvements, leaving the owner 45*l.* 4*s.* out of 100*l.*," that is to say, that 55 per cent. of the gross rent disappeared in outgoings. Such information as I have been able to obtain leads me to believe that these figures are too high for use as applicable to ordinary conditions in this country.   For one thing it must be remembered that they refer to a period of exceptional depression, and include a number of estates where the rents on the one hand were reduced and the expenditure on repairs well maintained, with the result that the percentage of outgoings was abnormally increased, whereas I think it is more generally true that the outgoings at the time of the depression were reduced to some extent to compensate for the reduced net income.

TABLE VII.

Year.	Gross Rental Received.	Cost of Repairs and Permanent Improvements.	Per Cent. of Gross Rent.	Net Income.*	Per Cent. of Gross Rent.
	£	£		£	
1872–76	357,487	96,404	27	204,209	57
'77–81	348,583	95,401	27	192,562	55
'82–86	322,413	89.227	27¼	171,698	53
'87–91	288,756	63,998	22	171,270	60
Total .	1,317,239	345,030	26	740,359	56

* This is the balance of the gross rent received, after deducting all outgoings, including permanent improvements.

[12] " Particulars of Expenditures and Outgoings on certain Estates in " Great Britain," Cd-8125, 1896.

For the fifteen years 1872-86 the cost for repairs and permanent improvements amounted to about 27 per cent., while in 1887-91 it fell to 22 per cent. The net income in the first fifteen years was about 55 per cent., but when rents were so largely reduced an effort was naturally made to reduce the outgoings, with the result that the net income was maintained at the same amount as before, but represented 60 per cent. of the gross. Over the twenty years, the repairs represent 26 per cent. of the rental, and the net income 56 per cent. of the gross.

On the large estates of the Ecclesiastical Commission, the repairs appear to fall only in part on the landlord, but with permanent improvements the cost amounted in thirteen years (1880-92)[13] to about 21·3 per cent., while the net income represented 62·7 of the gross. On certain of the Crown estates, where the conditions are approximately the same, the repairs and improvements in six years (1888-93) represented 21·5 per cent. and the net income 64·7 per cent. On one large estate of over 150,000 acres the expenditure on repairs and improvements has averaged 25⅓ per cent. during the last five years, but a similar calculation about the year 1852 showed the expenditure at that time to be 40 per cent. of the rent. On another estate of 45,000 acres, the outlay over forty years has averaged 23 per cent.

From these figures and from a number of enquiries I have made, I suggest 25 per cent. as a fair average figure for the cost of repairs and improvements in this country. No doubt in very many instances this figure is exceeded. One large landowner writes to me as follows: "Speaking roughly, there has never been less than 40 " and often 50 per cent. of the rental value returned to the estate in " improvements for the benefit of tenants; creation of farms and " farm-buildings to meet increased demands for stock consequent " upon the improvement of land. During the last forty years " the property has all been drained, and the drains constantly " require re-laying." Many similar instances are to be found in the publications of the Royal Commission.[14]

With regard to the balance of the gross rent left after paying all charges, the estates given in the table above show an average net income of 56 per cent. of the gross over twenty years, or 60 per cent. during the last five years, the estates of the Ecclesiastical Commissioners showed 62¾ per cent. and the Crown estates about 64¼ per cent. It would seem, therefore, that the net income ranges from 60 to 65 per cent. of the gross receipts. For the purposes of an average estimate applicable to England

[13] "Royal Commission on Agriculture, 1893," Evidence, vol. i, p. 420.
[14] Final Report, p. 287.

and Wales generally, it will I think be safer to take the higher figure; we may probably assume that most of these estates are dealt with somewhat liberally and it is almost certain that with reduced rents there has been a tendency to reduce expenses. I suggest, therefore, on the basis of these figures that the net income derived on the average from agricultural land in this country represents 65 per cent. of the gross rent, the difference being made up of 25 per cent. for repairs and permanent improvements and 10 per cent. for management, tithe and land tax, local and drainage rates, and other miscellaneous outgoings.

Estimate of the "Landlord's Capital" Invested in Buildings, Drainage, Fencing, &c.

John Stuart Mill drew a distinction between the rent defined by Ricardo as a payment for the use of "the natural and indestructible " powers of the soil," and that part of rent which is a payment for the landlords' improvements. "Under the name of rent," he says, " many payments are commonly included which are not a remunera- " tion for the original powers of the land itself, but for capital " expended on it," and the question which I now propose to consider is what is the amount of capital sunk in the land and what return the rent represents. Mill distinguished between "capital actually " sunk in improvements and not requiring periodical renewals, " but spent once for all in giving the land a permanent increase " in productiveness" (as in the case of the Bedford Level), the improvement of which, as he observes, cannot, after it is once done, be separated from the land itself, and capital represented by buildings, fences, &c., requiring renewal. The distinction is not one which it is always very easy to draw, and for my purpose I propose to consider what may roughly be assumed to be the cost of " making a farm," charging against it those obvious improvements which having involved an outlay of capital may fairly be expected to yield interest.

This is a question which was discussed in a very interesting paper, written by the late Mr. Albert Pell, on "The Making of the " Land in England,"[15] with the object of showing that the land as such was worth nothing, and that the rent represented a very small return on the capital expended in developing it.

In drawing attention to the considerable outlays which had been incurred in bringing the land from a state of nature, Mr. Pell included not only grubbing and clearing the land, but also the making of parish roads, as well as a charge for the provision of public worship; he also stated that the whole area with which he

---

[15] "Journal of the Royal Agricultural Society," 1887, p. 355.

was dealing was drained. In attempting to arrive at an average figure we cannot, however, charge drainage on the whole, as drainage is not necessary on every class of land. Moreover, for the purpose of considering the relation of rent to the capital invested in the land, we can only take, as Mill says, the cost of those improvements requiring periodical renewal. The provision of public roads must be put with other facilities for transit and advantages of position, which give land an economic value, and for which rent, as distinct from interest on capital is paid.

The sum arrived at by Mr. Pell was made up as follows :—

	Per Acre.
	£
Grubbing and preparing the land	5
Roads, fences, gates, drainage and various miscellaneous expenses . ... }	12
Buildings	9
	26

" For some such outlay[10] as this," Mr. Pell observes, " or its " equivalent, at the time when the several operations were carried " out, the open wild waste, denuded of its saleable timber, mere " rough naked land, in fact, has been converted into cleared and " levelled enclosures, ready for the occupancy of the cultivating " farmer and his staff."

Another estimate of the landlord's capital was made by Mr. Elias P. Squarey,[17] and this includes four different kinds of farms, as follows :—

Cost of Buildings, Cottages, Water Supply, Drainage (where necessary), Roads, and Fencing.

		Per Acre.		
	£	£	s.	d.
On a dairy farm of 200 acres mostly pasture............	4,050 =	20	5	–
On a mixed arable and pasture farm of 500 acres....	5,000 =	10	–	–
On a mixed upland, arable, and pasture farm of 1,000 acres .... }	7,350 =	7	7	–
On a grazing farm of 300 acres (without drainage)	2,600 =	7	10	–

The mean of these estimates is about 11l. 6s. per acre.

As the size of a holding diminishes, the average cost has usually a tendency to increase. An example of this occurs in the recent Report of the Small Holdings Committee. The cost of buildings on 30 acres is put by the Committee at 360l., or 12l. per acre, while

[16] The 12l. per acre includes 700l. per mile for parish roads, 200l. per mile for two boundary fences, 550l. for one mile of occupation road and its fences, 36 miles of quick fences at 112l. per mile, 200 gates at 40s. each, and 1,600 acres drained at 6l. 6s. per acre.

[17] " Journal of the Royal Agricultural Society," 1878, p. 431.

very similar buildings costing 400*l.* would serve for 50 acres; no proportionate reduction could, however, be secured for a 12-acre holding where the cost might run up to 20*l.* or 25*l.* per acre.

The very substantial difference between Mr. Pell's figures and those of Mr. Squarey is partly due to the inclusion by Mr. Pell of several items which cannot correctly be regarded as "capital "expenditure." A more accurate idea of the landlord's capital can perhaps be arrived at by taking some particulars which are available of the actual cost incurred in converting some mixed forest land on the Crown estates into cultivated land. These figures were supplied by Mr. John Clutton in a paper read by him before the Surveyors' Institution[18] in 1871, and are not estimates but actual results obtained by the disafforestation of portions of the Royal Forests of Hainault in Essex, Whichwood in Oxford, Whittlebury in Northampton, and Delamere in Cheshire between 1850 and 1860. The land was more or less heavily timbered, and the receipts from the sale of wood represented a substantial contribution towards the cost of the conversion, and also paid for the cost of public highways, legal expenses and some fencing.

The figures are as follows :—

	Hainault, 2,255 Acres.	Whichwood, 3,016 Acres.*	Whittlebury, 300 Acres.	Delamere, 1,554 Acres.
	£	£	£	£
Clearing and grubbing	18,730	6,233	1,714	9,214
Marling	—	—	—	19,451
Draining	22,618	520	1,602	1,417
Fencing	Included with draining	} 1,506	220	1,397
Farm roads	1,123	811	—	894
Farm-buildings and cottages	15,070	14,337	2,014	14,377
Miscellaneous	836	· -	—	—
	58,377	23,407	5,550	46,750
Receipts from timber	55,000	14,080	5,800	17,815

* Part of this area was already cultivated and provided with buildings.

The total cost of the conversion, therefore, was 134,084*l.,* towards which the timber contributed 92,695*l.* Where, however, land is covered with inferior timber or brushwood or is merely common or waste, the cost of preparing the land for cultivation, *i.e.,* grubbing or clearing, may easily involve a loss.

To arrive at an estimate on the principle explained above, I have excluded all charges for felling, clearing and grubbing the

18 " Surveyors' Institution, Transactions," vol. iv, p. 17, 1871-72.

land and also marling,[19] confining the outlay entirely to draining, fencing, buildings, and farm-road making. The total area affected was about 6,679 acres, and the sum expended was :—

	£		£	s.	d.
				Per Acre.	
Drainage and fencing	29,280	=	4	8	-
Farm buildings	45,798	=	6	17	-
Roads and other expenses	3,664	=	-	11	-
	78,742	=	11	16	-

There were about 13 farms and some small holdings. The farms were mostly arable, and varied a good deal in size.

Only a little over one-third of the land required draining, while the cost of fencing was partly charged against the timber. Owing to the character of the land, the cost of draining, however, so far as it was done, was above the average. The farms were well provided with buildings and cottages, and Mr. Clutton observes that the cost of building from various causes was somewhat high. The charge for roads, on the other hand, is low, as they are exclusively occupation roads, the expense of making public roads to serve the estates being put against the timber. It may be noted that the farms were all let at very low rents for the first two or three years.

For purposes of comparison, some particulars of the cost of the various operations in general is given below :—

Draining.—Pipe drainage costs from 5*l.* to 7*l.* per acre. The actual cost over 15,000 acres, including every variety of soil, was stated by Mr. Grantham to average 6*l.* per acre, while another surveyor gave as his experience in draining upwards of 90,000 acres the average cost as 5*l.* 15*s.* per acre.[20] As only a proportion of the land is drained, any estimate of the average outlay would have to be put much lower.

Fencing.—On fencing, the sum spent in the estates given above was 17*s.* per acre, but this was exclusive of outside fences round the estates. A hedge-and-ditch fence would cost a 1*s.* a yard or 88*l.* per mile.

Buildings.—The cost of erecting farm-houses and buildings was given by Mr. Bailey-Denton in about 1860 as averaging about 4*l.* 10*s.* per acre on 1,000-acre farms and upwards, 6*l.* per acre on mixed farms of 500 to 1,000 acres, and 7*l.* per acre on farms of 200 to 500 acres; but Mr. Tom Bright[21] says that under the more

---

[19] Marling is excluded as being an operation which improves the natural fertility of the soil.

[20] " Surveyors Institution, Transactions," 1871-72, pp. 66 and 102.

[21] " Agricultural Surveyor and Estate Agents Handbook," 1899.

economical systems of farm management of the present day the cost
may be as follows :—

Approximate Size of Holding.	Approximate Cost of Buildings.			Approximate Size of Holding.	Approximate Cost of Buildings.		
Acres.	Per Acre.			Acres.	Per Acre.		
	£	s.	£	s.		£	s.	£	s.
40	8	– to 11	10	375	3	– to 3	10
100	5	10 „ 6	10	500	3	– „ 3	15
150	4	15 „ 5	15	650	3	– „ 3	15
220	4	– „ 5	–				

This is exclusive of cottages, of which one or more must be allowed
per 100 acres, or an additional cost of, say, 2*l.* or 2*l.* 10*s.* per
acre.

Roads.—The cost of making a farm road may be put at 1*s.* a
square yard or about 350*l.* a mile, or say about 10*s.* per acre.

Another charge which has to be included is that for providing a
water supply.

It would seem from the foregoing that there is nothing exceptional in the outlay incurred on the Crown lands quoted by
Mr. Clutton, and on that general basis I suggest the following
estimate of landlord's capital as one which may be regarded as
broadly applicable to agricultural land in England and Wales
generally.

	£	s.	d.
Drainage and fencing	4	10	–
Roads....	–	10	–
Buildings, including cottages and water supply . ..	7	–	–
	12	–	–

It is perhaps a matter for consideration whether in view of the
number of small farms the estimate for buildings ought not to have
been put somewhat higher, but on the whole, I think 12*l.* per acre
may be taken as a reasonable average figure of the capital outlay
incurred by landowners throughout England in the equipment of
agricultural holdings.

Estimate of the " Economic Rent" of Agricultural Land.

If, then, we assume that the capital invested in the land in
improvements requiring renewal and repairs, such as buildings,
fences, gates, drainage, roads, &c., amounts on the average to 12*l.*
per acre, and that the average gross rent at the present time is
1*l.* per acre (see Appendix C) the gross return is $8\frac{1}{3}$ per cent.
Deducting 35 per cent. from the gross rent for repairs and upkeep,

the net return on the capital invested in buildings, &c., is 5*l*. 8*s*. 4*d*. per cent.   Or it may be put in this way :—

	Per Acre. £ s. d.		
Gross rent	1	-	-
Repairs, management and outgoings of all kinds, and sinking fund for new buildings, drainage, fencing, at 35 per cent. of the gross rent	-	7	-
Interest on 12*l*. capital invested in permanent improvements at 3½ per cent.	-	8	5
Balance representing rent of the land itself, *i.e*, the economic rent. ..	-	4	7

It will, of course, be understood that in speaking of the capital invested in the land I am referring solely to the average sum which the provision of drainage, fencing, gates, roads and buildings would cost to supply.   The capital invested in land when purchasing it represents all this, and also a payment for the "economic rent" which it may be expected to produce, as well as in many cases a payment for amenities appertaining to its possession.

If the above figures are accepted as of approximate accuracy, they would seem to show that the average rent of land in England and Wales, after deducting interest on capital, is about 4*s*. 6*d*. an acre, that is to say, that the net surplus remaining above the whole cost of production on 27,400,000 acres is about 6,300,000*l*.

This economic rent may be regarded as the net return which accrued to the nation at the end of the nineteenth century from the cultivation of the soil through its individual owners, and it is questionable whether it was not a lower figure than at any time in the previous hundred years, as the gross rent in 1815-30, which probably averaged about 20*s*. per acre, would undoubtedly have been subject to smaller deductions for repairs and interest than is the case with the gross rent in 1900.   In short, the progress of agricultural knowledge, the advance of science, the development of the country by road and rail, the increase in the population, the proximity of markets and the better equipment of farms, have not resulted, in the face of reduced prices, in obtaining as great a surplus as was got some seventy or eighty years earlier.

As a nation, the smaller return from the soil is compensated for by the cheapness of some of the principal articles of food, but the fact that the progress and improvement of agriculture in the past century have failed to increase the economic value of land cannot be regarded as satisfactory.   It suggests that those changes which are no doubt slowly taking place in our agricultural system must go much further before the full return to be expected from land so favourably situated as that of England can be obtained.

At the beginning of the nineteenth century, when " the agri-
" culture of the kingdom was the first of all its concerns, the
" foundation of all its prosperity," the growth in the population
demanded the increased cultivation of corn to feed the people,
and the formation of large farms was wisely urged as enabling
a maximum of production at a minimum cost.

The opening of the twentieth century, however, finds an
enormously increased population dependent for the greater proportion of its corn and meat on regions beyond the seas, and
the arguments which encouraged the large farm to the disadvantage
of the medium and small holding have no longer the same weight.

To split up a large farm is not, however, a change which a
landowner can lightly undertake. New buildings, fences, and
roads may be necessary, and without the prospect of a good
return the necessary money is not likely to be forthcoming.

But it is in a return to the conditions of earlier times, to a
more even distribution of the land in a larger number of holdings,
that we may perhaps anticipate more profitable results from the
utilisation of the soil. The medium farm, with a reasonable
proportion of still smaller holdings, favours and encourages the
growth of those products which can be produced as cheaply and
as well in this country as abroad. In milk, dairy produce, eggs,
pigs, calves, poultry, vegetables, and fruit, the farmers of this
country are at no disadvantage as regards climate or soil compared
with their principal competitors, while they have the advantage
of nearness to markets; and it is probably true that a greater
proportion of the soil of Great Britain could be advantageously
devoted to these products than is the case at present, without
interfering with large farms which, from soil or situation, are
especially suitable to the growth of grain, beef, mutton, or wool.

APPENDIX.

A.—*Average Rent per Acre of Agricultural Land on certain Estates in Lincoln, Essex, Hereford, and North Wales from 1800-1900.*

Year.	Acreage.	Average Rent per Acre.		Year.	Acreage.	Average Rent per Acre.	
		s.	d.			s.	d.
1801	62,655	11	8	1850	72,585	16	3
'02	62,655	10	10	'51	72,603	16	–
'03	62,655	10	11	'52	72,602	16	6
'04	62,655	11	2	'53	72,805	16	7
'05	62,655	11	2	'54	72,784	16	8
'06	63,325	11	2	'55	72,799	16	9
'07	63,620	11	3	'56	72,799	17	1
'08	64,320	11	8	'57	72,802	17	6
'09	64,320	11	8	'58	72,812	17	9
				'59	72,814	17	9
1810	64,320	12	3	1860	72,353	18	–
'11	65,320	13	6	'61	71,900	18	2
'12	65,320	14	6	'62	72,177	18	1
'13	66,320	14	11	'63	72,222	18	2
'14	66,320	15	–	'64	72,234	18	2
'15	66,320	15	2	'65	72,246	18	5
'16	66,320	14	7	'66	72,185	18	6
'17	67,348	14	5	'67	72,251	18	7
'18	67,348	15	11	'68	72,423	18	9
'19	67,349	15	5	'69	72,411	18	11
1820	67,349	15	5	1870	72,804	18	9
'21	67,349	14	10	'71	72,811	19	2
'22	67,549	13	7	'72	73,237	19	5
'23	67,750	14	10	'73	73,242	19	9
'24	67,950	16	1	'74	73,240	20	–
'25	68,150	16	9	'75	73,240	20	1
'26	68,350	14	11	'76	73,251	20	1
'27	68,550	15	–	'77	73,249	20	3
'28	68,750	15	5	'78	73,203	20	6
'29	68,950	14	10	'79	73,201	20	2
1830	69,150	15	3	1880	73,172	18	5
'31	69,251	15	10	'81	71,172	18	7
'32	69,376	15	2	'82	71,179	18	2
'33	69,595	15	3	'83	71,177	17	6
'34	69,832	15	2	'84	71,165	16	11
'35	70,025	15	6	'85	71,165	16	8
'36	70,225	15	3	'86	71,165	16	4
'37	70,365	15	9	'87	71,165	15	10
'38	70,465	15	9	'88	71,160	15	6
'39	70,678	15	4	'89	71,656	15	6
				1890	71,656	15	7
1840	70,878	15	7	'91	71,656	15	2
'41	71,261	16	6	'92	71,656	15	7
'42	71,472	16	3	'93	71,656	14	8
'43	71,568	16	5	'94	71,601	15	–
'44	71,667	16	8	'95	71,147	14	6
'45	71,911	16	8	'96	71,323	14	7
'46	72,019	17	1	'97	71,346	14	2
'47	72,168	16	8	'98	71,338	14	5
'48	72,414	17	3	'99	71,469	14	7
'49	72,538	16	1	1900	71,469	14	7

B.—*Average Rent per Acre of Agricultural Land on certain Estates in Lincoln, Hereford, Bucks, Beds, Cambridge, Essex, and North Wales from 1816-1900.*

Year.	Acreage.	Rent per Acre.		Year.	Acreage.	Rent per Acre.	
		s.	*d.*			*s.*	*d.*
1816	109,421	18	–	1860	121,949	23	–
'17	110,500	18	9	'61	121,545	23	5
'18	110,500	19	4	'62	121,784	23	4
'19	110,876	18	9	'63	121,126	23	6
				'64	122,145	23	4
1820	111,082	18	8	'65	122,222	23	2
'21	111,081	18	3	'66	122,140	23	4
'22	111.239	17	2	'67	122,258	23	9
'23	111,240	17	6	'68	122,463	24	7
'24	111,348	18	2	'69	122,340	24	10
'25	111,375	18	6				
'26	112,377	17	2				
'27	112,399	17	3	1870	122,805	24	–
'28	112,502	18	4	'71	122,889	24	4
'29	112,568	17	10	'72	123,419	24	10
				'73	124.776	25	3
1830	112,568	18	4	'74	125,000	25	6
'31	112,799	18	8	'75	125,014	25	6
'32	113,824	18	4	'76	125,323	25	5
'33	114,320	18	5	'77	125,463	26	1
'34	114,349	18	4	'78	125.351	26	5
'35	114,434	18	6	'79	125,368	19	9
'36	114,434	18	8				
'37	114,181	18	6				
'38	115,190	18	5	1880	125,337	21	4
'39	115,153	18	5	'81	121,424	20	6
				'82	119,423	23	6
1840	115,514	19	1	'83	117,158	23	3
'41	115,597	19	9	'84	116,204	22	4
'42	119,272	19	10	'85	116,405	18	–
'43	119,330	20	1	'86	116,405	20	11
'44	118,834	20	4	'87	116,418	17	–
'45	118,762	20	6	'88	116,332	19	6
'46	118,759	20	9	'89	116,821	20	1
'47	118,847	20	6				
'48	119,042	21	1				
'49	119,222	20	3	1890	116,868	19	6
				'91	116,868	19	6
1850	119,484	20	6	'92	119,068	18	6
'51	119,983	19	10	'93	118,823	17	–
'52	120,453	20	3	'94	119,149	15	11
'53	120,758	20	1	'95	118,790	16	1
'54	121,014	20	4	'96	119,299	17	0
'55	121,092	20	10	'97	119.022	16	11
'56	121,151	21	10	'98	118,990	17	0
'57	121.750	22	11	'99	119,144	17	1
'58	121,759	23	3	1900	119,178	17	2
'59	122,145	23	1				

C.—*Average Rent per Acre of Agricultural Land on certain Estates distributed throughout England and Wales from 1872-1900.*

Year.	Acreage.	Rent per Acre.		Year.	Acreage.	Rent per Acre.	
		s.	d.			s.	d.
1872 ..	415,003	28	6	1887 .	405,946	22	5
'73 .	416,749	28	10	'88 .	405,058	23	–
'74	418,650	29	–	'89 . .	404,414	23	4
'75	418,852	29	1				
'76 . . .	419,936	29	3	1890 ..	405,248	23	1
'77 . .	420,591	29	9	'91 . . .	402,310	23	–
'78	421,903	29	6	'92	402,152	22	5
'79 ..	421,654	26	8	'93 . . .	373,895	22	–
1880	420,045	26	4	'94	380,574	21	5
'81	416,941	25	11	'95 . .	381,479	21	4
'82 .	413.258	27	1	'96 .	390,021	20	10
'83 .	408,910	27	4	'97 .	390,482	20	6
'84	406.096	26	6	'98 .	390,044	20	6
'85	406.239	24	1	'99 .	398,920	20	0
'86	407,299	24	4	1900	399,167	20	1

D.—*Income Tax (Schedule A). Gross Income derived from the Ownership of Lands in England and Wales for the years 1843-1905.*

Year ending April	Amount in Thousands.	Percentage. 1867-77 = 100	Year ending April	Amount in Thousands.	Percentage. 1867-77 = 100.
	£			£	
1843	40,167	82	1874	49.906	102
'44	—	—	'75	50,125	102
'45	—	—	'76	50,218	103
'46	41,227	84	'77	51,811	106
'47	41,215	84	'78	51,722	106
'48	41,180	84	'79	51,658	105
'49	42,348	86	1880	51,799	106
1850	42,329	86	'81	51,599	105
'51	42,290	86	'82	51,182	104
'52	41,118	84	'83	48,403	99
'53	41,086	84	'84	47,955	98
'54	41,085	84	'85	47.594	97
'55	41,237	84	'86	45,994	94
'56	41,118	84	'87	45,376	93
'57	41,177	84	'88	44,472	91
'58	42,685	87	'89	42.274	86
'59	42.702	87	1890	41,796	85
1860	42.940	88	'91	41,379	84
'61	42.976	88	'92	41,130	84
'62	44,639	91	'93	40,805	83
'63	44,611	91	'94	40,066	82
'64	44.672	91	'95	39.680	81
'65	46,403	95	'96	39.366	80
'66	46,422	95	'97	38,806	79
'67	46,192	95	'98	38.143	78
'68	47,711	97	'99	37,296	76
'69	47,744	97	1900	37,111	76
1870	47,803	98	'01	36,942	75
'71	48,938	100	'02	36,804	75
'72	48,964	100	'03	36,624	75
'73	49,009	100	'04	36,923	75

E.—*Rent of certain Individual Farms.*

Farm of 204 Acres in Wilts.

Year.	Rent, less Abatements.	Remarks.
	£ s. d.	
1809 .	255 – –	Held on lease expiring in 1816.
'16	370 – –	⎧The rent was much below the average of rents during the war, and on the expiration of the lease, the farm was re-let on a yearly tenancy.
'17	325 – –	⎰Rent reduced in consequence of fall of prices on conclusion of peace.
'22 . .	288 – –	⎰Reduction 10 per cent. and allowance for damage by quarry.
'30	273 10 –	Abatement 10 per cent.
'31...............	267 5 –	,, 15 per cent.
'31-49	288 – –	
'50-53 .	259 – –	,, 10 per cent.
'54...............	288 – –	
'56 . .	289 10 –	⎱
'62....	291 2 –	⎬ Interest on draining added.
'63...............	295 – –	⎰
'64	333 10 –	⎧Farm re-let at an additional rent of 38*l.* 10*s.* the first year and a further 25*l.* in subsequent years, less 16*s.* for land taken for cottages.
'65-80	357 14 –	
'80-81 . . .	304 1 –	Abatement 15 per cent.
'81-86 .	307 14 –	,, of 50*l.* each year.
'86-1907	250 – –	

Note.—During the last forty-five years the landlord (besides paying half the labour and providing the materials for ordinary repairs) has expended on the buildings 535*l.* 16*s.* 9*d.*, and in draining (for which no interest was charged) since 1863 259*l.* 14*s.* 11*d.*

A Farm of 225 Acres in Norfolk.

Year.	Rent.	Year.	Rent.	Year.	Rent.
	£		£		£
1712-22	80	1799-1806	210	1876-80	450
'22-28 .	84	1806-14	200	'80-83	380
'28-57	100	'14-20 ...	700	'83-90	300
'57-70	120	'20-27 .	585	'90-93 ...	250
'70-86 ..	130	'27-34 ..	375	'93-94 ..	225
'86-92	170	'34-41	261	'94-97.......	210*
'92-99	190	'41-76 ...	500	'97-1906 ...	225*

* The landlord has paid the tithe since 1894. In 1905 this amounted to 64*l.* 3*s.* 8*d.*, so that if this is deducted from the rent of 225*l.*, the net rent in that year was 160*l.* 16*s.* 4*d.*

Note.—According to the agreement for this farm, the tenant pays the drainage rate and all other outgoings except land tax and property tax, and keeps in repair the windows, fixtures, gates, fences, &c., the house and buildings being repaired by the landlord. In 1822 a new bullock shed was erected and since that time the farm-house, barns, and other portions of the out-buildings have been re-built The tenant paid the tithe up to 1894.

E.—*Rent of certain Individual Farms — Contd.*

Four Typical Farms in the South Midlands.

Year.	Farm C.		Farm D.		Farm E.		Farm F.	
	Acreage.	Rent.	Acreage.	Rent.	Acreage.	Rent.	Acreage.	Rent.
		£		£		£		£
1807.........	352	399	122	103	—	—	454	524
'17.........	352	500	122	147	—	—	443	606
'27.........	356	434	121	127	—	—	448	494
'32.........	—	—	—	—	393	422	—	—
'37.........	360	390	121	110	—	—	472	500
'42..........	—	—	—	—	396	492	—	—
'47.........	356	442	120	122	396	492	478	526
'57	356	410	122	134	424	603*	475	739*
'67..	357	460*	122	152*	424	492*	475	626*
'77.	354	473*	122	198	416	570	500	800
'87†	354	225	122	79	416	285	487	350
'97.........	354	302	122	100	417	330	468	425
1907.........	359	302	122	100	417	330	467	420

* In these years the rent was partly a corn rent.

† In 1887 50 per cent. of the rent was remitted. The figure given is the sum actually paid.

Note.—Farm C is a grass farm; farm D is a heavy land arable farm; farm E is a mixed heavy and light land farm, half arable and half grass; farm F is a light limestone " turnip and barley " farm.

DISCUSSION on MR. R. J. THOMPSON'S PAPER.

THE CHAIRMAN (Major P. G. Craigie) said that it was his privilege, as Chairman of the evening, to present to Professor Edgeworth the Guy Medal in gold for his services to Statistical Science. This was an honour which was not very lavishly awarded by the Society, and there were only three gold medallists at the present time ; but they would all rejoice to know that the choice of the Council in selecting a fourth had fallen on so good an exponent of scientific statistical work as Professor Edgeworth. He was not only renowned as an economist, holding the professorship in his own University on that subject, but was known not only in this country but in many others as an interpreter of some of the difficult problems which faced the statistician in his work. Professor Edgeworth's work both in that Society in the larger sphere of scientific work, fully entitled him to recognition at the hands of the Fellows. In his presence and as an old personal friend, he could not say all that he should like to on such an occasion, beyond expressing much pleasure in handing him the medal, and wishing him long life to enjoy the distinction conferred on him by his colleagues.

THE GUY MEDAL in Gold was then presented to Professor Edgeworth.

Mr. R. H. REW said that Mr. Noel Humphreys, who it was hoped would have attended to receive a Silver Guy Medal on this occasion, was too unwell to attend, but it was hoped the presentation would be made at the next meeting.

Mr. R. J. THOMPSON then read his paper.

The CHAIRMAN, in inviting discussion, said that he would only indicate one or two of the aspects of the Paper to which he thought attention could most profitably be devoted. They were all agreed that Mr. Thompson was right in supplementing the mere customary calculation of agricultural rent from the official income tax returns by compiling a valuable series of direct returns from individual properties, such as those which had been laboriously got together for their study that evening. It would be well also they should welcome and discuss the details of the further data which had been put before them in the tables and in the form of a diagram with a view of showing how far and how closely rents and prices were correlated.

Sir FRANCIS S. POWELL, M.P., said the only remark which he would make was to refer to the great service rendered by this Paper in calling attention to the great difference between the prairie value of land and its value with all the improvements added to it. In many popular discussions which took place the amount which capital added to the natural value of the land appeared to be entirely ignored; and the land of commerce and of practical agriculture was spoken of as if it were the natural land of the country, whilst the owners and the occupiers and those who cultivated it were treated very unfairly in that class of discussion. It was owing to the industry of the farmer and the enterprise of the capitalist that the land of the country was what it was. Therefore, papers of this class were of very great value, apart from their statistical value, if they brought clearly before the public the very large proportion of the practical value of the land which was due to the application of capital and industry, and he was quite sure that the public mind was often misled by neglecting this consideration.

Mr. A. GODDARD (Secretary to the Surveyors' Institution) said he did not feel competent to discuss this Paper in any detail, as he had not had the advantage of seeing it beforehand; but it was evidently full of valuable research. He should like to associate himself with what had been said as to its value, not only to the statistician, but particularly to the profession which he represented. All land agents should have it in their hands; and every member of the Surveyors' Institution would find the figures and the deductions which the Author had drawn with so much ability, of very great service to them.

Mr. A. H. H. MATTHEWS (Secretary of the Central Chamber of Agriculture) said it would be rather ungracious to attempt to criticise a Paper like this, which had evidently cost the author so much research; and the only remark he would offer would be to emphasize what Sir Francis Powell had said. There was a certain class of individuals who believed, or affected to believe, that every penny of rent which the landowner—whether an individual or a corporation—collected went into their coffers. They forgot, or affected to forget, that there were large outgoings necessary for keeping up the estates. And he could not help feeling that the author in this Paper had somewhat under-estimated those outgoings. The author had referred to the difficulty he had had in getting sufficient data, and had been obliged, as one would expect, to collect his facts from the chief large estates of the country. But those facts would naturally give somewhat misleading estimates, because it was very much easier and more economical to keep up a large estate than a small one. He spoke with some practical experience of small estates (one particularly, an estate of some 2,000 acres), and with knowledge of a good many others, it cost much more proportionately to manage that than it would one of 40,000 or 50,000 acres. In the Paper the author said he thought it was more generally true that the outgoings at the time of depression were reduced to some extent to compensate for the reduced income; but he could not accept that, because he knew it would be found, particularly on small estates, that, instead of the outgoings being reduced as the rent fell, they were actually increased. The reason for this was that when farmers paid high rents and competed with

each other for any vacant farm, they were making big profits, and
the question of repairs to individual farmers did not matter so
much—therefore farmers did them themselves rather than trouble
their landlords about trifles; but these trifles added up to a considerable amount on an estate in the year. When the prices of
produce decreased and the rent decreased at the same time or
shortly afterwards, the farmer went to the landlord or his agent
for every trifling repair which was wanted. On many estates it
was the custom for the landlord to say that he would find the
materials for repairs and the tenant would find the labour; but, as
a matter of fact, it meant that during the last twenty-five years the
landlord had to find both material and labour. He meant these
remarks to apply to small estates, but probably in the aggregate
these would amount to a larger area than the big ones which the
author had dealt with. He also thought the author had omitted
one item, which on some estates was of considerable importance—
that of insurance.

Mr. E. J. HARPER, after congratulating the author on the value
of this Paper, said that what struck him most, as the outcome of this
long and careful consideration, was the fact that we had no exact
information as to the economic rent of this country. So far as
statistical information was concerned, the income tax returns and
the material which the author had obtained from so many different
sources all proceeded on the basis of rent as commonly understood,
not on the basis of its origin, as economic rent. When he came to
consider that point, he was reduced to estimates and calculations.
He was in hopes, some thirteen or fourteen years ago, when the
Agricultural Rating Act was passed, that there would be a scientific
valuation of agricultural rent; but, unfortunately, that was not done.
They knew that in arriving at the rateable value of agricultural land
for the purpose of that Act it was made to include the value of
improvements on the land; whereas, on the other hand, the separate
valuation of the buildings included the value of the land within the
same curtilage; and, consequently, there was no economic distinction, and no record whatever of the economic rent of this country.
He hoped it was not too late even now to start such a record. They
had heard of Valuation Bills; and, although they knew that they
were promoted for other purposes, he did not see why that Society
should not, as far as its influence went, make use of them to secure
that in the valuations to be made there should be something like a
scientific basis and a record of the true economic constituents that
went to make up the value of the land. He would point out that
it was in some sense, having regard to the enormous changes which
had taken place during the nineteenth century, satisfactory to find
that the value of agricultural land had not fallen more than it had.
When they saw what a very different proportion agriculture now
occupied to the total industry of the country from what it did at the
commencement of the century; and saw that in 1800 the valuation
of the houses in the Income Tax Returns (which, however, were
more misleading than he had time to explain) amounted to something

less than 7,000,000*l*. ; while at the end of the century it was in the neighbourhood of 150,000,000*l*. ; and that during the same century the value of agricultural land varied between 30,000,000*l*. at the beginning and 38,000,000*l*. at the end ; there was some slight ground for satisfaction there.

He would ask Mr. Thompson if he could give them any further information on a point which arose towards the end of the Paper, where he said that the economic rent of about 6,300,000*l*. might be regarded as the net return which accrued to the nation at the end of the nineteenth century from the cultivation of the soil. Would it not be, strictly speaking, more accurate to include there the amount of rates and taxes levied on the rent ? Did not those rates and taxes practically go to reduce only the item of economic rent, leaving the other items (interest on outlay, cost of repairs and management) untouched ? Because, if that were so, there should be an addition to the total return to the nation from the cultivation of the soil. The 6,3000,000*l*. represented the return enjoyed by the individual owner, but the rates and taxes certainly went to the benefit of the nation, probably in an even more direct form.

Mr. HOOKER congratulated Mr. Thompson upon his use of index numbers in reducing to order a mass of disconnected and disjointed data. Generally, in statistical inquiries, it was very desirable to give full information regarding the data employed. In this particular Paper it was part of the contract that nothing should be disclosed concerning individual estates, and the author was therefore precluded from giving precise data upon these points. Knowing how careful Mr. Thompson was, he was quite prepared to accept the results of the calculations, and he had no doubt that the author had given full consideration to all possible sources of error in comparing his material. He thought, however, that some definition of rent might have safely been given, or at all events some indication whether the area dealt with was held on different methods of tenure. The paper itself seemed to contain a hint that such was the case, as it seemed that on the estates of the Ecclesiastical Commissioners the outgoings averaged less than on the remainder, pointing to some difference in the conditions of tenure.

Mr. Hooker also thought that the author had given too much weight to the reasons he had adduced for not giving a second diagram showing the course of rents during the first half of the century. By comparing the rents of the smaller areas with those of the larger during, say, the first ten years of the period when the latter were available, the average difference in rent could be ascertained, and the earlier period "corrected" accordingly. This would give a curve that would be perfectly satisfactory for the main purpose, viz., to show the ups and downs during the period ; although the figures thus obtained might not be reliable as an indication of the actual rent in any particular year.

With regard to the author's statement that agriculture had made such progress in the first twenty years of the century as to contribute towards a rise in rents, he would like to ask him if he had much evidence in favour of that. He would not himself have expected to see much progress during an unsettled period of war. And he had noticed only the other day an article in " The Times " summarising estimates of the wheat harvest, and contemporaneous opinion there-upon, at intervals of ten years. According to " The Times," both 1807 and 1827 yielded about 20 bushels of wheat to the acre, and contemporaneous opinion described both, in almost the same words, as a large yield. After this period, however, such an amount soon got looked upon as only a moderate yield : this seemed to mark the following period as one of progress rather than the first two decades.

Mr. REW said he should like to take the opportunity of congratulating a colleague on his success. He thought that the proceedings of the Society would be enriched by Mr. Thompson's contribution. He did not intend to discuss the Paper, but one point might be mentioned. It appeared that the estimate, given towards the end of the paper, of the average cost of equipping land for farming purposes, was based mainly on the particulars given with regard to the disafforestation of land from 1850 to 1860 and on other estimates made about 1860. He thought that the cost of labour had probably increased since that time, and therefore he should be inclined to think that the estimate of 12*l.* per acre would have to be increased if it was applied to present conditions. Another point which interested him was that referred to by Mr. Hooker with regard to agricultural progress in the first twenty years of the century. He was disposed to agree that probably no very great improvement was made in the general cultivation of land in that period, but he thought that considerable improvement took place in the breeding and management of stock owing to the influence of men like Culley and Bakewell.

He had also been interested in Mr. Harper's remark that they might hope to get a valuation of the " economic" rent of land as distinguished from the commercial or competitive rent. Valuers were no doubt capable of doing almost anything, but he thought they would find it exceedingly difficult to fix a value which did not include anything which had been done to the land by the operation of man.

The CHAIRMAN, in moving a vote of thanks to Mr. Thompson, said he found much material for reflection in the parallel columns of Table VI, which brought into line certain things they were anxious to compare. But there was one figure there on which he should like, if the author could give a little explanation, namely : What was the reason for the special drop in the year 1887 and to some extent in 1885 in comparison with the neighbouring years ? In the first and second columns the rents of 120,000, and again of 400,000 acres, were in 1887 far below the standard level of the figures from 1869 to 1877, followed by a rise to something like the former value. In 1893, and thereafter, you come, no doubt, again to low figures, which had now tended to become stationary. The last column, the Sauerbeck's index number of prices, showed a similar fall. In connection with this, there was another point which should be borne in mind, that these prices were lumped together, both animal and vegetable products being combined in the index number, and he thought it would be interesting to separate those two factors, and see how far, over certain periods, the price of meat, milk and wool operated in one direction, and the price of grain and cereals in another. It would be well if they could have two separate columns, so as to give some comparison.

It was quite usual at their meetings to ask readers of Papers to give something more than they had given, so he would not apologise for saying he would have liked a comparison of the movement of rents under different conditions in relation to the character of the agriculture of the country, and perhaps some geographical comparison. That had, he fancied, been done in several instances, both by the Royal Commission of 1903-05 and by Sir James Caird at an earlier date, and in a very old Paper, which he well remembered being read at the Surveyors' Institute by the late Mr. Sturge in 1872. Most curiously divergent results were obtained in different parts of the country from a long and careful survey of prices and rents. The rise of rent in dairy and meat-producing districts was three or four times that which obtained on grain farms even at that time. These comparisons were made more than thirty years ago and could the author of this present Paper have continued their differential estimates, the present Paper, good as it was, would have been made still more valuable. He should himself hesitate a little about resting any elaborate conclusions on the figures for the very early years of the past century. Owing to the great fluctuations in the rates of the currency value to gold prices from year to year, he always found a difficulty in arriving at an absolute conclusion. With regard to the cost of equipment of land, he thought the author had made a useful and timely contribution to their knowledge. He had had occasion at several discussions to raise the point, often overlooked, of how very much of what was called the "rent" of the land was neither more nor less than interest on capital laid out by people within a comparatively recent date. Again, the question of the outlay on buildings and on the housing of the farmers was properly equipment. He was not quite sure if it was the case in some of these figures that the erection of dwelling houses was included, but proper equipment of a farm required the erection of a house, which was, in a sense, partly a factory, as well as of buildings for stock. He was glad to join with the previous speakers in thanking Mr. Thompson for giving them a really good original and lasting piece of work, which he believed would bear good fruit hereafter and induce people to look a little below the conventional surface data when dealing with figures as to rent and prices.

Mr. THOMPSON, in reply, said that there was no reason why the diagram should not, as Mr. Hooker suggested, be carried back to the year 1820. At that date the currency was settled on a gold basis; but during the previous twenty years there was considerable depreciation, so that the earlier figures were not altogether comparable.

Appendix B gave a continuous series of returns showing the rent of 120,000 acres land from 1816 to 1900, and he believed there had been practically no change worth speaking of in those estates over the whole century. Consequently, that rent would show very fairly the curve for the whole period. He had not carried the curve back earlier than the year 1846, because there were neither records of prices nor official figures of income tax with which it could be compared prior to that date.

With regard to the question whether any part of the rise in rent in the first twenty years of the century could properly be attributed to an improved knowledge of agriculture he would point out that it was in the period just before the beginning of the century that Bakewell and Culley, and other great agriculturists first introduced their improvements and discoveries in the breeding of live stock. It must also be remembered that this was the period of the illustrious Coke, of Holkham. The introduction of turnips and the four course rotation, also occurred in the previous century, but the date of their introduction was not identical with their coming into common use; it took many years before the knowledge spread, which it began to do in the early years of last century. Mr. Hooker asked also whether he could supply any information about the tenure on which the estates for which the rents were given were held. At the present time, it would be safe to assert that most or all of the farms would be held on annual tenancies. Since the fall in prices, the practice of leasing farms had gradually decayed, and was now very uncommon. As to how far the landlord carried out the repairs he was doubtful whether any definite statement could be made for the large area represented ; some would be held on one set of conditions, and some on another. On some farms the landowners would do the whole of the repairs, and on others only a part ; and although it might be specified in the lease that certain repairs should be done by the farmer, the actual practice varied very much. In favourable times, when the farmers were doing well, they did not ask their landlords to do so much ; they did more themselves ; but when times were bad the farmers insisted on all their rights, and asked for repairs or threatened to leave. On the whole, he should be inclined to say that generally the landlords carried out the bulk of the repairs at the present time. The item of insurance was included amongst the outgoings, although it was not specifically mentioned. Mr. Matthews had suggested that he had under-estimated the outgoings, on the ground that his figure were chiefly taken from large estates, but he would point out that the tables were derived from a very large acreage and covered a long period ; there was, therefore, a strong probability that they were substantially correct, in addition to which he was inclined to think that large estates were managed, if anything, on a more liberal basis than small ones. The figures were distinctly put forward as an average ; and individual estates would of course vary from it. With regard to Mr. Rew's suggestion that as the landlord's capital, which was put at 12*l.* per acre, was based on figures obtained some years ago the present figure might be somewhat different, he might say that he had arrived at the sum of 12*l.* by taking Mr. Clutton's outlay in 1860, which came to 11*l.* 16*s.*, and comparing it with estimates of expenses at the present day; and, as far as he was able to see, he did not think very much variation was necessary. Under the heading of "Building," he had quoted from an eminent surveyor, the author of the "Agricultural Surveyors' and Estate Agents' Handbook," whose estimates appeared to support the figures arrived at by Mr. Clutton. The only suggestion he could make with regard to the sudden drop in rents in 1887 was that prices in that year reached the lowest point since 1850-51, a time of great depression, and that this reduction was made to meet the cumulative effect of the fall in prices which had become very marked since 1884. As regards a geographical distribution of the changes in rents, he might say that it would not be possible to separate or split up the estates by counties, without giving the figures of individual estates separately, which he had pledged his informants not to do. Another difficulty would be, that in several returns given to him the estates were in several counties. The point raised by Mr. Harper was of some importance, and no doubt his suggestion was quite correct, although the net return which accrued to the nation at the end of the century was probably no greater than it was some seventy or eighty years earlier, yet the State, through local and imperial bodies, received from the land a very much larger sum in the form of rates and taxes.

The following were elected Fellows of the Society :—

Percy Ernest Braun, B.Sc.

Professor Jehangir Coyagi.

The Right Hon. the Earl of Cromer, O.M., G.C.B.

William Joseph Irvine.

MISCELLANEA.

CONTENTS :

PAGE

I.—Memorandum as to Birth-
Rates and Marriage-Rates
in England and Wales.
By THOMAS A. WELTON,
F.C.A. 625
II.—The Assize of Bread at
Oxford, 1794-1820. By
ADOLPHUS   BALLARD,
B.A., LL.B. (Lond.),
Hon. M.A. (Oxon.) 629

PAGE

III.—The Differential Law of
Wages. By HENRY L.
MOORE, Columbia Uni-
versity, New York 638
IV.—Agricultural Returns of
Great Britain, 1907 651
V.—The International Congress
on Tuberculosis, Wash-
ington, 1908 654

I.—*Memorandum as to Birth-Rates and Marriage-Rates in England and Wales.* By THOMAS A. WELTON, F.C.A.

THE new decennial volume of the Registrar-General, valuable as it is, would be worth more if it contained reliable data as to birth-rates and marriage-rates.

The ratios of births given are (no doubt in deference to the past) those for every 1,000 inhabitants, but there are now added those per 1,000 females aged 15—45, which, we must conclude, the Registrar-General thinks will best express the fertility of the sex.

We have but to think how few children are borne by unmarried mothers (in 1902, only 36,674 out of 940,509) to realise that for any scientific purpose the illegitimate births may be disregarded. And as to the married, out of 261,750 brides in 1902 only 20,132 were under 20 years of age, and a still smaller proportion could be expected to bear children before attaining that age. I think, therefore, that for the purpose of measuring fertility no measure can be satisfactory which comprehends more than the married at ages under 45, and I am inclined to think that index numbers representing the proportion of total births to married women under 35 years of age will be very interesting. I proceed to give these for a few subdivisions of the country :—

Groups of Registration Counties.	Births per 100 Married Women under 35.				
	1881.	1886.	1891.	1896.	1901.
Durham and Northumberland	50·9	49·2	49·0	46·0	45·8
Glamorgan, Monmouth, and Brecon	50·6	48·1	49·2	46·8	45·2
Stafford, Warwick, and Worcester .	51·6	49·6	48·7	45·9	43·6
Sussex	50·1	47·6	44·5	41·9	38·4
Hants and Berks	49·8	48·0	44·6	41·9	39·1
Leicester, Notts, and Derby ...	49·5	48·0	46·1	44·0	41·8
Lancashire and Cheshire	48·7	47·1	45·8	43·4	40·6
York	47·7	45·3	44·1	41·9	39·9
London, Surrey, Middlesex, Kent, Essex, and Herts	47·5	45·8	43·7	41·2	39·4
The remaining counties	53·4	51·7	48·9	46·6	43·1
England and Wales	49·8	47·9	46·2	43·7	41·4

It should be explained that the columns marked 1881, 1891, and 1901 represent averages for three years, 1880 to 1882 and so on, compared with the census population in the middle year, and those marked 1886 and 1896 represent averages for 1881-90 and 1891-1900 compared with the mean population shown by the censuses at either end of these periods.

The universal and important decline in birth-rates here shown might be illustrated in greater detail, but unfortunately the tables showing the civil condition of the inhabitants of registration districts which were given in the census volumes for 1881 and 1891 have no counterpart in the census publications for 1901. All that can be done is to frame estimates with the assistance of the figures which are given for counties and large boroughs. A short table founded[1] on such estimates is now supplied :—

Registration Districts and Groups. (Highest and lowest.)	Births per 100 Married Women under 35.				
	1881.	1886.	1891.	1896.	1901.
Yarmouth and Mutford (Lowestoft)	48·7	49·6	45·5	46·58	48·80
Wigan, Prescot, Warrington, Leigh, and Chorley	55·6	53·1	54·0	51·46	48·66
Wolverhampton, Dudley, and Stourbridge	53·4	52·4	53·1	51·00	48·61
Rotherham	50·8	48·3	49·7	48·12	48·23
Chester	53·8	49·9	48·3	47·16	47·25
Stoke-upon-Trent, Wolstanton, and Newcastle-under-Lyne	51·8	49·8	49·3	48·29	46·74
Middlesborough and Guisbrough	49·7	48·6	47·0	44·22	46·40
Walsall	53·9	51·7	51·7	47·92	46·17
Durham and Northumberland, excluding * 10 districts	50·5	48·7	48·8	45·72	45·77
Glamorgan, Monmouth, and Brecon, excluding 5 districts*	50·2	47·6	48·9	46·51	44·98
Portsmouth, Alverstoke, Fareham, and Havant	45·4	44·7	41·1	37·61	35·97
Burnley	48·8	45·8	43·1	41·41	35·94
Plymouth (3 towns) and Plympton St. Mary	45·9	43·1	40·5	37·09	35·28
Oldham	44·1	43·9	40·4	38·20	35·24
Christchurch (Bournemouth)	48·1	42·3	39·4	37·92	34·37
Bury	46·4	45·1	41·6	39·07	34·30
Hastings and Battle	47·7	44·7	41·0	38·02	34·00
Halifax	45·6	42·2	39·4	36·26	32·70
Bradford and North Bierley	44·9	41·6	39·1	36·66	32·50
Rochdale	41·8	39·2	36·6	34·83	31·85

* The excluded districts are largely agricultural.

Other places with low birth-rates in 1891 were Todmorden, Huddersfield, Dewsbury, and Nottingham.

With reference to marriage-rates, I have to point out that, in my opinion, the proportion of the male inhabitants enumerated as married at, say 35 to 40 years of age, gives a more reliable index of the tendency of a population towards the married state than the

[1] So far as concerns 1896 and 1901.

number of marriages celebrated per 1,000 inhabitants. Many marriages appear to take place at some distance from the locality where the married couple propose to reside.

In order to apply a rough measurement to this tendency to marry at a distance, let us assume for the moment that a given number of marriages during ten years will sustain a proportionate number of married people at ages under 35 at the end of that period. The number of marriages in England and Wales in 1881-90 was 2,047,428, and the number of married women under 35 years of age counted in 1891 was 1,936,890, the proportion being as 100 to 94·6. Again, the number of marriages in 1891-1900 was 2,394,105, and the married women under 35 counted in 1901 numbered 2,254,299, the proportion being as 100 to 94·16. If we apply these ratios to groups of counties, the following table is arrived at:—

Groups of Registration Counties	Married Women under 35.			
	1891.		1901.	
	In Excess	Deficient.	In Excess.	Deficient
Durham and Northumberland	6,913	—	10,719	—
Glamorgan, Monmouth, and Brecon .	4,798	—	6.558	—
Leicester, Notts, and Derby ...	4,933	--	4,719	—
London	13,179	—	18,207	—
York	5,074	—	3,965	—
Stafford, Warwick, and Worcester ...	1,207	—	2,670	—
Lancashire and Cheshire	2,190	—	245	—
Hants and Berks.	—	594	—	1,208
Sussex	—	274	—	1,608
The remaining counties	—	37,426	—	44,267

I am inclined to imagine that a more correct method might reduce these figures, but I am convinced that they represent facts to a great extent, and if so they show that local marriages do not represent correctly the demand for wives. Applying the identical method in selected localities, we have the following instructive figures:—

Registration District.	Marriages.		Married Women under 35.		1881.		1891.	
	1871-80.	1881-90.	1861.	1891.	In Excess.	De-ficient.	In Excess.	De-ficient.
Orsett (Tilbury) ...	715	1,202	1,071	2,038	649	—	901	—
St. Germans (near Plymouth)	635	685	930	1,070	354	—	421	—
Todmorden	1,786	1,716	2,481	2,384	861	—	761	—
Easthampstead (Berks)	551	563	695	714	195	—	181	—
Cheltenham	4,194	4,031	2,910	2,722	—	894	—	1,091
Canterbury	1,605	1,530	1,057	1,067	—	399	—	380
St. Asaph (Rhyl) ...	2,062	1,726	1,436	1,285	—	434	—	348
Macclesfield	5,438	4 460	3,945	3,578	—	987	—	641
Bath	6,189	5,660	3,917	4,116	—	1,696	—	1,237

In cases where a couple do not reside in the district in which they are married it is safe to say that they generally live at the husband's address. Deducting cases where whole families migrate, the residue of added wives may be held to represent an addition to the marriage rate of the district where they are found. I have given all large towns wide boundaries when investigating their social statistics, knowing that there is a large migration of entire families from central to outer districts.

I have again to deplore the absence of information as to the civil condition of the populations of registration districts in the Census tables for 1901, which would be of much use in this inquiry, the more so as the recent course of birth- and marriage-rates has lately become a matter of great interest to the public.

To illustrate the difficulty of arriving at a proper measure I will take the cases of the registration counties of Durham and Cardigan. The following tables show the principal facts :—

	Durham				Cardigan.			
Population.	1891.		1901.		1891.		1901.	
	Males.	Females.	Males.	Females.	Males.	Females	Males.	Females.
0—20 ..	253,616	250,415	280,686	278,355	18,127	18.777	16,260	16,632
20—25.....	47,620	45,665	57,425	56,547	2,598	4,032	2,733	3 988
25—30... } 30—35.... }	76,862	72,672	{ 52,071 { 43,044	50,797 41,303	} 4,335	6,615	{ 2,285 { 2,162	3,485 3,131
35 and upwards }	143,678	133,841	172,594	161,768	12,932	18,967	13,163	18.868
	521,776	502,593	605,820	588,770	37,992	48,391	36,603	46,104
Married People.								
0—20.	250	2,134	176	1,722	9	24	5	15
20—25.	10,473	19,598	11,588	21,939	278	557	260	480
25—30.... } 30....35 ... }	50,887	56,256	{ 29,635 { 31,852	35,356 33,509	} 2,176	2,958	{ 835 { 1,278	1,222 1,673
35 and upwards }	110,980	95,432	131,860	115,143	9,164	9,834	9,139	9,686
	172,590	173,420	205,111	207,669	11,627	13,373	11,517	13,076

In 1901 the proportion of Durham men aged 35—40 in the married state was 80·1 per cent., the similar figure for Cardigan being 67·7 per cent.

In 1891-1900 88,904 marriages were celebrated in Durham, 5,070 in Cardigan. If a proportion equal to 94·16 of these had been enumerated as married women under 35, there would have been 4,774 such women in Cardigan, 83,722 in Durham. But, in fact, 3,390 were enumerated in Cardigan (or 1,384 less, equal to 29 per cent.), and 92,526 in Durham, being 8,804 more, or about 10½ per cent.

If we compare the marriages with the mean number of unmarried

men aged 20—35 (including widowers) enumerated at the two ends
of the period, we have—

> 12·47 marriages per annum to each 100 men in Durham ;
> 10·92   „   „   Cardigan ;

but if we deduct from the Cardigan marriages 29 per cent. as really
belonging to other districts, and for the converse reason add.10½ per
cent. to the Durham rate, we arrive at—

> 13·78 marriages per 100 Durham men.
> 7·75   „   Cardigan „

Then, if we compare the marriages with the mean number of
unmarried women aged 20—35 (including widows), we have—

> 17·72 marriages per 100 Durham women.
> 7·07   „   Cardigan „

These last figures seem nearer to the true measure than any
others, yet I feel that the contrast is too strongly accentuated.

In the meantime, the ratios of persons married, calculated on
mean population, assuming the increase or decrease to be in arithmetical progression, would be—

> 16·03 Durham ; | 12·01 Cardigan ;

figures as clearly objectionable as any that could be chosen, since
they take nothing into account but the simple bulk of married and
unmarried people.   These last are in effect the Registrar-General's
figures, though, by a refinement assuming increase by geometrical
progression, he makes the Durham ratio a trifle higher, viz., 16·14·

II.—*The Assize of Bread at Oxford*, 1794-1820·   By ADOLPHUS
BALLARD, B.A., LL.B. (Lond.), Hon. M.A. (Oxon.).

THE following tables, compiled from *Jackson's Oxford Journal*, show
the prices of household bread fixed from week to week by the Vice-
Chancellor of the University of Oxford during the latter years of
the reign of George III.   In all municipal boroughs, except Oxford
and Cambridge, the Assize of Bread was set by the Mayor.   For
instance, during the first half of the seventeenth century, the Mayor
of Woodstock set the Assize of Bread and Beer to be observed by
the bakers, brewers, and victuallers within the Borough (see my
Chronicles of Woodstock, p. 141, where an assize is printed verbatim).
But in Oxford this business was gradually taken out of the hands of
the civic, and transferred to the University authorities.   In 1199
King John granted the City with all its liberties and appurtenances
to the citizens at fee farm, and under this grant the Assize of Bread
was set by the Mayor; but on 18th June, 1255, Henry III granted
a charter to the University providing the Chancellor should be
present at the Court when the Assize was set; and finally in 1355

Edward III granted the Assize of Bread, Beer, and Wine to the Chancellor, and thus took it out of the hands of the citizens.

That a power, which in other cities was exercised by the Mayor, should in Oxford be exercised by the University authorities was always a grievance, and during the period under review complaint was made that the University authorities exercised their power in a very oppressive manner, as was shown by the fact that on 7th November, 1801, they reckoned the average price of a bushel of wheat in the Oxford market as being 7s. 9d., whereas in reality it was 8s. 4¾d., thus causing a loss to the baker of 3s. 4d. on every sack of flour used by him. (*Oxford Journal*, 14th November, 1801.) And as evidence that this accusation was not entirely unfounded, it may be noted that the price of household bread in the city of Oxford was often 2d. or 3d. a peck less than that fixed by the Justices of the Hundred of Wootton, which adjoins the city on the north.

The records of punishment for breaches of the Assize are few, but this is probably because the doings of the local police courts were not then so fully reported as they are to-day. The *Oxford Journal* for 4th May, 1801, reports that :—

"On Monday last, two persons being convicted for selling hot bread, the penalty was laid out in bread and distributed to the poor of the parishes of St. Mary the Virgin and St. Peter-in-the-East, where the persons resided. The same day a baker was convicted for exposing to sale bread deficient in weight, 21 ounces in seven loaves ; and the forfeited bread and also the penalty were given to the poor of the parish of St. Giles of this city."

The former offence was in contravention of 40 Geo. III, c. 18, forbidding the sale of bread within twenty-four hours of its being baked.

Previously, on 18th July, 1795, it was reported that a baker was fined 5l. by the Vice-Chancellor for his bread being deficient 20 ounces.

The form in which the assize was set often appears in the newspaper as follows :—

"The second best price of a bushel of wheat being 12s. 6d., according to which price and a due allowance made to the baker, the assize and price of bread are as follows :—

		To Weigh			To be Sold for		
		lb.	oz.	dr.	s.	d.	
The 1d. loaf	standard wheaten ...	–	4	15	–	1	
	household	–	5	13	–	1	
The 2d. loaf	standard wheaten ...	–	9	15	–	2	
	household	–	11	9	–	2	
The peck loaf	standard wheaten	17	6	-	4	8	Avoirdupois weight.
	household	17	6	-	4	–	
The half peck	standard wheaten ..	8	11	..	2	4	
	household	8	11	–	2	–	
The quartern	standard wheaten	4	5	8	1	2	
	household	4	5	8	1	–	

"This assize took place on Wednesday, the 1st inst." (*Oxford Journal*, 4th January, 1800.)

But, in later years the price of the peck loaf (household) alone is given.

The dates in the table are those of the papers in which the price appears, and the dates of the various assizes are not given. In the example quoted above, the assize was set on the previous Wednesday, but after August, 1817, it was set on the previous Saturday. The paper appeared on Saturdays.

1794.		1795.		1796.		1797.	
Date.	Peck Loaf	Date.	Peck Loaf.	Date	Peck Loaf.	Date.	Peck Loaf.
	s. d.		s. d.		s. d.		s. d.
				Jan. 2	4 --		
				,, 16	4 --		
				Feb. 6	3 10		
				,, 13	3 8½		
Feb. 22	2 2						
		Feb. 28	2 6	,, 27	3 10		
				Mar. 5	4 2		
				,, 12	4 4		
				April 2	4 --		
				,, 9	3 5		
				,, 16	3 --		
				,, 30	3 2		
						May 13	2 1
				June 11	3 4		
				July 2	3 5		
		July 18	3 --			July 15	2 4
				,, 23	3 2		
				Aug. 6	3 --		
		Aug. 14	3 8				
				,, 27	2 8	Aug. 26	2 5
				Sept. 2	2 5		
		Sept. 12	3 2			Sept. 9	2 7
		,, 19	3 --			,, 16	2 8¾
		,, 26	3 2				
				Oct. 1	2 7		
		Oct. 9	3 3½				
		,, 24	3 6			Oct. 21	2 7¾
						Nov. 11	2 6
				Nov. 26	2 6		
		Dec. 5	3 5			Dec. 9	2 5
		,, 19	3 9				
Dec. 20	2 4						
				Dec. 31	2 4		
	2 3*		3 3*		3 4*		2 5½*

* Average for the year (calculated to nearest farthing).

1798.		1799.		1800.		1801.	
Date.	Peck Loaf	Date.	Peck Loaf.	Date.	Peck Loaf	Date.	Peck Loaf
	s. d.		s. d.		s. d.		s. d.
				Jan. 4	4 –	Jan. 3	5 10
						,, 10	5 6
						,, 17	5 8
						,, 24	5 9
				Feb. 1	4 4	,, 31	6 2
				,, 8	4 5	Feb. 7	5 10
		Feb. 16	2 2¾	,, 15	4 7	,, 14	6 4
				,, 22	4 9		
				Mar. 1	4 7		
Mar. 17	2 5					Mar. 14	7 –
,, 24	2 3½			,, 22	4 5		
,, 31	2 4			,, 29	4 7	,, 28	6 8
April 7	2 5	April 6	2 3½	April 5	4 8	April 4	6 4
		,, 27	2 4	,, 19	4 10	,, 18	5 8
				,, 26	5 1		
		May 11	2 7	May 3	5 4	May 2	5 3½
				,, 10	5 3	,, 9	4 8
				,, 17	5 2	,, 16	4 7
				,, 24	5 7		
June 2	2 3½			,, 31	4 9	,, 30	4 10
,, 9	2 2¾			June 7	5 1		
				,, 21	5 4		
				,, 28	5 5		
						July 18	5 2
July 28	2 1			July 26	4 11	,, 25	5 7
				Aug. 2	4 2	Aug. 1	5 5½
Aug. 11	2 –			,, 9	3 3½	,, 8	5 –
,, 18	2 2					,, 15	4 7½
				,, 23	3 7	,, 22	4 1
				,, 30	4 2	,, 29	3 6
				Sept. 6	4 7		
						Sept. 12	3 8½
				,, 20	4 4	,, 19	3 7
		Sept. 28	2 10	,, 27	3 2		
				Oct. 4	3 5	Oct. 2	3 2
		Oct. 12	3 2	,, 11	4 4	,, 10	2 10
Oct. 20	2 1	,, 19	3 5	,, 18	4 11	,, 17	2 7
				,, 25	5 4	,, 24	2 5
Nov. 10	2 2	Nov. 9	3 7			Nov. 7	2 7¾
,, 24	2 1	,, 23	3 9			,, 21	2 10
		,, 30	4 –			,, 28	3 –
				Dec. 6	5 2		
		Dec. 14	3 10	,, 13	5 4	Dec. 12	2 10
		,, 21	3 8	,, 20	5 7		
Dec. 29	2 2	,, 28	3 8	,, 27	5 11	,, 26	3 –
	2 2½*		3 2¼*		4 8½*		4 7¼*

* Average for the year (calculated to nearest farthing).

1802.		1803.		1804.		1805.	
Date.	Peck Loaf.	Date.	Peck Loaf.	Date.	Peck Loaf.	Date.	Peck Loaf.
	s. d.		s. d.		s. d.		s. d.
						Jan. 5	3 5
				Jan. 21	2 2	„ 19	3 6
Jan. 23	2 10					„ 26	3 8
						Feb. 9	3 10
				Mar. 17	2 1	Mar. 16	3 11
Mar. 20	3 -					„ 23	4 -
				„ 31	2 2		
April 3	2 10						
„ 10	2 7¾	April 9	2 3½			April 13	3 10
						„ 20	3 9
						„ 27	3 8
		May 28	2 4			May 18	3 7
						June 1	3 8
		June 4	2 6			„ 8	3 8½
						„ 29	3 7
		July 2	2 4			July 6	3 8½
				July 21	2 2	„ 20	3 8
				„ 28	2 3½		
						Aug. 3	4 1
Aug. 7	2 9½			Aug. 11	2 4		
						„ 17	4 -
„ 21	2 7¾			„ 25	2 9½	„ 24	3 11
„ 28	2 7					„ 31	3 8
				Sept. 15	2 7¾	Sept. 14	3 4
				„ 29	2 8½		
		Oct. 1	2 3½	Oct. 13	2 11	Oct. 5	3 5
						„ 19	3 4
Oct. 23	2 6			., 27	3 1	„ 26	3 3½
						Nov. 2	3 2
				Nov. 10	3 3½		
Nov. 13	2 5			„ 17	3 5		
						„ 23	3 1
		Dec. 10	2 2¾	Dec. 8	3 4	Dec. 7	2 11
Dec. 11	2 4					„ 14	2 10
„ 25	2 3½					„ 28	3 1
	2 7½*		2 4*		2 8*		3 6¾*

* Average for the year (calculated to nearest farthing).

1806.			1807.			1808.			1809.		
Date.	Peck Loaf.		Date.	Peck Loaf		Date.	Peck Loaf.		Date.	Peck Loaf.	
	s.	*d.*		*s.*	*d.*		*s.*	*d.*		*s.*	*d.*
			Jan. 3	3	4				Jan. 7	4	–
			,, 10	3	2¾				,, 14	3	10
			,, 17	3	4						
			,, 24	3	3½						
						Feb. 6	2	11			
						,, 13	2	10			
Feb. 22		2									
Mar. 1	3	2¾									
									Mar. 3	3	11
,, 15	3	2				Mar. 12	2	11			
						April 9	3	–	April 8	3	10
April 19	3	3½							,, 15	3	10
,, 26	3	6	April 25	3	2						
						May 7	3	1			
May 17	3	5									
									May 27	3	8½
June 7	3	4									
						June 11	3	2¾			
			June 27	3	1						
									July 15	3	6
July 26	3	4							,, 29	3	8½
			Aug. 8	2	11	Aug. 6	3	3½	Aug. 12	3	11
			,, 15	3	1						
									,, 26	4	1
						Sept. 3	3	5	Sept. 9	4	3
									,, 23	4	4
						,, 24	3	8	,, 30	4	7
			Oct. 3	2	9½				Oct. 7	4	9
									,, 14	4	7
			,, 17	2	7¼	Oct. 15	3	6	,, 21	4	6
						,, 22	3	8	,, 28	4	3
			,, 31	2	6	,, 29	3	8½			
						Nov. 5	3	11	Nov. 11	4	6
						,, 12	3	8½	,, 18	4	8
Nov. 22	3	2¾				,, 19	3	10	,, 25	4	9
,, 29	3	3½	Nov. 28	2	7						
			Dec. 5	2	8¾				Dec. 2	4	7
Dec. 13		4				Dec. 10	3	8	,, 9	4	9
,, 20	3	2¼	,, 19	2	10				,, 16	4	8
			,, 26	2	11				,, 23	4	9
						,, 31	3	10	,, 30	4	8
	3	3¼*		2	11½*		3	5*		4	3¼*

* Average for the year (calculated to nearest farthing).

1810.		1811.		1812.		1813.	
Date.	Peck Loaf	Date.	Peck Loaf	Date.	Peck Loaf	Date.	Peck Loaf
	s. d.		s. d.		s. d.		s. d.
Jan. 6	4 5	Jan. 5	3 10				
		,, 12	4 -	Jan. 11	4 6½	Jan. 9	5 1
,, 20	4 5½	,, 19	4 1				
		,, 26	3 11	,, 25	4 5	,, 30	5 -
				Feb. 1	4 6½		
		Feb. 9	4 -	,, 8	4 5½	Feb.. 6	5 1
Feb. 17	4 5½	,, 16	4 1				
				,, 22	4 7½	,, 20	5 2
Mar. 10	4 5	Mar. 2	4 -	Mar. 7	4 6½	Mar. 6	5 1
,, 24	4 6½	,, 23	4 -	,, 21	7	,, 20	5 2
		,, 30	4 1	,, 28	-		
April 7	4 9	April 6	4 -	April 4	4		
,, 14	4 6½	,, 13	3 10	,, 11	5	April 10	5 2
				,, 18	6		
,, 28	4 6½			,, 25	7	,, 24	5 3
				May 2	4	May 1	5 2
		May 11	3 9	,, 16	5 5		
				,, 23	5 4	,, 22	5 1
		,, 25	3 8			,, 29	5 -
May 26	4 9						
June 2	4 6¼	June 1	3 8½	June 13	5 6	June 12	5 1
		,, 8	3 8	,, 20	5 5		
		,, 15	3 7				
,, 23	4 6¼	,, 29	3 7				
,, 30	4 8						
July 14	4 10	July 13	3 6	July 4	5 7	July 3	5 -
,, 21	4 7			,, 11	5 10		
,, 28	4 9	,, 27	3 8				
Aug. 4	4 7½	Aug. 3	3 8½	Aug. 1	5 8	,, 31	4 11
		,, 10	3 10	,, 8	5 10	Aug. 7	4 10
		,, 17	4 -	,, 15	5 9		
		,, 24	4 3			,, 21	4 8
		Sept. 7	4 4	Sept. 12	5 5	Sept. 11	4 2
		,, 14	4 5½			,, 18	4 -
						,, 25	4 1
Sept. 29	4 7½			Oct. 3	5 3	Oct. 2	4 -
				,, 10	5 -	,, 9	4 1
Oct. 13	4 5	Oct. 19	4 6½	,, 17	4 7		
				,, 24	4 6½		
		Nov. 2	4 7	,, 31	4 7½	,, 30	4 -
		,, 16	4 8	Nov. 7	5 1	Nov. 6	3 10
		,, 23	4 9	,, 14	5 3	,, 13	3 8
		,, 30	4 8	,, 21	5 2	,, 20	3 6
Dec. 8	4 4					Dec. 4	3 4
,, 15	4 3	Dec. 14	4 7½			,, 11	3 2
,, 22	4 1					,, 18	3 4
,, 29	3 11					,, 24	3 7
	4 6*		4 -½*		5 1¼*		4 5½*

* Average for the year (calculated to nearest farthing).

1814.		1815.		1816.		1817.	
Date.	Peck Loaf.	Date.	Peck Loaf.	Date.	Peck Louf	Date.	Peck Loaf.
	s. d.		*s. d.*		*s. d.*		*s. d.*
Jan. 1	3 4			Jan. 6	2 7	Jan. 4	4 6
,, 8	3 6	Jan. 14	3 2			,, 11	4 7
,, 15	3 7	,, 21	2 11			,, 18	4 6
		,, 28	2 10	,, 27	2 8	,, 25	4 7
		Feb. 4	2 9	Feb. 3	2 9	Feb. 1	4 8
		,, 11	2 10				
Feb. 19	3 6	,, 18	3 2	,, 17	2 10	,, 15	4 7
,, 26	3 6	,, 25	3 5				
				Mar. 2	2 9	Mar. 1	4 8
Mar. 12	3 6	Mar. 11	3 6			,, 8	4 10
,, 19	3 7	,, 18	3 4				
,, 26	3 9	,, 25	3 5			,, 22	5 2
				,, 30	2 10	,, 29	5 5
April 9	3 5	April 1	3 3	April 6	2 9	April 5	5 2
,, 16	3 6	,, 8	3 4	,, 13	2 11	,, 12	5 3
,, 23	3 3	,, 15	3 5	,, 20	3 -	,, 19	5 -
,, 30	3 1	,, 22	3 4				
May 7	3 2			May 4	3 3	May 3	5 1
		May 13	3 5	,, 11	3 4		
,, 21	3 2	,, 20	3 4	,, 18	3 8	,, 17	5 -
,, 28	3 3	,, 27	3 2	,, 25	3 11	,, 31	5 1
June 4	3 4			June 1	3 8		
		June 10	3 3	,, 8	3 7	June 7	5 3
,, 18	3 3					,, 14	5 4
		,, 24	3 -	,, 22	3 7	,, 21	5 7
July 2	3 2			,, 29	3 6	,, 28	5 8
		July 8	3 2			July 5	5 5
		,, 15	3 -			,, 12	5 -
,, 23	3 4	,, 22	3 2	July 20	3 5	,, 19	4 8
		,, 29	3 1	,, 27	3 7	,, 26	4 4
Aug. 6	3 5					Aug. 2	4 -½
		Aug. 12	3 -	Aug. 10	3 8	,, 16	4 2
,, 20	3 8			,, 17	3 9	,, 23	3 11
,, 27	3 10	,, 26	3 -	,, 24	4 -	,, 30	3 10
Sept. 3	3 11	Sept. 2	2 10				
,, 10	3 10			Sept. 7	3 10	Sept. 6	4 1
,, 17	3 8			,, 14	3 8		
,, 24	3 10			,, 21	3 9	,, 20	3 4
		,, 30	2 9	,, 28	3 7		
Oct. 8	3 11	Oct. 7	2 11	Oct. 5	3 6	Oct. 4	3 5
,, 15	3 9	,, 14	2 10			,, 11	3 8
				,, 19	3 10		
,, 29	3 8	,, 28	2 9			,, 25	3 7
Nov. 5	3 8			Nov. 2	4 2		
,, 12	3 7	Nov. 11	2 8	,, 9	4 5	Nov. 8	3 8
,, 19	3 6	,, 18	2 9	,, 16	4 4	,, 15	3 9
,, 26	3 7	,, 25	2 8	,, 23	3 10	,, 29	3 10
Dec. 3	3 6			,, 30	4 2		
,, 10	3 7			Dec. 7	4 5	Dec. 6	3 9
,, 17	3 4	Dec. 16	2 9	,, 14	4 4		
,, 24	3 2			,, 21	4 2	,, 20	3 10
,, 31	3 3	,, 30	2 8	,, 28	4 4		
	3 6½*		3 0½*		3 8¼*		4 6¼*

* Average for the year (calculated to nearest farthing).

1818.		1819.		1820.	
Date.	Peck Loaf.	Date.	Peck Loaf.	Date.	Peck Loaf.
	s. d.		*s. d.*		*s. d.*
		Jan. 2.......	3 8	Jan. 1........	2 11
		,, 9.......	3 7	,, 8.......	3 –
Jan. 17	3 10	,, 16.......	3 8	,, 15.......	2 11
,, 24	3 11	,, 23.......	3 7	,, 22	3 –
				,, 29.......	3 1
Feb. 7	4 –				
· ,, 14	3 11			Feb. 12.......	3 1
,, 21	4 0			,, 19.......	3 3
,, 25	4 1	Feb. 27.......	3 6		
Mar. 7	3 11	Mar. 6.....	3 7	Mar. 4	3 4
				,, 11.......	3 5
,, 28	4 –			,, 25.......	3 7
April 4	4 1	April 3	3 8	April 1.......	3 4
,, 11	4 2	,, 10	3 6	,, 8.......	3 4
,, 18	4 3	,, 17.......	3 5	,, 15	3 3
,, 25	4 1	,, 24	3 4		
May 9	4 –				
,, 16	3 11				
		May 22.......	3 3		
,, 30	3 10	,, 29.......	3 1		
June 6	3 8	June 5.......	3 –		
,, 13	3 10	,, 12.......	3 –½		
,, 20	3 9				
,, 27	3 11			June 24.......	3 5
July 4	3 10	July 3........	3 4		
		,, 10.......	3 5		
,, 18	3 11	,, 17.......	3 6		
		,, 24	3 5		
Aug. 1	3 10			July 29.......	3 4
,, 8	3 7			Aug. 5.......	3 5
,, 15	3 8	Aug. 14.......	3 4	,, 12.......	3 4
,, 29	3 9				
Sept. 5	3 10	Sept. 4	3 3		
,, 12	3 11			Sept. 10.......	3 2
,, 26	4 –				
		Oct. 2	3 2	Oct. 7	2 11
Oct. 10	3 11			,, 14.......	2 9
		,, 16	3 3		
,, 24	3 10	,, 23........	3 2	,, 28.......	2 10
				Nov. 4.......	2 11
Nov. 14	3 10			,, 18.......	2 10
		Nov. 30.......	3 4	,, 25.......	2 9
		,, 27.......	3 3	Dec. 2.......	2 8
Dec. 5	3 8	Dec. 4.......	3 4	,, 9.......	2 10
,, 12	3 9	,, 11	3 2	,, 16.......	2 8
,, 19	3 8	,, 18.......	3 3		
,, 26	3 9	,, 25.......	3 1		
	3 10½*		3 4*		3 1*

* Average for the year (calculated to nearest farthing).

III.—*The Differential Law of Wages.* By Henry L. Moore,
Columbia University, New York.

In the present article I have tried to put a doctrine of pure
economics to a statistical test. Such an undertaking implies at
least three sources of error:—

(1.) Every doctrine of pure economics rests upon the assumption
of perfect mobility of the factors of production, while, in fact,
friction to an incalculable degree characterises the working of the
industrial mechanism.

(2.) The statistics available are incomplete, since, notwithstanding
great efficiency and honesty of purpose on the part of the Government officials charged with the collection and presentation of
material, the comparatively few accessible records are themselves
incomplete.

(3.) The two disciplines, statistics and pure economics, have
hitherto been so unrelated that a series of hypotheses must be made
in order to utilize the data and methods afforded by the one to
render effective the theories of the other.

There is obviously great danger, therefore, when working upon
a problem of this character, of introducing so many and such
complex hypotheses as to vitiate any conclusions that may be
reached. This danger has been constantly in mind as I have
attempted, at several points in this investigation, to connect fact
and theory, and special care has been taken, in the absence of full
and precise data, to preserve a befitting sobriety in the use of
hypotheses.

I.

The differential law of wages is the particular aspect of the
theory of wages which it is proposed to investigate. The expression
"theory of wages" may be understood to mean either of two things:
it may mean the theory of the causes and method of apportioning
the national dividend between capital and labour; or it may
mean the theory of the apportionment of aggregate wages among
subgroups of labourers, or among individual labourers. A complete
theory of wages would afford a law of the distribution of the total
product of industry between capital and labour, and a law of the
distribution among individual labourers of the aggregate product
going to labour as a whole. With the first part of the theory of
wages, as here stated, our study is not concerned; for purposes of
limiting the scope of the inquiry, it is assumed that this first part
of the general problem is already solved. The second part of the
theory, to which our investigation is confined, is, in substance, the
differential law of wages.

The statement of the differential law of wages by the most
approved authorities contains four leading propositions:—

(1,) The labour force in a country with varied industries is a
force of varying efficiency per labourer unit;

(2.) The character of the industrial organisation of a particular time and place determines the nature and degree of segregation of labour into groups of varying efficiency. The two most fundamental groups are those of skilled and unskilled labour;

(3.) The labourer of least efficiency in each group receives a wage which constitutes the minimum wage of the group. This minimum wage is at least equal to the highest wage that the least efficient labourer in the group could earn in the other forms of employment open to him;

(4.) The more efficient labourers within the group receive the minimum wage of the group plus a supplement proportionate to the excess of their efficiency over that of the least capable labourer in the group.

The theory composed of these four propositions is an important part of the doctrine frequently summarized in the statement that the labourer tends to get what he produces. It is very essential to observe that the differential law covers only a part of this general theory of wages; for, however large or however small the labour dividend, it may be apportioned among the labourers according to their efficiency, and consequently it is not allowable to conclude from the fact of labour being rewarded according to efficiency that therefore labour gets what it produces.

Because of our failure to put the theory of differential wages to any kind of empirical test it is generally expounded in a form in which, despite the valuable parts that will be utilised, it must be regarded as without significance so far as scientific uses are concerned. For unless the postulate stated above in the first proposition—that the labour force of a country with varied industries is a force of varying efficiency per labourer unit—is rounded out into the law of the variation of efficiency, it is very little scientific gain to arrive at the conclusion that wages are distributed according to a law about which we know nothing. Each of the last three propositions in the above analysis of this theory is to be interpreted in the light of the first proposition, and the law postulated in this proposition we confess we do not know.

If this law of wages is to be put to a statistical test, it is clear that two points must be settled: (1) Some hypothesis must be made as to the law of distribution of efficiency; (2) Some allowance must be made for the peculiar economic conditions of the particular time and place. This latter point is the subject of the second of the four propositions into which the statement of the differential law of wages has been analysed. Whatever assumption may seem probable as to the distribution of efficiency, we know that the distribution of income will not be exactly according to the assumed law of efficiency because of the strategic advantage in bargaining, due to organisation or other causes, enjoyed by some of the labourers and not by others. The character and extent of these disturbing conditions must be ascertained in each particular case by a direct study of the labour environment.

First, as to the distribution of efficiency among labourers. In making our hypothesis we shall proceed from the simple to the complex. As it is generally conceded that industrial efficiency is the result of a combination of physical, mental and moral qualities,[1] it is quite likely that we may receive light as to the distribution of efficiency from a consideration of the distribution of physical, mental, and moral qualities. Three-quarters of a century ago Quételet observed that physical qualities are distributed according to the normal or Gaussian law, and the most elaborate recent investigation of the subject ends with this conclusion: "We have very definite evidence that the normal curve suffices to describe within the limits of random sampling the distribution of the chief physical characters in man."[2]

The general conformity of the measurements of physical characters to the normal curve suggests the proper hypothesis affecting the distribution of mental and moral qualities. A number of years ago, Mr. Francis Galton began his studies of inheritance on the assumption that the latter qualities are distributed according to the same law as are physical characters. Professor Pearson's laborious investigation, which has just been brought to a close, proceeds upon the same assumption: "We have   .   .   . selected, as the normal scale of intelligence, that which would be given if the frequency distribution of intelligence followed the normal or Gaussian curve of errors."[3] It would seem, therefore, that a not unreasonable hypothesis as to the distribution of efficiency, which is itself a balance of physical, mental, and moral qualities, is that it is according to the normal law of error.

We come now to the second part of the problem, namely, the determining of the effect of the peculiar industrial environment in altering the results which might be expected from the law of efficiency of labour. In the early part of this paper it was observed that usually two large groups of labourers are distinguished: the group of unskilled, unorganised labour, and the group of skilled, organised labour. These two groups, which for our purpose constitute the whole of labour, share between them aggregate wages. The members of the latter group, in consequence of their strategic advantage in bargaining, are able to obtain a larger share than would be obtained if total wages were distributed according to the law of efficiency which has been assumed to exist. If the proposed statistical test is to be carried through, some way must be found for determining the extent to which this cause affects the working of

---

[1] "We have next to consider the conditions on which depend health and strength, physical, mental, and moral. They are the basis of industrial efficiency, on which the production of material wealth depends." Marshall, *Principles of Economics*, 4th edition, p. 272.

For a further consideration of this point see an article on "The Efficiency Theory of Wages" in the *Economic Journal*, December, 1907.

[2] Karl Pearson, F.R.S., and Alice Lee, D.Sc., "On the Laws of Inheritance in Man," *Biometrika*, vol. ii, part iv, 1903, p. 395.

[3] Karl Pearson, F.R.S., "On the Relationship of Intelligence to Size and Shape of Head, and to other Physical and Mental Characters," *Biometrika*, vol. v, parts i and ii, 1906, p. 106.

the law of reward according to efficiency. Later on the method employed in this study will be made clear. At this point a technical difficulty must be considered.

II.

It has been assumed that the distribution of efficiency follows the Gaussian law. But this law is a generalisation applying to an infinite number of measurements, whereas statistics of wages are available for only a finite number of labourers. Furthermore, the Gaussian law is a description of the arrangement of many small groups according to the group measurement, whereas the differential law of wages purports to be a law of distribution of wages according to differential efficiency. It is necessary, therefore, to know, not how groups indefinite in number, are arranged according to efficiency, but how much, in a finite group of individuals selected at random, the members of the group will, on the average, differ from each other. Although the properties of the law of error have been investigated for over a century and the law has been applied to human data during the greater part of this period, no analytical solution of this differential problem was given until five years ago.

In 1902 Mr. Francis Galton proposed to British mathematicians this problem: "A certain sum, say 100*l.*, is available for two prizes to be awarded at a forthcoming competition; the larger one for the first of the competitors, the smaller one for the second. How should the 100*l.* be most suitably divided between the two? What ratio should a first prize bear to that of a second one? Does it depend on the number of the competitors, and if so, in what way? Similar questions may be asked, but will not be answered here, when the number of prizes exceeds two. What should be the division of the 100*l.* when three prizes are given, or four, or any larger number?"[4]

Mr. Galton's own investigation suggested "that when only two prizes are given in any competition the first prize ought to be closely three times the value of the second." The novelty and interest of the problem led him to conclude: "I now commend the subject to mathematicians in the belief that those who are capable —which I am not—of treating it more thoroughly may find that further investigation may repay trouble in unexpected directions."

Professor Pearson answered the appeal to mathematicians and undertook the solution of the problem in this general form: "A random sample of n individuals is taken from a population of N members which, when N is very large, may be taken to obey any law of frequency expressed by the curve $y = N\phi(x)$, ydx being the total frequency of individuals with characters or organs lying between x and $x + dx$. It is required to find an expression for the average difference in character between the pth and the $(p + 1)^{th}$ individuals when the sample is arranged in order of magnitude of the character."

---

[4] Francis Galton, F.R.S., "The Most Suitable Proportion between the Values of First and Second Prizes," *Biometrika*, vol. i, part iv, p. 385.

" I propose to call this general problem *Francis Galton's Individual Difference Problem in Statistics*, or, more briefly, *Galton's Difference Problem.* It will be seen at once to carry us from the consideration of the means and standard deviations of mass aggregates and arrays to the average interval between individuals of those aggregates. We may still deal with *averages*, but we fix our attention no longer on the whole population, but on definite individuals in its ordered array. This I believe to be a real advance in statistical theory." The solution of the problem " provides us for the first time, I believe, with the most probable relationships between individuals forming a random sample."[5] .

One would suspect that this problem had been formulated and solved with a view to the application of the results to our problem of the differential law of wages! For the knowledge of the average difference in efficiency between each of 1,000 labourers and his less efficient neighbour, when the whole number are ranked according to their efficiency, would afford data for determining the average difference in efficiency of the 999 labourers over their least efficient associate. Moreover, if the 1,000 labourers were separated into two groups, the one composed of the less efficient, and the other the more efficient, thus giving rise to a minimum wage in each group, the knowledge of the average difference of efficiency in the population of 1,000 would suffice for the computation of the average difference in efficiency of the members in each group over that of the least efficient member of the same group. To handle our problem of wages, the first need is the construction of a standard population in which the average difference of efficiency is computed. Such a standard population, judiciously used, would supply the means with which to obtain a first approximation to the solution of several questions in the dynamics of wages.

It would be desirable to have a standard population containing at least 500 members, but the laborious calculations required for so large a population has rendered the undertaking of the work impossible at the present time. Table 1, the construction of which is described in detail in the Appendix, has been computed on the assumption that the distribution of efficiency is according to the Gaussian law. We find, for example, that in a population of 100 individuals, selected at random, the difference in ability between the ablest and the next ablest is, on the average, ·360964 times the standard deviation of the group from which the selection is made. We do not pretend to know the actual magnitude of the standard deviation, nor is the knowledge necessary for our problem.

III.

Having constructed our standard population, we have next to describe the concrete environment to which it is applied. A recent investigation of wages in the United States affords for the first time an ample collection of wages distributed according to the frequency

[5] Karl Pearson, " Note on Francis Galton's Problem," *Biometrika*, vol. i, part iv, p. 390—399.

of the different rates. In the second chapter of the report on *Employees and Wages* of the Twelfth Census, which is the product of an elaborate investigation of wages in the manufactures of the United States, an "Analysis of Occupational Comparison" is presented by considering the wages of labourers in 32 industries. By means of pay-rolls of a number of representative establishments in each industry, the actual distribution of wages of each industry is determined and set forth. As a result of this admirable inquiry we are able to state the proportion of labour in each of the 32 industries receiving wages between any assigned limits.

In order to obtain as general a view as possible of the distribution of wages in the manufacturing industries of the country, these wage schedules for the several industries, in 1900, have been combined in the same way that the wage schedules for the establishments were combined in the several industries. The figures used are those given in the "Wages" volume, in the case of each industry, under the heading: "Males 16 years and over; Rates per week; All sections; All occupations." It was believed that an investigation confined to this category would be most representative of the wage-earning conditions of labour employed in manufactures.

The wage schedules of 30 industries fulfilled the above requirements. The two industries omitted from the full number given in the census volume are "collars and cuffs," and "distilleries." The former is not included because no schedule is given of males 16 years and over, and the latter is omitted because the few figures tabulated relate only to the States of Kentucky and Ohio.

The 30 industries are: (1) carpet mills, (2) cotton mills, (3) dyeing and finishing textiles, (4) knitting mills, (5) woollen mills, (6) agricultural implements, (7) furniture, (8) lumber and planing mills, (9) pianos, (10) wagons and carriages, (11) car and railroad shops, (12) foundries and metal working, (13) iron and steel, (14) shipyards, (15) bakeries, (16) breweries, (17) candy, (18) chemicals, (19) cigars, (20) clothing, (21) flour mills, (22) glass, (23) paper mills, (24) potteries, (25) printing, (26) rubber, (27) shoes, (28) slaughtering, (29) tanneries, (30) tobacco.[6]

As a result of the combination of the census schedules we have the distribution of wages recorded in Table 2.

---

[6] The schedules may be found on the following pages of the Wages volume:—(1) carpet mills, p. 5; (2) cotton mills, p. 27; (3) dyeing and finishing textiles, p. 72; (4) knitting mills, p. 81; (5) woollen mills, p. 104; (6) agricultural implements, p. 143; (7) furniture, p. 169; (8) lumber and planing mills, p. 185; (9) pianos, p. 194; (10) wagons and carriages, p. 201; (11) car and railroad shops, p. 225; (12) foundries and metal working, p. 268; (13) iron and steel, p. 325; (14) shipyards, p. 353; (15) bakeries, p. 371; (16) breweries, p. 379; (17) candy, p. 391; (18) chemicals, p. 403; (19) cigars, p. 411; (20) clothing, p. 431; (21) flour mills, p. 461 (includes males under 16 years); (22) glass, p. 474; (23) paper mills, p. 497; (24) potteries, p. 510; (25) printing, p. 527; (26) rubber, p. 549; (27) shoes, p. 558; (28) slaughtering, p. 580; (29) tanneries, p. 591; (30) tobacco, p. 608.

IV.

How can these wage data be used to test the differential law of wages? Three difficulties must be solved before such a test can be made :—

(1.) The minimum wage to be assigned to the least efficient labourer in the standard population must be determined ;

(2.) The total amount to be divided between the 100 labourers in the standard population must be estimated;

(3.) Allowance must be made for the effect of the breaking up of the labour force into two groups of the unskilled, unorganised labour; and skilled, organised labour.

The following is offered as a solution of the first difficulty : The range of the efficiency of the standard population is about five times the standard deviation, that is, about two and a half times the standard deviation on each side of the mean. By referring to a table of the values of the normal probability integral corresponding to x/σ, it is found that 62 in 10,000 cases exceed two and a half times the standard deviation. Consequently from each end of the empirical series of wages given in Table 2 were subtracted 62 ten-thousandths of the total number of labourers. The resulting distribution of wages is given in Table 3. The minimum is therefore \$3.15.

The total amount divided between the 100 members of the standard population was regarded as one hundred times the average wage received by the labourers whose wages are given in Table 3. As the average wage in this case is \$11.43, the members of the standard population share between them \$1143.00.

The hypothesis which has been made to meet the third difficulty, namely, the effect in raising wages of the strategic advantage enjoyed by organised skilled labour, is that the more efficient 50 labourers in the standard population receive the same percentage of \$1143.00—the aggregate wages paid to the standard population —that the more efficient 50 per cent. of the labourers in actual industry receive of the aggregate wages paid to labour. This hypothesis is offered only as a first approximation in the absence of means of determining exactly the number of labourers directly and indirectly affected by organisation in the manufactures of the United States. From Table 3 it is found that the more efficient half of the labourers actually received 64·71 per cent. of the total amount of wages, and the less efficient half, the remaining 35·29 per cent. It was therefore assumed that the less efficient 50 members of the standard population received 35·29 per cent. of \$1143.00, and the more efficient half, the rest.

Our problem, now, is in this form : The wage received by the least efficient member of the standard population is \$3.15; the less efficient 50 members divide between them 35·29 per cent. of \$1143.00, that is, \$403.36 ; each of the 50 members receives the minimum wage and, in addition, a part of \$245.86—which equals \$403.36 minus 50 times \$3.15—determined by the excess of his efficiency over that of the man receiving the minimum wage. The more efficient 50 members divide between them 64·71 per cent. of \$1143.00, that is, \$739.64 ; each receives the highest wage paid in the group just described, namely, $10.30, and in addition a share of $224.64—which equals $739.64 minus 50 times $10.30—determined by the excess of his efficiency over that of the most efficient member of the less efficient group.

These 100 wage rates have been computed by means of Table 4. Columns I, II, V, VI have been taken from Table 1. Column III begins with the sum of the figures in column II. The meaning of this is that the difference in efficiency between the most able man in the standard population, and the fifty-first man is 2·526958 times the standard deviation. The second figure in column III is obtained by subtracting from the first figure in column III the first figure in column II. Since the difference between the ablest man, whom we call the first man, and the next ablest man, whom we call the second man, is ·360964 times the standard deviation, it follows that the difference between the second man and the fifty-first is 2·526958 − ·360964 = 2·165994 times the standard deviation. The other figures in column III are similarly determined by means of the figures in column II. The figure at the top of column IV, namely, 40·321478, is the sum of the figures in column III. Since the members of this more efficient of the two groups, which we shall call the first group, share the sum $224·64, according to the excess of their efficiency over the efficiency of the ablest member of the second group, it is necessary to express these 50 excesses or differences as percentages of the sum of the 50 differences. Column IV gives these percentages. For example, 2·526958 is 6·267 per cent. of 40·321478. As the wage received by the ablest member of the less efficient group is $10.30, and $224.64 is the sum divided by the members of the first group according to the excess of their efficiency over that of the ablest member of the second group, it follows that the wage of the ablest member of the standard population is $10.30 + (·06267)($224.64) = $10.30 + $14.08 = $24.38. In a like manner the wages of the remaining 49 members of the first group are determined by means of the percentages in column IV.

Columns VII and VIII are constructed from column VI in exactly the same way that columns III and IV were constructed from column II. The wage of the fifty-first man, who is the ablest member of the second group, is equal to the minimum wage of the group, $3.15 + (·029083) ($245.86) = $3.15 + $7.15 = $10.30. Similarly the wages of the other members of the second group are calculated.

In Table 5 the wages of the standard population, computed by the method which has just been described, are arranged in groups varying by $1, just as the wage data of the census report are arranged in Table 3.

On the accompanying chart the zig-zag line traces the percentage distribution of actual wages according to Table 3. The dashed curve, which has been computed by the method of moments from the data of Table 3, is the curve fitting best the observations. Its equation is given on the chart, the origin being at − 38·69. The distribution of the wages received by the standard population, which is also a percentage distribution, could likewise be given by

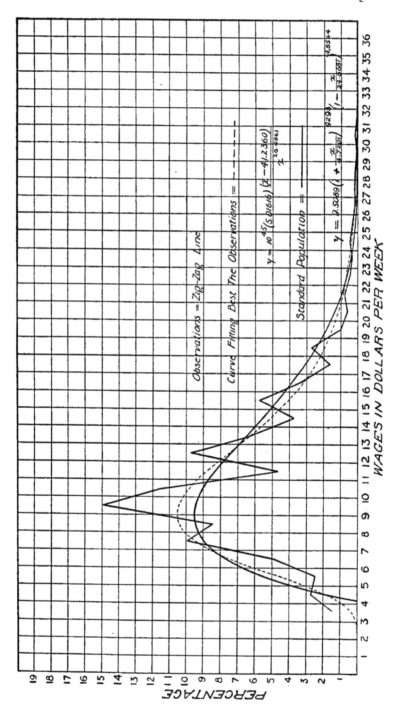

Observations = Zig-Zag Line

Curve Fitting Best The Observations = — · — · —

$$y = 10^{.45}(5.0i6i6)(\hat{x}-41.2360)$$
$$x^{2 \cdot .4861}$$

Standard Population = ————

$$y = 2.5089\left(1 + \frac{x}{4.7201}\right)^{.9291}\left(1 - \frac{x}{22.0081}\right)^{4.8554}$$

PERCENTAGE

WAGES IN DOLLARS PER WEEK

a zig-zag line. If this course were followed, however, inasmuch as the standard population is so small, we should get a very irregular distribution, which would give only an imperfect idea of the agreement of fact and theory. Instead, therefore, of crowding the chart with this line, a smooth curve has been computed by the method of moments from the data of Table 5, and is drawn on the chart. This curve, the equation to which is given on the chart (the origin being at 8·89), is the closest fit to the actual distribution of the wages of the standard population. It begins at $4.17, reaches a maximum at $8.89, and terminates at $33.56. The degree in which this continuous smooth curve approaches the dashed curve is the measure of the degree in which the differential law of wages receives an empirical verification in our statistical data.

This investigation has established :—

(1.) That, lacking a hypothesis as to the distribution of efficiency, the theory of reward according to efficiency is without significance so far as scientific uses are concerned ;

(2.) That the differential law of wages is only an important part of the productivity theory of wages, and that the establishment of the law of reward according to efficiency does not imply that the labourer receives what he produces ;

(3.) That by making a hypothesis as to the distribution of efficiency, and a reasonable allowance for the influence of the organisation of skilled labour, the differential law may be subjected to an empirical test ;

(4.) That when the particular hypothesis of this study is tested with the data afforded by the Wage census of 1900, we find a remarkable consilience of fact and theory.

APPENDIX.

The Construction of Table 1.   The Standard Population.

I. In computing the differences between the first six successive members of the standard population, Professor Pearson's formula,

$$\chi_p = s \frac{\sqrt{2\pi p}\; p^p e^{-p}}{\lfloor p} \frac{1}{n y_{,n}} \{1 + c_1 + c_2 + c_3\}$$ (where s is the standard

deviation), was used (*Biometrika*, vol. i, part iv, p. 396, formula xxvii).

II. Since, by Stirling's formula, when p is large, $\lfloor p = \sqrt{2\pi p}\; p^p e^{-p}$,

the factor $\dfrac{\sqrt{2\pi p}\; p^p e^{-p}}{\lfloor p}$, in the above formula for χ_p, approximates

to unity with increasing values of p. The last factor, $\{1 + c_1 + c_2 + c_3 + \}$, seems also to approach unity as p increases.

When p is 5, $\dfrac{\sqrt{2\pi p}\; p^p e^{-p}}{\lfloor p}\{1 + c_1 + c_2 + c_3\}$ is ·989794. It has

consequently been thought sufficient for the purposes of this article to compute χ_p by the formula $\chi_p = \dfrac{s}{n y_m}$ for values of p greater than 5 and less than 51.

III. The values of m, which are needed to obtain y_m, were computed from the formula $\dfrac{n - 2p}{n} = \sqrt{\dfrac{2}{\pi}} \displaystyle\int^{m} e^{-\frac{1}{2}x^2}\,dx.$ (*Ibid.*, p. 395, formula xii).

In making these computations the values of the probability integral, as given in *Merriman's Least Squares*, were used.

IV. The degree of accuracy of Table 1 is not so great as it appears to be, because, in the elevation of m, Barlow's tables were employed in calculating squares, and consequently only four figures were used. With this exception, the calculation has been carried to six decimals. The defect which has been described does not in any degree invalidate the theoretical result that has been reached, but it is noted here as a warning to others who, otherwise, might use the table for a purpose requiring greater precision.

TABLE 1.—*The Standard Population. Average Differences of Efficiency.*

p	$\dfrac{\chi_p}{s}$	p	$\dfrac{\chi_p}{s}$	p	$\dfrac{\chi_p}{s}$	p	$\dfrac{\chi_p}{s}$
1	·360964	26	·030822	51	·025074	76	·032160
2	·200664	27	·030247	52	·025098	77	·032937
3	·144746	28	·029710	53	·025137	78	·033769
4	·114680	29	·029207	54	·025192	79	·034686
5	·095994	30	·028755	55	·025266	80	·035700
6	·083843	31	·028347	56	·025354	81	·036854
7	·074499	32	·027967	57	·025458	82	·038131
8	·067258	33	·027614	58	·025583	83	·039512
9	·061599	34	·027287	59	·025732	84	·041081
10	·056909	35	·026994	60	·025881	85	·042871
11	·053146	36	·026725	61	·026061	86	·044913
12	·049990	37	·026486	62	·026260	87	·047250
13	·047250	38	·026260	63	·026486	88	·049990
14	·044913	39	·026061	64	·026725	89	·053146
15	·042871	40	·025881	65	·026994	90	·056909
16	·041081	41	·025732	66	·027287	91	·061599
17	·039512	42	·025583	67	·027614	92	·067258
18	·038131	43	·025458	68	·027967	93	·074499
19	·036854	44	·025354	69	·028347	94	·083843
20	·035700	45	·025266	70	·028755	95	·095994
21	·034686	46	·025192	71	·029207	96	·114680
22	·033769	47	·025137	72	·029710	97	·144746
23	·032937	48	·025098	73	·030247	98	·200664
24	·032160	49	·025074	74	·030822	99	·360964
25	·031479	50	·025066	75	·031479	100	—

Table 2.—*The Distribution of Wages in Manufactures of the United States in 1900, as represented by 30 Selected Industries.*

Rates per Week.	Number.	Rates per Week.	Number.
Below $2.00	21	$	
$		Between 27 and 28	362
Between 2 and 3	591	,, 28 ,, 29	300
,, 3 ,, 4	2,646	,, 29 ,, 30	175
,, 4 ,, 5	4,331	,, 30 ,, 31	359
,, 5 ,, 6	3,880	,, 31 ,, 32	107
,, 6 ,, 7	7,926	,, 32 ,, 33	131
,, 7 ,, 8	15,727	,, 33 ,, 34	103
,, 8 ,, 9	13,233	,, 34 ,, 35	104
,, 9 ,, 10	23,686	,, 35 ,, 36	73
,, 10 ,, 11	18,029	,, 36 ,, 37	51
,, 11 ,, 12	7,346	,, 37 ,, 38	115
,, 12 ,, 13	15,412	,, 38 ,, 39	195
,, 13 ,, 14	9,945	,, 39 ,, 40	198
,, 14 ,, 15	6,046	,, 40 ,, 41	53
,, 15 ,, 16	9,223	,, 41 ,, 42	41
,, 16 ,, 17	5,468	,, 42 ,, 43	36
,, 17 ,, 18	2,607	,, 43 ,, 44	25
,, 18 ,, 19	4,466	,, 44 ,, 45	23
,, 19 ,, 20	1,620	,, 45 ,, 46	20
,, 20 ,, 21	1,029	,, 46 ,, 47	12
,, 21 ,, 22	1,290	,, 47 ,, 48	16
,, 22 ,, 23	773	,, 48 ,, 49	23
,, 23 ,, 24	571	,, 49 ,, 50	12
,, 24 ,, 25	764	,, 50 ,, over	168
,, 25 ,, 26	520		
,, 26 ,, 27	224	Total	160,076

Table 3.—*The Percentage Distribution of Wages, between assigned Limits, in the Manufactures of the United States in 1900.*

Rates per Week.	Number.	Percentage.	Rates per Week.	Number.	Percentage.
$			$		
Between 3.15 and 4	2,266	1·43	Between 21 and 22	1,290	0·82
,, 4 ,, 5	4,331	2·74	,, 22 ,, 23	773	0·49
,, 5 ,, 6	3,880	2·45	,, 23 ,, 24	571	0·36
,, 6 ,, 7	7,926	5·01	,, 24 ,, 25	764	0·49
,, 7 ,, 8	15,727	9·95	,, 25 ,, 26	520	0·33
,, 8 ,, 9	13.233	8·38	,, 26 ,, 27	224	0·14
,, 9 ,, 10	23,686	14·98	,, 27 ,, 28	362	0·23
,, 10 ,, 11	18,029	11·41	,, 28 ,, 29	300	0·19
,, 11 ,, 12	7,346	4·64	,, 29 ,, 30	175	0·11
,, 12 ,, 13	15.412	9·75	,, 30 ,, 31	359	0·23
,, 13 ,, 14	9,945	6·29	,, 31 ,, 32	107	0·07
,, 14 ,, 15	6,046	3·83	,, 32 ,, 33	131	0·08
,, 15 ,, 16	9,223	5·83	,, 33 ,, 34	103	0·06
,, 16 ,, 17	5,468	3·46	,, 34 ,, 35	104	0·06
,, 17 ,, 18	2,607	1·65	,, 35 ,, 35.95	69	0·04
,, 18 ,, 19	4,466	2·82			
,, 19 ,, 20	1.620	1·03			
,, 20 ,, 21	1,029	0·65	Total	158,092	100·00

TABLE 4.—*Percentage Rates at which more Efficient Members of the Two Groups share the Excess over the Minimum Wage of the respective Groups.*

I. p	II. Difference $\dfrac{\chi_p}{s}$	III. Difference from the 51st Person.	IV. Percentage of 40·321478.	V. p	VI. Difference $\dfrac{\chi_p}{s}$	VII. Difference from the 100th Person	VIII. Percentage of 86·026422.
1	·360964	2·526958	·062670	51	·025074	2·501892	·029083
2	·200664	2·165994	·053718	52	·025098	2·476818	·028791
3	·144746	1·965330	·048741	53	·025137	2·451720	·028500
4	·114680	1·820584	·045152	54	·025192	2·426583	·028207
5	·095994	1·705904	·042308	55	·025266	2·401391	·027915
6	·083843	1·603910	·039927	56	·025354	2·376125	·027621
7	·074499	1·526067	·037847	57	·025458	2·350771	·027326
8	·067258	1·451568	·036000	58	·025583	2·325313	·027080
9	·061599	1·384310	·034332	59	·025732	2·299730	·026733
10	·056909	1·322711	·032804	60	·025881	2·273998	·026434
11	·053146	1·265802	·031393	61	·026061	2·248117	·026133
12	·049990	1·212656	·030075	62	·026260	2·222056	·025830
13	·047250	1·162666	·028835	63	·026486	2·195796	·025525
14	·044913	1·115416	·027663	64	·026725	2·169310	·025217
15	·042871	1·070503	·026549	65	·026994	2·142585	·024906
16	·041081	1·027632	·025486	66	·027287	2·115591	·024592
17	·039512	·986551	·024467	67	·027614	2·088304	·024275
18	·038131	·947039	·023487	68	·027967	2·060690	·023954
19	·036854	·908908	·022542	69	·028347	2·032723	·023629
20	·035700	·872054	·021628	70	·028755	2·004376	·023300
21	·034686	·836354	·020742	71	·029207	1·975621	·022965
22	·033769	·801668	·019882	72	·029710	1·946414	·022626
23	·032937	·767899	·019044	73	·030247	1·916704	·022280
24	·032160	·734962	·018228	74	·030822	1·886457	·021929
25	·031479	·702802	·017430	75	·031479	1·855635	·021571
26	·030822	·671323	·016649	76	·032160	1·824156	·021205
27	·030247	·640501	·015885	77	·032937	1·791996	·020831
28	·029710	·610254	·015135	78	·033769	1·759059	·020448
29	·029207	·580544	·014398	79	·034686	1·725290	·020055
30	·028755	·551337	·013674	80	·035700	1·690604	·019652
31	·028347	·522582	·012960	81	·036854	1·654904	·019237
32	·027967	·494235	·012257	82	·038131	1·618050	·018809
33	·027614	·466268	·011564	83	·039512	1·579919	·018366
34	·027287	·438654	·010879	84	·041081	1·540407	·017906
35	·026994	·411367	·010202	85	·042871	1·499326	·017429
36	·026725	·384373	·009533	86	·044913	1·456455	·016928
37	·026486	·357648	·008870	87	·047250	1·411542	·016408
38	·026260	·331162	·008213	88	·049990	1·364292	·015859
39	·026061	·304902	·007562	89	·053146	1·314302	·015278
40	·025881	·278841	·006915	90	·056909	1·261156	·014660
41	·025732	·252960	·006274	91	·061599	1·204247	·013999
42	·025583	·227228	·005635	92	·067258	1·142648	·013283
43	·025458	·201645	·005001	93	·074499	1·075390	·012501
44	·025354	·176187	·004370	94	·083843	1·000891	·011635
45	·025266	·150833	·003741	95	·095994	·917048	·010660
46	·025192	·125567	·003114	96	·114680	·821054	·009544
47	·025137	·100375	·002489	97	·144746	·706374	·008211
48	·025098	·075238	·001866	98	·200644	·561628	·006529
49	·025074	·050140	·001244	99	·360964	·360964	·004196
50	·025066	·025066	·000622				
Total	2·526958	40·321478	—	Total	2·501892	86·026422	—

TABLE 5.—*The Distribution of Wages of the Standard Population.*

Rates per Week.	Number.	Rates per Week.	Number.
$3.15	1	$	
$		Between 15 and 16	4
Between 4 and 5	2	,, 16 ,, 17 ..	4
,, 5 ,, 6	3	,, 17 ,, 18..	3
,, 6 ,, 7	6	,, 18 ,, 19	3
,, 7 ,, 8	9	,, 19 ,, 20.	2
,, 8 ,, 9	11	,, 20 ,, 21	1
,, 9 ,, 10	13	,, 21 ,, 22	1
,, 10 ,, 11	10	,, 22 ,, 23.	1
,, 11 ,, 12	7	,, 24 ,, 25	1
,, 12 ,, 13	6		
,, 13 ,, 14	6		
,, 14 ,, 15	6	Total	100

IV.—*Agricultural Returns of Great Britain, 1907.*

PRODUCE OF CROPS. *Preliminary Statement showing the Estimated Total Produce and Yield per Acre of the Corn, Pulse, and Hay Crops in Great Britain in the Year 1907, with Comparisons for 1906, and the Average Yield per Acre of the Ten Years 1897-1906.*

WHEAT.

	Estimated Total Produce.		Acreage.		Average Estimated Yield per Acre.		Average of the Ten Years 1897-1906.
	1907.	1906.	1907.	1906.	1907.	1906.	
	Quarters.	Quarters.	Acres.	Acres.	Bushels	Bushels	Bushels.
England	6,526,769	6,977,980	1,537,208	1,661,147	33·97	33·61	31·15
Wales	137,969	158,514	39,921	44,403	27·65	28·56	26·08
Scotland	236,428	249,977	48,307	50,059	39·15	39·95	38·83
Great Britain.	6,901,166	7,386,471	1,625,436	1,755,609	33·97	33·66	31·22

BARLEY.

England	6,290,730	6,246,063	1,411,163	1,439,708	35·66	34·71	32·88
Wales	349,622	377,576	90,622	92,834	30·86	32·54	31·27
Scotland	904,714	945,540	210,309	218,681	34·41	34·59	35·81
Great Britain.	7,545,066	7,569,179	1,712,094	1,751,223	35·26	34·58	33·14

OATS.

England	11,476,709	10,191,564	1.967,671	1,881,031	46·66	43·34	41·38
Wales	954,263	977,079	203.908	205,110	37·44	38·11	34·22
Scotland	4,369,313	4,254,462	951,011	956,816	36·76	35·57	36·38
Great Britain.	16,800,285	15,423,105	3,122,590	3,042,957	43·04	40·55	39·29

PRODUCE OF CROPS. *Preliminary Statement for Great Britain for* 1907—*Contd.*

BEANS.

	Estimated Total Produce.		Acreage.		Average Estimated Yield per Acre.		Average of the Ten Years 1897-1906.
	1907.	1906.	1907.	1906.	1907.	1906.	
	Quarters.	Quarters.	Acres.	Acres	Bushels	Bushels	Bushels.
England	1,270,988	1,190,807	295,129	274,779	34·45	34·67	29·28
Wales	5,635	4,756	1,572	1,300	28·68	29·27	25·84
Scotland	52,046	50,798	11,430	10,994	36·43	36·96	34·20
Great Britain.	1,328,669	1,246,361	308,131	287,073	34·50	34·73	29·50

PEAS.

England	587,788	559,417	159,431	148,034	29·49	30·23	27·15
Wales	2,214	2,911	845	858	20·95	27·15	21·41
Scotland	2,089	2,145	600	598	27·86	28·70	26·05
Great Britain.	592,091	564,473	160,876	149,490	29·44	30·21	27·10

HAY FROM CLOVER, SAINFOIN, &c.

	Tons	Tons			Cwts.	Cwts.	Cwts.
England	2,788,779	2,205,545	1,644,622	1,576,114	33·31	27·99	29·40
Wales	252,918	258,246	183,502	190,281	27·57	27·14	24·98
Scotland	717,934	737,178	422,195	425,192	34·01	34·68	32·34
Great Britain.	3,709,631	3,200,969	2,250,319	2,191,587	32·97	29·21	29·56

HAY FROM PERMANENT GRASS.

England	5,941,256	4,618,526	4,275,730	4,130,262	27·79	22·36	24·33
Wales	561,838	545,942	517,194	510,831	21·73	21·37	19·50
Scotland	216,163	219,096	143,011	142,767	30·23	30·69	29·59
Great Britain.	6,719,257	5,383,564	4,935,935	4,783,860	27·23	22·51	23·99

PRODUCE OF CROPS.   *Preliminary Statement giving the Estimated Yield of Potatoes, Turnips and Swedes, and Mangold in 1907.*

[The corresponding figures for 1906, and the Averages of the past ten years, are added for comparison.]

POTATOES.

	Estimated Total Produce.		Acreage.		Average Estimated Yield per Acre.		Average of the Ten Years 1897-1906.
	1907.	1906.	1907.	1906.	1907.	1906.	
	Tons.	Tons.	Acres	Acres.	Tons.	Tons.	Tons.
England	2,098,239	2,439,063	381,891	396,516	5·49	6·15	5·74
Wales	115,203	143,203	28,141	29,219	4·09	4·91	5·09
Scotland	764,468	846,228	138,888	140,186	5·50	6·04	5·93
Great Britain.	2,977,910	3,428,711	548,920	565,921	5·43	6·06	5·75

TURNIPS AND SWEDES.

England	14,651,158	14,104,146	1,058,292	1,082,821	13·84	13·03	12·19
Wales	881,936	934,997	58,496	59,143	15·08	15·81	14·81
Scotland	6,526,878	7,588,697	446,202	448,971	14·63	16·90	15·32
Great Britain.	22,059,972	22,627,840	1,562,990	1,590,935	14·11	14·22	13·15

MANGOLD.

England	8,689,323	8,288,300	436,193	418,415	19·92	19·81	19·24
Wales	203,864	203,385	11,056	10,621	18·44	19·15	16·93
Scotland	42,269	46,795	2,792	2,407	15·14	19·44	17·42
Great Britain.	8,935,456	8,538,480	450,041	431,443	19·85	19·79	19·17

Preliminary Statement showing the Estimated Total Production of Hops in the years 1907 and 1906, with the Acreage and Estimated Average Yield per Statute Acre in each County of England in which Hops were grown.

Counties, &c.	Estimated Total Produce.		Acreage Returned on 4th June.		Estimated Average Yield per Acre.	
	1907.	1906.	1907.	1906.	1907.	1906.
Kent—	Cwts.	Cwts.	Acres.	Acres.	Cwts.	Cwts.
East..	62,035	46,236	8,996	9,863	6·90	4·69
Mid	66,117	50,152	9,647	9,843	6·85	5·09
Weald......................	93,708	70,243	9,526	9,584	9 84	7·33
Total, Kent.......	221,860	166,631	28,169	29,296	7·88	5·69
Hants	17,865	10,263	1,842	1,939	9·70	5·29
Hereford.....	58,268	24,953	6,143	6,481	9·48	3·85
Salop	910	442	129	127	7·05	3·48
Surrey	7,089	3,399	744	777	9·53	4·37
Sussex	39,679	22,070	4,243	4,379	9·35	5·04
Worcester	28,216	17,893	3,622	3,672	7·79	4·87
Other counties*..........	242	37	46	51	5 25	0·72
Total	374,129	245,688	44,938	46,722	8·33	5·26

* Gloucester and Suffolk.

V.—*International Congress on Tuberculosis.*

AT the invitation of the National Association for the Study and Prevention of Tuberculosis, the International Congress on Tuberculosis will be held at Washington, D.C., from 21st September to 12th October, 1908. The section work of the Congress will be done in the week 28th September to 3rd October, but during the whole of the three weeks a Tuberculosis Exhibition will be open, and a course of Lectures by distinguished men will be in progress. Clinics and Demonstrations will be arranged for the whole period. The Departments of State, of the Treasury, of War, of the Navy, of the Interior, of Agriculture, and of Commerce and Labor of the United States have signified their intention of participating in the Congress.

The sectional work will be organised in seven sections : (1) Pathology and Bacteriology ; (2) Clinical Study and Therapy of Tuberculosis—Sanatoria, Hospitals and Dispensaries ; (3) Surgery and Orthopedics ; (4) Tuberculosis in Children—Etiology, Prevention and Treatment; (5) Hygienic, Social, Industrial and Economic Aspects of Tuberculosis; (6) State and Municipal Control of Tuberculosis ; (7) Tuberculosis in Animals and its relations to man. The papers announced in the official programme will be printed in advance, and distributed on the day of their presentation. The proceedings will be published within three months after adjournment.

The Exhibition will assemble illustrative materials from all parts of the civilized world. Members will find many opportunities to acquire or to increase, by exchange or otherwise, a valuable collection of illustrative objects. Literature forms an important part of many exhibits, and much of this can be obtained on the spot. Medals and money prizes are offered for specially meritorious exhibits.

There are two classes of Members : Active Members, who pay a subscription of $5, and receive, besides the ordinary privileges of membership, the full set of published transactions, without extra charge; Associate Members, who pay a subscription of $2, and receive the ordinary privileges of attendance at all meetings, etc., but do not receive the published transactions nor vote in the Congress.

Any Fellows of the Society who desire to see fuller particulars may refer to a copy of the " Preliminary Announcement " in the Library of the Society. The Secretary-General of the Congress is Dr. John S. Fulton, 810 Colorado Building, Washington.

NOTES ON ECONOMIC AND STATISTICAL WORKS.

CONTENTS :

PAGE

1.—Pearson (Karl). Further methods of determining correlation 655
2.—United States. Statistics of
women at work 656
3.—More (L. B.). Wage-earners'
budgets (New York) 659
4.—Rauchberg (H.). Die statistischen Unterlagen des Oester-
reichischen-Wahlreform 661
5.—Knibbs (G. H.). Classification of disease and causes
of death 662
6.—Australasia. Unification of
statistics 663
7.—Holmes (G. K). Meat
supply and surplus (U.S.A.) 664
8.—Heron (D.). Statistics of
insanity 667
9.—Agriculture, Board of, &c.
Wool production........................ 668

PAGE

10.—New York. Physical welfare
of school children........................ 670
11.—Tariff Commission. Vol. 3.
Agricultural report 671
12.—Levasseur (E.). Questions
ouvrières et industrielles en
France   674
13.—Foville (A. de). La monnaie 678
14.—Wampach (G.). L'impôt
sur le revenue en Allemagne .. 680
15.—Bremen. Wohnungen der
minder bemittelten Klassen.... 683
16.—Hull (W. H.). Practical problems in banking and currency.... 686
17.—Supino (C). Crisi econo-
miche 688
18.—Sundbärg(G.). Bevölkerungs-
statistik Schwedens (1750-1900) 690
19.— Correspondence 692
20.—Other new publications 693

1.—*On Further Methods of Determining Correlation.* By Karl Pearson,
F.R.S. 39 pp., 4to. London : Dulau and Co., 1907. Price 4s.

This memoir deals with some approximate methods for determining the correlation coefficient r between two variables, useful in
certain cases in lieu of the product-moment method. Thus r may
be expressed in terms of the standard-deviations of the two variables
and the standard-deviation of their difference; if the distribution
of frequency may be assumed to be normal, we may express the
standard-deviation of the difference in terms of the mean positive
difference, and thus shorten the work. If the means and standard-
deviations of the two variables are the same, as in certain symmetrical
tables, we have the further simplification—

$$ r = 1 - \pi \left[\frac{\Sigma(x - r)}{N . \sigma} \right]^2, $$

where the sum is taken for positive differences only. Professor Pearson
next proceeds to deal with "grade methods," as he terms them, *i.e.*,
methods based on that employed by Dr. Spearman, who obviated
the difficulty of dealing with the mental characters of children by
using the position of a child in class as the variable for correlation.
It is thus possible to deal with the correlations between the class
positions of a child in different subjects; and the method is
singularly simple, as the standard deviation σ is given by—

$$ \sigma^2 = \frac{1}{12} (N^2 - 1), $$

N being the number in class. Professor Pearson indicates errors in some approximate formulæ and in the probable errors given by Dr. Spearman, and points out that the correlation between the. *ranks* in two cases is not necessarily identical with the correlation between the values of the characters ranked. On the assumption of a normal distribution, Professor Pearson finds for the relation between the correlation of grades ρ and the correlation r between the values of the variables the singularly simple equation—

$$ r = 2 \sin \left(\frac{\pi}{6} \rho \right). $$

We do not concur with the writer, however, in his belief that "to make the rank into a unit itself cannot fail . . . . to lead to grave misconception." On the contrary, it seems to us a very important step in the simplification of methods of dealing with non-measurable characters. There is no such thing as "the true value of the variate" until some method of measurement has been agreed on; and there not only may, but should, be an indefinite number of correlations between variates, corresponding to one and the same correlation between ranks, until the method has been fixed, for the variable may be measured in an indefinite number of ways. G.U.Y.

2.—*Statistics of Women at Work; based on unpublished information derived from the Schedules of the Twelfth Census,* 1900. (Department of Commerce and Labor, Bureau of Census). 400 pp., 4to. Washington, 1907.

The statistics presented in this report on women employed in gainful occupations in the United States in 1900, like our own Census returns for 1901, are more usefully detailed and more readably presented than in previous years. Comparison with English conditions is rendered possible in many cases by the improvement on both sides. The American woman enters the labour market to a less extent than the English, Scotch, or Irish woman:—

Percentage of Women at Different Age-Periods in Gainful Occupations.

Age-Groups.	United States,* 1900.	England and Wales, 1901.	Scotland, 1901.	Ireland, 1901.
15 and under 25	30·6	60·8	64·7	43·6
25 „ 35	19·9	30·3	31·3	} 29·7†
35 „ 45	15·6	22·5	21·8	
45 „ 55	14·7	21·6	20·4	} 28 3†
55 „ 65	13·2	20·6	19·6	
65 and upwards . ..	9·1	13·2	14·3	30·5
15 and upwards ..	20·6	34·3*	35·4*	33·5*

* The figures for the United States include wives and daughters of farmers assisting in the work of the farm. These are not here included for the United Kingdom.

† The census for Ireland does not give returns for these two decades separately. The corresponding figures for Great Britain are:—

	England and Wales.	Scotland.
25 and under 45	26·9	27·2
45 „ 65	21·2	20·0

It may be suggested that the difference is due to the much greater proportion of rural population in the United States compared with the United Kingdom. But, apart from the fact that the percentage of women employed in Ireland at every age-group above 25 is higher than in the rest of the United Kingdom, the returns given for urban and rural districts in the United States Census and in the England and Wales Census show that the difference must be traced to other causes.

In the United States Report the occupations are tabulated separately for "cities with at least 50,000 inhabitants," and for "smaller cities and country districts." In the England and Wales report they are tabulated separately for *all* urban districts, however small, and for rural districts. It will be seen in the following table that even in our purely rural districts the percentage of women occupied is higher at every age-period than in the American mixed rural and small urban districts, and is higher than in American large towns, except between the ages of 25 and 45.

The United States figures refer to women of 16 years and upwards, those for England and Wales to women of 15 years and upwards. The percentage of girls of 15 years of age returned as occupied in the United States as a whole was only 21·4, of whom 5·1 were engaged in agricultural pursuits and 16·3 in other occupations (see *Child Labor in the United States*, p. 10). Were it possible to include them in the comparison the difference between the two countries would be even more apparent.

Percentage of Women Occupied.

Age-Period.	United States,* 1900.		England and Wales,* 1901.	
	Cities with at least 50,000 Inhabitants.	Small Cities and Rural Districts.	All Urban Districts.	Rural Districts.
16 and under 20	52·0	26·8	—	—
15 ,, 20	—	—	68·5	55·8
20 ,, 25	44·7	26·0	58·3	47·6
25 ,, 35	27·3	17·1	31·9	24·4
35 ,, 45	20·1	13·9	24·0	17·2
45 ,, 55	17·1	13·9	23·0	17·2
55 ,, 65	13·3	13·2	21·7	17·7
65 and upwards	7·5	9·5	13·3	13·0
16 ,,	28·3	18·0	—	—
15 ,,	—	—	36·5	27·2
	16 Years and Upwards.		15 Years and Upwards.	
Number of women living	5,840,321	17,572,077	9,005,620	2,513,195
Number occupied	1,653,518	3,162,418	3,286,428	683,996

* Relatives of farmers assisting in the work of the farm (so returned) are included in this table; in the rural districts of England and Wales they were 0·7 per cent. of the female population above 15 years.

In the United States, as in England and Wales, Scotland and Ireland, there was a decline in the proportion of domestic servants employed at every age-period. Notwithstanding this, the net result in the United States was an increase in the employment of women compared with 1890. If we subtract domestic servants from the total occupied, England and Wales still shows a decline, Scotland shows an increase, and Ireland is practically stationary.

Percentage of Women Occupied.

Age-Period.	1900.	1890.	Increase or Decrease on 1890.	1901.	1891.	Increase or Decrease on 1891.
	United States. Excluding "Servants and Waitresses."			England and Wales. Excluding "In-door Domestic Servants."		
15 and under 25	21·7	18·5	+ 3·2	38·0	35·9	+ 2·1
25 „ 35........	15·1	12·1	+ 3·0	20·2	21·7	− 1·5
35 „ 45......	12·7	10·1	+ 2·6	17·0	19·1	− 2·1
45 „ 55........	12·3	10·2	+ 2·1	17·1	20·3	− 3·2
55 „ 65........	11·3	9·7	+ 1·6	16·9	20·0	− 3·1
65 and upwards.....	7·8	6·5	+ 1·3	11·2	13·2	− 2·0
15 and upwards ..	15·6*	13·1*	+ 2·5	23·3*	24·4*	− 1·1

	1901.	1891.	Increase or Decrease on 1891.	1901.	1891.	Increase or Decrease on 1891.
	Scotland. Excluding "In-door Domestic Servants."			Ireland. Excluding "In-door Domestic Servants."		
15 and under 25 ...	46·7	43·3	+ 3·4	26·8	26·3	+ 0·5
25 „ 45...	20·2	20·1	+ 0·1	21·0	21·4	− 0·4
45 „ 65......	16·8	18·0	− 1·2	22·5	22·7	− 0·2
65 and upwards......	12·8	13·3	− 0·5	24·2	23·0	+ 1·2
15 and upwards...	26·5*	25·7*	+ 0·8	23·3*	23·4*	− 0·1

* In these comparative tables relatives of farmers assisting in the work of the farm are included for the United States but not for the United Kingdom.

So far as it is possible to compare the United States with England and Wales it would seem that the only important groups which show a greater employment of women in America than in England, are agriculture and clerical work. In the following table the names of the groups are selected from the United States census. Where the names differ from those in the English census, references are given to the latter :—

Number and Proportion of Women 15 Years and Upwards Occupied.

	United States, 1900.		England and Wales, 1901.		
	Number 15 and Upwards.	Per 1,000 of 15 and Upwards.	Number 15 and Upwards.	Per 1,000 of 15 and Upwards.	Reference to Census.
Agricultural pursuits	811,744	33·4	{ 38.45 ‡ 17,825*	{ 3·3 1·5*	
Housekeepers, janitors, servants and waitresses, laundresses and "other domestic and personal service" .	1,717,970	70·7	1,643,485	142·7	{ IV, 1, 2 and 3, and XX, 4 (sixth heading).
Teachers, professors, &c. (not music)	327,905	13 5	167,664	14·6	
Nurses and midwives	108,978	4·5	67,258	5·8	{ Sick nurses and midwives
Bookkeepers, accountants, clerks, stenographers, typewriters	243,458	10 0	54,445	4·7	Commercial clerks.
Telegraph and telephone operators	22,454	0·9	9,143	0·8	{ Telegraph and telephone service.
Dress, hat, shirtmakers, milliners, seamstresses, tailoresses, "other textile workers"	693,158	28·5	599,203	52·0	{ XIX, headings 2, 3, 4, 5, 7, 9, 10, 11.
Boot and shoe makers	38,285	1·6	40,905	3·6	
Textile mill operatives	250,376	10·3	532,869	46·3	XVIII, 1-6.
Tobacco and cigar factory operatives	40,325	1·7	17,663	1·5	{ Tobacco manufacture.
	4,254,653	175·1	3,188,914	276·8	
Other occupations ...	752,416	31·0	781,510	67·9	
Total occupied . .	5,007,069	206·1	3,970,424	344·7	

* Relatives of farmers returned as assisting in farm work.

C.E.C.

3.—*Wage-Earners' Budgets: a Study of Standards and Cost of Living in New York City.* By Louise Bolard More. xii + 280 pp., 8vo. New York: Henry Holt and Co. London: G. Bell and Sons, 1907.

The investigations on which this volume is based were undertaken by Mrs. More during the years 1903-05 on her appointment, by the "Greenwich House Committee on Social Investigations," to a resident Fellowship. Greenwich House is a social settlement on the lower west side of New York City, and the cordial relationship between the residents of Greenwich House and the people of the neighbourhood did much to render thorough enquiries possible. Frequent visits were made to each family during the time it was under observation, and every opportunity was taken of giving neighbourly help. The co-operation of charity and church visitors, teachers in kindergartens, nurses and others was also obtained, and some information collected through the members of a cookery class.

The facts as regards total income (for a year) and expenditure on food, rent, clothing, light and fuel, insurance and sundries were obtained for 200 families, and in 50 cases detailed budgets were kept for periods varying from one week to one year. The families are for the most part " wage-earners' families," but a few families of petty shopkeepers are included.

Greenwich is a district which is in a state of transition, exhibiting the extremes of housing conditions, from dignified, old-fashioned houses—owned for generations by the families still occupying them—to cheap tenements, tumble-down rear houses, and several disreputable courts and short streets. The population is very cosmopolitan ; of the heads of families investigated, 105 were born in the United States, 35 were Irish, 16 British, 17 German, 15 Italian, and the remaining 12 were distributed between France, Norway and Sweden, Switzerland, Austria, and Cuba. The trades and occupations of the heads of families (husband or wife) were very numerous ; but truckmen (22), long-shoremen (13), factory workers of various kinds (13), clerks (11), porters and casual labourers, janitors and washerwomen, were the most frequent. The Irish have the largest proportion of unskilled labourers, the Italians of skilled, and the Germans of the clerical class. The average size of "family"—*i.e.*, household including boarders—was 5·6. The incomes seem to have been estimated with considerable care, and it should be pointed out that any charity or gifts have been included. The actual household-incomes from all sources (not merely earnings of the head of the family) are as follows :—

Income.	Families.	Income.	Families.
$		$	
200—400 ..	11	800— 900	25
400—500 .	16	900—1,000	19
500—600 ...	16	1,000—1,200 . ..	28
600—700....	29	1,200—1,500 . ..	18
700—800...	27	1,500 and over	11

The average is $851.38, or roughly 170*l.* a year or 65*s.* a week, an income which Mrs. More regards as typical and representative. In those cases in which the head of the family was born in the United States, 69 per cent. of the income is derived from the husband's occupation, a percentage which falls to 58 for the English and Italians, 56 for the Germans, and 50 for the Irish. Taking the 200 families together, 43 per cent. (in round numbers) of the household income is spent on food, 19 per cent. on rent, 5 per cent. on fuel and light, 11 per cent. on clothing, 4 per cent. on insurance, 2·5 per cent. on intoxicating liquors, and the remainder on such miscellanea as recreation, car fares, &c. These percentages are very similar to those yielded by the 2,567 families throughout the United States for whom detailed particulars are given in the 18th Report of the U.S. Commissioner of Labor (1903), but exhibit, naturally, a higher proportionate expenditure on rent, which is compensated by a lower proportionate expenditure on clothing.

The detailed expenditure on food is given for 10 selected budgets. These budgets are not summarised or averaged, and consequently comparison with other food budgets, such as those given by the Board of Trade [Cd-2337, 1904] is difficult. The budgets are compared with each other by working out the "average cost per man," reducing women and children to their equivalent in men by Atwater's scale, the method used by Mr. Rowntree; this cost in the 10 budgets cited ranges from 17 to 31 cents, or, say, 8d. to 15d. These are, as would be expected, very high expenditures compared with those given in Mr. Rowntree's table for Class I, in York, in which the range is from 4·15d.—8·26d. only. Of the whole expenditure, 54 per cent. is expenditure on animal food, a figure which compares with about 50 per cent. on the average of the Board of Trade budgets for the United Kingdom, and 47 per cent. in London. Some interesting comparisons are made in Chapter VIII of the volume with the figures of Engel, Mr. Booth, and Mr. Rowntree, but for these we must refer to the work itself.

The value of such data as are here presented is very largely dependent on the opportunities which its workers are likely to possess of acquiring accurate information, and on the care with which such information is sifted and tested on the spot. So far as we can judge, the present work is in such respects satisfactory, and forms a valuable addition to the library on working-class budgets.

G.U.Y.

4.—*Die Statistischen Unterlagen der Oesterreichischen Wahlreform.* By Professor Dr. H. Rauchberg. 70 pp., 8vo. Brünn: F. Irrgang, 1907.

The recent reforms in the constitution of the Austrian electorate are of profound importance. The old complicated system with privileged classes of voters has been destroyed and (practically) adult male suffrage substituted in its place. Professor Rauchberg has collected a large quantity of electoral statistics and published them, with valuable comments, in the "Statistische Monatschrift." The most obviously interesting are those concerned with the representation of the different nationalities or groups of nationalities which compose the Empire of Austria. Roughly, the inhabitants are distributed locally by nationalities so that the minorities, who can never hope to have a national representative for the locality in which they live, are small, about 5 per cent. of the total population. The distribution of representatives amongst the separate nationalities is so interesting and important that the figures may be quoted here. Out of every hundred representatives there will be:—

	Per Cent.		Per Cent.
Germans	45·2	Slovenians	4·6
Czechs	20·7	Croats	2·5
Poles	15·9	Roumanians	1·0
Ruthenians	6·4	Italians	3·7

—from which it will be seen, first, that the Germans by themselves are in a minority; secondly, that the Slav block has just got a majority of the house, even if the Latin peoples combine with the Germans. But the balance is very even. If the figures are considered in greater detail we find that in four provinces (Upper and Lower Austria, Salzburg, and Vorarlberg) all the representatives will be German, and in five others (Styria, Carinthia, Tirol, Moravia, and Silesia) the majority of the representatives will be German. In Bohemia, as we should expect, the Czechs have a majority of representatives. In five provinces (Triest and district, Görz, and Gradiska, Istria, Galizia, and Dalmatia) there will be no German representatives; Germans, Ruthenians, and Roumanians are about equally represented in Bukowina; while Slovenians carry 90 per cent. of the seats in Carniola. Town dwellers have, as a whole, more representatives than countrymen, and this tells in favour of the Germans.

The interest of the figures is not confined to the points above mentioned, and this is not the place for a lengthened discussion of them in detail; it is only necessary to point out for the benefit of the readers of this *Journal* that Professor Rauchberg's statistics are a most useful mine in which those who are interested in electoral statistics may dig with profit.   C.P.S.

5.—*The Classification of Disease and Causes of Death, from the Standpoint of the Statistician.* By G. H. Knibbs, F.S.S., Commonwealth Statistician. (Reprinted from the *Intercolonial Medical Journal of Australasia* of 20th June, 1907.) 24 pp., 8vo. Melbourne, 1907.

This address deals in an interesting manner with the different systems of classifying diseases, from the standpoint of the statistician. Mr. Knibbs first discusses the essential features of nosology, pointing out that the scheme of any classification is determined by its specific aim, and that any classification based on medical knowledge must, in view of the rapid progress of medicine, be subject to occasional modifications. He then traces the history of classifications of disease, all of which in the English language are derived from Farr's original work. The considerations that Farr's groups of dietetic and miasmatic diseases would now be differently classified, and that the old division of diseases into local and general no longer holds good, sufficiently indicate the dangers of all classifications of disease; and it is regrettable that Mr. Knibbs has not boldly declared against all classifications in the sense of groupings of diseases, and stood by the paradoxical but true dictum which we may coin—the best classification is a mere enumeration.

This means that, apart from the vagaries of certificates of medical practitioners, which no system of classification will obviate, a mere enumeration of diseases and the number of deaths under each of them is much to be preferred to any grouping, however scientific it may appear. It leaves the individual investigator of vital statistics to make his own groupings, while not damaging the data for future use, however much nosological classifications may change. It should be added that there is no serious objection to the statement of group-headings, so long as the individual items are also fully stated. But it is the items which are valuable, not the grouped returns.

Mr. Knibbs leans to the use of the Bertillon system of classification, which fulfils the above conditions; as does likewise the system of the English Registrar-General, if the group-headings be ignored.

A.N.

6.— *Unification of Australasian Statistical Methods, and Co-ordination of the Work of the Commonwealth and State Bureaux.* Report of Conference, Melbourne, November—December, 1906. Fol. Melbourne, 1907.

The text of the last Presidential Address (November, 1907) was a plea for co-ordination of official statistics and statistical methods. In this Report, the arrival of which appears to be particularly opportune, we see what the Officials of Government Departments, who are not hampered by an excess of red-tape, can do when they tackle the question in a whole-hearted manner.

The Conference of last year was the eighth of a series, beginning in 1881, and the fact that uniformity has been the principal subject of discussion at six of the Conferences might be alleged as evidence of the hopelessness of ever achieving that aim. Circumstances have altered, however, since the beginning of the present century, in that the Commonwealth has been formed. The Report affords good reasons to hope that, under the guidance of the Statistician of the Commonwealth, the work of the Bureaux of the different States will be co-ordinated, and the various statistics collected and prepared on a uniform system. Inasmuch as the Statistician of New Zealand was a participant in the Conference, it may be anticipated that the system will spread to that Colony.

With the exception of one item, the scheme formulated in the Memorandum prepared by the Statistician of the Commonwealth was adopted unanimously by the Conference, as also were the tabular forms drawn up by him as representing the minimum of statistical data to be prepared by each State and the Commonwealth. The only point on which dissent was expressed was that of the manner of correcting the estimates of the populations. At present a system is in vogue of making allowances for unrecorded emigration and immigration. The Statistician of New South Wales was unable to give his adhesion to the system, as it had been found to give a steadily decreasing population for each State, an assumption which is contrary to practical experience.

It was agreed that the Bureaux of the States should furnish the Commonwealth with all information obtained in the ordinary routine of office work; that the former should abstain from publishing in their own reports information relating to the Commonwealth ; and that no departure should be made from the forms adopted by the Conference, except after any proposed variations had been submitted to and accepted by all the States.

It is interesting to note that multiplicity of areas without any system has grown up in Australia as in this country. The remedy suggested is to take the "police district" as the unit area, that body to be entrusted, it is proposed, with the collection of much of the information required.

Resolutions were adopted in favour of a quinquennial census, the intermediate one (as distinguished from the decennial at the usual date) to be limited to an enumeration of the people by sex and age. For the scheduling of causes of death Bertillon's system will be used, without alteration apparently. Further resolutions were agreed to with reference to the size of the reports and the order of sequence in which the different parts should be published.

From an examination of the 145 draft tables adopted by the Conference, we are of opinion that they will furnish all the data likely to be required by students in all branches of demography and sociology. The forms cover almost every conceivable variety of statistics—vital, economical, agricultural, commercial, judicial, etc., etc. We may be permitted to express the hope that great care will be taken in dividing the States into areas for purposes of tabulation. That very important matter was not dealt with at the Conference, but left to the decision of the Officers of the different States in consultation with the Statistician of the Commonwealth.

If the excellent system formulated by the Conference becomes really effective, a practical demonstration of the value of uniformity and co-ordinated action will be presented to us, which will, we hope, help to bring about those reforms in statistics of this country which have been so long desired.   R.D.

7.—*Meat Supply and Surplus, with Consideration of Consumption and Exports.* By George K. Holmes, Chief of the Division of Foreign Markets, United States Department of Agriculture. 100 pp., 8vo. Washington, 1907.

Compressed into the modest dimensions of one of the periodic Bulletins of the United States Bureau of Statistics, Mr. Holmes here presents the results of a very wide and laborious original investigation into the conditions of meat production and distribution. To the citizens of the States themselves the topic of their supply of animal food is always profoundly interesting, while there is in other lands a wide circle of consumers of American meat products gravely concerned in the dimensions and the destination of the surplus which remains, after satisfying the wants of a nation of 84,000,000 people. In the compass of a review it is not feasible to examine in detail the long array of compact tables, sixty-one in number, into which have been summarised all the various records and still more numerous estimates here presented. The method and sequence of the report may in parts leave room for some criticism ; and, of course, its author will be the last to deny, that some of the deductions made, and some of the data depended on, rather offer occasion for intelligent discussion than demand acceptance as authoritative facts.   The British reader also of these pages will stipulate for a little time for study of the author's language, in portions of the letterpress, for there is on this side of the Atlantic a want of familiarity with the phraseology, highly concentrated as it is, employed by American writers in dealing with the technicalities of the subject.   Moreover, even the warmest lover of figures accustomed to our relatively petty totals becomes timorous when he is confronted, as he is plentifully in these pages, with numerical aggregates expressed in thousands and tens of thousands of millions.   For this the smallness of the current units, alike of value and of weight, in the United States must be held responsible.

To the eye of many a statistician here a national meat production of 19,000,000,000 lbs., seven-eighths of which is consumed at home and one-eighth part exported, is bewilderingly huge, nor is the mind without reflection always ready to grasp that the value of the meat animals "on farms and ranges" in the United States is officially computed to exceed $2,000,000,000.   Much has to be added even to this figure to arrive at the aggregate capital employed.   Further estimates for animals "not on farms and ranges," for the value of the live stock farms and ranges themselves, for the machinery and implements they employ, and for the capital embarked in slaughtering, meat packing, lard refining, and oleomargarin establishments, carries the total to $10,625,059,223.   That vast estimate, we are reminded, reaches five-sixths of the value, put by the census authorities on the capital invested on all forms of manufacturing in the States, and is barely under the capitalisation estimate of the net earnings of steam railroads.

But it is necessary to trace the sequence of the leading subjects of this minutely detailed inquiry, commending it as we would do to the attention of the more active of our Fellows as offering more than one text for the discussion, not only of American, but of international problems.   Beginning with the estimates of capital embarked in the meat industry of the States and its relative proportion to other forms of wealth, Mr. Holmes at once passes to an exposition of the growth of the meat exports of his country, divided into what he calls the "historical" period of the trade, 1851-89, and the "recent" period, 1890-1906, culminating in what he regards as "the largest average" export of 2,200,000,000 lbs. He traces for twelve countries the share of each over the last seventeen years, reckoned in aggregate values and shown in numerous categories.   He specially calls attention to the "preferences" which he finds among foreign States for the purchase of fats, animal oils, and fat meat.   He, however, sets on one side the United Kingdom and Canada in this conclusion; in our own case because Great Britain is so dependent upon foreign food production as to be in a wholly abnormal position, and in the case of Canada because she is so nearly in a self-sufficient position.

Reviewing the world's live stock we are furnished with a table—which does not profess to be exhaustive, but which contains items that we have no means of checking here—wherein appear 424,500,000 cattle, of which 17·6 per cent. Mr. Holmes credits to his own country. The world's sheep are put at over 600,000,000, of which the United States own less than 9 per cent., while of an aggregate of 141,300,000 swine, 40 per cent., or no less than 56,600,000 head are in the States of the Union. Comparing meat animals and population within the United States, and excluding young stock under one year of age, it is shown, by an elaborate computation, whereby the meat equivalents of cattle, sheep and swine are merged in a statistical unit or "composite animal," that there was available 1·043 of such composite animal *per capita* of population in 1840, but only 0·709 of such an animal in 1900—a steadily declining ratio. This has been accompanied by increase in the exports of meat and its products, and the calculations made indicate that 12·68 per cent. of the meat produced in 1900 was exported, while ten years before it was only 8 per cent. Allowing for these exports, the conclusion is hazarded that if the "domestic consumption stock" bore to population in 1840 a ratio of 100, that of 1900 was little more than 59. In the latest period reviewed, 1890-1900, the domestic consumption stock of meat animals declined almost exactly one-fourth *per capita*.

One can only here commend to the study of agricultural statisticians the plan adopted in estimating yearly meat productions in the States—by direct enquiry from breeders, feeders, live-stock commission men, and slaughtering and meat-packing houses, large and small. The elaborate circular of inquiry, as to the numbers, and weights, and classes of animals, proceeds on the lines of the recent Reports of this Society, whose work is fully referred to here, although not made the basis of the American inquiry. In one section of the present report comparisons are offered dealing with meat consumption in the United Kingdom, in Germany, France, Italy, and elsewhere. Deferring, however, for a better occasion the reproduction of some of the many interesting tables here presented, it may be worth while to quote, as against the estimate of 121·8 lbs. per head as the consumption attributed to the people of the United Kingdom by this Society's investigation in 1903, that Mr. Holmes' report puts the United States average as high as 185·8 lbs. per head for dressed meat. He makes, it is true, another estimate of 220·5 lbs. for both "dressed and extra edible parts"; and yet again he quotes 182·6 lbs. as representing the "*edible, dressed, and extra edible parts.*"

Without a careful analysis of the items making up these varying descriptions of the aggregate of meat consumption, it is somewhat difficult to compare these statements, but we are helped to see what is meant by the explanation offered that of the three "aspects" of the supply, only the first—"dressed meat"—can be regarded as comparable with foreign estimates. This dressed weight is put down as the product of the annual slaughter of 93,502,000 animals (cattle, sheep, and swine) with a *live weight* totalling, we are told, 26,864,810,000 lbs., which afforded a dressed product of 16,549,921,000 lbs. But we are reminded, for the benefit of inquirers of another type, who are concerned, not with total weight, but with nutrition and dietetics, that 3,315,441,000 lbs. of the last quoted figure were "bones and non-edible trimmings," while, *per contra*, an item of 2,636,409,000 lbs., made up of parts outside of the conventional dressed weight, must, in a strict reckoning of eatable meat, be added to balance, these various corrections resulting in a "net meat weight" of 15,870,889,000 lbs., which, being expressed in our terser British phraseology, would mean more than 7,000,000 tons as the aggregate yearly ration of the inhabitants of the United States.

The report, in any case, with its incidental references to the course of prices, the rates of consumption by families, the consumers' meat bill, and the nutritive equivalents of meat and other foods, may be regarded as a mine waiting for the hand of the expert explorers of this class of statistics; and it will claim a very cordial word of thanks to its author for his most exhaustive investigation of a very difficult subject. P.G.C.

8.—*A First Study of the Statistics of Insanity and the Inheritance of the Insane Diathesis.* By David Heron, M.A., Galton Research Fellow in National Eugenics, University of London. 33 pp., 4to. London: Dulau and Co. Price 3s.

This investigation into the inheritance of insanity is founded on material provided by Dr. A. R. Urquhart, of the James Murray's Royal Asylum, Perth. The records consist of the family trees of 331 asylum patients, giving the brothers and sisters of the patient, and classifying each as insane, neurotic, epileptic, &c., or normal. Similar facts are given concerning the parents of the patient, and where possible concerning the grandparents and children also. These data refer, however, solely to tainted stocks, and to complete the investigation as to heredity it is necessary to form some estimate as to the number of living persons in Scotland who have at any time been insane; on various assumptions and by different persons this is estimated at two to four times the asylum population. The inheritance is very marked, the coefficient of correlation (calculated by Professor Pearson's fourfold table method) between the presence of insanity in parent and offspring lying between 0·52 and 0·62. The correlation between brothers is 0·44—0·51. Insane persons, it would seem, are slightly less fertile than normals, but the average size of family is no less than 5·18; the insane stocks, moreover, including the members who did not actually exhibit insanity, seem quite as fertile as normals, the average family being 5·97—infertile marriages apparently excluded in both cases. There seems to be a somewhat greater tendency for insanity to fall on the first-born than on those of later birth. The results generally are very similar to those obtained by Professor Pearson in his memoir on the inheritance of tuberculosis issued by the same publishers. Dr. Heron's work seems to us an interesting and valuable contribution to the subject. G.U.Y.

9.—*Board of Agriculture and Fisheries. Report on the Production of Wool in Great Britain in* 1905 *and* 1906. 59 pp., 8vo. London : Darling and Son, 1907.

Among the different signs, which have encouraged the British agriculturist of late to hope that the tide of depression has finally turned, a marked advance in the price of wool has been not the least conspicuous or important. As the Report before us states, "the rise which has taken place in the price of British wool since 1902 has probably surpassed in its rapidity and extent any change in agricultural values which has occurred during the whole period since what is usually termed the depression set in. It appears that in the short period of three or four years the value of the year's clip was enhanced by about 100 per cent." This decided rise, it would seem, has affected, "in varying degree, every variety " of wool ; and, while in the latter of the two years with which the present Report deals (*i.e.*, 1906), the " advance received," for a few months, "some check," "on the whole the upward movement continued," and the rise during the year amounted to nearly 1½*d.* per lb. Since 1902 it has been on the average about 6½*d.* per lb. (or 100 per cent.). It is possible that some portion of this increase of price may be due to a change which is now affecting prices generally in a direction opposite to that caused by the appreciation of gold which accompanied the earlier depression. It is also possible, and probable, that special influences, such as a temporary scarcity produced by serious drought diminishing the Australian output, may have contributed their particular force to the general movement ; and the total annual imports of wool from foreign countries and British possessions, which are given in a table of the Report, after rising from 468,000,000 lbs. for the triennial period, 1880-82, to 745,000,000 lbs. in 1895-97, fell gradually to 611,000,000 lbs. in 1904-06. It is interesting, and instructive to note, that the proportion of foreign wool to the total was about 13 per cent. in 1880-82, nearly 17 per cent. in 1887-89, 13 per cent. again in 1892-94, and 19 per cent. in 1904-06.

It is, accordingly, at an opportune moment that this new Report has been prepared and issued by the Board of Agriculture and Fisheries. A successful endeavour has been made to meet the previous deficiency of official information on the subject, and more definite particulars than have hitherto been available have now been collected from the Agricultural Correspondents and Market Reporters of the Board, as well as from flock-masters and wool-buyers in different localities. In 1905 two circulars of inquiry were issued, one to wool-growers and representative agriculturists, asking for an estimate of the average weight of fleece in their county for two classes of sheep (*i.e.*, breeding ewes and other sheep over 1 year), and the other to wool-buyers, asking for the number and total weight of fleeces of 1905 clip purchased, and of the districts and kinds of sheep from which they came, and for an opinion on the comparison of the clip of the year with the average. The replies to the first circular numbered 1,115 and to the second 104. But before the results were published the circulars of inquiry were repeated in 1906 in a slightly altered form, and were sent to all who had answered the earlier inquiry. The number of answers received from flock-masters this year was 791 and from wool-buyers 72. But, although the replies received were thus less numerous than in 1905, they could be used, with advantage, to check the earlier returns, and the Board of Agriculture and Fisheries now consider that data are available for forming a "fairly reliable basis for an estimate of the total quantity of wool annually grown in Great Britain." For each county in turn the Report furnishes information respecting the number of sheep, the chief breeds of which they consist, and the average weight of fleece. Supplementary information is also given respecting the prevalence or the reverse of washing.

About the advantage of this practice expert opinion seems divided ; and, although a rise, or the prospect of a rise, in price appears in many instances to turn the scale in favour of the practice, the most experienced flock-masters are by no means agreed on its advisability. It may be noticed, however, that on the other side of the question, which is presented in the opinions, also collected in the Report, of the wool-buyers, there seems to be a fairly general accord that carelessness is shown by British flock-masters in placing their wool upon the market, as contrasted with the methods followed with advantage by Colonial growers; and from this standpoint, even if washing be mainly dependent on the price secured, as many wool-buyers admit, the neglect of the practice possesses more significance. Colonial wool, it would appear, is graded, while British wool is generally mixed together ; by shearing the sheep on straw this unwelcome element makes its way into the fibre, and depreciates the wool; and the old practice of tying fleeces with cord or rope which leaves a little hemp behind operates to the same effect, and has not been abandoned by the farmers of some districts. These *obiter dicta* may serve to show that the Report is not a mere collection of statistical material, however valuable, but is both entertaining and instructive.

The Report does not pretend to furnish an exhaustive catalogue of the breeds of sheep or a complete census of their local distribution, but it supplies some contributory data. The number of separate breeds for which estimates of wool-production have been supplied is 29, the most widely-distributed being the Blackfaced and the Cheviots, and, in a somewhat less degree, the Border Leicesters. Of the English breeds five are prominent, namely, Hampshires, Shropshires, Oxford Downs, Southdowns, and Lincolns. The final estimate of the annual production of wool reached for the United Kingdom in the two years covered by the Report is 133,088,000 lbs., but the figure for Ireland alone, which was not comprised in the inquiries made directly by the Board, has been furnished by the Department of Agriculture and Technical Instruction for that country, and is 12,000,000 lbs. This total figure of 133,088,000 lbs. does not, it may be noticed, differ greatly from the commercial estimates published by the *Yorkshire Observer* for these two years. For 1905 the estimate was 130,529,000 lbs., and for 1906 it was

130,176,000.   Since 1872 the annual estimates given by that paper have, it may be remarked in conclusion, ranged from 128,000,000 lbs. in 1883 to 167,000,000 lbs. in 1874.   In 1858 Mr. E. Baines put the total clip at 175,000,000 lbs., in 1845 it was estimated by Professor Low at 157,000,000 lbs., in 1828 by Mr. James Hubbard and Sir George Goodwin at 111,161,000 lbs., and in 1800 by Mr. Luccock at 94,377,000 lbs.   The present Report is an important authoritative addition to these private calculations, which were quoted by Major Craigie in a paper read before the Statistical Society and published in this *Journal* in 1883.   L.L.P.

10.—*Physical Welfare of School Children.   An Examination of the Home Conditions of 1,400 New York School Children found by School Physicians to have Physical Defects.*   By New York Committee on Physical Welfare of School Children.   (*Quarterly Publications of the American Statistical Association*, new series, No. 78 (vol. x), June, 1907.)   44 pp., 8vo.   Boston : The Association, 1907.

The voluntary Committee above named was organised in May, 1906, funds having been provided for three years' work.   In organising their work the Committee very wisely substituted the word *welfare* for *condition*, to indicate their intention to use the facts obtained through investigation for improving home and school conditions prejudicial to child welfare.   They collected, to begin with, funds for three years' work, home investigation, investigation of schools, and investigation of school methods ; and the present report embodies the first year's work under the first of the above headings.   It discloses the facts as to physical defects and home conditions of 1,400 children of different nationalities found by school physicians to have defects of hearing, vision, breathing, teeth, nourishment.   A copy of the statistical card employed in the investigation is given.   The investigation was worked in conjunction with the school doctor's card report of physical defects found in the course of medical inspection of scholars at school.   The home investigators were also doctors.   The cost of the home investigation of the 1,400 cases was $2,416, not including supervision given by social workers on the Committee, &c.   Where material relief seemed to be needed the family apparently needing it was at once referred to another voluntary organisation.   During the year 271 out of 3,690 families visited were so referred, and received various forms of relief as needed—clothing, rent, food, eyeglasses, and medical care.   The "follow-up" work after these investigations is recognised as the real practical difficulty, and the Committee are unable to speak very definitely on this point, except in the cases referred as above. They comment similarly on the little use hitherto made by health or school officials of facts disclosed by physical examination of school children.   A more general system of informing the parents of the defects found in the children is evidently called for.

The most significant facts obtained from this study of home conditions affecting the physical welfare of school children are summarised in the report.   It is stated that if New York children are typical of school children in the United States, there must be in the schools of that country 12,000,000 children having physical defects needing attention from parents and doctors. Similarly, if the 1,400 children are representative of school children in New York city, there must be in that city 41,600 handicapped by malnutrition, 182,000 by enlarged glands, 382,800 by bad teeth, 236,400 by defective breathing. · It is noted that few of the defects can be corrected by nourishment alone, that neither race nor nationality affords proof against physical defects, and that only 7·8 per cent. of the children had failed to have a good start by being artificially fed from the beginning. The housing conditions of the children were generally bad, inadequate medical care was given to the children, and the employment of dentists was almost unknown. It is also noted that families with low incomes do not monopolise physical defects, though they show more than their proper share of these.

Many would incline to draw a sombre forecast from the above list of physical defects. That we are glad to note is not the view of this most valuable committee. They say : " The only new thing about the physical defects of school children is not their existence, but our recent awakening to their existence, their prevalence, their seriousness if neglected, and their cost to individual children, to school progress, to industry, and to social welfare." The first step towards improvement is knowledge of evils, and this step is being taken on both sides of the Atlantic. We commend this report to the notice of all social workers.   A.N.

11.—*The Tariff Commission.*   Vol. 3. *Report of the Agricultural Committee.* London : P. S. King and Son, 1906.

The investigations of Mr. Chamberlain's Tariff Commission possess a great interest, not only to supporters, but also to opponents of the changes to promote which its efforts are put forth. The report on agriculture possesses peculiar interest in many respects, and the conclusions and recommendations of the Committee which has examined this subject may be very instructively compared with the statement of the situation and the historical sketch which serve as a prelude. To these, rather than to the mass of detail contained in the bulky volume forming the report and appendix, attention must be confined in the brief space available here.

With the record of abandonment of wheat cultivation we are but too familiar; and the increasing dependence on imported supplies is patent. But the compilers of the report seem to have carried a mechanical process of calculation rather far when they declare that, in the first five years of the twentieth century, only 4·5 millions of the population were fed on home-grown wheat. The tables they give us show an average yield in those years of about 52 millions of bushels. The imports, on the assumed consumption of 5·5 bushels per head, may suffice for all but 4·5 millions of the population, but that scarcely justifies the conclusion that the 52 million bushels of the home crop, less seed, were consumed by that surplus of 4·5 millions. In fact, at the same rate of 5·5 bushels per head, the needs of the population would be about 235 million bushels, and of this amount the 52 millions of home-grown wheat form 22 per cent. How, then, demonstrate that only 10·6 per cent. of our people were fed on home-grown wheat? The realities of the case would have yielded a result reasonably satisfactory for the argument desired, and it seems a pity to proceed about the work with such strange contradictions at the outset. Moreover, on another page the home supplies are shown at about 19 per cent. of total consumption. It is, perhaps, also pertinent to the argument to call attention to the fact that, even assuming that the 2 millions of acres of wheat land, representing the reduction of wheat cultivation in thirty years, could be made to yield as high an average return as the land remaining under wheat, the addition to home supplies would be no more than 63 million bushels. Even with this addition, the need for imported wheat would be very great, for imports would still need to be considerably greater than home supplies. And at what cost could 30 bushels per acre be extracted from the land in question? The difference between the production of thirty years ago and of 1901-05 is not 63, but 42 millions of bushels, and as to the degrees in which the difference between these two amounts may be ascribed to improved cultivation of our day as compared with thirty years ago, and to the inferior quality of the soils withdrawn from wheat cultivation, the present writer ventures no opinion.

Turning to another point, we find in the report the statement that home-fed meats represent now 55 per cent. of the consumption as against 85 per cent. thirty years ago. The tables in the report show a growth of 23 per cent. in the consumption per head, which goes a long way towards accounting for the contrast of these figures. Further, the home supplies are calculated on the hypothesis that the annual meat yield of a given stock of animals has been unchanged in the thirty years. Is it safe to base, on such an assumption, the assertion that the increase of area given to pasture has practically had no effect on the food supply except to reduce the yield of corn, &c.? However difficult it may be to estimate the degree of change, is it very unlikely that, from a given number of mature animals, the meat yield year by year is greater now than formerly? In any case, the statement that dairy farmers have given more attention to milk production might be regarded as some explanation of a larger pasture area without much increase of meat yield. It is associated with an increase of 140 per cent. in imported dairy products, but the very association seems to suggest that the growing population has called for more dairy products, including milk, than were available without importation, and that, to meet the deficiency, those dairy products which could best be procured from a distance have shown increased imports.

Proceeding with the examination of the conclusions in the light of the reported evidence; we find that the volume of food imports is estimated to have increased nearly four times as much (per cent.) as the population. Now this result becomes much less striking, and may even have an altogether different significance if we read the facts from another standpoint. The increase of imports of food has been, in value, 81,000,000*l.*, comparing 1905 with 1875. The increase of population has been fully 10,000.000. Many indications suggest that the food consumption per head has increased in the interval, and it must not be forgotten that a significant change has occurred in the proportion of adults in the total population. Now, if the valuation of food supplies as made for the comparison of home and imported produce justify an estimate of total supply now at 8*l.* per head, the total will be about 344,000,000*l.*, and the home contribution 139,000,000*l.* If we could assume a consumption thirty years ago of one-eighth less per head, and also that prices are now 30 per cent. below the level then reached, the outlay per head would then have been 10*l.*, and the total about 330,000,000*l.*, of which the home contribution would be 206,000,000*l.* At a reduction of 30 per cent. in prices, this 206,000,000*l.* would now represent 144,000,000*l.* The comparison of this with the 139,000,000*l.*, estimated on the assumed basis for current production, shows little change in quantity produced, although the numbers engaged at the work are greatly diminished, and there are reduced areas under crop. The figures of this calculation are not put forward as ascertained and reliable figures, but they are more moderate in their estimate of outlay thirty years ago than the well-known figures of Sir Robert Giffen, though not as low as other estimates referring to the late seventies and early eighties. The figures of population have been taken roughly, but the object has been to show that, on assumptions not unreasonable in themselves, the assertion that the foreign producer has taken his market from the British farmer needs to be assigned a somewhat special meaning if it is to be true. As the assertion is made "especially of wheat and meat," the fact that meat production is admitted in the report not to have fallen off, but rather the contrary, seems to indicate that such a special meaning is attached to the phrase.

If anything like the results suggested by the above hypothesis be the actual facts, the decline in agriculture is a decline in values produced, and but in modest degree, if at all, in output. It seems hard to believe that one kind of produce can so largely have replaced others, but it is not inherently beyond belief.

The record of the past which forms part of the report is enriched by numerous small diagrams, many of which are devoted to comparing the price movement in England and on the Continent in the nineteenth century. The general result is to show that the price of wheat in England was higher than on the Continent up to about thirty years ago, and that since that time it has been lower, while prices in the chief Continental countries have not failed to fall at the same time as ours. Could it be more clearly shown that the price of the commodity is affected by tariff charges? And yet we are assured that the adoption of import duties here would not raise the prices of the dutiable goods!

Our space will not permit of an examination of the non-fiscal remedies proposed for the evils of the agricultural position. More might easily be said, and much profit derived from close attention to such remedies. The fiscal proposals seem strangely inadequate if we are to believe in the seriousness of the situation as sketched by the compilers of the report, and not regard the colours they use as unduly sombre. An import duty of 2*s.* per quarter, on the face of assurances that no price under 40*s.* will substantially affect the area under wheat, seems to suggest a belief that the duty is desirable even if it has no effect on British agriculture. Five per cent. on meat and 5 to 10 per cent. on other produce are figures which suggest but little belief either in the need of transforming the existing situation or in customs duties as an instrument for that purpose. It seems incredible that such small duties can be expected to solve such large problems, and if they produce little good to the agriculturist they might easily result in no small ill to the rest of the population.

The voluminous appendix to the report gives a summary of numerous opinions gathered by the Committee, as has been customary with preceding reports. It has seemed best in this notice to confine attention to the pronouncement of the Committee, as there was so much in it which called for comment.   A.W.F.

12.—*Questions Ouvrières et Industrielles en France sous la Troisième République.* Par E. Levasseur. lxxii + 968 pp., 8vo. Paris: Arthur Rousseau, 1907.

With this large volume, containing more than a thousand pages, the veteran French economist and statistician brings to a worthy close the monumental contribution he has made to the industrial history of his country. As he hints in the concluding paragraphs of his Preface, which have the peculiar interest attaching to autobiographical remarks, he has now earned by advancing years the right to lay aside the powerful armour he has worn to such effective purpose through so long and active a career. But he will perhaps allow us to observe that we cannot discover in these pages any indication of the failing strength which sometimes justifies retirement. M. Levasseur's judgment indeed on controversial matters in this as in his other writings has the ripeness and the weight which are the just prerogatives of age; and the rich stores of profound and accurate erudition he has accumulated by strenuous, protracted and extensive study are once again freely placed at the disposal of his readers. They, we are sure, will gratefully appreciate the practised skill which enables him to place before their attentive gaze a mass of various material arranged in such appropriate order that its significance can be grasped with ease and without delay. They will note with admiration the facility with which so accomplished and informed a statistician indicates the interpretation which can legitimately be drawn from the copious and diversified numerical data he has collected and examined for their benefit. But they will also find that the alert and vigilant eyes of the compiler of these exhaustive chapters have not allowed fresh material of the most recent date, which bears directly or indirectly on the topics which are here successively discussed, to escape attention or appraisement; and, while he does not attempt to hide the verdict he has formed on certain heretical opinions, such as those professed by collectivists, or refrain from the confident expression of his firm belief in the superior advantages shown by trade statistics to attach to the more free *régime* in fiscal matters established in his country during special periods of the history he narrates, yet his views are stated with a liberality and moderation that may fairly be regarded as sure symptoms of an openness of mind to new suggestions such as will be rarely found with men of more than middle age, whose convictions have naturally been definitively shaped into rigid moulds. The balanced temper, with which he affirms the mutual benefit that economic science and economic history may derive from one another, if pursued in harmony, and not in opposition, is happily a general characteristic of the calmer period, in which we are now fortunate enough to live, as contrasted with the stormy controversies of a preceding generation on the methods of economic study, and is not a peculiar feature of M. Levasseur's book alone. But it is typical of his mental attitude, and will be welcome to his readers.

He began his researches in French economic history more than half a century ago ; and the new editions of those special studies of the status and the fortunes of the working classes, to whom he has given so much of his attention since, which were published a few years ago, and were reviewed in 1904 in this *Journal*, were separated from their first editions by periods of little less considerable a length. In the first portion of his work, it will perhaps be remembered, he traced the history anterior to the Revolution, of which, as he remarks, privilege and authoritative regulation were the dominant characteristics in the sphere of industry. The second section of his work, which stretched from 1789 to the end of the second Empire, described a period when, by contrast, liberty, seconded by science, was conspicuous. Its termination indeed was not fixed by so natural or obvious or definite a limit as that set by the overthrow of the "ancien régime" at the Revolution ; and for that reason the third and concluding period, handled in the present final volume, exhibits to some extent the same outstanding features, for the results of scientific discovery have been applied to the development or transformation of industry with astonishing effects, and labour has secured in fuller and fuller measure the freedom it has sought. But other causes have interposed ; and the period, which has elapsed since 1870, has, he declares, been specially characterised by the study of those fresh problems which concern the organisation of the workers and the distribution of wealth. M. Levasseur admits of course that the conditions must be less favourable for forming a final judgment on contemporary events than they are for pronouncing a decision on the incidents and personages of the past. The necessary detachment is hard, if it is not impossible, to secure. Even narrators of past history, whether near or more remote, are rarely, if ever, immune from prejudice. But, as he himself does not and cannot attempt, dealing with so recent a period as that covered by the Third Republic, to place matters in their true historical perspective, he has adopted a method of arrangement different from that followed in the earlier sections of his work. Here indeed, as there, he has had recourse to original documents for his evidence ; but he has treated in successive chapters different topics, without aiming at a rigid chronological sequence. In the first instance he has dealt with the products of industry, and in the second with the producers. He first discusses things, and then he treats of men.

After an introduction, containing a sketch of the political history of the Third Republic, he traces the progress and vicissitudes of French industry since 1870, under the three main divisions of agricultural produce, preparatory industries, which are concerned with the extraction and preparation of materials, and industries which are more directly and immediately subservient to the requirements of personal consumption. The next chapter is devoted to the industries managed by the State; and the third deals with industrial legislation. In the fourth, the means of communication —with special reference to railway policy—and the domestic and foreign commerce of France under the Third Republic, are examined. The position and record of the Bank of France are reviewed, and the growth and development of Protection are described. With the following chapter M. Levasseur passes to the second main section of his treatise. He leaves behind him the products of industry and turns his attention henceforth to the producers. The population of France generally, and the industrial population in particular, are first discussed. Then education, primary and technical, is reviewed. Then an interesting sketch is given of the development of economic and social doctrines; then the laws affecting the working classes are investigated; then a careful estimate is made of the rate of wages and the cost of living; and, in a following chapter, a similar valuation is attempted of the wealth possessed by the French people. Chapters on strikes and the "syndicats," which correspond to our Trade Unions and Employers' Associations, on Co-operation and Trusts, on the provision made for future need, and the agencies formed for present help, on housing accommodation and charitable organisation, on the condition of the workers in the workshops and outside their work, complete this section of the book. And, finally, in a chapter described as an "epilogue," M. Levasseur summarises the main conclusions he has reached.

The summary description we have given of the contents of the various chapters will serve to show that this account of industrial questions in France under the Third Republic is no less interesting and exhaustive than the records of earlier history which were presented in the former portions of M. Levasseur's treatise noticed in this *Journal* three years ago. This large volume is in its turn a veritable storehouse of valuable information indispensable to the student of such questions. It abounds with suggestive observations and shrewd *aperçus;* it presents an immense ordered mass of exact and pertinent facts. The minute care which M. Levasseur has bestowed on each department of his subject is evident on every page. He has spared no pains to make his treatment complete in all respects. It would indeed be impossible within the necessary limits of the space at our disposal to render justice to the material which is here supplied for fruitful study; and we can only hope

that, by the few examples we .can give, we may whet the appetite of
the readers of this review, and send them to peruse M. Levasseur's
chapters for themselves.

His investigation of the population question is, for instance, of
peculiar interest. He shows that, sufficiently serious as it must be,
its real significance needs a more searching inquiry than has been
commonly bestowed, and does not justify the hasty undis-
criminating judgments which have frequently been formed. To
some extent the circumstances, which have become specially
prominent in France, are common to other European nations.
In fact, although population has decreased in certain districts, the
census returns, with the exception of that following the loss of
Alsace-Lorraine after the Franco-German War, have shown an
increase on each occasion since 1801. A steady decrease in the
number of births. has taken place ; but it was not more rapid in the
latter half of the nineteenth century than it had been in the earlier
fifty years, although France occupies the lowest place among
European nations in this matter. There has been, on the other hand,
in several of those nations a more extensive diminution of the
marriage-rate than that which has occurred in France. The
principal cause of the decrease of births must be sought in a
diminution in fecundity, and depopulation has been especially
evident in ten departments, all of which are agricultural ; and yet
a careful study of the statistical evidence available does not show
that the urban industrial population is generally more prolific than
are the agricultural districts. Such is the cautious and judicial
manner in which M. Levasseur handles this crucial interesting
problem.

With the same scrupulous regard for the strict truth he appends
to his recognition of the tendency shown in his country as elsewhere
to the consolidation of business, particularly perhaps of retail
enterprise, in large establishments, the qualifying commentary,
attested by authoritative facts, that smaller undertakings hold their
ground, or have made a fresh appearance, in many quarters. The
steady movement of the people into the large towns, and the great
development in the practical application of electricity, as of scientific
knowledge generally, to various forms of industrial action, are
noticeable features of recent history, which France has shared with
other countries ; and due prominence is given to them in these
pages. The pre-eminence of France in artistic production is by
contrast her peculiar privilege ; and it has been demonstrated in
many directions, appropriately noted by M. Levasseur. The
attention given to primary education by the Third Republic is
emphasised in a very interesting chapter where a fair and adequate
account is furnished of the outstanding incidents in the long
bitter controversies waged between the clerical party and successive Ministers of Education. Nor is a later chapter dealing
with industrial disputes of less immediate interest to the English
student who will observe that M. Levasseur regards English Trade
Unions as affording an example which French "syndicats" might
follow with advantage. These are but a few types of the wealth of

knowledge which may be discovered in this book ; and in conclusion
we can only hope that by citing these particular examples we have
succeeded in conveying some idea of the important place it will
take in the libraries of economists and statisticians.   M. Levasseur
is, we think, to be congratulated without reserve on the happy completion of his assiduous labours ; and we are confident that he will
earn a rich reward in the gratitude of his intelligent interested
countrymen.   In the bestowal of those merited thanks we would
claim a very considerable share for English students.   L.L.P.

13.—*La Monnaie.*   Par A. de Foville.   v + 242 pp., crown 8vo.
Paris : J. Cabalda et Cie., 1907.

The topic of money, treated with admirable dexterity for his
particular purpose by M. de Foville in this short but comprehensive
volume, enjoys perhaps a special advantage among those embraced
within the range of economic exposition.   On the one hand, its
obvious concern with some tangible object which continuously con-
fronts ordinary men in the daily business of their lives constitutes a
direct and powerful appeal to their interested curiosity, and is
calculated to retain their alert attention   On the other hand, the
apparent complications which inevitably appear whenever an attempt
is made to pass beyond the threshold of the subject seem no less
imperatively to demand the skilled assistance of a practised expert
if they are to be successfully unravelled.   Both these auspicious
circumstances are turned to good account in this small manual.
M. de Foville treats his subject with lucidity and verve, and he is
an acknowledged master of the successive topics with which he
deals both in their practical and in their theoretical developments.
It is true that many, if not most, contemporary economists would
admit that the ingenious work in this connection which proceeded
from the more subtle minds among the older authorities, like that of
Ricardo, has stood the searching test of time better than their discussions of other matters less completely adapted to their deductive
reasonings, such as wages, or profits, or distribution as a whole.
But even in the case of monetary theory later independent
investigation has recently shown with tolerable plainness that it
is not safe, with the older writers, to set aside the possible
influence exerted on the value of such inanimate commodities as
metal or paper by the feelings—the sympathies and the antipathies
—of the human agents who handle them in turn.   In monetary
practice at any rate the place of such a wayward force as the
imagination cannot be ignored without the risk of error, and on
this ground at least conceptions previously accepted without question may now need revision or addition.   One of the merits
accordingly of the little volume before us is what its author himself
describes as a combination of some new ideas with ancient maxims
which have won established fame.   His practical experience of
monetary fact derived from his administration of the Mint, his full
acquaintance with the data and technique of monetary statistics, which
has resulted in a clear and resolute appreciation of their necessary
limitations accompanied by no excessive or unmerited neglect of

their genuine possibilities, and his complete knowledge and discriminating approbation of the broad outlines and the nicer details
of monetary theory, have been happily united in the production of
this useful, authoritative, and interesting manual. It is one which
he who runs may read without the discouraging apprehension that
he will fail to understand its clear descriptions and its definite conclusions, or be unable to appreciate the significance of the appropriate
figures quoted or to recollect the bearing of its fresh suggestive
facts. It has in short in abundant measure the merits which should
properly belong to the popular treatment of a scientific subject.
For it is accurate without being dull; and it is terse without being
superficial.

Yet, on the other hand, neither the informed teacher nor the
advanced student, if they be wise, will forego the opportunities
afforded in the course of this general sketch of theory, past history and
present practice, for learning the judicial views which M. de Foville
has been prompted by a long and intimate contact with monetary
realities to form on disputed monetary problems. They may not
always agree with his conclusions but they will rarely, if ever, fail
to appreciate the force, and to approve the moderation, of his
arguments. He remarks, for instance, in his Preface that he has
taken care to reduce to its true proportions the quantitative theory;
but we cannot imagine that any competent economist will quarrel
seriously with the balanced statement of the necessary limitations
of that theory given on these pages. They will be the less disposed
to engage in such superfluous discussion because M. de Foville
carefully refrains from endorsing the more extravagant criticisms
brought against that theory. The same tone of judicious moderation characterises his treatment of index numbers; for, while he
does not attempt to hide their imperfections, he recognises without
reserve their important place as a tested and proved instrument
of scientific study. He pardonably congratulates himself on the
superior opportunity afforded by the special arrangements of the
French fiscal scheme for the construction of his own particular
variety of index number. Even bimetallists will probably allow in
their candid moments that his animadversions on the adequacy of
the system they would favour must be interpreted in the liberal
spirit shown by the frank acknowledgment, by which his criticism
is accompanied, of its past influence. An extreme monometallist,
we suppose, would unhesitatingly withhold this praise, or would
at any rate make the concession in a less ungrudging temper.
M. de Foville does not, however, conceal his decisive view that the
system could not have met unchanged the serious strain threatened
in 1873, when the Latin Union suspended the free coinage of silver,
and their bimetallism became " halting " or " limping." He regards
indeed the practice followed by England at the Resumption of Cash
Payments in 1819, when we adopted a single gold standard,
combined with subsidiary token currencies of silver and bronze, as
superior on its intrinsic merits to bimetallism and indeed to any
other monetary system. He considers that it is now destined to
become the universal system of the whole, or at any rate of the

civilised portion, of the globe; and he points, with the justification of accomplished fact, to the rebuttal of the confident prophecy advanced by the geologist Suess of an inadequate output of the yellow metal. It may be noticed by the way that his book contains a new and useful account, which is both brief and comprehensive, of the existing condition of the monetary systems of the world.

But these nice vexatious problems do not monopolise an excessive proportion of his space; and he duly observes, in the body of his book, the principles laid down in the Preface of avoiding the revival of ancient controversies. These questions indeed are discussed for the most part in his third section, which is appropriately entitled the "La vie économique des monnaies." In the preceding section he treats briefly of those details in the mechanism and products of coinage, of which he possesses a first-hand acquaintance, under the title of "monetary technique." In the first section he sets forth, more fully, the reasons which have led men to the common use of money, and traces in outline the long history of its past development, and of its gradual but steady and continuous improvement, under the title of "theory and legislation." The student, who has read the ordinary text-books, will find M. de Foville's restatement of accepted views in this connection attractive from its crispness and lucidity. But, like the plain citizen, approaching the matter without previous knowledge, he will also be entertained and instructed by fresh instances and new suggestions. A single example must suffice to illustrate this characteristic. M. de Foville is enabled, largely by the appropriate means of the useful collection, which he has been instrumental in forming, of the currencies of French Africa, to present a great diversity of novel types of primitive varieties of money. We think, indeed, that it would be difficult to improve upon the historical exposition of the growth of monetary systems which is furnished in this section; and we would repeat, in conclusion, the expression of gratitude, with which, in the interests both of the beginner, and of the more advanced student and the teacher, we welcome this opportune addition to the existing manuals of monetary economics. It possesses, as we have tried to show, certain qualities to which few or none of those can pretend; it is, in our opinion, admirably adapted to the purpose for which it has been written—the presentation in a popular but orderly shape of essential truths. And, finally, it may be justly considered "up to date."   L.L.P.

14.—*L'Impôt sur le Revenu en Allemagne.* Par Gaspard Wampach. 310 pp., crown 8vo. Paris: G. Cadet, 1907.

This interesting monograph was written primarily with a view to its immediate bearing on the financial politics of France, where proposals for an income tax have once again been recently put forward. The author accordingly does not neglect the opportunity afforded in the course of his investigations into the past history and present state of taxation of income in Germany to point a moral which is favourable to the employment of a similar fiscal instrument

in France. Of its efficiency as an engine for producing a large
revenue by means which can be easily and rapidly adapted to
changed requirements, and can without excessive pains be brought
into sufficient harmony with the legitimate demands of equity to
different classes of taxpayers, he feels no doubt, and his confidence
is justified by the illuminating detailed record which he furnishes
of the experience of such taxation. He would certainly lend
his powerful support to this particular reform, which occupies
no inconspicuous place among those favoured or projected by
the Ministry of M. Clémenceau ; and the main motive which
prompted him to undertake the book is openly acknowledged in the
preface.

But, if the primary object of the Essay is thus distinctly practical,
in the execution of his plan M. Wampach has succeeded, by the
comprehensiveness of his researches, by the penetration of his
judgment, and the lucidity of his arrangement, in producing a work
which is of more importance than could attach to any mere polemical
pamphlet adjusted to the transitory needs of a passing controversy.
He has unquestionably conceived and carried out his task in a
scientific spirit, and his facts and his conclusions will interest
English no less than French or German readers. As he states in
his preface, he chose Germany as the special field of his investigations, because that country presents a great variety of conditions,
and may, with some justice, claim in this matter the title commonly
bestowed on Belgium of being the " social laboratory " of the world.
In the second section of his treatise, where he examines the fiscal
arrangements made in this connection by the various other States
of the German Empire besides Prussia, this diversity of circumstance
is strikingly exhibited. From Bavaria, where agriculture is still
dominant, to industrial Saxony, and from the backward feudal
Duchies of Mecklenburg to the progressive and liberal state of
Baden, the interval traversed is considerable ; and abundant material
is offered for comparison. From Saxony, indeed, De Miquel
avowedly borrowed some of the reforms which he introduced in
Prussia in 1891 ; and the Prussian income tax, as arranged by this
law of 1891, modified by the new enactment of 1906, forms
the subject of exhaustive investigation in the first section of
M. Wampach's treatise. In successive chapters he inquires in turn
into the persons on whom the tax is levied, its incidence, the scale
on which it is arranged, the mode of its assessment, and the precautions taken to prevent evasion and provide redress against
injustice. He does not refrain from merited criticism of its shortcomings ; but he is ready to acknowledge freely the numerous good
points in the conception and administration of this important portion
of the machinery of the Prussian fiscal system.

He shows that in practice an income tax necessitates the fixing
of some limit of exemption, and that it is probable that in Prussia
this limit has now been placed too low. He allows that the irresistible attraction of tapping a productive source of revenue has led
Prussian financiers, by taxing joint stock companies, to increase the
probability of that double taxation, which can with difficulty be

duly limited in every system, and cannot be entirely avoided by any ingenious regulations about the domicile of the taxpayer or the like. Prussian administrators started with the notion, which seems carefully devised to meet the objection commonly alleged against an income tax that it is inquisitorial, of proceeding by criteria afforded by external evidence alone, but they have ended by making a declaration of income compulsory for those possessing more than a certain quota; and fault may be found with the detailed arrangement of the constitution and the action of the bodies charged with the assessment, while evidence which is forthcoming shows that dishonest declarations are not unknown, and that the methods of redress against unjust assessment fail to satisfy. Graduation, which fulfils the approved ideal of an equivalent sacrifice more completely than a fixed proportion taken from each taxpayer, only avoids the danger of confiscation by being exchanged in the Prussian system at the higher level of incomes for proportional taxation, and the rate by which below this point its increase has been regulated must in any event be open to the charge of being arbitrary, and in certain actual instances in Prussia seems to be excessive. Nor apparently is it easy, or perhaps is it possible, to give full effect to the general plan followed in Prussia of taxing income in the total mass, as opposed to the English practice of charging the different component portions of an income in distinct various schedules, without departures from consistency; and as a matter of fact the Prussian tax on income has been supplemented also by a tax on capital.

But nevertheless the Prussian financiers have been conspicuously successful in transforming within a recent period the whole basis of their financial system, and in thus meeting the imperative needs of an enlarged expenditure, by the skilful opportune employment of this particular productive fiscal instrument; and in the final chapter of his first section, where M. Wampach draws his general conclusions, his judgment is distinctly favourable. From the indications we have given of the material discussed, and of the mode of its discussion, it will be seen how informing is the narrative supplied, and the interest is sustained in the second and concluding section of the book. We have only space here to call special attention to the chapter in which M. Wampach shows how gradually but surely the Prussian ideas of finance have superseded those French arrangements which were found existing in the conquered provinces of Alsace-Lorraine; and to urge that English readers will find much to interest them in his pages. They will study with advantage the references given to English practice; they will derive no less instruction from the differences prevailing between the German systems and our own. For he would be a bold prophet who did not expect that changes would be introduced into our income tax in the future. The last Budget made some advance in that direction, and strenuous reformers have not failed to raise their voices in demands for further alterations. M. Wampach's book may, indeed, fittingly be read as a supplement to a recent official report issued in this country on Graduation as practised by foreign nations.

L.L.P.

15.—*Untersuchung der Wohnungen der minder bemittelten Klassen in Bremen: im Auftrage der Deputation wegen Wohnungsinspektion veranstaltet im April* 1904 *und bearbeitet vom Bremischen Statistischen Amt.* 122 pp., 8vo. Bremen : Franz Leuwer, 1905.

Bremen is a Hanse town, and a free city of the Empire, with a population of 215,000. Its State government and its City government are somewhat like the two chambers of an ordinary bicameral government. The burgomasters are, *ex-officio*, members of the Senate. The Senate, as a whole, is drawn from much the same body of men as the town council, and it is not extraordinary if the measures which appeal to the town council as desirable should also appear to the Senate as not altogether undesirable; and so the town council met with no opposition from its central government when it declared in favour of an inquiry into the dwellings of the less prosperous classes of Bremen.

The conduct of the inquiry was entrusted to a sub-commission; general instructions were given to it to extend the inquiry to every important aspect bearing upon the housing question, to the size of rooms, their air space, their allotment among the members of the family, the existing sleeping arrangements, the condition of the structure from the building and sanitary point of view. The inquiry was to be limited to certain streets occupied by the less prosperous classes, and definitely given over to residential and sleeping, not business, purposes. The alleys of the " Old-town " and " New-town " were eliminated from the inquiry, not because they did not come within its scope, but because "there was no difference of opinion that these houses must be dealt with by special regulations." It should be mentioned that the Old-town and the New-town are the London and Southwark of Bremen on either side of the Weser, and that the New-town dates from 1620. The inquiry was intensive rather than extensive.

The form of inquiry (a copy of which is attached to the report) was to be filled up in respect of every " dwelling," every " household " being reckoned as a dwelling. The criterion of a separate household, and so of a separate dwelling, was that it should have at least one room not used by the landlord, and that the most important of the furniture, especially the beds, crockery, &c., should be the property of the occupier. But if the occupier used the landlord's furniture, his room or rooms were not to constitute a separate household, but he was to be counted as a lodger in another man's household. Decision in the matter was not always easy.

With regard to the questions, the individual members of the household had to be set forth by name and according to age, sex, position in the household and occupation. The fact had to be noted if any were consumptive. In the case of married women, information had to be supplied whether they had formerly been domestic servants—a fact which would be of interest in judging of the internal economy of the household. The rooms for habitation were to be described individually in their size and the number and dimensions of the windows. In regard to the windows, the angle of light was required—an extraordinarily tedious item of inquiry and, in the result, of doubtful value. For each sleeping-room the number of persons (and which persons) sleeping in it had to be given, and the kind of sleeping-place (double bed, single bed, cot, cradle, sofa, &c.).

Broader ground still was taken by those questions which bore upon the social condition of the inhabitants. Inquiries were made into the income of all the members of the family. The questions were answered readily enough, though the persons questioned were often unable to estimate their income with much ability. In regard to health matters, the questions were asked, in addition to that above-mentioned as to whether any member of the household was consumptive, whether, and if so when, any connections of the family had died since the last census, and whether there had been any cases of diphtheria, scarlet fever, typhus or tuberculosis. Another question touched the care and feeding of any children in the house, and the preparation of meals.

The questions relating to the dwelling itself dealt with the rent paid, the kind and usefulness of the kitchen, the water supply, the scullery, &c. With regard to the closets, the only question asked was as to the number of persons using each. No more elaborate inquiry was made, because the whole domestic sanitary arrangements of Bremen were at the time in course of transformation.

Finally, in regard to lodgers, the questions were asked, how much they contributed to the rent, and what was done for them therefor.

It was taken for granted that such an inquiry could not be carried out either by voluntary enumerators or by persons who might be interested, but that only persons engaged in some building work or profession, who must be chosen specially for the task and paid, would be competent to settle any difficulties as they arose with the requisite technical knowledge.

No special authority was obtained calling upon the inhabitants to answer the questions. The authorities were of opinion that difficulties with the public would not arise, if the enumerators went about their work discreetly and courteously. The enumerators were to work in pairs, each pair consisting of a building expert and a clerk.

The cost of the inquiry had been estimated at 1,500 marks (75*l.*), and this amount was voted by the Senate.

Inquiry was made into the number of forms that could presumably be filled up per day, and it was found, from the experience of other cities, that it might be possible for each pair to fill up 20 forms in a day of eight hours. On this basis, remuneration was fixed at a rate of 50 pfennig (6*d.*) per form. But in view of the uncertainty of the data, a proviso was added to the effect that a higher rate would be adopted if it were found that the average of 20 forms per day could not be reached. On these terms, the services of 9 building experts were obtained; 7 were surveyors, 1 a certificated engineer, and 1 a carpenter. Practical builders did not apply, as building work was already in full swing at the date of the advertisement. To each was allotted a clerk, supplied by the Bureau for the Unemployed.

After several general conferences on the contents of the form of inquiry, and on the method of filling it up, and after public announcement of the inquiry in the newspapers, the enumeration itself was begun on the 27th April, 1904. On the day preceding the inquiry at each house a communication was sent to each house-holder explaining the objects of the inquiry and the confidential nature of the returns, and asking for his assistance. A special point was made that neither the police nor the taxation-committee had anything to do with the inquiry.

During the inquiry a "flying bureau" was established in the different parts of the town where the inquiry was being carried on. An officer of the Statistical Bureau attended at each, who settled all difficulties as they arose, and distributed the work. The enumerators handed in, every evening, the forms they had filled up during the day.

No opposition worth speaking of was encountered from the public. Even questions touching upon intimate personal relations were answered without parley. Only in four cases was information politely refused. No pressure was applied, as the houses in question were well represented in the inquiry. In the case of several dwellings in the heart of the city, the enumerators were unable, in spite of several attempts, to obtain entry, because the inhabitants left home too early and returned too late. These cases also were allowed to pass.

Even on the first day it was realised that the average expected output of 20 forms per day could not be reached. The most experienced of the officers only brought in 8 to 10 forms in the first days. As it was absolutely essential that the work should not be scamped, it was resolved to abolish payment by piece, and to substitute rates of pay which should vary, according to each enumerator's qualifications, and the number of returns he sent in, from 6 to 10 marks per day. For the clerks the Unemployment Bureau fixed a wage of 3 marks 50 pfennig (3s. 6d.) per day. The enumeration was practically completed in 10 days, during which 938 forms were filled up. Including some later additions, 1,044 forms were obtained, containing information as to 531 houses, 1,044 dwellings, 3,933 rooms, and 4,905 persons.

The whole value of the results of such a relatively small survey depends upon the skill with which the streets and houses were selected, in the extent, that is, to which the figures are typical. Only one with an intimate knowledge of the city can judge of this. If the figures are fairly typical, then some of the results are exceedingly interesting.

The size of the rooms may be taken as an interesting example of these results. Of the 3,933 rooms measured up, 890 were bedrooms only. The sizes of these rooms were as follows (taking 1 cubic metre = 35 cubic ft.) :—1 measured under 175 cubic ft., 28 between 175 and 350, 173 between 350 and 525, 273 between 525 and 700, 150 between 700 and 875, 113 between 875 and

1,050, 68 between 1,050 and 1,225, 60 between 1,225 and 1,400, 15 between 1,400 and 1,575, 2 between 1,575 and 1,750, and 7 over 1,750 cubic ft.

The superficial measurements of the same rooms were as follows (taking 1 square metre = 11 square ft.) :—25 measured under 44 square ft., 63 between 44 and 55, 179 between 55 and 66, 181 between 66 and 77, 75 between 77 and 88, 73 between 88 and 99, 81 between 99 and 110, 119 between 110 and 132, 83 between 132 and 165, 10 between 165 and 220, and 1 over 220 square ft.

Interesting statistics are given of the proportions of window-area to floor-area. In the houses surveyed there were 1,787 living rooms, excluding those in the basement and attic. In these rooms, the floor-area was less than twice the window-area in 28 cases, less than three times and more than twice in 418 cases, less than four times and more than three times in 636 cases, less than five times and more than four times in 367 cases, less than six times and more than five times in 177 cases, and more than six times in 161 cases. There was one case more than 40 times, one more than 50, and one more than 75. Of these 1,787 rooms, 1,145 had one window, 606 two windows, 28 three, and 8 four. In the case of eight of these rooms, we are told, the windows could not be opened.

None of the statistics are more interesting than those relating to the number of lodgers, with the amounts paid by them and the benefits they received for those payments, and those relating to children received for payment—children who in England (if under two years of age) come under the Infant Life Protection Act. Statistics were obtained with regard to 24 households which took children for payment. In 6 households the monthly payment was 10s., in 9 it was 12s., in 1 it was 14s., in 2 it was 15s., in 3 it was 18s., in 2 it was 20s., and in 1 it was 25s.

The volume abounds in photographs, vertical and horizontal sections of houses, and statistical tables. Throughout, the work bears every sign of the thoroughness for which German inves-tigators are famous. We are provided with numerous statistics of social facts and conditions, illustrating phases of life of which we have at present comparatively little statistical knowledge in England.

P.É.B.

16.—*Practical Problems in Banking and Currency.* Edited by Walter Henry Hull. xxvi. + 596 pp., 8vo. New York : The Macmillan Company, 1907.

This volume contains a series of papers and addresses on topics connected with banking, arranged so as to illustrate the principal problems actively discussed in recent years in the United States. It is, so far as the greater part of the matter included is concerned, not a discussion of matters relating to banking wherever conducted ; but it illustrates the opinions of thoughtful Americans on the situation of the United States, and on the best means of meeting the difficulties arising out of local conditions and the peculiar legislation touching banking, whether federal or state legislation. In the first division of the volume, it is true, some general banking problems are considered, and here there is, for the general English student, something more than a presentation of a position in which his interest is mainly that of an observer.

This first group of sixteen papers, forming the General Banking Section, deals with such important topics as the inspection of banks by state examiners, its possibilities and difficulties; the organisation of credit departments; the thorny question of interest on deposits; and advertising by banks. Some acute remarks on the conditions existing in the United States are, naturally, found in so varied a group of contributions from men of business experience. In view of recent events, the remark (p. 37) that "the connection between the managements of the banks in New York City and the great financial and speculative interests is very close, and if ever we have serious banking trouble, it will come from this fact," seems fully justified. The director who does not direct is, in another place, assigned with justice much responsibility for bank failures: "Where directors direct, defalcations are almost unknown" (p. 94).

Even in this section peculiarities of the banking arrangements in the United States affect the discussion in no small degree, but these features naturally dominate the remainder of the volume. Thus the second and largest section is concerned with Banking Reform and Currency. Here, in twenty-seven papers, the plans which have formed the subject of so much discussion among bankers in the United States are represented, and views on both sides respecting the merits of the proposals are included. The advocates and the opponents of branch banking are allowed space, though more is given to the former than to the latter. Similarly the Treasury system is not merely attacked, as is so common, but is also, and ably, defended. The introduction of what is known as "assets currency" is a very important feature of the discussions. The addition to the present paper currency of a supplement based, not on government bonds, but on general bank assets as security, or the substitution of such a currency for some part of the existing circulation of bank or government paper, is the point at issue. This proposition has especial interest when it becomes a question of "emergency circulation," or an issue to meet special temporary need, and intended to be promptly withdrawn as soon as the emergency has passed. A strange feature is the comparatively slight attention devoted to the means by which the withdrawal may be made prompt and certain. Most writers fail to present this as a vital point.

The third, or Trust Company Section, contains eighteen contributions dealing with the special problems raised by the activities of the trust companies, both in their special functions as trustees, etc., and in the banking part of their business, which has been so important a development of these corporations.

It is clearly impossible to discuss the views expressed in over sixty papers by half a hundred different contributors. The presentation of these papers, which represent very largely addresses delivered to state or national conventions of bankers in the last half-dozen years, may be regarded as timely in view of the interest certain to be developed in the question of possible reform in banking and currency law, reform not to exclude the trust company from its scope.   The facts presented by the different contributors are mostly trustworthy, though there is a tendency, natural in view of the origin of the papers, to reiteration of certain sets of figures.   In a few cases a common failing of writers and speakers in the United States, in not understanding fully old-world facts to which they make reference, is exemplified.   A case in point is found in references to the action of the Bank of England in regard to its note issue, on the three occasions when a government letter relieved the directors from responsibility for breach of the law. The fact that the law was not broken on two of the three occasions is entirely lost sight of, and it is a fact pertinent to discussions in which the matter is referred to.   These are but slight blemishes on the work before us, however, and its merits are very great, though some comprehension of the American situation is needed to assist the reader in understanding and enjoying the book.   This type of book, now being more and more introduced as an aid to students in their work on economic subjects, has much to be said in its favour.   A fully rounded discussion of principles is difficult to secure by the use of such books, but an air of reality is infused into theoretic discussions, and loss of interest through excessive formality of treatment is guarded against.   Is the field for their use in England yet wide enough to justify like issues here ?

A.W.F.

17.—*Le Crisi Economiche.*   Di Camillo Supino.   202 pp., la. 8vo. Milano : Ulrico Hoepli, 1907.

This work contains the text of a series of lectures delivered at the Bocconi Commercial University, Milan, in which the author has made a comprehensive survey of the views expressed by the leading British and foreign economists on the subject of commercial, industrial, and financial crises.   Economic crises, he points out, may always be traced to derangements of the equilibrium between production and consumption (or, in other words, between supply and demand), which spring originally from variation in consumption or in production as the case may be ; or from changes affecting the circulation of produce and money and the distribution of wealth and profits.   The actual causes of economic crises are thus classified into four categories accordingly as they arise from phenomena of consumption, of production, of circulation, or of distribution.

Among the circumstances affecting consumption, reference is made to the disastrous effects which changes of fashion have occasionally produced in certain industries, and such familiar examples are quoted as the distress of the Spitalfields weavers when silks were displaced by muslins, and the want of employment which occurred in Birmingham when shoe laces and stuff buttons ousted steel buckles and metal buttons.   In the same chapter mention is made of crises caused by variations in the relations between productive and unproductive consumption, by temporary increases and decreases of consumption, and by the effects of famines, wars, revolutions, and epidemics.

The chapter on the phenomena of production as causes of crises is devoted mainly to a discussion of the results of over-production, and to a criticism of the theory that a general excess of production is inconceivable. The doctrine of Mill, Say, and Ricardo, which denies the possibility of an over-supply of all commodities, is attacked on the ground that it assumes a stationary condition of society in which the total quantity of commodities produced will correspond at all times with the demand. This assumption, it is argued, ignores the condition of growing communities in which there is a surplus of commodities beyond the actual wants of the consumers, produced in anticipation of the increase in population. It presupposes that the exchange of products takes place directly by barter, or that sales are immediately followed by purchases, whereas these transactions take place through the agency of merchants and speculators who may overestimate the demands of the situation and thereby cause an excess of production. It overlooks the possibility of a superabundance of produce in one country which is not compensated by scarcity in another. It fails to take into account the fact that a State may artificially stimulate by bounties the over-production of commodities for which the demand may in the meantime be checked by the protectionist tariffs of other States. When these circumstances are taken into consideration it will be seen, the author holds, that there can be an excess of commodities above the demand, or an excess of supply in respect to the demand at remunerative prices. The arguments advanced in support of this point are the most interesting feature of the chapter, but while they go to show that there may be over-production of a particular commodity, or local superabundance of several commodities, they do not adequately meet the contention of Mill and others that a general over-supply of all commodities above the demand, so far as demand consists in means of payment, is an impossibility.

Crises caused by phenomena of circulation are discussed in reference to the effects of changes and improvements in the methods of transport and means of communication in disturbing the equilibrium between production and consumption. Attention is also directed under this head to crises caused by changes in the value and quantity of money and the weakening of credit, and by fluctuations in the relative values of gold and silver. The chapter on the phenomena of distribution deals with derangements of supply and demand caused by inequalities in the distribution of wealth or produce as between capital and labour, and with crises caused by the too rapid accumulation of capital and the diminution of profits.

The scope of the remaining chapters is indicated by their titles, viz.: the Course of Crises; Semiology of Crises, a chapter dealing with the movements of prices, imports and exports, bankers' clearances, bankers' reserves, the bank rate, and issues of notes, during certain periods of crises; Economic Depressions; Periodicity of Crises; Consequences of Crises and Remedies; Agrarian and Building Crises; Industrial and Commercial Crises; Stock Exchange Crises; Monetary and Credit Crises.

The utility of Signor Supino's work lies mainly in the thoroughness and lucidity with which he has reviewed the theories of other authorities, and in the examples he quotes in illustration of the points dealt with in the several chapters. But his interpretation of an "economic crisis" apparently embraces local and comparatively minor derangements of industries which would scarcely be regarded as falling within that category of serious and extensive upheavals usually designated as "crises" in this country. R.F.C.

18. *Bevolkerungsstatistik Schwedens* (1750-1900). By Gustav Sundbärg. 170 pp., 8vo. Stockholm: Norstedt and Söner, 1907.

Surely Sweden must be the envy of every student of population statistics. There is not another country in the world where official statistics of the main "vital" characteristics of a population strictly comparable for a period of upwards of one hundred and fifty years can be found. From about the year 1748 official information exists of the population each year, and apparently also of the age, sex, and conjugal condition at sufficiently frequent intervals throughout this period as to be practically continuous. This information is based mainly on Government enumerations, supplemented in some cases, however, by church registers, which appear to have been very carefully kept throughout the country. An important change in the form of the Swedish statistics appears to have been made by Fr. Th. Berg in 1860. The changes then introduced were rather in the nature of a complete reorganisation of the prevailing system of registration, to bring the materials collected by the church authorities and local bodies generally more in line with those collected by the periodic censuses, than a break in the continuity of the returns. The change was evolutionary, not revolutionary.

With such materials to work upon, Herr Gustav Sundbärg (of the Swedish Statistical Bureau), the well-known editor of that extraordinarily useful compilation known as *Aperçus Statistiques*, has laboured with remarkable success to exhibit some of the more important population phenomena in his country, and to deduce certain "laws" of population which, because they are based on materials of extraordinary fulness, are freer from probable errors than could be the case with the materials of any other country. To take one example, the Swedish statistics give a standard of population with subsidiary standards of age- and sex-distribution, and, more especially, of relative fertility of women at different ages, which must be of great advantage to statisticians all over the world. The "fertility" standard has already been utilised with effect by Drs. Newsholme and Stevenson in a Paper on the decline of the birth-rate, which he read before the Society in December, 1905.

Herr Sundbärg's first remarks, in the valuable critical introduction which precedes his elaborate tables, are directed to a comparison of various types of age-grouping in different countries, and he distinguishes three principal types as follows, per 1,000 of population :—

Ages.	Progressive	Stationary.	Retrogressive
0—14 .. .	400	265	200
15—49 ...	500	505	500
50—	100	230	300

It appears that in practically all civilised populations, whatever its character—progressive or retrogressive—about one-half of the entire population will be found between the ages of 15 and 50.   In a population increasing rapidly in numbers, both naturally and by immigration, such as the United States, about 40 per cent. of the population will be under 15, and $\frac{1}{10}$th will be aged 50 and over.   In a stationary population such as exists in France there will be rather more than one-fourth of the population under 15, and less than one-fourth at 50 and over.   In a retrogressive population like that of Ireland or some of the "departments" of France, the type is found to consist of 20 per cent. young people, and 30 per cent. old people.   It appears to follow from this that a much more satisfactory method of comparing the age-groupings of different populations than has been customary hitherto would be to express the numbers at different ages in proportion to the numbers between the ages 15 and 50; or what amounts to the same thing, it is necessary only to compare the proportions of those under 15 with those over 50.   This method was actually adopted (with very slight modification) in a paper on Jewish Vital Statistics read before this Society in 1905 to compare the age-distribution of Jews and general population in London.   A further advantage which this method enjoys results from the fact that the period 15 to 50 corresponds with the period of maximum economic usefulness in the case of men and roughly also to the child-bearing period of women.   The period is therefore one in which social and economic activity reaches a maximum.

The normal distribution in West European countries is one which lies exactly half-way between the progressive and stationary types, and consists of about one-third under 15, one-half aged 15 to 50, and one-sixth aged 50 and over, and examination of the Swedish statistics for the period 1805-75 shows that the Swedish population corresponds perfectly with this normal type.

Incidentally in this section Herr Sundbärg refutes two popular fallacies : (1) That the proportions of the populations under 15 in the different types are determined by the death-rates, and especially that the high proportions of those aged 50 and over indicate greater longevity.   The truth is that this high proportion of older people may be due as well to a small rate of natural increase as to a low death-rate.   (2) That the age-grouping is due to migration.   This statement is also untrue, for if the birth- and marriage-rates are normal, a large immigration is incapable of altering the proportions between the ages 15—50 ; but will rather, as in the United States, raise the proportions under 15. If the birth- and marriage-rates are low, the effect of a large immigration is to increase the proportions at the middle period.

An interesting method is adopted for exhibiting the annual fluctuations in the Swedish marriage- and birth-rates. Instead of fixing on a standard rate and comparing the annual rates with it, a movable standard is adopted, consisting of the average rate for the preceding twenty years. Thus in 1900 the marriage-rate in Sweden was 6·15 per 1,000 of the population ; the average rate for the preceding twenty years was 6·11 per 1,000, and the index of marriage variation for the year is therefore 101. Such a method appears to have the distinct advantage of eliminating altogether the effect of secular variation in the social habits and condition of the people, and assists the student to concentrate upon the phénomena of a single year. This method, for example, gives the same variation-index for the years 1851 and 1899, though in the earlier year the actual marriage-rate was nearly 20 per cent. higher.

An investigation of special interest is that which deals with the fertility of women at different ages. The result of this investigation is given in the following table :—

Age.	Fertility.	Fertility Index.	Age.	Fertility.	Fertility Index.
15—20 years....	0·560	1·628	40—45 years. .	0·155	0·451
20—25 ,, ..	0·474	1·378	45—50 ,, ...	0·025	0·059
25—30 ,, ...	0·389	1·131			
30—35 ,, ...	0·333	0·968			
35—40 ,, ...	0·266	0·773		0·344	1·000

The figures in the second column represent the average number of births per married woman per annum at each age-period. Those in the third column denote, in the case of Sweden, the relative fertility at each age-group, the general fertility at all ages being taken as unity. These proportions being assumed to hold for any other country, it is easy to correct for the birth-rates at different periods on account of the changes in age-grouping of the married women at different ages.

Herr Sundbärg has in this work succeeded in producing a work of the greatest importance to vital statisticians, comparable at once with the previous works in the same direction of Farr, Levasseur, and Bertillon.   S.R.

19.—CORRESPONDENCE.

To the Editors,

MESSIEURS,—Dans le numéro de Septembre du *Journal of the Royal Statistical Society* se trouve un compte rendu de l'*Album graphique de la Statistique générale de la France.* L'auteur du compte rendu veut bien adresser à cette publication des éloges dont je le remercie. Il y joint des critiques auxquelles il ne serait sans doute pas opportun de répondre. Toutefois l'une de ces critiques me semble le résultat d'une erreur, et c'est pourquoi je vous demande de bien vouloir attirer sur un point l'attention de l'auteur du compte rendu.

À la p. 490 il est dit : " The scale of shading is quite arbitrary; it differs from map to map, and the intervals are irregular . . . . No explanation is given of the principles by which those limits are determined."

Je crains que l'auteur n'ait pas remarqué les pages de texte placées en tête de l'Album. En effet, dans ces pages on a expliqué la méthode de graduation des cartogrammes et des diagrammes, méthode qui a pour objet de rendre comparables entre eux, soit les divers cartogrammes, soit les divers diagrammes, et d'éviter tout arbitraire dans la construction des échelles.

Comme j'attache une grande importance à cette question de comparabilité, et en raison de l'autorité particulière du *Journal*, je vous serais reconnaissant de bien vouloir communiquer mon observation à l'auteur du compte rendu.

En vous remerciant à l'avance, je vous prie d'agréer l'assurance de mes sentiments dévoués,   LUCIEN MARCH.

[The above communication has been submitted to the author of the note referred to, and he writes as follows :—

I greatly regret to find that I unwittingly fell into error in my account of this *Album*, pp. 489 and 490 of the September *Journal*, in the statement that "no explanation is given of the principles by which [the limits of the various shadings] are determined." In the preliminary matter of the *Album* it is stated that the various tints correspond throughout the cartograms to certain percentage variations from the average for the whole country; thus, Tint No. 1 is applied to Departments where the measurement of the phenomenon in question falls between 40 and 70 per cent. of the measurement for the whole of France. The maps are, accordingly, comparable with each other when the scale is grasped. But the scale is not given on each map, while the lowest or highest numbers actually occurring in a Department are printed; and some little appearance of arbitrariness arises if the preliminary explanation be overlooked, because the universal scale used changes at 70, 90, 110, 140, 200, 400, and 1,000 per cent., instead of in regular steps.]

20.—*Other New Publications.*

Adam (Edwin). Land values and taxation (social problems, series iv). 196 pp., 8vo. London : T. C. and E. C. Jack, 1907.

Anderson (Sir Robert). Criminals and crime : some facts and suggestions. 182 pp., 8vo. London : James Nisbet, 1907.
    [On the need for special dealing with professional as distinct from occasional criminals.]

Andersson (Thor). Social Sjukförsäkring. 152 pp., 8vo. Stockholm : Aktiebolajet Ljus, 1907.

Barratt (R. J.). Canada's century : progress and resources of the great Dominion. Introduction by the Rt. Hon. Lord Strathcona. 538 pp., la. 8vo. London : *Financier and Bullionist*, 1907.

Castberg (P. H.). Production : a study in economics. 382 pp., 8vo. London : Swan Sonnenschein, 1907.

De La Plaza (Victorino). Exposición contra el proteccionismo exagerado al azúcar, de producción interna. 84 pp., 8vo. Buenos Aires : Peuser, 1907.

Edwards (Clement), M.P. Railway nationalization. Preface by the Rt. Hon. Sir Charles W. Dilke, Bart., M.P. 2nd edition, 8vo. London : Methuen, 1907.
[1st edition, 1898.]

Elderton (Ethel M.). On the measure of the resemblance of first cousins. (Eugenics Laboratory Memoirs IV.) 54 pp., 4to. London : Dulau, 1907.

Esche (Arthur). Arbeitsordnung und Arbeiterausschuss (Neue Zeit- und Streitfragen). 46 pp., 8vo. Dresden : Zahn and Tansch, 1907.

Gilbart (J. W.). History, principles and practice of banking. New edition, revised by Ernest Sykes. 2 vols., 8vo. London : G. Bell and Sons, 1907.

Gnauck-Kuhne (Elisabeth). Die Deutsche Frau um die Jahrhundert- wende. Statistische Studie zur Frauenfrage. Zweite Auflage. 8vo. Berlin : Otto Liebmann, 1907.

Guyot (Yves). Sophismes socialistes et faits économiques. 352 pp., 8vo. Paris : Felix Alcan, 1908.

Kessler (Dr. Gerhard). Die deutschen Arbeitgeber-Verbände. Im Auftrag des Vereins für Socialpolitik herausgegeben. 386 pp., 8vo. Leipzig : Duncker and Humblot, 1907.

Lauder (Albert E.). The municipal manual. A description of the constitution and functions of urban local authorities. 292 pp., 8vo. London : P. S. King and Son, 1907.

Marx (Karl). Capital : a critique of political economy. Vol. 2. The process of circulation of capital. Edited by Frederick Engels. Translated from the 2nd German edition by Ernest Untermann. 8vo. London : Swan Sonnenschein, 1907.

Meyer (Hugo Richard). Public ownership and the telephone in Great Britain : restriction of the industry by the State and the municipalities. 386 pp., 8vo. New York : Macmillan, 1907.

——— British state telegraphs : a study of the problem of a large body of civil servants in a democracy. 408 pp., 8vo. New York : Macmillan, 1907.

Neymarck (Alfred). Finances contemporaines. iv, v, L'obsession fiscale, projects ministeriels et propositions dues à l'initiative parlementaire relatifs à la reforme de l'impôt, 1872-1907. i, 1872-1895. ii, 1896-1907. 2 vols., 8vo. Paris : Felix Alcan, 1907.

Nichols (John Benjamin). The numerical proportions of the sexes at birth. (Part 4 of vol. i of Memoirs of American Anthropological Association.) 51 pp., 8vo. Lancaster, Pa. : New Era Printing Company, 1907.
[A discussion, on the basis of international statistics, of sex proportions of living births, of the still-born, of legitimate and illegitimate, and of multiple births.]

Pedder (*D. C.*). Where men decay. A survey of present rural conditions. 152 pp., 8vo. London: A. C. Zifield, 1908.

Robertson (*William A.*) and *Ross* (*Frederick A.*). Actuarial theory. Notes for students on the subject-matter required in the second examinations of the Institute of Actuaries and Faculty of Actuaries in Scotland, with a prefatory note by Thomas G. Ackland. xxiv + 432 pp., 8vo. Edinburgh: Oliver and Boyd, 1907.

Schuster (*Edgar*). The promise of youth and performance of manhood: a statistical inquiry into the question whether success in the examination for the B.A. degree at Oxford is followed by success in professional life. (Eugenics Laboratory Memoirs III.) 16 pp., 4to. London: Dulau, 1907.
> [Of those who took first-class honours during a certain period, and subsequently entered the church, 68 per cent. afterwards obtained some form of distinction; of the second-class men, only 37 per cent.; of the third, 32 per cent.; of the fourth, 29 per cent.; of the pass degrees, 21 per cent.; of those who took no degrees, 9 per cent. Similar discussion for the bar.]

Scott (*W. R.*). The constitution and finance of an English copper mining company in the sixteenth and seventeenth centuries: an account of "The Society of the Mines Royal." (Sonderabdruck aus Vierteljahrschrift für Social- und Wirtschaftsgeschichte, 1907, 4. Heft.) 25 pp., 8vo. Stuttgart: W. Kohlhummer, 1907.

Sowray (*J. Russell*). British railway finance, with special reference to capital charges. 25 pp., 8vo. London: Edward Stanford, 1907.

Stein (-*Philipp*). Über Streiks und Aussperrungen. 24 pp., 8vo. Dresden: Zahn and Jaensch, 1907.

Sutherland (*William*). Old age pensions in theory and practice, with some foreign examples. 228 pp., 8vo. London: Methuen and Co., 1907.

Swan (*Charles Herbert*). Impersonal taxation: a discussion of some rights and wrongs of governmental revenue. 8vo. New York: American Academy of Political and Social Science, 1907.

Tarde (*Alfred de*). L'idée du juste prix. Essai de psychologie économique. 8vo. Paris: Félix Alcan, 1907.

Waghorn (*Thomas*). Traders and railways. (The traders' case.) 8vo. London: Effingham Wilson, 1907.

STATISTICAL AND ECONOMIC ARTICLES IN
RECENT PERIODICALS.

UNITED KINGDOM—

Accountants' Magazine, 1907—

November—The depreciation in investment securities and the prospects of improvement: *Walker (William).*

December—Negotiable instruments: *Hamilton (A. M.).*

Bankers' Magazine, 1907—

October—Consols—Their present position: *Palgrave (R. H. Inglis).* The Egyptian demand for gold. Canada's banking half-year: *Eckardt (H. M. P.).* Notes on colonial and foreign banking, finance, and commerce. Insurance and actuarial record.

November—A bankers' convention. Home railway stocks in relation to labour: *McDermott (Frederick).* The faculty of commerce of the University of Manchester: *Chapman (Prof. S. J.).* Old-age annuities: *Fatkin (Thomas).* American bankers' convention.

December—The unprecedented situation in the United States. The operations of the Imperial Bank of Germany from 1898 to 1906. The Limited Partnerships Act. Bank of the Netherlands, 1906-1907.

Journal of Institute of Bankers, 1907—

October—Bank Charter Act, 1844: *Tipper (Henry).*

December—The President's Inaugural Address: *Schuster (Sir Felix).* Financing the crops in Canada: *Echardt (H. M. P.).*

Economic Journal. December, 1907—The present position of political economy: *Ashley (Prof. W. J.).* The rise and tendencies of German Transatlantic enterprise: *Halle (E. von).* economic theory and proposals for a legal minimum wage: *Smith (H. B. Lees).* Government and public finance: *Cohn (Gustav).* Appreciation of mathematical theories: II: *Edgeworth (F. Y.).* Sugar and the tariff: *Cooke (Cozens E.).* The efficiency theory of wages: *Moore (Henry L.).* The Seventh Congress of the International Co-operative Alliance: *Gide (Charles).* Relation of the general supply curve to a "particular expenses" curve: *Bickerdike (C. F.).* Labour exchanges and unemployment: *Macgregor (D. H.).*

Economic Review. October, 1907—Back to the land: *Cunningham (Rev. Dr.).* Socialism in Italy: *Walter (Karl).* The control of sweating: *Hutchins (Miss B. L.).* The Elberfeld system: *Mason (F. B.).* The State and the children: *Lightbody (W. M.).* Two economic notes—1. Taxation of motor cars. 2. Cost of old-age pensions: *Allen (J. E.).* The economic position: *Fleming (Owen).* Legislation, parliamentary inquiries, and official returns: *Gough (G. W.).*

1907.]   *Statistical and Economic Articles in Recent Periodicals.*   697

UNITED KINGDOM—*Contd.*
Journal of the Board of Agriculture, 1907—
  September—The cost of food in the production of milk: *Speir (John).* Agricultural returns of 1907. Imports of grain in the cereal year 1906-07.
  October—Organisation of agricultural research. Changes in wages of agricultural labourers in 1906. Rental of farms in Scotland. Persons engaged in agriculture in different countries.
  November—The production of wool in Great Britain. Average mortality among horses. Price of wool. Earnings at corn harvest in 1907.
  December—Water supply for villages. The British Crops of 1907. The indebtedness of the peasant class on the Continent.
Journal of the Department of Agriculture, &c., for Ireland. October, 1907—Technical instruction in Ireland—Waterford. Cultivation of flax in Belgium and Holland. Crop report No. 4.—Mid-October. Irish fruit crop statistics.
Journal of the Institute of Actuaries. October, 1907—On extra premiums: *Lutt (Harold Edward William).* Notes on summation formulas of graduation, with certain new formulas for consideration: *King (George).*
Journal of the Royal Colonial Institute. December, 1907—"Twelve months of imperial evolution": *Jebb (Richard).* "The mineral wealth of New Zealand": *Bell (Dr. J. Mackintosh).*
Surveyors' Institution. Transactions. Session 1907-08—
  Part 1—The Opening Address. [On compensation questions.] *Wainwright (Thomas Taylor).*
  Part 2—The Agricultural Holdings Act, 1906: *Spencer (Aubrey J).*
Transactions of Manchester Statistical Society. Session 1906-07— A decade of Manchester banking: *Fraser (D. Drummond).* Some recent electoral statistics: *Corbett (J. Rooke).* Appreciation of municipal assets: *Burton (Francis G.).* Manchester municipal public libraries: *Butterworth (Councillor Walter).* Compensation under the Licensing Act, 1904. *Cooper (Fred. W.).*

UNITED STATES—
American Journal of Sociology. September, 1907 — Industrial Insurance. V. The Employers' Liability Law: *Henderson (Charles Richmond).* Are the social sciences answerable to common principles of method? *Small (Albion W.).* The opium trade in the Dutch East Indies. II: *Scheltema (J. F.).* Some permanent results of the Philadelphia upheaval of 1905-06: *Woodruff (Clinton Rogers).*
Bankers' Magazine (New York), 1907—
  September—Various theories of note circulation: *Hague (George).* Trust companies.—Their organization, growth and management: *Herrick (Clay).* Practical banking department.— Increasing a bank's business: *Bancker (E. A.).* Savings bank department.—Savings insurance in Massachusetts: *Coburn (Frederick W.).* Modern financial institutions and their equipment.

UNITED STATES—*Contd.*
　Bankers' Magazine (New York), 1907—*Contd.*
　　October—The Banking Act of Canada: *Hague (George).* Duties
　　and liabilities of trust companies acting in various capacities:
　　Herrick (Clay). Convention of the American bankers'
　　association.
　　November—The concentration of capital in New York and those
　　who manage it: *Conant (Charles A.).* Duties and liabilities
　　of trust companies acting in various capacities: *Herrick
　　(Clay).* Gold and silver production of the United States.
　　Mexico as a field for United States capital and enterprise.
　Bulletin of Bureau of Labor. July, 1907.—Wages and hours of
　　labor in manufacturing industries, 1890-1906. Retail prices of
　　food, 1890-1906. Digest of recent reports of State bureaus of
　　labor statistics. Digest of recent foreign statistical publications.
　　Decisions of courts affecting labor. Laws of various States
　　relating to labor, enacted since 1st January, 1904.
　Journal of Political Economy, 1907—
　　October—The transportation phrase of the oil industry:
　　Montague (Gilbert Holland). Socialistic tendencies in American
　　trade unions: *Kennedy (John Curtis).*
　　November—Municipal employment of unemployed women in
　　London: *Abbott (Edith).* Control of life insurance com-
　　panies: *Zartman (Lester W.).* Can industrial insurance be
　　cheapened ? · *Davenport (H. J.).* The failure of the tele-
　　graphers' strike: *Hoxie (Robert F.).* Side-lights on the
　　telegraphers' strike: *Kennedy (John C.).* The taxation of
　　dividends: *Davenport (H. J.).*
　Political Science Quarterly. September, 1907—Trade unions and
　　trusts: *Seager (Henry R.).* The workingmen's party of New
　　York: *Carlton (Frank T.).* Slave labor in the Charleston
　　district: *Phillips (Ulrich B.).* The education of voters:
　　Haynes (George H.). The ethics of Empire: *Ford (Henry
　　Jones).*
　Quarterly Journal of Economics. November, 1907—Mortgage taxa-
　　tion in Wisconsin: *Adams (T. S.).* The nature of capital:
　　a rejoinder: *Bohm-Bawerk (E.).* The rent concept, narrowed
　　and broadened: *Carlton (Frank T.).* An illustration of the
　　continuity of the openfield system. Appendix: court roll
　　of an Oxfordshire manor: *Vinsgradoff (P.).* The taxation of
　　the unearned increment in Germany. Appendix: The Cologne
　　ordinance levying an increment tax : *Brunhuber (Robert).* The
　　Texas stock and · bond law and its administration: *Miller
　　(E. T.).* Political economy and business economy: comments
　　on Fisher's Capital and Income: *Commons (J. R.).* The
　　meetings of British and of American economists: *Carver (T. N.).*
　　The Massachusetts inheritance tax of 1907: *Taussig (F. W.).*
　Yale Review. November, 1907—The new unearned increment
　　taxes in Germany: *Brooks (Robert C.).* An agricultural bank
　　for the Philippines: *Kemmerer (E. W.).* Distribution of
　　immigrants: *Fairchild (H. P.)*

UNITED STATES—*Contd.*
Annals of American Academy of Political and Social Science. 1907—
  September—Contains a series of papers by different authors on
    Bonds as investment securities.
  November—Contains a series of papers by different authors on
    social work of the church. Relation of the municipality to
    water supply.

AUSTRIA-HUNGARY—
Statistische Monatschrift, 1907—
  September—Die Grenzen der Kriminalstatistik: *Hoegel (Dr.).*
    Studentenstiftungen im Jahre 1906 : *Lorenz (Alfred).*
  October—Die Bearbeitung der gewerblichen Betriebszählung
    vom 2. Juni 1902 durch die statistische Zentralkommission :
    Schiff (Dr. Walter). Die finanzielle Gebarung der Kranken-
    kassen in den im Reichsrate vertretenen Königreichen und
    Ländern : *Bratassevic (Ed.).*
  November—Die Grundlagen der nationalen Bevölkerungsent-
    wicklung Steiermarks : *Pfaundler (Richard).* Die Zwangs-
    versteigerungen von Liegenschaften im Jahre 1905 : *Forcher
    (Dr.).* Konferenz für Landesstatistik : *Humbourg (Dr. v.).*

FRANCE—
Annales des Sciences Politiques. 1907—
  September — Le suffrage universel en Autriche : la loi du
    26 janvier, 1907 : *Beaumont (W.).* La France industrielle
    dans le dernier quart du XIXe siècle : *Viallate (A.).*
    Chronique internationale (1906) : *Dupius (Ch.).*
  November—La constitution et les réformes en Perse : *Savary
    (H. R.).* Le port de Rotterdam : *Lecarpentier (G.).* Les
    voies de pénétration et de communication en Afrique occi-
    dentale française : *Ferry (R.).* La vie politique en Allemagne
    (1906-07) : *Isambert (G.)* La vie politique en Angleterre
    (1906-07) : *Caudel (M.).* La vie politique aux États-Unis
    (1906-07) : *Viallate (A.).* La vie politique en Extrême-
    Orient (1906-07) : *Courant (M.).*
Bulletin de Statistique, Ministère des Finances, 1907—
  August—La situation financière des communes en 1906. La
    caisse nationale d'épargne en 1905. Les caisses d'épargne
    ordinaires en 1905. Les caisses de crédit agricole mutuel en
    1906. Les revenus de l'État.
  September—Produits des contributions indirectes pendant le
    1er semestre de 1907 et 1906. La caisse nationale des
    retraites pour la vieillesse en 1906. Allemagne.—L'impôt
    complémentaire en Prusse. (Loi du 19 juin, 1906.)
  October—Les octrois en 1906. Les successions en 1906.
  November—Lettre concernant l'impôt sur le revenu adressée
    par le Ministre des finances au Président de la commission
    des réformes fiscales de la Chambre des députés. Les contri-
    butions directes et les taxes assimilées. (Résultats définitifs
    de 1906.) Le commerce extérieur en 1906. (Résultats
    définitifs.) [France et Algérie.] Les revenus de l'État.

FRANCE—*Contd.*

Journal des Economistes, 1907—

September—La concentration des entreprises: *Pinard (André).*
Notes historiques sur le repos hebdomadaire: *Mossé (Armand).*
Mouvement scientifique et industriel: *Bellet (Daniel).* Revue
de l'Académie des sciences morales et politiques (du 15 mai
au 15 août, 1907): *Lefort (J.).* Travaux des chambres de
commerce: *Rouxel (M.).* Les finances du conseil de comté
de Londres: *Raffalovich (A.).* Icarie et son fondateur
Étienne Cabet: *Passy (Frédéric).*

October—Les travaux parlementaires de la Chambre des députés
(juin, 1906, à juillet, 1907): *Liesse (André).* Le Canada
économique: *Nouvion (Georges de).* La Crise de la Viti-
culture: *Bonnaud (Paul).* Mouvement financier et commercial: *Zablet (Maurice).* Revue des principales publications
économiques de l'étranger: *Breton (René)* et *Castelot (E.).*

November—Théorie de l'évolution: le monopole, la concurrence
productive ou économique: *Molinari (G. de).* L'économie
rurale actuelle de l'Angleterre: *Ryziger (F.).* L'impôt sur
les revenus immobiliers et la question des livres fonciers:
Henricet (J. G.). Mouvement agricole: *Molinari (Maurice de).*
Revue des principales publications économiques en langue
française: *Rouxel (M.).* La nouvelle loi anglaise sur les
compagnies par actions: *Raffalovich (A.).* Lettre des États-
Unis: *Tricoche (George N.).*

December—Le problème des chemins de fer aux État-Unis:
Tricoche (George Nestler). L'alcool et les peuples primitifs:
Nouet. Les opérations gagées à Paris et en banlieue sur
l'emprunt départemental: *Letourneur (E.).* Le libre échange
au point de vue anglais: *Holloway (William).* Mouvement
scientifique et industriel: *Bellet (Daniel).* Travaux des
chambres de commerce: *Rouxel.* Les banques d'émission
suisses: *François (G.).*

Journal de la Société de Statistique de Paris, 1907—

September—Les forces hydrauliques de la France et la houille
verte: *Barrat (M.).* Une nouvelle carte électorale de
l'empire allemand, d'après les élections du Reichstag de
1907: *Meuriot (Paul).* Chronique de statistique judiciaire:
Yvernès (Maurice). Chronique des questions ouvrières et des
assurances sur la vie: *Bellom (Maurice).*

October—Questions ouvrières et industrielles en France sous la
troisième République: *Levasseur (E.).* *Homo medius* (communication faite à l'Institut international de statistique,
session de Copenhague, août 1907): *Foville (A. de).* La
criminalité en Europe (Législation et statistique): *Yvernès
(Maurice).*

November—La xie session de l'Institut international de statistique
à Copenhague: *Neymarck (Alfred).* Le xive Congrès
d'hygiène et de démographie tenu à Berlin du 23 au 29
septembre 1907: *March (L.).* La Criminalité en Europe
(Législation et statistique): *Yvernès (Maurice).*

FRANCE—*Contd.*

La Réforme Sociale, 1907—
    1st October—L'habitation, le mobilier et le jardin de l'ouvrier :
        Rivière (Louis). Le syndicat mixte de l'industrie roubaisienne :
        Ernoult (François).
    16th October—L'union sociale de la femme dans l'industrie : les
        institutions patronales de la compagnie de Chatillon-Com-
        mentry : Cheysson (E.). Le Sixième congrès national des
        syndicats agricoles : Dufourmantelle (Maurice). Le monde
        du travail et le patronage industriel aux États-Unis : Escard
        (Paul). La semaine anglaise : Risler (Georges).
    1st November—La lutte contre l'alcoolisme dans l'industrie :
        Riémain (F.). L'évolution de l'économie politique : Boyenval
        (A.). La semaine sociale de France : Terrel (Jean).
    16th November—La participation aux bénéfices : Souchon (M.).
        L'activité industrielle et l'évolution sociale de la France :
        Blondel (Georges). Le monde du travail et le patronage
        industriel aux États-Unis : Escard (Paul). L'action sociale à
        la campagne, d'après le programme de l'union populaire des
        catholiques allemands : Hohn (Dr. W.). Le contrôle collectif
        de travail : Isaac (Auguste).
    1st December—L'héritage libre : Favière (A.). L'action sociale
        à la campagne, d'après le programme des catholiques alle-
        mands : Hohn (Dr. W.). Une institution patronale—La
        consultation de nourrissons et la goutte de lait de la com-
        pagnie des mines de Blanzy. Chronique du mouvement
        social.—France, Belgique et Suisse : Béchaux (Auguste).
    16th December—L'État-patron : Prévet (Charles). L'opération
        des domaines nationaux. Système économique et social :
        Cilleuls (Alfred des). L'Héritage libre : Favière (A.).

GERMANY—
    Archiv für Rassen- und Gesellschafts-Biologie. September-October,
        1907—Die Variabilität und die Artbildung nach dem Prinzip
        geographischer Formenketten bei den Cerion-Landschnecken
        der Bahama-Inseln. (Schluss) : Plate (Dr. L.). Die konstitu-
        tive Verderblichkeit der Monogamie und die Unentbehrlichkeit
        einer Sexualreform : Ehrenfels (Christian v.). Die soziologische
        Grundfrage : Lipps (Dr. Theodor). Soziologie, Psychologie und
        Ethik. Einige Bemerkungen zu der vorstehenden Abhandlung
        des Herrn Prof. Dr. Th. Lipps : Nordenholz (Dr. A.). Nord-
        amerikanische Bevölkerungs- und Rassenprobleme (Fortsetzung):
        Heiderich (Dr. Hans).
    Archiv für Sozialwissenschaft und Sozialpolitik, 1907—
        September—Neuere Geschichtsphilosophie. Kritische Analysen,
        I : Eulenburg (Dr. Franz). Der österreichisch-ungarische
        Ausgleich, II : Gaertner (Friedrich). Wertrechnung und
        Preisrechnung im Marx'schen System, III (Schluss) :
        Bortkiewicz (L. von). Kritische Bemerkungen zur Privatbeamten-
        bewegung : Vogelstein (Dr. Theodor). Neuere Finanzliteratur :
        Lotz (Dr. W.). Finanzwissenschaftliche Literatur, I :

GERMANY—*Contd.*

Archiv für Sozialwissenschaft und Sozialpolitik, 1907—Contd.

   September—Contd.

      Esslen (*Dr. Joseph*). Literatur aus dem Gebiete des
Gewerberechtes : *Schulz* (*M. v.*). Die italienische Literatur
über den Marxismus : *Michels* (*Robert*).

   November—Ethik und Sozialismus. Erster Artikel : *Tönnies*
(*Ferdinand*). Bodenspekulation und Wohnungsfrage : *Lederer*
(*Dr. Emil*). Zur Bewegung der technischen Privatbeamten :
Mertens (*Wilhelm*). Zur Literatur über die Wohnungsfrage :
Lindemann (*Dr. H.*). Neuere Versicherungsliteratur : *Zwiedi-
neck-Sudenhorst* (*O. von*).

Jahrbuch für Gesetzgebung, Verwaltung und Volkswirtschaft
(*Schmoller's*), *Heft* 4, 1907—Gustav Rümelin. Ein Lebensabriss
des schwäbischen Staatsmannes, Statistikers und Sozialphiloso-
phen : *Schmoller* (*G.*). Die Währungsfrage, vom Staate aus be-
trachtet : *Knapp* (*G. F.*). Der deutsche Geldmarkt : *Heiligenstadt*
(*C.*). Die österreichische Wahlreform. Beiträge zur Geschichte
ihrer Entstehung : *Garr* (*Max*). Was der preussischen Volks-
schule fehlt. Weinbau und Winzer im Rheingau. Ein Beitrag zu
den Agrarverhältnissen des Rheingaues, II : *Kayser* (*Emanuel*).
Englische Kartelle der Vergangenheit, II : *Levy* (*Hermann*).
Die wirtschaftliche Bedeutung der Binnenschiffahrtsabgabe :
Heubach (--). Die neuen Seeschiffahrtsgesetze Österreichs :
Inama-Sternegg (*Johann Paul von*). Zur ältesten Sozial- und
Wirtschaftsgeschichte der Germanen : *Rachfahl* (*Felix*). Augs-
burg, das einstige Geldreservoir des Platzes St. Gallen 1835-50.
Eine finanzgeschichtliche Studie : *Gygax* (*Paul*). Die Arbeits-
zeit in Wasch- und Plättanstalten : *Gnauck-Kühne* (*Elisabeth*).
Der Arbeitstarifvertrag im Deutschen Reiche : *Zimmermann*
(*Waldemar*). Zwanzig Jahre deutscher Kulturarbeit. Tätig-
keit und Aufgaben neupreussischer Kolonisation in West-
preussen und Posen : *Swart* (*F.*). Beiträge zur Frage der
Bodenspekulation und ihrer Gewinne : *Weber* (*Adolf*).

Jahrbücher für Nationalökonomie und Statistik (*Conrad's*), 1907—

   September—Der Rhein und die Schiffahrtsabgaben : *Wirminghaus*
(*A.*). Zur Berichtigung der grundlegenden theoretischen
Konstruktion von Marx im dritten Band des " Kapital " :
Bortkiewicz (*L. von*). Die neue Knappsche Geldtheorie und
das Wesen des Geldes : *Soda* (*Kiichiro*). Die Lohnklauseln
in den ausländischen und deutschen Submissionsbeding-
ungen : *Abelsdorff* (*Walter*). Die Ausdehnung der Arbeiter-
organisationen in der Gegenwart. Allgemeine öffentliche
Krankenhäuser im Königreich Sachsen : *Radestock* (—).
Die Automobilunfälle in Deutschland im Sommer 1906 :
Kuczynski (*R.*). Reformpläne im amerikanischen Versicherungswesen : *Brodnitz* (—). Der englische Getreidebau
im Jahre 1906. Die Streikbewegung der letzten Jahre.
Die Lohnverhältnisse der städtischen Arbeiter und die
Lebensmittelpreise in Dresden.

GERMANY—*Contd.*

Jahrbücher für Nationalökonomie und Statistik (Conrad's), 1907—*Contd.*

October — Australien als selbständiger Produktionsstaat : *Schachner* (*Robert*). Nationalökonomisches bei Voltaire : *Sakmann* (*P.*). Die wirtschaftliche Gesetzgebung der deutschen Bundesstaaten im Jahre 1906 (Fortsetzung) : *Hesse.* Die deutsche Segelschiffahrt und. ihre Entwickelung in der Zeit von 1875 bis 1905 : *Meltzing* (*Otto*). Die deutschen Grossbanken am Ende des Jahres 1906. Neuere Literatur über die äussere Handelspolitik : *Levy* (*Hermann*).

November—Die Scheckfrage und das Trennungsproblem im Bankwesen : *Heinemann* (*Ernst*). Die Organisation des Scheckverkehrs in Deutschland : *Warschauer* (*Otto*). Die neue Knappsche Geldtheorie und das Wesen des Geldes (Forsetzung und Schluss) : *Soda* (*Kiichiro*). Der Transithandel Russlands im 19. Jahrhundert : *Miller* (*Paul v.*). Das Internationale Statistische Institut in seiner XI. Tagung zu Kopenhagen 1907 : *Zimmermann* (*F. W. R.*). Literatur über gewerbliches Einigungswesen, Tarifverträge, Gewerkvereine : *Kestner* (*Fritz*).

December—Zur Methode, Technik und neuesten Phase der gewerblichen Produktionsstatistik : *Most* (*Otto*). Australien als selbständiger Produktionsstaat : *Schachner* (*Robert*). Die wirtschaftliche Gesetzgebung der deutschen Bundesstaaten im Jahre 1906. Die Entwickelung des Preisniveaus in den letzten Decennien und der deutsche und englische Getreidebedarf in den letzten Jahren. Durchschnittliche Monatslöhne der landwirtschaftlichen Arbeiter in Frankreich Ende 1904 : *Rudloff* (*Hans L.*). Gelbe Gewerkschaften : *Schellwien* (*Johs.*). Die Demographische Sektion des Int. Kongresses für Hygiene und Demographie, Berlin, 1907 : *Zimmermann* (*F. W. R.*).

Zeitschrift fur Socialwissenschaft, 1907—
Heft 9—Der Kosmopolitismus der Antike : *Schucking* (*Walter*). Die physiologischen Grundlagen der Arbeitsteilung, I : *Gerson* (*Adolf*). Die Pensionsversicherung der Privatangestellten : *Albin* (*Braf.*).
Heft 10—Die sociale Dreistufentheorie, I : *Goldstein* (*Ferdinand*). Die Monokultur in der Weltwirtschaft, I : *Schilder* (*Sigmund*). Zur Reform der konventionellen Geschlechtsmoral, I : *Stöcker* (*Helene*). Die physiologischen Grundlagen der Arbeitsteilung, II : *Gerson* (*Adolf*).
Heft 11—Die Zukunft der russischen Landwirtschaft. I : *Auhagen* (*Otto*). Die sociale Dreistufentheorie, II. (Schluss) : *Goldstein* (*Ferdinand*). Zur Reform der konventionellen Geschlechtsmoral, II. (Schluss) : *Stocker* (*Helene*). Die physiologischen Grundlagen der Arbeitsteilung, III : *Gerson* (*Adolf*). Die Monokultur in der Weltwirtschaft, II. (Schluss) : *Schilder* (*Sigmund*).

GERMANY—*Contd.*

Zeitschrift fur Socialwissenschaft, 1907—*Contd.*
Heft 12—Die Vorbildung der volkswirtschaftlichen Fach-
beamten: *Feld (Wilhelm)*. Am Tage nach der socialen
Revolution : *Oppenheimer (Franz)*. Die physiologischen
Grundlagen der Arbeitsteilung, IV. (Schluss): *Gerson (Adolf)*.
Die Zukunft der russischen Landwirtschaft, II. (Schluss):
Auhagen (Otto).
Zeitschrift für die gesamte Staatswissenschaft. *Heft* 4, 1907—
Der Parlamentarismus in der Lehre Benjamin Constants:
Dolmatowsky (A. M.). Die Steuern und Anleihen im öffent-
lichen Haushalt der Stadt Basel 1361-1500 : *Harms (Bernhard)*.
Eisenbahnüberschüsse und Steuern im preussischen Staatshaus-
halte : *Cohn (Gustav)*. Die französischen Aktienbanken : *Schmidt
(Fritz)*. Die xi. Tagung des Internationalen Statistischen
Instituts zu Kopenhagen 1907 : *Zimmermann (F. W. R.)*.
Zeitschrift für die gesamte Versicherungs-Wissenschaft. October, 1907—
Der Versicherungswert in der Feuerversicherung: *Hoppe (Ernst)*.
Zur neuesten Entwicklung der Frage der Arbeitslosenver-
sicherung : *Leo (Victor)*. Das Deckungskapital in der Lebens-
versicherung : *Engelbrecht (Georg)*. Die geschichtliche Entwick-
lung der Prämienbestimmung und Entschädigungsberechnung
in der deutschen Hagelversicherung : *Rohrbeck (Walter)*. Das
englische Postamt als Versicherungsbehörde : *Wolff (Henry W.)*.
Die neuen ungarischen Arbeitversicherungsgesetze : *Bokor
(Gustav)*. Chronische Mittelohreiterung und Lebensver-
sicherung : *Levy (Max)*.

ITALY—

Giornale degli Economisti, 1907—
September—La situazione finanziaria. La legge dei piccoli numeri:
Gini (C.). Della natalità e della fecondità: *Beneduce (A.)*.
Lo stato e le abitazioni popolari in Germania : *Badoglio (—)*.
Rassegna del movimento scientifico. Economia : *Ricci (U.)*.
October—Trattato di economia politica. Introduzione : *Salvioni
(G. B.)*. Della natalità e della fecondità : *Beneduce (A.)*.
Lo stato e le abitazioni popolari in Germania : *Badoglio (—)*.
Rassegna del movimento scientifico. Economia : *Ricci (U.)*.
November—Una visione cinematografica della scienza economica
(1870-1907): *Pantaleoni (M.)*. La tecnica finanziaria come
materia di indagine teorica e di studi storico-descrittivi :
Tangorra (V.). Della necessità di unificare la terminologia
economica : *Sella (E.)*. L' economia politica nell' insegnamento secondario : *Ricci (M.)*. Correlazioni e causalità nei
fatti economici : *Graziani (A.)*. Sulla statistica delle reli-
gioni : *Fornasari*. L' economia politica e il sistema delle
scienze : *Cossa*. Sull' uso delle formole empiriche nell'
economia applicata : *Benini (R.)*. Un teorema di economia
del lavoro : *Montemartini (G.)*. Le variazioni di mortalità
secondo gli anni di età : *Beneduce (A.)*. Cronaca del con-
gresso e verbali delle sedute della XIV sezione : *Ricci (U.)*.

ITALY—*Contd.*

La Riforma Sociale, 1907—

September-October—Gli inscritti nelle università e negli istituti superiori italiani nel quattordicennio scolastico dal 1893-94 al 1906-07 : *Ferraris (Carlo F.).* La politica industriale delle organizzazioni operaie.—A proposito di un contratto di lavoro in Italia : *Cabiati (Attilio).* La legge sul consorzio obbligatorio per le miniere di Sicilia e l'attuale momento dell' industria zolfifera siciliana : *Bruccoleri (Giuseppe).* Lo sviluppo delle società per azioni e il nostro sistema tributario : *Rocca (Eugenio Paolo).* A proposito di un trattato di economia politica : *Loria (Achille).*

November—La riforma agraria nell' Irlanda : *Dalla Volta (R.).* Prolegomeni ad uno studio sulla distribuzione topografica delle industrie : *Macchioro (Gino).* Il risorgimento coloniale del Congo : *Gorrini (Giovanni).* L'insegnamento industriale e commerciale in Italia : *Virgilii (Filippo).* Divagazioni economiche sulla funzione sociale del lusso : *Michels (Roberto).*

Rivista Italiana di Sociologia, 1907. *July-October*—L'Africa nuova e il diritto pubblico africano : *Catellani (E.).* La schiavitù medioevale e la sua influenza sui caratteri antropologici degli Italiani : *Livi (R.).* Il trattamento del delinquente e la scienza moderna : *Dorado (P.).* Di alcuni problemi della sociologia : *Squillace (F.).*

SWITZERLAND—

Journal de Statistique Suisse, 1907—

Lief. 6—Die Lohn- und Arbeitsverhältnisse in der Maschinenindustrie zu Winterthur : *Lotmar (Heinrich).*

Lief. 7—Examens pédagogiques des recrues en Valais de 1886 à 1906 : *Cucatrix (X. de).*

Lief. 8—Statistik der Todesfälle in der Gemeinde Bern in der fünfjährigen Periode 1891 bis 1895 : *Scharer (Gustav).* Notice sur l'Institut des sourds-muets, à Géronde (Valais) : *Bernalde (Rev. sœur).* Über Kinderzahl und jugendliche Sterblichkeit in früheren Zeiten : *Burckhardt (Dr. Albrecht).* État des étudiants et auditeurs des universités et académies suisses pendant l'hiver 1906-07. Die Organisation der amtlichen Statistik in der Schweiz. Mitteilungen über die Preise der wichtigsten Lebensmittel und anderer Bedarfsartikel im Oktober 1907. Preise der wichtigsten landwirtschaftlichen Erzeugnisse. Les épizooties en Valais : *Favre (Camille).* Der Armenspital in Leukerbad (Kanton Wallis) : *Bayard (Dr. A.).*

QUARTERLY LIST OF ADDITIONS TO THE LIBRARY.

During the Quarter ended 15th December, 1907, the Society has received the publications enumerated below. The titles are arranged alphabetically under the following heads :—(a) Foreign Countries; (b) India and Colonial Possessions; (c) United Kingdom and its Divisions; (d) Authors, &c.; (e) Societies, &c. (British); (f) Periodicals, &c. (British).

(a) Foreign Countries.

Argentine Republic—

Anuario de la Dirección general de estadística. Año 1905, Tomo ii. Año 1906, Tomo i. 2 vols., 8vo. 1906.07 .. .. } The Director-General of Statistics

Agricultura. Ministerio de, Boletín mensual de Estadística y Comercio. (Current numbers). 1907 } The Ministry of Agriculture

Bulletin démographique argentin. (Current numbers.) Fol. 1907 .... } The Oficina Demografica Nacional

Buenos Ayres (*Province*). Dirección General de Estadística. Boletín mensual. (Current numbers.) 1907 ..... } The Provincial Statistical Bureau

Buenos Ayres (*City*). Statistical Annuary of the City of Buenos Aires. 16th year, 1906. 8vo. 1907
Córdoba (*City*). Boletín mensual de estadística municipal. (Current numbers.) Fol. 1907 ......
Santa Fé. Boletín de estadística municipal. (Current numbers.) Fol. 1907 .... } The Municipal Statistical Bureau

Austria-Hungary—

Ackerbau-Ministeriums. Statistisches Jahrbuch des k.k., fur 1905. Heft 2, Bergswerksbetrieb Österreichs im Jahre 1905. Lieferung 3. 4to. 1907....
Ackerbau-Ministeriums. Statistisches Jahrbuch des k.k., für 1906. Heft 2, Bergwerksbetrieb Österreichs im Jahre 1906. Lieferung 2. 8vo. 1907 ... } The Ministry of Agriculture

Arbeitsstatistischen Amtes im Handelsministerium. Mitteilungen des k.k. (Current numbers.) 8vo. 1907 ......
Arbeit. Bleivergiftungen in hüttenmännischen und gewerblichen Betrieben, Ursachen und Bekämpfung. Teil 6, 4to. 1907 .... } The Austrian Labour Department

Landwirtschaftliche Betriebszählung vom 3. Juni, 1902. Bezirksübersichten für Böhmen, Mähren und Schlesien. 4to. 1907 .. .... } The I. and R. Central Statistical Commission

Mittheilungen des k.k. Finanzministeriums. (Current numbers.) La. 8vo. 1907 .... } The Ministry of Finance

Österreichisches Statistisches Handbuch. Jahrgang 25, 1906. 8vo. 1907. .. .. } The I. and R. Central Statistical Commission

Österreichisches Wirtschaftspolitisches Archiv (vormals "Austria"). (Current numbers.) 8vo. 1907 } The Ministry of Commerce

Rechtspflege. Ergebnisse der Zivilrechtspflege im Jahre 1905. 4to. 1907 ....
Rechtspflege. Statistische Nachweisungen über das zivilgerichtliche Depositenwesen, &c., im Jahre 1905. Fol. 1907 .... } The I. and R. Central Statistical Commission

(a) Foreign Countries—*Contd.*

Austria-Hungary—*Contd.*

Rechtspflege. Statistische Übersicht der Verhalt-⎤
nisse der österr. Strafanstalten, &c., im Jahre 1905. ⎟ The I. and R. Central
Fol. 1907 .... ⎟ Statistical Commis-
Sparkassen. Statistik der Sparkassen für 1905. Fol. 1907 ⎬ sion
Statistische Monatschrift. (Current numbers.) 1907 ⎟
Statistische Nachrichten aus dem Gesammtgebiete der ⎟
Landwirtschaft. (Current numbers.) 1907............⎦

Hungary—
Getreideproduktion der Welt im Jahre 1907. Her-⎤ The Ministry of
ausgegeben vom königl. ung. Ackerbauminister. ⎬ Agriculture
8vo. 1907 .... ⎦
Getreideproduktion der Welt im Jahre 1905, 1906. ⎱ Mr. F. R. Rutter
2 vols., 8vo. 1905-06 . ... ⎰
Budapest. Monatshefte des Budapester Communal-⎱ The Municipal Sta-
Statistischen Bureaus. (Current numbers.) 1907 ⎰ tistical Bureau

Belgium—
Annales des Mines. (Current numbers.) 8vo. 1907 { The Administration
of Mines

Travail. Annuaire de la législation du travail. Tables⎤
décennales des volumes i à x (1897-1906). 8vo. 1907 ⎟
Travail. Conseil supérieur du travail. Huitième ⎟
session 1906-1907. Fasc. ii. Repos du dimanche. ⎟
Demandes d'exceptions et d'autorisations en vertu ⎬ The Belgian Labour
de la loi du 17 juillet, 1905, sur le repos du ⎟ Department
dimanche. 4to. 1907 ..... ⎟
Travail. Rapport relatif à l'éxécution de la loi du ⎟
31 mars, 1898, sur les unions professionelles pendant ⎟
1902-1904. 8vo. 1907 ..... ⎦

Académie Royale de Belgique. Bulletin de la classe⎱ The Academy
des lettres . . . (Current numbers) 8vo. 1907 ⎰

Brazil—
The United States of Brazil. 64 pp., fol. 1907 ...... { The Brazilian Lega-
tion
Brazilian Review. (Current numbers.) Fol. 1907 .... The Editor

Bulgaria—
Mouvement commercial de la Bulgarie avec les pays⎤
étrangers, mouvement de la navigation par ports ⎟ The Statistical Bu-
et prix moyens dans les principales villes. (Current ⎬ reau
numbers.) 4to. 1907 ..... ⎦

China—
Customs Gazette. (Current numbers.) 4to. 1907....⎤ The Inspectorate-
Native customs trade returns. No. 3. Quinquennial ⎬ General of Cus-
reports and returns, 1902-06. 4to. 1907 ..... ⎦ toms, Shanghai

Cuba—
Boletín oficial de la Secretaria de Agricultura, In-⎤
dustria y Comercio. (Current numbers.) 8vo. 1907 ⎟
Estación central agronómica de Cuba. Boletín No. 8. ⎟
Sept., 1907. 8vo. 1907 ..... ⎟
Inmigración y movimiento de pasajeros en 1906-07. ⎬ The National Library
Fol. 1907 .... ⎟
Producción de azúcar en la Zafra de 1906-07, ⎟
comparada con la de 1905-06. 5 pp., fol. 1907 .... ⎟
Asociacion de dependientes del comercio de la Ha- ⎟
bana. [Account of its object and work.] 8vo. 1907⎦

(a) Foreign Countries—*Contd.*

Denmark—

Marine marchande et la navigation du Danemark, 1906. 4to. 1907	The State Statistical Bureau
Copenhagen. Aarsberetning angaaende Sundhedstilstanden for 1906. 4to. 1907	The Municipal Statistical Bureau

Egypt—

Navigation in Ports of Egypt and the Suez Canal. Quarterly Returns. (Current numbers.) 8vo. 1907	The Statistical Department, Ministry of Finance
Alexandria. Exercice 1906. Rapport de l'administrateur. Notes des divers services. Fol. 1907	The Registrar General of England

France—

Album graphique de la Statistique générale de France. 4to. 1907	The French Labour Department
Agriculture. Ministère de l'Agriculture. Bulletin mensuel de l'Office de Renseignements agricoles. (Current numbers.) 8vo. 1907	The Ministry of Agriculture
Commerce de la France. Documents statistiques [mensuels]. (Current numbers.) 8vo. 1907 Commerce. Tableau général du commerce et de la navigation. Année 1906. Vol. 1. 4to. 1907.	The Director-General of Customs
Finances. Ministère des Finances. Bulletin de Statistique et de Législation comparée. (Current numbers.) 1907	The Ministry of Finance
Travail. Statistique des grèves et des recours à la conciliation et à l'arbitrage survenus pendant 1906. 8vo. 1907	The French Labour Department
Revue d'Économie Politique. Jan.-Oct., 1907. 8vo. 1907	Messrs. Larose and Tenin

Germany—

Gesundheitsamtes, Veröffentlichungen des Kaiserlichen. (Current numbers.) 8vo. 1907	The Imperial Health Bureau
Handel. Monatliche Nachweise über den auswärtigen Handel Deutschlands. (Current numbers.) 8vo. 1907 Handel. Auswärtiger Handel im Jahre 1906. Hefte 8, 10, 11, 12, 13, 15, 17, 19, 22. 4to. 1907	The Imperial Statistical Bureau
Justiz-Statistik. Jahrgang 13. 8vo. 1907	The Imperial Judicial Bureau
Krankenversicherung im Jahre 1905. 4to. 1907 Reichstagswahlen von 1907, Statistik der. Teil 2. 4to. 1907 Stromgebiete des Deutschen Reichs. Teil 2a. Gebiet der Elbe. 4to. 1907 Vierteljahrshefte zur Statistik des Deutschen Reichs. (Current numbers.) 4to. 1907	The Imperial Statistical Bureau
Versicherungsamts. Amtliche Nachrichten des Reichs-, 1907. 1. Beiheft. Statistik der Heilbehandlung bei den Versicherungsanstalten und zugelassenen Kasseneinrichtungen der Invalidenversicherung für 1902-06. 4to. 1907	Imperial Insurance Bureau
Baden. Volkszählung vom 2. Dezember 1895. 4to. 1897	The Registrar-General of England
Prussia— Geburten, Eheschliessungen und Sterbefälle während 1905. (200.) Fol. 1906 Heilanstalten im preussischen Staate während 1905. (203.) Fol. 1907	The Royal Prussian Statistical Bureau

(a) Foreign Countries—*Contd.*

Germany—*Contd.*

Prussia—Contd.

Landwirtschaft. Statistik der, (Anbau, Saätenstand,⎫
Ernte, Hagelwetter und Wasserschäden) für ⎪
1906. (202.) Fol. 1907...... .... ⎪
Sterblichkeit nach Todesursachen und Altersklassen ⎪
der Gestorbenen während 1905. (199.) Fol. ⎪
1907 .... ⎪
Viehzählung vom 1. Dezember, 1904. Endgültigen ⎬ The Royal Prussian
Ergebnisse der. (201) Fol. 1907 .... ⎪   Statistical Bureau
Vieh- und Obstbaumzählung vom 1. Dezember ⎪
1900. Endgültigen Ergebnisse der. (172.) ⎪
Teil 2. Der Viehbesitzstand der Gehöfte. Teil 3. ⎪
Der Obstbaumbestand der Gehöfte. Fol. 1907 ⎪
Zeitschrift des K. Preussischen Statistischen ⎪
Landesamts. (Current numbers.) Fol. 1907.... ⎭

Saxony—

Medizinalwesen im Königreiche Sachsen. 37*ér* ⎫ The Régistrar-Gene-
Jahresbericht auf das Jahr 1905. 8vo. 1907 ... ⎰   ral of England
Zeitschrift des K. Sächsischen Statistischen ⎱ The Statistical Bu-
Landesamts. (Current numbers.) 4to. 1907.... ⎰   reau of Saxony

Berlin—

Bewegung der Bevölkerung der Stadt Berlin im⎫
Jahre 1906 und Erhebung über leerstehende ⎪
Wohnungen von Anfang 1907. 4 pp., fol. 1907 ⎪
Preis-Zusammenstellungen des Statistischen Amts ⎪
der Stadt Berlin. (Current monthly numbers.) ⎬ The Municipal Sta-
Sheets. 1907 .... ⎪   tistical Bureau
Bremen. Untersuchung der Wohnungen der minder ⎪
bemittelten Klassen in Bremen. 8vo. 1905........... ⎪
Dresden. Lohnverhältnisse der städtischen Arbeiter- ⎪
schaft in Dresden in 1904 und 1905. 8vo. 1907...⎭

Hamburg—

Hamburgs Handel und Schiffahrt, 1906. La. 4to. ⎱ The Commercial Sta-
1907 ... . ⎰   tistical Bureau
   [Another copy presented by the Consul-General
   for Germany.]
Medizinische Statistik des Hamburgischen Staates. ⎱ The Registrar-Gene-
Bericht für 1906. 4to. 1907 ... . ⎰   ral of England

Veröffentlichungen des Deutschen Vereins für Ver-
sicherungs-Wissenschaft—

Heft xii. Kulturaufgaben des Versicherungs-⎫
wesens. Vorlesungen von Dr. jur. *D. Bischoff.* ⎪
8vo. 1907 .... ⎪
Heft xiii. Überblick über die landesrechtlichen, ⎪
die Feuerversicherung betreffenden Vor- ⎬ The Society
schriften : *Karl Domizlaff.* 8vo. 1907 ...... ⎪
Heft xiv. Die rückwirkende Kraft des künftigen ⎪
Reichsgesetzes über den Versicherungsvertrag. ⎪
8vo. 1907 .... ⎭

Greece—

Bulletin trimestriel du commerce spécial de la Grèce avec ⎱ The   Bureau   of
les pays étrangers. (Current numbers.) 4to. 1907 ⎰   Statistics
Statistique du commerce spécial de la Grèce avec ⎫ The Ministry of
l'étranger, mouvement de la navigation en 1905. ⎬   Finance
4to. 1907 .... ⎭

Italy—

Annali di agricoltura. No. 252. Atti del consiglio ⎱ The Director-Gene-
di agricoltura. Sessioni 1905 e 1906. 8vo. 1907 ⎰   ral of Agriculture

(a) Foreign Countries—*Contd.*

Italy—*Contd.*

Cause di Morte, Statistica delle, nell' anno 1905 con
un' appendice sull' assistenza agli esposti nel quin-
quennio 1902-06. 8vo. 1907 ..... | The Director-Gene-
Movimento della popolazione secondo gli atti dello | ral of Statistics
stato civile nell' anno 1905. Con un' Appendice di
confronti internazionali. 8vo. 1907.................

La société " Umanitaria " de Milan.   Ce qu'elle est. }
Ce qu'elle fait. 8 pp., 8vo. 1907 .... } The Society

Mexico—

Boletín de Estadística fiscal.   (Current numbers.)
Fol. 1907 ....
Boletín de Estadística fiscal.   Primer semestre del
año fiscal de 1905-06. No. 292. Fol. 1907 ......
Censo y Division territorial, verificados en 1900. } The Director-Gene-
Estados de Guerrero (1 vol.) y de Oaxaca (2 vols.) | ral of Statistics
3 vols., fol. 1905-06....
Estadística fiscal. Datos relativos. (Current numbers.)
Fol. 1907 ....

Netherlands—

Armwezen over het jaar 1904. Statistik van het.
4to. 1907 ....
Justitiëele statistiek over het Jaar 1906. 4to. 1907 } The Central Statis-
Revue mensuelle du Bureau Central de Statistique. | tical Bureau
(Current numbers.) 8vo. 1907 ......
Statistiek van den In-, Uit-, en Doorvoer, 1906. }
Gedeelte 2. Fol. 1907................ } Ministry of Finance

Norway—

Agriculture et l'élève du bétail.   Divers renseigne-
ments statistiques pour 1901 à 1905.   8vo.   1907 ..
Aliénés.   Statistique des hospices d'Aliénés pour 1905.
8vo.   1907 ....
Chemins de fer publics. 1905-06.   8vo.   1906 ....
Chemins de fer.   Tableaux graphiques. 8vo.   1906....
Commerce pendant 1906.   Statistique du, 8vo.   1907
Enfants moralement abandonnés, Statistique con-
cernant le traitement des, 1900-03.   8vo.   1906 ...
Finances des Communes pendant 1904.   8vo.   1907....
Instruction publique.   Statistique pour 1904.   8vo.
1907 ....
Justice Criminelle pour 1903-04.   Statistique de la, |
8vo.   1907 ....
Lépreux en Norvège.   Rapport pour 1901 à 1905. } The Central Statisti-
8vo.   1907 ..... | cal Bureau
Mines et usines.   Statistique des, en 1904-05.   8vo.
1907 ....
Mouvement de la population pendant 1886 à 1900.
Aperçu general du, 8vo.   1906 . ...
Mouvement de la population pendant 1903-04.   8vo.
1907 ....
Prisons.   Annuaire de l'administration générale des
prisons, 1903-04   8vo.   1907 ....
Recrutement pour 1906.   Statistique du, 8vo.   1907
Sanitaire.   Rapport sur l'état sanitaire et médical pour
1904.   8vo.   1906 ....
Successions, faillites et biens pupillaires.   1903-04.
8vo.   1907 ....

(a) Foreign Countries—*Contd.*

Norway—*Contd.*

Tableaux des télégraphes et téléphones : Statistique
pour l'année budgetaire 1905-06. 8vo. 1906 ......
Vétérinaire, service, et inspection de la viande, 1905.
8vo. 1907 ....
Journal du Bureau Central de Statistique (24ᵉ année)
8vo. 1907 ....
Statistique sociale. V. Enfants illégitimes. VII.
Scieries et établissements de rabotage : Organisation et procédés du travail. Salaires. 8vo.
1907 ....

} The Central Statistical Bureau

Roumania—
Bulletin Statistique. (Current numbers.) 8vo. 1907 } The Statistical Bureau

Russia—

Agriculture. Year-Book of Department of Agricul-
ture for 1907. Part 3. (In Russian.) 8vo. 1907 } The Department of Agriculture

Prices of Grain at Ports. Return of (in Russian).
Sheets. (Current numbers.) 1907........................... } The Ministry of Finance

St. Petersburg. Bulletin du laboratoire biologique de
St. Pétersbourg. Tome 9, Livr. 1, 8vo. 1907 .... } The Laboratory

Kazan University. Bulletin of the. (Current
numbers.) (In Russian.) 8vo. 1907 .... } The University

Salvador—
Boletin del Consejo Superior de Salubridad. (Current
numbers.) 8vo. 1907 .... } The Board

Santo Domingo Republic—

Gaceto oficial 1907. Sheets ... .
Memoria con sus correspondientes anexos que al
cuidadano Presidente de la Republica presenta el
cuidadano secretario de estado en los despachos de
Hacienda y Comercio. 4to. 1907 ....
Revista de Agricultura. Julio y Agosto 1907. 2 parts,
8vo. 1907 . ...
Revista Judicial. Segunda epoca. 8vo. 1907 ....

} The Statistical Bureau

Spain—

Censo de la población de España, según el empadro-
namiento hecho en la Península é Islas adyacentes
en 31 de Diciembre de 1900. Vols. 2, 3, 4. 2 vols.,
4to. 1907 ....

} TheGeographicaland Statistical Institute

Estadística del impuesto de transportes por mar y á
la entrada y salida por las fronteras. (Current
numbers.) 8vo. 1907 . ...

} The Director-General of Customs

Sweden—

Bidrag till Sveriges Officiella Statistik. 4to. 1907—
H. Kungl. maj-ts Befallningsbafvandes Femars-
berattelser. Sammandrag for 1896-1900. 4to.
1907...................... ....
I. Telegrafväsendet, 1906. (Telegraphs.) 4to.
1907 ....
L. Statens järnvagstrafik, 1904. (Railways.) 4to.
1907.............
M. Postverket, 1906. (Postal.) 4to. 1907.......
P. Undervisningsväsendet, 1904-05. (Education.)
4to. 1907 ....
Q. Statens Domäner, 1905. (Forests.) 4to. 1907

} The Central Statistical Bureau

(a) Foreign Countries—*Contd.*
Sweden—*Contd.*

Försakringsinspektionens underdåniga berättelse . . . ⎫
beträffande försäkringsvasendet i riket År 1905. 2. ⎪
8vo. 1907 .... ⎬ University of Upsala
Meddelanden fran k. Kommerskollegii Afdelning for ⎪
Arbetsstatistik. Nr. 4, 1907. .8vo. 1907 ...... ⎭

Kapital-Konto till Riks-Hufvud-Boken for 1906. ⎫
4to. 1907 .... ⎪
Rikets In-, och Utforsel. (Current numbers.) 1907.... ⎪
Sammandrag af de enskilda sedelutgifvande bankernas. ⎪
(Current numbers.) 1907 .... ⎬ The Central Statis-
Sammandrag af Riksbankens Ställning. (Current ⎪   tical Bureau
numbers.) 1907 .... ⎪
Statistisk Tidskrift. (Current numbers.) 8vo. 1907 ⎪
Uppgifter om Hypoteksbanken och Hypoteksförenin- ⎪
garna för År 1906. 5 pp., 4to. 1907 .... ⎭

Yrkesinspektionens verksamhet Ar 1906. 8vo. 1907.... University of Upsala
Stockholm. Bulletin mensuel du Bureau de Statis- ⎫ The Municipal Sta-
tique de la ville. (Current numbers.) 8vo. 1907 ⎭ tistical Bureau

Switzerland—

Concordance de l'ancien répertoire statistique des ⎫
marchandises avec le nouveau tarif d'usage. 48 pp., ⎪
8vo. 1907 .... ⎪
Statistique du commerce avec l'étranger en 1906. ⎬ The Federal Customs
1ᵉ partie : Importation et exportation. 2ᵉ partie : ⎪   Bureau
Recettes de douanes. 2 vols., la. 4to. 1907 .... ⎪
Statistique du commerce suisse. Rapport annuel, ⎪
1906. Sm. 4to. 1907 .... ⎭

Schweizer. Handels- und Industrie-Verein. Bericht ⎫
über Handel und Industrie der Schweiz im Jahr ⎬ The Society
1906. 4to. 1907 .... ⎭

United States—
Agriculture. Department of—
Crop Reporter. (Current numbers.) Fol. 1907.... ⎫
Bureau of animal industry. Circular 114. Sanitary ⎪
milk production. 8vo. 1907 .... ⎪
Bureau of Statistics. Bulletins— ⎪
52. Imports of Farm and Forest Products, ⎪
1904.06, by countries from which consigned. ⎪
8vo. 1907 .... ⎪
53. Exports of farm and forest products, ⎪
1904-06, by countries to which consigned. ⎪
8vo. 1907 .... ⎪
54. Trade with noncontiguous possessions in ⎪
farm and forest products, 1904-06. 8vo. ⎬ The Department of
1907 .... ⎪   Agriculture
55. Meat supply and surplus, with consideration ⎪
of consumption and exports. 8vo. 1907 .... ⎪
67. Ocean freight rates and the conditions affect- ⎪
ing them. 8vo. 1907 .... ⎪
Yearbook of the United States Department of ⎪
Agriculture, 1905 and 1906. 2 vols., 8vo. ⎪
1906-07 .... ⎪
Foreign restrictions on American meat. [Reprint ⎪
from Yearbook of Department of Agriculture for ⎪
1906.] 8vo. 1907... .... ⎪
Freight costs and market values. [Reprint from ⎪
Yearbook of Department of Agriculture for 1906.] ⎪
8vo. 1907 .... ⎭

(a) **Foreign Countries**—*Contd.*
United States—*Contd.*
Census Bureau. Bulletins—

26. Illiteracy in the United States. 4to. 1905 ....
45. Statistics of cities having a population of 8,000 to 25,000, 1903. 4to. 1906 ....
69. Child labor in the United States, based on unpublished information derived from the schedules of the twelfth Census, 1900. 4to. 1907 ....
74. Census of Manufactures, 1905. Textiles. 4to. 1907 ....
75. Census of Manufactures, 1905. Agricultural implements. 4to. 1907 ....
77. Census of Manufactures, 1905. Lumber and timber products. 4to. 1907 ....
79. Census of Manufactures, 1905. Printing and publishing. 4to. 1907 ....
80. Census of Manufactures, 1905. Paper and wood pulp. 4to. 1907 ....
81. Census of Manufactures, 1905. Shipbuilding. 4to. 1907 ....
82. Census of Manufactures, 1905. Musical instruments, and materials. 4to. 1907 ....
83. Census of Manufactures, 1905. Slaughtering and meat packing, manufactured ice, and salt. 4to. 1907 ....
84. Census of Manufactures, 1905. Carriages and wagons, and the steam and street railroad car industry. 4to. 1907 ....
85. Census of Manufactures, 1905. Pens and pencils, buttons, needles, pins, and hooks and eyes, oilcloth and linoleum, and turpentine and rosin. 4to. 1907 ....
86. Census of Manufactures, 1905. Copper, lead, and zinc smelting and refining. 4to. 1907 ....
87. Census of Manufactures, 1905. Tobacco. 4to. 1907 ....
88. Census of Manufactures, 1905. Power employed in manufactures. 4to. 1907 ....

} The Census Bureau

Census Bureau. Bulletins, Census of Manufactures, 1905. 27, Maryland and District of Columbia. 41, New Hampshire and Vermont. 42, Connecticut. 43, Alabama. 44, Virginia and West Virginia. 46, Minnesota. 47, Kentucky and Tennessee. 4to. 1906 ....

Census Bureau. Statistics of women at work, based on unpublished information derived from the schedules of the twelfth Census, 1900. 4to. 1907 ....

Commerce and Finance. Monthly Summary. (Current numbers.) 4to. 1907 .... } Department of Commerce and Labor

Debt. Monthly Statements of Public Debt and Cash in Treasury. (Current numbers.) Sheets. 1907.... Gold, Silver, and Notes, &c., in Circulation. Monthly Statements. (Current numbers.) Sheets. 1907 .... } The Secretary of the Treasury

Labour. 21st Annual Report of Commissioner of Labor, 1906. Strikes and lock-outs. 8vo. 1907.... } The Bureau of Labor

California—

State Board of Health. Monthly Bulletins. 8vo. 1907. (Current numbers) ....
State Board of Health. 19th Biennial Report for 1904-06. 8vo. 1906 .... } The Board

(a) Foreign Countries—*Contd.*
United States—*Contd.*

Illinois. Bureau of Labor Statistics. 25th Annual ⎫
Coal Report, 1906. Also 8th Annual Report of ⎪ The Bureau
Illinois Free Employment Offices for 1905-06. 8vo. ⎬
1907 .... ⎭

Massachusetts—
Bureau of Statistics of Labor. 37th Annual ⎫
Report, January, 1907. 8vo. 1907 .... ⎪ The   Bureau   of
Labor Bulletin. (Current numbers.) 8vo. 1907.... ⎬ Statistics of Labor
Recent British legislation affecting working men. ⎪
8vo. 1907 .... ⎭
State Board of Health. 38th Annual Report for ⎫ The Board
1905-06. 8vo. 1907 .... ⎬

Nebraska. Bureau. Bulletin No. 11, Sept., 1907. ⎫
Acreage of Nebraska crops, 1907. Surplus com- ⎪ The Bureau
modities of Nebraska, 1906. Orchard Statistics, ⎬
1907. 8vo. 1907 .... ⎭

Boston—
Annual report of executive department for 1905. ⎫
2 parts, 8vo. 1907 .... ⎪ The Municipal Sta-
Monthly Bulletin of the Statistics Department. ⎬ tistical Bureau
(Current numbers.) 4to. 1907 .... ⎪
Municipal Register for 1907. 8vo. 1907............... ⎭

New York (City). Public Library. Bulletin. ⎫
(Current numbers.) 8vo. 1907............... ⎬ The Library

Commercial America. Published monthly. (Current ⎫ Philadelphia   Com-
numbers.) Fol. 1906 . ... ⎬ mercial Museum

Dun's Review. (Current numbers.) Fol. 1907........⎰ Messrs. R. G. Dun
                                                    ⎱ and Co.

Yale Law Journal. Vol. 16, No. 8. June, 1907. 8vo. ⎱
1907 . ... ⎰ The Editor

American anthropological and ethnological societies. ⎫
Memoirs. Vol. 1, Part 1. Materials for the physical ⎪ New Era Printing
anthropology of the eastern European Jews: *Maurice* ⎬ Co., U.S.A.
Fishberg. 8vo. 1905 .... ⎭

American Economic Association. Publications—
Vol. vii, No. 3. On collective phenomena and the ⎫
scientific value of statistical data : *Ernst G. F.* ⎪
Gryzanovski. With introduction : *Frederick* ⎪ The Association
Tuckerman. 8vo. 1906 .... ⎬
Vol. viii, No. 3. Labor legislation of Connecticut : ⎪
Alba M. Edwards. 8vo. 1907 .... ⎭

Smithsonian Institution—
Annual report of the Board of Regents for year ⎫
ending 30th June, 1906. 8vo. 1907. .... ⎪
Smithsonian Contributions to Knowledge. Part of ⎪ The   Smithsonian
vol. 35. No. 1718. 4to. 1907 .... ⎬ Institution
Smithsonian Miscellaneous Collections. Quarterly ⎪
issue. Vol. 4, part 2; and part of vol. 49. 8vo. ⎪
1907 .... ⎭

Uruguay—
Montevideo. Resumen anual de estadística muni- ⎱ Major P. G. Craigie,
cipal. Años 2 y 3, 1904 y 1905. 2 vols., 8vo. ⎰ C.B.
1905-06...............

International—
Bulletin International des Douanes. (Current ⎱ The Board of Trade
numbers.) 8vo. 1907 .... ⎰

(a) Foreign Countries—*Contd.*

International—*Contd.*

Fourth International Congress of delegated represen- ⎫
tatives of Master Cotton Spinners' and Manufac- ⎪
turers' Associations. Vienna. 1907 .... ⎬ Purchased
International Labour Office. Bulletin. Vol. 1, ⎪
Nos. 4, 5, 6, 7 and 8. 1906. 8vo. [1907] .... ⎭

International Congress on Tuberculosis, 1908. Pre- ⎫
liminary announcement. 8vo. 1907 .... ⎬ The Congress

---

(b) India and Colonies.

India, British—

Agricultural Statistics of India for 1901-02 to 1905-06. ⎫
2 vols., fol. 1907 .... ⎪
Cotton Spinning and Weaving. Monthly Statistics ⎪
of. (Current numbers.) 8vo. 1907.... . ... ⎬ The Director-Gene-
Indian Trade Journal. (Current numbers.) 4to. 1907 ⎪ ral of Commercial
Mint and Coinage Tables for 1906-07 and earlier ⎪ Intelligence
years. [Advance sheets.] Fol. 1907 .... ⎪
Prices and wages in India, Twenty-fourth issue. ⎪
Fol. 1907 .... ⎭

Trade. Review of Trade of India in 1906-07. ⎫
[Cd-3787.] 1907 . ... ⎪
Baluchistan District Gazeteer Series. Vol. 5. Quetta- ⎬ The India Office
Pishin District. 2 vols., 8vo. 1907 .... ⎭

Bengal—

Annual statement of sea-borne trade and navigation ⎫ The Collector of
with foreign countries and Indian ports for ⎬ Customs
1906-07. Fol. 1907..... .... ⎭

District Gazetteers. Balasore. 8vo. 1907..... .... ⎫
Central Provinces. District Gazetteers. Vol. A. ⎪
Descriptive. Districts of Betul, Saugor and Seoni. ⎪
3 vols, 8vo. 1907 .... ⎬ The India Office
Punjab. Gazetteer of the Chenab Colony. 1904. ⎪
La. 8vo. 1905.. .. .... ⎪
Travancore State Manual. 3 vols , la. 8vo. 1906 ⎭

East Indian Railway. Diagrams of traffic, audited ⎫
first half of 1907. and 123rd Report of the ⎬ The Company
Directors for first half-year of 1907. Fol. 1907.... ⎭

Australia, Commonwealth of—

Population and Vital Statistics. Bulletin No. 3, ⎫
Vital Statistics of the Commonwealth for quarter ⎪
ended 31st March, 1907. Fol. 1907 .... ⎪ The Commonwealth
Shipping and Oversea Migration of the Commonwealth ⎬ Bureau of Census
for 1906 Fol. 1907 ... . ⎪ and Statistics
Trade and Customs and Excise Revenue of the Com- ⎪
monwealth of Australia for 1906. Part II, fol. 1907 ⎭

Trade, Shipping, and oversea Migration of the Com- ⎫
monwealth. Official Bulletins. (Current numbers.) ⎬ The Commonwealth
Fol. 1907 .... ⎭ Statistician

Parliamentary Debates. Session 1907. (Current ⎫
numbers.) 8vo. 1907 .... ⎬ The Commonwealth

Proposed new Australian Customs Tariff. Issued by ⎫
the Manufacturers' Association of Great Britain. ⎬ Purchased
20 pp., fol. 1907 .... ⎭

"The Review," Vol. 8, No. 7, July, 1907. containing ⎫
an article by Mr. B. R. Gelling on "Idealism in ⎬ Mr. B. R. Gelling
life assurance." 4to. 1907 .... ⎭

(b) **India and Colonies**—*Contd.*

British South Africa—

First annual statement of the trade and shipping of the colonies and territories forming the South African Customs Union, 1906. Fol. 1907 .... } Major P. G. Craigie, C.B.

Canada, Dominion of—

Banks. Monthly Reports on Chartered. (Current numbers.) 4to. 1907 .... } The Deputy Minister of Finance

Labour. Report of Royal Commission on dispute respecting hours of employment between the Bell Telephone Co. of Canada, Ltd., and operators at Toronto, Ont. 102 pp., 8vo. 1907.....................
Labour. Report of Department of Labour for year ended 30th June, 1906. 8vo. 1906 .... } The Department of Labour

Alberta. Official handbook, containing reliable information concerning its resources. 60 pp., 8vo. 1907 } The Provincial Government

Manitoba—

Journals and sessional papers of the Legislative assembly. Session 1907. 8vo. 1907.....................
Orders and proclamations of the Lieutenant-Governor-in-Council having force of law. 8vo. 1907 .... } The King's Printer, Winnipeg

Report of Department of Public Works for 1906. 8vo. 1907 .... } The Department of Public Works

Ontario—

Department of Agriculture. Bulletin 161. The sheep industry in Ontario. 8vo. 1907 ....
Poultry Institute of the Province of Ontario. Second annual report, 1906-07. 8vo. 1907....... } The Department of Agriculture, Toronto

Saskatchewan. Annual Report of Department of Agriculture of the Province for 1905. 8vo. 1907 .... } The Department

Canadian Life and Resources. (Current numbers.) Fol. 1907 .... } The Superintendent of Emigration

Ceylon—

Administration reports, 1906. Part. II.—Revenue,
Railway. Report of the general manager for 1906. Fol. 1907 .... } The General Manager

New South Wales—

Prisons. Report of the Comptroller-General for 1906. Fol. 1907 .... } The Comptroller-General of Prisons

Public Finances [of New South Wales]. A six-years' retrospect . . . 40 pp., 8vo. [1907].............. } The Agent-General for N.S.W.

Railways and Tramways. Report of Chief Commissioner for year ended 30th June, 1907. Fol. 1907 } Chief Accountant, Railway Department

Statistical register for 1905 and previous years. 8vo. 1907 .... } The Agent-General for N.S.W.

Statistical register for 1906 and previous years. Part 1, Education, Science, and Art; 2, Population and Vital Statistics. Fol. 1907 .... } Director, Bureau of Statistics

New Zealand, Dominion of—

Labour. The Department of Labour, its organisation and work. 32 pp., 8vo. 1907.....................
Labour, Report of Department of, for year 1906-07. Fol. 1907 .... } The Department

(b) India and Colonies—*Contd.*

Orange River Colony—
Civil Service list of the Colony for 1907. 8vo. 1907 ⎫
Colonial Treasurer's annual accounts, 1905-06, and ⎬ The Government Li-
Auditor-General's report thereon. Fol. 1907........ ⎭ brarian

Queensland—
A B C of Queensland statistics, with appendix ⎫ The Agent-General
showing comparative Commonwealth and Austra- ⎬ for Queensland
lasian statistics, 1906. 44 pp., 8vo. 1906................ ⎭

Rhodesia—
Chamber of Mines. Monthly Reports of Executive ⎫
Committee, and Returns of Output of Gold, &c. │
(Current numbers.) Sheets. 1907 .... ⎬ The Chamber
Chamber of Mines. Twelfth Annual Report for year │
ended 31st March, 1907. 4to. 1907 .. .. ⎭

Information for Tourists and Sportsmen. 4to. 1907 { The British South Africa Co.

South Australia—
Agricultural and Live Stock Statistics. Season 1906- ⎫
1907. Preliminary Tables. 5 pp., 4to. 1907 . . . ⎬ The   Government
Births, Deaths, and Marriages. Annual Report of ⎬ Statist
Registrar-General for 1906. Fol. 1907 .... ⎭

Straits Settlements—
Supplements to the Perak Government Gazette, 1907. ⎫ The Government
(Current numbers.) Fol. 1907 .... ⎭ Secretary

Transvaal—
Agricultural Journal. (Current numbers.) 8vo. ⎫ The   Agricultural
1907 . ... ⎭ Department
Mines Department, Transvaal. Monthly Statistics. ⎫ The Department
(Current numbers.) Obl. 4to. 1907 .... ⎭
Johannesburg. Statistics. (Current numbers.) Fol. ⎫ The Town Statis-
1907 .... ⎭ tician
Transvaal Chamber of Mines. Monthly Analysis of ⎫ The Chamber
Gold Production. (Current numbers.) 1907 . ... ⎭

Victoria—
Friendly Societies. 29th Annual Report for 1906. ⎫ The Actuary for
Fol. 1906 .... ⎭ Friendly Societies
Friendly Societies. Report of the Registrar for 1906. ⎫ The   Registrar of
8 pp., fol. 1907 .... ⎭ Friendly Societies
Public library, museums, and national gallery of ⎫ The Trustees
Victoria. Report of trustees for 1906. Fol. 1907 ⎭
Statistical Register of the State for 1906. Parts 3. ⎫
Municipal statistics. 4. Accumulation. 5. Law, ⎬ The   Government
Crime, &c. 6. Social Condition. 7. Vital Statistics. ⎬ Statist
8. Population. Fol. 1907 .... ⎭

Western Australia—
Industrial Conciliation and Arbitration Act, 1902. ⎫ The Registrar of
6th Annual Report for 1906. Fol. 1907... .... ⎭ Friendly Societies
Mines. Report of Department of Mines for 1906. ⎫ The Agent-General
Fol. 1907 .... ⎭ for W. Australia
Monthly Statistical Abstract. (Current numbers.) ⎫ The Registrar-Gene-
Fol. 1907 .... │ ral and Govern-
Supplements to Government Gazette, containing ⎬ ment Statistician
Monthly Mining Statistics. (Current numbers.) 1907 ⎭

(c) United Kingdom and its several Divisions.

United Kingdom—

Board of Trade Journal. (Current numbers.) 1907 ...   The Board of Trade

Building Societies. 12th Annual Report by Chief
Registrar of Friendly Societies of proceedings of   Chief Registrar of
registrars under Building Societies Acts for 1906.   Friendly Societies
Part I, Report. (50.) 1907 ....

Coal Tables, 1906. (349.) 1907 ....   The Board of Trade

Factory and Workshop Act, 1901. Preliminary
tables of administration by local authorities in 1906
of the homework provisions of the Act. 15 pp.,   The Home Office
fol. 1907..................... .. ..

Friendly societies, workmen's compensation schemes,
industrial and provident societies, and trade unions.   Chief Registrar of
Reports of Chief Registrar, for 1906. Part A.   Friendly Societies
(49). 1907 ....

Labour. Eleventh abstract of labour statistics of
United Kingdom, 1905-06. [Cd-3690.]   8vo.
1907 ....

Labour. Conciliation and arbitration boards. Report
on rules of voluntary conciliation and arbitration
boards and joint committees. [Cd-3783]. 8vo.
1907 ....

Labour. Report on strikes and lock-outs and on conciliation and arbitration boards in United Kingdom   > The Board of Trade
in 1906. [Cd-3711.] 8vo. 1907 .. ..

Labour. Report on changes in rates of wages and
hours of labour in United Kingdom in 1906, with
comparative statistics for 1897-1905. [Cd-3713]
8vo. 1907 ... .

Merchant Shipping, 1906. Tables of progress of
merchant shipping in United Kingdom and principal
maritime countries. (348.) 1907 . ...

Mines and quarries : general report and statistics for
1906. Part ii.—Labour. [Cd-3770.] Part iii.—   > The Home Office
Output. [Cd-3774.] 1907 ... .

Railways. Summary of Statistics of Railways in
United Kingdom for 1896, 1902-06. Sheet. 1907.   > Mr. W. Bygate, York

Railway returns. Returns of capital, traffic, receipts,
and working expenditure of railway companies of
United Kingdom for 1906. [Cd-3705.] Fol.
1907 ....

Statistical abstract for the United Kingdom for
1892-1906. Fifty-fourth number. [Cd-3691.] 8vo.   > The Board of Trade
1907 . .. .

Statistical abstract for principal and other Foreign
Countries for 1895 to 1904-05. Thirty-third number.
[Cd-3291.] 8vo. 1907 ....

Trade of United Kingdom with Foreign Countries
and British Possessions, 1906. Supplement to
volumes I. & II. Abstract and detailed tables   The Statistical Office
showing countries of consignment of imports and   of Customs De-
countries of ultimate destination of exports.   partment
[Cd-3687.] 1907 ....
[Another copy presented by the Board of Trade.]

Woods, Forests, and Land Revenues. 85th Report
of Commissioners, dated 1907. (227.) 1907........ > The Commissioners

Wrecks. Abstracts of returns of shipping casualties
from 1st July, 1905 to 30th June, 1906. [Cd-3666.] > The Board of Trade
1907 ....

Australia Navigation Bill, 1907. [Cd-3826.] 1907 .... Purchased

(c) **United Kingdom and its Divisions**—*Contd.*
United Kingdom—*Contd.*

British Central Africa Protectorate. Report for⎫
1906-07. 8vo. 1907......................................

Canada. Papers relative to working of taxation of
unimproved value of Land in Canada. [Cd-3740.]
1907 ....

Canals and Waterways. Royal Commission on.
Vol. ii, Parts 1 and 2. [Cd-3716-17.] 1907 ....

Ceylon. Report on Mineral Survey in 1905-06. 8vo.
1907 ....

East India (Railways). Administration Report for
1906. [Cd-3634.] 1907 ....

Fiji. Correspondence *re* tenure of land in Fiji.
(120.) 1907. [Cd-3763.] 1907 ....

Home-work. Report of Select Committee with
minutes of evidence and appendix. (290.) 1907 ...

Horse breeding. 11th Report of Royal Commission.
[Cd-3712.] 1907 ...

Inebriates Acts, 1879-1900. Report of Inspector for
1906. [Cd-3685.] 1907 ....

Iron and Steel, 1906. (350.) 1907 ....

Labour. Conciliation (Trade Disputes) Act, 1896.
6th Report by Board of Trade, 1905-07 ....

Local Taxation Account, 1906-07. (317.) 1907 ... ...

Local Taxation Licences, &c., 1906-07. (298.) 1907

Lunacy. 61st Report of Commissioners for 1906.
(225.) 1907. 8vo. ....

Meteorological Committee. 2nd Annual Report for
1906-07. [Cd-3674.] 8vo. 1907..........

New South Wales. Papers relative to taxation of
unimproved value of land in N.S.W. [Cd-3761.] ⎬ Purchased
1907 ....

Police. Report of Commissioner of Police of Metropolis for 1906. [Cd-3771.] 1907 ....

Post-Office. 53rd Report of Postmaster-General for
1906-7. [Cd-3624.] 8vo. 1907 . ...

Prisons. Report of Commissioners of Prisons, &c.,
for 1906-7. [Cd-3738.] 8vo. 1907..............

Public General Acts, 7 Edward VII. 1907. 8vo.
1907 ....

Public Works Loan Board. 22nd Annual Report for
1906-07. (226.) 1907.. ....

Railways in British Protectorates. &c. (336.) 1907...

Railway servants (Hours of Labour). [Cd-3825.]
1907 ....

Reformatory and Industrial Schools of Great Britain.
Report for 1906. Part 2 [Cd-3759.] 8vo. 1907

Sanitary Officers in Rural Districts. (273.) 1907 ..

Servia. New Customs Tariff. Translation. [Cd-
3749.] 1907 ....

Steamship Subsidies. (359.) 1907 ....

Sugar. Brussels Sugar Convention, 1902. Additional
Act. [Cd-3780.] 1907 ......

Sugar (cost) (London, Paris and Berlin). (332). 1907

Taxes and Imposts. (281.) 1907 ....

Training of British Boy Seamen. Report of Departmental Committee. 1st Report. [Cd-3722.] 1907

Trustee Savings Banks. Return for 1906. (270.)
1907 ....

Unemployed Workmen Act, 1905. Report on Working of Act in 1906-07. (326.) 1907 ....⎭

(c) **United Kingdom and its Divisions**—*Contd.*
United Kingdom—*Contd.*

Women and Children in Public-houses. Return.⎫
[Cd-3813.] 1907 ....⎪
Workmen's Compensation Acts, 1897 and 1900. ⎬ Purchased
Statistics of Proceedings under the Acts during ⎪
1906. [Cd-3622.] 1907 ....⎭

Tariff Commission. The new Australian tariff.⎫
4to. 1907............... .... ⎬ The Commission

Great Britain—
Board of Agriculture and Fisheries—
Agricultural Statistics, 1906. Vol. xli, Part 4.⎫
Colonial and Foreign Statistics. [Cd-3832.]⎪
8vo. 1907 .... ⎪ Board of Agriculture
Agricultural Returns of Great Britain, 1907. (Pro- ⎬ and Fisheries
duce of Crop) (2 sheets.) Fol. 1907 . . .. ⎪
Report on production of wool in Great Britain in ⎪
1905 and 1906. 8vo. 1907 ....⎭
Journal of the Board. (Current numbers.) 8vo. 1907 ⎫
Leaflets. (Current numbers.) 8vo. 1907 ....⎪
Weekly Returns of Market Prices (of Cattle, Dead ⎬ The Board
Meat, Provisions, Fruit, and Vegetables, Hay and ⎪
Straw). (Current numbers.) Fol. 1907...........⎭
Report on Second International Dairy Congress, ⎫
held at Paris in October, 1905. [Cd-3689.] ⎬ Purchased
8vo. 1907 ....⎭

England and Wales—
Births, Deaths, and Marriages. Supplement to 55th ⎫
Annual Report of Registrar-General. Part 1. ⎬ Mr. R. J. Thompson
[Cd-7769.] 8vo. 1895 ....⎭
Local Government Board. 26th Annual Report for ⎫
1906-07. [Cd-3665.] 8vo. 1907 ....⎪
Local Government Board. Supplement to 35th annual ⎬ The Local Govern-
report, containing report of medical officer for ⎪ ment Board
1905-06. [Cd-3656.] 8vo. 1907 ....⎭
London County Council—
Housing of Working Classes. Tables showing ⎫
Rents, &c., for year 1906-07. Fol. 1907 ....⎬ Purchased
London Statistics, 1906-07. Vol. xvii. 8vo. ⎫
1907 ....⎪
Report of the Council for year 1905-06. 8vo. ⎪
1907 ....⎪
Report of Education Committee submitting report ⎬ The London County
of Medical Officer (education) for year ended ⎪ Council
31st March, 1907. Fol. 1907 ....⎪
London County Council Gazette. (Current num- ⎪
bers.) Fol. 1907 ....⎭
Wandsworth. Report of Council of the Metropolitan ⎫
Borough of Wandsworth for year ended 31st March, ⎬ Town Clerk
1907, to which is appended the annual report of the ⎪
Medical Officer of Health for 1906. 8vo. 1907 ...⎭
Blackburn. Annual Report on Health of Blackburn ⎫ The Medical Officer
for 1906. 8vo. 1907....... ....⎬ of Health
Manchester—
Abstract of Treasurer's Accounts for 1906-07. 8vo. ⎫
1907 ....⎪
Estimates for year 1907-08. 8vo. 1907.......... ⎬ The City Treasurer
Poor. Abstract of Accounts of the Guardians for ⎪
1906-07. 8vo. 1907.... .. ..⎭

(c) **United Kingdom and its Divisions**—*Contd.*
England and Wales—*Contd.*
Manchester—Contd.

Distress Committee. 2nd Annual Report of ⎫
Committee appointed under " Unemployed ⎪
Workmen Act, 1905." 1906-07. 8vo. 1907.... ⎬ The Corporation
Education Committee. 5th Annual Report of ⎪
Committee, 1906.07. 8vo. 1907.... .. .. ⎭

Tunbridge Wells. Abstracts of Accounts. Year ⎫ The Borough   Ac-
ended 31st March, 1907. 8vo. 1907..... .... ⎭ countant

Ireland—

Agricultural Statistics of Ireland, with detailed report ⎫
for 1906. [Cd-3794.] 8vo. 1907........................... ⎪
Agricultural statistics, Ireland, 1907. Abstracts ⎪
showing the acreage under crops and the numbers ⎪
of live stock in each county and province, 1906-07. ⎬ The Department of
[Cd-3769.] 8vo. 1907 .... ⎪ Agriculture
Banking, Railway, and Shipping Statistics, Ireland. ⎪
June, 1907. [Cd-3818.] 8vo. 1907 .... ⎪
Department of Agriculture and Technical Instruction. ⎪
Journal of the. (Current numbers) 8vo. 1907.... ⎭

Congestion in Ireland, Royal Commission on. ⎫
6th Report and Appendix. [Cd-3747-8]. 7th ⎪
Report and Appendices i and ii. [Cd-3784-5-6.] ⎪
1907 .... ⎪
Education. 73rd Report of Commissioners of Na- ⎪
tional Education for 1906-07. [Cd-3699.] 8vo. ⎪
1907 .... ⎪
Judicial Statistics, Ireland, 1906. Part 1. Criminal ⎪
Statistics. [Cd-3654.] 1907 .... ⎪
Land Act, 1903. Report of Estates Commissioners ⎪
for year ended March, 1907. [Cd-3692.] 1907 .. ⎪
Land Commission. Report for 1906.07. [Cd-3652.] ⎬ Purchase.
1907 .... ⎪
Local Government Board. Annual Report for 1906-07. ⎪
[Cd-3682.] 1907 .... ⎪
Lunacy. 56th Report of Inspection of Lunatics for ⎪
1906. [Cd-3745.] 8vo. 1907 .... ⎪
Prisons. 29th Report of General Prisons Board for ⎪
1906-07. [Cd-3698.] 8vo. 1907................... ⎪
Public Works, Ireland. 75th Report of Commis- ⎪
sioners, with Appendices, 1906-07. [Cd-3693]. ⎪
1907 .... ⎪
Reformatory and Industrial Schools. 45th Report ⎪
for 1906. [Cd-3623.] 8vo. 1907................ .... ⎭

Scotland—

Births, deaths, and marriages. 51st detailed annual ⎫ The Registrar-Gene-
report of Registrar-General. (Abstracts of 1905.) ⎬ ral for Scotland
[Cd-3650.] 8vo. 1907 .... ⎭

Deer Forests (Scotland). (344.) 1907 .... ⎫
House-letting in Scotland. Report of Departmental ⎪
Committee. Vol. 1. Report. [Cd-3715.] 1907 ⎬ Purchased
Occupiers of Farms (Scotland), numbers of occupiers ⎪
with gross rentals, 1906. (127–I.) 1907 .... ⎪
Teinds, &c. (Scotland). (146.) 1907 .... ⎭

Scotch Education Department—

Secondary education. Report for 1907, with appen- ⎫
dix. 8vo. 1907..... .... ⎬ The Scotch Educa-
Secondary education. Report for 1907. [Cd-3776.] ⎪ tion Department
8vo. 1907 .... ⎭

(c) **United Kingdom and its Divisions**—*Contd.*
Scotland—*Contd.*

Glasgow. Report of Medical Officer of Health for 1906. Fol. 1907 .... } The Medical Officer of Health

---

(d) **Authors, &c.**

Adam (Edwin). Land values and taxation (social problems, series iv). 8vo. 1907 .... } Purchased

Anderson (Sir Robert). Criminals and crime: some facts and suggestions. 8vo. 1907 .... } Messrs. James Nisbet and Co.

Andersson (Thor). Social Sjukförsäkring. 8vo. 1907.... The Author

Angier Brothers. Steam shipping reports, 1903, 1905, and 1906. Sheets, fol. 1903.06 .... } Messrs. Angier Brothers

Barrett (R. J.). Canada's century: progress and resources of the great Dominion. Introduction by Lord Strathcona. 538 pp., la. 8vo. 1907..................

Canto (Julio Perez). Economical and social progress of the Republic of Chile, 1906. La. 8vo. 1906 .... } The Author

Castberg (P. H.). Production: a study in economics. 8vo. 1907 .... } Messrs. Swan Sonnenschein and Co.

Cobbett (William). Rural rides . . . during 1821 to 1832: with economical and political observations. New edit., with notes by Pitt Cobbett. 2 vols., 8vo. 1893 .... } Purchased

Cooper (Joseph). Tabular guide, No. 2, to life assurance. November, 1907. 1907 .... } The Compiler

Cox (Harold). British Industries under Free Trade. Essays by experts, edited by Harold Cox. 2nd impression. 8vo. 1904 .... } Purchased

Davenport-Hill (Florence). Children of the State. Edited by Fanny Fowke. 2nd Edit. 8vo. 1889 ....

De La Plaza (Victorino). Exposición contra el proteccionismo exagerado al azúcar, de producción interna. 84 pp., 8vo. 1907 .... } The Author

Dyer (Henry). Evolution of Industry. 8vo. 1895 ....

Edwards (Clement, M.P.). Railway Nationalization. Preface by the Rt. Hon. Sir Charles W. Dilke, Bart., M.P. 2nd Edit., 8vo. 1907.... .... } Purchased

Elderton (Ethel M.). On the measure of the resemblance of first cousins. (Eugenics Laboratory Memoirs, IV.) 54 pp., 4to. 1907 ....

Esche (Arthur). Arbeitsordnung und Arbeiterausschuss (Neue Zeit- und Streitfragen). 46 pp., 8vo. 1907 .... } Messrs. Zahn and Jaensch

Ferraris (Carlo F.)—

Gli inscritti nelle università e negli istituti superiori Italiani nel 1893.94 al 1906-07. 13 pp., 8vo. 1907
La cassa nazionale di previdenza per la invalidità e per la vecchiaia degli operai. 44 pp., 8vo. 1907 .... } The Author

Flurscheim (Michael). Clue to the economic labyrinth. 8vo. [? 1900].............. .... } Purchased

Galton (Francis). Restrictions in marriage. Studies in national eugenics. Eugenics as a factor in religion. Followed by an abstract of an earlier memoir: Eugenics, its definition, scope and aims. Memoirs communicated to the Sociological Society. 8vo. 1905 .... } The Francis Galton Laboratory

Gilbart (J. W.). History, principles and practice of banking. New edition, revised by Ernest Sykes. 2 vols., 8vo. 1907 .... } Messrs. G. Bell and Sons

(d) **Authors, &c.**—*Contd.*

Gnauck-Kühne (Elisabeth). Die deutsche Frau um die Jahrhundertwende. Statistische Studie zur Frauenfrage. Zweite Auflage. 8vo. 1907 .... } M. Otto Liebmann

Guyot (Yves). Sophismes socialistes et faits économiques. 8vo. 1908 .... } The Author

Heron (David)—
Note on class incidence of cancer. (Reprinted from *British Medical Journal.*) 4 pp., 8vo. ... .
A first study of statistics of insanity and inheritance of insane diathesis. Eugenics Laboratory Memoirs, II. 33 pp., 4to. 1907 . ...} The Francis Galton Laboratory

Hopkins (J. Castell). The Canadian annual review of public affairs, 1906. Sixth year of issue. 8vo. 1907 .... } The Author

Hume (David). Essays and treatises on several subjects. Vol. I, containing essays, moral, political, and literary. A new edition. 8vo. 1793 .... } Purchased

Hutton (Charles). Mathematical tables containing common, hyperbolic, and logistic logarithms; also sines, tangents, secants, and versed sines, both natural and logarithmic. 8vo. 1860 .... } Mr. R. J. Thompson

Jebb (Eglantyne). Cambridge: a brief study in social questions. 8vo. 1906 .... } Messrs. Bowes and Bowes

Kessler (Dr. Gerhard). Die deutschen Arbeitgeber-Verbände. Im Auftrag des Vereins für Socialpolitik herausgegeben. 8vo. 1907..........................} Purchased

Laiglesia (F. de)—
Organizacion de la hacienda en la primera mitad del siglo xvi. 70 pp., 8vo. 1906 ....
Los gastos de la corona en el Império. 74 pp., 8vo. 1907 ....} The Author

Lauder (Albert E.). The Municipal Manual. A description of the constitution and functions of urban local authorities. 8vo. 1907 .. ..} P. S. King and Son

Livi (Dr. Ridolfo)—
Antropometria militare. Parte 1. 4to. 1896 .... Major P. G. Craigie
La schiavitù medioevale e la sua influenza sui caratteri antropologici degli Italiani. 28 pp., 8vo. 1907 .. } The Author

Mackay (Thomas) (Editor). Policy of Free Exchange. Essays by various writers on the economical and social aspects of free exchange and kindred subjects. 8vo. 1894 . . .. } Purchased

Marx (Karl). Capital: a critique of political economy. Vol. 2. The process of circulation of capital. Edited by Frederick Engels. Translated from the 2nd German edition by Ernest Untermann. 8vo. 1907 ...} Messrs. Swan Sonnenschein and Co.

Meyer (Hugo Richard)—
Public ownership and the telephone in Great Britain: restriction of the industry by the State and the municipalities. 8vo. 1907 ....
British State Telegraphs: a study of the problem of a large body of civil servants in a democracy. 8vo. 1907 . ... .. } Messrs. Macmillan and Co.

More (Louise Bolard). Wage-earners' budgets. A study of standards and cost of living in New York City. With a preface by Franklin H. Giddings. 8vo. 1907 ... . } Messrs. G. Bell and Sons

Neymarck (Alfred). Finances contemporaines. iv, v, L'obsession fiscale, projets ministeriels . . . relatifs à la reforme de l'impôt, 1872-1907. i, 1872-1895. ii, 1896-1907. 2 vols., 8vo. 1907 ....} Purchased

(d) **Authors, &c.**—*Contd.*

Nichols (John Benjamin). The numerical proportions of the sexes at birth. (Part 4 of vol. i of Memoirs of American Anthropological Association.) 51 pp., 8vo. 1907 .... } Major Craigie

Pearson (Karl)—

Mathematical contributions to theory of evolution. xiii. Theory of contingency and its relation to association and normal correlation. (Drapers' Company Research Memoirs. Biometric Series I.) 4to. 1907 Mathematical contributions to theory of evolution. xiv. General theory of skew correlation and non-linear regression. (Drapers' Company Research Memoirs, Biometric Series, II.) 4to. 1905 .... } The Francis Galton Laboratory

Mathematical contributions to theory of evolution. xvi. On further methods of determining correlation. (Drapers' Company Research Memoirs, Biometric Series, IV.) 4to. 1907 .... } Purchased

Pearson (Karl) and *Blakeman (John).* Mathematical contributions to theory of evolution. xv. A mathematical theory of random migration. (Drapers' Company Research Memoirs, Biometric Series, III.) 4to. 1906 .... } The Francis Galton Laboratory

Pedder (D. C.). Where men decay. A survey of present rural conditions. 8vo. 1908 .... } Mr. A. C. Fifield

Rauchberg (Prof. Dr. H.). Die statistischen Unterlagen der österreichischen Wahlreform. 71 pp., 8vo. 1907 } Mr. F. Irrgangs, Brünn

Robertson (William A.) and *Ross (Frederick A.).* Actuarial theory. Notes for students on subject-matter required in second examinations of Institute of Actuaries and Faculty of Actuaries in Scotland, with a prefatory note by Thomas G. Ackland. 8vo. 1907 .... } Messrs. Oliver and Boyd

Robertson (William Bell). The Slavery of Labour. A scientific demonstration of the identity of free and slave labour. Second edition. 8vo. (1906) .... } Messrs. Samuels and Taylor

Rousiers (Paul de). The Labour Question in Britain. With preface by Henri de Tourville. Translated by F. L. D. Herbertson. 8vo. 1896 .... } Purchased

Rozenraad (C.). Table comparing Gold and Silver Stock of principal Banks of Issue, bank-rate, &c., at end of Sept., 1907 and 1906. Sheet .... } The Compiler

Schoenhof (J.). History of Money and Prices. 8vo. 1896 .... } Purchased

Schoolmeesters (Herman). La mission de l'État. L'ordre économique. La réglementation du travail. 63 pp., 8vo. 1907 .... } M. Albert Dewit

Schuster (Edgar). Promise of youth and performance of manhood, a statistical inquiry into the question whether success in the examination for the B.A. degree at Oxford is followed by success in professional life. (Eugenics Laboratory Memoirs III.) 4to. 1907. .. } The Francis Galton Laboratory

Scott (W. R.). Constitution and finance of an English copper mining company in the sixteenth and seventeenth centuries : an account of "The Society of the Mines Royal." 8vo. 1907 .... } The Author

Sherwell (Arthur). Life in West London. A study and a contrast. 8vo. 1897 .... } Purchased

Smith (Charles William). Manifesto on International, Financial, and Commercial Gambling in "Options and Futures" (Marchés à terme) . . . 22 pp., fol. 1907 .... } The Author

(d) Authors, &c.—*Contd.*

Sowray (J. Russell). British railway finance, with special reference to capital charges. 25 pp., 8vo. 1907 .... } The Author

Stein (Philipp). Über Streiks und Aussperrungen (Neue Zeit- und Streitfragen). 24 pp., 8vo. 1907.... } Messrs. Zahn and Jaensch

Sundbärg (Gustav). Bevölkerungsstatistik Schwedens 1750-1900. Einige Hauptresultate. (XIV. Internationaler Kongress für Hygiene und Demographie, Berlin, September 1907.) 8vo. 1907 ... . } The Statistical Bureau of Sweden

Sutherland (William). Old age pensions in theory and practice, with some foreign examples. 8vo. 1907 .... } Messrs. Methuen and Co.

Swan (Charles Herbert). Impersonal taxation : a discussion of some rights and wrongs of governmental revenue (Annals of American Academy of Political and Social Science). 8vo. 1907 . ... } The Academy

Tarde (Alfred de). L'Idée du juste prix. Essai de psychologie économique. 8vo. 1907 .... } M. Félix Alcan

Taylor (Sedley). Profit-sharing between capital and labour. 8vo. 1884 .... } Purchased

Waghorn (Thomas). Traders and Railways (The Traders' Case). 8vo. 1907 . ... } Mr. Effingham Wilson

Wampach (Gaspard). L'impôt sur le revenu en Allemagne. 8vo. 1907 ...

Wines (Frederick Howard). Punishment and Reformation : an historical sketch of the rise of the penitentiary system. 8vo. 1895 .... } Purchased

---

(e) Societies, &c. (British).

Institution of Civil Engineers. Minutes of proceedings. Vol. 169. 8vo. 1907 .... } The Institution

London School of Economics and Political Science. (University of London.) Calendar 1907-08. 8vo. (1907) ..... } The Society

Manchester Statistical Society. Transactions. Session 1906-07. 8vo. 1907........ ... . } ,,

Royal Anthropological Institute. Journal. Vol. xxxvii. January to June, 1907. La. 8vo. 1907..... ... . } The Institute

Royal College of Physicians. Catalogue of accessions to Library in year 1906-07. 8vo. 1907 .... } The College

Royal College of Surgeons of England. Calendar. 1st August, 1907. 8vo. 1907 .... } ..

Royal Society of Edinburgh. Proceedings. Session 1906-07. Vol. 27, Nos. 3 and 4. (2 vols.) 8vo. 1907 .... } The Society

Society of Accountants and Auditors. Incorporated Accountants' Year-book . . . 1907-08. 8vo. 1907 .. } ,,

University of London. University College. Calendar. Session 1907-08. 8vo. 1907 .... } The University

---

(f) Periodicals, &c., and Miscellaneous (British).

Annual Register for 1906. New Series. 8vo. 1907 ...
Daily Mail Year Book for 1908 ....
Hazell's Annual for 1908 ... .
Whitaker's Almanack, 1908 ....
Who's Who, 1908 ......
Who's Who Year Book, 1908 ....
Year Book of Scientific and Learned Societies. 22nd Annual issue 1905. 23rd Annual issue. 1906 .... } Purchased

(f) Periodicals, &c. (British)—*Contd.*

Trades Union Congress. Report of proceedings at ⎫
fortieth Annual Congress, held at Bath, September │
2nd to 7th, 1907. 8vo. 1907 .. .. ⎬ Purchased
"The Times" Monthly Index. 8vo. 1907 .... ⎭

Agricultural Economist and Horticultural Review. ⎫
March, 1907. Fol. 1907 .... │
Bradshaw's Railway Manual, Shareholders' Guide and ⎬ The Editor
Official Directory, 1907. 59th Edition, edited by │
Herbert H. Bassett. 8vo. 1907 .... ⎭

Gas Works Directory and Statistics, 1907-08 (Revised ⎫ Hazell, Watson and
to July, 1907). Thirtieth issue. 8vo 1907 .... ⎭ Viney

The International. A review of the world's progress. ⎫
December, 1907. 8vo. 1907 ,..... .... ⎬ Mr. T. Fisher Unwin
⎭

Land Agents' Society. Journal. Vol. vi, Nos. 8—12. ⎫
8vo. 1907 .... ⎬ The Society
⎭

Lloyd's Register of British and Foreign Shipping. ⎫
Report of Society's operations during 1906-07. 15 þp., ⎬ The   Secretary,
8vo. 1907 ... . ⎭ Lloyd's

South Wales Coal Annual for 1907. Comprising steam, ⎫
bituminous, and anthracite coal, coke, and patent │
fuel. Wages, prices, freights, exports, docks, rail- ⎬ Joseph Davies, Esq.
ways, wagons, pitwood, and general statistics. Edited │
by Joseph Davies. 8vo. 1907 .... ⎭

The weekly, monthly, or quarterly issues of the following returns have also been received during the past quarter :—

Consular Reports—From United States and United Kingdom.

Labour Reports, &c.—From Austria-Hungary, Belgium, France, Germany, Italy, United States, Massachusetts and New York States, Canada, New Zealand, and United Kingdom.

Trade Returns—From Argentina, Austria-Hungary, Belgium, Bulgaria, China, Denmark, Egypt, France, Germany, Greece, Italy, Mexico, Netherlands, Norway, Roumania, Russia, Spain, Sweden, Switzerland, United States, India, and United Kingdom.

Vital Statistics—From Argentina, Egypt, Germany, Italy, Netherlands, Roumania, Switzerland, United States (Connecticut and Michigan only), Queensland, South Australia, and United Kingdom.

Vital Statistics of following Towns—Buenos Ayres, Buda-Pesth, Brünn, Prague, Brussels, Copenhagen, Berlin, Bucharest, Moscow, Madrid, Stockholm, London, Manchester, Dublin, Edinburgh, and Aberdeen.

The weekly, monthly, or quarterly issues of the following periodicals, &c., have also been received during the past quarter. They are arranged under the countries in which they are published :—

Denmark—Nationalökonomisk Tidsskrift.

France—Annales des Sciences Politiques. Économiste Français. Journal des Économistes. Monde Économique. Polybiblion, Parties Littéraire et Technique. Réforme Sociale. Le Rentier. Revue d'Économie Politique. Revue de Statistique. Journal de la Société de Statistique de Paris.

Germany—Allgemeines Statistisches Archiv. Archiv für Rassen- und Gesellschafts-Biologie. Archiv für Sozialwissenschaft und Sozialpolitik. Jahrbuch für Gesetzgebung, Verwaltung, und Volkswirtschaft. Jahrbücher für Nationalökonomie und Statistik. Kritische Blätter für die gesamten Socialwissenschaften. Zeitschrift für die gesamte Staatswissenschaft. Zeitschrift für die gesamte Versicherungs-Wissenschaft. Zeitschrift für Socialwissenschaft. Mittheilungen aus der Handelskammer Frankfurt a. M.

Italy—L'Economista. Giornale degli Economisti. Rivista Italiana di Sociologia. Riforma Sociale. Societa Umanitaria, Bollettino mensile.

Sweden—Ekonomisk Tidskrift.

Switzerland—Journal de Statistique suisse.

United States—Bankers' Magazine. Bradstreet's. Commercial and Financial Chronicle, with supplements. Duns' Review. Journal of Political Economy. Political Science Quarterly. Quarterly Journal of Economics. Yale Review. American Academy of Political and Social Science, Annals. American Economic Association, Publications. American Geographical Society, Bulletin. American Statistical Association, Quarterly Publications. American Philosophical Society, Proceedings and Transactions. Columbia University, Studies in History, &c.

Canada—The Chronicle: Insurance and Finance.

India—Indian Engineering.

New Zealand—Government Insurance Recorder. Trade Review and Price Current.

United Kingdom—The Accountant. Accountants' Magazine. Athenæum. Australian Trading World. Bankers' Magazine. Broomhalls' Corn Trade News. Browne's Export List. Colliery Guardian. Commercial World. Economic Journal. Economic Review. Economist. Fireman. Incorporated Accountants' Journal. Insurance Record. Investors' Monthly Manual. Investors' Review. Joint Stock Companies' Journal. Labour Co-partnership. Licensing World. Local Government Journal. Machinery Market. Nature. Navy League, Journal. Policy-Holder. Post Magazine. Produce Markets' Review. Public Health. Publishers' Circular. Sanitary Record. Shipping World. Statist. The Times. Anthropological Institute, Journal. Cobden Club, Leaflets. East India Association, Journal. Howard Association, Leaflets, &c. Institute of Actuaries, Journal. Institute of Bankers, Journal. Institution of Civil Engineers, Minutes of Proceedings. Iron and Steel Institute, Journal. Lloyd's Register of British and Foreign Shipping, Statistical Tables. London Chamber of Commerce, Journal London University Gazette. Manchester Literary and Philosophical Society, Memoirs and Proceedings. Royal Agricultural Society, Journal. Royal Colonial Institute, Proceedings and Journal. Royal Geographical Society, Geographical Journal. Royal Irish Academy, Proceedings and Transactions. Royal Meteorological Society, Meteorological Record and Quarterly Journal. Royal Society, Proceedings. Royal United Service Institution, Journal. Sanitary Institute, Journal. Society of Arts, Journal. Statistical and Social Inquiry Society of Ireland, Journal. Surveyors' Institution, Professional Notes and Transactions. Trade Circulars.

INDEX TO VOL. LXX,

YEAR 1907.

PAGE

ADAMS (W. G. S.). *Some Considerations relating to the Position of the Small Holding in the United Kingdom* **411-437**

Introduction. Deficiencies in the data. Purpose of the Paper. Definition of small holding, from 5 to 50 acres . . . 411
"Intense" culture excluded. Size and number of holdings in the United Kingdom. Irish returns of holdings include waste and rough grazing land, &c Not so the British returns . . 412
Summary showing number and size of holdings, 1905. Mr. Rew's Return giving further numbers of holdings according to size . 413
Average size of holdings in England, Scotland, and Wales; and by Counties 414
Small holdings in England are mainly near industrial centres; in Scotland they are in the Highlands. Statement showing number of holdings above 1 acre in Ireland, 1905, according to acreage, and the percentage of each class to the whole; total area of each class, and its percentage to the total area of Ireland . . 415
Average size of holdings in Ireland; and by Counties . . 416
Number and proportion of each class of holding in Ireland since 1841 418
Changes in agricultural economic conditions. *Table* showing decrease in area of tillage in the United Kingdom, 1867-1905 . . 419
Return of number, size, and percentage of crops in each class of holding in Ireland, 1864 and 1874 421
A similar return to date now being prepared. Number of live-stock, Great Britain and Ireland 422
Increase in agricultural imports 423
Table showing total value of certain produce imported into the United Kingdom, 1871-1906 424
Movements of agricultural prices. Home grain crops no longer profitable. Value of roots and green crops . . . 425
Prices of animal produce: beef, mutton, pork, dairy produce, eggs, and poultry 426
Good prospects for home beef of best grades: also for dairy produce, eggs and poultry, fruits, vegetables, and perishable produce. Conditions essential to the economic development of a small farm holding. Productive capacity of a 20-acre farm in Ireland. Requisites for success 428
Tenure and rent. Stocking and equipment 430
Organization of agriculture. Co-operative societies: (1) Purchasing; (2) Producing and marketing; and (3) Provident . . . 431
Agricultural education 433
Variety in type of holdings required 434
Appendix. Statement regarding a 20-acre farm of good average land, well cultivated 435

Discussion on Mr. W. G. S. Adams's Paper :

Eversley (Lord). Mr. Adams's paper a proper sequel to his own [see p. 267]. Number of small holdings over-estimated. An instance in Hampshire. Numbers given in the Census and in the agricultural returns. England, Scotland, and Ireland, compared. Small holdings mostly in pastoral districts. Conditions of profitable cultivation. Example in Cheshire. Aberdeen compared with S.E. Counties of Scotland as to people employed. Security of tenure . . . 438

Plunkett (Sir Horace). Problem of economic holdings in Ireland. Smaller size of the Irish holding. A question of the man rather than the land. Proper size of an economic holding not yet settled. Need for experimental colonies. Social life must be provided. Pressing need for education. Small holdings should be dealt with in groups. Co-operative organization essential . . . 440

PAGE

ADAMS (W. G. S.).   *Discussion on his Paper—Contd.*

Argyle (Jesse).   Personal qualities required for success as a small
   holder.   Progress of co-operation in Denmark   .   .   .   442
Winfrey (R.), M.P.   Land must first be provided to meet the demand.
   Tenancy preferable to ownership.   Experience of the Cambridge
   County Council.   The Act of 1891.   Higher assessment of small
   holdings.   Lincoln and Norfolk Small Holdings Association.
   Demand there for small farms   442
Craigie (Major).   Need for circumspection in creating small holdings.
   Number of small holdings.   Examples of success and of failure.
   A specimen parish in the Isle of Ely.   Need for experiments.
   Holdings should be of various types.   Men not always forthcoming.
   Numbers of small holdings in England and Germany compared.
   The hypothetical balance-sheet criticised   .   .   .   444
Bund (Willis).   No type of holding should be stereotyped.   Failure of
   whole-time small holders in Bromsgrove ; success of part-time
   in Worcestershire.   Special agricultural education not practicable
   in schools   446
Hiscock (W.).   Importance of the potato crop.   Co-operation   .   .   447
Adams (W. G. S.).   Number of existing small holdings.   Irish migra-
   tory labourers as landholders.   The hypothetical holding.   Records
   of milk production, and of hay and potatoes   .   .   .   447
ADDITIONS to the Library.   *See* LIBRARY.
AGRICULTURAL Labour in Great Britain.   Decline of.   *See* EVERSLEY
   (Lord).
———— Rent in England and Wales in the 19th Century.
   See THOMPSON (R. J).
———— Returns of Great Britain, 1907.   *Preliminary State-
   ment*   477
———— Produce of crops   .   .   651
ANNUAL General Meeting.   *See* GENERAL MEETING.
———— Report.   *See* REPORT.
ANTHROPOMETRIC Survey.   Deputation to the Prime Minister.   *See*
   REPORT OF COUNCIL.
ASSIZE of Bread at Oxford.   *See* BALLARD (A.).

BAILEY (A. H.).   Letter criticising the Paper by Messrs. Harris and
   Lake on Estimates of the Realisable Wealth of the United Kingdom;
   with reply by the authors of the paper   129–131
BALLARD (Adolphus).   *The Assize of Bread at Oxford, 1794-1820* .   629–637
   The tables compiled from *Jackson's Oxford Journal.*   The assize of
      bread set by the University authorities   .   .   .   629
   Breaches of the assize.   Form in which the assize was set   .   .   630
   Tables showing prices of the peck loaf by weeks, 1794-1820   .   .   631
BANK of England.   Weekly returns, 1906.   *See* PERIODICAL RETURNS.
BIBLIOGRAPHY of Cereals.   *See* REPORT of Council.
BIRTHS in 1906.   *See* PERIODICAL RETURNS.
BIRTH-RATES in England and Wales.   *See* WELTON (T. A.).
BOOKS.   Notes on Economic and Statistical Works :
   Agriculture (Board of).   Wool production   .   .   .   668
   Alden (P.) and Hayward (E. E.).   Housing   .   .   .   498
   Annuario statistico della città italiane.   335
   Ashley (P.).   Local and central government   .   .   .   148
   Australasia.   Unification of statistics   663
   Avebury (Lord).   Municipal and national trading   .   .   144
   Bailey (W. B.).   Modern social conditions (U.S.A.)   .   .   491
   Ballard (A).   Domesday inquest   368
   Barbour (J. S.).   William Paterson and the Darien Co.   .   515
   Berliner Statistik fur 1905.   Uebersichten 1907   .   .   491
   Bertillon (J.).   Fréquence des causes de décès à Paris   .   .   337
   Black (Clementina).   Sweated industry   349
   Boverat (R.).   Socialisme municipal en Angleterre   .   .   499
   Bray (R. A.).   The town child   495
   Bremin.   Wohnungen der minder bemittelten Klassen   .   .   683
   Burkett (C. W.) and Poe (C. H.).   Cotton   .   .   .   136
   Canada.   Census Bulletin I.   Wage-earners by occupations   .   .   486

PAGE

BOOKS. Notes on Economic and Statistical Works—*Contd.*

Chatterton-Hill (G.). Heredity and selection in sociology . . 492
Child labor in the United States 346
Collings (Jesse). Land reform 370
Condizioni della classe operaia in Milano 344
Devas (C. S.). Political economy 504
Dewsnup (E. R). Housing problem in England . . . 497
Elderton (W. P.). Frequency curves and correlation . . . 132
Fisher (Irving). Capital and income 351
Foville (A. de). La monnaie 678
France. Album graphique de la statistique générale . . . 489, 692
Gainsborough Commission. Life and labour in Germany . . 347
Galton (F.). Probability 335
Guyot (Yves). Science économique. 3rd ed. 1907 . . . 505
Halle (E. von). Die Weltwertschaft 358
Heron (D.) Statistics of insanity 667
Holmes (G. K.). Meat supply and surplus (U.S.A.) . . . 664
Holt (B. W.). Gold supply and prosperity 356
Hull (W. H.). Practical problems in banking and currency . . 686
Irish Imports and Exports, 1905. [Cd-3631.] 1907 . . . 481
Jacquart (C.). Mortalité infantile dans les Flandres . . . 494
———— Statistique et science sociale . . . 334
Jebb (L.). Small holdings in England 512
Knibbs (G. H.). Classification of disease and causes of death . 662
Lauterbach (E.). Staats- u. Kommunal-Besteuerung . . 355
Lescure (J.). Des crises générales et périodiques de surproduction . 138
Lethbridge, (Sir R). India and preference 366
Levasseur (E.). Questions ouvrières et industrielles en France . 674
Macgregor (H. D.). Industrial combination . . . 340
Mackenzie (W. L.) and Foster (A.). Physical condition of Glasgow
   school children. [Cd-3637.] 1907 485
Macrosty (H. W.). Trust movement 338
Martel (F.) and Grigaut (M.). Économie politique . . . 507
Martinez (A. B.). Argentine au 20e siècle 363
Meyer (H. R.). Municipal ownership in Great Britain . . . 146
Mombert (P.). Bevölkerungs bewegung in Deutschland . . 494
More (L. B.). Wage-earners' budgets (New York) . . . 659
Morison (T.). Industrial organisation of an Indian province . . 364
New York. Physical welfare of school-children . . . 670
Old Age Pensions. Tables [Cd-3618.]. 1907 . . . 423
Other new publications 153, 375, 519, 693
Pearson (K.). Further methods of determining correlation . . 655
———— Statistics of pulmonary tuberculosis . . . 331
Pigou (A. C.) Protective and preferential import duties . . 150
Porter (R. P.). Dangers of municipal trading . . . 501
Prinzing (F.). Handbook der Medizin. Statistik . . . 135
Punnett (R. C.). Mendelism 493
Rauchberg (H.). Die statistischen Unterlagen der österreich.
   Wahlreform 661
Registrar-General. Supplement to 65th Annual Report. [Cd-2618]. 1907 479
Sachet (A.). Assistance des vieillards 141
Schuster (E.). Inheritance of ability 336
Seager (H. R.). Introduction to economics. 3rd edit. . . 143
Simiand (F.). Salaire des ouvriers des mines de Charbon en France . 508
Slater (G.). The English peasantry 372
Sociological Society. Papers. Vol. iii 517
Spencer (M. G.) and Falk (H. J.). Employment pictures from the
   Census 134
Statistisches Handbuch fur das Deutsche Reich. Teil i . . 490
Sundbarg (G.). Bevölkerungsstatistik Schwedens (1750-1900) . 690
Supino (C.). Crisi economiche 688
Tariff Commission. Vol. 3. Agriculture report . . . 671
Thompson (H.). From cotton field to cotton mill . . . 136
Turot (H) and Bellamy (H.) Surpeuplement et habitations à bon-
   marché 499
United States. Statistics of women at work . . . 656
Wampach (G.). L'impôt sur le revenu en Allemagne . . 680
Welsford (J. W.). Strength of nations. 509
Wolff (H. W.). Co-operative banking 353
Yermoloff (A.). La Russie agricole 360

BREAD. Assize at Oxford. *See* BALLARD (A.).
BRITISH ASSOCIATION, Leicester, 1907. *Discussion on Modern
   Methods of treating Observations* 471–476
   Introduction 471
   Synopsis of a paper by W. Pulin Elderton dealing with methods of
   meteorological statistics. The "method of moments." Standard
   deviation. Correlation. Work of Prof. Pearson, and Miss A. Lee;
   and of Dr. G. T. Walker 471

3 c 2

PAGE

BRITISH ASSOCIATION, Leicester, 1907—*Contd.*

Shaw (Dr. W. N.). New methods of observation. Method of harmonic analysis. Prof. Schuster's "periodogram." Prof. Chrystal's "method of residuation." Diagrams prepared at the meteorological office showing the relation of the mean to frequency of occurrence of various values 473

Yule (G. U.). Applications of statistical methods. Limits in use of the arithmetical mean. Standard deviation. "Interquartile range." Correlation coefficient. Harmonic analysis not applicable in statistics 474

Hinks (A. R.). The theory of correlation as applied to astronomical statistics by Prof. Pearson. A dangerous application. Diagrammatic representations in the paper 475

Hooker (R. H.). Examples of practical use of the method of correlation. The weather and crops. Effect of rainfall and temperature on crops 475

Turner (Prof. H. H.). Illustration showing need of caution in interpreting statistics 475

Edgeworth (Prof.). The discussion falls under three heads : law, chance, and a mixture of the two. Statistics properly deal with plurality of causes. Prof. Pearson's method of representation falls under the third head. An empirical formula 476

Elderton (W. Palin). Reply to Mr. Hinks 476

CATALOGUE of Library. *See* REPORT OF THE COUNCIL.
CENSUS of Production Act (1906). *See* YULE (G. U.).
CEREALS. Bibliography. *See* REPORT OF COUNCIL.
CONSOLS. *See* PERIODICAL RETURNS.
CORN. Average prices. *See* PERIODICAL RETURNS.
—— Acreage under. *See* AGRICULTURAL RETURNS.
CORRELATION of the Weather and Crops. *See* HOOKER (R. H.).
COUNCIL. *See* REPORT of the Council.
CROPS and Weather. Correlation. *See* HOOKER (R. H.).
CROPS in 1907 651

DEATHS in 1906. *See* PERIODICAL RETURNS.
DECLINE in number of Agricultural Labourers in Great Britain. *See* EVERSLEY (Lord).
DIFFERENTIAL law of wages. *See* MOORE (H. L.).
DILKE (Sir Charles W.). *On official statistics. Presidential Address, delivered 19th November, 1907* 553–582

Chronicle of the Society for the year. Guy medal in gold awarded to Prof. Edgeworth; in silver to Mr. N. A. Humphreys . . . 553
Growth of bureaucracy. Report by M. Cheysson on the statistics of various countries. The Official Statistics Committee report, 1880. Action by Mr. W. H. Smith in 1877 554
Multiplication of independent official statistics Defective collation and indexing of parliamentary returns 555
Various termination of years adopted by the Inland Revenue, Post Office, Board of Trade, Local Government Board . . . 556
Report of the Select Committee in Official Publications, 1906. Financial advantage of co-ordination. Paralysis of the movement for reform since 1880. Organisation of statistics in Prussia in 1805, and recent German imperial statistics 557
The statistics of Austria-Hungary, Italy, the United States, Canada . 558
Central Statistical Commissions in many countries . . . 559
Formation of a French Superior Council of Statistics in 1885. Distinction between administrative statistics and that for social inquiry 560
The Census Committee of the Society. Co-ordination might be obtained through a representative advisory committee . . 561
Difficulty of collecting returns. Suggestion for a Department to index and explain the statistical returns of other Departments . 562
Economy of co-ordinating. Strong parliamentary demand necessary for reform. Lord Goschen's views. Mr. Bowley's address to the British Association . . . . [563

PAGE

DILKE (Sir Charles W.). *On official statistics—Contd.*

The "Official Publications" report, 1906 565
Select Committee on Publications, 1907. Overlapping of areas of
  Urban and Registration districts 566
True franchise statistics unattainable. War Office statistics. The
  Statistical, Colonial and Foreign Abstract . . . 567
Mr. Coghlan's Statistical account of Australia and New Zealand . 568
The scope of the Board of Trade Statistics. The Statistical Abstract
  compared with colonial publications 569
Criminal and civil judicial statistics. The work of Sir John
  Macdonell 570
Causes operating against co-ordination. Defects of local statistics.
  Urban and registration districts 572
L.G.B. and Board of Trade figures for local taxation . . . 573
Home Office and Census figures or occupations 574
Incompleteness of returns of particular trades. The Census of
  production. Necessity for a statistical department to deal with
  non-administrative statistics 575
Appendix A. Classification of Areas in returns by the Registrar-
  General and by the Local Government Board 577
—— B. Results of the Melbourne Conference on the unification of
  Australian statistical methods 582

Proceedings on the 19th November, 1907 ... . . . **583–585**
DUDFIELD (Dr. Reginald). *Note on the Mortality from Tuberculosis,*
1851-1905 . . . . **454–470**

Reason for beginning with 1851. Designations of the divisions of the
  disease 454
A. Mortality of all ages: Persons 455
Table showing rate of change in successive decennia . . . 456
B. Mortality at different ages: two sexes 456
Phthisis. Tabes mesenterica. Hydrocephalus 457
Scrofula 458
Table 1. Mortality at all ages 459
—— 2. England and Wales. Phthisis. Tabes mesenterica. Hydrocephalus. Scrofula. Mean rates per mille . . . 460–463
—— 2A. London. Phthisis. Tabes mesenterica. Hydrocephalus.
  Scrofula. Mean rates per mille 464–468
—— 3. England and Wales. Relative mortalities, under the four
  divisions 468
—— 3A. London. The same 469–470

ECONOMIC Articles in Recent Periodicals. *See* under STATISTICAL.
EDGEWORTH (Prof. F. Y.). *On the representation of statistical
frequency by a curve* **102–106**

The work of Professors Bruns, Charlier, and Thiele . . . 102
Coincidence of results obtained by the different methods of Charlier
  and Bruns 103
Comparison with the generalized law of error 104
Criticism of Mr. Elderton's "Frequency Curves" . . . 106

—————— Guy medal in gold awarded to Prof. Edgeworth . . 323
—————— Guy medal presented 617
ELDERTON (W. Palin). Summary of Paper on methods of meteoro-
logical statistics. *See* BRITISH ASSOCIATION.
EVERSLEY (Lord). *The Decline in Number of Agricultural
Labourers in Great Britain* **267–306**

Discussion at Political Economy Club. Mr. Rew's report on the
  decline in agricultural population, 1881-1901. Main decline took
  place 1861-81 267
Present paper covers period 1861-1901; its scope. Exaggeration as to
  extent of the decline. Quotation from Mr. Chamberlain . . 268
Table showing number of persons in England and Wales employed in
  agriculture. 1851-1901 269
After deducting women and males under 20, decline reduced from
  50 to 35 per cent. 270
Number of workers under 20 reduced by Education Acts of later years.
  Effect of new classification of the aged in 1881. . . . 271
Farmers' sons and relatives, in 1861 classed as engaged in agriculture.
  Effect of South African War on figures of 1901 . . . 272
Those engaged in "intense cultivation" not included. Tables
  showing increasing numbers of these 273

PAGE

Eversley (Lord). *Decline of Agricultural Labourers—Contd.*

Table A. Male persons employed in agriculture (classified) England
and Wales, 1861-1901 275
—— Male persons employed in agriculture (classified) Scotland . . 276
Comparisons of results, England and Scotland . . . 276
Table B. Occupation of land, England, Wales and Scotland . . 277
Number of farms over 20 acres in England, Wales and Scotland Com-
parison of actual decline in the two periods 1861-81 and 1881-1901 . 278
Table showing price of wheat, 1840-1900. Other prices of agricultural
produce 279
—— showing reduction of arable land 280
Rise of wages in towns, and on farms 280
Agricultural depression began 1879. Fall in prices and rents, but not
in wages 281
Reduction in cost of living. Report of Mr. W. Little in 1894, on
demand for labour 282
Proportion of arable to pasture land, 1881 and 1901. English counties
in groups, arable or pastoral 283
Table C. Percentage reduction of males above 20 employed in farms,
1861-1901, as distinct from labourers and "intense cultivators" . 284
Table D. Number of males above 20 and under 20 employed in farms
per 100 acres, 1861, 1881, 1891 284
Observations on various counties 286
Table comparing size of holdings in Aberdeen and South-eastern
Scotland 288
Decrease not due to enlargement of grass lands 289
Labour may be further economised. The hope for rural labour lies in
the growth of intense cultivation 290
Tables showing numbers of stock in various counties, 1881 and
1901 291
Question as to productiveness per acre as affected by decrease of
population. The disposal of the 130,000 labourers above 20, with-
drawn from farms 292
Economic causes. Conclusion 293
Appendix : Table I. Males employed in 3 counties where the
arable land is under 20 per cent. of the cultivated area : Derbyshire,
Westmoreland, Monmouth 294
—— —— II. In 5 counties . . . 20 and 30 per cent.
. . . . Lancashire, Leicester, Middlesex, Somerset, Staffordshire 295
—— —— III. In 12 counties . . . between 30 and 40 per
cent. . . . . Bucks, Cheshire, Dorset, Durham, Gloucester,
Hereford, Northants, Northumberland, Rutland, Salop, Warwick,
Worcester 296
—— —— IV. In 8 counties . . . between 40 and 50 per cent.
. . . . Cumberland, Devon, Kent, Surrey, Sussex, Wilts,
York (N. R.), York (W. R.) 297
—— —— V. In 7 counties . . . between 50 and 60 per cent.
. . . . Bedford, Berks, Cornwall, Hants, Huntingdon, Notts,
Oxford 298
—— —— VI. In 7 counties . . . over 60 per cent . . . .
Cambridge (76.3), Essex (62.2), Herts (63.5), Lincoln (67.1),
Norfolk (73), Suffolk (75.8), York (E. R.) (68.5) . . . 299
—— —— VII. In Wales 300
—— —— VIII. In counties where there has been little or no change
in the system of cultivation : Cornwall, Cheshire, Lancaster . 301–303
—— —— IX. In 5 counties of Scotland where there has been little
or no change in the system of cultivation : Ayrshire, Lanarkshire,
Roxburg, Berwick, Edinburgh, Aberdeen 304–306

Discussion on Lord Eversley's Paper :

Martin (Sir R. B.). Lord Eversley prevented from attending . . 307
Baines (Sir A.). Reads Lord Eversley's paper 307
Collings (Right Hon. Jesse). Agriculture prosperous, 1861-81 ; rise
of wages up to 1901 not substantial. Reduction in cost of living
not so great as the Paper stated. Prices in " the hungry forties "
in some respects lower than recently. Continued insufficiency of
wages. "Perquisites" and continuous employment in earlier
period. No "prospects" in this occupation. High qualities
required. Need for intense cultivation. Security of tenure a vague
expression. Ownership essential. The yeoman class necessary for
the country. The present system obsolete 307
Richards (Mr.). Royal Commission, 1892, agreed as to improvement in
condition of labourers. Importance of small holding facilities.
Agriculture as an industry compared with cotton manufacture.
Economy of labour inevitable. A prosperous agriculture to be
aimed at. Security of tenure essential. Need of State supervision
of cultivation. Small and large holdings might exist together . 309

PAGE

EVERSLEY (Lord).   *Discussion on his Paper—Contd.*

Longstaff (Dr.).   The State and "maximum rent" Decline of female labour not necessarily advantageous. Substitution of the town tradesman for the agricultural labourer in many occupations, *e.g.*, thatchers, hedgers, blacksmiths, drain-makers, threshers, buttermakers. Evenness of the decline over the country. Effect on the health of towns. Accuracy of agricultural returns questioned. Recent decrease less because rural population less .   .   .   310

Craigie (Major).   The present question statistical not political. Successive census figures for movement of population. Greatest reduction took place before 1881. Parallel movements in other countries. Female labour in America and in Denmark. Women suited to some kinds of agricultural labour. Effect on census occupation figures of including women. Details of local occupations should be compared with results ascertained for wages. Economic result of reduced cost of agricultural production. Number of horses not less than formerly. Approximate accuracy of Board of Agriculture returns of areas, crops, &c. .   .   .   312

Argyle (Jesse).   Omission of women employed in agriculture from census of 1871. Change in 1901. Earlier censuses returned landowners as agriculturists. Effects of machinery in farming. Creation of small village industries. Conditions of rural life .   314

Bund (Willis).   Fallacies in the census tables. Tradesmen possessing allotments would be returned as small holders .   .   .   315

Sansome (B.).   Cost of living in the forties less than now .   .   315

Lloyd (J.).   Burden of the tithe rent and other charges on the land .   316

Lawson (W. R.).   Census inconsistencies. The present question not the actual number of rural population, but its proportion to town population. The comparison should have been between the fifty years before and after 1846. The "agricultural towns" of Canada. How they were encouraged   316

Martin (Sir R. B.).   Proposes vote of thanks to Lord Eversley .   .   317

Eversley (Lord).   Communication on the discussion. Object of the paper to determine the real reduction in forty years; how far due to changes in system of cultivation. Improvement in conditions of living during forty years. Mr. Jesse Collings and cost of living in the "hungry forties." Fall in prices and rise in wages. Report on prices by Mr. William Little in 1894. Meat only excepted. Redundant labour in the early period. Deficiency at present. Substitution of urban for rural labour in fencing, slating, &c. Overcrowding in towns resulting from immigration of countrymen. Advantage of intense cultivation and small holdings .   .   .   318

FOREIGN Exchanges.   *See* PERIODICAL RETURNS.

GASTER (Leon).   *Roumania's forty years' progress*, 1866-1906   .   122-129

Population. Occupations   122
Live stock. Forests. Petroleum industry   .   .   .   123
Industries   124
Trade and commerce   125
Railways   Ports. Maritime service   126
Postal, telegraphs and telephones. Revenue and expenditure   .   127
National debt   127

GENERAL MEETING, 1907.   Proceedings   330
GOLD in 1906.   *See* PERIODICAL RETURNS.
GOSCHEN (Viscount).   Obituary notice   100-102

HARRIS (W. J.) and LAKE (Rev. K. A.).   Reply to Mr. Bailey's letter criticising their Paper on "Estimates of the realizable wealth of the United Kingdom."   *See* BAILEY (A. H.).

PAGE

HERRING fishery. *See* LARK (A. E.).

HOOKER (Reginald H.).   *Correlation of the weather and crops*   .   1–42

Introduction. Reference to paper by Dr. W. N. Shaw, connecting autumn rainfall and following wheat crop. Other crops now included   1

Also effects of variations of temperature. The district dealt with: Eastern England   2

Data used, average rainfall and accumulated temperature for periods of eight weeks   3–4

Meaning of correlation coefficients. Probable errors   .   .   .   5–8

Quantity only (not quality) of crops considered   9

Possible correlation between weather of two periods   .   .   .   10

Wheat   10–15

Advantage of dry September and October and dry warm winter   .   11

Conclusions of Gilberts and Lawes   12

Bulk and condition of seed differently affected   13

Periodicity in yield   14

Barley. Advantage of cool summer and dry January and February, and wet spring. Best brewing quality is early sown   .   .   15

Oats, similar to barley, but require spring rain. *Beans and Peas.* Condition of seed the chief factor   16–17

Potatoes. Advantage of dry summer. *Turnips and swedes* require wet sowing season and cool summer   17

Mangolds require cool and wet spring. Importance of conditions of seed   18–19

Hay. Advantage of heavy spring rain, and cool spring and summer   .   19

General results. Cool spring and summer good for most crops   .   21

Importance of condition of seed   22

Discussion whether better yield is obtained now than formerly   .   23

Comparisons : Eastern England, Scotland, Holland, France   .   .   24

Effect of reduction of cultivated areas   26

Variability of crops as measured by standard deviation.   .   .   27–29

Table I. Correlation coefficients between weather and crops: (*a*) Wheat; (*b*) Barley ; (*c*) Oats; (*d*) Beans: (*e*) Peas: (*f*) Potatoes; (*g*) Turnips and Swedes; (*h*) Mangolds; (*i*) Hay, from clover and rotation grass ; (*j*) Hay from permanent grass   30–39

—— II.   Average acreage and yield of crops, 1886–95 and 1896–1905 : (*a*) Eastern England ; (*b*) Scotland   40

—— III.   Average, range and standard deviation of certain crops in Eastern England, Scotland. and France, 1885–1905   .   .   41

—— IV.   Correlation coefficients between Rainfall and Accumulated Temperature above 42° F.   42

Discussion on Mr. R. H. Hooker's Paper :

Shaw (Dr. W. N.).   Advantage in having these results in numerical form. Meaning of correlation coefficients of low values. Relation between crops and subsequent temperatures. Question of a correlation between consecutive seasons. Abnormal seasons. Proposal to calculate combined coefficients between the crop and the several elements of the weather having high coefficients. Autumn rainfall and eleven-year periodicity   42

Edgeworth (Prof. F. Y.).   Deficiencies in the data. Computation of probable errors. Coefficients of double correlation. A variant method proposed   44

Craigie (Major P. G.).   Importance of connecting mathematical and practical methods. Unexpected results. The question of general progress in agriculture. A new field of investigation opened by Dr. Shaw and Mr. Hooker   45

Yule (G. U.).   Meaning of small correlation coefficients. Probable error of partial coefficient. Form of relationship between weather and crop. Importance of cool spring and summer. Apparent opposition between conditions needed for good seed and those for bulky crop. Alternation of good and bad crops. Advantage of specializing crops for seed and for food   46

Young (Sydney).   Plentiful harvest does not produce bad seed, but the following poor harvest caused by bad weather at sowing time. Dry weather required for sowing. The flowering time the most critical for wheat, i.e., June. The weather conditions required. Theory of eleven-year cycles not borne out   .   .   .   48

Rew (R. H.).   Importance of statistical treatment of practical agricultural subjects   49

Hooker (R. H.).   The critical value of 0·5. Correlation between successive seasons. Combined effects of two seasons in a crop. Abnormal seasons not rejected. Selection of districts. Alternation of good and bad crops. Specializing for seed   .   .   .   51

PAGE

HUMPHREYS (Noel A.).   *The alleged Increase of Insanity*   .   .   203–233

Deficiency of materials. General grounds for doubting increase   .   203
Articles in *The Times* alleging increase   204
Varying degrees of incompleteness of past returns   .   .   .   205
Greater accuracy of terms used in later schedules   .   .   .   206
Table A. Aggregate numbers of the Insane at the Censuses, 1871-1901 ;
  and those reported to the Lunacy Commissioners on 1st January
  of each year ; and percentage of deficiency in the Lunacy Com-
  missioners' numbers   207
—— B. Incidence rate of insanity per million of population at the
  Censuses, 1871-1901, on five groups of ages ; and increase or decrease
  of the rate in each intercensal period   208
Statistics of the Lunacy Commissioners   210
Table C. Mean annual ratio of certified cases of insanity (reported on
  by the Lunacy Commissioners) in quinquennial periods, per million
  of population ; and increase per cent. between the several periods   .   210
Accumulation of the insane   212
Table D. Annual rates of mortality in county and borough asylums,
  hospitals, and licensed houses in ten-year and five-year periods,
  1859-1905   213
Age distribution of the inmates of asylums   215
Table E. Proportional age-distribution of the enumerated inmates of
  lunatic asylums at each census, 1851-81   216
—— F. Proportional age-distribution of the inmates of lunatic
  asylums, hospitals, and licensed houses, 1894-1904, based on tables in
  the reports of the Lunacy Commissioners   217
—— G. Ratio of incidence of inmates of lunatic asylums, hospitals,
  and licensed houses in population, on five groups of ages, 1894 and
  1904. calculated from tables in reports of the Lunacy Commissioners   217
Age distribution of patients on admission to asylums, hospitals, and
  licensed houses for the insane   218
Table H. Average annual admissions to lunatic asylums, hospitals,
  and licensed houses ; proportional age distribution of admissions ;
  and rate of admissions to 10,000 population ; at five age-groups ; in
  five-year periods, 1890-94 and 1900-04   218
Effect of insanity upon the rate of mortality   222
Table I. Annual rate of mortality per 1,000 among the certified
  insane, at five age groups, compared with the rate of mortality in
  the general population at the same age groups in 1904   .   .   223
Metropolitan Asylums Board statistics   225
Table J. Average annual death rate in the Metropolitan Asylums for
  Idiots and Imbeciles in seven quinquennial periods, 1871-1905   .   226
—— K. Average annual death rate in the Metropolitan Asylums for
  Idiots and Imbeciles, 1904-05-06, at four age periods, compared with
  the death-rate in the general London population at the same ages
  and in the same years   227
Conclusion · Alleged increase deduced by fallacious reasoning .   .   228
Recapitulation—"Borderland" cases. Decline of unregistered cases.
  History of cases previous to admission not recorded   .   .   229
Changes in proportional age distribution. Accumulation. Certifi-
  cation of senile dementia cases   230
Need for scientific classification   231
No absolute proof of increase. Suggested improvement in statistics .   232

Discussion on Mr. Noel A. Humphreys' Paper :

Dudfield (Dr. R.). Supporting the writer's conclusions. Changes in
  the custody of the insane. Increase of recorded cases was among
  the very young and very old. Effect of transfer of asylums to
  County Councils. Public confidence in elected bodies. "Flat life" as
  partial cause of any increase. Senile dementia cases transferred from
  workhouses to asylums. Need for co-ordination in the statistics   .   234
Winslow (Dr. Forbes). Carlyle's views. Registration of temporary
  delirium undesirable. These should be treated in a "half-way
  house." Difficulty of certification. Asylums and workhouses.
  "Harmless" lunatics. Effects of civilisation.   .   .   .   234
Morrison (Dr. W. D.).   Asylums and workhouses. No proof of
  increase of insanity. Greater readiness now to attribute insanity.
  Increased pressure of living as a cause, balanced by better conditions   235
Dorington (Sir John). Increase not real. Greater care now taken of
  insane. Increased public confidence in asylum management.
  Treatment of the aged poor. Decrease of numbers in private
  institutions. Lunacy diminishing among the well-to-do. Causes
  of apparent increase   236
Tebb (Dr. Scott). The large proportion of insane to population. Large
  increase in Ireland ; scarcity of sane clergymen there. Mortality
  of the insane. Inheritance of insanity. Effects of compulsory
  education. Other causes   237

PAGE

HUMPHREYS (Noel A.).   *Discussion on his Paper—Contd.*

Mercièr (Dr.).   Urgent need for scientific definition.   Insanity not a medical, but a legal entity, including only cases requiring control. Greater numbers now treated than formerly   238

Martin (Sir R. B.).   Misleading character of crude returns, and importance of expert scrutiny.   Difficulty of determining the borderline of insanity   240

Humphreys (N. A.).   Decline of home industries as a cause of accumulation.   The increase in proportion of insane in Ireland.   Causes. Mortality of insane.   High mortality of the insane under 25 years of age.   Only the worst cases certified at that age . . .   240

———— Guy medal in silver awarded to Mr. Humphreys   .   323

INDEX-NUMBERS.   *See* SAUERBECK (A.).
INSANITY.   Alleged increase.   *See* HUMPHREYS (N. A.).
INTERNATIONAL Statistical Institute.   *See* STATISTICAL.

KÖRÖSY (Dr. Joseph).   Obituary notice   332

LABOUR, Agricultural.   Decline in Great Britain.   *See* EVERSLEY (Lord).
LAKE (Kenneth A.).   *See* HARRIS (W. J.) and LAKE (K. A.).
LARK (Albert E.).   *The Herring Fishery*   242-259

Introduction.   Antiquity of the herring fishery . . .   242
Districts   243
Table showing percentage of total catch of England by districts   .   244
Scotland   244
Table showing total quantities landed in Scotland, 1896-1905, by districts   245
Percentage of total quantities in Scotland by districts, 1896-1905   .   245
Table.   England and Wales: Quantities landed, by stations, and for the three coasts, 1896-1905   246
Note on the quantities landed at the various stations: England and Wales   247
Note on percentage of total catch table: England and Wales .   .   248
Table.   Aggregation of annual values of herrings landed in United Kingdom, 1896-1905   248
Percentages of total catch landed by stations, 1896-1905 . .   249
Table showing total catch and value of herrings landed in England and Wales, Scotland and Ireland, 1896-1905, taking the figures of 1896 as equivalent to 100   250
Export of herrings.   *Tables :* (*a*) Quantity ; (*b*) Value . .   251
Fish traffic by railways.   *Table :* Quantity of fish of all kinds carried by rail from the parts of the United Kingdom each year, 1896-1905 .   253
Imports of herrings.   Average value of herrings landed in England and Wales, Scotland and Ireland   254
As to the inexhaustibility of our fisheries and the alleged damage to spawn   255
Number and value of boats and gear, and numbers of fishermen and others engaged   257
The fishing fleet as an assistance to national prosperity and an aid to the navy   258

Discussion on Mr. A. E. Lark's Paper :

Hendriks (F.).   Magnitude of Yarmouth and Lowestoft fishery. Extent and value of the whole catch of the United Kingdom Value of the export trade.   Antiquity of herring trade . .   259

Towse (Wrench).   Methods of curing, British and German . .   260

Tabor (J. M.).   Weight of the "last."   Recent increase in value due to German meat tariff.   Reaction inevitable.   Competition between foreign distributing merchants.   Increase of German trade was in fresh not cured fish.   Moderate prices best for everybody.   Alleged destruction of fisheries.   No notable diminution . . .   261

Fryer (Mr.).   Apparent discrepancy between local and official returns. Increasing use of the trawl.   Its probable effects in developing other ports.   Other ports perhaps supplied English centres. Yarmouth and Lowestoft exporting.   Herring fishery fluctuating. Comparisons of different parts of coast and with Scotland .   .   262

PAGE

LARK (Albert E.). *Discussion on his Paper — Contd.*

Rew (R. H.). Fisheries and food supply. Work of the Royal Commission of 1863. Statistics and practical problems. Question of continuance of supply. Increased output balanced by increased fishing power, and greater extent of sea now fished. Growing attention of statisticians to fisheries. 263

Martin (Sir R. B.). Increased importance of fisheries. The destructive effects of trawls. Extent of sea now fished . . . 264

Lark (A. E.). Method of arriving at weights. Causes of price fluctuations. Various methods of curing. Effect of German tariff . 265

LIBRARY. List of additions . . . . $\left\{\begin{array}{l}165, 387 \\ 530, 706\end{array}\right.$

LIBRARY Catalogue. *See* REPORT OF THE COUNCIL.

MARRIAGES in 1906. *See* PERIODICAL RETURNS.

MARRIAGE-RATES in England and Wales. *See* WELTON (T. A.).

MOORE (Henry L.). *The Differential Law of Wages* . . . 638–651

The doctrine of pure economics put to a statistical test. Possible sources of error. Meaning of "theory of wages." The differential law defined 638
Conditions of making the statistical test. Distribution of efficiency among labourers. Effect of industrial environment . . . 639
Use of the Gaussian law. Mr. Galton's difference problem. Prof. Pearson's solution and its application to the law of wages . . 641
Standard population and environment 642
U.S.A. Report on employees and wages 643
The use of the wage data 644
The tables and chart explained 645
Chart 646
Results 647
Appendix. Construction of Table 1 647
Table 1. Standard population. Average difference of efficiency . 648
—— 2. Distribution of wages in manufactures of U.S.A. in 1900, as represented by 30 selected industries 649
—— 3. Percentage distribution of wages between assigned limits in the manufactures of U.S.A. in 1900 649
—— 4. Percentage rates at which more efficient members of the two groups share the excess over the minimum wage of the respective groups 650
—— 5. Distribution of wages of the standard population . . 651

MORTALITY from tuberculosis. *See* DUDFIELD (D. R.).

OLANESCO (Grégoire). Obituary notice 332

OXFORD. Assize of Bread. *See* BALLARD (A.).

PERIODICAL Returns, 1906 184–202

Registration of the United Kingdom, England and Wales . . 184
————————————————————— Scotland 189
————————————————————— Great Britain and Ireland . 191
Trade of the United Kingdom, 1906-05-04 192
Shipping 196
Gold and silver bullion and specie 197
Bank of England, weekly returns, 1906 198
Revenue 200
Foreign Exchanges 202

PERIODICALS. Statistical and economic articles. *See* STATISTICAL.

PRICES in 1906. *See* SAUERBECK (A.).

PRODUCTION Statistics. *See* YULE (G. U.).

REGISTRATION in 1906. *See* PERIODICAL RETURNS.

RENT, Agricultural, in England and Wales during the 19th Century. *See* THOMPSON (R. J.).

PAGE

REPORT of the Council for the financial year ended 31st December, 1906, and for the sessional year ending 18th June, 1907 . . 320–329

Number of Fellows, deaths, &c. 320
New Fellows elected 321
New investment 322
Ordinary meetings and papers read 322
Library report 323, 329
New Library Catalogue 323
Bibliography of Cereals 323
Deputation on an Anthropometric Survey . . . 323
2nd International Congress on School Hygiene . . . 323
Guy and Howard Medals 323
Officers of the Society, 1907-08 324
Financial statement 325
Auditors' report 327
Condition of the Society, 1882-1906 328

REPRESENTATION of statistical frequency by a curve. See EDGE-WORTH (Prof. F. Y.).
REVENUE of the United Kingdom, 1906. See PERIODICAL RETURNS.
REVIEWS. See BOOKS.
ROUMANIA. Forty years' progress. See GASTER (L.).
ROYAL STATISTICAL SOCIETY. See GENERAL MEETING; REPORT.

SAUERBECK (A.). Prices of Commodities in 1906 107–121

Summary of index-numbers, groups of articles . . . 107
Monthly fluctuations 108
Quarterly movements of prices 110
Silver, gold, rate of discount 111
Review of year 112
Movements of forty-five commodities in United Kingdom . 113
Total imports and exports and ratio of values . . . 114
Construction of tables of index-numbers 114
Table of average prices of commodities and index numbers, 1891-1905 . 116

SCHOOL Hygiene. 2nd International Congress on. See REPORT OF COUNCIL.
SHIPPING in 1906. See PERIODICAL RETURNS.
SILVER in 1906. See PERIODICAL RETURNS.
SMALL Holdings in United Kingdom. Position. See ADAMS (W. G. S.).

STATISTICAL and economic articles in recent periodicals . . { 156, 377 / 521, 696

———— Institute, International, Congress. Copenhagen, August, 1907 449–454

[An account of the general work of the Congress.]

STATISTICS. Modern methods of treating observations. See BRITISH ASSOCIATION.
———— The representation of statistical frequency by a curve. See EDGEWORTH (Prof. F. Y.).
———— Official. See DILKE (Sir C. W.).
———— of Production. See YULE (G. U.).

THOMPSON (Robert J.). An Inquiry into the Rents of Agricultural Land in England and Wales during the 19th Century . . . 587–616

Scarcity of statistics of rent. List of authorities . . . 587
This paper based on statements of 16 estates . . . 588
Changes in rent (a) 1801-20. Conditions favouring rise in rent . 589
Inquiry by the Board of Agriculture in 1804 . . . 589
Table I. Showing average rents 1801-20 . . . 590
McCulloch's figures 590
(b) 1820-45. Rise in prices 591
Table II. Rent of 110,000 acres, 1816-45 . . . 592
McCulloch's figures 592
(c) 1845-72. Higher standard of farming. Rising of rent . 593
Foundation of Royal Agriculture Society in 1839 . . 593
Effect of free trade 593
Table III. Rent of 12,000 acres, 1846-71 . . . 594

PAGE

THOMPSON (Robert J.).   *Rents of Agricultural Land—Contd.*

McCulloch and Caird's figures compared	594
(d) 1872-1900. Unfavourable seasons and low prices . . .	595
Table IV. Rent of about 41c,000 acres, 1872-92 . . .	595
—— V. Rent of about 380,000 acres, 1893-1900	596
Fall in rent. Other estimates compared	596
Comparison of figures of rent with Income Tax Returns and with prices of agricultural produce, 1845-1900	596
Four sets of figures available for comparison, including Sauerbeck's index numbers for food	596
Table VI. Comparison of the figures of rent, Income Tax returns and prices expressed as percentages	598
Diagram showing a comparison between the rent of agricultural land, the Income Tax returns of income from land, Sauerbeck's prices of animal and vegetable food (all expressed as percentages) . .	600
Estimate of the proportion of the gross rent expended in repairs, improvements and outgoings	602
Table VII. Gross rental, cost of repairs, net income, &c., 1872-91 .	603
Estimate of landlord's capital invested in buildings, drainage, fencing, &c.	605
John Stuart Mill on rent as including payment for improvements .	605
Mr. Albert Pell in the "Making of the Land in England"; his estimate of value of improvements per acre	605
Estimates by Mr. E. P. Squareys and Mr. John Clutton . .	606
Particulars of cost of various improvements: drainage, fencing, buildings, roads	607
Estimate of the economic rent of agricultural land . . .	609
The average rent of land in England 4s. 6d. per acre . . .	610
Definition of economic rent	610
Prospects for the 20th century	611
Appendix A. Average rent per acre of agricultural land in certain estates in Lincoln, Essex, Hereford, and North Wales, 1800-1900 .	612
—— B. Ditto in Lincoln, Hereford, Bucks, Beds, Cambridge, Essex, and North Wales. 1816-1900	613
—— C. Ditto in certain estates distributed throughout England and Wales, 1872-1900	614
—— D. Income Tax (Schedule A) gross income derived from the ownership of lands in England and Wales, 1843-1905 . . .	614
—— E. Rent of certain individual farmers in Wilts, Norfolk, and South Midlands	615

Discussion on Mr. R. J. Thompson's Paper :

Craigie (Major P. G.). Lines of discussion suggested . . .	617
Powell (Sir F. S.). Difference between "prairie" value and value of land improved by capital	617
Goddard (A.). Importance of the Paper to land-agents . . .	618
Matthews (A. H. H.). Large expenditure required in keeping up an estate. Lesser proportionate cost of large estates; influence of depression on outlay. Cost of insurance	618
Harper (E. J). Absence of exact information as to economic rent. The Agricultural Rating Act did not provide for this. Difference in rate of increase of house and land values. The amount of rates and taxes should be included in estimating the net return from the soil	619
Hooker (R. H.). The advantage of employing index-numbers. Possible error arising from varying methods of tenure. A second diagram might show the course of rents at the beginning of the century. Evidence of progress in agriculture at the middle of the century .	620
Rew (R. H.). Mr. Thompson's estimate of cost of working land based on estimate of about 1860. Increase since in cost of labour. Improvement in stock breeding at the beginning of the century, if not in cultivation of land	621
Craigie (Major P. G.). Fall in rents in 1887, as well as fall in prices. Rent movements according to the agricultural character of districts might have been shown. Rent as interest on capital. Cost of equipment	621
Thompson (R. J.). Difficulty of comparing early and later rents in the century. Increase of rent at beginning of century, and the improvement in stock breeding at that time. Annual tenure now prevalent. Repairs mostly done by landlords. Comparative outlay on larger estates. Increase in cost of labour. Mr. Clutton's estimate of amount of landlord's capital. The drop in rents in 1887. Geographical distribution of estates dealt with precluded. Inclusion of rates and taxes in the return from the soil . . .	622

PAGE

TRADE Returns, 1906. *See* PERIODICAL RETURNS.
TUBERCULOSIS, International Congress, Washington, 1908   .   .   654
———————— Mortality from. *See* DUDFIELD (Dr. R.).

UNITED Kingdom.   Official Statistics. *See* DILKE (Sir C. W.).

WAGES. Differential law. *See* MOORE (H. L.).
WEALTH of the United Kingdom. *See* BAILEY (A. H.).
WEATHER and Crops. Correlation. *See* HOOKER (R. H.).
WELTON (Thomas A.).   *Memorandum as to birth-rates and marriage
    rates in England and Wales*   625-629

> The Registrar-General's decennial report.   Index-numbers repre-
> senting proportion of total births to married women under 35, by
> counties   625
> Births per 100 married women under 35, by districts   .   .   626
> Effect of marriage at a distance from place of residence   .   .   627
> Married women under 35 by registration counties   .   .   .   627
> *Table* showing numbers of marriages and of married women under 35   627
> —— showing (1) male and female population, (2) married people of
> Durham and Cardigan, 1891-1901   628

YULE (G. Udny).   *Statistics of Production and the Census of Pro-
    duction Act* (1906)   52-87

> Introductory.   Definition of production   52
> Measurements taken in money value.   Risks of duplication   .   .   53
> Methods employed in U.S.A. Census of manufactures for eliminating
> duplication   54
> Value of an industry product is the value added to an article by the
> industry.   Value of materials and of contract work to be deducted
> from total production in each industry   56
> Limitation of the field to be covered   56
> Possible extension to include an industrial census   .   .   .   57
> II. Existing statistics of production.   In Europe these exist com-
> pletely only for agriculture and mining.   FRANCE .   .   .   57
> UNITED KINGDOM.   Statistics of the Home Office, Board of Trade,
> Board of Agriculture and Fisheries. Commissioners of Customs   .   58-60
> AUSTRALASIA.   Interstate conferences   60
> Commonwealth statistician appointed, 1905   61
> *New South Wales*   61
> *Victoria*   62
> *Queensland*   63
> *South Australia*   63
> *Western Australia*   63
> *Tasmania* , ...   64
> *New Zealand*.   64
> UNITED STATES.   History of census taking   64
> Scope of Industrial information given   65-69
> Special reports   66
> *Massachusetts*   69
> CANADA   71-74
> CAPE COLONY   74
> III.   The Census of Production Act.   Outline of provisions   .   75
> Comparison with the censuses of U.S.A. and Canada   .   .   .   76
> Comparative table of subjects covered.   No complete information
> to be provided as to quantities of materials, as distinct from values   78
> Separate wage census promised.   No information as to capital
> employed   79
> Use of voluntary information sanctioned.   Census intervals not
> determined (possibly biennial) ; advantages of quinquennial census   80
> A question of cost   81
> Omission of clause providing a centralized statistical bureau .   .   82
> *Appendix.*   Text of the Act   83-87

Discussion on Mr. G. U. Yule's Paper :

Magnus (Sir Philip).   Importance of the census in relation to the
    fiscal controversy.   Risks of duplication.   Exclusion of small
    industries.   Arrangements similar to that of other countries
    necessary for making correct comparisons.   Quantity of output
    would be useful as well as of value   87

PAGE

Yule (G. Udny).   *Discussion on his Paper—Contd.*

Schloss (D. F.).   Aggregate returns of associated companies to be treated as an individual return.   Consultation with manufacturers required.   Difficulty of carrying out this census.   Opinion of a French economist on its value   88

Birchenough (H.).   The importance of a census of production.   Difficulties would probably disappear with use.   Difficulty as to small trades.   The Act satisfactory for the present, and might be amended after each census.   Intercensal periods.   Population.   Industrial censuses should correspond—perhaps quinquennially . .   89

Coghlan (T. A.).   Practical difficulty of interpreting returns.   Need of expert scrutiny.   Short intercensal periods desirable.   An annual census in Australia.   Wage statistics easy to give, and should be given.   Quantities of production could not be given—only value. Need to distinguish raw material   90

Rosenbaum (S.).   Limitations of the Act.   Whole area of production not covered.   Absorption of small factories, or enlarge area in future.   Omission of agriculture.   Duplication not eliminated. Question of standard prices.   Determination of value.   Municipal undertakings not included   92

Macdonald (Mrs. J. R.).   Influence of the "new protection" policy on the Australian census.   Necessity for full returns there.   Intercensal periods.   Failure of annual returns of numbers employed in factories   94

Cannan (E.).   Net aggregate value of production could not be shown. This census really a census of products.   Amounts of income not to be deduced   94

Rew (R. H.).   The paper prepared at short notice.   Practical limits to collection of statistics.   The completeness not possible at once.   The present Act a great advance   95

Martin (Sir R. B.).   Subsidiary trades shall not be eliminated.   The returns should be as full as possible   95

Yule (G. U.).   Quinquennial periods, why suggested.   Full census impossible.   Small manufacturers not excluded by the Act.   The Board of Trade and the power of exemption.   Quantities not always obtainable.   Question of value added to product by transport. Reply to Mr. Cannan.   The census a return of total production in an intelligible form   96

Chisholm (G. G.).   Communication on Mr. Yule's paper.   The difficulty of dealing with value added by transport.   Importance of quantity returns where possible.   Effect of quantity on freights.   Collection of information as to motive power   97-99

LONDON:
HARRISON AND SONS, PRINTERS IN ORDINARY TO HIS MAJESTY,
ST. MARTIN'S LANE.

APPENDIX.

ROYAL STATISTICAL SOCIETY.

(FOUNDED 1834. INCORPORATED 1887.)

9, ADELPHI TERRACE,

STRAND, W.C., LONDON.

Contents.

	PAGE
COUNCIL AND OFFICERS, SESSION 1907-1908	ii
NOTICES TO FELLOWS	iii
CALENDAR FOR SESSION 1907-1908	iv
PROGRAMME OF THE SESSION 1907-1908	v
OBJECTS OF THE SOCIETY	vi
PUBLICATIONS OF THE SOCIETY	vii
LIST OF THE SOCIETY'S MEDALLISTS	viii and ix
NOTICE AS TO CANDIDATURE FOR FELLOWSHIP	x
LIST OF THE FORMER PATRON AND PRESIDENTS	xi
CONTENTS OF THE SOCIETY'S JOURNAL FOR 1907	xii
LIST OF FELLOWS	1
Do. HONORARY FELLOWS	42
CHARTER OF THE SOCIETY	50
INDEX TO BYE-LAWS AND RULES	54
BYE-LAWS AND RULES OF THE SOCIETY	55
REGULATIONS OF THE LIBRARY	59
DONORS TO THE LIBRARY DURING THE YEAR 1907	60
FORM OF BEQUEST	71

LONDON:

PRINTED FOR THE SOCIETY,

BY HARRISON AND SONS, 45, 46, AND 47, ST. MARTIN'S LANE,

Printers in Ordinary to His Majesty.

1907.

ROYAL STATISTICAL SOCIETY.

Patron.

HIS MOST GRACIOUS MAJESTY THE KING.

Honorary President.

H.R.H. THE PRINCE OF WALES, K.G.

COUNCIL AND OFFICERS.—1907-8.

Honorary Vice-Presidents
(having filled the Office of President).

RT. HON. LORD EVERSLEY.
RT. HON. LORD BRASSEY, G C.B.
SIR ROBERT GIFFEN, K.C B., LL.D., F.R.S.
RT. HON. CHARLES BOOTH, D.Sc., F.R.S.
SIR ALFRED E. BATEMAN, K.C.M.G.
RT. HON. LORD COURTNEY.

RT. HON. SIR H. H. FOWLER, G.C.S.I., M.P.
RT. HON. LORD AVEBURY, F.R.S.
MAJOR PATRICK GEORGE CRAIGIE, C.B.
SIR FRANCIS SHARP POWELL, BART., M.P.
RT. HON. THE EARL OF ONSLOW, G.C.M.G.
SIR RICHARD BIDDULPH MARTIN, BART.

President.
THE RIGHT HON. SIR CHARLES WENTWORTH DILKE, BART., M.P.

Vice-Presidents.

ARTHUR L BOWLEY, M.A.
SIR E. W. BRABROOK, C.B., V.-P.S.A.

TIMOTHY A. COGHLAN, I.O.S.
BERNARD MALLET.

Treasurer.
SIR RICHARD BIDDULPH MARTIN, BART.

Honorary Secretaries.
R. H. REW.   A. WILSON FOX, C.B.   G. UDNY YULE.

Honorary Foreign Secretary.
SIR J. ATHELSTANE BAINES, C.S.I.

Other Members of Council.

WILLIAM M. ACWORTH, M.A.
EDWARD BOND, M.A.
G. G. CHISHOLM, M.A., B.Sc., F.R G.S.
SIR ERNEST CLARKE, M.A., F.L.S., F.S.A.
NATHANIEL L. COHEN.
RICHARD F. CRAWFORD.
REGINALD DUDFIELD, M.A., M.B.
SIR WILLIAM C. DUNBAR, BART., C.B.
PROF. F. Y. EDGEWORTH, M.A., D.C.L.
SIR JOHN GLOVER, J.P.
EDGAR J. HARPER.

NOEL A. HUMPHREYS, I.S.O.
FREDERICK HENDRIKS, F.I.A.
ARTHUR W. WATERLOW KING, J.P.
PROF. C. S. LOCH, D.C.L.
THEODORE MORISON, M.A.
SIR SHIRLEY F. MURPHY, M.R.C.S.
FRANCIS G. P. NEISON, F.I.A.
GEORGE PAISH.
L. L. PRICE, M.A.
SIR LESLEY PROBYN, K.C.V.O.
DAVID A. THOMAS, M.A., M.P.

Assistant Secretary.
J. H. MAGEE, B.A.

Chief Clerk and Librarian.
JOHN A. P. MACKENZIE.

Bankers.—MESSRS. DRUMMOND, CHARING CROSS, S.W., LONDON.

Offices.—9, ADELPHI TERRACE, STRAND, W.C., LONDON.

ROYAL STATISTICAL SOCIETY.

No. 9, Adelphi Terrace, Strand, W.C., London.

NOTICES TO FELLOWS.

December, 1907.

The Council desire to call the attention of the Fellows to the fact that notwithstanding the change in the name of the Society by the addition of the word "Royal," they are still, in using letters after their names, signifying the membership of the Society, only entitled under Rule 6, to use the letters F.S.S.

Annual Subscriptions are due in advance, on the 1st of January in each year. A Form for authorising a Banker or Agent to pay the subscription Annually will be forwarded on application to the Assistant Secretary. When convenient, this mode of payment is recommended. Drafts should be made payable to the order of "The Royal Statistical Society," and crossed "*Drummond and Co.*"

In order to be included in the Ballot at any particular Ordinary Meeting, the nomination papers of candidates for Fellowship must be lodged at the Office of the Society at least six days before the date of such Meeting.

Fellows who may desire to receive special and separate notices of each paper to be read before the Society at the Ordinary Meetings, should indicate their wishes to the Assistant Secretary.

The Ordinary Meetings of the Society are held at 5 p.m., in most cases at The Society's Rooms, 9, Adelphi Terrace, W.C.

Particulars as to Papers to be read, and the time and place of Meeting, will be found advertised in "The Times" (on the page facing the leading articles) on the Saturday preceding the date of each Meeting; and in other London Daily Papers at the same time. The attention of Fellows is particularly directed to these announcements.

The *Journal* is issued on the last day of the months of March, June, September, and December in each year. Copies are delivered *carriage free* to all Fellows of the Society. Arrangements have been made for their delivery to those Fellows resident in London and the suburbs by Messrs. Carter Paterson & Co., and to most provincial Fellows by post. All copies for Colonial and Foreign Fellows are sent by mail. The *Journals* should reach British Fellows within the first ten days of the months of April, July, October, and January respectively, and those resident abroad somewhat later, on account of the time occupied in transmission. Addressees who fail to receive their *Journals* at the proper time are earnestly requested to communicate with the Assistant Secretary without delay, as the carriers cannot be expected to investigate complaints or be responsible for loss unless prompt notice be given.

The Library and the Reading Room are open daily for the use of Fellows from 10 a.m. to 5 p.m., excepting on Saturdays, when they are closed at 2 p.m.

It is requested that any change of address may be notified promptly to the ASSISTANT SECRETARY.

CALENDAR FOR THE SESSION 1907-08.

1907	MON.	TUES.	WED.	THURS.	FRI.	SATUR.	SUN.	1908	MON.	TUES.	WED.	THURS.	FRI.	SATUR.	SUN.
NOV.	...	...	...	...	1	2	3	MAY	...	...	...	...	1	2	3
	4	5	6	7	8	9	10		4	5	6	7	8	9	10
	11	12	13	14	15	16	17		11	12	13	14	15	16	17
	18	19	20	21	22	23	24		18	19	20	21	22	23	24
	25	26	27	28	29	30			25	26	27	28	29	30	31
DEC.	...	...	...	...	...	...	1	JUNE	1	2	3	4	5	6	7
	2	3	4	5	6	7	8		8	9	10	11	12	13	14
	9	10	11	12	13	14	15		15	16	17	18	19	20	21
	16	17	18	19	20	21	22		22	23	24	25	26	27	28
	23	24	25	26	27	28	29		29	30					
	30	31													
1908 JAN.	...	...	1	2	3	4	5	JULY	...	...	1	2	3	4	5
	6	7	8	9	10	11	12		6	7	8	9	10	11	12
	13	14	15	16	17	18	19		13	14	15	16	17	18	19
	20	21	22	23	24	25	26		20	21	22	23	24	25	26
	27	28	29	30	31				27	28	29	30	31		
FEB.	...	...	...	...	...	1	2	AUG.	...	...	...	...	...	1	2
	3	4	5	6	7	8	9		3	4	5	6	7	8	9
	10	11	12	13	14	15	16		10	11	12	13	14	15	16
	17	18	19	20	21	22	23		17	18	19	20	21	22	23
	24	25	26	27	28	29			24	25	26	27	28	29	30
									31						
MAR.	...	...	...	...	...	...	1	SEP.	...	1	2	3	4	5	6
	2	3	4	5	6	7	8		7	8	9	10	11	12	13
	9	10	11	12	13	14	15		14	15	16	17	18	19	20
	16	17	18	19	20	21	22		21	22	23	24	25	26	27
	23	24	25	26	27	28	29		28	29	30				
	30	31													
APR.	...	...	1	2	3	4	5	OCT.	...	...	...	1	2	3	4
	6	7	8	9	10	11	12		5	6	7	8	9	10	11
	13	14	15	16	17	18	19		12	13	14	15	16	17	18
	20	21	22	23	24	25	26		19	20	21	22	23	24	25
	27	28	29	30					26	27	28	29	30	31	

THE ANNUAL GENERAL MEETING

WILL BE HELD ON TUESDAY, THE 16TH JUNE 1908, AT THE SOCIETY'S ROOMS.

Programme of the Session 1907-8.

THE
ORDINARY MEETINGS

WILL BE HELD MONTHLY FROM NOVEMBER TO JUNE

IN MOST CASES AT THE SOCIETY'S ROOMS,

9, Adelphi Terrace, Strand, W.C., London.

The Chair will be taken at **5 p.m.** *on the following dates:—*

Tuesday, Jan. 21.	Tuesday, April 14.
„ Feb. 18.	„ May 19.
„ March 17.	„ June 16.

SEE NOTE ON THE OPPOSITE PAGE.

The following Papers have been read this Session:—

Presidential Address "On Official Statistics." (Delivered on 19th November, in the Lecture Room of the Society of Arts, John Street, Adelphi, W.C.) By the RT. HON. SIR CHARLES W. DILKE, BART., M.P.

"An Inquiry into the Rent of Agricultural Land in England and Wales during the 19th Century." By ROBERT J. THOMPSON. (Read 17th December, 1907.)

The following Papers have been offered; and from these and any others that may be offered, a selection will be made by the Council:—

"On Official Statistics." By ARTHUR L. BOWLEY, M.A.

"The Ratio of Home and Foreign Trade in the United Kingdom, Germany, and the United States." By GEORGE G. CHISHOLM, M.A., B.Sc., F.R.G.S.

"Some Unconsidered Factors affecting the Birth-rate." By REGINALD DUDFIELD, M.A., M.B.

"Railways and the Trade of Great Britain." By CHARLES LEWIS EDWARDS.

"A Method of estimating Capital Wealth from the Estate Duty statistics." By BERNARD MALLET.

"Statistics of Food Taxation in the Principal Countries. By SIMON ROSENBAUM, B.Sc.

"The Measurement of International Indebtedness." By J. W. SOWREY.

ROYAL STATISTICAL SOCIETY.

AN OUTLINE OF ITS OBJECTS.

THE *Royal Statistical Society* was founded on the 15th of March, 1834, in pursuance of a recommendation of the British Association for the Advancement of Science, its objects being the careful collection, arrangement, discussion and ,publication of facts bearing on and illustrating the complex relations of modern society in its social, economical, and political aspects, especially facts which can be stated numerically and arranged in tables; and also, the formation of a Statistical Library as rapidly as its funds would permit.

From its inception the Society has steadily progressed. It now possesses a valuable Library of about 50,000 volumes, and reading rooms. Monthly meetings are held from November to June, which are well attended, and cultivate among its Fellows an active spirit of investigation The Papers read at these meetings, with an abstract of the discussions thereon, are published in the *Journal*, which now consists of seventy annual volumes, and forms of itself a valuable library of reference.

The Society has originated and statistically conducted many special inquiries on subjects of economic or social interest, of which the results have been published in the *Journal*, or issued separately.

To enable the Society to extend its sphere of useful activity, and accomplish in a yet greater degree the various ends indicated, an increase in its numbers and revenue is desirable. With the desired increase in the number of Fellows, the Society will be enabled to publish standard works on Economic Science and Statistics, especially such as are out of print or scarce, and also greatly extend its collection of foreign works. Such a well-arranged Library for reference as would result does not at present exist in England, and is obviously a great *desideratum*.

The Society is cosmopolitan, and consists of Fellows and Honorary Fellows, together forming at the present time a body of about *one thousand* Members.

The annual subscription to the Society is *Two Guineas*, and at present there is no entrance fee. Fellows may, on joining the Society, or afterwards, compound for all future annual subscriptions by a payment of *Twenty Guineas*.

The Fellows of the Society receive gratuitously a copy of each part of the *Journal* as published quarterly, and have the privilege of purchasing back numbers at a reduced rate. The Library (reference and circulating), and the Reading Rooms are open daily, for the convenience of Members.

Nomination Forms, with any further information will be furnished, on application to the *Assistant Secretary, Royal Statistical Society*, 9, *Adelphi Terrace, Strand, W.C., London*.

ROYAL STATISTICAL SOCIETY.

LIST OF PUBLICATIONS.

Note.—Sets or separate numbers of the *Journal*, or of the other publications of the Society (if not out of print) can be obtained at the Offices of the Royal Statistical Society, 9, Adelphi Terrace, Strand, W.C., or through any bookseller. Fellows can purchase these publications at a reduced rate.

	Price.
Journal (published quarterly)— Vols. 1—70. 8vo. 1838-1907	5s. each part*
General Analytical Index to Vols. 1—50 of the Journal (1838-87). In 4 parts. 8vo.—	
(i) For Vols. 1—15 (1838-52)	7s. 6d.
(ii) For Vols. 16—25 (1853-62)	
(iii) For Vols. 26—35 (1863-72)	3s. 6d. each part
(iv) For Vols. 36—50 (1873-87)	
Subject-Index to the Journal, Vols. 28—57, 1865-94	1s. 6d.
First Report of a Committee on Beneficent Institutions. I. The Medical Charities of the Metropolis. 68 pp. 8vo. 1857	2s. 6d.
Statistics of the Farm School System of the Continent (reprinted from the *Journal*, with a Preface and Notes). 63 pp. 8vo. 1878...	1s.
Production and Consumption of Meat and Milk in the United Kingdom. Reports of Committee appointed 20th November, 1900, to Inquire into Statistics Available as a Basis for Estimating Production and Consumption of Meat and Milk in United Kingdom; with observations by Mr. R. H. Rew. 8vo. 1904	1s.
Catalogue of the Library— 573 pp. Cloth, super royal 8vo. 1884...... *A new edition is now in course of preparation.*	10s.
Index to the Catalogue of 1884— 372 pp. Cloth, super royal 8vo. 1886 ...	10s.
Jubilee Volume— xv + 372 pp. Cloth, 8vo. 1885	10s. 6d.
List of Fellows, Rules and Bye-Laws, Regulations of the Library, and Outline of the Objects of the Society, &c. Corrected annually to 31st December. 8vo.	Issued gratuitously

NOTE.—Several numbers of the *Journal* and Part ii of the Index are now out of print.

* Before 1870 the price varied.

LIST

OF THE

Society's Guy Medallists,

With the Date of the Awards.

Medals in GOLD *have been awarded as follows—*

1892. The Rt. Hon. CHARLES BOOTH, F.R.S.	1900. Sir J. ATHELSTANE BAINES, C.S.I.
1894. Sir ROBERT GIFFEN, F.R.S.	1907. Prof. F. Y. EDGEWORTH, D.C.L.

Medals in SILVER *have been awarded as follows—*

NAME.	TITLE OF PAPER.
1893. Sir JOHN GLOVER.	*Tonnage Statistics of the Decade, 1880–1890.*
1894. Mr. A. SAUERBECK.	*Prices of Commodities during the last Seven Years.*
1895. Mr. A. L. BOWLEY.	*Changes in Average Wages (Nominal and Real) in the United Kingdom between 1860 and 1891.*
1897. Mr. FRED. J. ATKINSON.	*Silver Prices in India.*
1899. Mr. CHARLES S. LOCH.	*Poor Relief in Scotland: its Statistics and Development, 1791-1891.*
1900. Mr. R. F. CRAWFORD.	*Notes on the Food Supply of the United Kingdom, Belgium. France, and Germany.*
1901. Mr. T. A. WELTON.	*Distribution of Population in England and Wales in the Period of Ninety Years from 1801 to 1891.*
1902. Mr. R. H. HOOKER.	*Suspension of the Berlin Produce Exchange, and its effect on Corn Prices.*
1903. M. YVES GUYOT.	*The Sugar Industry on the Continent.*
1904. Mr. D. A. THOMAS, M.P.	*The Growth and Direction of our Foreign Trade in Coal during the last Half Century.*
1905. Mr. R. HENRY REW.	*Reports of the Committee on Meat and Milk Production*
1906. Dr. W. N. SHAW, F.R.S.	*Seasons in the British Isles from 1878.*
1907. Mr. N. A. HUMPHREYS, I.S.O.	*The Alleged Increase of Insanity.*

---

* This paper was one of a series which now contains five decennial reviews.

LIST

OF THE

Society's Howard Medallists.

NAME.	SUBJECT OF COMPETITION.
1875. Mr. EDWARD SMITH.	*Influence of improved Dwellings of the Poor in Rural Districts of England.*
1876. Dr. J. C. STEELE.	*Past and Present Mortality of Hospitals in the United Kingdom.*
1878. Dr. JOHN MARTIN and Captain H. HILDYARD (extra Prize).*	*Effects of Health and Disease on Military and Naval Operations.*
1879. Miss B. JOURDAN.	*Improvements in Education of Children in Eighteenth and Nineteenth Centuries.*
1880. Mr. H. P. POTTER.	*The Oriental Plague. and Howard's Labours on the subject.*
1881. Dr. F. POLLARD.	*On the Jail Fever, from the earliest Black Assize to the latest Outbreak.*
1882. Mr. D. MANSON FRASER.	*State of English Prisons in the Eighteenth Century, and its relation to Small-Pox.*
1883. Dr. R. D. R. SWEETING.	*John Howard on Health of Inmates of Prisons, Workhouses, and other Public Institutions.*
1884. Dr. CLEMENT DUKES.	*Howard's Opinions on the Preservation of Health as affected by Personal Habits.*
1893. Dr. HUGH R. JONES.	*Perils and Protection of Infant Life.*
1895. Mr. JOHN WATSON.	*Reformatory and Industrial Schools.*
1897. Dr. JAMES KERR.	*School Hygiene.*
1899. Miss ROSA M. BARRETT.	*Sentences on, and Punishments of, Juvenile Offenders in Europe and the United States.*
1900. Dr J. F. J. SYKES.	*Housing of the Working Classes in London and other large Towns.*
1904. Mr. LEONARD WARD.	*Effects of State Regulation of Dangerous Trades on Health of Workers.*

NOTICE.—The subject appointed for the next "Howard Medal" Essay Competition (Session 1907-08) is: "The Cost, Conditions, and Results of Hospital Relief in London." The competition is open to the public, and a statement of the conditions may be obtained from the Assistant Secretary.

Royal Statistical Society.

THE ADVANTAGES OF FELLOWSHIP

Include—

The right to gratuitous COPIES OF THE SOCIETY'S "JOURNAL," which in the course of the year forms a volume of some 800 pages on current matters connected with the most modern statistics.

The use of the Society's LIBRARY AND READING ROOMS, with the right, under the Regulations, to take out volumes from the Library. The latter, comprising about 40,000 volumes, is one of the largest collections of statistical works in the world. In it will be found the latest issues of all important publications dealing with either British or foreign statistics.

The right to purchase such BACK ISSUES OF THE "JOURNAL" AND OTHER PUBLICATIONS of the Society as are in print at a discount, in many cases amounting to 40 per cent. off published price.

The right of ATTENDANCE AT THE ORDINARY MEETINGS OF THE SOCIETY, where, monthly, during each Session, papers on statistical subjects are read and discussed.

FELLOWSHIP OF THE SOCIETY IS ATTAINED BY ELECTION.

CANDIDATES must be proposed and seconded by Fellows of the Society, who, either from personal or general knowledge, vouch for the Candidate's qualification and eligibility.

There is at present no entrance fee and the SUBSCRIPTION is TWO GUINEAS per annum.

In lieu of the annual subscription, a composition of twenty guineas is accepted.

Further particulars, Lists of Fellows, Copies of the Rules, &c., may be obtained on application to

THE ASSISTANT SECRETARY,

ROYAL STATISTICAL SOCIETY,

9, Adelphi Terrace, Strand,

W.C., London.

ROYAL STATISTICAL SOCIETY.

Founded 15th March, 1834, Incorporated 31st January, 1887.

LIST OF THE FORMER

Patron and Presidents of the Society.

Patron.

Period.

HIS ROYAL HIGHNESS THE PRINCE CONSORT, K.G. 1840–61

Honorary President.

H.R.H. ALBERT EDWARD PRINCE OF WALES, K.G. .. 1872–1901

Presidents.

The Most Noble the Marquis of Lansdowne, K.G., F.R.S. {	1834–36 1842–43
Sir Charles Lemon, Bart., M.P., LL.D., F.R.S.	1836–38
The Rt.Hon.the Earl Fitzwilliam, F.R.S. 1838–40; 1847–49	1853–55
The Rt. Hon. the Viscount Sandon, M.P.	1840–42
The Rt. Hon. the Viscount Ashley, M.P.	1843–45
The Rt. Hon. the Lord Monteagle	1845–47
The Rt. Hon. the Earl of Harrowby, K.G., D.C.L.1849–51 .	1855–57
The Rt. Hon. the Lord Overstone	1851–53
The Rt. Hon. the Lord Stanley, M.P.	1857–59
The Rt. Hon. the Lord John Russell, M.P., F.R.S.........	1859–61
The Rt. Hon. Lord Hampton, G.C.B.	1861–63
Colonel W. H. Sykes, M.P., D.C.L.	1863–65
The Rt. Hon. the Lord Houghton. D.C.L., F.R.S.	1865–67
The Rt. Hon. W. E. Gladstone, M.P., D.C.L.	1867–69
W. Newmarch, F.R.S., Corr. Mem. Inst. of France	1869–71
William Farr, M.D., C.B., D.C.L., F.R.S................	1871–73
William A. Guy, M.B., F.R.S.....	1873–75
James Heywood, M.A., F.R.S., F.G.S...................	1875–77
The Rt. Hon. George Shaw-Lefevre, M.P..	1877–79
The Rt. Hon. Lord Brassey, K.C.B.	1879–80
The Rt. Hon. Sir James Caird, K.C.B., F.R.S.	1880–82
Sir Robert Giffen, K.C.B., LL.D , F.R.S	1882–84
Sir Rawson W. Rawson. K.C.M.G., C.B................	1884–86
The Rt. Hon. Viscount Goschen, F.R.S.................	1886–88
T. Graham Balfour, M.D., F.R.S.	1888–90
Frederic J. Monat, M.D., LL.D., F.R.C.S.	1890–92
The Rt. Hon. Charles Booth, D.Sc., F.R.S..............	1892–94
The Rt. Hon. the Lord Farrer	1894–96
John Biddulph Martin, M.A., F.Z.S.	1896–97
Sir Alfred Edmund Bateman, K.C.M.G.	1897
The Rt. Hon. Leonard H. Courtney, M.A., M.P.	1897–99
The Rt. Hon. Sir Henry H. Fowler, G.C.S.I., M.P.	1899–1900
The Rt. Hon. Lord Avebury, D.C.L., LL.D., F.R.S.	1900–02
Major Patrick George Craigie, C.B.	1902–04
Sir Francis Sharp Powell, Bart., M.P..................	1904–05
The Rt. Hon. the Earl of Onslow, G.C.M.G.	1905–06
Sir Richard Biddulph Martin, Bart..................	1906–07

CONTENTS OF RECENT ISSUES OF THE

JOURNAL OF THE ROYAL STATISTICAL SOCIETY.

Vol. LXX, Part I—*March*, 1907.   PAGE

Correlation of the Weather and Crops. By R. H. HOOKER,
F.R.Met.S. With Discussion .... 1— 51
Statistics of Production and the Census of Production Act (1906).
By G. UDNY YULE. With Discussion .... 52— 99
Miscellanea .... 100—131

Vol. LXX, Part II—*June*, 1907.

The Alleged Increase of Insanity. By NOEL A. HUMPHREYS, I.S.O.
With Discussion .... 203—241
The Herring Fishery. By ALBERT E. LARK, F.C.A. With Dis-
cussion .... 242—266
The Decline in Number of Agricultural Labourers in Great Britain.
By LORD EVERSLEY. With Discussion.... .... 267—319
Annual Report and Accounts, &c. .... 320—329
Proceedings of the Seventy-third Annual General Meeting 330, 331
Miscellanea .... 332—333

Vol. LXX, Part III—*September*, 1907.

Some Considerations relating to the Position of the Small Holding in
the United Kingdom. By W. G. S. ADAMS, M.A. With
Discussion .... 411—448
Miscellanea .... 449—478

Vol. LXX, Part IV—*December*, 1907.

The Presidential Address of THE RIGHT HON. SIR CHARLES W.
DILKE, BART., M.P., for the Session 1907-08. Delivered to the
Royal Statistical Society, 19th November, 1907.... .... 553—582
Proceedings on the 19th November, 1907 .... 583—586
An Inquiry into the Rent of Agricultural Land in England and Wales
during the Nineteenth Century. By ROBERT J. THOMPSON.
With Discussion .... 587—624
Miscellanea, including :—(1.) Memorandum as to Birth-rates and
Marriage-rates in England and Wales. By THOMAS A. WELTON,
F.C.A. (2.) The Assize of Bread at Oxford, 1794-1820. By
ADOLPHUS BALLARD, B A., LL.B. (Lond.), Hon. M.A. (Oxon.).
(3.) The Differential Law of Wages. By HENRY L. MOORE,
Columbia University, New York. (4.) Agricultural Returns of
Great Britain, 1907. (5.) The International Congress on Tuber-
culosis, Washington, 1908.... .... 625—654
Index to vol. lxx (1907) .... 729—743
Appendix. List of Fellows, Bye-Laws, Rules, &c. .... 1— 71

The *Journal* is published at the price of five shillings. It is obtainable by the general
public either at the offices of the Society, or through any bookseller. The postage of single
copies is usually threepence, and the subscription to non-members of the Society is one
guinea per annum. Fellows receive the current issues free.

LIST OF FELLOWS.

Those marked *c* have Served or are Serving on the Council.

   ,,   *d* have made Presentations to the Library.

   ,,   *p* have contributed Papers to the Society.

*Those marked thus * have compounded for their Annual Subscriptions.*

The names of Present Members of Council are printed in SMALL CAPITALS.

Year of Election.		
1904	*d*	*à Ababrelton, Robert, F.R.G.S., *Post Box 322, Pietermaritzburg, Natal.*
1907		*à Ababrelton, Robert R. de R., *Registry and Record Dept., India Office, S.W.*
1900		Ablett, Cecil Gerard, *1, Guardian Chambers, Port Elizabeth.*
1906		Abrahams, E. Goldsmid, *4, Albany Courtyard, Piccadilly, W.*
1888		Ackland, Thomas G., F.I.A. (*5 and 6, Clement's Inn*). *The Thatched House, Muswell-hill, Highgate, N.*
1888	*c d p*	Acland, The Right Hon. Arthur Herbert Dyke, M.A., *Westholme, Scarborough.*
1892	*c d p*	ACWORTH, WILLIAM MITCHELL, M.A., *The Albany, Piccadilly, W.*
1905	*d p*	Adams, W. G. S., M.A., *Dept. of Agri. and Tech. Instruction, Dublin.*
1891		Addington, Right Hon. Lord, *24, Prince's-gate, S.W.*
1902	*d*	Adeane, Charles Robert Whorwood, *Babraham Hall, near Cambridge.*
1884		Agius, Edward Tancred, *3, Belsize-grove, N.W.*
1888		*Airedale, Rt. Hon. Lord, *Gledhow Hall, Leeds.*

Year of Election.		
1879		Akers-Douglas, The Right Hon. Aretas. M.P., *Chilston-park, Maidstone, Kent.*
1896		Allen, George Berney. *Free Chase, Warminglid, Hayward's Heath.*
1899	*d*	Allen, Richard James (*Manchester Cotton Assoc.*), *St. Mary's-gate, Manchester.*
1898		Allen. William Henry, *Bromham House, Bromham, near Bedford.*
1880		*Allerton, The Right Hon. Lord, *Chapelallerton, Leeds.*
1893		Anderson, Herbert William, *S. W. Laboratory, 43, St. James's-rd., Kingston.*
1889		Anderson, John Andrew, *Faversham, Kent.*
1907		Andersson, Thor Erik Engelbreckt, Ph.D., *Regeringsgaten III., Stockholm.*
1886		Andras. Henry Walsingham, F.I.A., *50, Regent-street, W.*
1902	*d*	Angier, Sir Theodore Vivian Samuel, *Exchange Chambers, St. Mary Axe, E.C.*
1871		Angus, R. B.. *Montreal, Canada.*
1897		Anning, Edward Herbert, F.R.G.S., *78, Cheapside, E.C.*
1884		Anning. Edward James, *78, Cheapside, E.C.*
1906		Archer, Walter Edward, *17, Sloane-court, S. W.*
1872		*Archibald, William Frederick A., M.A., *114, Royal Courts of Justice, Strand, W.C.*
1892	*d*	Argyle, Jesse, *"Holmdale," 6, Northolme-rd., Highbury-pk., N.*
1906		Arkell, George E., *107. Ivanhoe-road, Denmark-park, S.E.*
1904		Arkövy, Richard, *65, Vaczi Utcza, Budapest.*
1888		Asch, William, *7, Lothbury, E.C.*
1900		Aston, William Henry, *46, Eagle Wharf-road, New North-road, N.*
1888	*d*	Atkinson, Charles, *56, Palewell-park, East Sheen.*
1893	*d p*	Atkinson, Frederic J. (*Deputy Auditor General*), *c/o King, King & Co., 45, Pall Mall, S.W.*
1865	*c d p*	AVEBURY, RIGHT HON. LORD, F.R.S. (*Honorary Vice-President*), *High Elms, Farnbro', R.S.O., Kent.*
1904		Avery, John, A.C.A., *23, St. Swithin's-lane, E.C.*
1893		*Aves, Ernest, M.A., *Lower Birtley, Witley, Surrey.*

Year of Election.	

1872   *c d*   *Babbage, Major-General Henry Prevost,
Mayfield, Lansdown, Cheltenham.

1892   Bacon, George Washington, F.R.G.S.,
127, Strand, W.C.

1855   *c d*   Bailey, Arthur Hutcheson, F.I.A.,
26, Mount Ephraim-road, Streatham, S.W.

1907   Bailey, Walter,
The Gobbins, Burton-road, Derby.

1900   Baily, James Thomas Herbert,
95, Temple Chambers, Temple-avenue, E.C.

1881   *c d p*   BAINES, SIR J ATHELSTANE, C.S.I. (*Hon. Foreign Secretary*),
Kidlington, Oxon.

1887   *Baldwin, Alfred, M.P.,
Wilden House, Stourport, Worcestershire.

1906   Baldwin-Wiseman, William Ralph,
165, Shirley-road, Southampton.

1878   Balfour, The Right Hon. Arthur J., M.P., F.R.S.,
4, Carlton-gardens, S.W.

1886   Balfour, The Right Hon. Gerald William,
3, Whitehall Court, S.W.

1907   Balleine, Arthur Edwin,
4, Whitehall-place, S.W.

1903   *d*   Bamber, Lieut.-Col. Charles James, D.P.H.,
Sanitary Comm. to Gov. of the Punjab, Lahore.

1904   *d*   Banaji, Khoshru Nowrosji,
"The Commercial Studio," Baroda, Bombay Presy.

1902   Barham, Sir George,
Snape, Wadhurst, Sussex; Danehurst, Hampstead.

1887   Barnes, Joseph Howard, F.I.A.,
70, Lombard-street, E.C.

1885   Barratt, Thomas J.,
75, New Oxford-street, W.

1887   *Barrett, Thomas Squire, F.Z.S., M.A.I., &c.,
Rose Cottage, Millfield-road, Widnes.

1888   *Bartlett, Frederick W.,
Paymaster General's Office, Whitehall, S.W.

1903   Barton, Edwin,
Beechwood, Heaton Moor Manchester.

1907   *d*   Bassett, Herbert Harry,
" Darent," Barnmead-road, Beckenham, Kent.

Year of Election		
1889	d	Bastable. Professor C. F., M.A., LL.D.,
		6, Trevelyan-trr., Brighton-rd., Rathgar, Dublin.
1877	c d p	BATEMAN, SIR ALFRED EDMUND, K.C.M.G. (Honorary Vice-President),
		Woodhouse, Wimbledon-park, S. W.
1877		Bayfield, Arthur,
		95, Colmore-row, Birmingham.
1873		*Baynes, Alfred Henry, F.R.G.S.,
		19, Furnival-street, Holborn, E.C.
1875	d	*Beardsall, Francis E. M.,
		42, Winifred-road, Urmston, nr. Manchester.
1875	d	*Beaufort, William Morris, F.R.A.S., F.R.G.S.,
		18, Piccadilly, W.
1905		Beaven, Edwin Sloper,
		5, Boreham-terrace, Warminster.
1882	d	*Beazeley. Michael Wornum, M.A.,
		Worting, Basingstoke.
1882	c d	*Beeton, Henry Ramie (18, Austin Friars, E.C.)
		9, Maresfield-gardens, Hampstead, N. W.
1899	d	Beeton, Mayson M., B.A.,
		Horsey Hall, Norfolk.
1886	d	Begg, Ferdinand Faithfull,
		Bartholomew House, E.C.
1890		Bell, Frederick, F.I.A.,
		47, Chancery-lane, W.C.
1892	d	Bell, Frederick William,
		P.O. Box 5,666, Johannesburg, Transvaal.
1884	d	Bell, James T.,
		330, Mansfield-road, Nottingham.
1901	d	Bellingham, Archer,
		Walcot, Burghley-road, Wimbledon.
1897		Bennett, William (City Mutual Life Ass. Soc.),
		475, Collins-street, Melbourne.
1888		*Benson, Godfrey R.,
		108, Eaton-square, S. W.
1884		*Bentley, Richard, F.R.G.S.,
		Upton, Slough. Bucks.
1907		Bernard, Major Francis T. H.,
		Cheursley Hall, Aylesbury.
1890		Berry, Arthur, M.A.,
		King's College, Cambridge.
1891		Berry, Oscar, C.C., F.C.A.,
		Monument House. Monument-square, E.C.
1869	p	*Beverley, The Hon. Mr. Justice Henry,
		Nascot Lodge, Watford.
1891	d	Biddle, Daniel, M.R.C.S., L.S.A.,
		St. Aubyns, Grove-cres., Kingston-on-Thames.
1888		Billinghurst, Henry F.,
		7, Oakcroft-road, Blackheath, S.E.
1899	c	Birchenough, Henry, C.M.G., M.A.,
		79, Eccleston-square, S. W.

Year of Election.		
1901		Bird, Harry, C.C., *Strathmore, Chingford, Essex.*
1881	d	Bishop, George, 113, *Powis-street, Woolwich.*
1902		Bisset-Smith, George Tulloch, 55, *Carlton-place, Aberdeen.*
1898		Blount, Edward Thomas Joseph, F.F.A., A.I.A., *Standard Insurance Co., Shanghai, China.*
1898	c d	*Blyth, Rt. Hon. Lord, *Stansted, Essex ; and 33, Portland-place, W.*
1907		Boddy, Henry Mitchell, *Rhodes Buildings, Cape Town.*
1884	d	Boileau, Lieut.-Col. John Peter H., M.A., M.D., &c., *Trowbridge, Wilts.*
1881		Bolitho, Thomas Robins, *Trengwainton, Hea Moor, R.S.O., Cornwall.*
1890		Bolton, Edward, J.P., 325, *Anlaby-road, Hull.*
1885	c d	*Bonar, James, M.A., LL.D., *The Mint, Ottawa, Canada.*
1887		BOND, EDWARD, 43. *Thurloe-square, S.W.*
1905		*Bonn, Max J., 43, *Park-lane, W.*
1885	c d p	BOOTH, RT. HON. CHARLES, D.C.L., D.Sc., F.R.S. (*Hon. Vice-President*), 8, *Adelphi-terrace, Strand, W.C.*
1907		Borrajo, Edward M., *Guildhall, E.C.* (*Representing the Library Committee of the Corporation of the City of London*).
1899	d	Bourne, Arthur, 131, *Seabank-road, Liscard, Cheshire.*
1894	c d p	BOWLEY, ARTHUR LYON, M.A. (*Vice-President*), *Northcourt-avenue, Reading.*
1879		Bowley, Edwin, 29, *Croftdown-road, Highgate-road, N.W.*
1894	c d p	BRABROOK, SIR EDWARD WILLIAM, C.B., V.P.S.A. (*Vice-President*), 178, *Bedford-hill, Balham, S.W.*
1883		Braby, Frederick, F.C.S., F.G.S., *Bushey Lodge, Teddington.*
1900		Branford, Victor Verasis, M.A , 5, *Old Queen-street, S.W.*
1873	c d p	BRASSEY, THE RIGHT HON. LORD, G.C.B. (*Honorary Vice-President*), 24, *Park-lane, W.*
1903	d p	Brassey, The Hon. Thomas A., *Park-gate, Battle.*
1907		Braun, Percy Ernest, B.Sc., *London County Council, Spring Gardens, S.W.*

Year of Election.		
1864		*Braye, The Right-Hon. Lord, *Stanford Hall, Market Harborough.*
1902	*d*	Broadbent, Albert, 257, *Deans Gate, Manchester.*
1906		Brook, Herbert E. J., *The Cottage, Hedon, East Yorks.*
1874		Broom, Andrew, A.C.A., *Eaglehurst, Staines, Middlesex*
1895	*d*	Broomhall, George James-Short, 17, *Goree Piazzas, Liverpool.*
1905		Brothers, Orlando Frank, *Box* 1163, *Johannesburg.*
1878		Brown, Sir Alexander Hargreaves, Bart., 12. *Grosvenor-gardens, S. W.*
1901		Brown, B. Hal., *London & Lancs. Life Ins.Co., Montreal, Canada.*
1896		*Brown, Daniel Maclaren, *P.O. Box* 187, *Carra Linn, Port Elizabeth.*
1893		Brown, James William Bray, F.S.A.A., *Prudential-bldgs., Corporation-st., Birmingham.*
1903	*d*	Brown, S. Stanley, *Hamilton House, Victoria Embankment, E.C.*
1875	*p*	Browne, Thomas Gillespie C., F.I.A.. 11, *Lombard-street, E.C.*
1903		Brownfoot. Harry Allison.
1886		*Brunner, The Rt. Hon. Sir John T., Bart., M.P.. *Druid's Cross, Wavertree, Liverpool.*
1880	*c d p*	*Burdett, Sir Henry Charles, K.C.B., *The Lodge, Porchester-square, W.*
1884	*d*	Burdett-Coutts, William, M.P., 1, *Stratton-street, Piccadilly, W.*
1902		Burgess, James Henry, F.S.A.A., *Bergen House, St. Catherine's, Lincoln.*
1897		Burke, David, A.I.A. *Royal Victoria Life Insurance Co., Montreal.*
1905		Burns, Thomas Robert, *Kingscourt, Wellington-place, Belfast.*
1895		Burrup, John Arthur Evans, *c/o Messrs. King, Hamilton & Co., Calcutta.*
1880		Burt, Frederick. F.R.G.S., *Pinewood, Stoke Poges,R.S.O.nr. Slough,Bucks.*
1901		Burt, George Stephen, *The Lancashire Watch Co., Ltd., Prescot.*
1872		*Burton, The Right Hon. Lord, *Chesterfield House, Mayfair, W*

1898		Burton, William,
		     c/o Colonial Mutual Life Association Society,
		     Queenstown, S. Africa.

1906		Bush, Joseph H.. " *Varaville," Cranbrook-road, Ilford.*

Year of Election.		
1892		Byworth, Charles Joseph, F.S.A.A., *Narford, Lyford-rd., Wandsworth Common, S.W.*
1902	d	Caillard, Sir Vincent Henry P., *42, Half Moon-street, W.*
1897		Cairnes, Frederick Evelyn, *Killester House, Raheny, Co. Dublin.*
1907		Calderón, Lieut.-Col. Guillermo Rafael, *Consul-Gen. for Republic of Colombia, 6, Holborn-viaduct, E.C.*
1903		Caldwell, William, *162, Bath-street, Glasgow.*
1896		Campbell, Charles William, C.M.G., *H B.M. Consulate General, Shanghai, China.*
1905	d	Campbell, Richardson, *37, Lansdowne-road, Crumpsall, Manchester.*
1879		Campbell-Colquhoun, Rev. John Erskine, *Chartwell, Westerham, Kent.*
1889	d p	Cannan, Edwin, M.A, LL.D, *46, Wellington-square, Oxford.*
1891	d	Cannon, Edwin, W. (*Chase National Bank*), *83, Cedar-street, New York, U.S.A.*
1900	d	Canovai, Commendatore Tito, *Bank of Italy, Rome.*
1904		Carrington, John Broyden, F.S.A.A., *20, Blomfield-road, Maida Vale, W.*
1890		*Carter, Eric Mackay, A.I.A., F.C.A., *33, Waterloo-street, Birmingham.*
1883	d	'Carter, Joseph Robert, *Courtfield, Ross-road, Wallington, Surrey.*
1881		Causton, Right Hon. Richard Knight, M.P., *12, Devonshire-place, Portland-place, W.*
1903		Cawson, Frederick Arthur, *80, Belmont-road, Liverpool.*
1907		*Chabot, Marius Taudin, *94, Haringvliet, Rotterdam, Holland.*
1884	d	*Chailley-Bert, Joseph, (*Union Coloniale Française*). *44, Chaussée d'Antin, Paris.*
1902		Chalmers, Patrick R., *9, Idol-lane, Eastcheap, E.C.*

Year of Election.		
1880	d	*Chamberlain, The Right Hon. Joseph, M.P., F.R.S., *Highbury, Moor Green, Birmingham.*
1901	d p	Chance, Sir William, Bart., J.P., *Orchards, near Godalming.*
1903		Channing, Sir Francis Allston, Bart., M.P., *40, Eaton-place, S.W.*
1886	d p	*Chapman, Samuel, *225—228, Gresham House, Old Broad-st., E.C.*
1903	d p	Chapman, Professor Sydney John, M.A., *Owen's College, Manchester.*
1901	d	Chapman, Walter William, *4, Mowbray House, Norfolk-street, Strand.*
1904		Charles, Thomas Edwin, *52, Sandrock-road, Lewisham, S.E.*
1892		*Chatham, James, F.I.A., F.F.A., *7, Belgrave-crescent, Edinburgh.*
1903	d	Chiozza-Money, Leo George, M.P., *3, Alexandra-court, Maida Vale, W.*
1886	c d p	*CHISHOLM, GEORGE GOUDIE, M.A., B.Sc., F.R.G.S., *59, Drakefield-road, Upper Tooting.*
1906		Choles, Herbert J., *Dept. of Agriculture; Pietermaritzburg, Natal.*
1904		Clark, Archibald Brown, *16, Comely Bank-street, Edinburgh.*
1901		Clark, William Henry, C.M.G., *13, Lower Belgrave-street, S.W.*
1888		Clarke, C. Goddard, J.P., *South Lodge, Champion-hill, S.E.*
1882	c d	*CLARKE, SIR ERNEST, *31. Tavistock-square, W.C.*
1877		*Clarke, Henry, L.R.C.P., *H.M. Prison, Wakefield, Yorks.*
1890		Clarke, Henry, J.P., *Cannon Hall, Hampstead, N.W.*
1899		Claughton, Gilbert H., *The Priory, Dudley.*
1907		Cleaver, Edgar John, F.A.A., *34, Dover-street, W.*
1907		Clements, Major Harry Charles, *Cheriton. Lismore-road, South Croydon.*
1853		Clirehugh, William Palin, F.I.A., *66, Cornhill, E.C.*
1893	c d p	COGHLAN, TIMOTHY AUGUSTINE, I.S.O. (*Vice-President*) (*Agent-General for New South Wales*), *4, Albert Gate-court, 124, Knightsbridge, W.*
1905		*Cohen, Charles Waley, M.A., *11, Hyde Park-terrace, W.*
1887	c d	COHEN, NATHANIEL LOUIS, *11, Hyde Park-terrace, W.*

Year of Election.		
1859		Coles, John, F.I.A.,
		39, *Throgmorton-street, E.C.*
1905		Coles, Richard John, F.C.I.S.,
		Addenbrooke's Hospital, Cambridge.
1892	*p*	*Collet, Miss Clara Elizabeth, M.A.,
		43, *Parliament-street, S.W.*
1895		Collins, Howard James,
		The General Hospital, Birmingham.
1906		Collins, Percy,
		81–83, *Cheapside, E.C.*
1882		*Collum, Rev. Hugh Robert, M.R.I.A., F.R.C.I.,
		35. *Oakley-street. Chelsea, S.W.*
1906		Contractor, Burjorjee Cawasjee,
		New Markers Buildings, Apollo-street, Bombay.
1903	*d*	Cook-Watson, Ralph,
		Standard Chambers, Neville-st., Newcastle-on-T.
1891	*d*	Cooper, Joseph,
		60, *Park-street, Farnworth, near Bolton.*
1906		Cornish, George Frederick,
		23, *St. Stephen's-road, North Bow, E.*
1889		Cornwallis. Fiennes Stanley Wykeham,
		Linton-park, Maidstone, Kent.
1899	*d*	Court, Stephen E.,
		High Commissioner's Office, Johannesburg.
1862	*c d p*	COURTNEY, RIGHT HON. LORD (*Hon. Vice-President*),
		15, *Cheyne Walk, Chelsea, S.W.*
1902		*Coxon, William,
		15, *Elsworthy-terrace, N.W.*
1907		Coyagi, Professor Jehangi,
		Wilson College, Bombay, India.
1871	*d*	Cozens-Smith, Edward,
		16, *Kensington-square, W.*
1874	*c d p*	CRAIGIE, MAJOR P. G., C.B. (*Hon. Vice-President*),
		West Wellow, Romsey. Hampshire.
1906		Craske. Harold,
		Kyle Lodge, Letchworth, Herts.
1902		Craven, Edward Joseph E. (*Poor Law Commission*),
		Scotland House, Victoria Embankment, S.W.
1890	*c d p*	CRAWFORD, RICHARD FREDERICK,
		Delamere, Hendon, N.W., & Custom House, E.C.
1891		*Crawley, Charles Edward,
		Lanhydrock Villa, Truro, Cornwall.
1878		Crewdson, Ernest,
		Castle Meadows, Kendal.
1892		Cripps, Charles Alfred, K.C.,
		1, *Essex-court, Temple, E.C.*
1890		Croal, David Octavius,
		Financial News, 11, Abchurch-lane, E.C.
1907		Cromer, The Rt. Hon. The Earl of, O.M., G.C.B.,
		6, *Wimpole-street, W.*

1904		Crotch, William Walter,
		199, *Piccadilly, W.*
1900		Crowley, Michael, F.C.A., F.S.A.A.,
		16, *College Green, Dublin*
1905		Cruce, Frederick George Landin,
		27, *Chetwynd-road, Southsea.*
1883	*c d*	Cunningham, The Venble. Archdeacon, **D.D.**,
		2, *St. Paul's-road, Cambridge.*
1879	*d*	Curtis, Robert Leabon, F.S.I., J.P..
		11—12, *Finsbury-square, E.C.*
1873		Czarnikow, Cæsar,
		29, *Mincing-lane, E.C.*
1900		Da Costa, José Simao G *arantia* (*amazona*).
		Belem do Para, Brazil.
1900		Dale, Charles Ernest, F.S.A.A.,
		Old Calabar, West Africa.
1888		Dangerfield, Athelstan, A.C.A.,
		56, *Cannon-street, E.C.*
1898	*d*	*Danson, Francis Chatillon,
		Liverpool and London Chambers, Liverpool.
1901	*d*	Danvers, Ernest, F.R.G.S.,
		475, *B. Mitre, Buenos Ayres.*
1897	*d p*	*Darwin. Major Leonard. R.E., F.R.G.S.,
		12, *Egerton-place, S.W.*
1905		Daugherty, Charles M., *Bureau of Statistics, Dept. of*
		Agriculture, Washington, D.C., U.S.A.
1901	*d*	Davar, Sohrab R., M.S.A.,
		53, *Esplanade-road, Fort, Bombay.*
1901		Davies, Dixon Henry.
		Great Central Ry., Marylebone Station, N.W.
1869		Davies, James Mair,
		168, *St Vincent-street, Glasgow.*
1888		Dawson, G. J Crosbie, M. Inst. C.E., F.G.S.,
		May-place, Newcastle, Staffs.

Year of Election.		
1899		Dawson, Miies Menander. F.A.S., F.I.A., 76, *William-street, New York, U.S.A.*
1903	*d*	Dawson Sidney Stanley, F.C.A F.C.I.S. 51, *North John-street, Liverpool.*
1905		D'Azevedo, Joas Lucio, 7, *Calçada do Sacramento, Lisbon.*
1897	*d*	Deane, Albert Bickerton, F.C.I.S., *Hillsbrook, Great Berkhamstead.*
1880		Debenham, Frank, 1, *Fitzjohn's-avenue, Hampstead, N.W.*
1885	*d*	De Broë, Emile Conrad De Bichin, *Walden Lodge, Carlisle-road, Eastbourne.*
1879		*De Ferrieres, The Baron Du Bois, *Bay's Hill House, Cheltenham.*
1898		Defries. Wolf, B.A., 147, *Houndsditch, E C.*
1900	*d*	De la Plaza, Victorino, LL.D. (*Buenos Ayres Ry. Co.*), *Poste Restante, Buenos Ayres.*
1907		Denman, Hon. Richard Douglas, 9, *Swan-walk, Chelsea, S.W.*
1891		Denne, William, *Phillimore, Wetherill-road, New Southgate, N.*
1873		Dent, Edward, 2, *Carlos-place, Grosvenor-square, W.*
1887		Dent, George Middlewood, 20, *Park-avenue, Southport.*
1889		De Rothschild. Leopold, D.L., 5, *Hamilton-place, Piccadilly, W.*
1892		De Smidt, Henry, C.M.G., "*Ravensworth*," *Claremont, South Africa.*
1906		De Vine, John M., *Royal National Hospital for Consumption, Ventnor, Isle of Wight.*
1892		Dewar, William Nimmo (*Standard Life Assurance Co.*), 28, *Elizabeth-street, Sydney, N.S.W.*
1900		Dewsnup, Professor Ernest Ritson, M.A., F.R.G.S., *University of Illinois, Urbana, Ill., U.S.A.*
1906	*d*	*Dick, Godfrey Watson, 197, *Stamford Hill-road, Durban, Natal.*
1903		Digby, William Pollard, 82, *Victoria-street, S.W.*
1866	*c d p*	*Dilke, The Right Hon. Sir Charles W., Bart., M.P. (*President*), 76, *Sloane-street, S.W.*
1889		Double, Alfred, C.C., 91, *Fore-street, E.C.*
1899	*d*	Dougharty, Harold, A.I.A., F.C.I.S., 91, *Gleneagle-road, Streatham, S.W.*
1894	*c d p*	Drage, Geoffrey, M.A., 29, *Cadogan-square, S.W.*

Year of Election.		
1897	*c d p*	Dudfield, Reginald, M.A., M.B., 19, *Blomfield-road, Maida Vale, W.*
1895	*c*	Dudley, The Right Hon. The Earl of, 7, *Carlton-gardens, S.W.*
1875	*d p*	Dun, John, *Parr's Bank, Bartholomew-lane, E.C.*
1902	*c d*	Dunbar, Sir William Cospatrick, Bart., C.B., *Somerset House, Strand, W.C.*
1878	*c*	*Dunraven, The Right Hon. the Earl of, K.P., C.M.G., *Kenry House, Putney Vale, S.W.*
1885		Dyer, William John, 17, *Montpelier-row, Blackheath, S.E.*
1905		Dyke, Arthur James, *Secretary's Office, Board of Customs, E.C.*
1904		Dymant, Arthur Francis, *Great Northern Railway, King's Cross Station, N.*

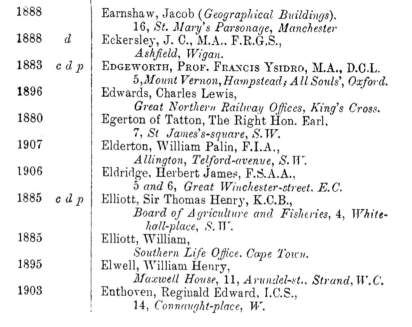

1888		Earnshaw, Jacob (*Geographical Buildings*), 16, *St. Mary's Parsonage, Manchester*
1888	*d*	Eckersley, J. C., M.A., F.R.G.S., *Ashfield, Wigan.*
1883	*c d p*	Edgeworth, Prof. Francis Ysidro, M.A., D.C.L. 5, *Mount Vernon, Hampstead; All Souls', Oxford.*
1896		Edwards, Charles Lewis, *Great Northern Railway Offices, King's Cross.*
1880		Egerton of Tatton, The Right Hon. Earl, 7, *St James's-square, S.W.*
1907		Elderton, William Palin, F.I.A., *Allington, Telford-avenue, S.W.*
1906		Eldridge, Herbert James, F.S.A.A., 5 and 6, *Great Winchester-street, E.C.*
1885	*c d p*	Elliott, Sir Thomas Henry, K.C.B., *Board of Agriculture and Fisheries, 4, Whitehall-place, S.W.*
1885		Elliott, William, *Southern Life Office, Cape Town.*
1895		Elwell, William Henry, *Maxwell House, 11, Arundel-st., Strand, W.C.*
1903		Enthoven, Reginald Edward, I.C.S., 14, *Connaught-place, W.*

Year of Election.		
1889	d	Erhardt, William,
		61¹, *Bismarckstr : Charlottenburg-Berlin.*
1905		Erlund, Cedric,
		Ashcroft, Wadhurst Sussex.
1896		Everett, Percy Winn,
		Oaklands, Elstree, Herts.
1877	c d p	EVERSLEY, RIGHT HON. LORD (*Hon. Vice-President*),
		18, *Bryanston-square, W.*
1892		Faber, Harald,
		Fiona, Lennard-road, Penge, S.E.
1905		Falk, Oswald Toynbee, B.A., A.I.A.,
		431, *Oxford-street, W.*
1888		Farlow, A. R. King,
		4, *King-street, Cheapside, E.C.*
1889	d	Farnworth, Edward James, F.S.A.A.
		26, *Winckley-square, Preston.*
1900		Farrer, The Right Hon. Lord,
		Abinger Hall, Dorking.
1890		Faulks, Joseph Ernest, B.A., F.I.A.,
		187. *Fleet-street, E.C.*
1893		*Fawcett, Mrs. Millicent Garrett,
		2, *Gower-street, W.C.*
1882		Fell, Arthur, M.A., M.P.,
		46, *Queen Victoria-street, E.C.*
1894		Fellows, Rowland Hill, F.I.A.,
		41, *Montrose-avenue, Kilburn, N.W.*
1899		Finch, Henry Hobson,
		Goff's Hill, Crawley, Sussex.
1889		*Finlay, Major Alexander,
		The Manor House, Little Brickhill, Bletchley.
1900	d	Fisher, Professor Irving, Ph D.,
		Yale University, New Haven, Conn., U.S.A.
1888		Fisher, Sir Walter Newton, F.C.A.,
		4, *Waterloo-street, Birmingham.*
1885		*Fitz-Gerald, Lt.-Col. Wm. G., M.A., F.R.Hist.S.,
1900	d	Fleming, Owen, Assoc. R.I.B.A.,
		3, *Warwick House-street, Charing Cross, S.W*
1893	d p	*Flux, Professor Alfred William, M.A.,
		McGill University, Montreal, Canada.

Year of Election.		
1882		Foley, Patrick James (*Pearl Insurance Company*), *Adelaide-place, London Bridge, E.C.*
1889		Foot, Alfred, *Hamilton, 14, Friends-road, Croydon.*
1898	*d*	Forster, John Walter, *18, Mountfield-gardens, Tunbridge Wells.*
1893		Fortune. David, J.P. (84, *Wilson-street, Glasgow*), and *19, Rowallon-gardens, Partick, Glasgow.*
1901		Foster, Harry Seymour, D.L., *Albert Mansions, 122, Victoria-street, S.W.*
1897		Fountain, H. *Board of Trade, Whitehall-gardens, S.W.*
1899	*c p*	FOWLER. THE RIGHT HON. SIR HENRY HARTLEY, G.C.S.I., M P. (*Honorary Vice-President*). *Reform Club, Pall Mall, S.W.*
1900	*c d p*	FOX, ARTHUR WILSON, C.B. (*Hon. Secretary*). *Board of Trade, 7, Whitehall-gardens, S.W.*
1903		Fox, Matthew Joseph, *c/o The National Mutual Life Office. Melbourne.*
1878	*c d*	Foxwell. Professor H. Somerton, M.A., *St. John's College, Cambridge (1, Harvey-road, Cambridge).*
1894		Francis, Joseph, *10, Finsbury-square, E.C.*
1887		Frankland, Frederick William. F.I.A., "*Okataina," Foxton, Manawata. N. Zealand.*
1899		Franklin. Arthur Ellis. *23, Pembridge-gardens. W*
1903		Fraser, Malcolm Alexander Clement. *Government Statistician, Perth. W. Australia.*
1887		Freeman, T. Kyffin, F.G.S.. *35, Whitehall-park, N.*
1890		Freestone, John, *328. East Park-road, Leicester.*
1902		Fremantle, Professor Henry Eardley Stephen, *University of South Africa. Cape Town.*
1905		Frings, Francis A.. *59, Bishopsgate-street Within, E.C.*
1886		Fuller, George Pargiter, *Neston-park, Corsham, Wilts.*
1878		Fuller, William Palmer, *Stone Lodge, Cheam, Surrey.*

Year of Election.		
1902		Gait, Edward Albert, I.C.S., C.I.E., *Writers-buildings, Calcutta.*
1852		Galsworthy, Sir Edwin Henry, J.P., *26, Sussex-place, Regent's-park, N.W.*
1860	c d p	Galton, Francis, F.R.S., D.C.L., D.Sc., *42, Rutland-gate, S.W.*
1887	d	Garcke, Emile, *Donington House, Norfolk-street, Strand, W.C.*
1904		*Gates, Chasemore Philip, *The Reed Cottage, Soham, Cambs.*
1880		*Gates, John Benjamin, A.C.A., *1 and 2, The Exchange, Southwark, S.E.*
1899		Gelling, Benjamin Richard, *Mutual Life Assn.of Australasia,Sydney,N.S.W.*
1907		Gemmill, William, F.I.A., *Statistician, Transvaal Chamber of Mines, P.O. Box 809, Johannesburg, S. Africa.*
1885		Gibb, Sir George S., *Hamilton House, Victoria Embankment, E.C.*
1867	c d p	*GIFFEN, SIR ROBERT, K.C.B., LL.D., F.R.S. (Hon. Vice-President), Chanctonbury, Hayward's Heath.*
1877		Gilbert, William H. S., *70, Queen-street, Cheapside, E.C.*
1900		Gladwell, Sydney William, *59, Palace-street, Victoria-street, S.W.*
1878		*Glanville, Silvanus Goring, *Lloyd's, Royal Exchange, E.C.*
1860	c p	GLOVER, SIR JOHN, J.P., *88, Bishopsgate-street Within, E.C.*
1888		Goad, Charles E., M. Am. and Can. Soc. C.E., *53, New Broad-st., E.C.; and Montreal, Canada.*
1901		Godfrey, Ernest Henry, *Census of Statistics Office, Dept. of Agriculture, Ottawa, Canada.*
1903		Goldman, Leopold, A.I.A., F.C.A., *N. American Life Assurance Co.*, 112–118, King-st. West, Toronto.
1897	c d p	Gomme, George Laurence, F.S.A., *24, Dorset-square, Marylebone, N.W.*
1884	d	*Gonner, Professor Edward C. K., M.A., *University College, Liverpool.*
1901		*Gooch, Henry Cubitt, *17, Oxford-square, W.*
1900	d	Goodsir, George (*Weddel & Co.*), *16, St. Helen's-place, E.C.*
1892		Goodwin, Alfred, M.A., *2, Charles-road, St. Leonards, Sussex.*
1899		Gordon, Charles H. F., *Pitlurg, Hindhead, Surrey.*
1887	.	Gover, Frederic Field, *10, Lee-park, Blackheath, S.E.*

Year of Election.		
1906		Graham, Major James Robert Douglas, *The Gables, Epping, Essex.*
1893		*Gray, The Hon. James McLaren, M.A., F.R.G.S., *c/o R. Todd, 1, York-buildings, Adelphi, W.C.*
1904		*Gray, Robert Kaye, 106, *Cannon-street, E.C.*
1895	d	Green, John Little. 2, *Belmont-park, Lee, S.E.*
1902		Green, Walford Davis, M.A., *High Garth, Balcombe, Sussex.*
1895		Gretton, John, *Stapleford Park, Melton-Mowbray.*
1868		Griffith, Col. Edward Clifton, *Reliance Office, 71, King William-street, E.C.*
1905		Gubbay, M. M. Simeon, B.A., *Custom House, Bombay.*
1878		Guthrie, Charles, F.C.A., *c/o London Bank of Australia, Melbourne.*
1887	d p	Guyot, Yves, 95, *Rue de Seine, Paris.*
1880		*Gwynne, James Eglinton A., J.P., F.S.A., *Folkington Manor, Polegate, Sussex.*
1887		Gwyther, John Howard, 13, *Lancaster-gate, W.*

1892	d	Hadfield, Robert A., *Parkhead House, Sheffield.*
1873	d	*Haggard, Frederick T., 1, *Broadwater Down, Tunbridge Wells.*
1903		*Haig, Edric Wolseley, M.A., LL.M., *Gatehampton, Goring, Oxon.*
1887		Haldeman, Donald Carmichael, " *Oakwood," Farquhar-rd., Up. Norwood, S.E.*
1897	d	Hall, Thomas, *Railway Commissioners' Offices, Sydney, N.S.W.*
1878		Hallett, Thomas George Palmer, M.A., *Claverton Lodge, Bath.*
1903		Hamilton, Charles Joseph, B.A., 88, *Twyford-avenue, Acton Hill, W.*

Year of Election.		
1887	d	Hamiltou, Sir Edward W., G.C.B., I.S.O., *The Treasury, Whitehall, S. W.*
1873	c d p	Hamilton, The Right Hon. Lord George F., G.C.S.I., 17, *Montagu-street, Portman-square, W.*
1884		*Hammersley. Hugh Greenwood, *The Grove, Hampstead, N. W.*
1885		*Hancock, Charles, M.A., 2, *Cloisters,Temple, E.C.; and Reform Club,S. W.*
1875		Hankey, Ernest Alers, *Notton, Lacock, Chippenham.*
1906		Hannon, Patrick J. H., *Dept. of Agriculture, Cape Town, S. Africa.*
1876		Hansard, Luke, , 68, *Lombard-street, E.C.*
1886		*Hardcastle, Basil William, 12, *Gainsborough-gardens, Hampstead, N. W.*
1883		Harding, G. P., 53, *Sunderland-road, Forest-hill, S.E.*
1900		Hardingham, Frederick Robert, 26, *East-parade, Leeds.*
1902		Hardy, Arthur Johnston, 52, *Lower Sackville-street, Dublin.*
1901	c d p	HARPER, EDGAR JOSIAH, *County Hall, Spring-gardens, S. W.*
1906		*Harper, Robarts, F.R.G.S.,
1893		Harrap, Thomas, 143, *Stamford-street, Ashton-under-Lyne, Lancs.*
1868		Harris. David, *Lyncombe Rise, Prior Park-road, Bath.*
1901		Harris, Frederic Ernest, *Met. Water Brd., Savoy Court, Strand, W.C.*
1897		Harris, Walter Fied., F.I.C.A., 16, *Parliament-street, Hull.*
1882	d p	Harris, William James, *Halwill Manor, Beaworthy, R.S.O. N. Devon.*
1900	p	Hartley, Edwin Leach, B.A., 1, *Paper-buildings, Temple, E.C.*
1896		Hawkins, Willoughby R., *Bute Docks, Cardiff.*
1897		Hayakawa. S. 69, *Nagatacho-Nichome, Tokio, Japan.*
1895	d •	Haynes, Thomas Henry, 1, *Endsleigh-terrace, Tavistock.*
1896		*Heaton-Armstrong, William Charles, M.P., J.P., 30, *Portland-place, W.*
1889		*Hemming, Arthur George, F.I.A. (*London Ass. Corporation*), 7, *Royal Exchange, E.C.*
1855	c d p	*HENDRIKS, FREDERICK, F.I.A., 7, *Vicarage-gate, Kensington, W.*

Year of Election.		
1906		Heron, David, M.A., *Galton Eugenics Laboratory.* 88, *Gower-st., W.C.*
1890	d	Hewins, W. A. S.. M A., 15, *Chartfield-avenue, Putney Hill, S. W*
1886		Hibbert, Sir Henry F., 8, *Park-road, Chorley, Lancashire.*
1892	c d p	*Higgs, Henry, LL.B , *The Treasury, Whitehall, S.W.*
1878		*Hill, Frederick Morley, 1, *The Terrace Camden-square, N.W.*
1904		Hill, William Edward. *Kenneth-chambers, Dogpole-court, Shrewsbury.*
1900		Hillingdon, The Right Hon. Lord. 67, *Lombard-street, E.C.*
1906		Hind, Robert, J.P. ("*Eastern Province Herald*"), *Port Elizabeth, S. Africa.*
1903		Hiscock, Elias John, 51, *Sotheby-road. Highbury, N.*
1904		Hobson, John Atkinson, *Elmstead, Limpsfield, Surrey.*
1905		Hodge, James Philp, A.C.A., *Hoole Park. Chester*
1897	d	Hodgson, William Gill, F.S.A.A., *Billagazine-lane, New Brighton, Cheshire.*
1888		Hollams, Sir John, 52, *Eaton-square, S.W.*
1895		Holland Hon. Lionel Raleigh. 75, *Eaton-square, S.W.*
1898		Holland, Robert Martin, 68, *Lombard-street, E C.*
1894	d p	Hollerith, Herman, Ph.D.. &c., 1054, 31*st-street, Washington, D.C., U.S.A.*
1900		Holliday, John, M.A.. F.I.A., A. "*Sul America*" *Compantna de Seguros de Vida,* 56, *Rua de Ouvidor, Rio de Janeiro.*
1901		Holmes, Richard Henry, J.P. (Alderman), 10, *Royal Arcade, Newcastle-on-Tyne.*
1891	d	Hooker, Sir Joseph Dalton. G C.S.I., F.R.S., &c.. *The Camp, Sunningdale.*
1895	d p	*Hooker, Reginald Hawthorn, M.A., 3, *Clement's Inn, W.C.*
1896		Hooper, Angus W., *Montreal, Canada.*
1906	d	Hooper, Frederick, *Board of Trade,* 73, *Basinghall-street, E.C.*
1904		Hooper, Frederick Tungate, 77—79. *New Briggate, Leeds.*
1879		Hooper, George Norgate. *Elmleigh, Hayne-road, Beckenham, Kent.*
1903	d	Hooper, William George, F.R.A.S. 51, *Musters-road, West Bridgford, Nottingham.*

Year of Election.		
1878	c d p	Hooper, Wynnard, *13, Sumner-place, Onslow-square, S. W.*
1887		Hopkins, John, *Little Boundes, Southborough, Kent.*
1899	d	Hopkins, John Castell, *90, Wellington-street West, Toronto.*
1902		Hopwood, Sir Francis John Stephen, K.C.B., K.C.M.G., *Colonial Office, S. W.*
1890		Howarth, William, *72, Endwell-road, Brockley, S.E.*
1883		Howell, Francis Buller, *Ethy, Lostwithiel, Cornwall.*
1897	p	Howell, Price, *Killara, near Sydney, N.S. W.*
1874	c d p	HUMPHREYS, NOEL ALGERNON, I.S.O., *Ravenhurst, Hook-road, Surbiton.*
1903		Hunt, Arthur Leonard, *West Heath Mount, Hermitage-lane, Hampstead, N.W.*
1883		Hunt, Richard Aldington, A.I.A., (*Wesleyan & Gen. Ass. Society*), *Steelhouse-lane, Birmingham.*
1903		Hunter, Arthur (*New York Life Ass. Co.*), 346, *Broadway, New York, U.S.A.*
1888		Hunter, Alderman George Burton, D.Sc. *Wallsend-on-Tyne.*
1902	d p	Hutchins, Miss Bessie Leigh, *The Glade, Branch-hill, Hampstead-heath, N.W.*
1888		Hyde, Clarendon G., M.P., *75, Gloucester-terrace, Hyde-park, W.*
1901		Hyde, Hugh Vivian (*Board of Agriculture & Fisheries*), *3, St James's-square, S. W.*
1893	d	Hyde, Hon. John, *130, Queen's Gate, S.W.*

Year of Election.		
1874	*d p*	*Ingall, William Thomas Fitzherbert Mackenzie, *Invermark, Limpsfield, Surrey.*
1869		*Inglis, Cornelius, M.D., *Athenæum Club, S. W.*
1903		Innes, Alfred Mitchell, *Under Sec. of State for Finance, Cairo, Egypt.*
1901	*d*	Ireland, Alleyne (c/o Dr. *Edward E. Thorpe*), 711, *Boylston-street, Boston, Mass., U.S.A.*
1887		Irvine, Somerset W. D'Arcy, J.P., *Equitable Life Assur. Soc. of U.S.A.,*91, *Queen Victoria-st., E.C.*
1907		Irvine, William Joseph, *Kensington-chambers, Ludgate-hill, E.C.*
1864		*Ivey, George Pearse, 7, *The Drive. Hove.*
1903		Jack, Robert Robertson, J.P., F.F.I.A., Australia, *Molesworth-street, Lismore. N.S.W.*
1902	*d*	Jagger, John William, *Cape Town.*
1906		James, Arthur Frederick Brodie,
1894	*d*	Jamieson, George, C.M.G., 180, *St. James'-court, Buckingham Gate, S.W.*
1872	*c d p*	Janson, Frederick Halsey, F.L.S., 8, *Fourth-avenue, Hove.*
1897	*d*	Jay, E. Aubrey Hastings, *Tower House. Woolwich.*
1881		*Jersey, The Right Hon. the Earl of, G.C.B., *Osterley-park, Isleworth.*
1907		Jevons, Herbert Stanley, M.A., B.Sc., *Llanishen, near Cardiff.*
1881		Johnson, E. Eltham, 110, *Cannon-street, E.C.*
1891	*d*	Johnson. George, 28, *Lockrt-road, Wealdstone.*
1878	*d*	Johnstone, Edward, *Queensbury, South-road, Clapham-park, S.W.*
1905		Jones, John Henry, 306, *Neath-road, Landore, Swansea.*
1877		Jones, Theodore Brooke, 70, *Gracechurch-street. E.C.*

Year of Election.		
1888	*d*	*Jordan, William Leighton,* *Royal Societies Club, St. James's-street, S.W.*
1889		Justican, Edwin, F.I.A., *St. Mildred's House, Poultry, E.C.*
1902		Kains-Jackson, Charles Philip Castle, *10, The Green, Richmond.*
1885		Keen, William Brock, *23, Queen Victoria-street, E.C.*
1884		Kelly, Edward Festus, *182—184, High Holborn, W.C.*
1883	*c d*	Keltie, John Scott, F.R.G.S., LL.D., *1, St. John's Wood Park, N.W.*
1884	*c d*	*Kennedy, Sir Charles Malcolm, K.C.M.G., C.B., *4, Louisa-terrace, Exmouth, South Devon.*
1878		Kennedy, J. Murray, *New University Club, St. James's-street, S.W.*
1901		*Kennedy, Pitt, *14, Pembridge-place, W.*
1898		Kent, Arthur C., *47, Buckingham Palace-road, S.W.*
1899		Kershaw, John Baker C., F.I.C., *West Lancs. Laboratory, Waterloo, Liverpool.*
1905		Keshishian, Agazar. *44, Broad-street, New York, U.S.A.*
1883	*d*	*Keynes, John Neville, M.A., D.Sc., *6, Harvey-road, Cambridge.*
1906		Khras, Minocher J. S., *Khras Bungalow, Middle Colaba, Bombay.*
1884		Kimber, Sir Henry, Bart., M.P., *79, Lombard-street, E.C.*
1898	*c d*	*KING, ARTHUR WILLIAM WATERLOW, J.P., *Orchard House, Gt. Smith-st., Westminster, S.W.*
1883	*p*	*King, Bolton, M.A., *Arden Lodge, Warwick.*
1894		*Kirkcaldy, William Melville, *Dunedin, Otago, New Zealand.*
1889		Kloetgen, W. J. H., *34, Gutter-lane, Cheapside, E.C.*
1906		Knibbs, George H., *Commonwealth Statistician, Melbourne, Victoria.*

Year of Election.		
1899	d	Knight, John Martin,
		Chrisdene, Wanstead Pk.-av., Wanstead Park, E.
1878		*Kusaka, Yoshio,
		First National Bank Tokio, Japan.
1902	d	Lahitte, Emilio.
		Departimento de Agricultura, Casa de Gobierno, Buenos Aires.
1901	d	Lakin-Smith, Herbert, F.C.A.,
		26, Waterloo-street, Birmingham.
1902	p	Lark, Albert Ernest, F.C.A.,
		2, South Quay, Great Yarmouth.
1885	d	Latham, Baldwin, M.Iust. C.E.,
		Parliament-mansions, Victoria-street, S.W.
1897	d	*Lawrence, Frederick William, M.A.,
		Mansfield House, Canning Town, E.
1890	d	Lawson, William Ramage,
		Finchley Lodge, North Finchley, N.
1883	d	*Leadam, Isaac Saunders, M.A.,
		1, The Cloisters, Temple, E.C.
1905	d	*Leake, Percy Dewe,
		25, Abchurch-lane, E.C.
1899	d	Lee, Arthur,
		37, Woodville-gardens, Ealing, W.
1879		*Leete, Joseph,
		36, St. Mary-at-hill, E.C.
1899		L'Estrange, Charles James,
		Delamere, Hendon, N.W.
1887		Leitch, Alexander (*Scottish Provident Institution*),
		3, Lombard-street, E.C.
1907		Lempfert, R. G. K., M.A.,
		Meteorological Office, 63, Victoria-street, S.W.
1892		Leon, Herbert Samuel,
		Bletchley-park, Bletchley, Bucks.
1905		Leonhardt, F. von,
		23, Austin Friars, E.C.
1888		*Le Poer-Trench, Col. The Hon. W., R.E., J.P.,
		3, Hyde Park-gardens, W.
1887		*Le Roy-Lewis, Lieut.-Colonel Herman, B.A., D.S.O.,
		Westbury House, Petersfield, Hants.

Year of Election.		
1898		Leveaux, Arthur Michael, A.I.A.,
		28, *Abingdon-street, Westminster, S.W.*
1903	*d*	Levy, Dr. Hermann,
		Kleinschmidtstr., 44, *Heidelberg, Germany.*
1862		Lewis, Robert,
		1, *Bartholomew-lane, E.C.*
1888		*Liberty, A. Lasenby,
		The Manor House, The Lee, near *Gt. Missenden.*
1884		*Lines, William Edward,
		c/o *Rev. H. Lines, Golant Vicarage, Par Station, Cornwall.*
1902		Litchfie'd, Frederick;
		16, *Woodfield-avenue, Ealing,* W
1898		Litkie. Valerian A.,
		39, *South-street, W.*
1892		Llewelyn, Sir John T. D., Bart.,
		Penllergaer, Swansea.
1903		Lloyd, Godfrey Isaac Howard,
		The University, Sheffield.
1879		Lloyd, Wilson, J.P., F.R.G.S.,
		Park Lane House, Wood-green, Wednesbury.
1888	*c d p*	Loch, Professor Charles S., D.C.L.,
		Drylaw Hatch, Oxshott, Leatherhead.
1882	*c d p*	*Longstaff, George Blundell. M.A., M.D., F.R.C.P.,
		Highlands, Putney Heath, S.W
1907		Lord, Samuel, A.S.A.A.,
		21. *Hereford-rd., Acton, W.*
1876		*Loruie, John Guthrie, J.P. (*of Birnam & Pitcastle*),
		Rosemount, Kirkcaldy, N.B.
1892	*d*	Lough, Thomas, M.P.,
		14, *Dean's-yard, Westminster, S.W.*
1886		*Low, Malcolm,
		22, *Roland-gardens, S.W.*
1895		Lowe, Thomas Enoch, F.S.A.A.,
		89, *Darlington-street, Wolverhampton.*
1906		Lucas, Thomas M.,
		4, *East Dulwich-grove, S.E.*
1903		Lunge, Ernest, LL.D.,
		18, *Southampton-mns., Southampton-row, W.C.*
1904		Lutterveld, Willem Margriet Johan van,
		Schiedamsche Singel, Rotterdam, Holland.
1905		Lynch, William Henry,
		Highfield, Loom-lane, Radlett.

Year of Election.		
1875		*Mabson, Richard Rous, *"Statist" Office*, 51, *Cannon-street, E.C.*
1894		Macaulay, Thomas Bassett, *Sun Life Assurance Co., Montreal, Canada.*
1888		McCankie, James, 63, *George-street, Edinburgh.*
1903		MacConochie, William Pitt, *Glengariff, New Barnet.*
1902		Macdonald, John Hutcheson, 10, *Victoria-street, Wesiminster, S.W.*
1897		MacDonald, Mrs. Margaret Ethel, 3, *Lincoln's Inn Fields, W.C.*
1898		*Macdonald, Robert Alexander, *Royal Bank of Scotland, Edinburgh.*
1872	c d p	Macdonell, Sir John, C.B., LL.D., *Room* 183, *Royal Courts of Justice, W.C.*
1873		*McEwen, Laurence T., c/o. *R. A. McLean,* 1, *Queen Victoria-st., E.C.*
1905		Macgregor, D. H., M.A., *Trinity College, Cambridge.*
1899	d	McHardy, Coghlan McLean, J.P., 1, *Grenville-place, Cromwell-road, S.W*
1906		Mackay, James John, 158, *Leadenhall-street, E.C.*
1900		Mackay, Thomas, *Sandwood, Nairn.*
1886		*Mackenzie, Colin, F.R.G.S.,
1878		McKewan, William, *Elmfield, Bickley, Kent.*
1876		*McLean, Robert Allan, F.R.G.S., 1, *Queen Victoria-street, E.C.*
1888	d	McNiel, Henry, 18, *Exchange-street, Manchester.*
1882		MacRosty, Alexander, *West Bank, Esher.*
1904		Macrosty, Henry William, B.A., 29, *Hervey-road. Blackheath, S.E.*
1899		*MacWharrie, Niel Matheson, *Conservative Club, St. James's, S.W.*
1906		Magnus, Sir Philip, M.P., 16, *Gloucester-terrace, Hyde Park, W.*
1891		Maidment, Thomas, *Insurance Chambers, King's-road, Southsea.*
1904	c d	Mallet, Bernard (*Vice-President*), *Inland Revenue, Somerset House, W.C.*
1902	d	Mandello, Professor Julius George, Ph.D. *Pozsony, Hungary.*
1884		*Manson, Frederick William, *Faircrouch, Wadhurst, Sussex.*

Year of Election.		
1888		Manuel, James,
		36, *Vittoria-street, Ottawa, Canada.*
1880	*c d p*	*Marshall, Professor Alfred, M.A.,
		Balliol Croft, Madingley-road, Cambridge.
1887		Marshall, W. Bayley, M.Inst.C.E., M.Inst.M.E.,
		21, *St. John's Wood-park, N.W.*
1887		Martin, James,
		4, *King-street, Cheapside, E.C.*
1899		Martin, John Roxburgh,
		Huntly, New Zealand.
1872	*c d p*	*MARTIN, SIR RICHARD BIDDULPH, BART. (Hon.
		Vice-President and Treasurer), Overbury-court,
		Tewkesbury, and 68, *Lombard-street, E.C.*
1884		Mason, William Arthur,
		31a, *Colmore-row, Birmingham.*
1898		Massingberd, Captain Stephen,
		Gunby Hall, Burgh, Lincolnshire.
1875		*Mathers, John Shackleton,
1903		Mayer, Dr. Clemens,
		27, *Potsdamerstrasse, Berlin, W. 35.*
1901		Meakin, George Healey, A.S.A.A.,
		Town Hall, Islington, N.
1882		Medhurst, John Thomas, F.S.A.A.,
		City of London College, Moorfields, E.C.
1901		Meredith, Hugh Owen,
		9, *Wolseley-place, Withington, Manchester.*
1884	*d*	Merton, Zachary,
		31, *Green-street, Park-lane, W.*
1907		Middleton, Professor Thomas Hudson, M.A.,
		4, *Whitehall-place, S.W.*
1900		Miller, John W.,
		Union Club, S.W.
1889		*Mills, Major Henry Farnsby,
1892	*c d*	Milner The Rt. Hon., Viscount, G.C.B., G.C.M.G.,
		47, *Duke-street, S.W.*
1882	*p*	Milnes, Alfred, M.A.,
		44, *Goldhurst-terrace, S. Hampstead, N.W.*
1907		*Mitchell, Frederick William,
		Star Life Assurance Soc., 32, Moorgate-st., E.C.
1906		Modi, Edalji Manakji, D.Sc., Litt. D.,
		Opposite Grant-rd. Station, Sleater-rd., Bombay.
1902		Molesworth, Sir Guilford Lindsey, K.C.I.E.,
		The Manor House, Bexley, Kent.
1888	*d*	*Molloy, William R. J., M.R.I.A.,
		78, *Kenilworth-square, Rathgar, Dublin.*
1899		*Moon, Edward Robert Pacy,
		6, *Onslow Gardens, W.*
1887		Moore, Arthur Chisholm,
		23, *Essex-street, Strand, W.C.*

Year of Election.		
1874		Moore, Charles Rendall,
		43, *Breakspears-road, St. Johns, S.E.*
1885		Moore, Harold É., F.S.I.,
		Oaklands, Beckenham.
1878		*Moore, John Byers Gunning,
		Loymount, Cookstown, Ireland.
1903		Moores, George,
		71, *Park-st., Chorlton-on-Medlock, Manchester.*
1893	*d*	Morgan, Percy Charlton,
		Queen Anne's Chambers, S.W.
1902	*p*	MORISON, THEODORE, M.A.,
		Ashleigh, St. George's-road, Weybridge.
1899		Morris, Thomas Morgan,
		12, *Green-street, Neath. South Wales.*
1891	*c d p*	Morrison, Rev. William Douglas, LL.D.,
		2, *Embankment-gardens, Chelsea, S.W.*
1904		Mosely, Alfred, C.M.G.,
		West Lodge, Hadley Wood, Barnet.
1885		*Mosley, Tonman,
		Bangors, Iver, Uxbridge.
1886	*c*	Mowbray, Sir Robert Gray Cornish, Bart.,
		10, *Little Stanhope-street, Mayfair, W.*
1886	*d*	Moxon, Thomas B.,
		Lancs. and Yorks. Bank, King-st., Manchester.
1904		Mudie-Smith, Richard,
		79, *Portsdown-rd., Maida Vale, W.*
1883		Muirhead, Henry James,
		Fairfield, Hythe, Kent; and Reform Club, S.W.
1899	*d*	Muirhead, James Muirhead Potter,
		Box 1161. 57, *St George's-street, Cape Town.*
1905		Muller, Osvald Valdemar, M.A.,
		Elphinstone College, Bombay; and Newquay, Cornwall.
1891	*c d*	MURPHY, SIR SHIRLEY FORSTER, M.R.C.S.,
		9, *Bentinck-terrace, Regent's-park, N.W.*
1878		*Nathan, Henry,
1907		Nathan, Sir Nathaniel, K.C.,
		Queen's House, St. James's Court, S.W.

Year of Election		
1869	c d p	NEISON, FRANCIS GUSTAVUS PAULUS, F.I.A.. 93, *Adelaide-road, South Hampstead, N. W*
1877		Nevill, Charles Henry, 1 *and* 2, *Great Winchester-street, E.C.*
1905		Nevill, Henry Rivers, *Allahabad, U.P., India.*
1900		Newcomb, Harry T., LL.M., *Room* 700, *Bond-buildings, Washington, D.C.*
1894		Newey, William Lewis, LL.D. 53, *Waverley-road, Small Heath, Birmingham.*
1889	d p	Newsholme, Arthur, M.D., 11, *Gloucester-place, Brighton.*
1895	c	*Nicholson, Charles Norris, M.P., 35, *Harrington-gardens, South Kensington, S.W.*
1878	d p	Nicholson, Professor .J. Shield, M.A., D.Sc., *University of Edinburgh.*
1858	d	Nightingale, Miss Florence, O.M., 10, *South-street, Park-lane, W.*
1871		*Noble, Benjamin, F.R.A.S., *Westmorland House, Low Fell, Gateshead.*
1902		Norman, Frederick Charles, *The Laurels, Carlton-la., Derwent-rd., Liverpool.*
1889		Northampton, The Most Hon. the Marquess of, 51, *Lennox-gardens, S. W.*
1888		Oakley, Sir Henry, 37, *Chester-terrace, Regent's-park, N.W.*
1886	d	O'Conor, James Edward, C.I.E., 144, *Church-road, Upper Norwood, S.E.*
1901		Offen, Charles Rose Witcher, *Bloomsbury House, Queen-square, W.C.*
1885	d	*Oldham, John (*River Plate Telegraph Co.*), 287, *San Martin, Buenos Aires.*
1905		Olivier, P. M., 4, *Rue du Parlement, Brussels.*
1904		Olmsted, Victor H., *The Plymouth, Washington, D.C., U.S.A.*
1892	c p	ONSLOW, THE RIGHT HON. THE EARL OF, G.C.M.G. (*Hon. Vice-President*), 7, *Richmond-terrace, Whitehall, S.W.*
1878		Oppenheim, Henry, 16, *Bruton-street, Bond-street, W.*

Year of Election.		
1899		Ormsby, John Yeaden,
		c/o Burnett, Ormsby Clapp & Co., 7, Melinda-street, Toronto.
1907		Osborne, R. Stanley,
		55, Clarendon-road, Holland-park, W.
1894	d	Owen, Edgar Theodore,
		Registrar of Friendly Societies, Perth, W.A.
1887	d	*Page, Edward D. (*Faulkner, Page, & Co.*),
		60, Worth-street, New York City.
1899	d	PAISH, GEORGE,
		"Statist" Office, 51, Cannon-street, E.C.
1866	c d p	*Palgrave, Robert Harry Inglis, F.R.S.,
		"Henstead Hall," Wrentham, Suffolk.
1906		Parish, Walter Woodbine,
		4, Neville-terrace, Onslow-gardens, S.W.
1901		Parisot, Oscar La Valette,
		H.H.The Nizam's Government,Hyderabad,India.
1878		Park, David Francis, C.A., F.F.A., A.I.A.,
		39, Lombard-street, E.C.
1903		Parker, Sir Gilbert, M.P.,
		20, Carlton House-terrace, S.W.
1883		Paterson, John,
		1, Walbrook, E.C.
1888		Pattullo, James Durie,
		65, London Wall, E.C.
1878	d	Paulin, David,
		6, Forres-street. Edinburgh.
1893	d	Payne, Alexander William, F.C.A.,
		70, Finsbury-pavement, E.C.
1884		*Peace, Sir Walter, K.C.M.G., I.S.O.
		83, Victoria-street, Westminster, S.W.
1895		Peixotto, M. Percy (*U.S. Equitable Life Office*),
		36, Avenue de l'Opéra, Paris.
1903		Pekelharing, Dr. G.,
		8, Zeemansstraat, Rotterdam.
1891	d	Penn-Lewis, William,
		"Cartref," Toller-road, Leicester.
1906		Perkins, Herbert H. W.,
		31, Marine-parade, Eastbourne.
1902	d	Peters, Edward T.,
		Bureau of Statistics, Dept. of Agriculture, Washington, D.C., U.S.A.

Year of Election.		
1890		Peters, John Wyatt,
		5, *King's-road, Southsea.*
1883		Petheram, Frederick William, F.C.A.,
		Moorfield-chmbrs., 95, Finsbury-pavement, E.C.
1886		Peto, Sir Henry, Bart., M.A.,
		Chedington Court, Misterton, Crewkerne.
1887		Phelps, Lieut.-General Arthur,
		23, *Augustus-road, Edgbaston, Birmingham.*
1886	d	*Phelps, Rev. Lancelot Ridley, M.A.,
		Oriel College, Oxford.
1871	d	*Pickering, John, F.R.G.S., F.S.A.,
		86, *Thicket-road, Anerley, S.E.*
1898		Pietersen, James Frederick G., L.R.C.P., M.R.C.S.,
		Ashwood House, Kingswinford, Dudley.
1900	d	*Pigou, Arthur Cecil, M.A.,
		King's College, Cambridge.
1904		Pilling, John Albert (c/o *Messrs. Deloitte and Co.*),
		5, *London Wall-buildings, Finsbury-circus, E.C.*
1878	d	*Pim, Joseph Todhunter,
		Rinnamara, Monkstown, Co. Dublin.
1886		Pink, J. Francis,
		62, *Chandos-street, Strand, W.C.*
1903		Pirrie, The Right Hon. Lord, LL.D..
		Downshire House, Belgrave-square, S.W.
1881		Planck, Deputy Surgeon-General Charles, M.R.C.S.,
		Lyden Croft, Edenbridge, Kent.
1902		Plant, Alfred Thomas,
		Accountant's Office, G.W.R., Paddington.
1895	d	Platt-Higgins, Frederick,
		Woodham-place, Horsell, Woking.
1901		Plender, William (c/o *Messrs. Deloitte and Co.*),
		5, *London Wall-buildings, Finsbury-circus, E.C.*
1861	c d	Plowden, Sir William Chicele, K.C.S.I.,
		5, *Park-crescent, Portland-place, W.*
1905		Pocock, Bernard George, A.S.A.A.,
		197, *High Holborn, W.C.*
1896		*Pontifex, Bryan, A.C.A..
		East India Railway House, Calcutta.
1891		Potter, Henry,
		276, *Queen's-road, New Cross Gate, S.E.*
1879	c d p	*POWELL, SIR FRANCIS SHARP, BART., M.P., (*Hono-rary Vice-President*), *Horton Old Hall, Bradford, and* 1, *Cambridge-square, Hyde-park, W.*
1877		*Prance, Reginald Heber,
		Frognal, Hampstead, N.W.
1867		*Pratt, Robert Lindsay,
		13, *Danesbury-terrace, Darlington.*
1896		Pretyman, Captain Ernest George,
		Orwell-park, Ipswich.

Year of Election.		
1887	c d p	*PRICE, L. L., M.A.,
		Oriel College, Oxford.
1887	c d p	PROBYN, SIR LESLEY, K.C.V.O.,
		79, *Onslow-square, S. W.*
1889		Probyn, Lieut.-Colonel Clifford,
		55, *Grosvenor-street, Grosvenor-square, W.*
1886	d	Provand, Andrew Dryburgh,
		2, *Whitehall-court, S. W.*
1896		Pryor, Edward Thomas,
		23, *Fore-street, E.C.*
1901		Quin, Stewart Blacker, F.C.A.,
		1, *Lombard-street, Belfast.*
1883		Rabbidge, Richard, F.C.A.,
		32, *Poultry, E.C.*
1872	d p	*Rabino, Joseph,
		Chief Manager, Imperial Bank of Persia, Teheran
1858		*Radstock, The Right Hon. Lord,
		Mayfield, Woolston, Southampton.
1885	c d	Rae, John, M.A.,
		1, *Rockland-road, Putney, S. W.*
1887	d p	Raffalovich, His Excellency Arthur,
		19, *Avenue Hoche, Paris.*
1880	c	Rankin, Sir James, Bart., M.P.,
		Bryngwyn, Hereford.
1897		Ranson, Albert,
		Tavern-street, Ipswich.
1903		Rathbone, Miss Eleanor F.,
		Green Bank, Liverpool.

Year of Election.		
1874	c d p	*Ravenstein, Ernest George, F.R.G.S.,
		2, *York-mansions Battersea-park, S. W.*
1877		*Rawlins, Thomas,
		45, *King William-street, E.C.*
1895		Rawlinson, Albert,
		22, *Ryder-street, St. James's, S. W.*
1893		Rea, Charles Herbert Edmund, F.R.A.S., A.I.A.,
		" *Holmesdale,*" *South Darenth, Kent.*
1889		*Reed, Thomas, F.C.A.,
		63, *King-street, South Shields.*
1903		Reilly, John,
		17, *Nassau-street, Dublin.*
1906		Rennie, James Stuart M.,
		Tanjong Pagar Dock Board, Singapore, S.S.
1888	c d p	REW, R. H. (*Hon. Secretary*),
		Board of Agriculture and Fisheries, 3, St. James's-square, S. W.
1888		Rhodes, George Webber,
		131, *Wool Exchange, E.C.*
1895		Richards, Roger C. (*Inner Temple*),
		14 D, *Hyde Pk. Mansions, Marylebone-rd., W.C.*
1903		Ripon, The Right Rev. the Lord Bishop of,
		The Palace, Ripon.
1873		Ripon, The Most Hon. the Marquess of, K.G., F R.S.,
		9, *Chelsea Embankment, S. W.*
1892		Rivington, Francis Hansard,
		44, *Connaught-square, W.*
1882		Roberts, Edward, I.S.O., F.R.A.S.,
		Park Lodge, Court-road, Eltham.
1894	d p	Robertson, James Barr,
		National Liberal Club, Whitehall-place, S.W.
1900		Robinson, James,
		Clarendon Ho., Clayton-st. W., Newcastle-on-Tyne.
1904		Rogers, Arthur George Liddon, M.A.,
		Board of Agriculture, &c., 4, Whitehall-place, S. W.
1880		*Ronald, Byron L.,
		14, *Upper Phillimore-gardens, W.*
1873	c	*Rosebery, The Rt. Hon. the Earl of, K.G., K.T., F.R.S.,
		38, *Berkeley-square, W.*
1904	d p	Rosenbaum, Simon, B.Sc.,
		" *Hauteville,*" 81, *Wavendon-av., Chiswick, W.*
1892	d	Ross, Charles Edmonstone, F.S.A.A.,
		Public Works Department, Chepauk, Madras.
1904		Routly, William Henry,
		Borough Accountant, Folkestone.
1899	d	Rowntree, Benjamin Seebohm,
		32, *St. Mary's, York & The Homestead, Clifton, York.*
1898	d p	Rozenraad, Cornelius,
		4, *Moreton-gardens, South Kensington, S. W.*
1890		Ruffer, Marc Armand, C.M.G., M.A., M.D., B.Sc.,
		Ramleh, Egypt.

Year of Election.		
1903		Runciman, Walter, M.P., *West Denton Hall, Scotswood-on-Tyne.*
1888	*d*	Rusher, Edward Arthur, F.I.A., *142, Holborn Bars, E.C.*
1886		Russell, Arthur B., F.C.A. (11, *Ludgate-hill, E.C.*), *17, Rosslyn-hill, Hampstead, N.W.*
1878	*d*	Russell, Richard F., *8, John-street, Adelphi, W.C.*
1907		Rutter. Frank Roy, *19, Lunham Road, Norwood, S.E.*
1902		Ruttkay, W. de, LL.D. (*Austro-Hungarian Consulate*), *22, Laurence Pountney-lane, E.C.*
1907		Ryder, John Joyce (*Bureau of Labor and Industrial Statistics*), *Lincoln, Neb., U.S.A.*
1907		Rye, Reginald A. (*Goldsmiths' Librarian*), *University of London, South Kensington, S.W.*
1894	*d*	Sachs, Edwin Otho, *3, Waterloo-place, Pall Mall, S.W.*
1898	*d*	Salmon, Richard George, F.I.A., *Sun Life Ass. Soc., Threadneedle-st., E.C.*
1875	*d*	*Salomons, Sir David Lionel, Bart., J.P., *Broom-hill, Tunbridge Wells.*
1899	*d*	Sanderson, Frank, M.A., *Canada Life Ass. Co., Toronto, Canada.*
1895		Sanger, Charles Percy, M.A., *58, Oakley-street, Chelsea, S.W.*
1891		*Sarda, Pandit Har Bilas, B.A., M.R.A.S., *Government College, Ajmere, India.*
1886	*d p*	Sauerbeck, Augustus (*Messrs. H. Schwartz & Co.*). *3 & 4, Moorgate-street-buildings, E.C.*
1887		*Scarth, Leveson, M.A., *12. York-buildings, Adelphi, W.C.*
1902		Schindler, Walter, *c/o Gebr Sulzer. Winterthur, Switzerland.*
1904		*Schlesinger. Louis G., *12A, Avenida Sur.16B, Guatemala.*
1891	*d p*	*Schloss, David F., M.A., *18, Hornton Court, Kensington, W.*

Year of Election.		
1895		Schmidt, Hermann, 9, *George-yard, Lombard-st., E.C.*
1891	*d p*	Schooling, John Holt, *Fotheringhay Ilse., Montpelier-row, Twickenham.*
1895		Schuurman, Willem H. A Elink, *Godelindeweg,* 10, *Hilversum, Holland.*
1883		*Schwann, John Frederick, *Oakfield, Wimbledon, S.W.*
1888		Scotter, Sir Charles, Bart., *Surbiton.*
1880		*Seeley, Sir Charles, Bart., *Sherwood Lodge, Nottingham.*
1905		Sellar, Alexander Smith, M.A., c/o *George King. Esq.,* 15, *Walbroo ,E.C.*
1899		Setchfield, George Beeby (*Refuge Ass. Co.*), *Beulah Kop,* 3, *Clarkson-street, Sheffield.*
1886	*d p*	Seyd, Ernest J. F., 38, *Lombard-street, E.C.*
1905	*d*	Seyd, Richard E. N. J., 38, *Lombard-street, E.C.*
1898	*c p*	Shaw, William Napier, D.Sc., F.R.S., 10, *Moreton-gardens, South Kensington, S.W.*
1898	*d*	Sherwell, Arthur, M.P., *Crossways House, Reigate-hill, Surrey.*
1888		Shillcock, Joshua, M.A., *Bank of England, Burlington-gardens, W.*
1907		Shimmell, James Edward, A.I.A., 96, *Oxford-road, Manchester.*
1904		Sidwell, Henry Thomas, *Hatfield, Herts.*
1905		Silva, N. P. da Motta E., 3, *Avenue du Trocadero, Paris.*
1905		Silversides, Charles William, *Trenholme, Hendon, N.W.*
1904		Sim, James Duncan Stuart, *Ravenscroft, Nutfield, Surrey.*
1907	*d*	Simon, André L., 24, *Mark-lane, E.C.*
1902		Sinclair, H. D., 19 *and* 20, *Silver-street, Wood-street, E.C.*
1892		*Sinclair, The Right Hon. John, M.P., 2, *Cambridge-square, W.*
1888		Slade, Alfred Thomas, *Wardrobe Chambers, Queen Victoria-street, E.C.*
1906		Smith, Charles, 11, *Winter-street, Sheffield.*
1878		*Smith, Charles, M.R.I.A., F.G.S., Assoc. C.E., Inst., "*Park View," Englfield-green, Surrey.*
1878	*d*	*Smith, George, LL.D., C.I.E., 10, *South Learmouth-gardens, Edinburgh.*

Year of Election.		
1889	d	Smith, George Armitage, M.A., D.Sc.,
		3, Albert-terrace, Regent's-park, N.W.
1904		*Smith, Hastmgs B. Lees, M.A.,
		Ruskin Colleye, Oxford.
1906		Smith, Horace A.
		Bureau of Statistics, Sydney, N.S.W.
1877		Smith, Howard S., A.I.A., F.F.A.,
		Bank Chambers,14,Waterloo-street,Birmingham.
1888	c d	Smith, Hubert Llewellyn, C.B., B.Sc.,
		Board of Trade, 7, Whitehall-gardens, S.W.
1891		Smith, Right Hon. James Parker,
		Jordanhill, Partick, N.B.
1901		Smith, Robert John, C.A.,
		163, West George-street, Glasgow.
1905		Smith, Stanley George,
		5, Grove Mansions, Stamford Grove West. Stoke Newington, N.E.
1890		Smith, William Alexander, J.P.,
		Arpafeelie, Moorebank, N.S.W.
1894		*Smith, The Hon. William Frederick Danvers, M.P.,
		3, Grosvenor-place, S.W.
1894		Smithers, Frederick Oldershaw,
		171, Adelaide-road, South Hampstead, N.W.
1900		*Somerville, William, M.A., D.Sc.,
		121, Banbury-road, Oxford.
1899		Sorley, James, F.I.A., F.F.A., F.R.S.E.,
		82, Onslow-gardens, S.W.
1904		Souter, John,
		c/o Mines Depart., P.O. Box 1132,Johannesburg.
1897		Southgate, Henry William,
		29, Hamilton-avenue, Chapletown, Leeds.
1895		Soward, Alfred Walter,
		28, Therapia-road, Honor Oak, S.E.
1855	d	Sowray, John Russell,
		" Fairlawn," Teston, Maidstone.
1904		Sowrey, John William,
		" Beaconsfield," Devonshire-road, Merton, S.W.
1896		Sparrow, Frederick Syer,
		c/o J. Wonfor,22, Yonge-pk., Seven Sisters-rd., N.
1904		Spencer, Frederick Herbert, LL.B.,
		" Elm Grove Cottage," Pinner, Middlesex.
1867		*Spencer, Robert James,
1892		Spender, John Alfred, M.A.,
		45, Sloane-street, S.W.
1897	d	Spensley, J. Calvert,
		3, Provost-road, S. Hampstead, N.W.
1883		Spicer, Sir Albert, Bart., M.P.,
		50, Upper Thames-street, E.C.
1898		Spicer, Edward Samuel,
		Grange Cottage, The Grange, Wimbledon.

Year of Election.		
1856	d	*Sprague, Thomas Bond, M.A., LL.D., F.I.A., 29, *Buckingham-terrace, Edinburgh.*
1882		Stack, Thomas Neville, 7, *Union-court, E.C.*
1901		Stallard, Charles Frampton, *P.O. Box 5156, Johannesburg.*
1907		Stanley of Alderley, The Right Hon. Lord, 18, *Mansfield-street, W.*
1889	d	Stanton, Arthur G., 13, *Rood-lane, E.C.*
1902		*Steel-Maitland, Arthur Herbert Drummond Ramsay, 72, *Cadogan-square, S.W.*
1905	d	Steiner, Dr. Maximilien, *Graben 16, Vienna.*
1899		Stenberg, Ernst Gottfried, *Government Statistician's Office, Perth, W.A.*
1882		*Stern, Sir Edward D., 4, *Carlton House-terrace, S.W.*
1885	d	*Stevens, Marshall, *Trafford Park, Manchester.*
1903	d	Stevens, William James, " *St. Clair." Tyson-road, Forest Hill, S.E.*
1906		*Stock, Edward James, A.I.A., 395, *Collins-st., Melbourne, Victoria, Australia.*
1902		Stott, Walter Grason,
1889		Stow, Major Harry Vane, 24, *Holborn, E.C.*
1872	d	Strachey, General Sir Richard, R.E., G.C.S.I., F.R.S. 67, *Belsize Park-gardens, Hampstead, N.W.*
1883	d	*Strathcona and Mount Royal, The Right Hon. Lord, G.C.M.G. (*High Commissioner for Canada*), 28, *Grosvenor-square, W.*
1880		Strutt, Hon. Frederick, *Milford House, near Derby.*
1884		*Sugden, Richard, *The Farre Close, Brighouse, Yorkshire.*
1895		Sutherland, J. Francis, M.D., 51, *Queen-street, Edinburgh.*
1902		Sutton, Martin John, J.P., *Holme Park, Sonning, Berks.*
1900		Swetenham, Charles C., *c/o Grindlay Groom & Co., Bombay, India.*
1900	d p	Sykes, John Frederick Joseph, M.D., D.Sc., 40, *Camden-square, N.W.*

Year of Election		
1904		Tatham, Basil St. John, *P.O. Box* 1558, *Johannesburg.*
1889	*d*	Tattersall, William, *Melbrook, Bowdon, Cheshire.*
1887	*d*	Taylor, R..Whately Cooke, 39, *Victoria-street, S.W.*
1888		*Taylor, Theodore Cooke, M.P., J.P., *Sunny Bank, Batley, Yorkshire.*
1905		Taylor, William B., B.A., LL.B , 112–118, *King-street West, Toronto.*
1907		Tebb, William Scott, M.A.. M.D. (Cantab.), F.I.C., " *Sandfield,*" *Putney Heath-lane, S.W.*
1893		Teece, Richard, F.I.A., F.F.A., *Actuary, A.M.P. Society, Sydney, N.S.W.*
1888	*d*	Temperley, William Angus, junr., 2, *St. Nicholas-buildings, Newcastle-on-Tyne.*
1906		Templeton,Col.JohnMontgomery,C.M.G.,V.D.,F.I.A., 395, *Collins-street, Melbourne, Victoria.*
1888		Theobald, John Wilson, 8, *Fairfield-road, Croydon.*
1889		Thodey, William Henry, 479, *Collins-street, Melbourne,Victoria.*
1888	*c d p*	THOMAS, DAVID ALFRED, M.A., M.P., *Llanwern, near Newport, Mon.*
1906		Thomas, Henry Charles, 160, *St. James's-street, Montreal, Canada.*
1887		Thomas, John Collette, *Trewince, Portscatho, Cornwall.*
1905		Thomas, Percy Scofield, 220, *Croydon-road, Anerley, S.E.*
1864		*Thompson, Henry Yates, 19, *Portman-square, W.*
1901	*d p*	Thompson. Robert John, *Board of Agriculture, &c.,* 8, *Whitehall-place, S.W.*
1889	*d*	Touche, George Alexander, 26, *Collingham-gardens,South Kensington, S.W.*
1868		*Treatt, Frank Burford, *Police Magistrate, Cobar, New South Wales.*
1868		Tritton, Joseph Herbert, 54, *Lombard-street, E.C.*
1903	*d*	Trivett, John Burt, *Registry of Friendly Societies, Sydney, N.S.W*
1903		Tryon, Captain George Clement, 45, *Eaton-place, S.W.*

Year of Election.		
1885		Turner, William (c/o *The Librarian*), *Free Public Library, Trinity-street, Cardiff.*
1892	d	Tyler, Edgar Alfred, 9, *Old Jewry Chambers, E.C.*
1903		Unstead, John Frederick, M.A., F.R.G.S., 5, *Wiverton-road, Sydenham, S.E.*
1903		*Vaizey, Ker George Russell, 10, *Lime-street, E.C.*
1888		Van Raalte, Marcus, 22, *Austin Friars, E.C.*
1903		Varley, Jesse, C.A., A.C.I.S., *Longleat, Albert-road, Wolverhampton.*
1889		*Venning, Charles Harrison, 25, *Lawrence-lane, Cheapside, E.C.*
1894		Verney, Frederick William, M.P., 12, *Connaught-place, Marble Arch, W.*
1886	c	Verulam, The Right Hon. the Earl of, *Gorhambury, St. Albans.*
1876		Vigers, Robert, 4, *Frederick's-place, Old Jewry, E.C.*
1905		Vigor, Harold Decimus, 23, *Islip-street, Kentish Town, N.W.*
1885		Vincent, Frederick James, A.I.A., *Insurance-buildings, Farringdon-street, E.C.*
1904		Vinter, James Odell, J.P., *Southfield, Trumpington, Cambs.*

D

Year of Election.		
1902		Wacha, Dinsha Edulji,
		84, *Hornby-road, Fort, Bombay.*
1905		Wadia, N. P. N., M.S.A.A.,
		Alice Buildings, Hornby-road, Fort, Bombay.
1904		Wagner, H. R.,
		71. *Broadway, New York, U.S.A.*
1900		Walford, Adolphus Augustus B. (*Frank Brown & Co.*),
		Finkle Chambers, Stockton-on-Tees.
1890	*d*	Walford, Ernest Leopold,
		47, *Hamilton-terrace, N. W.*
1906		Walker, William T.,
		79, *Gracechurch-street, E.C.*
1903	*d*	Wall, Edgar George,
		29, *Palliser-road, West Kensington, W.*
1904	*d*	Wall, Walter William,
		26, *Bradgate-road, Catford, S.E.*
1905		Wallis, B. Cotterell, F.C.P., B.Sc. (Econ.),
		43, *Tottenhall-road, Palmers Green, N.*
1868		Wallis, Charles James,
		Woodcroft, Battle, Sussex.
1880	*d*	Wallis, E. White,
		Upper Frognal Lodge, Hampstead, N. W.
1904		*Walsh, Correa Moylan,
		Bellport, Long Island, New York, U.S.A.
1899		Ward, Joseph Frederick,
		8, *Main-street, Port Elizabeth.*
1893		Ward, William Cullen, F.S.I.A.,
		113, *Pitt-street, Sydney, N.S. W.*
1888		Warren, Reginald Augustus, J.P.,
		Preston-place, near Worthing.
1865		Waterhouse, Edwin, A.I.A., F.C.A.,
		3. *Frederick-place, Old Jewry, E.C.*
1886	*p*	Waters, Alfred Charles,
		General Register Office, Somerset House, W.C.
1892		Wates, Charles Marshall,
		10, *Chinbrook-road, Grove-park, Lee, S.E.*
1902	*d*	Watson, Alfred William, F.I.A.,
		Wenhaston, Ebers-rd., Mapperley-pk., Notts.
1888		Webb, Henry Barlow,
		Holmdale, Dorking.

Year of Election.		
1904	d	Webb, The Hon. Mr. Montagu de Pomeroy, C.I.E.
		Karachi, India.
1893	d	Weedon, Thornhill,
		Govt. Statistician, Bryn-Mawr, Brisbane.
1873	c	*Welby, The Right Hon. Lord, G.C.B.,
		11, *Stratton-street. Piccadilly, W.*
1889		*Wells-Smith, Henry, F.C.A.,
		" *Hillcrest,*" *Blyth-grove, Worksop, Notts.*
1855	c d p	Welton, Thomas Abercrombie, F.C.A.,
		49, *Longridge-road, South Kensington, W.*
1902	d	Westall, George,
		87, *Chancery-lane, W.C.*
1879		*Westlake, John, K.C., LL.D.,
		The River House, 3, Chelsea Embankment, S.W.
1901		Weston, Sydney Frank,
		19, *Epperstone-rd., W. Bridgford, Nottingham.*
1882		*Whadcoat, John Henry, F.C.A.,
		Rockcliffe, Kirkcudbrightshire.
1878		Wharton, James,
		Edgehill, Netherhall-gds., Fitzjohn's-av., N.W.
1887		Whinney, Frederick,
		85, *Avenue-road, Regent's Park, N.W.*
1859		Whitbread, Samuel,
		Southill-park, Biggleswade, Beds.
1887		*White, The Rev. George Cecil, M.A.,
		Nursling Rectory, Southampton.
1905		White, Richard, F.C.I S.,
		Folkestone Chamber of Commerce, Folkestone.
1888	d	Whitehead, Sir James, Bart., J.P., D.L.,
		Wilmington Manor, near Dartford.
1895	d	Whitehead, The Hon. Thomas Henderson, M.L.C.,
		Chartered Bank of India, &c., Hong Kong.
1892	c d	Whitelegge, B. Arthur, C.B., M.D.,
		3, *Edwardes-place, Kensington, W.*
1895		Whittuck, Edward Arthur. M.A., B.C.L.,
		Claverton Manor, Bath.
1899		Wiener, Isidore,
		Colecroft, Kenley, Surrey.
1898		Wigham, Matthew Thomas, A.S.A.A., F.C.I.S.,
		826, *Salisbury House, London Wall, E.C.*
1884		Wightman, Charles,
		1, *Fenchurch-avenue, E.C.*
1895		Wilenkin, Gregory,
		1501, *Eighteenth-st., Washington, D.C., U.S.A.*
1904		Wilkins, Henry H. J.,
		St. Tydfil Chambers, Queen-street, Cardiff.
1860		Willans, John Wrigley,
		25, *King's-gardens, West End-lane, Hampstead.*
1901	d	Willcox, Walter F., Ph.D.,
		Cornell University, Ithaca, N.Y., U.S.A.

Year of Election.		
1896		*Williams, Major Charles Woolmer, 245, *Shaftesbury-avenue, New Oxford-st.*, *W.C.*
1906		Williams, David, *Bryn Awel, Allfarthing-lane, Wandsworth, S.W.*
1897		*Williams, Ernest E., *Ecclefechan, Lake-road, Wimbledon, S.W.*
1904		Williams, Frederick Alfred, A.I.A., *Louisiana Nat. Life Assurance Soc., New Orleans, La., U.S.A.*
1864		Williams, Frederic Bessant, F.S.A. (Scot.), 19, *Haymarket, S.W.*
1895		Williams, Harry Mallam, F.S.A. (Scot.), *Tilehurst, Priory-park, Kew.*
1907		Williams, J. Penry Cyril Clutton, B.A., 20, *Strand-road, Calcutta, India.*
1888		*Williams, Robert, M.P., 20, *Birchin-lane, E.C.*
1895		*Willis, J. G., B.A., *Board of Trade, Whitehall-gardens, S.W.*
1901		Wilson, George Thomson (*Equitable Life Ass. Soc. of U.S.*), 120, *Broadway, New York.*
1891		Wilson, Henry Joseph, M.P., *Osgathorpe Hills, Sheffield.*
1898		Wilson, Herbert Wrigley, 203, *Elgin-avenue, W.*
1884		Wilson, Hon. James, C.S.I., *Secretary to Government, Calcutta, India.*
1906		Wilson, Walter, 3, *East-parade, Leeds.*
1900	*d*	Wolfe, S. Herbert, 35, *Nassau-street, New York City, U.S.A.*
1900		Wolfenden, Henry, 1, *Palace-court, Hyde-park, W.*
1897	*d p*	Wood, George Henry, *Caerleon Ho., Oakfield-rd., Birkby, Huddersfield.*
1897		Woodd, Basil Aubrey Hollond, 59, *Drayton-gardens, S.W.*
1902		Woodhouse, Lister, A.C.A., *Westminster City Hall, Charing Cross-rd., W.C.*
1890		*Woollcombe, Robert Lloyd, LL.D., &c., 14, *Waterloo-road, Dublin.*
1903		Woolley, Ernest, 7, *Finch-lane, Cornhill, E.C.*
1895		Worsfold, Edward Mowll, F.C.A., *Market Square, Dover.*
1878		Worsfold, Rev. John Napper, M.A., *Hathelsey, 17, Alexandra-road, Worthing.*
1906		Wyldbore-Smith, Edmund C., H.M. *Vice-Consul, British Legation, Tangier, Morocco.*

Year of Election.		
1895	d	Yanagisawa, Count Yasutoshi,
		1, *Shiba Yamachi*, 8, *Chôme, Tokio, Japan.*
1886	c d p	Yerburgh, Robert Armstrong,
		25, *Kensington Gore, S. W.*
1900		Yerbury, John Edwin,
		24, *The Pryors, E. Heath-road, Hampstead, N. W.*
1888		*Yglesias, Miguel,
		2, *Tokenhouse-buildings, E.C.*
1877		*Youll, John Gibson,
		Jesmond-road, Newcastle-on-Tyne.
1898		Young, Sydney,
		The Corn Exchange, Mark-lane, E.C.
1895	c d p	YULE, GEORGE UDNY (*Hon Secretary*),
		City & Guilds Institute, Exhibition-road, S.W.;
		50, St. James's-court, Buckingham-gate, S.W.
1901		Zimmerman, Lawrence Wolff,
		282, Dickenson-road, Rusholme, Manchester.

. *The Honorary Secretaries request that any inaccuracy in the foregoing list, and all changes of address, may be notified to the* ASSISTANT SECRETARY.

HONORARY FELLOWS.

HIS MOST GRACIOUS MAJESTY THE KING,
Patron.

His Royal Highness the Prince of Wales, K.G.,
Honorary President.

Year of Election.		

Argentine Republic.

1890 | *d* | FRANCISCO LATZINA, **Calle Maipu, 982, Buenos Ayres.**
Director General of Statistics; Doctor *honoris causa* of the Faculty of Physical and Mathematical Sciences of the University of Cordoba; Knight of the Italian Order of S.S. Maurice and Lazare; Officer of the Academy of France; Member of the National Academy of Sciences, of the International Statistical Institute, of the Geographical and Statistical Societies of Paris, of the Society of Commercial Geography of Paris, and Corresponding Member of the National Historical Academy of Venezuela.

Austria-Hungary.

1890 | *d* | KARL THEODOR RITTER VON INAMA-STERNEGG, **Eliasbethstrasse 3, Innsbrück, Austria.**
Doctor of Political Economy; Member of the Austrian House of Lords; Ex-President of the Imperial and Royal Central Statistical Commission; Professor at the University of Vienna; President of the International Statistical Institute.

1893 | *d* | FRANZ RITTER VON JURASCHEK, **Kärnthnerstrasse, 55, Vienna.**
Doctor Juris et Philosophiæ; Hofrat; "K.K. Regierungsrath"; President of the Imperial and Royal Central Statistical Commission; Professor at the University of Vienna; Professor of Public Law and of Statistics at the Military Academies, Vienna; Knight of the Austrian Order of the Iron Crown (3rd Class); Officer of the Order of the Crown of Italy; Member of the Permanent Commission for Commercial Values; of the International Statistical Institute; and of the Royal Economic Society.

1904 | *d* | JULES DE VARGHA, **Budapest.**
Director of the Central Statistical Bureau of Hungary; President of the Commission for the preparation of the annual administration report on Hungary; Member of the International Statistical Institute.

Year of Election		

Belgium.

1904   *d*

EMILE WAXWEILER, Parc Leopold, Brussels.
Honorary Engineer of Roads and Bridges; Director of the Sociological Institute, Brussels; Professor of Economics and Finance at the University of Brussels; Superintendent of Statistical Section of Labour Department; Member of the International Statistical Institute.

China.

1890   *l*

SIR ROBERT HART, Baronet, G.C.M.G., LL.D., Peking.
Inspector-General of Imperial Maritime Customs, China.

Denmark.

1878   *d*

VIGAND ANDREAS FALBE-HANSEN, Copenhagen.
Director of the Statistical Bureau of the State; late Professor of Political Economy at the University of Copenhagen.

1900   *d p*

MARCUS RUBIN, Vendersgade 25a, Copenhagen.
Knight of the Order of the "Danebrog"; Director-General of Customs and Taxation; late Director of the Statistical Bureau of the State; President of the Danish Society of Political Economy and of the Board of the Danish Society of History; Member of the International Statistical Institute.

1907   *d p*

HARALD LUDWIG WESTERGAARD, The University, Copenhagen.
Professor of Statistics at the University of Copenhagen.

France.

1880   *d p*

JACQUES BERTILLON, M.D., 1, Avenue Victoria, Paris.
Chief of the Statistical Department of the City of Paris; Member of the Superior Council of Statistics; of the Consultative Committee of Public Hygiene of France; Past President of the Statistical Society of Paris; and Member of the International Statistical Institute, &c.

1879   *d*

ARTHUR CHERVIN, M.D., 82, Avenue Victor Hugo, Paris.
Doctor of Medicine and Surgery; Director of the Paris Institute for Stammerers; Vice-President of the Statistical Society of Paris; Member of the Superior Institute, &c.

1897   *d*

JEAN JACQUES ÉMILE CHEYSSON, 4, Rue Adolphe Yvon, Paris.
Inspector-General of Bridges and Highways; Member of the International Statistical Institute; Past President of the Statistical Society of Paris; late Director of the Creusot Iron Works, of Machinery at the Paris Exhibition of 1867, and of Graphic Statistics for the Ministry of Public Works.

Year of Election.		

France—*Contd.*

1890   *d p*   ALFRED DE FOVILLE, **3, Rue du Regard, Paris.**
Late Master of the Mint; Councillor of the Court of Accounts; Officer of the Legion of Honour; Member of the Institute of France: Past President of the Statistical Society of Paris; Member of the International Statistical Institute and of the Superior Council of Statistics.

1860   *d p*   PIERRE ÉMILE LEVASSEUR, **Collège de France, Paris.**
Member of the Institute of France; Professor at the College of France and at the Conservatoire of Arts and Trades; President of the Statistical Commission for Primary Instruction; Past President of the Statistical Society of Paris; Vice-President of the International Statistical Institute, of the Superior Council of Statistics, and of the Society of Political Economy, &c.

1887   DANIEL WILSON, **2, Avenue d'Jéna, Paris.**
Ex-Under-Secretary of State; Past President of the Statistical Society of Paris.

1876   *d*   THE PRESIDENT (for the time being) OF THE STATISTICAL SOCIETY OF PARIS, **28, Rue Danton, Paris.**

Germany.

1890   *d*   KARL JULIUS EMIL BLENCK, **Lindenstrasse, 28, Berlin, S.W.**
"Wirklicher Geheimer Ober-Regierungsrat;" Director of the Royal Statistical Bureau of Prussia, also Member of the Prussian Central Statistical Commission and of the Central Board of Control of the Survey of Prussia; Member of the International Statistical Institute; Honorary Member or Member of several learned Societies.

1896   *d*   CARL VICTOR BÖHMERT, **Hospitalstrasse, 4, Dresden.**
"Geheimer Regierungsrath;" Doctor Juris; Late Director of the Statistical Bureau of Saxony; Professor of Political Economy and Statistics in the Polytechnical High School of Dresden; Member of the International Statistical Institute.

1904   *d*   DR. WILHELM LEXIS, **Göttingen.**
Professor of Economics and Statistics at the University of Gottingen; Vice-President of the International Statistical Institute.

1877   *d*   GEORG VON MAYR, **Georgenstrasse, 38, Munich.**
Ex-Under Secretary of State in the Imperial Ministry for Alsace-Lorraine; formerly Director of the Royal Statistical Bureau of Bavaria; Honorary Member of the International Statistical Institute; Ordinary Professor of Statistics, Finances, and Political Economy at the University of Munich; Associate of the Statistical Society of Paris.

Year of Election		

1897 ADOLPH WAGNER, Ph.D, **51, Lessingstrasse, Berlin, N.W.**

Professor of Political Economy at the University of Berlin ; Member of the Statistical Bureau of Prussia, and of the International Statistical Institute.

1876 *d* THE PRESIDENT (for the time being) OF THE GEO-GRAPHICAL AND STATISTICAL SOCIETY OF FRANK-FORT, **Stadtbibliothek, Frankfort.**

Italy.

1874 *d* LUIGI BODIO, **153, Via Torino, Rome.**

Senator; Doctor of Laws ; Professor of Industrial Legis-lation and of Statistics at the Engineering College, Rome ; Councillor of State; formerly General Director of the Statistics of the Kingdom ; formerly Com-missioner-General of Emigration ; Member of the International Statistical Institute ; Member of the Royal Academy " dei Lincei"; Correspondent of the Institute of France (Academy of Moral and Political Sciences).

1899 *d* CARLO FRANCESCO FERRARIS, **Via 20 settembre, 7, Padua.**

Professor of Administrative Science and Law, and of Statistics at the Royal University of Padua ; Member of the Superior Council of Statistics and of the Superior Council of Public Education of Italy ; Member of the Academy " dei Lincei," of the Royal Institute of Science at Venice, of the International Statistical Institute, and Honorary Member of the Swiss Statistical Society; Ex-Minister of Public Works; Member of the Italian Parliament.

1907 *d* ENRICO RASERI, M.D., **Direction Générale de la Statis-tique du Royaume, Rome.**

Chief Director of the Division of Demographic Statistics of the Statistical Department of the Kingdom ; Secretary of the " Higher Council of Statistics.'

Mexico.

1895 *d* DON MANUEL FERNANDEZ LEAL, **Casa de Moneda, Mexico City.**

Director of the Mint; Late Secretary of State, Department of " Fomento," Colonization and Industry.

Year of Election		

𝕹𝖊𝖙𝖍𝖊𝖗𝖑𝖆𝖓𝖉𝖘.

1896   *d*   NICOLAAS GERARD PIERSON, **Académie Technique de Delft.**
> Minister of Finance; Late President of the "Commission Centrale de Statistique des Pays-Bas;" Late President of the Netherlands Bank; Late Professor of Political Economy at the University of Amsterdam; Member of the International Statistical Institute.

1904   *d*   C. A. VERRIJN STUART, **12, Nieuwe Parklaan, The Hague.**
> President of the "Commission Centrale de Statistique des Pays-Bas;" Professor of Political Economy and Commercial Law at the Académie Technique, Delft; Late Director of the Central Statistical Bureau of the Netherlands; Member of the Central Commission of Statistics; Corresponding Member of Statistical Society of Paris; Member of International Statistical Institute.

𝕹𝖔𝖗𝖜𝖆𝖞.

1858   *d*   THORKIL HALVORSEN ASCHEHOUG, **41, Josephinegade, Christiania.**
> Doctor of Laws; Professor of Political Economy at the University of Christiania; Assessor Extraordinary of the Supreme Court of Norway; Commander of the First Class of the Norwegian Order of St. Olave, of the Swedish Order of the North Star; and of the Danish Order of the "Dannebroge;" Corresponding Member of the Institute of France; Member of the Institute of International Law, of the International Statistical Institute, and of the Academies of Christiania, Stockholm, Trondhjem and Upsala, also of the Royal Historical Society of Denmark.

1874   *d*   ANDERS NICOLAI KIÆR, **Christiania.**
> Director of the Central Statistical Bureau of Norway; Associate of the Statistical Society of Paris; Member of the International Statistical Institute.

𝕽𝖚𝖘𝖘𝖎𝖆.

1873   *d*   HIS EXCELLENCY PIERRE SEMENOV, **St. Petersburg.**
> Senator; Privy Councillor to His Imperial Majesty; President of the Imperial Statistical Council; President of the Imperial Geographical Society; Honorary Member of the Academy of Sciences in St. Petersburg; Associate of the Statistical Society of Paris.

Year of Election		

Russia—*Contd.*

1890   *d*   HIS EXCELLENCY NICOLAS TROÏNITSKY, **Mohovaia 6, St. Petersburg.**
Former Governor; Senator; Privy Councillor; late Director of the Central Statistical Committee of the Ministry of the Interior; President of the Statistical Council, Life Member of the Imperial Geographical Society of Russia, Vice-President of the International Statistical Institute, and Member of the Statistical Society of Paris.

Sweden.

1890   *d*   ELIS SIDENBLADH., Ph.D., **Stockholm.**
Late Director in Chief of the Central Statistical Bureau of Sweden; Late President of the Royal Statistical Commission; Commander, Officer, and Knight of several Swedish and Foreign Orders; Member of the Royal Academies of Sciences and of Agriculture, at Stockholm, of the International Statistical Institute, and Honorary and Corresponding Member of several foreign learned Societies.

Switzerland.

1890   *d*   LOUIS GUILLAUME, **Bern.**
Doctor of Medicine; Director of the Federal Statistical Bureau; Secretary of the International Penitentiary Commission; Member of the International Statistical Institute.

United States.

1873   *d*   THE HON. WILLIAM BARNES, **The O'Conor-Barnes Homestead, On the Cliff, Nantucket Island, Mass., U.S.A.**
Lawyer; Ex-Superintendent of the Insurance Department, State of New York.

1881   *d*   JOHN SHAW BILLINGS, **New York Public Library, New York City.**
M.A., M.D., LL.D., Edinburgh and Harvard; D.C L., Oxon; Surgeon, U.S. Army; Member of the National Academy of Sciences, of the International Statistical Institute, &c.

1896   *d*   WORTHINGTON CHAUNCEY FORD, **Chevy Chase, Md., U.S.A.**
Late Chief of the Bureau of Statistics, Treasury Department; Chief of the Bureau of Statistics, Department of State; Member of the International Statistical Institute.

1870   *d*   THE HON. JOHN ELIOT SANFORD, **Taunton, Mass.**
Lawyer; Ex-Speaker of the House of Representatives; Ex-Insurance Commissioner; Ex-Chairman of the Board of Harbour and Land Commissioners; Chairman of the Board of Railroad Commissioners.

Year of Election.		

United States—*Contd.*

1893 | *d* | THE HON. CARROLL DAVIDSON WRIGHT, M.A., LL.D., **Clark College, Worcester, Mass., U.S.A.**

Late Commissioner of the U.S. Department of Labor; late Chief of the Massachusetts Bureau of Statistics of Labor; President of the Association for the promotion of Profit Sharing; late President and now Vice-President of the American Social Science Association; President of the American Statistical Association; Member of the American Economic Association, of the Royal Economic Society, and of the International Statistical Institute; Hon. Member of the Russian Imperial Academy of Sciences; Corresponding Member of the Institute of France; and Member of several other learned Societies.

1877 | *d* | EDWARD YOUNG, M.A., Ph.D., **207, Maryland Avenue, N.E., Washington, D.C.**

Late Consul of the United States; formerly Chief of the Bureau of Statistics, United States of America; Member of the Geographical Society of Paris.

𝕯ominion of 𝕮anada.

1894 | *d* | GEORGE JOHNSON, **Grand Pré, Nova Scotia.**

Late Statistician, Department of Agriculture, Ottawa, Canada.

𝕿asmania.

1894 | *d* | ROBERT MACKENZIE JOHNSTON, I.S.O., **Hobart.**

Registrar-General and Government Statistician; Fellow and Member of Council of the Royal Society of Tasmania; Member of Council and of Senate of the University of Tasmania; Fellow and Past President of Section F (*Economics* and *Statistics*) of the Australasian Association for the Advancement of Science; Fellow of the Royal Geographical Society of Australia; Honorary Foreign Corresponding Member of the Geological Society of Edinburgh; Fellow of the Linnean Society of London.

1876 | *d p* | EDWIN CRADOCK NOWELL, I.S.O., J.P., **Hobart.**

Clerk of Legislative Council of Tasmania; late Government Statistician; Clerk to the Federal Council of Australasia in its seven Sessions.

𝖁ictoria.

1858 | *d* | WILLIAM HENRY ARCHER. K.C.P., K.S.G., F.I.A., F.L.S., &c., **21, Hornby Street, Windsor, Melbourne.**

Barrister-at-Law.

Year of Election.		Great Britain and Ireland.
1876	d	THE PRESIDENT (for the time being) OF THE MAN-CHESTER STATISTICAL SOCIETY, **3, York Street, Manchester.**
1876	d	THE PRESIDENT (for the time being) OF THE STA-TISTICAL AND SOCIAL INQUIRY SOCIETY OF IRELAND, **35, Molesworth Street, Dublin.**

*** The Honorary Secretaries request that any inaccuracies in the List of HONORARY FELLOWS, and all changes of address, may be notified to the Assistant Secretary.

ROYAL STATISTICAL SOCIETY.

Copy of Charter.

𝕍𝕚𝕔𝕥𝕠𝕣𝕚𝕒, 𝕓𝕪 𝕥𝕙𝕖 𝔾𝕣𝕒𝕔𝕖 𝕠𝕗 𝔾𝕠𝕕 of the United Kingdom of Great Britain and Ireland Queen, Defender of the Faith.

𝕋𝕠 𝕒𝕝𝕝 𝕥𝕠 𝕨𝕙𝕠𝕞 these Presents shall come, Greeting :—

𝕎𝕙𝕖𝕣𝕖𝕒𝕤 Our Right trusty and entirely beloved cousin, Henry, Third Marquess of Lansdowne, Knight of the Most Noble Order of the Garter, Charles Babbage, Fellow of the Royal Society, John Elliott Drinkwater, Master of Arts, Henry Hallam, Fellow of the Royal Society, the Reverend Richard Jones, Master of Arts, and others of Our loving subjects, did, in the year One thousand eight hundred and thirty-four, establish a Society to collect, arrange, digest and publish facts, illustrating the condition and prospects of society in its material, social, and moral relations; these facts being for the most part arranged in tabular forms and in accordance with the principles of the numerical method, and the same Society is now called or known by the name of " The " Statistical Society."

𝔸𝕟𝕕 𝕎𝕙𝕖𝕣𝕖𝕒𝕤 it has been represented to Us that the same Society has, since its establishment, sedulously pursued such its proposed objects, and by its publications (including those of its transactions), and by promoting the discussion of legislative and other public measures from the statistical point of view, has greatly contributed to the progress of statistical and economical science.

𝔸𝕟𝕕 𝕎𝕙𝕖𝕣𝕖𝕒𝕤 distinguished individuals in foreign countries, as well as many eminent British subjects, have availed themselves of the facilities offered by the same Society for communicating important information largely extending statistical knowledge; and the general interest now felt in Statistics has been greatly promoted and fostered by this Society.

𝔸𝕟𝕕 𝕎𝕙𝕖𝕣𝕖𝕒𝕤 the same Society has, in aid of its objects, collected a large and valuable library of scientific works and charts, to which fresh accessions are constantly made; and the said Society has hitherto been supported by annual and other subscriptions and contributions to its funds, and has lately acquired leasehold premises in which the business of the said Society is carried on.

𝔸𝕟𝕕 𝕎𝕙𝕖𝕣𝕖𝕒𝕤 in order to secure the property of the said Society, to extend its operations, and to give it its due position among the Scientific Institutions of Our kingdom, We have been besought to grant to Sir Rawson William Rawson, Knight Com-

mander of the Most Distinguished Order of St. Michael and
St. George, and Companion of the Most Honourable Order of the
Bath, and to those who now are Members of the said Society, or
who shall from time to time be elected Fellows of the Royal
Statistical Society hereby incorporated, Our Royal Charter of
Incorporation for the purposes aforesaid.

1. **Now Know Ye** that We, being desirous of encouraging
a design so laudable and salutary, of Our especial grace, certain
knowledge and mere motion, have willed, granted, and declared
- and Do by these Presents, for Us, Our heirs and successors, will,
grant, and declare that the said Sir Rawson William Rawson,
Knight Commander of the Most Distinguished Order of St. Michael
and St. George, and Companion of the Most Honourable Order of
the Bath, and such other of Our loving subjects as now are
Members of the said Society, or shall from time to time be elected
Fellows of "The Royal Statistical Society" hereby incorporated
according to such regulations or bye laws as shall be hereafter
framed or enacted, and their successors, shall for ever hereafter be
by virtue of these presents one body politic and corporate, by the
name of "**The Royal Statistical Society,**" and for the
purposes aforesaid, and by the name aforesaid, shall have perpetual
succession and a common seal, with full power and authority to
alter, vary, break, and renew the same at their discretion, and by
the same name to sue and be sued, implead and be impleaded,
answer and be answered, unto and in every Court of Us, Our heirs
and successors.

2. **The** Royal Statistical Society, in this Charter hereinafter
called "The Society," may, notwithstanding the statutes of mortmain, take, purchase, hold and enjoy to them and their successors
a hall, or house, and any such messuages or hereditaments of
any tenure as may be necessary, for carrying out the purposes of
the Society, but so that the yearly value thereof to be computed
at the rack rent which might be gotten for the same at the time of
the purchase or other acquisition, and including the site of the
said hall, or house, do not exceed in the whole the sum of Two
thousand pounds.

3. **There** shall be a Council of the Society, and the said
Council and General Meetings of the Fellows to be held in
accordance with this Our Charter shall, subject to the provisions
of this Our Charter, have entire the management and direction of
the concerns of the Society.

4. **There** shall be a President, Vice-Presidents, a Treasurer
or Treasurers, and a Secretary or Secretaries of the Society. The
Council shall consist of the President, Vice-Presidents, and not

less than twenty Councillors; and the Treasurer or Treasurers and the Secretary or Secretaries if honorary.

5. **The** several persons who were elected to be the President, Vice-Presidents, and Members of the Council of the Statistical Society at the Annual Meeting held in the month of June, One thousand eight hundred and eighty-six, shall form the first Council of the Society, and shall continue in office until the first Election of officers is made under these presents as hereinafter provided.

6. **General** Meetings of the Fellows of the Society may be held from time to time, and at least one General Meeting shall be held in each year. Every General Meeting may be adjourned, subject to the provisions of the Bye Laws. The following business may be transacted by a General Meeting, viz.:—

> (*a.*) The Election of the President, Vice-Presidents, Treasurer or Treasurers, Secretary or Secretaries, and other Members of the Council of the Society.
>
> (*b.*) The making, repeal, or amendment of Bye Laws.
>
> (*c.*) The passing of any proper resolution respecting the affairs of the Society.

7. **Bye Laws** of the Society may be made for the following purposes, and subject to the following conditions, viz.:—

> (*a.*) For prescribing the qualification and condition of tenure of office of the President; the number, qualifications, functions, and conditions of tenure of office of the Vice-Presidents, Treasurers, Secretaries, and Members of Council, and Officers of the Society; for making regulations with respect to General Meetings and Meetings of the Council and proceedings thereat, and for the election of any persons to be Honorary Fellows or Associates of the Society, and defining their privileges (but such persons, if elected, shall not be Members of the Corporation), and for making regulations respecting the making, repeal and amendment of Bye Laws, and generally for the government of the Society and the management of its property and affairs.
>
> (*b.*) The first Bye Laws shall be made at the first General Meeting to be held under these presents, and shall (amongst other things) prescribe the time for holding the first election of officers under these presents.

8. **The** General Meetings and adjourned General Meetings of the Society shall take place (subject to the rules or bye laws of the Society, and to any power of convening or demanding a

Special General Meeting thereby given) at such times and places as may be fixed by the Council.

9. **The** existing rules of the Statistical Society, so far as not inconsistent with these presents, shall be in force as the Bye Laws of the Society until the first Bye Laws to be made under these presents shall come into operation.

10. **Subject** to these presents and the Bye Laws of the Society for the time being, the Council shall have the sole management of the income, funds, and property of the Society, and may manage and superintend all other affairs of the Society, and appoint and dismiss at their pleasure all salaried and other officers, attendants, and servants as they may think fit, and may do all such things as shall appear to them necessary or expedient for giving effect to the objects of the Society.

11. **The** Council shall once in every year present to a General Meeting a report of the proceedings of the Society, together with a statement of the receipts and expenditure, and of the financial position of the Society, and every Fellow of the Society may, at reasonable times to be fixed by the Council, examine the accounts of the Society.

12. **The** Council may, with the approval of a General Meeting, from time to time appoint fit persons to be Trustees of any part of the real or personal property of the Society, and may make or direct any transfer of such property so placed in trust necessary for the purposes of the trust, or may, at their discretion, take in the corporate name of the Society conveyances or transfers of any property capable of being held in that name. Provided that no sale, mortgage, incumbrance, or other disposition of any hereditaments belonging to the Society shall be made unless with the approval of a General Meeting.

13. **No** Rule, Bye Law, Resolution, or other proceeding shall be made or had by the Society, or any meeting thereof, or by the Council, contrary to the general scope or true intent and meaning of this Our Charter, or the laws or statutes of Our Realm, and anything done contrary to this present clause shall be void.

In witness whereof We have caused these Our Letters to be made Patent.

Witness Ourself, at Westminster, the thirty-first day of January, in the fiftieth year of Our Reign.

By Warrant under the Queen's Sign Manual,

MUIR MACKENZIE.

ROYAL STATISTICAL SOCIETY.

Index to Bye-Laws.

BYE-LAWS.

1. The Objects of the Society.
2. Society to consist of Fellows and Honorary Fellows.
3. Number of Fellows unlimited; Hon. Fellows not to exceed 70.
4. Fellows—Candidates to be proposed by two or more Fellows.
5. Do. to be elected by Ballot.
6. Do. on Admission may attach F.S.S. to their Names,
7. Honorary Fellows, Proposed by Council; Elected by Ballot.
8. Fellows, to pay an Annual Subscription or a Composition.
9. Do. how disqualified. Written notice of withdrawal required.
10. Do. and Honorary Fellows, Mode of Expulsion of.
11. Trustees. Property of Society, may be vested in Three.
12. President, Council, and Officers, Number and Particulars of.
13. Do. do. do. Election and Retirement of.
14. Do. do. do. Nomination of.
15. Do. do. do. Extraordinary Vacancies of.
16 Committees, may be appointed by Council.
17. Auditors, Appointment and Duties of.
18. Meetings, Ordinary and General, when to be held.
19. Ordinary Meetings, Business of. Strangers may be introduced.
20. Annual General Meeting, Business of.
21. Special General Meetings may be called.
22. President, Duties of. To have a Casting Vote.
23. Treasurer, Duties of, subject to the Council.
24. Honorary Secretaries, Duties of.
25. Vice-Presidents, Powers of.
26. Council, Duties of, in Publishing Papers and Expending Funds.
27. Do. may frame Regulations not inconsistent with Bye-laws.
28. Do. Duties of, with reference to the Common Seal.
29. Do. No Dividend, Gift, Division, or Bonus in Money to be made to Fellows, except as hereinafter provided for.
30. Do. to publish a Journal of the Transactions of the Society, and may remunerate Editors and their Assistants.
31. Do. Discretion of, as to Right of Property reserved in all Communications received.

BYE-LAWS OF THE ROYAL STATISTICAL SOCIETY.

Objects of the Society.

1. The objects of the Royal Statistical Society are to collect, arrange, digest and publish facts, illustrating the condition and prospects of society in its material, social and moral relations; these facts being for the most part arranged in tabular forms and in accordance with the principles of the numerical method.

The Society collects new materials, condenses, arranges, and publishes those already existing, whether unpublished or published in diffuse and expensive forms in the English or in any foreign language, and promotes the discussion of legislative and other public measures from the statistical point of view. These discussions form portions of the published Transactions of the Society.

Constitution of the Society.

2. The Society consists of Fellows and Honorary Fellows, elected in the manner hereinafter described.

Number of Fellows and Honorary Fellows.

3. The number of Fellows is unlimited. Foreigners or British subjects of distinction residing out of the United Kingdom may be admitted as Honorary Fellows, of whom the number shall not be more than seventy at any one time.

Proposal of Fellows.

4. Every Candidate for admission as a Fellow of the Society shall be proposed by two or more Fellows, who shall certify from their personal knowledge of him or of his works, that he is a fit person to be admitted a Fellow of the Society. Every such certificate having been read and approved of at a Meeting of the Council, shall be suspended in the office of the Society until the following Ordinary Meeting, at which the vote shall be taken.

Election of Fellows.

5. In the election of Fellows, the votes shall be taken by ballot. No person shall be admitted unless at least sixteen Fellows vote, and unless he have in his favour three-fourths of the Fellows voting.

Admission of Fellows.

6. Every Fellow elect is required to take the earliest opportunity of presenting himself for admission at an Ordinary Meeting of the Society.

The manner of admission shall be thus :—

Immediately after the reading of the minutes, the Fellow elect, having first paid his subscription for the current year or his composition, shall sign the obligation contained in the Fellowship-book, to the effect following :—

" We, who have underwritten our " names, do hereby undertake, each for " himself, that we will endeavour to " further the good of the Royal Statis-" tical Society for improving Statistical " Knowledge, and the ends for which " the same has been founded ; that we " will be present at the Meetings of the " Society as often as conveniently we " can, and that we will keep and fulfil " the Bye-laws and Orders of this " Society : provided that whensoever " any one of us shall make known, by " writing under his hand, to the Secre-" taries for the time being, that he " desires to withdraw from the Society, " he shall be free thenceforward from " this obligation."

Whereon the President, taking him by the hand, shall say,—" By the " authority, and in the name of the " Royal Statistical Society, I do admit " you a Fellow thereof."

Upon their admission Fellows shall have the right of attaching to their names the letters F.S.S., but not in connection with any trading or business advertisement other than the publication of any book or literary notice.

Admission of Honorary Fellows.

7. There shall be Two Meetings of the Society in the year, on such days as shall be hereafter fixed by the Council, at which Honorary Fellows may be elected.

No Honorary Fellow can be recommended for election but by the Council. At any Meeting of the Council any Member thereof may propose a Foreigner or

British subject of distinction residing out of the United Kingdom, delivering at the same time a written statement of the qualifications of, offices held by, and published works of, the person proposed; and ten days' notice at least shall be given to every Member of the Council, of the day on which the Council will vote by ballot on the question whether they will recommend to the Society the election of the person proposed. No such recommendation to the Society shall be adopted unless at least three-fourths of the votes are in favour thereof.

Notice of the recommendation shall be given from the chair at the Meeting of the Society next preceding that at which the vote shall be taken thereon. No person shall be elected an Honorary Fellow unless sixteen Fellows vote and three-fourths of the Fellows voting be in his favour.

The Council shall have power to elect as Honorary Fellows, the Presidents for the time being of the Statistical Societies of Dublin, Manchester, and Paris, and the President of any other Statistical Society at home or abroad.

Payments by Fellows.

8. Every Fellow of the Society shall pay a yearly subscription of Two Guineas, or may at any time compound for his future yearly payments by paying at once the sum of Twenty Guineas.* unless the Annual Subscription or Composition Fee shall be remitted by the Council; provided that the number of Fellows whose Annual Subscription or Composition Fee shall have been thus remitted, do not exceed five at any one time.

Every person elected to the Society shall pay his first subscription (or if he desire to become a Life Fellow, his composition) within three months at the latest of the date of his election, if he be resident in the United Kingdom. If he be resident abroad, this period shall be six months. If payment be not made within the time specified above, the election shall be void.

Defaulters.— Withdrawal of Fellows.

9. All yearly payments are due in advance on the 1st of January, and if any Fellow of the Society have not paid his subscription before the 1st of July, he shall be applied to in writing by the Secretaries, and if the same be not paid before the 1st of January of the second year, a written application shall again be made by the Secretaries, and the Fellow in arrear shall cease to receive the Society's publications, and shall not be entitled to any of the privileges of the Society until such arrears are paid; and if the subscription be not discharged before the 1st of February of the second year, the name of the Fellow thus in arrear shall be exhibited on a card suspended in the office of the Society; and if, at the next Annual General Meeting, the amount still remain unpaid, the defaulter shall, unless otherwise authorised by the Council, be announced to be no longer a Fellow of the Society, the reason for the same being at the same time assigned. No Fellow of the Society can withdraw his name from the Society's books, unless all arrears be paid; and no resignation will be deemed valid unless a written notice thereof be communicated to the Secretaries. No Fellow shall be entitled to vote at any Meeting of the Society until he shall have paid his subscription for the current year.

Expulsion of Fellows.

10. If any Fellow of the Society, or any Honorary Fellow, shall so demean himself that it would be for the dishonour of the Society that he longer continue to be a Fellow or Honorary Fellow thereof, the Council shall take the matter into consideration; and if the majority of the Members of the Council present at some Meeting (of which and of the matter in hand such Fellow or Honorary Fellow, and every Member of the Council, shall have due notice) shall decide by ballot to recommend that such Fellow or Honorary Fellow be expelled from the Society, the President shall at its next Ordinary Meeting announce to the Society the recommendation of the Council, and at the following Meeting the question shall be decided by ballot, and if at least three-fourths of the

* Cheques should be made payable to "The Royal Statistical Society," and crossed "Messrs " Drummond and Co."

number voting are in favour of the expulsion, the President shall forthwith cancel the name in the Fellowship-book, and shall say,—

" By the authority and in the name " of the Royal Statistical Society, I do " declare that A. B. (naming him) is no " longer a Fellow (or Honorary Fellow) " thereof."

And such Fellow or Honorary Fellow shall thereupon cease to be of the Society.

Trustees.

11. The property of the Society may be vested in three Trustees, chosen by the Fellows. The Trustees are eligible to any other offices in the Society.

President, Council, and Officers.

12. The Council shall consist of a President and thirty Members, together with the Honorary Vice-Presidents.

From the Council shall be chosen four Vice-Presidents, a Treasurer, the Honorary Secretaries, and a Foreign Secretary, who may be one of the Honorary Secretaries. The former Presidents who are continuing Fellows of the Society shall be Honorary Vice-Presidents. Any five of the Council shall be a quorum.

Election of President and Officers.

13. The President, Members of Council, Treasurer, and Honorary and Foreign Secretaries shall be chosen annually by the Fellows at the Annual General Meeting.

The Vice-Presidents shall be chosen annually from the Council by the President.

The President shall not be eligible for the office more than two years in succession.

Six Fellows, at least, who were not of the Council of the previous year, shall be annually elected; and of the Members retiring three at least shall be those who have served longest continuously on the Council, unless they hold office as Treasurer or Honorary or Foreign Secretary.

Nomination of President, Council, and Officers.

14. The Council shall, previously to the Annual General Meeting, nominate, by ballot, the Fellows whom they recommend to be the next President and

Council of the Society. They shall also recommend for election a Treasurer and the Secretaries (in accordance with Rule 12). Notice shall be sent to every Fellow whose residence is known to be within the limits of the metropolitan post, at least a fortnight before the Annual General Meeting, of the names of Fellows recommended by the Council.

Extraordinary Vacancies.

15. On any extraordinary vacancy occurring of the Office of President, or other Officer of the Society, the Honorary Secretaries shall summon the Council with as little delay as possible, and a majority of the Council, thereupon meeting in their usual place, shall, by ballot, and by a majority of those present, choose a new President, or other Officer of the Society, to be so until the next Annual General Meeting.

Committees.

16. The Council shall have power to appoint Committees of Fellows and also an Executive Committee of their own body. The Committees shall report their proceedings to the Council. No report shall be communicated to the Society except by the Council.

Auditors.

17. At the first Ordinary Meeting of each year, the Fellows shall choose two Fellows, not being Members of the Council, as Auditors, who, with one of the Council, chosen by the Council, shall audit the Treasurer's accounts for the past year, and report thereon to the Society, which report shall be presented at the Ordinary Meeting in February. The Auditors shall be empowered to examine into the particulars of all expenditure of the funds of the Society, and may report their opinion upon any part of it.

Meetings Ordinary and General.

18. The Ordinary Meetings of the Society shall be held monthly, or oftener, during the Session, which shall be from the 1st of November to the 1st of July in each year, both inclusive, on such days and at such hours as the Council shall declare. The Annual General Meeting shall be held on such day in the month of June of each year as shall be appointed by the Council for the time being.

Business of Ordinary Meetings.

19. The business of the Ordinary Meetings shall be to elect and admit Fellows, to read and hear reports, letters, and papers on subjects interesting to the Society. Nothing relating to the bye-laws or management of the Society shall be discussed at the Ordinary Meetings, except that the Auditors' Report shall be presented at the Ordinary Meeting in February, and that the Minutes of the Annual General Meeting, and of every Special General Meeting, shall be submitted for confirmation at the next Ordinary Meeting after the day of such Annual or Special General Meeting. Strangers may be introduced to the Ordinary Meetings, by any Fellow, with the leave of the President, Vice-President, or other Fellow presiding at the Meeting.

Business of Annual General Meeting.

20. The business of the Annual General Meeting shall be to elect the Officers of the Society, and to discuss questions on its bye-laws and management. No Fellow or Honorary Fellow shall be proposed at the Annual General Meeting. No Fellow shall propose any alteration of the rules or bye-laws of the Society at the Annual General Meeting, unless after three weeks' notice thereof given in writing to the Council, but amendments to any motion may be brought forward without notice, so that they relate to the same subject as the motion. The Council shall give fourteen days' notice to every Fellow of all questions of which such notice shall have been given to them.

Special General Meetings.

21. The Council may, at any time, call a Special General Meeting of the Society when it appears to them necessary. Any twenty Fellows may require a Special General Meeting to be called, by notice in writing signed by them, delivered to one of the Secretaries, specifying the questions to be moved. The Council shall, within one week of such notice, appoint a day for such Special General Meeting, and shall give at least one week's notice of every Special General Meeting, and of the questions to be moved, to every Fellow

within the limits of the metropolitan post, whose residence is known. No business shall be brought forward at any Special General Meeting other than that specified in the notice convening the same.

Duties of the President.

22. The President shall preside at all Meetings of the Society, Council, and Committees which he shall attend, and in case of an equality of votes, shall have a second or casting vote. He shall sign all diplomas of admission of Honorary Fellows. He shall admit and expel Fellows and Honorary Fellows, according to the bye-laws of the Society.

Duties of the Treasurer.

23. The Treasurer shall receive all moneys due to, and pay all moneys owing by, the Society, and shall keep an account of his receipts and payments. No sum exceeding Ten Pounds shall be paid but by order of the Council, excepting always any lawful demand for rates or taxes. The Treasurer shall invest the moneys of the Society in such manner as the Council shall from time to time direct.

Duties of the Honorary Secretaries.

24. The Honorary Secretaries shall, under the control of the Council, conduct the correspondence of the Society · they or one of them shall attend all Meetings of the Society and Council, and shall duly record the Minutes of the Proceedings. They shall issue the requisite notices, and read such papers to the Society as the Council may direct.

Powers of the Vice-Presidents.

25. A Vice-President, whether Honorary or nominated, in the chair, shall act with the power of the President in presiding and voting at any Meeting of the Society or Council, and in admitting Fellows; but no Vice-President shall be empowered to sign diplomas of admission of Honorary Fellows, or to expel Fellows or Honorary Fellows. In the absence of the President and Vice-Presidents, any Member of Council may be called upon by the Fellows then present, to preside at an Ordinary or Council Meeting, with the same power as a Vice-President.

Powers of the Council.

26. The Council shall have control over the papers and funds of the Society, and may, as they shall see fit, direct the publication of papers and the expenditure of the funds, in accordance with the provisions of the Charter.

27. The Council shall be empowered at any time to frame Regulations not inconsistent with these bye-laws, which shall be and remain in force until the next Annual General Meeting, at which they shall be either affirmed or annulled; but no Council shall have power to renew Regulations which have once been disapproved at an Annual General Meeting.

. 28. The Council shall have the custody of the Common Seal. The Common Seal shall not be affixed to any instrument, deed. or other document, except by order of the Council and in the presence of at least two Members of the Council and in accordance with such other regulations as the Council shall from time to time prescribe. The fact of the seal having been so affixed shall be entered on the minutes of the Council.

29. No Dividend, Gift, Division, of Bonus in money shall be made by the Society, unto or between any of the Fellows or Members, except as hereinafter provided.

30. The Council shall publish a Journal of the Transactions of the Society, and such other Statistical Publications as they may determine upon, and may from time to time pay such sums to Editors and their assistants whether Fellows of the Society or not as may be deemed advisable.

31. All communications to the Society are the property of the Society, unless the Council allow the right of property to be specially reserved by the Contributors.

REGULATIONS OF THE LIBRARY.

1. The Library and the Reading Room are open daily from 10 a.m. to 5 p.m. except on Saturdays, when they are closed at 2 p.m.

2. Every Fellow, whose subscription is not in arrear, is entitled to consult books and to use the Reading Room. Persons who are non-Fellows may be allowed to use the Library and Reading Room for a definite period on presentation to the Librarian of an introduction by a Member of Council. All cases in which temporary permission has been granted to non-Fellows shall be reported to the Library Committee at its next meeting. No books may be borrowed except by Fellows.

3. Fellows may borrow books from the Library on personal application, or by letter addressed to the Assistant Secretary or Librarian, all expenses for carriage being paid by them.

4. No Fellow may have more than ten volumes out at any one time or keep any book longer than one month. except by special authority from the Chairman of the Library Committee or an Honorary Secretary.

5. Cyclopædias, books of reference, and unbound scientific journals and periodicals may be borrowed only on the written order of an Honorary Secretary for a period not exceeding *four days*. If books so lent be not returned within the specified time, the borrower shall incur a fine of one shilling per day per volume for each day they are detained beyond the time specified.

6. Any Fellow who damages or loses a book, shall either replace the work or pay a fine equivalent to its value.

7. Readers are not themselves to replace books taken from the shelves, but to lay them on the Library table.

8. Any infringement of these regulations will involve the suspension of the right to the use of the Library, and shall be reported to the Library Committee at its next meeting.

DONORS TO THE LIBRARY.

DURING THE YEAR (ENDING 15TH SEPTEMBER) 1907.

(a) Foreign Countries.

Argentine Republic—
General Statistical Bureau.
Ministry of Agriculture.
" Oficina Demografica Nacional."
Buenos Ayres. Provincial and Municipal Statistical Bureaus.
Cordoba. Municipal Statistical Bureau.
Santa Fé. Statistical Bureau.

Austria-Hungary—
Central Statistical Commission.
Ministry of Agriculture.
     "   Finance.
     "   Railways.
Statistical Department of the Ministry of Commerce.
Austrian Labour Department.
Hungarian Statistical Bureau.
Bohemia. Statistical Bureau.
Bosnia and Herzegovina Statistical Bureau.
Bukowina. Statistical Bureau.
Agram Statistical Bureau.
Brünn. Statistical Bureau.
Budapest. Statistical Bureau.
Krakow. Statistical Bureau.
Prague. Statistical Bureau.
" Compass," The Editor.

Belgium—
Administration of Mines.
Army Medical Department.
Bureau of General Statistics.
Belgian Government.
     "   Labour Department.
     "   Legation, London.
     "   Chamber of Commerce.
Bruges. The Burgomaster.
Brussels. Bureau of Hygiene.
Hasselt. The Burgomaster.

Belgium—contd.
Royal Academy of Sciences.
Institute of Sociology.

Brazil—
Statistical Bureau.
" Brazilian Review," The Editor.

Bulgaria. Statistical Bureau.

Chile. The Central Statistical Bureau.

China. Imperial Maritime Customs.

Cuba—
National Library of Cuba.
Chamber of Commerce.
The " Secretaria de Hacienda."
Statistical Bureau.

Denmark—
State Statistical Bureau.
Copenhagen Statistical Bureau.
Political Economy Society.

Egypt—
Department of Public Health.
Director-General of Customs.
     "   Post Office.
Statistical Department, Ministry of Finance.
Comité de Conservation de Monuments de l'Art Arabe.
Public Debt Office.

France—
Director-General of Customs.
Director of the Mint.
Labour Department.
Colonial Office.
Ministry of Agriculture.
     "   Finance.
     "   Justice.

During the Year 1906-07—Contd.

(a) Foreign Countries—Contd.

France—Contd.

Ministry of Public Works.
Paris Statistical Bureau.
Economiste Français, The Editor.
Journal des Economistes, The Editor.
Monde Economique, The Editor
Polybiblion, Revue Bibliographique Universelle, The Editor.
Expansion Française.
Réforme Sociale, The Editor.
Rentier, Le, The Editor.
Revue d'Economie Politique, The Editor.
Revue de Statistique, The Publisher.
The Bank of France.
Statistical Society of Paris.

Germany—

Imperial Health Bureau.
　　　　,,　Insurance Bureau.
　　　　,,　Judicial Bureau.
　　　　,,　Statistical Bureau.
German Consul-General, London.
Prussian Royal Statistical Bureau.
Saxony Royal Statistical Bureau.
Berlin. Statistical Bureau.
Frankfort—
Chamber of Commerce.
Statistical Bureau.
Hamburg. Statistical Bureau.
Rheinische Creditbank.
Wiesbaden. Statistical Bureau.
Allgemeines Statistisches Archiv, The Editor.
Archiv für Rassen- und Gesellschafts-Biologie, The Editor.
Archiv für Soziale-wissenschaft und Sozialpolitik, &c., The Editor.
Jahrbuch für Gesetzgebung, &c., The Editor.
Jahrbücher für Nationalökonomie und Statistik, The Editor.

Germany—Contd.

Zeitschrift für die gesamte Staatswissenschaft, The Editor
Zeitschrift für Socialwissenschaft, The Editor.
Geographical and Statistical Society of Frankfort.
Metallgesellschaft, The.
Verein für Versicherungs-Wissenschaft.

Greece—

Statistical Bureau.
International Finance Commission.

Italy—

Commissioner of Emigration.
Director-General of Agriculture.
　　　　,,　　Customs.
　　　　,,　　Public Health.
　　　　,,　　Statistics.
Italian Labour Department.
Florence. Municipal Statistical Bureau.
Turin. Municipal Statistical Bureau.
Economista.
Giornale degli Economisti.
Rivista Italiana di Sociologia.
Società Umanitaria.

Japan—

Consul-General, London.
Bureau of General Statistics.
Department of Agriculture and Commerce.
Department of Finance.

Mexico. Statistical Bureau.

Netherlands—

Central Health Bureau.
　　,,　Statistical Bureau.
Ministry of Finance.
Director-General of Customs.

During the Year 1906-07—*Contd.*

(a) Foreign Countries—*Contd.*

Norway—
Central Statistical Bureau.
Christiania—
  Health Department.
  Statistical Bureau.

Paraguay. Statistical Bureau.

Portugal. General Statistical Bureau.

Roumania—
Statistical Bureau.
Bucharest. Municipal Statistical Bureau.

Russia—
Central Statistical Commission.
Controller of the Empire.
Customs Statistical Bureau.
Ministry of Agriculture.
    ,,   Finance.
    ,,   Justice.
Moscow. Statistical Bureau.
Finland—
  Statistical Bureau.
  Geographical Society.

Salvador—
Statistical Bureau.
Board of Health.

Servia. Statistical Bureau.

Spain—
Director-General of Customs.
Geographical and Statistical Institute.
The "Junta de Aranceles y de Valoraciones."
Ministry of Agriculture.
Statistical Bureau of Madrid.

Sweden—
Central Statistical Bureau.
Stockholm—
  Health Departmen .
  Statistical Bureau.
  Up a. Roy University.

Switzerland—
Federal Assurance Bureau.
  ,,   Statistical Bureau.
  ,,   Department of Customs.
"Régie fédérale des Alcools."
Bern Statistical Bureau.
Statistical Society of Switzerland.
Swiss Union of Commerce and Industry.

United States—
Bureau of Education.
  ,,   Immigration.
  ,,   the Mint.
  ,,   Navigation.
Census Bureau.
Comptroller of the Currency.
Department of Agriculture.
  ,,   Commerce and Labour.
Director of Geological Survey.
Interstate Commerce Commission.
Librarian of Congress.
Naval Observatory.
Secretary of the Treasury.
Surgeon-General, U. States Army.
Volta Bureau.
California—
  Bureau of Labor Statistics.
  State Board of Health.
Connecticut—
  State Board of Health.
  Bureau of Labor Statistics.
Illinois—
  Bureau of Labor Statistics.
  University.
Indiana. Department of Statistics.
Iowa. Bureau of Labor Statistics.
Kansas. Bureau of Labor Statistics.
Maine. Bureau of Labor and Industrial Statistics.
Maryland. Bureau of Statistics and Information.

During the Year 1906-07—*Contd.*

(a) Foreign Countries—*Contd.*

United States—*Contd.*

Massachusetts—
Board of Arbitration.
   ,,   Health, Lunacy, &c.
Bureau of Labor Statistics
Metropolitan Water Board.
Michigan—
Bureau of Labor Statistics.
Division of Vital Statistics.
Minnesota. Bureau of Labor Statistics.
Missouri. Bureau of Labor Statistics.
Nebraska—
State Bureau of Statistics.
University.
New Hampshire. Bureau of Labor Statistics.
New Jersey. Bureau of Labor Statistics.
New York State Library.
   ,,   Department of Labor.
   ,,   State University.
North Carolina. Bureau of Labor Statistics.
Ohio. Bureau of Labor Statistics.
Pennsylvania. Bureau of Industrial Statistics.
Wisconsin—
Bureau of Labor Statistics.
State Board of Health.
Boston—
Metropolitan Water and Sewerage Board.
Statistical Bureau.
Public Library.
Chicago. Board of Trade.
New York City. Public Library.

United States—*Contd.*

San Francisco. Relief and Red-Cross Funds.
Bankers' Magazine, The Editor.
Bradstreet's Journal, The Editor.
Commercial and Financial Chronicle, The Editor.
Commercial America, The Editor.
Journal of Political Economy, The Editor.
"Mineral Industry," Publishers of, New York.
Political Science Quarterly, Columbia University, The Editor.
Quarterly Journal of Economics, The Editor.
Yale Review, The Editor
Actuarial Society of America.
American Academy of Arts and Sciences.
American Academy of Political and Social Science.
American Economic Association.
American Geographical Society.
American Philosophical Society.
American Statistical Association.
Philadelphia Commercial Museum.
Columbia University, New York.
John Crerar Library.
Johns Hopkins University.
Smithsonian Institution.
Uruguay—
Statistical Bureau.
Montevideo Statistical Bureau.
International—
International Co-operative Alliance.
International Statistical Institute.

(b) India, and Colonial Possessions.

India, British—
Secretary of State in Council.
Chief Inspector of Mines.
Director-General of Commercial Intelligence.

India, British—*Contd.*
Lieutenant-Governor of Bengal.
Bengal, The Collector of Customs.
   ,,   Secretary, Judicial and General Department.

During the Year 1906-07—*Contd.*

(b) **India, and Colonial Possessions**—*Contd.*

India, British—*Contd.*

  Calcutta. Custom House.
  Sanitary Commissione for Punjab
  East India Railway Co.
  Indian Engineering, The Editor.

Canada—
  The Auditor-General.
  The High Commissioner.
  Census Commissioner.
  Clerk of House of Commons.
  Minister of Labour.
  Department of Agriculture.
  Deputy Minister of Finance.
  Finance Department.
  Superintendent of Emigration.
  British Columbia—
    Mining Record, The Editor.
    Department of Mines.
  Ontario—
    Agricultural and Experimental
      Union.
    Bureau of Industries.
    Department of Agriculture.
  Manitoba. The King's Printer.
  Saskatchewan. Department of
    Agriculture.
  Royal Society of Canada.
  The Royal Bank of Canada.

Cape of Good Hope—
  Agent-General for the Cape.
  Colonial Secretary.
  Registrar-General.

Ceylon—
  Ceylon Government.
  Lieut.-Governor and Colonial
    Secretary.
  General Manager of Government
    Railways.

Jamaica. Registrar-General.

Mauritius. The Colonial Secretary.

Natal. The Colonial Secretary

New South Wales—
  Bureau of Statistics.
  Acting Statistician.
  Agent-General, London.
  Controller-General of Prisons.
  Registrar-General.
  Registrar of Friendly Societies.
  Railway Commissioners, Sydney.

New Zealand—
  The High Commissioner, London.
  Registrar-General.
  Registrar of Friendly Societies.
  Insurance Department.
    „   Commissioner.
  Old Age Pension Department.
  Labour Department.
  New Zealand Institute.
  Trade Review, The Editor.
  Wellington Harbour Board.

Orange River Colony. Auditor-
  General.

Queensland—
  Agent-General, London.
  The Government Statistician.
  Registrar-General.

Rhodesia—
  British South Africa Company.
  Chamber of Mines.

South Australia—
  Agent-General, London.
  The Chief Secretary.
  The Registrar-General.
  Government Statist.
  Public Actuary.
  Public Library.

Straits Settlements. The Government Secretary, Perak.

Tasmania—
  The Agent-General, London.

During the Year 1906-07—Contd.

(b) India, and Colonial Possessions—Contd.

Tasmania—Contd.
Government of Tasmania.
Government Railways Department.
Government Statistician.
Royal Society of Tasmania.

Transvaal—
Agricultural Department.
Department of Mines.
Government Mining Engineer.
Johannesburg—
Town Statistician.
Chamber of Mines.
Chamber of Commerce.
Chamber of Trade.
Pretoria. Chamber of Commerce.
Statistical Society of S. Africa.

Transvaal and Orange River Colony—
The Auditor-General.
Secretary of the Inter-colonial Council.

Victoria—
Actuary for Friendly Societies.
Agent-General, London.
Government Statistician.
Registrar for Friendly Societies.
Public Library, &c., Melbourne.

Western Australia—
Agent-General, London.
The Government Actuary.
Acting Collector of Customs.
Registrar of Friendly Societies.
Registrar-General and Government Statistician.

Australia, Commonwealth of—
The Commonwealth Statistician.
Department of Trade and Customs.
Officer representing the Commonwealth, London.

(c) United Kingdom and its several Divisions.

United Kingdom—
Admiralty Medical Department.
Army Medical Department.
Board of Agriculture and Fisheries.
Board of Trade.
„ Labour Department.
„ Commercial Depart.
„ Marine Department.
British Museum.
Colonial Office.
Companies in Liquidation, Inspector-General of.
Customs, Commissioners of.
Factories and Workshops, Chief Inspector of.
Friendly Societies, Chief Registrar of.

United Kingdom—Contd.
Home Office.
India Office.
Inland Revenue, The Commissioners.
Inspector-General in Bankruptcy.
Joint Stock Companies, The Registrar of.
Local Government Board.
Royal Mint.
Woods, Forests, &c., Commissioners.
Tariff Commission.

England—
Registrar-General of England.
London County Council.
London County Council Education Committee.

During the Year 1906–07—*Contd.*

(c) United Kingdom and its several Divisions—*Contd.*

England—Contd.

London University.
Metropolitan Asylums Board.
„ Water „
Wandsworth Borough Council.
Birmingham City Treasurer.
Folkestone, Borough Accountant.
Leicester Borough Treasurer.
Manchester, The Town Clerk..
„ City Treasurer.
Mersey Conservancy.
Nottingham City Accountant.
Paddington Medical Officer of Health.
Poplar Medical Officer of Health.
Tunbridge Wells, The Borough Accountant.
West Hartlepool, The Borough Accountant.
The Medical Officer of Health of the Local Government Board

England—Contd.

and of the following towns :
Birmingham, Bradford, Bristol, Cardiff, Derby, Halifax, Huddersfield, Leicester, Liverpool, Manchester, Newcastle - on - Tyne, Norwich, Nottingham, Preston, West Hartlepool, Wigan, Wolverhampton.

Ireland—

Department of Agriculture.
Registrar-General of Ireland.

Scotland—

Education Department.
Registrar-General of Scotland.
Edinburgh City Chamberlain.
Aberdeen Medical Officer.
„ Sanitary Inspector.
Glasgow Medical Officer.

(d) Authors, Publishers, &c.

Alcan, M. Felix, Paris.
Angier Bros., London.
Babbage, Major-General H. P.
Bamber, Lieut.-Col. C. J., India.
Banaji, Khoshu, Bombay.
Barnes, Hon. William, U.S.A.
Barthe y Barthe, Andrés, Spain.
Bell, George, & Son, London.
Bellini, Augusto, Turin.
Bertillon, Dr. J., Paris.
Black, A. & C., Messrs., London.
Blackwood & Sons, Messrs.
Boutcher, Mortimore, & Co., London.
Boverat, Raymond.
Braun, M. G., Karlsruhe.
Broomhall, G. J. S., Liverpool.
Brown, Richard.
Buckley, T. J. W., London.
Bygate, W., York.
Chapman & Hall, London.

Clarendon Press, Oxford.
Coghlan, T. A., London.
Colesco, L., Roumania.
Colin, Librairie Armand, Paris.
Conrad, Dr. J., Jena.
Constable, A., & Co., London.
Cooper, Joseph, Farnworth.
Court, S. E., Johannesburg.
Courtney, J. M., Canada.
Craigie, Major P. G., C.B., London.
Dalla Volta, Riccardo, Florence.
Dawson, W., & Sons, Ltd., London.
Deane, Albert B., London.
Delagrave, M. Charles, Paris.
De la Plaza, V., Buenos Ayres.
Desclée, De Brouwer & Co., Brussels.
Dick, G. W., Natal.
Duckworth & Co., London.
Dudfield, Dr. R., London.

During the Year 1906-07—*Contd.*

(d) **Authors, &c.** —*Contd.*

Dun & Co., New York.
Duncker & Humblot, Leipzig.
Eaton, H. W., & Sons, London.
Ellison & Co., Liverpool.
Fahlbeck, Pontus.
Feldt, Wladimir, St. Petersburg.
Ferraris, Carlo F., Rome.
Fielding, Hon. W. S., M.P., Canada.
Figgis, S., & Co., London.
Fischer, Herr Gustav, Jena.
Fisher, Professor Irving, U.S.A.
Fleming, Owen, London.
Fornasari di Verce, E., Italy.
Forster, John W., Tunbridge-Wells.
Foville, A. de, Paris.
Fox, Morris, New Zealand.
Frowde, Henry, London.
Fry, T. Hallett, London.
Furnival, W. J.
Gabalda, J., & Co., Paris.
Garnier, Frères, Paris.
Gee & Co., London.
Ginn & Co., London.
Gooch, Thomas & Sons, London.
Gouge, H. Dillon, Adelaide.
Gow, Wilson, & Stanton, London.
Guillaume, Dr. Louis, Bern.
Guillaumin et Cie., Paris.
Guisti, Professor Ugo.
Guyot, Yves, Paris.
Hachette & Co., London.
Haggard, F. T., Tunbridge Wells.
Hall, Thomas, New South Wales.
Harper & Brothers, London.
Hart, Sir R., Bart., G.C.M.G., Peking.
Haynes, Mr. Thomas H , Tavistock.
Headley Bros., Messrs., London.
Heckscher, Mr. Eli F., Stockholm.
Helguero, Fernando de, Rome.
Helmuth Schwartz & Co., London.
Herold, C.
Hewins Prof. W. A. S., London.
Hodding, King & Co.
Hodges, Figgis & Co., London.
Hodgson, W. Gill, West Hartlepool.

Hoepli, Ulrico, Milan.
Holt, Henry, & Co., New York.
Hooper, Frederick.
Hopkins, J. Castell, Canada.
Hutchins, Miss B. L., London.
Hyde, Hon. John, U.S.A.
Inama-Sternegg, Dr. K. T., Vienna.
Jacquart, Camille, Brussels.
Jagger, Mr. J. W., Cape Town.
Johns Hopkins Press, Baltimore.
Johnson, Geo., Ottawa.
Johnston, R. M., Hobart.
Julin, M. Armand.
Juraschek, Dr. F. v., Vienna.
Kegan Paul & Co., London.
Keltie, J. Scott, London.
Kemp, John, London.
Kiær, A. N., Christiania.
King, A. W. W., London.
King, P. S., & Son, Westminster.
Lahitte, Emilio, Buenos Aires.
Lampertico, MM. D. & O.
Lancashire Publishing Company.
Larose & Tenin, Paris.
Latzina, Dr. F., Buenos Ayres.
Lawson, W. R., London.
Layton, C. & E., London.
Leake, Percy D., London.
Lee, Arthur, London.
Leroy-Beaulieu, Paul, Paris.
Levasseur, E., Paris.
Levy, Dr. H., Berlin.
Lexis, Prof. W., Germany.
Licht, Herr O., Magdeburg.
Lloyd's Register, London.
Loescher et Cie., Rome.
Longmans & Co., London.
MacDonald, Mr. Arthur.
Macmillan & Bowes, Cambridge.
Macmillan & Co., London.
Mallet, Bernard, London.
March, Lucien, Paris.
Mayr, Dr. G. von, Strassburg.
Methuen & Co., London.
Mitchell & Co., London.

During the Year 1906-07—Contd.

(d) Authors, &c.—*Contd.*

Mittler, E. S., & Sohn, Berlin.
Moody Corporation.
Morgan, Percy C., London.
Mortara, Mons. Giorgio.
Murray, John, London.
Neymarck, A., Paris.
Nicolai, Edmond, Brussels.
Nicholson, Prof. J. S., Edinburgh.
Oldham, J., Buenos Ayres.
Oliphant, Anderson & Co., London.
Oliver & Boyd, Edinburgh.
Owen, Edgar T., W. Australia.
Oxford University Press.
Page & Gwyther, London.
Penn-Lewis, W., Leicester.
Petersilie, Dr. A., Berlin.
Pierson, Israel C., New York.
Pinkus, Prof. Dr. N.
Pitman, Sir Isaac, & Sons, London.
Pixley & Abell, London.
Powell, Sir Francis S., Bart , M.P.
Powell, T. J., & Co., London.
Pratt, Edwin A., London.
Provand, A. D., U.S.A.
Raffalovich, Arthur, Paris.
Raseri, Dr. E., Italy.
Rauchberg, Dr. Heinrich, Austria.
Reimer, Mr. Georg, Berlin.
Renwick, Mr. J. P. A., London.
Rew, R. Henry, London.
Rider, D. J., London.
Ronald & Rodger, Liverpool.
Rosenbaum, S., London.
Rousseau, M. Arthur.
Routledge, G., & Sons, London.
Rowntree, Joseph, York.
Rozenraad, C., London.
Schäfer, Moritz.

Schmoller, Dr. G., Germany.
Schooling, J. Holt, London.
Sealey, Bryers & Walker, Dublin.
Seyd, Richard E., London.
Shaw & Sons, London.
Sherratt & Hughes, London.
Sidenbladh, Dr. K., Stockholm.
Simon, André, London.
Simpkin, Marshall & Co., London.
Smith, Elder & Co., London.
Smith, Mr. R. G.
Sundbårg, Gustav, Sweden.
Swan, Sonnenschein & Co., London.
Sweet & Maxwell, Ltd., London.
Tattersall, William, Manchester.
Teubner, Mr. B. G., Leipzig.
Thompson, Mr. R. J., London.
Thompson, W. J., & Co., London.
"Times, The," Manager.
Troïnitsky, M. N., St. Petersburg.
Unwin, T. Fisher, London.
Urmson, Elliot, & Co., Liverpool.
Vahlen, Franz, Berlin.
Vivian, Younger & Bond, London
Wagner, Henry R., London.
Walter Scott Publ'g Co., London.
Waxweiller, Prof. E., Brussels.
Weddel & Co., London.
Welton, Thomas A., London.
Whitelegge, B. Arthur, London.
Wiley, John, & Son, London.
Williams & Norgate, London.
Wilson, Effingham, London.
Wolfe, S. H., New York.
Wood, A. J., London.
Wright, Hon. C. D., Washington.
Yanagisawa, Count, Tokio.
Yule, G. Udny, London.

(e) Societies, &c. (British).

Accountants and Auditors, Society of.
Actuaries, Institute of.

Actuaries, Faculty of (Scotland).
Anthropological Institute.
Arts, Society of.

During the Year 1906-07—*Contd.*

(e) **Societies, &c. (British)**—*Contd.*

Bankers, Institute of.
Barnardo's (Dr.) Homes, The Sec.
Birmingham Chamber of Commerce.
British Association.
    „   Iron Trade Association.
    „   Weights and Measures
    Association.
Cambridge University Press.
Channel Tunnel Company.
Charity Organisation Society.
Chartered Accountants, Institute of.
    „ .   „   of Scotland.
Civil Engineers, Institution of.
Corporation of Foreign Bond-
    holders.
Council of the United Synagogue.
East India Association.
Glasgow Royal Philosophical
    Society.
Howard Association.
Imperial Institute.
Incorporated Accountants' Society.
Iron and Steel Institute.
Liverpool Chamber of Commerce.
    „   Lit. and Phil. Society.
    „   University.
London Chamber of Commerce.
    „   Hospital.
    „   Library.
    „   School of Economics.
Manchester Statistical Society.
Medical Officers of Health, Incor-
    porated Society of.
Middlesex Hospital.

National Liberal Club.
    „   Union of Teachers.
Navy League.
Peabody Donation Fund.
Royal Agricultural Society.
    „   Asiatic Society.
    „   College of Physicians.
    „   „   Surgeons.
    „   Colonial Institute.
    „   Economic Society.
    „   Geographical Society.
    „   Institution of Great Britain.
    „   Irish Academy.
    „   Meteorological Society.
    „   Philosophical Society, Glas-
    gow.
    „   Society, Edinburgh.
    „   „   London.
    „   United Service Institution.
St. Bartholomew's Hospital.
Sanitary Institute of Great Britain.
Scottish Automobile Club.
Seamen's Hospital Society.
Society of Comparative Legislation.
    „   for Propagation of the
    Gospel in Foreign Parts.
Sociological Society.
Statistical and Social Inquiry
    Society of Ireland.
Stock Exchange, London.
Surveyors' Institution.
Tariff Commission, London.
University College, London.

(f) **Periodicals, &c. (British).** *The Editors of*—

Accountant, The, London.
Appointments Gazette, Cambridge.
Athenæum, The, London.
Australian Trading World, The.
Bankers' Magazine, The, London.
Broomhall's Weekly Corn Trade
    News, Liverpool.

Browne's Export List, Newcastle-
    on-Tyne.
Colliery Guardian, The, London.
Commercial World, The, London.
Economic Review, The, London.
Economist, The, London.
Finance Chronicle, The, London.

F

During the Year 1906-07—*Contd.*

(f) Periodicals, &c. (British).   *The Editors of—Contd.*

Fireman, The, London.
Insurance Post, The, London.
„   Record, The, London.
Investors' Monthly Manual, The.
Joint Stock Companies Journal.
Labour Co-partnership, London.
Licensing World, The, London.
Lloyd's Register of Shipping.
Machinery Market, The, London.
National Telephone Journal, Editor
  of.

Nature, London.
Policy-Holder, The, Manchester.
Post Magazine, The, London.
„   Almanack, London.
Public Health, London.
Sanitary Record, The, London.
Shipping World, The, London.
Statesman's Year-book, Editor of.
Statist, The, London.

ROYAL STATISTICAL SOCIETY,

(9, ADELPHI TERRACE, STRAND, W.C., LONDON).

———————

THOSE persons who are inclined to benefit the Society by legacies are recommended to adopt the following

FORM OF BEQUEST.

I give and bequeath unto the " Royal Statistical Society," the sum of £   , such legacy to be paid out of such part of my personal estate, not specifically bequeathed, as the law permits to be appropriated by will to such a purpose.

———————

NOTE A.—All gifts by will to the Society of land, or of money secured on, or directed to be secured on, or to arise from the sale of, or directed to be laid out in the purchase of land, will be void. Gifts may be made by will of stock in the public funds, shares or debentures of railway or other joint-stock companies, or money to be paid out of the testator's pure personal estate, or of personal chattels.

NOTE B.—Bequests may be made either for the general purposes of the Society, or to the Society's "Building Fund."

LONDON :
HARRISON AND SONS, PRINTERS IN ORDINARY TO HIS MAJESTY,
ST. MARTIN'S LANE.